CORE STATUTES ON

The palgrave core statutes series:

Core EU Legislation	Rhona Smith
Core Statutes on Commercial & Consumer Law	Graham Stephenson
Core Statutes on Company Law	Cowan Ervine
Core Statutes on Contract, Tort & Restitution	Graham Stephenson
Core Statutes on Criminal Justice & Sentencing	Martin Wasik
Core Statutes on Criminal Law	Kate Cook, Mark James & Richard Lee
Core Statutes on Employment Law	Dominique Lauterburg
Core Statutes on Evidence	Christina McAlhone
Core Statutes on Family Law	Frances Burton
Core Statutes on Intellectual Property	Margaret Dowie-Whybrow
Core Statutes on Property Law	Peter Luther & Alan Moran
Core Statutes on Public Law & Civil Liberties	Rhona Smith, Eimear Spain & Richard Glancey
Core Documents on International Law	Karen Hulme
Core Documents on European/International Human Rights	Rhona Smith

CORE STATUTES ON COMPANY LAW

Cowan Ervine

macmillan education palgrave

First published 2015 by
PALGRAVE

Palgrave in the UK is an imprint of Macmillan Publishers Limited, registered in England, company number 785998, of 4 Crinan Street, London N1 9XW.

Palgrave Macmillan in the US is a division of St Martin's Press LLC, 175 Fifth Avenue, New York, NY 10010.

Palgrave is a global imprint of the above companies and is represented throughout the world.

Palgrave® and Macmillan® are registered trademarks in the United States, the United Kingdom, Europe and other countries.

ISBN 978–1–137–54506–0

This book is printed on paper suitable for recycling and made from fully managed and sustained forest sources. Logging, pulping and manufacturing processes are expected to conform to the environmental regulations of the country of origin.

A catalogue record for this book is available from the British Library.

PREFACE

The new edition includes the usual updating of existing material. In addition, there is a new statute, the Partnerships (Prosecution) (Scotland) Act 2013 which was enacted to close a loophole in the law. It makes a limited reform of Scots law on partnerships and prevents dissolution and change of membership from being technical obstacles to prosecution of partnerships. As ever, I am indebted to the Palgrave staff for their skill in seeing the book through the press.

Cowan Ervine
June 2015

CONTENTS

ALPHABETICAL LIST OF CONTENTS

PART I
STATUTES

PARTNERSHIP ACT 1890
(53 & 54 Vict., c. 39)

Nature of Partnership

1 Definition of partnership

(1) Partnership is the relation which subsists between persons carrying on a business in common with a view of profit.

(2) But the relation between members of any company or association which is—

(a) Registered under the Companies Act 2006; or

(b) Formed or incorporated by or in pursuance of any other Act of Parliament or letters patent, or Royal Charter:

is not a partnership within the meaning of this Act.

2 Rules for determining existence of partnership

In determining whether a partnership does or does not exist, regard shall be had to the following rules:

(1) Joint tenancy, tenancy in common, joint property, common property, or part ownership does not of itself create a partnership as to anything so held or owned, whether the tenants or owners do or do not share any profits made by the use thereof.

(2) The sharing of gross returns does not of itself create a partnership, whether the persons sharing such returns have or have not a joint or common right or interest in any property from which or from the use of which the returns are derived.

(3) The receipt by a person of a share of the profits of a business is prima facie evidence that he is a partner in the business, but the receipt of such a share, or of a payment contingent on or varying with the profits of a business, does not of itself make him a partner in the business; and in particular—

(a) The receipt by a person of a debt or other liquidated amount by instalments or otherwise out of the accruing profits of a business does not of itself make him a partner in the busines or liable as such:

(b) A contract for the remuneration of a servant or agent of a person engaged in a business by a share of the profits of the business does not of itself make the servant or agent a partner in the business or liable as such:

(c) A person being the widow, widower, surviving civil partner or child of a deceased partner, and receiving by way of annuity a portion of the profits made in the business in which the deceased person was a partner, is not by reason only of such receipt a partner in the business or liable as such:

(d) The advance of money by way of loan to a person engaged or about to engage in any business on a contract with that person that the lender shall receive a rate of interest varying with the profits, or shall receive a share of the profits arising from carrying on the business, does not of itself make the lender a partner with the person or persons carrying on the business or liable as such. Provided that the contract is in writing, and signed by or on behalf of all the parties thereto:

(e) A person receiving by way of annuity or otherwise a portion of the profits of a business in consideration of the sale by him of the goodwill of the business is not by reason only of such receipt a partner in the business or liable as such.

3 Postponement of rights of person lending or selling in consideration of share of profits in case of insolvency

In the event of any person to whom money has been advanced by way of loan upon such a contract as is mentioned in the last foregoing section, or of any buyer of a goodwill in consideration of a share of the profits of the business, being adjudged a bankrupt, entering into an arrangement to pay his creditors less than 100p in the pound, or dying in insolvent circumstances, the lender of the loan shall not be entitled to recover anything in respect of his loan, and the seller of the goodwill shall not be entitled to recover anything in respect of the share of profits contracted for, until the claims of the other creditors of the borrower or buyer for valuable consideration in money or money's worth have been satisfied.

4 Meaning of firm

(1) Persons who have entered into partnership with one another are for the purposes of this Act called collectively a firm, and the name under which their business is carried on is called the firm-name.

(2) In Scotland a firm is a legal person distinct from the partners of whom it is composed, but an individual partner may be charged on a decree or diligence directed against the firm, and on payment of the debts is entitled to relief pro rata from the firm and its other members.

Relations of Partners to persons dealing with them

5 Power of partner to bind the firm

Every partner is an agent of the firm and his other partners for the purpose of the business of the partnership; and the acts of every partner who does any act for carrying on in the usual way business of the kind carried on by the firm of which he is a member bind the firm and his partners, unless the partner so acting has in fact no authority to act for the firm in the particular matter, and the person with whom he is dealing either knows that he has no authority, or does not know or believe him to be a partner.

6 Partners bound by acts on behalf of firm

An act or instrument relating to the business of the firm done or executed in the firm-name, or in any other manner showing an intention to bind the firm, by any person thereto authorised, whether a partner or not, is binding on the firm and all the partners. Provided that this section shall not affect any general rule of law relating to the execution of deeds or negotiable instruments.

7 Partner using credit of firm for private purposes

Where one partner pledges the credit of the firm for a purpose apparently not connected with the firm's ordinary course of business, the firm is not bound, unless he is in fact specially authorised by the other partners; but this section does not affect any personal liability incurred by an individual partner.

8 Effect of notice that firm will not be bound by acts of partner

If it has been agreed between the partners that any restriction shall be placed on the power of any one or more of them to bind the firm, no act done in contravention of the agreement is binding on the firm with respect to persons having notice of the agreement.

9 Liability of partners

Every partner in a firm is liable jointly with the other partners, and in Scotland severally also, for all debts and obligations of the firm incurred while he is a partner; and after his death his estate is also severally liable in a due course of administration for such debts and obligations, so far as they remain unsatisfied, but subject in England or Ireland to the prior payment of his separate debts.

10 Liability of the firm for wrongs

Where, by any wrongful act or omission of any partner acting in the ordinary course of the business of the firm, or with the authority of his co-partners, loss or injury is caused to any person not being a partner in the firm, or any penalty is incurred, the firm is liable therefor to the same extent as the partner so acting or omitting to act.

11 Misapplication of money or property received for or in custody of the firm

In the following cases; namely—

(a) Where one partner acting within the scope of his apparent authority receives the money or property of a third person and misapplies it; and

(b) Where a firm in the course of its business receives money or property of a third person, and the money or property so received is misapplied by one or more of the partners while it is in the custody of the firm;

the firm is liable to make good the loss.

12 Liability for wrongs joint and several

Every partner is liable jointly with his co-partners and also severally for everything for which the firm while he is a partner therein becomes liable under either of the two last preceding sections.

13 Improper employment of trust-property for partnership purposes

If a partner, being a trustee, improperly employs trust-property in the business or on the account of the partnership, no other partner is liable for the trust property to the persons beneficially interested therein:

Provided as follows:—

(1) This section shall not affect any liability incurred by any partner by reason of his having notice of a breach of trust; and

(2) Nothing in this section shall prevent trust money from being followed and recovered from the firm if still in its possession or under its control.

14 Persons liable by "holding out"

(1) Every one who by words spoken or written or by conduct represents himself, or who knowingly suffers himself to be represented, as a partner in a particular firm, is liable as a partner to any one who has on the faith of any such representation given credit to the firm, whether the representation has or has not been made or communicated to the person so giving credit by or with the knowledge of the apparent partner making the representation or suffering it to be made.

(2) Provided that where after a partner's death the partnership business is continued in the old firm's name, the continued use of that name or of the deceased partner's name as part thereof shall not of itself make his executors or administrators estate or effects liable for any partnership debts contracted after his death.

15 Admissions and representations of partners

An admission or representation made by any partner concerning the partnership affairs, and in the ordinary course of its business, is evidence against the firm.

16 Notice to acting partner to be notice to the firm

Notice to any partner who habitually acts in the partnership business of any matter relating to partnership affairs operates as notice to the firm, except in the case of a fraud on the firm committed by or with the consent of that partner.

17 Liabilities of incoming and outgoing partners

(1) A person who is admitted as a partner into an existing firm does not thereby become liable to the creditors of the firm for anything done before he became a partner.

(2) A partner who retires from a firm does not thereby cease to be liable for partnership debts or obligations incurred before his retirement.

(3) A retiring partner may be discharged from any existing liabilities, by an agreement to that effect between himself and the members of the firm as newly constituted and the creditors, and this agreement may be either expressed or inferred as a fact from the course of dealing between the creditors and the firm as newly constituted.

18 Revocation of continuing guaranty by change in firm

A continuing guaranty or cautionary obligation given either to a firm or to a third person in respect of the transactions of a firm is, in the absence of agreement to the contrary, revoked as to future transactions by any change in the constitution of the firm to which, or of the firm in respect of the transactions of which, the guaranty or obligation was given.

Relations of Partners to one another

19 Variation by consent of terms of partnership

The mutual rights and duties of partners, whether ascertained by agreement or defined by this Act, may be varied by the consent of all the partners, and such consent may be either express or inferred from a course of dealing.

20 Partnership property

(1) All property and rights and interests in property originally brought into the partnership stock or acquired, whether by purchase or otherwise, on account of the firm, or for the purposes and in the course of the partnership business, are called in this Act partnership property, and must be held and applied by the partners exclusively for the purposes of the partnership and in accordance with the partnership agreement.

(2) Provided that the legal estate or interest in any land, or in Scotland the title to and interest in any heritable estate, which belongs to the partnership shall devolve according to the nature and tenure thereof, and the general rules of law thereto applicable, but in trust, so far as necessary, for the persons beneficially interested in the land under this section.

(3) Where co-owners of an estate or interest in any land, or in Scotland of any heritable estate, not being itself partnership property, are partners as to profits made by the use of that land or estate, and purchase other land or estate out of the profits to be used in like manner, the land or estate so purchased belongs to them, in the absence of an agreement to the contrary, not as partners, but as co-owners for the same respective estates and interests as are held by them in the land or estate first mentioned at the date of the purchase.

21 Property bought with partnership money

Unless the contrary intention appears, property bought with money belonging to the firm is deemed to have been bought on account of the firm.

22 Conversion into personal estate of land held as partnership property

Where land or any heritable interest therein has become partnership property, it shall, unless the contrary intention appears, be treated as between the partners (including the representatives of a deceased partner), and also as between the heirs of a deceased partner and his executors or administrators, as personal or moveable and not real or heritable estate.

Note: This section has been repealed in relation to England and Wales.

23 Procedure against partnership property for a partner's separate judgment debt

(1) A writ of execution shall not issue against any partnership property except on a judgment against the firm.

(2) The High Court, or a judge thereof, or the county court in England and Wales or a county court in Northern Ireland, may, on the application by summons of any judgment creditor of a partner, make an order charging that partner's interest in the partnership property and profits with payment of the amount of the judgment debt and interest thereon, and may by the same or a subsequent order appoint a receiver of that partner's share of profits (whether already declared or accruing), and of any other money which may be coming to him in respect of the partnership, and direct all accounts and inquiries, and give all other orders and directions which might have been directed or given if the charge had been made in favour of the judgment creditor by the partner, or which the circumstances of the case may require.

(3) The other partner or partners shall be at liberty at any time to redeem the interest charged, or in case of a sale being directed, to purchase the same.

(4) …

(5) This section shall not apply to Scotland.

24 Rules as to interests and duties of partners subject to special agreement

The interests of partners in the partnership property and their rights and duties in relation to the partnership shall be determined, subject to any agreement express or implied between the partners, by the following rules:

(1) All the partners are entitled to share equally in the capital and profits of the business, and must contribute equally towards the losses whether of capital or otherwise sustained by the firm.

(2) The firm must indemnify every partner in respect of payments made and personal liabilities incurred by him—

   (a) In the ordinary and proper conduct of the business of the firm; or,

   (b) In or about anything necessarily done for the preservation of the business or property of the firm.

(3) A partner making, for the purpose of the partnership, any actual payment or advance beyond the amount of capital which he has agreed to subscribe, is entitled to interest at the rate of five per cent. per annum from the date of the payment or advance.

(4) A partner is not entitled, before the ascertainment of profits, to interest on the capital subscribed by him.

(5) Every partner may take part in the management of the partnership business.
(6) No partner shall be entitled to remuneration for acting in the partnership business.
(7) No person may be introduced as a partner without the consent of all existing partners.
(8) Any difference arising as to ordinary matters connected with the partnership business may be decided by a majority of the partners, but no change may be made in the nature of the partnership business without the consent of all existing partners.
(9) The partnership books are to be kept at the place of business of the partnership (or the principal place, if there is more than one), and every partner may, when he thinks fit, have access to and inspect and copy any of them.

25 Expulsion of partner

No majority of the partners can expel any partner unless a power to do so has been conferred by express agreement between the partners.

26 Retirement from partnership at will

(1) Where no fixed term has been agreed upon for the duration of the partnership, any partner may determine the partnership at any time on giving notice of his intention so to do to all the other partners.
(2) Where the partnership has originally been constituted by deed, a notice in writing, signed by the partner giving it, shall be sufficient for this purpose.

27 Where partnership for term is continued over, continuance on old terms presumed

(1) Where a partnership entered into for a fixed term is continued after the term has expired, and without any express new agreement, the rights and duties of the partners remain the same as they were at the expiration of the term, so far as is consistent with the incidents of a partnership at will.
(2) A continuance of the business by the partners or such of them as habitually acted therein during the term, without any settlement or liquidation of the partnership affairs, is presumed to be a continuance of the partnership.

28 Duty of partners to render accounts, etc.

Partners are bound to render true accounts and full information of all things affecting the partnership to any partner or his legal representatives.

29 Accountability of partners for private profits

(1) Every partner must account to the firm for any benefit derived by him without the consent of the other partners from any transaction concerning the partnership, or from any use by him of the partnership property name or business connexion.
(2) This section applies also to transactions undertaken after a partnership has been dissolved by the death of a partner, and before the affairs thereof have been completely wound up, either by any surviving partner or by the representatives of the deceased partner.

30 Duty of partner not to compete with firm

If a partner, without the consent of the other partners, carries on any business of the same nature as and competing with that of the firm, he must account for and pay over to the firm all profits made by him in that business.

31 Rights of assignee of share in partnership

(1) An assignment by any partner of his share in the partnership, either absolute or by way of mortgage or redeemable charge, does not, as against the other partners, entitle the assignee, during the continuance of the partnership, to interfere in the management or administration of the partnership business or affairs, or to require any accounts of the partnership transactions, or to inspect the partnership books, but entitles the assignee only to receive the share of profits to which the assigning partner would otherwise be entitled, and the assignee must accept the account of profits agreed to by the partners.
(2) In case of a dissolution of the partnership, whether as respects all the partners or as respects the assigning partner, the assignee is entitled to receive the share of the partnership assets to which the assigning partner is entitled as between himself and the other partners, and, for the purpose of ascertaining that share, to an account as from the date of the dissolution.

Dissolution of Partnership, and its consequences

32 Dissolution by expiration or notice

Subject to any agreement between the partners, a partnership is dissolved—

(a) If entered into for a fixed term, by the expiration of that term:

(b) If entered into for a single adventure or undertaking, by the termination of that adventure or undertaking:

(c) If entered into for an undefined time, by any partner giving notice to the other or others of his intention to dissolve the partnership.

In the last-mentioned case the partnership is dissolved as from the date mentioned in the notice as the date of dissolution, or, if no date is so mentioned, as from the date of the communication of the notice.

33 Dissolution by bankruptcy, death, or charge

(1) Subject to any agreement between the partners, every partnership is dissolved as regards all the partners by the death or bankruptcy of any partner.

(2) A partnership may, at the option of the other partners, be dissolved if any partner suffers his share of the partnership property to be charged under this Act for his separate debt.

34 Dissolution by illegality of partnership

A partnership is in every case dissolved by the happening of any event which makes it unlawful for the business of the firm to be carried on or for the members of the firm to carry it on in partnership.

35 Dissolution by the Court

On application by a partner the Court may decree a dissolution of the partnership in any of the following cases:

(a) When a partner is found lunatic by inquisition, or in Scotland by cognition, or is shown to the satisfaction of the Court to be of permanently unsound mind, in either of which cases the application may be made as well on behalf of that partner by his committee or next friend or person having title to intervene as by any other partner:

(b) When a partner, other than the partner suing, becomes in any other way permanently incapable of performing his part of the partnership contract:

(c) When a partner, other than the partner suing, has been guilty of such conduct as, in the opinion of the Court, regard being had to the nature of the business, is calculated to prejudicially affect the carrying on of the business:

(d) When a partner, other than the partner suing, wilfully or persistently commits a breach of the partnership agreement, or otherwise so conducts himself in matters relating to the partnership business that it is not reasonably practicable for the other partner or partners to carry on the business in partnership with him:

(e) When the business of the partnership can only be carried on at a loss:

(f) Whenever in any case circumstances have arisen which, in the opinion of the Court, render it just and equitable that the partnership be dissolved.

Note: Paragraph (a) has been repealed in relation to England and Wales.

36 Rights of persons dealing with firm against apparent members of firm

(1) Where a person deals with a firm after a change in its constitution he is entitled to treat all apparent members of the old firm as still being members of the firm until he has notice of the change.

(2) An advertisement in the London Gazette as to a firm whose principal place of business is in England or Wales, in the Edinburgh Gazette as to a firm whose principal place of business is in Scotland, and in the Belfast Gazette as to a firm whose principal place of business is in Ireland, shall be notice as to persons who had not dealings with the firm before the date of the dissolution or change so advertised.

(3) The estate of a partner who dies, or who becomes bankrupt, or of a partner who, not having been known to the person dealing with the firm to be a partner, retires from the firm, is not liable for partnership debts contracted after the date of the death, bankruptcy, or retirement respectively.

37 Right of partners to notify dissolution

On the dissolution of a partnership or retirement of a partner any partner may publicly notify the same, and may require the other partner or partners to concur for that purpose in all necessary or proper acts, if any, which cannot be done without his or their concurrence.

38 Continuing authority of partners for purposes of winding up

After the dissolution of a partnership the authority of each partner to bind the firm, and the other rights and obligations of the partners, continue notwithstanding the dissolution so far as may be necessary to wind up the affairs of the partnership, and to complete transactions begun but unfinished at the time of the dissolution, and in relation to any prosecution of the partnership by virtue of section 1 of the Partnerships (Prosecution) (Scotland) Act 2013 but not otherwise.

Provided that the firm is in no case bound by the acts of a partner who has become bankrupt; but this proviso does not affect the liability of any person who has after the bankruptcy represented himself or knowingly suffered himself to be represented as a partner of the bankrupt.

39 Rights of partners as to application of partnership property

On the dissolution of a partnership every partner is entitled, as against the other partners in the firm, and all persons claiming through them in respect of their interests as partners, to have the property of the partnership applied in payment of the debts and liabilities of the firm, and to have the surplus assets after such payment applied in payment of what may be due to the partners respectively after deducting what may be due from them as partners to the firm; and for that purpose any partner or his representatives may on the termination of the partnership apply to the Court to wind up the business and affairs of the firm.

40 Apportionment of premium where partnership prematurely dissolved

Where one partner has paid a premium to another on entering into a partnership for a fixed term, and the partnership is dissolved before the expiration of that term otherwise than by the death of a partner, the Court may order the repayment of the premium, or of such part thereof as it thinks just, having regard to the terms of the partnership contract and to the length of time during which the partnership has continued; unless

(a) the dissolution is, in the judgment of the Court, wholly or chiefly due to the misconduct of the partner who paid the premium, or

(b) the partnership has been dissolved by an agreement containing no provision for a return of any part of the premium.

41 Rights where partnership dissolved for fraud or misrepresentation

Where a partnership contract is rescinded on the ground of the fraud or misrepresentation of one of the parties thereto, the party entitled to rescind is, without prejudice to any other right, entitled—

(a) to a lien on, or right of retention of, the surplus of the partnership assets, after satisfying the partnership liabilities, for any sum of money paid by him for the purchase of a share in the partnership and for any capital contributed by him, and is

(b) to stand in the place of the creditors of the firm for any payments made by him in respect of the partnership liabilities, and

(c) to be indemnified by the person guilty of the fraud or making the representation against all the debts and liabilities of the firm.

42 Right of out-going partner in certain cases to share profits made after dissolution

(1) Where any member of a firm has died or otherwise ceased to be a partner, and the surviving or continuing partners carry on the business of the firm with its capital or assets without any final settlement of accounts as between the firm and the outgoing partner or his estate, then, in the absence of any agreement to the contrary, the outgoing partner or his estate is entitled at the option of himself or his representatives to such share of the profits made since the dissolution as the Court may find to be attributable to the use of his share of the partnership assets, or to interest at the rate of five per cent. per annum on the amount of his share of the partnership assets.

(2) Provided that where by the partnership contract an option is given to surviving or continuing partners to purchase the interest of a deceased or outgoing partner, and that option is duly exercised, the estate of the deceased partner, or the outgoing partner or his estate, as the case may be, is not entitled to any further or other share of profits; but

if any partner assuming to act in exercise of the option does not in all material respects comply with the terms thereof, he is liable to account under the foregoing provisions of this section.

43 Retiring or deceased partner's share to be a debt

Subject to any agreement between the partners, the amount due from surviving or continuing partners to an outgoing partner or the representatives of a deceased partner in respect of the outgoing or deceased partner's share is a debt accruing at the date of the dissolution or death.

44 Rule for distribution of assets on final settlement of accounts

In settling accounts between the partners after a dissolution of partnership, the following rules shall, subject to any agreement, be observed:

(a) Losses, including losses and deficiencies of capital, shall be paid first out of profits, next out of capital, and lastly, if necessary, by the partners individually in the proportion in which they were entitled to share profits:

(b) The assets of the firm including the sums, if any, contributed by the partners to make up losses or deficiencies of capital, shall be applied in the following manner and order:

1 In paying the debts and liabilities of the firm to persons who are not partners therein:

2 In paying to each partner rateably what is due from the firm to him for advances as distinguished from capital:

3 In paying to each partner rateably what is due from the firm to him in respect of capital:

4 The ultimate residue, if any, shall be divided among the partners in the proportion in which profits are divisible.

Supplemental

45 Definitions of "court" and "business"

In this Act, unless the contrary intention appears,—

The expression "court" includes every court and judge having jurisdiction in the case:

The expression "business" includes every trade, occupation, or profession.

46 Saving for rules of equity and common law

The rules of equity and of common law applicable to partnership shall continue in force except so far as they are inconsistent with the express provisions of this Act.

47 Provision as to bankruptcy in Scotland

(1) In the application of this Act to Scotland the bankruptcy of a firm or of an individual shall mean sequestration under the Bankruptcy (Scotland) Acts, and also in the case of an individual the issue against him of a decree of cessio bonorum.

(2) Nothing in this Act shall alter the rules of the law of Scotland relating to the bankruptcy of a firm or of the individual partners thereof.

48, 49 ...

50 Short title

This Act may be cited as the Partnership Act 1890.

...

LIMITED PARTNERSHIPS ACT 1907
(1907, c. 23)

1 Short title

This Act may be cited for all purposes as the Limited Partnerships Act 1907.

2 ...

3 Interpretation of terms

In the construction of this Act the following words and expressions shall have the meanings respectively assigned to them in this section, unless there be something in the subject or context repugnant to such construction:—

"Firm," "firm name," and "business" have the same meanings as in the Partnership Act 1890:
"General partner" shall mean any partner who is not a limited partner as defined by this Act.

4 Definition and constitution of limited partnership

(1) Limited partnerships may be formed in the manner and subject to the conditions by this Act provided.

(2) A limited partnership must consist of one or more persons called general partners, who shall be liable for all debts and obligations of the firm, and one or more persons to be called limited partners, who shall at the time of entering into such partnership contribute thereto a sum or sums as capital or property valued at a stated amount, and who shall not be liable for the debts or obligations of the firm beyond the amount so contributed.

(3) A limited partner shall not during the continuance of the partnership, either directly or indirectly, draw out or receive back any part of his contribution, and if he does so draw out or receive back any such part shall be liable for the debts and obligations of the firm up to the amount so drawn out or received back.

(4) A body corporate may be a limited partner.

5 Registration of limited partnership required

Every limited partnership must be registered as such in accordance with the provisions of this Act.

6 Modifications of general law in case of limited partnerships

(1) A limited partner shall not take part in the management of the partnership business, and shall not have power to bind the firm:
Provided that a limited partner may by himself or his agent at any time inspect the books of the firm and examine into the state and prospects of the partnership business, and may advise with the partners thereon.
If a limited partner takes part in the management of the partnership business he shall be liable for all debts and obligations of the firm incurred while he so takes part in the management as though he were a general partner.

(2) A limited partnership shall not be dissolved by the death or bankruptcy of a limited partner, and the lunacy of a limited partner shall not be a ground for dissolution of the partnership by the court unless the lunatic's share cannot be otherwise ascertained and realised.

(3) In the event of the dissolution of a limited partnership its affairs shall be wound up by the general partners unless the court otherwise orders.

(4) ...

(5) Subject to any agreement expressed or implied between the partners—
   (a) Any difference arising as to ordinary matters connected with the partnership business may be decided by a majority of the general partners;
   (b) A limited partner may, with the consent of the general partners, assign his share in the partnership, and upon such an assignment the assignee shall become a limited partner with all the rights of the assignor;
   (c) The other partners shall not be entitled to dissolve the partnership by reason of any limited partner suffering his share to be charged for his separate debt;
   (d) A person may be introduced as a partner without the consent of the existing limited partners;
   (e) A limited partner shall not be entitled to dissolve the partnership by notice.

7 Law as to private partnerships to apply where not excluded by this Act

Subject to the provisions of this Act, the Partnership Act 1890, and the rules of equity and of common law applicable to partnerships, except so far as they are inconsistent with the express provisions of the last-mentioned Act, shall apply to limited partnerships.

8 Duty to register

The registrar shall register a limited partnership if an application is made to the registrar in accordance with section 8A.

8A Application for registration

(1) An application for registration must—
   (a) specify the firm name, complying with section 8B, under which the limited partnership is to be registered,

(b) contain the details listed in subsection (2),
(c) be signed or otherwise authenticated by or on behalf of each partner, and
(d) be made to the registrar for the part of the United Kingdom in which the principal place of business of the limited partnership is to be situated.

(2) The required details are—
(a) the general nature of the partnership business,
(b) the name of each general partner,
(c) the name of each limited partner,
(d) the amount of the capital contribution of each limited partner (and whether the contribution is paid in cash or in another specified form),
(e) the address of the proposed principal place of business of the limited partnership, and
(f) the term (if any) for which the limited partnership is to be entered into (beginning with the date of registration).

8B Name of limited partnership

(1) This section sets out conditions which must be satisfied by the firm name of a limited partnership as specified in the application for registration.

(2) The name must end with—
(a) the words "limited partnership" (upper or lower case, or any combination), or
(b) the abbreviation "LP" (upper or lower case, or any combination, with or without punctuation).

(3) But if the principal place of business of a limited partnership is to be in Wales, its firm name may end with—
(a) the words "partneriaeth cyfyngedig" (upper or lower case, or any combination), or
(b) the abbreviation "PC" (upper or lower case, or any combination, with or without punctuation).

8C Certificate of registration

(1) On registering a limited partnership the registrar shall issue a certificate of registration.

(2) The certificate must be—
(a) signed by the registrar, or
(b) authenticated with the registrar's seal.

(3) The certificate must state—
(a) the firm name of the limited partnership given in the application for registration,
(b) the limited partnership's registration number,
(c) the date of registration, and
(d) that the limited partnership is registered as a limited partnership under this Act.

(4) The certificate is conclusive evidence that a limited partnership came into existence on the date of registration.

9 Registration of changes in partnerships

(1) If during the continuance of a limited partnership any change is made or occurs in—
(a) the firm name,
(b) the general nature of the business,
(c) the principal place of business,
(d) the partners or the name of any partner,
(e) the term of character of the partnership,
(f) the sum contributed by any limited partner,
(g) the liability of any partner by reason of his becoming a limited instead of a general partner or a general instead of a limited partner,

a statement, signed by the firm, specifying the nature of the change, shall within seven days be sent by post or delivered to the registrar.

(2) If default is made in compliance with the requirements of this section each of the general partners shall, on conviction under the Magistrates' Courts Act 1952, be liable to a fine not exceeding one pound for each day during which the default continues.

10 Advertisement in Gazette of statement of general partner becoming a limited partner and of assignment of share of limited partner

(1) Notice of any arrangement or transaction under which any person will cease to be a general partner in any firm, and will become a limited partner in that firm, or under which the share of a limited partner in a firm will be assigned to any person, shall be forthwith advertised in the Gazette, and until notice of the arrangement or transaction is so advertised the arrangement or transaction shall, for the purposes of this Act, be deemed to be of no effect.

(2) For the purposes of this section, the expression "the Gazette" means —
In the case of a limited partnership registered in England, the London Gazette;
In the case of a limited partnership registered in Scotland, the Edinburgh Gazette;
In the case of a limited partnership registered in Northern Ireland , the Belfast Gazette .

11 ...

12 ...

13 Registrar to file statement and issue certificate of registration

On receiving any statement made in pursuance of this Act the registrar shall cause the same to be filed, and he shall send by post to the firm from whom such statement shall have been received a certificate of the registration thereof.

14 Register and index to be kept

The registrar shall keep, in proper books to be provided for the purpose, a register and an index of all the limited partnerships registered as aforesaid, and of all the statements registered in relation to such partnerships.

15 The registrar

(1) The registrar of companies is the registrar of limited partnerships.

(2) In this Act—

- (a) references to the registrar in relation to the registration of a limited partnership are to the registrar to whom the application for registration is to be made (see section 8A(1)(d));
- (b) references to registration in a particular part of the United Kingdom are to registration by the registrar for that part of the United Kingdom;
- (c) references to the registrar in relation to any other matter relating to a limited partnership are to the registrar for the part of the United Kingdom in which the partnership is registered.

16 Inspection of statements registered

(1) Any person may inspect the statements filed by the registrar; and any person may require a certificate of the registration of any limited partnership, or a copy of or extract from any registered statement, to be certified by the registrar.

(2) A certificate of registration, or a copy of or extract from any statement registered under this Act, if duly certified to be a true copy under the hand of the registrar (whom it shall not be necessary to prove to be the registrar) shall, in all legal proceedings, civil or criminal, and in all cases whatsoever be received in evidence.

17 Power to Board of Trade to make rules

The Board of Trade may make rules concerning any of the following matters:—

- (a) ...
- (b) The duties or additional duties to be performed by the registrar for the purposes of this Act;
- (c) The performance by assistant registrars and other officers of acts by this Act required to be done by the registrar;
- (d) The forms to be used for the purposes of this Act;
- (e) Generally the conduct and regulation of registration under this Act and any matters incidental thereto.

COMPANIES ACT 1985
(1985, c. 6)

PART XIV

INVESTIGATION OF COMPANIES AND THEIR AFFAIRS; REQUISITION OF DOCUMENTS

Appointment and functions of inspectors

431 Investigation of a company on its own application or that of its members

(1) The Secretary of State may appoint one or more competent inspectors to investigate the affairs of a company and to report the result of their investigations to him.

(2) The appointment may be made—

(a) in the case of a company having a share capital, on the application either of not less than 200 members or of members holding not less than one-tenth of the shares issued (excluding any shares held as treasury shares),

(b) in the case of a company not having a share capital, on the application of not less than one-fifth in number of the persons on the company's register of members, and

(c) in any case, on application of the company.

(3) The application shall be supported by such evidence as the Secretary of State may require for the purpose of showing that the applicant or applicants have good reason for requiring the investigation.

(4) The Secretary of State may, before appointing inspectors, require the applicant or applicants to give security, to an amount not exceeding £5,000, or such other sum as he may by order specify, for payment of the costs of the investigation.

An order under this subsection shall be made by statutory instrument subject to annulment in pursuance of a resolution of either House of Parliament.

432 Other company investigations

(1) The Secretary of State shall appoint one or more competent inspectors to investigate the affairs of a company and report the result of their investigations to him, if the court by order declares that its affairs out to be so investigated.

(2) The Secretary of State may make such an appointment if it appears to him that there are circumstances suggesting—

(a) that the company's affairs are being or have been conducted with intent to defraud its creditors or the creditors of any other person, or otherwise for a fraudulent or unlawful purpose, or in a manner which is unfairly prejudicial to some part of its members, or

(b) that any actual or proposed act or omission of the company (including an act or omission on its behalf) is or would be so prejudicial, or that the company was formed for any fraudulent or unlawful purpose, or

(c) that persons concerned with the company's formation or the management of its affairs have in connection therewith been guilty of fraud, misfeasance or other misconduct towards it or towards its members, or

(d) that the company's members have not been given all the information with respect to its affairs which they might reasonably expect.

(2A) Inspectors may be appointed under subsection (2) on terms that any report they may make is not for publication; and in such a case, the provisions of section 437(3) (availability and publication of inspectors' reports) do not apply.

(3) Subsections (1) and (2) are without prejudice to the powers of the Secretary of State under section 431; and the power conferred by subsection (2) is exercisable with respect to a body corporate notwithstanding that it is in course of being voluntarily wound up.

(4) The reference in subsection (2)(a) to a company's members includes any person who is not a member but to whom shares in the company have been transferred or transmitted by operation of law.

433 Inspectors' powers during investigation

(1) If inspectors appointed under section 431 or 432 to investigate the affairs of a company think it necessary for the purposes of their investigation to investigate also the affairs of another body corporate which is or at any relevant time has been the company's subsidiary

or holding company, or a subsidiary of its holding company or a holding company of its subsidiary, they have power to do so; and they shall report on the affairs of the other body corporate so far as they think that the results of their investigation of its affairs are relevant to the investigation of the affairs of the company first mentioned above.

...

434 Production of documents and evidence to inspectors

(1) When inspectors are appointed under section 431 or 432, it is the duty of all officers and agents of the company, and of all officers and agents of any other body corporate whose affairs are investigated under section 433(1)—

(a) to produce to the inspectors all documents of or relating to the company or, as the case may be, the other body corporate which are in their custody or power,

(b) to attend before the inspectors when required to do so, and

(c) otherwise to give the inspectors all assistance in connection with the investigation which they are reasonably able to give.

(2) If the inspectors consider that an officer or agent of the company or other body corporate, or any other person, is or may be in possession of information relating to a matter which they believe to be relevant to the investigation, they may require him—

(a) to produce to them any documents in his custody or power relating to that matter,

(b) to attend before them, and

(c) otherwise to give them all assistance in connection with the investigation which he is reasonably able to give; and it is that person's duty to comply with the requirement.

(3) An inspector may for the purposes of the investigation examine any person on oath, and may administer an oath accordingly.

(4) In this section a reference to officers or to agents includes past, as well as present, officers or agents (as the case may be); and "agents", in relation to a company or other body corporate, includes its bankers and solicitors and persons employed by it as auditors, whether these persons are or are not officers of the company or other body corporate.

(5) An answer given by a person to a question put to him in exercise of powers conferred by this section (whether as it has effect in relation to an investigation under any of sections 431 to 433, or as applied by any other section in this Part) may be used in evidence against him.

(5A) However, in criminal proceedings in which that person is charged with an offence to which this subsection applies—

(a) no evidence relating to the answer may be adduced, and

(b) no question relating to it may be asked,

by or on behalf of the prosecution, unless evidence relating to it is adduced, or a question relating to it is asked, in the proceedings by or on behalf of that person.

(5B) Subsection (5A) applies to any offence other than—

(a) an offence under section 2 or 5 of the Perjury Act 1911 (false statements made on oath otherwise than in judicial proceedings or made otherwise than on oath);

(b) an offence under section 44(1) or (2) of the Criminal Law (Consolidation) (Scotland) Act 1995 (false statements made on oath or otherwise than on oath); or

(c) an offence under Article 7 or 10 of the Pejury (Northern Ireland) Order 1979 (false statements made on oath otherwise than in judicial proceedings or made otherwise than on oath).

(6) In this section "document" includes information recorded in any form.

(7) The power under this section to require production of a document includes power, in the case of a document not in hard copy form, to require the production of a copy of the document—

(a) in hard copy form, or

(b) in a form from which a hard copy can be readily obtained.

(8) An inspector may take copies of or extracts from a document produced in pursuance of this section.

433 ...

436 Obstruction of inspectors treated as contempt of court

(1) If any person—

(a) fails to comply with section 434(1)(a) or (c),

(b) refuses to comply with a requirement under section 434(1)(b) or (2), or

(c) refuses to answer any question put to him by the inspectors for the purposes of the investigation,

the inspectors may certify that fact in writing to the court.

(3) The court may thereupon enquire into the case; and, after hearing any witnesses who may be produced against or on behalf of the alleged offender and after hearing any statement which may be offered in defence, the court may punish the offender in like manner as if he had been guilty of contempt of the court.

437 Inspectors' reports

(1) The inspectors may, and if so directed by the Secretary of State shall, make interim reports to the Secretary of State, and on the conclusion of their investigation shall make a final report to him.

(1A) Any persons who have been appointed under section 431 or 432 may at any time and, if the Secretary of State directs them to do so, shall inform him of any matters coming to their knowledge as a result of their investigations.

(2) If the inspectors were appointed under section 432 in pursuance of an order of the court, the Secretary of State shall furnish a copy of any report of theirs to the court.

(2A) If the company is registered under the Companies Act 2006 in Northern Ireland, the Secretary of State must send a copy of any interim or final report by the inspectors to the Department of Enterprise, Trade and Investment in Northern Ireland.

(3) In any case the Secretary of State may, if he thinks fit—

(a) forward a copy of any report made by the inspectors to the company's registered office,

(b) furnish a copy on request and on payment of the prescribed fee to—

(i) any member of the company or other body corporate which is the subject of the report,

(ii) any person whose conduct is referred to in the report,

(iii) the auditors of that company or body corporate,

(iv) the applicants for the investigation,

(v) any other person whose financial interests appear to the Secretary of State to be affected by the matters dealt with in the report, whether as a creditor of the company or body corporate, or otherwise, and

(c) cause any such report to be printed and published.

438 ...

439 Expenses of investigating a company's affairs

(1) The expenses of an investigation under any of the powers conferred by this Part shall be defrayed in the first instance by the Secretary of State, but he may recover those expenses from the persons liable in accordance with this section.

There shall be treated as expenses of the investigation, in particular, such reasonable sums as the Secretary of State may determine in respect of general staff costs and overheads.

(2) A person who is convicted on a prosecution instituted as a result of the investigation may in the same proceedings be ordered to pay those expenses to such extent as may be specified in the order.

(3) ...

(4) A body corporate dealt with by an inspectors' report, where the inspectors were appointed otherwise than of the Secretary of State's own motion, is liable except where it was the applicant for the investigation, and except so far as the Secretary of State otherwise directs.

(5) Where inspectors were appointed—

(a) under section 431, or

(b) on an application under section 442(3),

the applicant or applicants for the investigation is or are liable to such extent (if any) as the Secretary of State may direct.

(6) The report of inspectors appointed otherwise than of the Secretary of State's own motion may, if they think fit, and shall if the Secretary of State so directs, include a recommendation as to the directions (if any) which they think appropriate, in the light of their investigation, to be given under subsection (4) or (5) of this section.

...

(8) Any liability to repay the Secretary of State imposed by subsection (2) above is (subject to satisfaction of his right to repayment) a liability also to indemnify all persons against liability under subsections (4) and (5).

(9) A person liable under any one of those subsections is entitled to contribution from any other person liable under the same subsection, according to the amount of their respective liabilities under it.

(10) Expenses to be defrayed by the Secretary of State under this section shall, so far as not recovered under it, be paid out of money provided by Parliament.

440 ...

441 Inspectors' report to be evidence

(1) A copy of any report of inspectors appointed under this Part, certified by the Secretary of State to be a true copy, is admissible in any legal proceedings as evidence of the opinion of the inspectors in relation to any matter contained in the report and, in proceedings on an application under section 8 of the Company Directors Disqualification Act 1986 or Article 11 of the Company Directors Disqualification (Northern Ireland) Order 2002, as evidence of any fact stated therein.

(2) A document purporting to be such a certificate as is mentioned above shall be received in evidence and be deemed to be such a certificate, unless the contrary is proved.

Other powers of investigation available to the Secretary of State

442 Power to investigate company ownership

(1) Where it appears to the Secretary of State that there is good reason to do so, he may appoint one or more competent inspectors to investigate and report on the membership of any company, and otherwise with respect to the company, for the purpose of determining the true persons who are or have been financially interested in the success or failure (real or apparent) of the company or able to control or materially to influence its policy.

...

(3) If an application for investigation under this section with respect to particular shares or debentures of a company is made to the Secretary of State by members of the company, and the number of applicants or the amount of shares held by them is not less than that required for an application for the appointment of inspectors under section 431(2)(a) or (b), then, subject to the following provisions, the Secretary of State shall appoint inspectors to conduct the investigation applied for.

(3A) The Secretary of State shall not appoint inspectors if he is satisfied that the application is vexatious; and where inspectors are appointed their terms of appointment shall exclude any matter in so far as the Secretary of State is satisfied that it is unreasonable for it to be investigated.

(3B) The Secretary of State may, before appointing inspectors, require the applicant or applicants to give security, to an amount not exceeding £5,000, or such other sum as he may by order specify, for payment of the costs of the investigation.
An order under this subsection shall be made by statutory instrument which shall be subject to annulment in pursuance of a resolution of either House of Parliament.

(3C) If on an application under subsection (3) it appears to the Secretary of State that the powers conferred by section 444 are sufficient for the purposes of investigating the matters which inspectors would be appointed to investigate, he may instead conduct the investigation under that section.

(4) Subject to the terms of their appointment, the inspectors' powers extend to the investigation of any circumstances suggesting the existance of an arrangement or understanding which, though not legally binding, is or was observed or likely to be observed in practice and which is relevant to the purposes of the investigation.

443 Provisions applicable on investigation under section 442

(1) For purposes of an investigation under section 442, sections 433(1), 434, 436 and 437 apply with the necessary modifications of references to the affairs of the company or to those of any other body corporate, subject however to the following subsections.

(2) Those sections apply to—

(a) all persons who are or have been, or whom the inspector has reasonable cause to believe to be or have been, financially interested in the success or failure or the apparent success or failure of the company or any other body corporate whose membership is investigated with that of the company, or able to control or materially influence its policy (including persons concerned only on behalf of others), and

(b) any other person whom the inspector has reasonable cause to believe possesses information relevant to the investigation,

as they apply in relation to officers and agents of the company or the other body corporate (as the case may be).

(3) If the Secretary of State is of opinion that there is good reason for not divulging any part of a report made by virtue of section 442 and this section, he may under section 437 disclose the report with the omission of that part; and he may cause to be kept by the registrar of companies a copy of the report with that part omitted or, in the case of any other such report, a copy of the whole report.

444 Power to obtain information as to those interested in shares, etc.

(1) If it appears to the Secretary of State that there is good reason to investigate the ownership of any shares in or debentures of a company and that it is unnecessary to appoint inspectors for the purpose, he may require any person whom he has reasonable cause to believe to have or to be able to obtain any information as to the present and past interests in those shares or debentures and the names and addresses of the persons interested and of any persons who act or have acted on their behalf in relation to the shares or debentures to give any such information to the Secretary of State.

(2) For this purpose a person is deemed to have an interest in shares or debentures if he has any right to acquire or dispose of them or of any interest in them, or to vote in respect of them, or if his consent is necessary for the exercise of any of the rights of other persons interested in them, or if other persons interested in them can be required, or are accustomed, to exercise their rights in accordance with his instructions.

(3) A person who fails to give information required of him under this section, or who in giving such information makes any statement which he knows to be false in a material particular, or recklessly makes any statement which is false in a material particular, commits an offence.

(4) A person guilty of an offence under this section is liable—

(a) on conviction on indictment, to imprisonment for a term not exceeding two years or a fine (or both);

(b) on summary conviction—

(i) in England and Wales, to imprisonment for a term not exceeding twelve months or to a fine not exceeding the statutory maximum (or both) and, for continued contravention, a daily default fine not exceeding one- fiftieth of the greater of £5,000 or the amount corresponding to level 4 on the standard scale for summary offences;

(ii) in Scotland or Northern Ireland, to imprisonment for a term not exceeding six months, or to a fine not exceeding the statutory maximum (or both) and, for continued contravention, a daily default fine not exceeding one-fiftieth of the statutory maximum.

445 Power to impose restrictions on shares and debentures

(1) If in connection with an investigation under either section 442 or 444 it appears to the Secretary of State that there is difficulty in finding out the relevant facts about any shares (whether issued or to be issued), he may by order direct that the shares shall until further order be subject to the restrictions of Part XV of this Act.

(1A) If the Secretary of State is satisfied that an order under subsection (1) may unfairly affect the rights of third parties in respect of shares then the Secretary of State, for the purpose of protecting such rights and subject to such terms as he thinks fit, may direct that such acts by such persons or descriptions of persons and for such purposes as may be set out in the order, shall not constitute a breach of the restrictions of Part XV of this Act.

(2) This section, and Part XV in its application to orders under it, apply in relation to debentures as in relation to shares save that subsection (1A) shall not so apply.

446 …

446A General powers to give directions

(1) In exercising his functions an inspector shall comply with any direction given to him by the Secretary of State under this section.

(2) The Secretary of State may give an inspector appointed under section 431, 432(2) or 442(1) a direction—
  (a) as to the subject matter of his investigation (whether by reference to a specified area of a company's operation, a specified transaction, a period of time or otherwise), or
  (b) which requires the inspector to take or not to take a specified step in his investigation.

(3) The Secretary of State may give an inspector appointed under any provision of this Part a direction requiring him to secure that a specified report under section 437—
  (a) includes the inspector's views on a specified matter,
  (b) does not include any reference to a specified matter,
  (c) is made in a specified form or manner, or
  (d) is made by a specified date.

(4) A direction under this section—
  (a) may be given on an inspector's appointment,
  (b) may vary or revoke a direction previously given, and
  (c) may be given at the request of an inspector.

(5) In this section—
  (a) a reference to an inspector's investigation includes any investigation he undertakes, or could undertake, under section 433(1) (power to investigate affairs of holding company or subsidiary);
  (b) "specified" means specified in a direction under this section.

446B Direction to terminate investigation

(1) The Secretary of State may direct an inspector to take no further steps in his investigation.

(2) The Secretary of State may give a direction under this section to an inspector appointed under section 432(1) or 442(3) only on the grounds that it appears to him that—
  (a) matters have come to light in the course of the inspector's investigation which suggest that a criminal offence has been committed, and
  (b those matters have been referred to the appropriate prosecuting authority.

(3) Where the Secretary of State gives a direction under this section, any direction already given to the inspector under section 437(1) to produce an interim report, and any direction given to him under section 446A(3) in relation to such a report, shall cease to have effect.

(4) Where the Secretary of State gives a direction under this section, the inspector shall not make a final report to the Secretary of State unless—
  (a) the direction was made on the grounds mentioned in subsection (2) and the Secretary of State directs the inspector to make a final report to him, or
  (b) the inspector was appointed under section 432(1) (appointment in pursuance of order of the court).

(5) An inspector shall comply with any direction given to him under this section.

(6) In this section, a reference to an inspector's investigation includes any investigation he undertakes, or could undertake, under section 433(1) (power to investigate affairs of holding company or subsidiary).

Resignation, removal and replacement of inspectors

446C Resignation and revocation of appointment

(1) An inspector may resign by notice in writing to the Secretary of State.

(2) The Secretary of State may revoke the appointment of an inspector by notice in writing to the inspector.

446D Appointment of replacement inspectors

(1) Where—
  (a) an inspector resigns,
  (b) an inspector's appointment is revoked, or
  (c) an inspector dies,

the Secretary of State may appoint one or more competent inspectors to continue the investigation.

(2) An appointment under subsection (1) shall be treated for the purposes of this Part (apart from this section) as an appointment under the provision of this Part under which the former inspector was appointed.

(3) The Secretary of State must exercise his power under subsection (1) so as to secure that at least one inspector continues the investigation.

(4) Subsection (3) does not apply if—

(a) the Secretary of State could give any replacement inspector a direction under section 446B (termination of investigation), and

(b) such a direction would (under subsection (4) of that section) result in a final report not being made.

(5) In this section, references to an investigation include any investigation the former inspector conducted under section 433(1) (power to investigate affairs of holding company or subsidiary).

Power to obtain information from former inspectors etc.

446E Obtaining information from former inspectors etc.

(1) This section applies to a person who was appointed as an inspector under this Part—

(a) who has resigned, or

(b) whose appointment has been revoked.

(2) This section also applies to an inspector to whom the Secretary of State has given a direction under section 446B (termination of investigation).

(3) The Secretary of State may direct a person to whom this section applies to produce documents obtained or generated by that person during the course of his investigation to—

(a) the Secretary of State, or

(b) an inspector appointed under this Part.

(4) The power under subsection (3) to require production of a document includes power, in the case of a document not in hard copy form, to require the production of a copy of the document—

(a) in hard copy form, or

(b) in a form from which a hard copy can be readily obtained.

(5) The Secretary of State may take copies of or extracts from a document produced in pursuance of this section.

(6) The Secretary of State may direct a person to whom this section applies to inform him of any matters that came to that person's knowledge as a result of his investigation.

(7) A person shall comply with any direction given to him under this section.

(8) In this section—

(a) references to the investigation of a former inspector or inspector include any investigation he conducted under section 433(1) (power to investigate affairs of holding company or subsidiary), and

(b) "document" includes information recorded in any form.

447 Power to require production of documents

(1) The Secretary of State may act under subsections (2) and (3) in relation to a company.

(2) The Secretary of State may give directions to the company requiring it—

(a) to produce such documents (or documents of such description) as may be specified in the directions;

(b) to provide such information (or information of such description) as may be so specified.

(3) The Secretary of State may authorise a person (an investigator) to require the company or any other person—

(a) to produce such documents (or documents of such description) as the investigator may specify;

(b) to provide such information (or information of such description) as the investigator may specify.

(4) A person on whom a requirement under subsection (3) is imposed may require the investigator to produce evidence of his authority.

(5) A requirement under subsection (2) or (3) must be complied with at such time and place as may be specified in the directions or by the investigator (as the case may be).

(6) The production of a document in pursuance of this section does not affect any lien which a person has on the document.

(7) The Secretary of State or the investigator (as the case may be) may take copies of or extracts from a document produced in pursuance of this section.

(8) A "document" includes information recorded in any form.

(9) The power under this section to require production of a document includes power, in the case of a document not in hard copy form, to require the production of a copy of the document—

(a) in hard copy form, or

(b) in a form from which a hard copy can be readily obtained.

447A Information provided: evidence

(1) A statement made by a person in compliance with a requirement under section 447 may be used in evidence against him.

(2) But in criminal proceedings in which the person is charged with a relevant offence—

(a) no evidence relating to the statement may be adduced by or on behalf of the prosecution, and

(b) no question relating to it may be asked by or on behalf of the prosecution,

unless evidence relating to it is adduced or a question relating to it is asked in the proceedings by or on behalf of that person.

(3) A relevant offence is any offence other than the following––

(a) an offence under section 451,

(b) an offence under section 5 of the Perjury Act 1911 (false statement made otherwise than on oath),

(c) an offence under section 44(2) of the Criminal Law (Consolidation) (Scotland) Act 1995 (false statement made otherwise than on oath), or

(d) an offence under Article 10 of the Perjury (Northern Ireland) Order 1979 (false statements made otherwise than on oath).

448 Entry and search of premises

(1) A justice of the peace may issue a warrant under this section if satisfied on information on oath given by or on behalf of the Secretary of State, or by a person appointed or authorised to exercise powers under this Part, that there are reasonable grounds for believing that there are on any premises documents whose production has been required under this Part and which have not been produced in compliance with the requirement.

(2) A justice of the peace may also issue a warrant under this section if satisfied on information on oath given by or on behalf of the Secretary of State, or by a person appointed or authorised to exercise powers under this Part—

(a) that there are reasonable grounds for believing that an offence has been committed for which the penalty on conviction on indictment is imprisonment for a term of not less than two years and that there are on any premises documents relating to whether the offence has been committed,

(b) that the Secretary of State, or the person so appointed or authorised, has power to require the production of the documents under this Part, and

(c) that there are reasonable grounds for believing that if production was so required the documents would not be produced but would be removed from the premises, hidden, tampered with or destroyed.

(3) A warrant under this section shall authorise a constable, together with any other person named in it and any other constables—

(a) to enter the premises specified in the information, using such force as is reasonably necessary for the purpose;

(b) to search the premises and take possession of any documents appearing to be such documents as are mentioned in subsection (1) or (2), as the case may be, or to take, in relation to any such documents, any other steps which may appear to be necessary for preserving them or preventing interference with them;

(c) to take copies of any such documents; and

(d) to require any person named in the warrant to provide an explanation of them or to state where they may be found.

(4) If in the case of a warrant under subsection (2) the justice of the peace is satisfied on information on oath that there are reasonable grounds for believing that there are

also on the premises other documents relevant to the investigation, the warrant shall also authorise the actions mentioned in subsection (3) to be taken in relation to such documents.

(5) A warrant under this section shall continue in force until the end of the period of one month beginning with the day on which it is issued.

(6) Any documents of which possession is taken under this section may be retained—
(a) for a period of three months; or
(b) if within that period proceedings to which the documents are relevant are commenced against any person for any criminal offence, until the conclusion of those proceedings.

(7) Any person who intentionally obstructs the exercise of any rights conferred by a warrant issued under this section or fails without reasonable excuse to comply with any requirement imposed in accordance with subsection (3)(d) is guilty of an offence.

(7A) A person guilty of an offence under this section is liable—
(a) on conviction on indictment, to a fine;
(b) on summary conviction, to a fine not exceeding the statutory maximum.

(8) For the purposes of sections 449 and 451A (provision for security of information) documents obtained under this section shall be treated as if they had been obtained under the provision of this Part under which their production was or, as the case may be, could have been required.

(9) In the application of this section to Scotland for the references to a justice of the peace substitute references to a justice of the peace or a sheriff, and for the references to information on oath substitute references to evidence on oath.

(10) In this section "document" includes information recorded in any form.

448A Protection in relation to certain disclosures: information provided to Secretary of State

(1) A person who makes a relevant disclosure is not liable by reason only of that disclosure in any proceedings relating to a breach of an obligation of confidence.

(2) A relevant disclosure is a disclosure which satisfies each of the following conditions—
(a) it is made to the Secretary of State otherwise than in compliance with a requirement under this Part;
(b) it is of a kind that the person making the disclosure could be required to make in pursuance of this Part;
(c) the person who makes the disclosure does so in good faith and in the reasonable belief that the disclosure is capable of assisting the Secretary of State for the purposes of the exercise of his functions under this Part;
(d) the information disclosed is not more than is reasonably necessary for the purpose of assisting the Secretary of State for the purposes of the exercise of those functions;
(e) the disclosure is not one falling within subsection (3) or (4).

(3) A disclosure falls within this subsection if the disclosure is prohibited by virtue of any enactment whenever passed or made.

(4) A disclosure falls within this subsection if—
(a) it is made by a person carrying on the business of banking or by a lawyer, and
(b) it involves the disclosure of information in respect of which he owes an obligation of confidence in that capacity.

(5) In this section "enactment" has the meaning given by section 1293 of the Companies Act 2006.

449 Provision for security of information obtained

(1) This section applies to information (in whatever form) obtained—
(a) in pursuance of a requirement imposed under section 447;
(b) by means of a relevant disclosure within the meaning of section 448A(2);
(c) by an investigator in consequence of the exercise of his powers under section 453A.

(2) Such information must not be disclosed unless the disclosure—
(a) is made to a person specified in Schedule 15C, or
(b) is of a description specified in Schedule 15D.

(3) The Secretary of State may by order amend Schedules 15C and 15D.

(4) An order under subsection (3) must not—

(a) amend Schedule 15C by specifying a person unless the person exercises functions of a public nature (whether or not he exercises any other function);
(b) amend Schedule 15D by adding or modifying a description of disclosure unless the purpose for which the disclosure is permitted is likely to facilitate the exercise of a function of a public nature.

(5) An order under subsection (3) must be made by statutory instrument subject to annulment in pursuance of a resolution of either House of Parliament.

(6) A person who discloses any information in contravention of this section— is guilty of an offence.

(6A) A person guilty of an offence under this section is liable—
(a) on conviction on indictment, to imprisonment for a term not exceeding two years or a fine (or both);
(b) on summary conviction—
(i) in England and Wales, to imprisonment for a term not exceeding twelve months or to a fine not exceeding the statutory maximum (or both);
(ii) in Scotland or Northern Ireland, to imprisonment for a term not exceeding six months, or to a fine not exceeding the statutory maximum (or both).

...

(8) Any information which may by virtue of this section be disclosed to a person specified in Schedule 15C may be disclosed to any officer or employee of the person.

(9) This section does not prohibit the disclosure of information if the information is or has been available to the public from any other source.

(10) For the purposes of this section, information obtained by an investigator in consequence of the exercise of his powers under section 453A includes information obtained by a person accompanying the investigator in pursuance of subsection (4) of that section in consequence of that person's accompanying the investigator.

(11) Nothing in this section authorises the making of a disclosure in contravention of the Data Protection Act 1998.

450 Punishment for destroying, mutilating, etc. company documents

(1) An officer of a company who—
(a) destroys, mutilates or falsifies, or is privy to the destruction, mutilation or falsification of a document affecting, or relating to the company's property or affairs, or
(b) makes, or is privy to the making of, a false entry in such a document,

is guilty of an offence, unless he proves that he had no intention to conceal the state of affairs of the company or to defeat the law.

(1A) Subsection (1) applies to an officer of an authorised insurance company which is not a body corporate as it applies to an officer of a company.

(2) Such a person as above mentioned who fraudulently either parts with, alters or makes an omission in any such document or is privy to fraudulent parting with, fraudulent altering or fraudulent making of an omission in, any such document, is guilty of an offence.

(3) A person guilty of an offence under this section is liable—
(a) on conviction on indictment, to imprisonment for a term not exceeding seven years or a fine (or both);
(b) on summary conviction—
(i) in England and Wales, to imprisonment for a term not exceeding twelve months or to a fine not exceeding the statutory maximum (or both);
(ii) in Scotland or Northern Ireland, to imprisonment for a term not exceeding six months, or to a fine not exceeding the statutory maximum (or both).

...

(5) In this section "document" includes information recorded in any form.

451 Punishment for furnishing false information

(1) A person commits an offence if in purported compliance with a requirement under section 447 to provide information—
(a) he provides information which he knows to be false in a material particular;
(b) he recklessly provides information which is false in a material particular.

(2) A person guilty of an offence under this section is liable—
(a) on conviction on indictment, to imprisonment for a term not exceeding two years or a fine (or both);

(b) on summary conviction—
(i) in England and Wales, to imprisonment for a term not exceeding twelve months or to a fine not exceeding the statutory maximum (or both);
(ii) in Scotland or Northern Ireland, to imprisonment for a term not exceeding six months, or to a fine not exceeding the statutory maximum (or both).

451A Disclosure of information by Secretary of State or inspector

(1) This section applies to information obtained—
(a) under sections 434 to 446E;
(b) by an inspector in consequence of the exercise of his powers under section 453A.
(2) The Secretary of State may, if he thinks fit—
(a) disclose any information to which this section applies to any person to whom, or for any purpose for which, disclosure is permitted under section 449, or
(b) authorise or require an inspector appointed under this Part to disclose such information to any such person or for any such purpose.
(3) Information to which this section applies may also be disclosed by an inspector appointed under this Part to—
(a) another inspector appointed under this Part;
(b) a person appointed under—
(i) section 167 of the Financial Services and Markets Act 2000 (general investigations),
(ii) section 168 of that Act (investigations in particular cases),
(iii) section 169(1)(b) of that Act (investigation in support of overseas regulator);
(iv) section 284 of that Act (investigations into affairs of certain collective investment schemes), or
(v) regulations made as a result of section 262(2)(k) of that Act (investigations into open-ended investment companies),
to conduct an investigation; or
(c) a person authorised to exercise powers under—
(i) section 447 of this Act; or
(ii) section 84 of the Companies Act 1989 (exercise of powers to assist overseas regulatory authority).
(4) Any information which may by virtue of subsection (3) be disclosed to any person may be disclosed to any officer or servant of that person.
(5) The Secretary of State may, if he thinks fit, disclose any information obtained under section 444 to—
(a) the company whose ownership was the subject of the investigation,
(b) any member of the company,
(c) any person whose conduct was investigated in the course of the investigation,
(d) the auditors of the company, or
(e) any person whose financial interests appear to the Secretary of State to be affected by matters covered by the investigation.
(6) For the purposes of this section, information obtained by an inspector in consequence of the exercise of his powers under section 453A includes information obtained by a person accompanying the inspector in pursuance of subsection (4) of that section in consequence of that person's accompanying the inspector.
(7) The reference to an inspector in subsection (2)(b) above includes a reference to a person accompanying an inspector in pursuance of section 453A(4).

452 Privileged information

(1) Nothing in sections 431 to 446E compels the disclosure by any person to the Secretary of State or to an inspector appointed by him of information in respect of which in an action in the High Court a claim to legal professional privilege, or in an action in the Court of Session a claim to confidentiality of communications, could be maintained.
(1A) Nothing in section 434, 443 or 446 requires a person (except as mentioned in subsection (1B) below) to disclose information or produce documents in respect of which he owes an obligation of confidence by virtue of carrying on the business of banking unless—
(a) the person to whom the obligation of confidence is owed is the company or other body corporate under investigation,

(b) the person to whom the obligation of confidence is owed consents to the disclosure or production, or
(c) the making of the requirement is authorised by the Secretary of State.

(1B) Subsection (1A) does not apply where the person owing the obligation of confidence is the company or other body corporate under investigation under section 431, 432 or 433.

(2) Nothing in sections 447 to 451—
(a) compels the production by any person of a document or the disclosure by any person of information in respect of which in an action in the High Court a claim to legal professional privilege, or in an action in the Court of Session a claim to confidentiality of communications, could be maintained;
(b) authorises the taking of possession of any such document which is in the person's possession.

(3) The Secretary of State must not under section 447 require, or authorise a person to require—
(a) the production by a person carrying on the business of banking of a document relating to the affairs of a customer of his, or
(b) the disclosure by him of information relating to those affairs, unless one of the conditions in subsection (4) is met.

(4) The conditions are—
(a) the Secretary of State thinks it is necessary to do so for the purpose of investigating the affairs of the person carrying on the business of banking;
(b) the customer is a person on whom a requirement has been imposed under section 447;
(c) the customer is a person on whom a requirement to produce information or documents has been imposed by an investigator appointed by the Secretary of State in pursuance of section 171 or 173 of the Financial Services and Markets Act 2000 (powers of persons appointed under section 167 or as a result of section 168(2) to conduct an investigation).

(5) Despite subsections (1) and (2) a person who is a lawyer may be compelled to disclose the name and address of his client.

453 Investigation of overseas companies

(1) The provisions of this Part apply to bodies corporate incorporated outside Great Britain which are carrying on business in Great Britain, or have at any time carried on business there, as they apply to companies under this Act; but subject to the following exceptions, adaptations and modifications.

(1A) The following provisions do not apply to such bodies—
(a) section 431 (investigation on application of company or its members),
...
(c) sections 442 to 445 (investigation of company ownership and power to obtain information as to those interested in shares, &c.).

(1B) The other provisions of this Part apply to such bodies subject to such adaptations and modifications as may be specified by regulations made by the Secretary of State.

(2) Regulations under this section shall be made by statutory instrument subject to annulment in pursuance of a resolution of either House of Parliament.

453A Power to enter and remain on premises

(1) An inspector or investigator may act under subsection (2) in relation to a company if—
(a) he is authorised to do so by the Secretary of State, and
(b) he thinks that to do so will materially assist him in the exercise of his functions under this Part in relation to the company.

(2) An inspector or investigator may at all reasonable times—
(a) require entry to relevant premises, and
(b) remain there for such period as he thinks necessary for the purpose mentioned in subsection (1)(b).

(3) Relevant premises are premises which the inspector or investigator believes are used (wholly or partly) for the purposes of the company's business.

(4) In exercising his powers under subsection (2), an inspector or investigator may be accompanied by such other persons as he thinks appropriate.

(5) A person who intentionally obstructs a person lawfully acting under subsection (2) or (4) — is guilty of an offence.

(5A) A person guilty of an offence under this section is liable—
(a) on conviction on indictment, to a fine;
(b) on summary conviction, to a fine not exceeding the statutory maximum.

...

(7) An inspector is a person appointed under section 431, 432 or 442.
(8) An investigator is a person authorised for the purposes of section 447.

453B Power to enter and remain on premises: procedural

(1) This section applies for the purposes of section 453A.
(2) The requirements of subsection (3) must be complied with at the time an inspector or investigator seeks to enter relevant premises under section 453A(2)(a).
(3) The requirements are—
(a) the inspector or investigator must produce evidence of his identity and evidence of his appointment or authorisation (as the case may be);
(b) any person accompanying the inspector or investigator must produce evidence of his identity.
(4) The inspector or investigator must, as soon as practicable after obtaining entry, give to an appropriate recipient a written statement containing such information as to—
(a) the powers of the investigator or inspector (as the case may be) under section 453A;
(b) the rights and obligations of the company, occupier and the persons present on the premises, as may be prescribed by regulations.
(5) If during the time the inspector or investigator is on the premises there is no person present who appears to him to be an appropriate recipient for the purposes of subsection (8), the inspector or investigator must as soon as reasonably practicable send to the company—
(a) a notice of the fact and time that the visit took place, and
(b) the statement mentioned in subsection (4).
(6) As soon as reasonably practicable after exercising his powers under section 453A(2), the inspector or investigator must prepare a written record of the visit and—
(a) if requested to do so by the company he must give it a copy of the record;
(b) in a case where the company is not the sole occupier of the premises, if requested to do so by an occupier he must give the occupier a copy of the record.
(7) The written record must contain such information as may be prescribed by regulations.
(8) If the inspector or investigator thinks that the company is the sole occupier of the premises an appropriate recipient is a person who is present on the premises and who appears to the inspector or investigator to be—
(a) an officer of the company, or
(b) a person otherwise engaged in the business of the company if the inspector or investigator thinks that no officer of the company is present on the premises.
(9) If the inspector or investigator thinks that the company is not the occupier or sole occupier of the premises an appropriate recipient is—
(a) a person who is an appropriate recipient for the purposes of subsection (8), and (if different)
(b) a person who is present on the premises and who appears to the inspector or investigator to be an occupier of the premises or otherwise in charge of them.
(10) A statutory instrument containing regulations made under this section is subject to annulment in pursuance of a resolution of either House of Parliament.

453C Failure to comply with certain requirements

(1) This section applies if a person fails to comply with a requirement imposed by an inspector, the Secretary of State or an investigator in pursuance of either of the following provisions—
(a) section 447;
(b) section 453A.
(2) The inspector, Secretary of State or investigator (as the case may be) may certify the fact in writing to the court.
(3) If, after hearing—
(a) any witnesses who may be produced against or on behalf of the alleged offender;
(b) any statement which may be offered in defence,

the court is satisfied that the offender failed without reasonable excuse to comply with the requirement, it may deal with him as if he had been guilty of contempt of the court.

453D Offences by bodies corporate

Where an offence under any of sections 448, 449 to 451 and 453A is committed by a body corporate, every officer of the body who is in default also commits the offence. For this purpose—

(a) any person who purports to act as director, manager or secretary of the body is treated as an officer of the body, and

(b) if the body is a company, any shadow director is treated as an officer of the company.

PART XV
ORDERS IMPOSING RESTRICTIONS ON SHARES (SECTION 445)

454 Consequence of order imposing restrictions

(1) So long as any shares are directed to be subject to the restrictions of this Part then, subject to any directions made in relation to an order pursuant to sections 445(1A) or 456(1A)—

(a) any transfer of those shares or, in the case of unissued shares, any transfer of the right to be issued with them, and any issue of them, is void;

(b) no voting rights are exercisable in respect of the shares;

(c) no further shares shall be issued in right of them or in pursuance of any offer made to their holder; and

(d) except in a liquidation, no payment shall be made of any sums due from the company on the shares, whether in respect of capital or otherwise.

(2) Where shares are subject to the restrictions of subsection (1)(a), any agreement to transfer the shares or, in the case of unissued shares, the right to be issued with them is void (except such agreement or right as may be made or exercised under the terms of directions made by the Secretary of State or the court under section 445(1A) or 456(1A) or an agreement to transfer the shares on the making of an order under section 456(3)(b) below).

(3) Where shares are subject to the restrictions of subsection (1)(c) or (d), an agreement to transfer any right to be issued with other shares in right of those shares, or to receive any payment on them (otherwise than in a liquidation) is void (except such agreement or right as may be made or exercised under the terms of directions made by the Secretary of State or the court under section 445(1A), 456(1A) or an agreement to transfer any such right on the transfer of the shares on the making of an order under section 456(3)(b) below).

455 Punishment for attempted evasion of restrictions

(1) Subject to the terms of any directions made under section 445(1A) or 456 a person commits an offence if he—

(a) exercises or purports to exercise any right to dispose of any shares which, to his knowledge, are for the time being subject to the restrictions of this Part or of any right to be issued with any such shares, or

(b) votes in respect of any such shares (whether as holder or proxy), or appoints a proxy to vote in respect of them, or

(c) being the holder of any such shares, fails to notify of their being subject to those restrictions any person whom he does not know to be aware of that fact but does know to be entitled (apart from the restrictions) to vote in respect of those shares whether as holder or as proxy, or

(d) being the holder of any such shares, or being entitled to any right to be issued with other shares in right of them, or to receive any payment on them (otherwise than in a liquidation), enters into any agreement which is void under section 454(2) or (3).

(2) Subject to the terms of any directions made under section 445(1A) or 456 if shares in a company are issued in contravention of the restrictions, an offence is committed by—

(a) the company, and

(b) every officer of the company who is in default.

(2A) A person guilty of an offence under this section is liable—

(a) on conviction on indictment, to a fine;

(b) on summary conviction, to a fine not exceeding the statutory maximum.

456 Relaxation and removal of restrictions

(1) Where shares in a company are by order made subject to the restrictions of this Part, application may be made to the court for an order directing that the shares be no longer so subject.

(1A) Where the court is satisfied that an order subjecting the shares tothe restrictions of this Part unfairly affects the rights of third parties in respect of shares then the court, for the purpose of protecting such rights and subject to such terms as it thinks fit and in addition to any order it may make under subsection (1), may direct on an application made under that subsection that such acts by such persons or descriptions of persons and for such purposes, as may be set out in the order, shall not constitute a breach of the restrictions of Part XV of this Act.
Subsection (3) does not apply to an order made under this subsection.

(2) If the order applying the restrictions was made by the Secretary of State, or he has refused to make an order disapplying them, the application may be made by any person aggrieved.

(3) Subject as follows, an order of the court or the Secretary of State directing that shares shall cease to be subject to the restrictions may be made only if—
(a) the court or (as the case may be) the Secretary of State is satisfied that the relevant facts about the shares have been disclosed to the company and no unfair advantage has accrued to any person as a result of the earlier failure to make that disclosure, or
(b) the shares are to be transferred for valuable consideration and the court (in any case) or the Secretary of State (if the order was made under section 445) approves the transfer.

(4) Without prejudice to the power of the court to give directions under subsection (1A), where shares in a company are subject to the restrictions, the court may on application order the shares to be sold, subject to the court's approval as to the sale, and may also direct that the shares shall cease to be subject to the restrictions.
An application to the court under this subsection may be made by the Secretary of State, or by the company.

(5) Where an order has been made under subsection (4), the court may on application make such further order relating to the sale or transfer of the shares as it thinks fit.
An application to the court under this subsection may be made—
(a) by the Secretary of State, or
(b) by the company, or
(c) by the person appointed by or in pursuance of the order to effect the sale, or
(d) by any person interested in the shares.

(6) An order (whether of the Secretary of State or the court) directing that shares shall cease to be subject to the restrictions of this Part, if it is—
(a) expressed to be made with a view to permitting a transfer of the shares, or
(b) made under subsection (4) of this section,
may continue the restrictions mentioned in paragraphs (c) and (d) of section 454(1), either in whole or in part, so far as they relate to any right acquired or offer made before the transfer.

(7) Subsection (3) does not apply to an order directing that shares shall cease to be subject to any restrictions which have been continued in force in relation to those shares under subsection (6).

457 Further provisions on sale by court order of restricted shares

(1) Where shares are sold in pursuance of an order of the court under section 456(4) the proceeds of sale, less the costs of the sale, shall be paid into court for the benefit of the persons who are beneficially interested in the shares; and any such person may apply to the court for the whole or part of those proceeds to be paid to him.

(2) On application under subsection (1) the court shall (subject as provided below) order the payment to the applicant of the whole of the proceeds of sale together with any interest thereon or, if any other person had a beneficial interest in the shares at the time of their sale, such proportion of those proceeds and interest as is equal to the proportion which the value of the applicant's interest in the shares bears to the total value of the shares.

(3) On granting an application for an order under section 456(4) or (5) the court may order that the applicant's costs be paid out of the proceeds of sale; and if that order is made, the applicant is entitled to payment of his costs out of those proceeds before any person interested in the shares in question receives any part of those proceeds.

INSOLVENCY ACT 1986
(1986, c. 45)

THE FIRST GROUP OF PARTS
COMPANY INSOLVENCY; COMPANIES WINDING UP

PART I
COMPANY VOLUNTARY ARRANGEMENTS

The proposal

1 Those who may propose an arrangement

(1) The directors of a company (other than one which is in administration or being wound up) may make a proposal under this Part to the company and to its creditors for a composition in satisfaction of its debts or a scheme of arrangement of its affairs (from here on referred to, in either case, as a "voluntary arrangement").

(2) A proposal under this Part is one which provides for some person ("the nominee") to act in relation to the voluntary arrangement either as trustee or otherwise for the purpose of supervising its implementation; and the nominee must be a person who is qualified to act as an insolvency practitioner or authorised to act as nominee, in relation to the voluntary arrangement.

(3) Such a proposal may also be made—

(a) where the company is in administration, by the administrator, and

(b) where the company is being wound up, by the liquidator.

(4) In this Part "company" means—

(a) a company registered under the Companies Act 2006 in England and Wales or Scotland;

(b) a company incorporated in an EEA State other than the United Kingdom; or

(c) a company not incorporated in an EEA State but having its centre of main interests in a member State other than Denmark.

(5) In subsection (4), in relation to a company, "centre of main interests" has the same meaning as in the EC Regulation and, in the absence of proof to the contrary, is presumed to be the place of its registered office (within the meaning of that Regulation).

(6) If a company incorporated outside the United Kingdom has a principal place of business in Northern Ireland, no proposal under this Part shall be made in relation to it unless it also has a principal place of business in England and Wales or Scotland (or both in England and Wales or Scotland).

1A Moratorium

(1) Where the directors of an eligible company intend to make a proposal for a voluntary arrangement, they may take steps to obtain a moratorium for the company.

(2) The provisions of Schedule A1 to this Act have effect with respect to—

(a) companies eligible for a moratorium under this section,

(b) the procedure for obtaining such a moratorium,

(c) the effects of such a moratorium, and

(d) the procedure applicable (in place of sections 2 to 6 and 7) in relation to the approval and implementation of a voluntary arrangement where such a moratorium is or has been in force.

2 Procedure where nominee is not the liquidator or administrator

(1) This section applies where the nominee under section 1 is not the liquidator or administrator of the company and the directors do not propose to take steps to obtain a moratorium under section 1A for the company.

(2) The nominee shall, within 28 days (or such longer period as the court may allow) after he is given notice of the proposal for a voluntary arrangement, submit a report to the court stating—

(a) whether, in his opinion, the proposed voluntary arrangement has a reasonable prospect of being approved and implemented,

(aa) whether, in his opinion, meetings of the company and of its creditors should be summoned to consider the proposal, and

(b) if in his opinion such meetings should be summoned, the date on which, and time and place at which, he proposes the meetings should be held.

(3) For the purposes of enabling the nominee to prepare his report, the person intending to make the proposal shall submit to the nominee—

(a) a document setting out the terms of the proposed voluntary arrangement, and
(b) a statement of the company's affairs containing—
(i) such particulars of its creditors and of its debts and other liabilities and of its assets as may be prescribed, and
(ii) such other information as may be prescribed.

(4) The court may—
(a) on an application made by the person intending to make the proposal, in a case where the nominee has failed to submit the report required by this section or has died, or
(b) on an application made by that person or the nominee, in a case where it is impracticable or inappropriate for the nominee to continue to act as such,

direct that the nominee be replaced as such by another person qualified to act as an insolvency practitioner, or authorised to act as nominee, in relation to the voluntary arrangement.

3 Summoning of meetings

(1) Where the nominee under section 1 is not the liquidator or administrator, and it has been report to the court that such meetings as are mentioned in section 2(2) should be summoned, the person making the report shall (unless the court otherwise directs) summon those meetings for the time, date and place proposed in the report.
(2) Where the nominee is the liquidator or administrator, he shall summon meetings of the company and of its creditors to consider the proposal for such a time, date and place as he thinks fit.
(3) The persons to be summoned to a creditors' meeting under this section are every creditor of the company of whose claim and address the person summoning the meeting is aware.

Consideration and implementation of proposal

4 Decisions of meetings

(1) The meetings summoned under section 3 shall decide whether to approve the proposed voluntary arrangement (with or without modifications).
(2) The modifications may include one conferring the functions proposed to be conferred on the nominee on another person qualified to act as an insolvency practitioner or authorised to act as nominee, in relation to the voluntary arrangement.
But they shall not include any modification by virtue of which the proposal ceases to be a proposal such as is mentioned in section 1.
(3) A meeting so summoned shall not approve any proposal or modification which affects the right of a secured creditor of the company to enforce his security, except with the concurrence of the creditor concerned.
(4) Subject as follows, a meeting so summoned shall not approve any proposal or modification under which—
(a) any preferential debt of the company is to be paid otherwise than in priority to such of its debts as are not preferential debts,
(aa) any ordinary preferential debt of the company is to be paid otherwise than in priority to any secondary preferential debts that it may have,
(b) a preferential creditor of the company is to be paid an amount in respect of an ordinary preferential debt that bears to that debt a smaller proportion than is borne to another ordinary preferential debt by the amount that is to be paid in respect of that other debt, or
(c) a preferential creditor of the company is to be paid an amount in respect of a secondary preferential debt that bears to that debt a smaller proportion than is borne to another secondary preferential debt by the amount that is to be paid in respect of that other debt.

However, the meeting may approve such a proposal or modification with the concurrence of the preferential creditor concerned.
(5) Subject as above, each of the meetings shall be conducted in accordance with the rules.
(6) After the conclusion of either meeting in accordance with the rules, the chairman of the meeting shall report the result of the meeting to the court, and, immediately after reporting to the court, shall give notice of the result of the meeting to such persons as may be prescribed.

(7) References in this section to preferential debts, ordinary preferential debts, secondary preferential debts and preferential creditors are to be read in accordance with section 386 in Part XII of this Act.

4A Approval of arrangement

(1) This section applies to a decision, under section 4, with respect to the approval of a proposed voluntary arrangement.

(2) The decision has effect if, in accordance with the rules—

(a) it has been taken by both meetings summoned under section 3, or

(b) (subject to any order made under subsection (4)) it has been taken by the creditors' meeting summoned under that section.

(3) If the decision taken by the creditors' meeting differs from that taken by the company meeting, a member of the company may apply to the court.

(4) An application under subsection (3) shall not be made after the end of the period of 28 days beginning with—

(a) the day on which the decision was taken by the creditors' meeting, or

(b) where the decision of the company meeting was taken on a later day, that day.

(5) Where a member of a regulated company, within the meaning given by paragraph 44 of Schedule A1, applies to the court under subsection (3), the appropriate regulator is entitled to be heard on the application.

(5A) The "appropriate regulator" means—

(a) where the regulated company is a PRA-regulated company within the meaning of paragraph 44 of Schedule A1, the Financial Conduct Authority and the Prudential Regulation Authority, and

(b) in any other case, the Financial Conduct Authority.

(6) On an application under subsection (3), the court may—

(a) order the decision of the company meeting to have effect instead of the decision of the creditors' meeting, or

(b) make such other order as it thinks fit.

5 Effect of approval

(1) This section applies where a decision approving a voluntary arrangement has effect under section 4A.

(2) The voluntary arrangement—

(a) takes effect as if made by the company at the creditors' meeting, and

(b) binds every person who in accordance with the rules—

(i) was entitled to vote at that meeting (whether or not he was present or represented at it), or

(ii) would have been so entitled if he had had notice of it,

as if he were a party to the voluntary arrangement.

(2A) If—

when the arrangement ceases to have effect any amount payable under the arrangement to a person bound by virtue of subsection (2)(b)(ii) has not been paid, and

(b) the arrangement did not come to an end prematurely,

the company shall at that time become liable to pay to that person the amount payable under the arrangement.

(3) Subject as follows, if the company is being wound up or is in administration, the court may do one or both of the following, namely—

(a) by order stay or sist all proceedings in the winding up or provide for the appointment of the administrator to cease to have effect;

(b) give such directions with respect to the conduct of the winding up or the administration as it thinks appropriate for facilitating the implementation of the … voluntary arrangement.

(4) The court shall not make an order under subsection (3)(a)—

(a) at any time before the end of the period of 28 days beginning with the first day on which each of the reports required by section 4(6) has been made to the court, or

(b) at any time when an application under the next section or an appeal in respect of such an application is pending, or at any time in the period within which such an appeal may be brought.

(5) Where the company is in energy administration, the court shall not make an order or give a direction under subsection (3) unless—

(a) the court has given the Secretary of State or the Gas and Electricity Markets Authority a reasonable opportunity of making representations to it about the proposed order or direction; and

(b) the order or direction is consistent with the objective of the energy administration.

(6) In subsection (5) "in energy administration" and "objective of the energy administration" are to be construed in accordance with Schedule B1 to this Act, as applied by Part 1 of Schedule 20 to the Energy Act 2004.

6 Challenge of decisions

(1) Subject to this section, an application to the court may be made, by any of the persons specified below, on one or both of the following grounds, namely—

(a) that a voluntary arrangement which has effect under section 4A unfairly prejudices the interests of a creditor, member or contributory of the company;

(b) that there has been some material irregularity at or in relation to either of the meetings.

(2) The persons who may apply under subsection (1) are—

(a) a person entitled, in accordance with the rules, to vote at either of the meetings;

(aa) a person who would have been entitled, in accordance with the rules, to vote at the creditors' meeting if he had had notice of it;

(b) the nominee or any person who has replaced him under section 2(4) or 4(2); and

(c) if the company is being wound up or is in administration, the liquidator or administrator.

(2A) Subject to this section, where a voluntary arrangement in relation to a company in energy administration is approved at the meetings summoned under section 3, an application to the court may be made—

(a) by the Secretary of State, or

(b) with the consent of the Secretary of State, by the Gas and Electricity Markets Authority,

on the ground that the voluntary arrangement is not consistent with the achievement of the objective of the energy administration.

(3) An application under this section shall not be made—

(a) after the end of the period of 28 days beginning with the first day on which each of the reports required by section 4(6) has been made to the court, or

(b) in the case of a person who was not given notice of the creditors' meeting, after the end of the period of 28 days beginning with the day on which he became aware that the meeting had taken place,

but (subject to that) an application made by a person within subsection (2)(aa) on the ground that the voluntary arrangement prejudices his interests may be made after the arrangement has ceased to have effect, unless it came to an end prematurely.

(4) Where on such an application the court is satisfied as to either of the grounds mentioned in subsection (1) or, in the case of an application under subsection (2A), as to the ground mentioned in that subsection, it may do one or both of the following, namely—

(a) revoke or suspend any decision approving the voluntary arrangement which has effect under section 4A or, in a case falling within subsection (1)(b), any decision taken by the meeting in question which has effect under that section;

(b) give a direction to any person for the summoning of further meetings to consider any revised proposal the person who made the original proposal may make or, in a case falling within subsection (1)(b), a further company or (as the case may be) creditors' meeting to reconsider the original proposal.

(5) Where at any time after giving a direction under subsection (4)(b) for the summoning of meetings to consider a revised proposal the court is satisfied that the person who made the original proposal does not intend to submit a revised proposal, the court shall revoke the direction and revoke or suspend any decision approving the voluntary arrangement which has effect under section 4A.

(6) In a case where the court, on an application under this section with respect to any meeting—

(a) gives a direction under subsection (4)(b), or

(b) revokes or suspends an approval under subsection (4)(a) or (5),

the court may give such supplemental directions as it thinks fit and, in particular, directions with respect to things done under the voluntary arrangement since it took effect.

(7) Except in pursuance of the preceding provisions of this section, a decision taken at a meeting summoned under section 3 is not invalidated by any irregularity at or in relation to the meeting.

(8) In this section "in energy administration" and "objective of the energy administration" are to be construed in accordance with Schedule B1 to this Act, as applied by Part 1 of Schedule 20 to the Energy Act 2004.

6A False representations, etc.

(1) If, for the purpose of obtaining the approval of the members or creditors of a company to a proposal for a voluntary arrangement, a person who is an officer of the company—
  (a) makes any false representation, or
  (b) fraudulently does, or omits to do, anything, he commits an offence.
(2) Subsection (1) applies even if the proposal is not approved.
(3) For purposes of this section "officer" includes a shadow director.
(4) A person guilty of an offence under this section is liable to imprisonment or a fine, or both.

7 Implementation of proposal

(1) This section applies where a voluntary arrangement has effect under section 4A.
(2) The person who is for the time being carrying out in relation to the voluntary arrangement the functions conferred—
  (a) on the nominee by virtue of the approval given at one or both of the meetings summoned under section 3,
  (b) by virtue of section 2(4) or 4(2) on a person other than the nominee, shall be known as the supervisor of the voluntary arrangement.
(3) If any of the company's creditors or any other person is dissatisfied by any act, omission or decision of the supervisor, he may apply to the court; and on the application the court may—
  (a) confirm, reverse or modify any act or decision of the supervisor,
  (b) give him directions, or
  (c) make such other order as it thinks fit.
(4) The supervisor—
  (a) may apply to the court for directions in relation to any particular matter arising under the voluntary arrangement, and
  (b) is included among the persons who may apply to the court for the winding up of the company or for an administration order to be made in relation to it.
(5) The court may, whenever—
  (a) it is expedient to appoint a person to carry out the functions of the supervisor, and
  (b) it is inexpedient, difficult or impracticable for an appointment to be made without the assistance of the court,

  make an order appointing a person who is qualified to act as an insolvency practitioner or authorised to act as supervisor, in relation to the voluntary arrangement, either in substitution for the existing supervisor or to fill a vacancy.
(6) The power conferred by subsection (5) is exercisable so as to increase the number of persons exercising the functions of supervisor or, where there is more than one person exercising those functions, so as to replace one or more of those persons.

7A Prosecution of delinquent officers of company

(1) This section applies where a moratorium under section 1A has been obtained for a company or the approval of a voluntary arrangement in relation to a company has taken effect under section 4A or paragraph 36 of Schedule A1.
(2) If it appears to the nominee or supervisor that any past or present officer of the company has been guilty of any offence in connection with the moratorium or, as the case may be, voluntary arrangement for which he is criminally liable, the nominee or supervisor shall forthwith—
  (a) report the matter to the appropriate authority, and
  (b) provide the appropriate authority with such information and give the authority such access to and facilities for inspecting and taking copies of documents (being information or documents in the possession or under the control of the nominee or supervisor and relating to the matter in question) as the authority requires.

  In this subsection, "the appropriate authority" means—
    (i) in the case of a company registered in England and Wales, the Secretary of State, and
    (ii) in the case of a company registered in Scotland, the Lord Advocate.

(3) Where a report is made to the Secretary of State under subsection (2), he may, for the purpose of investigating the matter reported to him and such other matters relating to the affairs of the company as appear to him to require investigation, exercise any of the powers which are exercisable by inspectors appointed under section 431 or 432 of the Companies Act 1985 to investigate a company's affairs.

(4) For the purpose of such an investigation any obligation imposed on a person by any provision of the Companies Acts to produce documents or give information to, or otherwise to assist, inspectors so appointed is to be regarded as an obligation similarly to assist the Secretary of State in his investigation.

(5) An answer given by a person to a question put to him in exercise of the powers conferred by subsection (3) may be used in evidence against him.

(6) However, in criminal proceedings in which that person is charged with an offence to which this subsection applies—

(a) no evidence relating to the answer may be adduced, and

(b) no question relating to it may be asked,

by or on behalf of the prosecution, unless evidence relating to it is adduced, or a question relating to it is asked, in the proceedings by or on behalf of that person.

(7) Subsection (6) applies to any offence other than—

(a) an offence under section 2 or 5 of the Perjury Act 1911 (false statements made on oath otherwise than in judicial proceedings or made otherwise than on oath), or

(b) an offence under section 44(1) or (2) of the Criminal Law (Consolidation) (Scotland) Act 1995 (false statements made on oath or otherwise than on oath).

(8) Where a prosecuting authority institutes criminal proceedings following any report under subsection (2), the nominee or supervisor, and every officer and agent of the company past and present (other than the defendant or defender), shall give the authority all assistance in connection with the prosecution which he is reasonably able to give.

For this purpose—

"agent" includes any banker or solicitor of the company and any person employed by the company as auditor, whether that person is or is not an officer of the company,

"prosecuting authority" means the Director of Public Prosecutions, the Lord Advocate or the Secretary of State.

(9) The court may, on the application of the prosecuting authority, direct any person referred to in subsection (8) to comply with that subsection if he has failed to do so.

7B Arrangements coming to an end prematurely

For the purposes of this Part, a voluntary arrangement the approval of which has taken effect under section 4A or paragraph 36 of Schedule A1 comes to an end prematurely if, when it ceases to have effect, it has not been fully implemented in respect of all persons bound by the arrangement by virtue of section 5(2)(b)(i) or, as the case may be, paragraph 37(2)(b)(i) of Schedule A1.

PART II

ADMINISTRATION

8 Administration

Schedule B1 to this Act (which makes provision about the administrationof companies) shall have effect.

9-27 ...

PART III

RECEIVERSHIP

CHAPTER I

RECEIVERS AND MANAGERS (ENGLAND AND WALES)

Preliminary and general provisions

28 Extent of this Chapter

(1) In this Chapter "company" means a company registered under the Companies Act 2006 in England and Wales or Scotland.

(2) This Chapter does not apply to receivers appointed under Chapter 2 of this Part (Scotland).

29 Definitions

(1) It is hereby declared that, except where the context otherwise requires—

(a) any reference in this Act to a receiver or manager of the property of a company, or to a receiver of it, includes a receiver or manager, or (as the case may be) a receiver of part only of that property and a receiver only of the income arising from the property or from part of it; and

(b) any reference in this Act to the appointment of a receiver or manager under powers contained in an instrument includes an appointment made under powers which, by virtue of any enactment, are implied in and have effect as if contained in an instrument.

(2) In this Chapter "administrative receiver" means—

(a) a receiver or manager of the whole (or substantially the whole) of a company's property appointed by or on behalf of the holders of any debentures of the company secured by a charge which, as created, was a floating charge, or by such a charge and one or more other securities; or

(b) a person who would be such a receiver or manager but for the appointment of some other person as the receiver of part of the company's property.

30 Disqualification of body corporate from acting as receiver

A body corporate is not qualified for appointment as receiver of the property of a company, and any body corporate which acts as such a receiver is liable to a fine.

31 Disqualification of bankrupt or person in respect of whom a debt relief order is made

(1) A person commits an offence if he acts as receiver or manager of the property of a company on behalf of debenture holders while—

(a) he is an undischarged bankrupt,

(aa) a moratorium period under a debt relief order applies in relation to him, or

(b) a bankruptcy restrictions order or a debt relief restrictions order is in force in respect of him.

(2) A person guilty of an offence under subsection (1) shall be liable to imprisonment, a fine or both.

(3) This section does not apply to a receiver or manager acting under an appointment made by the court.

32 Power for court to appoint official receiver

Where application is made to the court to appoint a receiver on behalf of the debenture holders or other creditors of a company which is being wound up by the court, the official receiver may be appointed.

Receivers and managers appointed out of court

33 Time from which appointment is effective

(1) The appointment of a person as a receiver or manager of a company's property under powers contained in an instrument—

(a) is of no effect unless it is accepted by that person before the end of the business day next following that on which the instrument of appointment is received by him or on his behalf, and

(b) subject to this, is deemed to be made at the time at which the instrument of appointment is so received.

(2) This section applies to the appointment of two or more persons as joint receivers or managers of a company's property under powers contained in an instrument, subject to such modifications as may be prescribed by the rules.

34 Liability for invalid appointment

Where the appointment of a person as the receiver or manager of a company's property under powers contained in an instrument is discovered to be invalid (whether by virtue of the invalidity of the instrument or otherwise), the court may order the person by whom or on whose behalf the appointment was made to indemnify the person appointed against any liability which arises solely by reason of the invalidity of the appointment.

35 Application to court for directions

(1) A receiver or manager of the property of a company appointed under powers contained in an instrument, or the persons by whom or on whose behalf a receiver or manager has been so appointed, may apply to the court for directions in relation to any particular matter arising in connection with the performance of the functions of the receiver or manager.

(2) On such an application, the court may give such directions, or may make such order declaring the rights of persons before the court or otherwise, as it thinks just.

36 Court's power to fix remuneration

(1) The court may, on an application made by the liquidator of a company, by order fix the amount to be paid by way of remuneration to a person who, under powers contained in an instrument, has been appointed receiver or manager of the company's property.

(2) The court's power under subsection (1), where no previous order has been made with respect thereto under the subsection—

(a) extends to fixing the remuneration for any period before the making of the order or the application for it,

(b) is exercisable notwithstanding that the receiver or manager has died or ceased to act before the making of the order or the application, and

(c) where the receiver or manager has been paid or has retained for his remuneration for any period before the making of the order any amount in excess of that so fixed for that period, extends to requiring him or his personal representatives to account for the excess or such part of it as may be specified in the order.

But the power conferred by pararaph (c) shall not be exercised as respects any period before the making of the application for the order under this section, unless in the court's opinion there are special circumstances making it proper for the power to be exercised.

(3) The court may from time to time on an application made either by the liquidator or by the receiver or manager, vary or amend an order made under subsection (1).

37 Liability for contracts, etc.

(1) A receiver or manager appointed under powers contained in an instrument (other than an administrative receiver) is, to the same extent as if he had been appointed by order of the court—

(a) personally liable on any contract entered into by him in the performance of his functions (except in so far as the contract otherwise provides) and on any contract of employment adopted by him in the performance of those functions, and

(b) entitled in respect of that liability to indemnity out of the assets.

(2) For the purposes of subsection (1)(a), the receiver or manager is not to be taken to have adopted a contract of employment by reason of anything done or omitted to be done with 14 days after his appointment.

(3) Subsection (1) does not limit any right to indemnity which the receiver or manager would have apart from it, nor limit his liability on contracts entered into without authority, nor confer any right to indemnity in respect of that liability.

(4) Where at any time the receiver or manager so appointed vacates office—

(a) his remuneration and any expenses properly incurred by him, and

(b) any indemnity to which he is entitled out of the assets of the company,

shall be charged on and paid out of any property of the company which is in his custody or under his control at that time in priority to any charge or other security held by the person by or on whose behalf he was appointed.

38 Receivership accounts to be delivered to registrar

(1) Except in the case of an adminstrative receiver, every receiver or manager of a company's property who has been appointed under powers contained in an instrument shall deliver to the registrar of companies for registration the requisite accounts of his receipts and payments.

(2) The accounts shall be delivered within one month (or such longer period as the registrar may allow) after the expiration of 12 months from the date of his appointment and of every subsequent period of 6 months, and also within one month after he ceases to act as receiver or manager.

(3) The requisite accounts shall be an abstract in the prescribed form showing—
(a) receipts and payments during the relevant period of 12 or 6 months, or
(b) where the receiver or manager ceases to act, receipts and payments during the period from the end of the period of 12 or 6 months to which the last preceding abstract related (or, if no preceding abstract has been delivered under this section, from the date of his appointment) up to the date of his so ceasing, and the aggregate amount of receipts and payments during all preceding periods since his appointment.

(4) In this section "prescribed" means prescribed by regulations made by statutory instrument by the Secretary of State.

(5) A receiver or manager who makes default in complying with this section is liable to a fine and, for continued contravention, to a daily default fine.

Provisions applicable to every receivership

39 Notification that receiver or manager appointed

(1) Where a receiver or manager of the property of a company has been appointed—
(a) every invoice, order for goods or services, business letter or order form (whether in hard copy, electronic or any other form) issued by or on behalf of the company or the receiver or manager or the liquidator of the company; and
(b) all the company's websites,

must contain a statement that a receiver or manager has been appointed.

(2) If default is made in complying with this section, the company and any of the following persons, who knowingly and wilfully authorises or permits the default, namely, any officer of the company, any liquidator of the company and any receiver or manager, is liable to a fine.

40 Payment of debts out of assets subject to floating charge

(1) The following applies in the case of a company, where a receiver is appointed on behalf of the holders of any debentures of the company secured by a charge which, as created, was a floating charge.

(2) If the company is not at the time in course of being wound up, its preferential debts (within the meaning given to that expression by section 386 in Part XII) shall be paid out of the assets coming to the hands of the receiver in priority to any claims for principal or interest in respect of the debentures.

(3) Payments made under this section shall be recouped, as far as may be, out of the assets of the company available for payment of general creditors.

41 Enforcement of duty to make returns

(1) If a receiver or manager of a company's property—
(a) having made default in filing, delivering or making any return, account or other document, or in giving any notice, which a receiver or manager is by law required to file, deliver, make or give, fails to make good the default within 14 days after the service on him of a notice requiring him to do so, or
(b) having been appointed under powers contained in an instrument, has, after being required at any time by the liquidator of the company to do so, failed to render proper accounts of his receipts and payments and to vouch them and pay over to the liquidator the amount properly payable to him,

the court may, on an application made for the purpose, make an order directing the receiver or manager (as the case may be) to make good the default within such time as may be specified in the order.

(2) In the case of the default mentioned in subsection (1)(a), application to the court may be made by any member or creditor of the company or by the registrar of companies; and in the case of the default mentioned in subsection (1)(b), the application shall be made by the liquidator.

In either case the court's order may provide that all costs of and incidental to the application shall be borne by the receiver or manager, as the case may be.

(3) Nothing in this section prejudices the operation of any enactment imposing penalties on receivers in respect of any such default as is mentioned in subsection (1).

Administrative receivers: general

42 General powers

(1) The powers conferred on the administrative receiver of a company by the debentures by virtue of which he was appointed are deemed to include (except in so far as they are inconsistent with any of the provisions of those debentures) the powers specified in Schedule 1 to this Act.

(2) In the application of Schedule 1 to the administrative receiver of a company—

(a) the words "he" and "him" refer to the administrative receiver, and

(b) references to the property of the company are to the property of which he is or, but for the appointment of some other person as the receiver of part of the company's property, would be the receiver or manager.

(3) A person dealing with the administrative receiver in good faith and for value is not concerned to inquire whether the receiver is acting within his powers.

43 Power to dispose of charged property, etc.

(1) Where, on an application by the administrative receiver, the court is satisfied that the disposal (with or without other assets) of any relevant property which is subject to a security would be likely to promote a more advantageous realisation of the company's assets than would otherwise be effected, the court may by order authorise the administrative receiver to dispose of the property as if it were not subject to the security.

(2) Subsection (1) does not apply in the case of any security held by the person by or on whose behalf the administrative receiver was appointed, or of any security to which a security so held has priority.

(3) It shall be a condition of an order under this section that—

(a) the net proceeds of the disposal, and

(b) where those proceeds are less than such amount as may be determined by the court to be the net amount which would be realised on a sale of the property in the open market by a willing vendor, such sums as may be required to make good the deficiency,

shall be applied towards discharging the sums secured by the security.

(4) Where a condition imposed in pursuance of subsection (3) relates to two or more securities, that condition shall require the net proceeds of the disposal and, where paragraph (b) of that subsection applies, the sums mentioned in that paragraph to be applied towards discharging the sums secured by those securities in the order of their priorities.

(5) A copy of an order under this section shall, within 14 days of the making of the order, be sent by the administrative receiver to the registrar of companies.

(6) If the administrative receiver without reasonable excuse fails to comply with subsection (5), he is liable to a fine and, for continued contravention, to a daily default fine.

(7) In this section "relevant property", in relation to the administrative receiver, means the property of which he is or, but for the appointment of some other person as the receiver of part of the company's property, would be the receiver or manager.

44 Agency and liability for contracts

(1) The administrative receiver of a company—

(a) is deemed to be the company's agent, unless and until the company goes into liquidation;

(b) is personally liable on any contract entered into by him in the carrying out of his functions (except in so far as the contract otherwise provides) and, to the extent of any qualifying liability, on any contract of employment adopted by him in the carrying out of those functions; and

(c) is entitled in respect of that liability to an indemnity out of the assets of the company.

(2) For the purposes of subsection (1)(b) the administrative receiver is not to be taken to have adopted a contract of employment by reason of anything done or omitted to be done within 14 days after his appointment.

(2A) For the purposes of subsection (1)(b), a liability under a contract of employment is a qualifying liability if—

(a) it is a liability to pay a sum by way of wages or salary or contribution to an occupational pension scheme,

(b) it is incurred while the administrative receiver is in office, and

(c) it is in respect of services rendered wholly or partly after the adoption of the contract.

(2B) Where a sum payable in respect of a liability which is a qualifying liability for the purposes of subsection (1)(b) is payable in respect of services rendered partly before and partly after the adoption of the contract, liability under subsection (1)(b) shall only extend to so much of the sum as is payable in respect of services rendered after the adoption of the contract.

(2C) For the purposes of subsections (2A) and (2B)—

(a) wages or salary payable in respect of a period of holiday or absence from work through sickness or other good cause are deemed to be wages or (as the case may be) salary in respect of services rendered in that period, and

(b) a sum payable in lieu of holiday is deemed to be wages or (as the case may be) salary in respect of services rendered in the period by reference to which the holiday entitlement arose.

(2D) ...

(3) This section does not limit any right to indemnity which the administrative receiver would have apart from it, nor limit his liability on contracts entered into or adopted without authority, nor confer any right to indemnity in respect of that liability.

45 Vacation of office

(1) An administrative receiver of a company may at any time be removed from office by order of the court (but not otherwise) and may resign his office by giving notice of his resignation in the prescribed manner to such persons as may be prescribed.

(2) An administrative receiver shall vacate office if he ceases to be qualified to act as an insolvency practitioner in relation to the company.

(3) Where at any time an administrative receiver vacates office—

(a) his remuneration and any expenses properly incurred by him, and

(b) any indemnity to which he is entitled out of the assets of the company,

shall be charged on and paid out of any property of the company which is in his custody or under his control at that time in priority to any security held by the person by or on whose behalf he was appointed.

(4) Where an administrative receiver vacates office otherwise than by death, he shall, within 14 days after his vacation of office, send a notice to that effect to the registrar of companies.

(5) If an administrative receiver without reasonable excuse fails to comply with subsection (4), he is liable to a fine and, for continued contravention, to a daily default fine.

Administrative receivers: ascertainment and investigation of company's affairs

46 Information to be given by administrative receiver

(1) Where an administrative receiver is appointed, he shall—

(a) forthwith send to the company and publish in the prescribed manner a notice of his appointment, and

(b) within 28 days after his appointment, unless the court otherwise directs, send such a notice to all the creditors of the company (so far as he is aware of their addresses).

(2) This section and the next do not apply in relation to the appointment of an administrative receiver to act—

(a) with an existing administrative receiver, or

(b) in place of an administrative receiver dying or ceasing to act,

except that, where they apply to an administrative receiver who dies or ceases to act before they have been fully complied with, the references in this section and the next to the administrative receiver include (subject to the next subsection) his successor and any continuing administrative receiver.

(3) If the company is being wound up, this section and the next apply notwithstanding that the administrative receiver and the liquidator are the same person, but with any necessary modifications arising from that fact.

(4) If the administrative receiver without reasonable excuse fails to comply with this section, he is liable to a fine and, for continued contravention, to a daily default fine.

47 Statement of affairs to be submitted

(1) Where an administrative receiver is appointed, he shall forthwith require some or all of the persons mentioned below to make out and submit to him a statement in the prescribed form as to the affairs of the company.

(2) A statement submitted under this section shall be verified by a statement of truth by the persons required to submit it and shall show—
  (a) particulars of the company's assets, debts and liabilities;
  (b) the names and addresses of its creditors;
  (c) the securities held by them respectively;
  (d) the dates when the securities were respectively given; and
  (e) such further or other information as may be prescribed.

(3) The persons referred to in subsection (1) are—
  (a) those who are or have been officers of the company;
  (b) those who have taken part in the company's formation at any time within one year before the date of the appointment of the administrative receiver;
  (c) those who are in the company's employment, or have been in its employment within that year, and are in the administrative receiver's opinion capable of giving the information required;
  (d) those who are or have been within that year officers of or in the employment of a company which is, or within that year was, an officer of the company.

In this subsection "employment" includes employment under a contract for services.

(4) Where any persons are required under this section to submit a statement of affairs to the administrative receiver, they shall do so (subject to the next subsection) before the end of the period of 21 days beginning with the day after that on which the prescribed notice of the requirement is given to them by the administrative receiver.

(5) The administrative receiver, if he thinks fit, may—
  (a) at any time release a person from an obligation imposed on him under subsection (1) or (2), or
  (b) either when giving notice under subsection (4) or subsequently, extend the period so mentioned;

and where the administrative receiver has refused to exercise a power conferred by this subsection, the court, if it thinks fit, may exercise it.

(6) If a person without reasonable excuse fails to comply with any obligation imposed under this section, he is liable to a fine and, for continued contravention, to a daily default fine.

48 Report by administrative receiver

(1) Where an administrative receiver is appointed, he shall, within 3 months (or such longer period as the court may allow) after his appointment, send to the registrar of companies, to any trustees for secured creditors of the company and (so far as he is aware of their addresses) to all such creditors a report as to the following matters, namely—
  (a) the events leading up to his appointment, so far as he is aware of them;
  (b) the disposal or proposed disposal by him of any property of the company and the carrying on or proposed carrying on by him of any business of the company;
  (c) the amounts of principal and interest payable to the debenture holders by whom or on whose behalf he was appointed and the amounts payable to preferential creditors; and
  (d) the amount (if any) likely to be available for the payment of other creditors.

(2) The administrative receiver shall also, within 3 months (or such longer period as the court may allow) after his appointment, either—
  (a) send a copy of the report (so far as he is aware of their addresses) to all unsecured creditors of the company; or
  (b) publish in the prescribed manner a notice stating an address to which unsecured creditors of the company should write for copies of the report to be sent to them free of charge,

and (in either case), unless the court otherwise directs, lay a copy of the report before a meeting of the company's unsecured creditors summoned for the purpose on not less than 14 days' notice.

(3) The court shall not give a direction under subsection (2) unless—
  (a) the report states the intention of the administrative receiver to apply for the direction, and
  (b) a copy of the report is sent to the persons mentioned in paragraph (a) of that subsection, or a notice is published as mentioned in paragraph (b) of that subsection, not less than 14 days before the hearing of the application.

(4) Where the company has gone or goes into liquidation, the administrative receiver—
 (a) shall, within 7 days after his compliance with subsection (1) or, if later, the nomination or appointment of the liquidator, send a copy of the report to the liquidator, and
 (b) where he does so within the time limited for compliance with subsection (2), is not required to comply with that subsection.

(5) A report under this section shall include a summary of the statement of affairs made out and submitted to the administrative receiver under section 47 and of his comments (if any) upon it.

(6) Nothing in this section is to be taken as requiring any such report to include any information the disclosure of which would seriously prejudice the carrying out by the administrative receiver of his functions.

(7) Section 46(2) applies for the purposes of this section also.

(8) If the administrative receiver without reasonable excuse fails to comply with this section, he is liable to a fine and, for continued contravention, to a daily default fine.

49 Committee of creditors

(1) Where a meeting of creditors is summoned under section 48, the meeting may, if it thinks fit, establish a committee ("the creditors' committee") to exercise the functions conferred on it by or under this Act.

(2) If such a committee is established, the committee may, on giving not less than 7 days' notice, require the administrative receiver to attend before it at any reasonable time and furnish it with such information relating to the carrying out by him of his functions as it may reasonably require.

CHAPTER II
RECEIVERS (SCOTLAND)

50 Extent of this Chapter

This Chapter extends to Scotland only.

51 Power to appoint receiver

(1) It is competent under the law of Scotland for the holder of a floating charge over all or any part of the property (including uncalled capital), which may from time to time be comprised in the property and undertaking of an incorporated company (whether a company registered under the Companies Act 2006 or not)
 (a) which the Court of Session has jurisdiction to wind up; or
 (b) where paragraph (a) does not apply, in respect of which a court of a member state other than the United Kingdom has under the EU Regulation jurisdiction to open insolvency proceedings,

to appoint a receiver of such part of the property of the company as is subject to the charge.

(2) It is competent under the law of Scotland for the court, on the application of the holder of such a floating charge, to appoint a receiver of such part of the property of the company as is subject to the charge.

(2ZA) But, in relation to a company mentioned in subsection (1)(b), a receiver may be appointed under subsection (1) or (2) only in respect of property situated in Scotland.

(2A) Subsections (1) and (2) are subject to section 72A.

(3) The following are disqualified from being appointed as receiver—
 (a) a body corporate;
 (b) an undischarged bankrupt;
 (ba) a person subject to a bankruptcy restrictions order;
 (c) a firm according to the law of Scotland.

(4) A body corporate or a firm according to the law of Scotland which acts as a receiver is liable to a fine.

(5) An undischarged bankrupt or a person subject to a bankruptcy restrictions order who so acts is liable to imprisonment or a fine, or both.

(6) In this section, "receiver" includes joint receivers;

"bankruptcy restrictions order" means—
 (a) a bankruptcy restrictions order made under section 56A of the Bankruptcy (Scotland) Act 1985;
 (b) ...

(c) a bankruptcy restrictions order made under paragraph 1 of Schedule 4A to this Act; or
(d) a bankruptcy restrictions undertaking entered into under paragraph 7 of that Schedule.

"the EU Regulation" is the Regulation of the Council of the European Union published as Council Regulation (EC) No. 1346/2000 on insolvency proceedings;
"court" is to be construed in accordance with Article 2(d) of the EU Regulation; "insolvency proceedings" is to be construed in accordance with Article 2(a) of the EU Regulation.

52 Circumstances justifying appointment

(1) A receiver may be appointed under section 51(1) by the holder of the floating charge on the occurrence of any event which, by the provisions of the instrument creating the charge, entitles the holder of the charge to make that appointment and, in so far as not otherwise provided for by the instrument, on the occurrence of any of the following events, namely—
(a) the expiry of a period of 21 days after the making of a demand for payment of the whole or any part of the principal sum secured by the charge, without payment having been made;
(b) the expiry of a period of 2 months during the whole of which interest due and payable under the charge has been in arrears;
(c) the making of an order or the passing of a resolution to wind up the company;
(d) the appointment of a receiver by virtue of any other floating charge created by the company.

(2) A receiver may be appointed by the court under section 51(2) on the occurrence of any event which, by the provisions of the instrument creating the floating charge, entitles the holder of the charge to make that appointment and, in so far as not otherwise provided for by the instrument, on the occurrence of any of the following events, namely—
(a) where the court, on the application of the holder of the charge, pronounces itself satisfied that the position of the holder of the charge is likely to be prejudiced if no such appointment is made;
(b) any of the events referred to in paragraphs (a) to (c) of subsection (1).

53 Mode of appointment by holder of charge

(1) The appointment of a receiver by the holder of the floating charge under section 51(1) shall be by means of an instrument subscribed in accordance with the Requirements of Writing (Scotland) Act 1995 ("the instrument of appointment"), a copy (certified in the prescribed manner to be a correct copy) whereof shall be delivered by or on behalf of the person making the appointment to the registrar of companies for registration within 7 days of its execution and shall be accompanied by a notice in the prescribed form.

(2) If any person without reasonable excuse makes default in complying with the requirements of subsection (1), he is liable to a fine and, for continued contravention, to a daily default fine.

(3) ...

(4) If the receiver is to be appointed by the holders of a series of secured debentures, the instrument of appointment may be executed on behalf of the holders of the floating charge by any person authorised by resolution of the debenture-holders to execute the instrument.

(5) On receipt of the certified copy of the instrument of appointment in accordance with subsection (1), the registrar shall, on payment of the prescribed fee, enter the particulars of the appointment in the register.

(6) The appointment of a person as a receiver by an instrument of appointment in accordance with subsection (1)—
(a) is of no effect unless it is accepted by that person before the end of the business day next following that on which the instrument of appointment is received by him or on his behalf, and
(b) subject to paragraph (a), is deemed to be made on the day on and at the time at which the instrument of appointment is so received, as evidenced by a written docquet by that person or on his behalf;

and this subsection applies to the appointment of joint receivers subject to such modifications as may be prescribed.

(7) On the appointment of a receiver under this section, the floating charge by virtue of which he was appointed attaches to the property then subject to the charge; and such

attachment has effect as if the charge was a fixed security over the property to which it has attached.

54 Appointment by court

(1) Application for the appointment of a receiver by the court under section 51(2) shall be by petition to the court, which shall be served on the company.

(2) On such an application, the court shall, if it thinks fit, issue an interlocutor making the appointment of the receiver.

(3) A copy (certified by the clerk of the court to be a correct copy) of the court's interlocutor making the appointment shall be delivered by or on behalf of the petitioner to the registrar of companies for registration, accompanied by a notice in the prescribed form, within 7 days of the date of the interlocutor or much longer period as the court may allow.
If any person without reasonable excuse makes default in complying with the requirements of this subsection, he is liable to a fine and, for continued contravention, to a daily default fine.

(4) On receipt of the certified copy interlocutor in accordance with subsection (3), the registrar shall, on payment of the prescribed fee, enter the particulars of the appointment in the register.

(5) The receiver is to be regarded as having been appointed on the date of his being appointed by the court.

(6) On the appointment of a receiver under this section, the floating charge by virtue of which he was appointed attaches to the property then subject to the charge; and such attachment has effect as if the charge were a fixed security over the property to which it has attached.

(7) In making rules of court for the purposes of this section, the Court of Session shall have regard to the need for special provision for cases which appear to the court to require to be dealt with as a matter of urgency.

55 Powers of receiver

(1) Subject to the next subsection, a receiver has in relation to such part of the property of the company as is attached by the floating charge by virtue of which he was appointed, the powers, if any, given to him by the instrument creating that charge.

(2) In addition, the receiver has under this Chapter the powers as respects that property (in so far as these are not inconsistent with any provision contained in that instrument) which are specified in Schedule 2 to this Act.

(3) Subsections (1) and (2) apply—

(a) subject to the rights of any person who has effectually executed diligence on all or any part of the property of the company prior to the appointment of the receiver, and

(b) subject to the rights of any person who holds over all or any part of the property of the company a fixed security or floating charge having priority, over, or ranking pari passu with, the floating charge by virtue of which the receiver was appointed.

(4) A person dealing with a receiver in good faith and for value is not concerned to enquire whether the receiver is acting within his powers.

56 Precedence among receivers

(1) Where there are two or more floating charges subsisting over all or any part of the property of the company, a receiver may be appointed under this Chapter by virtue of each such charge; but a receiver appointed by, or on the application of, the holder of a floating charge having priority of ranking over any other floating charge by virtue of which a receiver has been appointed has the powers given to a receiver by section 55 and Schedule 2 to the exclusion of any other receiver.

(2) Where two or more floating charges rank with one another equally, and two or more receivers have been appointed by virtue of such charges, the receivers so appointed are deemed to have been appointed as joint receivers.

(3) Receivers appointed, or deemed to have been appointed, as joint receivers shall act jointly unless the instrument of appointment or respective instruments of appointment otherwise provide.

(4) Subject to subsection (5) below, the powers of a receiver appointed by, or on the application of, the holder of a floating charge are suspended by, and as from the date of, the appointment of a receiver by, or on the application of, the holder of a floating charge having priority of ranking over that charge to such extent as may be necessary to enable

the receiver second mentioned to exercise his powers under section 55 and Schedule 2; and any powers so suspended take effect again when the floating charge having priority of ranking ceases to attach to the property then subject to the charge, whether such cessation is by virtue of section 62(6) or otherwise.

(5) The suspension of the powers of a receiver under subsection (4) does not have the effect of requiring him to release any part of the property (including any letters or documents) of the company from his control until he receives from the receiver superseding him a valid indemnity (subject to the limit of the value of such part of the property of the company as is subject to the charge by virtue of which he was appointed) in respect of any expenses, charges and liabilities he may have incurred in the performance of his functions as receiver.

(6) The suspension of the powers of a receiver under subsection (4) does not cause the floating charge by virtue of which he was appointed to cease to attach to the property to which it attached by virtue of section 53(7) or 54(6).

(7) Nothing in this section prevents the same receiver being appointed by virtue of two or more floating charges.

57 Agency and liability of receiver for contracts

(1) A receiver is deemed to be the agent of the company in relation to such property of the company as is attached by the floating charge by virtue of which he was appointed.

(1A) Without prejudice to subsection (1), a receiver is deemed to be the agent of the company in relation to any contract of employment adopted by him in the carrying out of his functions.

(2) A receiver (including a receiver whose powers are subsequently suspended under section 56) is personally liable on any contract entered into by him in the performance of his functions, except in so far as the contract otherwise provides, and, to the extent of any qualifying liability, on any contract of employment adopted by him in the carrying out of those functions.

(2A) For the purposes of subsection (2), a liability under a contract of employment is a qualifying liability if—

- (a) it is a liability to pay a sum by way of wages or salary or contribution to an occupational pension scheme,
- (b) it is incurred while the receiver is in office, and
- (c) it is in respect of services rendered wholly or partly after the adoption of the contract.

(2B) Where a sum payable in respect of a liability which is a qualifying liability for the purposes of subsection (2) is payable in respect of services rendered partly before and partly after the adoption of the contract, liability under that subsection shall only extend to so much of the sum as is payable in respect of services rendered after the adoption of the contract.

(2C) For the purposes of subsections (2A) and (2B)—

- (a) wages or salary payable in respect of a period of holiday or absence from work through sickness or other good cause are deemed to be wages or (as the case may be) salary in respect of services rendered in that period, and
- (b) a sum payable in lieu of holiday is deemed to be wages or (as the case may be) salary in respect of services rendered in the period by reference to which the holiday entitlement arose.

(2D) In subsection (2C)(a), the reference to wages or salary payable in respect of a period of holiday includes any sums which, if they had been paid, would have been treated for the purposes of the enactments relating to social security as earnings in respect of that period.

(3) A receiver who is personally liable by virtue of subsection (2) is entitled to be indemnified out of the property in respect of which he was appointed.

(4) Any contract entered into by or on behalf of the company prior to the appointment of a receiver continues in force (subject to its terms) notwithstanding that appointment, but the receiver does not by virtue only of his appointment incur any personal liability on any such contract.

(5) For the purposes of subsection (2), a receiver is not to be taken to have adopted a contract of employment by reason of anything done or omitted to be done within 14 days after his appointment.

(6) This section does not limit any right to indemnity which the receiver would have apart from it, nor limit his liability on contracts entered into or adopted without authority, nor confer any right to indemnity in respect of that liability.

(7) Any contract entered into by a receiver in the performance of his functions continues in force (subject to its terms) although the powers of the receiver are subsequently suspended under section 56.

58 Remuneration of receiver

(1) The remuneration to be paid to a receiver is to be determined by agreement between the receiver and the holder of the floating charge by virtue of which he was appointed.

(2) Where the remuneration to be paid to the receiver has not been determined under subsection (1), or where it has been so determined but is disputed by any of the persons mentioned in paragraphs (a) to (d) below, it may be fixed instead by the Auditor of the Court of Session on application made to him by—

(a) the receiver;

(b) the holder of any floating charge or fixed security over all or any part of the property of the company;

(c) the company; or

(d) the liquidator of the company.

(3) Where the receiver has been paid or has retained for his remuneration for any period before the remuneration has been fixed by the Auditor of the Court of Session under subsection (2) any amount in excess of the remuneration so fixed for that period, the receiver or his personal representatives shall account for the excess.

59 Priority of debts

(1) Where a receiver is appointed and the company is not at the time of the appointment in course of being wound up, the debts which fall under subsection (2) of this section shall be paid out of any assets coming to the hands of the receiver in priority to any claim for principal or interest by the holder of the floating charge by virtue of which the receiver was appointed.

(2) Debts falling under this subsection are preferential debts (within the meaning given by section 386 in Part XII) which, by the end of a period of 6 months after advertisement by the receiver for claims in the Edinburgh Gazette and in a newspaper circulating in the district where the company carries on business either—

(i) have been intimated to him, or

(ii) have become known to him.

(3) Any payments made under this section shall be recouped as far as may be out of the assets of the company available for payment of ordinary creditors.

60 Distribution of moneys

(1) Subject to the next section, and to the rights of any of the following categories of persons (which rights shall, except to the extent otherwise provided in any instrument, have the following order of priority), namely—

(a) the holder of any fixed security which is over property subject to the floating charge and which ranks prior to, or pari passu with, the floating charge;

(b) all persons who have effectually executed diligence on any part of the property of the company which is subject to the charge by virtue of which the receiver was appointed;

(c) creditors in respect of all liabilities, charges and expenses incurred by or on behalf of the receiver;

(d) the receiver in respect of his liabilities, expenses and remuneration, and any indemnity to which he is entitled out of the property of the company; and

(e) the preferential creditors entitled to payment under section 59,

the receiver shall pay moneys received by him to the holder of the floating charge by virtue of which the receiver was appointed in or towards satisfaction of the debt secured by the floating charge.

(2) Any balance of moneys remaining after the provisions of subsection (1) and section 61 below have been satisfied shall be paid in accordance with their respective rights and interests to the following persons, as the case may require—

(a) any other receiver;

(b) the holder of a fixed security which is over property subject to the floating charge;

(c) the company or its liquidator, as the case may be.

(3) Where any question arises as to the person entitled to a payment under this section, or where a receipt or a discharge of a security cannot be obtained in respect of any such

payment, the receiver shall consign the amount of such payment in any joint stock bank of issue in Scotland in name of the Accountant of Court for behoof of the person or persons entitled thereto.

61 Disposal of interest in property

(1) Where the receiver sells or disposes, or is desirous of selling or disposing, or any property or interest in property of the company which is subject to the floating charge by virtue of which the receiver was appointed and which is—

(a) subject to any security or interest of, or burden or encumbrance in favour of, a creditor the ranking of which is prior to, or pari passu with, or postponed to the floating charge, or

(b) property or an interest in property affected or attached by effectual diligence executed by any person,

and the receiver is unable to obtain the consent of such creditor or, as the case may be, such person to such a sale or disposal, the receiver may apply to the court for authority to sell or dispose of the property or interest in property free of such security, interest, burden, encumbrance or diligence.

(1A) For the purposes of subsection (1) above, an inhibition which takes effect after the creation of the floating charge by virtue of which the receiver was appointed is not an effectual diligence.

(1B) For the purposes of subsection (1) above, an arrestment is an effectual diligence only where it is executed before the floating charge, by virtue of which the receiver was appointed, attaches to the property comprised in the company's property and undertaking.

(2) Subject to the next subsection, on such an application the court may, if it thinks fit, authorise the sale or disposal of the property or interest in question free of such security, interest, burden, encumbrance or diligence, and such authorisation may be on such terms or conditions as the court thinks fit.

(3) In the case of an application where a fixed security over the property or interest in question which ranks prior to the floating charge has not been met or provided for in full, the court shall not authorise the sale or disposal of the property or interest in question unless it is satisfied that the sale or disposal would be like to provide a more advantageous realisation of the company's assets than would otherwise be effected.

(4) It shall be a condition of an authorisation to which subsection (3) applies that—

(a) the net proceeds of the disposal, and

(b) where those proceeds are less than such amount as may be determined by the court to be the net amount which would be realised on a sale of the property or interest in the open market by a willing seller, such sums as may be required to make good the deficiency,

shall be applied towards discharging the sums secured by the fixed security.

(5) Where a condition imposed in pursuance of subsection (4) relates to two or more such fixed securities, that condition shall require the net proceeds of the disposal and, where paragraph (b) of that subsection applies, the sums mentioned in that paragraph to be applied towards discharging the sums secured by those fixed securities in the order of their priorities.

(6) A copy of an authorisation under subsection (2) shall, within 14 days of the granting of the authorisation, be sent by the receiver to the registrar of companies.

(7) If the receiver without reasonable excuse fails to comply with subsection (6), he is liable to a fine and, for continued contravention, to a daily default fine.

(8) Where any sale or disposal is effected in accordance with the authorisation of the court under subsection (2), the receiver shall grant to the purchaser or disponee an appropriate document of transfer or conveyance of the property or interest in question, and that document has the effect, or, where recording, intimation or registration of that document is a legal requirement for completion of title to the property or interest, then that recording, intimation or registration (as the case may be) has the effect, of—

(a) disencumbering the property or interest of the security, interest, burden or encumbrance affecting it, and

(b) freeing the property or interest from the diligence executed upon it.

(9) Nothing in this section prejudices the right of any creditor of the company to rank for his debt in the winding up of the company.

62 Cessation of appointment of receiver

(1) A receiver may be removed from office by the court under subsection (3) below and may resign his office by giving notice of his resignation in the prescribed manner to such persons as may be prescribed.

(2) A receiver shall vacate office if he ceases to be qualified to act as an insolvency practitioner in relation to the company.

(3) Subject to the next subsection, a receiver may, on application to the court by the holder of the floating charge by virtue of which he was appointed, be removed by the court on cause shown.

(4) Where at any time a receiver vacates office—

(a) his remuneration and any expenses properly incurred by him, and

(b) any indemnity to which he is entitled out of the property of the company,

shall be paid out of the property of the company which is subject to the floating charge and shall have priority as provided for in section 60(1).

(5) When a receiver ceases to act as such otherwise than by death he shall, and, when a receiver is removed by the court, the holder of the floating charge by virtue of which he was appointed shall, within 14 days of the cessation or removal (as the case may be) given the registrar of companies notice to that effect, and the registrar shall enter the notice in the register of charges.

If the receiver or the holder of the floating charge (as the case may require) makes default in complying with the requirements of this subsection, he is liable to a fine and, for continued contravention, to a daily default fine.

(6) If by the expiry of a period of one month following upon the removal of the receiver or his ceasing to act as such no other receiver has been appointed, the floating charge by virtue of which the receiver was appointed—

(a) thereupon ceases to attach to the property then subject to the charge, and

(b) again subsists as a floating charge;

and for the purposes of calculating the period of one month under this subsection no account shall be taken of any period during which the company is in administration under Part II of this Act.

63 Powers of court

(1) The court on the application of—

(a) the holder of a floating charge by virtue of which a receiver was appointed, or

(b) a receiver appointed under section 51,

may give directions to the receiver in respect of any matter arising in connection with the performance by him of his functions.

(2) Where the appointment of a person as a receiver by the holder of a floating charge is discovered to be invalid (whether by virtue of the invalidity of the instrument or otherwise), the court may order the holder of the floating charge to indemnify the person appointed against any liability which arises solely by reason of the invalidity of the appointment.

64 Notification that receiver appointed

(1) Where a receiver has been appointed—

(a) every invoice, order for goods or services, business letter or order form (whether in hard copy, electronic or any other form) issued by or on behalf of the company or the receiver or the liquidator of the company; and

(b) all the company's websites,

must contain a statement that a receiver has been appointed.

(2) If default is made in complying with the requirements of this section, the company and any of the following persons who knowingly and wilfully authorises or permits the default, namely any officer of the company, any liquidator of the company and any receiver, is liable to a fine.

65 Information to be given by receiver

(1) Where a receiver is appointed, he shall—

(a) forthwith send to the company and publish notice of his appointment, and

(b) within 28 days after his appointment, unless the court otherwise directs, send such notice to all the creditors of the company (so far as he is aware of their addresses).

(2) This section and the next do not apply in relation to the appointment of a receiver to act—

(a) with an existing receiver, or
(b) in place of a receiver who has died or ceased to act,

except that, where they apply to a receiver who dies or ceases to act before they have been fully complied with, the references in this section and the next to the receiver include (subject to subsection (3) of this section) his successor and any continuing receiver.

(3) If the company is being wound up, this section and the next apply notwithstanding that the receiver and the liquidator are the same person, but with any necessary modifications arising from that fact.

(4) If a person without reasonable excuse fails to comply with this section, he is liable to a fine and, for continued contravention, to a daily default fine.

66 Company's statement of affairs

(1) Where a receiver of a company is appointed, the receiver shall forthwith require some or all of the persons mentioned in subsection (3) below to make out and submit to him a statement in the prescribed form as to the affairs of the company.

(2) A statement submitted under this section shall be verified by affidavit by the persons required to submit it and shall show—
(a) particulars of the company's assets, debts and liabilities;
(b) the names and addresses of its creditors;
(c) the securities held by them respectively;
(d) the dates when the securities were respectively given; and
(e) such further or other information as may be prescribed.

(3) The persons referred to in subsection (1) are—
(a) those who are or have been officers of the company;
(b) those who have taken part in the company's formation at any time within one year before the date of the appointment of the receiver;
(c) those who are in the company's employment or have been in its employment within that year, and are in the receiver's opinion capable of giving the information required;
(d) those who are or have been within that year officers of or in the employment of a company which is, or within that year was, an officer of the company.

In this subsection "employment" includes employment under a contract for services.

(4) Where any persons are required under this section to submit a statement of affairs to the receiver they shall do so (subject to the next subsection) before the end of the period of 21 days beginning with the day after that on which the prescribed notice of the requirement is given to them by the receiver.

(5) The receiver, if he thinks fit, may—
(a) at any time release a person from an obligation imposed on him under subsection (1) or (2), or
(b) either when giving the notice mentioned in subsection (4) or subsequently extend the period so mentioned,

and where the receiver has refused to exercise a power conferred by this subsection, the court, if it thinks fit, may exercise it.

(6) If a person without reasonable excuse fails to comply with any obligation imposed under this section, he is liable to a fine and, for continued contravention to a daily default fine.

67 Report by receiver

(1) Where a receiver is appointed under section 51, he shall within 3 months (or such longer period as the court may allow) after his appointment, send to the registrar of companies, to the holder of the floating charge by virtue of which he was appointed and to any trustees for secured creditors of the company and (so far as he is aware of their addresses) to all such creditors a report as to the following matters, namely—
(a) the events leading up to his appointment, so far as he is aware of them;
(b) the disposal or proposed disposal by him of any property of the company and the carrying on or proposed carrying on by him of any business of the company;
(c) the amounts of principal and interest payable to the holder of the floating charge by virtue of which he was appointed and the amounts payable to preferential creditors; and
(d) the amount (if any) likely to be available for the payment of other creditors.

(2) The receiver shall also, within 3 months (or such longer period as the court may allow) after his appointment, either—

(a) send a copy of the report (so far as he is aware of their addresses) to all unsecured creditors of the company, or
(b) publish in the prescribed manner a notice stating an address to which unsecured creditors of the company should write for copies of the report to be sent to them free of charge,

and (in either case), unless the court otherwise directs, lay a copy of the report before a meeting of the company's unsecured creditors summoned for the purpose on not less than 14 days' notice.

(3) The court shall not give a direction under subsection (2) unless—
(a) the report states the intention of the receiver to apply for the direction, and
(b) a copy of the report is sent to the persons mentioned in paragraph (a) of that subsection, or a notice is published as mentioned in paragraph (b) of that subsection, not less than 14 days before the hearing of the application.

(4) Where the company has gone or goes into liquidation, the receiver—
(a) shall, within 7 days after his compliance with subsection (1) or, if later, the nomination or appointment of the liquidator, send a copy of the report to the liquidator, and
(b) where he does so within the time limited for compliance with subsection (2), is not required to comply with that subsection.

(5) A report under this section shall include a summary of the statement of affairs made out and submitted under section 66 and of his comments (if any) on it.

(6) Nothing in this section shall be taken as requiring any such report to include any information the disclosure of which would seriously prejudice the carrying out by the receiver of his functions.

(7) Section 65(2) applies for the purposes of this section also.

(8) If a person without reasonable excuse fails to comply with this section, he is liable to a fine and, for continued contravention, to a daily default fine.

(9) In this section "secured creditor", in relation to a company, means a creditor of the company who holds in respect of his debt a security over property of the company, and "unsecured creditor" shall be construed accordingly.

68 Committee of creditors

(1) Where a meeting of creditors is summoned under section 67, the meeting may, if it thinks fit, establish a committee ("the creditors' committee") to exercise the functions conferred on it by or under this Act.

(2) If such a committee is established, the committee may on giving not less than 7 days' notice require the receiver to attend before it at any reasonable time and furnish it with such information relating to the carrying out by him of his functions as it may reasonably require.

69 Enforcement of receiver's duty to make returns, etc.

(1) If any receiver—
(a) having made default in filing, delivering or making any return, account or other document, or in giving any notice, which a receiver is by law required to file, deliver, make or give, fails to make good the default within 14 days after the service on him of a notice requiring him to do so; or
(b) has, after being required at any time by the liquidator of the company so to do, failed to render proper accounts of his receipts and payments and to vouch the same and to pay over to the liquidator the amount properly payable to him, the court may, on an application made for the purpose, make an order directing the receiver to make good the default within such time as may be specified in the order.

(2) In the case of any such default as is mentioned in subsection (1)(a), an application for the purposes of this section may be made by any member or creditor of the company or by the registrar of companies; and, in the case of any such default as is mentioned in subsection (1)(b), the application shall be made by the liquidator; and, in either case, the order may provide that all expenses of and incidental to the application shall be borne by the receiver.

(3) Nothing in this section prejudices the operation of any enactments imposing penalties on receivers in respect of any such default as is mentioned in subsection (1).

70 Interpretation for Chapter II

(1) In this Chapter, unless the contrary intention appears, the following expressions have the following meanings respectively assigned to them—

"company" means an incorporated company (whether or not a company registered under the Companies Act 2006) which the Court of Session has jurisdiction to wind up;

"fixed security", in relation to any property of a company, means any security, other than a floating charge or a charge having the nature of a floating charge, which on the winding up of the company in Scotland would be treated as an effective security over that property, and (without prejudice to that generality) includes a security over that property, being a heritable security within the meaning of the Conveyancing and Feudal Reform (Scotland) Act 1970;

"instrument of appointment" has the meaning given by section 53(1);

"prescribed" means prescribed by regulations made under this Chapter by the Secretary of State;

"receiver" means a receiver of such part of the property of the company as is subject to the floating charge by virtue of which he has been appointed under section 51;

"register"has the meaning given by section 1080 of the Companies Act 2006;

"secured debenture" means a bond, debenture, debenture stock or other security which, either itself or by reference to any other instrument, creates a floating charge over all or any part of the property of the company, but does not include a security which creates no charge other than a fixed security; and

"series of secured debentures" means two or more secured debentures created as a series by the company in such a manner that the holders thereof are entitled pari passu to the benefit of the floating charge.

(2) Where a floating charge, secured debenture or series of secured debentures has been created by the company, then, except where the context otherwise requires, any reference in this Chapter to the holder of the floating charge shall—

(a) where the floating charge, secured debenture or series of secured debentures provides for a receiver to be appointed by any person or body, be construed as a reference to that person or body;

(b) where, in the case of a series of secured debentures, no such provision has been made therein but—

(i) there are trustees acting for the debenture-holders under and in accordance with a trust deed, be construed as a reference to those trustees, and

(ii) where no such trustees are acting, be construed as a reference to—

(aa) a majority in nominal value of those present or represented by proxy and voting at a meeting of debenture-holders at which the holders of at least one-third in nominal value of the outstanding debentures of the series are present or so represented, or

(bb) where no such meeting is held, the holders of at least one-half in nominal value of the outstanding debentures of the series.

(3) Any reference in this Chapter to a floating charge, secured debenture, series of secured debentures or instrument creating a charge includes, except where the context otherwise requires, a reference to that floating charge, debenture, series of debentures or instrument as varied by any instrument.

(4) References in this Chapter to the instrument by which a floating charge was created are, in the case of a floating charge created by words in a bond or other written acknowledgement, references to the bond or, as the case may be, the other written acknowledgement.

71 Prescription of forms, etc.; regulations

(1) The notice referred to in section 62(5), and the notice referred to in section 65(1)(a) shall be in such form as may be prescribed.

(2) Any power conferred by this Chapter on the Secretary of State to make regulations is exercisable by statutory instrument; and a statutory instrument made in the exercise of the power so conferred to prescribe a fee is subject to annulment in pursuance of a resolution of either House of Parliament.

CHAPTER III
RECEIVERS' POWERS IN GREAT BRITAIN AS A WHOLE

72 Cross-border operation of receivership provisions

(1) A receiver appointed under the law of either part of Great Britain in respect of the whole or any part of any property or undertaking of a company and in consequence of the company having created a charge which, as created, was a floating charge may exercise his powers in the other part of Great Britain so far as their exercise is not inconsistent with the law applicable there.

(2) In subsection (1) "receiver" includes a manager and a person who is appointed both receiver and manager.

CHAPTER IV
PROHIBITION OF APPOINTMENT OF ADMINISTRATIVE RECEIVER

72A Floating charge holder not to appoint administrative receiver

(1) The holder of a qualifying floating charge in respect of a company's property may not appoint an administrative receiver of the company.

(2) In Scotland, the holder of a qualifying floating charge in respect of a company's property may not appoint or apply to the court for the appointment of a receiver who on appointment would be an administrative receiver of property of the company.

(3) In subsections (1) and (2)—
"holder of a qualifying floating charge in respect of a company's property" has the same meaning as in paragraph 14 of Schedule B1 to this Act, and
"administrative receiver" has the meaning given by section 251.

(4) This section applies—
- (a) to a floating charge created on or after a date appointed by the Secretary of State by order made by statutory instrument, and
- (b) in spite of any provision of an agreement or instrument which purports to empower a person to appoint an administrative receiver (by whatever name).

(5) An order under subsection (4)(a) may—
- (a) make provision which applies generally or only for a specified purpose;
- (b) make different provision for different purposes;
- (c) make transitional provision.

(6) This section is subject to the exceptions specified in sections 72B to 72GA.

72B First exception: capital market

(1) Section 72A does not prevent the appointment of an administrative receiver in pursuance of an agreement which is or forms part of a capital market arrangement if—
- (a) a party incurs or, when the agreement was entered into was expected to incur, a debt of at least £50 million under the arrangement, and
- (b) the arrangement involves the issue of a capital market investment.

(2) In subsection (1)—
"capital market arrangement" means an arrangement of a kind described in paragraph 1 of Schedule 2A, and
"capital market investment" means an investment of a kind described in paragraph 2 or 3 of that Schedule.

72C Second exception: public-private partnership

(1) Section 72A does not prevent the appointment of an administrative receiver of a project company of a project which—
- (a) is a public-private partnership project, and
- (b) includes step-in rights.

(2) In this section "public-private partnership project" means a project—
- (a) the resources for which are provided partly by one or more public bodies and partly by one or more private persons, or
- (b) which is designed wholly or mainly for the purpose of assisting a public body to discharge a function.

(3) In this section—
"step-in rights" has the meaning given by paragraph 6 of Schedule 2A, and "project company" has the meaning given by paragraph 7 of that Schedule.

72D Third exception: utilities

(1) Section 72A does not prevent the appointment of an administrative receiver of a project company of a project which—
  (a) is a utility project, and
  (b) includes step-in rights.

(2) In this section—
  (a) "utility project" means a project designed wholly or mainly for the purpose of a regulated business,
  (b) "regulated business" means a business of a kind listed in paragraph 10 of Schedule 2A,
  (c) "step-in rights" has the meaning given by paragraph 6 of that Schedule, and
  (d) "project company" has the meaning given by paragraph 7 of that Schedule.

72DA Exception in respect of urban regeneration projects

(1) Section 72A does not prevent the appointment of an administrative receiver of a project company of a project which—
  (a) is designed wholly or mainly to develop land which at the commencement of the project is wholly or partly in a designated disadvantaged area outside Northern Ireland, and
  (b) includes step-in rights.

(2) In subsection (1) "develop" means to carry out—
  (a) building operations,
  (b) any operation for the removal of substances or waste from land and the levelling of the surface of the land, or
  (c) engineering operations in connection with the activities mentioned in paragraph (a) or (b).

(3) In this section—
"building" includes any structure or erection, and any part of a building as so defined, but does not include plant and machinery comprised in a building,
"building operations" includes—
  (a) demolition of buildings,
  (b) filling in of trenches,
  (c) rebuilding,
  (d) structural alterations of, or additions to, buildings and
  (e) other operations normally undertaken by a person carrying on business as a builder, "designated disadvantaged area" means an area designated as a disadvantaged area under section 92 of the Finance Act 2001,

"engineering operations" includes the formation and laying out of means of access to highways,
"project company" has the meaning given by paragraph 7 of Schedule 2A, "step-in rights" has the meaning given by paragraph 6 of that Schedule,
"substance" means any natural or artificial substance whether in solid or liquid form or in the form of a gas or vapour, and
"waste" includes any waste materials, spoil, refuse or other matter deposited on land.

72E Fourth exception: project finance

(1) Section 72A does not prevent the appointment of an administrative receiver of a project company of a project which—
  (a) is a financed project, and
  (b) includes step-in rights.

(2) In this section—
  (a) a project is "financed" if under an agreement relating to the project a project company incurs, or when the agreement is entered into is expected to incur, a debt of at least £50 million for the purposes of carrying out the project,
  (b) "project company" has the meaning given by paragraph 7 of Schedule 2A, and
  (c) "step-in rights" has the meaning given by paragraph 6 of that Schedule.

72F Fifth exception: financial market

Section 72A does not prevent the appointment of an administrative receiver of a company by virtue of—

(a) a market charge within the meaning of section 173 of the Companies Act 1989,
(b) a system-charge within the meaning of the Financial Markets and Insolvency Regulations 1996,
(c) a collateral security charge within the meaning of the Financial Markets and Insolvency (Settlement Finality) Regulations 1999.

72G Sixth exception: social landlords

Section 72A does not prevent the appointment of an administrative receiver of a companywhich is—

(a) a private registered provider of social housing, or
(b) registered as a social landlord under Part I of the Housing Act 1996 or under Part 2 of the Housing (Scotland) Act 2010.

72GA Exception in relation to protected railway companies etc.

Section 72A does not prevent the appointment of an administrative receiver of—

(a) a company holding an appointment under Chapter I of Part II of the Water Industry Act 1991,
(b) a protected railway company within the meaning of section 59 of the Railways Act 1993 (including that section as it has effect by virtue of section 19 of the Channel Tunnel Rail Link Act 1996, or
(c) a licence company within the meaning of section 26 of the Transport Act 2000.

72H Sections 72A to 72G: supplementary

(1) Schedule 2A (which supplements sections 72B to 72G) shall have effect.
(2) The Secretary of State may by order—
 (a) insert into this Act provision creating an additional exception to section 72A(1) or (2);
 (b) provide for a provision of this Act which creates an exception to section 72A(1) or (2) to cease to have effect;
 (c) amend section 72A in consequence of provision made under paragraph (a) or (b);
 (d) amend any of sections 72B to 72G;
 (e) amend Schedule 2A.
(3) An order under subsection (2) must be made by statutory instrument.
(4) An order under subsection (2) may make—
 (a) provision which applies generally or only for a specified purpose;
 (b) different provision for different purposes;
 (c) consequential or supplementary provision;
 (d) transitional provision.
(5) An order under subsection (2)—
 (a) in the case of an order under subsection (2)(e), shall be subject to annulment in pursuance of a resolution of either House of Parliament,
 (b) in the case of an order under subsection (2)(d) varying the sum specified in section 72B(1)(a) or 72E(2)(a) (whether or not the order also makes consequential or transitional provision), shall be subject to annulment in pursuance of a resolution of either House of Parliament, and
 (c) in the case of any other order under subsection (2)(a) to (d), may not be made unless a draft has been laid before and approved by resolution of each House of Parliament.

PART IV
WINDING UP OF COMPANIES REGISTERED UNDER THE COMPANIES ACTS

CHAPTER I
PRELIMINARY

Introductory

73 Scheme of this Part

(1) This Part applies to the winding up of a company registered under the Companies Act 2006 in England and Wales or Scotland.
(2) The winding up may be either—
 (a) voluntary (see Chapters 2 to 5), or
 (b) by the court (see Chapter 6).

(3) This Chapter and Chapters 7 to 10 relate to winding up generally, except where otherwise stated.

Contributories

74 Liability as contributories of present and past members

(1) When a company is wound up, every present and past member is liable to contribute to its assets to any amount sufficient for payment of its debts and liabilities, and the expenses of the winding up, and for the adjustment of the rights of the contributories among themselves.

(2) This is subject as follows—

(a) a past member is not liable to contribute if he has ceased to be a member for one year or more before the commencement of the winding up;

(b) a past member is not liable to contribute in respect of any debt or liability of the company contracted after he ceased to be a member;

(c) a past member is not liable to contribute, unless it appears to the court that the existing members are unable to satisfy the contributions required to be made by them;

(d) in the case of a company limited by shares, no contribution is required from any member exceeding the amount (if any) unpaid on the shares in respect of which he is liable as a present or past member;

(e) nothing in the Companies Act or this Act invalidates any provision contained in a policy of insurance or other contract whereby the liability of individual members on the policy or contract is restricted, or whereby the funds of the company are alone made liable in respect of the policy or contract;

(f) a sum due to any member of the company (in his character of a member) by way of dividends, profits or otherwise is not deemed to be a debt of the company, payable to that member in a case of competition between himself and any other creditor not a member of the company, but any such sum may be taken into account for the purpose of the final adjustment of the rights of the contributories among themselves.

(3) In the case of a company limited by guarantee, no contribution is required from any member exceeding the amount undertaken to be contributed by him to the company's assets in the event of its being wound up; but if it is a company with a share capital, every member of it is liable (in addition to the amount so undertaken to be contributed to the assets), to contribute to the extent of any sums unpaid on shares held by him.

75 ...

76 Liability of past directors and shareholders

(1) This section applies where a company is being wound up and—

(a) it has under Chapter 5 of Part 18 of the Companies Act 2006 (acquisition by limited company of its own shares: redemption or purchase by private company out of capital) made a payment out of capital in respect of the redemption or purchase of any of its own shares (the payment being referred to below as "the relevant payment"), and

(b) the aggregate amount of the company's assets and the amounts paid by way of contribution to its assets (apart from this section) is not sufficient for payment of its debts and liabilities, and the expenses of the winding up.

(2) If the winding up commenced within one year of the date on which the relevant payment was made, then—

(a) the person from whom the shares were redeemed or purchased, and

(b) the directors who signed the statement made in accordance with section 714(1) to (3) of the Companies Act 2006 for purposes of the redemption or purchase (except a director who shows that he had reasonable grounds for forming the opinion set out in the statement,

are, so as to enable that insufficiency to be met, liable to contribute to the following extent to the company's assets.

(3) A person from whom any of the shares were redeemed or purchased is liable to contribute an amount not exceeding so much of the relevant payment as was made by the company in respect of his shares; and the directors are jointly and severally liable with that person to contribute that amount.

(4) A person who has contributed any amount to the assets in pursuance of this section may apply to the court for an order directing any other person jointly and severally liable in respect of that amount to pay him such amount as the court thinks just and equitable.

(5) Sections 74 does not apply in relation to liability accruing by virtue of this section.

77 Limited company formerly unlimited

(1) This section applies in the case of a company being wound up which was at some former time registered as unlimited but has re-registered as a limited company.

(2) Notwithstanding section 74(2)(a) above, a past member of the company who was a member of it at the time of re-registration, if the winding up commences within the period of 3 years beginning with the day on which the company was re-registered, is liable to contribute to the assets of the company in respect of debts and liabilities contracted before that time.

(3) If no persons who were members of the company at that time are existing members of it, a person who at that time was a present or past member is liable to contribute as above notwithstanding that the existing members have satisfied the contributions required to be made by them.

This applies subject to section 74(2)(a) above and to subsection (2) of this section, but notwithstanding section 74(2)(c).

(4) Notwithstanding section 74(2)(d) and (3), there is no limit on the amount which a person who, at that time, was a past or present member of the company is liable to contribute as above.

78 Unlimited company formerly limited

(1) This section applies in the case of a company being wound up which was at some former time registered as limited but has been re-registered as unlimited.

(2) A person who, at the time when the application for the company to be re-registered was lodged, was a past member of the company and did not after that again become a member of it is not liable to contribute to the assets of the company more than he would have been liable to contribute had the company not been re-registered.

79 Meaning of "contributory"

(1) In this Act the expression "contributory" means every person liable to contribute to the assets of a company in the event of its being wound up, and for the purposes of all proceedings for determining, and all proceedings prior to the final determination of, the persons who are to be deemed contributories, includes any person alleged to be a contributory.

(2) The reference in subsection (1) to persons liable to contribute to the assets does not include a person so liable by virtue of a declaration by the court under section 213 (imputed responsibility for company's fraudulent trading) or section 214 (wrongful trading) in Chapter X of this Part.

(3) A reference in a company's articles to a contributory does not (unless the context requires) include a person who is a contributory only by virtue of section 76.

80 Nature of contributory's liability

The liability of a contributory creates a debt (in England and Wales in the nature of an ordinary contract debt) accruing due from him at the time when his liability commenced, but payable at the times when calls are made for enforcing the liability.

81 Contributories in case of death of a member

(1) If a contributory dies either before or after he has been placed on the list of contributories, his personal representatives, and the heirs and legatees of heritage of his heritable estate in Scotland, are liable in a due course of administration to contribute to the assets of the company in discharge of his liability and are contributories accordingly.

(2) Where the personal representatives are placed on the list of contributories, the heirs or legatees of heritage need not be added, but they may be added as and when the court thinks fit.

(3) If in England and Wales the personal representatives make default in paying any money ordered to be paid by them, proceedings may be taken for administering the estate of the deceased contributory and for compelling payment out of it of the money due.

82 Effect of contributory's bankruptcy

(1) The following applies if a contributory becomes bankrupt, either before or after he has been placed on the list of contributories.
(2) His trustee in bankruptcy represents him for all purposes of the winding up, and is a contributory accordingly.
(3) The trustee may be called on to admit to proof against the bankrupt's estate, or otherwise allow to be paid out of the bankrupt's assets in due course of law, any money due from the bankrupt in respect of his liability to contribute to the company's assets.
(4) There may be proved against the bankrupt's estate the estimated value of his liability to future calls as well as calls already made.

83 *omitted*

CHAPTER II
VOLUNTARY WINDING UP (INTRODUCTORY AND GENERAL)

Resolutions for, and commencement of, voluntary winding up

84 Circumstances in which company may be wound up voluntarily

(1) A company may be wound up voluntarily—
(a) when the period (if any) fixed for the duration of the company by the articles expires, or the event (if any) occurs, on the occurrence of which the articles provide that the company is to be dissolved, and the company in general meeting has passed a resolution requiring it be wound up voluntarily;
(b) if the company resolves by special resolution that it be wound up voluntarily;
(c) ...
(2) In this Act the expression "a resolution for voluntary winding up" means a resolution passed under either of the paragraphs of subsection (1).
(2A) Before a company passes a resolution for voluntary winding up it must give written notice of the resolution to the holder of any qualifying floating charge to which section 72A applies.
(2B) Where notice is given under subsection (2A) a resolution for voluntary winding up may be passed only—
(a) after the end of the period of five business days beginning with the day on which the notice was given, or
(b) if the person to whom the notice was given has consented in writing to the passing of the resolution.
(3) Chapter 3 of Part 3 of the Companies Act 2006 (resolutions affecting a company's constitution) applies to a resolution under paragraph (a) of subsection (1) as well as a special resolution under paragraph (b).
(4) This section has effect subject to section 43 of the Commonhold and Leasehold Reform Act 2002.

85 Notice of resolution to wind up

(1) When a company has passed a resolution for voluntary winding up, it shall, within 14 days after the passing of the resolution, give notice of the resolution by advertisement in the Gazette.
(2) If default is made in complying with this section, the company and every officer of it who is in default is liable to a fine and, for continued contravention, to a daily default fine.
For purposes of this subsection the liquidator is deemed an officer of the company.

86 Commencement of winding up

A voluntary winding up is deemed to commence at the time of the passing of the resolution for voluntary winding up.

Consequences of resolution to wind up

87 Effect on business and status of company

(1) In case of a voluntary winding up, the company shall from the commencement of the winding up cease to carry on its business, except so far as may be required for its beneficial winding up.

(2) However, the corporate state and corporate powers of the company, notwithstanding anything to the contrary in its articles, continue until the company is dissolved.

88 Avoidance of share transfers, etc. after winding-up resolution

Any transfer of shares, not being a transfer made to or with the sanction of the liquidator, and any alteration in the status of the company's members, made after the commencement of a voluntary winding up, is void.

Declaration of solvency

89 Statutory declaration of solvency

(1) Where it is proposed to wind up a company voluntarily, the directors (or, in the case of a company having more than two directors, the majority of them) may at a directors' meeting make a statutory declaration to the effect that they have made a full inquiry into the company's affairs and that, having done so, they have formed the opinion that the company will be able to pay its debts in full, together with interest at the official rate (as defined in section 251), within such period, not exceeding 12 months from the commencement of the winding up, as may be specified in the declaration.

(2) Such a declaration by the directors has no effect for purposes of this Act unless—

(a) it is made within the 5 weeks immediately preceding the date of the passing of the resolution for winding up, or on that date but before the passing of the resolution, and

(b) it embodies a statement of the company's assets and liabilities as at the latest practicable date before the making of the declaration.

(3) The declaration shall be delivered to the registrar of companies before the expiration of 15 days immediately following the date on which the resolution for winding up is passed.

(4) A director making a declaration under this section without having reasonable grounds for the opinion that the company will be able to pay its debts in full, together with interest at the official rate, within the period specified is liable to imprisonment or a fine, or both.

(5) If the company is wound up in pursuance of a resolution passed within 5 weeks after the making of the declaration, and its debts (together with interest at the official rate) are not paid or provided for in full within the period specified, it is to be presumed (unless the contrary is shown) that the director did not have reasonable grounds for his opinion.

(6) If a declaration required by subsection (3) to be delivered to the registrar is not so delivered within the time prescribed by that subsection, the company and every officer in default is liable to a fine and, for continued contravention, to a daily default fine.

90 Distinction between "members" and "creditors" voluntary winding up

A winding up in the case of which a directors' statutory declaration under section 89 has been made is a "members' voluntary winding up"; and a winding up in the case of which such a declaration has not been made is a "creditors' voluntary winding up".

CHAPTER III

MEMBERS' VOLUNTARY WINDING UP

91 Appointment of liquidator

(1) In a members' voluntary winding up, the company in general meeting shall appoint one or more liquidators for the purpose of winding up the company's affairs and distributing its assets.

(2) On the appointment of a liquidator all the powers of the directors cease, except so far as the company in general meeting or the liquidator sanctions their continuance.

92 Power to fill vacancy in office of liquidator

(1) If a vacancy occurs by death resignation or otherwise in the office of liquidator appointed by the company, the company in general meeting may, subject to any arrangement with its creditors, fill the vacancy.

(2) For that purpose a general meeting may be convened by any contributory or, if there were more liquidators than one, by the continuing liquidators.

(3) The meeting shall be held in manner provided by this Act or by the articles, or in such manner as may, on application by any contributory or by the continuing liquidators, be determined by the court.

92A Progress report to company at year's end (England and Wales)

(1) Subject to sections 96 and 102, where the company is registered in England and Wales continuing for more than one year, the liquidator must—
   (a) for each prescribed period produce a progress report relating to the prescribed matters; and
   (b) within such period commencing with the end of the period referred to in paragraph (a) as may be prescribed send a copy of the progress report to—
      (i) the members of the company; and
      (ii) such other persons as may be prescribed.

(2) A liquidator who fails to comply with this section is liable to a fine.

93 General company meeting at each year's end (Scotland)

(1) Subject to section 96, in the event of the winding up of a company registered in Scotland continuing for more than one year, the liquidator shall summon a general meeting of the company at the end of the first year from the commencement of the winding up, and of each succeeding year, or at the first convenient date within 3 months from the end of the year or such longer period as the Secretary of State may allow.

(2) The liquidator shall lay before the meeting an account of his acts and dealings, and of the conduct of the winding up, during the preceding year.

(3) If the liquidator fails to comply with this section, he is liable to a fine.

94 Final meeting prior to dissolution

(1) As soon as the company's affairs are fully wound up, the liquidator shall make up an account of the winding up showing how it has been conducted and the company's property has been disposed of, and thereupon shall call a general meeting of the company for the purpose of laying before it the account, and giving an explanation of it.

(2) The meeting shall be called by advertisement in the Gazette, specifying its time, place and object and published at least one month before the meeting.

(3) Within one week after the meeting, the liquidator shall send to the registrar of companies a copy of the account, and shall make a return to him of the holding of the meeting and of its date.

(4) If the copy is not sent or the return is not made in accordance with subsection (3), the liquidator is liable to a fine and, for continued contravention, to a daily default fine.

(5) If a quorum is not present at the meeting, the liquidator shall, in lieu of the return mentioned above, make a return that the meeting was duly summoned and that no quorum was present; and upon such a return being made, the provisions of subsection (3) as to the making of the return are deemed complied with.

(6) If the liquidator fails to call a general meeting of the company as required by subsection (1), he is liable to a fine.

95 Effect of company's insolvency

(1) This section applies where the liquidator is of the opinion that the company will be unable to pay its debts in full (together with interest at the official rate) within the period stated in the directors' declaration under section 89.

(2) In the case of the winding up of a company registered in Scotland, the liquidator shall—
   (a) summon a meeting of creditors for a day not later than the 28th day after the day on which he formed that opinion;
   (b) send notices of the creditors' meeting to the creditors by post not less than 7 days before the day on which that meeting is to be held;
   (c) cause notice of the creditors' meeting to be advertised once in the Gazette and once at least in 2 newspapers circulating in the relevant locality (that is to say the locality in which the company's principal place of business in Great Britain was situated during the relevant period); and
   (d) during the period before the day on which the creditors' meeting is to be held, furnish creditors free of charge with such information concerning the affairs of the company as they may reasonably require;

and the notice of the creditors' meeting shall state the duty imposed by paragraph (d) above.

(2A) In the case of the winding up of a company registered in England and Wales, the liquidator—

(a) shall summon a meeting of creditors for a day not later than the 28th day after the day on which he formed that opinion;

(b) shall send notices of the creditors' meeting to the creditors not less than 7 days before the day on which that meeting is to be held;

(c) shall cause notice of the creditors' meeting to be advertised once in the Gazette;

(d) may cause notice of the meeting to be advertised in such other manner as he thinks fit; and

(e) shall during the period before the day on which the creditors' meeting is to be held, furnish creditors free of charge with such information concerning the affairs of the company as they may reasonably require;

and the notice of the creditors' meeting shall state the duty imposed by paragraph (e) above.

(3) The liquidator shall also—

(a) make out a statement in the prescribed form as to the affairs of the company;

(b) lay that statement before the creditors' meeting; and

(c) attend and preside at that meeting.

(4) The statement as to the affairs of the company shall show—

(a) particulars of the company's assets, debts and liabilities;

(b) the names and addresses of the company's creditors;

(c) the securities held by them respectively;

(d) the dates when the securities were respectively given; and

(e) such further or other information as may be prescribed.

(4A) The statement as to the affairs of the company shall be verified by the liquidator—

(a) in the case of a winding up of a company registered in England and Wales, by a statement of truth; and

(b) in the case of a winding up of a company registered in Scotland, by affidavit.

(5) Where the company's principal place of business in Great Britain was situated in different localities at different times during the relevant period, the duty imposed by subsection (2)(c) applies separately in relation to each of those localities.

(6) Where the company had no place of business in Great Britain during the relevant period, references in subsections (2)(c) and (5) to the company's principal place of business in Great Britain are replaced by references to its registered office.

(7) In this section "the relevant period" means the period of 6 months immediately preceding the day on which were sent the notices summoning the company meeting at which it was resolved that the company be wound up voluntarily.

(8) If the liquidator without reasonable excuse fails to comply with this section, he is liable to a fine.

96 Conversion to creditors' voluntary winding up

As from the day on which the creditors' meeting is held under section 95, this Act has effect as if—

(a) the directors' declaration under section 89 had not been made; and

(b) the creditors' meeting and the company meeting at which it was resolved that the company be wound up voluntarily were the meetings mentioned in section 98 in the next Chapter;

and accordingly the winding up becomes a creditors' voluntary winding up.

CHAPTER IV

CREDITORS' VOLUNTARY WINDING UP

97 Application of this Chapter

(1) Subject as follows, this Chapter applies in relation to a creditors' voluntary winding up.

(2) Sections 98 and 99 do not apply where, under section 96 in Chapter III, a members' voluntary winding up has become a creditors' voluntary winding up.

98 Meeting of creditors

(1) In the case of the winding up of a company registered in Scotland, the company shall—

(a) cause a meeting of its creditorsto be summoned for a day not later than the 14th day after the day on which there is to be held the company meeting at which the resolution for voluntary winding up is to be proposed;

(b) cause the notices of the creditors' meeting to be sent by post to the creditors not less than 7 days before the day on which that meeting is to be held; and
(c) cause notice of the creditors' meeting to be advertised once in the Gazette and once at least in two newspapers circulating in the relevant locality (that is to say the locality in which the company's principal place of business in Great Britain was situated during the relevant period).

(1A) In the case of the winding up of a company registered in England and Wales, the company—
(a) shall cause a meeting of its creditors to be summoned for a day not later than the 14th day after the day on which there is to be held the company meeting at which the resolution for voluntary winding up is to be proposed;
(b) shall cause the notices of the creditors' meeting to be sent to the creditors not less than 7 days before the day on which that meeting is to be held;
(c) shall cause notice of the creditors' meeting to be advertised once in the Gazette; and
(d) may cause notice of the meeting to be advertised in such other manner as the directors think fit.

(2) The notice of the creditors' meeting shall state either—
(a) the name and address of a person qualified to act as an insolvency practitioner in relation to the company who, during the period before the day on which that meeting is to be held, will furnish creditors free of charge with such information concerning the company's affairs as they may reasonably require; or
(b) a place in the relevant locality where, on the two business days falling next before the day on which that meeting is to be held, a list of the names and addresses of the company's creditors will be available for inspection free of charge.

(3) Where the company's principal place of business in Great Britain was situated in different localities at different times during the relevant period, the duties imposed by subsections (1)(c) and (2)(b) above apply separately in relation to each of those localities.

(4) Where the company had no place of business in Great Britain during the relevant period, references in subsections (1)(c) and (3) to the company's principal place of business in Great Britain are replaced by references to its registered office.

(5) In this section "the relevant period" means the period of 6 months immediately preceding the day on which were sent the notices summoning the company meeting at which it was resolved that the company be wound up voluntarily.

(6) If the company without reasonable excuse fails to comply with subsection (1) or (2), it is guilty of an offence and liable to a fine.

99 Directors to lay statement of affairs before creditors

(1) The directors of the company shall—
(a) make out a statement in the prescribed formas to the affairs of the company;
(b) cause that statement to be laid before the creditors' meeting under section 98; and
(c) appoint one of their number to preside at that meeting;

and it is the duty of the director so appointed to attend the meeting and preside over it.

(2) The statement as to the affairs of the company shall show—
(a) particulars of the company's assets, debts and liabilities;
(b) the names and addresses of the company's creditors;
(c) the securities held by them respectively;
(d) the dates when the securities were respectively given; and
(e) such further or other information as may be prescribed.

(2A) The statement as to the affairs of the company shall be verified by some or all of the directors—
(a) in the case of a winding up of a company registered in England and Wales, by a statement of truth; and
(b) in the case of a winding up of a company registered in Scotland, by affidavit.

(3) If—
(a) the directors without reasonable excuse fail to comply with subsection (1), (2) or (2A); or
(b) any director without reasonable excuse fails to comply with subsection (1), so far as requiring him to attend and preside at the creditors' meeting,

the directors are or (as the case may be) the director is guilty of an offence and liable to a fine.

100 Appointment of liquidator

(1) The creditors and the company at their respective meetings mentioned in section 98 may nominate a person to be liquidator for the purpose of winding up the company's affairs and distributing its assets.

(2) The liquidator shall be the person nominated by the creditors or, where no person has been so nominated, the person (if any) nominated by the company.

(3) In the case of different persons being nominated, any director, member or creditor of the company may, within 7 days after the date on which the nomination was made by the creditors, apply to the court for an order either—

(a) directing that the person nominated as liquidator by the company shall be liquidator instead of or jointly with the person nominated by the creditors, or

(b) appointing some other person to be liquidator instead of the person nominated by the creditors.

101 Appointment of liquidation committee

(1) The creditors at the meeting to be held under section 98 or at any subsequent meeting may, if they think fit, appoint a committee ("the liquidation committee") of not more than 5 persons to exercise the functions conferred on it by or under this Act.

(2) If such a committee is appointed, the company may, either at the meeting at which the resolution for voluntary winding up is passed or at any time subsequently in general meeting, appoint such number of persons as they think fit to act as members of the committee, not exceeding 5.

(3) However, the creditors may, if they think fit, resolve that all or any of the persons so appointed by the company ought not to be members of the liquidation committee; and if the creditors so resolve—

(a) the persons mentioned in the resolution are not then, unless the court otherwise directs, qualified to act as members of the committee; and

(b) on any application to the court under this provision the court may, if it thinks fit, appoint other persons to act as such members in place of the persons mentioned in the resolution.

(4) In Scotland, the liquidation committee has, in addition to the powers and duties conferred and imposed on it by this Act, such of the powers and duties of commissioners on a bankrupt estate as may be conferred and imposed on liquidation committees by the rules.

102 Creditors' meeting where winding up converted under section 96

Where, in the case of a winding up which was under section 96 in Chapter III, converted to a creditors' voluntary winding up, a creditors' meeting is held in accordance with section 95, any appointment made or committee established by that meeting is deemed to have been made or established by a meeting held in accordance with section 98 in this Chapter.

103 Cesser of directors' powers

On the appointment of a liquidator, all the powers of the directors cease, except so far as the liquidation committee (or, if there is no such committee, the creditors) sanction their continuance.

104 Vacancy in office of liquidator

If a vacancy occurs, by death, resignation or otherwise, in the office of a liquidator (other than a liquidator appointed by, or by the direction of, the court), the creditors may fill the vacancy.

104A Progress report to company and creditors (England and Wales)

(1) If the winding up of a company registered in England and Wales continues for more than one year, the liquidator must—

(a) for each prescribed period produce a progress report relating to the prescribed matters; and

(b) within such period commencing with the end of the period referred to in paragraph (a) as may be prescribed send a copy of the progress report to—

(i) the members and creditors of the company; and
(ii) such other persons as may be prescribed.

(2) A liquidator who fails to comply with this section is liable to a fine.

105 Meetings of company and creditors at each year's end (Scotland)

(1) If the winding up of a company registered in Scotland continues for more than one year, the liquidator shall summon a general meeting of the company and a meeting of the creditors at the end of the first year from the commencement of the winding up, and of each succeeding year, or at the first convenient date within 3 months from the end of the year or such longer period as the Secretary of State may allow.

(2) The liquidator shall lay before each of the meetings an account of his acts and dealings and of the conduct of the winding up during the preceding year.

(3) If the liquidator fails to comply with this section, he is liable to a fine.

(4) Where under section 96 a members' voluntary winding up has become a creditors' voluntary winding up, and the creditors' meeting under section 95 is held 3 months or less before the end of the first year from the commencement of the winding up, the liquidator is not required by this section to summon a meeting of creditors at the end of that year.

106 Final meeting prior to dissolution

(1) As soon as the company's affairs are fully wound up, the liquidator shall make up an account of the winding up, showing how it has been conducted and the company's property has been disposed of, and thereupon shall call a general meeting of the company and a meeting of the creditors for the purpose of laying the account before the meetings and giving an explanation of it.

(2) Each such meeting shall be called by advertisement in the Gazette specifying the time, place and object of the meeting, and published at least one month before it.

(3) Within one week after the date of the meetings (or, if they are not held on the same date, after the date of the later one) the liquidator shall send to the registrar of companies a copy of the account, and shall make a return to him of the holding of the meetings and of their dates.

(4) If the copy is not sent or the return is not made in accordance with subsection (3), the liquidator is liable to a fine and, for continued contravention, to a daily default fine.

(5) However, if a quorum is not present at either such meeting, the liquidator shall, in lieu of the return required by subsection (3), make a return that the meeting was duly summoned and that no quorum was present; and upon such return being made the provisions of that subsection as to the making of the return are, in respect of that meeting, deemed complied with.

(6) If the liquidator fails to call a general meeting of the company or a meeting of the creditors as required by this section, he is liable to a fine.

CHAPTER V
PROVISIONS APPLYING TO BOTH KINDS OF VOLUNTARY WINDING UP

107 Distribution of company's property

Subject to the provisions of this Act as to preferential payments, the company's property in a voluntary winding up shall on the winding up be applied in satisfaction of the company's liabilities pari passu and, subject to that application, shall (unless the articles otherwise provide) be distributed among the members according to their rights and interests in the company.

108 Appointment or removal of liquidator by the court

(1) If from any cause whatever there is not liquidator acting, the court may appoint a liquidator.

(2) The court may, on cause shown, remove a liquidator and appoint another.

109 Notice by liquidator of his appointment

(1) The liquidator shall, within 14 days after his appointment, publish in the Gazette and deliver to the registrar of companies for registration a notice of his appointment in the form prescribed by statutory instrument made by the Secretary of State.

(2) If the liquidator fails to comply with this section, he is liable to a fine and, for continued contravention, to a daily default fine.

110 Acceptance of shares, etc., as consideration for sale of company property

(1) This section applies, in the case of a company proposed to be, or being, wound up voluntarily, where the whole or part of the company's business or property is proposed to be transferred or sold—

(a) to another company ("the transferee company"), whether or not the latter is a company registered under the Companies Act 2006, or

(b) to a limited liability partnership (the "transferee limited liability partnership").

(2) With the requisite sanction, the liquidator of the company being, or proposed to be, wound up ("the transferor company") may receive, in compensation or part compensation for the transfer or sale—

(a) in the case of the transferee company, shares, policies or other like interests in the company for distribution among the members of the transferor company, or

(b) in the case of the transferee limited liability partnership, membership in the limited liability partnership for distribution among the members of the transferor company.

(3) The sanction requisite under subsection (2) is—

(a) in the case of a members' voluntary winding up, that of a special resolution of the company, conferring either a general authority on the liquidator or an authority in respect of any particular arrangement, and

(b) in the case of a creditors' voluntary winding up, that of either the court or the liquidation committee.

(4) Alternatively to subsection (2), the liquidator may—

(a) in the case of the transferee company, in lieu of receiving cash, shares, policies or other like interests (or in addition thereto) participate in the profits of, or receive any other benefit from, the company, or

(b) in the case of the transferee limited liability partnership, in lieu of receiving cash, or membership (or in addition thereto) participate in some other way in the profits of, or receive any other benefit from, the limited liability partnership.

(5) A sale or arrangement in pursuance of this section is binding on members of the transferor company.

(6) A special resolution is not invalid for purposes of this section by reason that it is passed before or concurrently with a resolution for voluntary winding up or for appointing liquidators; but, if an order is made within a year for winding up the company by the court, the special resolution is not valid unless sanctioned by the court.

111 Dissent from arrangement under section 110

(1) This section applies in the case of a voluntary winding up where, for the purposes of section 110(2) or (4), there has been passed a special resolution of the transferor company providing the sanction requisite for the liquidator under that section.

(2) If a member of the transferor company who did not vote in favour of the special resolution expresses his dissent from it in writing, addressed to the liquidator and left at the company's registered office within 7 days after the passing of the resolution, he may require the liquidator either to abstain from carrying the resolution into effect or to purchase his interest at a price to be determined by agreement or by arbitration under this section.

(3) If the liquidator elects to purchase the member's interest, the purchase money must be paid before the company is dissolved and be raised by the liquidator in such manner as may be determined by special resolution.

(4) For purposes of an arbitration under this section, the provisions of the Companies Clauses Consolidation Act 1845 or, in the case of a winding up in Scotland, the Companies Clauses Consolidation (Scotland) Act 1845 with respect to the settlement of disputes by arbitration are incorporated with this Act, and—

(a) in the construction of those provisions this Act is deemed the special Act and "the company" means the transferor company, and

(b) any appointment by the incorporated provisions directed to be made under the hand of the secretary or any two of the directors may be made in writing by the liquidator (or, if there is more than one liquidator, then any two or more of them).

112 Reference of questions to court

(1) The liquidator or any contributory or creditor may apply to the court to determine any question arising in the winding up of a company, or to exercise, as respects the enforcing

of calls or any other matter, all or any of the powers which the court might exercise if the company were being wound up by the court.

(2) The court, if satisfied that the determination of the question or the required exercise of power will be just and beneficial, may accede wholly or partially to the application on such terms and conditions as it thinks fit, or may make such other order on the application as it thinks just.

(3) A copy of an order made by virtue of this section staying the proceedings in the winding up shall forthwith be forwarded by the company, or otherwise as may be prescribed, to the registrar of companies, who shall enter it in his records relating to the company.

113 Court's power to control proceedings (Scotland)

If the court, on the application of the liquidator in the winding up of a company registered in Scotland, so directs, no action or proceeding shall be proceeded with or commenced against the company except by leave of the court and subject to such terms as the court may impose.

114 No liquidator appointed or nominated by company

(1) This section applies where, in the case of a voluntary winding up, no liquidator has been appointed or nominated by the company.

(2) The powers of the directors shall not be exercised, except with the sanction of the court or (in the case of a creditors' voluntary winding up) so far as may be necessary to secure compliance with sections 98 (creditors' meeting) and 99 (statement of affairs), during the period before the appointment or nomination of a liquidator of the company.

(3) Subsection (2) does not apply in relation to the powers of the directors—

(a) to dispose of perishable goods and other goods the value of which is likely to diminish if they are not immediately disposed of, and

(b) to do all such other things as may be necessary for the protection of the company's assets.

(4) If the directors of the company without reasonable excuse fail to comply with this section, they are liable to a fine.

115 Expenses of voluntary winding up

All expenses properly incurred in the winding up, including the remuneration of the liquidator, are payable out of the company's assets in priority to all other claims.

116 Saving for certain rights

The voluntary winding up of a company does not bar the right of any creditor or contributory to have it wound up by the court; but in the case of an application by a contributory the court must be satisfied that the rights of the contributories will be prejudiced by a voluntary winding up.

CHAPTER VI
WINDING UP BY THE COURT

Jurisdiction (England and Wales)

117 High Court and county court jurisdiction

(1) The High Court has jurisdiction to wind up any company registered in England and Wales.

(2) Where in the case of a company registered in England and Wales the amount of its share capital paid up or credited as paid up does not exceed £120,000, then (subject to this section) the county court has concurrent jurisdiction with the High Court to wind up the company.

(2A) Despite subsection (2), proceedings for the exercise of the jurisdiction to wind up a company registered in England and Wales may be commenced only in the High Court if the place which has longest been the company's registered office during the 6 months immediately preceding the presentation of the petition for winding up is in the district that is the London insolvency district for the purposes of the second Group of Parts of this Act.

(3) The money sum for the time being specified in subsection (2) is subject to increase or reduction by order under section 416 in Part XV.

(4) …

(5) Every court in England and Wales having winding-up jurisdiction has for the purposes of that jurisdiction all the powers of the High Court; and every prescribed officer of the court shall perform any duties which an officer of the High Court may discharge by order of a judge of that court or otherwise in relation to winding up.

...

(7) This section is subject to Article 3 of the EC Regulation (jurisdiction under EC Regulation).

(8) The Lord Chief Justice may nominate a judicial office holder (as defined in section 109(4) of the Constitutional Reform Act 2005) to exercise his functions under this section.

118 Proceedings taken in wrong court

(1) Nothing in section 117 invalidates a proceeding by reason of its being taken in the wrong court.

(2) The winding up of a company by the court in England and Wales, or any proceedings in the winding up, may be retained in the court in which the proceedings were commenced, although it may not be the court in which they ought to have been commenced.

119 Proceedings in county court; case stated for High Court

(1) If any question arises in any winding-up proceedings in a county court which all the parties to the proceedings, or which one of them and the judge of the court, desire to have determined in the first instance in the High Court, the judge shall state the facts in the form of a special case for the opinion of the High Court.

(2) Thereupon the special case and the proceedings (or such of them as may be required) shall be transmitted to the High Court for the purposes of the determination.

Jurisdiction (Scotland)

120 Court of Session and sheriff court jurisdiction

(1) The Court of Session has jurisdiction to wind up any company registered in Scotland.

(2) When the Court of Session is in vacation, the jurisdiction conferred on that court by this section may (subject to the provisions of this Part) be exercised by the judge acting as vacation judge.

(3) Where the amount of a company's share capital paid up or credited as paid up does not exceed £120,000, the sheriff court of the sheriffdom in which the company's registered office is situated has concurrent jurisdiction with the Court of Session to wind up the company; but—

(a) the Court of Session may, if it thinks expedient having regard to the amount of the company's assets to do so—

(i) remit to a sheriff court any petition presented to the Court of Session for winding up such a company, or

(ii) require such a petition presented to a sheriff court to be remitted to the Court of Session; and

(b) the Court of Session may require any such petition as above mentioned presented to one sheriff court to be remitted to another sheriff court; and

(c) in a winding up in the sheriff court the sheriff may submit a stated case for the opinion of the Court of Session on any question of law arising in that winding up.

(4) For purposes of this section, the expression "registered office" means the place which has longest been the company's registered office during the 6 months immediately preceding the presentation of the petition for winding up.

(5) The money sum for the time being specified in subsection (3) is subject to increase or reduction by order under section 416 in Part XV.

(6) This section is subject to Article 3 of the EC Regulation (jurisdiction under EC Regulation).

121 Power to remit winding up to Lord Ordinary

(1) The Court of Session may, by Act of Sederunt, make provision for the taking of proceedings in a winding up before one of the Lords Ordinary; and, where provision is so made, the Lord Ordinary has, for the purposes of the winding up all the powers and jurisdiction of the court.

(2) However, the Lord Ordinary may report to the Inner House any matter which may arise in the course of a winding up.

Grounds and effect of winding-up petition

122 Circumstances in which company may be wound up by the court

(1) A company may be wound up by the court if—

(a) the company has by special resolution resolved that the company be wound up by the court,

(b) being a public company which was registered as such on its original incorporation, the company has not been issued with a trading certificate under section 761 of the Companies Act 2006 (requirement as to minimum share capital) and more than a year has expired since it was so registered,

(c) it is an old public company, within the meaning of Schedule 3 to the Companies Act 2006 (Consequential Amendments, Transitional Provisions and Savings) Order 2009,

(d) the company does not commence its business within a year from its incorporation or suspends its business for a whole year;

(e) ...

(f) the company is unable to pay its debts,

(fa) at the time at which a moratorium for the company under section 1A comes to an end, no voluntary arrangement approved under Part I has effect in relation to the company

(g) the court is of the opinion that it is just and equitable that the company should be wound up.

(2) In Scotland, a company which the Court of Session has jurisdiction to wind up may be wound up by the Court if there is subsisting a floating charge over property comprised in the company's property and undertaking, and the court is satisfied that the security of the creditor entitled to the benefit of the floating charge is in jeopardy.

For this purpose a creditor's security is deemed to be in jeopardy if the Court is satisfied that events have occurred or are about to occur which render it unreasonable in the creditor's interests that the company should retain power to dispose of the property which is subject to the floating charge.

123 Definition of inability to pay debts

(1) A company is deemed unable to pay its debts—

(a) if a creditor (by assignment or otherwise) to whom the company is indebted in a sum exceeding £750 then due has served on the company, by leaving it at the company's registered office, a written demand (in the prescribed form) requiring the company to pay the sum so due and the company has for 3 weeks thereafter neglected to pay the sum or to secure or compound for it to the reasonable satisfaction of the creditor, or

(b) if, in England and Wales, execution or other process issued on a judgment, decree or order of any court in favour of a creditor of the company is returned unsatisfied in whole or in part, or

(c) if, in Scotland, the induciae of a charge for payment on an extract decree, or an extract registered bond, or an extract registered protest, have expired without payment being made, or

(d) if, in Northern Ireland, a certificate of unenforceability has been granted in respect of a judgment against the company, or

(e) if it is proved to the satisfaction of the court that the company is unable to pay its debts as they fall due.

(2) A company is also deemed unable to pay its debts if it is proved to the satisfaction of the court that the value of the company's assets is less than the amount of its liabilities, taking into account its contingent and prospective liabilities.

(3) The money sum for the time being specified in subsection (1)(a) is subject to increase or reduction by order under section 416 in Part XV.

124 Application for winding up

(1) Subject to the provisions of this section, an application to the court for the winding up of a company shall be by petition presented either by the company, or the directors, or by any creditor or creditors (including any contingent or prospective creditor or creditors), contributory or contributories, or by a liquidator (within the meaning of Article 2(b) of the EC Regulation) appointed in proceedings by virtue of Article 3(1) of the EC Regulation

or a temporary administrator (within the meaning of Article 38 of the EC Regulation) or by the designated officer for a magistrates' court in the exercise of the power conferred by section 87A of the Magistrates' Courts Act 1980 (enforcement of fines imposed on companies), or by all or any of those parties, together or separately.

(2) Except as mentioned below, a contributory is not entitled to present a winding-up petition unless either—
(a) the number of members is reduced below 2, or
(b) the shares in respect of which he is a contributory, or some of them, either were originally allotted to him, or have been held by him, and registered in his name, for at least 6 months during the 18 months before the commencement of the winding up, or have devolved on him through the death of a former holder.

(3) A person who is liable under section 76 to contribute to a company's assets in the event of its being wound up may petition on either of the grounds set out in section 122(1)(f) and (g), and subsection (2) above does not then apply; but unless the person is a contributory otherwise than under section 76, he may not in his character as contributory petition on any other ground.

(3A) A winding-up petition on the ground set out in section 122(1)(fa) may only be presented by one or more creditors.

(4) A winding-up petition may be presented by the Secretary of State—
(a) if the ground of the petition is that in section 122(1)(b) or (c), or
(b) in a case falling within section 124A or 124B below.

(4AA) A winding up petition may be presented by the Financial Conduct Authority in a case falling within section 124C(1) or (2).

(4A) A winding-up petition may be presented by the Regulator of Community Interest Companies in a case falling within section 50 of the Companies (Audit, Investigations and Community Enterprise) Act 2004.

(5) Where a company is being wound up voluntarily in England and Wales, a winding-up petition may be presented by the official receiver attached to the court as well as by any other person authorised in that behalf under the other provisions of this section; but the court shall not make a winding-up order on the petition unless it is satisfied that the voluntary winding up cannot be continued with due regard to the interests of the creditors or contributories.

124A Petition for winding up on grounds of public interest

(1) Where it appears to the Secretary of State from—
(a) any report made or information obtained under Part XIV (except section 448A) of the Companies Act 1985 (company investigations, &c.),
(b) any report made by inspectors under—
(i) section 167, 168, 169 or 284 of the Financial Services and Markets Act 2000, or
(ii) where the company is an open-ended investment company (within the meaning of that Act), regulations made as a result of section 262(2)(k) of that Act;
(bb) any information or documents obtained under section 165, 171, 172, 173 or 175 of that Act,
(c) any information obtained under section 2 of the Criminal Justice Act 1987 or section 28 of the Criminal Law (Consolidation) (Scotland) Act 1995 (fraud investigations), or
(d) any information obtained under section 83 of the Companies Act 1989 (powers exercisable for purpose of assisting overseas regulatory authorities),

that it is expedient in the public interest that a company should be wound up, he may present a petition for it to be wound up if the court thinks it just and equitable for it to be so.

(2) This section does not apply if the company is already being wound up by the court.

124B Petition for winding up of SE

(1) Where—
(a) an SE whose registered office is in Great Britain is not in compliance with Article 7 of Council Regulation (EC) No 2157/2001 on the Statute for a European company (the "EC Regulation") (location of head office and registered office), and
(b) it appears to the Secretary of State that the SE should be wound up, he may present a petition for it to be wound up if the court thinks it is just and equitable for it to be so.

(2) This section does not apply if the SE is already being wound up by the court.
(3) In this section "SE" has the same meaning as in the EC Regulation.

124C *omitted*

125 Powers of court on hearing of petition

(1) On hearing a winding-up petition the court may dismiss it, or adjourn the hearing conditionally or unconditionally, or make an interim order, or any other order that it thinks fit; but the court shall not refuse to make a winding-up order on the ground only that the company's assets have been mortgaged to an amount equal to or in excess of those assets, or that the company has no assets.
(2) If the petition is presented by members of the company as contributories on the ground that it is just and equitable that the company should be wound up, the court, if it is of opinion—
(a) that the petitioners are entitled to relief either by winding up the company or by some other means, and
(b) that in the absence of any other remedy it would be just and equitable that the company should be wound up,

shall make a winding-up order; but this does not apply if the court is also of the opinion both that some other remedy is available to the petitioners and that they are acting unreasonably in seeking to have the company wound up instead of pursuing that other remedy.

126 Power to stay or restrain proceedings against company

(1) At any time after the presentation of a winding-up petition, and before a winding-up order has been made, the company, or any creditor or contributory, may—
(a) where any action or proceeding against the company is pending in the High Court or Court of Appeal in England and Wales or Northern Ireland, apply to the court in which the action or proceeding is pending for a stay of proceedings therein, and
(b) where any other action or proceeding is pending against the company, apply to the court having jurisdiction to wind up the company to restrain further proceedings in the action or proceeding;

and the court to which the application is so made may (as the case may be) stay, sist or restrain the proceedings accordingly on such terms as it thinks fit.
(2) In the case of a company registered but not formed under the Companies Act 2006, where the application to stay, sist or restrain is by a creditor, this section extends to actions and proceedings against any contributory of the company.

127 Avoidance of property dispositions, etc.

(1) In a winding up by the court, any disposition of the company's property, and any transfer of shares, or alteration in the status of the company's members, made after the commencement of the winding up is, unless the court otherwise orders, void.
(2) This section has no effect in respect of anything done by an administrator of a company while a winding-up petition is suspended under paragraph 40 of Schedule B1.

128 Avoidance of attachments, etc.

(1) Where a company registered in England and Wales is being wound up by the court, any attachment, sequestration, distress or execution put in force against the estate or effects of the company after the commencement of the winding up is void.
(2) This section, so far as relates to any estate or effects of the company situated in England and Wales, applies in the case of a company registered in Scotland as it applies in the case of a company registered in England and Wales.

Commencement of winding up

129 Commencement of winding up by the court

(1) If, before the presentation of a petition for the winding up of a company by the court, a resolution has been passed by the company for voluntary winding up, the winding up of the company is deemed to have commenced at the time of the passing of the resolution; and unless the court, on proof of fraud or mistake, directs otherwise, all proceedings taken in the voluntary winding up are deemed to have been validly taken.

(1A) Where the court makes a winding-up order by virtue of paragraph 13(1)(e) of Schedule B1, the winding up is deemed to commence on the making of the order.

(2) In any other case, the winding up of a company by the court is deemed to commence at the time of the presentation of the petition for winding up.

130 Consequences of winding-up order

(1) On the making of a winding-up order, a copy of the order must forthwith be forwarded by the company (or otherwise as may be prescribed) to the registrar of companies, who shall enter it in his records relating to the company.

(2) When a winding-up order has been made or a provisional liquidator has been appointed, no action or proceeding shall be proceeded with or commenced against the company or its property, except by leave of the court and subject to such terms as the court may impose.

(3) When an order has been made for winding up a company registered but not formed under the Companies Act 2006, no action or proceeding shall be commenced or proceeded with against the company or its property or any contributory of the company, in respect of any debt of the company, except by leave of the court, and subject to such terms as the court may impose.

(4) An order for winding up a company operates in favour of all the creditors and of all contributories of the company as if made on the joint petition of a creditor and of a contributory.

Investigation procedures

131 Company's statement of affairs

(1) Where the court has made a winding-up order or appointed a provisional liquidator, the official receiver may require some or all of the persons mentioned in subsection (3) below to make out and submit to him a statement in the prescribed form as to the affairs of the company.

(2) The statement shall show—
- (a) particulars of the company's assets, debts and liabilities;
- (b) the names and addresses of the company's creditors;
- (c) the securities held by them respectively;
- (d) the dates when the securities were respectively given; and
- (e) such further or other information as may be prescribed or as the official receiver may require.

(2A) The statement shall be verified by the persons required to submit it—
- (a) in the case of an appointment of a provisional liquidator or a winding up by the court in England and Wales, by a statement of truth; and
- (b) in the case of an appointment of a provisional liquidator or a winding up by the court in Scotland, by affidavit.

(3) The persons referred to in subsection (1) are—
- (a) those who are or have been officers of the company;
- (b) those who have taken part in the formation of the company at any time within one year before the relevant date;
- (c) those who are in the company's employment, or have been in its employment within that year, and are in the official receiver's opinion capable of giving the information required;
- (d) those who are or have been within that year officers of, or in the employment of, a company which is, or within that year was, an officer of the company.

(4) Where any persons are required under this section to submit a statement of affairs to the official receiver, they shall do so (subject to the next subsection) before the end of the period of 21 days beginning with the day after that on which the prescribed notice of the requirement is given to them by the official receiver.

(5) The official receiver, if he thinks fit, may—
- (a) at any time release a person from an obligation imposed on him under subsection (1) or (2) above; or
- (b) either when giving the notice mentioned in subsection (4) or subsequently, extend the period so mentioned;

and where the official receiver has refused to exercise a power conferred by this subsection, the court, if it thinks fit, may exercise it.

(6) In this section—
"employment" includes employment under a contract for services; and "the relevant date" means—
(a) in a case where a provisional liquidator is appointed, the date of his appointment; and
(b) in a case where no such appointment is made, the date of the winding-up order.
(7) If a person without reasonable excuse fails to comply with any obligation imposed under this section, he is liable to a fine and, for continued contravention, to a daily default fine.
(8) In the application of this section to Scotland references to the official receiver are to the liquidator or, in a case where a provisional liquidator is appointed, the provisional liquidator.

132 Investigation by official receiver

(1) Where a winding-up order is made by the court in England and Wales, it is the duty of the official receiver to investigate—
(a) if the company has failed, the causes of the failure; and
(b) generally, the promotion, formation, business, dealings and affairs of the company,
and to make such report (if any) to the court as he thinks fit.
(2) The report is, in any proceedings, prima facie evidence of the facts stated in it.

133 Public examination of officers

(1) Where a company is being wound up by the court, the official receiver or, in Scotland, the liquidator may at any time before the dissolution of the company apply to the court for the public examination of any person who—
(a) is or has been an officer of the company; or
(b) has acted as liquidator or administrator of the company or as receiver or manager or, in Scotland, receiver of its property; or
(c) not being a person falling within paragraph (a) or (b), is or has been concerned, or has taken part, in the promotion, formation or management of the company.
(2) Unless the court otherwise orders, the official receiver or, in Scotland, the liquidator shall make an application under subsection (1) if he is requested in accordance with the rules to do so by—
(a) one-half, in value, of the company's creditors; or
(b) three-quarters, in value, of the company's contributories.
(3) On an application under subsection (1), the court shall direct that a public examination of the person to whom the application relates shall be held on a day appointed by the court; and that person shall attend on that day and be publicly examined as to the promotion, formation or management of the company or as to the conduct of its business and affairs, or his conduct or dealings in relation to the company.
(4) The following may take part in the public examination of a person under this section and may question that person concerning the matters mentioned in subsection (3), namely—
(a) the official receiver;
(b) the liquidator of the company;
(c) any person who has been appointed as special manager of the company's property or business;
(d) any creditor of the company who has tendered a proof or, in Scotland, submitted a claim in the winding up;
(e) any contributory of the company.

134 Enforcement of section 133

(1) If a person without reasonable excuse fails at any time to attend his public examination under section 133, he is guilty of a contempt of court and liable to be punished accordingly.
(2) In a case where a person without reasonable excuse fails at any time to attend his examination under section 133 or there are reasonable grounds for believing that a person has absconded, or is about to abscond, with a view to avoiding or delaying his examination under that section, the court may cause a warrant to be issued to a constable or prescribed officer of the court—
(a) for the arrest of that person; and
(b) for the seizure of any books, papers, records, money or goods in that person's possession.

(3) In such a case the court may authorise the person arrested under the warrant to be kept in custody, and anything seized under such a warrant to be held, in accordance with the rules, until such time as the court may order.

Appointment of liquidator

135 Appointment and powers of provisional liquidator

(1) Subject to the provisions of this section, the court may, at any time after the presentation of a winding-up petition, appoint a liquidator provisionally.

(2) In England and Wales, the appointment of a provisional liquidator may be made at any time before the making of a winding-up order; and either the official receiver or any other fit person may be appointed.

(3) In Scotland, such an appointment may be made at any time before the first appointment of liquidators.

(4) The provisional liquidator shall carry out such functions as the court may confer on him.

(5) When a liquidator is provisionally appointed by the court, his powers may be limited by the order appointing him.

136 Functions of official receiver in relation to office of liquidator

(1) The following provisions of this section have effect, subject to section 140 below, on a winding-up order being made by the court in England and Wales.

(2) The official receiver, by virtue of his office, becomes the liquidator of the company and continues in office until another person becomes liquidator under the provisions of this Part.

(3) The official receiver is, by virtue of his office, the liquidator during any vacancy.

(4) At any time when he is the liquidator of the company, the official receiver may summon separate meetings of the company's creditors and contributories for the purpose of choosing a person to be liquidator of the company in place of the official receiver.

(5) It is the duty of the official receiver—

(a) as soon as practicable in the period of 12 weeks beginning with the day on which the winding-up order was made, to decide whether to exercise his power under sub- section (4) to summon meetings, and

(b) if in pursuance of paragraph (a) he decides not to exercise that power, to give notice of his decision, before the end of that period, to the court and to the company's creditors and contributories, and

(c) (whether or not he has decided to exercise that power) to exercise his power to summon meetings under subsection (4) if he is at any time requested, in accordance with rules, to do so by one-quarter, in value, of the company's creditors;

and accordingly, where the duty imposed by paragraph (c) arises before the official receiver has performed a duty imposed by paragraph (a) or (b), he is not required to perform the latter duty.

(6) A notice given under subsection (5)(b) to the company's creditors shall contain an explanation of the creditors' power under subsection (5)(c) to require the official receiver to summon meetings of the company's creditors and contributories.

137 Appointment by Secretary of State

(1) In a winding up by the court in England and Wales the official receiver may, at any time when he is the liquidator of the company, apply to the Secretary of State for the appointment of a person as liquidator in his place.

(2) If meetings are held in pursuance of a decision under section 136(5)(a), but no person is chosen to be liquidator as a result of those meetings, it is the duty of the official receiver to decide whether to refer the need for an appointment to the Secretary of State.

(3) On an application under subsection (1), or a reference made in pursuance of a decision under subsection (2), the Secretary of State shall either make an appointment or decline to make one.

(4) Where a liquidator has been appointed by the Secretary of State under subsection (3), the liquidator shall give notice of his appointment to the company's creditors or, if the court so allows, shall advertise his appointment in accordance with the directions of the court.

(5) In that notice or advertisement the liquidator shall—

(a) state whether he proposes to summon a general meeting of the company's creditors under section 141 below for the purpose of determining (together with any meeting of contributories) whether a liquidation committee should be established under that section, and

(b) if he does not propose to summon such a meeting, set out the power of the company's creditors under that section to require him to summon one.

138 Appointment of liquidator in Scotland

(1) Where a winding-up order is made by the court in Scotland, a liquidator shall be appointed by the court at the time when the order is made.

(2) The liquidator so appointed (here referred to as "the interim liquidator") continues in office until another person becomes liquidator in his place under this section or the next.

(3) The interim liquidator shall (subject to the next subsection) as soon as practicable in the period of 28 days beginning with the day on which the winding-up order was made or such longer period as the court may allow, summon separate meetings of the company's creditors and contributories for the purpose of choosing a person (who may be the person who is the interim liquidator) to be liquidator of the company in place of the interim liquidator.

(4) If it appears to the interim liquidator, in any case where a company is being wound up on grounds including its inability to pay its debts, that it would be inappropriate to summon under subsection (3) a meeting of the company's contributories, he may summon only a meeting of the company's creditors for the purpose mentioned in that subsection.

(5) If one or more meetings are held in pursuance of this section but no person is appointed or nominated by the meeting or meetings, the interim liquidator shall make a report to the court which shall appoint either the interim liquidator or some other person to be liquidator of the company.

(6) A person who becomes liquidator of the company in place of the interim liquidator shall, unless he is appointed by the court, forthwith notify the court of that fact.

139 Choice of liquidator at meetings of creditors and contributories

(1) This section applies where a company is being wound up by the court and separate meetings of the company's creditors and contributories are summoned for the purpose of choosing a person to be liquidator of the company.

(2) The creditors and the contributories at their respective meetings may nominate a person to be liquidator.

(3) The liquidator shall be the person nominated by the creditors or, where no person has been so nominated, the person (if any) nominated by the contributories.

(4) In the case of different persons being nominated, any contributory or creditor may, within 7 days after the date on which the nomination was made by the creditors, apply to the court for an order either—

(a) appointing the person nominated as liquidator by the contributories to be a liquidator instead of, or jointly with, the person nominated by the creditors; or

(b) appointing some other person to be liquidator instead of the person nominated by the creditors.

140 Appointment by the court following administration or voluntary arrangement

(1) Where a winding-up order is made immediately upon the appointment of an administrator ceasing to have effect, the court may appoint as liquidator of the company the person whose appointment as administrator has ceased to have effect.

(2) Where a winding-up order is made at a time when there is a supervisor of a voluntary arrangement approved in relation to the company under Part I, the court may appoint as liquidator of the company the person who is the supervisor at the time when the winding-up order is made.

(3) Where the court makes an appointment under this section, the official receiver does not become the liquidator as otherwise provided by section 136(2), and he has no duty under section 136(5)(a) or (b) in respect of the summoning of creditors' or contributories' meetings.

Liquidation committees

141 Liquidation committee (England and Wales)

(1) Where a winding-up order has been made by the court in England and Wales and separate meetings of creditors and contributories have been summoned for the purpose of choosing a person to be liquidator, those meetings may establish a committee ("the liquidation committee") to exercise the functions conferred on it by or under this Act.

(2) The liquidator (not being the official receiver) may at any time, if he thinks fit, summon separate general meetings of the company's creditors and contributories for the purpose of determining whether such a committee should be established and, if it is so determined, of establishing it.

The liquidator (not being the official receiver) shall summon such a meeting if he is requested, in accordance with the rules, to do so by one-tenth, in value, of the company's creditors.

(3) Where meetings are summoned under this section, or for the purpose of choosing a person to be liquidator, and either the meeting of creditors or the meeting of contributories decides that a liquidation committee should be established, but the other meeting does not so decide or decides that a committee should not be established, the committee shall be established in accordance with the rules, unless the court otherwise orders.

(4) The liquidation committee is not to be able or required to carry out its functions at any time when the official receiver is liquidator; but at any such time its functions are vested in the Secretary of State except to the extent that the rules otherwise provide.

(5) Where there is for the time being no liquidation committee, and the liquidator is a person other than the official receiver, the functions of such a committee are vested in the Secretary of State except to the extent that the rules otherwise provide.

142 Liquidation committee (Scotland)

(1) Where a winding-up order has been made by the court in Scotland and separate meetings of creditors and contributories have been summoned for the purpose of choosing a person to be liquidator or, under section 138(4), only a meeting of creditors has been summoned for that purpose, those meetings or (as the case may be) that meeting may establish a committee ("the liquidation committee") to exercise the functions conferred on it by or under this Act.

(2) The liquidator may at any time, if he thinks fit, summon separate general meetings of the company's creditors and contributories for the purpose of determining whether such a committee should be established and, if it is so determined, of establishing it.

(3) The liquidator, if appointed by the court otherwise than under section 139(4)(a), is required to summon meetings under subsection (2) if he is requested, in accordance with the rules, to do so by one-tenth, in value, of the company's creditors.

(4) Where meetings are summoned under this section, or for the purpose of choosing a person to be liquidator, and either the meeting of creditors or the meeting of contributories decides that a liquidation committee should be established, but the other meeting does not so decide or decides that a committee should not be established, the committee shall be established in accordance with the rules, unless the court otherwise orders.

(5) Where in the case of any winding up there is for the time being no liquidation committee, the functions of such a committee are vested in the court except to the extent that the rules otherwise provide.

(6) In addition to the powers and duties conferred and imposed on it by this Act, a liquidation committee has such of the powers and duties of commissioners in a sequestration as may be conferred and imposed on such committees by the rules.

The liquidator's functions

143 General functions in winding up by the court

(1) The functions of the liquidator of a company which is being wound up by the court are to secure that the assets of the company are got in, realised and distributed to the company's creditors and, if there is a surplus, to the persons entitled to it.

(2) It is the duty of the liquidator of a company which is being wound up by the court in England and Wales, if he is not the official receiver—

(a) to furnish the official receiver with such information,

(b) to produce to the official receiver, and permit inspection by the official receiver of, such books, papers and other records, and
(c) to give the official receiver such other assistance,

as the official receiver may reasonably require for the purposes of carrying out his functions in relation to the winding up.

144 Custody of company's property

(1) When a winding-up order has been made, or where a provisional liquidator has been appointed, the liquidator or the provisional liquidator (as the case may be) shall take into his custody or under his control all the property and things in action to which the company is or appears to be entitled.

(2) In a winding up by the court in Scotland, if and so long as there is no liquidator, all the property of the company is deemed to be in the custody of the court.

145 Vesting of company property in liquidator

(1) When a company is being wound up by the court, the court may on the application of the liquidator by order direct that all or any part of the property of whatsoever description belonging to the company or held by trustees on its behalf shall vest in the liquidator by his official name; and thereupon the property to which the order relates vests accordingly.

(2) The liquidator may, after giving such indemnity (if any) as the court may direct, bring or defend in his official name any action or other legal proceeding which relates to that property or which it is necessary to bring or defend for the purpose of effectually winding up the company and recovering its property.

146 Duty to summon final meeting

(1) Subject to the next subsection, if it appears to the liquidator of a company which is being wound up by the court that the winding up of the company is for practical purposes complete and the liquidator is not the official receiver, the liquidator shall summon a final general meeting of the company's creditors which—
(a) shall receive the liquidator's report of the winding up, and
(b) shall determine whether the liquidator should have his release under section 174 in Chapter VII of this Part.

(2) The liquidator may, if he thinks fit, give the notice summoning the final general meeting at the same time as giving notice of any final distribution of the company's property but, if summoned for an earlier date, that meeting shall be adjourned (and, if necessary, further adjourned) until a date on which the liquidator is able to report to the meeting that the winding up of the company is for practical purposes complete.

(3) In the carrying out of his functions in the winding up it is the duty of the liquidator to retain sufficient sums from the company's property to cover the expenses of summoning and holding the meeting required by this section.

General powers of court

147 Power to stay or sist winding up

(1) The court may at any time after an order for winding up, on the application either of the liquidator or the official receiver or any creditor or contributory, and on proof to the satisfaction of the court that all proceedings in the winding up ought to be stayed or sisted, make an order staying or sisting the proceedings, either altogether or for a limited time, on such terms and conditions as the court thinks fit.

(2) The court may, before making an order, require the official receiver to furnish to it a report with respect to any facts or matters which are in his opinion relevant to the application.

(3) A copy of every order made under this section shall forthwith be forwarded by the company, or otherwise as may be prescribed, to the registrar of companies, who shall enter it in his records relating to the company.

148 Settlement of list of contributories and application of assets

(1) As soon as may be after making a winding-up order, the court shall settle a list of contributories, with power to rectify the register of members in all cases where rectification is required, and shall cause the company's assets to be collected, and applied in discharge of its liabilities.

(2) If it appears to the court that it will not be necessary to make calls on or adjust the rights of contributories, the court may dispense with the settlement of a list of contributories.

(3) In settling the list, the court shall distinguish between persons who are contributories in their own right and persons who are contributories as being representatives of or liable for the debts of others.

149 Debts due from contributory to company

(1) The court may, at any time after making a winding-up order, make an order on any contributory for the time being on the list of contributories to pay, in manner directed by the order, any money due from him (or from the estate of the person who he represents) to the company, exclusive of any money payable by him or the estate by virtue of any call.

(2) The court in making such an order may—

(a) in the case of an unlimited company, allow to the contributory by way of set-off any money due to him or the estate which he represents from the company on any independent dealing or contract with the company, but not any money due to him as a member of the company in respect of any dividend or profit, and

(b) in the case of a limited company, make to any director or manager whose liability is unlimited or to his estate the like allowance.

(3) In the case of any company, whether limited or unlimited, when all the creditors are paid in full (together with interest at the official rate) any money due on any account whatever to a contributory from the company may be allowed to him by way of set-off against any subsequent call.

150 Power to make calls

(1) The court may, at any time after making a winding-up order, and either before or after it has ascertained the sufficiency of the company's assets, make calls on all or any of the contributories for the time being settled on the list of the contributories to the extent of their liability, for payment of any money which the court considers necessary to satisfy the company's debts and liabilities, and the expenses of winding up, and for the adjustment of the rights of the contributories among themselves, and make an order for payment of any calls so made.

(2) In making a call the court may take into consideration the probability that some of the contributories may partly or wholly fail to pay it.

151 Payment into bank of money due to company

(1) The court may order any contributory, purchaser or other person from whom money is due to the company to pay the amount due into the Bank of England (or any branch of it) to the account of the liquidator instead of to the liquidator, and such an order may be enforced in the same manner as if it had directed payment to the liquidator.

(2) All money and securities paid or delivered into the Bank of England (or branch) in the event of a winding up by the court are subject in all respects to the orders of the court.

152 Order on contributory to be conclusive evidence

(1) An order made by the court on a contributory is conclusive evidence that the money (if any) thereby appearing to be due or ordered to be paid is due, but subject to any right of appeal.

(2) All other pertinent matters stated in the order are to be taken as truly stated as against all persons and in all proceedings except proceedings in Scotland against the heritable estate of a deceased contributory; and in that case the order is only prima facie evidence for the purpose of charging his heritable estate, unless his heirs or legatees of heritage were on the list of contributories at the time of the order being made.

153 Power to exclude creditors not proving in time

The court may fix a time or times within which creditors are to prove their debts or claims or to be excluded from the benefit of any distribution made before those debts are proved.

154 Adjustment of rights of contributories

The court shall adjust the rights of the contributories among themselves and distribute any surplus among the persons entitled to it.

155 Inspection of books by creditors, etc.

(1) The court may, at any time after making a winding-up order, make such order for inspection of the company's books and papers by creditors and contributories as the court thinks just; and any books and papers in the company's possession may be inspected by creditors and contributories accordingly, but not further or otherwise.

(2) Nothing in this section excludes or restricts any statutory rights of a government department or person acting under the authority of a government department.

(3) For the purposes of subsection (2) above, references to a government department shall be construed as including references to any part of the Scottish Administration.

156 Payment of expenses of winding up

The court may, in the event of the assets being insufficient to satisfy the liabilities, make an order as to the payment out of the assets of the expenses incurred in the winding up in such order of priority as the court thinks just.

157 Attendance at company meetings (Scotland)

In the winding up by the court of a company registered in Scotland, the court has power to require the attendance of any officer of the company at any meeting of creditors or of contributories, or of a liquidation committee, for the purpose of giving information as to the trade, dealings, affairs or property of the company.

158 Power to arrest absconding contributory

The court, at any time either before or after making a winding-up order, on proof of probable cause for believing that a contributory is about to quit the United Kingdom or otherwise to abscond or to remove or conceal any of his property for the purpose of evading payment of calls, may cause the contributory to be arrested and his books and papers and moveable personal property to be seized and him and them to be kept safely until such time as the court may order.

159 Powers of court to be cumulative

Powers conferred on the court by this Act are in addition to, and not in restriction of, any existing powers of instituting proceedings against a contributory or debtor of the company, or the estate of any contributory or debtor, for the recovery of any call or other sums.

160 Delegation of powers to liquidator (England and Wales)

(1) Provision may be made by rules for enabling or requiring all or any of the powers and duties conferred and imposed on the court in England and Wales in respect of the following matters—

(a) the holding and conducting of meetings to ascertain the wishes of creditors and contributories,

(b) the settling of lists of contributories and the rectifying of the register of members where required, and the collection and application of the assets,

(c) the payment, delivery, conveyance, surrender or transfer of money, property, books or papers to the liquidator,

(d) the making of calls,

(e) the fixing of a time within which debts and claims must be proved,

to be exercised or performed by the liquidator as an officer of the court, and subject to the court's control.

(2) But the liquidator shall not, without the special leave of the court, rectify the register of members, and shall not make any call without either that special leave or the sanction of the liquidation committee.

Enforcement of, and appeal from, orders

161 Orders for calls on contributories (Scotland)

(1) In Scotland, where an order, interlocutor or decree has been made for winding up a company by the court, it is competent to the court, on production by the liquidators of a list certified by them of the names of the contributories liable in payment of any calls, and of the amount due by each contributory, and of the date when that amount became due, to pronounce forthwith a decree against those contributories for payment of the sums so certified to be due, with interest from that date until payment (at 5 per cent. per annum)

in the same way and to the same effect as if they had severally consented to registration for execution, on a charge of 6 days, of a legal obligation to pay those calls and interest.

(2) The decree may be extracted immediately, and no suspension of it is competent, except on caution or consignation, unless with special leave of the court.

162 Appeals from orders in Scotland

(1) Subject to the provision of this section and to rules of court, an appeal from any order or decision made or given in the winding up of a company by the court in Scotland under this Act lies in the same manner and subject to the same conditions as an appeal from an order or decision of the court in cases within its ordinary jurisdiction.

(2) In regard to orders of judgments pronounced by the judge acting as vacation judge—

(a) none of the orders specified in Part I of Schedule 3 to this Act are subject to review, reduction, suspension or stay of execution, and

(b) every other order or judgment (except as mentioned below) may be submitted to review by the Inner House by reclaiming motion enrolled within 14 days from the date of the order or judgment.

(3) However, an order being one of those specified in Part II of that Schedule shall, from the date of the order and notwithstanding that it has been submitted to review as above, be carried out and receive effect until the Inner House have disposed of the matter.

(4) In regard to orders or judgments pronounced in Scotland by a Lord Ordinary before whom proceedings in a winding up are being taken, any such order or judgment may be submitted to review by the Inner House by reclaiming motion enrolled within 14 days from its date; but should it not be so submitted to review during session, the provisions of this section in regard to orders or judgments pronounced by the judge acting as vacation judge apply.

(5) Nothing in this section affects provisions of the Companies Act or this Act in reference to decrees in Scotland for payment of calls in the winding up of companies, whether voluntary or by the court.

CHAPTER VII
LIQUIDATORS

Preliminary

163 Style and title of liquidators

The liquidator of a company shall be described—

(a) where a person other than the official receiver is liquidator, by the style of "the liquidator" of the particular company, or

(b) where the official receiver is liquidator, by the style of "the official receiver and liquidator" of the particular company;

And in neither case shall 1he be described by an individual name.

164 Corrupt inducement affecting appointment

A person who gives, or agrees or offers to give, to any member or creditor of a company any valuable consideration with a view to securing his own appointment or nomination, or to securing or preventing the appointment or nomination of some person other than himself, as the company's liquidator is liable to a fine.

Liquidator's powers and duties

165 Voluntary winding up

(1) This section has effect where a company is being wound up voluntarily, but subject to section 166 below in the case of a creditor's voluntary winding up.

(2) The liquidator may exercise any of the powers specified in Parts 1 to 3 of Schedule 4.

(3) ...

(4) The liquidator may—

(a) exercise the court's power of settling a list of contributories (which list is prima facie evidence of the liability of the persons named in it to be contributories),

(b) exercise the court's power of making calls,

(c) summon general meetings of the company for the purpose of obtaining its sanction by special resolution or for any other purpose he may think fit.

(5) The liquidator shall pay the company's debts and adjust the rights of the contributories among themselves.

(6) Where the liquidator in exercise of the powers conferred on him by this Act disposes of any property of the company to a person who is connected with the company (within the meaning of section 249 in Part VII), he shall, if there is for the time being a liquidation committee, give notice to the committee of that exercise of his powers.

166 Creditors' voluntary winding up

(1) This section applies where, in the case of a creditors' voluntary winding up, a liquidator has been nominated by the company.

(1A) The exercise by the liquidator of the power specified in paragraph 6 of Schedule 4 to this Act (power to sell any of the company's property) shall not be challengeable on the ground of any prior inhibition.

(2) The powers conferred on the liquidator by section 165 shall not be exercised, except with the sanction of the court, during the period before the holding of the creditors' meeting under section 98 in Chapter IV.

(3) Subsection (2) does not apply in relation to the power of the liquidator—

- (a) to take into his custody or under his control all the property to which the company is or appears to be entitled;
- (b) to dispose of perishable goods and other goods the value of which is likely to diminish if they are not immediately disposed of; and
- (c) to do all such other things as may be necessary for the protection of the company's assets.

(4) The liquidator shall attend the creditors' meeting held under section 98 and shall report to the meeting on any exercise by him of his powers (whether or not under this section or under section 112 or 165).

(5) If default is made—

- (a) by the company in complying with subsection (1), (1A) or (2) of section 98, or
- (b) by the directors in complying with subsection (1) or (2) of section 99,

the liquidator shall, within 7 days of the relevant day, apply to the court for directions as to the manner in which that default is to be remedied.

(6) "The relevant day" means the day on which the liquidator was nominated by the company or the day on which he first became aware of the default, whichever is the later.

(7) If the liquidator without reasonable excuse fails to comply with this section, he is liable to a fine.

167 Winding up by the court

(1) Where a company is being wound up by the court, the liquidator may exercise any of the powers specified in Parts 1 to 3 of Schedule 4.

(2) Where the liquidator (not being the official receiver), in exercise of the powers conferred on him by this Act—

- (a) disposes of any property of the company to a person who is connected with the company (within the meaning of section 249 in Part VII) or
- (b) employs a solicitor to assist him in the carrying out of his functions,

he shall, if there is for the time being a liquidation committee, give notice to the committee of that exercise of his powers.

(3) The exercise by the liquidator in a winding up by the court of the powers conferred by this section is subject to the control of the court, and any creditor or contributory may apply to the court with respect to any exercise or proposed exercise of any of those powers.

168 Supplementary powers (England and Wales)

(1) This section applies in the case of a company which is being wound up by the court in England and Wales.

(2) The liquidator may summon general metings of the creditors or contributories for the purpose of ascertaining their wishes; and it is his duty to summon meetings at such times as the creditors or contributories by resolution (either at the meeting appointing the liquidator or otherwise) may direct, or whenever requested in writing to do so by one-tenth in value of the creditors or contributories (as the case may be).

(3) The liquidator may apply to the court (in the prescribed manner) for directions in relation to any particular matter arising in the winding up.

(4) Subject to the provisions of this Act, the liquidator shall use his own discretion in the management of the assets and their distribution among the creditors.

(5) If any person is aggrieved by an act or decision of the liquidator, that person may apply to the court; and the court may confirm, reverse or modify the act or decision complained of, and make such order in the case as it thinks just.

(5A) Where at any time after a winding-up petition has been presented to the court against any person (including an insolvent partnership or other body which may be wound up under Part V of the Act as an unregistered company), whether by virtue of the provisions of the Insolvent Partnerships Order 1994 or not, the attention of the court is drawn to the fact that the person in question is a member of an insolvent partnership, the court may make an order as to the future conduct of the insolvency proceedings and any such order may apply any provisions of that Order with any necessary modifications.

(5B) Any order or directions under subsection (5A) may be made or given on the application of the official receiver, any responsible insolvency practitioner, the trustee of the partnership or any other interested person and may include provisions as to the administration of the joint estate of the partnership, and in particular how it and the separate estate of any member are to be administered.

(5C) Where the court makes an order for the winding up of an insolvent partnership under—

(a) section 72(1)(a) of the Financial Services Act 1986;

(b) section 92(1)(a) of the Banking Act 1987; or

(c) section 367(3)(a) of the Financial Services and Markets Act 2000,

the court may make an order as to the future conduct of the winding up proceedings, and any such order may apply any provisions of the Insolvent Partnerships Order 1994 with any necessary modifications

169 Supplementary powers (Scotland)

(1) ...

(2) In a winding up by the court in Scotland, the liquidator has (subject to the rules) the same powers as a trustee on a bankrupt estate.

170 Enforcement of liquidator's duty to make returns, etc.

(1) If a liquidator who has made any default—

(a) in filing, delivering or making any return, account or other document, or

(b) in giving any notice which he is by law required to file, deliver, make or give,

fails to make good the default within 14 days after the service on him of a notice requiring him to do so, the court has the following powers.

(2) On an application made by any creditor or contributory of the company, or by the registrar of companies, the court may make an order directing the liquidator to make good the default within such time as may be specified in the order.

(3) The court's order may provide that all costs of and incidental to the application shall be borne by the liquidator.

(4) Nothing in this section prejudices the operation of any enactment imposing penalties on a liquidator in respect of any such default as is mentioned above.

Removal; vacation of office

171 Removal, etc. (voluntary winding up)

(1) This section applies with respect to the removal from office and vacation of office of the liquidator of a company which is being wound up voluntarily.

(2) Subject to the next subsection, the liquidator may be removed from office only by an order of the court or—

(a) in the case of a members' voluntary winding up, by a general meeting of the company summoned specially for that puropose, or

(b) in the case of a creditors' voluntary winding up, by a general meeting of the company's creditors summoned specially for that purpose in accordance with the rules.

(3) Where the liquidator was appointed by the court under section 108 in Chapter V, a meeting such as is mentioned in subsection (2) above shall be summoned for the

purpose of replacing him only if he thinks fit or the court so directs or the meeting is requested, in accordance with the rules—

(a) in the case of a members' voluntary winding up, by members representing not less than one-half of the total voting rights of all the members having at the date of the request a right to vote at the meeting, or

(b) in the case of a creditors' voluntary winding up, by not less than one-half, in value, of the company's creditors.

(4) A liquidator shall vacate office if he ceases to be a person who is qualified to act as an insolvency practitioner in relation to the company.

(5) A liquidator may, in the prescribed circumstances, resign his office by giving notice of his resignation to the registrar of companies.

(6) Where—

(a) in the case of a members' voluntary winding up, a final meeting of the company has been held under section 94 in Chapter III, or

(b) in the case of a creditors' voluntary winding up, final meetings of the company and of the creditors have been held under section 106 in Chapter IV,

the liquidator whose report was considered at the meeting or meetings shall vacate office as soon as he has complied with subsection (3) of that section and has given notice to the registrar of companies that the meeting or meetings have been held and of the decisions (if any) of the meeting or meetings.

172 Removal, etc. (winding up by the court)

(1) This section applies with respect to the removal from office and vacationm of office of the liquidator of a company which is being wound up by the court, or of a provisional liquidator.

(2) Subject as follows, the liquidator may be removed from office only by an order of the court or by a general meeting of the company's creditors summoned specially for that purpose in accordance with the rules; and a provisional liquidator may be removed from office only by an order of the court.

(3) Where—

(a) the official receiver is liquidator otherwise than in succession under section 136(3) to a person who held office as a result of a nomination by a meeting of the company's creditors or contributories, or

(b) the liquidator was appointed by the court otherwise than under section 139(4)(a) or 140(1), or was appointed by the Secretary of State,

a general meeting of the company's creditors shall be summoned for the purpose of replacing him only if he thinks fit, or the court so directs, or the meeting is requested, in accordance with the rules, by not less than one-quarter, in value, of the creditors.

(4) If appointed by the Secretary of State, the liquidator may be removed from office by a direction of the Secretary of State.

(5) A liquidator or provisional liquidator, not being the official receiver, shall vacate office if he ceases to be a person who is qualified to act as an insolvency practitioner in relation to the company.

(6) A liquidator may, in the prescribed circumstances, resign his office by giving notice of his resignation to the court.

(7) Where an order is made under section 204 (early dissolution in Scotland) for the dissolution of the company, the liquidator shall vacate office when the dissolution of the company takes effect in accordance with that section.

(8) Where a final meeting has been held under section 146 (liquidator's report on completion of winding up), the liquidator whose report was considered at the meeting shall vacate office as soon as he has given notice to the court and the registrar of companies that the meeting has been held and of the decisions (if any) of the meeting.

Release of liquidator

173 Release (voluntary winding up)

(1) This section applies with respect to the release of the liquidator of a company which is being wound up voluntarily.

(2) A person who has ceased to be a liquidator shall have his release with effect from the following time, that is to say—

(a) in the case of a person who has been removed from office by a general meeting of the company or by a general meeting of the company's creditors that has not resolved against his release or who has died, the time at which notice is given to the registrar of companies in accordance with the rules that that person has ceased to hold office;

(b) in the case of a person who has been removed from office by a general meeting of the company's creditors that has resolved against his release, or by the court, or who has vacated office under section 171(4) above, such time as the Secretary of State may, on the application of that person, determine;

(c) in the case of a person who has resigned, such time as may be prescribed;

(d) in the case of a person who has vacated office under subsection (6)(a) of section 171, the time at which he vacated office;

(e) in the case of a person who has vacated office under subsection (6)(b) of that section—

(i) if the final meeting of the creditors referred to in that subsection has resolved against that person's release, such time as the Secretary of State may, on an application by that person, determine, and

(ii) if that meeting has not resolved against that person's release, the time at which he vacated office.

(3) In the application of subsection (2) to the winding up of a company registered in Scotland, the references to a determination by the Secretary of State as to the time from which a person who has ceased to be liquidator shall have his release are to be read as references to such a determination by the Accountant of Court.

(4) Where a liquidator has his release under subsection (2), he is, with effect from the time specified in that subsection, discharged from all liability both in respect of acts or omissions of his in the winding up and otherwise in relation to his conduct as liquidator. But nothing in this section prevents the exercise, in relation to a person who has had his release under subsection (2), of the court's powers under section 212 of this Act (summary remedy against delinquent directors, liquidators, etc.).

174 Release (winding up by the court)

(1) This section applies with respect to the release of the liquidator of a company which is being wound up by the court, or of a provisional liquidator.

(2) Where the official receiver has ceased to be liquidator and a person becomes liquidator in his stead, the official receiver has his release with effect from the following time, that is to say—

(a) in a case where that person was nominated by a general meeting of creditors or contributories, or was appointed by the Secretary of State, the time at which the official receiver gives notice to the court that he has been replaced;

(b) in a case where that person is appointed by the court, such time as the court may determine.

(3) If the official receiver while he is a liquidator gives notice to the Secretary of State that the winding up is for practical purposes complete, he has his release with effect from such time as the Secretary of State may determine.

(4) A person other than the official receiver who has ceased to be a liquidator has his release with efect from the following time, that is to say—

(a) in the case of a person who has been removed from office by a general meeting of creditors that has not resolved against his release or who has died, the time at which notice is given to the court in accordance with the rules that that person has ceased to hold office;

(b) in the case of a person who has been removed from office by a general meeting of creditors that has resolved against his release, or by the court or the Secretary of State, or who has vacated office under section 172(5) or (7), such time as the Secretary of State may, on an application by that person, determine;

(c) in the case of a person who has resigned, such time as may be prescribed;

(d) in the case of a person who has vacated office under section 172(8)—

(i) if the final meeting referred to in that subsection has resolved against that person's release, such time as the Secretary of State may, on an application by that person, determine, and

(ii) if that meeting has not so resolved, the time at which that person vacated office.

(5) A person who has ceased to hold office as a provisional liquidator has his release with effect from such time as the court may, on an application by him, determine.

(6) Where the official receiver or a liquidator or provisional liquidator has his release under this section, he is, with effect from the time specified in the preceding provisions of this section, discharged from all liability both in respect of acts or omissions of his in the winding up and otherwise in relation to his conduct as liquidator or provisional liquidator. But nothing in this section prevents the exercise, in relation to a person who has had his release under this section, of the court's powers under section 212 (summary remedy against delinquent directors, liquidators, etc.).

(7) In the application of this section to a case where the order for winding up has been made by the court in Scotland, the references to a determination by the Secretary of State as to the time from which a person who has ceased to be liquidator has his release are to such a determination by the Accountant of Court.

CHAPTER VIII
PROVISIONS OF GENERAL APPLICATION IN WINDING UP

Preferential debts

175 Preferential debts (general provision)

(1) In a winding up the company's preferential debts shall be paid in priority to all other debts.

(1A) Ordinary preferential debts rank equally among themselves after the expenses of the winding up and shall be paid in full, unless the assets are insufficient to meet them, in which case they abate in equal proportions.

(1B) Secondary preferential debts rank equally among themselves after the ordinary preferential debts and shall be paid in full, unless the assets are insufficient to meet them, in which case they abate in equal proportions.

(2) Preferential debts—

(a) ...

(b) so far as the assets of the company available for payment of general creditors are insufficient to meet them, have priority over the claims of holders of debentures secured by, or holders of, any floating charge created by the company, and shall be paid accordingly out of any property comprised in or subject to that charge.

(3) In this section "preferential debts", "ordinary preferential debts" and "secondary preferential debts" each has the meaning given in section 386 in Part 12.

176 Preferential charge on goods distrained

(1) This section applies where a company is being wound up by the court in England and Wales, and is without prejudice to section 128 (avoidance of attachments, etc.).

(2) Where any person (whether or not a landlord or person entitled to rent) has distrained upon the goods or effects of the company in the period of 3 months ending with the date of the winding-up order, those goods or effects, or the proceeds of their sale, shall be charged for the benefit of the company with the preferential debts of the company to the extent that the company's property is for the time being insufficient for meeting them.

(3) Where by virtue of a charge under subsection (2) any person surrenders any goods or effects to a company or makes a payment to a company, that person ranks, in respect of the amount of the proceeds of sale of those goods or effects by the liquidator or (as the case may be) the amount of the payment, as a preferential creditor of the company, except as against so much of the company's property as is available for the payment of preferential creditors by virtue of the surrender or payment.

Property subject to floating charge

176ZA Payment of expenses of winding up (England and Wales)

(1) The expenses of winding up in England and Wales, so far as the assets of the company available for payment of general creditors are insufficient to meet them, have priority over any claims to property comprised in or subject to any floating charge created by the company and shall be paid out of any such property accordingly.

(2) In subsection (1)—
  (a) the reference to assets of the company available for payment of general creditors does not include any amount made available under section 176A(2)(a);
  (b) the reference to claims to property comprised in or subject to a floating charge is to the claims of—
    (i) the holders of debentures secured by, or holders of, the floating charge, and
    (ii) any preferential creditors entitled to be paid out of that property in priority to them.

(3) Provision may be made by rules restricting the application of subsection (1), in such circumstances as may be prescribed, to expenses authorised or approved—
  (a) by the holders of debentures secured by, or holders of, the floating charge and by any preferential creditors entitled to be paid in priority to them, or
  (b) by the court.

(4) References in this section to the expenses of the winding up are to all expenses properly incurred in the winding up, including the remuneration of the liquidator.

176A Share of assets for unsecured creditors

(1) This section applies where a floating charge relates to property of a company—
  (a) which has gone into liquidation,
  (b) which is in administration,
  (c) of which there is a provisional liquidator, or
  (d) of which there is a receiver.

(2) The liquidator, administrator or receiver—
  (a) shall make a prescribed part of the company's net property available for the satisfaction of unsecured debts, and
  (b) shall not distribute that part to the proprietor of a floating charge except in so far as it exceeds the amount required for the satisfaction of unsecured debts.

(3) Subsection (2) shall not apply to a company if—
  (a) the company's net property is less than the prescribed minimum, and
  (b) the liquidator, administrator or receiver thinks that the cost of making a distribution to unsecured creditors would be disproportionate to the benefits.

(4) Subsection (2) shall also not apply to a company if or in so far as it is disapplied by—
  (a) a voluntary arrangement in respect of the company, or
  (b) a compromise or arrangement agreed under Part 26 of the Companies Act 2006 (arrangements and reconstructions).

(5) Subsection (2) shall also not apply to a company if—
  (a) the liquidator, administrator or receiver applies to the court for an order under this subsection on the ground that the cost of making a distribution to unsecured creditors would be disproportionate to the benefits, and
  (b) the court orders that subsection (2) shall not apply.

(6) In subsections (2) and (3) a company's net property is the amount of its property which would, but for this section, be available for satisfaction of claims of holders of debentures secured by, or holders of, any floating charge created by the company.

(7) An order under subsection (2) prescribing part of a company's net property may, in particular, provide for its calculation—
  (a) as a percentage of the company's net property, or
  (b) as an aggregate of different percentages of different parts of the company's net property.

(8) An order under this section—
  (a) must be made by statutory instrument, and
  (b) shall be subject to annulment pursuant to a resolution of either House of Parliament.

(9) In this section—
"floating charge" means a charge which is a floating charge on its creation and which is created after the first order under subsection (2)(a) comes into force, and "prescribed" means prescribed by order by the Secretary of State.

(10) An order under this section may include transitional or incidental provision.

Special managers

177 Power to appoint special manager

(1) Where a company has gone into liquidation or a provisional liquidator has been appointed, the court may, on an application under this section, appoint any person to be the special manager of the business or property of the company.

(2) The application may be made by the liquidator or provisional liquidator in any case where it appears to him that the nature of the business or property of the company, or the interests of the company's creditors or contributories or members generally, require the appointment of another to manage the company's business or property.

(3) The special manager has such powers as may be entrusted to him by the court.

(4) The court's power to entrust powers to the special manager includes power to direct that any provision of this Act that has effect in relation to the provisional liquidator or liquidator of a company shall have the like effect in relation to the special manager for the purposes of the carrying out by him of any of the functions of the provisional liquidator or liquidator.

(5) The special manager shall—

(a) give such security or, in Scotland, caution, as may be prescribed;

(b) prepare and keep such accounts as may be prescribed; and

(c) produce those accounts in accordance with the rules to the Secretary of State or to such other persons as may be prescribed.

Disclaimer (England and Wales only)

178 Power to disclaim onerous property

(1) This and the next two sections apply to a company that is being wound up in England and Wales.

(2) Subject as follows, the liquidator may, by the giving of the prescribed notice, disclaim any onerous property and may do so notwithstanding that he has taken possession of it, endeavoured to sell it, or otherwise exercised rights of ownership in relation to it.

(3) The following is onerous property for the purposes of this section—

(a) any unprofitable contract, and

(b) any other property of the company which is unsaleable or not readily saleable or is such that it may give rise to a liability to pay money or perform any other onerous act.

(4) A disclaimer under this section—

(a) operates so as to determine, as from the date of the disclaimer, the rights, interests and liabilities of the company in or in respect of the property disclaimed; but

(b) does not, except so far as is necessary for the purpose of releasing the company from any liability, affect the rights or liabilities of any other person.

(5) A notice of disclaimer shall not be given under this section in respect of any property if—

(a) a person interested in the property has applied in writing to the liquidator or one of his predecessors as liquidator requiring the liquidator or that predecessor to decide whether he will disclaim or not, and

(b) the period of 28 days beginning with the day on which that application was made, or such longer period as the court may allow, has expired without a notice of disclaimer having been given under this section in respect of that property.

(6) Any person sustaining loss or damage in consequence of the operation of a disclaimer under this section is deemed a creditor of the company to the extent of the loss or damage and accordingly may prove for the loss or damage in the winding up.

179 Disclaimer of leaseholds

(1) The disclaimer under section 178 of any property of a leasehold nature does not take effect unless a copy of the disclaimer has been served (so far as the liquidator is aware of their addresses) on every person claiming under the company as underlessee or mortgagee and either—

(a) no application under section 181 below is made with respect to that property before the end of the period of 14 days beginning with the day on which the last notice served under this subsection was served; or

(b) where such an application has been made, the court directs that the disclaimer shall take effect.

(2) Where the court gives a direction under subsection (1)(b) it may also, instead of or in addition to any order it makes under section 181, make such orders with respect to fixtures, tenant's improvements and other matters arising out of the lease as it thinks fit.

180 Land subject to rentcharge

(1) The following applies where, in consequence of the disclaimer under section 178 of any land subject to a rentcharge, that land vests by operation of law in the Crown or any other person (referred to in the next subsection as "the proprietor").

(2) The proprietor and the successors in title of the proprietor are not subject to any personal liability in respect of any sums becoming due under the rentcharge except sums becoming due after the proprietor, or some person claiming under or through the proprietor, has taken possession or control of the land or has entered into occupation of it.

181 Powers of court (general)

(1) This section and the next apply where the liquidator has disclaimed property under section 178.

(2) An application under this section may be made to the court by—
  (a) any person who claims an interest in the disclaimed property, or
  (b) any person who is under any liability in respect of the disclaimed property, not being a liability discharged by the disclaimer.

(3) Subject as follows, the court may on the application make an order, on such terms as it thinks fit, for the vesting of the disclaimed property in, or for its delivery to—
  (a) a person entitled to it or a trustee for such a person, or
  (b) a person subject to such a liability as is mentioned in subsection (2)(b) or a trustee for such a person.

(4) The court shall not make an order under subsection (3)(b) except where it appears to the court that it would be just to do so for the purpose of compensating the person subject to the liability in respect of the disclaimer.

(5) The effect of any order under this section shall be taken into account in assessing for the purpose of section 178(6) the extent of any loss or damage sustained by any person in consequence of the disclaimer.

(6) An order under this section vesting property in any person need not be completed by conveyance, assignment or transfer.

182 Powers of court (leaseholds)

(1) The court shall not make an order under section 181 vesting property of a leasehold nature in any person claiming under the company as underlessee or mortgagee except on terms making that person—
  (a) subject to the same liabilities and obligations as the company was subject to under the lease at the commencement of the winding up, or
  (b) if the court thinks fit, subject to the same liabilities and obligations as that person would be subject to if the lease had been assigned to him at the commencement of the winding up.

(2) For the purposes of an order under section 181 relating to only part of any property comprised in a lease, the requirements of subsection (1) apply as if the lease comprised only the property to which the order relates.

(3) Where subsection (1) applies and no person claiming under the company as underlessee or mortgagee is willing to accept an order under section 181 on the terms required by virtue of that subsection, the court may, by order under that section, vest the company's estate or interest in the property in any person who is liable (whether personally or in a representative capacity, and whether alone or jointly with the company) to perform the lessee's covenants in the lease.

The court may vest that estate and interest in such a person freed and discharged from all estates, incumbrances and interests created by the company.

(4) Where subsection (1) applies and a person claiming under the company as underlessee or mortgagee declines to accept an order under section 181, that person is excluded from all interest in the property.

Execution, attachment and the Scottish equivalents

183 Effect of execution or attachment (England and Wales)

(1) Where a creditor has issued execution against the goods or land of a company or has attached any debt due to it, and the company is subsequently wound up, he is not entitled to retain the benefit of the execution or attachment against the liquidator unless he has completed the execution or attachment before the commencement of the winding up.

(2) However—

(a) if a creditor has had notice of a meeting having been called at which a resolution for voluntary winding up is to be proposed, the date on which he had notice is substituted, for the purpose of subsection (1), for the date of commencement of the winding up;

(b) a person who purchases in good faith under a sale by the enforcement officer or other officer charged with the execution of the writ any goods of a company on which execution has been levied in all cases acquires a good title to them against the liquidator; and

(c) the rights conferred by subsection (1) on the liquidator may be set aside by the court in favour of the creditor to such extent and subject to such terms as the court thinks fit.

(3) For purposes of this Act—

(a) an execution against goods is completed by seizure and sale, or by making of a charging order under section 1 of the Charging Orders Act 1979;

(b) an attachment of a debt is completed by receipt of the debt; and

(c) an execution against land is completed by seizure, by the appointment of a receiver, or by the making of a charging order under section 1 of the Act above-mentioned.

(4) In this section "goods" includes all chattels personal; and "enforcement officer" means an individual who is authorised to act as an enforcement officer under the Courts Act 2003.

(5) This section does not apply in the case of a winding up in Scotland.

184 Duties of officers charged with execution of writs and other processes (England and Wales)

(1) The following applies where a company's goods are taken in execution and, before their sale or the completion of the execution (by the receipt or recovery of the full amount of the levy), notice is served on the enforcement officer, or other officer, charged with execution of the writ or other process, that a provisional liquidator has been appointed or that a winding-up order has been made, or that a resolution for voluntary winding up has been passed.

(2) The enforcement officer or other officer shall, on being so required, deliver the goods and any money seized or received in part satisfaction of the execution to the liquidator; but the costs of execution are a first charge on the goods or money so delivered, and the liquidator may sell the goods, or a sufficient part of them, for the purpose of satisfying the charge.

(3) If under an execution in respect of a judgment for a sum exceeding £500 a company's goods are sold or money is paid in order to avoid sale, the enforcement officer or other officer shall deduct the costs of the execution from the proceeds of sale or the money paid and retain the balance for 14 days.

(4) If within that time notice is served on the enforcement or other officer of a petition for the winding up of the company having been presented, or of a meeting having been called at which there is to be proposed a resolution for voluntary winding up, and an order is made or a resolution passed (as the case may be), the enforcement or other officer shall pay the balance to the liquidator, who is entitled to retain it as against the execution creditor.

(5) The rights conferred by this section on the liquidator may be set aside by the court in favour of the creditor to such extent and subject to such terms as the court thinks fit.

(6) In this section, "goods" includes all chattels personal; and "enforcement officer" means an individual who is authorised to act as an enforcement officer under the Courts Act 2003.

(7) The money sum for the time being specified in subsection (3) is subject to increase or reduction by order under section 416 in Part XV.

(8) This section does not apply in the case of a winding up in Scotland.

185 Effect of diligence (Scotland)

(1) In the winding up of a company registered in Scotland, the following provisions of the Bankruptcy (Scotland) Act 1985—
(a) subsections (1) to (6) of section 37 (effect of sequestration on diligence); and
(b) subsections (3), (4), (7) and (8) of section 39 (realisation of estate),
apply, so far as consistent with this Act, in like manner as they apply in the sequestration of a debtor's estate, with the substitutions specified below and with any other necessary modifications.

(2) The substitutions to be made in those sections of the Act of 1985 are as follows—
(a) for references to the debtor, substitute references to the company;
(b) for references to the sequestration, substitute references to the winding up;
(c) for references to the date of sequestration, substitute references to the commencement of the winding up of the company; and
(d) for references to the trustee, substitute references to the liquidator.

(3) In this section, "the commencement of the winding up of the company" means, where it is being wound up by the court, the day on which the winding-up order is made.

(4) This section, so far as relating to any estate or effects of the company situated in Scotland, applies in the case of a company registered in England and Wales as in the case of one registered in Scotland.

Miscellaneous matters

186 Rescission of contracts by the court

(1) The court may, on the application of a person who is, as against the liquidator, entitled to the benefit or subject to the burden of a contract made with the company, make an order rescinding the contract on such terms as to payment by or to either party of damages for the non-performance of the contract, or otherwise as the court thinks just.

(2) Any damages payable under the order to such a person may be proved by him as a debt in the winding up.

187 Power to make over assets to employees

(1) On the winding up of a company (whether by the court or voluntarily), the liquidator may, subject to the following provisions of this section, make any payment which the company has, before the commencement of the winding up, decided to make under section 247 of the Companies Act 2006 (power to provide for employees or former employees on cessation or transfer of business).

(2) The liquidator may, after the winding up has commenced, make any such provision as is mentioned in section 247(1) if—
(a) the company's liabilities have been fully satisfied and provision has been made for the expenses of the winding up,
(b) the exercise of the power has been sanctioned by a resolution of the company, and
(c) any requirements of the company's memorandum or articles as to the exercise of the power conferred by section 247(1) are complied with.

(3) Any payment which may be made by a company under this section (that is, a payment after the commencement of its winding up) may be made out of the company's assets which are available to the members on the winding up.

(4) On a winding up by the court, the exercise by the liquidator of his powers under this section is subject to the court's control, and any creditor or contributory may apply to the court with respect to any exercise or proposed exercise of the power.

(5) Subsections (1) and (2) above have effect notwithstanding anything in any rule of law or in section 107 of this Act (property of company after satisfaction of liabilities to be distributed among members).

188 Notification that company is in liquidation

(1) When a company is being wound up, whether by the court or voluntarily—
(a) every invoice, order for goods or services, business letter or order form (whether in hard copy, electronic or any other form) issued by or on behalf of the company, or a liquidator of the company or a receiver or manager of the company's property, and
(b) all the company's websites,
must contain a statement that the company is being wound up.

(2) If default is made in complying with this section, the company and any of the following persons who knowingly and wilfully authorises or permits the default, namely, any officer of the company, any liquidator of the company and any receiver or manager, is liable to a fine.

189 Interest on debts

(1) In a winding up interest is payable in accordance with this section on any debt proved in the winding up, including so much of any such debt as represents interest on the remainder.

(2) Any surplus remaining after the payment of the debts proved in a winding up shall, before being applied for any other purpose, be applied in paying interest on those debts in respect of the periods during which they have been outstanding since the company went into liquidation.

(3) All interest under this section ranks equally, whether or not the debts on which it is payable rank equally.

(4) The rate of interest payable under this section in respect of any debt ("the official rate" for the purposes of any provision of this Act in which that expression is used) is whichever is the greater of—

- (a) the rate specified in section 17 of the Judgments Act 1838 on the day on which the company went into liquidation, and
- (b) the rate applicable to that debt apart from the winding up.

(5) In the application of this section to Scotland—

- (a) references to a debt proved in a winding up have effect as references to a claim accepted in a winding up, and
- (b) the reference to section 17 of the Judgments Act 1838 has effect as a reference to the rules.

190, 191 *omitted*

192 Information as to pending liquidations

(1) If the winding up of a company is not concluded within one year after its commencement, the liquidator shall, at such intervals as may be prescribed, until the winding up is concluded, send to the registrar of companies a statement in the prescribed form and containing the prescribed particulars with respect to the proceedings in, and position of, the liquidation.

(2) If a liquidator fails to comply with this section, he is liable to a fine and, for continued contravention, to a daily default fine.

193 Unclaimed dividends (Scotland)

(1) The following applies where a company registered in Scotland has been wound up, and is about to be dissolved.

(2) The liquidator shall lodge in an appropriate bank or institution as defined in section 73(1) of the Bankruptcy (Scotland) Act 1985 (not being a bank or institution in or of which the liquidator is acting partner, manager, agent or cashier) in the name of the Accountant of Court the whole unclaimed dividends and unapplied or undistributable balances, and the deposit receipts shall be transmitted to the Accountant of Court.

(3) The provisions of section 58 of the Bankruptcy (Scotland) Act 1985 (so far as consistent with this Act and the Companies Acts) apply with any necessary modifications to sums lodged in a bank or institution under this section as they apply to sums deposited under section 57 of the Act first mentioned.

194 Resolutions passed at adjourned meetings

Where a resolution is passed at an adjourned meeting of a company's creditors or contributories, the resolution is treated for all purposes as having been passed on the date on which it was in fact passed, and not as having been passed on any earlier date.

195 Meetings to ascertain wishes of creditors or contributories

(1) The court may—

- (a) as to all matters relating to the winding up of a company, have regard to the wishes of the creditors or contributories (as proved to it by any sufficient evidence), and

(b) if it thinks fit, for the purpose of ascertaining those wishes, direct meetings of the creditors or contributories to be called, held and conducted in such manner as the court directs, and appoint a person to act as chairman of any such meeting and report the result of it to the court.

(2) In the case of creditors, regard shall be had to the value of each creditor's debt.

(3) In the case of contributories, regard shall be had to the number of votes conferred on each contributory.

196–200 *omitted*

CHAPER IX

DISSOLUTION OF COMPANIES AFTER WINDING UP

201 Dissolution (voluntary winding up)

(1) This section applies, in the case of a company wound up voluntarily, where the liquidator has sent to the registrar of companies his final account and return under section 94 (members' voluntary) or section 106 (creditors' voluntary).

(2) The registrar on receiving the account and return shall forthwith register them; and on the expiration of 3 months from the registration of the return the company is deemed to be dissolved.

(3) However, the court may, on the application of the liquidator or any other person who appears to the court to be interested, make an order deferring the date at which the dissolution of the company is to take effect for such time as the court thinks fit.

(4) It is the duty of the person on whose application an order of the court under this section is made within 7 days after the making of the order to deliver to the registrar a copy of the order for registration; and if that person fails to do so he is liable to a fine and, for continued contravention, to a daily default fine.

202 Early dissolution (England and Wales)

(1) This section applies where an order for the winding up of a company has been made by the court in England and Wales.

(2) The official receiver, if—

(a) he is the liquidator of the company, and

(b) it appears to him—

(i) that the realisable assets of the company are insufficient to cover the expenses of the winding up, and

(ii) that the affairs of the company do not require any further investigation,

may at any time apply to the registrar of companies for the early dissolution of the company.

(3) Before making that application, the official receiver shall give not less than 28 days' notice of his intention to do so to the company's creditors and contributories and, if there is an administrative receiver of the company, to that receiver.

(4) With the giving of that notice the official receiver ceases (subject to any directions under the next section) to be required to perform any duties imposed on him in relation to the company, its creditors or contributories by virtue of any provision of this Act, apart from a duty to make an application under subsection (2) of this section.

(5) On the receipt of the official receivers' application under subsection (2) the registrar shall forthwith register it and, at the end of the period of 3 months beginning with the day of the registration of the application, the company shall be dissolved.

However, the Secretary of State may, on the application of the official receiver or any other person who appears to the Secretary of State to be interested, give directions under section 203 at any time before the end of that period.

203 Consequence of notice under section 202

(1) Where a notice has been given under section 202(3), the official receiver or any creditor or contributory of the company, or the administrative receiver of the company (if there is one) may apply to the Secretary of State for directions under this section.

(2) The grounds on which that application may be made are—

(a) that the realisable assets of the company are sufficient to cover the expenses of the winding up;

(b) that the affairs of the company do require further investigation; or

(c) that for any other reason the early dissolution of the company is inappropriate.

(3) Directions under this section—

(a) are directions making such provision as the Secretary of State thinks fit for enabling the winding up of the company to proceed as if no notice had been given under section 202(3), and

(b) may, in the case of an application under section 202(5), include a direction deferring the date at which the dissolution of the company is to take effect for such period as the Secretary of State thinks fit.

(4) An appeal to the court lies from any decision of the Secretary of State on an application for directions under this section.

(5) It is the duty of the person on whose application any directions are given under this section, or in whose favour an appeal with respect to an application for such directions is determined, within 7 days after the giving of the directions or the determination of the appeal, to deliver to the registrar of companies for registration such a copy of the directions or determination as is prescribed.

(6) If a person without reasonable excuse fails to deliver a copy as required by subsection (5), he is liable to a fine and, for continued contravention, to a daily default fine.

204 Early dissolution (Scotland)

(1) This section applies where a winding-up order has been made by the court in Scotland.

(2) If after a meeting or meetings under section 138 (appointment of liquidator in Scotland) it appears to the liquidator that the realisable assets of the company are insufficient to cover the expenses of the winding up, he may apply to the court for an order that the company be dissolved.

(3) Where the liquidator makes that application, if the court is satisfied that the realisable assets of the company are insufficient to cover the expenses of the winding up and it appears to the court appropriate to do so, the court shall make an order that the company be dissolved in accordance with this section.

(4) A copy of the order shall within 14 days from its date be forwarded by the liquidator to the registrar of companies, who shall forthwith register it; and, at the end of the period of 3 months beginning with the day of the registration of the order, the company shall be dissolved.

(5) The court may, on an application by any person who appears to the court to have an interest, order that the date at which the dissolution of the company is to take effect shall be deferred for such period as the court thinks fit.

(6) It is the duty of the person on whose application an order is made under subsection (5), within 7 days after the making of the order, to deliver to the registrar of companies such a copy of the order as is prescribed.

(7) If the liquidator without reasonable excuse fails to comply with the requirements of subsection (4), he is liable to a fine and, for continued contravention, to a daily default fine.

(8) If a person without reasonable excuse fails to deliver a copy as required by subsection (6), he is liable to a fine and, for continued contravention, to a daily default fine.

205 Dissolution otherwise than under sections 202-204

(1) This section applies where the registrar of companies receives—

(a) a notice served for the purposes of section 172(8) (final meeting of creditors and vacation of office by liquidator), or

(b) a notice, from the official receiver that the winding up of a company by the court is complete.

(2) The registrar shall, on receipt of the notice, forthwith register it; and, subject, as follows, at the end of the period of 3 months beginning with the day of the registration of the notice, the company shall be dissolved.

(3) The Secretary of State may, on the application of the official receiver or any other person who appears to the Secretary of State to be interested, give a direction deferring the date at which the dissolution of the company is to take effect for such period as the Secretary of State thinks fit.

(4) An appeal to the court lies from any decision of the Secretary of State on an application for a direction under subsection (3).

(5) Subsection (3) does not apply in a case where the winding-up order was made by the court in Scotland, but in such a case the court may, on an application by any person

appearing to the court to have an interest, order that the date at which the dissolution of the company is to take effect shall be deferred for such period as the court thinks fit.

(6) It is the duty of the person—

(a) on whose application a direction is given under subsection (3);

(b) in whose favour an appeal with respect to an application for such a direction is determined; or

(c) on whose application an order is made under subsection (5),

within 7 days after the giving of the direction, the determination of the appeal or the making of the order, to deliver to the registrar for registration such a copy of the direction, determination or order as is prescribed.

(7) If a person without reasonable excuse fails to deliver a copy as required by subsection (6), he is liable to a fine and, for continued contravention, to a daily default fine.

CHAPTER X
MALPRACTICE BEFORE AND DURING LIQUIDATION; PENALISATION OF COMPANIES AND COMPANY OFFICERS; INVESTIGATIONS AND PROSECUTIONS

Offences of fraud, deception, etc.

206 Fraud, etc. in anticipation of winding up

(1) When a company is ordered to be wound up by the court, or passes a resolution for voluntary winding up, any person, being a past or present officer of the company, is deemed to have committed an offence if, within the 12 months immediately preceding the commencement of the winding up, he has—

(a) concealed any part of the company's property to the value of £500 or more, or concealed any debt due to or from the company, or

(b) fraudulently removed any part of the company's property to the value of £500 or more, or

(c) concealed, destroyed, mutilated or falsified any book or paper affecting or relating to the company's property or affairs, or

(d) made any false entry in any book or paper affecting or relating to the company's property or affairs, or

(e) fraudulently parted with, altered or made any omission in any document affecting or relating to the company's property or affairs, or

(f) pawned, pledged or disposed of any property of the company which has been obtained on credit and has not been paid for (unless the pawning, pledging or disposal was in the ordinary way of the company's business).

(2) Such a person is deemed to have committed an offence if within the period above mentioned he has been privy to the doing by others of any of the things mentioned in paragraphs (c), (d) and (e) of subsection (1); and he commits an offence if, at any time after the commencement of the winding up, he does any of the things mentioned in paragraphs (a) to (f) of that subsection, or is privy to the doing by others of any of the things mentioned in paragraphs (c) to (e) of it.

(3) For purposes of this section, "officer" includes a shadow director.

(4) It is a defence—

(a) for a person charged under paragraph (a) or (f) of subsection (1) (or under subsection (2) in respect of the things mentioned in either of those two paragraphs) to prove that he had no intent to defraud, and

(b) for a person charged under paragraph (c) or (d) of subsection (1) (or under subsection (2) in respect of the things mentioned in either of those two paragraphs) to prove that he had no intent to conceal the state of affairs of the company or to defeat the law.

(5) Where a person pawns, pledges or disposes of any property in circumstances which amount to an offence under subsection (1)(f), every person who takes in pawn or pledge, or otherwise receives, the property knowing it to be pawned, pledged or disposed of in such circumstances, is guilty of an offence.

(6) A person guilty of an offence under this section is liable to imprisonment or a fine, or both.

(7) The money sums specified in paragraphs (a) and (b) of subsection (1) are subject to increase or reduction by order under section 416 in Part XV.

207 Transactions in fraud of creditors

(1) When a company is ordered to be wound up by the court or passes a resolution for voluntary winding up, a person is deemed to have committed an offence if he, being at the time an officer of the company—

(a) has made or caused to be made any gift or transfer of, or charge on, or has caused or connived at the levying of any execution against, the company's property, or

(b) has concealed or removed any part of the company's property since, or within 2 months before, the date of any unsatisfied judgment or order for the payment of money obtained against the company.

(2) A person is not guilty of an offence under this section—

(a) by reason of conduct constituting an offence under subsection (1)(a) which occurred more than 5 years before the commencement of the winding up, or

(b) if he proves that, at the time of the conduct constituting the offence, he had no intent to defraud the company's creditors.

(3) A person guilty of an offence under this section is liable to imprisonment or a fine, or both.

208 Misconduct in course of winding up

(1) When a company is being wound up, whether by the court or voluntarily, any person, being a past or present officer of the company, commits an offence if he—

(a) does not to the best of his knowledge and belief fully and truly discover to the liquidator all the company's property, and how and to whom and for what consideration and when the company disposed of any part of that property (except such part as has been disposed of in the ordinary way of the company's business), or

(b) does not deliver up to the liquidator (or as he directs) all such part of the company's property as is in his custody or under his control, and which he is required by law to deliver up, or

(c) does not deliver up to the liquidator (or as he directs) all books and papers in his custody or under his control belonging to the company and which he is required by law to deliver up, or

(d) knowing or believing that a false debt has been proved by any person in the winding up, fails to inform the liquidator as soon as practicable, or

(e) after the commencement of the winding up, prevents the production of any book or paper affecting or relating to the company's property or affairs.

(2) Such a person commits an offence if after the commencement of the winding up he attempts to account for any part of the company's property by fictitious losses or expenses; and he is deemed to have committed that offence if he has so attempted at any meeting of the company's creditors within the 12 months immediately preceding the commencement of the winding up.

(3) For purposes of this section, "officer" includes a shadow director.

(4) It is a defence—

(a) for a person charged under paragraph (a), (b) or (c) of subsection (1) to prove that he had no intent to defraud, and

(b) for a person charged under paragraph (e) of that subsection to prove that he had no intent to conceal the state of affairs of the company or to defeat the law.

(5) A person guilty of an offence under this section is liable to imprisonment or a fine, or both.

209 Falsification of company's books

(1) When a company is being wound up, an officer or contributory of the company commits an offence if he destroys, multilates, alters or falsifies any books, papers or securities, or makes or is privy to the making of any false or fraudulent entry in any register, book of account or document belonging to the company with intent to defraud or deceive any person.

(2) A person guilty of an offence under this section is liable to imprisonment or a fine, or both.

210 Material omissions from statement relating to company's affairs

(1) When a company is being wound up, whether by the court or voluntarily, any person, being a past or present officer of the company, commits an offence if he makes any material omission in any statement relating to the company's affairs.

(2) When a company has been ordered to be wound up by the court, or has passed a resolution for voluntary winding up, any such person is deemed to have committed that offence if, prior to the winding up, he has made any material omission in any such statement.

(3) For purposes of this section, "officer" includes a shadow director.

(4) It is a defence for a person charged under this section to prove that he had no intent to defraud.

(5) A person guilty of an offence under this section is liable to imprisonment or a fine, or both.

211 False representations to creditors

(1) When a company is being wound up, whether by the court or voluntarily, any person, being a past or present officer of the company—

(a) commits an offence if he makes any false representation or commits any other fraud for the purpose of obtaining the consent of the company's creditors or any of them to an agreement with reference to the company's affairs or to the winding up, and

(b) is deemed to have committed that offence if, prior to the winding up, he has made any false representation, or committed any other fraud, for that purpose.

(2) For purposes of this section, "officer" includes a shadow director.

(3) A person guilty of an offence under this section is liable to imprisonment or a fine, or both.

Penalisation of directors and officers

212 Summary remedy against delinquent directors, liquidators, etc.

(1) This section applies if in the course of the winding up of a company it appears that a person who—

(a) is or has been an officer of the company,

(b) has acted as liquidator or administrative receiver of the company, or

(c) not being a person falling within paragraph (a) or (b), is or has been concerned, or has taken part, in the promotion, formation or management of the company,

has misapplied or retained, or become accountable for, any money or other property of the company, or been guilty of any misfeasance or breach of any fiduciary or other duty in relation to the company.

(2) The reference in subsection (1) to any misfeasance or breach of any fiduciary or other duty in relation to the company includes, in the case of a person who has acted as liquidator of the company, any misfeasance or breach of any fiduciary or other duty in connection with the carrying out of his functions as liquidator of the company.

(3) The court may, on the application of the offical receiver or the liquidator, or of any creditor or contributory, examine into the conduct of the person falling within subsection (1) and compel him—

(a) to repay, restore or account for the money or property or any part of it, with interest at such rate as the court thinks just, or

(b) to contribute such sum to the company's assets by way of compensation in respect of the misfeasance or breach of fiduciary or other duty as the court thinks just.

(4) The power to make an application under subsection (3) in relation to a person who has acted as liquidator of the company is not exerciseable, except with the leave of the court, after he has had his release.

(5) The power of a contributory to make an application under subsection (3) is not exercisable except with the leave of the court, but is exercisable notwithstanding that he will not benefit from any order the court may make on the application.

213 Fraudulent trading

(1) If in the course of the winding up of a company it appears that any business of the company has been carried on with intent to defraud creditors of the company or creditors of any other person, or for any fraudulent purpose, the following has effect.

(2) The court, on the application of the liquidator may declare that any persons who were knowingly parties to the carrying on of the business in the manner above-mentioned are to be liable to make such contributions (if any) to the company's assets as the court thinks proper.

214 Wrongful trading

(1) Subject to subsection (3) below, if in the course of the winding up of a company it appears that subsection (2) of this section applies in relation to a person who is or has been a director of the company, the court, on the application of the liquidator, may declare that that person is to be liable to make such contribution (if any) to the company's assets as the court thinks proper.

(2) This subsection applies in relation to a person if—

(a) the company has gone into insolvent liquidation,

(b) at some time before the commencement of the winding up of the company, that person knew or ought to have concluded that there was no reasonable prospect that the company would avoid going into insolvent liquidation, and

(c) that person was a director of the company at that time;

but the court shall not make a declaration under this section in any case where the time mentioned in paragraph (b) above was before 28th April 1986.

(3) The court shall not make a declaration under this section with respect to any person if it is satisfied that after the condition specified in subsection (2)(b) was first satisfied in relation to him that person took every step with a view to minimising the potential loss to the company's creditors as (assuming him to have known that there was no reasonable prospect that the company would avoid going into solvent liquidation) he ought to have taken.

(4) For the purposes of subsections (2) and (3), the facts which a director of a company ought to know or ascertain, the conclusions which he ought to reach and the steps which he ought to take are those which would be known or ascertained, or reached or taken, by a reasonably diligent person having both—

(a) the general knowledge, skill and experience that may reasonably be expected of a person carrying out the same functions as are carried out by that director in relation to the company, and

(b) the general knowledge, skill and experience that that director has.

(5) The reference in subsection (4) to the functions carried out in relation to a company by a director of the company includes any functions which he does not carry out but which have been entrusted to him.

(6) For the purposes of this section a company goes into insolvent liquidation if it goes into liquidation at a time when its assets are insufficient for the payment of its debts and other liabilities and the expenses of the winding up.

(7) In this section "director" includes a shadow director.

(8) This section is without prejudice to section 213.

214A *omitted*

215 Proceedings under sections 213, 214

(1) On the hearing of an application under section 213 or 214, the liquidator may himself give evidence or call witnesses.

(2) Where under either section the court makes a declaration, it may give such further directions as it thinks proper for giving effect to the declaration; and in particular, the court may—

(a) provide for the liability of any person under the declaration to be a charge on any debt or obligation due from the company to him, or on any mortgage or charge or any interest in a mortgage or charge on assets of the company held by or vested in him, or any person on his behalf, or any person claiming as assignee from or through the person liable or any person acting on his behalf, and

(b) from time to time make such further order as may be necessary for enforcing any charge imposed under this subsection.

(3) For the purposes of subsection (2), "assignee"—

(a) includes a person to whom or in whose favour, by the directions of the person made liable, the debt, obligation, mortgage or charge was created, issued or transferred or the interest created, but

(b) does not include an assignee for valuable consideration (not including consideration by way of marriage or the formation of a civil partnership) given in good faith and without notice of any of the matters on the ground of which the declaration is made.

(4) Where the court makes a declaration under either section in relation to a person who is a creditor of the company, it may direct that the whole or any part of any debt owed by the company to that person and any interest thereon shall rank in priority after all other debts owed by the company and after any interest on those debts.

(5) Sections 213 and 214 have effect notwithstanding that the person concerned may be criminally liable in respect of matters on the ground of which the declaration under the section is to be made.

216 Restriction on re-use of company names

(1) This section applies to a person where a company ("the liquidating company") has gone into insolvent liquidation on or after the appointed day and he was a director or shadow director of the company at any time in the period of 12 months ending with the day before it went into liquidation.

(2) For the purposes of this section, a name is a prohibited name in relation to such a person if—

(a) it is a name by which the liquidating company was known at any time in that period of 12 months, or

(b) it is a name which is so similar to a name falling within paragraph (a) as to suggest an association with that company.

(3) Except with leave of the court or in such circumstances as may be prescribed, a person to whom this section applies shall not at any time in the period of 5 years beginning with the day on which the liquidating company went into liquidation—

(a) be a director of any other company that is known by a prohibited name, or

(b) in any way, whether directly or indirectly, be concerned or take part in the promotion, formation or management of any such company, or

(c) in any way, whether directly or indirectly, be concerned or take part in the carrying on of a business carried on (otherwise than by a company) under a prohibited name.

(4) If a person acts in contravention of this section, he is liable to imprisonment or a fine, or both.

(5) In subsection (3) "the court" means any court having jurisdiction to wind up companies; and on an application for leave under that subsection, the Secretary of State or the official receiver may appear and call the attention of the court to any matters which seem to him to be relevant.

(6) References in this section, in relation to any time, to a name by which a company is known are to the name of the company at that time or to any name under which the company carries on business at that time.

(7) For the purposes of this section a company goes into insolvent liquidation if it goes into liquidation at at time when its assets are insufficient for the payment of its debts and other liabilities and the expenses of the winding up.

(8) In this section "company" includes a company which may be wound up under Part V of this Act.

217 Personal liability for debts, following contravention of section 216

(1) A person is personally responsible for all the relevant debts of a company if at any time—

(a) in contravention of section 216, he is involved in the management of the company, or

(b) as a person who is involved in the management of the company, he acts or is willing to act on instructions given (without the leave of the court) by a person whom he knows at that time to be in contravention in relation to the company of section 216.

(2) Where a person is personally responsible under this section for the relevant debts of a company, he is jointly and severally liable in respect of those debts with the company and any other person who, whether under this section or otherwise, is so liable.

(3) For the purposes of this section the relevant debts of a company are—

(a) in relation to a person who is personally responsible under paragraph (a) of subsection (1), such debts and other liabilities of the company as are incurred at a time when that person was involved in the management of the company, and

(b) in relation to a person who is personally responsible under paragraph (b) of that subsection, such debts and other liabilities of the company as are incurred at a time when that person was acting or was willing to act on instructions given as mentioned in that paragraph.

(4) For the purposes of this section, a person is involved in the management of a company if he is a director of the company or if he is concerned, whether directly or indirectly, or takes part, in the management of the company.

(5) For the purposes of this section a person who, as a person involved in the management of a company, has at any time acted on instructions given (without the leave of the court) by a person whom he knew at that time to be in contravention in relation to the company of section 216 is presumed, unless the contrary is shown, to have been willing at any time thereafter to act on any instructions given by that person.

(6) In this section "company" includes a company which may be wound up under Part V.

Investigation and prosecution of malpractice

218 Prosecution of delinquent officers and members of company

(1) If it appears to the court in the course of a winding up by the court that any past or present officer, or any member, of the company has been guilty of any offence in relation to the company for which he is criminally liable, the court may (either on the application of a person interested in the winding up or of its own motion) direct the liquidator to refer the matter

(a) in the case of a winding up in England and Wales, to the Secretary of State, and

(b) in the case of a winding up in Scotland, to the Lord Advocate

(2) …

(3) If in the case of a winding up by the court in England and Wales it appears to the liquidator, not being the official receiver, that any past or present officer of the company, or any member of it, has been guilty of an offence in relation to the company for which he is criminally liable, the liquidator shall report the matter to the official receiver.

(4) If it appears to the liquidator in the course of a voluntary winding up that any past or present officer of the company, or any member of it, has been guilty of an offence in relation to the company for which he is criminally liable, he shall forthwith report the matter—

(a) in the case of a winding up in England and Wales, to the Secretary of State, and

(b) in the case of a winding up in Scotland, to the Lord Advocate,

and shall furnish to the Secretary of State or (as the case may be) the Lord Advocate such information and give to him such access to and facilities for inspecting and taking copies of documents (being information or documents in the possession or under the control of the liquidator and relating to the matter in question) as the Secretary of State or (as the case may be) the Lord Advocate requires.

(5) Where a report is made to the Secretary of State under subsection (4) he may, for the purpose of investigating the matter reported to him and such other matters relating to the affairs of the company as appear to him to require investigation, exercise any of the powers which are exercisable by inspectors appointed under section 431 or 432 of the Companies Act 1985 to investigate a company's affairs.

(6) If it appears to the court in the course of a voluntary winding up that—

(a) any past or present officer of the company, or any member of it, has been guilty as above-mentioned, and

(b) no report with respect to the matter has been made by the liquidator under subsection (4),

the court may (on the application of any person interested in the winding up or of its own motion) direct the liquidator to make such a report.

On a report being made accordingly, this section has effect as though the report had been made in pursuance of subsection (4).

219 Obligations arising under section 218

(1) For the purpose of an investigation by the Secretary of State in consequence of a report made to him under section 218(4), any obligation imposed on a person by any provision of the Companies Act 1985 to produce documents or give information to, or otherwise to assist, inspectors appointed as mentioned in section 218(5) is to be regarded as an obligation similarly to assist the Secretary of State in his investigation.

(2) An answer given by a person to a question put to him in exercise of the powers conferred by section 218(5) may be used in evidence against him.

(2A) However, in criminal proceedings in which that person is charged with an offence to which this subsection applies—

(a) no evidence relating to the answer may be adduced, and

(b) no question relating to it may be asked,

by or on behalf of the prosecution, unless evidence relating to it is adduced, or a question relating to it is asked, in the proceedings by or on behalf of that person.

(2B) Subsection (2A) applies to any offence other than—

(a) an offence under section 2 or 5 of the Perjury Act 1911 (false statements made on oath otherwise than in judicial proceedings or made otherwise than on oath), or

(b) an offence under section 44(1) or (2) of the Criminal Law (Consolidation) (Scotland) Act 1995 (false statements made on oath or otherwise than on oath).

(3) Where criminal proceedings are instituted by the Director of Public Prosecutions, the Lord Advocate or the Secretary of State following any report or reference under section 218, it is the duty of the liquidator and every officer and agent of the company past and present (other than the defendant or defender) to give to the Director of Public Prosecutions, the Lord Advocate or the Secretary of State (as the case may be) all assistance in connection with the prosecution which he is reasonably able to give. For this purpose "agent" includes any banker or solicitor of the company and any person employed by the company as auditor, whether that person is or is not an officer of the company.

(4) If a person fails or neglects to give assistance in the manner required by subsection (3), the court may, on the application of the Director of Public Prosecutions, the Lord Advocate or the Secretary of State (as the case may be) direct the person to comply with that subsection; and if the application is made with respect to a liquidator, the court may (unless it appears that the failure or neglect to comply was due to the liquidator not having in his hands sufficient assets of the company to enable him to do so) direct that the costs shall be borne by the liquidator personally.

PART V
OMITTED

PART VI
MISCELLANEOUS PROVISIONS APPLYING TO COMPANIES WHICH ARE INSOLVENT OR IN LIQUIDATION

Office-holders

230 Holders of office to be qualified insolvency practitioners

(1) ...

(2) Where an administrative receiver of a company is appointed, he must be a person who is so qualified.

(3) Where a company goes into liquidation, the liquidator must be a person who is so qualified.

(4) Where a provisional liquidator is appointed, he must be a person who is so qualified.

(5) Subsections (3) and (4) are without prejudice to any enactment under which the official receiver is to be, or may be, liquidator or provisional liquidator.

231 Appointment to office of two or more persons

(1) This section applies if an appointment or nomination of any person to the office of administrative receiver, liquidator or provisional liquidator—

(a) relates to more than one person, or

(b) has the effect that the office is to be held by more than one person.

(2) The appointment or nomination shall declare whether any act required or authorised under any enactment to be done by the administrative receiver, liquidator or provisional liquidator is to be done by all or any one or more of the persons for the time being holding the office in question.

232 Validity of office-holder's acts

The acts of an individual as administrative receiver, liquidator or provisional liquidator of a company are valid notwithstanding any defect in his appointment, nomination or qualifications.

Management by administrators, liquidators, etc.

233 Supplies of gas, water, electricity, etc.

(1) This section applies in the case of a company where—
(a) the company enters administration, or
(b) an administrative receiver is appointed, or
(ba) a moratorium under section 1A is in force, or
(c) a voluntary arrangement approved under Part I, has taken effect, or
(d) the company goes into liquidation, or
(e) a provisional liquidator is appointed;
and "the office-holder" means the administrator, the administrative receiver, the nominee, the supervisor of the voluntary arrangement, the liquidator or the provisional liquidator, as the case may be.

(2) If a request is made by or with the concurrence of the office-holder for the giving, after the effective date, of any of the supplies mentioned in the next subsection, the supplier—
(a) may make it a condition of the giving of the supply that the office-holder personally guarantees the payment of any charges in respect of the supply, but
(b) shall not make it a condition of the giving of the supply, or do anything which has the effect of making it a condition of the giving of the supply, that any outstanding charges in respect of a supply given to the company before the effective date are paid.

(3) The supplies referred to in subsection (2) are—
(a) a supply of gas by a gas supplier within the meaning of Part I of the Gas Act 1986;
(aa) a supply of gas by a person within paragraph 1 of Schedule 2A to the Gas Act 1986
(b) a supply of electricity by an electricity supplier within the meaning of Part I of the Electricity Act 1989;
(ba) a supply of electricity by a class of person within Class A (small suppliers) or Class B (resale) of Schedule 4 to the Electricity (Class Exemptions from the Requirement for a Licence) Order 2001
(c) a supply of water by a water undertaker or, in Scotland, Scottish Water,
(ca) a supply of water by a water supply licensee within the meaning of the Water Industry Act 1991
(cb) a supply of water by a water services provider within the meaning of the Water Services etc. (Scotland) Act 2005
(cc) a supply of water by a person who has an interest in the premises to which the supply is given;
(d) a supply of communications services by a provider of a public electronic communications service;
(e) a supply of communications services by a person who carries on a business which includes giving such supplies;
(f) a supply of goods or services mentioned in subsection (3A) by a person who carries on a business which includes giving such supplies, where the supply is for the purpose of enabling or facilitating anything to be done by electronic means.

(3A) The goods and services referred to in subsection (3)(f) are—
(a) point of sale terminals;
(b) computer hardware and software;
(c) information, advice and technical assistance in connection with the use of information technology;
(d) data storage and processing;
(e) website hosting

(4) "The effective date" for the purposes of this section is whichever is applicable of the following dates—
(a) the date on which the company entered administration,
(b) the date on which the administrative receiver was appointed (or, if he was appointed in succession to another administrative receiver, the date on which the first of his predecessors was appointed),
(ba) the date on which the moratorium came into force,
(c) the date on which the voluntary arrangement took effect,
(d) the date on which the company went into liquidation,
(e) the date on which the provisional liquidator was appointed.

(5) The following applies to expressions used in subsection (3)—
(a)–(c) …
(d) "communications services" do not include electronic communications services to the extent that they are used to broadcast or otherwise transmit programme services (within the meaning of the Communications Act 2003).

233A Further protection of essential supplies

(1) An insolvency-related term of a contract for the supply of essential goods or services to a company ceases to have effect if—
(a) the company enters administration, or
(b) a voluntary arrangement approved under Part 1 takes effect in relation to the company.

(2) An insolvency-related term of a contract does not cease to have effect by virtue of subsection (1) to the extent that—
(a) it provides for the contract or the supply to terminate, or any other thing to take place, because the company becomes subject to an insolvency procedure other than administration or a voluntary arrangement;
(b) it entitles a supplier to terminate the contract or the supply, or do any other thing, because the company becomes subject to an insolvency procedure other than administration or a voluntary arrangement; or
(c) it entitles a supplier to terminate the contract or the supply because of an event that occurs, or may occur, after the company enters administration or the voluntary arrangement takes effect.

(3) Where an insolvency-related term of a contract ceases to have effect under this section the supplier may—
(a) terminate the contract, if the condition in subsection (4) is met;
(b) terminate the supply, if the condition in subsection (5) is met.

(4) The condition in this subsection is that—
(a) the insolvency office-holder consents to the termination of the contract,
(b) the court grants permission for the termination of the contract, or
(c) any charges in respect of the supply that are incurred after the company entered administration or the voluntary arrangement took effect are not paid within the period of 28 days beginning with the day on which payment is due.

The court may grant permission under paragraph (b) only if satisfied that the continuation of the contract would cause the supplier hardship.

(5) The condition in this subsection is that—
(a) the supplier gives written notice to the insolvency office-holder that the supply will be terminated unless the office-holder personally guarantees the payment of any charges in respect of the continuation of the supply after the company entered administration or the voluntary arrangement took effect, and
(b) the insolvency office-holder does not give that guarantee within the period of 14 days beginning with the day the notice is received.

(6) For the purposes of securing that the interests of suppliers are protected, where—
(a) an insolvency-related term of a contract (the "original term") ceases to have effect by virtue of subsection (1), and
(b) the company subsequently enters administration,

or a voluntary arrangement subsequently has effect in relation to it, the contract is treated for the purposes of subsections (1) to (5) as if, immediately before the subsequent administration is entered into or the subsequent voluntary arrangement takes effect, it included an insolvency-related term identical to the original term.

(7) A contract for the supply of essential goods or services is a contract for a supply mentioned in section 233(3).

(8) An insolvency-related term of a contract for the supply of essential goods or services to a company is a provision of the contract under which—
(a) the contract or the supply would terminate, or any other thing would take place, because the company enters administration or the voluntary arrangement takes effect,
(b) the supplier would be entitled to terminate the contract or the supply, or to do any other thing, because the company enters administration or the voluntary arrangement takes effect, or

(c) the supplier would be entitled to terminate the contract or the supply because of an event that occurred before the company enters administration or the voluntary arrangement takes effect.

(9) In this section "insolvency office-holder" means—
(a) in a case where a company enters administration, the administrator;
(b) in a case where a voluntary arrangement under Part 1 takes effect in relation to a company, the supervisor of the voluntary arrangement.

(10) Subsection (1) does not have effect in relation to a contract entered into before 1st October 2015.

234 Getting in the company's property

(1) This section applies in the case of a company where—
(a) the company enters administration, or
(b) an administrative receiver is appointed, or
(c) the company goes into liquidation, or
(d) a provisional liquidator is appointed;
and "the office-holder" means the administrator, the administrative receiver, the liquidator or the provisional liquidator, as the case may be.

(2) Where any person has in his possession or control any property, books, papers or records to which the company appears to be entitled, the court may require that person forthwith (or within such period as the court may direct) to pay, deliver, convey, surrender or transfer the property, books, papers or records to the office-holder.

(3) Where the office-holder—
(a) seizes or disposes of any property which is not property of the company, and
(b) at the time of seizure or disposal believes, and has reasonable grounds for believing, that he is entitled (whether in pursuance of an order of the court or otherwise) to seize or dispose of that property,
the next subsection has effect.

(4) In that case the office-holder—
(a) is not liable to any person in respect of any loss or damage resulting from the seizure or disposal except in so far as that loss or damage is caused by the office-holder's own negligence, and
(b) has a lien on the property, or the proceeds of its sale, for such expenses as were incurred in connection with the seizure or disposal.

235 Duty to co-operate with office-holder

(1) This section applies as does section 234; and it also applies, in the case of a company in respect of which a winding-up order has been made by the court in England and Wales, as if references to the office-holder included the official receiver, whether or not he is the liquidator.

(2) Each of the persons mentioned in the next subsection shall—
(a) give to the office-holder such information concerning the company and its promotion, formation, business, dealings, affairs or property as the office-holder may at any time after the effective date reasonably require, and
(b) attend on the office-holder at such times as the latter may reasonably require.

(3) The persons referred to above are—
(a) those who are or have at any time been officers of the company,
(b) those who have taken part in the formation of the company at any time within one year before the effective date,
(c) those who are in the employment of the company, or have been in its employment (including employment under a contract for services) within that year, and are in the office-holder's opinion capable of giving information which he requires,
(d) those who are, or have within that year been, officers of, or in the employment (including employment under a contract for services) of, another company which is, or within that year was, an officer of the company in question, and
(e) in the case of a company being wound up by the court, any person who has acted as administrator, administrative receiver or liquidator of the company.

(4) For the purposes of subsections (2) and (3), "the effective date" is whichever is applicable of the following dates—

(a) the date on which the company entered administration,
(b) the date on which the administrative receiver was appointed or, if he was appointed in succession to another administrative receiver, the date on which the first of his predecessors was appointed,
(c) the date on which the provisional liquidator was appointed, and
(d) the date on which the company went into liquidation.

(5) If a person without reasonable excuse fails to comply with any obligation imposed by this section, he is liable to a fine and, for continued contravention, to a daily default fine.

236 Inquiry into company's dealings, etc.

(1) This section applies as does section 234; and it also applies in the case of a company in respect of which a winding-up order has been made by the court in England and Wales as if references to the office-holder included the official receiver, whether or not he is the liquidator.

(2) The court may, on the application of the office-holder, summon to appear before it—
(a) any officer of the company,
(b) any person known or suspected to have in his possession any property of the company or supposed to be indebted to the company, or
(c) any person whom the court thinks capable of giving information concerning the promotion, formation, business, dealings, affairs or property of the company.

(3) The court may require any such person as is mentioned in subsection (2)(a) to (c) to submit to the court an account of his dealings with the company or to produce any books, papers or other records in his possession or under his control relating to the company or the matters mentioned in paragraph (c) of the subsection.

(3A) An account submitted to the court under subsection (3) must be contained in—
(a) a witness statement verified by a statement of truth (in England and Wales), and
(b) an affidavit (in Scotland).

(4) The following applies in a case where—
(a) a person without reasonable excuse fails to appear before the court when he is summoned to do so under this section, or
(b) there are reasonable grounds for believing that a person has absconded, or is about to abscond, with a view to avoiding his appearance before the court under this section.

(5) The court may, for the purpose of bringing that person and anything in his possession before the court, cause a warrant to be issued to a constable or prescribed officer of the court—
(a) for the arrest of that person, and
(b) for the seizure of any books, papers, records, money or goods in that person's possession.

(6) The court may authorise a person arrested under such a warrant to be kept in custody, and anything seized under such a warrant to be held, in accordance with the rules, until that person is brought before the court under the warrant or until such other time as the court may order.

237 Court's enforcement powers under section 236

(1) If it appears to the court, on consideration of any evidence obtained under section 236 or this section, that any person has in his possession any property of the company, the court may, on the application of the office-holder, order that person to deliver the whole or any part of the property to the office-holder at such time, in such manner and on such terms as the court thinks fit.

(2) If it appears to the court, on consideration of any evidence so obtained, that any person is indebted to the company, the court may, on the application of the office-holder, order that person to pay to the office holder,at such time and in such manner as the court may direct, the whole or any part of the amount due, whether in full discharge of the debt or otherwise, as the court thinks fit.

(3) The court may, if it thinks fit, order that any person who if within the jurisdiction of the court would be liable to be summoned to appear before it under section 236 or this section shall be examined in any part of the United Kingdom where he may for the time being be, or in a place outside the United Kingdom.

(4) Any person who appears or is brought before the court under section 236 or this section may be examined on oath, either orally or (except in Scotland) by interrogatories, concerning the company or the matters mentioned in section 236(2)(c).

Adjustment of prior transactions (administration and liquidation)

238 Transactions at an undervalue (England and Wales)

(1) This section applies in the case of a company where—

(a) the company enters administration, or

(b) the company goes into liquidation;

and "the office-holder" means the administrator or the liquidator, as the case may be.

(2) Where the company has at a relevant time (defined in section 240) entered into a transaction with any person at an undervalue, the office-holder may apply to the court for an order under this section.

(3) Subject as follows, the court shall, on such an application, make such order as it thinks fit for restoring the position to what it would have been if the company had not entered into that transaction.

(4) For the purposes of this section and section 241, a company enters into a transaction with a person at an undervalue if—

(a) the company makes a gift to that person or otherwise enters into a transaction with that person on terms that provide for the company to receive no consideration, or

(b) the company enters into a transaction with that person for a consideration the value of which, in money or money's worth, is significantly less than the value, in money or money's worth, of the consideration provided by the company.

(5) The court shall not make an order under this section in respect of a transaction at an undervalue if it is satisfied—

(a) that the company which entered into the transaction did so in good faith and for the purpose of carrying on its business, and

(b) that at the time it did so there were reasonable grounds for believing that the transaction would benefit the company.

239 Preferences (England and Wales)

(1) This section applies as does section 238.

(2) Where the company has at a relevant time (defined in the next section) given a preference to any person, the office-holder may apply to the court for an order under this section.

(3) Subject as follows, the court shall, on such an application, make such order as it thinks fit for restoring the position to what it would have been if the company had not given that preference.

(4) For the purposes of this section and section 241, a company gives a preference to a person if—

(a) that person is one of the company's creditors or a surety or guarantor for any of the company's debts or other liabilities, and

(b) the company does anything or suffers anything to be done which (in either case) has the effect of putting that person into a position which, in the event of the company going into insolvent liquidation, will be better than the position he would have been in if that thing had not been done.

(5) The court shall not make an order under this section in respect of a preference given to any person unless the company which gave the preference was influenced in deciding to give it by a desire to produce in relation to that person the effect mentioned in subsection (4)(b).

(6) A company which has given a preference to a person connected with the company (otherwise than by reason only of being its employee) at the time the preference was given is presumed, unless the contrary is shown, to have been influenced in deciding to give it by such a desire as is mentioned in subsection (5).

(7) The fact that something has been done in pursuance of the order of a court does not, without more, prevent the doing or suffering of that thing from constituting the giving of a preference.

240 "Relevant time" under sections 238, 239

(1) Subject to the next subsection, the time at which a company enters into a transaction at an undervalue or gives a preference is a relevant time if the transaction is entered into, or the preference given—

(a) in the case of a transaction at an undervalue or of a preference which is given to a person who is connected with the company (otherwise than by reason only of being its employee), at a time in the period of 2 years ending with the onset of insolvency (which expression is defined below),

(b) in the case of a preference which is not such a transaction and is not so given, at a time in the period of 6 months ending with the onset of insolvency,
(c) in either case, at a time between the making of an administration application in respect of the company and the making of an administration order on that application, and
(d) in either case, at a time between the filing with the court of a copy of notice of intention to appoint an administrator under paragraph 14 or 22 of Schedule B1 and the making of an appointment under that paragraph.

(2) Where a company enters into a transaction at an undervalue or gives a preference at a time mentioned in subsection (1)(a) or (b), that time is not a relevant time for the purposes of section 238 or 239 unless the company—
(a) is at that time unable to pay its debts within the meaning of section 123 in Chapter VI of Part IV, or
(b) becomes unable to pay its debts within the meaning of that section in consequence of the transaction or preference;

but the requirements of this subsection are presumed to be satisfied, unless the contrary is shown, in relation to any transaction at an undervalue which is entered into by a company with a person who is connected with the company.

(3) For the purposes of subsection (1), the onset of insolvency is—
(a) in a case where section 238 or 239 applies by reason of an administrator of a company being appointed by administration order, the date on which the administration application is made,
(b) in a case where section 238 or 239 applies by reason of an administrator of a company being appointed under paragraph 14 or 22 of Schedule B1 following filing with the court of a copy of a notice of intention to appoint under that paragraph, the date on which the copy of the notice is filed,
(c) in a case where section 238 or 239 applies by reason of an administrator of a company being appointed otherwise than as mentioned in paragraph (a) or (b), the date on which the appointment takes effect,
(d) in a case where section 238 or 239 applies by reason of a company going into liquidation either following conversion of administration into winding up by virtue of Article 37 of the EC Regulation or at the time when the appointment of an administrator ceases to have effect, the date on which the company entered administration (or, if relevant, the date on which the application for the administration order was made or a copy of the notice of intention to appoint was filed), and
(e) in a case where section 238 or 239 applies by reason of a company going into liquidation at any other time, the date of the commencement of the winding up.

241 Orders under sections 238, 239

(1) Without prejudice to the generality of sections 238(3) and 239(3), an order under either of those sections with respect to a transaction or preference entered into or given by a company may (subject to the next subsection)—
(a) require any property transferred as part of the transaction, or in connection with the giving of the preference, to be vested in the company,
(b) require any property to be so vested if it represents in any person's hands the application either of the proceeds of sale of property so transferred or of money so transferred,
(c) release or discharge (in whole or in part) any security given by the company,
(d) require any person to pay, in respect of benefits received by him from the company, such sums to the office-holder as the court may direct,
(e) provide for any surety or guarantor whose obligations to any person were released or discharged (in whole or in part) under the transaction, or by the giving of the preference, to be under such new or revived obligations to that person as the court thinks appropriate,
(f) provide for security to be provided for the discharge of any obligation imposed by or arising under the order, for such an obligation to be charged on any property and for the security or charge to have the same priority as a security or charge released or discharged (in whole or in part) under the transaction or by the giving of the preference, and

(g) provide for the extent to which any person whose property is vested by the order in the company, or on whom obligations are imposed by the order, is to be able to prove in the winding up of the company for debts or other liabilities which arose from, or were released or discharged (in whole or in part) under or by, the transaction or the giving of the preference.

(2) An order under section 238 or 239 may affect the property of, or impose any obligation on, any person whether or not he is the person with whom the company in question entered into the transaction or (as the case may be) the person to whom the preference was given; but such an order—

(a) shall not prejudice any interest in property which was acquired from a person other than the company and was acquired in good faith and for value, or prejudice any interest deriving from such an interest, and

(b) shall not require a person who received a benefit from the transaction or preference in good faith and for value to pay a sum to the office-holder, except where that person was a party to the transaction or the payment is to be in respect of a preference given to that person at a time when he was a creditor of the company.

(2A) Where a person has acquired an interest in property from a person other than the company in question, or has received a benefit from the transaction or preference, and at the time of that acquisition or receipt—

(a) he had notice of the relevant surrounding circumstances and of the relevant proceedings, or

(b) he was connected with, or was an associate of, either the company in question or the person with whom that company entered into the transaction or to whom that company gave the preference,

then, unless the contrary is shown, it shall be presumed for the purposes of paragraph (a) or (as the case may be) paragraph (b) of subsection (2) that the interest was acquired or the benefit was received otherwise than in good faith.

(3) For the purposes of subsection (2A)(a), the relevant surrounding circumstances are (as the case may require)—

(a) the fact that the company in question entered into the transaction at an undervalue; or

(b) the circumstances which amounted to the giving of the preference by the company in question;

and subsections (3A) to (3C) have effect to determine whether, for those purposes, a person has notice of the relevant proceedings.

(3A) Where section 238 or 239 applies by reason of a company's entering administration, a person has notice of the relevant proceedings if he has notice that—

(a) an administration application has been made,

(b) an administration order has been made,

(c) a copy of a notice of intention to appoint an administrator under paragraph 14 or 22 of Schedule B1 has been filed, or

(d) notice of the appointment of an administrator has been filed under paragraph 18 or 29 of that Schedule.

(3B) Where section 238 or 239 applies by reason of a company's going into liquidation at the time when the appointment of an administrator of the company ceases to have effect, a person has notice of the relevant proceedings if he has notice that—

(a) an administration application has been made,

(b) an administration order has been made,

(c) a copy of a notice of intention to appoint an administrator under paragraph 14 or 22 of Schedule B1 has been filed,

(d) notice of the appointment of an administrator has been filed under paragraph 18 or 29 of that Schedule, or

(e) the company has gone into liquidation.

(3C) In a case where section 238 or 239 applies by reason of the company in question going into liquidation at any other time, a person has notice of the relevant proceedings if he has notice—

(a) where the company goes into liquidation on the making of a winding-up order, of the fact that the petition on which the winding-up order is made has been presented or of the fact that the company has gone into liquidation;

(b) in any other case, of the fact that the company has gone into liquidation.

(4) The provisions of sections 238 to 241 apply without prejudice to the availability of any other remedy, even in relation to a transaction or preference which the company had no power to enter into or give.

242 Gratuitous alienations (Scotland)

(1) Where this subsection applies and—
  (a) the winding up of a company has commenced, an alienation by the company is challengeable by—
    (i) any creditor who is a creditor by virtue of a debt incurred on or before the date of such commencement, or
    (ii) the liquidator;
  (b) a company enters administration, an alienation by the company is challengeable by the administrator.

(2) Subsection (1) applies where—
  (a) by the alienation, whether before or after 1st April 1986 (the coming into force of section 75 of the Bankruptcy (Scotland) Act 1985), any part of the company's property is transferred or any claim or right of the company is discharged or renounced, and
  (b) the alienation takes place on a relevant day.

(3) For the purposes of subsection (2)(b), the day on which an alienation takes place is the day on which it becomes completely effectual; and in that subsection "relevant day" means, if the alienation has the effect of favouring—
  (a) a person who is an associate (within the meaning of the Bankruptcy (Scotland) Act 1985) of the company, a day not earlier than 5 years before the date on which—
    (i) the winding up of the company commences, or
    (ii) as the case may be, the company enters administration; or
  (b) any other person, a day not earlier than 2 years before that date.

(4) On a challenge being brought under subsection (1), the court shall grant decree of reduction or for such restoration of property to the company's assets or other redress as may be appropriate; but the court shall not grant such a decree if the person seeking to uphold the alienation establishes—
  (a) that immediately, or at any other time, after the alienation the company's assets were greater than its liabilities, or
  (b) that the alienation was made for adequate consideration, or
  (c) that the alienation—
    (i) was a birthday, Christmas or other conventional gift, or
    (ii) was a gift made, for a charitable purpose, to a person who is not an associate of the company, which, having regard to all the circumstances, it was reasonable for the company to make:

Provided that this subsection is without prejudice to any right or interest acquired in good faith and for value from or through the transferee in the alienation.

(5) In subsection (4) above, "charitable purpose" means any charitable, benevolent or philanthropic purpose, whether or not it is charitable within the meaning of any rule of law.

(6) For the purposes of the foregoing provisions of this section, an alienation in implementation of a prior obligation is deemed to be one for which there was no consideration or no adequate consideration to the extent that the prior obligation was undertaken for no consideration or no adequate consideration.

(7) A liquidator and an administrator have the same right as a creditor has under any rule of law to challenge an alienation of a company made for no consideration or no adequate consideration.

(8) This section applies to Scotland only.

243 Unfair preferences (Scotland)

(1) Subject to subsection (2) below, subsection (4) below applies to a transaction entered into by a company, whether before or after 1st April 1986, which has the effect of creating a preference in favour of a creditor to the prejudice of the general body of creditors, being a preference created not earlier than 6 months before the commencement of the winding up of the company or the company enters administration.

(2) Subsection (4) below does not apply to any of the following transactions—
  (a) a transaction in the ordinary course of trade or business;

(b) a payment in cash for a debt which when it was paid had become payable, unless the transaction was collusive with the purpose of prejudicing the general body of creditors;

(c) a transaction whereby the parties to it undertake reciprocal obligations (whether the performance by the parties of their respective obligations occurs at the same time or at different times) unless the transaction was collusive as aforesaid;

(d) the granting of a mandate by a company authorising an arrestee to pay over the arrested funds or part thereof to the arrester where—

(i) there has been a decree for payment or a warrant for summary diligence, and

(ii) the decree or warrant has been preceded by an arrestment on the dependence of the action or followed by an arrestment in execution.

(3) For the purposes of subsection (1) above, the day on which a preference was created is the day on which the preference became completely effectual.

(4) A transaction to which this subsection applies is challengeable by—

(a) in the case of a winding up—

(i) any creditor who is a creditor by virtue of a debt incurred on or before the date of commencement of the winding up, or

(ii) the liquidator; and

(b) where the company has entered administration, the administrator.

(5) On a challenge being brought under subsection (4) above, the court, if satisfied that the transaction challenged is a transaction to which this section applies, shall grant decree of reduction or for such restoration of property to the company's assets or other redress as may be appropriate;

Provided that this subsection is without prejudice to any right or interest acquired in good faith and for value from or through the creditor in whose favour the preference was created.

(6) A liquidator and an administrator have the same right as a creditor has under any rule of law to challenge a preference created by a debtor.

(7) This section applies to Scotland only.

244 Extortionate credit transactions

(1) This section applies as does section 238, and where the company is, or has been, a party to a transaction for, or involving, the provision of credit to the company.

(2) The court may, on the application of the office-holder, make an order with respect to the transaction if the transaction is or was extortionate and was entered into in the period of 3 years ending with the day on which the administration order was made or (as the case may be) the day on which the company entered administration or went into liquidation.

(3) For the purposes of this section a transaction is extortionate if, having regard to the risk accepted by the person providing the credit—

(a) the terms of it are or were such as to require grossly exorbitant payments to be made (whether unconditionally or in certain contingencies) in respect of the provision of the credit, or

(b) it otherwise grossly contravened ordinary principles of fair dealing;

and it shall be presumed, unless the contrary is proved, that a transaction with respect to which an application is made under this section is or, as the case may be, was extortionate.

(4) An order under this section with respect to any transaction may contain such one or more of the following as the court thinks fit, that is to say—

(a) provision setting aside the whole or part of any obligation created by the transaction,

(b) provision otherwise varying the terms of the transaction or varying the terms on which any security for the purposes of the transaction is held,

(c) provision requiring any person who is or was a party to the transaction to pay to the office-holder any sums paid to that person, by virtue of the transaction, by the company,

(d) provision requiring any person to surrender to the office-holder any property held by him as security for the purposes of the transaction,

(e) provision directing accounts to be taken between any persons.

(5) The powers conferred by this section are exercisable in relation to any transaction concurrently with any powers exercisable in relation to that transaction as a transaction at an undervalue or under section 242 (gratuitious alienations in Scotland).

245 Avoidance of certain floating charges

(1) This section applies as does section 238, but applies to Scotland as well as to England and Wales.

(2) Subject as follows, a floating charge on the company's undertaking or property created at a relevant time is invalid except to the extent of the aggregate of—

(a) the value of so much of the consideration for the creation of the charge as consists of money paid, or goods or services supplied, to the company at the same time as, or after, the creation of the charge,

(b) the value of so much of that consideration as consists of the discharge or reduction, at the same time as, or after, the creation of the charge, of any debt of the company, and

(c) the amount of such interest (if any) as is payable on the amount falling within paragraph (a) or (b) in pursuance of any agreement under which the money was so paid, the goods or services were so supplied or the debt was so discharged or reduced.

(3) Subject to the next subsection, the time at which a floating charge is created by a company is a relevant time for the purposes of this section if the charge is created—

(a) in the case of a charge which is created in favour of a person who is connected with the company, at a time in the period of 2 years ending with the onset of insolvency,

(b) in the case of a charge which is created in favour of any other person, at a time in the period of 12 months ending with the onset of insolvency,

(c) in either case, at a time between the making of an administration application in respect of the company and the making of an administration order on that application, or

(d) in either case, at a time between the filing with the court of a copy of notice of intention to appoint an administrator under paragraph 14 or 22 of Schedule B1 and the making of an appointment under that paragraph.

(4) Where a company creates a floating charge at a time mentioned in subsection (3)(b) and the person in favour of whom the charge is created is not connected with the company, that time is not a relevant time for the purposes of this section unless the company—

(a) is at that time unable to pay its debts within the meaning of section 123 in Chapter VI of Part IV, or

(b) becomes unable to pay its debts within the meaning of that section in consequence of the transaction under which the charge is created.

(5) For the purposes of subsection (3), the onset of insolvency is—

(a) in a case where this section applies by reason of an administrator of a company being appointed by administration order, the date on which the administration application is made,

(b) in a case where this section applies by reason of an administrator of a company being appointed under paragraph 14 or 22 of Schedule B1 following filing with the court of a copy of notice of intention to appoint under that paragraph, the date on which the copy of the notice is filed,

(c) in a case where this section applies by reason of an administrator of a company being appointed otherwise than as mentioned in paragraph (a) or (b), the date on which the appointment takes effect, and

(d) in a case where this section applies by reason of a company going into liquidation, the date of the commencement of the winding up.

(6) For the purposes of subsection (2)(a) the value of any goods or services supplied by way of consideration for a floating charge is the amount in money which at the time they were supplied could reasonably have been expected to be obtained for supplying the goods or services in the ordinary course of business and on the same terms (apart from the consideration) as those on which they were supplied to the company.

246 Unenforceability of liens on books, etc.

(1) This section applies in the case of a company where—

(a) the company enters administration, or

(b) the company goes into liquidation, or

(c) a provisional liquidator is appointed;

and "the office-holder" means the administrator, the liquidator or the provisional liquidator, as the case may be.

(2) Subject as follows, a lien or other right to retain possession of any of the books, papers or other records of the company is unenforceable to the extent that its enforcement would deny possession of any books, papers or other records to the office-holder.

(3) This does not apply to a lien on documents which give a title to property and are held as such.

246A Remote attendance at meetings

(1) Subject to subsection (2), this section applies to—
 (a) any meeting of the creditors of a company summoned under this Act or the rules, or
 (b) any meeting of the members or contributories of a company summoned by the office-holder under this Act or the rules, other than a meeting of the members of a company in a members' voluntary winding up.

(2) This section does not apply where—
 (a) a company is being wound up in Scotland, or
 (b) a receiver is appointed under section 51 in Chapter 2 of Part 3.

(3) Where the person summoning a meeting ("the convener") considers it appropriate, the meeting may be conducted and held in such a way that persons who are not present together at the same place may attend it.

(4) Where a meeting is conducted and held in the manner referred to in subsection (3), a person attends the meeting if that person is able to exercise any rights which that person may have to speak and vote at the meeting.

(5) For the purposes of this section—
 (a) a person is able to exercise the right to speak at a meeting when that person is in a position to communicate to all those attending the meeting, during the meeting, any information or opinions which that person has on the business of the meeting; and
 (b) a person is able to exercise the right to vote at a meeting when—
  (i) that person is able to vote, during the meeting, on resolutions put to the vote at the meeting, and
  (ii) that person's vote can be taken into account in determining whether or not such resolutions are passed at the same time as the votes of all the other persons attending the meeting.

(6) The convener of a meeting which is to be conducted and held in the manner referred to in subsection (3) shall make whatever arrangements the convener considers appropriate to—
 (a) enable those attending the meeting to exercise their rights to speak or vote, and
 (b) ensure the identification of those attending the meeting and the security of any electronic means used to enable attendance.

(7) Where in the reasonable opinion of the convener—
 (a) a meeting will be attended by persons who will not be present together at the same place, and
 (b) it is unnecessary or inexpedient to specify a place for the meeting,

any requirement under this Act or the rules to specify a place for the meeting may be satisfied by specifying the arrangements the convener proposes to enable persons to exercise their rights to speak or vote.

(8) In making the arrangements referred to in subsection (6) and in forming the opinion referred to in subsection (7)(b), the convener must have regard to the legitimate interests of the creditors, members or contributories and others attending the meeting in the efficient despatch of the business of the meeting.

(9) If—
 (a) the notice of a meeting does not specify a place for the meeting,
 (b) the convener is requested in accordance with the rules to specify a place for the meeting, and
 (c) that request is made—
  (i) in the case of a meeting of creditors or contributories, by not less than ten percent in value of the creditors or contributories, or
  (ii) in the case of a meeting of members, by members representing not less than ten percent of the total voting rights of all the members having at the date of the request a right to vote at the meeting,

it shall be the duty of the convener to specify a place for the meeting.

(10) In this section, "the office-holder", in relation to a company, means—
 (a) its liquidator, provisional liquidator, administrator, or administrative receiver, or

(b) where a voluntary arrangement in relation to the company is proposed or has taken effect under Part 1, the nominee or the supervisor of the voluntary arrangement.

246B Use of websites

(1) Subject to subsection (2), where any provision of this Act or the rules requires the office-holder to give, deliver, furnish or send a notice or other document or information to any person, that requirement is satisfied by making the notice, document or information available on a website—

(a) in accordance with the rules, and

(b) in such circumstances as may be prescribed.

(2) This section does not apply where—

(a) a company is being wound up in Scotland, or

(b) a receiver is appointed under section 51 in Chapter 2 of Part 3.

(3) In this section, "the office-holder" means—

(a) the liquidator, provisional liquidator, administrator, or administrative receiver of a company, or

(b) where a voluntary arrangement in relation to a company is proposed or has taken effect under Part 1, the nominee or the supervisor of the voluntary arrangement.

PART VII
INTERPRETATION FOR FIRST GROUP OF PARTS

247 "Insolvency" and "go into liquidation"

(1) In this Group of Parts, except in so far as the context otherwise requires, "insolvency", in relation to a company, includes the approval of a voluntary arrangement under Part I, or the appointment of an administrator or administrative receiver.

(2) For the purposes of any provision in this Group of Parts, a company goes into liquidation if it passes a resolution for voluntary winding up or an order for its winding up is made by the court at a time when it has not already gone into liquidation by passing such a resolution.

(3) The reference to a resolution for voluntary winding up in subsection (2) includes a reference to a resolution which is deemed to occur by virtue of—

(a) paragraph 83(6)(b) of Schedule B1, or

(b) an order made following conversion of administration or a voluntary arrangement into winding up by virtue of Article 37 of the EC Regulation.

248 "Secured creditor", etc.

In this Group of Parts, except in so far as the context otherwise requires—

(a) "secured creditor", in relation to a company, means a creditor of the company who holds in respect of his debt a security over property of the company, and "unsecured creditor" is to be read accordingly; and

(b) "security" means—

(i) in relation to England and Wales, any mortgage, charge, lien or other security, and

(ii) in relation to Scotland, any security (whether heritable or moveable), any floating charge and any right of lien or preference and any right of retention (other than a right of compensation or set off).

249 "Connected" with a company

For the purposes of any provision in this Group of Parts, a person is connected with a company if—

(a) he is a director or shadow director of the company or an associate of such a director or shadow director, or

(b) he is an associate of the company,

and "associate" has the meaning given by section 435 in Part XVIII of this Act.

250 "Member" of a company

For the purposes of any provision in this Group of Parts, a person who is not a member of a company but to whom shares in the company have been transferred, or transmitted by operation of law, is to be regarded as a member of the company, and references to a member or members are to be read accordingly.

251 Expressions used generally

In this Group of Parts, except in so far as the context otherwise requires—

"administrative receiver" means —

(a) an administrative receiver as defined by section 29(2) in Chapter I of Part III, or

(b) a receiver appointed under section 51 in Chapter II of that Part in a case where the whole (or substantially the whole) of the company's property is attached by the floating charge;

"agent" does not include a person's counsel acting as such;

"books and papers" and "books or papers" includes accounts, deeds, writing and documents;

"business day" means any day other than a Saturday, a Sunday, Christmas Day, Good Friday or a day which is a bank holiday in any part of Great Britain;

"chattel leasing agreement" means an agreement for the bailment or, in Scotland, the hiring of goods which is capable of subsisting for more than 3 months;

"contributory" has the meaning given by section 79;

"the court", in relation to a company, means a court having jurisdiction to wind up the company;

"director" includes any person occupying the position of director, by whatever name called; "document" includes summons, notice, order and other legal process, and registers; "floating charge" means a charge which, as created, was a floating charge and includes a floating charge within section 462 of the Companies Act (Scottish floating charges);

"the Gazette" means—

(a) as respects companies registered in England and Wales, the London Gazette;

(b) as respects companies registered in Scotland, the Edinburgh Gazette;

"officer", in relation to a body corporate, includes a director, manager or secretary;

"the official rate", in relation to interest, means the rate payable under section 189(4);

"prescribed" means prescribed by the rules;

"receiver", in the expression "receiver or manager", does not include a receiver appointed under section 51 in Chapter II of Part III;

"retention of title agreement" means an agreement for the sale of goods to a company, being an agreement—

(a) which does not constitute a charge on the goods, but

(b) under which, if the seller is not paid and the company is wound up, the seller will have priority over all other creditors of the company as respects the goods or any property representing the goods;

"the rules" means rules under section 411 in Part XV; and

"shadow director", in relation to a company, means a person in accordance with whose directions or instructions the directors of the company are accustomed to act (but so that a person is not deemed a shadow director by reason only that the directors act on advice given by him in a professional capacity).

PARTS VIII–XI

OMITTED

THE THIRD GROUP OF PARTS

MISCELLANEOUS MATTERS BEARING ON BOTH COMPANY AND INDIVIDUAL INSOLVENCY; GENERAL INTERPRETATION; FINAL PROVISIONS

PART XII

PREFERENTIAL DEBTS IN COMPANY AND INDIVIDUAL INSOLVENCY

386 Categories of preferential debts

(1) A reference in this Act to the preferential debts of a company or an individual is to the debts listed in Schedule 6 to this Act (contributions to occupational pension schemes; remuneration, &c. of employees; levies on coal and steel production; debts owed to the Financial Services Compensation Scheme; deposits covered by Financial Services Compensation Scheme; other deposits; and references to preferential creditors are to be read accordingly.

(1A) A reference in this Act to the "ordinary preferential debts" of a company or an individual is to the preferential debts listed in any of paragraphs 8 to 15B of Schedule 6 to this Act.

(1B) A reference in this Act to the "secondary preferential debts" of a company or an individual is to the preferential debts listed in paragraph 15BA or 15BB of Schedule 6 to this Act.

(2) In Schedule 6 "the debtor" means the company or the individual concerned.

(3) Schedule 6 is to be read with Schedule 4 to the Pension Schemes Act 1993 (occupational pension scheme contributions).

387 "The relevant date"

(1) This section explains references in Schedule 6 to the relevant date (being the date which determines the existence and amount of a preferential debt).

(2) For the purposes of section 4 in Part I (meetings to consider company voluntary arrangement), the relevant date in relation to a company which is not being wound up is—

(a) if the company is in administration, the date on which it entered administration, and

(b) if the company is not in administration, the date on which the voluntary arrangement takes effect.

(2A) For the purposes of paragraph 31 of Schedule A1 (meetings to consider company voluntary arrangement where a moratorium under section 1A is in force), the relevant date in relation to a company is the date of filing.

(3) In relation to a company which is being wound up, the following applies—

(a) if the winding up is by the court, and the winding-up order was made immediately upon the discharge of an administration order, the relevant date is the date on which the company entered administration;

(aa) if the winding up is by the court and the winding-up order was made following conversion of administration into winding up by virtue of Article 37 of the EC Regulation, the relevant date is the date on which the company entered administration;

(ab) if the company is deemed to have passed a resolution for voluntary winding up by virtue of an order following conversion of administration into winding up under Article 37 of the EC Regulation, the relevant date is the date on which the company entered administration;

(b) if the case does not fall within paragraph (a), (aa) or (ab) and the company—

(i) is being wound up by the court, and

(ii) had not commenced to be wound up voluntarily before the date of the making of the winding-up order,

the relevant date is the date of the appointment (or first appointment) of a provisional liquidator or, if no such appointment has been made, the date of the winding-up order;

(ba) if the case does not fall within paragraph (a), (aa), (ab) or (b) and the company is being wound up following administration pursuant to paragraph 83 of Schedule B1, the relevant date is the date on which the company entered administration;

(c) if the case does not fall within paragraph (a), (aa), (ab), (b) or (ba), the relevant date is the date of the passing of the resolution for the winding up of the company.

(3A) In relation to a company which is in administration (and to which no other provision of this section applies) the relevant date is the date on which the company enters administration.

(4) In relation to a company in receivership (where section 40 or, as the case may be, section 59 applies), the relevant date is—

(a) in England and Wales, the date of the appointment of the receiver by debenture-holders, and

(b) in Scotland, the date of the appointment of the receiver under section 53(6) or (as the case may be) 54(5).

(5) For the purposes of section 258 in Part VIII (individual voluntary arrangements), the relevant date is, in relation to a debtor who is not an undischarged bankrupt—
(a) where an interim order has been made under section 252 with respect to his proposal, the date of that order, and
(b) in any other case, the date on which the voluntary arrangement takes effect.
(6) In relation to a bankrupt, the following applies—
(a) where at the time the bankruptcy order was made there was an interim receiver appointed under section 286, the relevant date is the date on which the interim receiver was first appointed after the presentation of the bankruptcy petition;
(b) otherwise, the relevant date is the date of the making of the bankruptcy order.

PART XIII
INSOLVENCY PRACTITIONERS AND THEIR QUALIFICATION

Restrictions on unqualified persons acting as liquidator, trustee in bankruptcy, etc.

388 Meaning of "act as insolvency practitioner"

(1) A person acts as an insolvency practitioner in relation to a company by acting—
(a) as its liquidator, provisional liquidator, administrator or administrative receiver, or
(b) where a voluntary arrangement in relation to the company is proposed or approved under Part I, as nominee or supervisor.

...

(2B) In relation to a voluntary arrangement proposed under Part I or VIII, a person acts as nominee if he performs any of the functions conferred on nominees under the Part in question.

...

(4) In this section—
"administrative receiver" has the meaning given by section 251 in Part VII; "company" means—
(a) a company registered under the Companies Act 2006 in England and Wales or Scotland, or
(b) a company that may be wound up under Part 5 of this Act (unregistered companies);

...

(5) Nothing in this section applies to anything done by—
(a) the official receiver; or
(b) the Accountant in Bankruptcy (within the meaning of the Bankruptcy (Scotland) Act 1985).
(6) Nothing in this section applies to anything done (whether in the United Kingdom or elsewhere) in relation to insolvency proceedings under the EC Regulation in a member State other than the United Kingdom.

389 Acting without qualification an offence.

(1) A person who acts as an insolvency practitioner in relation to a company or an individual at a time when he is not qualified to do so is liable to imprisonment or a fine, or to both.
(1A) This section is subject to section 389A.
(2) This section does not apply to the official receiver or the Accountant in Bankruptcy (within the meaning of the Bankruptcy (Scotland) Act 1985).

389A Authorisation of nominees and supervisors

(1) Section 389 does not apply to a person acting, in relation to a voluntary arrangement proposed or approved under Part I or Part VIII, as nominee or supervisor if he is authorised so to act.
(2) For the purposes of subsection (1) and those Parts, an individual to whom subsection (3) does not apply is authorised to act as nominee or supervisor in relation to such an arrangement if—
(a) he is a member of a body recognised for the purpose by the Secretary of State, and
(b) there is in force security (in Scotland, caution) for the proper performance of his functions and that security or caution meets the prescribed requirements with respect to his so acting in relation to the arrangement.

(3) This subsection applies to a person if—
(a) he has been adjudged bankrupt or sequestration of his estate has been awarded and (in either case) he has not been discharged,
(b) he is subject to a disqualification order made or a disqualification undertaking accepted under the Company Directors Disqualification Act 1986 or the Company Directors Disqualification (Northern Ireland) Order 2002,
(c) he is a patient within the meaning of section 329(1) of the Mental Health (Care and Treatment) (Scotland) Act 2003, or
(d) he lacks capacity (within the meaning of the Mental Capacity Act 2005) to act as nominee or supervisor.

(4) The Secretary of State may by order declare a body which appears to him to fall within subsection (5) to be a recognised body for the purposes of subsection (2)(a).

...

389B *omitted*

390 Persons not qualified to act as insolvency practitioners

(1) A person who is not an individual is not qualified to act as an insolvency practitioner.

(2) A person is not qualified to act as an insolvency practitioner at any time unless at that time—
(a) he is authorised so to act by virtue of membership of a professional body recognised under section 391 below, being permitted so to act by or under the rules of that body, or
(b) he holds an authorisation granted by a competent authority under section 393; or
(c) he holds an authorisation granted by the Department of Enterprise, Trade and Investment for Northern Ireland under Article 352 of the Insolvency (Northern Ireland) Order 1989.

(3) A person is not qualified to act as an insolvency practitioner in relation to another person at any time unless—
(a) there is in force at that time security or, in Scotland, caution for the proper performance of his functions, and
(b) that security or caution meets the prescribed requirements with respect to his so acting in relation to that other person.

(4) A person is not qualified to act as an insolvency practitioner at any time if at that time—
(a) he has been adjudged bankrupt or sequestration of his estate has been awarded and (in either case) he has not been discharged,
(aa) a moratorium period under a debt relief order applies in relation of him,
(b) he is subject to a disqualification order made or a disqualification undertaking accepted under the Company Directors Disqualification Act 1986 or the Company Directors Disqualification (Northern Ireland) Order 2002,
(c) he is a patient within the meaning of section 329(1) of the Mental Health (Care and Treatment) (Scotland) Act 2003 or has had a guardian appointed to him under the Adults with Incapacity (Scotland) Act 2000, or
(d) he lacks capacity (within the meaning of the Mental Capacity Act 2005) to act as an insolvency practitioner.

(5) A person is not qualified to act as an insolvency practitioner while a bankruptcy restrictions order or a debt relief restrictions order is in force in respect of him.

391–398 *omitted*

PARTS XIV, XV
OMITTED

PART XVI
PROVISIONS AGAINST DEBT AVOIDANCE (ENGLAND AND WALES ONLY)

423 Transactions defrauding creditors

(1) This section relates to transactions entered into at an undervalue; and a person enters into such a transaction with another person if—
(a) he makes a gift to the other person or he otherwise enters into a transaction with the other on terms that provide for him to receive no consideration;

(b) he enters into a transaction with the other in consideration of marriage or the formation of a civil partnership ; or
(c) he enters into a transaction with the other for a consideration the value of which, in money or money's worth, is significantly less than the value, in money or money's worth, of the consideration provided by himself.

(2) Where a person has entered into such a transaction, the court may, if satisfied under the next subsection, make such order as it thinks fit for—
(a) restoring the position to what it would have been if the transaction had not been entered into, and
(b) protecting the interests of persons who are victims of the transaction.

(3) In the case of a person entering into such a transaction, an order shall only be made if the court is satisfied that it was entered into by him for the purpose—
(a) of putting assets beyond the reach of a person who is making, or may at some time make, a claim against him, or
(b) of otherwise prejudicing the interests of such a person in relation to the claim which he is making or may make.

(4) In this section "the court" means the High Court or—
(a) if the person entering into the transaction is an individual, any other court which would have jurisdiction in relation to a bankruptcy petition relating to him;
(b) if that person is a body capable of being wound up under Part IV or V of this Act, any other court having jurisdiction to wind it up.

(5) In relation to a transaction at an undervalue, references here and below to a victim of the transaction are to a person who is, or is capable of being, prejudiced by it; and in the following two sections the person entering into the transaction is referred to as "the debtor".

424 Those who may apply for an order under section 423

(1) An application for an order under section 423 shall not be made in relation to a transaction except—
(a) in a case where the debtor has been adjudged bankrupt or is a body corporate which is being wound up or which is in administration, by the official receiver, by the trustee of the bankrupt's estate or the liquidator or adminstrator of the body corporate or (with the leave of the court) by a victim of the transaction;
(b) in a case where a victim of the transaction is bound by a voluntary arrangement approved under Part I or Part VIII of this Act, by the supervisor of the voluntary arrangement or by any person who (whether or not so bound) is such a victim; or
(c) in any other case, by a victim of the transaction.

(2) An application made under any of the paragraphs of subsection (1) is to be treated as made on behalf of every victim of the transaction.

425 Provision which may be made by order under section 423

(1) Without prejudice to the generality of section 423, an order made under that section with respect to a transaction may (subject as follows)—
(a) require any property transferred as part of the transaction to be vested in any person, either absolutely or for the benefit of all the persons on whose behalf the application for the order is treated as made;
(b) require any property to be so vested if it represents, in any person's hands, the application either of the proceeds of sale of property so transferred or of the money so transferred;
(c) release or discharge (in whole or in part) any security given by the debtor;
(d) require any person to pay to any other person in respect of benefits received from the debtor such sums as the court may direct;
(e) provide for any surety or guarantor whose obligations to any person were released or discharged (in whole or in part) under the transaction to be under such new or revived obligations as the court thinks appropriate;
(f) provide for security to be provided for the discharge of any obligation imposed by or arising under the order, for such an obligation to be charged on any property and for such security or charge to have the same priority as a security or charge released or discharged (in whole or in part) under the transaction.

(2) An order under section 423 may affect the property of, or impose any obligation on, any person whether or not he is the person with whom the debtor entered into the transaction; but such an order—
   (a) shall not prejudice any interest in property which was acquired from a person other than the debtor and was acquired in good faith, for value and without notice of the relevant circumstances, or prejudice any interest deriving from such an interest, and
   (b) shall not require a person who received a benefit from the transaction in good faith, for value and without notice of the relevant circumstances to pay any sum unless he was a party to the transaction.

(3) For the purposes of this section the relevant circumstances in relation to a transaction are the circumstances by virtue of which an order under section 423 may be made in respect of the transaction.

(4) In this section "security" means any mortgage, charge, lien or other security.

PART XVII
MISCELLANEOUS AND GENERAL

426–429 *omitted*

430 Provision introducing Schedule of punishments

(1) Schedule 10 to this Act has effect with respect to the way in which offences under this Act are punishable on conviction.

(2) In relation to an offence under a provision of this Act specified in the first column of the Schedule (the general nature of the offence being described in the second column), the third column shows whether the offence is punishable on conviction on indictment, or on summary conviction, or either in the one way or the other.

(3) The fourth column of the Schedule shows, in relation to an offence, the maximum punishment by way of fine or imprisonment under this Act which may be imposed on a person convicted of the offence in the way specified in relation to it in the third column (that is to say, on indictment or summarily) a reference to a period of years or months being to a term of imprisonment of that duration.

(4) The fifth column shows (in relation to an offence for which there is an entry in that column) that a person convicted of the offence after continued contravention is liable to a daily default fine; that is to say, he is liable on a second or subsquent conviction of the offence to the fine specified in that column for each day on which the contravention is continued (instead of the penalty specified for the offence in the fourth column of the Schedule).

(5) For the purpose of any enactment in this Act whereby an officer of a company who is in default is liable to a fine or penalty, the expression "officer who is in default" means any officer of the company who knowingly and wilfully authorises or permits the default, refusal or contravention mentioned in the enactment.

431 Summary proceedings

(1) Summary proceedings for any offence under any of Parts I to VII of this Act may (without prejudice to any jurisdiction exercisable apart from this subsection) be taken against a body corporate at any place at which the body has a place of business, and against any other person at any place at which he is for the time being.

(2) Notwithstanding anything in section 127(1) of the Magistrates' Courts Act 1980, an information relating to such an offence which is triable by a magistrates' court in England and Wales may be so tried if it is laid at any time within 3 years after the commission of the offence and within 12 months after the date on which evidence sufficient in the opinion of the Director of Public Prosecutions or the Secretary of State (as the case may be) to justify the proceedings comes to his knowledge.

(3) Summary proceedings in Scotland for such an offence shall not be commenced after the expiration of 3 years from the commission of the offence.
Subject to this (and notwithstanding anything in section 136 of the Criminal Procdure (Scotland) Act 1995), such proceedings may (in Scotland) be commenced at any time within 12 months after the date on which evidence sufficient in the Lord Advocate's opinion to justify the proceedings came to his knowledge or, where such evidence was

reported to him by the Secretary of State, within 12 months after the date on which it came to the knowledge of the latter; and subsection (3) of that section applies for the purpose of this subsection as it applies for the purpose of that section.

(4) For purposes of this section, a certificate of the Director of Public Prosecutions, the Lord Advocate or the Secretary of State (as the case may be) as to the date on which such evidence as is referred to above came to his knowledge is conclusive evidence.

432 Offences by bodies corporate

(1) This section applies to offences under this Act other than those excepted by subsection (4).

(2) Where a body corporate is guilty of an offence to which this section applies and the offence is proved to have been committed with the consent or connivance of, or to be attributable to any neglect on the part of, any director, manager, secretary or other similar officer of the body corporate or any person who was purporting to act in any such capacity he, as well as the body corporate, is guilty of the offence and liable to be proceeded against and punished accordingly.

(3) Where the affairs of a body corporate are managed by its members, subsection (2) applies in relation to the acts and defaults of a member in connection with his functions of management as if he were a director of the body corporate.

(4) The offences excepted from this section are those under sections 30, 39, 51, 53, 54, 62, 64, 66, 85, 89, 164, 188, 201, 206, 207, 208, 209, 210 and 211 and those under paragraphs 16(2), 17(3)(a), 18(3)(a), 19(3)(a), 22(1) and 23(1)(a) of Schedule A1.

433 Admissibility in evidence of statements of affairs, etc.

(1) In any proceedings (whether or not under this Act)—

(a) a statement of affairs prepared for the purposes of any provision of this Act which is derived from the Insolvency Act 1985, and

(aa) a statement made in pursuance of a requirement imposed by or under Part 2 of the Banking Act 2009 (bank insolvency),

(ab) a statement made in pursuance of a requirement imposed by or under Part 3 of that Act (bank administration), and

(b) any other statement made in pursuance of a requirement imposed by or under any such provision or by or under rules made under this Act,

may be used in evidence against any person making or concurring in making the statement.

(2) However, in criminal proceedings in which any such person is charged with an offence to which this subsection applies—

(a) no evidence relating to the statement may be adduced, and

(b) no question relating to it may be asked,

by or on behalf of the prosecution, unless evidence relating to it is adduced, or a question relating to it is asked, in the proceedings by or on behalf of that person.

(3) Subsection (2) applies to any offence other than—

(a) an offence under section 22(6), 47(6), 48(8), 66(6), 67(8), 95(8), 98(6), 99(3)(a), 131(7), 192(2), 208(1)(a) or (d) or (2), 210, 235(5), 353(1), 354(1)(b) or (3) or 356(1) or (2)(a) or (b) or paragraph 4(3)(a) of Schedule 7;

(b) an offence which is—

(i) created by rules made under this Act, and

(ii) designated for the purposes of this subsection by such rules or by regulations made by the Secretary of State;

(c) an offence which is—

(i) created by regulations made under any such rules, and

(ii) designated for the purposes of this subsection by such regulations;

(d) an offence under section 1, 2 or 5 of the Perjury Act 1911 (false statements made on oath or made otherwise than on oath); or

(e) an offence under section 44(1) or (2) of the Criminal Law (Consolidation) (Scotland) Act 1995 (false statements made on oath or otherwise than on oath).

(4) Regulations under subsection (3)(b)(ii) shall be made by statutory instrument and, after being made, shall be laid before each House of Parliament.

434 Crown application

For the avoidance of doubt it is hereby declared that provisions of this Act which derive from the Insolvency Act 1985 bind the Crown so far as affecting or relating to the following matters, namely—

(a) remedies against, or against the property of, companies or individuals;
(b) priorities of debts;
(c) transactions at an undervalue or preferences;
(d) voluntary arrangements approved under Part I or Part VIII, and
(e) discharge from bankruptcy.

PART 17A
SUPPLEMENTARY PROVISIONS

434A Introductory

The provisions of this Part have effect for the purposes of—

(a) the First Group of Parts, and
(b) sections 411, 413, 414, 416 and 417 in Part 15.

434B Representation of corporations at meetings

(1) If a corporation is a creditor or debenture-holder, it may by resolution of its directors or other governing body authorise a person or persons to act as its representative or representatives—
(a) at any meeting of the creditors of a company held in pursuance of this Act or of rules made under it, or
(b) at any meeting of a company held in pursuance of the provisions contained in a debenture or trust deed.

(2) Where the corporation authorises only one person, that person is entitled to exercise the same powers on behalf of the corporation as the corporation could exercise if it were an individual creditor or debenture-holder.

(3) Where the corporation authorises more than one person, any one of them is entitled to exercise the same powers on behalf of the corporation as the corporation could exercise if it were an individual creditor or debenture-holder.

(4) Where the corporation authorises more than one person and more than one of them purport to exercise a power under subsection (3)—
(a) if they purport to exercise the power in the same way, the power is treated as exercised in that way;
(b) if they do not purport to exercise the power in the same way, the power is treated as not exercised.

434C Legal professional privilege

In proceedings against a person for an offence under this Act nothing in this Act is to be taken to require any person to disclose any information that he is entitled to refuse to disclose on grounds of legal professional privilege (in Scotland, confidentiality of communications).

434D Enforcement of company's filing obligations

(1) This section applies where a company has made default in complying with any obligation under this Act—
(a) to deliver a document to the registrar, or
(b) to give notice to the registrar of any matter.

(2) The registrar, or any member or creditor of the company, may give notice to the company requiring it to comply with the obligation.

(3) If the company fails to make good the default within 14 days after service of the notice, the registrar, or any member or creditor of the company, may apply to the court for an order directing the company, and any specified officer of it, to make good the default within a specified time.

(4) The court's order may provide that all costs (in Scotland, expenses) of or incidental to the application are to be borne by the company or by any officers of it responsible for the default.

(5) This section does not affect the operation of any enactment imposing penalties on a company or its officers in respect of any such default.

434E *omitted*

PART XVIII
INTERPRETATION

435 Meaning of "associate"

(1) For the purposes of this Act any question whether a person is an associate of another person is to be determined in accordance with the following provisions of this section (any provision that a person is an associate of another person being taken to mean that they are associates of each other).

(2) A person is an associate of an individual if that person is—
 (a) the individual's husband or wife or civil partner,
 (b) a relative of—
  (i) the individual, or
  (ii) the individual's husband or wife or civil partner, or
 (c) the husband or wife or civil partner of a relative of—
  (i) the individual, or
  (ii) the individual's husband or wife or civil partner.

(3) A person is an associate of any person with whom he is in partnership, and of the husband or wife or civil partner or a relative of any individual with whom he is in partnership; and a Scottish firm is an associate of any person who is a member of the firm.

(4) A person is an associate of any person whom he employs or by whom he is employed.

(5) A person in his capacity as trustee of a trust other than—
 (a) a trust arising under any of the second Group of Parts or the Bankruptcy (Scotland) Act 1985, or
 (b) a pension scheme or an employees' share scheme,

is an associate of another person if the beneficiaries of the trust include, or the terms of the trust confer a power that may be exercised for the benefit of, that other person or an associate of that other person.

(6) A company is an associate of another company—
 (a) if the same person has control of both, or a person has control of one and persons who are his associates, or he and persons who are his associates, have control of the other, or
 (b) if a group of two or more persons has control of each company, and the groups either consist of the same persons or could be regarded as consisting of the same persons by treating (in one or more cases) a member of either group as replaced by a person of whom he is an associate.

(7) A company is an associate of another person if that person has control of it or if that person and persons who are his associates together have control of it.

(8) For the purposes of this section a person is a relative of an individual if he is that individual's brother, sister, uncle, aunt, nephew, niece, lineal ancestor or lineal descendant, treating—
 (a) any relationship of the half blood as a relationship of the whole blood and the stepchild or adopted child of any person as his child, and
 (b) an illegitimate child as the legitimate child of his mother and reputed father;

and references in this section to a husband or wife include a former husband or wife and a reputed husband or wife and references to a civil partner include a former civil partner and a reputed civil partner.

(9) For the purposes of this section any director or other officer of a company is to be treated as employed by that company.

(10) For the purposes of this section a person is to be taken as having control of a company if—
 (a) the directors of the company or of another company which has control of it (or any of them) are accustomed to act in accordance with his directions or instructions, or
 (b) he is entitled to exercise, or control the exercise of, one third or more of the voting power at any general meeting of the company or of another company which has control of it;

and where two or more persons together satisfy either of the above conditions, they are to be taken as having control of the company.

(11) In this section "company" includes any body corporate (whether incorporated in Great Britain or elsewhere); and references to directors and other officers of a company and to voting power at any general meeting of a company have effect with any necessary modifications.

436 Expressions used generally

(1) In this Act, except in so far as the context otherwise requires (and subject to Parts VII and XI)—

"the appointed day" means the day on which this Act comes into force under section 443; "associate" has the meaning given by section 435;

"body corporate" includes a body incorporated outside Great Britain, but does not include—

(a) a corporation sole, or

(b) a partnership that, whether or not a legal person, is not regarded as a body corporate under the law by which it is governed;

"business" includes a trade or profession;

"the Companies Acts" means the Companies Acts (as defined in section 2 of the Companies Act 2006) as they have effect in Great Britain;

"conditional sale agreement" and "hire-purchase agreement" have the same meanings as in the Consumer Credit Act 1974;

"the EC Regulation" means Council Regulation (EC) No. 1346/2000;

"EEA State" means a state that is a Contracting Party to the Agreement on the European Economic Area signed at Oporto on 2nd May 1992 as adjusted by the Protocol signed at Brussels on 17th March 1993;

"employees' share scheme" means a scheme for encouraging or facilitating the holding of shares in or debentures of a company by or for the benefit of—

(a) the bona fide employees or former employees of—

(i) the company,

(ii) any subsidiary of the company, or

(iii) the company's holding company or any subsidiary of the company's holding company, or

(b) the spouses, civil partners, surviving spouses, surviving civil partners, or minor children or step-children of such employees or former employees;

"modifications" includes additions, alterations and omissions and cognate expressions shall be construed accordingly;

"property" includes money, goods, things in action, land and every description of property wherever situated and also obligations and every description of interest, whether present or future or vested or contingent, arising out of, or incidental to, property;

"records" includes computer records and other non-documentary records; "subordinate legislation" has the same meaning as in the Interpretation Act 1978; and

"transaction" includes a gift, agreement or arrangement, and references to entering into a transaction shall be construed accordingly.

(2) The following expressions have the same meaning in this Act as in the Companies Acts—

"articles", in relation to a company (see section 18 of the Companies Act 2006);

"debenture" (see section 738 of that Act);

"holding company" (see sections 1159 and 1160 of, and Schedule 6 to, that Act);

"the Joint Stock Companies Acts" (see section 1171 of that Act);

"overseas company" (see section 1044 of that Act);

"paid up" (see section 583 of that Act);

"private company" and "public company" (see section 4 of that Act);

"registrar of companies" (see section 1060 of that Act);

"share" (see section 540 of that Act);

"subsidiary" (see sections 1159 and 1160 of, and Schedule 6 to, that Act).

436A Proceedings under EC Regulations: modified definition of property

In the application of this Act to proceedings by virtue of Article 3 of the EC Regulation, a reference to property is a reference to property which may be dealt with in the proceedings.

436B References to things in writing

(1) A reference in this Act to a thing in writing includes that thing in electronic form.

(2) Subsection (1) does not apply to the following provisions—

(a) section 53 (mode of appointment by holder of charge),

(b) section 67(2) (report by receiver),

(c) section 70(4) (reference to instrument creating a charge),

(d) section 111(2) (dissent from arrangement under s. 110),
(e) in the case of a winding up of a company registered in Scotland, section 111(4),
(f) section 123(1) (definition of inability to pay debts),
(g) section 198(3) (duties of sheriff principal as regards examination),
(h) section 222(1) (inability to pay debts: unpaid creditor for £750 or more), and
(i) section 223 (inability to pay debts: debt remaining unsatisfied after action brought).

437–442 *omitted*

PART XIX
FINAL PROVISIONS

443 Commencement

This Act comes into force on the day appointed under section 236(2) of the Insolvency Act 1985 for the coming into force of Part III of that Act (individual insolvency and bankruptcy), immediately after that Part of that Act comes into force for England and Wales.

444 Citation

This Act may be cited as the Insolvency Act 1986.

SCHEDULE A1
MORATORIUM WHERE DIRECTORS PROPOSE VOLUNTARY ARRANGEMENT

Part I paras 1–5	INTRODUCTORY
Part II paras 6–11	OBTAINING A MORATORIUM
Part III paras 12–23	EFFECTS OF MORATORIUM
Part IV paras 24–28	NOMINEES
Part V paras 29–39	CONSIDERATION AND IMPLEMENTATION OF VOLUNTARY ARRANGEMENT
Part VI paras 40–45	MISCELLANEOUS

PART I
INTRODUCTORY

Interpretation

1. In this Schedule—

"the beginning of the moratorium" has the meaning given by paragraph 8(1),

"the date of filing" means the date on which the documents for the time being referred to in paragraph 7(1) are filed or lodged with the court,

"hire-purchase agreement" includes a conditional sale agreement, a chattel leasing agreement and a retention of title agreement,

"market contract" and "market charge" have the meanings given by Part VII of the Companies Act 1989,

"moratorium" means a moratorium under section 1A,

"the nominee" includes any person for the time being carrying out the functions of a nominee under this Schedule,

"the settlement finality regulations" means the Financial Markets and Insolvency (Settlement Finality) Regulations 1999,

"system-charge" has the meaning given by the Financial Markets and Insolvency Regulations 1996.

Eligible companies

2. (1) A company is eligible for a moratorium if it meets the requirements of paragraph 3, unless—
(a) it is excluded from being eligible by virtue of paragraph 4, or
(b) it falls within sub-paragraph (2).

(2) A company falls within this sub-paragraph if—
(a) it effects or carries out contracts of insurance, but is not exempt from the general prohibition, within the meaning of section 19 of the Financial Services and Markets Act 2000, in relation to that activity,

(b) it has permission under Part IV of that Act to accept deposits,
(bb) it has a liability in respect of a deposit which it accepted in accordance with the Banking Act 1979 or 1987,
(c) it is a party to a market contract or any of its property is subject to a market charge or a system-charge, or
(d) it is a participant (within the meaning of the settlement finality regulations) or any of its property is subject to a collateral security charge (within the meaning of those regulations).

(3) Paragraphs (a), (b) and (bb) of sub-paragraph (2) must be read with—
(a) section 22 of the Financial Services and Markets Act 2000;
(b) any relevant order under that section; and
(c) Schedule 2 to that Act.

3. (1) A company meets the requirements of this paragraph if the qualifying conditions are met—
(a) in the year ending with the date of filing, or
(b) in the financial year of the company which ended last before that date.

(2) For the purposes of sub-paragraph (1)—
(a) the qualifying conditions are met by a company in a period if, in that period, it satisfies two or more of the requirements for being a small company specified for the time being in section 382(3) of the Companies Act 2006, and
(b) a company's financial year is to be determined in accordance with that Act.

(3) Section 382(4), (5) and (6) of that Act apply for the purposes of this paragraph as they apply for the purposes of that section.

(4) A company does not meet the requirements of this paragraph if it is a parent company of a group of companies which does not qualify as a small group or a medium-sized group in relation to the financial year of the company which ended last before the date of filing.

(5) For the purposes of sub-paragraph (4)—
(a) "group" has the same meaning as in Part 15 of the Companies Act 2006 (see section 474(1) of that Act); and
(b) a group qualifies as small in relation to a financial year if it so qualifies under section 383(2) to (7) of that Act, and qualifies as medium-sized in relation to a financial year if it so qualifies under section 466(2) to (7) of that Act.

(6) Expressions used in this paragraph that are defined expressions in Part 15 of the Companies Act 2006 (accounts and reports) have the same meaning in this paragraph as in that Part.

4. (1) A company is excluded from being eligible for a moratorium if, on the date of filing—
(a) the company is in administration,
(b) the company is being wound up,
(c) there is an administrative receiver of the company,
(d) a voluntary arrangement has effect in relation to the company,
(e) there is a provisional liquidator of the company,
(f) a moratorium has been in force for the company at any time during the period of 12 months ending with the date of filing and—
(i) no voluntary arrangement had effect at the time at which the moratorium came to an end, or
(ii) a voluntary arrangement which had effect at any time in that period has come to an end prematurely,
(fa) an administrator appointed under paragraph 22 of Schedule B1 has held office in the period of 12 months ending with the date of filing, or
(g) a voluntary arrangement in relation to the company which had effect in pursuance of a proposal under section 1(3) has come to an end prematurely and, during the period of 12 months ending with the date of filing, an order under section 5(3)(a) has been made.

(2) Sub-paragraph (1)(b) does not apply to a company which, by reason of a winding-up order made after the date of filing, is treated as being wound up on that date.

Capital market arrangement

4A. A company is also excluded from being eligible for a moratorium if, on the date of filing, it is a party to an agreement which is or forms part of a capital market arrangement under which—

(i) a party has incurred, or when the agreement was entered into was expected to incur, a debt of at least £10 million under the arrangement, and
(ii) the arrangement involves the issue of a capital market investment.

Public private partnership

4B. A company is also excluded from being eligible for a moratorium if, on the date of filing, it is a project company of a project which—
(i) is a public-private partnership project, and
(ii) includes step-in rights.

Liability under an arrangement

4C. (1) A company is also excluded from being eligible for a moratorium if, on the date of filing, it has incurred a liability under an agreement of £10 million or more.
(2) Where the liability in sub-paragraph (1) is a contingent liability under or by virtue of a guarantee or an indemnity or security provided on behalf of another person, the amount of that liability is the full amount of the liability in relation to which the guarantee, indemnity or security is provided.
(3) In this paragraph—
(a) the reference to "liability" includes a present or future liability whether, in either case, it is certain or contingent,
(b) the reference to "liability" includes a reference to a liability to be paid wholly or partly in foreign currency (in which case the sterling equivalent shall be calculated as at the time when the liability is incurred).

Interpretation of capital market arrangement

4D. (1) For the purposes of paragraph 4A an arrangement is a capital market arrangement if—
(a) it involves a grant of security to a person holding it as trustee for a person who holds a capital market investment issued by a party to the arrangement, or
(b) at least one party guarantees the performance of obligations of another party, or
(c) at least one party provides security in respect of the performance of obligations of another party, or
(d) the arrangement involves an investment of a kind described in articles 83 to 85 of the Financial Services and Markets Act 2000 (Regulated Activities) Order 2001 (SI 2001/544) (options, futures and contracts for differences).
(2) For the purposes of sub-paragraph (1)—
(a) a reference to holding as trustee includes a reference to holding as nominee or agent,
(b) a reference to holding for a person who holds a capital market investment includes a reference to holding for a number of persons at least one of whom holds a capital market investment, and
(c) a person holds a capital market investment if he has a legal or beneficial interest in it.
(3) In paragraph 4A, 4C, 4J and this paragraph—
"agreement" includes an agreement or undertaking effected by—
(a) contract,
(b) deed, or
(c) any other instrument intended to have effect in accordance with the law of England and Wales, Scotland or another jurisdiction, and
"party" to an arrangement includes a party to an agreement which—
(a) forms part of the arrangement,
(b) provides for the raising of finance as part of the arrangement, or
(c) is necessary for the purposes of implementing the arrangement.

Capital market investment

4E. (1) For the purposes of paragraphs 4A and 4D, an investment is a capital market investment if—
(a) it is within article 77 or 77A of the Financial Services and Markets Act 2000 (Regulated Activities) Order 2001 (debt instruments) and
(b) it is rated, listed or traded or designed to be rated, listed or traded.

(2) In sub-paragraph (1)—
"listed" means admitted to the official list within the meaning given by section 103(1) of the Financial Services and Markets Act 2000 (interpretation),
"rated" means rated for the purposes of investment by an internationally recognised rating agency,
"traded" means admitted to trading on a market established under the rules of a recognised investment exchange or on a foreign market.

(3) In sub-paragraph (2)—
"foreign market" has the same meaning as "relevant market" in article 67(2) of the Financial Services and Markets Act 2000 (Financial Promotion) Order 2001 (foreign markets),
"recognised investment exchange" has the meaning given by section 285 of the Financial Services and Markets Act 2000 (recognised investment exchange).

4F. (1) For the purposes of paragraphs 4A and 4D an investment is also a capital market investment if it consists of a bond or commercial paper issued to one or more of the following—
(a) an investment professional within the meaning of article 19(5) of the Financial Services and Markets Act 2000 (Financial Promotion) Order 2001,
(b) a person who is, when the agreement mentioned in paragraph 4A is entered into, a certified high net worth individual in relation to a communication within the meaning of article 48(2) of that order,
(c) a person to whom article 49(2) of that order applies (high net worth company, &c.),
(d) a person who is, when the agreement mentioned in paragraph 4A is entered into, a certified sophisticated investor in relation to a communication within the meaning of article 50(1) of that order, and
(e) a person in a State other than the United Kingdom who under the law of that State is not prohibited from investing in bonds or commercial paper.

(2) For the purposes of sub-paragraph (1)—
(a) in applying article 19(5) of the Financial Services and Markets Act 2000 (Financial Promotion) Order 2001 for the purposes of sub-paragraph (1)(a)—
(i) in article 19(5)(b), ignore the words after "exempt person",
(ii) in article 19(5)(c)(i), for the words from "the controlled activity" to the end substitute "a controlled activity", and
(iii) in article 19(5)(e) ignore the words from "where the communication" to the end, and
(b) in applying article 49(2) of that order for the purposes of sub-paragraph (1)(c), ignore article 49(2)(e).

(3) In sub-paragraph (1)—
"bond" shall be construed in accordance with article 77 of the Financial Services and Markets Act 2000 (Regulated Activities) Order 2001 and includes any instrument falling within article 77A of that Order, and
"commercial paper" has the meaning given by article 9(3) of that order.

Debt

4G. The debt of at least £10 million referred to in paragraph 4A—
(a) may be incurred at any time during the life of the capital market arrangement, and
(b) may be expressed wholly or partly in a foreign currency (in which case the sterling equivalent shall be calculated as at the time when the arrangement is entered into).

Interpretation of project company

4H. (1) For the purposes of paragraph 4B a company is a "project company" of a project if—
(a) it holds property for the purpose of the project,
(b) it has sole or principal responsibility under an agreement for carrying out all or part of the project,
(c) it is one of a number of companies which together carry out the project,
(d) it has the purpose of supplying finance to enable the project to be carried out, or
(e) it is the holding company of a company within any of paragraphs (a) to (d).

(2) But a company is not a "project company" of a project if—
(a) it performs a function within sub-paragraph (1)(a) to (d) or is within sub-paragraph (1)(e), but
(b) it also performs a function which is not—
(i) within sub-paragraph (1)(a) to (d),
(ii) related to a function within sub-paragraph (1)(a) to (d), or
(iii) related to the project.
(3) For the purposes of this paragraph a company carries out all or part of a project whether or not it acts wholly or partly through agents.

Public-private partnership project

4I. (1) In paragraph 4B "public-private partnership project" means a project—
(a) the resources for which are provided partly by one or more public bodies and partly by one or more private persons, or
(b) which is designed wholly or mainly for the purpose of assisting a public body to discharge a function.
(2) In sub-paragraph (1) "resources" includes—
(a) funds (including payment for the provision of services or facilities),
(b) assets,
(c) professional skill,
(d) the grant of a concession or franchise, and
(e) any other commercial resource.
(3) In sub-paragraph (1) "public body" means—
(a) a body which exercises public functions,
(b) a body specified for the purposes of this paragraph by the Secretary of State, and
(c) a body within a class specified for the purposes of this paragraph by the Secretary of State.
(4) A specification under sub-paragraph (3) may be—
(a) general, or
(b) for the purpose of the application of paragraph 4B to a specified case.

Step-in rights

4J. (1) For the purposes of paragraph 4B a project has "step-in rights" if a person who provides finance in connection with the project has a conditional entitlement under an agreement to—
(i) assume sole or principal responsibility under an agreement for carrying out all or part of the project, or
(ii) make arrangements for carrying out all or part of the project.
(2) In sub-paragraph (1) a reference to the provision of finance includes a reference to the provision of an indemnity.

"Person"

4K. For the purposes of paragraphs 4A to 4J, a reference to a person includes a reference to a partnership or another unincorporated group of persons.
5. The Secretary of State may by regulations modify the qualifications for eligibility of a company for a moratorium.

PART II
OBTAINING A MORATORIUM

6. (1) Where the directors of a company wish to obtain a moratorium, they shall submit to the nominee—
(a) a document setting out the terms of the proposed voluntary arrangement,
(b) a statement of the company's affairs containing—
(i) such particulars of its creditors and of its debts and other liabilities and of its assets as may be prescribed, and
(ii) such other information as may be prescribed, and
(c) any other information necessary to enable the nominee to comply with sub-paragraph (2) which he requests from them.

(2) The nominee shall submit to the directors a statement in the prescribed form indicating whether or not, in his opinion—
  (a) the proposed voluntary arrangement has a reasonable prospect of being approved and implemented,
  (b) the company is likely to have sufficient funds available to it during the proposed moratorium to enable it to carry on its business, and
  (c) meetings of the company and its creditors should be summoned to consider the proposed voluntary arrangement.

(3) In forming his opinion on the matters mentioned in sub-paragraph (2), the nominee is entitled to rely on the information submitted to him under sub-paragraph (1) unless he has reason to doubt its accuracy.

(4) The reference in sub-paragraph (2)(b) to the company's business is to that business as the company proposes to carry it on during the moratorium.

7. (1) To obtain a moratorium the directors of a company must file (in Scotland, lodge) with the court—
  (a) a document setting out the terms of the proposed voluntary arrangement,
  (b) a statement of the company's affairs containing—
    (i) such particulars of its creditors and of its debts and other liabilities and of its assets as may be prescribed, and
    (ii) such other information as may be prescribed,
  (c) a statement that the company is eligible for a moratorium,
  (d) a statement from the nominee that he has given his consent to act, and
  (e) a statement from the nominee that, in his opinion—
    (i) the proposed voluntary arrangement has a reasonable prospect of being approved and implemented,
    (ii) the company is likely to have sufficient funds available to it during the proposed moratorium to enable it to carry on its business, and
    (iii) meetings of the company and its creditors should be summoned to consider the proposed voluntary arrangement.

(2) Each of the statements mentioned in sub-paragraph (1)(b) to (e), except so far as it contains the particulars referred to in paragraph (b)(i), must be in the prescribed form.

(3) The reference in sub-paragraph (1)(e)(ii) to the company's business is to that business as the company proposes to carry it on during the moratorium.

(4) The Secretary of State may by regulations modify the requirements of this paragraph as to the documents required to be filed (in Scotland, lodged) with the court in order to obtain a moratorium.

Duration of moratorium

8. (1) A moratorium comes into force when the documents for the time being referred to in paragraph 7(1) are filed or lodged with the court and references in this Schedule to "the beginning of the moratorium" shall be construed accordingly.

(2) A moratorium ends at the end of the day on which the meetings summoned under paragraph 29(1) are first held (or, if the meetings are held on different days, the later of those days), unless it is extended under paragraph 32.

(3) If either of those meetings has not first met before the end of the period of 28 days beginning with the day on which the moratorium comes into force, the moratorium ends at the end of the day on which those meetings were to be held (or, if those meetings were summoned to be held on different days, the later of those days), unless it is extended under paragraph 32.

(4) If the nominee fails to summon either meeting within the period required by paragraph 29(1), the moratorium ends at the end of the last day of that period.

(5) If the moratorium is extended (or further extended) under paragraph 32, it ends at the end of the day to which it is extended (or further extended).

(6) Sub-paragraphs (2) to (5) do not apply if the moratorium comes to an end before the time concerned by virtue of—
  (a) paragraph 25(4) (effect of withdrawal by nominee of consent to act),
  (b) an order under paragraph 26(3), 27(3) or 40 (challenge of actions of nominee or directors), or
  (c) a decision of one or both of the meetings summoned under paragraph 29.

(7) If the moratorium has not previously come to an end in accordance with sub-paragraphs (2) to (6), it ends at the end of the day on which a decision under paragraph 31 to approve a voluntary arrangement takes effect under paragraph 36.

(8) The Secretary of State may by order increase or reduce the period for the time being specified in sub-paragraph (3).

Notification of beginning of moratorium

9. (1) When a moratorium comes into force, the directors shall notify the nominee of that fact forthwith.

(2) If the directors without reasonable excuse fail to comply with sub-paragraph (1), each of them is liable to imprisonment or a fine, or both.

10. (1) When a moratorium comes into force, the nominee shall, in accordance with the rules—

(a) advertise that fact forthwith, and

(b) notify the registrar of companies, the company and any petitioning creditor of the company of whose claim he is aware of that fact.

(2) In sub-paragraph (1)(b), "petitioning creditor" means a creditor by whom a winding-up petition has been presented before the beginning of the moratorium, as long as the petition has not been dismissed or withdrawn.

(3) If the nominee without reasonable excuse fails to comply with sub-paragraph (1)(a) or (b), he is liable to a fine.

Notification of end of moratorium

11. (1) When a moratorium comes to an end, the nominee shall, in accordance with the rules—

(a) advertise that fact forthwith, and

(b) notify the court, the registrar of companies, the company and any creditor of the company of whose claim he is aware of that fact.

(2) If the nominee without reasonable excuse fails to comply with sub-paragraph (1)(a) or (b), he is liable to a fine.

PART III
EFFECTS OF MORATORIUM

Effect on creditors, etc.

12. (1) During the period for which a moratorium is in force for a company—

(a) no petition may be presented for the winding up of the company,

(b) no meeting of the company may be called or requisitioned except with the consent of the nominee or the leave of the court and subject (where the court gives leave) to such terms as the court may impose,

(c) no resolution may be passed or order made for the winding up of the company,

(d) no administration application may be made in respect of the company,

(da) no administrator of the company may be appointed under paragraph 14 or 22 of Schedule B1,

(e) no administrative receiver of the company may be appointed,

(f) no landlord or other person to whom rent is payable may exercise any right of forfeiture by peaceable re-entry in relation to premises let to the company in respect of a failure by the company to comply with any term or condition of its tenancy of such premises, except with the leave of the court and subject to such terms as the court may impose,

(g) no other steps may be taken to enforce any security over the company's property, or to repossess goods in the company's possession under any hire-purchase agreement, except with the leave of the court and subject to such terms as the court may impose, and

(h) no other proceedings and no execution or other legal process may be commenced or continued, and no distress may be levied, against the company or its property except with the leave of the court and subject to such terms as the court may impose.

(2) Where a petition, other than an excepted petition, for the winding up of the company has been presented before the beginning of the moratorium, section 127 shall not apply in relation to any disposition of property, transfer of shares or alteration in status made during the moratorium or at a time mentioned in paragraph 37(5)(a).

(3) In the application of sub-paragraph (1)(h) to Scotland, the reference to execution being commenced or continued includes a reference to diligence being carried out or continued, and the reference to distress being levied is omitted.

(4) Paragraph (a) of sub-paragraph (1) does not apply to an excepted petition and, where such a petition has been presented before the beginning of the moratorium or is presented during the moratorium, paragraphs (b) and (c) of that sub-paragraph do not apply in relation to proceedings on the petition.

(5) For the purposes of this paragraph, "excepted petition" means a petition under—

(a) section 124A or 124B of this Act,

(b) section 72 of the Financial Services Act 1986 on the ground mentioned in subsection (1)(b) of that section, or

(c) section 92 of the Banking Act 1987 on the ground mentioned in subsection (1)(b) of that section.

(d) section 367 of the Financial Services and Markets Act 2000 on the ground mentioned in subsection (3)(b) of that section.

13. (1) This paragraph applies where there is an uncrystallised floating charge on the property of a company for which a moratorium is in force.

(2) If the conditions for the holder of the charge to give a notice having the effect mentioned in sub-paragraph (4) are met at any time, the notice may not be given at that time but may instead be given as soon as practicable after the moratorium has come to an end.

(3) If any other event occurs at any time which (apart from this sub-paragraph) would have the effect mentioned in sub-paragraph (4), then—

(a) the event shall not have the effect in question at that time, but

(b) if notice of the event is given to the company by the holder of the charge as soon as is practicable after the moratorium has come to an end, the event is to be treated as if it had occurred when the notice was given.

(4) The effect referred to in sub-paragraphs (2) and (3) is—

(a) causing the crystallisation of the floating charge, or

(b) causing the imposition, by virtue of provision in the instrument creating the charge, of any restriction on the disposal of any property of the company.

(5) Application may not be made for leave under paragraph 12(1)(g) or (h) with a view to obtaining—

(a) the crystallisation of the floating charge, or

(b) the imposition, by virtue of provision in the instrument creating the charge, of any restriction on the disposal of any property of the company.

14. Security granted by a company at a time when a moratorium is in force in relation to the company may only be enforced if, at that time, there were reasonable grounds for believing that it would benefit the company.

Effect on company

15. (1) Paragraphs 16 to 23 apply in relation to a company for which a moratorium is in force.

(2) The fact that a company enters into a transaction in contravention of any of paragraphs 16 to 22 does not—

(a) make the transaction void, or

(b) make it to any extent unenforceable against the company.

Company invoices, etc.

16. (1) Every invoice, order for goods or services, business letter or order form (whether in hard copy, electronic or any other form) issued by or on behalf of the company, and all the company's websites, must also contain the nominee's name and a statement that the moratorium is in force for the company.

(2) If default is made in complying with sub-paragraph (1), the company and (subject to sub-paragraph (3)) any officer of the company is liable to a fine.

(3) An officer of the company is only liable under sub-paragraph (2) if, without reasonable excuse, he authorises or permits the default.

Obtaining credit during moratorium

17. (1) The company may not obtain credit to the extent of £250 or more from a person who has not been informed that a moratorium is in force in relation to the company.
(2) The reference to the company obtaining credit includes the following cases—
(a) where goods are bailed (in Scotland, hired) to the company under a hire-purchase agreement, or agreed to be sold to the company under a conditional sale agreement, and
(b) where the company is paid in advance (whether in money or otherwise) for the supply of goods or services.
(3) Where the company obtains credit in contravention of sub-paragraph (1)—
(a) the company is liable to a fine, and
(b) if any officer of the company knowingly and wilfully authorised or permitted the contravention, he is liable to imprisonment or a fine, or both.
(4) The money sum specified in sub-paragraph (1) is subject to increase or reduction by order under section 417A in Part XV.

Disposals and payments

18. (1) Subject to sub-paragraph (2), the company may only dispose of any of its property if—
(a) there are reasonable grounds for believing that the disposal will benefit the company, and
(b) the disposal is approved by the committee established under paragraph 35(1) or, where there is no such committee, by the nominee.
(2) Sub-paragraph (1) does not apply to a disposal made in the ordinary way of the company's business.
(3) If the company makes a disposal in contravention of sub-paragraph (1) otherwise than in pursuance of an order of the court—
(a) the company is liable to a fine, and
(b) if any officer of the company authorised or permitted the contravention, without reasonable excuse, he is liable to imprisonment or a fine, or both.

19. (1) Subject to sub-paragraph (2), the company may only make any payment in respect of any debt or other liability of the company in existence before the beginning of the moratorium if—
(a) there are reasonable grounds for believing that the payment will benefit the company, and
(b) the payment is approved by the committee established under paragraph 35(1) or, where there is no such committee, by the nominee.
(2) Sub-paragraph (1) does not apply to a payment required by paragraph 20(6).
(3) If the company makes a payment in contravention of sub-paragraph (1) otherwise than in pursuance of an order of the court—
(a) the company is liable to a fine, and
(b) if any officer of the company authorised or permitted the contravention, without reasonable excuse, he is liable to imprisonment or a fine, or both.

Disposal of charged property, etc.

20. (1) This paragraph applies where—
(a) any property of the company is subject to a security, or
(b) any goods are in the possession of the company under a hire-purchase agreement.
(2) If the holder of the security consents, or the court gives leave, the company may dispose of the property as if it were not subject to the security.
(3) If the owner of the goods consents, or the court gives leave, the company may dispose of the goods as if all rights of the owner under the hire-purchase agreement were vested in the company.
(4) Where property subject to a security which, as created, was a floating charge is disposed of under sub-paragraph (2), the holder of the security has the same priority in respect of any property of the company directly or indirectly representing the property disposed of as he would have had in respect of the property subject to the security.

(5) Sub-paragraph (6) applies to the disposal under sub-paragraph (2) or (as the case may be) sub-paragraph (3) of—
(a) any property subject to a security other than a security which, as created, was a floating charge, or
(b) any goods in the possession of the company under a hire-purchase agreement.
(6) It shall be a condition of any consent or leave under sub-paragraph (2) or (as the case may be) sub-paragraph (3) that—
(a) the net proceeds of the disposal, and
(b) where those proceeds are less than such amount as may be agreed, or determined by the court, to be the net amount which would be realised on a sale of the property or goods in the open market by a willing vendor, such sums as may be required to make good the deficiency,
shall be applied towards discharging the sums secured by the security or payable under the hire-purchase agreement.
(7) Where a condition imposed in pursuance of sub-paragraph (6) relates to two or more securities, that condition requires—
(a) the net proceeds of the disposal, and
(b) where paragraph (b) of sub-paragraph (6) applies, the sums mentioned in that paragraph,
to be applied towards discharging the sums secured by those securities in the order of their priorities.
(8) Where the court gives leave for a disposal under sub-paragraph (2) or (3), the directors shall, within 14 days after leave is given, send an office copy of the order giving leave to the registrar of companies.
(9) If the directors without reasonable excuse fail to comply with sub-paragraph (8), they are liable to a fine.

21. (1) Where property is disposed of under paragraph 20 in its application to Scotland, the company shall grant to the disponee an appropriate document of transfer or conveyance of the property, and
(a) that document, or
(b) where any recording, intimation or registration of the document is a legal requirement for completion of title to the property, that recording, intimation or registration,
has the effect of disencumbering the property of, or (as the case may be) freeing the property from, the security.
(2) Where goods in the possession of the company under a hire-purchase agreement are disposed of under paragraph 20 in its application to Scotland, the disposal has the effect of extinguishing, as against the disponee, all rights of the owner of the goods under the agreement.

22. (1) If the company—
(a) without any consent or leave under paragraph 20, disposes of any of its property which is subject to a security otherwise than in accordance with the terms of the security,
(b) without any consent or leave under paragraph 20, disposes of any goods in the possession of the company under a hire-purchase agreement otherwise than in accordance with the terms of the agreement, or
(c) fails to comply with any requirement imposed by paragraph 20 or 21, it is liable to a fine.
(2) If any officer of the company, without reasonable excuse, authorises or permits any such disposal or failure to comply, he is liable to imprisonment or a fine, or both.

Market contracts, etc.

23. (1) If the company enters into any transaction to which this paragraph applies—
(a) the company is liable to a fine, and
(b) if any officer of the company, without reasonable excuse, authorised or permitted the company to enter into the transaction, he is liable to imprisonment or a fine, or both.
(2) A company enters into a transaction to which this paragraph applies if it—
(a) enters into a market contract,
(b) gives a transfer order,

(c) grants a market charge or a system-charge, or
(d) provides any collateral security.

(3) The fact that a company enters into a transaction in contravention of this paragraph does not—
(a) make the transaction void, or
(b) make it to any extent unenforceable by or against the company.

(4) Where during the moratorium a company enters into a transaction to which this paragraph applies, nothing done by or in pursuance of the transaction is to be treated as done in contravention of paragraphs 12(1)(g), 14 or 16 to 22.

(5) Paragraph 20 does not apply in relation to any property which is subject to a market charge, a system-charge or a collateral security charge.

(6) In this paragraph, "transfer order", "collateral security" and "collateral security charge" have the same meanings as in the settlement finality regulations.

PART IV
NOMINEES

Monitoring of company's activities

24. (1) During a moratorium, the nominee shall monitor the company's affairs for the purpose of forming an opinion as to whether—
(a) the proposed voluntary arrangement or, if he has received notice of proposed modifications under paragraph 31(7), the proposed arrangement with those modifications has a reasonable prospect of being approved and implemented, and
(b) the company is likely to have sufficient funds available to it during the remainder of the moratorium to enable it to continue to carry on its business.

(2) The directors shall submit to the nominee any information necessary to enable him to comply with sub-paragraph (1) which he requests from them.

(3) In forming his opinion on the matters mentioned in sub-paragraph (1), the nominee is entitled to rely on the information submitted to him under sub-paragraph (2) unless he has reason to doubt its accuracy.

(4) The reference in sub-paragraph (1)(b) to the company's business is to that business as the company proposes to carry it on during the remainder of the moratorium.

Withdrawal of consent to act

25. (1) The nominee may only withdraw his consent to act in the circumstances mentioned in this paragraph.

(2) The nominee must withdraw his consent to act if, at any time during a moratorium—
(a) he forms the opinion that—
(i) the proposed voluntary arrangement or, if he has received notice of proposed modifications under paragraph 31(7), the proposed arrangement with those modifications no longer has a reasonable prospect of being approved or implemented, or
(ii) the company will not have sufficient funds available to it during the remainder of the moratorium to enable it to continue to carry on its business,
(b) he becomes aware that, on the date of filing, the company was not eligible for a moratorium, or
(c) the directors fail to comply with their duty under paragraph 24(2).

(3) The reference in sub-paragraph (2)(a)(ii) to the company's business is to that business as the company proposes to carry it on during the remainder of the moratorium.

(4) If the nominee withdraws his consent to act, the moratorium comes to an end.

(5) If the nominee withdraws his consent to act he must, in accordance with the rules, notify the court, the registrar of companies, the company and any creditor of the company of whose claim he is aware of his withdrawal and the reason for it.

(6) If the nominee without reasonable excuse fails to comply with sub-paragraph (5), he is liable to a fine.

Challenge of nominee's actions, etc.

26. (1) If any creditor, director or member of the company, or any other person affected by a moratorium, is dissatisfied by any act, omission or decision of the nominee during the moratorium, he may apply to the court.

(2) An application under sub-paragraph (1) may be made during the moratorium or after it has ended.

(3) On an application under sub-paragraph (1) the court may—
(a) confirm, reverse or modify any act or decision of the nominee,
(b) give him directions, or
(c) make such other order as it thinks fit.

(4) An order under sub-paragraph (3) may (among other things) bring the moratorium to an end and make such consequential provision as the court thinks fit.

27. (1) Where there are reasonable grounds for believing that—
(a) as a result of any act, omission or decision of the nominee during the moratorium, the company has suffered loss, but
(b) the company does not intend to pursue any claim it may have against the nominee,
any creditor of the company may apply to the court.

(2) An application under sub-paragraph (1) may be made during the moratorium or after it has ended.

(3) On an application under sub-paragraph (1) the court may—
(a) order the company to pursue any claim against the nominee,
(b) authorise any creditor to pursue such a claim in the name of the company, or
(c) make such other order with respect to such a claim as it thinks fit,
unless the court is satisfied that the act, omission or decision of the nominee was in all the circumstances reasonable.

(4) An order under sub-paragraph (3) may (among other things)—
(a) impose conditions on any authority given to pursue a claim,
(b) direct the company to assist in the pursuit of a claim,
(c) make directions with respect to the distribution of anything received as a result of the pursuit of a claim,
(d) bring the moratorium to an end and make such consequential provision as the court thinks fit.

(5) On an application under sub-paragraph (1) the court shall have regard to the interests of the members and creditors of the company generally.

Replacement of nominee by court

28. (1) The court may—
(a) on an application made by the directors in a case where the nominee has failed to comply with any duty imposed on him under this Schedule or has died, or
(b) on an application made by the directors or the nominee in a case where it is impracticable or inappropriate for the nominee to continue to act as such,
direct that the nominee be replaced as such by another person qualified to act as an insolvency practitioner, or authorised to act as nominee, in relation to the voluntary arrangement.

(2) A person may only be appointed as a replacement nominee under this paragraph if he submits to the court a statement indicating his consent to act.

PART V
CONSIDERATION AND IMPLEMENTATION OF VOLUNTARY ARRANGEMENT

Summoning of meetings

29. (1) Where a moratorium is in force, the nominee shall summon meetings of the company and its creditors for such a time, date (within the period for the time being specified in paragraph 8(3)) and place as he thinks fit.

(2) The persons to be summoned to a creditors' meeting under this paragraph are every creditor of the company of whose claim the nominee is aware.

Conduct of meetings

30. (1) Subject to the provisions of paragraphs 31 to 35, the meetings summoned under paragraph 29 shall be conducted in accordance with the rules.

(2) A meeting so summoned may resolve that it be adjourned (or further adjourned).

(3) After the conclusion of either meeting in accordance with the rules, the chairman of the meeting shall report the result of the meeting to the court, and, immediately after reporting to the court, shall give notice of the result of the meeting to such persons as may be prescribed.

Approval of voluntary arrangement

31. (1) The meetings summoned under paragraph 29 shall decide whether to approve the proposed voluntary arrangement (with or without modifications).

(2) The modifications may include one conferring the functions proposed to be conferred on the nominee on another person qualified to act as an insolvency practitioner, or authorised to act as nominee, in relation to the voluntary arrangement.

(3) The modifications shall not include one by virtue of which the proposal ceases to be a proposal such as is mentioned in section 1.

(4) A meeting summoned under paragraph 29 shall not approve any proposal or modification which affects the right of a secured creditor of the company to enforce his security, except with the concurrence of the creditor concerned.

(5) Subject to sub-paragraph (6), a meeting so summoned shall not approve any proposal or modification under which—

(a) any preferential debt of the company is to be paid otherwise than in priority to such of its debts as are not preferential debts,

(aa) any ordinary preferential debt of the company is to be paid otherwise than in priority to any secondary preferential debts that it may have,

(b) a preferential creditor of the company is to be paid an amount in respect of an ordinary preferential debt that bears to that debt a smaller proportion than is borne to another ordinary preferential debt by the amount that is to be paid in respect of that other debt, or

(c) a preferential creditor of the company is to be paid an amount in respect of a secondary preferential debt that bears to that debt a smaller proportion than is borne to another secondary preferential debt by the amount that is to be paid in respect of that other debt.

(6) The meeting may approve such a proposal or modification with the concurrence of the preferential creditor concerned.

(7) The directors of the company may, before the beginning of the period of seven days which ends with the meetings (or either of them) summoned under paragraph 29 being held, give notice to the nominee of any modifications of the proposal for which the directors intend to seek the approval of those meetings.

(8) References in this paragraph to preferential debts, ordinary preferential debts, secondary preferential debts and preferential creditors are to be read in accordance with section 386 in Part XII of this Act.

Extension of moratorium

32. (1) Subject to sub-paragraph (2), a meeting summoned under paragraph 29 which resolves that it be adjourned (or further adjourned) may resolve that the moratorium be extended (or further extended), with or without conditions.

(2) The moratorium may not be extended (or further extended) to a day later than the end of the period of two months which begins—

(a) where both meetings summoned under paragraph 29 are first held on the same day, with that day,

(b) in any other case, with the day on which the later of those meetings is first held.

(3) At any meeting where it is proposed to extend (or further extend) the moratorium, before a decision is taken with respect to that proposal, the nominee shall inform the meeting—

(a) of what he has done in order to comply with his duty under paragraph 24 and the cost of his actions for the company, and

(b) of what he intends to do to continue to comply with that duty if the moratorium is extended (or further extended) and the expected cost of his actions for the company.

(4) Where, in accordance with sub-paragraph (3)(b), the nominee informs a meeting of the expected cost of his intended actions, the meeting shall resolve whether or not to approve that expected cost.

(5) If a decision not to approve the expected cost of the nominee's intended actions has effect under paragraph 36, the moratorium comes to an end.

(6) A meeting may resolve that a moratorium which has been extended (or further extended) be brought to an end before the end of the period of the extension (or further extension).

(7) The Secretary of State may by order increase or reduce the period for the time being specified in sub-paragraph (2).

33. (1) The conditions which may be imposed when a moratorium is extended (or further extended) include a requirement that the nominee be replaced as such by another person qualified to act as an insolvency practitioner, or authorised to act as nominee, in relation to the voluntary arrangement.

(2) A person may only be appointed as a replacement nominee by virtue of sub-paragraph (1) if he submits to the court a statement indicating his consent to act.

(3) At any meeting where it is proposed to appoint a replacement nominee as a condition of extending (or further extending) the moratorium—

(a) the duty imposed by paragraph 32(3)(b) on the nominee shall instead be imposed on the person proposed as the replacement nominee, and

(b) paragraphs 32(4) and (5) and 36(1)(e) apply as if the references to the nominee were to that person.

34. (1) If a decision to extend, or further extend, the moratorium takes effect under paragraph 36, the nominee shall, in accordance with the rules, notify the registrar of companies and the court.

(2) If the moratorium is extended, or further extended, by virtue of an order under paragraph 36(5), the nominee shall, in accordance with the rules, send a copy of the order to the registrar of companies.

(3) If the nominee without reasonable excuse fails to comply with this paragraph, he is liable to a fine.

Moratorium committee

35. (1) A meeting summoned under paragraph 29 which resolves that the moratorium be extended (or further extended) may, with the consent of the nominee, resolve that a committee be established to exercise the functions conferred on it by the meeting.

(2) The meeting may not so resolve unless it has approved an estimate of the expenses to be incurred by the committee in the exercise of the proposed functions.

(3) Any expenses, not exceeding the amount of the estimate, incurred by the committee in the exercise of its functions shall be reimbursed by the nominee.

(4) The committee shall cease to exist when the moratorium comes to an end.

Effectiveness of decisions

36. (1) Sub-paragraph (2) applies to references to one of the following decisions having effect, that is, a decision, under paragraph 31, 32 or 35, with respect to—

(a) the approval of a proposed voluntary arrangement,

(b) the extension (or further extension) of a moratorium,

(c) the bringing of a moratorium to an end,

(d) the establishment of a committee, or

(e) the approval of the expected cost of a nominee's intended actions.

(2) The decision has effect if, in accordance with the rules—

(a) it has been taken by both meetings summoned under paragraph 29, or

(b) (subject to any order made under sub-paragraph (5)) it has been taken by the creditors' meeting summoned under that paragraph.

(3) If a decision taken by the creditors' meeting under any of paragraphs 31, 32 or 35 with respect to any of the matters mentioned in sub-paragraph (1) differs from one so taken by the company meeting with respect to that matter, a member of the company may apply to the court.

(4) An application under sub-paragraph (3) shall not be made after the end of the period of 28 days beginning with—

(a) the day on which the decision was taken by the creditors' meeting, or

(b) where the decision of the company meeting was taken on a later day, that day.

(5) On an application under sub-paragraph (3), the court may—
(a) order the decision of the company meeting to have effect instead of the decision of the creditors' meeting, or
(b) make such other order as it thinks fit.

Effect of approval of voluntary arrangement

37. (1) This paragraph applies where a decision approving a voluntary arrangement has effect under paragraph 36.
(2) The approved voluntary arrangement—
(a) takes effect as if made by the company at the creditors' meeting, and
(b) binds every person who in accordance with the rules—
(i) was entitled to vote at that meeting (whether or not he was present or represented at it), or
(ii) would have been so entitled if he had had notice of it, as if he were a party to the voluntary arrangement.
(3) If—
(a) when the arrangement ceases to have effect any amount payable under the arrangement to a person bound by virtue of sub-paragraph (2)(b)(ii) has not been paid, and
(b) the arrangement did not come to an end prematurely,
the company shall at that time become liable to pay to that person the amount payable under the arrangement.
(4) Where a petition for the winding up of the company, other than an excepted petition within the meaning of paragraph 12, was presented before the beginning of the moratorium, the court shall dismiss the petition.
(5) The court shall not dismiss a petition under sub-paragraph (4)—
(a) at any time before the end of the period of 28 days beginning with the first day on which each of the reports of the meetings required by paragraph 30(3) has been made to the court, or
(b) at any time when an application under paragraph 38 or an appeal in respect of such an application is pending, or at any time in the period within which such an appeal may be brought.

Challenge of decisions

38. (1) Subject to the following provisions of this paragraph, any of the persons mentioned in sub- paragraph (2) may apply to the court on one or both of the following grounds—
(a) that a voluntary arrangement approved at one or both of the meetings summoned under paragraph 29 and which has taken effect unfairly prejudices the interests of a creditor, member or contributory of the company,
(b) that there has been some material irregularity at or in relation to either of those meetings.
(2) The persons who may apply under this paragraph are—
(a) a person entitled, in accordance with the rules, to vote at either of the meetings,
(b) a person who would have been entitled, in accordance with the rules, to vote at the creditors' meeting if he had had notice of it, and
(c) the nominee.
(3) An application under this paragraph shall not be made—
(a) after the end of the period of 28 days beginning with the first day on which each of the reports required by paragraph 30(3) has been made to the court, or
(b) in the case of a person who was not given notice of the creditors' meeting, after the end of the period of 28 days beginning with the day on which he became aware that the meeting had taken place,
but (subject to that) an application made by a person within sub-paragraph (2)(b) on the ground that the arrangement prejudices his interests may be made after the arrangement has ceased to have effect, unless it came to an end prematurely.
(4) Where on an application under this paragraph the court is satisfied as to either of the grounds mentioned in sub-paragraph (1), it may do any of the following—
(a) revoke or suspend—
(i) any decision approving the voluntary arrangement which has effect under paragraph 36, or

(ii) in a case falling within sub-paragraph (1)(b), any decision taken by the meeting in question which has effect under that paragraph,

(b) give a direction to any person—

(i) for the summoning of further meetings to consider any revised proposal for a voluntary arrangement which the directors may make, or

(ii) in a case falling within sub-paragraph (1)(b), for the summoning of a further company or (as the case may be) creditors' meeting to reconsider the original proposal.

(5) Where at any time after giving a direction under sub-paragraph (4)(b)(i) the court is satisfied that the directors do not intend to submit a revised proposal, the court shall revoke the direction and revoke or suspend any decision approving the voluntary arrangement which has effect under paragraph 36.

(6) Where the court gives a direction under sub-paragraph (4)(b), it may also give a direction continuing or, as the case may require, renewing, for such period as may be specified in the direction, the effect of the moratorium.

(7) Sub-paragraph (8) applies in a case where the court, on an application under this paragraph—

(a) gives a direction under sub-paragraph (4)(b), or

(b) revokes or suspends a decision under sub-paragraph (4)(a) or (5).

(8) In such a case, the court may give such supplemental directions as it thinks fit and, in particular, directions with respect to—

(a) things done under the voluntary arrangement since it took effect, and

(b) such things done since that time as could not have been done if a moratorium had been in force in relation to the company when they were done.

(9) Except in pursuance of the preceding provisions of this paragraph, a decision taken at a meeting summoned under paragraph 29 is not invalidated by any irregularity at or in relation to the meeting.

Implementation of voluntary arrangement

39. (1) This paragraph applies where a voluntary arrangement approved by one or both of the meetings summoned under paragraph 29 has taken effect.

(2) The person who is for the time being carrying out in relation to the voluntary arrangement the functions conferred—

(a) by virtue of the approval of the arrangement, on the nominee, or

(b) by virtue of paragraph 31(2), on a person other than the nominee, shall be known as the supervisor of the voluntary arrangement.

(3) If any of the company's creditors or any other person is dissatisfied by any act, omission or decision of the supervisor, he may apply to the court.

(4) On an application under sub-paragraph (3) the court may—

(a) confirm, reverse or modify any act or decision of the supervisor,

(b) give him directions, or

(c) make such other order as it thinks fit.

(5) The supervisor—

(a) may apply to the court for directions in relation to any particular matter arising under the voluntary arrangement, and

(b) is included among the persons who may apply to the court for the winding up of the company or for an administration order to be made in relation to it.

(6) The court may, whenever—

(a) it is expedient to appoint a person to carry out the functions of the supervisor, and

(b) it is inexpedient, difficult or impracticable for an appointment to be made without the assistance of the court,

make an order appointing a person who is qualified to act as an insolvency practitioner, or authorised to act as supervisor, in relation to the voluntary arrangement, either in substitution for the existing supervisor or to fill a vacancy.

(7) The power conferred by sub-paragraph (6) is exercisable so as to increase the number of persons exercising the functions of supervisor or, where there is more than one person exercising those functions, so as to replace one or more of those persons.

PART VI
MISCELLANEOUS

Challenge of directors' actions

40. (1) This paragraph applies in relation to acts or omissions of the directors of a company during a moratorium.

(2) A creditor or member of the company may apply to the court for an order under this paragraph on the ground—

(a) that the company's affairs, business and property are being or have been managed by the directors in a manner which is unfairly prejudicial to the interests of its creditors or members generally, or of some part of its creditors or members (including at least the petitioner), or

(b) that any actual or proposed act or omission of the directors is or would be so prejudicial.

(3) An application for an order under this paragraph may be made during or after the moratorium.

(4) On an application for an order under this paragraph the court may—

(a) make such order as it thinks fit for giving relief in respect of the matters complained of,

(b) adjourn the hearing conditionally or unconditionally, or

(c) make an interim order or any other order that it thinks fit.

(5) An order under this paragraph may in particular—

(a) regulate the management by the directors of the company's affairs, business and property during the remainder of the moratorium,

(b) require the directors to refrain from doing or continuing an act complained of by the petitioner, or to do an act which the petitioner has complained they have omitted to do,

(c) require the summoning of a meeting of creditors or members for the purpose of considering such matters as the court may direct,

(d) bring the moratorium to an end and make such consequential provision as the court thinks fit.

(6) In making an order under this paragraph the court shall have regard to the need to safeguard the interests of persons who have dealt with the company in good faith and for value.

(7) Sub-paragraph (8) applies where—

(a) the appointment of an administrator has effect in relation to the company and that appointment was in pursuance of—

(i) an administration application made, or

(ii) a notice of intention to appoint filed, before the moratorium came into force, or

(b) the company is being wound up in pursuance of a petition presented before the moratorium came into force.

(8) No application for an order under this paragraph may be made by a creditor or member of the company; but such an application may be made instead by the administrator or (as the case may be) the liquidator.

Offences

41. (1) This paragraph applies where a moratorium has been obtained for a company.

(2) If, within the period of 12 months ending with the day on which the moratorium came into force, a person who was at the time an officer of the company—

(a) did any of the things mentioned in paragraphs (a) to (f) of sub-paragraph (4), or

(b) was privy to the doing by others of any of the things mentioned in paragraphs (c), (d) and (e) of that sub-paragraph,

he is to be treated as having committed an offence at that time.

(3) If, at any time during the moratorium, a person who is an officer of the company—

(a) does any of the things mentioned in paragraphs (a) to (f) of sub-paragraph (4), or

(b) is privy to the doing by others of any of the things mentioned in paragraphs (c), (d) and (e) of that sub-paragraph,

he commits an offence.

(4) Those things are—

(a) concealing any part of the company's property to the value of £500 or more, or concealing any debt due to or from the company, or

(b) fraudulently removing any part of the company's property to the value of £500 or more, or
(c) concealing, destroying, mutilating or falsifying any book or paper affecting or relating to the company's property or affairs, or
(d) making any false entry in any book or paper affecting or relating to the company's property or affairs, or
(e) fraudulently parting with, altering or making any omission in any document affecting or relating to the company's property or affairs, or
(f) pawning, pledging or disposing of any property of the company which has been obtained on credit and has not been paid for (unless the pawning, pledging or disposal was in the ordinary way of the company's business).

(5) For the purposes of this paragraph, "officer" includes a shadow director.

(6) It is a defence—
(a) for a person charged under sub-paragraph (2) or (3) in respect of the things mentioned in paragraph (a) or (f) of sub-paragraph (4) to prove that he had no intent to defraud, and
(b) for a person charged under sub-paragraph (2) or (3) in respect of the things mentioned in paragraph (c) or (d) of sub-paragraph (4) to prove that he had no intent to conceal the state of affairs of the company or to defeat the law.

(7) Where a person pawns, pledges or disposes of any property of a company in circumstances which amount to an offence under sub-paragraph (2) or (3), every person who takes in pawn or pledge, or otherwise receives, the property knowing it to be pawned, pledged or disposed of in circumstances which—
(a) would, if a moratorium were obtained for the company within the period of 12 months beginning with the day on which the pawning, pledging or disposal took place, amount to an offence under sub-paragraph (2), or
(b) amount to an offence under sub-paragraph (3), commits an offence.

(8) A person guilty of an offence under this paragraph is liable to imprisonment or a fine, or both.

(9) The money sums specified in paragraphs (a) and (b) of sub-paragraph (4) are subject to increase or reduction by order under section 417A in Part XV.

42\. (1) If, for the purpose of obtaining a moratorium, or an extension of a moratorium, for a company, a person who is an officer of the company—
(a) makes any false representation, or
(b) fraudulently does, or omits to do, anything, he commits an offence.

(2) Sub-paragraph (1) applies even if no moratorium or extension is obtained.

(3) For the purposes of this paragraph, "officer" includes a shadow director.

(4) A person guilty of an offence under this paragraph is liable to imprisonment or a fine, or both.

Void provisions in floating charge documents

43\. (1) A provision in an instrument creating a floating charge is void if it provides for—
(a) obtaining a moratorium, or
(b) anything done with a view to obtaining a moratorium (including any preliminary decision or investigation),

to be an event causing the floating charge to crystallise or causing restrictions which would not otherwise apply to be imposed on the disposal of property by the company or a ground for the appointment of a receiver.

(2) In sub-paragraph (1), "receiver" includes a manager and a person who is appointed both receiver and manager.

Functions of the Financial Conduct Authority and Prudential Regulation Authority

44\. (1) This Schedule has effect in relation to a moratorium for a regulated company with the modifications in sub-paragraphs (2) to (16) below.

(2) Any notice or other document required by virtue of this Schedule to be sent to a creditor of a regulated company must also be sent to the appropriate regulator.

(3) The appropriate regulator is entitled to be heard on any application to the court for leave under paragraph 20(2) or 20(3) (disposal of charged property, etc.).

(4) Where paragraph 26(1) (challenge of nominee's actions, etc.) applies, the persons who may apply to the court include the appropriate regulator.
(5) If a person other than a regulator applies to the court under that paragraph, the appropriate regulator is entitled to be heard on the application.
(6) Where paragraph 27(1) (challenge of nominee's actions, etc.) applies, the persons who may apply to the court include the appropriate regulator.
(7) If a person other than a regulator applies to the court under that paragraph, the appropriate regulator is entitled to be heard on the application.
(8) The persons to be summoned to a creditors' meeting under paragraph 29 include the appropriate regulator.
(9) A person appointed for the purpose by the appropriate regulator is entitled to attend and participate in (but not to vote at)—
   (a) any creditors' meeting summoned under that paragraph,
   (b) any meeting of a committee established under paragraph 35 (moratorium committee).
(10) The appropriate regulator is entitled to be heard on any application under paragraph 36(3) (effectiveness of decisions).
(11) Where paragraph 38(1) (challenge of decisions) applies, the persons who may apply to the court include the appropriate regulator.
(12) If a person other than a regulator applies to the court under that paragraph, the appropriate regulator is entitled to be heard on the application.
(13) Where paragraph 39(3) (implementation of voluntary arrangement) applies, the persons who may apply to the court include the appropriate regulator.
(14) If a person other than a regulator applies to the court under that paragraph, the appropriate regulator is entitled to be heard on the application.
(15) Where paragraph 40(2) (challenge of directors' actions) applies, the persons who may apply to the court include the appropriate regulator.
(16) If a person other than a regulator applies to the court under that paragraph, the appropriate regulator is entitled to be heard on the application.
(16A) If either regulator makes an application to the court under any of the provisions mentioned in sub-paragraphs (5), (7), (12), (14) or (16) in relation to a PRA-regulated company, the other regulator is entitled to be heard on the application.
(17) This paragraph does not prejudice any right the appropriate regulator has (apart from this paragraph) as a creditor of a regulated company.
(17A) The "appropriate regulator" means—
   (a) for the purposes of sub-paragraphs (2) to (8) and (10) to (17)—
      (i) where the regulated company is a PRA-regulated company, each of the Financial Conduct Authority and the Prudential Regulation Authority, and
      (ii) in any other case, the Financial Conduct Authority;
   (b) for the purposes of sub-paragraph (9)—
      (i) where the regulated company is a PRA-regulated company, the Financial Conduct Authority or the Prudential Regulation Authority, and
      (ii) in any other case, the Financial Conduct Authority.
(18) In this paragraph—
"PRA-authorised person" has the meaning given by section 2B(5) of the Financial Services and Markets Act 2000;
"PRA-regulated activity" has the meaning given by section 22A of the Financial Services and Markets Act 2000;
"PRA-regulated company" means a regulated company which—
   (a) is, or has been, a PRA-authorised person,
   (b) is, or has been, an appointed representative within the meaning given by section 39 of the Financial Services and Markets Act 2000, whose principal (or one of whose principals) is, or was, a PRA-authorised person, or
   (c) is carrying on, or has carried on, a PRA-regulated activity in contravention of the general prohibition;
"regulated company" means a company which—
   (a) is, or has been, an authorised person within the meaning given by section 31 of the Financial Services and Markets Act 2000,
   (b) is, or has been, an appointed representative within the meaning given by section 39 of that Act, or

(c) is carrying on, or has carried on, a regulated activity, within the meaning given by section 22 of that Act, in contravention of the general prohibition within the meaning given by section 19 of that Act; and

"regulator" means the Financial Conduct Authority or the Prudential Regulation Authority.

Subordinate legislation

45. (1) Regulations or an order made by the Secretary of State under this Schedule may make different provision for different cases.

(2) Regulations so made may make such consequential, incidental, supplemental and transitional provision as may appear to the Secretary of State necessary or expedient.

(3) Any power of the Secretary of State to make regulations under this Schedule may be exercised by amending or repealing any enactment contained in this Act (including one contained in this Schedule) or contained in the Company Directors Disqualification Act 1986.

(4) Regulations (except regulations under paragraph 5) or an order made by the Secretary of State under this Schedule shall be made by statutory instrument subject to annulment in pursuance of a resolution of either House of Parliament.

(5) Regulations under paragraph 5 of this Schedule are to be made by statutory instrument and shall only be made if a draft containing the regulations has been laid before and approved by resolution of each House of Parliament.

SCHEDULE B1
ADMINISTRATION
ARRANGEMENT OF SCHEDULE

Nature of administration	Paragraphs 1 to 9
Appointment of administrator by court	Paragraphs 10 to 13
Appointment of administrator by holder of floating charge	Paragraphs 14 to 21
Appointment of administrator by company or directors	Paragraphs 22 to 34
Administration application: special cases	Paragraphs 35 to 39
Effect of administration	Paragraphs 40 to 45
Process of administration	Paragraphs 46 to 58
Functions of administrator	Paragraphs 59 to 75
Ending administration	Paragraphs 76 to 86
Replacing administrator	Paragraphs 87 to 99
General	Paragraphs 100 to 116

NATURE OF ADMINISTRATION

Administration

1. (1) For the purposes of this Act "administrator" of a company means a person appointed under this Schedule to manage the company's affairs, business and property.

(2) For the purposes of this Act—

(a) a company is "in administration" while the appointment of an administrator of the company has effect,

(b) a company "enters administration" when the appointment of an administrator takes effect,

(c) a company ceases to be in administration when the appointment of an administrator of the company ceases to have effect in accordance with this Schedule, and

(d) a company does not cease to be in administration merely because an administrator vacates office (by reason of resignation, death or otherwise) or is removed from office.

2. A person may be appointed as administrator of a company—

(a) by administration order of the court under paragraph 10,

(b) by the holder of a floating charge under paragraph 14, or
(c) by the company or its directors under paragraph 22.

Purpose of administration

3. (1) The administrator of a company must perform his functions with the objective of—
(a) rescuing the company as a going concern, or
(b) achieving a better result for the company's creditors as a whole than would be likely if the company were wound up (without first being in administration), or
(c) realising property in order to make a distribution to one or more secured or preferential creditors.
(2) Subject to sub-paragraph (4), the administrator of a company must perform his functions in the interests of the company's creditors as a whole.
(3) The administrator must perform his functions with the objective specified in sub-paragraph (1)(a) unless he thinks either—
(a) that it is not reasonably practicable to achieve that objective, or
(b) that the objective specified in sub-paragraph (1)(b) would achieve a better result for the company's creditors as a whole.
(4) The administrator may perform his functions with the objective specified in sub-paragraph (1)(c) only if—
(a) he thinks that it is not reasonably practicable to achieve either of the objectives specified in sub-paragraph (1)(a) and (b), and
(b) he does not unnecessarily harm the interests of the creditors of the company as a whole.

4. The administrator of a company must perform his functions as quickly and efficiently as is reasonably practicable.

Status of administrator

5. An administrator is an officer of the court (whether or not he is appointed by the court).

General restrictions

6. A person may be appointed as administrator of a company only if he is qualified to act as an insolvency practitioner in relation to the company.

7. A person may not be appointed as administrator of a company which is in administration (subject to the provisions of paragraphs 90 to 97 and 100 to 103 about replacement and additional administrators).

8. (1) A person may not be appointed as administrator of a company which is in liquidation by virtue of—
(a) a resolution for voluntary winding up, or
(b) a winding-up order.
(2) Sub-paragraph (1)(a) is subject to paragraph 38.
(3) Sub-paragraph (1)(b) is subject to paragraphs 37 and 38.

9. (1) A person may not be appointed as administrator of a company which—
(a) has a liability in respect of a deposit which it accepted in accordance with the Banking Act 1979 or 1987, but
(b) is not an authorised deposit taker.
(2) A person may not be appointed as administrator of a company which effects or carries out contracts of insurance.
(3) But sub-paragraph (2) does not apply to a company which—
(a) is exempt from the general prohibition in relation to effecting or carrying out contracts of insurance, or
(b) is an authorised deposit taker effecting or carrying out contracts of insurance in the course of a banking business.
(4) In this paragraph—
"authorised deposit taker" means a person with permission under Part IV of the Financial Services and Markets Act 2000 to accept deposits, and
"the general prohibition" has the meaning given by section 19 of that Act.
(5) This paragraph shall be construed in accordance with—
(a) section 22 of the Financial Services and Markets Act 2000 (classes of regulated activity and categories of investment),

(b) any relevant order under that section, and
(c) Schedule 2 to that Act (regulated activities).

APPOINTMENT OF ADMINISTRATOR BY COURT

Administration order

10. An administration order is an order appointing a person as the administrator of a company.

Conditions for making order

11. The court may make an administration order in relation to a company only if satisfied—
(a) that the company is or is likely to become unable to pay its debts, and
(b) that the administration order is reasonably likely to achieve the purpose of administration.

Administration application

12. (1) An application to the court for an administration order in respect of a company (an "administration application") may be made only by—
(a) the company,
(b) the directors of the company,
(c) one or more creditors of the company,
(d) the designated officer for a magistrates' court in the exercise of the power conferred by section 87A of the Magistrates' Courts Act 1980 (c. 43) (fine imposed on company), or
(e) a combination of persons listed in paragraphs (a) to (d).
(2) As soon as is reasonably practicable after the making of an administration application the applicant shall notify—
(a) any person who has appointed an administrative receiver of the company,
(b) any person who is or may be entitled to appoint an administrative receiver of the company,
(c) any person who is or may be entitled to appoint an administrator of the company under paragraph 14, and
(d) such other persons as may be prescribed.
(3) An administration application may not be withdrawn without the permission of the court.
(4) In sub-paragraph (1) "creditor" includes a contingent creditor and a prospective creditor.
(5) Sub-paragraph (1) is without prejudice to section 7(4)(b).

Powers of court

13. (1) On hearing an administration application the court may—
(a) make the administration order sought;
(b) dismiss the application;
(c) adjourn the hearing conditionally or unconditionally;
(d) make an interim order;
(e) treat the application as a winding-up petition and make any order which the court could make under section 125;
(f) make any other order which the court thinks appropriate.
(2) An appointment of an administrator by administration order takes effect—
(a) at a time appointed by the order, or
(b) where no time is appointed by the order, when the order is made.
(3) An interim order under sub-paragraph (1)(d) may, in particular—
(a) restrict the exercise of a power of the directors or the company;
(b) make provision conferring a discretion on the court or on a person qualified to act as an insolvency practitioner in relation to the company.
(4) This paragraph is subject to paragraph 39.

APPOINTMENT OF ADMINISTRATOR BY HOLDER OF FLOATING CHARGE

Power to appoint

14. (1) The holder of a qualifying floating charge in respect of a company's property may appoint an administrator of the company.

(2) For the purposes of sub-paragraph (1) a floating charge qualifies if created by an instrument which—
(a) states that this paragraph applies to the floating charge,
(b) purports to empower the holder of the floating charge to appoint an administrator of the company,
(c) purports to empower the holder of the floating charge to make an appointment which would be the appointment of an administrative receiver within the meaning given by section 29(2), or
(d) purports to empower the holder of a floating charge in Scotland to appoint a receiver who on appointment would be an administrative receiver.

(3) For the purposes of sub-paragraph (1) a person is the holder of a qualifying floating charge in respect of a company's property if he holds one or more debentures of the company secured—
(a) by a qualifying floating charge which relates to the whole or substantially the whole of the company's property,
(b) by a number of qualifying floating charges which together relate to the whole or substantially the whole of the company's property, or
(c) by charges and other forms of security which together relate to the whole or substantially the whole of the company's property and at least one of which is a qualifying floating charge.

Restrictions on power to appoint

15. (1) A person may not appoint an administrator under paragraph 14 unless—
(a) he has given at least two business days' written notice to the holder of any prior floating charge which satisfies paragraph 14(2), or
(b) the holder of any prior floating charge which satisfies paragraph 14(2) has consented in writing to the making of the appointment.

(2) One floating charge is prior to another for the purposes of this paragraph if—
(a) it was created first, or
(b) it is to be treated as having priority in accordance with an agreement to which the holder of each floating charge was party.

(3) Sub-paragraph (2) shall have effect in relation to Scotland as if the following were substituted for paragraph (a)—
"(a) it has priority of ranking in accordance with section 464(4)(b) of the Companies Act 1985,".

16. An administrator may not be appointed under paragraph 14 while a floating charge on which the appointment relies is not enforceable.

17. An administrator of a company may not be appointed under paragraph 14 if—
(a) a provisional liquidator of the company has been appointed under section 135, or
(b) an administrative receiver of the company is in office.

Notice of appointment

18. (1) A person who appoints an administrator of a company under paragraph 14 shall file with the court—
(a) a notice of appointment, and
(b) such other documents as may be prescribed.

(2) The notice of appointment must include a statutory declaration by or on behalf of the person who makes the appointment—
(a) that the person is the holder of a qualifying floating charge in respect of the company's property,
(b) that each floating charge relied on in making the appointment is (or was) enforceable on the date of the appointment, and
(c) that the appointment is in accordance with this Schedule.

(3) The notice of appointment must identify the administrator and must be accompanied by a statement by the administrator—
(a) that he consents to the appointment,
(b) that in his opinion the purpose of administration is reasonably likely to be achieved, and
(c) giving such other information and opinions as may be prescribed.

(4) For the purpose of a statement under sub-paragraph (3) an administrator may rely on information supplied by directors of the company (unless he has reason to doubt its accuracy).

(5) The notice of appointment and any document accompanying it must be in the prescribed form.

(6) A statutory declaration under sub-paragraph (2) must be made during the prescribed period.

(7) A person commits an offence if in a statutory declaration under sub-paragraph (2) he makes a statement—

(a) which is false, and

(b) which he does not reasonably believe to be true.

Commencement of appointment

19. The appointment of an administrator under paragraph 14 takes effect when the requirements of paragraph 18 are satisfied.

20. A person who appoints an administrator under paragraph 14—

(a) shall notify the administrator and such other persons as may be prescribed as soon as is reasonably practicable after the requirements of paragraph 18 are satisfied, and

(b) commits an offence if he fails without reasonable excuse to comply with paragraph (a).

Invalid appointment: indemnity

21. (1) This paragraph applies where—

(a) a person purports to appoint an administrator under paragraph 14, and

(b) the appointment is discovered to be invalid.

(2) The court may order the person who purported to make the appointment to indemnify the person appointed against liability which arises solely by reason of the appointment's invalidity.

APPOINTMENT OF ADMINISTRATOR BY COMPANY OR DIRECTORS

Power to appoint

22. (1) A company may appoint an administrator.

(2) The directors of a company may appoint an administrator.

Restrictions on power to appoint

23. (1) This paragraph applies where an administrator of a company is appointed—

(a) under paragraph 22, or

(b) on an administration application made by the company or its directors.

(2) An administrator of the company may not be appointed under paragraph 22 during the period of 12 months beginning with the date on which the appointment referred to in sub- paragraph (1) ceases to have effect.

24. (1) If a moratorium for a company under Schedule A1 ends on a date when no voluntary arrangement is in force in respect of the company, this paragraph applies for the period of 12 months beginning with that date.

(2) This paragraph also applies for the period of 12 months beginning with the date on which a voluntary arrangement in respect of a company ends if—

(a) the arrangement was made during a moratorium for the company under Schedule A1, and

(b) the arrangement ends prematurely (within the meaning of section 7B).

(3) While this paragraph applies, an administrator of the company may not be appointed under paragraph 22.

25. An administrator of a company may not be appointed under paragraph 22 if—

(a) a petition for the winding up of the company has been presented and is not yet disposed of,

(b) an administration application has been made and is not yet disposed of, or

(c) an administrative receiver of the company is in office.

25A (1) Paragraph 25(a) does not prevent the appointment of an administrator of a company if the petition for the winding up of the company was presented after the person proposing to make the appointment filed the notice of intention to appoint with the court under paragraph 27.

(2) But sub-paragraph (1) does not apply if the petition was presented under a provision mentioned in paragraph 42(4).

Notice of intention to appoint

26. (1) A person who proposes to make an appointment under paragraph 22 shall give at least five business days' written notice to—

(a) any person who is or may be entitled to appoint an administrative receiver of the company, and

(b) any person who is or may be entitled to appoint an administrator of the company under paragraph 14.

(2) A person who proposes to make an appointment under paragraph 22 shall also give such notice as may be prescribed to such other persons as may be prescribed.

(3) A notice under this paragraph must—

(a) identify the proposed administrator, and

(b) be in the prescribed form.

27. (1) A person who gives notice of intention to appoint under paragraph 26 shall file with the court as soon as is reasonably practicable a copy of—

(a) the notice, and

(b) any document accompanying it.

(2) The copy filed under sub-paragraph (1) must be accompanied by a statutory declaration made by or on behalf of the person who proposes to make the appointment—

(a) that the company is or is likely to become unable to pay its debts,

(b) that the company is not in liquidation, and

(c) that, so far as the person making the statement is able to ascertain, the appointment is not prevented by paragraphs 23 to 25, and

(d) to such additional effect, and giving such information, as may be prescribed.

(3) A statutory declaration under sub-paragraph (2) must—

(a) be in the prescribed form, and

(b) be made during the prescribed period.

(4) A person commits an offence if in a statutory declaration under sub-paragraph (2) he makes a statement—

(a) which is false, and

(b) which he does not reasonably believe to be true.

28. (1) An appointment may not be made under paragraph 22 unless the person who makes the appointment has complied with any requirement of paragraphs 26 and 27 and—

(a) the period of notice specified in paragraph 26(1) has expired, or

(b) each person to whom notice has been given under paragraph 26(1) has consented in writing to the making of the appointment.

(2) An appointment may not be made under paragraph 22 after the period of ten business days beginning with the date on which the notice of intention to appoint is filed under paragraph 27(1).

Notice of appointment

29. (1) A person who appoints an administrator of a company under paragraph 22 shall file with the court—

(a) a notice of appointment, and

(b) such other documents as may be prescribed.

(2) The notice of appointment must include a statutory declaration by or on behalf of the person who makes the appointment—

(a) that the person is entitled to make an appointment under paragraph 22,

(b) that the appointment is in accordance with this Schedule, and

(c) that, so far as the person making the statement is able to ascertain, the statements made and information given in the statutory declaration filed with the notice of intention to appoint remain accurate.

(3) The notice of appointment must identify the administrator and must be accompanied by a statement by the administrator—
(a) that he consents to the appointment,
(b) that in his opinion the purpose of administration is reasonably likely to be achieved, and
(c) giving such other information and opinions as may be prescribed.
(4) For the purpose of a statement under sub-paragraph (3) an administrator may rely on information supplied by directors of the company (unless he has reason to doubt its accuracy).
(5) The notice of appointment and any document accompanying it must be in the prescribed form.
(6) A statutory declaration under sub-paragraph (2) must be made during the prescribed period.
(7) A person commits an offence if in a statutory declaration under sub-paragraph (2) he makes a statement—
(a) which is false, and
(b) which he does not reasonably believe to be true.

30. In a case in which no person is entitled to notice of intention to appoint under paragraph 26(1) (and paragraph 28 therefore does not apply)—
(a) the statutory declaration accompanying the notice of appointment must include the statements and information required under paragraph 27(2), and
(b) paragraph 29(2)(c) shall not apply.

Commencement of appointment

31. The appointment of an administrator under paragraph 22 takes effect when the requirements of paragraph 29 are satisfied.

32. A person who appoints an administrator under paragraph 22—
(a) shall notify the administrator and such other persons as may be prescribed as soon as is reasonably practicable after the requirements of paragraph 29 are satisfied, and
(b) commits an offence if he fails without reasonable excuse to comply with paragraph (a).

33. If before the requirements of paragraph 29 are satisfied the company enters administration by virtue of an administration order or an appointment under paragraph 14—
(a) the appointment under paragraph 22 shall not take effect, and
(b) paragraph 32 shall not apply.

Invalid appointment: indemnity

34 . (1) This paragraph applies where—
(a) a person purports to appoint an administrator under paragraph 22, and
(b) the appointment is discovered to be invalid.
(2) The court may order the person who purported to make the appointment to indemnify the person appointed against liability which arises solely by reason of the appointment's invalidity.

ADMINISTRATION APPLICATION — SPECIAL CASES

Application by holder of floating charge

35. (1) This paragraph applies where an administration application in respect of a company—
(a) is made by the holder of a qualifying floating charge in respect of the company's property, and
(b) includes a statement that the application is made in reliance on this paragraph.
(2) The court may make an administration order—
(a) whether or not satisfied that the company is or is likely to become unable to pay its debts, but
(b) only if satisfied that the applicant could appoint an administrator under paragraph 14.

Intervention by holder of floating charge

36. (1) This paragraph applies where—
(a) an administration application in respect of a company is made by a person who is not the holder of a qualifying floating charge in respect of the company's property, and

(b) the holder of a qualifying floating charge in respect of the company's property applies to the court to have a specified person appointed as administrator (and not the person specified by the administration applicant).

(2) The court shall grant an application under sub-paragraph (1)(b) unless the court thinks it right to refuse the application because of the particular circumstances of the case.

Application where company in liquidation

37. (1) This paragraph applies where the holder of a qualifying floating charge in respect of a company's property could appoint an administrator under paragraph 14 but for paragraph 8(1)(b).

(2) The holder of the qualifying floating charge may make an administration application.

(3) If the court makes an administration order on hearing an application made by virtue of sub-paragraph (2)—

(a) the court shall discharge the winding-up order,
(b) the court shall make provision for such matters as may be prescribed,
(c) the court may make other consequential provision,
(d) the court shall specify which of the powers under this Schedule are to be exercisable by the administrator, and
(e) this Schedule shall have effect with such modifications as the court may specify.

38. (1) The liquidator of a company may make an administration application.

(2) If the court makes an administration order on hearing an application made by virtue of sub-paragraph (1)—

(a) the court shall discharge any winding-up order in respect of the company,
(b) the court shall make provision for such matters as may be prescribed,
(c) the court may make other consequential provision,
(d) the court shall specify which of the powers under this Schedule are to be exercisable by the administrator, and
(e) this Schedule shall have effect with such modifications as the court may specify.

Effect of administrative receivership

39. (1) Where there is an administrative receiver of a company the court must dismiss an administration application in respect of the company unless—

(a) the person by or on behalf of whom the receiver was appointed consents to the making of the administration order,
(b) the court thinks that the security by virtue of which the receiver was appointed would be liable to be released or discharged under sections 238 to 240 (transaction at undervalue and preference) if an administration order were made,
(c) the court thinks that the security by virtue of which the receiver was appointed would be avoided under section 245 (avoidance of floating charge) if an administration order were made, or
(d) the court thinks that the security by virtue of which the receiver was appointed would be challengeable under section 242 (gratuitous alienations) or 243 (unfair preferences) or under any rule of law in Scotland.

(2) Sub-paragraph (1) applies whether the administrative receiver is appointed before or after the making of the administration application.

EFFECT OF ADMINISTRATION

Dismissal of pending winding-up petition

40. (1) A petition for the winding up of a company—

(a) shall be dismissed on the making of an administration order in respect of the company, and
(b) shall be suspended while the company is in administration following an appointment under paragraph 14.

(2) Sub-paragraph (1)(b) does not apply to a petition presented under—

(a) section 124A (public interest),
(aa) section 124B (SEs), or
(b) section 367 of the Financial Services and Markets Act 2000 (petition by Financial Conduct or Prudential Regulation Authority).

(3) Where an administrator becomes aware that a petition was presented under a provision referred to in sub-paragraph (2) before his appointment, he shall apply to the court for directions under paragraph 63.

Dismissal of administrative or other receiver

41. (1) When an administration order takes effect in respect of a company any administrative receiver of the company shall vacate office.

(2) Where a company is in administration, any receiver of part of the company's property shall vacate office if the administrator requires him to.

(3) Where an administrative receiver or receiver vacates office under sub-paragraph (1) or (2)—

(a) his remuneration shall be charged on and paid out of any property of the company which was in his custody or under his control immediately before he vacated office, and

(b) he need not take any further steps under section 40 or 59.

(4) In the application of sub-paragraph (3)(a)—

(a) "remuneration" includes expenses properly incurred and any indemnity to which the administrative receiver or receiver is entitled out of the assets of the company,

(b) the charge imposed takes priority over security held by the person by whom or on whose behalf the administrative receiver or receiver was appointed, and

(c) the provision for payment is subject to paragraph 43.

Moratorium on insolvency proceedings

42. (1) This paragraph applies to a company in administration.

(2) No resolution may be passed for the winding up of the company.

(3) No order may be made for the winding up of the company.

(4) Sub-paragraph (3) does not apply to an order made on a petition presented under—

(a) section 124A (public interest), (aa) section 124B (SEs), or

(b) section 367 of the Financial Services and Markets Act 2000 (petition by Financial Conduct Authority or Prudential Regulation Authority).

(5) If a petition presented under a provision referred to in sub-paragraph (4) comes to the attention of the administrator, he shall apply to the court for directions under paragraph 63.

Moratorium on other legal process

43. (1) This paragraph applies to a company in administration.

(2) No step may be taken to enforce security over the company's property except—

(a) with the consent of the administrator, or

(b) with the permission of the court.

(3) No step may be taken to repossess goods in the company's possession under a hire-purchase agreement except—

(a) with the consent of the administrator, or

(b) with the permission of the court.

(4) A landlord may not exercise a right of forfeiture by peaceable re-entry in relation to premises let to the company except—

(a) with the consent of the administrator, or

(b) with the permission of the court.

(5) In Scotland, a landlord may not exercise a right of irritancy in relation to premises let to the company except—

(a) with the consent of the administrator, or

(b) with the permission of the court.

(6) No legal process (including legal proceedings, execution, distress and diligence) may be instituted or continued against the company or property of the company except—

(a) with the consent of the administrator, or

(b) with the permission of the court.

(6A) An administrative receiver of the company may not be appointed.

(7) Where the court gives permission for a transaction under this paragraph it may impose a condition on or a requirement in connection with the transaction.

(8) In this paragraph "landlord" includes a person to whom rent is payable.

Interim moratorium

44. (1) This paragraph applies where an administration application in respect of a company has been made and—
(a) the application has not yet been granted or dismissed, or
(b) the application has been granted but the administration order has not yet taken effect.
(2) This paragraph also applies from the time when a copy of notice of intention to appoint an administrator under paragraph 14 is filed with the court until—
(a) the appointment of the administrator takes effect, or
(b) the period of five business days beginning with the date of filing expires without an administrator having been appointed.
(3) Sub-paragraph (2) has effect in relation to a notice of intention to appoint only if it is in the prescribed form.
(4) This paragraph also applies from the time when a copy of notice of intention to appoint an administrator is filed with the court under paragraph 27(1) until—
(a) the appointment of the administrator takes effect, or
(b) the period specified in paragraph 28(2) expires without an administrator having been appointed.
(5) The provisions of paragraphs 42 and 43 shall apply (ignoring any reference to the consent of the administrator).
(6) If there is an administrative receiver of the company when the administration application is made, the provisions of paragraphs 42 and 43 shall not begin to apply by virtue of this paragraph until the person by or on behalf of whom the receiver was appointed consents to the making of the administration order.
(7) This paragraph does not prevent or require the permission of the court for—
(a) the presentation of a petition for the winding up of the company under a provision mentioned in paragraph 42(4),
(b) the appointment of an administrator under paragraph 14,
(c) the appointment of an administrative receiver of the company, or
(d) the carrying out by an administrative receiver (whenever appointed) of his functions.

Publicity

45. (1) While a company is in administration every business document issued by or on behalf of the company or the administrator and all the company's websites must state—
(a) the name of the administrator, and
(b) that the affairs, business and property of the company are being managed by him.
(2) Any of the following commits an offence if without reasonable excuse he authorises or permits a contravention of sub-paragraph (1)—
(a) the administrator,
(b) an officer of the company, and
(c) the company.
(3) In sub-paragraph (1) "business document" means—
(a) an invoice,
(b) an order for goods or services,
(c) a business letter, and
(d) an order form,
whether in hard copy, electronic or any other form.

PROCESS OF ADMINISTRATION

Announcement of administrator's appointment

46. (1) This paragraph applies where a person becomes the administrator of a company.
(2) As soon as is reasonably practicable the administrator shall—
(a) send a notice of his appointment to the company, and
(b) publish a notice of his appointment in the prescribed manner.
(3) As soon as is reasonably practicable the administrator shall—
(a) obtain a list of the company's creditors, and
(b) send a notice of his appointment to each creditor of whose claim and address he is aware.

(4) The administrator shall send a notice of his appointment to the registrar of companies before the end of the period of 7 days beginning with the date specified in sub-paragraph (6).

(5) The administrator shall send a notice of his appointment to such persons as may be prescribed before the end of the prescribed period beginning with the date specified in sub-paragraph (6).

(6) The date for the purpose of sub-paragraphs (4) and (5) is—

(a) in the case of an administrator appointed by administration order, the date of the order,
(b) in the case of an administrator appointed under paragraph 14, the date on which he receives notice under paragraph 20, and
(c) in the case of an administrator appointed under paragraph 22, the date on which he receives notice under paragraph 32.

(7) The court may direct that sub-paragraph (3)(b) or (5)—

(a) shall not apply, or
(b) shall apply with the substitution of a different period.

(8) A notice under this paragraph must—

(a) contain the prescribed information, and
(b) be in the prescribed form.

(9) An administrator commits an offence if he fails without reasonable excuse to comply with a requirement of this paragraph.

Statement of company's affairs

47. (1) As soon as is reasonably practicable after appointment the administrator of a company shall by notice in the prescribed form require one or more relevant persons to provide the administrator with a statement of the affairs of the company.

(2) The statement must—

(a) be verified by a statement of truth in accordance with Civil Procedure Rules,
(b) be in the prescribed form,
(c) give particulars of the company's property, debts and liabilities,
(d) give the names and addresses of the company's creditors,
(e) specify the security held by each creditor,
(f) give the date on which each security was granted, and
(g) contain such other information as may be prescribed.

(3) In sub-paragraph (1) "relevant person" means—

(a) a person who is or has been an officer of the company,
(b) a person who took part in the formation of the company during the period of one year ending with the date on which the company enters administration,
(c) a person employed by the company during that period, and
(d) a person who is or has been during that period an officer or employee of a company which is or has been during that year an officer of the company.

(4) For the purpose of sub-paragraph (3) a reference to employment is a reference to employment through a contract of employment or a contract for services.

(5) In Scotland, a statement of affairs under sub-paragraph (1) must be a statutory declaration made in accordance with the Statutory Declarations Act 1835 (and sub-paragraph (2)(a) shall not apply).

48. (1) A person required to submit a statement of affairs must do so before the end of the period of 11 days beginning with the day on which he receives notice of the requirement.

(2) The administrator may—

(a) revoke a requirement under paragraph 47(1), or
(b) extend the period specified in sub-paragraph (1) (whether before or after expiry).

(3) If the administrator refuses a request to act under sub-paragraph (2)—

(a) the person whose request is refused may apply to the court, and
(b) the court may take action of a kind specified in sub-paragraph (2).

(4) A person commits an offence if he fails without reasonable excuse to comply with a requirement under paragraph 47(1).

Administrator's proposals

49. (1) The administrator of a company shall make a statement setting out proposals for achieving the purpose of administration.

(2) A statement under sub-paragraph (1) must, in particular—
(a) deal with such matters as may be prescribed, and
(b) where applicable, explain why the administrator thinks that the objective mentioned in paragraph 3(1)(a) or (b) cannot be achieved.
(3) Proposals under this paragraph may include—
(a) a proposal for a voluntary arrangement under Part I of this Act (although this paragraph is without prejudice to section 4(3));
(b) a proposal for a compromise or arrangement to be sanctioned under Part 26 of the Companies Act 2006 (arrangements and reconstructions).
(4) The administrator shall send a copy of the statement of his proposals—
(a) to the registrar of companies,
(b) to every creditor of the company of whose claim and address he is aware, and
(c) to every member of the company of whose address he is aware.
(5) The administrator shall comply with sub-paragraph (4)—
(a) as soon as is reasonably practicable after the company enters administration, and
(b) in any event, before the end of the period of eight weeks beginning with the day on which the company enters administration.
(6) The administrator shall be taken to comply with sub-paragraph (4)(c) if he publishes in the prescribed manner a notice undertaking to provide a copy of the statement of proposals free of charge to any member of the company who applies in writing to a specified address.
(7) An administrator commits an offence if he fails without reasonable excuse to comply with sub-paragraph (5).
(8) A period specified in this paragraph may be varied in accordance with paragraph 107.

Creditors' meeting

50. (1) In this Schedule "creditors' meeting" means a meeting of creditors of a company summoned by the administrator—
(a) in the prescribed manner, and
(b) giving the prescribed period of notice to every creditor of the company of whose claim and address he is aware.
(2) A period prescribed under sub-paragraph (1)(b) may be varied in accordance with paragraph 107.
(3) A creditors' meeting shall be conducted in accordance with the rules.

Requirement for initial creditors' meeting

51. (1) Each copy of an administrator's statement of proposals sent to a creditor under paragraph 49(4)(b) must be accompanied by an invitation to a creditors' meeting (an "initial creditors' meeting").
(2) The date set for an initial creditors' meeting must be—
(a) as soon as is reasonably practicable after the company enters administration, and
(b) in any event, within the period of ten weeks beginning with the date on which the company enters administration.
(3) An administrator shall present a copy of his statement of proposals to an initial creditors' meeting.
(4) A period specified in this paragraph may be varied in accordance with paragraph 107.
(5) An administrator commits an offence if he fails without reasonable excuse to comply with a requirement of this paragraph.

52. (1) Paragraph 51(1) shall not apply where the statement of proposals states that the administrator thinks—
(a) that the company has sufficient property to enable each creditor of the company to be paid in full,
(b) that the company has insufficient property to enable a distribution to be made to unsecured creditors other than by virtue of section 176A(2)(a), or
(c) that neither of the objectives specified in paragraph 3(1)(a) and (b) can be achieved.
(2) But the administrator shall summon an initial creditors' meeting if it is requested—
(a) by creditors of the company whose debts amount to at least 10% of the total debts of the company,

(b) in the prescribed manner, and
(c) in the prescribed period.

(3) A meeting requested under sub-paragraph (2) must be summoned for a date in the prescribed period.

(4) The period prescribed under sub-paragraph (3) may be varied in accordance with paragraph 107.

Business and result of initial creditors' meeting

53. (1) An initial creditors' meeting to which an administrator's proposals are presented shall consider them and may—
(a) approve them without modification, or
(b) approve them with modification to which the administrator consents.

(2) After the conclusion of an initial creditors' meeting the administrator shall as soon as is reasonably practicable report any decision taken to—
(a) the court,
(b) the registrar of companies, and
(c) such other persons as may be prescribed.

(3) An administrator commits an offence if he fails without reasonable excuse to comply with sub-paragraph (2).

Revision of administrator's proposals

54. (1) This paragraph applies where—
(a) an administrator's proposals have been approved (with or without modification) at an initial creditors' meeting,
(b) the administrator proposes a revision to the proposals, and
(c) the administrator thinks that the proposed revision is substantial.

(2) The administrator shall—
(a) summon a creditors' meeting,
(b) send a statement in the prescribed form of the proposed revision with the notice of the meeting sent to each creditor,
(c) send a copy of the statement, within the prescribed period, to each member of the company of whose address he is aware, and
(d) present a copy of the statement to the meeting.

(3) The administrator shall be taken to have complied with sub-paragraph (2)(c) if he publishes a notice undertaking to provide a copy of the statement free of charge to any member of the company who applies in writing to a specified address.

(4) A notice under sub-paragraph (3) must be published—
(a) in the prescribed manner, and
(b) within the prescribed period.

(5) A creditors' meeting to which a proposed revision is presented shall consider it and may—
(a) approve it without modification, or
(b) approve it with modification to which the administrator consents.

(6) After the conclusion of a creditors' meeting the administrator shall as soon as is reasonably practicable report any decision taken to—
(a) the court,
(b) the registrar of companies, and
(c) such other persons as may be prescribed.

(7) An administrator commits an offence if he fails without reasonable excuse to comply with sub-paragraph (6).

Failure to obtain approval of administrator's proposals

55. (1) This paragraph applies where an administrator reports to the court that—
(a) an initial creditors' meeting has failed to approve the administrator's proposals presented to it, or
(b) a creditors' meeting has failed to approve a revision of the administrator's proposals presented to it.

(2) The court may—

(a) provide that the appointment of an administrator shall cease to have effect from a specified time;
(b) adjourn the hearing conditionally or unconditionally;
(c) make an interim order;
(d) make an order on a petition for winding up suspended by virtue of paragraph 40(1)(b);
(e) make any other order (including an order making consequential provision) that the court thinks appropriate.

Further creditors' meetings

56. (1) The administrator of a company shall summon a creditors' meeting if—
(a) it is requested in the prescribed manner by creditors of the company whose debts amount to at least 10% of the total debts of the company, or
(b) he is directed by the court to summon a creditors' meeting.
(2) An administrator commits an offence if he fails without reasonable excuse to summon a creditors' meeting as required by this paragraph.

Creditors' committee

57. (1) A creditors' meeting may establish a creditors' committee.
(2) A creditors' committee shall carry out functions conferred on it by or under this Act.
(3) A creditors' committee may require the administrator—
(a) to attend on the committee at any reasonable time of which he is given at least seven days' notice, and
(b) to provide the committee with information about the exercise of his functions.

Correspondence instead of creditors' meeting

58. (1) Anything which is required or permitted by or under this Schedule to be done at a creditors' meeting may be done by correspondence between the administrator and creditors—
(a) in accordance with the rules, and
(b) subject to any prescribed condition.
(2) A reference in this Schedule to anything done at a creditors' meeting includes a reference to anything done in the course of correspondence in reliance on sub-paragraph (1).
(3) A requirement to hold a creditors' meeting is satisfied by conducting correspondence in accordance with this paragraph.

FUNCTIONS OF ADMINISTRATOR

General powers

59. (1) The administrator of a company may do anything necessary or expedient for the management of the affairs, business and property of the company.
(2) A provision of this Schedule which expressly permits the administrator to do a specified thing is without prejudice to the generality of sub-paragraph (1).
(3) A person who deals with the administrator of a company in good faith and for value need not inquire whether the administrator is acting within his powers.
60. The administrator of a company has the powers specified in Schedule 1 to this Act.
60A (1) The Secretary of State may by regulations make provision for—
(a) prohibiting, or
(b) imposing requirements or conditions in relation to,
the disposal, hiring out or sale of property of a company by the administrator to a connected person in circumstances specified in the regulations.
(2) Regulations under this paragraph may in particular require the approval of, or provide for the imposition of requirements or conditions by—
(a) creditors of the company,
(b) the court, or
(c) a person of a description specified in the regulations.
(3) In sub-paragraph (1), "connected person", in relation to a company, means—
(a) a relevant person in relation to the company, or
(b) a company connected with the company.

(4) For the purposes of sub-paragraph (3)—
(a) "relevant person", in relation to a company, means—
(i) a director or other officer, or shadow director, of the company;
(ii) a non-employee associate of such a person;
(iii) a non-employee associate of the company;
(b) a company is connected with another if any relevant person of one is or has been a relevant person of the other.
(5) In sub-paragraph (4), "non-employee associate" of a person means a person who is an associate of that person otherwise than by virtue of employing or being employed by that person.
(6) Subsection (10) of section 435 (extended definition of company) applies for the purposes of sub-paragraphs (3) to (5) as it applies for the purposes of that section.
(7) Regulations under this paragraph may—
(a) make different provision for different purposes;
(b) make incidental, consequential, supplemental and transitional provision.
(8) Regulations under this paragraph are to be made by statutory instrument.
(9 Regulations under this paragraph may not be made unless a draft of the statutory instrument containing the regulations has been laid before Parliament and approved by a resolution of each House of Parliament.
(10) This paragraph expires at the end of the period of 5 years beginning with the day on which it comes into force unless the power conferred by it is exercised during that period.

61. The administrator of a company—
(a) may remove a director of the company, and
(b) may appoint a director of the company (whether or not to fill a vacancy).

62. The administrator of a company may call a meeting of members or creditors of the company.

63. The administrator of a company may apply to the court for directions in connection with his functions.

64. (1) A company in administration or an officer of a company in administration may not exercise a management power without the consent of the administrator.
(2) For the purpose of sub-paragraph (1)—
(a) "management power" means a power which could be exercised so as to interfere with the exercise of the administrator's powers,
(b) it is immaterial whether the power is conferred by an enactment or an instrument, and
(c) consent may be general or specific.

Distribution

65. (1) The administrator of a company may make a distribution to a creditor of the company.
(2) Section 175 shall apply in relation to a distribution under this paragraph as it applies in relation to a winding up.
(3) A payment may not be made by way of distribution under this paragraph to a creditor of the company who is neither secured nor preferential unless the court gives permission.

66. The administrator of a company may make a payment otherwise than in accordance with paragraph 65 or paragraph 13 of Schedule 1 if he thinks it likely to assist achievement of the purpose of administration.

General duties

67. The administrator of a company shall on his appointment take custody or control of all the property to which he thinks the company is entitled.

68. (1) Subject to sub-paragraph (2), the administrator of a company shall manage its affairs, business and property in accordance with—
(a) any proposals approved under paragraph 53,
(b) any revision of those proposals which is made by him and which he does not consider substantial, and
(c) any revision of those proposals approved under paragraph 54.
(2) If the court gives directions to the administrator of a company in connection with any aspect of his management of the company's affairs, business or property, the administrator shall comply with the directions.
(3) The court may give directions under sub-paragraph (2) only if—

(a) no proposals have been approved under paragraph 53,
(b) the directions are consistent with any proposals or revision approved under paragraph 53 or 54,
(c) the court thinks the directions are required in order to reflect a change in circumstances since the approval of proposals or a revision under paragraph 53 or 54, or
(d) the court thinks the directions are desirable because of a misunderstanding about proposals or a revision approved under paragraph 53 or 54.

Administrator as agent of company

69 In exercising his functions under this Schedule the administrator of a company acts as its agent.

Charged property: floating charge

70. (1) The administrator of a company may dispose of or take action relating to property which is subject to a floating charge as if it were not subject to the charge.
(2) Where property is disposed of in reliance on sub-paragraph (1) the holder of the floating charge shall have the same priority in respect of acquired property as he had in respect of the property disposed of.
(3) In sub-paragraph (2) "acquired property" means property of the company which directly or indirectly represents the property disposed of.

Charged property: non-floating charge

71. (1) The court may by order enable the administrator of a company to dispose of property which is subject to a security (other than a floating charge) as if it were not subject to the security.
(2) An order under sub-paragraph (1) may be made only—
(a) on the application of the administrator, and
(b) where the court thinks that disposal of the property would be likely to promote the purpose of administration in respect of the company.
(3) An order under this paragraph is subject to the condition that there be applied towards discharging the sums secured by the security—
(a) the net proceeds of disposal of the property, and
(b) any additional money required to be added to the net proceeds so as to produce the amount determined by the court as the net amount which would be realised on a sale of the property at market value.
(4) If an order under this paragraph relates to more than one security, application of money under sub-paragraph (3) shall be in the order of the priorities of the securities.
(5) An administrator who makes a successful application for an order under this paragraph shall send a copy of the order to the registrar of companies before the end of the period of 14 days starting with the date of the order.
(6) An administrator commits an offence if he fails to comply with sub-paragraph (5) without reasonable excuse.

Hire-purchase property

72. (1) The court may by order enable the administrator of a company to dispose of goods which are in the possession of the company under a hire-purchase agreement as if all the rights of the owner under the agreement were vested in the company.
(2) An order under sub-paragraph (1) may be made only—
(a) on the application of the administrator, and
(b) where the court thinks that disposal of the goods would be likely to promote the purpose of administration in respect of the company.
(3) An order under this paragraph is subject to the condition that there be applied towards discharging the sums payable under the hire-purchase agreement—
(a) the net proceeds of disposal of the goods, and
(b) any additional money required to be added to the net proceeds so as to produce

the amount determined by the court as the net amount which would be realised on a sale of the goods at market value.

(4) An administrator who makes a successful application for an order under this paragraph shall send a copy of the order to the registrar of companies before the end of the period of 14 days starting with the date of the order.

(5) An administrator commits an offence if he fails without reasonable excuse to comply with sub-paragraph (4).

Protection for secured or preferential creditor

73. (1) An administrator's statement of proposals under paragraph 49 may not include any action which—

(a) affects the right of a secured creditor of the company to enforce his security,

(b) would result in a preferential debt of the company being paid otherwise than in priority to its non-preferential debts,

(bb) would result in an ordinary preferential debt of the company being paid otherwise than in priority to any secondary preferential debts that it may have,

(c) would result in one preferential creditor of the company being paid a smaller proportion of an ordinary preferential debt than another, or

(d) would result in one preferential creditor of the company being paid a smaller proportion of a secondary preferential debt than another.

(2) Sub-paragraph (1) does not apply to—

(a) action to which the relevant creditor consents,

(b) a proposal for a voluntary arrangement under Part I of this Act (although this sub-paragraph is without prejudice to section 4(3)),

(c) a proposal for a compromise or arrangement to be sanctioned under Part 26 of the Companies Act 2006 (arrangements and reconstructions), or

(d) a proposal for a cross-border merger within the meaning of regulation 2 of the Companies (Cross-Border Mergers) Regulations 2007.

(3) The reference to a statement of proposals in sub-paragraph (1) includes a reference to a statement as revised or modified.

Challenge to administrator's conduct of company

74. (1) A creditor or member of a company in administration may apply to the court claiming that—

(a) the administrator is acting or has acted so as unfairly to harm the interests of the applicant (whether alone or in common with some or all other members or creditors), or

(b) the administrator proposes to act in a way which would unfairly harm the interests of the applicant (whether alone or in common with some or all other members or creditors).

(2) A creditor or member of a company in administration may apply to the court claiming that the administrator is not performing his functions as quickly or as efficiently as is reasonably practicable.

(3) The court may—

(a) grant relief;

(b) dismiss the application;

(c) adjourn the hearing conditionally or unconditionally;

(d) make an interim order;

(e) make any other order it thinks appropriate.

(4) In particular, an order under this paragraph may—

(a) regulate the administrator's exercise of his functions;

(b) require the administrator to do or not do a specified thing;

(c) require a creditors' meeting to be held for a specified purpose;

(d) provide for the appointment of an administrator to cease to have effect;

(e) make consequential provision.

(5) An order may be made on a claim under sub-paragraph (1) whether or not the action complained of—

(a) is within the administrator's powers under this Schedule;

(b) was taken in reliance on an order under paragraph 71 or 72.

(6) An order may not be made under this paragraph if it would impede or prevent the implementation of—
(a) a voluntary arrangement approved under Part I,
(b) a compromise or arrangement sanctioned under Part 26 of the Companies Act 2006 (arrangements and reconstructions),
(ba) a cross-border merger within the meaning of regulation 2 of the Companies (Cross-Border Mergers) Regulations 2007, or
(c) proposals or a revision approved under paragraph 53 or 54 more than 28 days before the day on which the application for the order under this paragraph is made.

Misfeasance

75. (1) The court may examine the conduct of a person who—
(a) is or purports to be the administrator of a company, or
(b) has been or has purported to be the administrator of a company.
(2) An examination under this paragraph may be held only on the application of—
(a) the official receiver,
(b) the administrator of the company,
(c) the liquidator of the company,
(d) a creditor of the company, or
(e) a contributory of the company.
(3) An application under sub-paragraph (2) must allege that the administrator—
(a) has misapplied or retained money or other property of the company,
(b) has become accountable for money or other property of the company,
(c) has breached a fiduciary or other duty in relation to the company, or
(d) has been guilty of misfeasance.
(4) On an examination under this paragraph into a person's conduct the court may order him—
(a) to repay, restore or account for money or property;
(b) to pay interest;
(c) to contribute a sum to the company's property by way of compensation for breach of duty or misfeasance.
(5) In sub-paragraph (3) "administrator" includes a person who purports or has purported to be a company's administrator.
(6) An application under sub-paragraph (2) may be made in respect of an administrator who has been discharged under paragraph 98 only with the permission of the court.

ENDING ADMINISTRATION

Automatic end of administration

76. (1) The appointment of an administrator shall cease to have effect at the end of the period of one year beginning with the date on which it takes effect.
(2) But—
(a) on the application of an administrator the court may by order extend his term of office for a specified period, and
(b) an administrator's term of office may be extended for a specified period not exceeding six months by consent.

77. (1) An order of the court under paragraph 76—
(a) may be made in respect of an administrator whose term of office has already been extended by order or by consent, but
(b) may not be made after the expiry of the administrator's term of office.
(2) Where an order is made under paragraph 76 the administrator shall as soon as is reasonably practicable notify the registrar of companies.
(3) An administrator who fails without reasonable excuse to comply with sub-paragraph (2) commits an offence.

78. (1) In paragraph 76(2)(b) "consent" means consent of—
(a) each secured creditor of the company, and
(b) if the company has unsecured debts, creditors whose debts amount to more than 50% of the company's unsecured debts, disregarding debts of any creditor who does not respond to an invitation to give or withhold consent.

(2) But where the administrator has made a statement under paragraph 52(1)(b) "consent" means—
(a) consent of each secured creditor of the company, or
(b) if the administrator thinks that a distribution may be made to preferential creditors, consent of—
(i) each secured creditor of the company, and
(ii) preferential creditors whose debts amount to more than 50% of the preferential debts of the company, disregarding debts of any creditor who does not respond to an invitation to give or withhold consent.
(3) Consent for the purposes of paragraph 76(2)(b) may be—
(a) written, or
(b) signified at a creditors' meeting.
(4) An administrator's term of office—
(a) may be extended by consent only once,
(b) may not be extended by consent after extension by order of the court, and
(c) may not be extended by consent after expiry.
(5) Where an administrator's term of office is extended by consent he shall as soon as is reasonably practicable—
(a) file notice of the extension with the court, and
(b) notify the registrar of companies.
(6) An administrator who fails without reasonable excuse to comply with sub-paragraph (5) commits an offence.

Court ending administration on application of administrator

79. (1) On the application of the administrator of a company the court may provide for the appointment of an administrator of the company to cease to have effect from a specified time.
(2) The administrator of a company shall make an application under this paragraph if—
(a) he thinks the purpose of administration cannot be achieved in relation to the company,
(b) he thinks the company should not have entered administration, or
(c) a creditors' meeting requires him to make an application under this paragraph.
(3) The administrator of a company shall make an application under this paragraph if—
(a) the administration is pursuant to an administration order, and
(b) the administrator thinks that the purpose of administration has been sufficiently achieved in relation to the company.
(4) On an application under this paragraph the court may—
(a) adjourn the hearing conditionally or unconditionally;
(b) dismiss the application;
(c) make an interim order;
(d) make any order it thinks appropriate (whether in addition to, in consequence of or instead of the order applied for).

Termination of administration where objective achieved

80. (1) This paragraph applies where an administrator of a company is appointed under paragraph 14 or 22.
(2) If the administrator thinks that the purpose of administration has been sufficiently achieved in relation to the company he may file a notice in the prescribed form—
(a) with the court, and
(b) with the registrar of companies.
(3) The administrator's appointment shall cease to have effect when the requirements of sub- paragraph (2) are satisfied.
(4) Where the administrator files a notice he shall within the prescribed period send a copy to every creditor of the company of whose claim and address he is aware.
(5) The rules may provide that the administrator is taken to have complied with sub-paragraph
(4) if before the end of the prescribed period he publishes in the prescribed manner a notice undertaking to provide a copy of the notice under sub-paragraph (2) to any creditor of the company who applies in writing to a specified address.

(6) An administrator who fails without reasonable excuse to comply with sub-paragraph (4) commits an offence.

Court ending administration on application of creditor

81. (1) On the application of a creditor of a company the court may provide for the appointment of an administrator of the company to cease to have effect at a specified time.
(2) An application under this paragraph must allege an improper motive—
(a) in the case of an administrator appointed by administration order, on the part of the applicant for the order, or
(b) in any other case, on the part of the person who appointed the administrator.
(3) On an application under this paragraph the court may—
(a) adjourn the hearing conditionally or unconditionally;
(b) dismiss the application;
(c) make an interim order;
(d) make any order it thinks appropriate (whether in addition to, in consequence of or instead of the order applied for).

Public interest winding-up

82. (1) This paragraph applies where a winding-up order is made for the winding up of a company in administration on a petition presented under—
(a) section 124A (public interest), (aa) section 124B (SEs), or
(b) section 367 of the Financial Services and Markets Act 2000 (petition by Financial Conduct or Prudential Regulation Authority).
(2) This paragraph also applies where a provisional liquidator of a company in administration is appointed following the presentation of a petition under any of the provisions listed in sub-paragraph (1).
(3) The court shall order—
(a) that the appointment of the administrator shall cease to have effect, or
(b) that the appointment of the administrator shall continue to have effect.
(4) If the court makes an order under sub-paragraph (3)(b) it may also—
(a) specify which of the powers under this Schedule are to be exercisable by the administrator, and
(b) order that this Schedule shall have effect in relation to the administrator with specified modifications.

Moving from administration to creditors' voluntary liquidation

83. (1) This paragraph applies in England and Wales where the administrator of a company thinks—
(a) that the total amount which each secured creditor of the company is likely to receive has been paid to him or set aside for him, and
(b) that a distribution will be made to unsecured creditors of the company (if there are any).
(2) This paragraph applies in Scotland where the administrator of a company thinks—
(a) that each secured creditor of the company will receive payment in respect of his debt, and
(b) that a distribution will be made to unsecured creditors (if there are any).
(3) The administrator may send to the registrar of companies a notice that this paragraph applies.
(4) On receipt of a notice under sub-paragraph (3) the registrar shall register it.
(5) If an administrator sends a notice under sub-paragraph (3) he shall as soon as is reasonably practicable—
(a) file a copy of the notice with the court, and
(b) send a copy of the notice to each creditor of whose claim and address he is aware.
(6) On the registration of a notice under sub-paragraph (3)—
(a) the appointment of an administrator in respect of the company shall cease to have effect, and
(b) the company shall be wound up as if a resolution for voluntary winding up under section 84 were passed on the day on which the notice is registered.

(7) The liquidator for the purposes of the winding up shall be—
(a) a person nominated by the creditors of the company in the prescribed manner and within the prescribed period, or
(b) if no person is nominated under paragraph (a), the administrator.

(8) In the application of Part IV to a winding up by virtue of this paragraph—
(a) section 85 shall not apply,
(b) section 86 shall apply as if the reference to the time of the passing of the resolution for voluntary winding up were a reference to the beginning of the date of registration of the notice under sub-paragraph (3),
(c) section 89 does not apply,
(d) sections 98, 99 and 100 shall not apply,
(e) section 129 shall apply as if the reference to the time of the passing of the resolution for voluntary winding up were a reference to the beginning of the date of registration of the notice under sub-paragraph (3), and
(f) any creditors' committee which is in existence immediately before the company ceases to be in administration shall continue in existence after that time as if appointed as a liquidation committee under section 101.

Moving from administration to dissolution

84. (1) If the administrator of a company thinks that the company has no property which might permit a distribution to its creditors, he shall send a notice to that effect to the registrar of companies.

(2) The court may on the application of the administrator of a company disapply sub-paragraph (1) in respect of the company.

(3) On receipt of a notice under sub-paragraph (1) the registrar shall register it.

(4) On the registration of a notice in respect of a company under sub-paragraph (1) the appointment of an administrator of the company shall cease to have effect.

(5) If an administrator sends a notice under sub-paragraph (1) he shall as soon as is reasonably practicable—
(a) file a copy of the notice with the court, and
(b) send a copy of the notice to each creditor of whose claim and address he is aware.

(6) At the end of the period of three months beginning with the date of registration of a notice in respect of a company under sub-paragraph (1) the company is deemed to be dissolved.

(7) On an application in respect of a company by the administrator or another interested person the court may—
(a) extend the period specified in sub-paragraph (6),
(b) suspend that period, or
(c) disapply sub-paragraph (6).

(8) Where an order is made under sub-paragraph (7) in respect of a company the administrator shall as soon as is reasonably practicable notify the registrar of companies.

(9) An administrator commits an offence if he fails without reasonable excuse to comply with sub-paragraph (5).

Discharge of administration order where administration ends

85. (1) This paragraph applies where—
(a) the court makes an order under this Schedule providing for the appointment of an administrator of a company to cease to have effect, and
(b) the administrator was appointed by administration order.

(2) The court shall discharge the administration order.

Notice to Companies Registrar where administration ends

86. (1) This paragraph applies where the court makes an order under this Schedule providing for the appointment of an administrator to cease to have effect.

(2) The administrator shall send a copy of the order to the registrar of companies within the period of 14 days beginning with the date of the order.

(3) An administrator who fails without reasonable excuse to comply with sub-paragraph (2) commits an offence.

REPLACING ADMINISTRATOR

Resignation of administrator

87. (1) An administrator may resign only in prescribed circumstances.
(2) Where an administrator may resign he may do so only—
(a) in the case of an administrator appointed by administration order, by notice in writing to the court,
(b) in the case of an administrator appointed under paragraph 14, by notice in writing to holder of the floating charge by virtue of which the appointment was made,
(c) in the case of an administrator appointed under paragraph 22(1), by notice in writing to the company, or
(d) in the case of an administrator appointed under paragraph 22(2), by notice in writing to the directors of the company.

Removal of administrator from office

88. The court may by order remove an administrator from office.

Administrator ceasing to be qualified

89. (1) The administrator of a company shall vacate office if he ceases to be qualified to act as an insolvency practitioner in relation to the company.
(2) Where an administrator vacates office by virtue of sub-paragraph (1) he shall give notice in writing—
(a) in the case of an administrator appointed by administration order, to the court,
(b) in the case of an administrator appointed under paragraph 14, to the holder of the floating charge by virtue of which the appointment was made,
(c) in the case of an administrator appointed under paragraph 22(1), to the company, or
(d) in the case of an administrator appointed under paragraph 22(2), to the directors of the company.
(3) An administrator who fails without reasonable excuse to comply with sub-paragraph (2) commits an offence.

Supplying vacancy in office of administrator

90. Paragraphs 91 to 95 apply where an administrator—
(a) dies,
(b) resigns,
(c) is removed from office under paragraph 88, or
(d) vacates office under paragraph 89.

91. (1) Where the administrator was appointed by administration order, the court may replace the administrator on an application under this sub-paragraph made by—
(a) a creditors' committee of the company,
(b) the company,
(c) the directors of the company,
(d) one or more creditors of the company, or
(e) where more than one person was appointed to act jointly or concurrently as the administrator, any of those persons who remains in office.
(2) But an application may be made in reliance on sub-paragraph (1)(b) to (d) only where—
(a) there is no creditors' committee of the company,
(b) the court is satisfied that the creditors' committee or a remaining administrator is not taking reasonable steps to make a replacement, or
(c) the court is satisfied that for another reason it is right for the application to be made.

92. Where the administrator was appointed under paragraph 14 the holder of the floating charge by virtue of which the appointment was made may replace the administrator.

93. (1) Where the administrator was appointed under paragraph 22(1) by the company it may replace the administrator.
(2) A replacement under this paragraph may be made only—
(a) with the consent of each person who is the holder of a qualifying floating charge in respect of the company's property, or

(b) where consent is withheld, with the permission of the court.

94. (1) Where the administrator was appointed under paragraph 22(2) the directors of the company may replace the administrator.

(2) A replacement under this paragraph may be made only—

(a) with the consent of each person who is the holder of a qualifying floating charge in respect of the company's property, or

(b) where consent is withheld, with the permission of the court.

95. The court may replace an administrator on the application of a person listed in paragraph 91(1) if the court—

(a) is satisfied that a person who is entitled to replace the administrator under any of paragraphs 92 to 94 is not taking reasonable steps to make a replacement, or

(b) that for another reason it is right for the court to make the replacement.

Substitution of administrator: competing floating charge-holder

96. (1) This paragraph applies where an administrator of a company is appointed under paragraph 14 by the holder of a qualifying floating charge in respect of the company's property.

(2) The holder of a prior qualifying floating charge in respect of the company's property may apply to the court for the administrator to be replaced by an administrator nominated by the holder of the prior floating charge.

(3) One floating charge is prior to another for the purposes of this paragraph if—

(a) it was created first, or

(b) it is to be treated as having priority in accordance with an agreement to which the holder of each floating charge was party.

(4) Sub-paragraph (3) shall have effect in relation to Scotland as if the following were substituted for paragraph (a)—

"(a) it has priority of ranking in accordance with section 464(4)(b) of the Companies Act 1985,".

Substitution of administrator appointed by company or directors: creditors' meeting

97. (1) This paragraph applies where—

(a) an administrator of a company is appointed by a company or directors under paragraph 22, and

(b) there is no holder of a qualifying floating charge in respect of the company's property.

(2) A creditors' meeting may replace the administrator.

(3) A creditors' meeting may act under sub-paragraph (2) only if the new administrator's written consent to act is presented to the meeting before the replacement is made.

Vacation of office: discharge from liability

98. (1) Where a person ceases to be the administrator of a company (whether because he vacates office by reason of resignation, death or otherwise, because he is removed from office or because his appointment ceases to have effect) he is discharged from liability in respect of any action of his as administrator.

(2) The discharge provided by sub-paragraph (1) takes effect—

(a) in the case of an administrator who dies, on the filing with the court of notice of his death,

(b) in the case of an administrator appointed under paragraph 14 or 22, at a time appointed by resolution of the creditors' committee or, if there is no committee, by resolution of the creditors, or

(c) in any case, at a time specified by the court.

(3) For the purpose of the application of sub-paragraph (2)(b) in a case where the administrator has made a statement under paragraph 52(1)(b), a resolution shall be taken as passed if (and only if) passed with the approval of—

(a) each secured creditor of the company, or

(b) if the administrator has made a distribution to preferential creditors or thinks that a distribution may be made to preferential creditors—

(i) each secured creditor of the company, and

(ii) preferential creditors whose debts amount to more than 50% of the preferential debts of the company, disregarding debts of any creditor who does not respond to an invitation to give or withhold approval.

(4) Discharge—

(a) applies to liability accrued before the discharge takes effect, and

(b) does not prevent the exercise of the court's powers under paragraph 75.

Vacation of office: charges and liabilities

99. (1) This paragraph applies where a person ceases to be the administrator of a company (whether because he vacates office by reason of resignation, death or otherwise, because he is removed from office or because his appointment ceases to have effect).

(2) In this paragraph—
"the former administrator" means the person referred to in sub-paragraph (1), and "cessation" means the time when he ceases to be the company's administrator.

(3) The former administrator's remuneration and expenses shall be—

(a) charged on and payable out of property of which he had custody or control immediately before cessation, and

(b) payable in priority to any security to which paragraph 70 applies.

(4) A sum payable in respect of a debt or liability arising out of a contract entered into by the former administrator or a predecessor before cessation shall be—

(a) charged on and payable out of property of which the former administrator had custody or control immediately before cessation, and

(b) payable in priority to any charge arising under sub-paragraph (3).

(5) Sub-paragraph (4) shall apply to a liability arising under a contract of employment which was adopted by the former administrator or a predecessor before cessation; and for that purpose—

(a) action taken within the period of 14 days after an administrator's appointment shall not be taken to amount or contribute to the adoption of a contract,

(b) no account shall be taken of a liability which arises, or in so far as it arises, by reference to anything which is done or which occurs before the adoption of the contract of employment, and

(c) no account shall be taken of a liability to make a payment other than wages or salary.

(6) In sub-paragraph (5)(c) "wages or salary" includes—

(a) a sum payable in respect of a period of holiday (for which purpose the sum shall be treated as relating to the period by reference to which the entitlement to holiday accrued),

(b) a sum payable in respect of a period of absence through illness or other good cause,

(c) a sum payable in lieu of holiday, and

(e) a contribution to an occupational pension scheme.

GENERAL

Joint and concurrent administrators

100. (1) In this Schedule—

(a) a reference to the appointment of an administrator of a company includes a reference to the appointment of a number of persons to act jointly or concurrently as the administrator of a company, and

(b) a reference to the appointment of a person as administrator of a company includes a reference to the appointment of a person as one of a number of persons to act jointly or concurrently as the administrator of a company.

(2) The appointment of a number of persons to act as administrator of a company must specify—

(a) which functions (if any) are to be exercised by the persons appointed acting jointly, and

(b) which functions (if any) are to be exercised by any or all of the persons appointed.

101. (1) This paragraph applies where two or more persons are appointed to act jointly as the administrator of a company.

(2) A reference to the administrator of the company is a reference to those persons acting jointly.

(3) But a reference to the administrator of a company in paragraphs 87 to 99 of this Schedule is a reference to any or all of the persons appointed to act jointly.

(4) Where an offence of omission is committed by the administrator, each of the persons appointed to act jointly—

(a) commits the offence, and

(b) may be proceeded against and punished individually.

(5) The reference in paragraph 45(1)(a) to the name of the administrator is a reference to the name of each of the persons appointed to act jointly.

(6) Where persons are appointed to act jointly in respect of only some of the functions of the administrator of a company, this paragraph applies only in relation to those functions.

102. (1) This paragraph applies where two or more persons are appointed to act concurrently as the administrator of a company.

(2) A reference to the administrator of a company in this Schedule is a reference to any of the persons appointed (or any combination of them).

103. (1) Where a company is in administration, a person may be appointed to act as administrator jointly or concurrently with the person or persons acting as the administrator of the company.

(2) Where a company entered administration by administration order, an appointment under sub-paragraph (1) must be made by the court on the application of—

(a) a person or group listed in paragraph 12(1)(a) to (e), or

(b) the person or persons acting as the administrator of the company.

(3) Where a company entered administration by virtue of an appointment under paragraph 14, an appointment under sub-paragraph (1) must be made by—

(a) the holder of the floating charge by virtue of which the appointment was made, or

(b) the court on the application of the person or persons acting as the administrator of the company.

(4) Where a company entered administration by virtue of an appointment under paragraph 22(1), an appointment under sub-paragraph (1) above must be made either by the court on the application of the person or persons acting as the administrator of the company or—

(a) by the company, and

(b) with the consent of each person who is the holder of a qualifying floating charge in respect of the company's property or, where consent is withheld, with the permission of the court.

(5) Where a company entered administration by virtue of an appointment under paragraph 22(2), an appointment under sub-paragraph (1) must be made either by the court on the application of the person or persons acting as the administrator of the company or—

(a) by the directors of the company, and

(b) with the consent of each person who is the holder of a qualifying floating charge in respect of the company's property or, where consent is withheld, with the permission of the court.

(6) An appointment under sub-paragraph (1) may be made only with the consent of the person or persons acting as the administrator of the company.

Presumption of validity

104. An act of the administrator of a company is valid in spite of a defect in his appointment or qualification.

Majority decision of directors

105. A reference in this Schedule to something done by the directors of a company includes a reference to the same thing done by a majority of the directors of a company.

Penalties

106. (1) A person who is guilty of an offence under this Schedule is liable to a fine (in accordance with section 430 and Schedule 10).

(2) A person who is guilty of an offence under any of the following paragraphs of this Schedule is liable to a daily default fine (in accordance with section 430 and Schedule 10)—
(a) paragraph 20,
(b) paragraph 32,
(c) paragraph 46,
(d) paragraph 48,
(e) paragraph 49,
(f) paragraph 51,
(g) paragraph 53,
(h) paragraph 54,
(i) paragraph 56,
(j) paragraph 71,
(k) paragraph 72,
(l) paragraph 77,
(m) paragraph 78,
(n) paragraph 80,
(o) paragraph 84,
(p) paragraph 86, and
(q) paragraph 89.

Extension of time limit

107. (1) Where a provision of this Schedule provides that a period may be varied in accordance with this paragraph, the period may be varied in respect of a company—
(a) by the court, and
(b) on the application of the administrator.
(2) A time period may be extended in respect of a company under this paragraph—
(a) more than once, and
(b) after expiry.

108. (1) A period specified in paragraph 49(5), 50(1)(b) or 51(2) may be varied in respect of a company by the administrator with consent.
(2) In sub-paragraph (1) “consent” means consent of—
(a) each secured creditor of the company, and
(b) if the company has unsecured debts, creditors whose debts amount to more than 50% of the company’s unsecured debts, disregarding debts of any creditor who does not respond to an invitation to give or withhold consent.
(3) But where the administrator has made a statement under paragraph 52(1)(b) “consent” means—
(a) consent of each secured creditor of the company, or
(b) if the administrator thinks that a distribution may be made to preferential creditors, consent of—
(i) each secured creditor of the company, and
(ii) preferential creditors whose debts amount to more than 50% of the total preferential debts of the company, disregarding debts of any creditor who does not respond to an invitation to give or withhold consent.
(4) Consent for the purposes of sub-paragraph (1) may be—
(a) written, or
(b) signified at a creditors’ meeting.
(5) The power to extend under sub-paragraph (1)—
(a) may be exercised in respect of a period only once,
(b) may not be used to extend a period by more than 28 days,
(c) may not be used to extend a period which has been extended by the court, and
(d) may not be used to extend a period after expiry.

109. Where a period is extended under paragraph 107 or 108, a reference to the period shall be taken as a reference to the period as extended.

Amendment of provision about time

110. (1) The Secretary of State may by order amend a provision of this Schedule which—
(a) requires anything to be done within a specified period of time,

(b) prevents anything from being done after a specified time, or
(c) requires a specified minimum period of notice to be given.

(2) An order under this paragraph—
(a) must be made by statutory instrument, and
(b) shall be subject to annulment in pursuance of a resolution of either House of Parliament.

Interpretation

111. (1) In this Schedule—
"administrative receiver" has the meaning given by section 251,
"administrator" has the meaning given by paragraph 1 and, where the context requires, includes a reference to a former administrator,
"correspondence" includes correspondence by telephonic or other electronic means,
"creditors' meeting" has the meaning given by paragraph 50,
"enters administration" has the meaning given by paragraph 1,
"floating charge" means a charge which is a floating charge on its creation,
"in administration" has the meaning given by paragraph 1,
"hire-purchase agreement" includes a conditional sale agreement, a chattel leasing agreement and a retention of title agreement,
"holder of a qualifying floating charge" in respect of a company's property has the meaning given by paragraph 14,
"market value" means the amount which would be realised on a sale of property in the open market by a willing vendor,
"the purpose of administration" means an objective specified in paragraph 3, and
"unable to pay its debts" has the meaning given by section 123.

(1A) In this Schedule, "company" means—
(a) a company registered under the Companies Act 2006 in England and Wales or Scotland,
(b) a company incorporated in an EEA State other than the United Kingdom, or
(c) a company not incorporated in an EEA State but having its centre of main interests in a member State other than Denmark.

(1B) In sub-paragraph (1A), in relation to a company, "centre of main interests" has the same meaning as in the EC Regulation and, in the absence of proof to the contrary, is presumed to be the place of its registered office (within the meaning of that Regulation).

...

(3) In this Schedule a reference to action includes a reference to inaction.

Non-UK companies

111A. A company incorporated outside the United Kingdom that has a principal place of business in Northern Ireland may not enter administration under this Schedule unless it also has a principal place of business in England and Wales or Scotland (or both in England and Wales and in Scotland).

Scotland

112. In the application of this Schedule to Scotland—
(a) a reference to filing with the court is a reference to lodging in court, and
(b) a reference to a charge is a reference to a right in security.

113. Where property in Scotland is disposed of under paragraph 70 or 71, the administrator shall grant to the disponee an appropriate document of transfer or conveyance of the property, and—
(a) that document, or
(b) recording, intimation or registration of that document (where recording, intimation or registration of the document is a legal requirement for completion of title to the property),

has the effect of disencumbering the property of or, as the case may be, freeing the property from, the security.

114. In Scotland, where goods in the possession of a company under a hire-purchase agreement are disposed of under paragraph 72, the disposal has the effect of extinguishing as against the disponee all rights of the owner of the goods under the agreement.

115. (1) In Scotland, the administrator of a company may make, in or towards the satisfaction of the debt secured by the floating charge, a payment to the holder of a floating charge which has attached to the property subject to the charge.

(1A) In Scotland, sub-paragraph (1B) applies in connection with the giving by the court of permission as provided for in paragraph 65(3)(b).

(1B) On the giving by the court of such permission, any floating charge granted by the company shall, unless it has already so attached, attach to the property which is subject to the charge.

(2) In Scotland, where the administrator thinks that the company has insufficient property to enable a distribution to be made to unsecured creditors other than by virtue of section 176A(2)(a), he may file a notice to that effect with the registrar of companies.

(3) On delivery of the notice to the registrar of companies, any floating charge granted by the company shall, unless it has already so attached, attach to the property which is subject to the charge.

(4) Attachment of a floating charge under sub-paragraph (1B) or (3) has effect as if the charge is a fixed security over the property to which it has attached.

116. In Scotland, the administrator in making any payment in accordance with paragraph 115 shall make such payment subject to the rights of any of the following categories of persons (which rights shall, except to the extent provided in any instrument, have the following order of priority)—

(a) the holder of any fixed security which is over property subject to the floating charge and which ranks prior to, or pari passu with, the floating charge,

(b) creditors in respect of all liabilities and expenses incurred by or on behalf of the administrator,

(c) the administrator in respect of his liabilities, expenses and remuneration and any indemnity to which he is entitled out of the property of the company,

(d) the preferential creditors entitled to payment in accordance with paragraph 65,

(e) the holder of the floating charge in accordance with the priority of that charge in relation to any other floating charge which has attached, and

(f) the holder of a fixed security, other than one referred to in paragraph (a), which is over property subject to the floating charge.

SCHEDULE 1 **Sections 14, 42**

POWERS OF ADMINISTRATOR OR ADMINISTRATIVE RECEIVER

1. Power to take possession of, collect and get in the property of the company and, for that purpose, to take such proceedings as may seem to him expedient.
2. Power to sell or otherwise dispose of the property of the company by public auction or private contract or, in Scotland, to sell, hire out or otherwise dispose of the property of the company by public roup or private bargain.
3. Power to raise or borrow money and grant security therefor over the property of the company.
4. Power to appoint a solicitor or accountant or other professionally qualified person to assist him in the performance of his functions.
5. Power to bring or defend any action or other legal proceedings in the name and on behalf of the company.
6. Power to refer to arbitration any question affecting the company.
7. Power to effect and maintain insurances in respect of the business and property of the company.
8. Power to use the company's seal.
9. Power to do all acts and to execute in the name and on behalf of the company any deed, receipt or other document.
10. Power to draw, accept, make and endorse any bill of exchange or promissory note in the name and on behalf of the company.
11. Power to appoint any agent to do any business which he is unable to do himself or which can more conveniently be done by an agent and power to employ and dismiss employees.
12. Power to do all such things (including the carrying out of works) as may be necessary for the realisation of the property of the company.

13. Power to make any payment which is necessary or incidental to the performance of his functions.
14. Power to carry on the business of the company.
15. Power to establish subsidiaries of the company.
16. Power to transfer to subsidiaries of the company the whole or any part of the business and property of the company.
17. Power to grant or accept a surrender of a lease or tenancy of any of the property of the company, and to take a lease or tenancy of any property required or convenient for the business of the company.
18. Power to make any arrangement or compromise on behalf of the company.
19. Power to call up any uncalled capital of the company.
20. Power to rank and claim in the bankruptcy, insolvency, sequestration or liquidation of any person indebted to the company and to receive dividends, and to accede to trust deeds for the creditors of any such person.
21. Power to present or defend a petition for the winding up of the company.
22. Power to change the situation of the company's registered office.
23. Power to do all other things incidental to the exercise of the foregoing powers.

SCHEDULE 2 **Section 55**

POWERS OF A SCOTTISH RECEIVER (ADDITIONAL TO THOSE CONFERRED ON HIM BY THE INSTRUMENT OF CHARGE)

1. Power to take possession of, collect and get in the property from the company or a liquidator thereof or any other person, and for that purpose, to take such proceedings as may seem to him expedient.
2. Power to sell, hire out or otherwise dispose of the property by public roup or private bargain and with or without advertisement.
3. Power to raise or borrow money and grant security therefor over the property.
4. Power to appoint a solicitor or accountant or other professionally qualified person to assist him in the performance of his functions.
5. Power to bring or defend any action or other legal proceedings in the name and on behalf of the company.
6. Power to refer to arbitration all questions affecting the company.
7. Power to effect and maintain insurances in respect of the business and property of the company.
8. Power to use the company's seal.
9. Power to do all acts and to execute in the name and on behalf of the company any deed, receipt or other document.
10. Power to to draw, accept, make and endorse any bill of exchange or promissory note in the name and on behalf of the company.
11. Power to to appoint any agent to do any business which he is unable to do himself or which can more conveniently be done by an agent, and power to employ and dismiss employees.
12. Power to do all such things (including the carrying out of works), as may be necessary for the realisation of the property.
13. Power to make any payment which is necessary or incidental to the performance of his functions.
14. Power to carry on the business of the company or any part of it.
15. Power to grant or accept a surrender of a lease or tenancy of any of the property, and to take a lease or tenancy of any property required or convenient for the business of the company.
16. Power to make any arrangement or compromise on behalf of the company.
17. Power to call up any uncalled capital of the company.
18. Power to to establish subsidiaries of the company.
19. Power to to transfer to subsidiaries of the company the business of the company or any part of it and any of the property.
20. Power to rank and claim in the bankruptcy, insolvency, sequestration or liquidation of any person or company indebted to the company and to receive dividends, and to accede to trust deeds for creditors of any such person.
21. Power to present or defend a petition for the winding up of the company.
22. Power to change the situation of the company's registered office.
23. Power to do all other things incidental to the exercise of the powers mentioned in section 55(1) of this Act or above in this Schedule.

SCHEDULE 2A

EXCEPTIONS TO PROHIBITION ON APPOINTMENT OF ADMINISTRATIVE RECEIVER: SUPPLEMENTARY PROVISIONS

Capital market arrangement

1. (1) For the purposes of section 72B an arrangement is a capital market arrangement if—
   (a) it involves a grant of security to a person holding it as trustee for a person who holds a capital market investment issued by a party to the arrangement, or
   (aa) it involves a grant of security to—
      (i) a party to the arrangement who issues a capital market investment, or
      (ii) a person who holds the security as trustee for a party to the arrangement in connection with the issue of a capital market investment, or
   (ab) it involves a grant of security to a person who holds the security as trustee for a party to the arrangement who agrees to provide finance to another party, or
   (b) at least one party guarantees the performance of obligations of another party, or
   (c) at least one party provides security in respect of the performance of obligations of another party, or
   (d) the arrangement involves an investment of a kind described in articles 83 to 85 of the Financial Services and Markets Act 2000 (Regulated Activities) Order 2001 (options, futures and contracts for differences).
   (2) For the purposes of sub-paragraph (1)—
   (a) a reference to holding as trustee includes a reference to holding as nominee or agent,
   (b) a reference to holding for a person who holds a capital market investment includes a reference to holding for a number of persons at least one of whom holds a capital market investment,
   (c) a person holds a capital market investment if he has a legal or beneficial interest in it, and
   (d) the reference to the provision of finance includes the provision of an indemnity.
   (3) In section 72B(1) and this paragraph "party" to an arrangement includes a party to an agreement which—
   (a) forms part of the arrangement,
   (b) provides for the raising of finance as part of the arrangement, or
   (c) is necessary for the purposes of implementing the arrangement.

Capital market investment

2. (1) For the purposes of section 72B an investment is a capital market investment if it—
   (a) is within article 77 or 77A of the Financial Services and Markets Act 2000 (Regulated Activities) Order 2001 (debt instruments), and
   (b) is rated, listed or traded or designed to be rated, listed or traded.
   (2) In sub-paragraph (1)—
   "rated" means rated for the purposes of investment by an internationally recognised rating agency,
   "listed" means admitted to the official list within the meaning given by section 103(1) of the Financial Services and Markets Act 2000 (interpretation), and
   "traded" means admitted to trading on a market established under the rules of a recognised investment exchange or on a foreign market.
   (3) In sub-paragraph (2)—
   "recognised investment exchange" has the meaning given by section 285 of the Financial Services and Markets Act 2000 (recognised investment exchange), and
   "foreign market" has the same meaning as "relevant market" in article 67(2) of the Financial Services and Markets Act 2000 (Financial Promotion) Order 2001 (foreign markets).
3. (1) An investment is also a capital market investment for the purposes of section 72B if it consists of a bond or commercial paper issued to one or more of the following—
   (a) an investment professional within the meaning of article 19(5) of the Financial Services and Markets Act 2000 (Financial Promotion) Order 2001,
   (b) a person who is, when the agreement mentioned in section 72B(1) is entered into, a certified high net worth individual in relation to a communication within the meaning of article 48(2) of that order,

(c) a person to whom article 49(2) of that order applies (high net worth company, &c.),
(d) a person who is, when the agreement mentioned in section 72B(1) is entered into, a certified sophisticated investor in relation to a communication within the meaning of article 50(1) of that order, and
(e) a person in a State other than the United Kingdom who under the law of that State is not prohibited from investing in bonds or commercial paper.

(2) In sub-paragraph (1)—
"bond" shall be construed in accordance with article 77 of the Financial Services and Markets Act 2000 (Regulated Activities) Order 2001 and includes any instrument falling within Article 77A of that Order, and
"commercial paper" has the meaning given by article 9(3) of that order.

(3) For the purposes of sub-paragraph (1)—
(a) in applying article 19(5) of the Financial Promotion Order for the purposes of sub-paragraph (1)(a)—
(i) in article 19(5)(b), ignore the words after "exempt person",
(ii) in article 19(5)(c)(i), for the words from "the controlled activity" to the end substitute "a controlled activity", and
(iii) in article 19(5)(e) ignore the words from "where the communication" to the end, and
(b) in applying article 49(2) of that order for the purposes of sub-paragraph (1)(c), ignore article 49(2)(e).

"Agreement"

4. For the purposes of sections 72B and 72E and this Schedule "agreement" includes an agreement or undertaking effected by—
(a) contract,
(b) deed, or
(c) any other instrument intended to have effect in accordance with the law of England and Wales, Scotland or another jurisdiction.

Debt

5. The debt of at least £50 million referred to in section 72B(1)(a) or 72E(2)(a)—
(a) may be incurred at any time during the life of the capital market arrangement or financed project, and
(b) may be expressed wholly or partly in foreign currency (in which case the sterling equivalent shall be calculated as at the time when the arrangement is entered into or the project begins).

Step-in rights

6. (1) For the purposes of sections 72C to 72E a project has "step-in rights" if a person who provides finance in connection with the project has a conditional entitlement under an agreement to—
(a) assume sole or principal responsibility under an agreement for carrying out all or part of the project, or
(b) make arrangements for carrying out all or part of the project.

(2) In sub-paragraph (1) a reference to the provision of finance includes a reference to the provision of an indemnity.

Project company

7. (1) For the purposes of sections 72C to 72E a company is a "project company" of a project if—
(a) it holds property for the purpose of the project,
(b) it has sole or principal responsibility under an agreement for carrying out all or part of the project,
(c) it is one of a number of companies which together carry out the project,
(d) it has the purpose of supplying finance to enable the project to be carried out, or
(e) it is the holding company of a company within any of paragraphs (a) to (d).

(2) But a company is not a "project company" of a project if—
(a) it performs a function within sub-paragraph (1)(a) to (d) or is within sub-paragraph (1)(e), but
(b) it also performs a function which is not—
(i) within sub-paragraph (1)(a) to (d),
(ii) related to a function within sub-paragraph (1)(a) to (d), or
(iii) related to the project.
(3) For the purposes of this paragraph a company carries out all or part of a project whether or not it acts wholly or partly through agents.

"Resources"

8. In section 72C "resources" includes—
(a) funds (including payment for the provision of services or facilities),
(b) assets,
(c) professional skill,
(d) the grant of a concession or franchise, and
(e) any other commercial resource.

"Public body"

9. (1) In section 72C "public body" means—
(a) a body which exercises public functions,
(b) a body specified for the purposes of this paragraph by the Secretary of State, and
(c) a body within a class specified for the purposes of this paragraph by the Secretary of State.
(2) A specification under sub-paragraph (1) may be—
(a) general, or
(b) for the purpose of the application of section 72C to a specified case.

Regulated business

10. (1) For the purposes of section 72D a business is regulated if it is carried on—
(a) ...
(b) in reliance on a licence under section 7 or 7A of the Gas Act 1986 (transport and supply of gas),
(c) in reliance on a licence granted by virtue of section 41C of that Act (power to prescribe additional licensable activity),
(d) in reliance on a licence under section 6 of the Electricity Act 1989 (supply of electricity),
(e) by a water undertaker,
(f) by a sewerage undertaker,
(g) by a universal service provider within the meaning of Part 3 of the Postal Services Act 2011,
(h) by the Post Office company within the meaning of Part 1 of that Act,
(i) ...
(j) in reliance on a licence under section 8 of the Railways Act 1993 (railway services),
(k) in reliance on a licence exemption under section 7 of that Act (subject to sub-paragraph (2) below),
(l) by the operator of a system of transport which is deemed to be a railway for a purpose of Part I of that Act by virtue of section 81(2) of that Act (tramways, &c.),
(m) by the operator of a vehicle carried on flanged wheels along a system within paragraph (l), or
(n) in reliance on a European licence granted pursuant to a provision contained in any instrument made for the purpose of implementing Council Directive 1995/18/EC dated 19th June 1995 on the licensing of railway undertakings, as amended by

Directive 2001/13/EC dated 26th February 2001 and Directive 2004/49/EC dated 29th April 2004, both of the European Parliament and of the Council, or pursuant to any action taken by an EEA State for that purpose.

(2) Sub-paragraph (1)(k) does not apply to the operator of a railway asset on a railway unless on some part of the railway there is a permitted line speed exceeding 40 kilometres per hour.

(2A) For the purposes of section 72D a business is also regulated to the extent that it consists in the provision of a public electronic communications network or a public electronic communications service.

(2B) In sub-paragraph (1)(n), an "EEA State" means a member State, Norway, Iceland or Liechtenstein.

"Person"

11. A reference to a person in this Schedule includes a reference to a partnership or another unincorporated group of persons.

SCHEDULE 3
OMITTED

SCHEDULE 4 **Sections 165, 167**

POWERS OR LIQUIDATOR IN A WINDING UP

1. Power to pay any class of creditors in full.
2. Power to make any compromise or arrangement with creditors or persons claiming to be creditors, or having or alleging themselves to have any claim (present or future, certain or contingent, ascertained or sounding only in damages) against the company, or whereby the company may be rendered liable.
3. Power to compromise, on such terms as may be agreed—
   (a) all calls and liabilities to calls, all debts and liabilities capable of resulting in debts, and all claims (present or future, certain or contingent, ascertained or sounding only in damages) subsisting or supposed to subsist between the company and a contributory or alleged contributory or other debtor or person apprehending liability to the company, and
   (b) all questions in any way relating to or affecting the assets or the winding up of the company, and take any security for the discharge of any such call, debt, liability or claim and give a complete discharge in respect of it.

3A. Power to bring legal proceedings under section 213, 214, 238, 239, 242, 243 or 423.
4. Power to bring or defend any action or other legal proceeding in the name annd on behalf of the company.
5. Power to carry on the business of the company so far as may be necessary for its beneficial winding up.
6. Power to sell any of the company's property by public auction or private contract with power to transfer the whole of it to any person or to sell the same in parcels.

6A. …

7. Power to do all acts and execute, in the name and on behalf of the company, all deeds, receipts and other documents and for that purpose to use, when necessary, the company's seal.
8. Power to prove, rank and claim in the bankruptcy, insolvency or sequestration of any contributory for any balance against his estate, and to receive dividends in the bankruptcy, insolvency or sequestration in respect of that balance, as a separate debt due from the bankrupt or insolvent, and rateably with the other separate creditors.
9. Power to draw, accept, make and indorse any bill of exchange or promissory note in the name and on behalf of the company, with the same effect with respect to the company's liability as if the bill or note had been drawn, accepted, made or indorsed by or on behalf of the company in the course of its business.
10. Power to raise on the security of the assets of the company any money requisite.
11. Power to take out in his official name letters of administration to any deceased contributory, and to do in his official name any other act necessary for obtaining payment of any money due from a contributory or his estate which cannot conveniently be done in the name of the company.
    In all such cases the money due is deemed, for the purpose of enabling the liquidator to take out the letters of administration or recover the money, to be due to the liquidator himself.

12. Power to appoint an agent to do any business which the liquidator is unable to do himself.
13. Power to do all such other things as may be necessary for winding up the company's affairs and distributing its assets.

SCHEDULES 4ZA–5
OMITTED

SCHEDULE 6 **Section 386**
THE CATEGORIES OF PREFERENTIAL DEBTS

. . .

Category 4: Contributions to occupational pension schemes, etc

8. Any sum which is owed by the debtor and is a sum to which Schedule 4 to the Pension Schemes Act 1993 applies (contributions to occupational pension schemes and state scheme premiums).

Category 5: Remuneration, etc, of employees

9. So much of any amount which—
 (a) is owed by the debtor to a person who is or has been an employee of the debtor, and
 (b) is payable by way of remuneration in respect of the whole or any part of the period of 4 months next before the relevant date,

as does not exceed so much as may be prescribed by order made by the Secretary of State.
10. An amount owed by way of accrued holiday remuneration, in respect of any period of employment before the relevant date, to a person whose employment by the debtor has been terminated, whether before, on or after that date.
11. So much of any sum owed in respect of money advanced for the purpose as has been applied for the payment of a debt which, if it had not been paid, would have been a debt falling within paragraph 9 or 10.
12. So much of any amount which—
 (a) is ordered (whether before or after the relevant date) to be paid by the debtor under the Reserve Forces (Safeguard of Employment) Act 1985, and
 (b) is so ordered in respect of a default made by the debtor before that date in the discharge of his obligations under that Act,

as does no exceed such amount as may be prescribed by order made by the Secretary of State.

Interpretation for Category 5

13. (1) For the purposes of paragraphs 9 to 12, a sum is payable by the debtor to a person by way of remuneration in respect of any period if—
 (a) it is paid as wages or salary (whether payable for time or for piece work or earned wholly or partly by way of commission) in respect of services rendered to the debtor in that period, or
 (b) it is an amount falling within the following sub-paragraph and is payable by the debtor in respect of that period.

(2) An amount falls within this sub-paragraph if it is—
 (a) a guarantee payment under Part III of the Employment Rights Act 1996 (employee without work to do);
 (b) any payment for time off under section 53 (time off to look for work or arrange training) or section 56 (time off for ante-natal care) of that Act or under section 169 of the Trade Union and Labour Relations (Consolidation) Act 1992 (time off for carrying out trade union duties etc);
 (c) remuneration on suspension on medical grounds, or on maternity grounds, under Part VII of the Employment Rights Act 1996; or

(d) remuneration under a protective award under section 189 of the Trade Union and Labour Relations (Consolidation) Act 1992 (redundancy dismissal with compensation).

14. (1) This paragraph relates to a case in which a person's employment has been terminated by or in consequence of his employer going into liquidation or being adjudged bankrupt or (his employer being a company not in liquidation) by or in consequence of—

(a) a receiver being appointed as mentioned in section 40 of this Act (debenture-holders secured by floating charge), or

(b) the appointment of a receiver under section 53(6) or 54(5) of this Act (Scottish company with property subject to floating charge), or

(c) the taking of possession by debenture-holders (so secured), as mentioned in section 754 of the Companies Act 2006.

(2) For the purposes of paragraphs 9 to 12, holiday remuneration is deemed to have accrued to that person in respect of any period of employment if, by virtue of his contract of employment or of any enactment that remuneration would have accrued in respect of that period if his employment had continued until he became entitled to be allowed the holiday.

(3) The reference in sub-paragraph (2) to any enactment includes an order or direction made under an enactment.

15. Without prejudice to paragraphs 13 and 14—

(a) any remuneration payable by the debtor to a person in respect of a period of holiday or of absence from work through sickness or other good cause is deemed to be wages or (as the case may be) salary in respect of services rendered to the debtor in that period, and

(b) references here and in those paragraphs to remuneration in respect of a period of holiday include any sums which, if they had been paid, would have been treated for the purposes of the enactments to social security as earnings in respect of that period.

Category 6: Levies on coal and steel production

15A. Any sums due at the relevant date from the debtor in respect of—

(a) the levies on the production of coal and steel referred to in Articles 49 and 50 of the ECSC Treaty, or

(b) any surcharge for delay provided for in Article 50(3) of that Treaty and Article 6 of Decision 3/52 of the High Authority of the Coal and Steel Community.

Category 6A: Debts owed to the Financial Services Compensation Scheme

15AA. Any debt owed by the debtor to the scheme manager of the Financial Services Compensation Scheme under section 215(2A) of the Financial Services and Markets Act 2000.

Category 7: Deposits covered by Financial Services Compensation Scheme

15B. So much of any amount owed at the relevant date by the debtor in respect of an eligible deposit as does not exceed the compensation that would be payable in respect of the deposit under the Financial Services Compensation Scheme to the person or persons to whom the amount is owed.

Category 8: Other deposits

15BA. So much of any amount owed at the relevant date by the debtor to one or more eligible persons in respect of an eligible deposit as exceeds any compensation that would be payable in respect of the deposit under the Financial Services Compensation Scheme to that person or those persons.

15BB. An amount owed at the relevant date by the debtor to one or more eligible persons in respect of a deposit that—

(a) was made through a non-EEA branch of a credit institution authorised by the competent authority of an EEA state, and

(b) would have been an eligible deposit if it had been made through an EEA branch of that credit institution.

Interpretation for categories 6A, 7 and 8

15C. (A1) In paragraph 15AA "the scheme manager" has the meaning given in section 212(1) of the Financial Services and Markets Act 2000.

(1) In paragraphs 15B to 15BB "eligible deposit" means a deposit in respect of which the person, or any of the persons, to whom it is owed would be eligible for compensation under the Financial Services Compensation Scheme.

(2) For the purposes of those paragraphs and this paragraph a "deposit" means rights of the kind described in—

(a) paragraph 22 of Schedule 2 to the Financial Services and Markets Act 2000 (deposits), or

(b) section 1(2)(b) of the Dormant Bank and Building Society Accounts Act 2008 (balances transferred under that Act to authorised reclaim fund).

(3) In paragraphs 15BA and 15BB, "eligible person" means—

(a) an individual, or

(b) a micro-enterprise, a small enterprise or a medium-sized enterprise, each of those terms having the meaning given in Article 2.1(107) of Directive 2014/59/EU of 15th May 2014 establishing a framework for the recovery and resolution of credit institutions and investment firms.

(4) In paragraph 15BB—

(a) "credit institution" has the meaning given in Article 4.1(1) of the capital requirements regulation;

(b) "EEA branch" means a branch, as defined in Article 4.1(17) of the capital requirements regulation, which is established in an EEA state;

(c) "non-EEA branch" means a branch, as so defined, which is established in a country which is not an EEA state;

and for this purpose "the capital requirements regulation" means Regulation (EU) No 575/2013 of the European Parliament and of the Council of 26th June 2013 on prudential requirements for credit institutions and investment firms and amending Regulation (EU) No 648/2012.

Orders

16. An order under paragraph 9 or 12—

(a) may contain such transitional provisions as may appear to the Secretary of State necessary or expedient;

(b) shall be made by statutory instrument subject to annulment in pursuance of a resolution of either House of Parliament.

SCHEDULES 7–11
OMITTED

COMPANY DIRECTORS DISQUALIFICATION ACT 1986 (1986, c. 46)

Preliminary

1 Disqualification orders: general

(1) In the circumstances specified below in this Act a court may, and under section 6 and 9A shall, make against a person a disqualification order, that is to say an order that for a period specified in the order—

(b) he shall not act as an insolvency practitioner.

(2) In each section of this Act which gives to a court power or, as the case may be, imposes on it the duty to make a disqualification order there is specified the maximum (and, in section 6, the minimum) period of disqualification which may or (as the case may be) must be imposed by means of the order and, unless the court otherwise orders, the period of disqualification so imposed shall begin at the end of the period of 21 days beginning with the date of the order.

(3) Where a disqualification order is made against a person who is already subject to such an order or to a disqualification undertaking, the periods specified in those orders or, as the case may be, in the order and the undertaking shall run concurrently.

(4) A disqualification order may be made on grounds which are or include matters other than criminal convictions, notwithstanding that the person in respect of whom it is to be made may be criminally liable in respect of those matters.

1A Disqualification undertakings: general

(1) In the circumstances specified in sections 7 and 8 the Secretary of State may accept a disqualification undertaking, that is to say an undertaking by any person that, for a period specified in the undertaking, the person—

(a) will not be a director of a company, act as receiver of a company's property or in any way, whether directly or indirectly, be concerned or take part in the promotion, formation or management of a company unless (in each case) he has the leave of a court, and

(b) will not act as an insolvency practitioner.

(2) The maximum period which may be specified in a disqualification undertaking is 15 years; and the minimum period which may be specified in a disqualification undertaking under section 7 is two years.

(3) Where a disqualification undertaking by a person who is already subject to such an undertaking or to a disqualification order is accepted, the periods specified in those undertakings or (as the case may be) the undertaking and the order shall run concurrently.

(4) In determining whether to accept a disqualification undertaking by any person, the Secretary of State may take account of matters other than criminal convictions, notwithstanding that the person may be criminally liable in respect of those matters.

Disqualification for general misconduct in connection with companies

2 Disqualification on conviction of indictable offence

(1) The court may make a disqualification order against a person where he is convicted of an indictable offence (whether on indictment or summarily) in connection with the promotion, formation, management liquidation or striking off of a company with the receivership of a company's property or with his being an administrative receiver of a company.

(2) "The court" for this purpose means—

(a) any court having jurisdiction to wind up the company in relation to which the offence was committed, or

(b) the court by or before which the person is convicted of the offence, or

(c) in the case of a summary conviction in England and Wales, any other magistrates' court acting in the same local justice area;

and for the purposes of this section the definition of "indictable offence" in Schedule 1 to the Interpretation Act 1978 applies for Scotland as it does for England and Wales.

(3) The maximum period of disqualification under this section is—

(a) where the disqualification order is made by a court of summary jurisdiction, 5 years, and

(b) in any other case, 15 years.

3 Disqualification for persistent breaches of companies legislation

(1) The court may made a disqualification order against a person where it appears to it that he has been persistently in default in relation to provisions of the companies legislation requiring any return, account or other document to be filed with, delivered or sent, or notice of any matter to be given, to the registrar of companies.

(2) On an application to the court for an order to be made under this section, the fact that a person has been persistently in default in relation to such provisions as are mentioned above may (without prejudice to its proof in any other manner) be conclusively proved by showing that in the 5 years ending with the date of the application he has been adjudged guilty (whether or not on the same occasion) of three or more defaults in relation to those provisions.

(3) A person is to be treated under subsection (2) as being adjudged guilty of a default in relation to any provision of that legislation if—
(a) he is convicted (whether on indictment or summarily) of an offence consisting in a contravention of or failure to comply with that provision (whether on his own part or on the part of any company), or
(b) a default order is made against him, that is to say an order under any of the following provisions—
(i) section 452 of the Companies Act 2006 (order requiring delivery of company accounts),
(ia) section 456 of that Act (order requiring preparation of revised accounts),
(ii) section 1113 of that Act (enforcement of company's filing obligations),
(iii) section 41 of the Insolvency Act 1986 (enforcement of receiver's or manager's duty to make returns), or
(iv) section 170 of that Act (corresponding provision for liquidator in winding up), in respect of any such contravention of or failure to comply with that provision (whether on his own part or on the part of any company).
(4) In this section "the court" means any court having jurisdiction to wind up any of the companies in relation to which the offence or other default has been or is alleged to have been committed.
(4A) In this section "the companies legislation" means the Companies Acts and Parts 1 to 7 of the Insolvency Act 1986 (company insolvency and winding up).
(5) The maximum period of disqualification under this section is 5 years.

4 Disqualification for fraud, etc., in winding up

(1) The court may make a disqualification order against a person if, in the course of the winding up of a company, it appears that he—
(a) has been guilty of an offence for which he is liable (whether he has ben convicted or not) under section 993 of the Companies Act 2006 (fraudulent trading), or
(b) has otherwise been guilty, while an officer or liquidator of the company receiver of the company's property or administrative receiver of the company, of any fraud in relation to the company or of any breach of his duty as such officer, liquidator, receiver or administrative receiver.
(2) In this section "the court" means any court having jurisdiction to wind up any of the companies in relation to which the offence or other default has been or is alleged to have been committed; and "officer" includes a shadow director.
(3) The maximum period of disqualification under this section is 15 years.

5 Disqualification on summary conviction

(1) An offence counting for the purposes of this section is one of which a person is convicted (either on indictment or summarily) in consequence of a contravention of, or failure to comply with, any provision of the companies legislation requiring a return, account or other document to be filed with, delivered or sent, or notice of any matter to be given, to the registrar of companies (whether the contravention or failure is on the person's own part or on the part of any company).
(2) Where a person is convicted of a summary offence counting for those purposes, the court by which he is convicted (or, in England and Wales, any other magistrates' court acting in the same local justice area) may make a disqualification order against him if the circumstances specified in the next subsection are present.
(3) Those circumstances are that, during the 5 years ending with the date of the conviction, the person has had made against him, or has been convicted of, in total not less than 3 default orders and offences counting for the purposes of this section; and those offences may include that of which he is convicted as mentioned in subsection (2) and any other offence of which he is convicted on the same occasion.
(4) For the purposes of this section—
(a) the definition of "summary offence" in Schedule 1 to the Interpretation Act 1978 applies for Scotland as for England and Wales, and
(b) "default order" means the same as in section 3(3)(b).

(4A) In this section "the companies legislation" means the Companies Acts and Parts 1 to 7 of the Insolvency Act 1986 (company insolvency and winding up).

(5) The maximum period of disqualification under this section is 5 years.

Disqualification for unfitness

6 Duty of court to disqualify unfit directors of insolvent companies

(1) The court shall make a disqualification order against a person in any case where, on an application under this section, it is satisfied—

(a) that he is or has been a director of a company which has at any time become insolvent (whether while he was a director or subsequently), and

(b) that his conduct as a director of that company (either taken alone or taken together with his conduct as a director of any other company or companies) makes him unfit to be concerned in the management of a company.

(2) For the purposes of this section and the next, a company becomes insolvent if—

(a) the company goes into liquidation at a time when its assets are insufficient for the payment of its debts and other liabilities and the expenses of the winding up,

(b) the company enters administration, or

(c) an administrative receiver of the company is appointed;

and references to a person's conduct as a director of any company or companies include, where that company or any of those companies has become insolvent, that person's conduct in relation to any matter connected with or arising out of the insolvency of that company.

(3) In this section and section 7(2), "the court" means—

(a) where the company in question is being or has been wound up by the court, that court,

(b) where the company in question is being or has been wound up voluntarily, any court which has or (as the case may be) had jurisdiction to wind it up,

(c) where neither paragraph (a) nor (b) applies but an administrator or administrative receiver has at any time been appointed in respect of the company in question, any court which has jurisdiction to wind it up

(3A) Sections 117 and 120 of the Insolvency Act 1986 (jurisdiction) shall apply for the purposes of subsection (3) as if the references in the definitions of "registered office" to the presentation of the petition for winding up were references—

(a) in a case within paragraph (b) of that subsection, to the passing of the resolution for voluntary winding up,

(b) in a case within paragraph (c) of that subsection, to the appointment of the administrator or (as the case may be) administrative receiver.

(3B) Nothing in subsection (3) invalidates any proceedings by reason of their being taken in the wrong court; and proceedings—

(a) for or in connection with a disqualification order under this section, or

(b) in connection with a disqualification undertaking accepted under section 7,

may be retained in the court in which the proceedings were commenced, although it may not be the court in which they ought to have been commenced.

(3C) In this section and section 7, "director" includes a shadow director

(4) Under this section the minimum period of disqualification is 2 years, and the maximum period is 15 years.

7 Disqualification order or undertaking; and reporting provisions

(1) If it appears to the Secretary of State that it is expedient in the public interest that a disqualification order under section 6 should be made against any person, an application for the making of such an order against that person may be made—

(a) by the Secretary of State, or

(b) if the Secretary of State so directs in the case of a person who is or has been a director of a company which is being or has been wound up by the court in England and Wales, by the official receiver.

(2) Except with the leave of the court, an application for the making under that section of a disqualification order against any person shall not be made after the end of the period of 2 years beginning with the day on which the company of which that person is or has been a director became insolvent.

(2A) If it appears to the Secretary of State that the conditions mentioned in section 6(1) are satisfied as respects any person who has offered to give him a disqualification undertaking, he may accept the undertaking if it appears to him that it is expedient in the public interest that he should do so (instead of applying, or proceeding with an application, for a disqualification order).

(3) If it appears to the office-holder responsible under this section, that is to say—

(a) in the case of a company which is being wound up by the court in England and Wales, the official receiver,

(b) in the case of a company which is being wound up otherwise, the liquidator,

(c) in the case of a company which is in administration, the administrator, or

(d) in the case of a company of which there is an administrative receiver, that receiver,

that the conditions mentioned in section 6(1) are satisfied as respects a person who is or has been a director of that company, the office-holder shall forthwith report the matter to the Secretary of State.

(4) The Secretary of State or the official receiver may require the liquidator, administrator or administrative receiver of a company, or the former liquidator, administrator or administrative receiver of a company—

(a) to furnish him with such information with respect to any person's conduct as a director of the company, and

(b) to produce and permit inspection of such books, papers and other records relevant to that person's conduct as such a director,

as the Secretary of State or the official receiver may reasonably require for the purpose of determining whether to exercise, or of exercising, any function of his under this section.

8 Disqualification after investigation of company

(1) If it appears to the Secretary of State from investigative material that it is expedient in the public interest that a disqualification order should be made against a person who is, or has been, a director or shadow director of a company, he may apply to the court for such an order.

(1A) "Investigative material" means—

(a) a report made by inspectors under—

(i) section 437 of the Companies Act 1985;

(ii) section 167, 168, 169 or 284 of the Financial Services and Markets Act 2000; and

(b) information or documents obtained under—

(i) section 437, 446E, 447, 448, 451A or 453A of the Companies Act 1985;

(ii) section 2 of the Criminal Justice Act 1987;

(iii) section 28 of the Criminal Law (Consolidation) (Scotland) Act 1995;

(iv) section 83 of the Companies Act 1989; or

(v) section 165, 171, 172, 173 or 175 of the Financial Services and Markets Act 2000.

(2) The court may make a disqualification order against a person where, on an application under this section, it is satisfied that his conduct in relation to the company makes him unfit to be concerned in the management of a company.

(2A) Where it appears to the Secretary of State from such report, information or documents that, in the case of a person who has offered to give him a disqualification undertaking—

(a) the conduct of the person in relation to a company of which the person is or has been a director or shadow director makes him unfit to be concerned in the management of a company, and

(b) it is expedient in the public interest that he should accept the undertaking (instead of applying, or proceeding with an application, for a disqualification order),

(3) In this section "the court" means the High Court or, in Scotland, the Court of Session.

(4) The maximum period of disqualification under this section is 15 years.

8A Variation etc. of disqualification undertaking

(1) The court may, on the application of a person who is subject to a disqualification undertaking—

(a) reduce the period for which the undertaking is to be in force, or

(b) provide for it to cease to be in force.

(2) On the hearing of an application under subsection (1), the Secretary of State shall appear and call the attention of the court to any matters which seem to him to be relevant, and may himself give evidence or call witnesses.

(2A) Subsection (2) does not apply to an application in the case of an undertaking given under section 9B, and in such a case on the hearing of the application whichever of the Competition and Markets Authority or a specified regulator (within the meaning of section 9E) accepted the undertaking—

(a) must appear and call the attention of the court to any matters which appear to it or him (as the case may be) to be relevant;

(b) may give evidence or call witnesses

(3) In this section "the court"—

(a) in the case of an undertaking given under section 9B means the High Court or (in Scotland) the Court of Session;

(b) in any other case has the same meaning as in section 7(2) or 8 (as the case may be).

9 Matters for determining unfitness of directors

(1) Where it falls to a court to determine whether a person's conduct as a director of ny particular company or companies makes him unfit to be concerned in the management of a company, the court shall, as respects his conduct as a director of that company or, as the case may be, each of those companies, have regard in particular—

(a) to the matters mentioned in Part I of Schedule 1 to this Act, and

(b) here the company has become insolvent, to the matters mentioned in Part II of that Schedule;

and references in that Schedule to the director and the company are to be read accordingly.

(1A) In determining whether he may accept a disqualification undertaking from any person the Secretary of State shall, as respects the person's conduct as a director of any company concerned, have regard in particular—

(a) to the matters mentioned in Part I of Schedule 1 to this Act, and

(b) where the company has become insolvent, to the matters mentioned in Part II of that Schedule;

and references in that Schedule to the director and the company are to be read accordingly.

(2) Section 6(2) applies for the purposes of this section and Schedule 1 as it applies for the purposes of sections 6 and 7 and in this section and that Schedule "director" includes a shadow director.

...

(4) The Secretary of State may by order modify any of the provisions of Schedule 1; and such an order may contain such transitional provisions as may appear to the Secretary of State necessary or expedient.

(5) The power to make orders under this section is exercisable by statutory instrument subject to annulment in pursuance of a resolution of either House of Parliament.

Disqualification for competition infringements

9A Competition disqualification order

(1) The court must make a disqualification order against a person if the following two conditions are satisfied in relation to him.

(2) The first condition is that an undertaking which is a company of which he is a director commits a breach of competition law.

(3) The second condition is that the court considers that his conduct as a director makes him unfit to be concerned in the management of a company.

(4) An undertaking commits a breach of competition law if it engages in conduct which infringes any of the following—

(a) the Chapter 1 prohibition (within the meaning of the Competition Act 1998) (prohibition on agreements, etc. preventing, restricting or distorting competition);

(b) the Chapter 2 prohibition (within the meaning of that Act) (prohibition on abuse of a dominant position);

(c) Article 101 of the Treaty on the Functioning of the European Union (prohibition on agreements, etc. preventing, restricting or distorting competition);
(d) Article 102 of that Treaty (prohibition on abuse of a dominant position).

(5) For the purpose of deciding under subsection (3) whether a person is unfit to be concerned in the management of a company the court—
(a) must have regard to whether subsection (6) applies to him;
(b) may have regard to his conduct as a director of a company in connection with any other breach of competition law;
(c) must not have regard to the matters mentioned in Schedule 1.

(6) This subsection applies to a person if as a director of the company—
(a) his conduct contributed to the breach of competition law mentioned in subsection (2);
(b) his conduct did not contribute to the breach but he had reasonable grounds to suspect that the conduct of the undertaking constituted the breach and he took no steps to prevent it;
(c) he did not know but ought to have known that the conduct of the undertaking constituted the breach.

(7) For the purposes of subsection (6)(a) it is immaterial whether the person knew that the conduct of the undertaking constituted the breach.

(8) For the purposes of subsection (4)(a) or (c) references to the conduct of an undertaking are references to its conduct taken with the conduct of one or more other undertakings.

(9) The maximum period of disqualification under this section is 15 years.

(10) An application under this section for a disqualification order may be made by the the Competition and Markets Authority or by a specified regulator.

(11) Section 60 of the Competition Act 1998 (consistent treatment of questions arising under United Kingdom and EU law) applies in relation to any question arising by virtue of subsection (4)(a) or (b) above as it applies in relation to any question arising under Part 1 of that Act.

9B Competition undertakings

(1) This section applies if—
(a) the Competition and Markets Authority or a specified regulator thinks that in relation to any person an undertaking which is a company of which he is a director has committed or is committing a breach of competition law,
(b) the Competition and Markets Authority or the specified regulator thinks that the conduct of the person as a director makes him unfit to be concerned in the management of a company, and
(c) the person offers to give the Competition and Markets Authority or the specified regulator (as the case may be) a disqualification undertaking.

(2) The Competition and Markets Authority or the specified regulator (as the case may be) may accept a disqualification undertaking from the person instead of applying for or proceeding with an application for a disqualification order.

(3) A disqualification undertaking is an undertaking by a person that for the period specified in the undertaking he will not—
(a) be a director of a company;
(b) act as receiver of a company's property;
(c) in any way, whether directly or indirectly, be concerned or take part in the promotion, formation or management of a company;
(d) act as an insolvency practitioner.

(4) But a disqualification undertaking may provide that a prohibition falling within subsection (3)(a) to (c) does not apply if the person obtains the leave of the court.

(5) The maximum period which may be specified in a disqualification undertaking is 15 years.

(6) If a disqualification undertaking is accepted from a person who is already subject to a disqualification undertaking under this Act or to a disqualification order the periods specified in those undertakings or the undertaking and the order (as the case may be) run concurrently.

(7) Subsections (4) to (8) of section 9A apply for the purposes of this section as they apply for the purposes of that section but in the application of subsection (5) of that section the

reference to the court must be construed as a reference to the Competition and Markets Authority or a specified regulator (as the case may be).

9C Competition investigations

(1) If the Competition and Markets Authority or a specified regulator has reasonable grounds for suspecting that a breach of competition law has occurred it or he (as the case may be) may carry out an investigation for the purpose of deciding whether to make an application under section 9A for a disqualification order.

(2) For the purposes of such an investigation sections 26 to 30 of the Competition Act 1998 apply to the Competition and Markets Authority and the specified regulators as they apply to the Competition and Markets Authority for the purposes of an investigation under section 25 of that Act.

(3) Subsection (4) applies if as a result of an investigation under this section the Competition and Markets Authority or a specified regulator proposes to apply under section 9A for a disqualification order.

(4) Before making the application the Competition and Markets Authority or regulator (as the case may be) must—

(a) give notice to the person likely to be affected by the application, and

(b) give that person an opportunity to make representations.

9D Co-ordination

(1) The Secretary of State may make regulations for the purpose of co-ordinating the performance of functions under sections 9A to 9C (relevant functions) which are exercisable concurrently by two or more persons.

(2) Section 54(5) to (7) of the Competition Act 1998 applies to regulations made under this section as it applies to regulations made under that section and for that purpose in that section—

(a) references to Part 1 functions must be read as references to relevant functions;

(b) references to a regulator must be read as references to a specified regulator;

(ba) the reference in subsection (6A)(b) to notice under section 31(1) of the Competition Act 1998 that the regulator proposes to make a decision within the meaning given by section 31(2) of that Act is to be read as notice under section 9C(4) that the specified regulator proposes to apply under section 9A for a disqualification order;

(c) a competent person also includes any of the specified regulators.

(3) The power to make regulations under this section must be exercised by statutory instrument subject to annulment in pursuance of a resolution of either House of Parliament.

(4) Such a statutory instrument may—

(a) contain such incidental, supplemental, consequential and transitional provision as the Secretary of State thinks appropriate;

(b) make different provision for different cases.

9E Interpretation

(1) This section applies for the purposes of sections 9A to 9D.

(2) Each of the following is a specified regulator for the purposes of a breach of competition law in relation to a matter in respect of which he or it has a function—

(a) the Office of Communications;

(b) the Gas and Electricity Markets Authority;

(c) the Water Services Regulation Authority;

(d) the Office of Rail Regulation;

(e) the Civil Aviation Authority;

(f) Monitor;

(g) the Payment Systems Regulator established under section 40 of the Financial Services (Banking Reform) Act 2013;

(h) the Financial Conduct Authority.

(3) The court is the High Court or (in Scotland) the Court of Session.

(4) Conduct includes omission.

(5) Director includes shadow director.

10 Participation in wrongful trading

(1) Where the court makes a declaration under section 213 or 214 of the Insolvency Act 1986 that a person is liable to make a contribution to a company's assets, then, whether

or not an application for such an order is made by any person, the court may, if it thinks fit, also make a disqualification order against the person to whom the declaration relates.

(2) The maximum period of disqualification under this section is 15 years.

11 Undischarged bankrupts

(1) It is an offence for a person who is an undischarged bankrupt to act as director of, or directly or indirectly to take part in or be concerned in the promotion, formation or management of, a company, except with the leave of the court.

(1) It is an offence for a person to act as director of a company or directly or indirectly to take part in or be concerned in the promotion, formation or management of a company, without the leave of the court, at a time when—

(a) he is an undischarged bankrupt,

(aa) a moratorium period under a debt relief order applies in relation to him, or

(b) a bankruptcy restrictions order or a debt relief restrictions order is in force in respect of him.

Note: The italicised subsection (1) applies only to England and Wales.

(2) "The court" for this purpose is the court by which the person was adjudged bankrupt or, in Scotland, sequestration of his estates was awarded.

(3) In England and Wales, the leave of the court shall not be given unless notice of intention to apply for it has been served on the official receiver; and it is the latter's duty, if he is of opinion that it is contrary to the public interest that the application should be granted, to attend on the hearing of the application and oppose it.

(4) In this section "company" includes a company incorporated outside Great Britain that has an established place of business in Great Britain.

12 Failure to pay under county court administration order

(1) The following has effect where a court under section 429 of the Insolvency Act 1986 revokes an administration order under Part VI of the County Courts Act 1984.

(2) A person to whom that section applies by virtue of the order under section 429(2)(b) shall not, except with the leave of the court which made the order, act as director or liquidator of, or directly or indirectly take part or be concerned in the promotion, formation or management of, a company.

12A Northern Irish disqualification orders

A person subject to a disqualification order under the Company Directors Disqualification (Northern Ireland) Order 2002—

(a) shall not be a director of a company, act as receiver of a company's property or in any way, whether directly or indirectly, be concerned or take part in the promotion, formation or management of a company unless (in each case) he has the leave of the High Court of Northern Ireland, and

(b) shall not act as an insolvency practitioner.

12B Northern Irish disqualification undertakings

A person subject to a disqualification undertaking under the Company Directors Disqualification (Northern Ireland) Order 2002—

(a) shall not be a director of a company, act as receiver of a company's property or in any way, whether directly or indirectly, be concerned or take part in the promotion, formation or management of a company unless (in each case) he has the leave of the High Court of Northern Ireland, and

(b) shall not act as an insolvency practitioner.

Consequences of contravention

13 Criminal penalties

If a person acts in contravention of a disqualification order or disqualification undertaking or in contravention of section 12(2) 12A or 12B, or is guilty of an offence under section 11, he is liable—

(a) on conviction on indictment, to imprisonment for not more than 2 years or a fine, or both; and

(b) on summary conviction, to imprisonment for not more than 6 months or a fine not exceeding the statutory maximum, or both.

14 Offences by body corporate

(1) Where a body corporate is guilty of an offence of acting in contravention of a disqualification order or disqualification undertaking or in contravention of section 12A or 12B, it is proved that the offence occurred with the consent or connivance of, or was attributable to any neglect on the part of any director, manager, secretary or other similar officer of the body corporate, or any person who was purporting to act in any such capacity he, as well as the body corporate, is guilty of the offence and liable to be proceeded against and punished accordingly.

(2) Where the affairs of a body corporate are managed by its members, subsection (1) applies in relation to the acts and defaults of a member in connection with his functions of management as if he were a director of the body corporate.

15 Personal liability for company's debts where person acts while disqualified

(1) A person is personally responsible for all the relevant debts of a company if at any time—

- (a) in contravention of a disqualification order or disqualification undertaking or in contravention of section 11, 12A or 12B of this Act he is involved in the management of the company, or
- (b) as a person who is involved in the management of the company, he acts or is willing to act on instructions given without the leave of the court by a person whom he knows at that time—
  - (i) to be the subject of a disqualification order made or disqualification undertaking accepted under this Act or under the Company Directors Disqualification (Northern Ireland) Order 2002, or
  - (ii) to be an undischarged bankrupt.

(2) Where a person is personally responsible under this section for the relevant debts of a company, he is jointly and severally liable in respect of those debts with the company and any other person who, whether under this section or otherwise, is so liable.

(3) For the purposes of this section the relevant debts of a company are—

- (a) in relation to a person who is personally responsible under paragraph (a) of subsection (1), such debts and other liabilities of the company as are incurred at a time when that person was involved in the management of the company, and
- (b) in relation to a person who is personally responsible under paragraph (b) of that subsection, such debts and other liabilities of the company as are incurred at a time when that person was acting or was willing to act on instructions given as mentioned in that paragraph.

(4) For the purposes of this section, a person is involved in the management of a company if he is a director of the company or if he is concerned, whether directly or indirectly, or takes part, in the management of the company.

(5) For the purposes of this section a person who, as a person involved in the management of a company, has at any time acted on instructions given without the leave of the court by a person whom he knew at that time—

- (a) to be the subject of a disqualification order made or disqualification undertaking accepted under this Act or under the Company Directors Disqualification (Northern Ireland) Order 2002, or
- (b) to be an undischarged bankrupt,

is presumed, unless the contrary is shown, to have been willing at any time thereafter to act on any instructions given by that person.

Supplementary provisions

16 Application for disqualification order

(1) A person intending to apply for the making of a disqualification order by the court having jurisdiction to wind up a company shall give not less than 10 days' notice of his intention to the person against whom the order is sought; and on the hearing of the application the last-mentioned person may appear and himself give evidence or call witnesses.

(2) An application to a court with jurisdiction to wind up companies for the making against any person of a disqualification order under any of sections 2 to 4 may be made by the Secretary of State or the official receiver, or by the liquidator or any past or present

member or creditor of any company in relation to which that person has committed or is alleged to have committed an offence or other default.

(3) On the hearing of any application under this Act made by a person falling within subsection (4), the applicant shall appear and call the attention of the court to any matters which seem to him to be relevant, and may himself give evidence or call witnesses.

(4) The following fall within this subsection—

(a) the Secretary of State;

(b) the official receiver;

(c) the Competition and Markets Authority;

(d) the liquidator;

(e) a specified regulator (within the meaning of section 9E).

17 Application for leave under an order or undertaking

(1) Where a person is subject to a disqualification order made by a court having jurisdiction to wind up companies, any application for leave for the purposes of section 1(1)(a) shall be made to that court.

(2) Where—

(a) a person is subject to a disqualification order made under section 2 by a court other than a court having jurisdiction to wind up companies, or

(b) a person is subject to a disqualification order made under section 5,

any application for leave for the purposes of section 1(1)(a) shall be made to any court which, when the order was made, had jurisdiction to wind up the company (or, if there is more than one such company, any of the companies) to which the offence (or any of the offences) in question related.

(3) Where a person is subject to a disqualification undertaking accepted at any time under section 7 or 8, any application for leave for the purposes of section 1A(1)(a) shall be made to any court to which, if the Secretary of State had applied for a disqualification order under the section in question at that time, his application could have been made.

(3A) Where a person is subject to a disqualification undertaking accepted at any time under section 9B any application for leave for the purposes of section 9B(4) must be made to the High Court or (in Scotland) the Court of Session.

(4) But where a person is subject to two or more disqualification orders or undertakings (or to one or more disqualification orders and to one or more disqualification undertakings), any application for leave for the purposes of section 1(1)(a) or 1A(1)(a) shall be made to any court to which any such application relating to the latest order to be made, or undertaking to be accepted, could be made.

(5) On the hearing of an application for leave for the purposes of section 1(1)(a) or 1A(1)(a), the Secretary of State shall appear and call the attention of the court to any matters which seem to him to be relevant, and may himself give evidence or call witnesses.

(6) Subsection (5) does not apply to an application for leave for the purposes of section 1(1)(a) if the application for the disqualification order was made under section 9A.

(7) In such a case and in the case of an application for leave for the purposes of section 9B(4) on the hearing of the application whichever of the Competition and Markets Authority or a specified regulator (within the meaning of section 9E) applied for the order or accepted the undertaking (as the case may be)—

(a) must appear and draw the attention of the court to any matters which appear to it or him (as the case may be) to be relevant;

(b) may give evidence or call witnesses.

18 Register of disqualification orders and undertakings

(1) The Secretary of State may make regulations requiring officers of courts to furnish him with such particulars as the regulations may specify of cases in which—

(a) a disqualification order is made, or

(b) any action is taken by a court in consequence of which such an order or a disqualification undertaking is varied or ceases to be in force, or

(c) leave is granted by a court for a person subject to such an order to do any thing which otherwise the order prohibits him from doing; or

(d) leave is granted by a court for a person subject to such an undertaking to do anything which otherwise the undertaking prohibits him from doing;

and the regulations may specify the time within which, and the form and manner in which, such particulars are to be furnished.

(2) The Secretary of State shall, from the particulars so furnished, continue to maintain the register of orders, and of cases in which leave has been granted as mentioned in subsection (1)(c).

(2A) The Secretary of State must include in the register such particulars as he considers appropriate of—

(a) disqualification undertakings accepted by him under section 7 or 8;

(b) disqualification undertakings accepted by the Competition and Markets Authority or a specified regulator under section 9B;

(c) cases in which leave has been granted as mentioned in subsection (1)(d).

(3) When an order or undertaking of which entry is made in the register ceases to be in force, the Secretary of State shall delete the entry from the register and all particulars relating to it which have been furnished to him under this section or any previous corresponding provision and, in the case of a disqualification undertaking, any other particulars he has included in the register.

(4) The register shall be open to inspection on payment of such fee as may be specified by the Secretary of State in regulations.

(4A) Regulations under this section may extend the preceding provisions of this section, to such extent and with such modifications as may be specified in the regulations, to disqualification orders.

(5) Regulations under this section shall be made by statutory instrument subject to annulment in pursuance of a resolution of either House of Parliament.

19 Special savings from repealed enactments

Schedule 2 to this Act has effect—

(a) in connection with certain transitional cases arising under sections 93 and 94 of the Companies Act 1981, so as to limit the power to make a disqualification order, or to restrict the duration of an order, by reference to events occurring or things done before those sections came into force,

(b) to preserve orders made under section 28 of the Companies Act 1976 (repealed by the Act of 1981), and

(c) to preclude any applications for a disqualification order under section 6 or 8, where the relevant company went into liquidation before 28th April 1986.

Miscellaneous and general

20 Admissibility in evidence of statements

(1) In any proceedings (whether or not under this Act), any statement made in pursuance of a requirement imposed by or under sections 6 to 10, 15 or 19(c) of, or Schedule 1 to, this Act, or by or under rules made for the purposes of this Act under the Insolvency Act, may be used in evidence against any person making or concurring in making the statement.

(2) However, in criminal proceedings in which any such person is charged with an offence to which this subsection applies—

(a) no evidence relating to the statement may be adduced, and

(b) no question relating to it may be asked,

by or on behalf of the prosecution, unless evidence relating to it is adduced, or a question relating to it is asked, in the proceedings by or on behalf of that person.

(3) Subsection (2) applies to any offence other than—

(a) an offence which is—

(i) created by rules made for the purposes of this Act under the Insolvency Act 1986, and

(ii) designated for the purposes of this subsection by such rules or by regulations made by the Secretary of State;

(b) an offence which is—

(i) created by regulations made under any such rules, and

(ii) designated for the purposes of this subsection by such regulations;

(c) an offence under section 5 of the Perjury Act 1911 (false statements made otherwise than on oath); or

(d) an offence under section 44(2) of the Criminal Law (Consolidation) (Scotland) Act 1995 (false statements made otherwise than on oath).

(4) Regulations under subsection (3)(a)(ii) shall be made by statutory instrument and, after being made, shall be laid before each House of Parliament.

20A Legal professional privilege

In proceedings against a person for an offence under this Act nothing in this Act is to be taken to require any person to disclose any information that he is entitled to refuse to disclose on grounds of legal professional privilege (in Scotland, confidentiality of communications).

21 Interaction with Insolvency Act 1986

(1) References in this Act to the official receiver, in relation to the winding up of a company or the bankruptcy of an individual, are to any person who, by virtue of section 399 of the Insolvency Act 1986, is authorised to act as the official receiver in relation to that winding up or bankruptcy; and, in accordance with section 401(2) of that Act, references in this Act to an official receiver includes a person appointed as his deputy.

(2) Sections 1A, 6 to 10, 13, 14, 15, 19(c) and 20 of, and Schedule 1 to, this Act and sections 1 and 17 of this Act as they apply for the purposes of those provisions are deemed included in Parts I to VII of the Insolvency Act 1986 for the purposes of the following sections of that Act—

section 411 (power to make insolvency rules);

section 414 (fees orders);

section 420 (orders extending provisions about insolvent companies to insolvent partnerships);

section 422 (modification of such provisions in their application to recognised banks);

(3) Section 434 of that Act (Crown application) applies to sect ons 1A, 6 to 10, 13, 14, 15, 19(c) and 20 of, and Schedule 1 to, this Act and sections 1 and 17 of this Act as they apply for the purposes of those provisionsas it does to the provisions of that Act which are there mentioned.

(4) For the purposes of summary proceedings in Scotland, section 431 of that Act applies to summary proceedings for an offence under section 11 or 13 of this Act as it applies to summary proceedings for an offence under Parts I to VII of the Act.

22 Interpretation

(1) This section has effect with respect to the meaning of expressions used in this Act, and applies unless the context otherwise requires.

(2) "Company" means—

(a) a company registered under the Companies Act 2006 in Great Britain, or

(b) a company that may be wound up under Part 5 of the Insolvency Act 1986 (unregistered companies).

(3) Section 247 in Part VII of the Insolvency Act 1986 (interpretation for the first Group of Parts of that Act) applies as regards references to a company's insolvency and to its going into liquidation; and "administrative receiver" has the meaning given by section 251 of that Act and references to acting as an insolvency practitioner are to be read in accordance with section 388 of that Act.

(4) "Director" includes any person occupying the position of director, by whatever name called.

(5) "Shadow director", in relation to a company, means a person in accordance with whose directions or instructions the directors of the company are accustomed to act, but so that a person is not deemed a shadow director by reason only that the directors act—

- (a) on advice given by that person in a professional capacity;
- (b) in accordance with instructions, a direction, guidance or advice given by that person in the exercise of a function conferred by or under an enactment;
- (c) in accordance with guidance or advice given by that person in that person's capacity as a Minister of the Crown (within the meaning of the Ministers of the Crown Act 1975).

(6) "Body corporate" and "officer" have the same meaning as in the Companies Acts (see section 1173(1) of the Companies Act 2006).

(7) "The Companies Acts" has the meaning given by section 2(1) of the Companies Act 2006.

(8) Any reference to provisions, or a particular provision, of the Companies Acts or the Insolvency Act 1986 includes the corresponding provisions or provision of corresponding earlier legislation.

(9) Subject to the provisions of this section, expressions that are defined for the purposes of the Companies Acts (see section 1174 of, and Schedule 8 to, the Companies Act 2006) have the same meaning in this Act.

(10) Any reference to acting as receiver—

(a) includes acting as manager or as both receiver and manager, but

(b) does not include acting as administrative receiver;

and "receivership" is to be read accordingly.

23 Transitional provisions, savings, repeals

(1) The transitional provisions and savings in Schedule 3 to this Act have effect, and are without prejudice to anything in the Interpretation Act 1978 with regard to the effect of repeals.

(2) The enactments specified in the second column of Schedule 4 to this Act are repealed to the extent specified in the third column of that Schedule.

24 Extent

(1) This Act extends to England and Wales and to Scotland.

(2) Nothing in this Act extends to Northern Ireland.

25 Commencement

This Act comes into force simultaneously with the Insolvency Act 1986.

26 Citation

This Act may be cited as the Company Directors Disqualification Act 1986.

SCHEDULES

SCHEDULE 1 **Section 9**

MATTERS FOR DETERMINING UNFITNESS OF DIRECTORS

PART I

MATTERS APPLICABLE IN ALL CASES

1. Any misfeasance or breach of any fiduciary or other duty by the director in relation to the company, including in particular any breach by the director of a duty under Chapter 2 of Part 10 of the Companies Act 2006 (general duties of directors) owed to the company.
2. Any misapplication or retention by the director of, or any conduct by the director giving rise to an obligation to account for, any money or other property of the company.
3. The extent of the director's responsibility for the company entering into any transaction liable to be set aside under Part XVI of the Insolvency Act 1986 (provisions against debt avoidance).
4. The extent of the director's responsibility for any failure by the company to comply with any of the following provisions of the Companies Act 2006—
   (a) section 113 (register of members);
   (b) section 114 (register to be kept available for inspection);
   (c) section 162 (register of directors);
   (d) section 165 (register of directors' residential addresses);
   (e) section 167 (duty to notify registrar of changes: directors);
   (f) section 275 (register of secretaries);
   (g) section 276 (duty to notify registrar of changes: secretaries);
   (h) section 386 (duty to keep accounting records);
   (i) section 388 (where and for how long accounting records to be kept);
   (j) section 854 (duty to make annual returns);
   (k) section 860 (duty to register charges);
   (l) section 878 (duty to register charges: companies registered in Scotland).
5. The extent of the director's responsibility for any failure by the directors of the company to comply with the following provisions of the Companies Act 2006—
   (a) section 394 or 399 (duty to prepare annual accounts);
   (b) section 414 or 450 (approval and signature of abbreviated accounts); or
   (c) section 433 (name of signatory to be stated in published copy of accounts).

PART II
MATTERS APPLICABLE WHERE COMPANY HAS BECOME INSOLVENT

6. The extent of the director's responsibility for the causes of the company becoming insolvent.
7. The extent of the director's responsibility for any failure by the company to supply any goods or services which have been paid for (in whole or in part).
8. The extent of the director's responsibility for the company entering into any transaction or giving any preference, being a transaction or preference—
   (a) liable to be set aside under section 127 or sections 238 to 240 of the Insolvency Act 1986, or
   (b) challengeable under section 242 or 243 of that Act or under any rule of law in Scotland.
9. The extent of the director's responsibility for any failure by the directors of the company to comply with section 98 of the Insolvency Act 1986 (duty to call creditors' meeting in creditors' voluntary winding up).
10. Any failure by the director to comply with any obligation imposed on him by or under any of the following provisions of the Insolvency Act—
   (a) paragraph 47 of Schedule B1 (company's statement of affairs in administration);
   (b) section 47 (statement of affairs to administrative receiver);
   (c) section 66 (statement of affairs in Scottish receivership);
   (d) section 99 (directors' duty to attend meeting; statement of affairs in creditors' voluntary winding up);
   (e) section 131 (statement of affairs in winding up by the court);
   (f) section 234 (duty of any one with company property to deliver it up);
   (g) section 235 (duty to co-operate with liquidator, etc.).

SCHEDULES 2–4
OMITTED

CRIMINAL JUSTICE ACT 1993
(1993, c. 36)

PART V
INSIDER DEALING

The offence of insider dealing

52 The offence

(1) An individual who has information as an insider is guilty of insider dealing if, in the circumstances mentioned in subsection (3), he deals in securities that are price-affected securities in relation to the information.

(2) An individual who has information as an insider is also guilty of insider dealing if—
   (a) he encourages another person to deal in securities that are (whether or not that other knows it) price-affected securities in relation to the information, knowing or having reasonable cause to believe that the dealing would take place in the circumstances mentioned in subsection (3); or
   (b) he discloses the information, otherwise than in the proper performance of the functions of his employment, office or profession, to another person.

(3) The circumstances referred to above are that the acquisition or disposal in question occurs on a regulated market, or that the person dealing relies on a professional intermediary or is himself acting as a professional intermediary.

(4) This section has effect subject to section 53.

53 Defences

(1) An individual is not guilty of insider dealing by virtue of dealing in securities if he shows—
   (a) that he did not at the time expect the dealing to result in a profit attributable to the fact that the information in question was price-sensitive information in relation to the securities, or
   (b) that at the time he believed on reasonable grounds that the information had been disclosed widely enough to ensure that none of those taking part in the dealing would be prejudiced by not having the information, or

(c) that he would have done what he did even if he had not had the information.

(2) An individual is not guilty of insider dealing by virtue of encouraging another person to deal in securities if he shows—

(a) that he did not at the time expect the dealing to result in a profit attributable to the fact that the information in question was price-sensitive information in relation to the securities, or

(b) that at the time he believed on reasonable grounds that the information had been or would be disclosed widely enough to ensure that none of those taking part in the dealing would be prejudiced by not having the information, or

(c) that he would have done what he did even if he had not had the information.

(3) An individual is not guilty of insider dealing by virtue of a disclosure of information if he shows—

(a) that he did not at the time expect any person, because of the disclosure, to deal in securities in the circumstances mentioned in subsection (3) of section 52; or

(b) that, although he had such an expectation at the time, he did not expect the dealing to result in a profit attributable to the fact that the information was price-sensitive information in relation to the securities.

(4) Schedule 1 (special defences) shall have effect.

(5) The Treasury may by order amend Schedule 1.

(6) In this section references to a profit include references to the avoidance of a loss.

Interpretation

54 Securities to which Part V applies

(1) This Part applies to any security which—

(a) falls within any paragraph of Schedule 2; and

(b) satisfies any conditions applying to it under an order made by the Treasury for the purposes of this subsection;

and in the provisions of this Part (other than that Schedule) any reference to a security is a reference to a security to which this Part applies.

(2) The Treasury may by order amend Schedule 2.

55 "Dealing" in securities

(1) For the purposes of this Part, a person deals in securities if—

(a) he acquires or disposes of the securities (whether as principal or agent); or

(b) he procures, directly or indirectly, an acquisition or disposal of the securities by any other person.

(2) For the purposes of this Part, "acquire", in relation to a security, includes—

(a) agreeing to acquire the security; and

(b) entering into a contract which creates the security.

(3) For the purposes of this Part, "dispose", in relation to a security, includes—

(a) agreeing to dispose of the security; and

(b) bringing to an end a contract which created the security.

(4) For the purposes of subsection (1), a person procures an acquisition or disposal of a security if the security is acquired or disposed of by a person who is—

(a) his agent,

(b) his nominee, or

(c) a person who is acting at his direction, in relation to the acquisition or disposal.

(5) Subsection (4) is not exhaustive as to the circumstances in which one person may be regarded as procuring an acquisition or disposal of securities by another.

56 "Inside information", etc.

(1) For the purposes of this section and section 57, "inside information" means information which—

(a) relates to particular securities or to a particular issuer of securities or to particular issuers of securities and not to securities generally or to issuers of securities generally;

(b) is specific or precise;

(c) has not been made public; and

(d) if it were made public would be likely to have a significant effect on the price of any securities.

(2) For the purposes of this Part, securities are "price-affected securities" in relation to inside information, and inside information is "price-sensitive information" in relation

to securities, if and only if the information would, if made public, be likely to have a significant effect on the price of the securities.

(3) For the purposes of this section "price" includes value.

57 "Insiders"

(1) For the purposes of this Part, a person has information as an insider if and only if—
   (a) it is, and he knows that it is, inside information, and
   (b) he has it, and knows that he has it, from an inside source.

(2) For the purposes of subsection (1), a person has information from an inside source if and only if—
   (a) he has it through—
      (i) being a director, employee or shareholder of an issuer of securities; or
      (ii) having access to the information by virtue of his employment, office or profession; or
   (b) the direct or indirect source of his information is a person within paragraph (a).

58 Information "made public"

(1) For the purposes of section 56, "made public", in relation to information, shall be construed in accordance with the following provisions of this section; but those provisions are not exhaustive as to the meaning of that expression.

(2) Information is made public if—
   (a) it is published in accordance with the rules of a regulated market for the purpose of informing investors and their professional advisers;
   (b) it is contained in records which by virtue of any enactment are open to inspection by the public;
   (c) it can be readily acquired by those likely to deal in any securities—
      (i) to which the information relates, or
      (ii) of an issuer to which the information relates; or
   (d) it is derived from information which has been made public.

(3) Information may be treated as made public even though—
   (a) it can be acquired only by persons exercising diligence or expertise;
   (b) it is communicated to a section of the public and not to the public at large;
   (c) it can be acquired only by observation;
   (d) it is communicated only on payment of a fee; or
   (e) it is published only outside the United Kingdom.

59 "Professional intermediary"

(1) For the purposes of this Part, a "professional intermediary" is a person—
   (a) who carries on a business consisting of an activity mentioned in subsection (2) and who holds himself out to the public or any section of the public (including a section of the public constituted by persons such as himself) as willing to engage in any such business; or
   (b) who is employed by a person falling within paragraph (a) to carry out any such activity.

(2) The activities referred to in subsection (1) are—
   (a) acquiring or disposing of securities (whether as principal or agent); or
   (b) acting as an intermediary between persons taking part in any dealing in securities.

(3) A person is not to be treated as carrying on a business consisting of an activity mentioned in subsection (2)—
   (a) if the activity in question is merely incidental to some other activity not falling within subsection (2); or
   (b) merely because he occasionally conducts one of those activities.

(4) For the purposes of section 52, a person dealing in securities relies on a professional intermediary if and only if a person who is acting as a professional intermediary carries out an activity mentioned in subsection (2) in relation to that dealing.

60 Other interpretation provisions

(1) For the purposes of this Part, "regulated market" means any market, however operated, which, by an order made by the Treasury, is identified (whether by name or by reference to criteria prescribed by the order) as a regulated market for the purposes of this Part.

(2) For the purposes of this Part an "issuer", in relation to any securities, means any company, public sector body or individual by which or by whom the securities have been or are to be issued.

(3) For the purposes of this Part—

(a) "company" means any body (whether or not incorporated and wherever incorporated or constituted) which is not a public sector body; and

(b) "public sector body" means—

(i) the government of the United Kingdom, of Northern Ireland or of any country or territory outside the United Kingdom;

(ii) a local authority in the United Kingdom or elsewhere;

(iii) any international organisation the members of which include the United Kingdom or another member state;

(iv) the Bank of England; or

(v) the central bank of any sovereign State.

(4) For the purposes of this Part, information shall be treated as relating to an issuer of securities which is a company not only where it is about the company but also where it may affect the company's business prospects.

Miscellaneous

61 Penalties and prosecution

(1) An individual guilty of insider dealing shall be liable—

(a) on summary conviction, to a fine not exceeding the statutory maximum or imprisonment for a term not exceeding six months or to both; or

(b) on conviction on indictment, to a fine or imprisonment for a term not exceeding seven years or to both.

(2) Proceedings for offences under this Part shall not be instituted in England and Wales except by or with the consent of—

(a) the Secretary of State; or

(b) the Director of Public Prosecutions.

(3) In relation to proceedings in Northern Ireland for offences under this Part, subsection (2) shall have effect as if the reference to the Director of Public Prosecutions were a reference to the Director of Public Prosecutions for Northern Ireland.

61A Summary proceedings: venue and time limit for proceedings

(1) Summary proceedings for an offence of insider dealing may (without prejudice to any jurisdiction exercisable apart from this subsection) be brought against an individual at any place at which the individual is for the time being.

(2) An information relating to an offence of insider dealing that is triable by a magistrates' court in England and Wales may be so tried if it is laid—

(a) at any time within three years after the commission of the offence, and

(b) within twelve months after the date on which evidence sufficient in the opinion of the Director of Public Prosecutions or the Secretary of State (as the case may be) to justify the proceedings comes to that person's knowledge.

(3) Summary proceedings in Scotland for an offence of insider dealing—

(a) must not be commenced after the expiration of three years from the commission of the offence;

(b) subject to that, may be commenced at any time—

(i) within twelve months after the date on which evidence sufficient in the Lord Advocate's opinion to justify the proceedings came to that person's knowledge, or

(ii) where such evidence was reported to the Lord Advocate by the Secretary of State, within twelve months after the date on which it came to the knowledge of the latter.

Section 136(3) of the Criminal Procedure (Scotland) Act 1995 (date when proceedings deemed to be commenced) applies for the purposes of this subsection as for the purposes of that section.

(4) A magistrates' court in Northern Ireland has jurisdiction to hear and determine a complaint charging the commission of a summary offence of insider dealing provided that the complaint is made—

(a) within three years from the time when the offence was committed, and

(b) within twelve months from the date on which evidence sufficient in the opinion of the Director of Public Prosecutions for Northern Ireland or the Secretary of State (as the case may be) to justify the proceedings comes to that person's knowledge.

(5) For the purposes of this section a certificate of the Director of Public Prosecutions, the Lord Advocate, the Director of Public Prosecutions for Northern Ireland or the Secretary of State (as the case may be) as to the date on which such evidence as is referred to above came to that person's notice is conclusive evidence.

62 Territorial scope of offence of insider dealing

(1) An individual is not guilty of an offence falling within subsection (1) of section 52 unless—

(a) he was within the United Kingdom at the time when he is alleged to have done any act constituting or forming part of the alleged dealing;

(b) the regulated market on which the dealing is alleged to have occurred is one which, by an order made by the Treasury, is identified (whether by name or by reference to criteria prescribed by the order) as being, for the purposes of this Part, regulated in the United Kingdom; or

(c) the professional intermediary was within the United Kingdom at the time when he is alleged to have done anything by means of which the offence is alleged to have been committed.

(2) An individual is not guilty of an offence falling within subsection (2) of section 52 unless—

(a) he was within the United Kingdom at the time when he is alleged to have disclosed the information or encouraged the dealing; or

(b) the alleged recipient of the information or encouragement was within the United Kingdom at the time when he is alleged to have received the information or encouragement.

63 Limits on section 52

(1) Section 52 does not apply to anything done by an individual acting on behalf of a public sector body in pursuit of monetary policies or policies with respect to exchange rates or the management of public debt or foreign exchange reserves.

(2) No contract shall be void or unenforceable by reason only of section 52.

64 Orders

(1) Any power under this Part to make an order shall be exercisable by statutory instrument.

(2) No order shall be made under this Part unless a draft of it has been laid before and approved by a resolution of each House of Parliament.

(3) An order under this Part—

(a) may make different provision for different cases; and

(b) may contain such incidental, supplemental and transitional provisions as the Treasury consider expedient.

SCHEDULE 1 — Section 53(4)

SPECIAL DEFENCES

Market makers

1. (1) An individual is not guilty of insider dealing by virtue of dealing in securities or encouraging another person to deal if he shows that he acted in good faith in the course of—

(a) his business as a market maker, or

(b) his employment in the business of a market maker.

(2) A market maker is a person who—

(a) holds himself out at all normal times in compliance with the rules of a regulated market or an approved organisation as willing to acquire or dispose of securities; and

(b) is recognised as doing so under those rules.

(3) In this paragraph "approved organisation" means an international securities self-regulating organisation approved by the Treasury under any relevant order under section 22 of the Financial Services and Markets Act 2000.

Market information

2. (1) An individual is not guilty of insider dealing by virtue of dealing in securities or encouraging another person to deal if he shows that—

(a) the information which he had as an insider was market information; and
(b) it was reasonable for an individual in his position to have acted as he did despite having that information as an insider at the time.

(2) In determining whether it is reasonable for an individual to do any act despite having market information at the time, there shall, in particular, be taken into account—
(a) the content of the information;
(b) the circumstances in which he first had the information and in what capacity; and
(c) the capacity in which he now acts.

3. An individual is not guilty of insider dealing by virtue of dealing in securities or encouraging another person to deal if he shows—
(a) that he acted—
(i) in connection with an acquisition or disposal which was under consideration or the subject of negotiation, or in the course of a series of such acquisitions or disposals; and
(ii) with a view to facilitating the accomplishment of the acquisition or disposal or the series of acquisitions or disposals; and
(b) that the information which he had as an insider was market information arising directly out of his involvement in the acquisition or disposal or series of acquisitions or disposals.

4. For the purposes of paragraphs 2 and 3 market information is information consisting of one or more of the following facts—
(a) that securities of a particular kind have been or are to be acquired or disposed of, or that their acquisition or disposal is under consideration or the subject of negotiation;
(b) that securities of a particular kind have not been or are not to be acquired or disposed of;
(c) the number of securities acquired or disposed of or to be acquired or disposed of or whose acquisition or disposal is under consideration or the subject of negotiation;
(d) the price (or range of prices) at which securities have been or are to be acquired or disposed of or the price (or range of prices) at which securities whose acquisition or disposal is under consideration or the subject of negotiation may be acquired or disposed of;
(e) the identity of the persons involved or likely to be involved in any capacity in an acquisition or disposal.

Price stabilisation

5. (1) An individual is not guilty of insider dealing by virtue of dealing in securities or encouraging another person to deal if he shows that he acted in conformity with the price stabilisation rules or with the relevant provisions of Commission Regulation (EC) No 2273/2003 of 22 December 2003 implementing Directive 2003/6/EC of the European Parliament and of the Council as regards exemptions for buy-back programmes and stabilisation of financial instruments.

(2) "Price stabilisation rules" means rules made under section 144(1) of the Financial Services and Markets Act 2000.

SCHEDULE 2 **Section 54**
SECURITIES

Shares

1. Shares and stock in the share capital of a company ("shares").

Debt securities

2. Any instrument creating or acknowledging indebtedness which is issued by a company or public sector body, including, in particular, debentures, debenture stock, loan stock, bonds and certificates of deposit ("debt securities").

Warrants

3. Any right (whether conferred by warrant or otherwise) to subscribe for shares or debt securities ("warrants").

Depositary receipts

4. (1) The rights under any depositary receipt.
(2) For the purposes of sub-paragraph (1) a "depositary receipt" means a certificate or other record (whether or not in the form of a document)—
(a) which is issued by or on behalf of a person who holds any relevant securities of a particular issuer; and
(b) which acknowledges that another person is entitled to rights in relation to the relevant securities or relevant securities of the same kind.
(3) In sub-paragraph (2) "relevant securities" means shares, debt securities and warrants.

Options

5. Any option to acquire or dispose of any security falling within any other paragraph of this Schedule.

Futures

6. (1) Rights under a contract for the acquisition or disposal of relevant securities under which delivery is to be made at a future date and at a price agreed when the contract is made.
(2) In sub-paragraph (1)—
(a) the references to a future date and to a price agreed when the contract is made include references to a date and a price determined in accordance with terms of the contract; and
(b) "relevant securities" means any security falling within any other paragraph of this Schedule.

Contracts for differences

7. (1) Rights under a contract which does not provide for the delivery of securities but whose purpose or pretended purpose is to secure a profit or avoid a loss by reference to fluctuations in—
(a) a share index or other similar factor connected with relevant securities;
(b) the price of particular relevant securities; or
(c) the interest rate offered on money placed on deposit.
(2) In sub-paragraph (1) "relevant securities" means any security falling within any other paragraph of this Schedule.

FINANCIAL SERVICES AND MARKETS ACT 2000
(2000, c. 8)

PART IA
THE REGULATORS

CHAPTER 1
THE FINANCIAL CONDUCT AUTHORITY

The Financial Conduct Authority

1A The Financial Conduct Authority

(1) The body corporate previously known as the Financial Services Authority is renamed as the Financial Conduct Authority.
(2) The Financial Conduct Authority is in this Act referred to as "the FCA".
(3) *omitted*

1B–1T *omitted*

CHAPTER 2
THE PRUDENTIAL REGULATION AUTHORITY

The Prudential Regulation Authority

2A The Prudential Regulation Authority

(1) The body corporate originally incorporated as the Prudential Regulation Authority Limited is renamed as the Prudential Regulation Authority.

(2) The Prudential Regulation Authority is in this Act referred to as “the PRA”.
(3) *omitted*

2B–18 *omitted*

PART II
REGULATED AND PROHIBITED ACTIVITIES

The general prohibition

19 The general prohibition

(1) No person may carry on a regulated activity in the United Kingdom, or purport to do so, unless he is—
  (a) an authorised person; or
  (b) an exempt person.
(2) The prohibition is referred to in this Act as the general prohibition.

Requirement for permission

20 Authorised persons acting without permission

(1) If an authorised person other than a PRA-authorised person carries on a regulated activity in the United Kingdom, or purports to do so, otherwise than in accordance with permission—
  (a) given to that person under Part 4A, or
  (b) resulting from any other provision of this Act,
  he is to be taken to have contravened a requirement imposed on him by the FCA under this Act.
(1A) If a PRA-authorised person carries on a regulated activity in the United Kingdom, or purports to do so, otherwise than in accordance with permission given to the person under Part 4A or resulting from any other provision of this Act, the person is to be taken to have contravened—
  (a) a requirement imposed by the FCA, and
  (b) a requirement imposed by the PRA.
(2) A contravention within subsection (1) or (1A)—
  (a) does not, except as provided by section 23(1A), make a person guilty of an offence,
  (b) does not, except as provided by section 26A, make any transaction void or unenforceable, and
  (c) does not, except as provided by subsection (3), give rise to any right of action for breach of statutory duty.
(3) In prescribed cases a contravention within subsection (1) or (1A) is actionable at the suit of a person who suffers loss as a result of the contravention, subject to the defences and other incidents applying to actions for breach of statutory duty.
(4) Subsections (1) and (1a) are subject to section 39(1D).
(5) References in this Act to an authorised person acting in contravention of this section are references to the person acting in a way that results in a contravention within subsection (1) or (1A).

Financial promotion

21 Restrictions on financial promotion

(1) A person (“A”) must not, in the course of business, communicate an invitation or inducement to engage in investment activity.
(2) But subsection (1) does not apply if—
  (a) A is an authorised person; or
  (b) the content of the communication is approved for the purposes of this section by an authorised person.
(3) In the case of a communication originating outside the United Kingdom, subsection (1) applies only if the communication is capable of having an effect in the United Kingdom.
(4) The Treasury may by order specify circumstances in which a person is to be regarded for the purposes of subsection (1) as—
  (a) acting in the course of business;
  (b) not acting in the course of business.

(5) The Treasury may by order specify circumstances (which may include compliance with financial promotion rules) in which subsection (1) does not apply.

(6) An order under subsection (5) may, in particular, provide that subsection (1) does not apply in relation to communications—
  (a) of a specified description;
  (b) originating in a specified country or territory outside the United Kingdom;
  (c) originating in a country or territory which falls within a specified description of country or territory outside the United Kingdom; or
  (d) originating outside the United Kingdom.

(7) The Treasury may by order repeal subsection (3).

(8) "Engaging in investment activity" means—
  (a) entering or offering to enter into an agreement the making or performance of which by either party constitutes a controlled activity; or
  (b) exercising any rights conferred by a controlled investment to acquire, dispose of, underwrite or convert a controlled investment.

(9) An activity is a controlled activity if—
  (a) it is an activity of a specified kind or one which falls within a specified class of activity; and
  (b) it relates to an investment of a specified kind, or to one which falls within a specified class of investment.

(10) An investment is a controlled investment if it is an investment of a specified kind or one which falls within a specified class of investment.

(11) Schedule 2 (except paragraph 26) applies for the purposes of subsections (9) and (10) with references to section 22 being read as references to each of those subsections.

(12) Nothing in Schedule 2, as applied by subsection (11), limits the powers conferred by subsection (9) or (10).

(13) "Communicate" includes causing a communication to be made.

(14) "Investment" includes any asset, right or interest.

(15) "Specified" means specified in an order made by the Treasury.

Regulated activities

22 Regulated activities

(1) An activity is a regulated activity for the purposes of this Act if it is an activity of a specified kind which is carried on by way of business and—
  (a) relates to an investment of a specified kind; or
  (b) in the case of an activity of a kind which is also specified for the purposes of this paragraph, is carried on in relation to property of any kind.

(1A) An activity is also a regulated activity for the purposes of this Act if it is an activity of a specified kind which is carried on by way of business and relates to—
  (a) information about a person's financial standing, or
  (b) the setting of a specified benchmark.

(2) Schedule 2 makes provision supplementing this section.

(3) Nothing in Schedule 2 limits the powers conferred by subsection (1) or (1A).

(4) "Investment" includes any asset, right or interest.

(5) "Specified" means specified in an order made by the Treasury.

(6) "Benchmark" means an index, rate or price that—
  (a) is determined from time to time by reference to the state of the market,
  (b) is made available to the public (whether free of charge or on payment), and
  (c) is used for reference for purposes that include one or more of the following—
    (i) determining the interest payable, or other sums due, under loan agreements or under other contracts relating to investments;
    (ii) determining the price at which investments may be bought or sold or the value of investments;
    (iii) measuring the performance of investments.

22A Designation of activities requiring prudential regulation by PRA

(1) The Treasury may by order specify the regulated activities that are "PRA-regulated activities" for the purposes of this Act.

(2)–(4) *omitted*

22B *omitted*

23 Contravention of the general prohibition or section 20(1) or (1A)

(1) A person who contravenes the general prohibition is guilty of an offence and liable—
   (a) on summary conviction, to imprisonment for a term not exceeding six months or a fine not exceeding the statutory maximum, or both;
   (b) on conviction on indictment, to imprisonment for a term not exceeding two years or a fine, or both.

(1A) An authorised person ("A") is guilty of an offence if A carries on a credit-related regulated activity in the United Kingdom, or purports to do so, otherwise than in accordance with permission—
   (a) given to that person under Part 4A, or
   (b) resulting from any other provision of this Act.

(1B) In this Act "credit-related regulated activity" means a regulated activity of a kind designated by the Treasury by order.

(1C) The Treasury may designate a regulated activity under subsection (1B) only if the activity involves a person—
   (a) entering into or administering an agreement under which the person provides another person with credit,
   (b) exercising or being able to exercise the rights of the lender under an agreement under which another person provides a third party with credit, or
   (c) taking steps to procure payment of debts due under an agreement under which another person is provided with credit.

(1D) But a regulated activity may not be designated under subsection (1B) if the agreement in question is one under which the obligation of the borrower is secured on land.

(1E) "Credit" includes any cash loan or other financial accommodation.

(1F) A person guilty of an offence under subsection (1A) is liable—
   (a) on summary conviction, to imprisonment for a term not exceeding the applicable maximum term or a fine not exceeding the statutory maximum, or both;
   (b) on conviction on indictment, to imprisonment for a term not exceeding two years, or a fine, or both.

(1G) The "applicable maximum term" is—
   (a) in England and Wales, 12 months (or 6 months, if the offence was committed before the commencement of section 154(1) of the Criminal Justice Act 2003);
   (b) in Scotland, 12 months;
   (c) in Northern Ireland, 6 months.

(2) In this Act "an authorisation offence" means an offence under this section.

(3) In proceedings for an authorisation offence it is a defence for the accused to show that he took all reasonable precautions and exercised all due diligence to avoid committing the offence.

(4) Subsection (1A) is subject to section 39(1D).

(5) No proceedings may be brought against a person in respect of an offence under subsection (1A) in a case where either regulator has taken action under section 205, 206 or 206A in relation to the alleged contravention within section 20(1) or (1A).

23A *omitted*

24 False claims to be authorised or exempt

(1) A person who is neither an authorised person nor, in relation to the regulated activity in question, an exempt person is guilty of an offence if he—
   (a) describes himself (in whatever terms) as an authorised person;
   (b) describes himself (in whatever terms) as an exempt person in relation to the regulated activity; or
   (c) behaves, or otherwise holds himself out, in a manner which indicates (or which is reasonably likely to be understood as indicating) that he is—
      (i) an authorised person; or
      (ii) an exempt person in relation to the regulated activity.

(2) In proceedings for an offence under this section it is a defence for the accused to show that he took all reasonable precautions and exercised all due diligence to avoid committing the offence.

(3) A person guilty of an offence under this section is liable on summary conviction to imprisonment for a term not exceeding six months or a fine not exceeding level 5 on the standard scale, or both.

(4) ...

25 Contravention of section 21

(1) A person who contravenes section 21(1) is guilty of an offence and liable—

(a) on summary conviction, to imprisonment for a term not exceeding six months or a fine not exceeding the statutory maximum, or both;

(b) on conviction on indictment, to imprisonment for a term not exceeding two years or a fine, or both.

(2) In proceedings for an offence under this section it is a defence for the accused to show—

(a) that he believed on reasonable grounds that the content of the communication was prepared, or approved for the purposes of section 21, by an authorised person; or

(b) that he took all reasonable precautions and exercised all due diligence to avoid committing the offence.

Enforceability of agreements

26 Agreements made by unauthorised persons

(1) An agreement made by a person in the course of carrying on a regulated activity in contravention of the general prohibition is unenforceable against the other party.

(2) The other party is entitled to recover—

(a) any money or other property paid or transferred by him under the agreement; and

(b) compensation for any loss sustained by him as a result of having parted with it.

(3) "Agreement" means an agreement—

(a) made after this section comes into force; and

(b) the making or performance of which constitutes, or is part of, the regulated activity in question.

(4) This section does not apply if the regulated activity is accepting deposits.

26A *omitted*

27 Agreements made through unauthorised persons

(1) This section applies to an agreement that—

(a) is made by an authorised person ("the provider") in the course of carrying on a regulated activity,

(b) is not made in contravention of the general prohibition,

(c) if it relates to a credit-related regulated activity, is not made in contravention of section 20, and

(d) is made in consequence of something said or done by another person ("the third party") in the course of—

(i) a regulated activity carried on by the third party in contravention of the general prohibition, or

(ii) a credit-related regulated activity carried on by the third party in contravention of section 20.

(1A) The agreement is unenforceable against the other party.

(2) The other party is entitled to recover—

(a) any money or other property paid or transferred by him under the agreement; and

(b) compensation for any loss sustained by him as a result of having parted with it.

(3) "Agreement" means an agreement—

(a) made after this section comes into force; and

(b) the making or performance of which constitutes, or is part of, the regulated activity in question carried on by the provider.

(4) This section does not apply if the regulated activity is accepting deposits.

28 Agreements made unenforceable by section 26 or 27: general cases

(1) This section applies to an agreement which is unenforceable because of section 26 or 27, other than an agreement entered into in the course of carrying on a credit-related regulated activity.

(2) The amount of compensation recoverable as a result of that section is—

(a) the amount agreed by the parties; or

(b) on the application of either party, the amount determined by the court.

(3) If the court is satisfied that it is just and equitable in the circumstances of the case, it may allow—
(a) the agreement to be enforced; or
(b) money and property paid or transferred under the agreement to be retained.

(4) In considering whether to allow the agreement to be enforced or (as the case may be) the money or property paid or transferred under the agreement to be retained the court must—
(a) if the case arises as a result of section 26, have regard to the issue mentioned in subsection (5); or
(b) if the case arises as a result of section 27, have regard to the issue mentioned in subsection (6).

(5) The issue is whether the person carrying on the regulated activity concerned reasonably believed that he was not contravening the general prohibition by making the agreement.

(6) The issue is whether the provider knew that the third party was (in carrying on the regulated activity) contravening the general prohibition.

(7) If the person against whom the agreement is unenforceable—
(a) elects not to perform the agreement, or
(b) as a result of this section, recovers money paid or other property transferred by him under the agreement,

he must repay any money and return any other property received by him under the agreement.

(8) If property transferred under the agreement has passed to a third party, a reference in section 26 or 27 or this section to that property is to be read as a reference to its value at the time of its transfer under the agreement.

(9) The commission of an authorisation offence does not make the agreement concerned illegal or invalid to any greater extent than is provided by section 26 or 27.

28A, 28B *omitted*

29 Accepting deposits in breach of general prohibition

(1) This section applies to an agreement between a person ("the depositor") and another person ("the deposit-taker") made in the course of the carrying on by the deposit-taker of accepting deposits in contravention of the general prohibition.

(2) If the depositor is not entitled under the agreement to recover without delay any money deposited by him, he may apply to the court for an order directing the deposit-taker to return the money to him.

(3) The court need not make such an order if it is satisfied that it would not be just and equitable for the money deposited to be returned, having regard to the issue mentioned in subsection (4).

(4) The issue is whether the deposit-taker reasonably believed that he was not contravening the general prohibition by making the agreement.

(5) "Agreement" means an agreement—
(a) made after this section comes into force; and
(b) the making or performance of which constitutes, or is part of, accepting deposits.

30 Enforceability of agreements resulting from unlawful communications

(1) In this section—

"unlawful communication" means a communication in relation to which there has been a contravention of section 21(1);

"controlled agreement" means an agreement the making or performance of which by either party constitutes a controlled activity for the purposes of that section; and

"controlled investment" has the same meaning as in section 21.

(2) If in consequence of an unlawful communication a person enters as a customer into a controlled agreement, it is unenforceable against him and he is entitled to recover—
(a) any money or other property paid or transferred by him under the agreement; and
(b) compensation for any loss sustained by him as a result of having parted with it.

(3) If in consequence of an unlawful communication a person exercises any rights conferred by a controlled investment, no obligation to which he is subject as a result of exercising them is enforceable against him and he is entitled to recover—
(a) any money or other property paid or transferred by him under the obligation; and
(b) compensation for any loss sustained by him as a result of having parted with it.

(4) But the court may allow—
(a) the agreement or obligation to be enforced, or
(b) money or property paid or transferred under the agreement or obligation to be retained,

if it is satisfied that it is just and equitable in the circumstances of the case.

(5) In considering whether to allow the agreement or obligation to be enforced or (as the case may be) the money or property paid or transferred under the agreement to be retained the court must have regard to the issues mentioned in subsections (6) and (7).

(6) If the applicant made the unlawful communication, the issue is whether he reasonably believed that he was not making such a communication.

(7) If the applicant did not make the unlawful communication, the issue is whether he knew that the agreement was entered into in consequence of such a communication.

(8) "Applicant" means the person seeking to enforce the agreement or obligation or retain the money or property paid or transferred.

(9) Any reference to making a communication includes causing a communication to be made.

(10) The amount of compensation recoverable as a result of subsection (2) or (3) is—
(a) the amount agreed between the parties; or
(b) on the application of either party, the amount determined by the court.

(11) If a person elects not to perform an agreement or an obligation which (by virtue of subsection (2) or (3)) is unenforceable against him, he must repay any money and return any other property received by him under the agreement.

(12) If (by virtue of subsection (2) or (3)) a person recovers money paid or property transferred by him under an agreement or obligation, he must repay any money and return any other property received by him as a result of exercising the rights in question.

(13) If any property required to be returned under this section has passed to a third party, references to that property are to be read as references to its value at the time of its receipt by the person required to return it.

PARTS III–V
OMITTED

PART VI
OFFICIAL LISTING

The competent authority

72, 73 …

Rules

73A Part 6 Rules

(1) The FCA may make rules ("Part 6 rules") for the purposes of this Part.

(2) Provisions of Part 6 rules expressed to relate to the official list are referred to in this Part as "listing rules".

(3) Provisions of Part 6 rules expressed to relate to disclosure of information in respect of financial instruments which have been admitted to trading on a regulated market or for which a request for admission to trading on such a market has been made, are referred to in this Part as "disclosure rules".

(4) Provisions of Part 6 rules expressed to relate to transferable securities are referred to in this Part as "prospectus rules".

(5) In relation to prospectus rules, the purposes of this Part include the purposes of the prospectus directive.

(6) Transparency rules and corporate governance rules are not listing rules, disclosure rules or prospectus rules, but are Part 6 rules.

The official list

74 The official list

(1) The FCA must maintain the official list.

(2) The FCA may admit to the official list such securities and other things as it considers appropriate.

(3) But—
  (a) nothing may be admitted to the official list except in accordance with this Part; and
  (b) the Treasury may by order provide that anything which falls within a description or category specified in the order may not be admitted to the official list.

(4) …

(5) In the following provisions of this Part—
"listing" means being included in the official list in accordance with this Part.

Listing

75 Applications for listing

(1) Admission to the official list may be granted only on an application made to the FCA in such manner as may be required by listing rules.

(2) No application for listing may be entertained by the FCA unless it is made by, or with the consent of, the issuer of the securities concerned.

(3) No application for listing may be entertained by the FCA in respect of securities which are to be issued by a body of a prescribed kind.

(4) The FCA may not grant an application for listing unless it is satisfied that—
  (a) the requirements of listing rules (so far as they apply to the application), and
  (b) any other requirements imposed by the authority in relation to the application, are complied with.

(5) An application for listing may be refused if, for a reason relating to the issuer, the FCA considers that granting it would be detrimental to the interests of investors.

(6) An application for listing securities which are already officially listed in another EEA State may be refused if the issuer has failed to comply with any obligations to which he is subject as a result of that listing.

76 Decision on application

(1) The FCA must notify the applicant of its decision on an application for listing—
  (a) before the end of the period of six months beginning with the date on which the application is received; or
  (b) if within that period the FCA has required the applicant to provide further information in connection with the application, before the end of the period of six months beginning with the date on which that information is provided.

(2) If the FCA fails to comply with subsection (1), it is to be taken to have decided to refuse the application.

(3) If the FCA decides to grant an application for listing, it must give the applicant written notice.

(4) If the FCA proposes to refuse an application for listing, it must give the applicant a warning notice.

(5) If the FCA decides to refuse an application for listing, it must give the applicant a decision notice.

(6) If the FCA decides to refuse an application for listing, the applicant may refer the matter to the Tribunal.

(7) If securities are admitted to the official list, their admission may not be called in question on the ground that any requirement or condition for their admission has not been complied with.

77 Discontinuance and suspension of listing

(1) The FCA may, in accordance with listing rules, discontinue the listing of any securities if satisfied that there are special circumstances which preclude normal regular dealings in them.

(2) The FCA may, in accordance with listing rules, suspend the listing of any securities.

(2A) The FCA may discontinue under subsection (1) or suspend under subsection (2) the listing of any securities on its own initiative or on the application of the issuer of those securities.

(3) If securities are suspended under subsection (2) they are to be treated, for the purposes of sections 96 and 99, as still being listed.

(4) This section applies to securities whenever they were admitted to the official list.

(5) If the FCA discontinues or suspends the listing of any securities, on its own initiative, the issuer may refer the matter to the Tribunal.

78 Discontinuance or suspension: procedure

(1) A discontinuance or suspension by the FCA on its own initiative takes effect—
(a) immediately, if the notice under subsection (2) states that that is the case;
(b) in any other case, on such date as may be specified in that notice.

(2) If on its own initiative the FCA—
(a) proposes to discontinue or suspend the listing of securities, or
(b) discontinues or suspends the listing of securities with immediate effect,
it must give the issuer of the securities written notice.

(3) The notice must—
(a) give details of the discontinuance or suspension;
(b) state the FCA's reasons for the discontinuance or suspension and for choosing the date on which it took effect or takes effect;
(c) inform the issuer of the securities that he may make representations to the FCA within such period as may be specified in the notice (whether or not he has referred the matter to the Tribunal);
(d) inform him of the date on which the discontinuance or suspension took effect or will take effect; and
(e) inform him of his right to refer the matter to the Tribunal.

(4) The FCA may extend the period within which representations may be made to it.

(5) If, having considered any representations made by the issuer of the securities, the FCA decides—
(a) to discontinue or suspend the listing of the securities, or
(b) if the discontinuance or suspension has taken effect, not to cancel it, the FCA must give the issuer of the securities written notice.

(6) A notice given under subsection (5) must inform the issuer of the securities of his right to refer the matter to the Tribunal.

(7) If a notice informs a person of his right to refer a matter to the Tribunal, it must give an indication of the procedure on such a reference.

(8) If the FCA decides—
(a) not to discontinue or suspend the listing of the securities, or
(b) if the discontinuance or suspension has taken effect, to cancel it, the FCA must give the issuer of the securities written notice.

(9) The effect of cancelling a discontinuance is that the securities concerned are to be readmitted, without more, to the official list.

(10) If—
(a) the FCA has suspended the listing of securities on its own initiative, or securities have been suspended by the Bank of England under section 19, 39B or 48L of the Banking Act 2009, and
(b) the FCA proposes to refuse an application by the issuer of the securities for the cancellation of the suspension,
the FCA must give the issuer a warning notice.

(11) The FCA must, having considered any representations made in response to the warning notice—
(a) if it decides to refuse the application, give the issuer of the securities a decision notice;
(b) if it grants the application, give him written notice of its decision.

(12) If the FCA decides to refuse an application for the cancellation of the suspension of listed securities, the applicant may refer the matter to the Tribunal.

(13) "Discontinuance" means a discontinuance of listing under section 77(1).

(14) "Suspension" means a suspension of listing under section 77(2) and in subsections (10) and (12), includes a suspension of listing under section 19, 39B or 48L of the Banking Act 2009.

78A Discontinuance or suspension at the request of the issuer: procedure

(1) A discontinuance or suspension by the FCA on the application of the issuer of the securities takes effect—
(a) immediately, if the notice under subsection (2) states that this is the case;
(b) in any other case, on such date as may be specified in that notice.

(2) If the FCA discontinues or suspends the listing of securities on the application of the issuer of the securities it must give him written notice.

(3) The notice must—

(a) give details of the discontinuance or suspension;

(b) inform the issuer of the securities of the date on which the discontinuance or suspension took effect or will take effect; and

(c) inform the issuer of his right to apply for the cancellation of the suspension.

(4) If the FCA proposes to refuse an application by the issuer of the securities for the discontinuance or suspension of the listing of the securities, it must give him a warning notice.

(5) The FCA must, having considered any representations made in response to the warning notice, if it decides to refuse the application, give the issuer of the securities a decision notice.

(6) If the FCA decides to refuse an application by the issuer of the securities for the discontinuance or suspension of the listing of the securities, the issuer may refer the matter to the Tribunal.

(7) If the FCA has suspended the listing of securities on the application of the issuer of the securities and proposes to refuse an application by the issuer for the cancellation of the suspension, it must give him a warning notice.

(8) The FCA must, having considered any representations made in response to the warning notice—

(a) if it decides to refuse the application for the cancellation of the suspension, give the issuer of the securities a decision notice;

(b) if it grants the application, give him written notice of its decision.

(9) If the FCA decides to refuse an application for the cancellation of the suspension of listed securities, the applicant may refer the matter to the Tribunal.

(10) "Discontinuance" means a discontinuance of listing under section 77(1).

(11) "Suspension" means a suspension of listing under section 77(2).

Listing particulars

79 Listing particulars and other documents

(1) Listing rules may provide that securities of a kind specified in the rules may not be admitted to the official list unless—

(a) listing particulars have been submitted to, and approved by, the FCA and published; or

(b) in such cases as may be specified by listing rules, such document (other than listing particulars or a prospectus of a kind required by listing rules) as may be so specified has been published.

(2) "Listing particulars" means a document in such form and containing such information as may be specified in listing rules.

(3) For the purposes of this Part, the persons responsible for listing particulars are to be determined in accordance with regulations made by the Treasury.

(3A) Listing rules made under subsection (1) may not specify securities of a kind for which an approved prospectus is required as a result of section 85.

(4) Nothing in this section affects the FCA's general power to make listing rules.

80 General duty of disclosure in listing particulars

(1) Listing particulars submitted to the FCA under section 79 must contain all such information as investors and their professional advisers would reasonably require, and reasonably expect to find there, for the purpose of making an informed assessment of—

(a) the assets and liabilities, financial position, profits and losses, and prospects of the issuer of the securities; and

(b) the rights attaching to the securities.

(2) That information is required in addition to any information required by—

(a) listing rules, or

(b) the FCA,

as a condition of the admission of the securities to the official list.

(3) Subsection (1) applies only to information—

(a) within the knowledge of any person responsible for the listing particulars; or

(b) which it would be reasonable for him to obtain by making enquiries.

(4) In determining what information subsection (1) requires to be included in listing particulars, regard must be had (in particular) to—

(a) the nature of the securities and their issuer;
(b) the nature of the persons likely to consider acquiring them;
(c) the fact that certain matters may reasonably be expected to be within the knowledge of professional advisers of a kind which persons likely to acquire the securities may reasonably be expected to consult; and
(d) any information available to investors or their professional advisers as a result of requirements imposed on the issuer of the securities by a recognised investment exchange, by listing rules or by or under any other enactment.

81 Supplementary listing particulars

(1) If at any time after the preparation of listing particulars which have been submitted to the FCA under section 79 and before the commencement of dealings in the securities concerned following their admission to the official list—
(a) there is a significant change affecting any matter contained in those particulars the inclusion of which was required by—
(i) section 80,
(ii) listing rules, or
(iii) the FCA, or
(b) a significant new matter arises, the inclusion of information in respect of which would have been so required if it had arisen when the particulars were prepared,

the issuer must, in accordance with listing rules, submit supplementary listing particulars of the change or new matter to the FCA, for its approval and, if they are approved, publish them.

(2) "Significant" means significant for the purpose of making an informed assessment of the kind mentioned in section 80(1).
(3) If the issuer of the securities is not aware of the change or new matter in question, he is not under a duty to comply with subsection (1) unless he is notified of the change or new matter by a person responsible for the listing particulars.
(4) But it is the duty of any person responsible for those particulars who is aware of such a change or new matter to give notice of it to the issuer.
(5) Subsection (1) applies also as respects matters contained in any supplementary listing particulars previously published under this section in respect of the securities in question.

82 Exemptions from disclosure

(1) The FCA may authorise the omission from listing particulars of any information, the inclusion of which would otherwise be required by section 80 or 81, on the ground—
(a) that its disclosure would be contrary to the public interest;
(b) that its disclosure would be seriously detrimental to the issuer; or
(c) in the case of securities of a kind specified in listing rules, that its disclosure is unnecessary for persons of the kind who may be expected normally to buy or deal in securities of that kind.
(2) But—
(a) no authority may be granted under subsection (1)(b) in respect of essential information; and
(b) no authority granted under subsection (1)(b) extends to any such information.
(3) The Secretary of State or the Treasury may issue a certificate to the effect that the disclosure of any information (including information that would otherwise have to be included in listing particulars for which they are themselves responsible) would be contrary to the public interest.
(4) The FCA is entitled to act on any such certificate in exercising its powers under subsection (1)(a).
(5) This section does not affect any powers of the FCA under listing rules made as a result of section 101(2).
(6) "Essential information" means information which a person considering acquiring securities of the kind in question would be likely to need in order not to be misled about any facts which it is essential for him to know in order to make an informed assessment.
(7) "Listing particulars" includes supplementary listing particulars.

83 ...

Transferable securities: public offers and admission to trading

84 Matters which may be dealt with by prospectus rules

(1) Prospectus rules may make provision as to—
  (a) the required form and content of a prospectus (including a summary);
  (b) the cases in which a summary need not be included in a prospectus;
  (c) the languages which may be used in a prospectus (including a summary);
  (d) the determination of the persons responsible for a prospectus;
  (e) the manner in which applications to the FCA for the approval of a prospectus are to be made.

(2) Prospectus rules may also make provision as to—
  (a) the period of validity of a prospectus;
  (b) the disclosure of the maximum price or of the criteria or conditions according to which the final offer price is to be determined, if that information is not contained in a prospectus;
  (c) the disclosure of the amount of the transferable securities which are to be offered to the public or of the criteria or conditions according to which that amount is to be determined, if that information is not contained in a prospectus;
  (d) the required form and content of other summary documents (including the languages which may be used in such a document);
  (e) the ways in which a prospectus that has been approved by the FCA may be made available to the public;
  (f) the disclosure, publication or other communication of such information as the FCA may reasonably stipulate;
  (g) the principles to be observed in relation to advertisements in connection with an offer of transferable securities to the public or admission of transferable securities to trading on a regulated market and the enforcement of those principles;
  (h) the suspension of trading in transferable securities where continued trading would be detrimental to the interests of investors;
  (i) elections under section 87 or under Article 2.1(m)(iii) of the prospectus directive as applied for the purposes of this Part by section 102C

(3) Prospectus rules may also make provision as to—
  (a) access to the register of investors maintained under section 87R; and
  (b) the supply of information from that register.

(4) Prospectus rules may make provision for the purpose of dealing with matters arising out of or related to any provision of the prospectus directive.

(5) In relation to cases where the home State in relation to an issuer of transferable securities is an EEA State other than the United Kingdom, prospectus rules may make provision for the recognition of elections made in relation to such securities under the law of that State in accordance with Article 1.3 or 2.1(m)(iii) of the prospectus directive.

(6) In relation to a document relating to transferable securities issued by an issuer incorporated in a non-EEA State and drawn up in accordance with the law of that State, prospectus rules may make provision as to the approval of that document as a prospectus.

(7) Nothing in this section affects the FCA's general power to make prospectus rules.

85 Prohibition of dealing etc in transferable securities without approved prospectus

(1) It is unlawful for transferable securities to which this subsection applies to be offered to the public in the United Kingdom unless an approved prospectus has been made available to the public before the offer is made.

(2) It is unlawful to request the admission of transferable securities to which this subsection applies to trading on a regulated market situated or operating in the United Kingdom unless an approved prospectus has been made available to the public before the request is made.

(3) A person who contravenes subsection (1) or (2) is guilty of an offence and liable—
  (a) on summary conviction, to imprisonment for a term not exceeding 3 months or a fine not exceeding the statutory maximum or both;
  (b) on conviction on indictment, to imprisonment for a term not exceeding 2 years or a fine or both.

(4) A contravention of subsection (1) or (2) is actionable, at the suit of a person who suffers loss as a result of the contravention, subject to the defences and other incidents applying to actions for breach of statutory duty.

(5) Subsection (1) applies to all transferable securities other than—
(a) those listed in Schedule 11A;
(b) such other transferable securities as may be specified in prospectus rules.

(6) Subsection (2) applies to all transferable securities other than—
(a) those listed in Part 1 of Schedule 11A;
(b) such other transferable securities as may be specified in prospectus rules.

(7) "Approved prospectus" means, in relation to transferable securities to which this section applies, a prospectus approved by the competent authority of the home State in relation to the issuer of the securities.

86 Exempt offers to the public

(1) A person does not contravene section 85(1) if—
(a) the offer is made to or directed at qualified investors only;
(b) the offer is made to or directed at fewer than 150 persons, other than qualified investors, per EEA State;
(c) the minimum consideration which may be paid by any person for transferable securities acquired by him pursuant to the offer is at least 100,000 euros (or an equivalent amount);
(d) the transferable securities being offered are denominated in amounts of at least 100,000 euros (or equivalent amounts);
(e) the total consideration for the transferable securities being offered in the EEA States cannot exceed 100,000 euros (or an equivalent amount); or
(f) the offer falls within subsection (1A).

(1A) An offer ("the current offer") falls within this subsection if the transferable securities are being sold or placed through a financial intermediary where—
(a) the transferable securities have previously been the subject of one or more offers to the public;
(b) in respect of one or more of those previous offers any of paragraphs (a) to (e) of subsection (1) applied;
(c) a prospectus is available for the securities which has been approved by the FCA and meets either of the conditions in subsection (1B); and
(d) the issuer or other person who was responsible for drawing up the prospectus has given written consent to the use of the prospectus for the purpose of the current offer.

(1B) The conditions referred to in subsection (1A)(c) are—
(a) that the prospectus was approved by the FCA no earlier than 12 months before the date the current offer is made, and is supplemented by every supplementary prospectus which was required to be submitted under section 87G; or
(b) in the case of non-equity transferable securities falling within Article 5(4)(b) of the prospectus directive, that the securities concerned have not ceased to be issued in a continuous or repeated manner.

(2) Where—
(a) a person who is not a qualified investor ("the client") has engaged a qualified investor falling within point (1) of Section I of Annex II to the markets in financial instruments directive to act as his agent, and
(b) the terms on which the qualified investor is engaged enable him to make decisions concerning the acceptance of offers of transferable securities on the client's behalf without reference to the client,

an offer made to or directed at the qualified investor is not to be regarded for the purposes of subsection (1) as also having been made to or directed at the client.

(3) For the purposes of subsection (1)(b), the making of an offer of transferable securities to—
(a) trustees of a trust,
(b) members of a partnership in their capacity as such, or
(c) two or more persons jointly,

is to be treated as the making of an offer to a single person.

(4) In determining whether subsection (1)(e) is satisfied in relation to an offer ("offer A"), offer A is to be taken together with any other offer of transferable securities of the same class made by the same person which—

(a) was open at any time within the period of 12 months ending with the date on which offer A is first made; and
(b) had previously satisfied subsection (1)(e).

(5) For the purposes of this section, an amount (in relation to an amount denominated in euros) is an "equivalent amount" if it is an amount of equal value denominated wholly or partly in another currency or unit of account.

(6) The equivalent is to be calculated at the latest practicable date before (but in any event not more than 3 working days before) the date on which the offer is first made.

(7) "Qualified investor", in relation to an offer of transferable securities, means—
(a) a person described in points (1) to (4) of Section I of Annex II to the markets in financial instruments directive, other than a person who, before the making of the offer, has agreed in writing with the relevant firm (or each of the relevant firms) to be treated as a non-professional client in accordance with the final paragraph of Section I of Annex II to that directive;
(b) a person who has made a request to one or more relevant firms to be treated as a professional client in accordance with Section II of Annex II to that directive and has not subsequently, but before the making of the offer, agreed in writing with that relevant firm (or each of those relevant firms) to be treated as a non-professional client in accordance with the final paragraph of Section I of Annex II to that directive;
(c) a person who is an eligible counterparty in accordance with Article 24 of that directive and has not, before the making of the offer, agreed in writing with the relevant firm (or each of the relevant firms) to be treated as a non-professional client in accordance with the final paragraph of Section I of Annex II to that directive; or
(d) a person whom any relevant firm is authorised to continue to treat as a professional client in accordance with Article 71(6) of that directive.

(8) In subsection (7) "relevant firm" means an investment firm or credit institution acting in connection with the offer.

(9) Investment firms and credit institutions which are authorised persons must communicate their classification of their clients as being or not being qualified investors on request to an issuer subject to complying with the Data Protection Act 1998 or any directly applicable EU legislation relating to data protection.

(10) In subsections (8) and (9), "credit institution" means—
(a) a credit institution authorised under the capital requirements directive; or
(b) an institution which would satisfy the requirements for authorisation as a credit institution under that directive if it had its registered office (or if it does not have one, its head office) in an EEA State.

87 Election to have prospectus

(1) A person who proposes—
(a) to issue transferable securities to which this section applies,
(b) to offer to the public transferable securities to which this section applies, or
(c) to request the admission to a regulated market of transferable securities to which this section applies,

may elect, in accordance with prospectus rules, to have a prospectus in relation to the securities.

(2) If a person makes such an election, the provisions of this Part and of prospectus rules apply in relation to those transferable securities as if, in relation to an offer of the securities to the public or the admission of the securities to trading on a regulated market, they were transferable securities for which an approved prospectus would be required as a result of section 85.

(3) Listing rules made under section 79 do not apply to securities which are the subject of an election.

(4) The transferable securities to which this section applies are those which fall within any of the following paragraphs of Schedule 11A—
(a) paragraph 2,
(b) paragraph 4,
(c) paragraph 8, or
(d) paragraph 9,

where the United Kingdom is the home State in relation to the issuer of the securities.

Approval of prospectus

87A Criteria for approval of prospectus by FCA

(1) The FCA may not approve a prospectus unless it is satisfied that—
   (a) the United Kingdom is the home State in relation to the issuer of the transferable securities to which it relates,
   (b) the prospectus contains the necessary information, and
   (c) all of the other requirements imposed by or in accordance with this Part or the prospectus directive have been complied with (so far as those requirements apply to a prospectus for the transferable securities in question).

(2) The necessary information is the information necessary to enable investors to make an informed assessment of—
   (a) the assets and liabilities, financial position, profits and losses, and prospects of the issuer of the transferable securities and of any guarantor; and
   (b) the rights attaching to the transferable securities.

(3) The necessary information must be presented in a form which is comprehensible and easy to analyse.

(4) The necessary information must be prepared having regard to the particular nature of the transferable securities and their issuer.

(5) The prospectus must include a summary (unless the transferable securities in question are ones in relation to which prospectus rules provide that a summary is not required).

(6) The summary must, briefly and in non-technical language, convey the essential characteristics of, and risks associated with, the issuer, any guarantor and the transferable securities to which the prospectus relates.

(7) Where the prospectus for which approval is sought does not include the final offer price or the amount of transferable securities to be offered to the public, the applicant must inform the FCA in writing of that information as soon as that element is finalised.

(7A) ...

(8) "Prospectus" (except in subsection (5)) includes a supplementary prospectus.

(9) "The key information" means the information which is essential to enable investors to understand the transferable securities to which the prospectus relates and to decide whether to consider the offer further.

(10) The key information must include—
   (a) the essential characteristics of, and risks associated with, the issuer and any guarantor, including their assets, liabilities and financial positions;
   (b) the essential characteristics of, and risks associated with, investment in the transferable securities, including any rights attaching to the securities;
   (c) the general terms of the offer, including an estimate of the expenses charged to an investor by the issuer and the person offering the securities to the public, if not the issuer;
   (d) details of the admission to trading; and
   (e) the reasons for the offer and proposed use of the proceeds.

87B Exemptions from disclosure

(1) The FCA may authorise the omission from a prospectus of any information, the inclusion of which would otherwise be required, on the ground—
   (a) that its disclosure would be contrary to the public interest;
   (b) that its disclosure would be seriously detrimental to the issuer, provided that the omission would be unlikely to mislead the public with regard to any facts or circumstances which are essential for an informed assessment of the kind mentioned in section 87A(2); or
   (c) that the information is only of minor importance for a specific offer to the public or admission to trading on a regulated market and unlikely to influence an informed assessment of the kind mentioned in section 87A(2).

(2) The Secretary of State or the Treasury may issue a certificate to the effect that the disclosure of any information would be contrary to the public interest.

(3) The FCA is entitled to act on any such certificate in exercising its powers under subsection (1)(a).

(4) This section does not affect any powers of the FCA under prospectus rules.

(5) "Prospectus" includes a supplementary prospectus.

87C Consideration of application for approval

(1) The FCA must notify the applicant of its decision on an application for approval of a prospectus before the end of the period for consideration.

(2) The period for consideration—
- (a) begins with the first working day after the date on which the application is received; but
- (b) if the FCA gives a notice under subsection (4), is to be treated as beginning with the first working day after the date on which the notice is complied with.

(3) The period for consideration is—
- (a) except in the case of a new issuer, 10 working days; or
- (b) in that case, 20 working days.

(4) The FCA may by notice in writing require a person who has applied for approval of a prospectus to provide—
- (a) specified documents or documents of a specified description, or
- (b) specified information or information of a specified description.

(5) No notice under subsection (4) may be given after the end of the period, beginning with the first working day after the date on which the application is received, of—
- (a) except in the case of a new issuer, 10 working days; or
- (b) in that case, 20 working days.

(6) Subsection (4) applies only to information and documents reasonably required in connection with the exercise by the FCA of its functions in relation to the application.

(7) The FCA may require any information provided under this section to be provided in such form as it may reasonably require.

(8) The FCA may require—
- (a) any information provided, whether in a document or otherwise, to be verified in such manner, or
- (b) any document produced to be authenticated in such manner, as it may reasonably require.

(9) The FCA must notify the applicant of its decision on an application for approval of a supplementary prospectus before the end of the period of 7 working days beginning with the date on which the application is received; and subsections (4) and (6) to (8) apply to such an application as they apply to an application for approval of a prospectus.

(10) The FCA's failure to comply with subsection (1) or (9) does not constitute approval of the application in question.

(11) "New issuer" means an issuer of transferable securities which—
- (a) does not have transferable securities admitted to trading on any regulated market; and
- (b) has not previously offered transferable securities to the public.

87D Procedure for decision on application for approval

(1) If the FCA approves a prospectus, it must give the applicant written notice.

(2) If the FCA proposes to refuse to approve a prospectus, it must give the applicant written notice.

(3) The notice must state the FCA's reasons for the proposed refusal.

(4) If the FCA decides to refuse to approve a prospectus, it must give the applicant written notice.

(5) The notice must—
- (a) give the FCA's reasons for refusing the application; and
- (b) inform the applicant of his right to refer the matter to the Tribunal.

(6) If the FCA refuses to approve a prospectus, the applicant may refer the matter to the Tribunal.

(7) In this section "prospectus" includes a supplementary prospectus.

Transfer of application for approval of a prospectus

87E Transfer by FCA of application for approval

(1) The FCA may transfer an application for the approval of a prospectus or a supplementary prospectus to the competent authority of another EEA State ("the transferee authority").

(2) Before doing so, the FCA must obtain the agreement of the transferee authority.

(3) The FCA must inform the applicant of the transfer within 3 working days beginning with the first working day after the date of the transfer.

(4) On making a transfer under subsection (1), the FCA ceases to have functions under this Part in relation to the application transferred.

87F Transfer to FCA of application for approval

(1) Where the FCA agrees to the transfer to it of an application for the approval of a prospectus made to the competent authority of another EEA State—

(a) the United Kingdom is to be treated for the purposes of this Part as the home State in relation to the issuer of the transferable securities to which the prospectus relates, and

(b) this Part applies to the application as if it had been made to the FCA but with the modification in subsection (2).

(2) Section 87C applies as if the date of the transfer were the date on which the application was received by the FCA.

87FA Final terms

Final terms issued in relation to a prospectus must only contain information that relates to the securities note and must not be used to supplement the prospectus.

Supplementary prospectus

87G Supplementary prospectus

(1) Subsection (2) applies if, during the relevant period, there arises or is noted a significant new factor, material mistake or inaccuracy relating to the information included in a prospectus approved by the FCA.

(2) The person on whose application the prospectus was approved must, in accordance with prospectus rules, submit a supplementary prospectus containing details of the new factor, mistake or inaccuracy to the FCA for its approval.

(3) The relevant period begins when the prospectus is approved and ends—

(a) with the closure of the offer of the transferable securities to which the prospectus relates; or

(b) when trading in those securities on a regulated market begins.

(3A) But where the prospectus relates both to an offer of transferable securities to the public and the admission of those securities to trading on a regulated market, subsection (3) does not apply and the relevant period begins when the prospectus is approved and ends with the later of—

(a) the closure of the offer to the public to which the prospectus relates, or

(b) the time when trading in those securities on a regulated markets begins.

(4) "Significant" means significant for the purposes of making an informed assessment of the kind mentioned in section 87A(2).

(5) Any person responsible for the prospectus who is aware of any new factor, mistake or inaccuracy which may require the submission of a supplementary prospectus in accordance with subsection (2) must give notice of it to—

(a) the issuer of the transferable securities to which the prospectus relates, and

(b) the person on whose application the prospectus was approved.

(6) A supplementary prospectus must provide sufficient information to correct any mistake or inaccuracy which gave rise to the need for it.

(7) Subsection (1) applies also to information contained in any supplementary prospectus published under this section.

Passporting

87H Prospectus approved in another EEA State

(1) A prospectus approved by the competent authority of an EEA State other than the United Kingdom is not an approved prospectus for the purposes of section 85 unless that authority has notified ESMA and provided the FCA with—

(a) a certificate of approval;

(b) a copy of the prospectus as approved; and

(c) if requested by the FCA, a translation of the summary of the prospectus.

(2) A document is not a certificate of approval unless it states that the prospectus—

(a) has been drawn up in accordance with the prospectus directive; and

(b) has been approved, in accordance with that directive, by the competent authority providing the certificate.

(3) A document is not a certificate of approval unless it states whether (and, if so, why) the competent authority providing it authorised, in accordance with the prospectus directive, the omission from the prospectus of information which would otherwise have been required to be included.

(3A) The FCA must publish on its website a list of certificates of approval provided to it in accordance with this section.
(3B) The list referred to in subsection (3A) must—
(a) be kept up-to-date,
(b) retain items on it for a period of at least 12 months, and
(c) include hyperlinks to any certificate of approval and prospectus published on the website of—
(i) the competent authority of the EEA State which provided the certificate,
(ii) the issuer, or
(iii) the regulated market where admission to trading is sought.
(4) "Prospectus" includes a supplementary prospectus.

87I Provision of information to host Member State

(1) The FCA must, if requested to do so, supply the competent authority of a specified EEA State with—
(a) a certificate of approval;
(b) a copy of the specified prospectus (as approved by the FCA); and
(c) a translation of the summary of the specified prospectus (if the request states that one has been requested by the competent authority).
(1A) If the FCA supplies a certificate of approval to the competent authority of the specified EEA State, it must also supply a copy of that certificate to—
(a) the person who made the request under this section; and
(b) ESMA.
(2) Only the following may make a request under this section—
(a) the issuer of the transferable securities to which the specified prospectus relates;
(b) a person who wishes to offer the transferable securities to which the specified prospectus relates to the public in an EEA State other than (or as well as) the United Kingdom;
(c) a person requesting the admission of the transferable securities to which the specified prospectus relates to a regulated market situated or operating in an EEA State other than (or as well as) the United Kingdom.
(3) A certificate of approval must state that the prospectus—
(a) has been drawn up in accordance with this Part and the prospectus directive; and
(b) has been approved, in accordance with those provisions, by the FCA.
(4) A certificate of approval must state whether (and, if so, why) the FCA authorised, in accordance with section 87B, the omission from the prospectus of information which would otherwise have been required to be included.
(5) The FCA must comply with a request under this section—
(a) if the prospectus has been approved before the request is made, within 3 working days beginning with the date the request is received; or
(b) if the request is submitted with an application for the approval of the prospectus, on the first working day after the date on which it approves the prospectus.
(6) "Prospectus" includes a supplementary prospectus.
(7) "Specified" means specified in a request made for the purposes of this section.

Transferable securities: powers of FCA

87J Requirements imposed as condition of approval

(1) As a condition of approving a prospectus, the competent authority may by notice in writing—
(a) require the inclusion in the prospectus of such supplementary information necessary for investor protection as the FCA may specify;
(b) require a person controlling, or controlled by, the applicant to provide specified information or documents;
(c) require an auditor or manager of the applicant to provide specified information or documents;
(d) require a financial intermediary commissioned to assist either in carrying out the offer to the public of the transferable securities to which the prospectus relates or in requesting their admission to trading on a regulated market, to provide specified information or documents.

(2) "Specified" means specified in the notice.
(3) "Prospectus" includes a supplementary prospectus.

87K Power to suspend or prohibit offer to the public

(1) This section applies where a person ("the offeror") has made an offer of transferable securities to the public ("the offer").
(2) If the FCA has reasonable grounds for suspecting that an applicable provision has been infringed, it may—
 (a) require the offeror to suspend the offer for a period not exceeding 10 working days;
 (b) require a person not to advertise the offer, or to take such steps as the authority may specify to suspend any existing advertisement of the offer, for a period not exceeding 10 working days.
(3) If the FCA has reasonable grounds for suspecting that it is likely that an applicable provision will be infringed, it may require the offeror to withdraw the offer.
(4) If the FCA finds that an applicable provision has been infringed, it may require the offeror to withdraw the offer.
(5) "An applicable provision" means—
 (a) a provision of this Part,
 (b) a provision contained in prospectus rules,
 (c) any other provision made in accordance with the prospectus directive,
 applicable in relation to the offer.

87L Power to suspend or prohibit admission to trading on a regulated market

(1) This section applies where a person has requested the admission of transferable securities to trading on a regulated market.
(2) If the FCA has reasonable grounds for suspecting that an applicable provision has been infringed and the securities have not yet been admitted to trading on the regulated market in question, it may—
 (a) require the person requesting admission to suspend the request for a period not exceeding 10 working days;
 (b) require a person not to advertise the securities to which it relates, or to take such steps as the authority may specify to suspend any existing advertisement in connection with those securities, for a period not exceeding 10 working days.
(3) If the FCA has reasonable grounds for suspecting that an applicable provision has been infringed and the securities have been admitted to trading on the regulated market in question, it may—
 (a) require the market operator to suspend trading in the securities for a period not exceeding 10 working days;
 (b) require a person not to advertise the securities, or to take such steps as the FCA may specify to suspend any existing advertisement in connection with those securities, for a period not exceeding 10 working days.
(4) If the FCA finds that an applicable provision has been infringed, it may require the market operator to prohibit trading in the securities on the regulated market in question.
(5) "An applicable provision" means—
 (a) a provision of this Part,
 (b) a provision contained in prospectus rules,
 (c) any other provision made in accordance with the prospectus directive,
 applicable in relation to the admission of the transferable securities to trading on the regulated market in question.

87M Public censure of issuer

(1) If the FCA finds that—
 (a) an issuer of transferable securities,
 (b) a person offering transferable securities to the public, or
 (c) a person requesting the admission of transferable securities to trading on a regulated market, is failing or has failed to comply with his obligations under an applicable provision, it may publish a statement to that effect.
(2) If the FCA proposes to publish a statement, it must give the person a warning notice setting out the terms of the proposed statement.
(3) If, after considering any representations made in response to the warning notice, the FCA decides to make the proposed statement, it must give the person a decision notice setting out the terms of the statement.

(4) "An applicable provision" means—
(a) a provision of this Part,
(b) a provision contained in prospectus rules,
(c) any other provision made in accordance with the prospectus directive, applicable to a prospectus in relation to the transferable securities in question.
(5) "Prospectus" includes a supplementary prospectus.

87N Right to refer matters to the Tribunal

(1) A person to whom a decision notice is given under section 87M may refer the matter to the Tribunal.
(2) A person to whom a notice is given under section 87O may refer the matter to the Tribunal.

87O Procedure under sections 87K and 87L

(1) A requirement under section 87K or 87L takes effect—
(a) immediately, if the notice under subsection (2) states that that is the case;
(b) in any other case, on such date as may be specified in that notice.
(2) If the FCA—
(a) proposes to exercise the powers in section 87K or 87L in relation to a person, or
(b) exercises any of those powers in relation to a person with immediate effect, it must give that person written notice.
(3) The notice must—
(a) give details of the FCA's action or proposed action;
(b) state the FCA's reasons for taking the action in question and choosing the date on which it took effect or takes effect;
(c) inform the recipient that he may make representations to the FCA within such period as may be specified by the notice (whether or not he has referred the matter to the Tribunal);
(d) inform him of the date on which the action took effect or takes effect; and
(e) inform him of his right to refer the matter to the Tribunal.
(4) The FCA may extend the period within which representations may be made to it.
(5) If, having considered any representations made to it, the FCA decides to maintain, vary or revoke its earlier decision, it must give written notice to that effect to the person mentioned in subsection (2).
(6) A notice given under subsection (5) must inform that person, where relevant, of his right to refer the matter to the Tribunal.
(7) If a notice informs a person of his right to refer a matter to the Tribunal, it must give an indication of the procedure on such a reference.
(8) If a notice under this section relates to the exercise of the power conferred by section 87L(3), the notice must also be given to the person at whose request the transferable securities were admitted to trading on the regulated market.

87P Exercise of powers at request of competent authority of another EEA State

(1) This section applies if—
(a) the competent authority of an EEA State other than the United Kingdom has approved a prospectus,
(b) the transferable securities to which the prospectus relates have been offered to the public in the United Kingdom or their admission to trading on a regulated market has been requested, and
(c) that competent authority makes a request that the competent authority assist it in the performance of its functions under the law of that State in connection with the prospectus directive.
(2) For the purpose of complying with the request mentioned in subsection (1)(c), the powers conferred by sections 87K and 87L may be exercised as if the prospectus were one which had been approved by the FCA.
(3) Section 87N does not apply to an exercise of those powers as a result of this section.
(4) Section 87O does apply to such an exercise of those powers but with the omission of subsections (3)(e), (6) and (7).

Rights of investors

87Q Right of investor to withdraw

(1) Where a person agrees to buy or subscribe for transferable securities in circumstances where the final offer price or the amount of transferable securities to be offered to the public is not included in the prospectus, he may withdraw his acceptance before the end of the withdrawal period.

(2) The withdrawal period—

(a) begins with the investor's acceptance; and

(b) ends at the end of the second working day after the date on which the FCA is informed of the information in accordance with section 87A(7).

(3) Subsection (1) does not apply if the prospectus contains—

(a) in the case of the amount of transferable securities to be offered to the public, the criteria or conditions (or both) according to which that element will be determined, or

(b) in the case of price, the criteria or conditions (or both) according to which that element will be determined or the maximum price.

(4) Where a supplementary prospectus has been published and, prior to the publication, a person agreed to buy or subscribe for transferable securities to which it relates, he may withdraw his acceptance before the end of the period of 2 working days beginning with the first working day after the date on which the supplementary prospectus was published.

Registered investors

87R ...

88 Sponsors

(1) Listing rules may require a person to make arrangements with a sponsor for the performance by the sponsor of such services in relation to him as may be specified in the rules.

(2) "Sponsor" means a person approved by the FCA for the purposes of the rules.

(3) Listing rules made by virtue of subsection (1) may—

(a) provide for the FCA to maintain a list of sponsors;

(b) specify services which must be performed by a sponsor;

(c) impose requirements on a sponsor in relation to the provision of services or specified services;

(d) specify the circumstances in which a person is qualified for being approved as a sponsor.

(4) If the FCA proposes—

(a) to refuse a person's application under sponsor rules,

(aa) to impose limitations or other restrictions on the services to which a person's approval relates, or

(b) to cancel a person's approval as a sponsor, otherwise than at his request it must give him a warning notice.

(5) If, after considering any representations made in response to the warning notice, the FCA decides—

(a) to grant the application under sponsor rules,

(aa) not to impose limitations or other restrictions on the services to which a person's approval relates, or

(b) not to cancel the approval,

it must give the person concerned, and any person to whom a copy of the warning notice was given, written notice of its decision.

(6) If, after considering any representations made in response to the warning notice, the FCA decides—

(a) to refuse to grant the application under sponsor rules,

(aa) to impose limitations or other restrictions on the services to which a person's approval relates, or

(b) to cancel the approval,

it must give the person concerned a decision notice.

(7) A person to whom a decision notice is given under this section may refer the matter to the Tribunal.

(8) In this section any reference to an application under sponsor rules means—
(a) an application for approval as a sponsor,
(b) an application for the suspension of an approval as a sponsor,
(c) an application for the withdrawal of the suspension of an approval as a sponsor, or
(d) an application for the withdrawal or variation of a limitation or other restriction on the services to which a sponsor's approval relates.

88A Disciplinary powers: contravention of s 88(3)(c) or (e)

(1) The FCA may take action against a sponsor under this section if it considers that the sponsor has contravened a requirement or restriction imposed on the sponsor by rules made as a result of section 88(3)(c) or (e).
(2) If the FCA is entitled to take action under this section against a sponsor, it may do one or more of the following—
(a) impose a penalty on the sponsor of such amount as it considers appropriate;
(b) suspend, for such period as it considers appropriate, the sponsor's approval;
(c) impose, for such period as it considers appropriate, such limitations or other restrictions in relation to the performance of services to which the sponsor's approval relates as it considers appropriate;
(d) publish a statement to the effect that the sponsor has contravened a requirement or restriction imposed on the sponsor by rules made as a result of section 88(3)(c) or (e).
(3) The period for which a suspension or restriction is to have effect may not exceed 12 months.
(4) A suspension may relate only to the performance in specified circumstances of a service to which the approval relates.
(5) A restriction may, in particular, be imposed so as to require the sponsor to take, or refrain from taking, specified action.
(6) The FCA may—
(a) withdraw a suspension or restriction; or
(b) vary a suspension or restriction so as to reduce the period for which it has effect or otherwise to limit its effect.
(7) The FCA may not take action against a sponsor under this section after the end of the limitation period unless, before the end of that period, it has given a warning notice to the sponsor under section 88B(1).
(8) "The limitation period" means the period of 3 years beginning with the first day on which the FCA knew that the sponsor had contravened the requirement or restriction.
(9) For this purpose the FCA is to be treated as knowing that a sponsor has contravened a requirement or restriction if it has information from which that can reasonably be inferred.

88B Action under s 88A: procedure and right to refer to Tribunal

(1) If the FCA proposes to take action against a sponsor under section 88A, it must give the sponsor a warning notice.
(2) A warning notice about a proposal to impose a penalty must state the amount of the penalty.
(3) A warning notice about a proposal—
(a) to suspend an approval, or
(b) to impose a restriction in relation to the performance of a service, must state the period for which the suspension or restriction is to have effect.
(4) A warning notice about a proposal to publish a statement must set out the terms of the statement.
(5) If the FCA decides to take action against a sponsor under section 88A, it must give the sponsor a decision notice.
(6) A decision notice about the imposition of a penalty must state the amount of the penalty.
(7) A decision notice about—
(a) the suspension of an approval, or
(b) the imposition of a restriction in relation to the performance of a service, must state the period for which the suspension or restriction is to have effect.
(8) A decision notice about the publication of a statement must set out the terms of the statement.
(9) If the FCA decides to take action against a sponsor under section 88A, the sponsor may refer the matter to the Tribunal.

88C–88E *omitted*

89 ...

Transparency obligations

89A Transparency rules

(1) The FCA may make rules for the purposes of the transparency obligations directive.
(2) The rules may include provision for dealing with any matters arising out of or related to any provision of the transparency obligations directive.
(3) The FCA may also make rules—
  (a) for the purpose of ensuring that voteholder information in respect of voting shares traded on a UK market other than a regulated market is made public or notified to the FCA;
  (b) providing for persons who hold comparable instruments (see section 89F(1)(c)) in respect of voting shares to be treated, in the circumstances specified in the rules, as holding some or all of the voting rights in respect of those shares.
(4) Rules under this section may, in particular, make provision—
  (a) specifying how the proportion of—
    (i) the total voting rights in respect of shares in an issuer, or
    (ii) the total voting rights in respect of a particular class of shares in an issuer, held by a person is to be determined;
  (b) specifying the circumstances in which, for the purposes of any determination of the voting rights held by a person ("P") in respect of voting shares in an issuer, any voting rights held, or treated by virtue of subsection (3)(b) as held, by another person in respect of voting shares in the issuer are to be regarded as held by P;
  (c) specifying the nature of the information which must be included in any notification;
  (d) about the form of any notification;
  (e) requiring any notification to be given within a specified period;
  (f) specifying the manner in which any information is to be made public and the period within which it must be made public;
  (g) specifying circumstances in which any of the requirements imposed by rules under this section does not apply.
(5) Rules under this section are referred to in this Part as "transparency rules".
(6) Nothing in sections 89B to 89G affects the generality of the power to make rules under this section.

89B Provision of voteholder information

(1) Transparency rules may make provision for voteholder information in respect of voting shares to be notified, in circumstances specified in the rules—
  (a) to the issuer, or
  (b) to the public, or to both.
(2) Transparency rules may make provision for voteholder information notified to the issuer to be notified at the same time to the FCA.
(3) In this Part "voteholder information" in respect of voting shares means information relating to the proportion of voting rights held by a person in respect of the shares.
(4) Transparency rules may require notification of voteholder information relating to a person—
  (a) initially, not later than such date as may be specified in the rules for the purposes of the first indent of Article 30.2 of the transparency obligations directive, and
  (b) subsequently, in accordance with the following provisions.
(5) Transparency rules under subsection (4)(b) may require notification of voteholder information relating to a person only where there is a notifiable change in the proportion of—
  (a) the total voting rights in respect of shares in the issuer, or
  (b) the total voting rights in respect of a particular class of share in the issuer, held by the person.
(6) For this purpose there is a "notifiable change" in the proportion of voting rights held by a person when the proportion changes—
  (a) from being a proportion less than a designated proportion to a proportion equal to or greater than that designated proportion,

(b) from being a proportion equal to a designated proportion to a proportion greater or less than that designated proportion, or
(c) from being a proportion greater than a designated proportion to a proportion equal to or less than that designated proportion.

(7) In subsection (6) "designated" means designated by the rules.

89C Provision of information by issuers of transferable securities

(1) Transparency rules may make provision requiring the issuer of transferable securities, in circumstances specified in the rules—
(a) to make public information to which this section applies, or
(b) to notify to the FCA information to which this section applies, or to do both.

(2) In the case of every issuer, this section applies to—
(a) information required by Article 4 of the transparency obligations directive;
(b) information relating to the rights attached to the transferable securities, including information about the terms and conditions of those securities which could indirectly affect those rights; and
(c) information about new loan issues and about any guarantee or security in connection with any such issue.

(3) In the case of an issuer of debt securities, this section also applies to information required by Article 5 of the transparency obligations directive.

(4) In the case of an issuer of shares, this section also applies to—
(a) information required by Article 5 of the transparency obligations directive;
(b) information required by Article 6 of that directive;
(c) voteholder information—
(i) notified to the issuer, or
(ii) relating to the proportion of voting rights held by the issuer in respect of shares in the issuer;
(d) information relating to the issuer's capital; and
(e) information relating to the total number of voting rights in respect of shares or shares of a particular class.

89D Notification of voting rights held by issuer

(1) Transparency rules may require notification of voteholder information relating to the proportion of voting rights held by an issuer in respect of voting shares in the issuer—
(a) initially, not later than such date as may be specified in the rules for the purposes of the second indent of Article 30.2 of the transparency obligations directive, and
(b) subsequently, in accordance with the following provisions.

(2) Transparency rules under subsection (1)(b) may require notification of voteholder information relating to the proportion of voting rights held by an issuer in respect of voting shares in the issuer only where there is a notifiable change in the proportion of—
(a) the total voting rights in respect of shares in the issuer, or
(b) the total voting rights in respect of a particular class of share in the issuer,
held by the issuer.

(3) For this purpose there is a "notifiable change" in the proportion of voting rights held by a person when the proportion changes—
(a) from being a proportion less than a designated proportion to a proportion equal to or greater than that designated proportion,
(b) from being a proportion equal to a designated proportion to a proportion greater or less than that designated proportion, or
(c) from being a proportion greater than a designated proportion to a proportion equal to or less than that designated proportion.

(4) In subsection (3) "designated" means designated by the rules.

89E Notification of proposed amendment of issuer's constitution

Transparency rules may make provision requiring an issuer of transferable securities that are admitted to trading on a regulated market to notify a proposed amendment to its constitution—
(a) to the FCA, and
(b) to the market on which the issuer's securities are admitted,
at times and in circumstances specified in the rules.

89F Transparency rules: interpretation etc.

(1) For the purposes of sections 89A to 89G—
  (a) the voting rights in respect of any voting shares are the voting rights attached to those shares,
  (b) a person is to be regarded as holding the voting rights in respect of the shares—
    (i) if, by virtue of those shares, he is a shareholder within the meaning of Article 2.1(e) of the transparency obligations directive;
    (ii) if, and to the extent that, he is entitled to acquire, dispose of or exercise those voting rights in one or more of the cases mentioned in Article 10(a) to (h) of the transparency obligations directive;
    (iii) if he holds, directly or indirectly, a financial instrument which results in an entitlement to acquire the shares and is an Article 13 instrument, and
  (c) a person holds a "comparable instrument" in respect of voting shares if he holds, directly or indirectly, a financial instrument in relation to the shares which has similar economic effects to an Article 13 instrument (whether or not the financial instrument results in an entitlement to acquire the shares).

(2) Transparency rules under section 89A(3)(b) may make different provision for different descriptions of comparable instrument.

(3) For the purposes of sections 89A to 89G two or more persons may, at the same time, each be regarded as holding the same voting rights.

(4) In those sections—
"Article 13 instrument" means a financial instrument of a type determined by the European Commission under Article 13.2 of the transparency obligations directive;
"financial instrument" has the meaning given in Article 4.1(17) of Directive 2004/39/EC on markets in financial instruments;
"UK market" means a market that is situated or operating in the United Kingdom; "voting shares" means shares of an issuer to which voting rights are attached.

89G Transparency rules: other supplementary provisions

(1) Transparency rules may impose the same obligations on a person who has applied for the
admission of transferable securities to trading on a regulated market without the issuer's consent as they impose on an issuer of transferable securities.

(2) Transparency rules that require a person to make information public may include provision authorising the FCA to make the information public in the event that the person fails to do so.

(3) The FCA may make public any information notified to the FCA in accordance with transparency rules.

(4) Transparency rules may make provision by reference to any provision of any rules made by the Panel on Takeovers and Mergers under Part 28 of the Companies Act 2006.

(5) Sections 89A to 89F and this section are without prejudice to any other power conferred by this Part to make Part 6 rules.

89H FCA's power to call for information

(1) The FCA may by notice in writing given to a person to whom this section applies require him—
  (a) to provide specified information or information of a specified description, or
  (b) to produce specified documents or documents of a specified description.

(2) This section applies to—
  (a) an issuer in respect of whom transparency rules have effect;
  (b) a voteholder;
  (c) an auditor of—
    (i) an issuer to whom this section applies, or
    (ii) a voteholder;
  (d) a person who controls a voteholder;
  (e) a person controlled by a voteholder;
  (f) a director or other similar officer of an issuer to whom this section applies;
  (g) a director or other similar officer of a voteholder or, where the affairs of a voteholder are managed by its members, a member of the voteholder.

(3) This section applies only to information and documents reasonably required in connection with the exercise by the FCA of functions conferred on it by or under sections 89A to 89G (transparency rules).

(4) Information or documents required under this section must be provided or produced—
  (a) before the end of such reasonable period as may be specified, and
  (b) at such place as may be specified.

(5) If a person claims a lien on a document, its production under this section does not affect the lien.

89I Requirements in connection with call for information

(1) The FCA may require any information provided under section 89H to be provided in such form as it may reasonably require.

(2) The FCA may require—
  (a) any information provided, whether in a document or otherwise, to be verified in such manner as it may reasonably require;
  (b) any document produced to be authenticated in such manner as it may reasonably require.

(3) If a document is produced in response to a requirement imposed under section 89H, the FCA may—
  (a) take copies of or extracts from the document; or
  (b) require the person producing the document, or any relevant person, to provide an explanation of the document.

(4) In subsection (3)(b) "relevant person", in relation to a person who is required to produce a document, means a person who—
  (a) has been or is a director or controller of that person;
  (b) has been or is an auditor of that person;
  (c) has been or is an actuary, accountant or lawyer appointed or instructed by that person; or
  (d) has been or is an employee of that person.

(5) If a person who is required under section 89H to produce a document fails to do so, the FCA may require him to state, to the best of his knowledge and belief, where the document is.

89J Power to call for information: supplementary provisions

(1) The FCA may require an issuer to make public any information provided to the authority under section 89H.

(2) If the issuer fails to comply with a requirement under subsection (1), the FCA may, after seeking representations from the issuer, make the information public.

(3) In sections 89H and 89I (power of FCA to call for information)—
"control" and "controlled" have the meaning given by subsection (4) below; "specified" means specified in the notice;
"voteholder" means a person who—
  (a) holds voting rights in respect of any voting shares for the purposes of sections 89A to 89G (transparency rules), or
  (b) is treated as holding such rights by virtue of rules under section 89A(3)(b).

(4) For the purposes of those sections a person ("A") controls another person ("B") if—
  (a) A holds a majority of the voting rights in B,
  (b) A is a member of B and has the right to appoint or remove a majority of the members of the board of directors (or, if there is no such board, the equivalent management body) of B,
  (c) A is a member of B and controls alone, pursuant to an agreement with other shareholders or members, a majority of the voting rights in B, or
  (d) A has the right to exercise, or actually exercises, dominant influence or control over B.

(5) For the purposes of subsection (4)(b)—
  (a) any rights of a person controlled by A, and
  (b) any rights of a person acting on behalf of A or a person controlled by A,

are treated as held by A.

Powers exercisable in case of infringement of transparency obligation

89K Public censure of issuer

(1) If the FCA finds that an issuer of securities admitted to trading on a regulated market is failing or has failed to comply with an applicable transparency obligation, it may publish a statement to that effect.

(2) If the FCA proposes to publish a statement, it must give the issuer a warning notice setting out the terms of the proposed statement.

(3) If, after considering any representations made in response to the warning notice, the FCA decides to make the proposed statement, it must give the issuer a decision notice setting out the terms of the statement.

(4) A notice under this section must inform the issuer of his right to refer the matter to the Tribunal (see section 89N) and give an indication of the procedure on such a reference.

(5) In this section "transparency obligation" means an obligation under—

(a) a provision of transparency rules, or

(b) any other provision made in accordance with the transparency obligations directive.

(6) In relation to an issuer whose home State is a member State other than the United Kingdom, any reference to an applicable transparency obligation must be read subject to section 100A(2).

89L Power to suspend or prohibit trading of securities

(1) This section applies to securities admitted to trading on a regulated market.

(2) If the FCA has reasonable grounds for suspecting that an applicable transparency obligation has been infringed by an issuer, it may—

(a) suspend trading in the securities for a period not exceeding 10 days,

(b) prohibit trading in the securities, or

(c) make a request to the operator of the market on which the issuer's securities are traded—

(i) to suspend trading in the securities for a period not exceeding 10 days, or

(ii) to prohibit trading in the securities.

(3) If the FCA has reasonable grounds for suspecting that a provision required by the transparency obligations directive has been infringed by a voteholder of an issuer, it may—

(a) prohibit trading in the securities, or

(b) make a request to the operator of the market on which the issuer's securities are traded to prohibit trading in the securities.

(4) If the FCA finds that an applicable transparency obligation has been infringed, it may require the market operator to prohibit trading in the securities.

(5) In this section "transparency obligation" means an obligation under—

(a) a provision contained in transparency rules, or

(b) any other provision made in accordance with the transparency obligations directive.

(6) In relation to an issuer whose home State is a member State other than the United Kingdom, any reference to an applicable transparency obligation must be read subject to section 100A(2).

89M Procedure under section 89L

(1) A requirement under section 89L takes effect—

(a) immediately, if the notice under subsection (2) states that that is the case;

(b) in any other case, on such date as may be specified in the notice.

(2) If the FCA—

(a) proposes to exercise the powers in section 89L in relation to a person, or

(b) exercises any of those powers in relation to a person with immediate effect, it must give that person written notice.

(3) The notice must—

(a) give details of the FCA's action or proposed action;

(b) state the competent authority's reasons for taking the action in question and choosing the date on which it took effect or takes effect;

(c) inform the recipient that he may make representations to the FCA within such period as may be specified by the notice (whether or not he had referred the matter to the Tribunal);

(d) inform him of the date on which the action took effect or takes effect;

(e) inform him of his right to refer the matter to the Tribunal (see section 89N) and give an indication of the procedure on such a reference.

(4) The FCA may extend the period within which representations may be made to it.

(5) If, having considered any representations made to it, the FCA decides to maintain, vary or revoke its earlier decision, it must give written notice to that effect to the person mentioned in subsection (2).

89N Right to refer matters to the Tribunal

A person—

(a) to whom a decision notice is given under section 89K (public censure), or

(b) to whom a notice is given under section 89M (procedure in connection with suspension or prohibition of trading),

may refer the matter to the Tribunal.

Corporate governance

89O Corporate governance rules

(1) The FCA may make rules ("corporate governance rules")—

(a) for the purpose of implementing, enabling the implementation of or dealing with matters arising out of or related to, any EU obligation relating to the corporate governance of issuers who have requested or approved admission of their securities to trading on a regulated market;

(b) about corporate governance in relation to such issuers for the purpose of implementing, or dealing with matters arising out of or related to, any EU obligation.

(2) "Corporate governance", in relation to an issuer, includes—

(a) the nature, constitution or functions of the organs of the issuer;

(b) the manner in which organs of the issuer conduct themselves;

(c) the requirements imposed on organs of the issuer;

(d) the relationship between the different organs of the issuer;

(e) the relationship between the organs of the issuer and the members of the issuer or holders of the issuer's securities.

(3) The burdens and restrictions imposed by rules under this section on foreign-traded issuers must not be greater than the burdens and restrictions imposed on UK-traded issuers by—

(a) rules under this section, and

(b) listing rules.

(4) For this purpose—

— "foreign-traded issuer" means an issuer who has requested or approved admission of the issuer's securities to trading on a regulated market situated or operating outside the United Kingdom;

— "UK-traded issuer" means an issuer who has requested or approved admission of the issuer's securities to trading on a regulated market situated or operating in the United Kingdom.

(5) This section is without prejudice to any other power conferred by this Part to make Part 6 rules.

Primary information providers

89P Primary information providers

(1) Part 6 rules may require issuers of financial instruments to use primary information providers for the purpose of giving information of a specified description to a market of a specified description.

(2) "Primary information provider" means a person approved by the FCA for the purposes of this section.

(3) "Specified" means specified in the Part 6 rules.

(4) Part 6 rules made by virtue of subsection (1) may—

(a) provide for the FCA to maintain a list of providers;

(b) impose requirements on a provider in relation to the giving of information or of information of a specified description;

(c) specify the circumstances in which a person is qualified for being approved as a provider;

(d) provide for limitations or other restrictions to be imposed on the giving of information to which an approval relates (whether or not the approval has already been granted);
(e) provide for the approval of a provider to be suspended on the application of the provider.

(5) If the FCA proposes—
(a) to refuse a person's application under information provider rules,
(b) to impose limitations or other restrictions on the giving of information to which a person's approval relates, or
(c) to cancel a person's approval as a provider otherwise than at the person's request,
it must give the person a warning notice.

(6) If the FCA decides—
(a) to grant the application under information provider rules,
(b) not to impose limitations or other restrictions on the giving of information to which a person's approval relates, or
(c) not to cancel the approval,
it must give the person concerned written notice of its decision.

(7) If the FCA decides—
(a) to refuse to grant the application under information provider rules,
(b) to impose limitations or other restrictions on the giving of information to which a person's approval relates, or
(c) to cancel the approval,
it must give the person concerned a decision notice.

(8) A person to whom a decision notice is given under this section may refer the matter to the Tribunal.

(9) In this section any reference to an application under information provider rules means—
(a) an application for approval as a provider,
(b) an application for the suspension of an approval as a provider,
(c) an application for the withdrawal of the suspension of an approval as a provider, or
(d) an application for the withdrawal or variation of a limitation or other restriction on the giving of information to which a provider's approval relates.

89Q Disciplinary powers: contravention of s 89P(4)(b) or (d)

(1) The FCA may take action against a provider under this section if it considers that the provider has contravened a requirement or restriction imposed on the provider by rules made as a result of section 89P(4)(b) or (d).

(2) If the FCA is entitled to take action under this section against a provider, it may do one or more of the following—
(a) impose a penalty on the provider of such amount as it considers appropriate;
(b) suspend, for such period as it considers appropriate, the provider's approval;
(c) impose, for such period as it considers appropriate, such limitations or other restrictions in relation to the giving by the provider of information as it considers appropriate;
(d) publish a statement to the effect that the provider has contravened a requirement or restriction imposed on the provider by rules made as a result of section 89P(4)(b) or (d).

(3) The period for which a suspension or restriction is to have effect may not exceed 12 months.

(4) A suspension may relate only to the giving of information in specified circumstances.

(5) A restriction may, in particular, be imposed so as to require the provider to take, or refrain from taking, specified action.

(6) The FCA may—
(a) withdraw a suspension or restriction, or
(b) vary a suspension or restriction so as to reduce the period for which it has effect or otherwise to limit its effect.

(7) The FCA may not take action against a provider under this section after the end of the limitation period unless, before the end of that period, it has given a warning notice to the provider under section 89R(1).

(8) "The limitation period" means the period of 3 years beginning with the first day on which the FCA knew that the provider had contravened the requirement or restriction.

(9) For this purpose the FCA is to be treated as knowing that a provider has contravened a requirement or restriction if it has information from which that can reasonably be inferred.

89R Action under s 89Q: procedure and right to refer to Tribunal

(1) If the FCA proposes to take action against a provider under section 89Q, it must give the provider a warning notice.

(2) A warning notice about a proposal to impose a penalty must state the amount of the penalty.

(3) A warning notice about a proposal—
(a) to suspend an approval, or
(b) to impose a restriction in relation to the giving of information,
must state the period for which the suspension or restriction is to have effect.

(4) A warning notice about a proposal to publish a statement must set out the terms of the statement.

(5) If the FCA decides to take action against a provider under section 89Q, it must give the provider a decision notice.

(6) A decision notice about the imposition of a penalty must state the amount of the penalty.

(7) A decision notice about—
(a) the suspension of an approval, or
(b) the imposition of a restriction in relation to the giving of information, must state the period for which the suspension or restriction is to have effect.

(8) A decision notice about the publication of a statement must set out the terms of the statement.

(9) If the FCA decides to take action against a provider under section 89Q, the provider may refer the matter to the Tribunal.

89S Action under s 89Q: statement of policy

(1) The FCA must prepare and issue a statement of its policy with respect to—
(a) the imposition of penalties, suspensions or restrictions under section 89Q,
(b) the amount of penalties under that section,
(c) the period for which suspensions or restrictions under that section are to have effect, and
(d) the matters in relation to which suspensions or restrictions under that section are to have effect.

(2) The FCA's policy in determining what the amount of a penalty should be, or what the period for which a suspension or restriction is to have effect should be, must include having regard to—
(a) the seriousness of the contravention in question in relation to the nature of the requirement concerned,
(b) the extent to which that contravention was deliberate or reckless, and
(c) whether the provider concerned is an individual.

(3) The FCA may at any time alter or replace a statement issued under this section.

(4) If a statement issued under this section is altered or replaced, the FCA must issue the altered or replacement statement.

(5) In exercising, or deciding whether to exercise, its power under section 89Q in the case of any particular contravention, the FCA must have regard to any statement of policy published under this section and in force at a time when the contravention in question occurred.

(6) A statement issued under this section must be published by the FCA in the way appearing to the FCA to be best calculated to bring it to the attention of the public.

(7) The FCA may charge a reasonable fee for providing a person with a copy of the statement.

(8) The FCA must, without delay, give the Treasury a copy of any statement which it publishes under this section.

89T–89V *omitted*

Compensation for false or misleading statements etc.

90 Compensation for statements in listing particulars or prospectus

(1) Any person responsible for listing particulars is liable to pay compensation to a person who has—

(a) acquired securities to which the particulars apply; and
(b) suffered loss in respect of them as a result of—
(i) any untrue or misleading statement in the particulars; or
(ii) the omission from the particulars of any matter required to be included by section 80 or 81.

(2) Subsection (1) is subject to exemptions provided by Schedule 10.

(3) If listing particulars are required to include information about the absence of a particular matter, the omission from the particulars of that information is to be treated as a statement in the listing particulars that there is no such matter.

(4) Any person who fails to comply with section 81 is liable to pay compensation to any person who has—
(a) acquired securities of the kind in question; and
(b) suffered loss in respect of them as a result of the failure.

(5) Subsection (4) is subject to exemptions provided by Schedule 10.

(6) This section does not affect any liability which may be incurred apart from this section.

(7) References in this section to the acquisition by a person of securities include references to his contracting to acquire them or any interest in them.

(8) No person shall, by reason of being a promoter of a company or otherwise, incur any liability for failing to disclose information which he would not be required to disclose in listing particulars in respect of a company's securities—
(a) if he were responsible for those particulars; or
(b) if he is responsible for them, which he is entitled to omit by virtue of section 82.

(9) The reference in subsection (8) to a person incurring liability includes a reference to any other person being entitled as against that person to be granted any civil remedy or to rescind or repudiate an agreement.

(10) "Listing particulars", in subsection (1) and Schedule 10, includes supplementary listing particulars.

(11) This section applies in relation to a prospectus as it applies to listing particulars, with the following modifications—
(a) references in this section or in Schedule 10 to listing particulars, supplementary listing particulars or sections 80, 81 or 82 are to be read, respectively, as references to a prospectus, supplementary prospectus and sections 87A, 87G and 87B;
(b) references in Schedule 10 to admission to the official list are to be read as references to admission to trading on a regulated market;
(c) in relation to a prospectus, "securities" means "transferable securities".

(12) A person is not to be subject to civil liability solely on the basis of a summary in a prospectus unless the summary, when read with the rest of the prospectus—
(a) is misleading, inaccurate or inconsistent; or
(b) does not provide key information (as defined in section 87A(9) and (10)), and in this subsection a summary includes any translation of it.

90ZA Liability for key investor information

(1) A person is not to be subject to civil liability solely on the basis of the key investor information produced in relation to a collective investment scheme or a sub-fund of such a scheme in accordance with rules or other provisions implementing Chapter IX of the UCITS directive, or of any translation of that information, unless the key investor information is misleading, inaccurate or inconsistent with the relevant parts of the prospectus published for that collective investment scheme or sub-fund in accordance with rules made by the FCA under section 248 or 261J of this Act.

(2) In this section, a reference to a sub-fund of a collective investment scheme is a reference to a part of the property of the collective investment scheme which forms a separate pool where—
(a) the collective investment scheme provides arrangements for separate pooling of the contributions of the participants and the profits and income out of which payments are made to them; and
(b) the participants are entitled to exchange rights in one pool for rights in another.

90A Liability of issuers in connection with published information

Schedule 10A makes provision about the liability of issuers of securities to pay compensation to persons who have suffered loss as a result of—
(a) a misleading statement or dishonest omission in certain published information relating to the securities, or

(b) a dishonest delay in publishing such information.

90B Power to make further provision about liability for published information

(1) The Treasury may by regulations make provision about the liability of issuers of securities traded on a regulated market, and other persons, in respect of information published to holders of securities, to the market or to the public generally.

(2) Regulations under this section may amend any primary or subordinate legislation, including any provision of, or made under, this Act.

Penalties

91 Penalties for breach of Part 6 rules

(1) If the FCA considers that—

(a) an issuer of listed securities, or

(b) an applicant for listing,

has contravened any provision of listing rules, it may impose on him a penalty of such amount as it considers appropriate.

(1ZA) If the FCA considers that—

(a) an issuer who has requested or approved the admission of a financial instrument to trading on a regulated market,

(b) a person discharging managerial responsibilities within such an issuer, or

(c) a person connected with such a person discharging managerial responsibilities, has contravened any provision of disclosure rules, it may impose on him a penalty of such amount as it considers appropriate.

(1A) If the FCA considers that—

(a) an issuer of transferable securities,

(b) a person offering transferable securities to the public or requesting their admission to trading on a regulated market,

(c) an applicant for the approval of a prospectus in relation to transferable securities,

(d) a person on whom a requirement has been imposed under section 87K or 87L, or

(e) any other person to whom a provision of the prospectus directive applies,

has contravened a provision of this Part or of prospectus rules, or a provision otherwise made in accordance with the prospectus directive or a requirement imposed on him under such a provision, it may impose on him a penalty of such amount as it considers appropriate.

(1B) If the FCA considers—

(a) that a person has contravened—

(i) a provision of transparency rules or a provision otherwise made in accordance with the transparency obligations directive, or

(ii) a provision of corporate governance rules, or

(b) that a person on whom a requirement has been imposed under section 89L (power to suspend or prohibit trading of securities in case of infringement of applicable transparency obligation), has contravened that requirement,

it may impose on the person a penalty of such amount as it considers appropriate.

(2) If, in the case of a contravention by a person referred to in subsection (1), (1ZA)(a), (1A) or (1B) ("P"), the FCA considers that another person who was at the material time a director of P was knowingly concerned in the contravention, it may impose upon him a penalty of such amount as it considers appropriate.

(3) If the FCA is entitled to impose a penalty on a person under this section in respect of a particular matter it may, instead of imposing a penalty on him in respect of that matter, publish a statement censuring him.

(4) Nothing in this section prevents the FCA from taking any other steps which it has power to take under this Part.

(5) A penalty under this section is payable to the FCA.

(6) The FCA may not take action against a person under this section after the end of the period of two years beginning with the first day on which it knew of the contravention unless proceedings against that person, in respect of the contravention, were begun before the end of that period.

(7) For the purposes of subsection (6)—

(a) the FCA is to be treated as knowing of a contravention if it has information from which the contravention can reasonably be inferred; and

(b) proceedings against a person in respect of a contravention are to be treated as begun when a warning notice is given to him under section 92.

92 Procedure

(1) If the FCA proposes to take action against a person under section 91, it must give him a warning notice.
(2) A warning notice about a proposal to impose a penalty must state the amount of the proposed penalty.
(3) A warning notice about a proposal to publish a statement must set out the terms of the proposed statement.
(4) If the FCA decides to take action against a person under section 91, it must give him a decision notice.
(5) A decision notice about the imposition of a penalty must state the amount of the penalty.
(6) A decision notice about the publication of a statement must set out the terms of the statement.
(7) If the FCA decides to take action against a person under section 91, he may refer the matter to the Tribunal.

93 Statement of policy

(1) The FCA must prepare and issue a statement ("its policy statement") of its policy with respect to—
 (a) the imposition of penalties under section 91; and
 (b) the amount of penalties under that section.
(2) The FCA's policy in determining what the amount of a penalty should be must include having regard to—
 (a) the seriousness of the contravention in question in relation to the nature of the requirement contravened;
 (b) the extent to which that contravention was deliberate or reckless; and
 (c) whether the person on whom the penalty is to be imposed is an individual.
(3) The FCA may at any time alter or replace its policy statement.
(4) If its policy statement is altered or replaced, the FCA must issue the altered or replacement statement.
(5) In exercising, or deciding whether to exercise, its power under section 91 in the case of any particular contravention, the FCA must have regard to any policy statement published under this section and in force at the time when the contravention in question occurred.
(6)–(8) *omitted*

94, 95 ...

96 Obligations of issuers of listed securities

(1) Listing rules may—
 (a) specify requirements to be complied with by issuers of listed securities; and
 (b) make provision with respect to the action that may be taken by the FCA in the event of non-compliance.
(2) If the rules require an issuer to publish information, they may include provision authorising the FCA to publish it in the event of his failure to do so.
(3) This section applies whenever the listed securities were admitted to the official list.

96A Disclosure of information requirements

(1) Disclosure rules must include provision specifying the disclosure of information requirements to be complied with by—
 (a) issuers who have requested or approved admission of their financial instruments to trading on a regulated market in the United Kingdom;
 (b) persons acting on behalf of or for the account of such issuers;
 (c) persons discharging managerial responsibilities within an issuer—
  (i) who is registered in the United Kingdom and who has requested or approved admission of its shares to trading on a regulated market; or
  (ii) who is not registered in the United Kingdom or any other EEA State but who has requested or approved admission of its shares to trading on a regulated market and whose home state is the United Kingdom;

(d) persons connected to such persons discharging managerial responsibilities.

(2) The rules must in particular—

(a) require an issuer to publish specified inside information;

(b) require an issuer to publish any significant change concerning information it has already published in accordance with paragraph (a);

(c) allow an issuer to delay the publication of inside information in specified circumstances;

(d) require an issuer (or a person acting on his behalf or for his account) who discloses inside information to a third party to publish that information without delay in specified circumstances;

(e) require an issuer (or person acting on his behalf or for his account) to draw up a list of those persons working for him who have access to inside information relating directly or indirectly to that issuer; and

(f) require persons discharging managerial responsibilities within an issuer falling within subsection (1)(c)(i) or (ii), and persons connected to such persons discharging managerial responsibilities, to disclose transactions conducted on their own account in shares of the issuer, or derivatives or any other financial instrument relating to those shares.

(3) Disclosure rules may make provision with respect to the action that may be taken by the FCA in respect of non-compliance.

96B Disclosure rules: persons responsible for compliance

(1) For the purposes of the provisions of this Part relating to disclosure rules, a "person discharging managerial responsibilities within an issuer" means—

(a) a director of an issuer falling within section 96A(1)(c)(i) or (ii); or

(b) a senior executive of such an issuer who—

(i) has regular access to inside information relating, directly or indirectly, to the issuer, and

(ii) has power to make managerial decisions affecting the future development and business prospects of the issuer.

(2) Schedule 11B (connected persons) has effect for the purposes of the provisions of this Part relating to disclosure rules.

96C Suspension of trading

(1) The FCA may, in accordance with disclosure rules, suspend trading in a financial instrument.

(2) If the FCA does so, the issuer of that financial instrument may refer the matter to the Tribunal.

(3) The provisions relating to suspension of listing of securities in section 78 apply to the suspension of trading in a financial instrument and the references to listing and securities are to be read as references to trading and financial instruments respectively for the purposes of this section.

97 Appointment by FCA of persons to carry out investigations

(1) Subsection (2) applies if it appears to the FCA that there are circumstances suggesting that—

(a) there may have been a contravention of—

(i) a provision of this Part or of Part 6 rules, or

(ii) a provision otherwise made in accordance with the prospectus directive or the transparency obligations directive;

(b) a person who was at the material time a director of a person mentioned in section 91(1), (1ZA)(a), (1A) or (1B) has been knowingly concerned in a contravention by that person of—

(i) a provision of this Part or of Part 6 rules, or

(ii) a provision otherwise made in accordance with the prospectus directive or the transparency obligations directive;

...

(d) there may have been a contravention of section 85 or 87G.

(2) The FCA may appoint one or more competent persons to conduct an investigation on its behalf.
(3) Part XI applies to an investigation under subsection (2) as if—
(a) the investigator were appointed under section 167(1);
(b) references to the investigating authority in relation to him were to the FCA;
(c) references to the offences mentioned in section 168 were to those mentioned in subsection (1)(d);
(d) references to an authorised person were references to the person under investigation.

98–100 ...

100A Exercise of powers where UK is host member state

(1) This section applies to the exercise by the FCA of any power under this Part exercisable in case of infringement of—
(a) a provision of prospectus rules or any other provision made in accordance with the prospectus directive, or
(b) a provision of transparency rules or any other provision made in accordance with the transparency obligations directive,
in relation to an issuer whose home State is a member State other than the United Kingdom.
(2) The FCA may act in such a case only in respect of the infringement of a provision required by the relevant directive.
Any reference to an applicable provision or applicable transparency obligation shall be read accordingly.
(3) If the FCA finds that there has been such an infringement, it must—
(a) give a notice to that effect to the competent authority of the person's home State requesting it—
(i) to take all appropriate measures for the purpose of ensuring that the person remedies the situation that has given rise to the notice, and
(ii) to inform the FCA of the measures it proposes to take or has taken or the reasons for not taking such measures, and
(b) notify ESMA.
(4) The FCA may not act further unless satisfied—
(a) that the competent authority of the person's home State has failed or refused to take measures for the purpose mentioned in subsection (3)(a), or
(b) that the measures taken by that authority have proved inadequate for that purpose.
This does not affect exercise of the powers under section 87K(2), 87L(2) or (3) or 89L(2) or (3) (powers to protect market).
(5) If the FCA is so satisfied, it must, after informing the competent authority of the person's home State and ESMA, take all appropriate measures to protect investors.
(6) In such a case the FCA must inform the Commission and ESMA of the measures at the earliest opportunity.

101 Part 6 rules: general provisions

(1) ...
(2) Part 6 rules may authorise the FCA to dispense with or modify the application of the rules in particular cases and by reference to any circumstances.
(3)–(8) ...

102 ...

Interpretative provisions

102A Meaning of "securities" etc.

(1) This section applies for the purposes of this Part.
(2) "Securities" means (except in section 74(2) and the expression "transferable securities") anything which has been, or may be, admitted to the official list.

(3) "Transferable securities" means anything which is a transferable security for the purposes of the investment services directive, other than money-market instruments for the purposes of that directive which have a maturity of less than 12 months.

(3A) "Debt securities" has the meaning given in Article 2.1(b) of the transparency obligations directive.

(4) "Financial instrument" has except in section 89F the meaning given in Article 1.3 of Directive 2003/6/EC of the European Parliament and of the Council of 28 January 2003 on insider dealing and market manipulation (as modified by Article 69 of Directive 2004/39/EC on markets in financial instruments).

(5) "Non-equity transferable securities" means all transferable securities that are not equity securities; and for this purpose "equity securities" has the meaning given in Article 2.1(b) of the prospectus directive.

(6) "Issuer"

(a) in relation to an offer of transferable securities to the public or admission of transferable securities to trading on a regulated market for which an approved prospectus is required as a result of section 85, means a legal person who issues or proposes to issue the transferable securities in question,

(aa) in relation to transparency rules, means a legal person whose securities are admitted to trading on a regulated market or whose voting shares are admitted to trading on a UK market other than a regulated market, and in the case of depository receipts representing securities, the issuer is the issuer of the securities represented;

(b) in relation to anything else which is or may be admitted to the official list, has such meaning as may be prescribed by the Treasury, and

(c) in any other case, means a person who issues financial instruments.

102B Meaning of "offer of transferable securities to the public" etc.

(1) For the purposes of this Part there is an offer of transferable securities to the public if there is a communication to any person which presents sufficient information on—

(a) the transferable securities to be offered, and

(b) the terms on which they are offered, to enable an investor to decide to buy or subscribe for the securities in question.

(2) For the purposes of this Part, to the extent that an offer of transferable securities is made to a person in the United Kingdom it is an offer of transferable securities to the public in the United Kingdom.

(3) The communication may be made—

(a) in any form;

(b) by any means.

(4) Subsection (1) includes the placing of securities through a financial intermediary.

(5) Subsection (1) does not include a communication in connection with trading on—

(a) a regulated market;

(b) a multilateral trading facility; or

(c) a market prescribed by an order under section 130A(3).

(6) "Multilateral trading facility" means a multilateral system, operated by an investment firm ... or a market operator, which brings together multiple third-party buying and selling interests in financial instruments in accordance with non-discretionary rules so as to result in a contract.

102C Meaning of "home State" in relation to transferable securities

In this Part, in relation to an issuer of transferable securities, the "home-State" is the EEA State which is the "home Member State" for the purposes of the prospectus directive (which is to be determined in accordance with Article 2.1(m) of that directive).

103 Interpretation of this Part

(1) In this Part, save where the context otherwise requires—

"disclosure rules" has the meaning given in section 73A;

"inside information" has the meaning given in section 118C;

"listed securities" means anything which has been admitted to the official list;

"listing" has the meaning given in section 74(5);

"listing particulars" has the meaning given in section 79(2);

"listing rules" has the meaning given in section 73A;

"market operator" means a person who manages or operates the business of a regulated market;

"offer of transferable securities to the public" has the meaning given in section 102B;
"the official list" means the list maintained by the FCA as that list has effect for the time being;
"Part 6 rules" has the meaning given in section 73A;
"the prospectus directive" means Directive 2003/71/EC of the European Parliament and of the Council of 4 November 2003 on the prospectus to be published when securities are offered to the public or admitted to trading;
"prospectus rules" has the meaning given in section 73A;
"regulated market" has the meaning given in Article 4.1(14) of Directive 2004/39/EC of the European Parliament and of the Council on markets in financial instruments;
"supplementary prospectus" has the meaning given in section 87G;
"the transparency obligations directive" means Directive 2004/109/EC of the European Parliament and of the Council relating to the harmonisation of transparency requirements in relation to information about issuers whose securities are admitted to trading on a regulated market as amended by Directive 2010/73/EU of the European Parliament and of the Council of 24 November 2010 and by Directive 2010/78/EU of the European Parliament and of the Council of 24 November 2010;
"transparency rules" has the meaning given by section 89A(5);
"voteholder information" has the meaning given by section 89B(3);
"working day" means any day other that a Saturday, a Sunday, Christmas Day, Good Friday or a day which is a bank holiday under the Banking and Financial Dealings Act 1971 in any part of the United Kingdom.

(1A) The definition of "the transparency obligations directive" in subsection (1) applies for the purposes of sections 89A(1) and (2) and 89C(2)(aa) as if, at the end of the definition, there were inserted "and by Directive 2013/50/EU of the European Parliament and of the Council of 22 October 2013.

(2), (3) …

PART VII
OMITTED

PART VIII
PENALTIES FOR MARKET ABUSE

118 Market abuse

(1) For the purposes of this Act, market abuse is behaviour (whether by one person alone or by two or more persons jointly or in concert) which—
  (a) occurs in relation to—
    (i) qualifying investments admitted to trading on a prescribed market,
    (ii) qualifying investments in respect of which a request for admission to trading on such a market has been made, or
    (iii) in the case of subsection (2) or (3) behaviour, investments which are related investments in relation to such qualifying investments, and
  (b) falls within any one or more of the types of behaviour set out in subsections (2) to (8).

(2) …

(3) The second is where an insider discloses inside information to another person otherwise than in the proper course of the exercise of his employment, profession or duties.

(4) The third is where the behaviour (not falling within subsection (2) or (3))—
  (a) is based on information which is not generally available to those using the market but which, if available to a regular user of the market, would be, or would be likely to be, regarded by him as relevant when deciding the terms on which transactions in qualifying investments should be effected, and
  (b) is likely to be regarded by a regular user of the market as a failure on the part of the person concerned to observe the standard of behaviour reasonably expected of a person in his position in relation to the market.

(5) The fourth is where the behaviour consists of effecting transactions or orders to trade (otherwise than for legitimate reasons and in conformity with accepted market practices on the relevant market) which—
  (a) give, or are likely to give, a false or misleading impression as to the supply of, or demand for, or as to the price of, one or more qualifying investments, or
  (b) secure the price of one or more such investments at an abnormal or artificial level.

(6) The fifth is where the behaviour consists of effecting transactions or orders to trade which employ fictitious devices or any other form of deception or contrivance.

(7) The sixth is where the behaviour consists of the dissemination of information by any means which gives, or is likely to give, a false or misleading impression as to a qualifying investment by a person who knew or could reasonably be expected to have known that the information was false or misleading.

(8) The seventh is where the behaviour (not falling within subsection (5), (6) or (7))—

(a) is likely to give a regular user of the market a false or misleading impression as to the supply of, demand for or price or value of, qualifying investments, or

(b) would be, or would be likely to be, regarded by a regular user of the market as behaviour that would distort, or would be likely to distort, the market in such an investment,

and the behaviour is likely to be regarded by a regular user of the market as a failure on the part of the person concerned to observe the standard of behaviour reasonably expected of a person in his position in relation to the market.

(9) Subsection (4) ceases to have effect on 31 December 2014 and subsections (2) and (3) of section 118A are then to be read as no longer referring to that subsection.

(10) Subsection (8) and the definition of "regular user" in section 130A(3) cease to have effect on 3 July 2016 and the reference in subsection (1)(b) to that subsection is then to be read as a reference to subsection (7)

118A Supplementary provision about certain behaviour

(1) Behaviour is to be taken into account for the purposes of this Part only if it occurs—

(a) in the United Kingdom, or

(b) in relation to—

(i) qualifying investments which are admitted to trading on a prescribed market situated in, or operating in, the United Kingdom,

(ii) qualifying investments for which a request for admission to trading on such a prescribed market has been made, or

(iii) in the case of section 118(2) and (3), investments which are related investments in relation to such qualifying investments.

(2) For the purposes of subsection (1), as it applies in relation to section 118(4) and (8), a prescribed market accessible electronically in the United Kingdom is to be treated as operating in the United Kingdom.

(3) For the purposes of section 118(4) and (8), the behaviour that is to be regarded as occurring in relation to qualifying investments includes behaviour which—

(a) occurs in relation to anything that is the subject matter, or whose price or value is expressed by reference to the price or value of the qualifying investments, or

(b) occurs in relation to investments (whether or not they are qualifying investments) whose subject matter is the qualifying investments.

(4) For the purposes of section 118(7), the dissemination of information by a person acting in the capacity of a journalist is to be assessed taking into account the codes governing his profession unless he derives, directly or indirectly, any advantage or profits from the dissemination of the information.

(5) Behaviour does not amount to market abuse for the purposes of this Act if—

(a) it conforms with a rule which includes a provision to the effect that behaviour conforming with the rule does not amount to market abuse,

(b) it conforms with the relevant provisions of Commission Regulation (EC) No 2273/2003 of 22 December 2003 implementing Directive 2003/6/EC of the European Parliament and of the Council as regards exemptions for buy-back programmes and stabilisation of financial instruments, or

(c) it is done by a person acting on behalf of a public authority in pursuit of monetary policies or policies with respect to exchange rates or the management of public debt or foreign exchange reserves.

(6) Subsections (2) and (3) cease to have effect on 3 July 2016.

118B Insiders

For the purposes of this Part an insider is any person who has inside information—

(a) as a result of his membership of an administrative, management or supervisory body of an issuer of qualifying investments,

(b) as a result of his holding in the capital of an issuer of qualifying investments,
(c) as a result of having access to the information through the exercise of his employment, profession or duties,
(d) as a result of his criminal activities, or
(e) which he has obtained by other means and which he knows, or could reasonably be expected to know, is inside information.

118C Inside information

(1) This section defines "inside information" for the purposes of this Part.
(2) In relation to qualifying investments, or related investments, which are not commodity derivatives, inside information is information of a precise nature which—
(a) is not generally available,
(b) relates, directly or indirectly, to one or more issuers of the qualifying investments or to one or more of the qualifying investments, and
(c) would, if generally available, be likely to have a significant effect on the price of the qualifying investments or on the price of related investments.
(3) In relation to qualifying investments or related investments which are commodity derivatives, inside information is information of a precise nature which—
(a) is not generally available,
(b) relates, directly or indirectly, to one or more such derivatives, and
(c) users of markets on which the derivatives are traded would expect to receive in accordance with any accepted market practices on those markets.
(4) In relation to a person charged with the execution of orders concerning any qualifying investments or related investments, inside information includes information conveyed by a client and related to the client's pending orders which—
(a) is of a precise nature,
(b) is not generally available,
(c) relates, directly or indirectly, to one or more issuers of qualifying investments or to one or more qualifying investments, and
(d) would, if generally available, be likely to have a significant effect on the price of those qualifying investments or the price of related investments.
(5) Information is precise if it—
(a) indicates circumstances that exist or may reasonably be expected to come into existence or an event that has occurred or may reasonably be expected to occur, and
(b) is specific enough to enable a conclusion to be drawn as to the possible effect of those circumstances or that event on the price of qualifying investments or related investments.
(6) Information would be likely to have a significant effect on price if and only if it is information of a kind which a reasonable investor would be likely to use as part of the basis of his investment decisions.
(7) For the purposes of subsection (3)(c), users of markets on which investments in commodity derivatives are traded are to be treated as expecting to receive information relating directly or indirectly to one or more such derivatives in accordance with any accepted market practices, which is—
(a) routinely made available to the users of those markets, or
(b) required to be disclosed in accordance with any statutory provision, market rules, or contracts or customs on the relevant underlying commodity market or commodity derivatives market.
(8) Information which can be obtained by research or analysis conducted by, or on behalf of, users of a market is to be regarded, for the purposes of this Part, as being generally available to them.

119 The code

(1) The FCA must prepare and issue a code containing such provisions as the FCA considers will give appropriate guidance to those determining whether or not behaviour amounts to market abuse.
(2) The code may among other things specify—
(a) descriptions of behaviour that, in the opinion of the FCA, amount to market abuse;
(b) descriptions of behaviour that, in the opinion of the FCA, do not amount to market abuse;
(c) factors that, in the opinion of the FCA, are to be taken into account in determining whether or not behaviour amounts to market abuse.

(d) descriptions of behaviour that are accepted market practices in relation to one or more specified markets;
(e) descriptions of behaviour that are not accepted market practices in relation to one or more specified markets.

(2A) In determining, for the purposes of subsections (2)(d) and (2)(e) or otherwise, what are and what are not accepted market practices, the FCA must have regard to the factors and procedures laid down in Articles 2 and 3 respectively of Commission Directive 2004/72/EC of 29 April 2004 implementing Directive 2003/6/EC of the European Parliament and of the Council.

(3) The code may make different provision in relation to persons, cases or circumstances of different descriptions.

(4) The FCA may at any time alter or replace the code.

(5) If the code is altered or replaced, the altered or replacement code must be issued by the FCA.

(6) A code issued under this section must be published by the FCA in the way appearing to the FCA to be best calculated to bring it to the attention of the public.

(7) The FCA must, without delay, give the Treasury a copy of any code published under this section.

(8) The FCA may charge a reasonable fee for providing a person with a copy of the code.

120 Provisions included in the FCA's code by reference to the City Code

(1) The FCA may include in a code issued by it under section 119 ("the FCA's code") provision to the effect that in its opinion behaviour conforming with the City Code—
(a) does not amount to market abuse;
(b) does not amount to market abuse in specified circumstances; or
(c) does not amount to market abuse if engaged in by a specified description of person.

(2) But the Treasury's approval is required before any such provision may be included in the FCA's code.

(3) If the FCA's code includes provision of a kind authorised by subsection (1), the FCA must keep itself informed of the way in which the Panel on Takeovers and Mergers interprets and administers the relevant provisions of the City Code.

(4) "City Code" means the City Code on Takeovers and Mergers issued by the Panel as it has effect at the time when the behaviour occurs.

(5) "Specified" means specified in the FCA's code.

121 *omitted*

122 Effect of the code

(1) If a person behaves in a way which is described (in the code in force under section 119 at the time of the behaviour) as behaviour that, in the FCA's opinion, does not amount to market abuse that behaviour of his is to be taken, for the purposes of this Act, as not amounting to market abuse.

(2) Otherwise, the code in force under section 119 at the time when particular behaviour occurs may be relied on so far as it indicates whether or not that behaviour should be taken to amount to market abuse.

123 Power to impose penalties in cases of market abuse

(1) If the FCA is satisfied that a person ("A")—
(a) is or has engaged in market abuse, or
(b) by taking or refraining from taking any action has required or encouraged another person or persons to engage in behaviour which, if engaged in by A, would amount to market abuse,

it may impose on him a penalty of such amount as it considers appropriate.

(2) But the FCA may not impose a penalty on a person if, having considered any representations made to it in response to a warning notice, there are reasonable grounds for it to be satisfied that—
(a) he believed, on reasonable grounds, that his behaviour did not fall within paragraph (a) or (b) of subsection (1), or
(b) he took all reasonable precautions and exercised all due diligence to avoid behaving in a way which fell within paragraph (a) or (b) of that subsection.

(3) If the FCA is entitled to impose a penalty on a person under this section it may, instead of imposing a penalty on him, publish a statement to the effect that he has engaged in market abuse.

124, 125 *omitted*

126 Warning notices

(1) If the FCA proposes to take action against a person under section 123, it must give him a warning notice.

(2) A warning notice about a proposal to impose a penalty must state the amount of the proposed penalty.

(3) A warning notice about a proposal to publish a statement must set out the terms of the proposed statement.

127, 128 *omitted*

Miscellaneous

129 Power of court to impose penalty in cases of market abuse

(1) The FCA may on an application to the court under section 381 or 383 request the court to consider whether the circumstances are such that a penalty should be imposed on the person to whom the application relates.

(2) The court may, if it considers it appropriate, make an order requiring the person concerned to pay to the FCA a penalty of such amount as it considers appropriate.

130 Guidance

(1) The Treasury may from time to time issue written guidance for the purpose of helping relevant authorities to determine the action to be taken in cases where behaviour occurs which is behaviour—

(a) with respect to which the power in section 123 appears to be exercisable; and

(b) which appears to involve the commission of an offence under Part 7 of the Financial Services Act 2012 or Part V of the Criminal Justice Act 1993 (insider dealing).

(2) The Treasury must obtain the consent of the Attorney General and the Secretary of State before issuing any guidance under this section.

(3) In this section "relevant authorities" —

(a) in relation to England and Wales, means the Secretary of State, the FCA, the Director of the Serious Fraud Office and the Director of Public Prosecutions;

(b) in relation to Northern Ireland, means the Secretary of State, the FCA, the Director of the Serious Fraud Office and the Director of Public Prosecutions for Northern Ireland.

(4) Subsection (1) to (3) do not apply to Scotland.

(5) In relation to Scotland, the Lord Advocate may from time to time, after consultation with the Treasury, issue written guidance for the purpose of helping the FCA to determine the action to be taken in cases where behaviour mentioned in subsection (1) occurs.

130A Interpretation and supplementary provision

(1) The Treasury may by order specify (whether by name or description)—

(a) the markets which are prescribed markets for the purposes of specified provisions of this Part, and

(b) the investments that are qualifying investments in relation to the prescribed markets.

(2) An order may prescribe different investments or descriptions of investment in relation to different markets or descriptions of market.

(3) In this Part—

"accepted market practices" means practices that are reasonably expected in the financial market or markets in question and are accepted by the FCA or, in the case of a market situated in another EEA State, the competent authority of that EEA State within the meaning of Directive 2003/6/EC of the European Parliament and of the Council of 28 January 2003 on insider dealing and market manipulation (market abuse),

"behaviour" includes action or inaction,

"dealing", in relation to an investment, means acquiring or disposing of the investment whether as principal or agent or directly or indirectly, and includes agreeing to acquire or dispose of the investment, and entering into and bringing to an end a contract creating it,

"investment" is to be read with section 22 and Schedule 2,
"regular user", in relation to a particular market, means a reasonable person who regularly deals on that market in investments of the kind in question,
"related investment", in relation to a qualifying investment, means an investment whose price or value depends on the price or value of the qualifying investment.

(4) Any reference in this Act to a person engaged in market abuse is to a person engaged in market abuse either alone or with one or more other persons.

131 Effect on transactions

The imposition of a penalty under this Part does not make any transaction void or unenforceable.

131A Protected Disclosures

(1) A disclosure which satisfies the following three conditions is not to be taken to breach any restriction on the disclosure of information (however imposed).

(2) The first condition is that the information or other matter—
(a) causes the person making the disclosure (the discloser) to know or suspect, or
(b) gives him reasonable grounds for knowing or suspecting, that another person has engaged in market abuse.

(3) The second condition is that the information or other matter disclosed came to the discloser in the course of his trade, profession, business or employment.

(4) The third condition is that the disclosure is made to the FCA or to a nominated officer as soon as is practicable after the information or other matter comes to the discloser.

(5) A disclosure to a nominated officer is a disclosure which is made to a person nominated by the discloser's employer to receive disclosures under this section, and is made in the course of the discloser's employment and in accordance with the procedure established by the employer for the purpose.

(6) For the purposes of this section, references to a person's employer include any body, association or organisation (including a voluntary organisation) in connection with whose activities the person exercises a function (whether or not for gain or reward) and references to employment must be construed accordingly.

PARTS IX–XXIV
OMITTED

PART XXV
INJUNCTIONS AND RESTITUTION

Injunctions

380 Injunctions

(1) If, on the application of the appropriate regulator or the Secretary of State, the court is satisfied—
(a) that there is a reasonable likelihood that any person will contravene a relevant requirement, or
(b) that any person has contravened a relevant requirement and that there is a reasonable likelihood that the contravention will continue or be repeated,
the court may make an order restraining (or in Scotland an interdict prohibiting) the contravention.

(2) If on the application of the appropriate regulator or the Secretary of State the court is satisfied—
(a) that any person has contravened a relevant requirement, and
(b) that there are steps which could be taken for remedying the contravention,
the court may make an order requiring that person, and any other person who appears to have been knowingly concerned in the contravention, to take such steps as the court may direct to remedy it.

(3) If, on the application of the appropriate regulator or the Secretary of State, the court is satisfied that any person may have—
(a) contravened a relevant requirement, or
(b) been knowingly concerned in the contravention of such a requirement,

it may make an order restraining (or in Scotland an interdict prohibiting) him from disposing of, or otherwise dealing with, any assets of his which it is satisfied he is reasonably likely to dispose of or otherwise deal with.

(4) The jurisdiction conferred by this section is exercisable by the High Court and the Court of Session.

(5) In subsection (2), references to remedying a contravention include references to mitigating its effect.

(6) "Relevant requirement"—

(a) in relation to an application by the appropriate regulator, means a requirement—

(i) which is imposed by or under this Act or by a qualifying EU provision specified, or of a description specified, for the purposes of this subsection by the Treasury by order;

(ii) which is imposed by or under any other Act and whose contravention constitutes an offence mentioned in section 402(1); or

(iii) which is imposed by the Alternative Investment Fund Managers Regulations 2013;

(b) in relation to an application by the Secretary of State, means a requirement which is imposed by or under this Act and whose contravention constitutes an offence which the Secretary of State has power to prosecute under this Act.

(7) In the application of subsection (6) to Scotland—

(a) ...

(b) in paragraph (b) omit "which the Secretary of State has power to prosecute under this Act".

(8) The PRA is the "appropriate regulator" in the case of a contravention of—

(a) a requirement that is imposed by the PRA under any provision of this Act,

(b) a requirement under section 56(6) where the authorised person concerned is a PRA-authorised person and the prohibition order concerned is made by the PRA, or

(c) a requirement under section 59(1) or (2) where the authorised person concerned is a PRA-authorised person and the approval concerned falls to be given by the PRA.

(9) In the case of a contravention of a requirement that is imposed by a qualifying EU provision, "the appropriate regulator" is whichever of the PRA or the FCA (or both) is specified by the Treasury by order in relation to the qualifying EU provision for the purposes of this section.

(10) In the case of a contravention of a requirement where the contravention constitutes an offence under this Act, the "appropriate regulator" is whichever of the PRA or the FCA has power to prosecute the offence (see section 401).

(11) The FCA is the "appropriate regulator" in the case of a contravention of any other requirement.

(12) The Treasury may by order amend the definition of "appropriate regulator".

381 Injunctions in cases of market abuse

(1) If, on the application of the FCA, the court is satisfied—

(a) that there is a reasonable likelihood that any person will engage in market abuse, or

(b) that any person is or has engaged in market abuse and that there is a reasonable likelihood that the market abuse will continue or be repeated,

the court may make an order restraining (or in Scotland an interdict prohibiting) the market abuse.

(2) If on the application of the FCA the court is satisfied—

(a) that any person is or has engaged in market abuse, and

(b) that there are steps which could be taken for remedying the market abuse,

the court may make an order requiring him to take such steps as the court may direct to remedy it.

(3) Subsection (4) applies if, on the application of the FCA, the court is satisfied that any person—

(a) may be engaged in market abuse; or

(b) may have been engaged in market abuse.

(4) The court may make an order restraining (or in Scotland an interdict prohibiting) the person concerned from disposing of, or otherwise dealing with, any assets of his which it is satisfied that he is reasonably likely to dispose of, or otherwise deal with.

(5) The jurisdiction conferred by this section is exercisable by the High Court and the Court of Session.

(6) In subsection (2), references to remedying any market abuse include references to mitigating its effect.

382 Restitution orders

(1) The court may, on the application of the appropriate regulator or the Secretary of State, make an order under subsection (2) if it is satisfied that a person has contravened a relevant requirement, or been knowingly concerned in the contravention of such a requirement, and—

(a) that profits have accrued to him as a result of the contravention; or

(b) that one or more persons have suffered loss or been otherwise adversely affected as a result of the contravention.

(2) The court may order the person concerned to pay to the regulator concerned such sum as appears to the court to be just having regard—

(a) in a case within paragraph (a) of subsection (1), to the profits appearing to the court to have accrued;

(b) in a case within paragraph (b) of that subsection, to the extent of the loss or other adverse effect;

(c) in a case within both of those paragraphs, to the profits appearing to the court to have accrued and to the extent of the loss or other adverse effect.

(3) Any amount paid to the regulator concerned in pursuance of an order under subsection (2) must be paid by it to such qualifying person or distributed by it among such qualifying persons as the court may direct.

(4) On an application under subsection (1) the court may require the person concerned to supply it with such accounts or other information as it may require for any one or more of the following purposes—

(a) establishing whether any and, if so, what profits have accrued to him as mentioned in paragraph (a) of that subsection;

(b) establishing whether any person or persons have suffered any loss or adverse effect as mentioned in paragraph (b) of that subsection and, if so, the extent of that loss or adverse effect; and

(c) determining how any amounts are to be paid or distributed under subsection (3).

(5) The court may require any accounts or other information supplied under subsection (4) to be verified in such manner as it may direct.

(6) The jurisdiction conferred by this section is exercisable by the High Court and the Court of Session.

(7) Nothing in this section affects the right of any person other than the appropriate regulator or the Secretary of State to bring proceedings in respect of the matters to which this section applies.

(8) "Qualifying person" means a person appearing to the court to be someone—

(a) to whom the profits mentioned in subsection (1)(a) are attributable; or

(b) who has suffered the loss or adverse effect mentioned in subsection (1)(b).

(9) "Relevant requirement"—

(a) in relation to an application by the appropriate regulator, means a requirement—

(i) which is imposed by or under this Act or by a qualifying EU provision specified, or of a description specified, for the purposes of this subsection by the Treasury by order;

(ii) which is imposed by or under any other Act and whose contravention constitutes an offence mentioned in section 402(1);

(iii) which is imposed by the Alternative Investment Fund Managers Regulations 2013;

(iv) which is imposed by Part 7 of the Financial Services Act 2012 (offences relating to financial services) and whose contravention constitutes an offence under that Part;

(b) in relation to an application by the Secretary of State, means a requirement which is imposed by or under this Act and whose contravention constitutes an offence which the Secretary of State has power to prosecute under this Act.

(10) In the application of subsection (9) to Scotland—

(a) ...

(b) in paragraph (b) omit "which the Secretary of State has power to prosecute under this Act".

(11) The PRA is the "appropriate regulator" in the case of a contravention of—
(a) a requirement that is imposed by the PRA under any provision of this Act,
(b) a requirement under section 56(6) where the authorised person concerned is a PRA-authorised person and the prohibition order concerned is made by the PRA, or
(c) a requirement under section 59(1) or (2) where the authorised person concerned is a PRA-authorised person and the approval concerned falls to be given by the PRA.

(12) In the case of a contravention of a requirement that is imposed by a qualifying EU provision, "the appropriate regulator" is whichever of the PRA or the FCA (or both) is specified by the Treasury by order in relation to the qualifying EU provision for the purposes of this section.

(13) In the case of a contravention of a requirement where the contravention constitutes an offence under this Act, the "appropriate regulator" is the regulator which has power to prosecute the offence (see section 401).

(14) The FCA is the "appropriate regulator" in the case of a contravention of any other requirement.

(15) The Treasury may by order amend the definition of "appropriate regulator".

383 Restitution orders in cases of market abuse

(1) The court may, on the application of the FCA, make an order under subsection (4) if it is satisfied that a person ("the person concerned")—
(a) has engaged in market abuse, or
(b) by taking or refraining from taking any action has required or encouraged another person or persons to engage in behaviour which, if engaged in by the person concerned, would amount to market abuse,

and the condition mentioned in subsection (2) is fulfilled.

(2) The condition is—
(a) that profits have accrued to the person concerned as a result; or
(b) that one or more persons have suffered loss or been otherwise adversely affected as a result.

(3) But the court may not make an order under subsection (4) if it is satisfied that—
(a) the person concerned believed, on reasonable grounds, that his behaviour did not fall within paragraph (a) or (b) of subsection (1); or
(b) he took all reasonable precautions and exercised all due diligence to avoid behaving in a way which fell within paragraph (a) or (b) of subsection (1).

(4) The court may order the person concerned to pay to the FCA such sum as appears to the court to be just having regard—
(a) in a case within paragraph (a) of subsection (2), to the profits appearing to the court to have accrued;
(b) in a case within paragraph (b) of that subsection, to the extent of the loss or other adverse effect;
(c) in a case within both of those paragraphs, to the profits appearing to the court to have accrued and to the extent of the loss or other adverse effect.

(5) Any amount paid to the FCA in pursuance of an order under subsection (4) must be paid by it to such qualifying person or distributed by it among such qualifying persons as the court may direct.

(6) On an application under subsection (1) the court may require the person concerned to supply it with such accounts or other information as it may require for any one or more of the following purposes—
(a) establishing whether any and, if so, what profits have accrued to him as mentioned in subsection (2)(a);
(b) establishing whether any person or persons have suffered any loss or adverse effect as mentioned in subsection (2)(b) and, if so, the extent of that loss or adverse effect; and
(c) determining how any amounts are to be paid or distributed under subsection (5).

(7) The court may require any accounts or other information supplied under subsection (6) to be verified in such manner as it may direct.

(8) The jurisdiction conferred by this section is exercisable by the High Court and the Court of Session.

(9) Nothing in this section affects the right of any person other than the FCA to bring proceedings in respect of the matters to which this section applies.

(10) "Qualifying person" means a person appearing to the court to be someone—
(a) to whom the profits mentioned in paragraph (a) of subsection (2) are attributable; or
(b) who has suffered the loss or adverse effect mentioned in paragraph (b) of that subsection.

Restitution required by FCA or PRA

384 Power of FCA or PRA to require restitution

(1) The appropriate regulator may exercise the power in subsection (5) if it is satisfied that an authorised person or recognised investment exchange ("the person concerned") has contravened a relevant requirement, or been knowingly concerned in the contravention of such a requirement, and—
(a) that profits have accrued to him as a result of the contravention; or
(b) that one or more persons have suffered loss or been otherwise adversely affected as a result of the contravention.

(2) The FCA may exercise the power in subsection (5) if it is satisfied that a person ("the person concerned")—
(a) has engaged in market abuse, or
(b) by taking or refraining from taking any action has required or encouraged another person or persons to engage in behaviour which, if engaged in by the person concerned, would amount to market abuse,

and the condition mentioned in subsection (3) is fulfilled.

(3) The condition is—
(a) that profits have accrued to the person concerned as a result of the market abuse; or
(b) that one or more persons have suffered loss or been otherwise adversely affected as a result of the market abuse.

(4) But the FCA may not exercise that power as a result of subsection (2) if, having considered any representations made to it in response to a warning notice, there are reasonable grounds for it to be satisfied that—
(a) the person concerned believed, on reasonable grounds, that his behaviour did not fall within paragraph (a) or (b) of that subsection; or
(b) he took all reasonable precautions and exercised all due diligence to avoid behaving in a way which fell within paragraph (a)or (b) of that subsection.

(5) The power referred to in subsections (1) and (2) is a power to require the person concerned, in accordance with such arrangements as the regulator exercising the power ("the regulator concerned") considers appropriate, to pay to the appropriate person or distribute among the appropriate persons such amount as appears to the regulator concerned to be just having regard—
(a) in a case within paragraph (a) of subsection (1) or (3), to the profits appearing to the regulator concerned to have accrued;
(b) in a case within paragraph (b) of subsection (1) or (3), to the extent of the loss or other adverse effect;
(c) in a case within paragraphs (a) and (b) of subsection (1) or (3), to the profits appearing to the regulator concerned to have accrued and to the extent of the loss or other adverse effect.

(6) "Appropriate person" means a person appearing to the regulator concerned to be someone—
(a) to whom the profits mentioned in paragraph (a) of subsection (1) or (3) are attributable; or
(b) who has suffered the loss or adverse effect mentioned in paragraph (b) of subsection (1) or (3).

(7) "Relevant requirement" means—
(a) a requirement imposed by or under this Act or by a qualifying EU provision specified, or of a description specified, for the purposes of this subsection by the Treasury by order; and
(b) a requirement which is imposed by or under any other Act and whose contravention constitutes an offence mentioned in section 402(1).

(8) …

(9) The PRA is the "appropriate regulator" in the case of a contravention of—
(a) a requirement that is imposed by the PRA under any provision of this Act,
(b) a requirement under section 56(6) where the authorised person concerned is a PRA-authorised person and the prohibition order concerned is made by the PRA, or

(c) a requirement under section 59(1) or (2) where the authorised person concerned is a PRA-authorised person and the approval concerned falls to be given by the PRA.

(10) In the case of a contravention of a requirement that is imposed by a qualifying EU provision, "the appropriate regulator" is whichever of the PRA or the FCA (or both) is specified by the Treasury by order in relation to the qualifying EU provision for the purposes of this section.

(11) In the case of a contravention of a requirement where the contravention constitutes an offence under this Act, the "appropriate regulator" is the regulator which has power to prosecute the offence (see section 401).

(12) The FCA is the "appropriate regulator" in the case of a contravention of any other requirement.

(13) The Treasury may by order amend the definition of "appropriate regulator".

385 Warning notices

(1) If a regulator proposes to exercise the power under section 384(5) in relation to a person, it must give him a warning notice.

(2) A warning notice under this section must specify the amount which the regulator proposes to require the person concerned to pay or distribute as mentioned in section 384(5).

386 Decision notices

(1) If the regulator decides to exercise the power under section 384(5), it must give a decision notice to the person in relation to whom the power is exercised.

(2) The decision notice must—

(a) state the amount that he is to pay or distribute as mentioned in section 384(5);

(b) identify the person or persons to whom that amount is to be paid or among whom that amount is to be distributed; and

(c) state the arrangements in accordance with which the payment or distribution is to be made.

(3) If the regulator decides to exercise the power under section 384(5), the person in relation to whom it is exercised may refer the matter to the Tribunal.

PART XXVI–XXVIII
OMITTED

PART XXIX
INTERPRETATION

417 Definitions

(1) In this Act—

"AIF" has the meaning given in regulation 3 of the Alternative Investment Fund Managers Regulations 2013;

"appointed representative" has the meaning given in section 39(2);

"auditors and actuaries rules" means rules made under section 340;

"authorisation offence" has the meaning given in section 23(2);

"authorised open-ended investment company" has the meaning given in section 237(3);

"authorised person" has the meaning given in section 31(2);

"body corporate" includes a body corporate constituted under the law of a country or territory outside the United Kingdom;

"capital requirements directive" means Directive 2013/36/EU of the European Parliament and of the Council of 26 June 2013 on access to the activity of credit institutions and the prudential supervision of credit institutions and investment firms, amending Directive 2002/87/EC and repealing Directives 2006/48/EC and 2006/49/EC;

"capital requirements regulation" means Regulation (EU) No 575/2013 of the European Parliament and of the Council of 26 June 2013 on prudential requirements for credit institutions and investment firms and amending Regulation (EU) No 648/2012;

"chief executive"—

(a) in relation to a body corporate whose principal place of business is within the United Kingdom, means an employee of that body who, alone or jointly with one or more others, is responsible under the immediate authority of the directors, for the conduct of the whole of the business of that body; and

(b) in relation to a body corporate whose principal place of business is outside the United Kingdom,

means the person who, alone or jointly with one or more others, is responsible for the conduct of its business within the United Kingdom;

"claim", in relation to the Financial Services Compensation Scheme under Part XV, is to be construed in accordance with section 214(1B);

"collective investment scheme" has the meaning given in section 235;

"the Commission" means the European Commission;

"the compensation scheme" has the meaning given in section 213(2);

"control of information rules" has the meaning given in section 137P;

"credit-related activity" has the meaning given in section 23(1B);

"the CSD regulation" means Regulation (EU) No 909/2014 of the European Parliament and of the Council of 23 July 2014 on improving securities settlement in the European Union and on central securities depositories;

"director", in relation to a body corporate, includes—

(a) a person occupying in relation to it the position of a director (by whatever name called); and

(b) a person in accordance with whose directions or instructions (not being advice given in a professional capacity) the directors of that body are accustomed to act;

"documents" includes information recorded in any form and, in relation to information recorded otherwise than in legible form, references to its production include references to producing a copy of the information in legible form, or in a form from which it can readily be produced in visible and legible form;

"EBA" means the European Banking Authority established by Regulation (EU) No. 1093/2010 of the European Parliament and of the Council of 24 November 2010 establishing a European Supervisory Authority (European Banking Authority);

"electronic commerce directive" means Directive 2000/31/EC of the European Parliament and the Council of 8 June 2000 on certain legal aspects of information society services, in particular electronic commerce, in the Internal Market (Directive on electronic commerce); "ESMA" means the European Securities and Markets Authority established by Regulation (EU) No. 1095/2010 of the European Parliament and of the Council of 24 November 2010 establishing a European Supervisory Authority (European Securities and Markets Authority);

"exempt person", in relation to a regulated activity, means a person who is exempt from the general prohibition in relation to that activity as a result of an exemption order made under section 38(1) or as a result of section 39(1) or 285(2) or (3);

"FCA" means the Financial Conduct Authority;

"financial promotion rules" means rules made under section 137R;

"friendly society" means an incorporated or registered friendly society;

"full-scope UK AIFM" has the meaning given in regulation 2(1) of the Alternative Investment Fund Managers Regulations 2013;

"general prohibition" has the meaning given in section 19(2); "general rules"—

(a) in relation to the FCA, has the meaning given in section 137A(2), and

(b) in relation to the PRA, has the meaning given in section 137G(2);

"incorporated friendly society" means a society incorporated under the Friendly Societies Act 1992;

"information society service" means an information society service within the meaning of Article 2 a) of the electronic commerce directive;

"insurance undertaking" has the meaning given in Article 13(1) of the Solvency 2 Directive;

"investment services and activities" has the meaning given in Article 4.1.2 of the markets in financial instruments directive, read with—

(a) Chapter VI of Commission Regulation 1287/2006 of 10 August 2006,

(b) Article 52 of Commission Directive 2006/73/EC of 10 August 2006; and

(c) Article 6(5) of the emission allowance auctioning regulation;

"market abuse" has the meaning given in section 118;

"minimum capital requirement" means—

(a) in relation to an insurance undertaking or reinsurance undertaking, requirements imposed by or under this Act in pursuance of Section 5 of Chapter 6 of Title 1 of the Solvency 2 Directive;

(b) in relation to a third-country insurance undertaking, requirements imposed by or under this Act in pursuance of those provisions and Article 166 of the Solvency 2 Directive.

"Minister of the Crown" has the same meaning as in the Ministers of the Crown Act 1975;

"the ombudsman scheme" has the meaning given in section 225(3);

"open-ended investment company" has the meaning given in section 236; "Part 4A permission" has the meaning given in section 55A(5);

"partnership" includes a partnership constituted under the law of a country or territory outside the United Kingdom;

"the PRA" means the Prudential Regulation Authority;

"PRA-authorised person" has the meaning given in section 2B(5); "PRA-regulated activity" has the meaning given in section 22A;

"prescribed" (where not otherwise defined) means prescribed in regulations made by the Treasury;

"reinsurance undertaking" has the meaning given in Article 13(4) of the Solvency 2 Directive;

"price stabilising rules" means rules made under section 137Q;

"principal" in relation to an appointed representative, is to be read in accordance with section 39;

"private company" has the same meaning as in the Companies Acts (see section 4 of the Companies Act 2006);

"prohibition order" has the meaning given in section 56(2);

"recognised clearing house" and "recognised investment exchange" have the meaning given in section 285;

"registered friendly society" means a society which is—

(a) a friendly society within the meaning of section 7(1)(a) of the Friendly Societies Act 1974; and

(b) registered within the meaning of that Act;

"registered society" (except where otherwise indicated) means—

(a) a registered society within the meaning of the Co-operative and Community Benefit Societies Act 2014, or

(b) a society registered or deemed to be registered under the Industrial and Provident Societies Act (Northern Ireland) 1969;

"regulated activity" has the meaning given in section 22;

"regulating provisions" has the meaning given in section 140A;

"regulator" has the meaning given in section 3A(2);

"rule" means a rule made by the FCA or the PRA under this Act;

"rule-making instrument" has the meaning given in section 138G;

"the scheme manager" has the meaning given in section 212(1);

"the scheme operator" has the meaning given in section 225(2);

"scheme particulars rules" has the meaning given in section 248(1);

"Seventh Company Law Directive" means the European Council Seventh Company Law Directive of 13 June 1983 on consolidated accounts (No 83/349/EEC);

"short selling regulation" means Regulation (EU) No 236/2012 of the European Parliament and of the Council of 14 March 2012 on short selling and certain aspects of credit default swaps;

"solvency capital requirement" means—

(a) in relation to an insurance undertaking or reinsurance undertaking, requirements imposed by or under this Act in pursuance of Section 4 of Chapter 6 of Title 1 of the Solvency 2 Directive;

(b) in relation to a third-country insurance undertaking, requirements imposed by or under this Act in pursuance of those provisions and Article 166 of the Solvency 2 Directive.

"Takeovers Directive" means Directive 2004/25/EC of the European Parliament and of the Council;

"third-country insurance undertaking" means an undertaking that has received authorisation under Article 162 of the Solvency 2 Directive from the PRA or the FCA;

"threshold conditions", in relation to a regulated activity, has the meaning given in section 55B(1);

"the Treaty" means the Treaty on the Functioning of the European Union; "the Tribunal" means the Upper Tribunal;

"trust scheme rules" has the meaning given in section 247(1);
"UK authorised person" has the meaning given in section 191G(1);
"the UK financial system" has the meaning given in section 11; and
"unit trust scheme" has the meaning given in section 237.

(2) In the application of this Act to Scotland, references to a matter being actionable at the suit of a person are to be read as references to the matter being actionable at the instance of that person.

(3) For the purposes of any provision of this Act (other than a provision of Part 6) authorising or requiring a person to do anything within a specified number of days no account is to be taken of any day which is a public holiday in any part of the United Kingdom.

(4) For the purposes of this Act—
(a) an information society service is provided from an EEA State if it is provided from an establishment in that State;
(b) an establishment, in connection with an information society service, is the place at which the provider of the service (being a national of an EEA State or a company or firm as mentioned in Article 54 of the Treaty) effectively pursues an economic activity for an indefinite period;
(c) the presence or use in a particular place of equipment or other technical means of providing an information society service does not, of itself, constitute that place as an establishment of the kind mentioned in paragraph (b);
(d) where it cannot be determined from which of a number of establishments a given information society service is provided, that service is to be regarded as provided from the establishment where the provider has the centre of his activities relating to the service.

418–432 *omitted*

PART XXX
SUPPLEMENTAL

433 Short title

This Act may be cited as the Financial Services and Markets Act 2000.

SCHEDULES 1–9
OMITTED

SCHEDULE 10 **Section 90(2) and (5)**
COMPENSATION: EXEMPTIONS

Statements believed to be true

1. (1) In this paragraph "statement" means—
(a) any untrue or misleading statement in listing particulars; or
(b) the omission from listing particulars of any matter required to be included by section 80 or 81.

(2) A person does not incur any liability under section 90(1) for loss caused by a statement if he satisfies the court that, at the time when the listing particulars were submitted to the FCA, he reasonably believed (having made such enquiries, if any, as were reasonable) that—
(a) the statement was true and not misleading, or
(b) the matter whose omission caused the loss was properly omitted,
and that one or more of the conditions set out in sub-paragraph (3) are satisfied.

(3) The conditions are that—
(a) he continued in his belief until the time when the securities in question were acquired;
(b) they were acquired before it was reasonably practicable to bring a correction to the attention of persons likely to acquire them;
(c) before the securities were acquired, he had taken all such steps as it was reasonable for him to have taken to secure that a correction was brought to the attention of those persons;
(d) he continued in his belief until after the commencement of dealings in the securities

following their admission to the official list and they were acquired after such a lapse of time that he ought in the circumstances to be reasonably excused.

Statements by experts

2. (1) In this paragraph "statement" means a statement included in listing particulars which—
(a) purports to be made by, or on the authority of, another person as an expert; and
(b) is stated to be included in the listing particulars with that other person's consent.
(2) A person does not incur any liability under section 90(1) for loss in respect of any securities caused by a statement if he satisfies the court that, at the time when the listing particulars were submitted to the FCA, he reasonably believed that the other person—
(a) was competent to make or authorise the statement, and
(b) had consented to its inclusion in the form and context in which it was included, and that one or more of the conditions set out in sub-paragraph (3) are satisfied.
(3) The conditions are that—
(a) he continued in his belief until the time when the securities were acquired;
(b) they were acquired before it was reasonably practicable to bring the fact that the expert was not competent, or had not consented, to the attention of persons likely to acquire the securities in question;
(c) before the securities were acquired he had taken all such steps as it was reasonable for him to have taken to secure that that fact was brought to the attention of those persons;
(d) he continued in his belief until after the commencement of dealings in the securities following their admission to the official list and they were acquired after such a lapse of time that he ought in the circumstances to be reasonably excused.

Corrections of statements

3. (1) In this paragraph "statement" has the same meaning as in paragraph 1.
(2) A person does not incur liability under section 90(1) for loss caused by a statement if he satisfies the court—
(a) that before the securities in question were acquired, a correction had been published in a manner calculated to bring it to the attention of persons likely to acquire the securities; or
(b) that he took all such steps as it was reasonable for him to take to secure such publication and reasonably believed that it had taken place before the securities were acquired.
(3) Nothing in this paragraph is to be taken as affecting paragraph 1.

Corrections of statements by experts

4. (1) In this paragraph "statement" has the same meaning as in paragraph 2.
(2) A person does not incur liability under section 90(1) for loss caused by a statement if he satisfies the court—
(a) that before the securities in question were acquired, the fact that the expert was not competent or had not consented had been published in a manner calculated to bring it to the attention of persons likely to acquire the securities; or
(b) that he took all such steps as it was reasonable for him to take to secure such publication and reasonably believed that it had taken place before the securities were acquired.
(3) Nothing in this paragraph is to be taken as affecting paragraph 2.

Official statements

5. A person does not incur any liability under section 90(1) for loss resulting from—
(a) a statement made by an official person which is included in the listing particulars, or
(b) a statement contained in a public official document which is included in the listing particulars,
if he satisfies the court that the statement is accurately and fairly reproduced.

False or misleading information known about

6. A person does not incur any liability under section 90(1) or (4) if he satisfies the court that the person suffering the loss acquired the securities in question with knowledge—
(a) that the statement was false or misleading,
(b) of the omitted matter, or

(c) of the change or new matter,

as the case may be.

Belief that supplementary listing particulars not called for

7. A person does not incur any liability under section 90(4) if he satisfies the court that he reasonably believed that the change or new matter in question was not such as to call for supplementary listing particulars.

Meaning of "expert"

8. "Expert" includes any engineer, valuer, accountant or other person whose profession, qualifications or experience give authority to a statement made by him.

SCHEDULE 10A
LIABILITY OF ISSUERS IN CONNECTION WITH PUBLISHED INFORMATION

PART 1
SCOPE OF THIS SCHEDULE

Securities to which this Schedule applies

1. (1) This Schedule applies to securities that are, with the consent of the issuer, admitted to trading on a securities market, where—
   (a) the market is situated or operating in the United Kingdom, or
   (b) the United Kingdom is the issuer's home State.

(2) For the purposes of this Schedule—
   (a) an issuer of securities is not taken to have consented to the securities being admitted to trading on a securities market by reason only of having consented to their admission to trading on another market as a result of which they are admitted to trading on the first-mentioned market;
   (b) an issuer who has accepted responsibility (to any extent) for any document prepared for the purposes of the admission of the securities to trading on a securities market (such as a prospectus or listing particulars) is taken to have consented to their admission to trading on that market.

(3) For the purposes of this Schedule the United Kingdom is the home State of an issuer—
   (a) in the case of securities in relation to which the transparency obligations directive applies, if the United Kingdom is the home Member State for the purposes of that directive (see Article 2.1 of the directive);
   (b) in any other case, if the issuer has its registered office (or, if it does not have a registered office, its head office) in the United Kingdom.

Published information to which this Schedule applies

2. (1) This Schedule applies to information published by the issuer of securities to which this Schedule applies—
   (a) by recognised means, or
   (b) by other means where the availability of the information has been announced by the issuer by recognised means.

(2) It is immaterial whether the information is required to be published (by recognised means or otherwise).

(3) The following are "recognised means"—
   (a) a recognised information service;
   (b) other means required or authorised to be used to communicate information to the market in question, or to the public, when a recognised information service is unavailable.

(4) A "recognised information service" means—
   (a) in relation to a securities market situated or operating in the EEA, a service used for the dissemination of information in accordance with Article 21 of the transparency obligations directive;
   (b) in relation to a securities market situated or operating outside the EEA, a service used for the dissemination of information corresponding to that required to be disclosed under that directive; or

(c) in relation to any securities market, any other service used by issuers of securities for the dissemination of information required to be disclosed by the rules of the market.

PART 2
LIABILITY IN CONNECTION WITH PUBLISHED INFORMATION

Liability of issuer for misleading statement or dishonest omission

3. (1) An issuer of securities to which this Schedule applies is liable to pay compensation to a person who—
   (a) acquires, continues to hold or disposes of the securities in reliance on published information to which this Schedule applies, and
   (b) suffers loss in respect of the securities as a result of—
      (i) any untrue or misleading statement in that published information, or
      (ii) the omission from that published information of any matter required to be included in it.
   (2) The issuer is liable in respect of an untrue or misleading statement only if a person discharging managerial responsibilities within the issuer knew the statement to be untrue or misleading or was reckless as to whether it was untrue or misleading.
   (3) The issuer is liable in respect of the omission of any matter required to be included in published information only if a person discharging managerial responsibilities within the issuer knew the omission to be a dishonest concealment of a material fact.
   (4) A loss is not regarded as suffered as a result of the statement or omission unless the person suffering it acquired, continued to hold or disposed of the relevant securities—
   (a) in reliance on the information in question, and
   (b) at a time when, and in circumstances in which, it was reasonable for him to rely on it.

4. An issuer of securities to which this Schedule applies is not liable under paragraph 3 to pay compensation to a person for loss suffered as a result of an untrue or misleading statement in, or omission from, published information to which this Schedule applies if—
   (a) the published information is contained in listing particulars or a prospectus (or supplementary listing particulars or a supplementary prospectus), and
   (b) the issuer is liable under section 90 (compensation for statements in listing particulars or prospectus) to pay compensation to the person in respect of the statement or omission.

Liability of issuer for dishonest delay in publishing information

5 (1) An issuer of securities to which this Schedule applies is liable to pay compensation to a person who—
   (a) acquires, continues to hold or disposes of the securities, and
   (b) suffers loss in respect of the securities as a result of delay by the issuer in publishing information to which this Schedule applies.
   (2) The issuer is liable only if a person discharging managerial responsibilities within the issuer acted dishonestly in delaying the publication of the information.

Meaning of dishonesty

6. For the purposes of paragraphs 3(3) and 5(2) a person's conduct is regarded as dishonest if (and only if)—
   (a) it is regarded as dishonest by persons who regularly trade on the securities market in question, and
   (b) the person was aware (or must be taken to have been aware) that it was so regarded.

Exclusion of certain other liabilities

7 (1) The issuer is not subject—
   (a) to any liability other than that provided for by paragraph 3 in respect of loss suffered as a result of reliance by any person on—
      (i) an untrue or misleading statement in published information to which this Schedule applies, or

(ii) the omission from any such published information of any matter required to be included in it;

(b) to any liability other than that provided for by paragraph 5 in respect of loss suffered as a result of delay in the publication of information to which this Schedule applies.

(2) A person other than the issuer is not subject to any liability, other than to the issuer, in respect of any such loss.

(3) This paragraph does not affect—

(a) civil liability—

(i) under section 90 (compensation for statements in listing particulars or prospectus),

(ii) under rules made by virtue of section 954 of the Companies Act 2006 (compensation),

(iii) for breach of contract,

(iv) under the Misrepresentation Act 1967, or

(v) arising from a person's having assumed responsibility, to a particular person for a particular purpose, for the accuracy or completeness of the information concerned;

(b) liability to a civil penalty; or

(c) criminal liability.

(4) This paragraph does not affect the powers conferred by sections 382 and 384 (powers of the court to make a restitution order and of the Authority to require restitution).

(5) References in this paragraph to liability, in relation to a person, include a reference to another person being entitled as against that person to be granted any civil remedy or to rescind or repudiate an agreement.

PART 3
SUPPLEMENTARY PROVISIONS

Interpretation

8. (1) In this Schedule—

(a) "securities" means transferable securities within the meaning of Article 4.1.18 of the markets in financial instruments directive, other than money-market instruments as defined in Article 4.1.19 of that directive that have a maturity of less than 12 months (and includes instruments outside the EEA);

(b) "securities market" means—

(i) a regulated market as defined in Article 4.1.14 of the markets in financial instruments directive,

(ii) a multilateral trading facility as defined in Article 4.1.15 of the markets in financial instruments directive, or

(iii) a market or facility of a corresponding description outside the EEA.

(2) References in this Schedule to the issuer of securities are—

(a) in relation to a depositary receipt, derivative instrument or other financial instrument representing securities where the issuer of the securities represented has consented to the admission of the instrument to trading as mentioned in paragraph 1(1), to the issuer of the securities represented;

(b) in any other case, to the person who issued the securities.

(3) References in this Schedule to the acquisition or disposal of securities include—

(a) acquisition or disposal of any interest in securities, or

(b) contracting to acquire or dispose of securities or of any interest in securities, except where what is acquired or disposed of (or contracted to be acquired or disposed of) is a depositary receipt, derivative instrument or other financial instrument representing securities.

(4) References to continuing to hold securities have a corresponding meaning.

(5) For the purposes of this Schedule the following are persons "discharging managerial responsibilities" within an issuer—

(a) any director of the issuer (or person occupying the position of director, by whatever name called);

(b) in the case of an issuer whose affairs are managed by its members, any member of the issuer;

(c) in the case of an issuer that has no persons within paragraph (a) or (b), any senior executive of the issuer having responsibilities in relation to the information in question or its publication.

(6) The following definitions (which apply generally for the purposes of Part 6 of this Act) do not apply for the purposes of this Schedule:

(a) section 102A(1), (2) and (6) (meaning of "securities" and "issuer");

(b) section 102C (meaning of "home State" in relation to transferable securities).

SCHEDULE 11A
TRANSFERABLE SECURITIES

PART 1

1. Units (within the meaning in section 237(2)) in an open-ended collective investment scheme.

2. Non-equity transferable securities issued by

(a) the government of an EEA State;

(b) a local or regional authority of an EEA State;

(c) a public international body of which an EEA State is a member;

(d) the European Central Bank;

(e) the central bank of an EEA State.

3. Shares in the share capital of the central bank of an EEA State.

4. Transferable securities unconditionally and irrevocably guaranteed by the government, or a local or regional authority, of an EEA State.

5. (1) Non-equity transferable securities, issued in a continuous or repeated manner by a credit institution, which satisfy the conditions in sub-paragraph (2).

(2) The conditions are that the transferable securities—

(a) are not subordinated, convertible or exchangeable;

(b) do not give a right to subscribe to or acquire other types of securities and are not linked to a derivative instrument;

(c) materialise reception of repayable deposits; and

(d) are covered by a deposit guarantee under directive 94/19/EC of the European Parliament and of the Council on deposit-guarantee schemes.

6. Non-fungible shares of capital—

(a) the main purpose of which is to provide the holder with a right to occupy any immoveable property, and

(b) which cannot be sold without that right being given up.

PART 2

7. (1) Transferable securities issued by a body specified in sub-paragraph (2) if, and only if, the proceeds of the offer of the transferable securities to the public will be used solely for the purposes of the issuer's objectives.

(2) The bodies are—

(a) a charity—

(i) as defined by section 1(1) of the Charities Act 2011, or

(ii) within the meaning of section 35 of the Charities Act (Northern Ireland) 1964;

(b) a body entered in the Scottish Charity Register;

(c) a housing association within the meaning of—

(i) section 5(1) of the Housing Act 1985,

(ii) section 1 of the Housing Associations Act 1985, or

(iii) Article 3 of the Housing (Northern Ireland) Order 1992;

(d) an industrial and provident society registered in accordance with—

(i) section 1(2)(b) of the Industrial and Provident Societies Act 1965, or

(ii) section 1(2)(b) of the Industrial and Provident Societies Act (Northern Ireland) 1969;

(e) a non-profit making association or body recognised by an EEA State with objectives similar to those of a body falling within any of sub-paragraphs (a) to (d).

8. (1) Non-equity transferable securities, issued in a continuous or repeated manner by a credit institution, which satisfy the conditions in sub-paragraph (2).

(2) The conditions are—

(a) that the total consideration for the transferable securities being offered in the EEA States is less than 75,000,000 euros (or an equivalent amount); and

(b) those mentioned in paragraph 5(2)(a) and (b).

(3) In determining whether sub-paragraph (2)(a) is satisfied in relation to an offer ("offer A"), offer A is to be taken together with any other offer of transferable securities of the same class made by the same person which—

(a) was open at any time within the period of 12 months ending with the date on which offer A is first made; and

(b) had previously satisfied sub-paragraph (2)(a).

(4) For the purposes of this paragraph, an amount (in relation to an amount denominated in euros) is an "equivalent amount" if it is an amount of equal value denominated wholly or partly in another currency or unit of account.

(5) The equivalent is to be calculated at the latest practicable date before (but in any event not more than 3 working days before) the date on which the offer is first made.

(6) "Credit institution" means a credit institution as defined in Article 4(1) of the capital requirements regulation.

9. (1) Transferable securities included in an offer where the total consideration for the transferable securities being offered in the EEA States is less than 5,000,000 euros (or an equivalent amount).

(2) Sub-paragraphs (3) to (5) of paragraph 8 apply for the purposes of this paragraph but with the references in sub-paragraph (3) to "sub-paragraph (2)(a)" being read as references to "paragraph 9(1)".

LIMITED LIABILITY PARTNERSHIPS ACT 2000
(2000, c. 12)

Introductory

1 Limited liability partnerships

(1) There shall be a new form of legal entity to be known as a limited liability partnership.

(2) A limited liability partnership is a body corporate (with legal personality separate from that of its members) which is formed by being incorporated under this Act; and—

(a) in the following provisions of this Act (except in the phrase "oversea limited liability partnership"), and

(b) in any other enactment (except where provision is made to the contrary or the context otherwise requires),

references to a limited liability partnership are to such a body corporate.

(3) A limited liability partnership has unlimited capacity.

(4) The members of a limited liability partnership have such liability to contribute to its assets in the event of its being wound up as is provided for by virtue of this Act.

(5) Accordingly, except as far as otherwise provided by this Act or any other enactment, the law relating to partnerships does not apply to a limited liability partnership.

(6) The Schedule (which makes provision about the names and registered offices of limited liability partnerships) has effect.

Incorporation

2 Incorporation document etc.

(1) For a limited liability partnership to be incorporated—

(a) two or more persons associated for carrying on a lawful business with a view to profit must have subscribed their names to an incorporation document,

(b) the incorporation document or a copy of it must have been delivered to the registrar, and

(c) there must have been so delivered a statement made by either a solicitor engaged in the formation of the limited liability partnership or anyone who subscribed his name to the incorporation document, that the requirement imposed by paragraph (a) has been complied with.

(2) The incorporation document must—

...

(b) state the name of the limited liability partnership,
(c) state whether the registered office of the limited liability partnership is to be situated in England and Wales, in Wales, in Scotland or in Northern Ireland,
(d) state the address of that registered office,
(e) give the required particulars of each of the persons who are to be members of the limited liability partnership on incorporation, and
(f) either specify which of those persons are to be designated members or state that every person who from time to time is a member of the limited liability partnership is a designated member.

(2ZA) The required particulars mentioned in subsection (2)(e) are the particulars required to be stated in the LLP's register of members and register of members' residential addresses.

...

(3) If a person makes a false statement under subsection (1)(c) which he—
(a) knows to be false, or
(b) does not believe to be true, he commits an offence.

(4) A person guilty of an offence under subsection (3) is liable—
(a) on summary conviction, to imprisonment for a period not exceeding six months or a fine not exceeding the statutory maximum, or to both, or
(b) on conviction on indictment, to imprisonment for a period not exceeding two years or a fine, or to both.

3 Incorporation by registration

(1) The registrar, if satisfied that the requirements of section 2 are complied with, shall—
(a) register the documents delivered under that section, and
(b) give a certificate that the limited liability partnership is incorporated.

(1A) The certificate must state—
(a) the name and registered number of the limited liability partnership,
(b) the date of its incorporation, and
(c) whether the limited liability partnership's registered office is situated in England and Wales (or in Wales), in Scotland or in Northern Ireland.

(2) The registrar may accept the statement delivered under paragraph (c) of subsection (1) of section 2 as sufficient evidence that the requirement imposed by paragraph (a) of that subsection has been complied with.

(3) The certificate shall either be signed by the registrar or be authenticated by his official seal.

(4) The certificate is conclusive evidence that the requirements of section 2 are complied with and that the limited liability partnership is incorporated by the name specified in the incorporation document.

Membership

4 Members

(1) On the incorporation of a limited liability partnership its members are the persons who subscribed their names to the incorporation document (other than any who have died or been dissolved).

(2) Any other person may become a member of a limited liability partnership by and in accordance with an agreement with the existing members.

(3) A person may cease to be a member of a limited liability partnership (as well as by death or dissolution) in accordance with an agreement with the other members or, in the absence of agreement with the other members as to cessation of membership, by giving reasonable notice to the other members.

(4) A member of a limited liability partnership shall not be regarded for any purpose as employed by the limited liability partnership unless, if he and the other members were partners in a partnership, he would be regarded for that purpose as employed by the partnership.

4A Minimum membership for carrying on business

(1) This section applies where a limited liability partnership carries on business without having at least two members, and does so for more than 6 months.

(2) A person who, for the whole or any part of the period that it so carries on business after those 6 months—

(a) is a member of the limited liability partnership, and

(b) knows that it is carrying on business with only one member,

is liable (jointly and severally with the limited liability partnership) for the payment of the limited liability partnership's debts contracted during the period or, as the case may be, that part of it.

5 Relationship of members etc.

(1) Except as far as otherwise provided by this Act or any other enactment, the mutual rights and duties of the members of a limited liability partnership, and the mutual rights and duties of a limited liability partnership and its members, shall be governed—

(a) by agreement between the members, or between the limited liability partnership and its members, or

(b) in the absence of agreement as to any matter, by any provision made in relation to that matter by regulations under section 15(c).

(2) An agreement made before the incorporation of a limited liability partnership between the persons who subscribe their names to the incorporation document may impose obligations on the limited liability partnership (to take effect at any time after its incorporation).

6 Members as agents

(1) Every member of a limited liability partnership is the agent of the limited liability partnership.

(2) But a limited liability partnership is not bound by anything done by a member in dealing with a person if—

(a) the member in fact has no authority to act for the limited liability partnership by doing that thing, and

(b) the person knows that he has no authority or does not know or believe him to be a member of the limited liability partnership.

(3) Where a person has ceased to be a member of a limited liability partnership, the former member is to be regarded (in relation to any person dealing with the limited liability partnership) as still being a member of the limited liability partnership unless—

(a) the person has notice that the former member has ceased to be a member of the limited liability partnership, or

(b) notice that the former member has ceased to be a member of the limited liability partnership has been delivered to the registrar.

(4) Where a member of a limited liability partnership is liable to any person (other than another member of the limited liability partnership) as a result of a wrongful act or omission of his in the course of the business of the limited liability partnership or with its authority, the limited liability partnership is liable to the same extent as the member.

7 Ex-members

(1) This section applies where a member of a limited liability partnership has either ceased to be a member or—

(a) has died,

(b) has become bankrupt or had his estate sequestrated or has been wound up,

(c) has granted a trust deed for the benefit of his creditors, or

(d) has assigned the whole or any part of his share in the limited liability partnership (absolutely or by way of charge or security).

(2) In such an event the former member or—

(a) his personal representative,

(b) his trustee in bankruptcy or permanent or interim trustee (within the meaning of the Bankruptcy (Scotland) Act 1985) or liquidator,

(c) his trustee under the trust deed for the benefit of his creditors, or

(d) his assignee,

may not interfere in the management or administration of any business or affairs of the limited liability partnership.

(3) But subsection (2) does not affect any right to receive an amount from the limited liability partnership in that event.

8 Designated members

(1) If the incorporation document specifies who are to be designated members—
(a) they are designated members on incorporation, and
(b) any member may become a designated member by and in accordance with an agreement with the other members, and a member may cease to be a designated member in accordance with an agreement with the other members.
(2) But if there would otherwise be no designated members, or only one, every member is a designated member.
(3) If the incorporation document states that every person who from time to time is a member of the limited liability partnership is a designated member, every member is a designated member.
(4) A limited liability partnership may at any time deliver to the registrar—
(a) notice that specified members are to be designated members, or
(b) notice that every person who from time to time is a member of the limited liability partnership is a designated member,
and, once it is delivered, subsection (1) (apart from paragraph (a)) and subsection (2), or subsection (3), shall have effect as if that were stated in the incorporation document.
...
(6) A person ceases to be a designated member if he ceases to be a member.

9 Registration of membership changes

(1) A limited liability partnership must ensure that—
(a) where a person becomes or ceases to be a member or designated member, notice is delivered to the registrar within fourteen days, and
(b) where there is any change in the particulars contained in its register of members or its register of members' residential addresses, notice is delivered to the registrar within 14 days.
(2) Where all the members from time to time of a limited liability partnership are designated members, subsection (1)(a) does not require notice that a person has become or ceased to be a designated member as well as a member.
(3) A notice delivered under subsection (1) that relates to a person becoming a member or designated member must contain—
(a) a statement that the member or designated member consents to acting in that capacity, and
(b) in the case of a person becoming a member, a statement of the particulars of the new member that are required to be included in the limited liability partnership's register of members and its register of residential addresses.
(3ZA) Where—
(a) a limited liability partnership gives notice of a change of a member's service address as stated in its register of members, and
(b) the notice is not accompanied by notice of any resulting change in the particulars contained in its register of members' residential addresses,
the notice must be accompanied by a statement that no such change is required.
(4) If a limited liability partnership fails to comply with subsection (1), the partnership and every designated member commits an offence.
(5) But it is a defence for a designated member charged with an offence under subsection (4) to prove that he took all reasonable steps for securing that subsection (1) was complied with.
(6) A person guilty of an offence under subsection (4) is liable on summary conviction to a fine not exceeding level 5 on the standard scale.

10–13 *omitted*

Regulations

14 Insolvency and winding up

(1) Regulations shall make provision about the insolvency and winding up of limited liability partnerships by applying or incorporating, with such modifications as appear appropriate—

(a) in relation to a limited liability partnership registered in Great Britain, Parts 1 to 4, 6 and 7 of the Insolvency Act 1986;
(b) in relation to a limited liability partnership registered in Northern Ireland, Parts 2 to 5 and 7 of the Insolvency (Northern Ireland) Order 1989, and so much of Part 1 of that Order as applies for the purposes of those Parts.

(2) Regulations may make other provision about the insolvency and winding up of limited liability partnerships, and provision about the insolvency and winding up of oversea limited liability partnerships, by—
(a) applying or incorporating, with such modifications as appear appropriate, any law relating to the insolvency or winding up of companies or other corporations which would not otherwise have effect in relation to them, or
(b) providing for any law relating to the insolvency or winding up of companies or other corporations which would otherwise have effect in relation to them not to apply to them or to apply to them with such modifications as appear appropriate.

(3) In this Act "oversea limited liability partnership" means a body incorporated or otherwise established outside the United Kingdom and having such connection with the United Kingdom, and such other features, as regulations may prescribe.

15 Application of company law etc.

Regulations may make provision about limited liability partnerships and oversea limited liability partnerships (not being provision about insolvency or winding up) by—
(a) applying or incorporating, with such modifications as appear appropriate, any law relating to companies or other corporations which would not otherwise have effect in relation to them,
(b) providing for any law relating to companies or other corporations which would otherwise have effect in relation to them not to apply to them or to apply to them with such modifications as appear appropriate, or
(c) applying or incorporating, with such modifications as appear appropriate, any law relating to partnerships.

16 Consequential amendments

(1) Regulations may make in any enactment such amendments or repeals as appear appropriate in consequence of this Act or regulations made under it.

(2) The regulations may, in particular, make amendments and repeals affecting companies or other corporations or partnerships.

17 General

(1) In this Act "regulations" means regulations made by the Secretary of State by statutory instrument.

(2) Regulations under this Act may in particular—
(a) make provision for dealing with non-compliance with any of the regulations (including the creation of criminal offences),
(b) impose fees (which shall be paid into the Consolidated Fund), and
(c) provide for the exercise of functions by persons prescribed by the regulations.

(3) Regulations under this Act may—
(a) contain any appropriate consequential, incidental, supplementary or transitional provisions or savings, and
(b) make different provision for different purposes.

(4) No regulations to which this subsection applies shall be made unless a draft of the statutory instrument containing the regulations (whether or not together with other provisions) has been laid before, and approved by a resolution of, each House of Parliament.

(5) Subsection (4) applies to—
(a) regulations under section 14(2) not consisting entirely of the application or incorporation (with or without modifications) of provision contained in or made under the Insolvency Act 1986 or the Insolvency (Northern Ireland) Order 1989,
(b) regulations under section 15 not consisting entirely of the application or incorporation (with or without modifications) of provisions contained in or made under the following provisions of the Companies Act 2006—
Part 4 (a company's capacity and related matters);

Part 5 (a company's name);
Part 6 (a company's registered office);
Chapters 1 and 8 of Part 10 (register of directors);
Part 15 (accounts and reports);
Part 16 (audit);
Part 19 (debentures);
Part 21 (certification and transfer of securities);
Part 24 (a company's annual return);
Part 25 (company charges);
Part 26 (arrangements and reconstructions);
Part 29 (fraudulent trading);
Part 30 (protection of members against unfair prejudice);
Part 31 (dissolution and restoration to the register);
Part 35 (the registrar of companies);
Part 36 (offences under the Companies Acts);
Part 37 (supplementary provisions);
Part 38 (interpretation).

(c) regulations under section 14 or 15 making provision about oversea limited liability partnerships, and

(d) regulations under section 16.

(6) A statutory instrument containing regulations under this Act shall (unless a draft of it has been approved by a resolution of each House of Parliament) be subject to annulment in pursuance of a resolution of either House of Parliament.

Supplementary

18 Interpretation

In this Act—

"business" includes every trade, profession and occupation,

"designated member" shall be construed in accordance with section 8,

"enactment" includes subordinate legislation (within the meaning of the Interpretation Act 1978),

"incorporation document" shall be construed in accordance with section 2,

"limited liability partnership" has the meaning given by section 1(2),

"member" shall be construed in accordance with section 4,

"modifications" includes additions and omissions,

"name", in relation to a member of a limited liability partnership, means—

(a) if an individual, his forename and surname (or, in the case of a peer or other person usually known by a title, his title instead of or in addition to either or both his forename and surname), and

(b) if a corporation or Scottish firm, its corporate or firm name,

"oversea limited liability partnership" has the meaning given by section 14(3),

"the registrar" means—

(a) if the registered office of the limited liability partnership is, or is to be, in England and Wales (or Wales), the registrar of companies for England and Wales,

(b) if the registered office of the limited liability partnership is, or is to be, in Scotland, the registrar of companies for Scotland, and

(c) if the registered office of the limited liability partnership is, or is to be, in Northern Ireland, the registrar of companies for Northern Ireland;

"regulations" has the meaning given by section 17(1).

19 Commencement, extent and short title

(1) The preceding provisions of this Act shall come into force on such day as the Secretary of State may by order made by statutory instrument appoint; and different days may be appointed for different purposes.

(2) The Secretary of State may by order made by statutory instrument make any transitional provisions and savings which appear appropriate in connection with the coming into force of any provision of this Act.

(3) For the purposes of the Scotland Act 1998 this Act shall be taken to be a pre-commencement enactment within the meaning of that Act.

(4) This Act extends to the whole of the United Kingdom.
(5) This Act may be cited as the Limited Liability Partnerships Act 2000.

SCHEDULE

NAMES AND REGISTERED OFFICES PART I

NAMES

Index of names

1. …

Name to indicate status

2. (1) The name of a limited liability partnership must end with—
   (a) the expression "limited liability partnership", or
   (b) the abbreviation "llp" or "LLP".
   (2) But if the incorporation document for a limited liability partnership states that the registered office is to be situated in Wales, its name must end with—
   (a) one of the expressions "limited liability partnership" and "partneriaeth atebolrwydd cyfyngedig", or
   (b) one of the abbreviations "llp", "LLP", "pac" and "PAC".
3. …

Change of name

4. (1) A limited liability partnership may change its name at any time.
   (2) The name of a limited liability partnership may also be changed—
   (a) on the determination of a new name by a company names adjudicator under section 73 of the Companies Act 2006 as applied to limited liability partnerships (powers of adjudicator on upholding objection to name);
   (b) on the determination of a new name by the court under section 74 of the Companies Act 2006 as so applied (appeal against decision of company names adjudicator);
   (c) under section 1033 as so applied (name on restoration to the register).

Notification of change of name

5. (1) Where a limited liability partnership changes its name it shall deliver notice of the change to the registrar.
   …
   (3) Where the registrar receives notice of a change of name he shall (unless the new name is one by which a limited liability partnership may not be registered)—
   (a) enter the new name on the register in place of the former name, and
   (b) issue a certificate of the change of name.
   (4) The change of name has effect from the date on which the certificate is issued.

Effect of change of name

6. A change of name by a limited liability partnership does not—
   (a) affect any of its rights or duties,
   (b) render defective any legal proceedings by or against it,
   and any legal proceedings that might have been commenced or continued against it by its former name may be commenced or continued against it by its new name.

Improper use of "limited liability partnership" etc.

7. (1) If any person carries on a business under a name or title which includes as the last words—
   (a) the expression "limited liability partnership" or "partneriaeth atebolrwydd cyfyngedig", or
   (b) any contraction or imitation of either of those expressions, that person, unless a limited liability partnership or oversea limited liability partnership, commits an offence.

(2) A person guilty of an offence under sub-paragraph (1) is liable on summary conviction to a fine not exceeding level 3 on the standard scale.

...

COMPANIES ACT 2006
(2006, c. 46)

Power of authorised person to require documents etc

459 Power of authorised person to require documents, information and explanations
460 Restrictions on disclosure of information obtained under compulsory powers
461 Permitted disclosure of information obtained under compulsory powers
462 Power to amend categories of permitted disclosure

CHAPTER 12
SUPPLEMENTARY PROVISIONS

Liability for false or misleading statements in reports

463 Liability for false or misleading statements in reports

Accounting and reporting standards

464 Accounting standards

Companies qualifying as medium-sized

465 Companies qualifying as medium-sized: general
466 Companies qualifying as medium-sized: parent companies
467 Companies excluded from being treated as medium-sized

General power to make further provision about accounts and reports

468 General power to make further provision about accounts and reports

Other supplementary provisions

469 Preparation and filing of accounts in euros
470 *omitted*
471 Meaning of "annual accounts" and related expressions
472 Notes to the accounts
472A Meaning of "corporate governance statement" etc
473 *omitted*
474 Minor definitions

PART 16
AUDIT

CHAPTER 1
REQUIREMENT FOR AUDITED ACCOUNTS

Requirement for audited accounts

475 Requirement for audited accounts
476 Right of members to require audit

Exemption from audit: small companies

477 Small companies: conditions for exemption from audit
478 Companies excluded from small companies exemption
479 Availability of small companies exemption in case of group company
479A Subsidiary companies: conditions for exemption from audit
479B Companies excluded from the subsidiary companies audit exemption
479C Subsidiary companies audit exemption: parent undertaking declaration of guarantee

Exemption from audit: dormant companies

480 Dormant companies: conditions for exemption from audit
481 Companies excluded from dormant companies exemption

Companies subject to public sector audit

482, 483 *omitted*

General power of amendment by regulations

484 *omitted*

CHAPTER 2
APPOINTMENT OF AUDITORS

Private companies

485 Appointment of auditors of private company: general
486 Appointment of auditors of private company: default power of Secretary of State
487 Term of office of auditors of private company
488 Prevention by members of deemed re-
Public companies
489 Appointment of auditors of public company: general
490 Appointment of auditors of public company: default power of Secretary of State
491 Term of office of auditors of public company

General provisions

492 Fixing of auditor's remuneration
493 Disclosure of terms of audit appointment
494 Disclosure of services provided by auditor or associates and related remuneration

CHAPTER 3
FUNCTIONS OF AUDITOR

Auditor's report

495 Auditor's report on company's annual accounts
496 Auditor's report on 'strategic report and directors' report
497 Auditor's report on auditable part of directors' remuneration report
497A Auditor's report on separate corporate governance statement

Duties and rights of auditors

498 Duties of auditor

PART 1
GENERAL INTRODUCTORY PROVISIONS

Companies and Companies Acts

1 **Companies**

(1) In the Companies Acts, unless the context otherwise requires—
"company" means a company formed and registered under this Act, that is—
(a) a company so formed and registered after the commencement of this Part, or
(b) a company that immediately before the commencement of this Part—
(i) was formed and registered under the Companies Act 1985 or the Companies (Northern Ireland) Order 1986, or
(ii) was an existing company for the purposes of that Act or that Order,
(which is to be treated on commencement as if formed and registered under this Act).
(2) Certain provisions of the Companies Acts apply to—
(a) companies registered, but not formed, under this Act (see Chapter 1 of Part 33), and
(b) bodies incorporated in the United Kingdom but not registered under this Act (see Chapter 2 of that Part).
(3) For provisions applying to companies incorporated outside the United Kingdom, see Part 34 (overseas companies).

2 **The Companies Acts**

(1) In this Act "the Companies Acts" means—
(a) the company law provisions of this Act,
(b) Part 2 of the Companies (Audit, Investigations and Community Enterprise) Act 2004 (community interest companies), and
(c) the provisions of the Companies Act 1985 and the Companies Consolidation (Consequential Provisions) Act 1985 that remain in force.
(2) The company law provisions of this Act are—
(a) the provisions of Parts 1 to 39 of this Act, and
(b) the provisions of Parts 45 to 47 of this Act so far as they apply for the purposes of those Parts.

Types of company

3 **Limited and unlimited companies**

(1) A company is a "limited company" if the liability of its members is limited by its constitution. It may be limited by shares or limited by guarantee.
(2) If their liability is limited to the amount, if any, unpaid on the shares held by them, the company is "limited by shares".
(3) If their liability is limited to such amount as the members undertake to contribute to the assets of the company in the event of its being wound up, the company is "limited by guarantee".
(4) If there is no limit on the liability of its members, the company is an "unlimited company".

4 **Private and public companies**

(1) A "private company" is any company that is not a public company.
(2) A "public company" is a company limited by shares or limited by guarantee and having a share capital—
(a) whose certificate of incorporation states that it is a public company, and
(b) in relation to which the requirements of this Act, or the former Companies Acts, as to registration or re-registration as a public company have been complied with on or after the relevant date.
(3) For the purposes of subsection (2)(b) the relevant date is—
(a) in relation to registration or re-registration in Great Britain, 22nd December 1980;
(b) in relation to registration or re-registration in Northern Ireland, 1st July 1983.
(4) For the two major differences between private and public companies, see Part 20.

5 **Companies limited by guarantee and having share capital**

(1) A company cannot be formed as, or become, a company limited by guarantee with a share capital.

(2) Provision to this effect has been in force—
  (a) in Great Britain since 22nd December 1980, and
  (b) in Northern Ireland since 1st July 1983.
(3) Any provision in the constitution of a company limited by guarantee that purports to divide the company's undertaking into shares or interests is a provision for a share capital. This applies whether or not the nominal value or number of the shares or interests is specified by the provision.

6 Community interest companies

(1) In accordance with Part 2 of the Companies (Audit, Investigations and Community Enterprise) Act 2004—
  (a) a company limited by shares or a company limited by guarantee and not having a share capital may be formed as or become a community interest company, and
  (b) a company limited by guarantee and having a share capital may become a community interest company.
(2) The other provisions of the Companies Acts have effect subject to that Part.

PART 2
COMPANY FORMATION

General

7 Method of forming company

(1) A company is formed under this Act by one or more persons—
  (a) subscribing their names to a memorandum of association (see section 8), and
  (b) complying with the requirements of this Act as to registration (see sections 9 to 13).
(2) A company may not be so formed for an unlawful purpose.

8 Memorandum of association

(1) A memorandum of association is a memorandum stating that the subscribers—
  (a) wish to form a company under this Act, and
  (b) agree to become members of the company and, in the case of a company that is to have a share capital, to take at least one share each.
(2) The memorandum must be in the prescribed form and must be authenticated by each subscriber.

Requirements for registration

9 Registration documents

(1) The memorandum of association must be delivered to the registrar together with an application for registration of the company, the documents required by this section and a statement of compliance.
(2) The application for registration must state—
  (a) the company's proposed name,
  (b) whether the company's registered office is to be situated in England and Wales (or in Wales), in Scotland or in Northern Ireland,
  (c) whether the liability of the members of the company is to be limited, and if so whether it is to be limited by shares or by guarantee, and
  (d) whether the company is to be a private or a public company.
(3) If the application is delivered by a person as agent for the subscribers to the memorandum of association, it must state his name and address.
(4) The application must contain—
  (a) in the case of a company that is to have a share capital, a statement of capital and initial shareholdings (see section 10);
  (b) in the case of a company that is to be limited by guarantee, a statement of guarantee (see section 11);
  (c) a statement of the company's proposed officers (see section 12).
(5) The application must also contain—
  (a) a statement of the intended address of the company's registered office; and
  (b) a copy of any proposed articles of association (to the extent that these are not supplied by the default application of model articles: see section 20).

(6) The application must be delivered—
  (a) to the registrar of companies for England and Wales, if the registered office of the company is to be situated in England and Wales (or in Wales);
  (b) to the registrar of companies for Scotland, if the registered office of the company is to be situated in Scotland;
  (c) to the registrar of companies for Northern Ireland, if the registered office of the company is to be situated in Northern Ireland.

10 Statement of capital and initial shareholdings

(1) The statement of capital and initial shareholdings required to be delivered in the case of a company that is to have a share capital must comply with this section.
(2) It must state—
  (a) the total number of shares of the company to be taken on formation by the subscribers to the memorandum of association,
  (b) the aggregate nominal value of those shares,
  (c) for each class of shares—
    (i) prescribed particulars of the rights attached to the shares,
    (ii) the total number of shares of that class, and
    (iii) the aggregate nominal value of shares of that class, and
  (d) the amount to be paid up and the amount (if any) to be unpaid on each share (whether on account of the nominal value of the share or by way of premium).
(3) It must contain such information as may be prescribed for the purpose of identifying the subscribers to the memorandum of association.
(4) It must state, with respect to each subscriber to the memorandum—
  (a) the number, nominal value (of each share) and class of shares to be taken by him on formation, and
  (b) the amount to be paid up and the amount (if any) to be unpaid on each share (whether on account of the nominal value of the share or by way of premium).
(5) Where a subscriber to the memorandum is to take shares of more than one class, the information required under subsection (4)(a) is required for each class.

11 Statement of guarantee

(1) The statement of guarantee required to be delivered in the case of a company that is to be limited by guarantee must comply with this section.
(2) It must contain such information as may be prescribed for the purpose of identifying the subscribers to the memorandum of association.
(3) It must state that each member undertakes that, if the company is wound up while he is a member, or within one year after he ceases to be a member, he will contribute to the assets of the company such amount as may be required for—
  (a) payment of the debts and liabilities of the company contracted before he ceases to be a member,
  (b) payment of the costs, charges and expenses of winding up, and
  (c) adjustment of the rights of the contributories among themselves,
not exceeding a specified amount.

12 Statement of proposed officers

(1) The statement of the company's proposed officers required to be delivered to the registrar must contain the required particulars of—
  (a) the person who is, or persons who are, to be the first director or directors of the company;
  (b) in the case of a company that is to be a private company, any person who is (or any persons who are) to be the first secretary (or joint secretaries) of the company;
  (c) in the case of a company that is to be a public company, the person who is (or the persons who are) to be the first secretary (or joint secretaries) of the company.
(2) The required particulars are the particulars that will be required to be stated—
  (a) in the case of a director, in the company's register of directors and register of directors' residential addresses (see sections 162 to 166);
  (b) in the case of a secretary, in the company's register of secretaries (see sections 277 to 279).

(3) The statement must also contain a consent by each of the persons named as a director, as secretary or as one of joint secretaries, to act in the relevant capacity. If all the partners in a firm are to be joint secretaries, consent may be given by one partner on behalf of all of them.

13 Statement of compliance

(1) The statement of compliance required to be delivered to the registrar is a statement that the requirements of this Act as to registration have been complied with.

(2) The registrar may accept the statement of compliance as sufficient evidence of compliance.

Registration and its effect

14 Registration

If the registrar is satisfied that the requirements of this Act as to registration are complied with, he shall register the documents delivered to him.

15 Issue of certificate of incorporation

(1) On the registration of a company, the registrar of companies shall give a certificate that the company is incorporated.

(2) The certificate must state—

- (a) the name and registered number of the company,
- (b) the date of its incorporation,
- (c) whether it is a limited or unlimited company, and if it is limited whether it is limited by shares or limited by guarantee,
- (d) whether it is a private or a public company, and
- (e) whether the company's registered office is situated in England and Wales (or in Wales), in Scotland or in Northern Ireland.

(3) The certificate must be signed by the registrar or authenticated by the registrar's official seal.

(4) The certificate is conclusive evidence that the requirements of this Act as to registration have been complied with and that the company is duly registered under this Act.

16 Effect of registration

(1) The registration of a company has the following effects as from the date of incorporation.

(2) The subscribers to the memorandum, together with such other persons as may from time to time become members of the company, are a body corporate by the name stated in the certificate of incorporation.

(3) That body corporate is capable of exercising all the functions of an incorporated company.

(4) The status and registered office of the company are as stated in, or in connection with, the application for registration.

(5) In the case of a company having a share capital, the subscribers to the memorandum become holders of the shares specified in the statement of capital and initial shareholdings.

(6) The persons named in the statement of proposed officers—

- (a) as director, or
- (b) as secretary or joint secretary of the company, are deemed to have been appointed to that office.

PART 3
A COMPANY'S CONSTITUTION

CHAPTER 1
INTRODUCTORY

17 A company's constitution

Unless the context otherwise requires, references in the Companies Acts to a company's constitution include—

- (a) the company's articles, and
- (b) any resolutions and agreements to which Chapter 3 applies (see section 29).

CHAPTER 2
ARTICLES OF ASSOCIATION

General

18 Articles of association

(1) A company must have articles of association prescribing regulations for the company.
(2) Unless it is a company to which model articles apply by virtue of section 20 (default application of model articles in case of limited company), it must register articles of association.
(3) Articles of association registered by a company must—
    (a) be contained in a single document, and
    (b) be divided into paragraphs numbered consecutively.
(4) References in the Companies Acts to a company's "articles" are to its articles of association.

19 Power of Secretary of State to prescribe model articles

(1) The Secretary of State may by regulations prescribe model articles of association for companies.
(2) Different model articles may be prescribed for different descriptions of company.
(3) A company may adopt all or any of the provisions of model articles.
(4) Any amendment of model articles by regulations under this section does not affect a company registered before the amendment takes effect. "Amendment" here includes addition, alteration or repeal.
(5) Regulations under this section are subject to negative resolution procedure.

20 Default application of model articles

(1) On the formation of a limited company—
    (a) if articles are not registered, or
    (b) if articles are registered, in so far as they do not exclude or modify the relevant model articles,

    the relevant model articles (so far as applicable) form part of the company's articles in the same manner and to the same extent as if articles in the form of those articles had been duly registered.
(2) The "relevant model articles" means the model articles prescribed for a company of that description as in force at the date on which the company is registered.

Alteration of articles

21 Amendment of articles

(1) A company may amend its articles by special resolution.
(2) In the case of a company that is a charity, this is subject to—
    (a) in England and Wales, sections 197 and 198 of the Charities Act 2011;
    (b) in Northern Ireland, Article 9 of the Charities (Northern Ireland) Order 1987.
(3) In the case of a company that is registered in the Scottish Charity Register, this is subject to—
    (a) section 112 of the Companies Act 1989, and
    (b) section 16 of the Charities and Trustee Investment (Scotland) Act 2005.

22 Entrenched provisions of the articles

(1) A company's articles may contain provision ("provision for entrenchment") to the effect that specified provisions of the articles may be amended or repealed only if conditions are met, or procedures are complied with, that are more restrictive than those applicable in the case of a special resolution.

...

(3) Provision for entrenchment does not prevent amendment of the company's articles—
    (a) by agreement of all the members of the company, or
    (b) by order of a court or other authority having power to alter the company's articles.
(4) Nothing in this section affects any power of a court or other authority to alter a company's articles.

23 Notice to registrar of existence of restriction on amendment of articles

(1) Where a company's articles—
  (a) on formation contain provision for entrenchment,
  (b) are amended so as to include such provision, or
  (c) are altered by order of a court or other authority so as to restrict or exclude the power of the company to amend its articles,

the company must give notice of that fact to the registrar.

(2) Where a company's articles—
  (a) are amended so as to remove provision for entrenchment, or
  (b) are altered by order of a court or other authority—
    (i) so as to remove such provision, or
    (ii) so as to remove any other restriction on, or any exclusion of, the power of the company to amend its articles,

the company must give notice of that fact to the registrar.

24 Statement of compliance where amendment of articles restricted

(1) This section applies where a company's articles are subject—
  (a) to provision for entrenchment, or
  (b) to an order of a court or other authority restricting or excluding the company's power to amend the articles.

(2) If the company—
  (a) amends its articles, and
  (b) is required to send to the registrar a document making or evidencing the amendment,

the company must deliver with that document a statement of compliance.

(3) The statement of compliance required is a statement certifying that the amendment has been made in accordance with the company's articles and, where relevant, any applicable order of a court or other authority.

(4) The registrar may rely on the statement of compliance as sufficient evidence of the matters stated in it.

25 Effect of alteration of articles on company's members

(1) A member of a company is not bound by an alteration to its articles after the date on which he became a member, if and so far as the alteration—
  (a) requires him to take or subscribe for more shares than the number held by him at the date on which the alteration is made, or
  (b) in any way increases his liability as at that date to contribute to the company's share capital or otherwise to pay money to the company.

(2) Subsection (1) does not apply in a case where the member agrees in writing, either before or after the alteration is made, to be bound by the alteration.

26 Registrar to be sent copy of amended articles

(1) Where a company amends its articles it must send to the registrar a copy of the articles as amended not later than 15 days after the amendment takes effect.

(2) This section does not require a company to set out in its articles any provisions of model articles that—
  (a) are applied by the articles, or
  (b) apply by virtue of section 20 (default application of model articles).

(3) If a company fails to comply with this section an offence is committed by—
  (a) the company, and
  (b) every officer of the company who is in default.

(4) A person guilty of an offence under this section is liable on summary conviction to a fine not exceeding level 3 on the standard scale and, for continued contravention, a daily default fine not exceeding one-tenth of level 3 on the standard scale.

27 Registrar's notice to comply in case of failure with respect to amended articles

(1) If it appears to the registrar that a company has failed to comply with any enactment requiring it—
  (a) to send to the registrar a document making or evidencing an alteration in the company's articles, or

(b) to send to the registrar a copy of the company's articles as amended, the registrar may give notice to the company requiring it to comply.

(2) The notice must—

(a) state the date on which it is issued, and

(b) require the company to comply within 28 days from that date.

(3) If the company complies with the notice within the specified time, no criminal proceedings may be brought in respect of the failure to comply with the enactment mentioned in subsection (1).

(4) If the company does not comply with the notice within the specified time, it is liable to a civil penalty of £200.

This is in addition to any liability to criminal proceedings in respect of the failure mentioned in subsection (1).

(5) The penalty may be recovered by the registrar and is to be paid into the Consolidated Fund.

Supplementary

28 Existing companies: provisions of memorandum treated as provisions of articles

(1) Provisions that immediately before the commencement of this Part were contained in a company's memorandum but are not provisions of the kind mentioned in section 8 (provisions of new-style memorandum) are to be treated after the commencement of this Part as provisions of the company's articles.

(2) This applies not only to substantive provisions but also to provision for entrenchment (as defined in section 22).

(3) The provisions of this Part about provision for entrenchment apply to such provision as they apply to provision made on the company's formation, except that the duty under section 23(1)(a) to give notice to the registrar does not apply.

CHAPTER 3

RESOLUTIONS AND AGREEMENTS AFFECTING A COMPANY'S CONSTITUTION

29 Resolutions and agreements affecting a company's constitution

(1) This Chapter applies to—

(a) any special resolution;

(b) any resolution or agreement agreed to by all the members of a company that, if not so agreed to, would not have been effective for its purpose unless passed as a special resolution;

(c) any resolution or agreement agreed to by all the members of a class of shareholders that, if not so agreed to, would not have been effective for its purpose unless passed by some particular majority or otherwise in some particular manner;

(d) any resolution or agreement that effectively binds all members of a class of shareholders though not agreed to by all those members;

(e) any other resolution or agreement to which this Chapter applies by virtue of any enactment.

(2) References in subsection (1) to a member of a company, or of a class of members of a company, do not include the company itself where it is such a member by virtue only of its holding shares as treasury shares.

30 Copies of resolutions or agreements to be forwarded to registrar

(1) A copy of every resolution or agreement to which this Chapter applies, or (in the case of a resolution or agreement that is not in writing) a written memorandum setting out its terms, must be forwarded to the registrar within 15 days after it is passed or made.

(2) If a company fails to comply with this section, an offence is committed by—

(a) the company, and

(b) every officer of it who is in default.

(3) A person guilty of an offence under this section is liable on summary conviction to a fine not exceeding level 3 on the standard scale and, for continued contravention, a daily default fine not exceeding one-tenth of level 3 on the standard scale.

(4) For the purposes of this section, a liquidator of the company is treated as an officer of it.

CHAPTER 4
MISCELLANEOUS AND SUPPLEMENTARY PROVISIONS

Statement of company's objects

31 Statement of company's objects

(1) Unless a company's articles specifically restrict the objects of the company, its objects are unrestricted.

(2) Where a company amends its articles so as to add, remove or alter a statement of the company's objects—
  (a) it must give notice to the registrar,
  (b) on receipt of the notice, the registrar shall register it, and
  (c) the amendment is not effective until entry of that notice on the register.

(3) Any such amendment does not affect any rights or obligations of the company or render defective any legal proceedings by or against it.

(4) In the case of a company that is a charity, the provisions of this section have effect subject to—
  (a) in England and Wales, sections 197 and 198 of the Charities Act 2011;
  (b) in Northern Ireland, Article 9 of the Charities (Northern Ireland) Order 1987.

(5) In the case of a company that is entered in the Scottish Charity Register, the provisions of this section have effect subject to the provisions of the Charities and Trustee Investment (Scotland) Act 2005.

Other provisions with respect to a company's constitution

32 Constitutional documents to be provided to members

(1) A company must, on request by any member, send to him the following documents—
  (a) an up-to-date copy of the company's articles;
  (b) a copy of any resolution or agreement relating to the company to which Chapter 3 applies (resolutions and agreements affecting a company's constitution) and that is for the time being in force;
  (c) a copy of any document required to be sent to the registrar under—
    (i) section 34(2) (notice where company's constitution altered by enactment), or
    (ii) section 35(2)(a) (notice where order of court or other authority alters company's constitution);
  (d) a copy of any court order under section 899 (order sanctioning compromise or arrangement) or section 900 (order facilitating reconstruction or amalgamation);
  (e) a copy of any court order under section 996 (protection of members against unfair prejudice: powers of the court) that alters the company's constitution;
  (f) a copy of the company's current certificate of incorporation, and of any past certificates of incorporation;
  (g) in the case of a company with a share capital, a current statement of capital;
  (h) in the case of a company limited by guarantee, a copy of the statement of guarantee.

(2) The statement of capital required by subsection (1)(g) is a statement of—
  (a) the total number of shares of the company,
  (b) the aggregate nominal value of those shares,
  (c) for each class of shares—
    (i) prescribed particulars of the rights attached to the shares,
    (ii) the total number of shares of that class, and
    (iii) the aggregate nominal value of shares of that class, and
  (d) the amount paid up and the amount (if any) unpaid on each share (whether on account of the nominal value of the share or by way of premium).

(3) If a company makes default in complying with this section, an offence is committed by every officer of the company who is in default.

(4) A person guilty of an offence under this section is liable on summary conviction to a fine not exceeding level 3 on the standard scale.

33 Effect of company's constitution

(1) The provisions of a company's constitution bind the company and its members to the same extent as if there were covenants on the part of the company and of each member to observe those provisions.

(2) Money payable by a member to the company under its constitution is a debt due from him to the company.
In England and Wales and Northern Ireland it is of the nature of an ordinary contract debt.

34 Notice to registrar where company's constitution altered by enactment

(1) This section applies where a company's constitution is altered by an enactment, other than an enactment amending the general law.

(2) The company must give notice of the alteration to the registrar, specifying the enactment, not later than 15 days after the enactment comes into force. In the case of a special enactment the notice must be accompanied by a copy of the enactment.

(3) If the enactment amends—
(a) the company's articles, or
(b) a resolution or agreement to which Chapter 3 applies (resolutions and agreements affecting a company's constitution),
the notice must be accompanied by a copy of the company's articles, or the resolution or agreement in question, as amended.

(4) A "special enactment" means an enactment that is not a public general enactment, and includes—
(a) an Act for confirming a provisional order,
(b) any provision of a public general Act in relation to the passing of which any of the standing orders of the House of Lords or the House of Commons relating to Private Business applied, or
(c) any enactment to the extent that it is incorporated in or applied for the purposes of a special enactment.

(5) If a company fails to comply with this section an offence is committed by—
(a) the company, and
(b) every officer of the company who is in default.

(6) A person guilty of an offence under this section is liable on summary conviction to a fine not exceeding level 3 on the standard scale and, for continued contravention, a daily default fine not exceeding one-tenth of level 3 on the standard scale.

35 Notice to registrar where company's constitution altered by order

(1) Where a company's constitution is altered by an order of a court or other authority, the company must give notice to the registrar of the alteration not later than 15 days after the alteration takes effect.

(2) The notice must be accompanied by—
(a) a copy of the order, and
(b) if the order amends—
(i) the company's articles, or
(ii) a resolution or agreement to which Chapter 3 applies (resolutions and agreements affecting the company's constitution),
a copy of the company's articles, or the resolution or agreement in question, as amended.

(3) If a company fails to comply with this section an offence is committed by—
(a) the company, and
(b) every officer of the company who is in default.

(4) A person guilty of an offence under this section is liable on summary conviction to a fine not exceeding level 3 on the standard scale and, for continued contravention, a daily default fine not exceeding one-tenth of level 3 on the standard scale.

(5) This section does not apply where provision is made by another enactment for the delivery to the registrar of a copy of the order in question.

36 Documents to be incorporated in or accompany copies of articles issued by company

(1) Every copy of a company's articles issued by the company must be accompanied by—
(a) a copy of any resolution or agreement relating to the company to which Chapter 3 applies (resolutions and agreements affecting a company's constitution),

(b) where the company has been required to give notice to the registrar under section 34(2) (notice where company's constitution altered by enactment), a statement that the enactment in question alters the effect of the company's constitution,
(c) where the company's constitution is altered by a special enactment (see section 34(4)), a copy of the enactment, and
(d) a copy of any order required to be sent to the registrar under section 35(2)(a) (order of court or other authority altering company's constitution).

(2) This does not require the articles to be accompanied by a copy of a document or by a statement if—
(a) the effect of the resolution, agreement, enactment or order (as the case may be) on the company's constitution has been incorporated into the articles by amendment, or
(b) the resolution, agreement, enactment or order (as the case may be) is not for the time being in force.

(3) If the company fails to comply with this section, an offence is committed by every officer of the company who is in default.

(4) A person guilty of an offence under this section is liable on summary conviction to a fine not exceeding level 3 on the standard scale for each occasion on which copies are issued, or, as the case may be, requested.

(5) For the purposes of this section, a liquidator of the company is treated as an officer of it.

Supplementary provisions

37 Right to participate in profits otherwise than as member void

In the case of a company limited by guarantee and not having a share capital any provision in the company's articles, or in any resolution of the company, purporting to give a person a right to participate in the divisible profits of the company otherwise than as a member is void.

38 Application to single member companies of enactments and rules of law

Any enactment or rule of law applicable to companies formed by two or more persons or having two or more members applies with any necessary modification in relation to a company formed by one person or having only one person as a member.

PART 4
A COMPANY'S CAPACITY AND RELATED MATTERS

Capacity of company and power of directors to bind it

39 A company's capacity

(1) The validity of an act done by a company shall not be called into question on the ground of lack of capacity by reason of anything in the company's constitution.

(2) This section has effect subject to section 42 (companies that are charities).

40 Power of directors to bind the company

(1) In favour of a person dealing with a company in good faith, the power of the directors to bind the company, or authorise others to do so, is deemed to be free of any limitation under the company's constitution.

(2) For this purpose—
(a) a person "deals with" a company if he is a party to any transaction or other act to which the company is a party,
(b) a person dealing with a company—
(i) is not bound to enquire as to any limitation on the powers of the directors to bind the company or authorise others to do so,
(ii) is presumed to have acted in good faith unless the contrary is proved, and
(iii) is not to be regarded as acting in bad faith by reason only of his knowing that an act is beyond the powers of the directors under the company's constitution.

(3) The references above to limitations on the directors' powers under the company's constitution include limitations deriving—
(a) from a resolution of the company or of any class of shareholders, or
(b) from any agreement between the members of the company or of any class of shareholders.

(4) This section does not affect any right of a member of the company to bring proceedings to restrain the doing of an action that is beyond the powers of the directors. But no such proceedings lie in respect of an act to be done in fulfilment of a legal obligation arising from a previous act of the company.

(5) This section does not affect any liability incurred by the directors, or any other person, by reason of the directors' exceeding their powers.

(6) This section has effect subject to—

section 41 (transactions with directors or their associates), and
section 42 (companies that are charities).

41 Constitutional limitations: transactions involving directors or their associates

(1) This section applies to a transaction if or to the extent that its validity depends on section 40 (power of directors deemed to be free of limitations under company's constitution in favour of person dealing with company in good faith).

Nothing in this section shall be read as excluding the operation of any other enactment or rule of law by virtue of which the transaction may be called in question or any liability to the company may arise.

(2) Where—

(a) a company enters into such a transaction, and
(b) the parties to the transaction include—
(i) a director of the company or of its holding company, or
(ii) a person connected with any such director,

the transaction is voidable at the instance of the company.

(3) Whether or not it is avoided, any such party to the transaction as is mentioned in subsection (2)(b)(i) or (ii), and any director of the company who authorised the transaction, is liable—

(a) to account to the company for any gain he has made directly or indirectly by the transaction, and
(b) to indemnify the company for any loss or damage resulting from the transaction.

(4) The transaction ceases to be voidable if—

(a) restitution of any money or other asset which was the subject matter of the transaction is no longer possible, or
(b) the company is indemnified for any loss or damage resulting from the transaction, or
(c) rights acquired bona fide for value and without actual notice of the directors' exceeding their powers by a person who is not party to the transaction would be affected by the avoidance, or
(d) the transaction is affirmed by the company.

(5) A person other than a director of the company is not liable under subsection (3) if he shows that at the time the transaction was entered into he did not know that the directors were exceeding their powers.

(6) Nothing in the preceding provisions of this section affects the rights of any party to the transaction not within subsection (2)(b)(i) or (ii). But the court may, on the application of the company or any such party, make an order affirming, severing or setting aside the transaction on such terms as appear to the court to be just.

(7) In this section—

(a) "transaction" includes any act; and
(b) the reference to a person connected with a director has the same meaning as in Part 10 (company directors).

42 Constitutional limitations: companies that are charities

(1) Sections 39 and 40 (company's capacity and power of directors to bind company) do not apply to the acts of a company that is a charity except in favour of a person who—

(a) does not know at the time the act is done that the company is a charity, or
(b) gives full consideration in money or money's worth in relation to the act in question and does not know (as the case may be)—
(i) that the act is not permitted by the company's constitution, or
(ii) that the act is beyond the powers of the directors.

(2) Where a company that is a charity purports to transfer or grant an interest in property, the fact that (as the case may be)—
(a) the act was not permitted by the company's constitution, or
(b) the directors in connection with the act exceeded any limitation on their powers under the company's constitution,

does not affect the title of a person who subsequently acquires the property or any interest in it for full consideration without actual notice of any such circumstances affecting the validity of the company's act.

(3) In any proceedings arising out of subsection (1) or (2) the burden of proving—
(a) that a person knew that the company was a charity, or
(b) that a person knew that an act was not permitted by the company's constitution or was beyond the powers of the directors,

lies on the person asserting that fact.

(4) In the case of a company that is a charity the affirmation of a transaction to which section 41 applies (transactions with directors or their associates) is ineffective without the prior written consent of—
(a) in England and Wales, the Charity Commission;
(b) in Northern Ireland, the Department for Social Development.

(5) This section does not extend to Scotland (but see section 112 of the Companies Act 1989).

Formalities of doing business under the law of England and Wales or Northern Ireland

43 Company contracts

(1) Under the law of England and Wales or Northern Ireland a contract may be made—
(a) by a company, by writing under its common seal, or
(b) on behalf of a company, by a person acting under its authority, express or implied.

(2) Any formalities required by law in the case of a contract made by an individual also apply, unless a contrary intention appears, to a contract made by or on behalf of a company.

44 Execution of documents

(1) Under the law of England and Wales or Northern Ireland a document is executed by a company—
(a) by the affixing of its common seal, or
(b) by signature in accordance with the following provisions.

(2) A document is validly executed by a company if it is signed on behalf of the company—
(a) by two authorised signatories, or
(b) by a director of the company in the presence of a witness who attests the signature.

(3) The following are "authorised signatories" for the purposes of subsection (2)—
(a) every director of the company, and
(b) in the case of a private company with a secretary or a public company, the secretary (or any joint secretary) of the company.

(4) A document signed in accordance with subsection (2) and expressed, in whatever words, to be executed by the company has the same effect as if executed under the common seal of the company.

(5) In favour of a purchaser a document is deemed to have been duly executed by a company if it purports to be signed in accordance with subsection (2).
A "purchaser" means a purchaser in good faith for valuable consideration and includes a lessee, mortgagee or other person who for valuable consideration acquires an interest in property.

(6) Where a document is to be signed by a person on behalf of more than one company, it is not duly signed by that person for the purposes of this section unless he signs it separately in each capacity.

(7) References in this section to a document being (or purporting to be) signed by a director or secretary are to be read, in a case where that office is held by a firm, as references to its being (or purporting to be) signed by an individual authorised by the firm to sign on its behalf.

(8) This section applies to a document that is (or purports to be) executed by a company in the name of or on behalf of another person whether or not that person is also a company.

45 Common seal

(1) A company may have a common seal, but need not have one.
(2) A company which has a common seal shall have its name engraved in legible characters on the seal.
(3) If a company fails to comply with subsection (2) an offence is committed by—
  (a) the company, and
  (b) every officer of the company who is in default.
(4) An officer of a company, or a person acting on behalf of a company, commits an offence if he uses, or authorises the use of, a seal purporting to be a seal of the company on which its name is not engraved as required by subsection (2).
(5) A person guilty of an offence under this section is liable on summary conviction to a fine not exceeding level 3 on the standard scale.
(6) This section does not form part of the law of Scotland.

46 Execution of deeds

(1) A document is validly executed by a company as a deed for the purposes of section 1(2)(b) of the Law of Property (Miscellaneous Provisions) Act 1989 and for the purposes of the law of Northern Ireland if, and only if—
  (a) it is duly executed by the company, and
  (b) it is delivered as a deed.
(2) For the purposes of subsection (1)(b) a document is presumed to be delivered upon its being executed, unless a contrary intention is proved.

47 Execution of deeds or other documents by attorney

(1) Under the law of England and Wales or Northern Ireland a company may, by instrument executed as a deed, empower a person, either generally or in respect of specified matters, as its attorney to execute deeds or other documents on its behalf.
(2) A deed or other document so executed, whether in the United Kingdom or elsewhere, has effect as if executed by the company.

Formalities of doing business under the law of Scotland

48 Execution of documents by companies

(1) The following provisions form part of the law of Scotland only.
(2) Notwithstanding the provisions of any enactment, a company need not have a company seal.
(3) For the purposes of any enactment—
  (a) providing for a document to be executed by a company by affixing its common seal, or
  (b) referring (in whatever terms) to a document so executed,

a document signed or subscribed (or, in the case of an electronic document, authenticated) by or on behalf of the company in accordance with the provisions of the Requirements of Writing (Scotland) Act 1995 has effect as if so executed.

Other matters

49 Official seal for use abroad

(1) A company that has a common seal may have an official seal for use outside the United Kingdom.
(2) The official seal must be a facsimile of the company's common seal, with the addition on its face of the place or places where it is to be used.
(3) The official seal when duly affixed to a document has the same effect as the company's common seal.
This subsection does not extend to Scotland.
(4) A company having an official seal for use outside the United Kingdom may—
  (a) by writing under its common seal, or
  (b) as respects Scotland, by writing subscribed or authenticated in accordance with the Requirements of Writing (Scotland) Act 1995,

authorise any person appointed for the purpose to affix the official seal to any deed or other document to which the company is party.
(5) As between the company and a person dealing with such an agent, the agent's authority continues—

(a) during the period mentioned in the instrument conferring the authority, or
(b) if no period is mentioned, until notice of the revocation or termination of the agent's authority has been given to the person dealing with him.

(6) The person affixing the official seal must certify in writing on the deed or other document to which the seal is affixed the date on which, and place at which, it is affixed.

50 Official seal for share certificates etc.

(1) A company that has a common seal may have an official seal for use—
(a) for sealing securities issued by the company, or
(b) for sealing documents creating or evidencing securities so issued.

(2) The official seal—
(a) must be a facsimile of the company's common seal, with the addition on its face of the word "Securities", and
(b) when duly affixed to the document has the same effect as the company's common seal.

51 Pre-incorporation contracts, deeds and obligations

(1) A contract that purports to be made by or on behalf of a company at a time when the company has not been formed has effect, subject to any agreement to the contrary, as one made with the person purporting to act for the company or as agent for it, and he is personally liable on the contract accordingly.

(2) Subsection (1) applies—
(a) to the making of a deed under the law of England and Wales or Northern Ireland, and
(b) to the undertaking of an obligation under the law of Scotland, as it applies to the making of a contract.

52 Bills of exchange and promissory notes

A bill of exchange or promissory note is deemed to have been made, accepted or endorsed on behalf of a company if made, accepted or endorsed in the name of, or by or on behalf or on account of, the company by a person acting under its authority.

PART 5
A COMPANY'S NAME

CHAPTER 1
GENERAL REQUIREMENTS

Prohibited names

53 Prohibited names

A company must not be registered under this Act by a name if, in the opinion of the Secretary of State—
(a) its use by the company would constitute an offence, or
(b) it is offensive.

Sensitive words and expressions

54 Names suggesting connection with government or public authority

(1) The approval of the Secretary of State is required for a company to be registered under this Act by a name that would be likely to give the impression that the company is connected with—
(a) Her Majesty's Government, any part of the Scottish administration, the Welsh Government or Her Majesty's Government in Northern Ireland,
(b) a local authority, or
(c) any public authority specified for the purposes of this section by regulations made by the Secretary of State.

(2) For the purposes of this section— "local authority" means—
(a) a local authority within the meaning of the Local Government Act 1972, the Common Council of the City of London or the Council of the Isles of Scilly,
(b) a council constituted under section 2 of the Local Government etc. (Scotland) Act 1994, or

(c) a district council in Northern Ireland;

"public authority" includes any person or body having functions of a public nature.

(3) Regulations under this section are subject to affirmative resolution procedure.

55 Other sensitive words or expressions

(1) The approval of the Secretary of State is required for a company to be registered under this Act by a name that includes a word or expression for the time being specified in regulations made by the Secretary of State under this section.

(2) Regulations under this section are subject to approval after being made.

56 Duty to seek comments of government department or other specified body

(1) The Secretary of State may by regulations under—

(a) section 54 (name suggesting connection with government or public authority), or

(b) section 55 (other sensitive words or expressions),

require that, in connection with an application for the approval of the Secretary of State under that section, the applicant must seek the view of a specified Government department or other body.

(2) Where such a requirement applies, the applicant must request the specified department or other body (in writing) to indicate whether (and if so why) it has any objections to the proposed name.

(3) Where a request under this section is made in connection with an application for the registration of a company under this Act, the application must—

(a) include a statement that a request under this section has been made, and

(b) be accompanied by a copy of any response received.

(4) Where a request under this section is made in connection with a change in a company's name, the notice of the change sent to the registrar must be accompanied by—

(a) a statement by a director or secretary of the company that a request under this section has been made, and

(b) a copy of any response received.

(5) In this section "specified" means specified in the regulations.

Permitted characters etc

57 Permitted characters etc

(1) The Secretary of State may make provision by regulations—

(a) as to the letters or other characters, signs or symbols (including accents and other diacritical marks) and punctuation that may be used in the name of a company registered under this Act; and

(b) specifying a standard style or format for the name of a company for the purposes of registration.

(2) The regulations may prohibit the use of specified characters, signs or symbols when appearing in a specified position (in particular, at the beginning of a name).

(3) A company may not be registered under this Act by a name that consists of or includes anything that is not permitted in accordance with regulations under this section.

(4) Regulations under this section are subject to negative resolution procedure.

(5) In this section "specified" means specified in the regulations.

CHAPTER 2
INDICATIONS OF COMPANY TYPE OR LEGAL FORM

Required indications for limited companies

58 Public limited companies

(1) The name of a limited company that is a public company must end with "public limited company" or "p.l.c.".

(2) In the case of a Welsh company, its name may instead end with "cwmni cyfyngedig cyhoeddus" or "c.c.c.".

(3) This section does not apply to community interest companies (but see section 33(3) and (4) of the Companies (Audit, Investigations and Community Enterprise) Act 2004).

59 Private limited companies

(1) The name of a limited company that is a private company must end with "limited" or "ltd.".
(2) In the case of a Welsh company, its name may instead end with "cyfyngedig" or "cyf.".
(3) Certain companies are exempt from this requirement (see section 60).
(4) This section does not apply to community interest companies (but see section 33(1) and (2) of the Companies (Audit, Investigations and Community Enterprise) Act 2004).

60 Exemption from requirement as to use of "limited"

(1) A private company is exempt from section 59 (requirement to have name ending with "limited" or permitted alternative) if—
  (a) it is a charity,
  (b) it is exempted from the requirement of that section by regulations made by the Secretary of State, or
  (c) it meets the conditions specified in—
    section 61 (continuation of existing exemption: companies limited by shares), or
    section 62 (continuation of existing exemption: companies limited by guarantee).
(2) The registrar may refuse to register a private limited company by a name that does not include the word "limited" (or a permitted alternative) unless a statement has been delivered to him that the company meets the conditions for exemption.
(3) The registrar may accept the statement as sufficient evidence of the matters stated in it.
(4) Regulations under this section are subject to negative resolution procedure.

61 Continuation of existing exemption: companies limited by shares

(1) This section applies to a private company limited by shares—
  (a) that on 25th February 1982—
    (i) was registered in Great Britain, and
    (ii) had a name that, by virtue of a licence under section 19 of the Companies Act 1948 (or corresponding earlier legislation), did not include the word "limited" or any of the permitted alternatives, or
  (b) that on 30th June 1983—
    (i) was registered in Northern Ireland, and
    (ii) had a name that, by virtue of a licence under section 19 of the Companies Act (Northern Ireland) 1960 (or corresponding earlier legislation), did not include the word "limited" or any of the permitted alternatives.
(2) A company to which this section applies is exempt from section 59 (requirement to have name ending with "limited" or permitted alternative) so long as—
  (a) it continues to meet the following two conditions, and
  (b) it does not change its name.
(3) The first condition is that the objects of the company are the promotion of commerce, art, science, education, religion, charity or any profession, and anything incidental or conducive to any of those objects.
(4) The second condition is that the company's articles—
  (a) require its income to be applied in promoting its objects,
  (b) prohibit the payment of dividends, or any return of capital, to its members, and
  (c) require all the assets that would otherwise be available to its members generally to be transferred on its winding up either—
    (i) to another body with objects similar to its own, or
    (ii) to another body the objects of which are the promotion of charity and anything incidental or conducive thereto,
  (whether or not the body is a member of the company).

62 Continuation of existing exemption: companies limited by guarantee

(1) A private company limited by guarantee that immediately before the commencement of this Part—
  (a) was exempt by virtue of section 30 of the Companies Act 1985 or Article 40 of the Companies (Northern Ireland) Order 1986 from the requirement to have a name including the word "limited" or a permitted alternative, and
  (b) had a name that did not include the word "limited" or any of the permitted alternatives,

is exempt from section 59 (requirement to have name ending with "limited" or permitted alternative) so long as it continues to meet the following two conditions and does not change its name.

(2) The first condition is that the objects of the company are the promotion of commerce, art, science, education, religion, charity or any profession, and anything incidental or conducive to any of those objects.

(3) The second condition is that the company's articles—
 (a) require its income to be applied in promoting its objects,
 (b) prohibit the payment of dividends to its members, and
 (c) require all the assets that would otherwise be available to its members generally to be transferred on its winding up either—
  (i) to another body with objects similar to its own, or
  (ii) to another body the objects of which are the promotion of charity and anything incidental or conducive thereto,

(whether or not the body is a member of the company).

63 Exempt company: restriction on amendment of articles

(1) A private company—
 (a) that is exempt under section 61 or 62 from the requirement to use "limited" (or a permitted alternative) as part of its name, and
 (b) whose name does not include "limited" or any of the permitted alternatives,

must not amend its articles so that it ceases to comply with the conditions for exemption under that section.

(2) If subsection (1) above is contravened an offence is committed by—
 (a) the company, and
 (b) every officer of the company who is in default.

For this purpose a shadow director is treated as an officer of the company.

Version applying to England and Wales

(3) A person guilty of an offence under this section is liable on summary conviction to a fine not exceeding level 5 on the standard scale and, for continued contravention, a daily default fine not exceeding one-tenth of the greater of £5,000 or level 4

Version applying to Scotland

(3) A person guilty of an offence under this section is liable on summary conviction to a fine not exceeding level 5 on the standard scale and, for continued contravention, a daily default fine not exceeding one-tenth of level 5 on the standard scale.

(4) Where immediately before the commencement of this section—
 (a) a company was exempt by virtue of section 30 of the Companies Act 1985 or Article 40 of the Companies (Northern Ireland) Order 1986 from the requirement to have a name including the word "limited" (or a permitted alternative), and
 (b) the company's memorandum or articles contained provision preventing an alteration of them without the approval of—
  (i) the Board of Trade or a Northern Ireland department (or any other department or Minister), or
  (ii) the Charity Commission,

that provision, and any condition of any such licence as is mentioned in section 61(1)(a)(ii) or (b)(ii) requiring such provision, shall cease to have effect.

This does not apply if, or to the extent that, the provision is required by or under any other enactment.

(5) It is hereby declared that any such provision as is mentioned in subsection (4)(b) formerly contained in a company's memorandum was at all material times capable, with the appropriate approval, of being altered or removed under section 17 of the Companies Act 1985 or Article 28 of the Companies (Northern Ireland) Order 1986 (or corresponding earlier enactments).

64 Power to direct change of name in case of company ceasing to be entitled to exemption

(1) If it appears to the Secretary of State that a company whose name does not include "limited" or any of the permitted alternatives—
 (a) has ceased to be entitled to exemption under section 60(1)(a) or (b), or
 (b) in the case of a company within section 61 or 62 (which impose conditions as to the objects and articles of the company)—

(i) has carried on any business other than the promotion of any of the objects mentioned in subsection (3) of section 61 or, as the case may be, subsection (2) of section 62, or

(ii) has acted inconsistently with the provision required by subsection (4)(a) or (b) of section 61 or, as the case may be, subsection (3)(a) or (b) of section 62,

the Secretary of State may direct the company to change its name so that it ends with "limited" or one of the permitted alternatives.

(2) The direction must be in writing and must specify the period within which the company is to change its name.

(3) A change of name in order to comply with a direction under this section may be made by resolution of the directors.
This is without prejudice to any other method of changing the company's name.

(4) Where a resolution of the directors is passed in accordance with subsection (3), the company must give notice to the registrar of the change.
Sections 80 and 81 apply as regards the registration and effect of the change.

(5) If the company fails to comply with a direction under this section an offence is committed by—
(a) the company, and
(b) every officer of the company who is in default.

Version applying to Scotland

(6) A person guilty of an offence under this section is liable on summary conviction to a fine not exceeding level 5 on the standard scale and, for continued contravention, a daily default fine not exceeding one-tenth of level 5 on the standard scale.

Version applying to England and Wales

(6) A person guilty of an offence under this section is liable on summary conviction to a fine not exceeding level 5 on the standard scale and, for continued contravention, a daily default fine not exceeding one-tenth of the greater of £5,000 or level 4 on the standard scale.

(7) A company that has been directed to change its name under this section may not, without the approval of the Secretary of State, subsequently change its name so that it does not include "limited" or one of the permitted alternatives.
This does not apply to a change of name on re-registration or on conversion to a community interest company.

Inappropriate use of indications of company type or legal form

65 Inappropriate use of indications of company type or legal form

(1) The Secretary of State may make provision by regulations prohibiting the use in a company name of specified words, expressions or other indications —
(a) that are associated with a particular type of company or form of organisation, or
(b) that are similar to words, expressions or other indications associated with a particular type of company or form of organisation.

(2) The regulations may prohibit the use of words, expressions or other indications—
(a) in a specified part, or otherwise than in a specified part, of a company's name;
(b) in conjunction with, or otherwise than in conjunction with, such other words, expressions or indications as may be specified.

(3) A company must not be registered under this Act by a name that consists of or includes anything prohibited by regulations under this section.

(4) In this section "specified" means specified in the regulations.

(5) Regulations under this section are subject to negative resolution procedure.

CHAPTER 3
SIMILARITY TO OTHER NAMES

Similarity to other name on registrar's index

66 Name not to be the same as another in the index

(1) A company must not be registered under this Act by a name that is the same as another name appearing in the registrar's index of company names.

(2) The Secretary of State may make provision by regulations supplementing this section.

(3) The regulations may make provision—
(a) as to matters that are to be disregarded, and
(b) as to words, expressions, signs or symbols that are, or are not, to be regarded as the same,
for the purposes of this section.
(4) The regulations may provide—
(a) that registration by a name that would otherwise be prohibited under this section is permitted—
(i) in specified circumstances, or
(ii) with specified consent, and
(b) that if those circumstances obtain or that consent is given at the time a company is registered by a name, a subsequent change of circumstances or withdrawal of consent does not affect the registration.
(5) Regulations under this section are subject to negative resolution procedure.
(6) In this section "specified" means specified in the regulations.

67 Power to direct change of name in case of similarity to existing name

(1) The Secretary of State may direct a company to change its name if it has been registered in a name that is the same as or, in the opinion of the Secretary of State, too like—
(a) a name appearing at the time of the registration in the registrar's index of company names, or
(b) a name that should have appeared in that index at that time.
(2) The Secretary of State may make provision by regulations supplementing this section.
(3) The regulations may make provision—
(a) as to matters that are to be disregarded, and
(b) as to words, expressions, signs or symbols that are, or are not, to be regarded as the same,
for the purposes of this section.
(4) The regulations may provide—
(a) that no direction is to be given under this section in respect of a name—
(i) in specified circumstances, or
(ii) if specified consent is given, and
(b) that a subsequent change of circumstances or withdrawal of consent does not give rise to grounds for a direction under this section.
(5) Regulations under this section are subject to negative resolution procedure.
(6) In this section "specified" means specified in the regulations.

68 Direction to change name: supplementary provisions

(1) The following provisions have effect in relation to a direction under section 67 (power to direct change of name in case of similarity to existing name).
(2) Any such direction—
(a) must be given within twelve months of the company's registration by the name in question, and
(b) must specify the period within which the company is to change its name.
(3) The Secretary of State may by a further direction extend that period.
Any such direction must be given before the end of the period for the time being specified.
(4) A direction under section 67 or this section must be in writing.
(5) If a company fails to comply with the direction, an offence is committed by—
(a) the company, and
(b) every officer of the company who is in default.
For this purpose a shadow director is treated as an officer of the company.
(6) A person guilty of an offence under this section is liable on summary conviction to a fine not exceeding level 3 on the standard scale and, for continued contravention, a daily default fine not exceeding one-tenth of level 3 on the standard scale.

Similarity to other name in which person has goodwill

69 Objection to company's registered name

(1) A person ("the applicant") may object to a company's registered name on the ground—
(a) that it is the same as a name associated with the applicant in which he has goodwill, or

(b) that it is sufficiently similar to such a name that its use in the United Kingdom would be likely to mislead by suggesting a connection between the company and the applicant.

(2) The objection must be made by application to a company names adjudicator (see section 70).

(3) The company concerned shall be the primary respondent to the application.
Any of its members or directors may be joined as respondents.

(4) If the ground specified in subsection (1)(a) or (b) is established, it is for the respondents to show—

(a) that the name was registered before the commencement of the activities on which the applicant relies to show goodwill; or

(b) that the company—

(i) is operating under the name, or

(ii) is proposing to do so and has incurred substantial start-up costs in preparation, or

(iii) was formerly operating under the name and is now dormant;or

(c) that the name was registered in the ordinary course of a company formation business and the company is available for sale to the applicant on the standard terms of that business; or

(d) that the name was adopted in good faith; or

(e) that the interests of the applicant are not adversely affected to any significant extent. If none of those is shown, the objection shall be upheld.

(5) If the facts mentioned in subsection (4)(a), (b) or (c) are established, the objection shall nevertheless be upheld if the applicant shows that the main purpose of the respondents (or any of them) in registering the name was to obtain money (or other consideration) from the applicant or prevent him from registering the name.

(6) If the objection is not upheld under subsection (4) or (5), it shall be dismissed.

(7) In this section "goodwill" includes reputation of any description.

70 Company names adjudicators

(1) The Secretary of State shall appoint persons to be company names adjudicators.

(2) The persons appointed must have such legal or other experience as, in the Secretary of State's opinion, makes them suitable for appointment.

(3)–(6) *omitted*

71 *omitted*

72 Decision of adjudicator to be made available to public

(1) A company names adjudicator must, within 90 days of determining an application under section 69, make his decision and his reasons for it available to the public.

(2) He may do so by means of a website or by such other means as appear to him to be appropriate.

73 Order requiring name to be changed

(1) If an application under section 69 is upheld, the adjudicator shall make an order—

(a) requiring the respondent company to change its name to one that is not an offending name, and

(b) requiring all the respondents—

(i) to take all such steps as are within their power to make, or facilitate the making, of that change, and

(ii) not to cause or permit any steps to be taken calculated to result in another company being registered with a name that is an offending name.

(2) An "offending name" means a name that, by reason of its similarity to the name associated with the applicant in which he claims goodwill, would be likely—

(a) to be the subject of a direction under section 67 (power of Secretary of State to direct change of name), or

(b) to give rise to a further application under section 69.

(3) The order must specify a date by which the respondent company's name is to be changed and may be enforced—

(a) in England and Wales or Northern Ireland, in the same way as an order of the High Court;

(b) in Scotland, in the same way as a decree of the Court of Session.

(4) If the respondent company's name is not changed in accordance with the order by the specified date, the adjudicator may determine a new name for the company.

(5) If the adjudicator determines a new name for the respondent company he must give notice of his determination—

(a) to the applicant,

(b) to the respondents, and

(c) to the registrar.

(6) For the purposes of this section a company's name is changed when the change takes effect in accordance with section 81(1) (on the issue of the new certification of incorporation).

74 Appeal from adjudicator's decision

(1) An appeal lies to the court from any decision of a company names adjudicator to uphold or dismiss an application under section 69.

(2)–(6) *omitted*

CHAPTER 4
OTHER POWERS OF THE SECRETARY OF STATE

75 Provision of misleading information etc.

(1) If it appears to the Secretary of State—

(a) that misleading information has been given for the purposes of a company's registration by a particular name, or

(b) that an undertaking or assurance has been given for that purpose and has not been fulfilled,

the Secretary of State may direct the company to change its name.

(2) Any such direction—

(a) must be given within five years of the company's registration by that name, and

(b) must specify the period within which the company is to change its name.

(3) The Secretary of State may by a further direction extend the period within which the company is to change its name.

Any such direction must be given before the end of the period for the time being specified.

(4) A direction under this section must be in writing.

(5) If a company fails to comply with a direction under this section, an offence is committed by—

(a) the company, and

(b) every officer of the company who is in default.

For this purpose a shadow director is treated as an officer of the company.

(6) A person guilty of an offence under this section is liable on summary conviction to a fine not exceeding level 3 on the standard scale and, for continued contravention, a daily default fine not exceeding one-tenth of level 3 on the standard scale.

76 Misleading indication of activities

(1) If in the opinion of the Secretary of State the name by which a company is registered gives so misleading an indication of the nature of its activities as to be likely to cause harm to the public, the Secretary of State may direct the company to change its name.

(2) The direction must be in writing.

(3) The direction must be complied with within a period of six weeks from the date of the direction or such longer period as the Secretary of State may think fit to allow.

This does not apply if an application is duly made to the court under the following provisions.

(4) The company may apply to the court to set the direction aside.

The application must be made within the period of three weeks from the date of the direction.

(5) The court may set the direction aside or confirm it.

If the direction is confirmed, the court shall specify the period within which the direction is to be complied with.

(6) If a company fails to comply with a direction under this section, an offence is committed by—
  (a) the company, and
  (b) every officer of the company who is in default.

For this purpose a shadow director is treated as an officer of the company.

(7) A person guilty of an offence under this section is liable on summary conviction to a fine not exceeding level 3 on the standard scale and, for continued contravention, a daily default fine not exceeding one-tenth of level 3 on the standard scale.

CHAPTER 5
CHANGE OF NAME

77 Change of name

(1) A company may change its name—
  (a) by special resolution (see section 78), or
  (b) by other means provided for by the company's articles (see section 79).

(2) The name of a company may also be changed—
  (a) by resolution of the directors acting under section 64 (change of name to comply with direction of Secretary of State under that section);
  (b) on the determination of a new name by a company names adjudicator under section 73 (powers of adjudicator on upholding objection to company name);
  (c) on the determination of a new name by the court under section 74 (appeal against decision of company names adjudicator);
  (d) under section 1033 (company's name on restoration to the register).

78 Change of name by special resolution

(1) Where a change of name has been agreed to by a company by special resolution, the company must give notice to the registrar.

This is in addition to the obligation to forward a copy of the resolution to the registrar.

(2) Where a change of name by special resolution is conditional on the occurrence of an event, the notice given to the registrar of the change must—
  (a) specify that the change is conditional, and
  (b) state whether the event has occurred.

(3) If the notice states that the event has not occurred—
  (a) the registrar is not required to act under section 80 (registration and issue of new certificate of incorporation) until further notice,
  (b) when the event occurs, the company must give notice to the registrar stating that it has occurred, and
  (c) the registrar may rely on the statement as sufficient evidence of the matters stated in it.

79 Change of name by means provided for in company's articles

(1) Where a change of a company's name has been made by other means provided for by its articles—
  (a) the company must give notice to the registrar, and
  (b) the notice must be accompanied by a statement that the change of name has been made by means provided for by the company's articles.

(2) The registrar may rely on the statement as sufficient evidence of the matters stated in it.

80 Change of name: registration and issue of new certificate of incorporation

(1) This section applies where the registrar receives notice of a change of a company's name.

(2) If the registrar is satisfied—
  (a) that the new name complies with the requirements of this Part, and
  (b) that the requirements of the Companies Acts, and any relevant requirements of the company's articles, with respect to a change of name are complied with,

the registrar must enter the new name on the register in place of the former name.

(3) On the registration of the new name, the registrar must issue a certificate of incorporation altered to meet the circumstances of the case.

81 Change of name: effect

(1) A change of a company's name has effect from the date on which the new certificate of incorporation is issued.
(2) The change does not affect any rights or obligations of the company or render defective any legal proceedings by or against it.
(3) Any legal proceedings that might have been continued or commenced against it by its former name may be continued or commenced against it by its new name.

CHAPTER 6
TRADING DISCLOSURES

82 Requirement to disclose company name etc.

(1) The Secretary of State may by regulations make provision requiring companies—
  (a) to display specified information in specified locations,
  (b) to state specified information in specified descriptions of document or communication, and
  (c) to provide specified information on request to those they deal with in the course of their business.
(2) The regulations—
  (a) must in every case require disclosure of the name of the company, and
  (b) may make provision as to the manner in which any specified information is to be displayed, stated or provided.
(3) The regulations may provide that, for the purposes of any requirement to disclose a company's name, any variation between a word or words required to be part of the name and a permitted abbreviation of that word or those words (or vice versa) shall be disregarded.
(4) In this section "specified" means specified in the regulations.
(5) Regulations under this section are subject to affirmative resolution procedure.

83 Civil consequences of failure to make required disclosure

(1) This section applies to any legal proceedings brought by a company to which section 82 applies (requirement to disclose company name etc) to enforce a right arising out of a contract made in the course of a business in respect of which the company was, at the time the contract was made, in breach of regulations under that section.
(2) The proceedings shall be dismissed if the defendant (in Scotland, the defender) to the proceedings shows—
  (a) that he has a claim against the claimant (pursuer) arising out of the contract that he has been unable to pursue by reason of the latter's breach of the regulations, or
  (b) that he has suffered some financial loss in connection with the contract by reason of the claimant's (pursuer's) breach of the regulations,

  unless the court before which the proceedings are brought is satisfied that it is just and equitable to permit the proceedings to continue.
(3) This section does not affect the right of any person to enforce such rights as he may have against another person in any proceedings brought by that person.

84 Criminal consequences of failure to make required disclosures

(1) Regulations under section 82 may provide—
  (a) that where a company fails, without reasonable excuse, to comply with any specified requirement of regulations under that section an offence is committed by—
    (i) the company, and
    (ii) every officer of the company who is in default;
  (b) that a person guilty of such an offence is liable on summary conviction to a fine not exceeding level 3 on the standard scale and, for continued contravention, a daily default fine not exceeding one-tenth of level 3 on the standard scale.
(2) The regulations may provide that, for the purposes of any provision made under subsection (1), a shadow director of the company is to be treated as an officer of the company.
(3) In subsection (1)(a) "specified" means specified in the regulations.

85 Minor variations in form of name to be left out of account

(1) For the purposes of this Chapter, in considering a company's name no account is to be taken of—
  (a) whether upper or lower case characters (or a combination of the two) are used,
  (b) whether diacritical marks or punctuation are present or absent,
  (c) whether the name is in the same format or style as is specified under section 57(1)(b) for the purposes of registration,

provided there is no real likelihood of names differing only in those respects being taken to be different names.

(2) This does not affect the operation of regulations under section 57(1)(a) permitting only specified characters, diacritical marks or punctuation.

PART 6
A COMPANY'S REGISTERED OFFICE

General

86 A company's registered office

A company must at all times have a registered office to which all communications and notices may be addressed.

87 Change of address of registered office

(1) A company may change the address of its registered office by giving notice to the registrar.

(2) The change takes effect upon the notice being registered by the registrar, but until the end of the period of 14 days beginning with the date on which it is registered a person may validly serve any document on the company at the address previously registered.

(3) For the purposes of any duty of a company—
  (a) to keep available for inspection at its registered office any register, index or other document, or
  (b) to mention the address of its registered office in any document,

a company that has given notice to the registrar of a change in the address of its registered office may act on the change as from such date, not more than 14 days after the notice is given, as it may determine.

(4) Where a company unavoidably ceases to perform at its registered office any such duty as is mentioned in subsection (3)(a) in circumstances in which it was not practicable to give prior notice to the registrar of a change in the address of its registered office, but—
  (a) resumes performance of that duty at other premises as soon as practicable, and
  (b) gives notice accordingly to the registrar of a change in the situation of its registered office within 14 days of doing so,

it is not to be treated as having failed to comply with that duty.

Welsh companies

88 Welsh companies

(1) In the Companies Acts a "Welsh company" means a company as to which it is stated in the register that its registered office is to be situated in Wales.

(2) A company—
  (a) whose registered office is in Wales, and
  (b) as to which it is stated in the register that its registered office is to be situated in England and Wales,

may by special resolution require the register to be amended so that it states that the company's registered office is to be situated in Wales.

(3) A company—
  (a) whose registered office is in Wales, and
  (b) as to which it is stated in the register that its registered office is to be situated in Wales,

may by special resolution require the register to be amended so that it states that the company's registered office is to be situated in England and Wales.

(4) Where a company passes a resolution under this section it must give notice to the registrar, who shall—

(a) amend the register accordingly, and
(b) issue a new certificate of incorporation altered to meet the circumstances of the case.

PART 7
RE-REGISTRATION AS A MEANS OF ALTERING A COMPANY'S STATUS

Introductory

89 Alteration of status by re-registration

A company may by re-registration under this Part alter its status—

(a) from a private company to a public company (see sections 90 to 96);
(b) from a public company to a private company (see sections 97 to 101);
(c) from a private limited company to an unlimited company (see sections 102 to 104);
(d) from an unlimited private company to a limited company (see sections 105 to 108);
(e) from a public company to an unlimited private company (see sections 109 to 111).

Private company becoming public

90 Re-registration of private company as public

(1) A private company (whether limited or unlimited) may be re-registered as a public company limited by shares if—

(a) a special resolution that it should be so re-registered is passed,
(b) the conditions specified below are met, and
(c) an application for re-registration is delivered to the registrar in accordance with section 94, together with—
(i) the other documents required by that section, and
(ii) a statement of compliance.

(2) The conditions are—

(a) that the company has a share capital;
(b) that the requirements of section 91 are met as regards its share capital;
(c) that the requirements of section 92 are met as regards its net assets;
(d) if section 93 applies (recent allotment of shares for non-cash consideration), that the requirements of that section are met; and
(e) that the company has not previously been re-registered as unlimited.

(3) The company must make such changes—

(a) in its name, and
(b) in its articles,

as are necessary in connection with its becoming a public company.

(4) If the company is unlimited it must also make such changes in its articles as are necessary in connection with its becoming a company limited by shares.

91 Requirements as to share capital

(1) The following requirements must be met at the time the special resolution is passed that the company should be re-registered as a public company—

(a) the nominal value of the company's allotted share capital must be not less than the authorised minimum;
(b) each of the company's allotted shares must be paid up at least as to one-quarter of the nominal value of that share and the whole of any premium on it;
(c) if any shares in the company or any premium on them have been fully or partly paid up by an undertaking given by any person that he or another should do work or perform services (whether for the company or any other person), the undertaking must have been performed or otherwise discharged;
(d) if shares have been allotted as fully or partly paid up as to their nominal value or any premium on them otherwise than in cash, and the consideration for the allotment consists of or includes an undertaking to the company (other than one to which paragraph (c) applies), then either—
(i) the undertaking must have been performed or otherwise discharged, or
(ii) there must be a contract between the company and some person pursuant to which the undertaking is to be performed within five years from the time the special resolution is passed.

(2) For the purpose of determining whether the requirements in subsection (1)(b), (c) and (d) are met, the following may be disregarded—
  (a) shares allotted—
    (i) before 22nd June 1982 in the case of a company then registered in Great Britain, or
    (ii) before 31st December 1984 in the case of a company then registered in Northern Ireland;
  (b) shares allotted in pursuance of an employees' share scheme by reason of which the company would, but for this subsection, be precluded under subsection (1)(b) (but not otherwise) from being re-registered as a public company.

(3) No more than one-tenth of the nominal value of the company's allotted share capital is to be disregarded under subsection (2)(a).
For this purpose the allotted share capital is treated as not including shares disregarded under subsection (2)(b).

(4) Shares disregarded under subsection (2) are treated as not forming part of the allotted share capital for the purposes of subsection (1)(a).

(5) A company must not be re-registered as a public company if it appears to the registrar that—
  (a) the company has resolved to reduce its share capital,
  (b) the reduction—
    (i) is made under section 626 (reduction in connection with redenomination of share capital),
    (ii) is supported by a solvency statement in accordance with section 643, or
    (iii) has been confirmed by an order of the court under section 648, and
  (c) the effect of the reduction is, or will be, that the nominal value of the company's allotted share capital is below the authorised minimum.

92 Requirements as to net assets

(1) A company applying to re-register as a public company must obtain—
  (a) a balance sheet prepared as at a date not more than seven months before the date on which the application is delivered to the registrar,
  (b) an unqualified report by the company's auditor on that balance sheet, and
  (c) a written statement by the company's auditor that in his opinion at the balance sheet date the amount of the company's net assets was not less than the aggregate of its called-up share capital and undistributable reserves.

(2) Between the balance sheet date and the date on which the application for re-registration is delivered to the registrar, there must be no change in the company's financial position that results in the amount of its net assets becoming less than the aggregate of its called- up share capital and undistributable reserves.

(3) In subsection (1)(b) an "unqualified report" means—
  (a) if the balance sheet was prepared for a financial year of the company, a report stating without material qualification the auditor's opinion that the balance sheet has been properly prepared in accordance with the requirements of this Act;
  (b) if the balance sheet was not prepared for a financial year of the company, a report stating without material qualification the auditor's opinion that the balance sheet has been properly prepared in accordance with the provisions of this Act which would have applied if it had been prepared for a financial year of the company.

(4) For the purposes of an auditor's report on a balance sheet that was not prepared for a financial year of the company, the provisions of this Act apply with such modifications as are necessary by reason of that fact.

(5) For the purposes of subsection (3) a qualification is material unless the auditor states in his report that the matter giving rise to the qualification is not material for the purpose of determining (by reference to the company's balance sheet) whether at the balance sheet date the amount of the company's net assets was not less than the aggregate of its called- up share capital and undistributable reserves.

(6) In this Part "net assets" and "undistributable reserves" have the same meaning as in section 831 (net asset restriction on distributions by public companies).

93 Recent allotment of shares for non-cash consideration

(1) This section applies where—

(a) shares are allotted by the company in the period between the date as at which the balance sheet required by section 92 is prepared and the passing of the resolution that the company should re-register as a public company, and
(b) the shares are allotted as fully or partly paid up as to their nominal value or any premium on them otherwise than in cash.

(2) The registrar shall not entertain an application by the company for re-registration as a public company unless—
(a) the requirements of section 593(1)(a) and (b) have been complied with (independent valuation of non-cash consideration; valuer's report to company not more than six months before allotment), or
(b) the allotment is in connection with—
(i) a share exchange (see subsections (3) to (5) below), or
(ii) a proposed merger with another company (see subsection (6) below).

(3) An allotment is in connection with a share exchange if—
(a) the shares are allotted in connection with an arrangement under which the whole or part of the consideration for the shares allotted is provided by—
(i) the transfer to the company allotting the shares of shares (or shares of a particular class) in another company, or
(ii) the cancellation of shares (or shares of a particular class) in another company; and
(b) the allotment is open to all the holders of the shares of the other company in question (or, where the arrangement applies only to shares of a particular class, to all the holders of the company's shares of that class) to take part in the arrangement in connection with which the shares are allotted.

(4) In determining whether a person is a holder of shares for the purposes of subsection (3), there shall be disregarded—
(a) shares held by, or by a nominee of, the company allotting the shares;
(b) shares held by, or by a nominee of—
(i) the holding company of the company allotting the shares,
(ii) a subsidiary of the company allotting the shares, or
(iii) a subsidiary of the holding company of the company allotting the shares.

(5) It is immaterial, for the purposes of deciding whether an allotment is in connection with a share exchange, whether or not the arrangement in connection with which the shares are allotted involves the issue to the company allotting the shares of shares (or shares of a particular class) in the other company.

(6) There is a proposed merger with another company if one of the companies concerned proposes to acquire all the assets and liabilities of the other in exchange for the issue of its shares or other securities to shareholders of the other (whether or not accompanied by a cash payment).
"Another company" includes any body corporate.

(7) For the purposes of this section—
(a) the consideration for an allotment does not include any amount standing to the credit of any of the company's reserve accounts, or of its profit and loss account, that has been applied in paying up (to any extent) any of the shares allotted or any premium on those shares; and
(b) "arrangement" means any agreement, scheme or arrangement, (including an arrangement sanctioned in accordance with—
(i) Part 26 of this Act (arrangements and reconstructions), or
(ii) section 110 of the Insolvency Act 1986 or Article 96 of the Insolvency (Northern Ireland) Order 1989 (liquidator in winding up accepting shares as consideration for sale of company's property)).

94 Application and accompanying documents

(1) An application for re-registration as a public company must contain—
(a) a statement of the company's proposed name on re-registration; and
(b) in the case of a company without a secretary, a statement of the company's proposed secretary (see section 95).

(2) The application must be accompanied by—
(a) a copy of the special resolution that the company should re-register as a public company (unless a copy has already been forwarded to the registrar under Chapter 3 of Part 3);

(b) a copy of the company's articles as proposed to be amended;
(c) a copy of the balance sheet and other documents referred to in section 92(1); and
(d) if section 93 applies (recent allotment of shares for non-cash consideration), a copy of the valuation report (if any) under subsection (2)(a) of that section.

(3) The statement of compliance required to be delivered together with the application is a statement that the requirements of this Part as to re-registration as a public company have been complied with.

(4) The registrar may accept the statement of compliance as sufficient evidence that the company is entitled to be re-registered as a public company.

95 Statement of proposed secretary

(1) The statement of the company's proposed secretary must contain the required particulars of the person who is or the persons who are to be the secretary or joint secretaries of the company.

(2) The required particulars are the particulars that will be required to be stated in the company's register of secretaries (see sections 277 to 279).

(3) The statement must also contain a consent by the person named as secretary, or each of the persons named as joint secretaries, to act in the relevant capacity.
If all the partners in a firm are to be joint secretaries, consent may be given by one partner on behalf of all of them.

96 Issue of certificate of incorporation on re-registration

(1) If on an application for re-registration as a public company the registrar is satisfied that the company is entitled to be so re-registered, the company shall be re-registered accordingly.

(2) The registrar must issue a certificate of incorporation altered to meet the circumstances of the case.

(3) The certificate must state that it is issued on re-registration and the date on which it is issued.

(4) On the issue of the certificate—
(a) the company by virtue of the issue of the certificate becomes a public company,
(b) the changes in the company's name and articles take effect, and
(c) where the application contained a statement under section 95 (statement of proposed secretary), the person or persons named in the statement as secretary or joint secretary of the company are deemed to have been appointed to that office.

(5) The certificate is conclusive evidence that the requirements of this Act as to re-registration have been complied with.

Public company becoming private

97 Re-registration of public company as private limited company

(1) A public company may be re-registered as a private limited company if—
(a) a special resolution that it should be so re-registered is passed,
(b) the conditions specified below are met, and
(c) an application for re-registration is delivered to the registrar in accordance with section 100, together with—
(i) the other documents required by that section, and
(ii) a statement of compliance.

(2) The conditions are that—
(a) where no application under section 98 for cancellation of the resolution has been made—
(i) having regard to the number of members who consented to or voted in favour of the resolution, no such application may be made, or
(ii) the period within which such an application could be made has expired, or
(b) where such an application has been made—
(i) the application has been withdrawn, or
(ii) an order has been made confirming the resolution and a copy of that order has been delivered to the registrar.

(3) The company must make such changes—
(a) in its name, and
(b) in its articles,

as are necessary in connection with its becoming a private company limited by shares or, as the case may be, by guarantee.

98 Application to court to cancel resolution

(1) Where a special resolution by a public company to be re-registered as a private limited company has been passed, an application to the court for the cancellation of the resolution may be made—

(a) by the holders of not less in the aggregate than 5% in nominal value of the company's issued share capital or any class of the company's issued share capital (disregarding any shares held by the company as treasury shares);

(b) if the company is not limited by shares, by not less than 5% of its members; or

(c) by not less than 50 of the company's members;

but not by a person who has consented to or voted in favour of the resolution.

(2) The application must be made within 28 days after the passing of the resolution and may be made on behalf of the persons entitled to make it by such one or more of their number as they may appoint for the purpose.

(3) On the hearing of the application the court shall make an order either cancelling or confirming the resolution.

(4) The court may—

(a) make that order on such terms and conditions as it thinks fit,

(b) if it thinks fit adjourn the proceedings in order that an arrangement may be made to the satisfaction of the court for the purchase of the interests of dissentient members, and

(c) give such directions, and make such orders, as it thinks expedient for facilitating or carrying into effect any such arrangement.

(5) The court's order may, if the court thinks fit—

(a) provide for the purchase by the company of the shares of any of its members and for the reduction accordingly of the company's capital; and

(b) make such alteration in the company's articles as may be required in consequence of that provision.

(6) The court's order may, if the court thinks fit, require the company not to make any, or any specified, amendments to its articles without the leave of the court.

(7) In this section and section 99(3) "the court", in England and Wales, means the High Court.

99 Notice to registrar of court application or order

(1) On making an application under section 98 (application to court to cancel resolution) the applicants, or the person making the application on their behalf, must immediately give notice to the registrar.

This is without prejudice to any provision of rules of court as to service of notice of the application.

(2) On being served with notice of any such application, the company must immediately give notice to the registrar.

(3) Within 15 days of the making of the court's order on the application, or such longer period as the court may at any time direct, the company must deliver to the registrar a copy of the order.

(4) If a company fails to comply with subsection (2) or (3) an offence is committed by—

(a) the company, and

(b) every officer of the company who is in default.

(5) A person guilty of an offence under this section is liable on summary conviction to a fine not exceeding level 3 on the standard scale and, for continued contravention, a daily default fine not exceeding one-tenth of level 3 on the standard scale.

100 Application and accompanying documents

(1) An application for re-registration as a private limited company must contain a statement of the company's proposed name on re-registration.

(2) The application must be accompanied by—

(a) a copy of the resolution that the company should re-register as a private limited company (unless a copy has already been forwarded to the registrar under Chapter 3 of Part 3); and

(b) a copy of the company's articles as proposed to be amended.

(3) The statement of compliance required to be delivered together with the application is a statement that the requirements of this Part as to re-registration as a private limited company have been complied with.

(4) The registrar may accept the statement of compliance as sufficient evidence that the company is entitled to be re-registered as a private limited company.

101 Issue of certificate of incorporation on re-registration

(1) If on an application for re-registration as a private limited company the registrar is satisfied that the company is entitled to be so re-registered, the company shall be re-registered accordingly.

(2) The registrar must issue a certificate of incorporation altered to meet the circumstances of the case.

(3) The certificate must state that it is issued on re-registration and the date on which it is issued.

(4) On the issue of the certificate—

(a) the company by virtue of the issue of the certificate becomes a private limited company, and

(b) the changes in the company's name and articles take effect.

(5) The certificate is conclusive evidence that the requirements of this Act as to re-registration have been complied with.

Private limited company becoming unlimited

102 Re-registration of private limited company as unlimited

(1) A private limited company may be re-registered as an unlimited company if—

(a) all the members of the company have assented to its being so re-registered,

(b) the condition specified below is met, and

(c) an application for re-registration is delivered to the registrar in accordance with section 103, together with—

(i) the other documents required by that section, and

(ii) a statement of compliance.

(2) The condition is that the company has not previously been re-registered as limited.

(3) The company must make such changes in its name and its articles—

(a) as are necessary in connection with its becoming an unlimited company; and

(b) if it is to have a share capital, as are necessary in connection with its becoming an unlimited company having a share capital.

(4) For the purposes of this section—

(a) a trustee in bankruptcy of a member of the company is entitled, to the exclusion of the member, to assent to the company's becoming unlimited; and

(b) the personal representative of a deceased member of the company may assent on behalf of the deceased.

(5) In subsection (4)(a), "a trustee in bankruptcy of a member of the company" includes—

(a) a permanent trustee or an interim trustee (within the meaning of the Bankruptcy (Scotland) Act 1985 on the sequestrated estate of a member of the company;

(b) a trustee under a protected trustee deed (within the meaning of the Bankruptcy (Scotland) Act 1985) granted by a member of the company.

103 Application and accompanying documents

(1) An application for re-registration as an unlimited company must contain a statement of the company's proposed name on re-registration.

(2) The application must be accompanied by—

(a) the prescribed form of assent to the company's being registered as an unlimited company, authenticated by or on behalf of all the members of the company;

(b) a copy of the company's articles as proposed to be amended.

(3) The statement of compliance required to be delivered together with the application is a statement that the requirements of this Part as to re-registration as an unlimited company have been complied with.

(4) The statement must contain a statement by the directors of the company—

(a) that the persons by whom or on whose behalf the form of assent is authenticated constitute the whole membership of the company, and

(b) if any of the members have not authenticated that form themselves, that the directors have taken all reasonable steps to satisfy themselves that each person who authenticated it on behalf of a member was lawfully empowered to do so.

(5) The registrar may accept the statement of compliance as sufficient evidence that the company is entitled to be re-registered as an unlimited company.

104 Issue of certificate of incorporation on re-registration

(1) If on an application for re-registration of a private limited company as an unlimited company the registrar is satisfied that the company is entitled to be so re-registered, the company shall be re-registered accordingly.

(2) The registrar must issue a certificate of incorporation altered to meet the circumstances of the case.

(3) The certificate must state that it is issued on re-registration and the date on which it is issued.

(4) On the issue of the certificate—

(a) the company by virtue of the issue of the certificate becomes an unlimited company, and

(b) the changes in the company's name and articles take effect.

(5) The certificate is conclusive evidence that the requirements of this Act as to re-registration have been complied with.

Unlimited private company becoming limited

105 Re-registration of unlimited company as limited

(1) An unlimited company may be re-registered as a private limited company if—

(a) a special resolution that it should be so re-registered is passed,

(b) the condition specified below is met, and

(c) an application for re-registration is delivered to the registrar in accordance with section 106, together with—

(i) the other documents required by that section, and

(ii) a statement of compliance.

(2) The condition is that the company has not previously been re-registered as unlimited.

(3) The special resolution must state whether the company is to be limited by shares or by guarantee.

(4) The company must make such changes—

(a) in its name, and

(b) in its articles,

as are necessary in connection with its becoming a company limited by shares or, as the case may be, by guarantee.

106 Application and accompanying documents

(1) An application for re-registration as a limited company must contain a statement of the company's proposed name on re-registration.

(2) The application must be accompanied by—

(a) a copy of the resolution that the company should re-register as a private limited company (unless a copy has already been forwarded to the registrar under Chapter 3 of Part 3);

(b) if the company is to be limited by guarantee, a statement of guarantee;

(c) a copy of the company's articles as proposed to be amended.

(3) The statement of guarantee required to be delivered in the case of a company that is to be limited by guarantee must state that each member undertakes that, if the company is wound up while he is a member, or within one year after he ceases to be a member, he will contribute to the assets of the company such amount as may be required for—

(a) payment of the debts and liabilities of the company contracted before he ceases to be a member,

(b) payment of the costs, charges and expenses of winding up, and

(c) adjustment of the rights of the contributories among themselves, not exceeding a specified amount.

(4) The statement of compliance required to be delivered together with the application is a statement that the requirements of this Part as to re-registration as a limited company have been complied with.

(5) The registrar may accept the statement of compliance as sufficient evidence that the company is entitled to be re-registered as a limited company.

107 Issue of certificate of incorporation on re-registration

(1) If on an application for re-registration of an unlimited company as a limited company the registrar is satisfied that the company is entitled to be so re-registered, the company shall be re-registered accordingly.

(2) The registrar must issue a certificate of incorporation altered to meet the circumstances of the case.

(3) The certificate must state that it is issued on re-registration and the date on which it is so issued.

(4) On the issue of the certificate—
- (a) the company by virtue of the issue of the certificate becomes a limited company, and
- (b) the changes in the company's name and articles take effect.

(5) The certificate is conclusive evidence that the requirements of this Act as to re-registration have been complied with.

108 Statement of capital required where company already has share capital

(1) A company which on re-registration under section 107 already has allotted share capital must within 15 days after the re-registration deliver a statement of capital to the registrar.

(2) This does not apply if the information which would be included in the statement has already been sent to the registrar in—
- (a) a statement of capital and initial shareholdings (see section 10), or
- (b) a statement of capital contained in an annual return (see section 856(2)).

(3) The statement of capital must state with respect to the company's share capital on re- registration—
- (a) the total number of shares of the company,
- (b) the aggregate nominal value of those shares,
- (c) for each class of shares—
  - (i) prescribed particulars of the rights attached to the shares,
  - (ii) the total number of shares of that class, and
  - (iii) the aggregate nominal value of shares of that class, and
- (d) the amount paid up and the amount (if any) unpaid on each share (whether on account of the nominal value of the share or by way of premium).

(4) If default is made in complying with this section, an offence is committed by—
- (a) the company, and
- (b) every officer of the company who is in default.

(5) A person guilty of an offence under this section is liable on summary conviction to a fine not exceeding level 3 on the standard scale and, for continued contravention, a daily default fine not exceeding one-tenth of level 3 on the standard scale.

Public company becoming private and unlimited

109 Re-registration of public company as private and unlimited

(1) A public company limited by shares may be re-registered as an unlimited private company with a share capital if—
- (a) all the members of the company have assented to its being so re-registered,
- (b) the condition specified below is met, and
- (c) an application for re-registration is delivered to the registrar in accordance with section 110, together with—
  - (i) the other documents required by that section, and
  - (ii) a statement of compliance.

(2) The condition is that the company has not previously been re-registered—
- (a) as limited, or
- (b) as unlimited.

(3) The company must make such changes—
- (a) in its name, and
- (b) in its articles,

as are necessary in connection with its becoming an unlimited private company.

(4) For the purposes of this section—
- (a) a trustee in bankruptcy of a member of the company is entitled, to the exclusion of the member, to assent to the company's re-registration; and
- (b) the personal representative of a deceased member of the company may assent on behalf of the deceased.

(5) In subsection (4)(a), "a trustee in bankruptcy of a member of the company" includes—
(a) a permanent trustee or an interim trustee (within the meaning of the Bankruptcy (Scotland) Act 1985) on the sequestrated estate of a member of the company;
(b) a trustee under a protected trustee deed (within the meaning of the Bankruptcy (Scotland) Act 1985) granted by a member of the company.

110 Application and accompanying documents

(1) An application for re-registration of a public company as an unlimited private company must contain a statement of the company's proposed name on re-registration.
(2) The application must be accompanied by—
(a) the prescribed form of assent to the company's being registered as an unlimited company, authenticated by or on behalf of all the members of the company, and
(b) a copy of the company's articles as proposed to be amended.
(3) The statement of compliance required to be delivered together with the application is a statement that the requirements of this Part as to re-registration as an unlimited private company have been complied with.
(4) The statement must contain a statement by the directors of the company—
(a) that the persons by whom or on whose behalf the form of assent is authenticated constitute the whole membership of the company, and
(b) if any of the members have not authenticated that form themselves, that the directors have taken all reasonable steps to satisfy themselves that each person who authenticated it on behalf of a member was lawfully empowered to do so.
(5) The registrar may accept the statement of compliance as sufficient evidence that the company is entitled to be re-registered as an unlimited private company.

111 Issue of certificate of incorporation on re-registration

(1) If on an application for re-registration of a public company as an unlimited private company the registrar is satisfied that the company is entitled to be so re-registered, the company shall be re-registered accordingly.
(2) The registrar must issue a certificate of incorporation altered to meet the circumstances of the case.
(3) The certificate must state that it is issued on re-registration and the date on which it is so issued.
(4) On the issue of the certificate—
(a) the company by virtue of the issue of the certificate becomes an unlimited private company, and
(b) the changes in the company's name and articles take effect.
(5) The certificate is conclusive evidence that the requirements of this Act as to re-registration have been complied with.

PART 8
A COMPANY'S MEMBERS

CHAPTER 1
THE MEMBERS OF A COMPANY

112 The members of a company

(1) The subscribers of a company's memorandum are deemed to have agreed to become members of the company, and on its registration become members and must be entered as such in its register of members.
(2) Every other person who agrees to become a member of a company, and whose name is entered in its register of members, is a member of the company.

CHAPTER 2
REGISTER OF MEMBERS

General

113 Register of members

(1) Every company must keep a register of its members.

(2) There must be entered in the register—
(a) the names and addresses of the members,
(b) the date on which each person was registered as a member, and
(c) the date at which any person ceased to be a member.
(3) In the case of a company having a share capital, there must be entered in the register, with the names and addresses of the members, a statement of—
(a) the shares held by each member, distinguishing each share—
(i) by its number (so long as the share has a number), and
(ii) where the company has more than one class of issued shares, by its class, and
(b) the amount paid or agreed to be considered as paid on the shares of each member.
(4) If the company has converted any of its shares into stock, and given notice of the conversion to the registrar, the register of members must show the amount and class of stock held by each member instead of the amount of shares and the particulars relating to shares specified above.
(5) In the case of joint holders of shares or stock in a company, the company's register of members must state the names of each joint holder.
In other respects joint holders are regarded for the purposes of this Chapter as a single member (so that the register must show a single address).
(6) In the case of a company that does not have a share capital but has more than one class of members, there must be entered in the register, with the names and addresses of the members, a statement of the class to which each member belongs.
(7) If a company makes default in complying with this section an offence is committed by—
(a) the company, and
(b) every officer of the company who is in default.
(8) A person guilty of an offence under this section is liable on summary conviction to a fine not exceeding level 3 on the standard scale and, for continued contravention, a daily default fine not exceeding one-tenth of level 3 on the standard scale.

114 Register to be kept available for inspection

(1) A company's register of members must be kept available for inspection—
(a) at its registered office, or
(b) at a place specified in regulations under section 1136.
(2) A company must give notice to the registrar of the place where its register of members is kept available for inspection and of any change in that place.
(3) No such notice is required if the register has, at all times since it came into existence (or, in the case of a register in existence on the relevant date, at all times since then) been kept available for inspection at the company's registered office.
(4) The relevant date for the purposes of subsection (3) is—
(a) 1st July 1948 in the case of a company registered in Great Britain, and
(b) 1st April 1961 in the case of a company registered in Northern Ireland.
(5) If a company makes default for 14 days in complying with subsection (2), an offence is committed by—
(a) the company, and
(b) every officer of the company who is in default.
(6) A person guilty of an offence under this section is liable on summary conviction to a fine not exceeding level 3 on the standard scale and, for continued contravention, a daily default fine not exceeding one-tenth of level 3 on the standard scale.

115 Index of members

(1) Every company having more than 50 members must keep an index of the names of the members of the company, unless the register of members is in such a form as to constitute in itself an index.
(2) The company must make any necessary alteration in the index within 14 days after the date on which any alteration is made in the register of members.
(3) The index must contain, in respect of each member, a sufficient indication to enable the account of that member in the register to be readily found.
(4) The index must be at all times kept available for inspection at the same place as the register of members.
(5) If default is made in complying with this section, an offence is committed by—

(a) the company, and
(b) every officer of the company who is in default.

(6) A person guilty of an offence under this section is liable on summary conviction to a fine not exceeding level 3 on the standard scale and, for continued contravention, a daily default fine not exceeding one-tenth of level 3 on the standard scale.

116 Rights to inspect and require copies

(1) The register and the index of members' names must be open to the inspection—
(a) of any member of the company without charge, and
(b) of any other person on payment of such fee as may be prescribed.

(2) Any person may require a copy of a company's register of members, or of any part of it, on payment of such fee as may be prescribed.

(3) A person seeking to exercise either of the rights conferred by this section must make a request to the company to that effect.

(4) The request must contain the following information—
(a) in the case of an individual, his name and address;
(b) in the case of an organisation, the name and address of an individual responsible for making the request on behalf of the organisation;
(c) the purpose for which the information is to be used; and
(d) whether the information will be disclosed to any other person, and if so—
(i) where that person is an individual, his name and address,
(ii) where that person is an organisation, the name and address of an individual responsible for receiving the information on its behalf, and
(iii) the purpose for which the information is to be used by that person.

117 Register of members: response to request for inspection or copy

(1) Where a company receives a request under section 116 (register of members: right to inspect and require copy), it must within five working days either—
(a) comply with the request, or
(b) apply to the court.

(2) If it applies to the court it must notify the person making the request.

(3) If on an application under this section the court is satisfied that the inspection or copy is not sought for a proper purpose—
(a) it shall direct the company not to comply with the request, and
(b) it may further order that the company's costs (in Scotland, expenses) on the application be paid in whole or in part by the person who made the request, even if he is not a party to the application.

(4) If the court makes such a direction and it appears to the court that the company is or may be subject to other requests made for a similar purpose (whether made by the same person or different persons), it may direct that the company is not to comply with any such request.
The order must contain such provision as appears to the court appropriate to identify the requests to which it applies.

(5) If on an application under this section the court does not direct the company not to comply with the request, the company must comply with the request immediately upon the court giving its decision or, as the case may be, the proceedings being discontinued.

118 Register of members: refusal of inspection or default in providing copy

(1) If an inspection required under section 116 (register of members: right to inspect and require copy) is refused or default is made in providing a copy required under that section, otherwise than in accordance with an order of the court, an offence is committed by—
(a) the company, and
(b) every officer of the company who is in default.

(2) A person guilty of an offence under this section is liable on summary conviction to a fine not exceeding level 3 on the standard scale and, for continued contravention, a daily default fine not exceeding one-tenth of level 3 on the standard scale.

(3) In the case of any such refusal or default the court may by order compel an immediate inspection or, as the case may be, direct that the copy required be sent to the person requesting it.

119 Register of members: offences in connection with request for or disclosure of information

(1) It is an offence for a person knowingly or recklessly to make in a request under section 116 (register of members: right to inspect or require copy) a statement that is misleading, false or deceptive in a material particular.

(2) It is an offence for a person in possession of information obtained by exercise of either of the rights conferred by that section—
  (a) to do anything that results in the information being disclosed to another person, or
  (b) to fail to do anything with the result that the information is disclosed to another person,

knowing, or having reason to suspect, that person may use the information for a purpose that is not a proper purpose.

(3) A person guilty of an offence under this section is liable—
  (a) on conviction on indictment, to imprisonment for a term not exceeding two years or a fine (or both);
  (b) on summary conviction—
    (i) in England and Wales, to imprisonment for a term not exceeding twelve months or to a fine not exceeding the statutory maximum (or both);
    (ii) in Scotland or Northern Ireland, to imprisonment for a term not exceeding six months, or to a fine not exceeding the statutory maximum (or both).

120 Information as to state of register and index

(1) When a person inspects the register, or the company provides him with a copy of the register or any part of it, the company must inform him of the most recent date (if any) on which alterations were made to the register and there were no further alterations to be made.

(2) When a person inspects the index of members' names, the company must inform him whether there is any alteration to the register that is not reflected in the index.

(3) If a company fails to provide the information required under subsection (1) or (2), an offence is committed by—
  (a) the company, and
  (b) every officer of the company who is in default.

(4) A person guilty of an offence under this section is liable on summary conviction to a fine not exceeding level 3 on the standard scale.

121 Removal of entries relating to former members

An entry relating to a former member of the company may be removed from the register after the expiration of ten years from the date on which he ceased to be a member.

Special cases

122 Share warrants

(1) Until a share warrant issued by a company is surrendered the following are deemed to be the particulars required to be entered in the register of members in respect of the warrant—
  (a) the fact of the issue of the warrant,
  (b) a statement of the shares included in the warrant, distinguishing each share by its number so long as the share has a number, and
  (c) the date of the issue of the warrant, and

(2) ...

(3) The bearer of a share warrant may, if the articles of the company so provide, be deemed a member of the company within the meaning of this Act, either to the full extent or for any purposes defined in the articles.

(4) ...

(5) The company is responsible for any loss incurred by any person by reason of the company entering in the register the name of a bearer of a share warrant in respect of the shares specified in it without the warrant being surrendered and cancelled.

(6) On the surrender of a share warrant, the date of the surrender must be entered in the register.

123 Single member companies

(1) If a limited company is formed under this Act with only one member there shall be entered in the company's register of members, with the name and address of the sole member, a statement that the company has only one member.

(2) If the number of members of a limited company falls to one, or if an unlimited company with only one member becomes a limited company on re-registration, there shall upon the occurrence of that event be entered in the company's register of members, with the name and address of the sole member—

(a) a statement that the company has only one member, and

(b) the date on which the company became a company having only one member.

(3) If the membership of a limited company increases from one to two or more members, there shall upon the occurrence of that event be entered in the company's register of members, with the name and address of the person who was formerly the sole member—

(a) a statement that the company has ceased to have only one member, and

(b) the date on which that event occurred.

(4) If a company makes default in complying with this section, an offence is committed by—

(a) the company, and

(b) every officer of the company who is in default.

(5) A person guilty of an offence under this section is liable on summary conviction to a fine not exceeding level 3 on the standard scale and, for continued contravention, a daily default fine not exceeding one-tenth of level 3 on the standard scale.

124 Company holding its own shares as treasury shares

(1) Where a company purchases its own shares in circumstances in which section 724 (treasury shares) applies—

(a) the requirements of section 113 (register of members) need not be complied with if the company cancels all of the shares forthwith after the purchase, and

(b) if the company does not cancel all of the shares forthwith after the purchase, any share that is so cancelled shall be disregarded for the purposes of that section.

(2) Subject to subsection (1), where a company holds shares as treasury shares the company must be entered in the register as the member holding those shares.

Supplementary

125 Power of court to rectify register

(1) If—

(a) the name of any person is, without sufficient cause, entered in or omitted from a company's register of members, or

(b) default is made or unnecessary delay takes place in entering on the register the fact of any person having ceased to be a member,

the person aggrieved, or any member of the company, or the company, may apply to the court for rectification of the register.

(2) The court may either refuse the application or may order rectification of the register and payment by the company of any damages sustained by any party aggrieved.

(3) On such an application the court may decide any question relating to the title of a person who is a party to the application to have his name entered in or omitted from the register, whether the question arises between members or alleged members, or between members or alleged members on the one hand and the company on the other hand, and generally may decide any question necessary or expedient to be decided for rectification of the register.

(4) In the case of a company required by this Act to send a list of its members to the registrar of companies, the court, when making an order for rectification of the register, shall by its order direct notice of the rectification to be given to the registrar.

126 Trusts not to be entered on register

No notice of any trust, expressed, implied or constructive, shall be entered on the register of members of a company registered in England and Wales or Northern Ireland, or be receivable by the registrar.

127 Register to be evidence

The register of members is prima facie evidence of any matters which are by this Act directedor authorised to be inserted in it.

128 Time limit for claims arising from entry in register

(1) Liability incurred by a company—
   (a) from the making or deletion of an entry in the register of members, or
   (b) from a failure to make or delete any such entry,
   is not enforceable more than ten years after the date on which the entry was made or deleted or, as the case may be, the failure first occurred.

(2) This is without prejudice to any lesser period of limitation (and, in Scotland, to any rule that the obligation giving rise to the liability prescribes before the expiry of that period).

CHAPTER 3
OMITTED

CHAPTER 4
PROHIBITION ON SUBSIDIARY BEING MEMBER OF ITS HOLDING COMPANY

General prohibition

136 Prohibition on subsidiary being a member of its holding company

(1) Except as provided by this Chapter—
   (a) a body corporate cannot be a member of a company that is its holding company, and
   (b) any allotment or transfer of shares in a company to its subsidiary is void.

(2) The exceptions are provided for in—
   section 138 (subsidiary acting as personal representative or trustee), and
   section 141 (subsidiary acting as authorised dealer in securities).

137 Shares acquired before prohibition became applicable

(1) Where a body corporate became a holder of shares in a company—
   (a) before the relevant date, or
   (b) on or after that date and before the commencement of this Chapter in circumstances in which the prohibition in section 23(1) of the Companies Act 1985 or Article 33(1) of the Companies (Northern Ireland) Order 1986 (or any corresponding earlier enactment), as it then had effect, did not apply, or
   (c) on or after the commencement of this Chapter in circumstances in which the prohibition in section 136 did not apply,
   it may continue to be a member of the company.

(2) The relevant date for the purposes of subsection (1)(a) is—
   (a) 1st July 1948 in the case of a company registered in Great Britain, and
   (b) 1st April 1961 in the case of a company registered in Northern Ireland.

(3) So long as it is permitted to continue as a member of a company by virtue of this section, an allotment to it of fully paid shares in the company may be validly made by way of capitalisation of reserves of the company.

(4) But, so long as the prohibition in section 136 would (apart from this section) apply, it has no right to vote in respect of the shares mentioned in subsection (1) above, or any shares allotted as mentioned in subsection (3) above, on a written resolution or at meetings of the company or of any class of its members.

Subsidiary acting as personal representative or trustee

138 Subsidiary acting as personal representative or trustee

(1) The prohibition in section 136 (prohibition on subsidiary being a member of its holding company) does not apply where the subsidiary is concerned only—
   (a) as personal representative, or
   (b) as trustee,
   unless, in the latter case, the holding company or a subsidiary of it is beneficially interested under the trust.

(2) For the purpose of ascertaining whether the holding company or a subsidiary is so interested, there shall be disregarded—
   (a) any interest held only by way of security for the purposes of a transaction entered

into by the holding company or subsidiary in the ordinary course of a business that includes the lending of money;

(b) any interest within—

section 139 (interests to be disregarded: residual interest under pension scheme or employees' share scheme), or

section 140 (interests to be disregarded: employer's rights of recovery under pension scheme or employees' share scheme);

(c) any rights that the company or subsidiary has in its capacity as trustee, including in particular—

(i) any right to recover its expenses or be remunerated out of the trust property, and

(ii) any right to be indemnified out of the trust property for any liability incurred by reason of any act or omission in the performance of its duties as trustee.

139 Interests to be disregarded: residual interest under pension scheme or employees' share scheme

(1) Where shares in a company are held on trust for the purposes of a pension scheme or employees' share scheme, there shall be disregarded for the purposes of section 138 any residual interest that has not vested in possession.

(2) A "residual interest" means a right of the company or subsidiary ("the residual beneficiary") to receive any of the trust property in the event of—

(a) all the liabilities arising under the scheme having been satisfied or provided for, or

(b) the residual beneficiary ceasing to participate in the scheme, or

(c) the trust property at any time exceeding what is necessary for satisfying the liabilities arising or expected to arise under the scheme.

(3) In subsection (2)—

(a) the reference to a right includes a right dependent on the exercise of a discretion vested by the scheme in the trustee or another person, and

(b) the reference to liabilities arising under a scheme includes liabilities that have resulted, or may result, from the exercise of any such discretion.

(4) For the purposes of this section a residual interest vests in possession—

(a) in a case within subsection (2)(a), on the occurrence of the event mentioned there (whether or not the amount of the property receivable pursuant to the right is ascertained);

(b) in a case within subsection (2)(b) or (c), when the residual beneficiary becomes entitled to require the trustee to transfer to him any of the property receivable pursuant to the right.

(5) In this section "pension scheme" means a scheme for the provision of benefits consisting of or including relevant benefits for or in respect of employees or former employees.

(6) In subsection (5)—

(a) "relevant benefits" means any pension, lump sum, gratuity or other like benefit given or to be given on retirement or on death or in anticipation of retirement or, in connection with past service, after retirement or death; and

(b) "employee" shall be read as if a director of a company were employed by it.

140 Interests to be disregarded: employer's rights of recovery under pension scheme or employees' share scheme

(1) Where shares in a company are held on trust for the purposes of a pension scheme or employees' share scheme, there shall be disregarded for the purposes of section 138 any charge or lien on, or set-off against, any benefit or other right or interest under the scheme for the purpose of enabling the employer or former employer of a member of the scheme to obtain the discharge of a monetary obligation due to him from the member.

(2) In the case of a trust for the purposes of a pension scheme there shall also be disregarded any right to receive from the trustee of the scheme, or as trustee of the scheme to retain, an amount that can be recovered or retained, under section 61 of the Pension Schemes Act 1993 or section 57 of the Pension Schemes (Northern Ireland) Act 1993 (deduction of contributions equivalent premium from refund of scheme contributions) or otherwise, as reimbursement or partial reimbursement for any contributions equivalent premium paid in connection with the scheme under Part 3 of that Act.

(3) In this section "pension scheme" means a scheme for the provision of benefits consisting of or including relevant benefits for or in respect of employees or former employees. "Relevant benefits" here means any pension, lump sum, gratuity or other like benefit given or to be given on retirement or on death or in anticipation of retirement or, in connection with past service, after retirement or death.

(4) In this section "employer" and "employee" shall be read as if a director of a company were employed by it.

Subsidiary acting as dealer in securities

141 Subsidiary acting as authorised dealer in securities

(1) The prohibition in section 136 (prohibition on subsidiary being a member of its holding company) does not apply where the shares are held by the subsidiary in the ordinary course of its business as an intermediary.

(2) For this purpose a person is an intermediary if he—
- (a) carries on a bona fide business of dealing in securities,
- (b) is a member of or has access to a regulated market, and
- (c) does not carry on an excluded business.

(3) The following are excluded businesses—
- (a) a business that consists wholly or mainly in the making or managing of investments;
- (b) a business that consists wholly or mainly in, or is carried on wholly or mainly for the purposes of, providing services to persons who are connected with the person carrying on the business;
- (c) a business that consists in insurance business;
- (d) a business that consists in managing or acting as trustee in relation to a pension scheme, or that is carried on by the manager or trustee of such a scheme in connection with or for the purposes of the scheme;
- (e) a business that consists in operating or acting as trustee in relation to a collective investment scheme, or that is carried on by the operator or trustee of such a scheme in connection with and for the purposes of the scheme.

(4) For the purposes of this section—
- (a) the question whether a person is connected with another shall be determined in accordance with section 1122 of the Corporation Tax Act 2010;
- (b) "collective investment scheme" has the meaning given in section 235 of the Financial Services and Markets Act 2000;
- (c) "insurance business" means business that consists in the effecting or carrying out of contracts of insurance;
- (d) "securities" includes—
  - (i) options,
  - (ii) futures, and
  - (iii) contracts for differences,

  and rights or interests in those investments;
- (e) "trustee" and "the operator" in relation to a collective investment scheme shall be construed in accordance with section 237(2) of the Financial Services and Markets Act 2000.

(5) Expressions used in this section that are also used in the provisions regulating activities under the Financial Services and Markets Act 2000 have the same meaning here as they do in those provisions.
See section 22 of that Act, orders made under that section and Schedule 2 to that Act.

142 Protection of third parties in other cases where subsidiary acting as dealer in securities

(1) This section applies where—
- (a) a subsidiary that is a dealer in securities has purportedly acquired shares in its holding company in contravention of the prohibition in section 136, and
- (b) a person acting in good faith has agreed, for value and without notice of the contravention, to acquire shares in the holding company—

(i) from the subsidiary, or
(ii) from someone who has purportedly acquired the shares after their disposal by the subsidiary.

(2) A transfer to that person of the shares mentioned in subsection (1)(a) has the same effect as it would have had if their original acquisition by the subsidiary had not been in contravention of the prohibition.

Supplementary

143 Application of provisions to companies not limited by shares

In relation to a company other than a company limited by shares, the references in this Chapter to shares shall be read as references to the interest of its members as such, whatever the form of that interest.

144 Application of provisions to nominees

The provisions of this Chapter apply to a nominee acting on behalf of a subsidiary as to the subsidiary itself.

PART 9
EXERCISE OF MEMBERS' RIGHTS

Effect of provisions in company's articles

145 Effect of provisions of articles as to enjoyment or exercise of members' rights

(1) This section applies where provision is made by a company's articles enabling a member to nominate another person or persons as entitled to enjoy or exercise all or any specified rights of the member in relation to the company.

(2) So far as is necessary to give effect to that provision, anything required or authorised by any provision of the Companies Acts to be done by or in relation to the member shall instead be done, or (as the case may be) may instead be done, by or in relation to the nominated person (or each of them) as if he were a member of the company.

(3) This applies, in particular, to the rights conferred by—
(a) sections 291 and 293 (right to be sent proposed written resolution);
(b) section 292 (right to require circulation of written resolution);
(c) section 303 (right to require directors to call general meeting);
(d) section 310 (right to notice of general meetings);
(e) section 314 (right to require circulation of a statement);
(ea) section 319A (right to ask question at meeting of traded company);
(f) section 324 (right to appoint proxy to act at meeting);
(g) section 338 (right to require circulation of resolution for AGM of public company);
(ga) section 338A (traded companies: members' power to include matters in business dealt with at AGM); and
(h) section 423 (right to be sent a copy of annual accounts and reports).

(4) This section and any such provision as is mentioned in subsection (1)—
(a) do not confer rights enforceable against the company by anyone other than the member, and
(b) do not affect the requirements for an effective transfer or other disposition of the whole or part of a member's interest in the company.

Information rights

146 Traded companies: nomination of persons to enjoy information rights

(1) This section applies to a company whose shares are admitted to trading on a regulated market.

(2) A member of such a company who holds shares on behalf of another person may nominate that person to enjoy information rights.

(3) "Information rights" means—
(a) the right to receive a copy of all communications that the company sends to its members generally or to any class of its members that includes the person making the nomination, and

(b) the rights conferred by—
(i) section 431 or 432 (right to require copies of accounts and reports), and
(ii) section 1145 (right to require hard copy version of document or information provided in another form).

(4) The reference in subsection (3)(a) to communications that a company sends to its members generally includes the company's annual accounts and reports.
For the application of section 426 (option to provide summary financial statement) in relation to a person nominated to enjoy information rights, see subsection (5) of that section.

(5) A company need not act on a nomination purporting to relate to certain information rights only.

147 Information rights: form in which copies to be provided

(1) This section applies as regards the form in which copies are to be provided to a person nominated under section 146 (nomination of person to enjoy information rights).

(2) If the person to be nominated wishes to receive hard copy communications, he must—
(a) request the person making the nomination to notify the company of that fact, and
(b) provide an address to which such copies may be sent. This must be done before the nomination is made.

(3) If having received such a request the person making the nomination—
(a) notifies the company that the nominated person wishes to receive hard copy communications, and
(b) provides the company with that address,
the right of the nominated person is to receive hard copy communications accordingly.

(4) This is subject to the provisions of Parts 3 and 4 of Schedule 5 (communications by company) under which the company may take steps to enable it to communicate in electronic form or by means of a website.

(5) If no such notification is given (or no address is provided), the nominated person is taken to have agreed that documents or information may be sent or supplied to him by the company by means of a website.

(6) That agreement—
(a) may be revoked by the nominated person, and
(b) does not affect his right under section 1145 to require a hard copy version of a document or information provided in any other form.

148 Termination or suspension of nomination

(1) The following provisions have effect in relation to a nomination under section 146 (nomination of person to enjoy information rights).

(2) The nomination may be terminated at the request of the member or of the nominated person.

(3) The nomination ceases to have effect on the occurrence in relation to the member or the nominated person of any of the following—
(a) in the case of an individual, death or bankruptcy;
(b) in the case of a body corporate, dissolution or the making of an order for the winding up of the body otherwise than for the purposes of reconstruction.

(4) In subsection (3)—
(a) the reference to bankruptcy includes—
(i) the sequestration of a person's estate, and
(ii) a person's estate being the subject of a protected trust deed (within the meaning of the Bankruptcy (Scotland) Act 1985); and
(b) the reference to the making of an order for winding up is to—
(i) the making of such an order under the Insolvency Act 1986 or the Insolvency (Northern Ireland) Order 1989, or
(ii) any corresponding proceeding under the law of a country or territory outside the United Kingdom.

(5) The effect of any nominations made by a member is suspended at any time when there are more nominated persons than the member has shares in the company.

(6) Where—
(a) the member holds different classes of shares with different information rights, and
(b) there are more nominated persons than he has shares conferring a particular right,
the effect of any nominations made by him is suspended to the extent that they confer that right.

(7) Where the company—
(a) enquires of a nominated person whether he wishes to retain information rights, and
(b) does not receive a response within the period of 28 days beginning with the date on which the company's enquiry was sent,

the nomination ceases to have effect at the end of that period.

Such an enquiry is not to be made of a person more than once in any twelve-month period.

(8) The termination or suspension of a nomination means that the company is not required to act on it.

It does not prevent the company from continuing to do so, to such extent or for such period as it thinks fit.

149 Information as to possible rights in relation to voting

(1) This section applies where a company sends a copy of a notice of a meeting to a person nominated under section 146 (nomination of person to enjoy information rights)

(2) The copy of the notice must be accompanied by a statement that—
(a) he may have a right under an agreement between him and the member by whom he was nominated to be appointed, or to have someone else appointed, as a proxy for the meeting, and
(b) if he has no such right or does not wish to exercise it, he may have a right under such an agreement to give instructions to the member as to the exercise of voting rights.

(3) Section 325 (notice of meeting to contain statement of member's rights in relation to appointment of proxy) does not apply to the copy, and the company must either—
(a) omit the notice required by that section, or
(b) include it but state that it does not apply to the nominated person.

150 Information rights: status of rights

(1) This section has effect as regards the rights conferred by a nomination under section 146 (nomination of person to enjoy information rights).

(2) Enjoyment by the nominated person of the rights conferred by the nomination is enforceable against the company by the member as if they were rights conferred by the company's articles.

(3) Any enactment, and any provision of the company's articles, having effect in relation to communications with members has a corresponding effect (subject to any necessary adaptations) in relation to communications with the nominated person.

(4) In particular—
(a) where under any enactment, or any provision of the company's articles, the members of a company entitled to receive a document or information are determined as at a date or time before it is sent or supplied, the company need not send or supply it to a nominated person—
(i) whose nomination was received by the company after that date or time, or
(ii) if that date or time falls in a period of suspension of his nomination; and
(b) where under any enactment, or any provision of the company's articles, the right of a member to receive a document or information depends on the company having a current address for him, the same applies to any person nominated by him.

(5) The rights conferred by the nomination—
(a) are in addition to the rights of the member himself, and
(b) do not affect any rights exercisable by virtue of any such provision as is mentioned in section 145 (provisions of company's articles as to enjoyment or exercise of members' rights).

(6) A failure to give effect to the rights conferred by the nomination does not affect the validity of anything done by or on behalf of the company.

(7) References in this section to the rights conferred by the nomination are to—
(a) the rights referred to in section 146(3) (information rights), and
(b) where applicable, the rights conferred by section 147(3) (right to hard copy communications) and section 149 (information as to possible voting rights).

151 Information rights: power to amend

(1) The Secretary of State may by regulations amend the provisions of sections 146 to 150 (information rights) so as to—

(a) extend or restrict the classes of companies to which section 146 applies,
(b) make other provision as to the circumstances in which a nomination may be made under that section, or
(c) extend or restrict the rights conferred by such a nomination.

(2) The regulations may make such consequential modifications of any other provisions of this Part, or of any other enactment, as appear to the Secretary of State to be necessary.

(3) Regulations under this section are subject to affirmative resolution procedure.

Exercise of rights where shares held on behalf of others

152 Exercise of rights where shares held on behalf of others: exercise in different ways

(1) Where a member holds shares in a company on behalf of more than one person—
(a) rights attached to the shares, and
(b) rights under any enactment exercisable by virtue of holding the shares,
need not all be exercised, and if exercised, need not all be exercised in the same way.

(2) A member who exercises such rights but does not exercise all his rights, must inform the company to what extent he is exercising the rights.

(3) A member who exercises such rights in different ways must inform the company of the ways in which he is exercising them and to what extent they are exercised in each way.

(4) If a member exercises such rights without informing the company—
(a) that he is not exercising all his rights, or
(b) that he is exercising his rights in different ways,
the company is entitled to assume that he is exercising all his rights and is exercising them in the same way.

153 Exercise of rights where shares held on behalf of others: members' requests

(1) This section applies for the purposes of—
(a) section 314 (power to require circulation of statement),
(b) section 338 (public companies: power to require circulation of resolution for AGM),
(ba) section 338A (traded companies: members' power to include matters in business dealt with at AGM),
(c) section 342 (power to require independent report on poll), and
(d) section 527 (power to require website publication of audit concerns).

(2) A company is required to act under any of those sections if it receives a request in relation to which the following conditions are met—
(a) it is made by at least 100 persons;
(b) it is authenticated by all the persons making it;
(c) in the case of any of those persons who is not a member of the company, it is accompanied by a statement—
(i) of the full name and address of a person ("the member") who is a member of the company and holds shares on behalf of that person,
(ii) that the member is holding those shares on behalf of that person in the course of a business,
(iii) of the number of shares in the company that the member holds on behalf of that person,
(iv) of the total amount paid up on those shares,
(v) that those shares are not held on behalf of anyone else or, if they are, that the other person or persons are not among the other persons making the request,
(vi) that some or all of those shares confer voting rights that are relevant for the purposes of making a request under the section in question, and
(vii) that the person has the right to instruct the member how to exercise those rights;
(d) in the case of any of those persons who is a member of the company, it is accompanied by a statement—
(i) that he holds shares otherwise than on behalf of another person, or
(ii) that he holds shares on behalf of one or more other persons but those persons are not among the other persons making the request;

(e) it is accompanied by such evidence as the company may reasonably require of the matters mentioned in paragraph (c) and (d);

(f) the total amount of the sums paid up on—

(i) shares held as mentioned in paragraph (c), and

(ii) shares held as mentioned in paragraph (d),

divided by the number of persons making the request, is not less than £100;

(g) the request complies with any other requirements of the section in question as to contents, timing and otherwise.

PART 10
A COMPANY'S DIRECTORS

CHAPTER 1
APPOINTMENT AND REMOVAL OF DIRECTORS

Requirement to hab ve directors

154 Companies required to have directors

(1) A private company must have at least one director.

(2) A public company must have at least two directors.

155 Companies required to have at least one director who is a natural person

(1) A company must have at least one director who is a natural person.

(2) This requirement is met if the office of director is held by a natural person as a corporation sole or otherwise by virtue of an office.

156 Direction requiring company to make appointment

(1) If it appears to the Secretary of State that a company is in breach of—

section 154 (requirements as to number of directors), or

section 155 (requirement to have at least one director who is a natural person),

the Secretary of State may give the company a direction under this section.

(2) The direction must specify—

(a) the statutory requirement the company appears to be in breach of,

(b) what the company must do in order to comply with the direction, and

(c) the period within which it must do so.

That period must be not less than one month or more than three months after the date on which the direction is given.

(3) The direction must also inform the company of the consequences of failing to comply.

(4) Where the company is in breach of section 154 or 155 it must comply with the direction by—

(a) making the necessary appointment or appointments, and

(b) giving notice of them under section 167,

before the end of the period specified in the direction.

(5) If the company has already made the necessary appointment or appointments (or so far as it has done so), it must comply with the direction by giving notice of them under section 167 before the end of the period specified in the direction.

(6) If a company fails to comply with a direction under this section, an offence is committed by—

(a) the company, and

(b) every officer of the company who is in default.

For this purpose a shadow director is treated as an officer of the company.

Version applying in Scotland

(7) A person guilty of an offence under this section is liable on summary conviction to a fine not exceeding level 5 on the standard scale and, for continued contravention, a daily default fine not exceeding one-tenth of level 5 on the standard scale.

Version applying in England and Wales

(7) A person guilty of an offence under this section is liable on summary conviction to a fine not exceeding level 5 on the standard scale and, for continued contravention, a daily default fine not exceeding one-tenth of the greater of £5,000 or level 4 on the standard scale.

Appointment

157 Minimum age for appointment as director

(1) A person may not be appointed a director of a company unless he has attained the age of 16 years.

(2) This does not affect the validity of an appointment that is not to take effect until the person appointed attains that age.

(3) Where the office of director of a company is held by a corporation sole, or otherwise by virtue of another office, the appointment to that other office of a person who has not attained the age of 16 years is not effective also to make him a director of the company until he attains the age of 16 years.

(4) An appointment made in contravention of this section is void.

(5) Nothing in this section affects any liability of a person under any provision of the Companies Acts if he—

(a) purports to act as director, or

(b) acts as a shadow director,

although he could not, by virtue of this section, be validly appointed as a director.

(6) This section has effect subject to section 158 (power to provide for exceptions from minimum age requirement).

158 Power to provide for exceptions from minimum age requirement

(1) The Secretary of State may make provision by regulations for cases in which a person who has not attained the age of 16 years may be appointed a director of a company.

(2) The regulations must specify the circumstances in which, and any conditions subject to which, the appointment may be made.

(3) If the specified circumstances cease to obtain, or any specified conditions cease to be met, a person who was appointed by virtue of the regulations and who has not since attained the age of 16 years ceases to hold office.

(4) The regulations may make different provision for different parts of the United Kingdom. This is without prejudice to the general power to make different provision for different cases.

(5) Regulations under this section are subject to negative resolution procedure.

159 Existing under-age directors

(1) This section applies where—

(a) a person appointed a director of a company before section 157 (minimum age for appointment as director) comes into force has not attained the age of 16 when that section comes into force, or

(b) the office of director of a company is held by a corporation sole, or otherwise by virtue of another office, and the person appointed to that other office has not attained the age of 16 years when that section comes into force,

and the case is not one excepted from that section by regulations under section 158.

(2) That person ceases to be a director on section 157 coming into force.

(3) The company must make the necessary consequential alteration in its register of directors but need not give notice to the registrar of the change.

(4) If it appears to the registrar (from other information) that a person has ceased by virtue of this section to be a director of a company, the registrar shall note that fact on the register.

160 Appointment of directors of public company to be voted on individually

(1) At a general meeting of a public company a motion for the appointment of two or more persons as directors of the company by a single resolution must not be made unless a resolution that it should be so made has first been agreed to by the meeting without any vote being given against it.

(2) A resolution moved in contravention of this section is void, whether or not its being so moved was objected to at the time.

But where a resolution so moved is passed, no provision for the automatic reappointment of retiring directors in default of another appointment applies.

(3) For the purposes of this section a motion for approving a person's appointment, or for nominating a person for appointment, is treated as a motion for his appointment.

(4) Nothing in this section applies to a resolution amending the company's articles.

161 Validity of acts of directors

(1) The acts of a person acting as a director are valid notwithstanding that it is afterwards discovered—
  (a) that there was a defect in his appointment;
  (b) that he was disqualified from holding office;
  (c) that he had ceased to hold office;
  (d) that he was not entitled to vote on the matter in question.

(2) This applies even if the resolution for his appointment is void under section 160 (appointment of directors of public company to be voted on individually).

Register of directors, etc

162 Register of directors

(1) Every company must keep a register of its directors.

(2) The register must contain the required particulars (see sections 163, 164 and 166) of each person who is a director of the company.

(3) The register must be kept available for inspection—
  (a) at the company's registered office, or
  (b) at a place specified in regulations under section 1136.

(4) The company must give notice to the registrar—
  (a) of the place at which the register is kept available for inspection, and
  (b) of any change in that place,

unless it has at all times been kept at the company's registered office.

(5) The register must be open to the inspection—
  (a) of any member of the company without charge, and
  (b) of any other person on payment of such fee as may be prescribed.

(6) If default is made in complying with subsection (1), (2) or (3) or if default is made for 14 days in complying with subsection (4), or if an inspection required under subsection (5) is refused, an offence is committed by—
  (a) the company, and
  (b) every officer of the company who is in default.

For this purpose a shadow director is treated as an officer of the company.

Version applying in Scotland

(7) A person guilty of an offence under this section is liable on summary conviction to a fine not exceeding level 5 on the standard scale and, for continued contravention, a daily default fine not exceeding one-tenth of level 5 on the standard scale.

Version applying in England and Wales

(7) A person guilty of an offence under this section is liable on summary conviction to a fine not exceeding level 5 on the standard scale and, for continued contravention, a daily default fine not exceeding one-tenth of the greater of £5,000 or level 4 on the standard scale.

(8) In the case of a refusal of inspection of the register, the court may by order compel an immediate inspection of it.

163 Particulars of directors to be registered: individuals

(1) A company's register of directors must contain the following particulars in the case of an individual—
  (a) name and any former name;
  (b) a service address;
  (c) the country or state (or part of the United Kingdom) in which he is usually resident;
  (d) nationality;
  (e) business occupation (if any);
  (f) date of birth.

(2) For the purposes of this section "name" means a person's Christian name (or other forename) and surname, except that in the case of—
  (a) a peer, or
  (b) an individual usually known by a title,

the title may be stated instead of his Christian name (or other forename) and surname or in addition to either or both of them.

(3) For the purposes of this section a "former name" means a name by which the individual was formerly known for business purposes.

Where a person is or was formerly known by more than one such name, each of them must be stated.

(4) It is not necessary for the register to contain particulars of a former name in the following cases—
 (a) in the case of a peer or an individual normally known by a British title, where the name is one by which the person was known previous to the adoption of or succession to the title;
 (b) in the case of any person, where the former name—
  (i) was changed or disused before the person attained the age of 16 years, or
  (ii) has been changed or disused for 20 years or more.
(5) A person's service address may be stated to be "The company's registered office".

164 Particulars of directors to be registered: corporate directors and firms

A company's register of directors must contain the following particulars in the case of a body corporate, or a firm that is a legal person under the law by which it is governed—
 (a) corporate or firm name;
 (b) registered or principal office;
 (c) in the case of an EEA company to which the First Company Law Directive (68/151/EEC) applies, particulars of—
  (i) the register in which the company file mentioned in Article 3 of that Directive is kept (including details of the relevant state), and
  (ii) the registration number in that register;
 (d) in any other case, particulars of—
  (i) the legal form of the company or firm and the law by which it is governed, and
  (ii) if applicable, the register in which it is entered (including details of the state) and its registration number in that register.

165 Register of directors' residential addresses

(1) Every company must keep a register of directors' residential addresses.
(2) The register must state the usual residential address of each of the company's directors.
(3) If a director's usual residential address is the same as his service address (as stated in the company's register of directors), the register of directors' residential addresses need only contain an entry to that effect.
This does not apply if his service address is stated to be "The company's registered office".
(4) If default is made in complying with this section, an offence is committed by—
 (a) the company, and
 (b) every officer of the company who is in default.
For this purpose a shadow director is treated as an officer of the company.

Version applying in Scotland

(5) A person guilty of an offence under this section is liable on summary conviction to a fine not exceeding level 5 on the standard scale and, for continued contravention, a daily default fine not exceeding one-tenth of level 5 on the standard scale.

Version applying in England and Wales

(5) A person guilty of an offence under this section is liable on summary conviction to a fine not exceeding level 5 on the standard scale and, for continued contravention, a daily default fine not exceeding one-tenth of the greater of £5,000 or level 4 on the standard scale.
(6) This section applies only to directors who are individuals, not where the director is a body corporate or a firm that is a legal person under the law by which it is governed.

166 *omitted*

167 Duty to notify registrar of changes

(1) A company must, within the period of 14 days from—
 (a) a person becoming or ceasing to be a director, or
 (b) the occurrence of any change in the particulars contained in its register of directors or its register of directors' residential addresses,
give notice to the registrar of the change and of the date on which it occurred.
(2) Notice of a person having become a director of the company must—
 (a) contain a statement of the particulars of the new director that are required to be included in the company's register of directors and its register of directors' residential addresses, and

(b) be accompanied by a consent, by that person, to act in that capacity.

(3) Where—

(a) a company gives notice of a change of a director's service address as stated in the company's register of directors, and

(b) the notice is not accompanied by notice of any resulting change in the particulars contained in the company's register of directors' residential addresses,

the notice must be accompanied by a statement that no such change is required.

(4) If default is made in complying with this section, an offence is committed by—

(a) the company, and

(b) every officer of the company who is in default.

For this purpose a shadow director is treated as an officer of the company.

Version applying in Scotland

(5) A person guilty of an offence under this section is liable on summary conviction to a fine not exceeding level 5 on the standard scale and, for continued contravention, a daily default fine not exceeding one-tenth of level 5 on the standard scale.

Version applying in England and Wales

(5) A person guilty of an offence under this section is liable on summary conviction to a fine not exceeding level 5 on the standard scale and, for continued contravention, a daily default fine not exceeding one-tenth of the greater of £5,000 or level 4 on the standard scale.

Removal

168 Resolution to remove director

(1) A company may by ordinary resolution at a meeting remove a director before the expiration of his period of office, notwithstanding anything in any agreement between it and him.

(2) Special notice is required of a resolution to remove a director under this section or to appoint somebody instead of a director so removed at the meeting at which he is removed.

(3) A vacancy created by the removal of a director under this section, if not filled at the meeting at which he is removed, may be filled as a casual vacancy.

(4) A person appointed director in place of a person removed under this section is treated, for the purpose of determining the time at which he or any other director is to retire, as if he had become director on the day on which the person in whose place he is appointed was last appointed a director.

(5) This section is not to be taken—

(a) as depriving a person removed under it of compensation or damages payable to him in respect of the termination of his appointment as director or of any appointment terminating with that as director, or

(b) as derogating from any power to remove a director that may exist apart from this section.

169 Director's right to protest against removal

(1) On receipt of notice of an intended resolution to remove a director under section 168, the company must forthwith send a copy of the notice to the director concerned.

(2) The director (whether or not a member of the company) is entitled to be heard on the resolution at the meeting.

(3) Where notice is given of an intended resolution to remove a director under that section, and the director concerned makes with respect to it representations in writing to the company (not exceeding a reasonable length) and requests their notification to members of the company, the company shall, unless the representations are received by it too late for it to do so—

(a) in any notice of the resolution given to members of the company state the fact of the representations having been made; and

(b) send a copy of the representations to every member of the company to whom notice of the meeting is sent (whether before or after receipt of the representations by the company).

(4) If a copy of the representations is not sent as required by subsection (3) because received too late or because of the company's default, the director may (without prejudice to his right to be heard orally) require that the representations shall be read out at the meeting.

(5) Copies of the representations need not be sent out and the representations need not be read out at the meeting if, on the application either of the company or of any other person who claims to be aggrieved, the court is satisfied that the rights conferred by this section are being abused.

(6) The court may order the company's costs (in Scotland, expenses) on an application under subsection (5) to be paid in whole or in part by the director, notwithstanding that he is not a party to the application.

CHAPTER 2
GENERAL DUTIES OF DIRECTORS

Introductory

170 Scope and nature of general duties

(1) The general duties specified in sections 171 to 177 are owed by a director of a company to the company.

(2) A person who ceases to be a director continues to be subject—

(a) to the duty in section 175 (duty to avoid conflicts of interest) as regards the exploitation of any property, information or opportunity of which he became aware at a time when he was a director, and

(b) to the duty in section 176 (duty not to accept benefits from third parties) as regards things done or omitted by him before he ceased to be a director.

To that extent those duties apply to a former director as to a director, subject to any necessary adaptations.

(3) The general duties are based on certain common law rules and equitable principles as they apply in relation to directors and have effect in place of those rules and principles as regards the duties owed to a company by a director.

(4) The general duties shall be interpreted and applied in the same way as common law rules or equitable principles, and regard shall be had to the corresponding common law rules and equitable principles in interpreting and applying the general duties.

(5) The general duties apply to a shadow director of a company where and to the extent that they are capable of so applying.

The general duties

171 Duty to act within powers

A director of a company must—

(a) act in accordance with the company's constitution, and

(b) only exercise powers for the purposes for which they are conferred.

172 Duty to promote the success of the company

(1) A director of a company must act in the way he considers, in good faith, would be most likely to promote the success of the company for the benefit of its members as a whole, and in doing so have regard (amongst other matters) to—

(a) the likely consequences of any decision in the long term,

(b) the interests of the company's employees,

(c) the need to foster the company's business relationships with suppliers, customers and others,

(d) the impact of the company's operations on the community and the environment,

(e) the desirability of the company maintaining a reputation for high standards of business conduct, and

(f) the need to act fairly as between members of the company.

(2) Where or to the extent that the purposes of the company consist of or include purposes other than the benefit of its members, subsection (1) has effect as if the reference to promoting the success of the company for the benefit of its members were to achieving those purposes.

(3) The duty imposed by this section has effect subject to any enactment or rule of law requiring directors, in certain circumstances, to consider or act in the interests of creditors of the company.

173 Duty to exercise independent judgment

(1) A director of a company must exercise independent judgment.
(2) This duty is not infringed by his acting—
 (a) in accordance with an agreement duly entered into by the company that restricts the future exercise of discretion by its directors, or
 (b) in a way authorised by the company's constitution.

174 Duty to exercise reasonable care, skill and diligence

(1) A director of a company must exercise reasonable care, skill and diligence.
(2) This means the care, skill and diligence that would be exercised by a reasonably diligent person with—
 (a) the general knowledge, skill and experience that may reasonably be expected of a person carrying out the functions carried out by the director in relation to the company, and
 (b) the general knowledge, skill and experience that the director has.

175 Duty to avoid conflicts of interest

(1) A director of a company must avoid a situation in which he has, or can have, a direct or indirect interest that conflicts, or possibly may conflict, with the interests of the company.
(2) This applies in particular to the exploitation of any property, information or opportunity (and it is immaterial whether the company could take advantage of the property, information or opportunity).
(3) This duty does not apply to a conflict of interest arising in relation to a transaction or arrangement with the company.
(4) This duty is not infringed—
 (a) if the situation cannot reasonably be regarded as likely to give rise to a conflict of interest; or
 (b) if the matter has been authorised by the directors.
(5) Authorisation may be given by the directors—
 (a) where the company is a private company and nothing in the company's constitution invalidates such authorisation, by the matter being proposed to and authorised by the directors; or
 (b) where the company is a public company and its constitution includes provision enabling the directors to authorise the matter, by the matter being proposed to and authorised by them in accordance with the constitution.
(6) The authorisation is effective only if—
 (a) any requirement as to the quorum at the meeting at which the matter is considered is met without counting the director in question or any other interested director, and
 (b) the matter was agreed to without their voting or would have been agreed to if their votes had not been counted.
(7) Any reference in this section to a conflict of interest includes a conflict of interest and duty and a conflict of duties.

176 Duty not to accept benefits from third parties

(1) A director of a company must not accept a benefit from a third party conferred by reason of—
 (a) his being a director, or
 (b) his doing (or not doing) anything as director.
(2) A "third party" means a person other than the company, an associated body corporate or a person acting on behalf of the company or an associated body corporate.
(3) Benefits received by a director from a person by whom his services (as a director or otherwise) are provided to the company are not regarded as conferred by a third party.
(4) This duty is not infringed if the acceptance of the benefit cannot reasonably be regarded as likely to give rise to a conflict of interest.
(5) Any reference in this section to a conflict of interest includes a conflict of interest and duty and a conflict of duties.

177 Duty to declare interest in proposed transaction or arrangement

(1) If a director of a company is in any way, directly or indirectly, interested in a proposed transaction or arrangement with the company, he must declare the nature and extent of that interest to the other directors.

(2) The declaration may (but need not) be made—
(a) at a meeting of the directors, or
(b) by notice to the directors in accordance with—
(i) section 184 (notice in writing), or
(ii) section 185 (general notice).
(3) If a declaration of interest under this section proves to be, or becomes, inaccurate or incomplete, a further declaration must be made.
(4) Any declaration required by this section must be made before the company enters into the transaction or arrangement.
(5) This section does not require a declaration of an interest of which the director is not aware or where the director is not aware of the transaction or arrangement in question.
For this purpose a director is treated as being aware of matters of which he ought reasonably to be aware.
(6) A director need not declare an interest—
(a) if it cannot reasonably be regarded as likely to give rise to a conflict of interest;
(b) if, or to the extent that, the other directors are already aware of it (and for this purpose the other directors are treated as aware of anything of which they ought reasonably to be aware); or
(c) if, or to the extent that, it concerns terms of his service contract that have been or are to be considered—
(i) by a meeting of the directors, or
(ii) by a committee of the directors appointed for the purpose under the company's constitution.

Supplementary provisions

178 Civil consequences of breach of general duties

(1) The consequences of breach (or threatened breach) of sections 171 to 177 are the same as would apply if the corresponding common law rule or equitable principle applied.
(2) The duties in those sections (with the exception of section 174 (duty to exercise reasonable care, skill and diligence)) are, accordingly, enforceable in the same way as any other fiduciary duty owed to a company by its directors.

179 Cases within more than one of the general duties

Except as otherwise provided, more than one of the general duties may apply in any given case.

180 Consent, approval or authorisation by members

(1) In a case where—
(a) section 175 (duty to avoid conflicts of interest) is complied with by authorisation by the directors, or
(b) section 177 (duty to declare interest in proposed transaction or arrangement) is complied with,

the transaction or arrangement is not liable to be set aside by virtue of any common law rule or equitable principle requiring the consent or approval of the members of the company. This is without prejudice to any enactment, or provision of the company's constitution, requiring such consent or approval.
(2) The application of the general duties is not affected by the fact that the case also falls within Chapter 4 (transactions requiring approval of members) or 4A, except that where either of those Chapters applies and—
(a) approval is given under the Chapter concerned, or
(b) the matter is one as to which it is provided that approval is not needed,

it is not necessary also to comply with section 175 (duty to avoid conflicts of interest) or section 176 (duty not to accept benefits from third parties).
(3) Compliance with the general duties does not remove the need for approval under any applicable provision of Chapter 4 (transactions requiring approval of members) or 4A.
(4) The general duties—
(a) have effect subject to any rule of law enabling the company to give authority, specifically or generally, for anything to be done (or omitted) by the directors, or any of them, that would otherwise be a breach of duty, and

(b) where the company's articles contain provisions for dealing with conflicts of interest, are not infringed by anything done (or omitted) by the directors, or any of them, in accordance with those provisions.

(5) Otherwise, the general duties have effect (except as otherwise provided or the context otherwise requires) notwithstanding any enactment or rule of law.

181 Modification of provisions in relation to charitable companies

(1) In their application to a company that is a charity, the provisions of this Chapter have effect subject to this section.

(2) Section 175 (duty to avoid conflicts of interest) has effect as if—

(a) for subsection (3) (which disapplies the duty to avoid conflicts of interest in the case of a transaction or arrangement with the company) there were substituted—

"(3) This duty does not apply to a conflict of interest arising in relation to a transaction or arrangement with the company if or to the extent that the company's articles allow that duty to be so disapplied, which they may do only in relation to descriptions of transaction or arrangement specified in the company's articles.";

(b) for subsection (5) (which specifies how directors of a company may give authority under that section for a transaction or arrangement) there were substituted—

"(5) Authorisation may be given by the directors where the company's constitution includes provision enabling them to authorise the matter, by the matter being proposed to and authorised by them in accordance with the constitution.".

(3) Section 180(2)(b) (which disapplies certain duties under this Chapter in relation to cases excepted from requirement to obtain approval by members under Chapter 4) applies only if or to the extent that the company's articles allow those duties to be so disapplied, which
they may do only in relation to descriptions of transaction or arrangement specified in the company's articles.

(4) …

(5) This section does not extend to Scotland.

CHAPTER 3
DECLARATION OF INTEREST IN EXISTING TRANSACTION OR ARRANGEMENT

182 Declaration of interest in existing transaction or arrangement

(1) Where a director of a company is in any way, directly or indirectly, interested in a transaction or arrangement that has been entered into by the company, he must declare the nature and extent of the interest to the other directors in accordance with this section.
This section does not apply if or to the extent that the interest has been declared under section 177 (duty to declare interest in proposed transaction or arrangement).

(2) The declaration must be made—

(a) at a meeting of the directors, or

(b) by notice in writing (see section 184), or

(c) by general notice (see section 185).

(3) If a declaration of interest under this section proves to be, or becomes, inaccurate or incomplete, a further declaration must be made.

(4) Any declaration required by this section must be made as soon as is reasonably practicable.
Failure to comply with this requirement does not affect the underlying duty to make the declaration.

(5) This section does not require a declaration of an interest of which the director is not aware or where the director is not aware of the transaction or arrangement in question.
For this purpose a director is treated as being aware of matters of which he ought reasonably to be aware.

(6) A director need not declare an interest under this section—

(a) if it cannot reasonably be regarded as likely to give rise to a conflict of interest;

(b) if, or to the extent that, the other directors are already aware of it (and for this purpose the other directors are treated as aware of anything of which they ought reasonably to be aware); or

(c) if, or to the extent that, it concerns terms of his service contract that have been or are to be considered—
  (i) by a meeting of the directors, or
  (ii) by a committee of the directors appointed for the purpose under the company's constitution.

183 Offence of failure to declare interest

(1) A director who fails to comply with the requirements of section 182 (declaration of interest in existing transaction or arrangement) commits an offence.

(2) A person guilty of an offence under this section is liable—
  (a) on conviction on indictment, to a fine;
  (b) on summary conviction, to a fine not exceeding the statutory maximum.

184 Declaration made by notice in writing

(1) This section applies to a declaration of interest made by notice in writing.

(2) The director must send the notice to the other directors.

(3) The notice may be sent in hard copy form or, if the recipient has agreed to receive it in electronic form, in an agreed electronic form.

(4) The notice may be sent—
  (a) by hand or by post, or
  (b) if the recipient has agreed to receive it by electronic means, by agreed electronic means.

(5) Where a director declares an interest by notice in writing in accordance with this section—
  (a) the making of the declaration is deemed to form part of the proceedings at the next meeting of the directors after the notice is given, and
  (b) the provisions of section 248 (minutes of meetings of directors) apply as if the declaration had been made at that meeting.

185 General notice treated as sufficient declaration

(1) General notice in accordance with this section is a sufficient declaration of interest in relation to the matters to which it relates.

(2) General notice is notice given to the directors of a company to the effect that the director—
  (a) has an interest (as member, officer, employee or otherwise) in a specified body corporate or firm and is to be regarded as interested in any transaction or arrangement that may, after the date of the notice, be made with that body corporate or firm, or
  (b) is connected with a specified person (other than a body corporate or firm) and is to be regarded as interested in any transaction or arrangement that may, after the date of the notice, be made with that person.

(3) The notice must state the nature and extent of the director's interest in the body corporate or firm or, as the case may be, the nature of his connection with the person.

(4) General notice is not effective unless—
  (a) it is given at a meeting of the directors, or
  (b) the director takes reasonable steps to secure that it is brought up and read at the next meeting of the directors after it is given.

186 Declaration of interest in case of company with sole director

(1) Where a declaration of interest under section 182 (duty to declare interest in existing transaction or arrangement) is required of a sole director of a company that is required to have more than one director—
  (a) the declaration must be recorded in writing,
  (b) the making of the declaration is deemed to form part of the proceedings at the next meeting of the directors after the notice is given, and
  (c) the provisions of section 248 (minutes of meetings of directors) apply as if the declaration had been made at that meeting.

(2) Nothing in this section affects the operation of section 231 (contract with sole member who is also a director: terms to be set out in writing or recorded in minutes).

187 Declaration of interest in existing transaction by shadow director

(1) The provisions of this Chapter relating to the duty under section 182 (duty to declare interest in existing transaction or arrangement) apply to a shadow director as to a director, but with the following adaptations.

(2) Subsection (2)(a) of that section (declaration at meeting of directors) does not apply.
(3) In section 185 (general notice treated as sufficient declaration), subsection (4) (notice to be given at or brought up and read at meeting of directors) does not apply.
(4) General notice by a shadow director is not effective unless given by notice in writing in accordance with section 184.

CHAPTER 4
TRANSACTIONS WITH DIRECTORS REQUIRING APPROVAL OF MEMBERS

Service contracts

188 Directors' long-term service contracts: requirement of members' approval

(1) This section applies to provision under which the guaranteed term of a director's employment—
  (a) with the company of which he is a director, or
  (b) where he is the director of a holding company, within the group consisting of that company and its subsidiaries,
is, or may be, longer than two years.
(2) A company may not agree to such provision unless it has been approved—
  (a) by resolution of the members of the company, and
  (b) in the case of a director of a holding company, by resolution of the members of that company.
(3) The guaranteed term of a director's employment is—
  (a) the period (if any) during which the director's employment—
    (i) is to continue, or may be continued otherwise than at the instance of the company (whether under the original agreement or under a new agreement entered into in pursuance of it), and
    (ii) cannot be terminated by the company by notice, or can be so terminated only in specified circumstances, or
  (b) in the case of employment terminable by the company by notice, the period of notice required to be given, or, in the case of employment having a period within paragraph (a) and a period within paragraph (b), the aggregate of those periods.
(4) If more than six months before the end of the guaranteed term of a director's employment the company enters into a further service contract (otherwise than in pursuance of a right conferred, by or under the original contract, on the other party to it), this section applies as if there were added to the guaranteed term of the new contract the unexpired period of the guaranteed term of the original contract.
(5) A resolution approving provision to which this section applies must not be passed unless a memorandum setting out the proposed contract incorporating the provision is made available to members—
  (a) in the case of a written resolution, by being sent or submitted to every eligible member at or before the time at which the proposed resolution is sent or submitted to him;
  (b) in the case of a resolution at a meeting, by being made available for inspection by members of the company both—
    (i) at the company's registered office for not less than 15 days ending with the date of the meeting, and
    (ii) at the meeting itself.
(6) No approval is required under this section on the part of the members of a body corporate that—
  (a) is not a UK-registered company, or
  (b) is a wholly-owned subsidiary of another body corporate.
(7) In this section "employment" means any employment under a director's service contract.

189 Directors' long-term service contracts: civil consequences of contravention

If a company agrees to provision in contravention of section 188 (directors' long-term service contracts: requirement of members' approval)—
  (a) the provision is void, to the extent of the contravention, and
  (b) the contract is deemed to contain a term entitling the company to terminate it at any time by the giving of reasonable notice.

Substantial property transactions

190 Substantial property transactions: requirement of members' approval

(1) A company may not enter into an arrangement under which—

(a) a director of the company or of its holding company, or a person connected with such a director, acquires or is to acquire from the company (directly or indirectly) a substantial non-cash asset, or

(b) the company acquires or is to acquire a substantial non-cash asset (directly or indirectly) from such a director or a person so connected,

unless the arrangement has been approved by a resolution of the members of the company or is conditional on such approval being obtained.

For the meaning of "substantial non-cash asset" see section 191.

(2) If the director or connected person is a director of the company's holding company or a person connected with such a director, the arrangement must also have been approved by a resolution of the members of the holding company or be conditional on such approval being obtained.

(3) A company shall not be subject to any liability by reason of a failure to obtain approval required by this section.

(4) No approval is required under this section on the part of the members of a body corporate that—

(a) is not a UK-registered company, or

(b) is a wholly-owned subsidiary of another body corporate.

(5) For the purposes of this section—

(a) an arrangement involving more than one non-cash asset, or

(b) an arrangement that is one of a series involving non-cash assets,

shall be treated as if they involved a non-cash asset of a value equal to the aggregate value of all the non-cash assets involved in the arrangement or, as the case may be, the series.

(6) This section does not apply to a transaction so far as it relates—

(a) to anything to which a director of a company is entitled under his service contract, or

(b) to payment for loss of office as defined in section 215 (payments to which the requirements of Chapter 4 or 4A apply).

191 Meaning of "substantial"

(1) This section explains what is meant in section 190 (requirement of approval for substantial property transactions) by a "substantial" non-cash asset.

(2) An asset is a substantial asset in relation to a company if its value—

(a) exceeds 10% of the company's asset value and is more than £5,000, or

(b) exceeds £100,000.

(3) For this purpose a company's "asset value" at any time is—

(a) the value of the company's net assets determined by reference to its most recent statutory accounts, or

(b) if no statutory accounts have been prepared, the amount of the company's called-up share capital.

(4) A company's "statutory accounts" means its annual accounts prepared in accordance with Part 15, and its "most recent" statutory accounts means those in relation to which the time for sending them out to members (see section 424) is most recent.

(5) Whether an asset is a substantial asset shall be determined as at the time the arrangement is entered into.

192 Exception for transactions with members or other group companies

Approval is not required under section 190 (requirement of members' approval for substantial property transactions)—

(a) for a transaction between a company and a person in his character as a member of that company, or

(b) for a transaction between—

(i) a holding company and its wholly-owned subsidiary, or

(ii) two wholly-owned subsidiaries of the same holding company.

193 Exception in case of company in winding up or administration

(1) This section applies to a company—

(a) that is being wound up (unless the winding up is a members' voluntary winding up), or

(b) that is in administration within the meaning of Schedule B1 to the Insolvency Act 1986 or the Insolvency (Northern Ireland) Order 1989.

(2) Approval is not required under section 190 (requirement of members' approval for substantial property transactions)—

(a) on the part of the members of a company to which this section applies, or

(b) for an arrangement entered into by a company to which this section applies.

194 Exception for transactions on recognised investment exchange

(1) Approval is not required under section 190 (requirement of members' approval for substantial property transactions) for a transaction on a recognised investment exchange effected by a director, or a person connected with him, through the agency of a person who in relation to the transaction acts as an independent broker.

(2) For this purpose—

(a) "independent broker" means a person who, independently of the director or any person connected with him, selects the person with whom the transaction is to be effected; and

(b) "recognised investment exchange" has the same meaning as in Part 18 of the Financial Services and Markets Act 2000.

195 Property transactions: civil consequences of contravention

(1) This section applies where a company enters into an arrangement in contravention of section 190 (requirement of members' approval for substantial property transactions).

(2) The arrangement, and any transaction entered into in pursuance of the arrangement (whether by the company or any other person), is voidable at the instance of the company, unless—

(a) restitution of any money or other asset that was the subject matter of the arrangement or transaction is no longer possible,

(b) the company has been indemnified in pursuance of this section by any other persons for the loss or damage suffered by it, or

(c) rights acquired in good faith, for value and without actual notice of the contravention by a person who is not a party to the arrangement or transaction would be affected by the avoidance.

(3) Whether or not the arrangement or any such transaction has been avoided, each of the persons specified in subsection (4) is liable—

(a) to account to the company for any gain that he has made directly or indirectly by the arrangement or transaction, and

(b) (jointly and severally with any other person so liable under this section) to indemnify the company for any loss or damage resulting from the arrangement or transaction.

(4) The persons so liable are—

(a) any director of the company or of its holding company with whom the company entered into the arrangement in contravention of section 190,

(b) any person with whom the company entered into the arrangement in contravention of that section who is connected with a director of the company or of its holding company,

(c) the director of the company or of its holding company with whom any such person is connected, and

(d) any other director of the company who authorised the arrangement or any transaction entered into in pursuance of such an arrangement.

(5) Subsections (3) and (4) are subject to the following two subsections.

(6) In the case of an arrangement entered into by a company in contravention of section 190 with a person connected with a director of the company or of its holding company, that director is not liable by virtue of subsection (4)(c) if he shows that he took all reasonable steps to secure the company's compliance with that section.

(7) In any case—

(a) a person so connected is not liable by virtue of subsection (4)(b), and

(b) a director is not liable by virtue of subsection (4)(d),

if he shows that, at the time the arrangement was entered into, he did not know the relevant circumstances constituting the contravention.

(8) Nothing in this section shall be read as excluding the operation of any other enactment or rule of law by virtue of which the arrangement or transaction may be called in question or any liability to the company may arise.

196 Property transactions: effect of subsequent affirmation

Where a transaction or arrangement is entered into by a company in contravention of section 190 (requirement of members' approval) but, within a reasonable period, it is affirmed—

(a) in the case of a contravention of subsection (1) of that section, by resolution of the members of the company, and

(b) in the case of a contravention of subsection (2) of that section, by resolution of the members of the holding company,

the transaction or arrangement may no longer be avoided under section 195.

Loans, quasi-loans and credit transactions

197 Loans to directors: requirement of members' approval

(1) A company may not—

(a) make a loan to a director of the company or of its holding company, or

(b) give a guarantee or provide security in connection with a loan made by any person to such a director,

unless the transaction has been approved by a resolution of the members of the company.

(2) If the director is a director of the company's holding company, the transaction must also have been approved by a resolution of the members of the holding company.

(3) A resolution approving a transaction to which this section applies must not be passed unless a memorandum setting out the matters mentioned in subsection (4) is made available to members—

(a) in the case of a written resolution, by being sent or submitted to every eligible member at or before the time at which the proposed resolution is sent or submitted to him;

(b) in the case of a resolution at a meeting, by being made available for inspection by members of the company both—

(i) at the company's registered office for not less than 15 days ending with the date of the meeting, and

(ii) at the meeting itself.

(4) The matters to be disclosed are—

(a) the nature of the transaction,

(b) the amount of the loan and the purpose for which it is required, and

(c) the extent of the company's liability under any transaction connected with the loan.

(5) No approval is required under this section on the part of the members of a body corporate that—

(a) is not a UK-registered company, or

(b) is a wholly-owned subsidiary of another body corporate.

198 Quasi-loans to directors: requirement of members' approval

(1) This section applies to a company if it is—

(a) a public company, or

(b) a company associated with a public company.

(2) A company to which this section applies may not—

(a) make a quasi-loan to a director of the company or of its holding company, or

(b) give a guarantee or provide security in connection with a quasi-loan made by any person to such a director,

unless the transaction has been approved by a resolution of the members of the company.

(3) If the director is a director of the company's holding company, the transaction must also have been approved by a resolution of the members of the holding company.

(4) A resolution approving a transaction to which this section applies must not be passed unless a memorandum setting out the matters mentioned in subsection (5) is made available to members—

(a) in the case of a written resolution, by being sent or submitted to every eligible member at or before the time at which the proposed resolution is sent or submitted to him;

(b) in the case of a resolution at a meeting, by being made available for inspection by members of the company both—

(i) at the company's registered office for not less than 15 days ending with the date of the meeting, and
(ii) at the meeting itself.

(5) The matters to be disclosed are—
(a) the nature of the transaction,
(b) the amount of the quasi-loan and the purpose for which it is required, and
(c) the extent of the company's liability under any transact on connected with the quasi- loan.

(6) No approval is required under this section on the part of the members of a body corporate that—
(a) is not a UK-registered company, or
(b) is a wholly-owned subsidiary of another body corporate.

199 Meaning of "quasi-loan" and related expressions

(1) A "quasi-loan" is a transaction under which one party ("the creditor") agrees to pay, or pays otherwise than in pursuance of an agreement, a sum for another ("the borrower") or agrees to reimburse, or reimburses otherwise than in pursuance of an agreement, expenditure incurred by another party for another ("the borrower")—
(a) on terms that the borrower (or a person on his behalf) will reimburse the creditor; or
(b) in circumstances giving rise to a liability on the borrower to reimburse the creditor.

(2) Any reference to the person to whom a quasi-loan is made is a reference to the borrower.

(3) The liabilities of the borrower under a quasi-loan include the liabilities of any person who has agreed to reimburse the creditor on behalf of the borrower.

200 Loans or quasi-loans to persons connected with directors: requirement of members' approval

(1) This section applies to a company if it is—
(a) a public company, or
(b) a company associated with a public company.

(2) A company to which this section applies may not—
(a) make a loan or quasi-loan to a person connected with a director of the company or of its holding company, or
(b) give a guarantee or provide security in connection with a loan or quasi-loan made by any person to a person connected with such a director,

unless the transaction has been approved by a resolution of the members of the company.

(3) If the connected person is a person connected with a director of the company's holding company, the transaction must also have been approved by a resolution of the members of the holding company.

(4) A resolution approving a transaction to which this section applies must not be passed unless a memorandum setting out the matters mentioned in subsection (5) is made available to members—
(a) in the case of a written resolution, by being sent or submitted to every eligible member at or before the time at which the proposed resolution is sent or submitted to him;
(b) in the case of a resolution at a meeting, by being made available for inspection by members of the company both—
(i) at the company's registered office for not less than 15 days ending with the date of the meeting, and
(ii) at the meeting itself.

(5) The matters to be disclosed are—
(a) the nature of the transaction,
(b) the amount of the loan or quasi-loan and the purpose for which it is required, and
(c) the extent of the company's liability under any transaction connected with the loan or quasi-loan.

(6) No approval is required under this section on the part of the members of a body corporate that—
(a) is not a UK-registered company, or
(b) is a wholly-owned subsidiary of another body corporate.

201 Credit transactions: requirement of members' approval

(1) This section applies to a company if it is—
(a) a public company, or
(b) a company associated with a public company.

(2) A company to which this section applies may not—
(a) enter into a credit transaction as creditor for the benefit of a director of the company or of its holding company, or a person connected with such a director, or
(b) give a guarantee or provide security in connection with a credit transaction entered into by any person for the benefit of such a director, or a person connected with such a director,

unless the transaction (that is, the credit transaction, the giving of the guarantee or the provision of security, as the case may be) has been approved by a resolution of the members of the company.

(3) If the director or connected person is a director of its holding company or a person connected with such a director, the transaction must also have been approved by a resolution of the members of the holding company.

(4) A resolution approving a transaction to which this section applies must not be passed unless a memorandum setting out the matters mentioned in subsection (5) is made available to members—
(a) in the case of a written resolution, by being sent or submitted to every eligible member at or before the time at which the proposed resolution is sent or submitted to him;
(b) in the case of a resolution at a meeting, by being made available for inspection by members of the company both—
(i) at the company's registered office for not less than 15 days ending with the date of the meeting, and
(ii) at the meeting itself.

(5) The matters to be disclosed are—
(a) the nature of the transaction,
(b) the value of the credit transaction and the purpose for which the land, goods or services sold or otherwise disposed of, leased, hired or supplied under the credit transaction are required, and
(c) the extent of the company's liability under any transaction connected with the credit transaction.

(6) No approval is required under this section on the part of the members of a body corporate that—
(a) is not a UK-registered company, or
(b) is a wholly-owned subsidiary of another body corporate.

202 Meaning of "credit transaction"

(1) A "credit transaction" is a transaction under which one party ("the creditor")—
(a) supplies any goods or sells any land under a hire-purchase agreement or a conditional sale agreement,
(b) leases or hires any land or goods in return for periodical payments, or
(c) otherwise disposes of land or supplies goods or services on the understanding that payment (whether in a lump sum or instalments or by way of periodical payments or otherwise) is to be deferred.

(2) Any reference to the person for whose benefit a credit transaction is entered into is to the person to whom goods, land or services are supplied, sold, leased, hired or otherwise disposed of under the transaction.

(3) In this section—
"conditional sale agreement" has the same meaning as in the Consumer Credit Act 1974; and
"services" means anything other than goods or land.

203 Related arrangements: requirement of members' approval

(1) A company may not—
(a) take part in an arrangement under which—
(i) another person enters into a transaction that, if it had been entered into by the company, would have required approval under section 197, 198, 200 or 201, and

(ii) that person, in pursuance of the arrangement, obtains a benefit from the company or a body corporate associated with it, or

(b) arrange for the assignment to it, or assumption by it, of any rights, obligations or liabilities under a transaction that, if it had been entered into by the company, would have required such approval,

unless the arrangement in question has been approved by a resolution of the members of the company.

(2) If the director or connected person for whom the transaction is entered into is a director of its holding company or a person connected with such a director, the arrangement must also have been approved by a resolution of the members of the holding company.

(3) A resolution approving an arrangement to which this section applies must not be passed unless a memorandum setting out the matters mentioned in subsection (4) is made available to members—

(a) in the case of a written resolution, by being sent or submitted to every eligible member at or before the time at which the proposed resolution is sent or submitted to him;

(b) in the case of a resolution at a meeting, by being made available for inspection by members of the company both—

(i) at the company's registered office for not less than 15 days ending with the date of the meeting, and

(ii) at the meeting itself.

(4) The matters to be disclosed are—

(a) the matters that would have to be disclosed if the company were seeking approval of the transaction to which the arrangement relates,

(b) the nature of the arrangement, and

(c) the extent of the company's liability under the arrangement or any transaction connected with it.

(5) No approval is required under this section on the part of the members of a body corporate that—

(a) is not a UK-registered company, or

(b) is a wholly-owned subsidiary of another body corporate.

(6) In determining for the purposes of this section whether a transaction is one that would have required approval under section 197, 198, 200 or 201 if it had been entered into by the company, the transaction shall be treated as having been entered into on the date of the arrangement.

204 Exception for expenditure on company business

(1) Approval is not required under section 197, 198, 200 or 201 (requirement of members' approval for loans etc) for anything done by a company—

(a) to provide a director of the company or of its holding company, or a person connected with any such director, with funds to meet expenditure incurred or to be incurred by him—

(i) for the purposes of the company, or

(ii) for the purpose of enabling him properly to perform his duties as an officer of the company, or

(b) to enable any such person to avoid incurring such expenditure.

(2) This section does not authorise a company to enter into a transaction if the aggregate of—

(a) the value of the transaction in question, and

(b) the value of any other relevant transactions or arrangements,

exceeds £50,000.

205 Exception for expenditure on defending proceedings etc.

(1) Approval is not required under section 197, 198, 200 or 201 (requirement of members' approval for loans etc) for anything done by a company—

(a) to provide a director of the company or of its holding company with funds to meet expenditure incurred or to be incurred by him—

(i) in defending any criminal or civil proceedings in connection with any alleged negligence, default, breach of duty or breach of trust by him in relation to the company or an associated company, or

(ii) in connection with an application for relief (see subsection (5)), or

(b) to enable any such director to avoid incurring such expenditure, if it is done on the following terms.

(2) The terms are—

(a) that the loan is to be repaid, or (as the case may be) any liability of the company incurred under any transaction connected with the thing done is to be discharged, in the event of—

(i) the director being convicted in the proceedings,

(ii) judgment being given against him in the proceedings, or

(iii) the court refusing to grant him relief on the application; and

(b) that it is to be so repaid or discharged not later than—

(i) the date when the conviction becomes final,

(ii) the date when the judgment becomes final, or

(iii) the date when the refusal of relief becomes final.

(3) For this purpose a conviction, judgment or refusal of relief becomes final—

(a) if not appealed against, at the end of the period for bringing an appeal;

(b) if appealed against, when the appeal (or any further appeal) is disposed of.

(4) An appeal is disposed of—

(a) if it is determined and the period for bringing any further appeal has ended, or

(b) if it is abandoned or otherwise ceases to have effect.

(5) The reference in subsection (1)(a)(ii) to an application for relief is to an application for relief under—

section 661(3) or (4) (power of court to grant relief in case of acquisition of shares by innocent nominee), or

section 1157 (general power of court to grant relief in case of honest and reasonable conduct).

206 Exception for expenditure in connection with regulatory action or investigation

Approval is not required under section 197, 198, 200 or 201 (requirement of members' approval for loans etc) for anything done by a company—

(a) to provide a director of the company or of its holding company with funds to meet expenditure incurred or to be incurred by him in defending himself—

(i) in an investigation by a regulatory authority, or

(ii) against action proposed to be taken by a regulatory authority,

in connection with any alleged negligence, default, breach of duty or breach of trust by him in relation to the company or an associated company, or

(b) to enable any such director to avoid incurring such expenditure.

207 Exceptions for minor and business transactions

(1) Approval is not required under section 197, 198 or 200 for a company to make a loan or quasi-loan, or to give a guarantee or provide security in connection with a loan or quasi-loan, if the aggregate of—

(a) the value of the transaction, and

(b) the value of any other relevant transactions or arrangements, does not exceed £10,000.

(2) Approval is not required under section 201 for a company to enter into a credit transaction, or to give a guarantee or provide security in connection with a credit transaction, if the aggregate of—

(a) the value of the transaction (that is, of the credit transaction, guarantee or security), and

(b) the value of any other relevant transactions or arrangements, does not exceed £15,000.

(3) Approval is not required under section 201 for a company to enter into a credit transaction, or to give a guarantee or provide security in connection with a credit transaction, if—

(a) the transaction is entered into by the company in the ordinary course of the company's business, and

(b) the value of the transaction is not greater, and the terms on which it is entered into are not more favourable, than it is reasonable to expect the company would have offered to, or in respect of, a person of the same financial standing but unconnected with the company.

208 Exceptions for intra-group transactions

(1) Approval is not required under section 197, 198 or 200 for—
- (a) the making of a loan or quasi-loan to an associated body corporate, or
- (b) the giving of a guarantee or provision of security in connection with a loan or quasi-loan made to an associated body corporate.

(2) Approval is not required under section 201—
- (a) to enter into a credit transaction as creditor for the benefit of an associated body corporate, or
- (b) to give a guarantee or provide security in connection with a credit transaction entered into by any person for the benefit of an associated body corporate.

209 Exceptions for money-lending companies

(1) Approval is not required under section 197, 198 or 200 for the making of a loan or quasi-loan, or the giving of a guarantee or provision of security in connection with a loan or quasi-loan, by a money-lending company if—
- (a) the transaction (that is, the loan, quasi-loan, guarantee or security) is entered into by the company in the ordinary course of the company's business, and
- (b) the value of the transaction is not greater, and its terms are not more favourable, than it is reasonable to expect the company would have offered to a person of the same financial standing but unconnected with the company.

(2) A "money-lending company" means a company whose ordinary business includes the making of loans or quasi-loans, or the giving of guarantees or provision of security in connection with loans or quasi-loans.

(3) The condition specified in subsection (1)(b) does not of itself prevent a company from making a home loan—
- (a) to a director of the company or of its holding company, or
- (b) to an employee of the company,

if loans of that description are ordinarily made by the company to its employees and the terms of the loan in question are no more favourable than those on which such loans are ordinarily made.

(4) For the purposes of subsection (3) a "home loan" means a loan—
- (a) for the purpose of facilitating the purchase, for use as the only or main residence of the person to whom the loan is made, of the whole or part of any dwelling-house together with any land to be occupied and enjoyed with it,
- (b) for the purpose of improving a dwelling-house or part of a dwelling-house so used or any land occupied and enjoyed with it, or
- (c) in substitution for any loan made by any person and falling within paragraph (a) or (b).

210 Other relevant transactions or arrangements

(1) This section has effect for determining what are "other relevant transactions or arrangements" for the purposes of any exception to section 197, 198, 200 or 201.

In the following provisions "the relevant exception" means the exception for the purposes of which that falls to be determined.

(2) Other relevant transactions or arrangements are those previously entered into, or entered into at the same time as the transaction or arrangement in question in relation to which the following conditions are met.

(3) Where the transaction or arrangement in question is entered into—
- (a) for a director of the company entering into it, or
- (b) for a person connected with such a director,

the conditions are that the transaction or arrangement was (or is) entered into for that director, or a person connected with him, by virtue of the relevant exception by that company or by any of its subsidiaries.

(4) Where the transaction or arrangement in question is entered into—
- (a) for a director of the holding company of the company entering into it, or
- (b) for a person connected with such a director,

the conditions are that the transaction or arrangement was (or is) entered into for that director, or a person connected with him, by virtue of the relevant exception by the holding company or by any of its subsidiaries.

(5) A transaction or arrangement entered into by a company that at the time it was entered into—
(a) was a subsidiary of the company entering into the transaction or arrangement in question, or
(b) was a subsidiary of that company's holding company,
is not a relevant transaction or arrangement if, at the time the question arises whether the transaction or arrangement in question falls within a relevant exception, it is no longer such a subsidiary.

211 The value of transactions and arrangements

(1) For the purposes of sections 197 to 214 (loans etc)—
(a) the value of a transaction or arrangement is determined as follows, and
(b) the value of any other relevant transaction or arrangement is taken to be the value so determined reduced by any amount by which the liabilities of the person for whom the transaction or arrangement was made have been reduced.
(2) The value of a loan is the amount of its principal.
(3) The value of a quasi-loan is the amount, or maximum amount, that the person to whom the quasi-loan is made is liable to reimburse the creditor.
(4) The value of a credit transaction is the price that it is reasonable to expect could be obtained for the goods, services or land to which the transaction relates if they had been supplied (at the time the transaction is entered into) in the ordinary course of business and on the same terms (apart from price) as they have been supplied, or are to be supplied, under the transaction in question.
(5) The value of a guarantee or security is the amount guaranteed or secured.
(6) The value of an arrangement to which section 203 (related arrangements) applies is the value of the transaction to which the arrangement relates.
(7) If the value of a transaction or arrangement is not capable of being expressed as a specific sum of money—
(a) whether because the amount of any liability arising under the transaction or arrangement is unascertainable, or for any other reason, and
(b) whether or not any liability under the transaction or arrangement has been reduced,
its value is deemed to exceed £50,000.

212 The person for whom a transaction or arrangement is entered into

For the purposes of sections 197 to 214 (loans etc) the person for whom a transaction or arrangement is entered into is—
(a) in the case of a loan or quasi-loan, the person to whom it is made;
(b) in the case of a credit transaction, the person to whom goods, land or services are supplied, sold, hired, leased or otherwise disposed of under the transaction;
(c) in the case of a guarantee or security, the person for whom the transaction is made in connection with which the guarantee or security is entered into;
(d) in the case of an arrangement within section 203 (related arrangements), the person for whom the transaction is made to which the arrangement relates.

213 Loans etc: civil consequences of contravention

(1) This section applies where a company enters into a transaction or arrangement in contravention of section 197, 198, 200, 201 or 203 (requirement of members' approval for loans etc).
(2) The transaction or arrangement is voidable at the instance of the company, unless—
(a) restitution of any money or other asset that was the subject matter of the transaction or arrangement is no longer possible,
(b) the company has been indemnified for any loss or damage resulting from the transaction or arrangement, or
(c) rights acquired in good faith, for value and without actual notice of the contravention by a person who is not a party to the transaction or arrangement would be affected by the avoidance.
(3) Whether or not the transaction or arrangement has been avoided, each of the persons specified in subsection (4) is liable—
(a) to account to the company for any gain that he has made directly or indirectly by the transaction or arrangement, and

(b) (jointly and severally with any other person so liable under this section) to indemnify the company for any loss or damage resulting from the transaction or arrangement.

(4) The persons so liable are—

(a) any director of the company or of its holding company with whom the company entered into the transaction or arrangement in contravention of section 197, 198, 201 or 203,

(b) any person with whom the company entered into the transaction or arrangement in contravention of any of those sections who is connected with a director of the company or of its holding company,

(c) the director of the company or of its holding company with whom any such person is connected, and

(d) any other director of the company who authorised the transaction or arrangement.

(5) Subsections (3) and (4) are subject to the following two subsections.

(6) In the case of a transaction or arrangement entered into by a company in contravention of section 200, 201 or 203 with a person connected with a director of the company or of its holding company, that director is not liable by virtue of subsection (4)(c) if he shows that he took all reasonable steps to secure the company's compliance with the section concerned.

(7) In any case—

(a) a person so connected is not liable by virtue of subsection (4)(b), and

(b) a director is not liable by virtue of subsection (4)(d),

if he shows that, at the time the transaction or arrangement was entered into, he did not know the relevant circumstances constituting the contravention.

(8) Nothing in this section shall be read as excluding the operation of any other enactment or rule of law by virtue of which the transaction or arrangement may be called in question or any liability to the company may arise.

214 Loans etc: effect of subsequent affirmation

Where a transaction or arrangement is entered into by a company in contravention of section 197, 198, 200, 201 or 203 (requirement of members' approval for loans etc) but, within a reasonable period, it is affirmed—

(a) in the case of a contravention of the requirement for a resolution of the members of the company, by a resolution of the members of the company, and

(b) in the case of a contravention of the requirement for a resolution of the members of the company's holding company, by a resolution of the members of the holding company,

the transaction or arrangement may no longer be avoided under section 213.

Payments for loss of office

215 Payments for loss of office

(1) In this Chapter a "payment for loss of office" means a payment made to a director or past director of a company—

(a) by way of compensation for loss of office as director of the company,

(b) by way of compensation for loss, while director of the company or in connection with his ceasing to be a director of it, of—

(i) any other office or employment in connection with the management of the affairs of the company, or

(ii) any office (as director or otherwise) or employment in connection with the management of the affairs of any subsidiary undertaking of the company,

(c) as consideration for or in connection with his retirement from his office as director of the company, or

(d) as consideration for or in connection with his retirement, while director of the company or in connection with his ceasing to be a director of it, from—

(i) any other office or employment in connection with the management of the affairs of the company, or

(ii) any office (as director or otherwise) or employment in connection with the management of the affairs of any subsidiary undertaking of the company.

(2) The references to compensation and consideration include benefits otherwise than in cash and references in this Chapter to payment have a corresponding meaning.

(3) For the purposes of sections 217 to 221 (payments requiring members' approval)—

(a) payment to a person connected with a director, or

(b) payment to any person at the direction of, or for the benefit of, a director or a person connected with him,

is treated as payment to the director.

(4) References in those sections to payment by a person include payment by another person at the direction of, or on behalf of, the person referred to.

(5) Nothing in this section or sections 216 to 222 applies in relation to a payment for loss of office to a director of a quoted company other than a payment to which section 226C does not apply by virtue of section 226D(6).

216 Amounts taken to be payments for loss of office

(1) This section applies where in connection with any such transfer as is mentioned in section 218 or 219 (payment in connection with transfer of undertaking, property or shares) a director of the company—

(a) is to cease to hold office, or

(b) is to cease to be the holder of—

(i) any other office or employment in connection with the management of the affairs of the company, or

(ii) any office (as director or otherwise) or employment in connection with the management of the affairs of any subsidiary undertaking of the company.

(2) If in connection with any such transfer—

(a) the price to be paid to the director for any shares in the company held by him is in excess of the price which could at the time have been obtained by other holders of like shares, or

(b) any valuable consideration is given to the director by a person other than the company,

the excess or, as the case may be, the money value of the consideration is taken for the purposes of those sections to have been a payment for loss of office.

217 Payment by company: requirement of members' approval

(1) A company may not make a payment for loss of office to a director of the company unless the payment has been approved by a resolution of the members of the company.

(2) A company may not make a payment for loss of office to a director of its holding company unless the payment has been approved by a resolution of the members of each of those companies.

(3) A resolution approving a payment to which this section applies must not be passed unless a memorandum setting out particulars of the proposed payment (including its amount) is made available to the members of the company whose approval is sought—

(a) in the case of a written resolution, by being sent or submitted to every eligible member at or before the time at which the proposed resolution is sent or submitted to him;

(b) in the case of a resolution at a meeting, by being made available for inspection by the members both—

(i) at the company's registered office for not less than 15 days ending with the date of the meeting, and

(ii) at the meeting itself.

(4) No approval is required under this section on the part of the members of a body corporate that—

(a) is not a UK-registered company, or

(b) is a wholly-owned subsidiary of another body corporate.

218 Payment in connection with transfer of undertaking etc: requirement of members' approval

(1) No payment for loss of office may be made by any person to a director of a company in connection with the transfer of the whole or any part of the undertaking or property of the company unless the payment has been approved by a resolution of the members of the company.

(2) No payment for loss of office may be made by any person to a director of a company in connection with the transfer of the whole or any part of the undertaking or property of a subsidiary of the company unless the payment has been approved by a resolution of the members of each of the companies.

(3) A resolution approving a payment to which this section applies must not be passed unless a memorandum setting out particulars of the proposed payment (including its amount) is made available to the members of the company whose approval is sought—
(a) in the case of a written resolution, by being sent or submitted to every eligible member at or before the time at which the proposed resolution is sent or submitted to him;
(b) in the case of a resolution at a meeting, by being made available for inspection by the members both—
(i) at the company's registered office for not less than 15 days ending with the date of the meeting, and
(ii) at the meeting itself.
(4) No approval is required under this section on the part of the members of a body corporate that—
(a) is not a UK-registered company, or
(b) is a wholly-owned subsidiary of another body corporate.
(5) A payment made in pursuance of an arrangement—
(a) entered into as part of the agreement for the transfer in question, or within one year before or two years after that agreement, and
(b) to which the company whose undertaking or property is transferred, or any person to whom the transfer is made, is privy,
is presumed, except in so far as the contrary is shown, to be a payment to which this section applies.

219 Payment in connection with share transfer: requirement of members' approval

(1) No payment for loss of office may be made by any person to a director of a company in connection with a transfer of shares in the company, or in a subsidiary of the company, resulting from a takeover bid unless the payment has been approved by a resolution of the relevant shareholders.
(2) The relevant shareholders are the holders of the shares to which the bid relates and any holders of shares of the same class as any of those shares.
(3) A resolution approving a payment to which this section applies must not be passed unless a memorandum setting out particulars of the proposed payment (including its amount) is made available to the members of the company whose approval is sought—
(a) in the case of a written resolution, by being sent or submitted to every eligible member at or before the time at which the proposed resolution is sent or submitted to him;
(b) in the case of a resolution at a meeting, by being made available for inspection by the members both—
(i) at the company's registered office for not less than 15 days ending with the date of the meeting, and
(ii) at the meeting itself.
(4) Neither the person making the offer, nor any associate of his (as defined in section 988), is entitled to vote on the resolution, but—
(a) where the resolution is proposed as a written resolution, they are entitled (if they would otherwise be so entitled) to be sent a copy of it, and
(b) at any meeting to consider the resolution they are entitled (if they would otherwise be so entitled) to be given notice of the meeting, to attend and speak and if present (in person or by proxy) to count towards the quorum.
(5) If at a meeting to consider the resolution a quorum is not present, and after the meeting has been adjourned to a later date a quorum is again not present, the payment is (for the purposes of this section) deemed to have been approved.
(6) No approval is required under this section on the part of shareholders in a body corporate that—
(a) is not a UK-registered company, or
(b) is a wholly-owned subsidiary of another body corporate.
(7) A payment made in pursuance of an arrangement—
(a) entered into as part of the agreement for the transfer in question, or within one year before or two years after that agreement, and
(b) to which the company whose shares are the subject of the bid, or any person to whom the transfer is made, is privy,

is presumed, except in so far as the contrary is shown, to be a payment to which this section applies.

220 Exception for payments in discharge of legal obligations etc.

(1) Approval is not required under section 217, 218 or 219 (payments requiring members' approval) for a payment made in good faith—
 (a) in discharge of an existing legal obligation (as defined below),
 (b) by way of damages for breach of such an obligation,
 (c) by way of settlement or compromise of any claim arising in connection with the termination of a person's office or employment, or
 (d) by way of pension in respect of past services.

(2) In relation to a payment within section 217 (payment by company) an existing legal obligation means an obligation of the company, or any body corporate associated with it, that was not entered into in connection with, or in consequence of, the event giving rise to the payment for loss of office.

(3) In relation to a payment within section 218 or 219 (payment in connection with transfer of undertaking, property or shares) an existing legal obligation means an obligation of the person making the payment that was not entered into for the purposes of, in connection with or in consequence of, the transfer in question.

(4) In the case of a payment within both section 217 and section 218, or within both section 217 and section 219, subsection (2) above applies and not subsection (3).

(5) A payment part of which falls within subsection (1) above and part of which does not is treated as if the parts were separate payments.

221 Exception for small payments

(1) Approval is not required under section 217, 218 or 219 (payments requiring members' approval) if—
 (a) the payment in question is made by the company or any of its subsidiaries, and
 (b) the amount or value of the payment, together with the amount or value of any other relevant payments, does not exceed £200.

(2) For this purpose "other relevant payments" are payments for loss of office in relation to which the following conditions are met.

(3) Where the payment in question is one to which section 217 (payment by company) applies, the conditions are that the other payment was or is paid—
 (a) by the company making the payment in question or any of its subsidiaries,
 (b) to the director to whom that payment is made, and
 (c) in connection with the same event.

(4) Where the payment in question is one to which section 218 or 219 applies (payment in connection with transfer of undertaking, property or shares), the conditions are that the other payment was (or is) paid in connection with the same transfer—
 (a) to the director to whom the payment in question was made, and
 (b) by the company making the payment or any of its subsidiaries.

222 Payments made without approval: civil consequences

(1) If a payment is made in contravention of section 217 (payment by company)—
 (a) it is held by the recipient on trust for the company making the payment, and
 (b) any director who authorised the payment is jointly and severally liable to indemnify the company that made the payment for any loss resulting from it.

(2) If a payment is made in contravention of section 218 (payment in connection with transfer of undertaking etc), it is held by the recipient on trust for the company whose undertaking or property is or is proposed to be transferred.

(3) If a payment is made in contravention of section 219 (payment in connection with share transfer)—
 (a) it is held by the recipient on trust for persons who have sold their shares as a result of the offer made, and
 (b) the expenses incurred by the recipient in distributing that sum amongst those persons shall be borne by him and not retained out of that sum.

(4) If a payment is in contravention of section 217 and section 218, subsection (2) of this section applies rather than subsection (1).

(5) If a payment is in contravention of section 217 and section 219, subsection (3) of this section applies rather than subsection (1), unless the court directs otherwise.

Supplementary

223 Transactions requiring members' approval: application of provisions to shadow directors

(1) For the purposes of—
  (a) sections 188 and 189 (directors' service contracts),
  (b) sections 190 to 196 (property transactions),
  (c) sections 197 to 214 (loans etc), and
  (d) sections 215 to 222 (payments for loss of office), a shadow director is treated as a director.

(2) Any reference in those provisions to loss of office as a director does not apply in relation to loss of a person's status as a shadow director.

224 Approval by written resolution: accidental failure to send memorandum

(1) Where—
  (a) approval under this Chapter is sought by written resolution, and
  (b) a memorandum is required under this Chapter to be sent or submitted to every eligible member before the resolution is passed,

any accidental failure to send or submit the memorandum to one or more members shall be disregarded for the purpose of determining whether the requirement has been met.

(2) Subsection (1) has effect subject to any provision of the company's articles.

225 Cases where approval is required under more than one provision

(1) Approval may be required under more than one provision of this Chapter.
(2) If so, the requirements of each applicable provision must be met.
(3) This does not require a separate resolution for the purposes of each provision.

226 ...

CHAPTER 4A
DIRECTORS OF QUOTED COMPANIES: SPECIAL PROVISION

Interpretation

226A Key definitions

(1) In this Chapter—

"directors' remuneration policy" means the policy of a quoted company with respect to the making of remuneration payments and payments for loss of office;

"quoted company" has the same meaning as in Part 15 of this Act;

"remuneration payment" means any form of payment or other benefit made to or otherwise conferred on a person as consideration for the person—
  (a) holding, agreeing to hold or having held office as director of a company, or
  (b) holding, agreeing to hold or having held, during a period when the person is or was such a director—
    (i) any other office or employment in connection with the management of the affairs of the company, or
    (ii) any office (as director or otherwise) or employment in connection with the management of the affairs of any subsidiary undertaking of the company,

other than a payment for loss of office;

"payment for loss of office" has the same meaning as in Chapter 4 of this Part.

(2) Subsection (3) applies where, in connection with a relevant transfer, a director of a quoted company is—
  (a) to cease to hold office as director, or
  (b) to cease to be the holder of—
    (i) any other office or employment in connection with the management of the affairs of the company, or
    (ii) any office (as director or otherwise) or employment in connection with the management of the affairs of any subsidiary undertaking of the company.

(3) If in connection with the transfer—

(a) the price to be paid to the director for any shares in the company held by the director is in excess of the price which could at the time have been obtained by other holders of like shares, or
(b) any valuable consideration is given to the director by a person other than the company,

the excess or, as the case may be, the money value of the consideration is taken for the purposes of section 226C to have been a payment for loss of office.

(4) In subsection (2), "relevant transfer" means—
(a) a transfer of the whole or any part of the undertaking or property of the company or a subsidiary of the company;
(b) a transfer of shares in the company, or in a subsidiary of the company, resulting from a takeover bid.

(5) References in this Chapter to the making of a remuneration payment or to the making of a payment for loss of office are to be read in accordance with this section.

(6) References in this Chapter to a payment by a company include a payment by another person at the direction of, or on behalf of, the company.

(7) References in this Chapter to a payment to a person ("B") who is, has been or is to be a director of a company include—
(a) a payment to a person connected with B, or
(b) a payment to a person at the direction of, or for the benefit of, B or a person connected with B.

(8) Section 252 applies for the purposes of determining whether a person is connected with a person who has been, or is to be, a director of a company as it applies for the purposes of determining whether a person is connected with a director.

(9) References in this Chapter to a director include a shadow director but references to loss of office as a director do not include loss of a person's status as a shadow director.

Restrictions relating to remuneration or loss of office payments

226B Remuneration payments

(1) A quoted company may not make a remuneration payment to a person who is, or is to be or has been, a director of the company unless—
(a) the payment is consistent with the approved directors' remuneration policy, or
(b) the payment is approved by resolution of the members of the company.

(2) The approved directors' remuneration policy is the most recent remuneration policy to have been approved by a resolution passed by the members of the company in general meeting.

226C Loss of office payments

(1) No payment for loss of office may be made by any person to a person who is, or has been, a director of a quoted company unless—
(a) the payment is consistent with the approved directors' remuneration policy, or
(b) the payment is approved by resolution of the members of the company.

(2) The approved directors' remuneration policy is the most recent remuneration policy to have been approved by a resolution passed by the members of the company in general meeting.

226D Sections 226B and 226C: supplementary

(1) A resolution approving a payment for the purposes of section 226B(1)(b) or 226C(1)(b) must not be passed unless a memorandum setting out particulars of the proposed payment (including its amount) is made available for inspection by the members of the company—
(a) at the company's registered office for not less than 15 days ending with the date of the meeting at which the resolution is to be considered, and
(b) at that meeting itself.

(2) The memorandum must explain the ways in which the payment is inconsistent with the approved directors' remuneration policy (within the meaning of the section in question).

(3) The company must ensure that the memorandum is made available on the company's website from the first day on which the memorandum is made available for inspection under subsection (1) until its next accounts meeting.

(4) Failure to comply with subsection (3) does not affect the validity of the meeting at which a resolution is passed approving a payment to which the memorandum relates or the validity of anything done at the meeting.
(5) Nothing in section 226B or 226C authorises the making of a remuneration payment or (as the case may be) a payment for loss of office in contravention of the articles of the company concerned.
(6) Nothing in section 226B or 226C applies in relation to a remuneration payment or (as the case may be) a payment for loss of office made to a person who is, or is to be or has been, a director of a quoted company before the earlier of—
(a) the end of the first financial year of the company to begin on or after the day on which it becomes a quoted company, and
(b) the date from which the company's first directors' remuneration policy to be approved under section 439A takes effect.
(7) In this section the "company's website" is the website on which the company makes material available under section 430.

Supplementary

226E Payments made without approval: civil consequences

(1) An obligation (however arising) to make a payment which would be in contravention of section 226B or 226C has no effect.
(2) If a payment is made in contravention of section 226B or 226C—
(a) it is held by the recipient on trust for the company or other person making the payment, and
(b) in the case of a payment by a company, any director who authorised the payment is jointly and severally liable to indemnify the company that made the payment for any loss resulting from it.
(3) If a payment for loss of office is made in contravention of section 226C to a director of a quoted company in connection with the transfer of the whole or any part of the undertaking or property of the company or a subsidiary of the company—
(a) subsection (2) does not apply, and
(b) the payment is held by the recipient on trust for the company whose undertaking or property is or is proposed to be transferred.
(4) If a payment for loss of office is made in contravention of section 226C to a director of a quoted company in connection with a transfer of shares in the company, or in a subsidiary of the company, resulting from a takeover bid—
(a) subsection (2) does not apply,
(b) the payment is held by the recipient on trust for persons who have sold their shares as a result of the offer made, and
(c) the expenses incurred by the recipient in distributing that sum amongst those persons shall be borne by the recipient and not retained out of that sum.
(5) If in proceedings against a director for the enforcement of a liability under subsection (2)(b)—
(a) the director shows that he or she has acted honestly and reasonably, and
(b) the court considers that, having regard to all the circumstances of the case, the director ought to be relieved of liability, the court may relieve the director, either wholly or in part, from liability on such terms as the court thinks fit.

226F Relationship with requirements under Chapter 4

(1) This Chapter does not affect any requirement for approval by a resolution of the members of a company which applies in relation to the company under Chapter 4.
(2) Where the making of a payment to which section 226B or 226C applies requires approval by a resolution of the members of the company concerned under Chapter 4, approval obtained for the purposes of that Chapter is to be treated as satisfying the requirements of section 226B(1)(b) or (as the case may be) 226C(1)(b).

CHAPTER 5
DIRECTORS' SERVICE CONTRACTS

227 Directors' service contracts

(1) For the purposes of this Part a director's "service contract", in relation to a company, means a contract under which—

(a) a director of the company undertakes personally to perform services (as director or otherwise) for the company, or for a subsidiary of the company, or
(b) services (as director or otherwise) that a director of the company undertakes personally to perform are made available by a third party to the company, or to a subsidiary of the company.

(2) The provisions of this Part relating to directors' service contracts apply to the terms of a person's appointment as a director of a company.
They are not restricted to contracts for the performance of services outside the scope of the ordinary duties of a director.

228 Copy of contract or memorandum of terms to be available for inspection

(1) A company must keep available for inspection—
(a) a copy of every director's service contract with the company or with a subsidiary of the company, or
(b) if the contract is not in writing, a written memorandum setting out the terms of the contract.

(2) All the copies and memoranda must be kept available for inspection at—
(a) the company's registered office, or
(b) a place specified in regulations under section 1136.

(3) The copies and memoranda must be retained by the company for at least one year from the date of termination or expiry of the contract and must be kept available for inspection during that time.

(4) The company must give notice to the registrar—
(a) of the place at which the copies and memoranda are kept available for inspection, and
(b) of any change in that place,
unless they have at all times been kept at the company's registered office.

(5) If default is made in complying with subsection (1), (2) or (3), or default is made for 14 days in complying with subsection (4), an offence is committed by every officer of the company who is in default.

(6) A person guilty of an offence under this section is liable on summary conviction to a fine not exceeding level 3 on the standard scale and, for continued contravention, a daily default fine not exceeding one-tenth of level 3 on the standard scale.

(7) The provisions of this section apply to a variation of a director's service contract as they apply to the original contract.

229 Right of member to inspect and request copy

(1) Every copy or memorandum required to be kept under section 228 must be open to inspection by any member of the company without charge.

(2) Any member of the company is entitled, on request and on payment of such fee as may be prescribed, to be provided with a copy of any such copy or memorandum.
The copy must be provided within seven days after the request is received by the company.

(3) If an inspection required under subsection (1) is refused, or default is made in complying with subsection (2), an offence is committed by every officer of the company who is in default.

(4) A person guilty of an offence under this section is liable on summary conviction to a fine not exceeding level 3 on the standard scale and, for continued contravention, a daily default fine not exceeding one-tenth of level 3 on the standard scale.

(5) In the case of any such refusal or default the court may by order compel an immediate inspection or, as the case may be, direct that the copy required be sent to the person requiring it.

230 Directors' service contracts: application of provisions to shadow directors

A shadow director is treated as a director for the purposes of the provisions of this Chapter.

CHAPTER 6

CONTRACTS WITH SOLE MEMBERS WHO ARE DIRECTORS

231 Contract with sole member who is also a director

(1) This section applies where—
(a) a limited company having only one member enters into a contract with the sole member,

(b) the sole member is also a director of the company, and
(c) the contract is not entered into in the ordinary course of the company's business.

(2) The company must, unless the contract is in writing, ensure that the terms of the contract are either—
(a) set out in a written memorandum, or
(b) recorded in the minutes of the first meeting of the directors of the company following the making of the contract.

(3) If a company fails to comply with this section an offence is committed by every officer of the company who is in default.

(4) A person guilty of an offence under this section is liable on summary conviction to a fine not exceeding level 5 on the standard scale.

(5) For the purposes of this section a shadow director is treated as a director.

(6) Failure to comply with this section in relation to a contract does not affect the validity of the contract.

(7) Nothing in this section shall be read as excluding the operation of any other enactment or rule of law applying to contracts between a company and a director of the company.

CHAPTER 7
DIRECTORS' LIABILITIES

Provision protecting directors from liability

232 Provisions protecting directors from liability

(1) Any provision that purports to exempt a director of a company (to any extent) from any liability that would otherwise attach to him in connection with any negligence, default, breach of duty or breach of trust in relation to the company is void.

(2) Any provision by which a company directly or indirectly provides an indemnity (to any extent) for a director of the company, or of an associated company, against any liability attaching to him in connection with any negligence, default, breach of duty or breach of trust in relation to the company of which he is a director is void, except as permitted by—
(a) section 233 (provision of insurance),
(b) section 234 (qualifying third party indemnity provision), or
(c) section 235 (qualifying pension scheme indemnity provision).

(3) This section applies to any provision, whether contained in a company's articles or in any contract with the company or otherwise.

(4) Nothing in this section prevents a company's articles from making such provision as has previously been lawful for dealing with conflicts of interest.

233 Provision of insurance

Section 232(2) (voidness of provisions for indemnifying directors) does not prevent a company from purchasing and maintaining for a director of the company, or of an associated company, insurance against any such liability as is mentioned in that subsection.

234 Qualifying third party indemnity provision

(1) Section 232(2) (voidness of provisions for indemnifying directors) does not apply to qualifying third party indemnity provision.

(2) Third party indemnity provision means provision for indemnity against liability incurred by the director to a person other than the company or an associated company.
Such provision is qualifying third party indemnity provision if the following requirements are met.

(3) The provision must not provide any indemnity against—
(a) any liability of the director to pay—
(i) a fine imposed in criminal proceedings, or
(ii) a sum payable to a regulatory authority by way of a penalty in respect of non-compliance with any requirement of a regulatory nature (however arising); or
(b) any liability incurred by the director—
(i) in defending criminal proceedings in which he is convicted, or
(ii) in defending civil proceedings brought by the company, or an associated company, in which judgment is given against him, or
(iii) in connection with an application for relief (see subsection (6)) in which the court refuses to grant him relief.

(4) The references in subsection (3)(b) to a conviction, judgment or refusal of relief are to the final decision in the proceedings.

(5) For this purpose—

(a) a conviction, judgment or refusal of relief becomes final—

(i) if not appealed against, at the end of the period for bringing an appeal, or

(ii) if appealed against, at the time when the appeal (or any further appeal) is disposed of; and

(b) an appeal is disposed of—

(i) if it is determined and the period for bringing any further appeal has ended, or

(ii) if it is abandoned or otherwise ceases to have effect.

(6) The reference in subsection (3)(b)(iii) to an application for relief is to an application for relief under—

section 661(3) or (4) (power of court to grant relief in case of acquisition of shares by innocent nominee), or

section 1157 (general power of court to grant relief in case of honest and reasonable conduct).

235 Qualifying pension scheme indemnity provision

(1) Section 232(2) (voidness of provisions for indemnifying directors) does not apply to qualifying pension scheme indemnity provision.

(2) Pension scheme indemnity provision means provision indemnifying a director of a company that is a trustee of an occupational pension scheme against liability incurred in connection with the company's activities as trustee of the scheme.

Such provision is qualifying pension scheme indemnity provision if the following requirements are met.

(3) The provision must not provide any indemnity against—

(a) any liability of the director to pay—

(i) a fine imposed in criminal proceedings, or

(ii) a sum payable to a regulatory authority by way of a penalty in respect of non-compliance with any requirement of a regulatory nature (however arising); or

(b) any liability incurred by the director in defending criminal proceedings in which he is convicted.

(4) The reference in subsection (3)(b) to a conviction is to the final decision in the proceedings.

(5) For this purpose—

(a) a conviction becomes final—

(i) if not appealed against, at the end of the period for bringing an appeal, or

(ii) if appealed against, at the time when the appeal (or any further appeal) is disposed of; and

(b) an appeal is disposed of—

(i) if it is determined and the period for bringing any further appeal has ended, or

(ii) if it is abandoned or otherwise ceases to have effect.

(6) In this section "occupational pension scheme" means an occupational pension scheme as defined in section 150(5) of the Finance Act 2004 that is established under a trust.

236 Qualifying indemnity provision to be disclosed in directors' report

(1) This section requires disclosure in the directors' report of—

(a) qualifying third party indemnity provision, and

(b) qualifying pension scheme indemnity provision.

Such provision is referred to in this section as "qualifying indemnity provision".

(2) If when a directors' report is approved any qualifying indemnity provision (whether made by the company or otherwise) is in force for the benefit of one or more directors of the company, the report must state that such provision is in force.

(3) If at any time during the financial year to which a directors' report relates any such provision was in force for the benefit of one or more persons who were then directors of the company, the report must state that such provision was in force.

(4) If when a directors' report is approved qualifying indemnity provision made by the company is in force for the benefit of one or more directors of an associated company, the report must state that such provision is in force.

(5) If at any time during the financial year to which a directors' report relates any such provision was in force for the benefit of one or more persons who were then directors of an associated company, the report must state that such provision was in force.

237 Copy of qualifying indemnity provision to be available for inspection

(1) This section has effect where qualifying indemnity provision is made for a director of a company, and applies—
   (a) to the company of which he is a director (whether the provision is made by that company or an associated company), and
   (b) where the provision is made by an associated company, to that company.

(2) That company or, as the case may be, each of them must keep available for inspection—
   (a) a copy of the qualifying indemnity provision, or
   (b) if the provision is not in writing, a written memorandum setting out its terms.

(3) The copy or memorandum must be kept available for inspection at—
   (a) the company's registered office, or
   (b) a place specified in regulations under section 1136.

(4) The copy or memorandum must be retained by the company for at least one year from the date of termination or expiry of the provision and must be kept available for inspection during that time.

(5) The company must give notice to the registrar—
   (a) of the place at which the copy or memorandum is kept available for inspection, and
   (b) of any change in that place,

   unless it has at all times been kept at the company's registered office.

(6) If default is made in complying with subsection (2), (3) or (4), or default is made for 14 days in complying with subsection (5), an offence is committed by every officer of the company who is in default.

(7) A person guilty of an offence under this section is liable on summary conviction to a fine not exceeding level 3 on the standard scale and, for continued contravention, a daily default fine not exceeding one-tenth of level 3 on the standard scale.

(8) The provisions of this section apply to a variation of a qualifying indemnity provision as they apply to the original provision.

(9) In this section "qualifying indemnity provision" means—
   (a) qualifying third party indemnity provision, and
   (b) qualifying pension scheme indemnity provision.

238 Right of member to inspect and request copy

(1) Every copy or memorandum required to be kept by a company under section 237 must be open to inspection by any member of the company without charge.

(2) Any member of the company is entitled, on request and on payment of such fee as may be prescribed, to be provided with a copy of any such copy or memorandum.

   The copy must be provided within seven days after the request is received by the company.

(3) If an inspection required under subsection (1) is refused, or default is made in complying with subsection (2), an offence is committed by every officer of the company who is in default.

(4) A person guilty of an offence under this section is liable on summary conviction to a fine not exceeding level 3 on the standard scale and, for continued contravention, a daily default fine not exceeding one-tenth of level 3 on the standard scale.

(5) In the case of any such refusal or default the court may by order compel an immediate inspection or, as the case may be, direct that the copy required be sent to the person requiring it.

Ratification of acts giving rise to liability

239 Ratification of acts of directors

(1) This section applies to the ratification by a company of conduct by a director amounting to negligence, default, breach of duty or breach of trust in relation to the company.

(2) The decision of the company to ratify such conduct must be made by resolution of the members of the company.

(3) Where the resolution is proposed as a written resolution neither the director (if a member of the company) nor any member connected with him is an eligible member.

(4) Where the resolution is proposed at a meeting, it is passed only if the necessary majority is obtained disregarding votes in favour of the resolution by the director (if a member of the company) and any member connected with him.

This does not prevent the director or any such member from attending, being counted towards the quorum and taking part in the proceedings at any meeting at which the decision is considered.

(5) For the purposes of this section—

(a) "conduct" includes acts and omissions;

(b) "director" includes a former director;

(c) a shadow director is treated as a director; and

(d) in section 252 (meaning of "connected person"), subsection (3) does not apply (exclusion of person who is himself a director).

(6) Nothing in this section affects—

(a) the validity of a decision taken by unanimous consent of the members of the company, or

(b) any power of the directors to agree not to sue, or to settle or release a claim made by them on behalf of the company.

(7) This section does not affect any other enactment or rule of law imposing additional requirements for valid ratification or any rule of law as to acts that are incapable of being ratified by the company.

CHAPTER 8
DIRECTORS' RESIDENTIAL ADDRESSES: PROTECTION FROM DISCLOSURE

240 Protected information

(1) This Chapter makes provision for protecting, in the case of a company director who is an individual—

(a) information as to his usual residential address;

(b) the information that his service address is his usual residential address.

(2) That information is referred to in this Chapter as "protected information".

(3) Information does not cease to be protected information on the individual ceasing to be a director of the company.

References in this Chapter to a director include, to that extent, a former director.

241 Protected information: restriction on use or disclosure by company

(1) A company must not use or disclose protected information about any of its directors, except—

(a) for communicating with the director concerned,

(b) in order to comply with any requirement of the Companies Acts as to particulars to be sent to the registrar, or

(c) in accordance with section 244 (disclosure under court order).

(2) Subsection (1) does not prohibit any use or disclosure of protected information with the consent of the director concerned.

242 Protected information: restriction on use or disclosure by registrar

(1) The registrar must omit protected information from the material on the register that is available for inspection where—

(a) it is contained in a document delivered to him in which such information is required to be stated, and

(b) in the case of a document having more than one part, it is contained in a part of the document in which such information is required to be stated.

(2) The registrar is not obliged—

(a) to check other documents or (as the case may be) other parts of the document to ensure the absence of protected information, or

(b) to omit from the material that is available for public inspection anything registered before this Chapter comes into force.

(3) The registrar must not use or disclose protected information except—
(a) as permitted by section 243 (permitted use or disclosure by registrar), or
(b) in accordance with section 244 (disclosure under court order).

243 Permitted use or disclosure by the registrar

(1) The registrar may use protected information for communicating with the director in question.
(2) The registrar may disclose protected information—
(a) to a public authority specified for the purposes of this section by regulations made by the Secretary of State, or
(b) to a credit reference agency.
(3) The Secretary of State may make provision by regulations—
(a) specifying conditions for the disclosure of protected information in accordance with this section, and
(b) providing for the charging of fees.
(4) The Secretary of State may make provision by regulations requiring the registrar, on application, to refrain from disclosing protected information relating to a director to a credit reference agency.
(5) Regulations under subsection (4) may make provision as to—
(a) who may make an application,
(b) the grounds on which an application may be made,
(c) the information to be included in and documents to accompany an application, and
(d) how an application is to be determined.
(6) Provision under subsection (5)(d) may in particular—
(a) confer a discretion on the registrar;
(b) provide for a question to be referred to a person other than the registrar for the purposes of determining the application.
(7) In this section—
"credit reference agency" means a person carrying on a business comprising the furnishing of information relevant to the financial standing of individuals, being information collected by the agency for that purpose; and
"public authority" includes any person or body having functions of a public nature.
(8) Regulations under this section are subject to negative resolution procedure.

244 Disclosure under court order

(1) The court may make an order for the disclosure of protected information by the company or by the registrar if—
(a) there is evidence that service of documents at a service address other than the director's usual residential address is not effective to bring them to the notice of the director, or
(b) it is necessary or expedient for the information to be provided in connection with the enforcement of an order or decree of the court,
and the court is otherwise satisfied that it is appropriate to make the order.
(2) An order for disclosure by the registrar is to be made only if the company—
(a) does not have the director's usual residential address, or
(b) has been dissolved.
(3) The order may be made on the application of a liquidator, creditor or member of the company, or any other person appearing to the court to have a sufficient interest.
(4) The order must specify the persons to whom, and purposes for which, disclosure is authorised.

245 Circumstances in which registrar may put address on the public record

(1) The registrar may put a director's usual residential address on the public record if—
(a) communications sent by the registrar to the director and requiring a response within a specified period remain unanswered, or
(b) there is evidence that service of documents at a service address provided in place of the director's usual residential address is not effective to bring them to the notice of the director.

(2) The registrar must give notice of the proposal—
(a) to the director, and
(b) to every company of which the registrar has been notified that the individual is a director.
(3) The notice must—
(a) state the grounds on which it is proposed to put the director's usual residential address on the public record, and
(b) specify a period within which representations may be made before that is done.
(4) It must be sent to the director at his usual residential address, unless it appears to the registrar that service at that address may be ineffective to bring it to the individual's notice, in which case it may be sent to any service address provided in place of that address.
(5) The registrar must take account of any representations received within the specified period.
(6) What is meant by putting the address on the public record is explained in section 246.

246 Putting the address on the public record

(1) The registrar, on deciding in accordance with section 245 that a director's usual residential address is to be put on the public record, shall proceed as if notice of a change of registered particulars had been given—
(a) stating that address as the director's service address, and
(b) stating that the director's usual residential address is the same as his service address.
(2) The registrar must give notice of having done so—
(a) to the director, and
(b) to the company.
(3) On receipt of the notice the company must—
(a) enter the director's usual residential address in its register of directors as his service address, and
(b) state in its register of directors' residential addresses that his usual residential address is the same as his service address.
(4) If the company has been notified by the director in question of a more recent address as his usual residential address, it must—
(a) enter that address in its register of directors as the director's service address, and
(b) give notice to the registrar as on a change of registered particulars.
(5) If a company fails to comply with subsection (3) or (4), an offence is committed by—
(a) the company, and
(b) every officer of the company who is in default.

Version applying in Scotland

(6) A person guilty of an offence under subsection (5) is liable on summary conviction to a fine not exceeding level 5 on the standard scale and, for continued contravention, a daily default fine not exceeding one-tenth of level 5 on the standard scale.

Version applying in England and Wales

(6) A person guilty of an offence under subsection (5) is liable on summary conviction to a fine not exceeding level 5 on the standard scale and, for continued contravention, a daily default fine not exceeding one-tenth of the greater of £5,000 or level 4 on the standard scale.
(7) A director whose usual residential address has been put on the public record by the registrar under this section may not register a service address other than his usual residential address for a period of five years from the date of the registrar's decision.

CHAPTER 9
SUPPLEMENTARY PROVISIONS

Provision for employees on cessation or transfer of business

247 Power to make provision for employees on cessation or transfer of business

(1) The powers of the directors of a company include (if they would not otherwise do so) power to make provision for the benefit of persons employed or formerly employed by

the company, or any of its subsidiaries, in connection with the cessation or the transfer to any person of the whole or part of the undertaking of the company or that subsidiary.

(2) This power is exercisable notwithstanding the general duty imposed by section 172 (duty to promote the success of the company).

(3) In the case of a company that is a charity it is exercisable notwithstanding any restrictions on the directors' powers (or the company's capacity) flowing from the objects of the company.

(4) The power may only be exercised if sanctioned—
  (a) by a resolution of the company, or
  (b) by a resolution of the directors,
in accordance with the following provisions.

(5) A resolution of the directors—
  (a) must be authorised by the company's articles, and
  (b) is not sufficient sanction for payments to or for the benefit of directors, former directors or shadow directors.

(6) Any other requirements of the company's articles as to the exercise of the power conferred by this section must be complied with.

(7) Any payment under this section must be made—
  (a) before the commencement of any winding up of the company, and
  (b) out of profits of the company that are available for dividend.

Records of meetings of directors

248 Minutes of directors' meetings

(1) Every company must cause minutes of all proceedings at meetings of its directors to be recorded.

(2) The records must be kept for at least ten years from the date of the meeting.

(3) If a company fails to comply with this section, an offence is committed by every officer of the company who is in default.

(4) A person guilty of an offence under this section is liable on summary conviction to a fine not exceeding level 3 on the standard scale and, for continued contravention, a daily default fine not exceeding one-tenth of level 3 on the standard scale.

249 Minutes as evidence

(1) Minutes recorded in accordance with section 248, if purporting to be authenticated by the chairman of the meeting or by the chairman of the next directors' meeting, are evidence (in Scotland, sufficient evidence) of the proceedings at the meeting.

(2) Where minutes have been made in accordance with that section of the proceedings of a meeting of directors, then, until the contrary is proved—
  (a) the meeting is deemed duly held and convened,
  (b) all proceedings at the meeting are deemed to have duly taken place, and
  (c) all appointments at the meeting are deemed valid.

Meaning of "director" and "shadow director"

250 "Director"

In the Companies Acts "director" includes any person occupying the position of director, by whatever name called.

251 "Shadow director"

(1) In the Companies Acts "shadow director", in relation to a company, means a person in accordance with whose directions or instructions the directors of the company are accustomed to act.

(2) A person is not to be regarded as a shadow director by reason only that the directors act—
  (a) on advice given by that person in a professional capacity;
  (b) in accordance with instructions, a direction, guidance or advice given by that person in the exercise of a function conferred by or under an enactment;
  (c) in accordance with guidance or advice given by that person in that person's

capacity as a Minister of the Crown (within the meaning of the Ministers of the Crown Act 1975).

(3) A body corporate is not to be regarded as a shadow director of any of its subsidiary companies for the purposes of—

Chapter 2 (general duties of directors),

Chapter 4 (transactions requiring members' approval), or Chapter 6 (contract with sole member who is also a director),

by reason only that the directors of the subsidiary are accustomed to act in accordance with its directions or instructions.

Other definitions

252 Persons connected with a director

(1) This section defines what is meant by references in this Part to a person being "connected" with a director of a company (or a director being "connected" with a person).

(2) The following persons (and only those persons) are connected with a director of a company—

(a) members of the director's family (see section 253);

(b) a body corporate with which the director is connected (as defined in section 254);

(c) a person acting in his capacity as trustee of a trust—

(i) the beneficiaries of which include the director or a person who by virtue of paragraph (a) or (b) is connected with him, or

(ii) the terms of which confer a power on the trustees that may be exercised for the benefit of the director or any such person,

other than a trust for the purposes of an employees' share scheme or a pension scheme;

(d) a person acting in his capacity as partner—

(i) of the director, or

(ii) of a person who, by virtue of paragraph (a), (b) or (c), is connected with that director;

(e) a firm that is a legal person under the law by which it is governed and in which—

(i) the director is a partner,

(ii) a partner is a person who, by virtue of paragraph (a), (b) or (c) is connected with the director, or

(iii) a partner is a firm in which the director is a partner or in which there is a partner who, by virtue of paragraph (a), (b) or (c), is connected with the director.

(3) References in this Part to a person connected with a director of a company do not include a person who is himself a director of the company.

253 Members of a director's family

(1) This section defines what is meant by references in this Part to members of a director's family.

(2) For the purposes of this Part the members of a director's family are—

(a) the director's spouse or civil partner;

(b) any other person (whether of a different sex or the same sex) with whom the director lives as partner in an enduring family relationship;

(c) the director's children or step-children;

(d) any children or step-children of a person within paragraph (b) (and who are not children or step-children of the director) who live with the director and have not attained the age of 18;

(e) the director's parents.

(3) Subsection (2)(b) does not apply if the other person is the director's grandparent or grandchild, sister, brother, aunt or uncle, or nephew or niece.

254 Director "connected with" a body corporate

(1) This section defines what is meant by references in this Part to a director being "connected with" a body corporate.

(2) A director is connected with a body corporate if, but only if, he and the persons connected with him together—
  (a) are interested in shares comprised in the equity share capital of that body corporate of a nominal value equal to at least 20% of that share capital, or
  (b) are entitled to exercise or control the exercise of more than 20% of the voting power at any general meeting of that body.
(3) The rules set out in Schedule 1 (references to interest in shares or debentures) apply for the purposes of this section.
(4) References in this section to voting power the exercise of which is controlled by a director include voting power whose exercise is controlled by a body corporate controlled by him.
(5) Shares in a company held as treasury shares, and any voting rights attached to such shares, are disregarded for the purposes of this section.
(6) For the avoidance of circularity in the application of section 252 (meaning of "connected person")—
  (a) a body corporate with which a director is connected is not treated for the purposes of this section as connected with him unless it is also connected with him by virtue of subsection (2)(c) or (d) of that section (connection as trustee or partner); and
  (b) a trustee of a trust the beneficiaries of which include (or may include) a body corporate with which a director is connected is not treated for the purposes of this section as connected with a director by reason only of that fact.

255 Director "controlling" a body corporate

(1) This section defines what is meant by references in this Part to a director "controlling" a body corporate.
(2) A director of a company is taken to control a body corporate if, but only if—
  (a) he or any person connected with him—
    (i) is interested in any part of the equity share capital of that body, or
    (ii) is entitled to exercise or control the exercise of any part of the voting power at any general meeting of that body, and
  (b) he, the persons connected with him and the other directors of that company, together—
    (i) are interested in more than 50% of that share capital, or
    (ii) are entitled to exercise or control the exercise of more than 50% of that voting power.
(3) The rules set out in Schedule 1 (references to interest in shares or debentures) apply for the purposes of this section.
(4) References in this section to voting power the exercise of which is controlled by a director include voting power whose exercise is controlled by a body corporate controlled by him.
(5) Shares in a company held as treasury shares, and any voting rights attached to such shares, are disregarded for the purposes of this section.
(6) For the avoidance of circularity in the application of section 252 (meaning of "connected person")—
  (a) a body corporate with which a director is connected is not treated for the purposes of this section as connected with him unless it is also connected with him by virtue of subsection (2)(c) or (d) of that section (connection as trustee or partner); and
  (b) a trustee of a trust the beneficiaries of which include (or may include) a body corporate with which a director is connected is not treated for the purposes of this section as connected with a director by reason only of that fact.

256 Associated bodies corporate

For the purposes of this Part—
  (a) bodies corporate are associated if one is a subsidiary of the other or both are subsidiaries of the same body corporate, and
  (b) companies are associated if one is a subsidiary of the other or both are subsidiaries of the same body corporate.

257 References to company's constitution

(1) References in this Part to a company's constitution include—
  (a) any resolution or other decision come to in accordance with the constitution, and
  (b) any decision by the members of the company, or a class of members, that is treated by virtue of any enactment or rule of law as equivalent to a decision by the company.

(2) This is in addition to the matters mentioned in section 17 (general provision as to matters contained in company's constitution).

General

258 Power to increase financial limits

(1) The Secretary of State may by order substitute for any sum of money specified in this Part a larger sum specified in the order.
(2) An order under this section is subject to negative resolution procedure.
(3) An order does not have effect in relation to anything done or not done before it comes into force.
Accordingly, proceedings in respect of any liability incurred before that time may be continued or instituted as if the order had not been made.

259 Transactions under foreign law

For the purposes of this Part it is immaterial whether the law that (apart from this Act) governs an arrangement or transaction is the law of the United Kingdom, or a part of it, or not.

PART 11
DERIVATIVE CLAIMS AND PROCEEDINGS BY MEMBERS

CHAPTER 1
DERIVATIVE CLAIMS IN ENGLAND AND WALES OR NORTHERN IRELAND

260 Derivative claims

(1) This Chapter applies to proceedings in England and Wales or Northern Ireland by a member of a company—
  (a) in respect of a cause of action vested in the company, and
  (b) seeking relief on behalf of the company.
  This is referred to in this Chapter as a "derivative claim".
(2) A derivative claim may only be brought—
  (a) under this Chapter, or
  (b) in pursuance of an order of the court in proceedings under section 994 (proceedings for protection of members against unfair prejudice).
(3) A derivative claim under this Chapter may be brought only in respect of a cause of action arising from an actual or proposed act or omission involving negligence, default, breach of duty or breach of trust by a director of the company.
  The cause of action may be against the director or another person (or both).
(4) It is immaterial whether the cause of action arose before or after the person seeking to bring or continue the derivative claim became a member of the company.
(5) For the purposes of this Chapter—
  (a) "director" includes a former director;
  (b) a shadow director is treated as a director; and
  (c) references to a member of a company include a person who is not a member but to whom shares in the company have been transferred or transmitted by operation of law.

261 Application for permission to continue derivative claim

(1) A member of a company who brings a derivative claim under this Chapter must apply to the court for permission (in Northern Ireland, leave) to continue it.
(2) If it appears to the court that the application and the evidence filed by the applicant in support of it do not disclose a prima facie case for giving permission (or leave), the court—
  (a) must dismiss the application, and
  (b) may make any consequential order it considers appropriate.
(3) If the application is not dismissed under subsection (2), the court—
  (a) may give directions as to the evidence to be provided by the company, and
  (b) may adjourn the proceedings to enable the evidence to be obtained.

(4) On hearing the application, the court may—
- (a) give permission (or leave) to continue the claim on such terms as it thinks fit,
- (b) refuse permission (or leave) and dismiss the claim, or
- (c) adjourn the proceedings on the application and give such directions as it thinks fit.

262 Application for permission to continue claim as a derivative claim

(1) This section applies where—
- (a) a company has brought a claim, and
- (b) the cause of action on which the claim is based could be pursued as a derivative claim under this Chapter.

(2) A member of the company may apply to the court for permission (in Northern Ireland, leave) to continue the claim as a derivative claim on the ground that—
- (a) the manner in which the company commenced or continued the claim amounts to an abuse of the process of the court,
- (b) the company has failed to prosecute the claim diligently, and
- (c) it is appropriate for the member to continue the claim as a derivative claim.

(3) If it appears to the court that the application and the evidence filed by the applicant in support of it do not disclose a prima facie case for giving permission (or leave), the court—
- (a) must dismiss the application, and
- (b) may make any consequential order it considers appropriate.

(4) If the application is not dismissed under subsection (3), the court—
- (a) may give directions as to the evidence to be provided by the company, and
- (b) may adjourn the proceedings to enable the evidence to be obtained.

(5) On hearing the application, the court may—
- (a) give permission (or leave) to continue the claim as a derivative claim on such terms as it thinks fit,
- (b) refuse permission (or leave) and dismiss the application, or
- (c) adjourn the proceedings on the application and give such directions as it thinks fit.

263 Whether permission to be given

(1) The following provisions have effect where a member of a company applies for permission (in Northern Ireland, leave) under section 261 or 262.

(2) Permission (or leave) must be refused if the court is satisfied—
- (a) that a person acting in accordance with section 172 (duty to promote the success of the company) would not seek to continue the claim, or
- (b) where the cause of action arises from an act or omission that is yet to occur, that the act or omission has been authorised by the company, or
- (c) where the cause of action arises from an act or omission that has already occurred, that the act or omission—
  - (i) was authorised by the company before it occurred, or
  - (ii) has been ratified by the company since it occurred.

(3) In considering whether to give permission (or leave) the court must take into account, in particular—
- (a) whether the member is acting in good faith in seeking to continue the claim;
- (b) the importance that a person acting in accordance with section 172 (duty to promote the success of the company) would attach to continuing it;
- (c) where the cause of action results from an act or omission that is yet to occur, whether the act or omission could be, and in the circumstances would be likely to be—
  - (i) authorised by the company before it occurs, or
  - (ii) ratified by the company after it occurs;
- (d) where the cause of action arises from an act or omission that has already occurred, whether the act or omission could be, and in the circumstances would be likely to be, ratified by the company;
- (e) whether the company has decided not to pursue the claim;
- (f) whether the act or omission in respect of which the claim is brought gives rise to a cause of action that the member could pursue in his own right rather than on behalf of the company.

(4) In considering whether to give permission (or leave) the court shall have particular regard to any evidence before it as to the views of members of the company who have no personal interest, direct or indirect, in the matter.

(5) The Secretary of State may by regulations—

(a) amend subsection (2) so as to alter or add to the circumstances in which permission (or leave) is to be refused;

(b) amend subsection (3) so as to alter or add to the matters that the court is required to take into account in considering whether to give permission (or leave).

(6) Before making any such regulations the Secretary of State shall consult such persons as he considers appropriate.

(7) Regulations under this section are subject to affirmative resolution procedure.

264 Application for permission to continue derivative claim brought by another member

(1) This section applies where a member of a company ("the claimant")—

(a) has brought a derivative claim,

(b) has continued as a derivative claim a claim brought by the company, or

(c) has continued a derivative claim under this section.

(2) Another member of the company ("the applicant") may apply to the court for permission (in Northern Ireland, leave) to continue the claim on the ground that—

(a) the manner in which the proceedings have been commenced or continued by the claimant amounts to an abuse of the process of the court,

(b) the claimant has failed to prosecute the claim diligently, and

(c) it is appropriate for the applicant to continue the claim as a derivative claim.

(3) If it appears to the court that the application and the evidence filed by the applicant in support of it do not disclose a prima facie case for giving permission (or leave), the court—

(a) must dismiss the application, and

(b) may make any consequential order it considers appropriate.

(4) If the application is not dismissed under subsection (3), the court—

(a) may give directions as to the evidence to be provided by the company, and

(b) may adjourn the proceedings to enable the evidence to be obtained.

(5) On hearing the application, the court may—

(a) give permission (or leave) to continue the claim on such terms as it thinks fit,

(b) refuse permission (or leave) and dismiss the application, or

(c) adjourn the proceedings on the application and give such directions as it thinks fit.

CHAPTER 2

DERIVATIVE PROCEEDINGS IN SCOTLAND

265 Derivative proceedings

(1) In Scotland, a member of a company may raise proceedings in respect of an act or omission specified in subsection (3) in order to protect the interests of the company and obtain a remedy on its behalf.

(2) A member of a company may raise such proceedings only under subsection (1).

(3) The act or omission referred to in subsection (1) is any actual or proposed act or omission involving negligence, default, breach of duty or breach of trust by a director of the company.

(4) Proceedings may be raised under subsection (1) against (either or both)—

(a) the director referred to in subsection (3), or

(b) another person.

(5) It is immaterial whether the act or omission in respect of which the proceedings are to be raised or, in the case of continuing proceedings under section 267 or 269, are raised, arose before or after the person seeking to raise or continue them became a member of the company.

(6) This section does not affect—

(a) any right of a member of a company to raise proceedings in respect of an act or omission specified in subsection (3) in order to protect his own interests and obtain a remedy on his own behalf, or
(b) the court's power to make an order under section 996(2)(c) or anything done under such an order.
(7) In this Chapter—
(a) proceedings raised under subsection (1) are referred to as "derivative proceedings",
(b) the act or omission in respect of which they are raised is referred to as the "cause of action",
(c) "director" includes a former director,
(d) references to a director include a shadow director, and
(e) references to a member of a company include a person who is not a member but to whom shares in the company have been transferred or transmitted by operation of law.

266 Requirement for leave and notice

(1) Derivative proceedings may be raised by a member of a company only with the leave of the court.
(2) An application for leave must—
(a) specify the cause of action, and
(b) summarise the facts on which the derivative proceedings are to be based.
(3) If it appears to the court that the application and the evidence produced by the applicant in support of it do not disclose a prima facie case for granting it, the court—
(a) must refuse the application, and
(b) may make any consequential order it considers appropriate.
(4) If the application is not refused under subsection (3)—
(a) the applicant must serve the application on the company,
(b) the court—
(i) may make an order requiring evidence to be produced by the company, and
(ii) may adjourn the proceedings on the application to enable the evidence to be obtained, and
(c) the company is entitled to take part in the further proceedings on the application.
(5) On hearing the application, the court may—
(a) grant the application on such terms as it thinks fit,
(b) refuse the application, or
(c) adjourn the proceedings on the application and make such order as to further procedure as it thinks fit.

267 Application to continue proceedings as derivative proceedings

(1) This section applies where—
(a) a company has raised proceedings, and
(b) the proceedings are in respect of an act or omission which could be the basis for derivative proceedings.
(2) A member of the company may apply to the court to be substituted for the company in the proceedings, and for the proceedings to continue in consequence as derivative proceedings, on the ground that—
(a) the manner in which the company commenced or continued the proceedings amounts to an abuse of the process of the court,
(b) the company has failed to prosecute the proceedings diligently, and
(c) it is appropriate for the member to be substituted for the company in the proceedings.
(3) If it appears to the court that the application and the evidence produced by the applicant in support of it do not disclose a prima facie case for granting it, the court—
(a) must refuse the application, and
(b) may make any consequential order it considers appropriate.
(4) If the application is not refused under subsection (3)—
(a) the applicant must serve the application on the company,
(b) the court—
(i) may make an order requiring evidence to be produced by the company, and

(ii) may adjourn the proceedings on the application to enable the evidence to be obtained, and

(c) the company is entitled to take part in the further proceedings on the application.

(5) On hearing the application, the court may—

(a) grant the application on such terms as it thinks fit,

(b) refuse the application, or

(c) adjourn the proceedings on the application and make such order as to further procedure as it thinks fit.

268 Granting of leave

(1) The court must refuse leave to raise derivative proceedings or an application under section 267 if satisfied—

(a) that a person acting in accordance with section 172 (duty to promote the success of the company) would not seek to raise or continue the proceedings (as the case may be), or

(b) where the cause of action is an act or omission that is yet to occur, that the act or omission has been authorised by the company, or

(c) where the cause of action is an act or omission that has already occurred, that the act or omission—

(i) was authorised by the company before it occurred, or

(ii) has been ratified by the company since it occurred.

(2) In considering whether to grant leave to raise derivative proceedings or an application under section 267, the court must take into account, in particular—

(a) whether the member is acting in good faith in seeking to raise or continue the proceedings (as the case may be),

(b) the importance that a person acting in accordance with section 172 (duty to promote the success of the company) would attach to raising or continuing them (as the case may be),

(c) where the cause of action is an act or omission that is yet to occur, whether the act or omission could be, and in the circumstances would be likely to be—

(i) authorised by the company before it occurs, or

(ii) ratified by the company after it occurs,

(d) where the cause of action is an act or omission that has already occurred, whether the act or omission could be, and in the circumstances would be likely to be, ratified by the company,

(e) whether the company has decided not to raise proceedings in respect of the same cause of action or to persist in the proceedings (as the case may be),

(f) whether the cause of action is one which the member could pursue in his own right rather than on behalf of the company.

(3) In considering whether to grant leave to raise derivative proceedings or an application under section 267, the court shall have particular regard to any evidence before it as to the views of members of the company who have no personal interest, direct or indirect, in the matter.

(4) The Secretary of State may by regulations—

(a) amend subsection (1) so as to alter or add to the circumstances in which leave or an application is to be refused,

(b) amend subsection (2) so as to alter or add to the matters that the court is required to take into account in considering whether to grant leave or an application.

(5) Before making any such regulations the Secretary of State shall consult such persons as he considers appropriate.

(6) Regulations under this section are subject to affirmative resolution procedure.

269 Application by member to be substituted for member pursuing derivative proceedings

(1) This section applies where a member of a company ("the claimant")—

(a) has raised derivative proceedings,

(b) has continued as derivative proceedings raised by the company, or

(c) has continued derivative proceedings under this section.

(2) Another member of the company ("the applicant") may apply to the court to be substituted for the claimant in the action on the ground that—

(a) the manner in which the proceedings have been commenced or continued by the claimant amounts to an abuse of the process of the court,
(b) the claimant has failed to prosecute the proceedings diligently, and
(c) it is appropriate for the applicant to be substituted for the claimant in the proceedings.

(3) If it appears to the court that the application and the evidence produced by the applicant in support of it do not disclose a prima facie case for granting it, the court—
(a) must refuse the application, and
(b) may make any consequential order it considers appropriate.

(4) If the application is not refused under subsection (3)—
(a) the applicant must serve the application on the company,
(b) the court—
(i) may make an order requiring evidence to be produced by the company, and
(ii) may adjourn the proceedings on the application to enable the evidence to be obtained, and
(c) the company is entitled to take part in the further proceedings on the application.

(5) On hearing the application, the court may—
(a) grant the application on such terms as it thinks fit,
(b) refuse the application, or
(c) adjourn the proceedings on the application and make such order as to further procedure as it thinks fit.

PART 12
COMPANY SECRETARIES

Private companies

270 Private company not required to have secretary

(1) A private company is not required to have a secretary.

(2) References in the Companies Acts to a private company "without a secretary" are to a private company that for the time being is taking advantage of the exemption in subsection (1); and references to a private company "with a secretary" shall be construed accordingly.

(3) In the case of a private company without a secretary—
(a) anything authorised or required to be given or sent to, or served on, the company by being sent to its secretary—
(i) may be given or sent to, or served on, the company itself, and
(ii) if addressed to the secretary shall be treated as addressed to the company; and
(b) anything else required or authorised to be done by or to the secretary of the company may be done by or to—
(i) a director, or
(ii) a person authorised generally or specifically in that behalf by the directors.

Public companies

271 Public company required to have secretary

A public company must have a secretary.

272 Direction requiring public company to appoint secretary

(1) If it appears to the Secretary of State that a public company is in breach of section 271 (requirement to have secretary), the Secretary of State may give the company a direction under this section.

(2) The direction must state that the company appears to be in breach of that section and specify—
(a) what the company must do in order to comply with the direction, and
(b) the period within which it must do so.

That period must be not less than one month or more than three months after the date on which the direction is given.

(3) The direction must also inform the company of the consequences of failing to comply.

(4) Where the company is in breach of section 271 it must comply with the direction by—
  (a) making the necessary appointment, and
  (b) giving notice of it under section 276,

before the end of the period specified in the direction.

(5) If the company has already made the necessary appointment, it must comply with the direction by giving notice of it under section 276 before the end of the period specified in the direction.

(6) If a company fails to comply with a direction under this section, an offence is committed by—
  (a) the company, and
  (b) every officer of the company who is in default.

For this purpose a shadow director is treated as an officer of the company.

Version applying to Scotland

(7) A person guilty of an offence under this section is liable on summary conviction to a fine not exceeding level 5 on the standard scale and, for continued contravention, a daily default fine not exceeding one-tenth of level 5 on the standard scale.

Version applying to England and Wales

(7) A person guilty of an offence under this section is liable on summary conviction to a fine not exceeding level 5 on the standard scale and, for continued contravention, a daily default fine not exceeding one-tenth of level 5 on the standard scale.

273 Qualifications of secretaries of public companies

(1) It is the duty of the directors of a public company to take all reasonable steps to secure that the secretary (or each joint secretary) of the company—
  (a) is a person who appears to them to have the requisite knowledge and experience to discharge the functions of secretary of the company, and
  (b) has one or more of the following qualifications.

(2) The qualifications are—
  (a) that he has held the office of secretary of a public company for at least three of the five years immediately preceding his appointment as secretary;
  (b) that he is a member of any of the bodies specified in subsection (3);
  (c) that he is a barrister, advocate or solicitor called or admitted in any part of the United Kingdom;
  (d) that he is a person who, by virtue of his holding or having held any other position or his being a member of any other body, appears to the directors to be capable of discharging the functions of secretary of the company.

(3) The bodies referred to in subsection (2)(b) are—
  (a) the Institute of Chartered Accountants in England and Wales;
  (b) the Institute of Chartered Accountants of Scotland;
  (c) the Association of Chartered Certified Accountants;
  (d) the Institute of Chartered Accountants in Ireland;
  (e) the Institute of Chartered Secretaries and Administrators;
  (f) the Chartered Institute of Management Accountants;
  (g) the Chartered Institute of Public Finance and Accountancy.

Provisions applying to private companies with a secretary and to public companies

274 Discharge of functions where office vacant or secretary unable to act

Where in the case of any company the office of secretary is vacant, or there is for any other reason no secretary capable of acting, anything required or authorised to be done by or to the secretary may be done—
  (a) by or to an assistant or deputy secretary (if any), or
  (b) if there is no assistant or deputy secretary or none capable of acting, by or to any person authorised generally or specifically in that behalf by the directors.

275 Duty to keep register of secretaries

(1) A company must keep a register of its secretaries.

(2) The register must contain the required particulars (see sections 277 to 279) of the person who is, or persons who are, the secretary or joint secretaries of the company.

(3) The register must be kept available for inspection—
  (a) at the company's registered office, or

(b) at a place specified in regulations under section 1136.

(4) The company must give notice to the registrar—

(a) of the place at which the register is kept available for inspection, and

(b) of any change in that place,

unless it has at all times been kept at the company's registered office.

(5) The register must be open to the inspection—

(a) of any member of the company without charge, and

(b) of any other person on payment of such fee as may be prescribed.

(6) If default is made in complying with subsection (1), (2) or (3), or if default is made for 14 days in complying with subsection (4), or if an inspection required under subsection (5) is refused, an offence is committed by—

(a) the company, and

(b) every officer of the company who is in default.

For this purpose a shadow director is treated as an officer of the company.

Version applying in Scotland

(7) A person guilty of an offence under this section is liable on summary conviction to a fine not exceeding level 5 on the standard scale and, for continued contravention, a daily default fine not exceeding one-tenth of level 5 on the standard scale.

Version applying in England and Wales

(7) A person guilty of an offence under this section is liable on summary conviction to a fine not exceeding level 5 on the standard scale and, for continued contravention, a daily default fine not exceeding one-tenth of the greater of £5,000 or level 4 on the standard scale.

(8) In the case of a refusal of inspection of the register, the court may by order compel an immediate inspection of it.

276 Duty to notify registrar of changes

(1) A company must, within the period of 14 days from—

(a) a person becoming or ceasing to be its secretary or one of its joint secretaries, or

(b) the occurrence of any change in the particulars contained in its register of secretaries,

give notice to the registrar of the change and of the date on which it occurred.

(2) Notice of a person having become secretary, or one of joint secretaries, of the company must be accompanied by a consent by that person to act in the relevant capacity.

(3) If default is made in complying with this section, an offence is committed by every officer of the company who is in default.

For this purpose a shadow director is treated as an officer of the company.

Version applying in Scotland

(4) A person guilty of an offence under this section is liable on summary conviction to a fine not exceeding level 5 on the standard scale and, for continued contravention, a daily default fine not exceeding one-tenth of level 5 on the standard scale.

Version applying in England and Wales

(4) A person guilty of an offence under this section is liable on summary conviction to a fine not exceeding level 5 on the standard scale and, for continued contravention, a daily default fine not exceeding one-tenth of the greater of £5,000 or level 4 on the standard scale.

277 Particulars of secretaries to be registered: individuals

(1) A company's register of secretaries must contain the following particulars in the case of an individual—

(a) name and any former name;

(b) address.

(2) For the purposes of this section "name" means a person's Christian name (or other forename) and surname, except that in the case of—

(a) a peer, or

(b) an individual usually known by a title,

the title may be stated instead of his Christian name (or other forename) and surname or in addition to either or both of them.

(3) For the purposes of this section a "former name" means a name by which the individual was formerly known for business purposes.

Where a person is or was formerly known by more than one such name, each of them must be stated.

(4) It is not necessary for the register to contain particulars of a former name in the following cases—

(a) in the case of a peer or an individual normally known by a British title, where the name is one by which the person was known previous to the adoption of or succession to the title;

(b) in the case of any person, where the former name—

(i) was changed or disused before the person attained the age of 16 years, or

(ii) has been changed or disused for 20 years or more.

(5) The address required to be stated in the register is a service address.
This may be stated to be "The company's registered office".

278 Particulars of secretaries to be registered: corporate secretaries and firms

(1) A company's register of secretaries must contain the following particulars in the case of a body corporate, or a firm that is a legal person under the law by which it is governed—

(a) corporate or firm name;

(b) registered or principal office;

(c) in the case of an EEA company to which the First Company Law Directive (68/151/EEC) applies, particulars of—

(i) the register in which the company file mentioned in Article 3 of that Directive is kept (including details of the relevant state), and

(ii) the registration number in that register;

(d) in any other case, particulars of—

(i) the legal form of the company or firm and the law by which it is governed, and

(ii) if applicable, the register in which it is entered (including details of the state) and its registration number in that register.

(2) If all the partners in a firm are joint secretaries it is sufficient to state the particulars that would be required if the firm were a legal person and the firm had been appointed secretary.

279 Particulars of secretaries to be registered: power to make regulations

(1) The Secretary of State may make provision by regulations amending—

section 277 (particulars of secretaries to be registered: individuals), or

section 278 (particulars of secretaries to be registered: corporate secretaries and firms),

so as to add to or remove items from the particulars required to be contained in a company's register of secretaries.

(2) Regulations under this section are subject to affirmative resolution procedure.

280 Acts done by person in dual capacity

A provision requiring or authorising a thing to be done by or to a director and the secretary of a company is not satisfied by its being done by or to the same person acting both as director and as, or in place of, the secretary.

PART 13
RESOLUTIONS AND MEETINGS

CHAPTER 1
GENERAL PROVISIONS ABOUT RESOLUTIONS

281 Resolutions

(1) A resolution of the members (or of a class of members) of a private company must be passed—

(a) as a written resolution in accordance with Chapter 2, or

(b) at a meeting of the members (to which the provisions of Chapter 3 apply).

(2) A resolution of the members (or of a class of members) of a public company must be passed at a meeting of the members (to which the provisions of Chapter 3 and, where relevant, Chapter 4 apply).

(3) Where a provision of the Companies Acts—

(a) requires a resolution of a company, or of the members (or a class of members) of a company, and

(b) does not specify what kind of resolution is required,
what is required is an ordinary resolution unless the company's articles require a higher majority (or unanimity).

(4) Nothing in this Part affects any enactment or rule of law as to—
(a) things done otherwise than by passing a resolution,
(b) circumstances in which a resolution is or is not treated as having been passed, or
(c) cases in which a person is precluded from alleging that a resolution has not been duly passed.

282 Ordinary resolutions

(1) An ordinary resolution of the members (or of a class of members) of a company means a resolution that is passed by a simple majority.

(2) A written resolution is passed by a simple majority if it is passed by members representing a simple majority of the total voting rights of eligible members (see Chapter 2).

(3) A resolution passed at a meeting on a show of hands is passed by a simple majority of the votes cast by those entitled to vote.

(4) A resolution passed on a poll taken at a meeting is passed by a simple majority if it is passed by members representing a simple majority of the total voting rights of members who (being entitled to do so) vote in person, by proxy or in advance (see section 322A) on the resolution.

(5) Anything that may be done by ordinary resolution may also be done by special resolution.

283 Special resolutions

(1) A special resolution of the members (or of a class of members) of a company means a resolution passed by a majority of not less than 75%.

(2) A written resolution is passed by a majority of not less than 75% if it is passed by members representing not less than 75% of the total voting rights of eligible members (see Chapter 2).

(3) Where a resolution of a private company is passed as a written resolution—
(a) the resolution is not a special resolution unless it stated that it was proposed as a special resolution, and
(b) if the resolution so stated, it may only be passed as a special resolution.

(4) A resolution passed at a meeting on a show of hands is passed by a majority of not less than 75% if it is passed by not less than 75% of the votes cast by those entitled to vote.

(5) A resolution passed on a poll taken at a meeting is passed by a majority of not less than 75% if it is passed by members representing not less than 75% of the total voting rights of the members who (being entitled to do so) vote in person or by proxy on the resolution.

(6) Where a resolution is passed at a meeting—
(a) the resolution is not a special resolution unless the notice of the meeting included the text of the resolution and specified the intention to propose the resolution as a special resolution, and
(b) if the notice of the meeting so specified, the resolution may only be passed as a special resolution.

284 Votes: general rules

(1) On a vote on a written resolution—
(a) in the case of a company having a share capital, every member has one vote in respect of each share or each £10 of stock held by him, and
(b) in any other case, every member has one vote.

(2) On a vote on a resolution on a show of hands at a meeting, each member present in person has one vote.

(3) On a vote on a resolution on a poll taken at a meeting—
(a) in the case of a company having a share capital, every member has one vote in respect of each share or each £10 of stock held by him, and
(b) in any other case, every member has one vote.

(4) The provisions of this section have effect subject to any provision of the company's articles.

(5) Nothing in this section is to be read as restricting the effect of— section 152 (exercise of rights by nominees),
section 285 (voting by proxy),
section 322 (exercise of voting rights on poll),

section 322A (voting on a poll: votes cast in advance), or
section 323 (representation of corporations at meetings).

285 Voting by proxy

(1) On a vote on a resolution on a show of hands at a meeting, every proxy present who has been duly appointed by one or more members entitled to vote on the resolution has one vote.
This is subject to subsection (2).

(2) On a vote on a resolution on a show of hands at a meeting, a proxy has one vote for and one vote against the resolution if—
(a) the proxy has been duly appointed by more than one member entitled to vote on the resolution, and
(b) the proxy has been instructed by one or more of those members to vote for the resolution and by one or more other of those members to vote against it.

(3) On a poll taken at a meeting of a company all or any of the voting rights of a member may be exercised by one or more duly appointed proxies.

(4) Where a member appoints more than one proxy, subsection (3) does not authorise the exercise by the proxies taken together of more extensive voting rights than could be exercised by the member in person.

(5) Subsections (1) and (2) have effect subject to any provision of the company's articles.

285A Voting rights on poll or written resolution

In relation to a resolution required or authorised by an enactment, if a private company's articles provide that a member has a different number of votes in relation to a resolution when it is passed as a written resolution and when it is passed on a poll taken at a meeting—
(a) the provision about how many votes a member has in relation to the resolution passed on a poll is void, and
(b) a member has the same number of votes in relation to the resolution when it is passed on a poll as the member has when it is passed as a written resolution.

286 Votes of joint holders of shares

(1) In the case of joint holders of shares of a company, only the vote of the senior holder who votes (and any proxies duly authorised by him) may be counted by the company.

(2) For the purposes of this section, the senior holder of a share is determined by the order in which the names of the joint holders appear in the register of members.

(3) Subsections (1) and (2) have effect subject to any provision of the company's articles.

287 Saving for provisions of articles as to determination of entitlement to vote

Nothing in this Chapter affects—
(a) any provision of a company's articles—
(i) requiring an objection to a person's entitlement to vote on a resolution to be made in accordance with the articles, and
(ii) for the determination of any such objection to be final and conclusive, or
(b) the grounds on which such a determination may be questioned in legal proceedings.

CHAPTER 2
WRITTEN RESOLUTIONS

General provisions about written resolutions

288 Written resolutions of private companies

(1) In the Companies Acts a "written resolution" means a resolution of a private company proposed and passed in accordance with this Chapter.

(2) The following may not be passed as a written resolution—
(a) a resolution under section 168 removing a director before the expiration of his period of office;
(b) a resolution under section 510 removing an auditor before the expiration of his term of office.

(3) A resolution may be proposed as a written resolution—
(a) by the directors of a private company (see section 291), or
(b) by the members of a private company (see sections 292 to 295).

(4) References in enactments passed or made before this Chapter comes into force to—
(a) a resolution of a company in general meeting, or
(b) a resolution of a meeting of a class of members of the company,
have effect as if they included references to a written resolution of the members, or of a class of members, of a private company (as appropriate).
(5) A written resolution of a private company has effect as if passed (as the case may be)—
(a) by the company in general meeting, or
(b) by a meeting of a class of members of the company,
and references in enactments passed or made before this section comes into force to a meeting at which a resolution is passed or to members voting in favour of a resolution shall be construed accordingly.

289 Eligible members

(1) In relation to a resolution proposed as a written resolution of a private company, the eligible members are the members who would have been entitled to vote on the resolution on the circulation date of the resolution (see section 290).
(2) If the persons entitled to vote on a written resolution change during the course of the day that is the circulation date of the resolution, the eligible members are the persons entitled to vote on the resolution at the time that the first copy of the resolution is sent or submitted to a member for his agreement.

Circulation of written resolutions

290 Circulation date

References in this Part to the circulation date of a written resolution are to the date on which copies of it are sent or submitted to members in accordance with this Chapter (or if copies are sent or submitted to members on different days, to the first of those days).

291 Circulation of written resolutions proposed by directors

(1) This section applies to a resolution proposed as a written resolution by the directors of the company.
(2) The company must send or submit a copy of the resolution to every eligible member.
(3) The company must do so—
(a) by sending copies at the same time (so far as reasonably practicable) to all eligible members in hard copy form, in electronic form or by means of a website, or
(b) if it is possible to do so without undue delay, by submitting the same copy to each eligible member in turn (or different copies to each of a number of eligible members in turn),
or by sending copies to some members in accordance with paragraph (a) and submitting a copy or copies to other members in accordance with paragraph (b).
(4) The copy of the resolution must be accompanied by a statement informing the member—
(a) how to signify agreement to the resolution (see section 296), and
(b) as to the date by which the resolution must be passed if it is not to lapse (see section 297).
(5) In the event of default in complying with this section, an offence is committed by every officer of the company who is in default.
(6) A person guilty of an offence under this section is liable—
(a) on conviction on indictment, to a fine;
(b) on summary conviction, to a fine not exceeding the statutory maximum.
(7) The validity of the resolution, if passed, is not affected by a failure to comply with this section.

292 Members' power to require circulation of written resolution

(1) The members of a private company may require the company to circulate a resolution that may properly be moved and is proposed to be moved as a written resolution.
(2) Any resolution may properly be moved as a written resolution unless—
(a) it would, if passed, be ineffective (whether by reason of inconsistency with any enactment or the company's constitution or otherwise),
(b) it is defamatory of any person, or
(c) it is frivolous or vexatious.

(3) Where the members require a company to circulate a resolution they may require the company to circulate with it a statement of not more than 1,000 words on the subject matter of the resolution.

(4) A company is required to circulate the resolution and any accompanying statement once it has received requests that it do so from members representing not less than the requisite percentage of the total voting rights of all members entitled to vote on the resolution.

(5) The "requisite percentage" is 5% or such lower percentage as is specified for this purpose in the company's articles.

(6) A request—
   (a) may be in hard copy form or in electronic form,
   (b) must identify the resolution and any accompanying statement, and
   (c) must be authenticated by the person or persons making it.

293 Circulation of written resolution proposed by members

(1) A company that is required under section 292 to circulate a resolution must send or submit to every eligible member—
   (a) a copy of the resolution, and
   (b) a copy of any accompanying statement.

This is subject to section 294(2) (deposit or tender of sum in respect of expenses of circulation) and section 295 (application not to circulate members' statement).

(2) The company must do so—
   (a) by sending copies at the same time (so far as reasonably practicable) to all eligible members in hard copy form, in electronic form or by means of a website, or
   (b) if it is possible to do so without undue delay, by submitting the same copy to each eligible member in turn (or different copies to each of a number of eligible members in turn),

or by sending copies to some members in accordance with paragraph (a) and submitting a copy or copies to other members in accordance with paragraph (b).

(3) The company must send or submit the copies (or, if copies are sent or submitted to members on different days, the first of those copies) not more than 21 days after it becomes subject to the requirement under section 292 to circulate the resolution.

(4) The copy of the resolution must be accompanied by guidance as to—
   (a) how to signify agreement to the resolution (see section 296), and
   (b) the date by which the resolution must be passed if it is not to lapse (see section 297).

(5) In the event of default in complying with this section, an offence is committed by every officer of the company who is in default.

(6) A person guilty of an offence under this section is liable—
   (a) on conviction on indictment, to a fine;
   (b) on summary conviction, to a fine not exceeding the statutory maximum.

(7) The validity of the resolution, if passed, is not affected by a failure to comply with this section.

294 Expenses of circulation

(1) The expenses of the company in complying with section 293 must be paid by the members who requested the circulation of the resolution unless the company resolves otherwise.

(2) Unless the company has previously so resolved, it is not bound to comply with that section unless there is deposited with or tendered to it a sum reasonably sufficient to meet its expenses in doing so.

295 Application not to circulate members' statement

(1) A company is not required to circulate a members' statement under section 293 if, on an application by the company or another person who claims to be aggrieved, the court is satisfied that the rights conferred by section 292 and that section are being abused.

(2) The court may order the members who requested the circulation of the statement to pay the whole or part of the company's costs (in Scotland, expenses) on such an application, even if they are not parties to the application.

Agreeing to written resolutions

296 Procedure for signifying agreement to written resolution

(1) A member signifies his agreement to a proposed written resolution when the company receives from him (or from someone acting on his behalf) an authenticated document—

(a) identifying the resolution to which it relates, and

(b) indicating his agreement to the resolution.

(2) The document must be sent to the company in hard copy form or in electronic form.

(3) A member's agreement to a written resolution, once signified, may not be revoked.

(4) A written resolution is passed when the required majority of eligible members have signified their agreement to it.

297 Period for agreeing to written resolution

(1) A proposed written resolution lapses if it is not passed before the end of—

(a) the period specified for this purpose in the company's articles, or

(b) if none is specified, the period of 28 days beginning with the circulation date.

(2) The agreement of a member to a written resolution is ineffective if signified after the expiry of that period.

Supplementary

298 Sending documents relating to written resolutions by electronic means

(1) Where a company has given an electronic address in any document containing or accompanying a proposed written resolution, it is deemed to have agreed that any document or information relating to that resolution may be sent by electronic means to that address (subject to any conditions or limitations specified in the document).

(2) In this section "electronic address" means any address or number used for the purposes of sending or receiving documents or information by electronic means.

299 Publication of written resolution on website

(1) This section applies where a company sends—

(a) a written resolution, or

(b) a statement relating to a written resolution, to a person by means of a website.

(2) The resolution or statement is not validly sent for the purposes of this Chapter unless the resolution is available on the website throughout the period beginning with the circulation date and ending on the date on which the resolution lapses under section 297.

300 Relationship between this Chapter and provisions of company's articles

A provision of the articles of a private company is void in so far as it would have the effect that a resolution that is required by or otherwise provided for in an enactment could not be proposed and passed as a written resolution.

CHAPTER 3
RESOLUTIONS AT MEETINGS

General provisions about resolutions at meetings

301 Resolutions at general meetings

A resolution of the members of a company is validly passed at a general meeting if—

(a) notice of the meeting and of the resolution is given, and

(b) the meeting is held and conducted,

in accordance with the provisions of this Chapter (and, where relevant, Chapter 4) and the company's articles.

Calling meetings

302 Directors' power to call general meetings

The directors of a company may call a general meeting of the company.

303 Members' power to require directors to call general meeting

(1) The members of a company may require the directors to call a general meeting of the company.

(2) The directors are required to call a general meeting once the company has received requests to do so from—
   (a) members representing at least 5% of such of the paid-up capital of the company as carries the right of voting at general meetings of the company (excluding any paid- up capital held as treasury shares); or
   (b) in the case of a company not having a share capital, members who represent at least 5% of the total voting rights of all the members having a right to vote at general meetings.

...

(4) A request—
   (a) must state the general nature of the business to be dealt with at the meeting, and
   (b) may include the text of a resolution that may properly be moved and is intended to be moved at the meeting.

(5) A resolution may properly be moved at a meeting unless—
   (a) it would, if passed, be ineffective (whether by reason of inconsistency with any enactment or the company's constitution or otherwise),
   (b) it is defamatory of any person, or
   (c) it is frivolous or vexatious.

(6) A request—
   (a) may be in hard copy form or in electronic form, and
   (b) must be authenticated by the person or persons making it.

304 Directors' duty to call meetings required by members

(1) Directors required under section 303 to call a general meeting of the company must call a meeting—
   (a) within 21 days from the date on which they become subject to the requirement, and
   (b) to be held on a date not more than 28 days after the date of the notice convening the meeting.

(2) If the requests received by the company identify a resolution intended to be moved at the meeting, the notice of the meeting must include notice of the resolution.

(3) The business that may be dealt with at the meeting includes a resolution of which notice is given in accordance with this section.

(4) If the resolution is to be proposed as a special resolution, the directors are treated as not having duly called the meeting if they do not give the required notice of the resolution in accordance with section 283.

305 Power of members to call meeting at company's expense

(1) If the directors—
   (a) are required under section 303 to call a meeting, and
   (b) do not do so in accordance with section 304,

   the members who requested the meeting, or any of them representing more than one half of the total voting rights of all of them, may themselves call a general meeting.

(2) Where the requests received by the company included the text of a resolution intended to be moved at the meeting, the notice of the meeting must include notice of the resolution.

(3) The meeting must be called for a date not more than three months after the date on which the directors become subject to the requirement to call a meeting.

(4) The meeting must be called in the same manner, as nearly as possible, as that in which meetings are required to be called by directors of the company.

(5) The business which may be dealt with at the meeting includes a resolution of which notice is given in accordance with this section.

(6) Any reasonable expenses incurred by the members requesting the meeting by reason of the failure of the directors duly to call a meeting must be reimbursed by the company.

(7) Any sum so reimbursed shall be retained by the company out of any sums due or to become due from the company by way of fees or other remuneration in respect of the services of such of the directors as were in default.

306 Power of court to order meeting

(1) This section applies if for any reason it is impracticable—
   (a) to call a meeting of a company in any manner in which meetings of that company may be called, or
   (b) to conduct the meeting in the manner prescribed by the company's articles or this Act.

(2) The court may, either of its own motion or on the application—
(a) of a director of the company, or
(b) of a member of the company who would be entitled to vote at the meeting, order a meeting to be called, held and conducted in any manner the court thinks fit.
(3) Where such an order is made, the court may give such ancillary or consequential directions as it thinks expedient.
(4) Such directions may include a direction that one member of the company present at the meeting be deemed to constitute a quorum.
(5) A meeting called, held and conducted in accordance with an order under this section is deemed for all purposes to be a meeting of the company duly called, held and conducted.

Notice of meetings

307 Notice required of general meeting

(A1) This section applies to—
(a) a general meeting of a company that is not a traded company; and
(b) a general meeting of a traded company that is an opted-in company (as defined by section 971(1)), where—
(i) the meeting is held to decide whether to take any action that might result in the frustration of a takeover bid for the company; or
(ii) the meeting is held by virtue of section 969 (power of offeror to require general meeting to be held).
(A2) For corresponding provision in relation to general meetings of traded companies (other than meetings within subsection (A1)(b)), see section 307A.
(1) A general meeting of a private company (other than an adjourned meeting) must be called by notice of at least 14 days.
(2) A general meeting of a public company (other than an adjourned meeting) must be called by notice of—
(a) in the case of an annual general meeting, at least 21 days, and
(b) in any other case, at least 14 days.
(3) The company's articles may require a longer period of notice than that specified in subsection (1) or (2).
(4) A general meeting may be called by shorter notice than that otherwise required if shorter notice is agreed by the members.
(5) The shorter notice must be agreed to by a majority in number of the members having a right to attend and vote at the meeting, being a majority who—
(a) together hold not less than the requisite percentage in nominal value of the shares giving a right to attend and vote at the meeting (excluding any shares in the company held as treasury shares), or
(b) in the case of a company not having a share capital, together represent not less than the requisite percentage of the total voting rights at that meeting of all the members.
(6) The requisite percentage is—
(a) in the case of a private company, 90% or such higher percentage (not exceeding 95%) as may be specified in the company's articles;
(b) in the case of a public company, 95%.
(7) Subsections (5) and (6) do not apply to an annual general meeting of a public company (see instead section 337(2)).

307A Notice required of general meeting: certain meetings of traded companies

(1) A general meeting of a traded company must be called by notice of—
(a) in a case where conditions A to C (set out below) are met, at least 14 days;
(b) in any other case, at least 21 days.
(2) Condition A is that the general meeting is not an annual general meeting.
(3) Condition B is that the company offers the facility for members to vote by electronic means accessible to all members who hold shares that carry rights to vote at general meetings. This condition is met if there is a facility, offered by the company and accessible to all such members, to appoint a proxy by means of a website.

(4) Condition C is that a special resolution reducing the period of notice to not less than 14 days has been passed—
(a) at the immediately preceding annual general meeting, or
(b) at a general meeting held since that annual general meeting.
(5) In the case of a company which has not yet held an annual general meeting, condition C is that a special resolution reducing the period of notice to not less than 14 days has been passed at a general meeting.
(6) The company's articles may require a longer period of notice than that specified in subsection (1).
(7) Where a general meeting is adjourned, the adjourned meeting may be called by shorter notice than required by subsection (1).
But in the case of an adjournment for lack of a quorum this subsection applies only if—
(a) no business is to be dealt with at the adjourned meeting the general nature of which was not stated in the notice of the original meeting, and
(b) the adjourned meeting is to be held at least 10 days after the original meeting.
(8) Nothing in this section applies in relation to a general meeting of a kind mentioned in section 307(A1)(b) (certain meetings regarding takeover of opted-in company).

308 Manner in which notice to be given

Notice of a general meeting of a company must be given—
(a) in hard copy form,
(b) in electronic form, or
(c) by means of a website (see section 309),
or partly by one such means and partly by another.

309 Publication of notice of meeting on website

(1) Notice of a meeting is not validly given by a company by means of a website unless it is given in accordance with this section.
(2) When the company notifies a member of the presence of the notice on the website the notification must—
(a) state that it concerns a notice of a company meeting,
(b) specify the place, date and time of the meeting, and
(c) in the case of a public company, state whether the meeting will be an annual general meeting.
(3) The notice must be available on the website throughout the period beginning with the date of that notification and ending with the conclusion of the meeting.

310 Persons entitled to receive notice of meetings

(1) Notice of a general meeting of a company must be sent to—
(a) every member of the company, and
(b) every director.
(2) In subsection (1), the reference to members includes any person who is entitled to a share in consequence of the death or bankruptcy of a member, if the company has been notified of their entitlement.
(3) In subsection (2), the reference to the bankruptcy of a member includes—
(a) the sequestration of the estate of a member;
(b) a member's estate being the subject of a protected trust deed (within the meaning of the Bankruptcy (Scotland) Act 1985).
(4) This section has effect subject to—
(a) any enactment, and
(b) any provision of the company's articles.

311 Contents of notices of meetings

(1) Notice of a general meeting of a company must state—
(a) the time and date of the meeting, and
(b) the place of the meeting.
(2) Notice of a general meeting of a company must state the general nature of the business to be dealt with at the meeting.
In relation to a company other than a traded company, this subsection has effect subject to any provision of the company's articles.

(3) Notice of a general meeting of a traded company must also include—
   (a) a statement giving the address of the website on which the information required by section 311A (traded companies: publication of information in advance of general meeting) is published;
   (b) a statement—
      (i) that the right to vote at the meeting is determined by reference to the register of members, and
      (ii) of the time when that right will be determined in accordance with section 360B(2) (traded companies: share dealings before general meetings);
   (c) a statement of the procedures with which members must comply in order to be able to attend and vote at the meeting (including the date by which they must comply);
   (d) a statement giving details of any forms to be used for the appointment of a proxy;
   (e) where the company offers the facility for members to vote in advance (see section 322A) or by electronic means (see section 360A), a statement of the procedure for doing so (including the date by which it must be done, and details of any forms to be used); and
   (f) a statement of the right of members to ask questions in accordance with section 319A (traded companies: questions at meetings).

311A Traded companies: publication of information in advance of general meeting

(1) A traded company must ensure that the following information relating to a general meeting of the company is made available on a website—
   (a) the matters set out in the notice of the meeting;
   (b) the total numbers of—
      (i) shares in the company, and
      (ii) shares of each class,
   in respect of which members are entitled to exercise voting rights at the meeting;
   (c) the totals of the voting rights that members are entitled to exercise at the meeting in respect of the shares of each class;
   (d) members' statements, members' resolutions and members' matters of business received by the company after the first date on which notice of the meeting is given.
(2) The information must be made available on a website that—
   (a) is maintained by or on behalf of the company, and
   (b) identifies the company.
(3) Access to the information on the website, and the ability to obtain a hard copy of the information from the website, must not be conditional on payment of a fee or otherwise restricted.
(4) The information—
   (a) must be made available—
      (i) in the case of information required by subsection (1)(a) to (c), on or before the first date on which notice of the meeting is given, and
      (ii) in the case of information required by subsection (1)(d), as soon as reasonably practicable, and
   (b) must be kept available throughout the period of two years beginning with the date on which it is first made available on a website in accordance with this section.
(5) A failure to make information available throughout the period specified in subsection (4)(b) is disregarded if—
   (a) the information is made available on the website for part of that period, and
   (b) the failure is wholly attributable to circumstances that it would not be reasonable to have expected the company to prevent or avoid.
(6) The amounts mentioned in subsection (1)(b) and (c) must be ascertained at the latest practicable time before the first date on which notice of the meeting is given.
(7) Failure to comply with this section does not affect the validity of the meeting or of anything done at the meeting.
(8) If this section is not complied with as respects any meeting, an offence is committed by every officer of the company who is in default.

(9) A person guilty of an offence under this section is liable on summary conviction to a fine not exceeding level 3 on the standard scale.

312 Resolution requiring special notice

(1) Where by any provision of the Companies Acts special notice is required of a resolution, the resolution is not effective unless notice of the intention to move it has been given to the company at least 28 days before the meeting at which it is moved.

(2) The company must, where practicable, give its members notice of any such resolution in the same manner and at the same time as it gives notice of the meeting.

(3) Where that is not practicable, the company must give its members notice at least 14 days before the meeting—

- (a) by advertisement in a newspaper having an appropriate circulation, or
- (b) in any other manner allowed by the company's articles.

(4) If, after notice of the intention to move such a resolution has been given to the company, a meeting is called for a date 28 days or less after the notice has been given, the notice is deemed to have been properly given, though not given within the time required.

313 Accidental failure to give notice of resolution or meeting

(1) Where a company gives notice of—

- (a) a general meeting, or
- (b) a resolution intended to be moved at a general meeting,

any accidental failure to give notice to one or more persons shall be disregarded for the purpose of determining whether notice of the meeting or resolution (as the case may be) is duly given.

(2) Except in relation to notice given under—

- (a) section 304 (notice of meetings required by members),
- (b) section 305 (notice of meetings called by members), or
- (c) section 339 (notice of resolutions at AGMs proposed by members), subsection (1) has effect subject to any provision of the company's articles.

Members' statements

314 Members' power to require circulation of statements

(1) The members of a company may require the company to circulate, to members of the company entitled to receive notice of a general meeting, a statement of not more than 1,000 words with respect to—

- (a) a matter referred to in a proposed resolution to be dealt with at that meeting, or
- (b) other business to be dealt with at that meeting.

(2) A company is required to circulate a statement once it has received requests to do so from—

- (a) members representing at least 5% of the total voting rights of all the members who have a relevant right to vote (excluding any voting rights attached to any shares in the company held as treasury shares), or
- (b) at least 100 members who have a relevant right to vote and hold shares in the company on which there has been paid up an average sum, per member, of at least £100.

See also section 153 (exercise of rights where shares held on behalf of others).

(3) In subsection (2), a "relevant right to vote" means—

- (a) in relation to a statement with respect to a matter referred to in a proposed resolution, a right to vote on that resolution at the meeting to which the requests relate, and
- (b) in relation to any other statement, a right to vote at the meeting to which the requests relate.

(4) A request—

- (a) may be in hard copy form or in electronic form,
- (b) must identify the statement to be circulated,
- (c) must be authenticated by the person or persons making it, and
- (d) must be received by the company at least one week before the meeting to which it relates.

315 Company's duty to circulate members' statement

(1) A company that is required under section 314, to circulate a statement must send a copy of it to each member of the company entitled to receive notice of the meeting—
   (a) in the same manner as the notice of the meeting, and
   (b) at the same time as, or as soon as reasonably practicable after, it gives notice of the meeting.

(2) Subsection (1) has effect subject to section 316(2) (deposit or tender of sum in respect of expenses of circulation) and section 317 (application not to circulate members' statement).

(3) In the event of default in complying with this section, an offence is committed by every officer of the company who is in default.

(4) A person guilty of an offence under this section is liable—
   (a) on conviction on indictment, to a fine;
   (b) on summary conviction, to a fine not exceeding the statutory maximum.

316 Expenses of circulating members' statement

(1) The expenses of the company in complying with section 315 need not be paid by the members who requested the circulation of the statement if—
   (a) the meeting to which the requests relate is an annual general meeting of a public company, and
   (b) requests sufficient to require the company to circulate the statement are received before the end of the financial year preceding the meeting.

(2) Otherwise—
   (a) the expenses of the company in complying with that section must be paid by the members who requested the circulation of the statement unless the company resolves otherwise, and
   (b) unless the company has previously so resolved, it is not bound to comply with that section unless there is deposited with or tendered to it, not later than one week before the meeting, a sum reasonably sufficient to meet its expenses in doing so.

317 Application not to circulate members' statement

(1) A company is not required to circulate a members' statement under section 315 if, on an application by the company or another person who claims to be aggrieved, the court is satisfied that the rights conferred by section 314 and that section are being abused.

(2) The court may order the members who requested the circulation of the statement to pay the whole or part of the company's costs (in Scotland, expenses) on such an application, even if they are not parties to the application.

Procedure at meetings

318 Quorum at meetings

(1) In the case of a company limited by shares or guarantee and having only one member, one qualifying person present at a meeting is a quorum.

(2) In any other case, subject to the provisions of the company's articles, two qualifying persons present at a meeting are a quorum, unless—
   (a) each is a qualifying person only because he is authorised under section 323 to act as the representative of a corporation in relation to the meeting, and they are representatives of the same corporation; or
   (b) each is a qualifying person only because he is appointed as proxy of a member in relation to the meeting, and they are proxies of the same member.

(3) For the purposes of this section a "qualifying person" means—
   (a) an individual who is a member of the company,
   (b) a person authorised under section 323 (representation of corporations at meetings) to act as the representative of a corporation in relation to the meeting, or
   (c) a person appointed as proxy of a member in relation to the meeting.

319 Chairman of meeting

(1) A member may be elected to be the chairman of a general meeting by a resolution of the company passed at the meeting.

(2) Subsection (1) is subject to any provision of the company's articles that states who may or may not be chairman.

319A Traded companies: questions at meetings

(1) At a general meeting of a traded company, the company must cause to be answered any question relating to the business being dealt with at the meeting put by a member attending the meeting.

(2) No such answer need be given—

(a) if to do so would—

(i) interfere unduly with the preparation for the meeting, or

(ii) involve the disclosure of confidential information;

(b) if the answer has already been given on a website in the form of an answer to a question; or

(c) if it is undesirable in the interests of the company or the good order of the meeting that the question be answered.

320 Declaration by chairman on a show of hands

(1) On a vote on a resolution at a meeting on a show of hands, a declaration by the chairman that the resolution—

(a) has or has not been passed, or

(b) passed with a particular majority,

is conclusive evidence of that fact without proof of the number or proportion of the votes recorded in favour of or against the resolution.

(2) An entry in respect of such a declaration in minutes of the meeting recorded in accordance with section 355 is also conclusive evidence of that fact without such proof.

(3) This section does not have effect if a poll is demanded in respect of the resolution (and the demand is not subsequently withdrawn).

321 Right to demand a poll

(1) A provision of a company's articles is void in so far as it would have the effect of excluding the right to demand a poll at a general meeting on any question other than—

(a) the election of the chairman of the meeting, or

(b) the adjournment of the meeting.

(2) A provision of a company's articles is void in so far as it would have the effect of making ineffective a demand for a poll on any such question which is made—

(a) by not less than 5 members having the right to vote on the resolution; or

(b) by a member or members representing not less than 10% of the total voting rights of all the members having the right to vote on the resolution (excluding any voting rights attached to any shares in the company held as treasury shares); or

(c) by a member or members holding shares in the company conferring a right to vote on the resolution, being shares on which an aggregate sum has been paid up equal to not less than 10% of the total sum paid up on all the shares conferring that right (excluding shares in the company conferring a right to vote on the resolution which are held as treasury shares).

322 Voting on a poll

On a poll taken at a general meeting of a company, a member entitled to more than one vote need not, if he votes, use all his votes or cast all the votes he uses in the same way.

322A Voting on a poll: votes cast in advance

(1) A company's articles may contain provision to the effect that on a vote on a resolution on a poll taken at a meeting, the votes may include votes cast in advance.

(2) In the case of a traded company any such provision in relation to voting at a general meeting may be made subject only to such requirements and restrictions as are—

(a) necessary to ensure the identification of the person voting, and

(b) proportionate to the achievement of that objective.

Nothing in this subsection affects any power of a company to require reasonable evidence of the entitlement of any person who is not a member to vote.

(3) Any provision of a company's articles is void in so far as it would have the effect of requiring any document casting a vote in advance to be received by the company or another person earlier than the following time—

(a) in the case of a poll taken more than 48 hours after it was demanded, 24 hours before the time appointed for the taking of the poll;

(b) in the case of any other poll, 48 hours before the time for holding the meeting or adjourned meeting.

(4) In calculating the periods mentioned in subsection (3), no account is to be taken of any part of a day that is not a working day.

323 Representation of corporations at meetings

(1) If a corporation (whether or not a company within the meaning of this Act) is a member of a company, it may by resolution of its directors or other governing body authorise a person or persons to act as its representative or representatives at any meeting of the company.

(2) A person authorised by a corporation is entitled to exercise (on behalf of the corporation) the same powers as the corporation could exercise if it were an individual member of the company.
Where a corporation authorises more than one person, this subsection is subject to subsections (3) and (4).

(3) On a vote on a resolution on a show of hands at a meeting of the company, each authorised person has the same voting rights as the corporation would be entitled to.

(4) Where subsection (3) does not apply and more than one authorised person purport to exercise a power under subsection (2) in respect of the same shares—
   (a) if they purport to exercise the power in the same way as each other, the power is treated as exercised in that way;
   (b) if they do not purport to exercise the power in the same way as each other, the power is treated as not exercised.

Proxies

324 Rights to appoint proxies

(1) A member of a company is entitled to appoint another person as his proxy to exercise all or any of his rights to attend and to speak and vote at a meeting of the company.

(2) In the case of a company having a share capital, a member may appoint more than one proxy in relation to a meeting, provided that each proxy is appointed to exercise the rights attached to a different share or shares held by him, or (as the case may be) to a different £10, or multiple of £10, of stock held by him.

324A Obligation of proxy to vote in accordance with instructions

A proxy must vote in accordance with any instructions given by the member by whom the proxy is appointed.

325 Notice of meeting to contain statement of rights

(1) In every notice calling a meeting of a company there must appear, with reasonable prominence, a statement informing the member of—
   (a) his rights under section 324, and
   (b) any more extensive rights conferred by the company's articles to appoint more than one proxy.

(2) Failure to comply with this section does not affect the validity of the meeting or of anything done at the meeting.

(3) If this section is not complied with as respects any meeting, an offence is committed by every officer of the company who is in default.

(4) A person guilty of an offence under this section is liable on summary conviction to a fine not exceeding level 3 on the standard scale.

326 Company-sponsored invitations to appoint proxies

(1) If for the purposes of a meeting there are issued at the company's expense invitations to members to appoint as proxy a specified person or a number of specified persons, the invitations must be issued to all members entitled to vote at the meeting.

(2) Subsection (1) is not contravened if—
   (a) there is issued to a member at his request a form of appointment naming the proxy or a list of persons willing to act as proxy, and
   (b) the form or list is available on request to all members entitled to vote at the meeting.

(3) If subsection (1) is contravened as respects a meeting, an offence is committed by every officer of the company who is in default.

(4) A person guilty of an offence under this section is liable on summary conviction to a fine not exceeding level 3 on the standard scale.

327 Notice required of appointment of proxy etc.

(A1) In the case of a traded company—
- (a) the appointment of a person as proxy for a member must be notified to the company in writing;
- (b) where such an appointment is made, the company may require reasonable evidence of—
  - (i) the identity of the member and of the proxy,
  - (ii) the member's instructions (if any) as to how the proxy is to vote, and
  - (iii) where the proxy is appointed by a person acting on behalf of the member, authority of that person to make the appointment;

  but may not require to be provided with anything else relating to the appointment.

(1) The following provisions apply in the case of traded companies and other companies as regards—
- (a) the appointment of a proxy, and
- (b) any document necessary to show the validity of, or otherwise relating to, the appointment of a proxy.

(2) Any provision of the company's articles is void in so far as it would have the effect of requiring any such appointment or document to be received by the company or another person earlier than the following time—
- (a) in the case of a meeting or adjourned meeting, 48 hours before the time for holding the meeting or adjourned meeting;
- (b) in the case of a poll taken more than 48 hours after it was demanded, 24 hours before the time appointed for the taking of the poll;

(3) In calculating the periods mentioned in subsection (2) no account shall be taken of any part of a day that is not a working day.

328 Chairing meetings

(1) A proxy may be elected to be the chairman of a general meeting by a resolution of the company passed at the meeting.

(2) Subsection (1) is subject to any provision of the company's articles that states who may or who may not be chairman.

329 Right of proxy to demand a poll

(1) The appointment of a proxy to vote on a matter at a meeting of a company authorises the proxy to demand, or join in demanding, a poll on that matter.

(2) In applying the provisions of section 321(2) (requirements for effective demand), a demand by a proxy counts—
- (a) for the purposes of paragraph (a), as a demand by the member;
- (b) for the purposes of paragraph (b), as a demand by a member representing the voting rights that the proxy is authorised to exercise;
- (c) for the purposes of paragraph (c), as a demand by a member holding the shares to which those rights are attached.

330 Notice required of termination of proxy's authority

(A1) In the case of a traded company the termination of the authority of a person to act as proxy must be notified to the company in writing.

(1) The following provisions apply in the case of traded companies and other companies as regards notice that the authority of a person to act as proxy is terminated ("notice of termination").

(2) The termination of the authority of a person to act as proxy does not affect—
- (a) whether he counts in deciding whether there is a quorum at a meeting,
- (b) the validity of anything he does as chairman of a meeting, or
- (c) the validity of a poll demanded by him at a meeting,

unless the company receives notice of the termination before the commencement of the meeting.

(3) The termination of the authority of a person to act as proxy does not affect the validity of a vote given by that person unless the company receives notice of the termination—
- (a) before the commencement of the meeting or adjourned meeting at which the vote is given, or
- (b) in the case of a poll taken more than 48 hours after it is demanded, before the time appointed for taking the poll.

(4) If the company's articles require or permit members to give notice of termination to a person other than the company, the references above to the company receiving notice have effect as if they were or (as the case may be) included a reference to that person.

(5) Subsections (2) and (3) have effect subject to any provision of the company's articles which has the effect of requiring notice of termination to be received by the company or another person at a time earlier than that specified in those subsections.
This is subject to subsection (6).

(6) Any provision of the company's articles is void in so far as it would have the effect of requiring notice of termination to be received by the company or another person earlier than the following time—
(a) in the case of a meeting or adjourned meeting, 48 hours before the time for holding the meeting or adjourned meeting;
(b) in the case of a poll taken more than 48 hours after it was demanded, 24 hours before the time appointed for the taking of the poll;

(7) In calculating the periods mentioned in subsections (3)(b) and (6) no account shall be taken of any part of a day that is not a working day.

331 Saving for more extensive rights conferred by articles

Nothing in sections 324 to 330 (proxies) prevents a company's articles from conferring more extensive rights on members or proxies than are conferred by those sections.

Adjourned meetings

332 Resolution passed at adjourned meeting

Where a resolution is passed at an adjourned meeting of a company, the resolution is for all purposes to be treated as having been passed on the date on which it was in fact passed, and is not to be deemed passed on any earlier date.

Electronic communications

333 Sending documents relating to meetings etc in electronic form

(1) Where a company has given an electronic address in a notice calling a meeting, it is deemed to have agreed that any document or information relating to proceedings at the meeting may be sent by electronic means to that address (subject to any conditions or limitations specified in the notice).

(2) Where a company has given an electronic address—
(a) in an instrument of proxy sent out by the company in relation to the meeting, or
(b) in an invitation to appoint a proxy issued by the company in relation to the meeting, it is deemed to have agreed that any document or information relating to proxies for that meeting may be sent by electronic means to that address (subject to any conditions or limitations specified in the notice).

(3) In subsection (2), documents relating to proxies include—
(a) the appointment of a proxy in relation to a meeting,
(b) any document necessary to show the validity of, or otherwise relating to, the appointment of a proxy, and
(c) notice of the termination of the authority of a proxy.

(4) In this section "electronic address" means any address or number used for the purposes of sending or receiving documents or information by electronic means.

333A Traded company: duty to provide electronic address for receipt of proxies etc

(1) A traded company must provide an electronic address for the receipt of any document or information relating to proxies for a general meeting.

(2) The company must provide the address either—
(a) by giving it when sending out an instrument of proxy for the purposes of the meeting or issuing an invitation to appoint a proxy for those purposes; or
(b) by ensuring that it is made available, throughout the period beginning with the first date on which notice of the meeting is given and ending with the conclusion of the meeting, on the website on which the information required by section 311A(1) is made available.

(3) The company is deemed to have agreed that any document or information relating to proxies for the meeting may be sent by electronic means to the address provided (subject to any limitations specified by the company when providing the address).

(4) In this section—
  (a) documents relating to proxies include—
    (i) the appointment of a proxy for a meeting,
    (ii) any document necessary to show the validity of, or otherwise relating to, the appointment of a proxy, and
    (iii) notice of the termination of the authority of a proxy;
  (b) "electronic address" has the meaning given by section 333(4).

Application to class meetings

334 Application to class meetings

(1) The provisions of this Chapter apply (with necessary modifications) in relation to a meeting of holders of a class of shares as they apply in relation to a general meeting.
This is subject to subsections (2) to (3).

(2) The following provisions of this Chapter do not apply in relation to a meeting of holders of a class of shares–
  (a) sections 303 to 305 (members' power to require directors to call general meeting),
  (b) section 306 (power of court to order meeting), and
  (c) sections 311(3), 311A, 319A, 327(A1), 330(A1) and 333A (additional requirements relating to traded companies).

(2A) Section 307(1) to (6) apply in relation to a meeting of holders of a class of shares in a traded company as they apply in relation to a meeting of holders of a class of shares in a company other than a traded company (and, accordingly, section 307A does not apply in relation to such a meeting).

(3) The following provisions (in addition to those mentioned in subsection (2)) do not apply in relation to a meeting in connection with the variation of rights attached to a class of shares (a "variation of class rights meeting")—
  (a) section 318 (quorum), and
  (b) section 321 (right to demand a poll).

(4) The quorum for a variation of class rights meeting is—
  (a) for a meeting other than an adjourned meeting, two persons present holding at least one-third in nominal value of the issued shares of the class in question (excluding any shares of that class held as treasury shares);
  (b) for an adjourned meeting, one person present holding shares of the class in question.

(5) For the purposes of subsection (4), where a person is present by proxy or proxies, he is treated as holding only the shares in respect of which those proxies are authorised to exercise voting rights.

(6) At a variation of class rights meeting, any holder of shares of the class in question present may demand a poll.

(7) For the purposes of this section—
  (a) any amendment of a provision contained in a company's articles for the variation of the rights attached to a class of shares, or the insertion of any such provision into the articles, is itself to be treated as a variation of those rights, and
  (b) references to the variation of rights attached to a class of shares include references to their abrogation.

335 Application to class meetings: companies without a share capital

(1) The provisions of this Chapter apply (with necessary modifications) in relation to a meeting of a class of members of a company without a share capital as they apply in relation to a general meeting.
This is subject to subsections (2) and (3).

(2) The following provisions of this Chapter do not apply in relation to a meeting of a class of members—
  (a) sections 303 to 305 (members' power to require directors to call general meeting), and
  (b) section 306 (power of court to order meeting).

(3) The following provisions (in addition to those mentioned in subsection (2)) do not apply in relation to a meeting in connection with the variation of the rights of a class of members (a "variation of class rights meeting")—
(a) section 318 (quorum), and
(b) section 321 (right to demand a poll).
(4) The quorum for a variation of class rights meeting is—
(a) for a meeting other than an adjourned meeting, two members of the class present (in person or by proxy) who together represent at least one-third of the voting rights of the class;
(b) for an adjourned meeting, one member of the class present (in person or by proxy).
(5) At a variation of class rights meeting, any member present (in person or by proxy) may demand a poll.
(6) For the purposes of this section—
(a) any amendment of a provision contained in a company's articles for the variation of the rights of a class of members, or the insertion of any such provision into the articles, is itself to be treated as a variation of those rights, and
(b) references to the variation of rights of a class of members include references to their abrogation.

CHAPTER 4
PUBLIC COMPANIES AND TRADED COMPANIES: ADDITIONAL REQUIREMENTS FOR AGMS

336 Public companies and traded companies: annual general meeting

(1) Every public company must hold a general meeting as its annual general meeting in each period of 6 months beginning with the day following its accounting reference date (in addition to any other meetings held during that period).
(1A) Every private company that is a traded company must hold a general meeting as its annual general meeting in each period of 9 months beginning with the day following its accounting reference date (in addition to any other meetings held during that period).
(2) A company that fails to comply with subsection (1) or (1A) as a result of giving notice under section 392 (alteration of accounting reference date)—
(a) specifying a new accounting reference date, and
(b) stating that the current accounting reference period or the previous accounting reference period is to be shortened,
shall be treated as if it had complied with subsection (1) or (1A) if it holds a general meeting as its annual general meeting within 3 months of giving that notice.
(3) If a company fails to comply with subsection (1) or (1A), an offence is committed by every officer of the company who is in default.
(4) A person guilty of an offence under this section is liable—
(a) on conviction on indictment, to a fine;
(b) on summary conviction, to a fine not exceeding the statutory maximum.

337 Public companies and traded companies: notice of AGM

(1) A notice calling an annual general meeting of a public company or a private company that is a traded company must state that the meeting is an annual general meeting.
(2) An annual general meeting of a public company that is not a traded company may be called by shorter notice than that required by section 307(2) or by the company's articles (as the case may be), if all the members entitled to attend and vote at the meeting agree to the shorter notice.
(3) Where a notice calling an annual general meeting of a traded company is given more than 6 weeks before the meeting, the notice must include—
(a) if the company is a public company, a statement of the right under section 338 to require the company to give notice of a resolution to be moved at the meeting, and
(b) whether or not the company is a public company, a statement of the right under section 338A to require the company to include a matter in the business to be dealt with at the meeting.

338 Public companies: members' power to require circulation of resolutions for AGMs

(1) The members of a public company may require the company to give, to members of the company entitled to receive notice of the next annual general meeting, notice of a resolution which may properly be moved and is intended to be moved at that meeting.

(2) A resolution may properly be moved at an annual general meeting unless—
- (a) it would, if passed, be ineffective (whether by reason of inconsistency with any enactment or the company's constitution or otherwise),
- (b) it is defamatory of any person, or
- (c) it is frivolous or vexatious.

(3) A company is required to give notice of a resolution once it has received requests that it do so from—
- (a) members representing at least 5% of the total voting rights of all the members who have a right to vote on the resolution at the annual general meeting to which the requests relate (excluding any voting rights attached to any shares in the company held as treasury shares), or
- (b) at least 100 members who have a right to vote on the resolution at the annual general meeting to which the requests relate and hold shares in the company on which there has been paid up an average sum, per member, of at least £100.

See also section 153 (exercise of rights where shares held on behalf of others).

(4) A request—
- (a) may be in hard copy form or in electronic form,
- (b) must identify the resolution of which notice is to be given,
- (c) must be authenticated by the person or persons making it, and
- (d) must be received by the company not later than—
  - (i) 6 weeks before the annual general meeting to which the requests relate, or
  - (ii) if later, the time at which notice is given of that meeting.

338A Traded companies: members' power to include other matters in business dealt with at AGM

(1) The members of a traded company may request the company to include in the business to be dealt with at an annual general meeting any matter (other than a proposed resolution) which may properly be included in the business.

(2) A matter may properly be included in the business at an annual general meeting unless–
- (a) it is defamatory of any person, or
- (b) it is frivolous or vexatious.

(3) A company is required to include such a matter once it has received requests that it do so from—
- (a) members representing at least 5% of the total voting rights of all the members who have a right to vote at the meeting, or
- (b) at least 100 members who have a right to vote at the meeting and hold shares in the company on which there has been paid up an average sum, per member, of at least £100.

See also section 153 (exercise of rights where shares held on behalf of others).

(4) A request—
- (a) may be in hard copy form or in electronic form,
- (b) must identify the matter to be included in the business,
- (c) must be accompanied by a statement setting out the grounds for the request, and
- (d) must be authenticated by the person or persons making it.

(5) A request must be received by the company not later than—
- (a) 6 weeks before the meeting, or
- (b) if later, the time at which notice of the meeting is given.

339 Public companies: company's duty to circulate members' resolutions for AGMs

(1) A company that is required under section 338 to give notice of a resolution must send a copy of it to each member of the company entitled to receive notice of the annual general meeting—
- (a) in the same manner as notice of the meeting, and
- (b) at the same time as, or as soon as reasonably practicable after, it gives notice of the meeting.

(2) Subsection (1) has effect subject to section 340(2) (deposit or tender of sum in respect of expenses of circulation).
(3) The business which may be dealt with at an annual general meeting includes a resolution of which notice is given in accordance with this section.
(4) In the event of default in complying with this section, an offence is committed by every officer of the company who is in default.
(5) A person guilty of an offence under this section is liable—
  (a) on conviction on indictment, to a fine;
  (b) on summary conviction, to a fine not exceeding the statutory maximum.

340 Public companies: expenses of circulating members' resolutions for AGM

(1) The expenses of the company in complying with section 339 need not be paid by the members who requested the circulation of the resolution if requests sufficient to require the company to circulate it are received before the end of the financial year preceding the meeting.
(2) Otherwise—
  (a) the expenses of the company in complying with that section must be paid by the members who requested the circulation of the resolution unless the company resolves otherwise, and
  (b) unless the company has previously so resolved, it is not bound to comply with that section unless there is deposited with or tendered to it, not later than—
    (i) six weeks before the annual general meeting to which the requests relate, or
    (ii) if later, the time at which notice is given of that meeting,
  a sum reasonably sufficient to meet its expenses in complying with that section.

340A Traded companies: duty to circulate members' matters for AGM

(1) A company that is required under section 338A to include any matter in the business to be dealt with at an annual general meeting must—
  (a) give notice of it to each member of the company entitled to receive notice of the annual general meeting—
    (i) in the same manner as notice of the meeting, and
    (ii) at the same time as, or as soon as reasonably practicable after, it gives notice of the meeting, and
  (b) publish it on the same website as that on which the company published the information required by section 311A.
(2) Subsection (1) has effect subject to section 340B(2) (deposit or tender of sum in respect of expenses of circulation).
(3) In the event of default in complying with this section, an offence is committed by every officer of the company who is in default.
(4) A person guilty of an offence under this section is liable—
  (a) on conviction on indictment, to a fine;
  (b) on summary conviction, to a fine not exceeding the statutory maximum.

340B Traded companies: expenses of circulating members' matters to be dealt with at AGM

(1) The expenses of the company in complying with section 340A need not be paid by the members who requested the inclusion of the matter in the business to be dealt with at the annual general meeting if requests sufficient to require the company to include the matter are received before the end of the financial year preceding the meeting.
(2) Otherwise—
  (a) the expenses of the company in complying with that section must be paid by the members who requested the inclusion of the matter unless the company resolves otherwise, and
  (b) unless the company has previously so resolved, it is not bound to comply with that section unless there is deposited with or tendered to it, not later than—
    (i) six weeks before the annual general meeting to which the requests relate, or
    (ii) if later, the time at which notice is given of that meeting,
  a sum reasonably sufficient to meet its expenses in complying with that section.

CHAPTER 5
ADDITIONAL REQUIREMENTS FOR QUOTED COMPANIES AND TRADED COMPANIES

Website publication of poll results

341 Results of poll to be made available on website

(1) Where a poll is taken at a general meeting of a quoted company, the company must ensure that the following information is made available on a website—
- (a) the date of the meeting,
- (b) the text of the resolution or, as the case may be, a description of the subject matter of the poll,
- (c) the number of votes cast in favour, and
- (d) the number of votes cast against.

(1A) Where a poll is taken at a general meeting of a traded company, the company must ensure that the following information is made available on a website—
- (a) the date of the meeting,
- (b) the text of the resolution or, as the case may be, a description of the subject matter of the poll,
- (c) the number of votes validly cast,
- (d) the proportion of the company's issued share capital (determined at the time at which the right to vote is determined under section 360B(2)) represented by those votes,
- (e) the number of votes cast in favour,
- (f) the number of votes cast against, and
- (g) the number of abstentions (if counted).

(1B) A traded company must comply with subsection (1A) by—
- (a) the end of 16 days beginning with the day of the meeting, or
- (b) if later, the end of the first working day after the day on which the result of the poll is declared.

(2) The provisions of section 353 (requirements as to website availability) apply.

(3) In the event of default in complying with this section (or with the requirements of section 353 as it applies for the purposes of this section), an offence is committed by every officer of the company who is in default.

(4) A person guilty of an offence under subsection (3) is liable on summary conviction to a fine not exceeding level 3 on the standard scale.

(5) Failure to comply with this section (or the requirements of section 353) does not affect the validity of—
- (a) the poll, or
- (b) the resolution or other business (if passed or agreed to) to which the poll relates.

(6) This section only applies to polls taken after this section comes into force.

Independent report on poll

342 Members' power to require independent report on poll

(1) The members of a quoted company may require the directors to obtain an independent report on any poll taken, or to be taken, at a general meeting of the company.

(2) The directors are required to obtain an independent report if they receive requests to do so from—
- (a) members representing not less than 5% of the total voting rights of all the members who have a right to vote on the matter to which the poll relates (excluding any voting rights attached to any shares in the company held as treasury shares), or
- (b) not less than 100 members who have a right to vote on the matter to which the poll relates and hold shares in the company on which there has been paid up an average sum, per member, of not less than £100.

See also section 153 (exercise of rights where shares held on behalf of others).

(3) Where the requests relate to more than one poll, subsection (2) must be satisfied in relation to each of them.

(4) A request—
- (a) may be in hard copy form or in electronic form,
- (b) must identify the poll or polls to which it relates,
- (c) must be authenticated by the person or persons making it, and
- (d) must be received by the company not later than one week after the date on which the poll is taken.

343 Appointment of independent assessor

(1) Directors who are required under section 342 to obtain an independent report on a poll or polls must appoint a person they consider to be appropriate (an "independent assessor") to prepare a report for the company on it or them.

(2) The appointment must be made within one week after the company being required to obtain the report.

(3) The directors must not appoint a person who—

(a) does not meet the independence requirement in section 344, or

(b) has another role in relation to any poll on which he is to report (including, in particular, a role in connection with collecting or counting votes or with the appointment of proxies).

(4) In the event of default in complying with this section, an offence is committed by every officer of the company who is in default.

(5) A person guilty of an offence under this section is liable on summary conviction to a fine not exceeding level 5 on the standard scale.

(6) If at the meeting no poll on which a report is required is taken—

(a) the directors are not required to obtain a report from the independent assessor, and

(b) his appointment ceases (but without prejudice to any right to be paid for work done before the appointment ceased).

344 Independence requirement

(1) A person may not be appointed as an independent assessor—

(a) if he is—

(i) an officer or employee of the company, or

(ii) a partner or employee of such a person, or a partnership of which such a person is a partner;

(b) if he is—

(i) an officer or employee of an associated undertaking of the company, or

(ii) a partner or employee of such a person, or a partnership of which such a person is a partner;

(c) if there exists between—

(i) the person or an associate of his, and

(ii) the company or an associated undertaking of the company,

a connection of any such description as may be specified by regulations made by the Secretary of State.

(2) An auditor of the company is not regarded as an officer or employee of the company for this purpose.

(3) In this section—

"associated undertaking" means—

(a) a parent undertaking or subsidiary undertaking of the company, or

(b) a subsidiary undertaking of a parent undertaking of the company; and

"associate" has the meaning given by section 345.

(4) Regulations under this section are subject to negative resolution procedure.

345 Meaning of "associate"

(1) This section defines "associate" for the purposes of section 344 (independence requirement).

(2) In relation to an individual, "associate" means—

(a) that individual's spouse or civil partner or minor child or step-child,

(b) any body corporate of which that individual is a director, and

(c) any employee or partner of that individual.

(3) In relation to a body corporate, "associate" means—

(a) any body corporate of which that body is a director,

(b) any body corporate in the same group as that body, and

(c) any employee or partner of that body or of any body corporate in the same group.

(4) In relation to a partnership that is a legal person under the law by which it is governed, "associate" means—

(a) any body corporate of which that partnership is a director,

(b) any employee of or partner in that partnership, and

(c) any person who is an associate of a partner in that partnership.

(5) In relation to a partnership that is not a legal person under the law by which it is governed, “associate” means any person who is an associate of any of the partners.
(6) In this section, in relation to a limited liability partnership, for “director” read “member”.

346 Effect of appointment of a partnership

(1) This section applies where a partnership that is not a legal person under the law by which it is governed is appointed as an independent assessor.
(2) Unless a contrary intention appears, the appointment is of the partnership as such and not of the partners.
(3) Where the partnership ceases, the appointment is to be treated as extending to—
(a) any partnership that succeeds to the practice of that partnership, or
(b) any other person who succeeds to that practice having previously carried it on in partnership.
(4) For the purposes of subsection (3)—
(a) a partnership is regarded as succeeding to the practice of another partnership only if the members of the successor partnership are substantially the same as those of the former partnership, and
(b) a partnership or other person is regarded as succeeding to the practice of a partnership only if it or he succeeds to the whole or substantially the whole of the business of the former partnership.
(5) Where the partnership ceases and the appointment is not treated under subsection (3) as extending to any partnership or other person, the appointment may with the consent of the company be treated as extending to a partnership, or other person, who succeeds to—
(a) the business of the former partnership, or
(b) such part of it as is agreed by the company is to be treated as comprising the appointment.

347 The independent assessor's report

(1) The report of the independent assessor must state his opinion whether—
(a) the procedures adopted in connection with the poll or polls were adequate;
(b) the votes cast (including proxy votes) were fairly and accurately recorded and counted;
(c) the validity of members' appointments of proxies was fairly assessed;
(d) the notice of the meeting complied with section 325 (notice of meeting to contain statement of rights to appoint proxy);
(e) section 326 (company-sponsored invitations to appoint proxies) was complied with in relation to the meeting.
(2) The report must give his reasons for the opinions stated.
(3) If he is unable to form an opinion on any of those matters, the report must record that fact and state the reasons for it.
(4) The report must state the name of the independent assessor.

348 Rights of independent assessor: right to attend meeting etc.

(1) Where an independent assessor has been appointed to report on a poll, he is entitled to attend—
(a) the meeting at which the poll may be taken, and
(b) any subsequent proceedings in connection with the poll.
(2) He is also entitled to be provided by the company with a copy of—
(a) the notice of the meeting, and
(b) any other communication provided by the company in connection with the meeting to persons who have a right to vote on the matter to which the poll relates.
(3) The rights conferred by this section are only to be exercised to the extent that the independent assessor considers necessary for the preparation of his report.
(4) If the independent assessor is a firm, the right under subsection (1) to attend the meeting and any subsequent proceedings in connection with the poll is exercisable by an individual authorised by the firm in writing to act as its representative for that purpose.

349 Rights of independent assessor: right to information

(1) The independent assessor is entitled to access to the company's records relating to—

(a) any poll on which he is to report;
(b) the meeting at which the poll or polls may be, or were, taken.

(2) The independent assessor may require anyone who at any material time was—
(a) a director or secretary of the company,
(b) an employee of the company,
(c) a person holding or accountable for any of the company's records,
(d) a member of the company, or
(e) an agent of the company,
to provide him with information or explanations for the purpose of preparing his report.

(3) For this purpose "agent" includes the company's bankers, solicitors and auditor.

(4) A statement made by a person in response to a requirement under this section may not be used in evidence against him in criminal proceedings except proceedings for an offence under section 350 (offences relating to provision of information).

(5) A person is not required by this section to disclose information in respect of which a claim to legal professional privilege (in Scotland, to confidentiality of communications) could be maintained in legal proceedings.

350 Offences relating to provision of information

(1) A person who fails to comply with a requirement under section 349 without delay commits an offence unless it was not reasonably practicable for him to provide the required information or explanation.

(2) A person guilty of an offence under subsection (1) is liable on summary conviction to a fine not exceeding level 3 on the standard scale.

(3) A person commits an offence who knowingly or recklessly makes to an independent assessor a statement (oral or written) that—
(a) conveys or purports to convey any information or explanations which the independent assessor requires, or is entitled to require, under section 349, and
(b) is misleading, false or deceptive in a material particular.

(4) A person guilty of an offence under subsection (3) is liable—
(a) on conviction on indictment, to imprisonment for a term not exceeding two years or a fine (or both);
(b) on summary conviction—
(i) in England and Wales, to imprisonment for a term not exceeding twelve months or to a fine not exceeding the statutory maximum (or both);
(ii) in Scotland or Northern Ireland, to imprisonment for a term not exceeding six months, or to a fine not exceeding the statutory maximum (or both).

(5) Nothing in this section affects any right of an independent assessor to apply for an injunction (in Scotland, an interdict or an order for specific performance) to enforce any of his rights under section 348 or 349.

351 Information to be made available on website

(1) Where an independent assessor has been appointed to report on a poll, the company must ensure that the following information is made available on a website—
(a) the fact of his appointment,
(b) his identity,
(c) the text of the resolution or, as the case may be, a description of the subject matter of the poll to which his appointment relates, and
(d) a copy of a report by him which complies with section 347.

(2) The provisions of section 353 (requirements as to website availability) apply.

(3) In the event of default in complying with this section (or with the requirements of section 353 as it applies for the purposes of this section), an offence is committed by every officer of the company who is in default.

(4) A person guilty of an offence under subsection (3) is liable on summary conviction to a fine not exceeding level 3 on the standard scale.

(5) Failure to comply with this section (or the requirements of section 353) does not affect the validity of—
(a) the poll, or
(b) the resolution or other business (if passed or agreed to) to which the poll relates.

Supplementary

352 Application of provisions to class meetings

(1) The provisions of section 341 (results of poll to be made available on website) apply (with any necessary modifications) in relation to a meeting of holders of a class of shares of a quoted company or traded company in connection with the variation of the rights attached to such shares as they apply in relation to a general meeting of the company.

(1A) The provisions of section 342 to 351 (independent report on poll) apply (with any necessary modifications) in relation to a meeting of holders of a class of shares of a quoted company in connection with the variation of the rights attached to such shares as they apply in relation to a general meeting of the company.

(2) For the purposes of this section—

(a) any amendment of a provision contained in a company's articles for the variation of the rights attached to a class of shares, or the insertion of any such provision into the articles, is itself to be treated as a variation of those rights, and

(b) references to the variation of rights attached to a class of shares include references to their abrogation.

353 Requirements as to website availability

(1) The following provisions apply for the purposes of—

section 341 (results of poll to be made available on website), and

section 351 (report of independent observer to be made available on website).

(2) The information must be made available on a website that—

(a) is maintained by or on behalf of the company, and

(b) identifies the company in question.

(3) Access to the information on the website, and the ability to obtain a hard copy of the information from the website, must not be conditional on the payment of a fee or otherwise restricted.

(4) The information—

(a) must be made available as soon as reasonably practicable, and

(b) must be kept available throughout the period of two years beginning with the date on which it is first made available on a website in accordance with this section.

(5) A failure to make information available on a website throughout the period specified in subsection (4)(b) is disregarded if—

(a) the information is made available on the website for part of that period, and

(b) the failure is wholly attributable to circumstances that it would not be reasonable to have expected the company to prevent or avoid.

354 Power to limit or extend the types of company to which provisions of this Chapter apply

(1) The Secretary of State may by regulations—

(a) limit the types of company to which some or all of the provisions of this Chapter apply, or

(b) extend some or all of the provisions of this Chapter to additional types of company.

(2) Regulations under this section extending the application of any provision of this Chapter are subject to affirmative resolution procedure.

(3) Any other regulations under this section are subject to negative resolution procedure.

(4) Regulations under this section may—

(a) amend the provisions of this Chapter (apart from this section);

(b) repeal and re-enact provisions of this Chapter with modifications of form or arrangement, whether or not they are modified in substance;

(c) contain such consequential, incidental and supplementary provisions (including provisions amending, repealing or revoking enactments) as the Secretary of State thinks fit.

CHAPTER 6
RECORDS OF RESOLUTIONS AND MEETINGS

355 Records of resolutions and meetings etc.

(1) Every company must keep records comprising—

(a) copies of all resolutions of members passed otherwise than at general meetings,

(b) minutes of all proceedings of general meetings, and
(c) details provided to the company in accordance with section 357 (decisions of sole member).

(2) The records must be kept for at least ten years from the date of the resolution, meeting or decision (as appropriate).

(3) If a company fails to comply with this section, an offence is committed by every officer of the company who is in default.

(4) A person guilty of an offence under this section is liable on summary conviction to a fine not exceeding level 3 on the standard scale and, for continued contravention, a daily default fine not exceeding one-tenth of level 3 on the standard scale.

356 Records as evidence of resolutions etc.

(1) This section applies to the records kept in accordance with section 355.

(2) The record of a resolution passed otherwise than at a general meeting, if purporting to be signed by a director of the company or by the company secretary, is evidence (in Scotland, sufficient evidence) of the passing of the resolution.

(3) Where there is a record of a written resolution of a private company, the requirements of this Act with respect to the passing of the resolution are deemed to be complied with unless the contrary is proved.

(4) The minutes of proceedings of a general meeting, if purporting to be signed by the chairman of that meeting or by the chairman of the next general meeting, are evidence (in Scotland, sufficient evidence) of the proceedings at the meeting.

(5) Where there is a record of proceedings of a general meeting of a company, then, until the contrary is proved—
(a) the meeting is deemed duly held and convened,
(b) all proceedings at the meeting are deemed to have duly taken place, and
(c) all appointments at the meeting are deemed valid.

357 Records of decisions by sole member

(1) This section applies to a company limited by shares or by guarantee that has only one member.

(2) Where the member takes any decision that—
(a) may be taken by the company in general meeting, and
(b) has effect as if agreed by the company in general meeting,
he must (unless that decision is taken by way of a written resolution) provide the company with details of that decision.

(3) If a person fails to comply with this section he commits an offence.

(4) A person guilty of an offence under this section is liable on summary conviction to a fine not exceeding level 2 on the standard scale.

(5) Failure to comply with this section does not affect the validity of any decision referred to in subsection (2).

358 Inspection of records of resolutions and meetings

(1) The records referred to in section 355 (records of resolutions etc) relating to the previous ten years must be kept available for inspection—
(a) at the company's registered office, or
(b) at a place specified in regulations under section 1136.

(2) The company must give notice to the registrar—
(a) of the place at which the records are kept available for inspection, and
(b) of any change in that place,
unless they have at all times been kept at the company's registered office.

(3) The records must be open to the inspection of any member of the company without charge.

(4) Any member may require a copy of any of the records on payment of such fee as may be prescribed.

(5) If default is made for 14 days in complying with subsection (2) or an inspection required under subsection (3) is refused, or a copy requested under subsection (4) is not sent, an offence is committed by every officer of the company who is in default.

(6) A person guilty of an offence under this section is liable on summary conviction to a fine not exceeding level 3 on the standard scale and, for continued contravention, a daily default fine not exceeding one-tenth of level 3 on the standard scale.

(7) In a case in which an inspection required under subsection (3) is refused or a copy requested under subsection (4) is not sent, the court may by order compel an immediate inspection of the records or direct that the copies required be sent to the persons who requested them.

359 Records of resolutions and meetings of class of members

The provisions of this Chapter apply (with necessary modifications) in relation to resolutions and meetings of—

(a) holders of a class of shares, and

(b) in the case of a company without a share capital, a class of members,

as they apply in relation to resolutions of members generally and to general meetings.

CHAPTER 7
SUPPLEMENTARY PROVISIONS

360 Computation of periods of notice etc: clear day rule

(1) This section applies for the purposes of the following provisions of this Part—

section 307(1) and (2) (notice required of general meeting),

section 307A(1), (4), (5) and (7)(b) (notice required of general meeting of traded company),

section 312(1) and (3) (resolution requiring special notice),

section 314(4)(d) (request to circulate members' statement),

section 316(2)(b) (expenses of circulating statement to be deposited or tendered before meeting),

section 337(3) (contents of notice of AGM of traded company),

section 338(4)(d)(i) (request to circulate member's resolution at AGM of public company),

section 338A(5) (request to include matter in the business to be dealt with at AGM of traded company),

section 340(2)(b)(i) (expenses of circulating statement to be deposited or tendered before meeting), and

section 340B(2)(b) (traded companies: duty to circulate members' matters for AGM).

(2) Any reference in those provisions to a period of notice, or to a period before a meeting by which a request must be received or sum deposited or tendered, is to a period of the specified length excluding—

(a) the day of the meeting, and

(b) the day on which the notice is given, the request received or the sum deposited or tendered.

360A Electronic meetings and voting

(1) Nothing in this Part is to be taken to preclude the holding and conducting of a meeting in such a way that persons who are not present together at the same place may by electronic means attend and speak and vote at it.

(2) In the case of a traded company the use of electronic means for the purpose of enabling members to participate in a general meeting may be made subject only to such requirements and restrictions as are—

(a) necessary to ensure the identification of those taking part and the security of the electronic communication, and

(b) proportionate to the achievement of those objectives.

(3) Nothing in subsection (2) affects any power of a company to require reasonable evidence of the entitlement of any person who is not a member to participate in the meeting.

360B Traded companies: requirements for participating in and voting at general meetings

(1) Any provision of a traded company's articles is void in so far as it would have the effect of—

(a) imposing a restriction on a right of a member to participate in and vote at a general meeting of the company unless the member's shares have (after having been acquired by the member and before the meeting) been deposited with, or transferred to, or registered in the name of another person, or

(b) imposing a restriction on the right of a member to transfer shares in the company during the period of 48 hours before the time for the holding of a general meeting of the company if that right would not otherwise be subject to that restriction.

(2) A traded company must determine the right to vote at a general meeting of the company by reference to the register of members as at a time (determined by the company) that is not more than 48 hours before the time for the holding of the meeting.

(3) In calculating the period mentioned in subsection (1)(b) or (2), no account is to be taken of any part of a day that is not a working day.

(4) Nothing in this section affects—

(a) the operation of—

(i) Part 22 of this Act (information about interests in a company's shares),

(ii) Part 15 of the Companies Act 1985 (orders imposing restrictions on shares), or

(iii) any provision in a company's articles relating to the application of any provision of either of those Parts; or

(b) the validity of articles prescribed, or to the same effect as articles prescribed, under section 19 of this Act (power of Secretary of State to prescribe model articles).

360C Meaning of "traded company"

In this Part, "traded company" means a company any shares of which—

(a) carry rights to vote at general meetings, and

(b) are admitted to trading on a regulated market in an EEA State by or with the consent of the company.

361 Meaning of "quoted company"

In this Part "quoted company" has the same meaning as in Part 15 of this Act.

PART 14
CONTROL OF POLITICAL DONATIONS AND EXPENDITURE

Introductory

362 Introductory

This Part has effect for controlling—

(a) political donations made by companies to political parties, to other political organisations and to independent election candidates, and

(b) political expenditure incurred by companies.

Donations and expenditure to which this Part applies

363 Political parties, organisations etc to which this Part applies

(1) This Part applies to a political party if—

(a) it is registered under Part 2 of the Political Parties, Elections and Referendums Act 2000, or

(b) it carries on, or proposes to carry on, activities for the purposes of or in connection with the participation of the party in any election or elections to public office held in a member State other than the United Kingdom.

(2) This Part applies to an organisation (a "political organisation") if it carries on, or proposes to carry on, activities that are capable of being reasonably regarded as intended—

(a) to affect public support for a political party to which, or an independent election candidate to whom, this Part applies, or

(b) to influence voters in relation to any national or regional referendum held under the law of the United Kingdom or another member State.

(3) This Part applies to an independent election candidate at any election to public office held in the United Kingdom or another member State.

(4) Any reference in the following provisions of this Part to a political party, political organisation or independent election candidate, or to political expenditure, is to a party, organisation, independent candidate or expenditure to which this Part applies.

364 Meaning of "political donation"

(1) The following provisions have effect for the purposes of this Part as regards the meaning of "political donation".

(2) In relation to a political party or other political organisation—

(a) "political donation" means anything that in accordance with sections 50 to 52 of the Political Parties, Elections and Referendums Act 2000—

(i) constitutes a donation for the purposes of Chapter 1 of Part 4 of that Act (control of donations to registered parties), or

(ii) would constitute such a donation reading references in those sections to a registered party as references to any political party or other political organisation,

and

(b) section 53 of that Act applies, in the same way, for the purpose of determining the value of a donation.

(3) In relation to an independent election candidate—

(a) "political donation" means anything that, in accordance with sections 50 to 52 of that Act, would constitute a donation for the purposes of Chapter 1 of Part 4 of that Act (control of donations to registered parties) reading references in those sections to a registered party as references to the independent election candidate,

and

(b) section 53 of that Act applies, in the same way, for the purpose of determining the value of a donation.

(4) For the purposes of this section, sections 50 and 53 of the Political Parties, Elections and Referendums Act 2000 (definition of "donation" and value of donations) shall be treated as if the amendments to those sections made by the Electoral Administration Act 2006 (which remove from the definition of "donation" loans made otherwise than on commercial terms) had not been made.

365 Meaning of "political expenditure"

(1) In this Part "political expenditure", in relation to a company, means expenditure incurred by the company on—

(a) the preparation, publication or dissemination of advertising or other promotional or publicity material—

(i) of whatever nature, and

(ii) however published or otherwise disseminated,

that, at the time of publication or dissemination, is capable of being reasonably regarded as intended to affect public support for a political party or other political organisation, or an independent election candidate, or

(b) activities on the part of the company that are capable of being reasonably regarded as intended—

(i) to affect public support for a political party or other political organisation, or an independent election candidate, or

(ii) to influence voters in relation to any national or regional referendum held under the law of a member State.

(2) For the purposes of this Part a political donation does not count as political expenditure.

Authorisation required for donations or expenditure

366 Authorisation required for donations or expenditure

(1) A company must not—

(a) make a political donation to a political party or other political organisation, or to an independent election candidate, or

(b) incur any political expenditure,

unless the donation or expenditure is authorised in accordance with the following provisions.

(2) The donation or expenditure must be authorised—

(a) in the case of a company that is not a subsidiary of another company, by a resolution of the members of the company;

(b) in the case of a company that is a subsidiary of another company by—

(i) a resolution of the members of the company, and

(ii) a resolution of the members of any relevant holding company.

(3) No resolution is required on the part of a company that is a wholly-owned subsidiary of a UK-registered company.

(4) For the purposes of subsection (2)(b)(ii) a "relevant holding company" means a company that, at the time the donation was made or the expenditure was incurred—

(a) was a holding company of the company by which the donation was made or the expenditure was incurred,

(b) was a UK-registered company, and

(c) was not a subsidiary of another UK-registered company.

(5) The resolution or resolutions required by this section—

(a) must comply with section 367 (form of authorising resolution), and

(b) must be passed before the donation is made or the expenditure incurred.

(6) Nothing in this section enables a company to be authorised to do anything that it could not lawfully do apart from this section.

367 Form of authorising resolution

(1) A resolution conferring authorisation for the purposes of this Part may relate to—

(a) the company passing the resolution,

(b) one or more subsidiaries of that company, or

(c) the company passing the resolution and one or more subsidiaries of that company.

(2) A resolution may be expressed to relate to all companies that are subsidiaries of the company passing the resolution—

(a) at the time the resolution is passed, or

(b) at any time during the period for which the resolution has effect, without identifying them individually.

(3) The resolution may authorise donations or expenditure under one or more of the following heads—

(a) donations to political parties or independent election candidates;

(b) donations to political organisations other than political parties;

(c) political expenditure.

(4) The resolution must specify a head or heads—

(a) in the case of a resolution under subsection (2), for all of the companies to which it relates taken together;

(b) in the case of any other resolution, for each company to which it relates.

(5) The resolution must be expressed in general terms conforming with subsection (2) and must not purport to authorise particular donations or expenditure.

(6) For each of the specified heads the resolution must authorise donations or, as the case may be, expenditure up to a specified amount in the period for which the resolution has effect (see section 368).

(7) The resolution must specify such amounts—

(a) in the case of a resolution under subsection (2), for all of the companies to which it relates taken together;

(b) in the case of any other resolution, for each company to which it relates.

368 Period for which resolution has effect

(1) A resolution conferring authorisation for the purposes of this Part has effect for a period of four years beginning with the date on which it is passed unless the directors determine, or the articles require, that it is to have effect for a shorter period beginning with that date.

(2) The power of the directors to make a determination under this section is subject to any provision of the articles that operates to prevent them from doing so.

Remedies in case of unauthorised donations or expenditure

369 Liability of directors in case of unauthorised donation or expenditure

(1) This section applies where a company has made a political donation or incurred political expenditure without the authorisation required by this Part.

(2) The directors in default are jointly and severally liable—

(a) to make good to the company the amount of the unauthorised donation or expenditure, with interest, and

(b) to compensate the company for any loss or damage sustained by it as a result of the unauthorised donation or expenditure having been made.

(3) The directors in default are—
(a) those who, at the time the unauthorised donation was made or the unauthorised expenditure was incurred, were directors of the company by which the donation was made or the expenditure was incurred, and
(b) where—
(i) that company was a subsidiary of a relevant holding company, and
(ii) the directors of the relevant holding company failed to take all reasonable steps to prevent the donation being made or the expenditure being incurred,
the directors of the relevant holding company.
(4) For the purposes of subsection (3)(b) a "relevant holding company" means a company that, at the time the donation was made or the expenditure was incurred—
(a) was a holding company of the company by which the donation was made or the expenditure was incurred,
(b) was a UK-registered company, and
(c) was not a subsidiary of another UK-registered company.
(5) The interest referred to in subsection (2)(a) is interest on the amount of the unauthorised donation or expenditure, so far as not made good to the company—
(a) in respect of the period beginning with the date when the donation was made or the expenditure was incurred, and
(b) at such rate as the Secretary of State may prescribe by regulations.
Section 379(2) (construction of references to date when donation made or expenditure incurred) does not apply for the purposes of this subsection.
(6) Where only part of a donation or expenditure was unauthorised, this section applies only to so much of it as was unauthorised.

370 Enforcement of directors' liabilities by shareholder action

(1) Any liability of a director under section 369 is enforceable—
(a) in the case of a liability of a director of a company to that company, by proceedings brought under this section in the name of the company by an authorised group of its members;
(b) in the case of a liability of a director of a holding company to a subsidiary, by proceedings brought under this section in the name of the subsidiary by—
(i) an authorised group of members of the subsidiary, or
(ii) an authorised group of members of the holding company.
(2) This is in addition to the right of the company to which the liability is owed to bring proceedings itself to enforce the liability.
(3) An "authorised group" of members of a company means—
(a) the holders of not less than 5% in nominal value of the company's issued share capital,
(b) if the company is not limited by shares, not less than 5% of its members, or
(c) not less than 50 of the company's members.
(4) The right to bring proceedings under this section is subject to the provisions of section 371.
(5) Nothing in this section affects any right of a member of a company to bring or continue proceedings under Part 11 (derivative claims or proceedings).

371 Enforcement of directors' liabilities by shareholder action: supplementary

(1) A group of members may not bring proceedings under section 370 in the name of a company unless—
(a) the group has given written notice to the company stating—
(i) the cause of action and a summary of the facts on which the proceedings are to be based,
(ii) the names and addresses of the members comprising the group, and
(iii) the grounds on which it is alleged that those members constitute an authorised group; and
(b) not less than 28 days have elapsed between the date of the giving of the notice to the company and the bringing of the proceedings.
(2) Where such a notice is given to a company, any director of the company may apply to the court within the period of 28 days beginning with the date of the giving of the notice for an order directing that the proposed proceedings shall not be brought, on one or more of the following grounds—
(a) that the unauthorised amount has been made good to the company;

(b) that proceedings to enforce the liability have been brought, and are being pursued with due diligence, by the company;
(c) that the members proposing to bring proceedings under this section do not constitute an authorised group.

(3) Where an application is made on the ground mentioned in subsection (2)(b), the court may as an alternative to directing that the proposed proceedings under section 370 are not to be brought, direct—
(a) that such proceedings may be brought on such terms and conditions as the court thinks fit, and
(b) that the proceedings brought by the company—
(i) shall be discontinued, or
(ii) may be continued on such terms and conditions as the court thinks fit.

(4) The members by whom proceedings are brought under section 370 owe to the company in whose name they are brought the same duties in relation to the proceedings as would be owed by the company's directors if the proceedings were being brought by the company.
But proceedings to enforce any such duty may be brought by the company only with the permission of the court.

(5) Proceedings brought under section 370 may not be discontinued or settled by the group except with the permission of the court, which may be given on such terms as the court thinks fit.

372 Costs of shareholder action

(1) This section applies in relation to proceedings brought under section 370 in the name of a company ("the company") by an authorised group ("the group").

(2) The group may apply to the court for an order directing the company to indemnify the group in respect of costs incurred or to be incurred by the group in connection with the proceedings.
The court may make such an order on such terms as it thinks fit.

(3) The group is not entitled to be paid any such costs out of the assets of the company except by virtue of such an order.

(4) If no such order has been made with respect to the proceedings, then—
(a) if the company is awarded costs in connection with the proceedings, or it is agreed that costs incurred by the company in connection with the proceedings should be paid by any defendant, the costs shall be paid to the group; and
(b) if any defendant is awarded costs in connection with the proceedings, or it is agreed that any defendant should be paid costs incurred by him in connection with the proceedings, the costs shall be paid by the group.

(5) In the application of this section to Scotland for "costs" read "expenses" and for "defendant" read "defender".

373 Information for purposes of shareholder action

(1) Where proceedings have been brought under section 370 in the name of a company by an authorised group, the group is entitled to require the company to provide it with all information relating to the subject matter of the proceedings that is in the company's possession or under its control or which is reasonably obtainable by it.

(2) If the company, having been required by the group to do so, refuses to provide the group with all or any of that information, the court may, on an application made by the group, make an order directing—
(a) the company, and
(b) any of its officers or employees specified in the application,
to provide the group with the information in question in such form and by such means as the court may direct.

Exemptions

374 Trade unions

(1) A donation to a trade union, other than a contribution to the union's political fund, is not a political donation for the purposes of this Part.

(2) A trade union is not a political organisation for the purposes of section 365 (meaning of "political expenditure").

(3) In this section—

"trade union" has the meaning given by section 1 of Trade Union and Labour Relations (Consolidation) Act 1992 or Article 3 of the Industrial Relations (Northern Ireland) Order 1992;

"political fund" means the fund from which payments by a trade union in the furtherance of political objects are required to be made by virtue of section 82(1)(a) of that Act or Article 57(2)(a) of that Order.

375 Subscription for membership of trade association

(1) A subscription paid to a trade association for membership of the association is not a political donation for the purposes of this Part.

(2) For this purpose—

"trade association" means an organisation formed for the purpose of furthering the trade interests of its members, or of persons represented by its members, and

"subscription" does not include a payment to the association to the extent that it is made for the purpose of financing any particular activity of the association.

376 All-party parliamentary groups

(1) An all-party parliamentary group is not a political organisation for the purposes of this Part.

(2) An "all-party parliamentary group" means an all-party group composed of members of one or both of the Houses of Parliament (or of such members and other persons).

377 Political expenditure exempted by order

(1) Authorisation under this Part is not needed for political expenditure that is exempt by virtue of an order of the Secretary of State under this section.

(2) An order may confer an exemption in relation to—

(a) companies of any description or category specified in the order, or

(b) expenditure of any description or category so specified (whether framed by reference to goods, services or other matters in respect of which such expenditure is incurred or otherwise),

or both.

(3) If or to the extent that expenditure is exempt from the requirement of authorisation under this Part by virtue of an order under this section, it shall be disregarded in determining what donations are authorised by any resolution of the company passed for the purposes of this Part.

(4) An order under this section is subject to affirmative resolution procedure.

378 Donations not amounting to more than £5,000 in any twelve month period

(1) Authorisation under this Part is not needed for a donation except to the extent that the total

amount of—

(a) that donation, and

(b) other relevant donations made in the period of 12 months ending with the date on which that donation is made,

exceeds £5,000.

(2) In this section—

"donation" means a donation to a political party or other political organisation or to an independent election candidate; and

"other relevant donations" means—

(a) in relation to a donation made by a company that is not a subsidiary, any other donations made by that company or by any of its subsidiaries;

(b) in relation to a donation made by a company that is a subsidiary, any other donations made by that company, by any holding company of that company or by any other subsidiary of any such holding company.

(3) If or to the extent that a donation is exempt by virtue of this section from the requirement of authorisation under this Part, it shall be disregarded in determining what donations are authorised by any resolution passed for the purposes of this Part.

Supplementary provisions

379 Minor definitions

(1) In this Part—

"director" includes shadow director; and
"organisation" includes any body corporate or unincorporated association and any combination of persons.

(2) Except as otherwise provided, any reference in this Part to the time at which a donation is made or expenditure is incurred is, in a case where the donation is made or expenditure incurred in pursuance of a contract, any earlier time at which that contract is entered into by the company.

PART 15
ACCOUNTS AND REPORTS

CHAPTER 1
INTRODUCTION

General

380 Scheme of this Part

(1) The requirements of this Part as to accounts and reports apply in relation to each financial year of a company.
(2) In certain respects different provisions apply to different kinds of company.
...

Companies subject to the small companies regime

381 Companies subject to the small companies regime

The small companies regime applies to a company for a financial year in relation to which the company—
(a) qualifies as small (see sections 382 and 383), and
(b) is not excluded from the regime (see section 384).

382 Companies qualifying as small: general

(1) A company qualifies as small in relation to its first financial year if the qualifying conditions are met in that year.
(1A) Subject to subsection (2), a company qualifies as small in relation to a subsequent financial year if the qualifying conditions are met in that year.
(2) In relation to a subsequent financial year, where on its balance sheet date a company meets or ceases to meet the qualifying conditions, that affects its qualification as a small company only if it occurs in two consecutive financial years.
(3) The qualifying conditions are met by a company in a year in which it satisfies two or more of the following requirements—

1. Turnover	Not more than £10.2 million
2. Balance sheet total	Not more than £5.1 million
3. Number of employees	Not more than 50

(4) For a period that is a company's financial year but not in fact a year the maximum figures for turnover must be proportionately adjusted.
(5) The balance sheet total means the aggregate of the amounts shown as assets in the company's balance sheet.
(6) The number of employees means the average number of persons employed by the company in the year, determined as follows—
(a) find for each month in the financial year the number of persons employed under contracts of service by the company in that month (whether throughout the month or not),
(b) add together the monthly totals, and
(c) divide by the number of months in the financial year.
(7) This section is subject to section 383 (companies qualifying as small: parent companies).

383 Companies qualifying as small: parent companies

(1) A parent company qualifies as a small company in relation to a financial year only if the group headed by it qualifies as a small group.
(2) A group qualifies as small in relation to the parent company's first financial year if the qualifying conditions are met in that year.

(2A) Subject to subsection (3), a group qualifies as small in relation to a subsequent financial year of the parent company if the qualifying conditions are met in that year.

(3) In relation to a subsequent financial year of the parent company, where on the parent company's balance sheet date the group meets or ceases to meet the qualifying conditions, that affects the group's qualification as a small group only if it occurs in two consecutive financial years.

(4) The qualifying conditions are met by a group in a year in which it satisfies two or more of the following requirements—

1. Aggregate turnover	Not more than £10.2 million net (or £12.2 million gross)
2. Aggregate balance sheet total	Not more than £5.1 million net (or £6.1 million gross)
3. Aggregate number of employees	Not more than 50

(5) The aggregate figures are ascertained by aggregating the relevant figures determined in accordance with section 382 for each member of the group.

(6) In relation to the aggregate figures for turnover and balance sheet total—
"net" means after any set-offs and other adjustments made to eliminate group transactions—
(a) in the case of Companies Act accounts, in accordance with regulations under section 404,
(b) in the case of IAS accounts, in accordance with international accounting standards; and
"gross" means without those set-offs and other adjustments.
A company may satisfy any relevant requirement on the basis of either the net or the gross figure.

(7) The figures for each subsidiary undertaking shall be those included in its individual accounts for the relevant financial year, that is—
(a) if its financial year ends with that of the parent company, that financial year, and
(b) if not, its financial year ending last before the end of the financial year of the parent company.
If those figures cannot be obtained without disproportionate expense or undue delay, the latest available figures shall be taken.

384 Companies excluded from the small companies regime

(1) The small companies regime does not apply to a company that was at any time within the financial year to which the accounts relate—
(a) a traded company,
(b) a company that—
(i) is an authorised insurance company, a banking company, an e-money issuer, a MiFID investment firm or a UCITS management company, or
(ii) carries on insurance market activity, or
(c) a member of an ineligible group.

(2) A group is ineligible if any of its members is—
(a) a public company,
(b) a body corporate (other than a company) whose shares are admitted to trading on a regulated market in an EEA State,
(c) a person (other than a small company) who has permission under Part 4A of the Financial Services and Markets Act 2000 to carry on a regulated activity,
(ca) an e-money issuer,
(d) a small company that is an authorised insurance company, a banking company, an e-money issuer, a MiFID investment firm or a UCITS management company, or
(e) a person who carries on insurance market activity.

(3) A company is a small company for the purposes of subsection (2) if it qualified as small in relation to its last financial year ending on or before the end of the financial year to which the accounts relate.

384A Companies qualifying as micro-entities

(1) A company qualifies as a micro-entity in relation to its first financial year if the qualifying conditions are met in that year.

(2) Subject to subsection (3), a company qualifies as a micro-entity in relation to a subsequent financial year if the qualifying conditions are met in that year.

(3) In relation to a subsequent financial year, where on its balance sheet date a company meets or ceases to meet the qualifying conditions, that affects its qualification as a micro-entity only if it occurs in two consecutive financial years.

(4) The qualifying conditions are met by a company in a year in which it satisfies two or more of the following requirements—

1.	Turnover	Not more than £632,000
2.	Balance sheet total	Not more than £316,000
3.	Number of employees	Not more than 10

(5) For a period that is a company's financial year but not in fact a year the maximum figures for turnover must be proportionately adjusted.

(6) The balance sheet total means the aggregate of the amounts shown as assets in the company's balance sheet.

(7) The number of employees means the average number of persons employed by the company in the year, determined as follows—

(a) find for each month in the financial year the number of persons employed under contracts of service by the company in that month (whether throughout the month or not),

(b) add together the monthly totals, and

(c) divide by the number of months in the financial year.

(8) In the case of a company which is a parent company, the company qualifies as a micro-entity in relation to a financial year only if—

(a) the company qualifies as a micro-entity in relation to that year, as determined by subsections (1) to (7), and

(b) the group headed by the company qualifies as a small group, as determined by section 383(2) to (7).

384B Companies excluded from being treated as micro-entities

(1) The micro-entity provisions do not apply in relation to a company's accounts for a particular financial year if the company was at any time within that year—

(a) a company excluded from the small companies regime by virtue of section 384,

(b) an investment undertaking as defined in Article 2(14) of Directive 2013/34/EU of 26 June 2013 on the annual financial statements etc. of certain types of undertakings,

(c) a financial holding undertaking as defined in Article 2(15) of that Directive,

(d) a credit institution as defined in Article 4 of Directive 2006/48/EC of the European Parliament and of the Council of 14 June 2006 relating to the taking up and pursuit of the business of credit institutions, other than one referred to in Article 2 of that Directive,

(e) an insurance undertaking as defined in Article 2(1) of Council Directive 91/674/EEC of 19 December 1991 on the annual accounts of insurance undertakings, or

(f) a charity.

(2) The micro-entity provisions also do not apply in relation to a company's accounts for a financial year if —

(a) the company is a parent company which prepares group accounts for that year as permitted by section 398, or

(b) the company is not a parent company but its accounts are included in consolidated group accounts for that year.

Quoted and unquoted companies

385 Quoted and unquoted companies

(1) For the purposes of this Part a company is a quoted company in relation to a financial year if it is a quoted company immediately before the end of the accounting reference period by reference to which that financial year was determined.

(2) A "quoted company" means a company whose equity share capital—

(a) has been included in the official list in accordance with the provisions of Part 6 of the Financial Services and Markets Act 2000, or

(b) is officially listed in an EEA State, or
(c) is admitted to dealing on either the New York Stock Exchange or the exchange known as Nasdaq. In paragraph (a) "the official list" has the meaning given by section 103(1) of the Financial Services and Markets Act 2000.

(3) An "unquoted company" means a company that is not a quoted company.
(4) The Secretary of State may by regulations amend or replace the provisions of subsections (1) to (2) so as to limit or extend the application of some or all of the provisions of this Part that are expressed to apply to quoted companies.
(5) Regulations under this section extending the application of any such provision of this Part are subject to affirmative resolution procedure.
(6) Any other regulations under this section are subject to negative resolution procedure.

CHAPTER 2
ACCOUNTING RECORDS

386 Duty to keep accounting records

(1) Every company must keep adequate accounting records.
(2) Adequate accounting records means records that are sufficient—
(a) to show and explain the company's transactions,
(b) to disclose with reasonable accuracy, at any time, the financial position of the company at that time, and
(c) to enable the directors to ensure that any accounts required to be prepared comply with the requirements of this Act (and, where applicable, of Article 4 of the IAS Regulation).

(3) Accounting records must, in particular, contain—
(a) entries from day to day of all sums of money received and expended by the company and the matters in respect of which the receipt and expenditure takes place, and
(b) a record of the assets and liabilities of the company.

(4) If the company's business involves dealing in goods, the accounting records must contain—
(a) statements of stock held by the company at the end of each financial year of the company,
(b) all statements of stocktakings from which any statement of stock as is mentioned in paragraph (a) has been or is to be prepared, and
(c) except in the case of goods sold by way of ordinary retail trade, statements of all goods sold and purchased, showing the goods and the buyers and sellers in sufficient detail to enable all these to be identified.

(5) A parent company that has a subsidiary undertaking in relation to which the above requirements do not apply must take reasonable steps to secure that the undertaking keeps such accounting records as to enable the directors of the parent company to ensure that any accounts required to be prepared under this Part comply with the requirements of this Act (and, where applicable, of Article 4 of the IAS Regulation).

387 Duty to keep accounting records: offence

(1) If a company fails to comply with any provision of section 386 (duty to keep accounting records), an offence is committed by every officer of the company who is in default.
(2) It is a defence for a person charged with such an offence to show that he acted honestly and that in the circumstances in which the company's business was carried on the default was excusable.
(3) A person guilty of an offence under this section is liable—
(a) on conviction on indictment, to imprisonment for a term not exceeding two years or a fine (or both);
(b) on summary conviction—
(i) in England and Wales, to imprisonment for a term not exceeding twelve months or to a fine not exceeding the statutory maximum (or both);
(ii) in Scotland or Northern Ireland, to imprisonment for a term not exceeding six months, or to a fine not exceeding the statutory maximum (or both).

388 Where and for how long records to be kept

(1) A company's accounting records—
  (a) must be kept at its registered office or such other place as the directors think fit, and
  (b) must at all times be open to inspection by the company's officers.

(2) If accounting records are kept at a place outside the United Kingdom, accounts and returns with respect to the business dealt with in the accounting records so kept must be sent to, and kept at, a place in the United Kingdom, and must at all times be open to such inspection.

(3) The accounts and returns to be sent to the United Kingdom must be such as to—
  (a) disclose with reasonable accuracy the financial position of the business in question at intervals of not more than six months, and
  (b) enable the directors to ensure that the accounts required to be prepared under this Part comply with the requirements of this Act (and, where applicable, of Article 4 of the IAS Regulation).

(4) Accounting records that a company is required by section 386 to keep must be preserved by it—
  (a) in the case of a private company, for three years from the date on which they are made;
  (b) in the case of a public company, for six years from the date on which they are made.

(5) Subsection (4) is subject to any provision contained in rules made under section 411 of the Insolvency Act 1986 (company insolvency rules) or Article 359 of the Insolvency (Northern Ireland) Order 1989.

389 Where and for how long records to be kept: offences

(1) If a company fails to comply with any provision of subsections (1) to (3) of section 388 (requirements as to keeping of accounting records), an offence is committed by every officer of the company who is in default.

(2) It is a defence for a person charged with such an offence to show that he acted honestly and that in the circumstances in which the company's business was carried on the default was excusable.

(3) An officer of a company commits an offence if he—
  (a) fails to take all reasonable steps for securing compliance by the company with subsection (4) of that section (period for which records to be preserved), or
  (b) intentionally causes any default by the company under that subsection.

(4) A person guilty of an offence under this section is liable—
  (a) on conviction on indictment, to imprisonment for a term not exceeding two years or a fine (or both);
  (b) on summary conviction—
    (i) in England and Wales, to imprisonment for a term not exceeding twelve months or to a fine not exceeding the statutory maximum (or both);
    (ii) in Scotland or Northern Ireland, to imprisonment for a term not exceeding six months, or to a fine not exceeding the statutory maximum (or both).

CHAPTER 3
A COMPANY'S FINANCIAL YEAR

390 A company's financial year

(1) A company's financial year is determined as follows.

(2) Its first financial year—
  (a) begins with the first day of its first accounting reference period, and
  (b) ends with the last day of that period or such other date, not more than seven days before or after the end of that period, as the directors may determine.

(3) Subsequent financial years—
  (a) begin with the day immediately following the end of the company's previous financial year, and
  (b) end with the last day of its next accounting reference period or such other date, not more than seven days before or after the end of that period, as the directors may determine.

(4) In relation to an undertaking that is not a company, references in this Act to its financial year are to any period in respect of which a profit and loss account of the undertaking is required to be made up (by its constitution or by the law under which it is established), whether that period is a year or not.

(5) The directors of a parent company must secure that, except where in their opinion there are good reasons against it, the financial year of each of its subsidiary undertakings coincides with the company's own financial year.

391 Accounting reference periods and accounting reference date

(1) A company's accounting reference periods are determined according to its accounting reference date in each calendar year.

(2) The accounting reference date of a company incorporated in Great Britain before 1st April 1996 is—

(a) the date specified by notice to the registrar in accordance with section 224(2) of the Companies Act 1985 (notice specifying accounting reference date given within nine months of incorporation), or

(b) failing such notice—

(i) in the case of a company incorporated before 1st April 1990, 31st March, and

(ii) in the case of a company incorporated on or after 1st April 1990, the last day of the month in which the anniversary of its incorporation falls.

(3) The accounting reference date of a company incorporated in Northern Ireland before 22nd August 1997 is—

(a) the date specified by notice to the registrar in accordance with article 232(2) of the Companies (Northern Ireland) Order 1986 (notice specifying accounting reference date given within nine months of incorporation), or

(b) failing such notice—

(i) in the case of a company incorporated before the coming into operation of Article 5 of the Companies (Northern Ireland) Order 1990, 31st March, and

(ii) in the case of a company incorporated after the coming into operation of that Article, the last day of the month in which the anniversary of its incorporation falls.

(4) The accounting reference date of a company incorporated—

(a) in Great Britain on or after 1st April 1996 and before the commencement of this Act,

(b) in Northern Ireland on or after 22nd August 1997 and before the commencement of this Act, or

(c) after the commencement of this Act,

is the last day of the month in which the anniversary of its incorporation falls.

(5) A company's first accounting reference period is the period of more than six months, but not more than 18 months, beginning with the date of its incorporation and ending with its accounting reference date.

(6) Its subsequent accounting reference periods are successive periods of twelve months beginning immediately after the end of the previous accounting reference period and ending with its accounting reference date.

(7) This section has effect subject to the provisions of section 392 (alteration of accounting reference date).

392 Alteration of accounting reference date

(1) A company may by notice given to the registrar specify a new accounting reference date having effect in relation to—

(a) the company's current accounting reference period and subsequent periods, or

(b) the company's previous accounting reference period and subsequent periods.

A company's "previous accounting reference period" means the one immediately preceding its current accounting reference period.

(2) The notice must state whether the current or previous accounting reference period—

(a) is to be shortened, so as to come to an end on the first occasion on which the new accounting reference date falls or fell after the beginning of the period, or

(b) is to be extended, so as to come to an end on the second occasion on which that date falls or fell after the beginning of the period.

(3) A notice extending a company's current or previous accounting reference period is not effective if given less than five years after the end of an earlier accounting reference period of the company that was extended under this section.
This does not apply—
(a) to a notice given by a company that is a subsidiary undertaking or parent undertaking of another EEA undertaking if the new accounting reference date coincides with that of the other EEA undertaking or, where that undertaking is not a company, with the last day of its financial year, or
(b) where the company is in administration under Part 2 of the Insolvency Act 1986 or Part 3 of the Insolvency (Northern Ireland) Order 1989, or
(c) where the Secretary of State directs that it should not apply, which he may do with respect to a notice that has been given or that may be given.
(4) A notice under this section may not be given in respect of a previous accounting reference period if the period for filing accounts and reports for the financial year determined by reference to that accounting reference period has already expired.
(5) An accounting reference period may not be extended so as to exceed 18 months and a notice under this section is ineffective if the current or previous accounting reference period as extended in accordance with the notice would exceed that limit.
This does not apply where the company is in administration under Part 2 of the Insolvency Act 1986 or Part 3 of the Insolvency (Northern Ireland) Order 1989.
(6) In this section "EEA undertaking" means an undertaking established under the law of any part of the United Kingdom or the law of any other EEA State.

CHAPTER 4
ANNUAL ACCOUNTS

General

393 Accounts to give true and fair view

(1) The directors of a company must not approve accounts for the purposes of this Chapter unless they are satisfied that they give a true and fair view of the assets, liabilities, financial position and profit or loss—
(a) in the case of the company's individual accounts, of the company;
(b) in the case of the company's group accounts, of the undertakings included in the consolidation as a whole, so far as concerns members of the company.
(1A) The following provisions apply to the directors of a company which qualifies as a micro-entity in relation to a financial year (see sections 384A and 384B) in their consideration of whether the Companies Act individual accounts of the company for that year give a true and fair view as required by subsection (1)(a)—
(a) where the accounts comprise only micro-entity minimum accounting items, the directors must disregard any provision of an accounting standard which would require the accounts to contain information additional to those items,
(b) in relation to a micro-entity minimum accounting item contained in the accounts, the directors must disregard any provision of an accounting standard which would require theaccounts to contain further information in relation to that item, and
(c) where the accounts contain an item of information additional to the micro-entity minimum accounting items, the directors must have regard to any provision of an accounting standard which relates to that item.
(2) The auditor of a company in carrying out his functions under this Act in relation to the company's annual accounts must have regard to the directors' duty under subsection (1).

Individual accounts

394 Duty to prepare individual accounts

The directors of every company must prepare accounts for the company for each of its financial years unless the company is exempt from that requirement under section 394A.
Those accounts are referred to as the company's "individual accounts".

394A Individual accounts: exemption for dormant subsidiaries

(1) A company is exempt from the requirement to prepare individual accounts for a financial year if—

(a) it is itself a subsidiary undertaking,
(b) it has been dormant throughout the whole of that year, and
(c) its parent undertaking is established under the law of an EEA State.

(2) Exemption is conditional upon compliance with all of the following conditions—
(a) all members of the company must agree to the exemption in respect of the financial year in question,
(b) the parent undertaking must give a guarantee under section 394C in respect of that year,
(c) the company must be included in the consolidated accounts drawn up for that year or to an earlier date in that year by the parent undertaking in accordance with—
(i) the provisions of Directive 2013/34/EU of the European Parliament and of the Council on the annual financial statements, consolidated financial statements and related reports of certain types of undertakings, or
(ii) international accounting standards,
(d) the parent undertaking must disclose in the notes to the consolidated accounts that the company is exempt from the requirement to prepare individual accounts by virtue of this section, and
(e) the directors of the company must deliver to the registrar within the period for filing the company's accounts and reports for that year—
(i) a written notice of the agreement referred to in subsection (2)(a),
(ii) the statement referred to in section 394C(1),
(iii) a copy of the consolidated accounts referred to in subsection (2)(c),
(iv) a copy of the auditor's report on those accounts, and
(v) a copy of the consolidated annual report drawn up by the parent undertaking.

394B Companies excluded from the dormant subsidiaries exemption

A company is not entitled to the exemption conferred by section 394A (dormant subsidiaries) if it was at any time within the financial year in question—
(a) a traded company,
(b) a company that—
(i) is an authorised insurance company, a banking company, an e-money issuer, a MiFID investment firm or a UCITS management company, or
(ii) carries on insurance market activity, or
(c) a special register body as defined in section 117(1) of the Trade Union and Labour Relations (Consolidation) Act 1992 or an employers' association as defined in section 122 of that Act or Article 4 of the Industrial Relations (Northern Ireland) Order 1992.

394C Dormant subsidiaries exemption: parent undertaking declaration of guarantee

(1) A guarantee is given by a parent undertaking under this section when the directors of the subsidiary company deliver to the registrar a statement by the parent undertaking that it guarantees the subsidiary company under this section.

(2) The statement under subsection (1) must be authenticated by the parent undertaking and must specify—
(a) the name of the parent undertaking,
(b) if the parent undertaking is incorporated in the United Kingdom, its registered number (if any),
(c) if the parent undertaking is incorporated outside the United Kingdom and registered in the country in which it is incorporated, the identity of the register on which it is registered and the number with which it is so registered,
(d) the name and registered number of the subsidiary company in respect of which the guarantee is being given,
(e) the date of the statement, and
(f) the financial year to which the guarantee relates.

(3) A guarantee given under this section has the effect that—
(a) the parent undertaking guarantees all outstanding liabilities to which the subsidiary company is subject at the end of the financial year to which the guarantee relates, until they are satisfied in full, and

(b) the guarantee is enforceable against the parent undertaking by any person to whom the subsidiary company is liable in respect of those liabilities.

395 Individual accounts: applicable accounting framework

(1) A company's individual accounts may be prepared—

(a) in accordance with section 396 ("Companies Act individual accounts"), or

(b) in accordance with international accounting standards ("IAS individual accounts").

This is subject to the following provisions of this section and to section 407 (consistency of financial reporting within group).

(2) The individual accounts of a company that is a charity must be Companies Act individual accounts.

(3) After the first financial year in which the directors of a company prepare IAS individual accounts ("the first IAS year"), all subsequent individual accounts of the company must be prepared in accordance with international accounting standards unless there is a relevant change of circumstance. This is subject to subsection (4A).

(4) There is a relevant change of circumstance if, at any time during or after the first IAS year—

(a) the company becomes a subsidiary undertaking of another undertaking that does not prepare IAS individual accounts,

(aa) the company ceases to be a subsidiary undertaking,

(b) the company ceases to be a company with securities admitted to trading on a regulated market in an EEA State, or

(c) a parent undertaking of the company ceases to be an undertaking with securities admitted to trading on a regulated market in an EEA State.

(4A) After a financial year in which the directors of a company prepare IAS individual accounts for the company, the directors may change to preparing Companies Act individual accounts for a reason other than a relevant change of circumstance provided they have not changed to Companies Act individual accounts in the period of five years preceding the first day of that financial year.

(4B) In calculating the five year period for the purpose of subsection (4A), no account should be taken of a change due to a relevant change of circumstance.

(5) If, having changed to preparing Companies Act individual accounts, the directors again prepare IAS individual accounts for the company, subsections (3) and (4) apply again as if the first financial year for which such accounts are again prepared were the first IAS year.

396 Companies Act individual accounts

(A1) Companies Act individual accounts must state—

(a) the part of the United Kingdom in which the company is registered,

(b) the company's registered number,

(c) whether the company is a public or a private company and whether it is limited by shares or by guarantee,

(d) the address of the company's registered office, and

(e) where appropriate, the fact that the company is being wound-up.

(1) Companies Act individual accounts must comprise—

(a) a balance sheet as at the last day of the financial year, and

(b) a profit and loss account.

(2) The accounts must—

(a) in the case of the balance sheet, give a true and fair view of the state of affairs of the company as at the end of the financial year, and

(b) in the case of the profit and loss account, give a true and fair view of the profit or loss of the company for the financial year.

(2A) In the case of the individual accounts of a company which qualifies as a micro-entity in relation to the financial year (see sections 384A and 384B), the micro-entity minimum accounting items included in the company's accounts for the year are presumed to give the true and fair view required by subsection (2).

(3) The accounts must comply with provision made by the Secretary of State by regulations as to—

(a) the form and content of the balance sheet and profit and loss account, and

(b) additional information to be provided by way of notes to the accounts.

(4) If compliance with the regulations, and any other provision made by or under this Act as to the matters to be included in a company's individual accounts or in notes to those accounts, would not be sufficient to give a true and fair view, the necessary additional information must be given in the accounts or in a note to them.

(5) If in special circumstances compliance with any of those provisions is inconsistent with the requirement to give a true and fair view, the directors must depart from that provision to the extent necessary to give a true and fair view.
Particulars of any such departure, the reasons for it and its effect must be given in a note to the accounts.

(6) Subsections (4) and (5) do not apply in relation to the micro-entity minimum accounting items included in the individual accounts of a company for a financial year in relation to which the company qualifies as a micro-entity.

397 IAS individual accounts

(1) IAS individual accounts must state—
   (a) the part of the United Kingdom in which the company is registered,
   (b) the company's registered number,
   (c) whether the company is a public or a private company and whether it is limited by shares or by guarantee,
   (d) the address of the company's registered office, and
   (e) where appropriate, the fact that the company is being wound-up.

(2) The notes to the accounts must state that the accounts have been prepared in accordance with international accounting standards.

Group accounts: small companies

398 Option to prepare group accounts

If at the end of a financial year a company subject to the small companies regime is a parent company the directors, as well as preparing individual accounts for the year, may prepare group accounts for the year.

Group accounts: other companies

399 Duty to prepare group accounts

(1) This section applies to companies that are not subject to the small companies regime.

(2) If at the end of a financial year the company is a parent company the directors, as well as preparing individual accounts for the year, must prepare group accounts for the year unless the company is exempt from that requirement.

(2A) A company is exempt from the requirement to prepare group accounts if—
   (a) it would be subject to the small companies regime but for being a public company, and
   (b) it is not a traded company.

(3) There are further exemptions under–
   section 400 (company included in EEA accounts of larger group),
   section 401 (company included in non-EEA accounts of larger group), and
   section 402 (company none of whose subsidiary undertakings need be included in the consolidation).

(4) A company to which this section applies but which is exempt from the requirement to prepare group accounts, may do so.

400 Exemption for company included in EEA group accounts of larger group

(1) A company is exempt from the requirement to prepare group accounts if it is itself a subsidiary undertaking and its immediate parent undertaking is established under the law of an EEA State, in the following cases—
   (a) where the company is a wholly-owned subsidiary of that parent undertaking;
   (b) where that parent undertaking holds 90% or more of the allotted shares in the company and the remaining shareholders have approved the exemption;
   (c) where that parent undertaking holds more than 50% (but less than 90%) of the allotted shares in the company and notice requesting the preparation of group accounts has not been served on the company by the shareholders holding in aggregate at least 5% of the allotted shares in the company. Such notice must be served at least six months before the end of the financial year to which it relates.

Such notice must be served not later than six months after the end of the financial year before that to which it relates.

(2) Exemption is conditional upon compliance with all of the following conditions—
  (a) the company must be included in consolidated accounts for a larger group drawn up to the same date, or to an earlier date in the same financial year, by a parent undertaking established under the law of an EEA State;
  (b) those accounts must be drawn up and audited, and that parent undertaking's annual report must be drawn up, according to that law—
    (i) in accordance with the provisions of Directive 2013/34/EU of the European Parliament and of the Council on the annual financial statements, consolidated financial statements and related reports of certain types of undertakings, or
    (ii) in accordance with international accounting standards;
  (c) the company must disclose in the notes to its individual accounts that it is exempt from the obligation to prepare and deliver group accounts;
  (d) the company must state in its individual accounts the name of the parent undertaking that draws up the group accounts referred to above and—
    (i) the address of the undertaking's registered office (whether in or outside the United Kingdom), or
    (ii) if it is unincorporated, the address of its principal place of business;
  (e) the company must deliver to the registrar, within the period for filing its accounts and reports for the financial year in question, copies of—
    (i) those group accounts, and
    (ii) the parent undertaking's annual report, together with the auditor's report on them;
  (f) any requirement of Part 35 of this Act as to the delivery to the registrar of a certified translation into English must be met in relation to any document comprised in the accounts and reports delivered in accordance with paragraph (e).

(3) For the purposes of subsection (1)(b) and (c) shares held by a wholly-owned subsidiary of the parent undertaking, or held on behalf of the parent undertaking or a wholly-owned subsidiary, shall be attributed to the parent undertaking.

(4) The exemption does not apply to a company which is a traded company.

(5) Shares held by directors of a company for the purpose of complying with any share qualification requirement shall be disregarded in determining for the purposes of this section whether the company is a wholly-owned subsidiary.

401 Exemption for company included in non-EEA group accounts of larger group

(1) A company is exempt from the requirement to prepare group accounts if it is itself a subsidiary undertaking and its parent undertaking is not established under the law of an EEA State, in the following cases—
  (a) where the company is a wholly-owned subsidiary of that parent undertaking;
  (b) where that parent undertaking holds 90% or more of the allotted shares in the company and the remaining shareholders have approved the exemption; or
  (c) where that parent undertaking holds more than 50% (but less than 90%) of the allotted shares in the company and notice requesting the preparation of group accounts has not been served on the company by the shareholders holding in aggregate at least 5% of the allotted shares in the company.

Such notice must be served at least six months before the end of the financial year to which it relates.

(2) Exemption is conditional upon compliance with all of the following conditions—
  (a) the company and all of its subsidiary undertakings must be included in consolidated accounts for a larger group drawn up to the same date, or to an earlier date in the same financial year, by a parent undertaking;
  (b) those accounts and, where appropriate, the group's annual report, must be drawn up—
    (i) in accordance with the provisions of Directive 2013/34/EU of the European Parliament and of the Council of 26 June 2013 on the annual financial statements, consolidated financial statements and related reports of certain types of undertakings,

(ii) in a manner equivalent to consolidated accounts and consolidated reports so drawn up,

(iii) in accordance with international accounting standards adopted pursuant to the IAS Regulation, or

(iv) in accordance with accounting standards which are equivalent to such international accounting standards, as determined pursuant to Commission Regulation (EC) No. 1569/2007 of 21 December 2007 establishing a mechanism for the determination of equivalence of accounting standards applied by third country issuers of securities pursuant to Directives 2003/71/EC and 2004/109/EC of the European Parliament and of the Council;

(c) the group accounts must be audited by one or more persons authorised to audit accounts under the law under which the parent undertaking which draws them up is established;

(d) the company must disclose in its individual accounts that it is exempt from the obligation to prepare and deliver group accounts;

(e) the company must state in its individual accounts the name of the parent undertaking which draws up the group accounts referred to above and—

(i) the address of the undertaking's registered office (whether in or outside the United Kingdom), or

(ii) if it is unincorporated, the address of its principal place of business;

(f) the company must deliver to the registrar, within the period for filing its accounts and reports for the financial year in question, copies of—

(i) the group accounts, and

(ii) where appropriate, the consolidated annual report, together with the auditor's report on them;

(g) any requirement of Part 35 of this Act as to the delivery to the registrar of a certified translation into English must be met in relation to any document comprised in the accounts and reports delivered in accordance with paragraph (f).

(3) For the purposes of subsection (1)(b) and (c), shares held by a wholly-owned subsidiary of the parent undertaking, or held on behalf of the parent undertaking or a wholly-owned subsidiary, are attributed to the parent undertaking.

(4) The exemption does not apply to a company which is a traded company.

(5) Shares held by directors of a company for the purpose of complying with any share qualification requirement shall be disregarded in determining for the purposes of this section whether the company is a wholly-owned subsidiary.

402 Exemption if no subsidiary undertakings need be included in the consolidation

A parent company is exempt from the requirement to prepare group accounts if under section 405 all of its subsidiary undertakings could be excluded from consolidation in Companies Act group accounts.

Group accounts: general

403 Group accounts: applicable accounting framework

(1) The group accounts of certain parent companies are required by Article 4 of the IAS Regulation to be prepared in accordance with international accounting standards ("IAS group accounts").

(2) The group accounts of other companies may be prepared—

(a) in accordance with section 404 ("Companies Act group accounts"), or

(b) in accordance with international accounting standards ("IAS group accounts"). This is subject to the following provisions of this section.

(3) The group accounts of a parent company that is a charity must be Companies Act group accounts.

(4) After the first financial year in which the directors of a parent company prepare IAS group accounts ("the first IAS year"), all subsequent group accounts of the company must be prepared in accordance with international accounting standards unless there is a relevant change of circumstance. This is subject to subsection (5A).

(5) There is a relevant change of circumstance if, at any time during or after the first IAS year—

(a) the company becomes a subsidiary undertaking of another undertaking that does not prepare IAS group accounts,
(b) the company ceases to be a company with securities admitted to trading on a regulated market in an EEA State, or
(c) a parent undertaking of the company ceases to be an undertaking with securities admitted to trading on a regulated market in an EEA State.

(5A) After a financial year in which the directors of a parent company prepare IAS group accounts for the company, the directors may change to preparing Companies Act group accounts for a reason other than a relevant change of circumstance provided they have not changed to Companies Act group accounts in the period of five years preceding the first day of that financial year.

(5B) In calculating the five year period for the purpose of subsection (5A), no account should be taken of a change due to a relevant change of circumstance.

(6) If, having changed to preparing Companies Act group accounts, the directors again prepare IAS group accounts for the company, subsections (4) and (5) apply again as if the first financial year for which such accounts are again prepared were the first IAS year.

404 Companies Act group accounts

(A1) Companies Act group accounts must state, in respect of the parent company—
(a) the part of the United Kingdom in which the company is registered,
(b) the company's registered number,
(c) whether the company is a public or a private company and whether it is limited by shares or by guarantee,
(d) the address of the company's registered office, and
(e) where appropriate, the fact that the company is being wound-up.

(1) Companies Act group accounts must comprise—
(a) a consolidated balance sheet dealing with the state of affairs of the parent company and its subsidiary undertakings, and
(b) a consolidated profit and loss account dealing with the profit or loss of the parent company and its subsidiary undertakings.

(2) The accounts must give a true and fair view of the state of affairs as at the end of the financial year, and the profit or loss for the financial year, of the undertakings included in the consolidation as a whole, so far as concerns members of the company.

(3) The accounts must comply with provision made by the Secretary of State by regulations as to—
(a) the form and content of the consolidated balance sheet and consolidated profit and loss account, and
(b) additional information to be provided by way of notes to the accounts.

(4) If compliance with the regulations, and any other provision made by or under this Act as to the matters to be included in a company's group accounts or in notes to those accounts, would not be sufficient to give a true and fair view, the necessary additional information must be given in the accounts or in a note to them.

(5) If in special circumstances compliance with any of those provisions is inconsistent with the requirement to give a true and fair view, the directors must depart from that provision to the extent necessary to give a true and fair view.
Particulars of any such departure, the reasons for it and its effect must be given in a note to the accounts.

405 Companies Act group accounts: subsidiary undertakings included in the consolidation

(1) Where a parent company prepares Companies Act group accounts, all the subsidiary undertakings of the company must be included in the consolidation, subject to the following exceptions.

(2) A subsidiary undertaking may be excluded from consolidation if its inclusion is not material for the purpose of giving a true and fair view (but two or more undertakings may be excluded only if they are not material taken together).

(3) A subsidiary undertaking may be excluded from consolidation where—
(a) severe long-term restrictions substantially hinder the exercise of the rights of the parent company over the assets or management of that undertaking, or

(b) extremely rare circumstances mean that the information necessary for the preparation of group accounts cannot be obtained without disproportionate expense or undue delay, or

(c) the interest of the parent company is held exclusively with a view to subsequent resale.

(4) The reference in subsection (3)(a) to the rights of the parent company and the reference in subsection (3)(c) to the interest of the parent company are, respectively, to rights and interests held by or attributed to the company for the purposes of the definition of "parent undertaking" (see section 1162) in the absence of which it would not be the parent company.

406 IAS group accounts

(1) IAS group accounts must state—

(a) the part of the United Kingdom in which the company is registered,

(b) the company's registered number,

(c) whether the company is a public or a private company and whether it is limited by shares or by guarantee,

(d) the address of the company's registered office, and

(e) where appropriate, the fact that the company is being wound-up.

(2) The notes to the accounts must state that the accounts have been prepared in accordance with international accounting standards.

407 Consistency of financial reporting within group

(1) The directors of a parent company must secure that the individual accounts of—

(a) the parent company, and

(b) each of its subsidiary undertakings,

are all prepared using the same financial reporting framework, except to the extent that in their opinion there are good reasons for not doing so.

(2) Subsection (1) does not apply if the directors do not prepare group accounts for the parent company.

(3) Subsection (1) only applies to accounts of subsidiary undertakings that are required to be prepared under this Part.

(4) Subsection (1) does not require accounts of undertakings that are charities to be prepared using the same financial reporting framework as accounts of undertakings which are not charities.

(5) Subsection (1)(a) does not apply where the directors of a parent company prepare IAS group accounts and IAS individual accounts.

408 Individual profit and loss account where group accounts prepared

(1) This section applies where—

(a) a company prepares group accounts in accordance with this Act, and

(b) the company's individual balance sheet shows the company's profit and loss for the financial year determined in accordance with this Act.

(2) …

(3) The company's individual profit and loss account must be approved in accordance with section 414(1) (approval by directors) but may be omitted from the company's annual accounts for the purposes of the other provisions of the Companies Acts.

(4) The exemption conferred by this section is conditional upon its being disclosed in the company's annual accounts that the exemption applies.

Information to be given in notes to the accounts

409 Information about related undertakings

(1) The Secretary of State may make provision by regulations requiring information about related undertakings to be given in notes to a company's annual accounts.

(2) The regulations—

(a) may make different provision according to whether or not the company prepares group accounts, and

(b) may specify the descriptions of undertaking in relation to which they apply, and make different provision in relation to different descriptions of related undertaking.

(3) The regulations may provide that information need not be disclosed with respect to an undertaking that—
   (a) is established under the law of a country outside the United Kingdom, or
   (b) carries on business outside the United Kingdom, if the following conditions are met.

(4) The conditions are—
   (a) that in the opinion of the directors of the company the disclosure would be seriously prejudicial to the business of—
      (i) that undertaking,
      (ii) the company,
      (iii) any of the company's subsidiary undertakings, or
      (iv) any other undertaking which is included in the consolidation;
   (b) that the Secretary of State agrees that the information need not be disclosed.

(5) Where advantage is taken of any such exemption, that fact must be stated in a note to the company's annual accounts.

410 ...

410A Information about off-balance sheet arrangements

(1) If in any financial year—
   (a) a company is or has been party to arrangements that are not reflected in its balance sheet, and
   (b) at the balance sheet date the risks or benefits arising from those arrangements are material,

the information required by this section must be given in the notes to the company's annual accounts.

(2) The information required is—
   (a) the nature and business purpose of the arrangements, and
   (b) the financial impact of the arrangements on the company.

(3) The information need only be given to the extent necessary for enabling the financial position of the company to be assessed.

(4) If the company is subject to the small companies regime in relation to the financial year (see section 381), it need not comply with subsection (2)(b).

(5) This section applies in relation to group accounts as if the undertakings included in the consolidation were a single company.

411 Information about employee numbers and costs

(1) The notes to a company's annual accounts must disclose the average number of persons employed by the company in the financial year.

(1A) In the case of a company not subject to the small companies regime, the notes to the company's accounts must also disclose the average number of persons within each category of persons so employed.,

(2) The categories by reference to which the number required to be disclosed by subsection (1A) is to be determined must be such as the directors may select having regard to the manner in which the company's activities are organised.

(3) The average number required by subsection (1) or (1A) is determined by dividing the relevant annual number by the number of months in the financial year.

(4) The relevant annual number is determined by ascertaining for each month in the financial year—
   (a) for the purposes of subsection (1), the number of persons employed under contracts of service by the company in that month (whether throughout the month or not);
   (b) for the purposes of subsection (1A), the number of persons in the category in question of persons so employed;

and adding together all the monthly numbers.

(5) Except in the case of a company subject to the small companies regime, the notes to the company's annual accounts or the profit and loss account must disclose, with reference to all persons employed by the company during the financial year, the total staff costs of the company relating to the financial year broken down between—
   (a) wages and salaries paid or payable in respect of that year to those persons,
   (b) social security costs incurred by the company on their behalf, and
   (c) other pension costs so incurred.

(6) In subsection (5)—
"pension costs" includes any costs incurred by the company in respect of—
(a) any pension scheme established for the purpose of providing pensions for persons currently or formerly employed by the company,
(b) any sums set aside for the future payment of pensions directly by the company to current or former employees, and
(c) any pensions paid directly to such persons without having first been set aside;
"social security costs" means any contributions by the company to any state social security or pension scheme, fund or arrangement.
(7) This section applies in relation to group accounts as if the undertakings included in the consolidation were a single company.

412 Information about directors' benefits: remuneration

(1) The Secretary of State may make provision by regulations requiring information to be given in notes to a company's annual accounts about directors' remuneration.
(2) The matters about which information may be required include—
(a) gains made by directors on the exercise of share options;
(b) benefits received or receivable by directors under long-term incentive schemes;
(c) payments for loss of office (as defined in section 215);
(d) benefits receivable, and contributions for the purpose of providing benefits, in respect of past services of a person as director or in any other capacity while director;
(e) consideration paid to or receivable by third parties for making available the services of a person as director or in any other capacity while director.
(3) Without prejudice to the generality of subsection (1), regulations under this section may make any such provision as was made immediately before the commencement of this Part by Part 1 of Schedule 6 to the Companies Act 1985.
(4) For the purposes of this section, and regulations made under it, amounts paid to or receivable by—
(a) a person connected with a director, or
(b) a body corporate controlled by a director, are treated as paid to or receivable by the director.
The expressions "connected with" and "controlled by" in this subsection have the same meaning as in Part 10 (company directors).
(5) It is the duty of—
(a) any director of a company, and
(b) any person who is or has at any time in the preceding five years been a director of the company,
to give notice to the company of such matters relating to himself as may be necessary for the purposes of regulations under this section.
(6) A person who makes default in complying with subsection (5) commits an offence and is liable on summary conviction to a fine not exceeding level 3 on the standard scale.

413 Information about directors' benefits: advances, credit and guarantees

(1) In the case of a company that does not prepare group accounts, details of—
(a) advances and credits granted by the company to its directors, and
(b) guarantees of any kind entered into by the company on behalf of its directors, must be shown in the notes to its individual accounts.
(2) In the case of a parent company that prepares group accounts, details of—
(a) advances and credits granted to the directors of the parent company, by that company or by any of its subsidiary undertakings, and
(b) guarantees of any kind entered into on behalf of the directors of the parent company, by that company or by any of its subsidiary undertakings,
must be shown in the notes to the group accounts.
(3) The details required of an advance or credit are—
(a) its amount,
(b) an indication of the interest rate,
(c) its main conditions,
(d) any amounts repaid,
(e) any amounts written off, and
(f) any amounts waived

(4) The details required of a guarantee are—
(a) its main terms,
(b) the amount of the maximum liability that may be incurred by the company (or its subsidiary), and
(c) any amount paid and any liability incurred by the company (or its subsidiary) for the purpose of fulfilling the guarantee (including any loss incurred by reason of enforcement of the guarantee).
(5) There must also be stated in the notes to the accounts the totals—
(a) of amounts stated under subsection (3)(a),
(b) of amounts stated under subsection (3)(d),
(ba) of amounts stated under subsection 3(e),
(bb) of amounts stated under subsection 3(f),
(c) of amounts stated under subsection (4)(b), and
(d) of amounts stated under subsection (4)(c).
(6) References in this section to the directors of a company are to the persons who were directors at any time in the financial year to which the accounts relate.
(7) The requirements of this section apply in relation to every advance, credit or guarantee subsisting at any time in the financial year to which the accounts relate—
(a) whenever it was entered into,
(b) whether or not the person concerned was a director of the company in question at the time it was entered into, and
(c) in the case of an advance, credit or guarantee involving a subsidiary undertaking of that company, whether or not that undertaking was such a subsidiary undertaking at the time it was entered into.
(8) Banking companies and the holding companies of credit institutions need only state the details required by subsection (5)(a) and (c).

Approval and signing of accounts

414 Approval and signing of accounts

(1) A company's annual accounts must be approved by the board of directors and signed on behalf of the board by a director of the company.
(2) The signature must be on the company's balance sheet.
(3) If the accounts are prepared in accordance with the small companies regime, the balance sheet must contain, in a prominent position above the signature—
(a) in the case of individual accounts prepared in accordance with the micro-entity provisions, a statement to that effect, or
(b) in the case of accounts not prepared as mentioned in paragraph (a), a statement to the effect that the accounts have been prepared in accordance with the provisions applicable to companies subject to the small companies regime.
(4) If annual accounts are approved that do not comply with the requirements of this Act (and, where applicable, of Article 4 of the IAS Regulation), every director of the company who—
(a) knew that they did not comply, or was reckless as to whether they complied, and
(b) failed to take reasonable steps to secure compliance with those requirements or, as the case may be, to prevent the accounts from being approved,

commits an offence.
(5) A person guilty of an offence under this section is liable—
(a) on conviction on indictment, to a fine;
(b) on summary conviction, to a fine not exceeding the statutory maximum.

CHAPTER 4A
STRATEGIC REPORT

414A Duty to prepare strategic report

(1) The directors of a company must prepare a strategic report for each financial year of the company.
(2) Subsection (1) does not apply if the company is entitled to the small companies exemption.
(3) For a financial year in which—
(a) the company is a parent company, and

(b) the directors of the company prepare group accounts, the strategic report must be a consolidated report (a "group strategic report") relating to the undertakings included in the consolidation.

(4) A group strategic report may, where appropriate, give greater emphasis to the matters that are significant to the undertakings included in the consolidation, taken as a whole.

(5) In the case of failure to comply with the requirement to prepare a strategic report, an offence is committed by every person who—

(a) was a director of the company immediately before the end of the period for filing accounts and reports for the financial year in question, and

(b) failed to take all reasonable steps for securing compliance with that requirement.

(6) A person guilty of an offence under this section is liable—

(a) on conviction on indictment, to a fine;

(b) on summary conviction, to a fine not exceeding the statutory maximum.

414B Strategic report: small companies exemption

A company is entitled to the small companies exemption in relation to the strategic report for a financial year if—

(a) it is entitled to prepare accounts for the year in accordance with the small companies regime, or

(b) it would be so entitled but for being or having been a member of an ineligible group.

414C Contents of strategic report

(1) The purpose of the strategic report is to inform members of the company and help them assess how the directors have performed their duty under section 172 (duty to promote the success of the company).

(2) The strategic report must contain—

(a) a fair review of the company's business, and

(b) a description of the principal risks and uncertainties facing the company.

(3) The review required is a balanced and comprehensive analysis of—

(a) the development and performance of the company's business during the financial year, and

(b) the position of the company's business at the end of that year, consistent with the size and complexity of the business.

(4) The review must, to the extent necessary for an understanding of the development, performance or position of the company's business, include—

(a) analysis using financial key performance indicators, and

(b) where appropriate, analysis using other key performance indicators, including information relating to environmental matters and employee matters.

(5) In subsection (4), "key performance indicators" means factors by reference to which the development, performance or position of the company's business can be measured effectively.

(6) Where a company qualifies as medium-sized in relation to a financial year (see sections 465 to 467), the review for the year need not comply with the requirements of subsection (4) so far as they relate to non-financial information.

(7) In the case of a quoted company the strategic report must, to the extent necessary for an understanding of the development, performance or position of the company's business, include—

(a) the main trends and factors likely to affect the future development, performance and position of the company's business, and

(b) information about—

(i) environmental matters (including the impact of the company's business on the environment),

(ii) the company's employees, and

(iii) social, community and human rights issues, including information about any policies of the company in relation to those matters and the effectiveness of those policies. If the report does not contain information of each kind mentioned in paragraphs (b)(i), (ii) and (iii), it must state which of those kinds of information it does not contain.

(8) In the case of a quoted company the strategic report must include—

(a) a description of the company's strategy,

(b) a description of the company's business model,

(c) a breakdown showing at the end of the financial year—
 (i) the number of persons of each sex who were directors of the company;
 (ii) the number of persons of each sex who were senior managers of the company (other than persons falling within sub-paragraph (i)); and
 (iii) the number of persons of each sex who were employees of the company.

(9) In subsection (8), "senior manager" means a person who—
 (a) has responsibility for planning, directing or controlling the activities of the company, or a strategically significant part of the company, and
 (b) is an employee of the company.

(10) In relation to a group strategic report—
 (a) the reference to the company in subsection (8)(c)(i) is to the parent company; and
 (b) the breakdown required by subsection (8)(c)(ii) must include the number of persons of each sex who were the directors of the undertakings included in the consolidation.

(11) The strategic report may also contain such of the matters otherwise required by regulations made under section 416(4) to be disclosed in the directors' report as the directors consider are of strategic importance to the company.

(12) The report must, where appropriate, include references to, and additional explanations of, amounts included in the company's annual accounts.

(13) Subject to paragraph (10), in relation to a group strategic report this section has effect as if the references to the company were references to the undertakings included in the consolidation.

(14) Nothing in this section requires the disclosure of information about impending developments or matters in the course of negotiation if the disclosure would, in the opinion of the directors, be seriously prejudicial to the interests of the company.

414D Approval and signing of strategic report

(1) The strategic report must be approved by the board of directors and signed on behalf of the board by a director or the secretary of the company.

(2) If a strategic report is approved that does not comply with the requirements of this Act, every director of the company who—
 (a) knew that it did not comply, or was reckless as to whether it complied, and
 (b) failed to take reasonable steps to secure compliance with those requirements or, as the case may be, to prevent the report from being approved, commits an offence.

(3) A person guilty of an offence under this section is liable—
 (a) on conviction on indictment, to a fine;
 (b) on summary conviction, to a fine not exceeding the statutory maximum.

CHAPTER 5
DIRECTORS' REPORT

Directors' report

415 Duty to prepare directors' report

(1) The directors of a company must prepare a directors' report for each financial year of the company.

(1A) Subsection (1) does not apply if the company qualifies as a micro-entity (see sections 384A and 384B).

(2) For a financial year in which—
 (a) the company is a parent company, and
 (b) the directors of the company prepare group accounts,
 the directors' report must be a consolidated report (a "group directors' report") relating to the undertakings included in the consolidation.

(3) A group directors' report may, where appropriate, give greater emphasis to the matters that are significant to the undertakings included in the consolidation, taken as a whole.

(4) In the case of failure to comply with the requirement to prepare a directors' report, an offence is committed by every person who—
 (a) was a director of the company immediately before the end of the period for filing accounts and reports for the financial year in question, and
 (b) failed to take all reasonable steps for securing compliance with that requirement.

(5) A person guilty of an offence under this section is liable—

(a) on conviction on indictment, to a fine;
(b) on summary conviction, to a fine not exceeding the statutory maximum.

415A Directors' report: small companies exemption

(1) A company is entitled to small companies exemption in relation to the directors' report for a financial year if—
(a) it is entitled to prepare accounts for the year in accordance with the small companies regime, or
(b) it would be so entitled but for being or having been a member of an ineligible group.

(2) The exemption is relevant to—
section 416(3) (contents of report: statement of amount recommended by way of dividend), and
sections 444 to 446 (filing obligations of different descriptions of company).

416 Contents of directors' report: general

(1) The directors' report for a financial year must state—
(a) the names of the persons who, at any time during the financial year, were directors of the company.

(2) …

(3) Except in the case of a company entitled to the small companies exemption, the report must state the amount (if any) that the directors recommend should be paid by way of dividend.

(4) The Secretary of State may make provision by regulations as to other matters that must be disclosed in a directors' report.
Without prejudice to the generality of this power, the regulations may make any such provision as was formerly made by Schedule 7 to the Companies Act 1985.

417 …

418 Contents of directors' report: statement as to disclosure to auditors

(1) This section applies to a company unless—
(a) it is exempt for the financial year in question from the requirements of Part 16 as to audit of accounts, and
(b) the directors take advantage of that exemption.

(2) The directors' report must contain a statement to the effect that, in the case of each of the persons who are directors at the time the report is approved—
(a) so far as the director is aware, there is no relevant audit information of which the company's auditor is unaware, and
(b) he has taken all the steps that he ought to have taken as a director in order to make himself aware of any relevant audit information and to establish that the company's auditor is aware of that information.

(3) "Relevant audit information" means information needed by the company's auditor in connection with preparing his report.

(4) A director is regarded as having taken all the steps that he ought to have taken as a director in order to do the things mentioned in subsection (2)(b) if he has—
(a) made such enquiries of his fellow directors and of the company's auditors for that purpose, and
(b) taken such other steps (if any) for that purpose,
as are required by his duty as a director of the company to exercise reasonable care, skill and diligence.

(5) Where a directors' report containing the statement required by this section is approved but the statement is false, every director of the company who—
(a) knew that the statement was false, or was reckless as to whether it was false, and
(b) failed to take reasonable steps to prevent the report from being approved, commits an offence.

(6) A person guilty of an offence under subsection (5) is liable—
(a) on conviction on indictment, to imprisonment for a term not exceeding two years or a fine (or both);
(b) on summary conviction—

(i) in England and Wales, to imprisonment for a term not exceeding twelve months or to a fine not exceeding the statutory maximum (or both);
(ii) in Scotland or Northern Ireland, to imprisonment for a term not exceeding six months, or to a fine not exceeding the statutory maximum (or both).

419 Approval and signing of directors' report

(1) The directors' report must be approved by the board of directors and signed on behalf of the board by a director or the secretary of the company.
(2) If in preparing the report advantage is taken of the small companies exemption, it must contain a statement to that effect in a prominent position above the signature.
(3) If a directors' report is approved that does not comply with the requirements of this Act, every director of the company who—
(a) knew that it did not comply, or was reckless as to whether it complied, and
(b) failed to take reasonable steps to secure compliance with those requirements or, as the case may be, to prevent the report from being approved,
commits an offence.
(4) A person guilty of an offence under this section is liable—
(a) on conviction on indictment, to a fine;
(b) on summary conviction, to a fine not exceeding the statutory maximum.

419A Approval and signing of separate corporate governance statement

Any separate corporate governance statement must be approved by the board of directors and signed on behalf of the board by a director or the secretary of the company.

CHAPTER 6
QUOTED COMPANIES: DIRECTORS' REMUNERATION REPORT

420 Duty to prepare directors' remuneration report

(1) The directors of a quoted company must prepare a directors' remuneration report for each financial year of the company.
(2) In the case of failure to comply with the requirement to prepare a directors' remuneration report, every person who—
(a) was a director of the company immediately before the end of the period for filing accounts and reports for the financial year in question, and
(b) failed to take all reasonable steps for securing compliance with that requirement, commits an offence.
(3) A person guilty of an offence under this section is liable—
(a) on conviction on indictment, to a fine;
(b) on summary conviction, to a fine not exceeding the statutory maximum.

421 Contents of directors' remuneration report

(1) The Secretary of State may make provision by regulations as to—
(a) the information that must be contained in a directors' remuneration report,
(b) how information is to be set out in the report, and
(c) what is to be the auditable part of the report.
(2) Without prejudice to the generality of this power, the regulations may make any such provision as was made, immediately before the commencement of this Part, by Schedule 7A to the Companies Act 1985.
(2A) The regulations must provide that any information required to be included in the report as to the policy of the company with respect to the making of remuneration payments and payments for loss of office (within the meaning of Chapter 4A of Part 10) is to be set out in a separate part of the report.
(3) It is the duty of—
(a) any director of a company, and
(b) any person who is or has at any time in the preceding five years been a director of the company,
to give notice to the company of such matters relating to himself as may be necessary for the purposes of regulations under this section.

(4) A person who makes default in complying with subsection (3) commits an offence and is liable on summary conviction to a fine not exceeding level 3 on the standard scale.

422 Approval and signing of directors' remuneration report

(1) The directors' remuneration report must be approved by the board of directors and signed on behalf of the board by a director or the secretary of the company.

(2) If a directors' remuneration report is approved that does not comply with the requirements of this Act, every director of the company who—

(a) knew that it did not comply, or was reckless as to whether it complied, and

(b) failed to take reasonable steps to secure compliance with those requirements or, as the case may be, to prevent the report from being approved,

commits an offence.

(3) A person guilty of an offence under this section is liable—

(a) on conviction on indictment, to a fine;

(b) on summary conviction, to a fine not exceeding the statutory maximum.

422A Revisions to directors' remuneration policy

(1) The directors' remuneration policy contained in a company's directors' remuneration report may be revised.

(2) Any such revision must be approved by the board of directors.

(3) The policy as so revised must be set out in a document signed on behalf of the board by a director or the secretary of the company.

(4) Regulations under section 421(1) may make provision as to—

(a) the information that must be contained in a document setting out a revised rectors' remuneration policy, and

(b) how information is to be set out in the document.

(5) Sections 422(2) and (3), 454, 456 and 463 apply in relation to such a document as they apply in relation to a directors' remuneration report.

(6) In this section, "directors' remuneration policy" means the policy of a company with respect to the matters mentioned in section 421(2A).

CHAPTER 7
PUBLICATION OF ACCOUNTS AND REPORTS

Duty to circulate copies of accounts and reports

423 Duty to circulate copies of annual accounts and reports

(1) Every company must send a copy of its annual accounts and reports for each financial year to—

(a) every member of the company,

(b) every holder of the company's debentures, and

(c) every person who is entitled to receive notice of general meetings.

(2) Copies need not be sent to a person for whom the company does not have a current address.

(3) A company has a "current address" for a person if—

(a) an address has been notified to the company by the person as one at which documents may be sent to him, and

(b) the company has no reason to believe that documents sent to him at that address will not reach him.

(4) In the case of a company not having a share capital, copies need not be sent to anyone who is not entitled to receive notices of general meetings of the company.

(5) Where copies are sent out over a period of days, references in the Companies Acts to the day on which copies are sent out shall be read as references to the last day of that period.

(6) This section has effect subject to section 426 (option to provide strategic report with supplemental material).

424 Time allowed for sending out copies of accounts and reports

(1) The time allowed for sending out copies of the company's annual accounts and reports is as follows.

(2) A private company must comply with section 423 not later than—
(a) the end of the period for filing accounts and reports, or
(b) if earlier, the date on which it actually delivers its accounts and reports to the registrar.
(3) A public company must comply with section 423 at least 21 days before the date of the relevant accounts meeting.
(4) If in the case of a public company copies are sent out later than is required by subsection (3), they shall, despite that, be deemed to have been duly sent if it is so agreed by all the members entitled to attend and vote at the relevant accounts meeting.
(5) Whether the time allowed is that for a private company or a public company is determined by reference to the company's status immediately before the end of the accounting reference period by reference to which the financial year for the accounts in question was determined.
(6) In this section the "relevant accounts meeting" means the accounts meeting of the company at which the accounts and reports in question are to be laid.

425 Default in sending out copies of accounts and reports: offences

(1) If default is made in complying with section 423 or 424, an offence is committed by—
(a) the company, and
(b) every officer of the company who is in default.
(2) A person guilty of an offence under this section is liable—
(a) on conviction on indictment, to a fine;
(b) on summary conviction, to a fine not exceeding the statutory maximum.

Option to provide strategic report with supplemental material

426 Option to provide strategic report with supplemental material

(1) A company may—
(a) in such cases as may be specified by regulations made by the Secretary of State, and
(b) provided any conditions so specified are complied with,
provide a copy of the strategic report together with the supplementary material described in section 426A instead of copies of the accounts and reports required to be sent out in accordance with section 423.
(2) Copies of those accounts and reports must, however, be sent to any person entitled to be sent them in accordance with that section and who wishes to receive them.
(3) The Secretary of State may make provision by regulations as to the manner in which it is to be ascertained, whether before or after a person becomes entitled to be sent a copy of those accounts and reports, whether he wishes to receive them.
(4) ...
(5) This section applies to copies of accounts and reports required to be sent out by virtue of section 146 to a person nominated to enjoy information rights as it applies to copies of accounts and reports required to be sent out in accordance with section 423 to a member of the company.
(6) Regulations under this section are subject to negative resolution procedure.

426A Supplementary material

(1) The supplementary material referred to in section 426 must be prepared in accordance with this section.
(2) The supplementary material must—
(a) contain a statement that the strategic report is only part of the company's annual accounts and reports;
(b) state how a person entitled to them can obtain a full copy of the company's annual accounts and reports;
(c) state whether the auditor's report on the annual accounts was unqualified or qualified and, if it was qualified, set out the report in full together with any further material needed to understand the qualification;
(d) state whether, in that report, the auditor's statement under section 496 (whether strategic report and directors' report consistent with the accounts) was unqualified or qualified and, if it was qualified, set out the qualified statement in full together with any further material needed to understand the qualification;

(e) in the case of a quoted company, contain a copy of that part of the directors' remuneration report which sets out the single total figure table in respect of the company's directors' remuneration in accordance with the requirements of Schedule 8 to the Large and Medium-sized Companies (Accounts and Reports) Regulations 2008.

427–429 ...

Quoted companies: requirements as to website publication

430 Quoted companies: annual accounts and reports to be made available on website

(1) A quoted company must ensure that its annual accounts and reports—
(a) are made available on a website, and
(b) remain so available until the annual accounts and reports for the company's next financial year are made available in accordance with this section.

(2) The annual accounts and reports must be made available on a website that—
(a) is maintained by or on behalf of the company, and
(b) identifies the company in question.

(2A) If the directors' remuneration policy of a quoted company is revised in accordance with section 422A, the company must ensure that the revised policy is made available on the website on which its annual accounts and reports are made available.

(2B) If a person ceases to be a director of a quoted company, the company must ensure that the following information is made available on the website on which its annual accounts and reports are made available—
(a) the name of the person concerned,
(b) particulars of any remuneration payment (within the meaning of Chapter 4A of Part 10) made or to be made to the person after ceasing to be a director, including its amount and how it was calculated, and
(c) particulars of any payment for loss of office (within the meaning of that Chapter) made or to be made to the person, including its amount and how it was calculated.

(3) Access to the material made available on the website under subsections (1) to (2B), and the ability to obtain a hard copy of such material from the website, must not be–
(a) conditional on the payment of a fee, or
(b) otherwise restricted, except so far as necessary to comply with any enactment or regulatory requirement (in the United Kingdom or elsewhere).

(4) The annual accounts and reports–
(a) must be made available as soon as reasonably practicable, and
(b) must be kept available throughout the period specified in subsection (1)(b). (4A) Where subsection (2A) or (2B) applies, the material in question—
(a) must be made available as soon as reasonably practicable, and
(b) must be kept available until the next directors' remuneration report of the company is made available on the website.

(5) A failure to make material available on a website throughout the period mentioned in subsection (4) or (as the case may be) (4A) is disregarded if—
(a) the material is made available on the website for part of that period, and
(b) the failure is wholly attributable to circumstances that it would not be reasonable to have expected the company to prevent or avoid.

(6) In the event of default in complying with this section, an offence is committed by every officer of the company who is in default.

(7) A person guilty of an offence under subsection (6) is liable on summary conviction to a fine not exceeding level 3 on the standard scale.

Right of member or debenture holder to demand copies of accounts and reports

431 Right of member or debenture holder to copies of accounts and reports: unquoted companies

(1) A member of, or holder of debentures of, an unquoted company is entitled to be provided, on demand and without charge, with a copy of—
(a) the company's last annual accounts,
(aa) the strategic report (if any) for the last financial year,

(b) the last directors' report, and
(c) the auditor's report on those accounts (including the statement on that report and (where applicable) on the strategic report).

(2) The entitlement under this section is to a single copy of those documents, but that is in addition to any copy to which a person may be entitled under section 423.

(3) If a demand made under this section is not complied with within seven days of receipt by the company, an offence is committed by—
(a) the company, and
(b) every officer of the company who is in default.

(4) A person guilty of an offence under this section is liable on summary conviction to a fine not exceeding level 3 on the standard scale and, for continued contravention, a daily default fine not exceeding one-tenth of level 3 on the standard scale.

432 Right of member or debenture holder to copies of accounts and reports: quoted companies

(1) A member of, or holder of debentures of, a quoted company is entitled to be provided, on demand and without charge, with a copy of—
(a) the company's last annual accounts,
(b) the last directors' remuneration report,
(ba) the strategic report (if any) for the last financial year,
(c) the last directors' report, and
(d) the auditor's report on those accounts (including the report on the directors' remuneration report, on the strategic report (where this is covered by the auditor's report) and on the directors' report).

(2) The entitlement under this section is to a single copy of those documents, but that is in addition to any copy to which a person may be entitled under section 423.

(3) If a demand made under this section is not complied with within seven days of receipt by the company, an offence is committed by—
(a) the company, and
(b) every officer of the company who is in default.

(4) A person guilty of an offence under this section is liable on summary conviction to a fine not exceeding level 3 on the standard scale and, for continued contravention, a daily default fine not exceeding one-tenth of level 3 on the standard scale.

Requirements in connection with publication of accounts and reports

433 Name of signatory to be stated in published copies of accounts and reports

(1) Every copy of a document to which this section applies that is published by or on behalf of the company must state the name of the person who signed it on behalf of the board.

(2) In the case of an unquoted company, this section applies to copies of—
(a) the company's balance sheet,
(aa) the strategic report, and
(b) the directors' report.

(3) In the case of a quoted company, this section applies to copies of—
(a) the company's balance sheet,
(b) the directors' remuneration report, (ba) the strategic report, and
(c) the directors' report.

(4) If a copy is published without the required statement of the signatory's name, an offence is committed by—
(a) the company, and
(b) every officer of the company who is in default.

(5) A person guilty of an offence under this section is liable on summary conviction to a fine not exceeding level 3 on the standard scale.

434 Requirements in connection with publication of statutory accounts

(1) If a company publishes any of its statutory accounts, they must be accompanied by the auditor's report on those accounts (unless the company is exempt from audit and the directors have taken advantage of that exemption).

(2) A company that prepares statutory group accounts for a financial year must not publish its statutory individual accounts for that year without also publishing with them its statutory group accounts.

(3) A company's "statutory accounts" are its accounts for a financial year as required to be delivered to the registrar under section 441.

(4) If a company contravenes any provision of this section, an offence is committed by—
 (a) the company, and
 (b) every officer of the company who is in default.

(5) A person guilty of an offence under this section is liable on summary conviction to a fine not exceeding level 3 on the standard scale.

435 Requirements in connection with publication of non-statutory accounts

(1) If a company publishes non-statutory accounts, it must publish with them a statement indicating—
 (a) that they are not the company's statutory accounts,
 (b) whether statutory accounts dealing with any financial year with which the non-statutory accounts purport to deal have been delivered to the registrar, and
 (c) whether an auditor's report has been made on the company's statutory accounts for any such financial year, and if so whether the report—
  (i) was qualified or unqualified, or included a reference to any matters to which the auditor drew attention by way of emphasis without qualifying the report, or
  (ii) contained a statement under section 498(2) (accounting records or returns inadequate or accounts or directors' remuneration report not agreeing with records and returns), or section 498(3) (failure to obtain necessary information and explanations).

(2) The company must not publish with non-statutory accounts the auditor's report on the company's statutory accounts.

(3) References in this section to the publication by a company of "non-statutory accounts" are to the publication of—
 (a) any balance sheet or profit and loss account relating to, or purporting to deal with, a financial year of the company, or
 (b) an account in any form purporting to be a balance sheet or profit and loss account for a group headed by the company relating to, or purporting to deal with, a financial year of the company,

otherwise than as part of the company's statutory accounts.

(4) In subsection (3)(b) "a group headed by the company" means a group consisting of the company and any other undertaking (regardless of whether it is a subsidiary undertaking of the company) other than a parent undertaking of the company.

(5) If a company contravenes any provision of this section, an offence is committed by—
 (a) the company, and
 (b) every officer of the company who is in default.

(6) A person guilty of an offence under this section is liable on summary conviction to a fine not exceeding level 3 on the standard scale.

436 Meaning of "publication" in relation to accounts and reports

(1) This section has effect for the purposes of—
section 433 (name of signatory to be stated in published copies of accounts and reports),
section 434 (requirements in connection with publication of statutory accounts), and
section 435 (requirements in connection with publication of non-statutory accounts).

(2) For the purposes of those sections a company is regarded as publishing a document if it publishes, issues or circulates it or otherwise makes it available for public inspection in a manner calculated to invite members of the public generally, or any class of members of the public, to read it.

CHAPTER 8

PUBLIC COMPANIES: LAYING OF ACCOUNTS AND REPORTS BEFORE GENERAL MEETING

437 Public companies: laying of accounts and reports before general meeting

(1) The directors of a public company must lay before the company in general meeting copies of its annual accounts and reports.

(2) This section must be complied with not later than the end of the period for filing the accounts and reports in question.

(3) In the Companies Acts "accounts meeting", in relation to a public company, means a general meeting of the company at which the company's annual accounts and reports are (or are to be) laid in accordance with this section.

438 Public companies: offence of failure to lay accounts and reports

(1) If the requirements of section 437 (public companies: laying of accounts and reportsefore general meeting) are not complied with before the end of the period allowed, every person who immediately before the end of that period was a director of the company commits an offence.

(2) It is a defence for a person charged with such an offence to prove that he took all reasonable steps for securing that those requirements would be complied with before the end of that period.

(3) It is not a defence to prove that the documents in question were not in fact prepared as required by this Part.

Version applying in Scotland

(4) A person guilty of an offence under this section is liable on summary conviction to a fine not exceeding level 5 on the standard scale and, for continued contravention, a daily default fine not exceeding one-tenth of the greater of £5,000 or level 4 on the standard scale.

Version applying in England and Wales

(4) A person guilty of an offence under this section is liable on summary conviction to a fine not exceeding level 5 on the standard scale and, for continued contravention, a daily default fine not exceeding one-tenth of the greater of £5,000 or level 4 on the standard scale.

CHAPTER 9

QUOTED COMPANIES: MEMBERS' APPROVAL OF DIRECTORS' REMUNERATION REPORT

439 Quoted companies: members' approval of directors' remuneration report

(1) A quoted company must, prior to the accounts meeting, give to the members of the company entitled to be sent notice of the meeting notice of the intention to move at the meeting, as an ordinary resolution, a resolution approving the directors' remuneration report for the financial year.

(2) The notice may be given in any manner permitted for the service on the member of notice of the meeting.

(3) The business that may be dealt with at the accounts meeting includes the resolution. This is so notwithstanding any default in complying with subsection (1) or (2).

(4) The existing directors must ensure that the resolution is put to the vote of the meeting.

(5) No entitlement of a person to remuneration is made conditional on the resolution being passed by reason only of the provision made by this section.

(6) In this section—
"the accounts meeting" means the general meeting of the company before which the company's annual accounts for the financial year are to be laid; and
"existing director" means a person who is a director of the company immediately before that meeting.

439A Quoted companies: members' approval of directors' remuneration policy

(1) A quoted company must give notice of the intention to move, as an ordinary resolution, a resolution approving the relevant directors' remuneration policy—
  (a) at the accounts meeting held in the first financial year which begins on or after the day on which the company becomes a quoted company, and
  (b) at an accounts or other general meeting held no later than the end of the period of three financial years beginning with the first financial year after the last accounts or other general meeting in relation to which notice is given under this subsection.

(2) A quoted company must give notice of the intention to move at an accounts meeting, as an ordinary resolution, a resolution approving the relevant directors' remuneration policy if—
  (a) a resolution required to be put to the vote under section 439 was not passed at the last accounts meeting of the company, and

(b) no notice under this section was given in relation to that meeting or any other general meeting held before the next accounts meeting.

(3) Subsection (2) does not apply in relation to a quoted company before the first meeting in relation to which it gives notice under subsection (1).

(4) A notice given under subsection (2) is to be treated as given under subsection (1) for the purpose of determining the period within which the next notice under subsection (1) must be given.

(5) Notice of the intention to move a resolution to which this section applies must be given, prior to the meeting in question, to the members of the company entitled to be sent notice of the meeting.

(6) Subsections (2) to (4) of section 439 apply for the purposes of a resolution to which this section applies as they apply for the purposes of a resolution to which section 439 applies, with the modification that, for the purposes of a resolution relating to a general meeting other than an accounts meeting, subsection (3) applies as if for "accounts meeting" there were substituted "general meeting".

(7) For the purposes of this section, the relevant directors' remuneration policy is—

(a) in a case where notice is given in relation to an accounts meeting, the remuneration policy contained in the directors' remuneration report in respect of which a resolution under section 439 is required to be put to the vote at that accounts meeting;

(b) in a case where notice is given in relation to a general meeting other than an accounts meeting—

(i) the remuneration policy contained in the directors' remuneration report in respect of which such a resolution was required to be put to the vote at the last accounts meeting to be held before that other general meeting, or

(ii) where that policy has been revised in accordance with section 422A, the policy as so revised.

(8) In this section—

(a) "accounts meeting" means a general meeting of the company before which the company's
annual accounts for a financial year are to be laid;

(b) "directors' remuneration policy" means the policy of the company with respect to the matters mentioned in section 421(2A).

440 Quoted companies: offences in connection with procedure for approval

(1) In the event of default in complying with section 439(1) (notice to be given of resolution for approval of directors' remuneration report or policy) or 439A(1) or (2), an offence is committed by every officer of the company who is in default.

(2) If the resolution is not put to the vote of the meeting to which it relates, an offence is committed by each existing director.

(3) It is a defence for a person charged with an offence under subsection (2) to prove that he took all reasonable steps for securing that the resolution was put to the vote of the meeting.

(4) A person guilty of an offence under this section is liable on summary conviction to a fine not exceeding level 3 on the standard scale.

(5) In this section—
"existing director" means a person who is a director of the company immediately before that meeting.

CHAPTER 10
FILING OF ACCOUNTS AND REPORTS

Duty to file accounts and reports

441 Duty to file accounts and reports with the registrar

(1) The directors of a company must deliver to the registrar for each financial year the accounts and reports required by—
section 444 (filing obligations of companies subject to small companies regime),
section 444A (filing obligations of companies entitled to small companies exemption in relation to directors' report),
section 445 (filing obligations of medium-sized companies), section 446 (filing obligations of unquoted companies), or section 447 (filing obligations of quoted companies).

(2) This is subject to section 448 (unlimited companies exempt from filing obligations), and section 448A (dormant subsidiaries exempt from filing obligations).

442 Period allowed for filing accounts

(1) This section specifies the period allowed for the directors of a company to comply with their obligation under section 441 to deliver accounts and reports for a financial year to the registrar.

This is referred to in the Companies Acts as the "period for filing" those accounts and reports.

(2) The period is—

(a) for a private company, nine months after the end of the relevant accounting reference period, and

(b) for a public company, six months after the end of that period.

This is subject to the following provisions of this section.

(3) If the relevant accounting reference period is the company's first and is a period of more than twelve months, the period is—

(a) nine months or six months, as the case may be, from the first anniversary of the incorporation of the company, or

(b) three months after the end of the accounting reference period,

whichever last expires.

(4) Subject to subsection (5A), if the relevant accounting reference period is treated as shortened by virtue of a notice given by the company under section 392 (alteration of accounting reference date), the period is—

(a) that applicable in accordance with the above provisions, or

(b) three months from the date of the notice under that section, whichever last expires.

(5) If for any special reason the Secretary of State thinks fit he may, on an application made before the expiry of the period otherwise allowed, by notice in writing to a company extend that period by such further period as may be specified in the notice.

(5A) Any such extension must not have the effect of extending the period for filing to more than twelve months after the end of the relevant accounting reference period.

(6) Whether the period allowed is that for a private company or a public company is determined by reference to the company's status immediately before the end of the relevant accounting reference period.

(7) In this section "the relevant accounting reference period" means the accounting reference period by reference to which the financial year for the accounts in question was determined.

443 Calculation of period allowed

(1) This section applies for the purposes of calculating the period for filing a company's accounts and reports which is expressed as a specified number of months from a specified date or after the end of a specified previous period.

(2) Subject to the following provisions, the period ends with the date in the appropriate month corresponding to the specified date or the last day of the specified previous period.

(3) If the specified date, or the last day of the specified previous period, is the last day of a month, the period ends with the last day of the appropriate month (whether or not that is the corresponding date).

(4) If—

(a) the specified date, or the last day of the specified previous period, is not the last day of a month but is the 29th or 30th, and

(b) the appropriate month is February,

the period ends with the last day of February.

(5) "The appropriate month" means the month that is the specified number of months after the month in which the specified date, or the end of the specified previous period, falls.

Filing obligations of different descriptions of company

444 Filing obligations of companies subject to small companies regime

(1) The directors of a company subject to the small companies regime—

(a) must deliver to the registrar for each financial year a copy of the balance sheet drawn up as at the last day of that year, and

(b) may also deliver to the registrar—

(i) a copy of the company's profit and loss account for that year, and
(ii) a copy of the directors' report for that year.

(2) Where the directors deliver to the registrar a copy of the company's profit and loss account under subsection (1)(b)(i), the directors must also deliver to the registrar a copy of the auditor's report on the accounts (and any directors' report) that it delivers.

This does not apply if the company is exempt from audit and the directors have taken advantage of that exemption.

(2A) Where the balance sheet or profit and loss account is abridged pursuant to paragraph 1A of Schedule 1 to the Small Companies and Groups (Accounts and Directors' Report) Regulations, the directors must also deliver to the registrar a statement by the company that all the members of the company have consented to the abridgement.

(3) The copies of accounts and reports delivered to the registrar must be copies of the company's annual accounts and reports.

(3A) – (4) …

(5) Where the directors of a company subject to the small companies regime –
(a) do not deliver to the registrar a copy of the company's profit and loss account, or
(b) do not deliver to the registrar a copy of the directors' report,

the copy of the balance sheet delivered to the registrar must contain in a prominent position a statement that the company's annual accounts and reports have been delivered in accordance with the provisions applicable to companies subject to the small companies regime.

(5A) Subject to subsection (5C), where the directors of a company subject to the small companies regime do not deliver to the registrar a copy of the company's profit and loss account—
(a) the copy of the balance sheet delivered to the registrar must disclose that fact, and
(b) unless the company is exempt from audit and the directors have taken advantage of that exemption, the notes to the balance sheet delivered must satisfy the requirements in subsection (5B).

(5B) Those requirements are that the notes to the balance sheet must—
(a) state whether the auditor's report was qualified or unqualified,
(b) where that report was qualified, disclose the basis of the qualification (reproducing any statement under section 498(2)(a) or (b) or section 498(3), if applicable),
(c) where that report was unqualified, include a reference to any matters to which the auditor drew attention by way of emphasis, and
(d) state—
(i) the name of the auditor and (where the auditor is a firm) the name of the person who signed the auditor's report as senior statutory auditor, or
(ii) if the conditions in section 506 (circumstances in which names may be omitted) are met, that a resolution has been passed and notified to the Secretary of State in accordance with that section.

(5C) Subsection (5A) does not apply in relation to a company if—
(a) the company qualifies as a micro-entity (see sections 384A and 384B) in relation to a financial year, and
(b) the company's accounts are prepared for that year in accordance with any of the micro-entity provisions.

(6) The copies of the balance sheet and any directors' report delivered to the registrar under this section must state the name of the person who signed it on behalf of the board.

(7) The copy of the auditor's report delivered to the registrar under this section must–
(a) state the name of the auditor and (where the auditor is a firm) the name of the person who signed it as senior statutory auditor, or
(b) if the conditions in section 506 (circumstances in which names may be omitted) are met, state that a resolution has been passed and notified to the Secretary of State in accordance with that section.

444A Filing obligations of companies entitled to small companies exemption in relation to directors' report

(1) The directors of a company that is entitled to small companies exemption in relation to the directors' report for a financial year—
(a) must deliver to the registrar a copy of the company's annual accounts for that year, and
(b) may also deliver to the registrar a copy of the directors' report.

(2) The directors must also deliver to the registrar a copy of the auditor's report on the accounts (and any directors' report) that it delivers.
This does not apply if the company is exempt from audit and the directors have taken advantage of that exception.
(3) The copies of the balance sheet and directors' report delivered to the registrar under this section must state the name of the person who signed it on behalf of the board.
(4) The copy of the auditor's report delivered to the registrar under this section must—
(a) state the name of the auditor and (where the auditor is a firm) the name of the person who signed it as senior statutory auditor, and
(b) be signed by the auditor or (where the auditor is a firm) in the name of the firm by a person authorised to sign on its behalf,
or, if the conditions in section 506 (circumstances in which names may be omitted) are met, state that a resolution has been passed and notified to the Secretary of State in accordance with that section.
(5) This section does not apply to companies within section 444 (filing obligations of companies subject to the small companies regime).

445 Filing obligations of medium-sized companies

(1) The directors of a company that qualifies as a medium-sized company in relation to a financial year (see sections 465 to 467) must deliver to the registrar a copy of—
(a) the company's annual accounts, (aa) the strategic report, and
(b) the directors' report.
(2) They must also deliver to the registrar a copy of the auditor's report on those accounts (and on the strategic report and the directors' report).
This does not apply if the company is exempt from audit and the directors have taken advantage of that exemption.
(3)-(4) ...
(5) The copies of the balance sheet, strategic report and directors' report delivered to the registrar under this section must state the name of the person who signed it on behalf of the board.
(6) The copy of the auditor's report delivered to the registrar under this section must—
(a) state the name of the auditor and (where the auditor is a firm) the name of the person who signed it as senior statutory auditor, or
(b) if the conditions in section 506 (circumstances in which names may be omitted) are met, state that a resolution has been passed and notified to the Secretary of State in accordance with that section.
(7) This section does not apply to companies within—
(a) section 444 (filing obligations of companies subject to the small companies regime), or
(b) section 444A (filing obligations of companies entitled to small companies exemption in relation to directors' report).

446 Filing obligations of unquoted companies

(1) The directors of an unquoted company must deliver to the registrar for each financial year of the company a copy of—
(a) the company's annual accounts,
(aa) the strategic report,
(b) the directors' report, and
(c) any separate governance statement.
(2) The directors must also deliver to the registrar a copy of the auditor's report on those accounts (and the strategic report where this is covered by the auditor's report, the directors' report and any separate governance statement).
This does not apply if the company is exempt from audit and the directors have taken advantage of that exemption.
(3) The copies of the balance sheet, the strategic report and directors' report delivered to the registrar under this section must state the name of the person who signed it on behalf of the board.
(4) The copy of the auditor's report delivered to the registrar under this section must—
(a) state the name of the auditor and (where the auditor is a firm) the name of the person who signed it as senior statutory auditor, or
(b) if the conditions in section 506 (circumstances in which names may be omitted) are met, state that a resolution has been passed and notified to the Secretary of State in accordance with that section.

(5) This section does not apply to companies within—
(a) section 444 (filing obligations of companies subject to the small companies regime),
(aa) section 444A (filing obligations of companies entitled to small companies exemption in relation to directors' report), or
(b) section 445 (filing obligations of medium-sized companies).

447 Filing obligations of quoted companies

(1) The directors of a quoted company must deliver to the registrar for each financial year of the company a copy of—
(a) the company's annual accounts,
(b) the directors' remuneration report, (ba) the strategic report,
(c) the directors' report, and
(d) any separate corporate governance statement.
(2) They must also deliver a copy of the auditor's report on those accounts (and on the directors' remuneration report, the strategic report where this is covered by the auditor's report, the directors' report and any separate corporate governance statement).
(3) The copies of the balance sheet, the directors' remuneration report and the directors' report delivered to the registrar under this section must state the name of the person who signed it on behalf of the board.
(4) The copy of the auditor's report delivered to the registrar under this section must—
(a) state the name of the auditor and (where the auditor is a firm) the name of the person who signed it as senior statutory auditor, or
(b) if the conditions in section 506 (circumstances in which names may be omitted) are met, state that a resolution has been passed and notified to the Secretary of State in accordance with that section.

448 Unlimited companies exempt from obligation to file accounts

(1) The directors of an unlimited company are not required to deliver accounts and reports to the registrar in respect of a financial year if the following conditions are met.
(2) The conditions are that at no time during the relevant accounting reference period—
(a) has the company been, to its knowledge, a subsidiary undertaking of an undertaking which was then limited, or
(b) have there been, to its knowledge, exercisable by or on behalf of two or more undertakings which were then limited, rights which if exercisable by one of them would have made the company a subsidiary undertaking of it, or
(c) has the company been a parent company of an undertaking which was then limited.

The references above to an undertaking being limited at a particular time are to an undertaking (under whatever law established) the liability of whose members is at that time limited.
(3) The exemption conferred by this section does not apply if—
(a) the company is a banking or insurance company or the parent company of a banking or insurance group, or
(b) each of the members of the company is—
(i) a limited company,
(ii) another unlimited company each of whose members is a limited company,
(iii) a Scottish partnership which is not a limited partnership, each of whose members is a limited company, or
(iv) a Scottish partnership which is a limited partnership, each of whose general partners is a limited company.

The references in paragraph (b) to a limited company, another unlimited company, a Scottish partnership which is not a limited partnership or a Scottish partnership which is a limited partnership include a comparable undertaking incorporated in or formed under the law of a country or territory outside the United Kingdom.
(4) Where a company is exempt by virtue of this section from the obligation to deliver accounts—
(a) section 434(3) (requirements in connection with publication of statutory accounts: meaning of "statutory accounts") has effect with the substitution for the words "as required to be delivered to the registrar under section 441" of the words "as prepared in accordance with this Part and approved by the board of directors"; and

(b) section 435(1)(b) (requirements in connection with publication of non-statutory accounts: statement whether statutory accounts delivered) has effect with the substitution for the words from “whether statutory accounts” to “have been delivered to the registrar” of the words “that the company is exempt from the requirement to deliver statutory accounts”.

(5) In this section—

“general partner” means—

(a) in relation to a Scottish partnership which is a limited partnership, a person who is a general partner within the meaning of the Limited Partnerships Act 1907; and

(b) in relation to an undertaking incorporated in or formed under the law of any country or territory outside the United Kingdom and which is comparable to a Scottish partnership which is a limited partnership, a person comparable to such a general partner;

“limited partnership” means a partnership registered under the Limited Partnerships Act 1907; and

the “relevant accounting reference period”, in relation to a financial year, means the accounting reference period by reference to which that financial year was determined.

448A Dormant subsidiaries exempt from obligation to file accounts

(1) The directors of a company are not required to deliver a copy of the company’s individual accounts to the registrar in respect of a financial year if—

(a) the company is a subsidiary undertaking,

(b) it has been dormant throughout the whole of that year, and

(c) its parent undertaking is established under the law of an EEA State.

(2) Exemption is conditional upon compliance with all of the following conditions—

(a) all members of the company must agree to the exemption in respect of the financial year in question,

(b) the parent undertaking must give a guarantee under section 448C in respect of that year,

(c) the company must be included in the consolidated accounts drawn up for that year or to an earlier date in that year by the parent undertaking in accordance with—

(i) the provisions of Directive 2013/34/EU of the European Parliament and of the Council on the annual financial statements, consolidated financial statements and related reports of certain types of undertakings, or

(ii) international accounting standards,

(d) the parent undertaking must disclose in the notes to the consolidated accounts that the directors of the company are exempt from the requirement to deliver a copy of the company’s individual accounts to the registrar by virtue of this section, and

(e) the directors of the company must deliver to the registrar within the period for filing the company’s accounts and reports for that year—

(i) a written notice of the agreement referred to in subsection (2)(a),

(ii) the statement referred to in section 448C(1),

(iii) a copy of the consolidated accounts referred to in subsection (2)(c),

(iv) a copy of the auditor’s report on those accounts, and

(v) a copy of the consolidated annual report drawn up by the parent undertaking.

448B Companies excluded from the dormant subsidiaries exemption

The directors of a company are not entitled to the exemption conferred by section 448A (dormant subsidiaries) if the company was at any time within the financial year in question—

(a) a traded company,

(b) a company that—

(i) is an authorised insurance company, a banking company, an e-Money issuer, a MiFID investment firm or a UCITS management company, or

(ii) carries on insurance market activity, or

(c) a special register body as defined in section 117(1) of the Trade Union and Labour Relations (Consolidation) Act 1992 or an employers’ association as defined in section 122 of that Act or Article 4 of the Industrial Relations (Northern Ireland) Order 1992.

448C Dormant subsidiaries filing exemption: parent undertaking declaration of guarantee

(1) A guarantee is given by a parent undertaking under this section when the directors of the subsidiary company deliver to the registrar a statement by the parent undertaking that it guarantees the subsidiary company under this section.

(2) The statement under subsection (1) must be authenticated by the parent undertaking and must specify—

(a) the name of the parent undertaking,

(b) if the parent undertaking is incorporated in the United Kingdom, its registered number (if any),

(c) if the parent undertaking is incorporated outside the United Kingdom and registered in the country in which it is incorporated, the identity of the register on which it is registered and the number with which it is so registered,

(d) the name and registered number of the subsidiary company in respect of which the guarantee is being given,

(e) the date of the statement, and

(f) the financial year to which the guarantee relates.

(3) A guarantee given under this section has the effect that—

(a) the parent undertaking guarantees all outstanding liabilities to which the subsidiary company is subject at the end of the financial year to which the guarantee relates, until they are satisfied in full, and

(b) the guarantee is enforceable against the parent undertaking by any person to whom the subsidiary company is liable in respect of those liabilities.

449, 450 ...

Failure to file accounts and reports

451 Default in filing accounts and reports: offences

(1) If the requirements of section 441 (duty to file accounts and reports) are not complied with in relation to a company's accounts and reports for a financial year before the end of the period for filing those accounts and reports, every person who immediately before the end of that period was a director of the company commits an offence.

(2) It is a defence for a person charged with such an offence to prove that he took all reasonable steps for securing that those requirements would be complied with before the end of that period.

(3) It is not a defence to prove that the documents in question were not in fact prepared as required by this Part.

(4) A person guilty of an offence under this section is liable on summary conviction to a fine not exceeding level 5 on the standard scale and, for continued contravention, a daily default fine not exceeding one-tenth of level 5 on the standard scale.

452 Default in filing accounts and reports: court order

(1) If—

(a) the requirements of section 441 (duty to file accounts and reports) are not complied with in relation to a company's accounts and reports for a financial year before the end of the period for filing those accounts and reports, and

(b) the directors of the company fail to make good the default within 14 days after the service of a notice on them requiring compliance,

the court may, on the application of any member or creditor of the company or of the registrar, make an order directing the directors (or any of them) to make good the default within such time as may be specified in the order.

(2) The court's order may provide that all costs (in Scotland, expenses) of and incidental to the application are to be borne by the directors.

453 Civil penalty for failure to file accounts and reports

(1) Where the requirements of section 441 are not complied with in relation to a company's accounts and reports for a financial year before the end of the period for filing those accounts and reports, the company is liable to a civil penalty.

This is in addition to any liability of the directors under section 451.

(2) The amount of the penalty shall be determined in accordance with regulations made by the Secretary of State by reference to—
   (a) the length of the period between the end of the period for filing the accounts and reports in question and the day on which the requirements are complied with, and
   (b) whether the company is a private or public company.
(3) The penalty may be recovered by the registrar and is to be paid into the Consolidated Fund.
(4) It is not a defence in proceedings under this section to prove that the documents in question were not in fact prepared as required by this Part.
(5) Regulations under this section having the effect of increasing the penalty payable in any case are subject to affirmative resolution procedure.
Otherwise, the regulations are subject to negative resolution procedure.

CHAPTER 11
REVISION OF DEFECTIVE ACCOUNTS AND REPORTS

Voluntary revision

454 Voluntary revision of accounts etc

(1) If it appears to the directors of a company that—
   (a) the company's annual accounts,
   (b) the directors' remuneration report or the directors' report, or
   (c) a strategic report of the company,
   did not comply with the requirements of this Act (or, where applicable, of Article 4 of the IAS Regulation), they may prepare revised accounts or a revised report or statement.
(2) Where copies of the previous accounts or report have been sent out to members, delivered to the registrar or (in the case of a public company) laid before the company in general meeting, the revisions must be confined to—
   (a) the correction of those respects in which the previous accounts or report did not comply with the requirements of this Act (or, where applicable, of Article 4 of the IAS Regulation), and
   (b) the making of any necessary consequential alterations.
(3) The Secretary of State may make provision by regulations as to the application of the provisions of this Act in relation to—
   (a) revised annual accounts,
   (b) a revised directors' remuneration report or directors' report, or
   (c) a revised strategic report of the company.
(4) The regulations may, in particular—
   (a) make different provision according to whether the previous accounts, report or statement are replaced or are supplemented by a document indicating the corrections to be made;
   (b) make provision with respect to the functions of the company's auditor in relation to the revised accounts or report;
   (c) require the directors to take such steps as may be specified in the regulations where the previous accounts or report have been—
      (i) sent out to members and others under section 423,
      (ii) laid before the company in general meeting, or
      (iii) delivered to the registrar,
      or where a strategic report and supplementary material containing information derived from the previous accounts or report have been sent to members under section 426;
   (d) apply the provisions of this Act (including those creating criminal offences) subject to such additions, exceptions and modifications as are specified in the regulations.
(5) Regulations under this section are subject to negative resolution procedure.

Secretary of State's notice

455 Secretary of State's notice in respect of accounts or reports

(1) This section applies where—

(a) copies of a company's annual accounts, strategic report or directors' report have been sent out under section 423, or
(b) a copy of a company's annual accounts, strategic report or directors' report have been delivered to the registrar or (in the case of a public company) laid before the company in general meeting,

and it appears to the Secretary of State that there is, or may be, a question whether the accounts or report comply with the requirements of this Act (or, where applicable, of Article 4 of the IAS Regulation).

(2) The Secretary of State may give notice to the directors of the company indicating the respects in which it appears that such a question arises or may arise.

(3) The notice must specify a period of not less than one month for the directors to give an explanation of the accounts or report or prepare revised accounts or a revised report.

(4) If at the end of the specified period, or such longer period as the Secretary of State may allow, it appears to the Secretary of State that the directors have not—
(a) given a satisfactory explanation of the accounts or report, or
(b) revised the accounts or report so as to comply with the requirements of this Act (or, where applicable, of Article 4 of the IAS Regulation),

the Secretary of State may apply to the court.

(5) The provisions of this section apply equally to revised annual accounts, revised strategic reports and revised directors' reports, in which case they have effect as if the references to revised accounts or reports were references to further revised accounts or reports.

Application to court

456 Application to court in respect of defective accounts or reports

(1) An application may be made to the court—
(a) by the Secretary of State, after having complied with section 455, or
(b) by a person authorised by the Secretary of State for the purposes of this section, for a declaration (in Scotland, a declarator) that the annual accounts of a company do not comply, or a strategic report or a directors' report does not comply, with the requirements of this Act (or, where applicable, of Article 4 of the IAS Regulation) and for an order requiring the directors of the company to prepare revised accounts or a revised report.

(2) Notice of the application, together with a general statement of the matters at issue in the proceedings, shall be given by the applicant to the registrar for registration.

(3) If the court orders the preparation of revised accounts, it may give directions as to—
(a) the auditing of the accounts,
(b) the revision of any directors' remuneration report, strategic report and supplementary material or, directors' report, and
(c) the taking of steps by the directors to bring the making of the order to the notice of persons likely to rely on the previous accounts,

and such other matters as the court thinks fit.

(4) If the court orders the preparation of a revised strategic report or directors' report it may give directions as to—
(a) the review of the report by the auditors,
(b) …
(c) the taking of steps by the directors to bring the making of the order to the notice of persons likely to rely on the previous report, and
(d) such other matters as the court thinks fit.

(5) If the court finds that the accounts or report did not comply with the requirements of this Act (or, where applicable, of Article 4 of the IAS Regulation) it may order that all or part of—
(a) the costs (in Scotland, expenses) of and incidental to the application, and
(b) any reasonable expenses incurred by the company in connection with or in consequence of the preparation of revised accounts or a revised report,

are to be borne by such of the directors as were party to the approval of the defective accounts or report.

For this purpose every director of the company at the time of the approval of the accounts or report shall be taken to have been a party to the approval unless he shows that he took all reasonable steps to prevent that approval.

(6) Where the court makes an order under subsection (5) it shall have regard to whether the directors party to the approval of the defective accounts or report knew or ought to have known that the accounts or report did not comply with the requirements of this Act (or, where applicable, of Article 4 of the IAS Regulation), and it may exclude one or more directors from the order or order the payment of different amounts by different directors.

(7) On the conclusion of proceedings on an application under this section, the applicant must send to the registrar for registration a copy of the court order or, as the case may be, give notice to the registrar that the application has failed or been withdrawn.

(8) The provisions of this section apply equally to revised annual accounts, revised strategic reports and revised directors' reports, in which case they have effect as if the references to revised accounts or reports were references to further revised accounts or reports.

457 Other persons authorised to apply to the court

(1) The Secretary of State may by order (an "authorisation order") authorise for the purposes of section 456 any person appearing to him—

(a) to have an interest in, and to have satisfactory procedures directed to securing, compliance by companies with the requirements of this Act (or, where applicable, of Article 4 of the IAS Regulation) relating to accounts, strategic reports and directors' reports,

(b) to have satisfactory procedures for receiving and investigating complaints about companies' annual accounts, strategic reports and directors' reports, and

(c) otherwise to be a fit and proper person to be authorised.

(2) A person may be authorised generally or in respect of particular classes of case, and different persons may be authorised in respect of different classes of case.

(3) The Secretary of State may refuse to authorise a person if he considers that his authorisation is unnecessary having regard to the fact that there are one or more other persons who have been or are likely to be authorised.

(4) If the authorised person is an unincorporated association, proceedings brought in, or in connection with, the exercise of any function by the association as an authorised person may be brought by or against the association in the name of a body corporate whose constitution provides for the establishment of the association.

(5) An authorisation order may contain such requirements or other provisions relating to the exercise of functions by the authorised person as appear to the Secretary of State to be appropriate.

No such order is to be made unless it appears to the Secretary of State that the person would, if authorised, exercise his functions as an authorised person in accordance with the provisions proposed.

(6) Where authorisation is revoked, the revoking order may make such provision as the Secretary of State thinks fit with respect to pending proceedings.

(7) An order under this section is subject to negative resolution procedure.

458 Disclosure of information by tax authorities

(1) The Commissioners for Her Majesty's Revenue and Customs may disclose information to a person authorised under section 457 for the purpose of facilitating—

(a) the taking of steps by that person to discover whether there are grounds for an application to the court under section 456 (application in respect of defective accounts etc), or

(b) a decision by the authorised person whether to make such an application.

(2) This section applies despite any statutory or other restriction on the disclosure of information.

Provided that, in the case of personal data within the meaning of the Data Protection Act 1998, information is not to be disclosed in contravention of that Act.

(3) Information disclosed to an authorised person under this section—

(a) may not be used except in or in connection with—

(i) taking steps to discover whether there are grounds for an application to the court under section 456, or

(ii) deciding whether or not to make such an application,

or in, or in connection with, proceedings on such an application; and

(b) must not be further disclosed except—

(i) to the person to whom the information relates, or
(ii) in, or in connection with, proceedings on any such application to the court.

(4) A person who contravenes subsection (3) commits an offence unless—
(a) he did not know, and had no reason to suspect, that the information had been disclosed under this section, or
(b) he took all reasonable steps and exercised all due diligence to avoid the commission of the offence.

(5) A person guilty of an offence under subsection (4) is liable—
(a) on conviction on indictment, to imprisonment for a term not exceeding two years or a fine (or both);
(b) on summary conviction—
(i) in England and Wales, to imprisonment for a term not exceeding twelve months or to a fine not exceeding the statutory maximum (or both);
(ii) in Scotland or Northern Ireland, to imprisonment for a term not exceeding six months, or to a fine not exceeding the statutory maximum (or both).

(6) Where an offence under this section is committed by a body corporate, every officer of the body who is in default also commits the offence.For this purpose—
(a) any person who purports to act as director, manager or secretary of the body is treated as an officer of the body, and
(b) if the body is a company, any shadow director is treated as an officer of the company.

Power of authorised person to require documents etc

459 Power of authorised person to require documents, information and explanations

(1) This section applies where it appears to a person who is authorised under section 457 that there is, or may be, a question whether a company's annual accounts, strategic report or directors' report complies with the requirements of this Act (or, where applicable, of Article 4 of the IAS Regulation).

(2) The authorised person may require any of the persons mentioned in subsection (3) to produce any document, or to provide him with any information or explanations, that he may reasonably require for the purpose of—
(a) discovering whether there are grounds for an application to the court under section 456, or
(b) deciding whether to make such an application.

(3) Those persons are—
(a) the company;
(b) any officer, employee, or auditor of the company;
(c) any persons who fell within paragraph (b) at a time to which the document or information required by the authorised person relates.

(4) If a person fails to comply with such a requirement, the authorised person may apply to the court.

(5) If it appears to the court that the person has failed to comply with a requirement under subsection (2), it may order the person to take such steps as it directs for securing that the documents are produced or the information or explanations are provided.

(6) A statement made by a person in response to a requirement under subsection (2) or an order under subsection (5) may not be used in evidence against him in any criminal proceedings.

(7) Nothing in this section compels any person to disclose documents or information in respect of which a claim to legal professional privilege (in Scotland, to confidentiality of communications) could be maintained in legal proceedings.

(8) In this section "document" includes information recorded in any form.

460 Restrictions on disclosure of information obtained under compulsory powers

(1) This section applies to information (in whatever form) obtained in pursuance of a requirement or order under section 459 (power of authorised person to require documents etc) that relates to the private affairs of an individual or to any particular business.

(2) No such information may, during the lifetime of that individual or so long as that business continues to be carried on, be disclosed without the consent of that individual or the person for the time being carrying on that business.

(3) This does not apply—
 (a) to disclosure permitted by section 461 (permitted disclosure of information obtained under compulsory powers), or
 (b) to the disclosure of information that is or has been available to the public from another source.

(4) A person who discloses information in contravention of this section commits an offence, unless—
 (a) he did not know, and had no reason to suspect, that the information had been disclosed under section 459, or
 (b) he took all reasonable steps and exercised all due diligence to avoid the commission of the offence.

(5) A person guilty of an offence under this section is liable—
 (a) on conviction on indictment, to imprisonment for a term not exceeding two years or a fine (or both);
 (b) on summary conviction—
  (i) in England and Wales, to imprisonment for a term not exceeding twelve months or to a fine not exceeding the statutory maximum (or both);
  (ii) in Scotland or Northern Ireland, to imprisonment for a term not exceeding six months, or to a fine not exceeding the statutory maximum (or both).

(6) Where an offence under this section is committed by a body corporate, every officer of the body who is in default also commits the offence.For this purpose—
 (a) any person who purports to act as director, manager or secretary of the body is treated as an officer of the body, and
 (b) if the body is a company, any shadow director is treated as an officer of the company.

461 Permitted disclosure of information obtained under compulsory powers

(1) The prohibition in section 460 of the disclosure of information obtained in pursuance of a requirement or order under section 459 (power of authorised person to require documents etc) that relates to the private affairs of an individual or to any particular business has effect subject to the following exceptions.

(2) It does not apply to the disclosure of information for the purpose of facilitating the carrying out by the authorised person of his functions under section 456.

(3) It does not apply to disclosure to—
 (a) the Secretary of State,
 (b) the Department of Enterprise, Trade and Investment for Northern Ireland,
 (c) the Treasury,
 (d) the Bank of England,
 (e) the Financial Conduct Authority,
 (ea) the Prudential Regulation Authority, or
 (f) the Commissioners for Her Majesty's Revenue and Customs.

(4) It does not apply to disclosure—
 (a) for the purpose of assisting a body designated by an order under section 1252 (delegation of functions of the Secretary of State) to exercise its functions under Part 42 of that Act;
 (aa) for the purpose of facilitating the carrying out of inspections under paragraph 23 of Schedule 10 (arrangements for independent monitoring of audits of listed companies and other major bodies);
 (b) with a view to the institution of, or otherwise for the purposes of, disciplinary proceedings relating to the performance by an accountant or auditor of his professional duties;
 (c) for the purpose of enabling or assisting the Secretary of State or the Treasury to exercise any of their functions under any of the following—
  (i) the Companies Acts,
  (ii) Part 5 of the Criminal Justice Act 1993 (insider dealing),
  (iii) the Insolvency Act 1986 or the Insolvency (Northern Ireland) Order 1989,
  (iv) the Company Directors Disqualification Act 1986 or the Company Directors Disqualification (Northern Ireland) Order 2002,

(v) the Financial Services and Markets Act 2000;

(d) for the purpose of enabling or assisting the Department of Enterprise, Trade and Investment for Northern Ireland to exercise any powers conferred on it by the enactments relating to companies, directors' disqualification or insolvency;

(e) for the purpose of enabling or assisting the Bank of England to exercise its functions;

(f) for the purpose of enabling or assisting the Commissioners for Her Majesty's Revenue and Customs to exercise their functions;

(g) for the purpose of enabling or assisting the Financial Conduct Authority or the Prudential Regulation Authority to exercise its functions under any of the following—

(i) the legislation relating to friendly societies or to industrial and provident societies,

(ii) the Building Societies Act 1986,

(iii) Part 7 of the Companies Act 1989,

(iv) the Financial Services and Markets Act 2000; or

(h) in pursuance of any EU obligation.

(5) It does not apply to disclosure to a body exercising functions of a public nature under legislation in any country or territory outside the United Kingdom that appear to the authorised person to be similar to his functions under section 456 for the purpose of enabling or assisting that body to exercise those functions.

(6) In determining whether to disclose information to a body in accordance with subsection (5), the authorised person must have regard to the following considerations—

(a) whether the use which the body is likely to make of the information is sufficiently important to justify making the disclosure;

(b) whether the body has adequate arrangements to prevent the information from being used or further disclosed other than—

(i) for the purposes of carrying out the functions mentioned in that subsection, or

(ii) for other purposes substantially similar to those for which information disclosed to the authorised person could be used or further disclosed.

(7) Nothing in this section authorises the making of a disclosure in contravention of the Data Protection Act 1998.

462 Power to amend categories of permitted disclosure

(1) The Secretary of State may by order amend section 461(3), (4) and (5).

(2) An order under this section must not—

(a) amend subsection (3) of that section (UK public authorities) by specifying a person unless the person exercises functions of a public nature (whether or not he exercises any other function);

(b) amend subsection (4) of that section (purposes for which disclosure permitted) by adding or modifying a description of disclosure unless the purpose for which the disclosure is permitted is likely to facilitate the exercise of a function of a public nature;

(c) amend subsection (5) of that section (overseas regulatory authorities) so as to have the effect of permitting disclosures to be made to a body other than one that exercises functions of a public nature in a country or territory outside the United Kingdom.

(3) An order under this section is subject to negative resolution procedure.

CHAPTER 12
SUPPLEMENTARY PROVISIONS

Liability for false or misleading statements in reports

463 Liability for false or misleading statements in reports

(1) The reports to which this section applies are—

(a) the directors' report,

(za) the strategic report,

(b) the directors' remuneration report,

(c) …

(2) A director of a company is liable to compensate the company for any loss suffered by it as a result of—
(a) any untrue or misleading statement in a report to which this section applies, or
(b) the omission from a report to which this section applies of anything required to be included in it.
(3) He is so liable only if—
(a) he knew the statement to be untrue or misleading or was reckless as to whether it was untrue or misleading, or
(b) he knew the omission to be dishonest concealment of a material fact.
(4) No person shall be subject to any liability to a person other than the company resulting from reliance, by that person or another, on information in a report to which this section applies.
(5) The reference in subsection (4) to a person being subject to a liability includes a reference to another person being entitled as against him to be granted any civil remedy or to rescind or repudiate an agreement.
(6) This section does not affect—
(a) liability for a civil penalty, or
(b) liability for a criminal offence.

Accounting and reporting standards

464 Accounting standards

(1) In this Part "accounting standards" means statements of standard accounting practice issued by such body or bodies as may be prescribed by regulations.
(2) References in this Part to accounting standards applicable to a company's annual accounts are to such standards as are, in accordance with their terms, relevant to the company's circumstances and to the accounts.
(3) Regulations under this section may contain such transitional and other supplementary and incidental provisions as appear to the Secretary of State to be appropriate.

Companies qualifying as medium-sized

465 Companies qualifying as medium-sized: general

(1) A company qualifies as medium-sized in relation to its first financial year if the qualifying conditions are met in that year.
(2) A company qualifies as medium-sized in relation to a subsequent financial year—
(a) if the qualifying conditions are met in that year and the preceding financial year;
(b) if the qualifying conditions are met in that year and the company qualified as medium-sized in relation to the preceding financial year;
(c) if the qualifying conditions were met in the preceding financial year and the company qualified as medium-sized in relation to that year.
(3) The qualifying conditions are met by a company in a year in which it satisfies two or more of the following requirements—

1.	Turnover	Not more than £36 million
2.	Balance sheet total	Not more than £18 million
3.	Number of employees	Not more than 250

(4) For a period that is a company's financial year but not in fact a year the maximum figures for turnover must be proportionately adjusted.
(5) The balance sheet total means the aggregate of the amounts shown as assets in the company's balance sheet.
(6) The number of employees means the average number of persons employed by the company in the year, determined as follows—
(a) find for each month in the financial year the number of persons employed under contracts of service by the company in that month (whether throughout the month or not),
(b) add together the monthly totals, and
(c) divide by the number of months in the financial year.
(7) This section is subject to section 466 (companies qualifying as medium-sized: parent companies).

466 Companies qualifying as medium-sized: parent companies

(1) A parent company qualifies as a medium-sized company in relation to a financial year only if the group headed by it qualifies as a medium-sized group.

(2) A group qualifies as medium-sized in relation to the parent company's first financial year if the qualifying conditions are met in that year.

(3) A group qualifies as medium-sized in relation to a subsequent financial year of the parent company—

(a) if the qualifying conditions are met in that year and the preceding financial year;

(b) if the qualifying conditions are met in that year and the group qualified as medium-sized in relation to the preceding financial year;

(c) if the qualifying conditions were met in the preceding financial year and the group qualified as medium-sized in relation to that year.

(4) The qualifying conditions are met by a group in a year in which it satisfies two or more of the following requirements—

1.	Aggregate turnover	Not more than £36 million net (or £43.2 million gross)
2.	Aggregate balance sheet total	Not more than £18 million net (or £21.6 million gross)
3.	Aggregate number of employees	Not more than 250

(5) The aggregate figures are ascertained by aggregating the relevant figures determined in accordance with section 465 for each member of the group.

(6) In relation to the aggregate figures for turnover and balance sheet total—

"net" means after any set-offs and other adjustments made to eliminate group transactions—

(a) in the case of Companies Act accounts, in accordance with regulations under section 404,

(b) in the case of IAS accounts, in accordance with international accounting standards; and

"gross" means without those set-offs and other adjustments.

A company may satisfy any relevant requirement on the basis of either the net or the gross figure.

(7) The figures for each subsidiary undertaking shall be those included in its individual accounts for the relevant financial year, that is—

(a) if its financial year ends with that of the parent company, that financial year, and

(b) if not, its financial year ending last before the end of the financial year of the parent company.

If those figures cannot be obtained without disproportionate expense or undue delay, the latest available figures shall be taken.

467 Companies excluded from being treated as medium-sized

(1) A company is not entitled to take advantage of any of the provisions of this Part relating to companies qualifying as medium-sized if it was at any time within the financial year in question—

(a) a traded company,

(b) a company that—

(i) has permission under Part 4A of the Financial Services and Markets Act 2000 to carry on a regulated activity, or

(ii) carries on insurance market activity,

(ba) an e-money issuer, or

(c) a member of an ineligible group.

(2) A group is ineligible if any of its members is—

(a) a public company,

(b) a body corporate (other than a company) whose shares are admitted to trading on a regulated market,

(c) a person (other than a small company) who has permission under Part 4A of the Financial Services and Markets Act 2000 to carry on a regulated activity,

(ca) an e-money issuer, or

(d) a small company that is an authorised insurance company, a banking company, an e-money issuer, a MiFID investment firm or a UCITS management company, or

(e) a person who carries on insurance market activity.

(3) A company is a small company for the purposes of subsection (2) if it qualified as small in relation to its last financial year ending on or before the end of the financial year in question.

(4) This section does not prevent a company from taking advantage of section 417(7) (business review: non-financial information) by reason only of its having been a member of an ineligible group at any time within the financial year in question.

General power to make further provision about accounts and reports

468 General power to make further provision about accounts and reports

(1) The Secretary of State may make provision by regulations about—
  (a) the accounts and reports that companies are required to prepare;
  (b) the categories of companies required to prepare accounts and reports of any description;
  (c) the form and content of the accounts and reports that companies are required to prepare;
  (d) the obligations of companies and others as regards—
    (i) the approval of accounts and reports,
    (ii) the sending of accounts and reports to members and others,
    (iii) the laying of accounts and reports before the company in general meeting,
    (iv) the delivery of copies of accounts and reports to the registrar, and
    (v) the publication of accounts and reports.

(2) The regulations may amend this Part by adding, altering or repealing provisions.

(3) But they must not amend (other than consequentially)—
  (a) section 393 (accounts to give true and fair view), or
  (b) the provisions of Chapter 11 (revision of defective accounts and reports).

(4) The regulations may create criminal offences in cases corresponding to those in which an offence is created by an existing provision of this Part.
The maximum penalty for any such offence may not be greater than is provided in relation to an offence under the existing provision.

(5) The regulations may provide for civil penalties in circumstances corresponding to those within section 453(1) (civil penalty for failure to file accounts and reports).
The provisions of section 453(2) to (5) apply in relation to any such penalty.

Other supplementary provisions

469 Preparation and filing of accounts in euros

(1) The amounts set out in the annual accounts of a company may also be shown in the same accounts translated into euros.

(2) When complying with section 441 (duty to file accounts and reports), the directors of a company may deliver to the registrar an additional copy of the company's annual accounts in which the amounts have been translated into euros.

(3) In both cases—
  (a) the amounts must have been translated at the exchange rate prevailing on the date to which the balance sheet is made up, and
  (b) that rate must be disclosed in the notes to the accounts.

(3A) Subsection (3)(b) does not apply to the Companies Act individual accounts of a company for a financial year in which the company qualifies as a micro-entity (see sections 384A and 384B).

(4) For the purposes of sections 434 and 435 (requirements in connection with published accounts) any additional copy of the company's annual accounts delivered to the registrar under subsection (2) above shall be treated as statutory accounts of the company.
In the case of such a copy, references in those sections to the auditor's report on the company's annual accounts shall be read as references to the auditor's report on the annual accounts of which it is a copy.

470 *omitted*

471 Meaning of "annual accounts" and related expressions

(1) In this Part a company's "annual accounts", in relation to a financial year, means—
  (a) any individual accounts prepared by the company for that year (see section 394), and

(b) any group accounts prepared by the company for that year (see sections 398 and 399).

This is subject to section 408 (option to omit individual profit and loss account from annual accounts where information given in group accounts).

(2) In the case of an unquoted company, its "annual accounts and reports" for a financial year are—

(a) its annual accounts,

(aa) the strategic report (if any),

(b) the directors' report, and

(c) the auditor's report on those accounts, the strategic report (where this is covered by the auditor's report) and the directors' report (unless the company is exempt from audit).

(3) In the case of a quoted company, its "annual accounts and reports" for a financial year are—

(a) its annual accounts,

(b) the directors' remuneration report, (ba) the strategic report (if any),

(c) the directors' report, and

(d) the auditor's report on those accounts, on the auditable part of the directors' remuneration report, on the strategic report (where this is covered by the auditor's report) and on the directors' report.

472 Notes to the accounts

(1) ...

(1A) In the case of a company which qualifies as a micro-entity in relation to a financial year (see sections 384A and 384B), the notes to the accounts for that year required by section 413 of this Act and regulation 5A of, and paragraph 57 of Part 3 of Schedule 1 to, the Small Companies and Groups (Accounts and Directors' Report) Regulations 2008 must be included at the foot of the balance sheet.

(2) References in this Part to a company's annual accounts, or to a balance sheet or profit and loss account, include notes to the accounts giving information which is required by any provision of this Act or international accounting standards, and required or allowed by any such provision to be given in a note to company accounts.

472A Meaning of "corporate governance statement" etc.

(1) In this Part "corporate governance statement" means the statement required by rules 7.2.1 to 7.2.11 in the Disclosure Rules and Transparency Rules sourcebook issued by the Financial Conduct Authority.

(2) Those rules were inserted by Annex C of the Disclosure Rules and Transparency Rules Sourcebook (Corporate Governance Rules) Instrument 2008 made by the Authority on 26th June 2008 (FSA 2008/32).

(3) A "separate" corporate governance statement means one that is not included in the directors' report.

473 *omitted*

474 Minor definitions

(1) In this Part—

"e-money issuer" means—

(a) an electronic money institution, within the meaning of the Electronic Money Regulations 2011, or

(b) a person who has permission under Part 4A of the Financial Services and Markets Act 2000 to carry on the activity of issuing electronic money within the meaning of article 9B of the Financial Services and Markets Act 2000 (Regulated Activities) Order 2001;

"group" means a parent undertaking and its subsidiary undertakings;

"IAS Regulation" means EC Regulation No. 1606/2002 of the European Parliament and of the Council of 19 July 2002 on the application of international accounting standards;

"included in the consolidation", in relation to group accounts, or "included in consolidated group accounts", means that the undertaking is included in the accounts by the method of full (and not proportional) consolidation, and references to an undertaking excluded from consolidation shall be construed accordingly;

"international accounting standards" means the international accounting standards, within the meaning of the IAS Regulation, adopted from time to time by the European Commission in accordance with that Regulation;

"micro-entity minimum accounting item" means an item of information required by this Part or by regulations under this Part to be contained in the Companies Act individual accounts of a company for a financial year in relation to which it qualifies as a micro-entity (see sections 384A and 384B);

"micro-entity provisions" means any provisions of this Part, Part 16 or regulations under this Part relating specifically to the individual accounts of a company which qualifies as a micro-entity;

"MiFID investment firm" means an investment firm within the meaning of Article 4.1.1 of Directive 2004/39/EC of the European Parliament and of the Council of 21 April 2004 on markets in financial instruments, other than—

(a) a company to which that Directive does not apply by virtue of Article 2 of that Directive,

(b) a company which is an exempt investment firm within the meaning of regulation 4A(3) of the Financial Services and Markets Act 2000 (Markets in Financial Instruments) Regulations 2007, and

(c) any other company which fulfils all the requirements set out in regulation 4C(3) of those Regulations;

"profit and loss account", in relation to a company that prepares IAS accounts, includes an income statement or other equivalent financial statement required to be prepared by international accounting standards;

"qualified", in relation to an auditor's report, means that the report does not state the auditor's unqualified opinion that the accounts have been properly prepared in accordance with this Act;

"regulated activity" has the meaning given in section 22 of the Financial Services and Markets Act 2000, except that it does not include activities of the kind specified in any of the following provisions of the Financial Services and Markets Act 2000 (Regulated Activities) Order 2001—

(a) article 25A (arranging regulated mortgage contracts),

(b) article 25B (arranging regulated home reversion plans),

(c) article 25C (arranging regulated home purchase plans),

(ca) article 25E (arranging regulated sale and rent back agreements),

(d) article 39A (assisting administration and performance of a contract of insurance),

(e) article 53A (advising on regulated mortgage contracts),

(f) article 53B (advising on regulated home reversion plans),

(g) article 53C (advising on regulated home purchase plans),

(ga) article 53D (advising on regulated sale and rent back agreements),

(h) article 21 (dealing as agent), article 25 (arranging deals in investments) or article 53 (advising on investments) where the activity concerns relevant investments that are not contractually based investments (within the meaning of article 3 of that Order), or

(i) article 64 (agreeing to carry on a regulated activity of the kind mentioned in paragraphs (a) to (h));

"traded company" means a company any of whose transferable securities are admitted to trading on a regulated market;

"turnover", in relation to a company, means the amounts derived from the provision of goods and services, after deduction of—

(a) trade discounts,

(b) value added tax, and

(c) any other taxes based on the amounts so derived;

"UCITS management company" has the meaning given by the Glossary forming part of the Handbook made by the Financial Conduct Authority under the Financial Services and Markets Act 2000.

(2) In the case of an undertaking not trading for profit, any reference in this Part to a profit and loss account is to an income and expenditure account.

References to profit and loss and, in relation to group accounts, to a consolidated profit and loss account shall be construed accordingly.

PART 16
AUDIT

CHAPTER 1
REQUIREMENT FOR AUDITED ACCOUNTS

Requirement for audited accounts

475 Requirement for audited accounts

(1) A company's annual accounts for a financial year must be audited in accordance with this Part unless the company—
- (a) is exempt from audit under—
  section 477 (small companies),
  section 479A (subsidiary companies), or section 480 (dormant companies);

  or
- (b) is exempt from the requirements of this Part under section 482 (non-profit-making companies subject to public sector audit).

(2) A company is not entitled to any such exemption unless its balance sheet contains a statement by the directors to that effect.

(3) A company is not entitled to exemption under any of the provisions mentioned in subsection (1)(a) unless its balance sheet contains a statement by the directors to the effect that—
- (a) the members have not required the company to obtain an audit of its accounts for the year in question in accordance with section 476, and
- (b) the directors acknowledge their responsibilities for complying with the requirements of this Act with respect to accounting records and the preparation of accounts.

(4) The statement required by subsection (2) or (3) must appear on the balance sheet above the signature required by section 414.

476 Right of members to require audit

(1) The members of a company that would otherwise be entitled to exemption from audit under any of the provisions mentioned in section 475(1)(a) may by notice under this section require it to obtain an audit of its accounts for a financial year.

(2) The notice must be given by—
- (a) members representing not less in total than 10% in nominal value of the company's issued share capital, or any class of it, or
- (b) if the company does not have a share capital, not less than 10% in number of the members of the company.

(3) The notice may not be given before the financial year to which it relates and must be given not later than one month before the end of that year.

Exemption from audit: small companies

477 Small companies: conditions for exemption from audit

(1) A company that qualifies as a small company in relation to a financial year is exempt from the requirements of this Act relating to the audit of accounts for that year.

(2), (3) ...

(4) For the purposes of this section—
- (a) whether a company qualifies as a small company shall be determined in accordance with section 382(1) to (6),
- (b) ...

(5) This section has effect subject to—
  section 475(2) and (3) (requirements as to statements to be contained in balance sheet),
  section 476 (right of members to require audit),
  section 478 (companies excluded from small companies exemption), and
  section 479 (availability of small companies exemption in case of group company).

478 Companies excluded from small companies exemption

A company is not entitled to the exemption conferred by section 477 (small companies) if it was at any time within the financial year in question—

(a) a public company,
(b) a company that—
(i) is an authorised insurance company, a banking company, an e-money issuer, not more than £3.26 million, a MiFID investment firm or a UCITS management company, or
(ii) carries on insurance market activity, or
(c) a special register body as defined in section 117(1) of the Trade Union and Labour Relations (Consolidation) Act 1992 or an employers' association as defined in section 122 of that Act or Article 4 of the Industrial Relations (Northern Ireland) Order 1992.

479 Availability of small companies exemption in case of group company

(1) A company is not entitled to the exemption conferred by section 477 (small companies) in respect of a financial year during any part of which it was a group company unless—
(a) the group—
(i) qualifies as a small group in relation to that financial year, and
(ii) was not at any time in that year an ineligible group, or
(b) subsection (3) applies.
(2) ...
(3) A company is not excluded by subsection (1) if, throughout the whole of the period or periods during the financial year when it was a group company, it was both a subsidiary undertaking and dormant.
(4) In this section—
(a) "group company" means a company that is a parent company or a subsidiary undertaking, and
(b) "the group", in relation to a group company, means that company together with all its associated undertakings.
For this purpose undertakings are associated if one is a subsidiary undertaking of the other or both are subsidiary undertakings of a third undertaking.
(5) For the purposes of this section—
(a) whether a group qualifies as small shall be determined in accordance with section 383 (companies qualifying as small: parent companies);
(b) "ineligible group" has the meaning given by section 384(2) and (3).
(c)–(e) ...
(6) The provisions mentioned in subsection (5) apply for the purposes of this section as if all the bodies corporate in the group were companies.

479A Subsidiary companies: conditions for exemption from audit

(1) A company is exempt from the requirements of this Act relating to the audit of individual accounts for a financial year if—
(a) it is itself a subsidiary undertaking, and
(b) its parent undertaking is established under the law of an EEA State.
(2) Exemption is conditional upon compliance with all of the following conditions—
(a) all members of the company must agree to the exemption in respect of the financial year in question,
(b) the parent undertaking must give a guarantee under section 479C in respect of that year,
(c) the company must be included in the consolidated accounts drawn up for that year or to an earlier date in that year by the parent undertaking in accordance with—
(i) the provisions of Directive 2013/34/EU of the European Parliament and of the Council on the annual financial statements, consolidated statements and related reports of certain types of undertakings, or
(ii) international accounting standards,
(d) the parent undertaking must disclose in the notes to the consolidated accounts that the company is exempt from the requirements of this Act relating to the audit of individual accounts by virtue of this section, and
(e) the directors of the company must deliver to the registrar on or before the date that they file the accounts for that year—

(i) a written notice of the agreement referred to in subsection (2)(a),
(ii) the statement referred to in section 479C(1),
(iii) a copy of the consolidated accounts referred to in subsection (2)(c),
(iv) a copy of the auditor's report on those accounts, and
(v) a copy of the consolidated annual report drawn up by the parent undertaking.

(3) This section has effect subject to—
section 475(2) and (3) (requirements as to statements contained in balance sheet), and
section 476 (right of members to require audit).

479B Companies excluded from the subsidiary companies audit exemption

A company is not entitled to the exemption conferred by section 479A (subsidiary companies) if it was at any time within the financial year in question—

(a) a traded company as defined in section 474(1),
(b) a company that—
(i) is an authorised insurance company, a banking company, an e-money issuer, a MiFID investment firm or a UCITS management company, or
(ii) carries on insurance market activity, or
(c) a special register body as defined in section 117(1) of the Trade Union and Labour Relations (Consolidation) Act 1992 or an employers' association as defined in section 122 of that Act or Article 4 of the Industrial Relations (Northern Ireland) Order 1992.

479C Subsidiary companies audit exemption: parent undertaking declaration of guarantee

(1) A guarantee is given by a parent undertaking under this section when the directors of the subsidiary company deliver to the registrar a statement by the parent undertaking that it guarantees the subsidiary company under this section.

(2) The statement under subsection (1) must be authenticated by the parent undertaking and must specify—
(a) the name of the parent undertaking,
(b) if the parent undertaking is incorporated in the United Kingdom, its registered number (if any),
(c) if the parent undertaking is incorporated outside the United Kingdom and registered in the country in which it is incorporated, the identity of the register on which it is registered and the number with which it is so registered,
(d) the name and registered number of the subsidiary company in respect of which the guarantee is being given,
(e) the date of the statement, and
(f) the financial year to which the guarantee relates.

(3) A guarantee given under this section has the effect that—
(a) the parent undertaking guarantees all outstanding liabilities to which the subsidiary company is subject at the end of the financial year to which the guarantee relates, until they are satisfied in full, and
(b) the guarantee is enforceable against the parent undertaking by any person to whom the subsidiary company is liable in respect of those liabilities.

Exemption from audit: dormant companies

480 Dormant companies: conditions for exemption from audit

(1) A company is exempt from the requirements of this Act relating to the audit of accounts in respect of a financial year if—
(a) it has been dormant since its formation, or
(b) it has been dormant since the end of the previous financial year and the following conditions are met.

(2) The conditions are that the company—
(a) as regards its individual accounts for the financial year in question—
(i) is entitled to prepare accounts in accordance with the small companies regime (see sections 381 to 384), or
(ii) would be so entitled but for having been a public company or a member of an ineligible group, and

(b) is not required to prepare group accounts for that year.

(3) This section has effect subject to—

section 475(2) and (3) (requirements as to statements to be contained in balance sheet),

section 476 (right of members to require audit), and

section 481 (companies excluded from dormant companies exemption).

481 Companies excluded from dormant companies exemption

A company is not entitled to the exemption conferred by section 480 (dormant companies) if it was at any time within the financial year in question a company that—

(za) is a traded company as defined in section 474(1),

(a) is an authorised insurance company, a banking company, an e-money issuer, a MiFID investment firm or a UCITS management company, or

(b) carries on insurance market activity.

Companies subject to public sector audit

482, 483 *omitted*

General power of amendment by regulations

484 *omitted*

CHAPTER 2
APPOINTMENT OF AUDITORS

Private companies

485 Appointment of auditors of private company: general

(1) An auditor or auditors of a private company must be appointed for each financial year of the company, unless the directors reasonably resolve otherwise on the ground that audited accounts are unlikely to be required.

(2) For each financial year for which an auditor or auditors is or are to be appointed (other than the company's first financial year), the appointment must be made before the end of the period of 28 days beginning with—

(a) the end of the time allowed for sending out copies of the company's annual accounts and reports for the previous financial year (see section 424), or

(b) if earlier, the day on which copies of the company's annual accounts and reports for the previous financial year are sent out under section 423.

This is the "period for appointing auditors".

(3) The directors may appoint an auditor or auditors of the company—

(a) at any time before the company's first period for appointing auditors,

(b) following a period during which the company (being exempt from audit) did not have any auditor, at any time before the company's next period for appointing auditors, or

(c) to fill a casual vacancy in the office of auditor.

(4) The members may appoint an auditor or auditors by ordinary resolution—

(a) during a period for appointing auditors,

(b) if the company should have appointed an auditor or auditors during a period for appointing auditors but failed to do so, or

(c) where the directors had power to appoint under subsection (3) but have failed to make an appointment.

(5) An auditor or auditors of a private company may only be appointed—

(a) in accordance with this section, or

(b) in accordance with section 486 (default power of Secretary of State).

This is without prejudice to any deemed re-appointment under section 487.

486 Appointment of auditors of private company: default power of Secretary of State

(1) If a private company fails to appoint an auditor or auditors in accordance with section 485, the Secretary of State may appoint one or more persons to fill the vacancy.

(2) Where subsection (2) of that section applies and the company fails to make the necessary appointment before the end of the period for appointing auditors, the company must within one week of the end of that period give notice to the Secretary of State of his power having become exercisable.

(3) If a company fails to give the notice required by this section, an offence is committed by—
   (a) the company, and
   (b) every officer of the company who is in default.

(4) A person guilty of an offence under this section is liable on summary conviction to a fine not exceeding level 3 on the standard scale and, for continued contravention, a daily default fine not exceeding one-tenth of level 3 on the standard scale.

487 Term of office of auditors of private company

(1) An auditor or auditors of a private company hold office in accordance with the terms of their appointment, subject to the requirements that—
   (a) they do not take office until any previous auditor or auditors cease to hold office, and
   (b) they cease to hold office at the end of the next period for appointing auditors unless re-appointed.

(2) Where no auditor has been appointed by the end of the next period for appointing auditors, any auditor in office immediately before that time is deemed to be re-appointed at that time, unless—
   (a) he was appointed by the directors, or
   (b) the company's articles require actual re-appointment, or
   (c) the deemed re-appointment is prevented by the members under section 488, or
   (d) the members have resolved that he should not be re-appointed, or
   (e) the directors have resolved that no auditor or auditors should be appointed for the financial year in question.

(3) This is without prejudice to the provisions of this Part as to removal and resignation of auditors.

(4) No account shall be taken of any loss of the opportunity of deemed re-appointment under this section in ascertaining the amount of any compensation or damages payable to an auditor on his ceasing to hold office for any reason.

488 Prevention by members of deemed re-appointment of auditor

(1) An auditor of a private company is not deemed to be re-appointed under section 487(2) if the company has received notices under this section from members representing at least the requisite percentage of the total voting rights of all members who would be entitled to vote on a resolution that the auditor should not be re-appointed.

(2) The "requisite percentage" is 5%, or such lower percentage as is specified for this purpose in the company's articles.

(3) A notice under this section—
   (a) may be in hard copy or electronic form,
   (b) must be authenticated by the person or persons giving it, and
   (c) must be received by the company before the end of the accounting reference period immediately preceding the time when the deemed re-appointment would have effect.

Public companies

489 Appointment of auditors of public company: general

(1) An auditor or auditors of a public company must be appointed for each financial year of the

company, unless the directors reasonably resolve otherwise on the ground that audited accounts are unlikely to be required.

(2) For each financial year for which an auditor or auditors is or are to be appointed (other than the company's first financial year), the appointment must be made before the end of the accounts meeting of the company at which the company's annual accounts and reports for the previous financial year are laid.

(3) The directors may appoint an auditor or auditors of the company—
(a) at any time before the company's first accounts meeting;
(b) following a period during which the company (being exempt from audit) did not have any auditor, at any time before the company's next accounts meeting;
(c) to fill a casual vacancy in the office of auditor.
(4) The members may appoint an auditor or auditors by ordinary resolution—
(a) at an accounts meeting;
(b) if the company should have appointed an auditor or auditors at an accounts meeting but failed to do so;
(c) where the directors had power to appoint under subsection (3) but have failed to make an appointment.
(5) An auditor or auditors of a public company may only be appointed—
(a) in accordance with this section, or
(b) in accordance with section 490 (default power of Secretary of State).

490 Appointment of auditors of public company: default power of Secretary of State

(1) If a public company fails to appoint an auditor or auditors in accordance with section 489, the Secretary of State may appoint one or more persons to fill the vacancy.
(2) Where subsection (2) of that section applies and the company fails to make the necessary appointment before the end of the accounts meeting, the company must within one week of the end of that meeting give notice to the Secretary of State of his power having become exercisable.
(3) If a company fails to give the notice required by this section, an offence is committed by—
(a) the company, and
(b) every officer of the company who is in default.
(4) A person guilty of an offence under this section is liable on summary conviction to a fine not exceeding level 3 on the standard scale and, for continued contravention, a daily default fine not exceeding one-tenth of level 3 on the standard scale.

491 Term of office of auditors of public company

(1) The auditor or auditors of a public company hold office in accordance with the terms of their appointment, subject to the requirements that—
(a) they do not take office until the previous auditor or auditors have ceased to hold office, and
(b) they cease to hold office at the conclusion of the accounts meeting next following their appointment, unless re-appointed.
(2) This is without prejudice to the provisions of this Part as to removal and resignation of auditors.

General provisions

492 Fixing of auditor's remuneration

(1) The remuneration of an auditor appointed by the members of a company must be fixed by the members by ordinary resolution or in such manner as the members may by ordinary resolution determine.
(2) The remuneration of an auditor appointed by the directors of a company must be fixed by the directors.
(3) The remuneration of an auditor appointed by the Secretary of State must be fixed by the Secretary of State.
(4) For the purposes of this section "remuneration" includes sums paid in respect of expenses.
(5) This section applies in relation to benefits in kind as to payments of money.

493 Disclosure of terms of audit appointment

(1) The Secretary of State may make provision by regulations for securing the disclosure of the terms on which a company's auditor is appointed, remunerated or performs his duties. Nothing in the following provisions of this section affects the generality of this power.
(2) The regulations may—

(a) require disclosure of—
(i) a copy of any terms that are in writing, and
(ii) a written memorandum setting out any terms that are not in writing;
(b) require disclosure to be at such times, in such places and by such means as are specified in the regulations;
(c) require the place and means of disclosure to be stated—
(i) in a note to the company's annual accounts (in the case of its individual accounts) or in such manner as is specified in the regulations (in the case of group accounts),
(ii) in the directors' report, or
(iii) in the auditor's report on the company's annual accounts.

(3) The provisions of this section apply to a variation of the terms mentioned in subsection (1) as they apply to the original terms.

(4) Regulations under this section are subject to affirmative resolution procedure.

494 Disclosure of services provided by auditor or associates and related remuneration

(1) The Secretary of State may make provision by regulations for securing the disclosure of—
(a) the nature of any services provided for a company by the company's auditor (whether in his capacity as auditor or otherwise) or by his associates;
(b) the amount of any remuneration received or receivable by a company's auditor, or his associates, in respect of any such services.

Nothing in the following provisions of this section affects the generality of this power.

(2) The regulations may provide—
(a) for disclosure of the nature of any services provided to be made by reference to any class or description of services specified in the regulations (or any combination of services, however described);
(b) for the disclosure of amounts of remuneration received or receivable in respect of services of any class or description specified in the regulations (or any combination of services, however described);
(c) for the disclosure of separate amounts so received or receivable by the company's auditor or any of his associates, or of aggregate amounts so received or receivable by all or any of those persons.

(3) The regulations may—
(a) provide that "remuneration" includes sums paid in respect of expenses;
(b) apply to benefits in kind as well as to payments of money, and require the disclosure of the nature of any such benefits and their estimated money value;
(c) apply to services provided for associates of a company as well as to those provided for a company;
(d) define "associate" in relation to an auditor and a company respectively.

(4) The regulations may provide that any disclosure required by the regulations is to be made—
(a) in a note to the company's annual accounts (in the case of its individual accounts) or in such manner as is specified in the regulations (in the case of group accounts),
(b) in the directors' report, or
(c) in the auditor's report on the company's annual accounts.

(5) If the regulations provide that any such disclosure is to be made as mentioned in subsection (4)(a) or (b), the regulations may require the auditor to supply the directors of the company with any information necessary to enable the disclosure to be made.

(6) Regulations under this section are subject to negative resolution procedure.

CHAPTER 3
FUNCTIONS OF AUDITOR

Auditor's report

495 Auditor's report on company's annual accounts

(1) A company's auditor must make a report to the company's members on all annual accounts of the company of which copies are, during his tenure of office—
(a) in the case of a private company, to be sent out to members under section 423;

(b) in the case of a public company, to be laid before the company in general meeting under section 437.

(2) The auditor's report must include—

(a) an introduction identifying the annual accounts that are the subject of the audit and the financial reporting framework that has been applied in their preparation, and

(b) a description of the scope of the audit identifying the auditing standards in accordance with which the audit was conducted.

(3) The report must state clearly whether, in the auditor's opinion, the annual accounts—

(a) give a true and fair view—

(i) in the case of an individual balance sheet, of the state of affairs of the company as at the end of the financial year,

(ii) in the case of an individual profit and loss account, of the profit or loss of the company for the financial year,

(iii) in the case of group accounts, of the state of affairs as at the end of the financial year and of the profit or loss for the financial year of the undertakings included in the consolidation as a whole, so far as concerns members of the company;

(b) have been properly prepared in accordance with the relevant financial reporting framework; and

(c) have been prepared in accordance with the requirements of this Act (and, where applicable, Article 4 of the IAS Regulation).

Expressions used in this subsection that are defined for the purposes of Part 15 (see section 474) have the same meaning as in that Part.

(4) The auditor's report—

(a) must be either unqualified or qualified, and

(b) must include a reference to any matters to which the auditor wishes to draw attention by way of emphasis without qualifying the report.

496 Auditor's report on strategic report and directors' report

In his report on the company's annual accounts, the auditor must—

(a) state whether, in his opinion, based on the work undertaken in the course of the audit—

(i) the information given in the strategic report (if any) and the directors' report for the financial year for which the accounts are prepared is consistent with those accounts, and

(ii) any such strategic report and the directors' report have been prepared in accordance with applicable legal requirements,

(b) state whether, in the light of the knowledge and understanding of the company and its environment obtained in the course of the audit, he has identified material misstatements in the strategic report (if any) and the directors' report, and

(c) if applicable, give an indication of the nature of each of the misstatements referred to in paragraph (b).

497 Auditor's report on auditable part of directors' remuneration report

(1) If the company is a quoted company, the auditor, in his report on the company's annual accounts for the financial year, must—

(a) report to the company's members on the auditable part of the directors' remuneration report, and

(b) state whether in his opinion that part of the directors' remuneration report has been properly prepared in accordance with this Act.

(2) For the purposes of this Part, "the auditable part" of a directors' remuneration report is the part identified as such by regulations under section 421.

497A Auditor's report on separate corporate governance statement

Where the company prepares a separate corporate governance statement in respect of a financial year, the auditor must, in his report of the company's annual accounts for that year—

(a) state whether, in his opinion, based on the work undertaken in the course of the audit, the information given in the statement in compliance with rules 7.2.5 and 7.2.6 in the Disclosure Rules and Transparency Rules sourcebook made

by the Financial Conduct Authority (information about internal control and risk management systems in relation to financial reporting processes and about share capital structures)—
(i) is consistent with those accounts, and
(ii) has been prepared in accordance with applicable legal requirements,
(b) state whether, in the light of the knowledge and understanding of the company and its environment obtained in the course of the audit, he has identified material misstatements in the information in the statement referred to in paragraph (a),
(c) if applicable, give an indication of the nature of each of the misstatements referred to in paragraph (b), and
(d) state whether, in his opinion, based on the work undertaken in the course of the audit, rules 7.2.2, 7.2.3 and 7.2.7 in the Disclosure Rules and Transparency Rules sourcebook made by the Financial Conduct Authority (information about the company's corporate governance code and practices and about its administrative, management and supervisory bodies and their committees) have been complied with, if applicable.

Duties and rights of auditors

498 Duties of auditor

(1) A company's auditor, in preparing his report, must carry out such investigations as will enable him to form an opinion as to—
(a) whether adequate accounting records have been kept by the company and returns adequate for their audit have been received from branches not visited by him, and
(b) whether the company's individual accounts are in agreement with the accounting records and returns, and
(c) in the case of a quoted company, whether the auditable part of the company's directors' remuneration report is in agreement with the accounting records and returns.

(2) If the auditor is of the opinion—
(a) that adequate accounting records have not been kept, or that returns adequate for their audit have not been received from branches not visited by him, or
(b) that the company's individual accounts are not in agreement with the accounting records and returns, or
(c) in the case of a quoted company, that the auditable part of its directors' remuneration report is not in agreement with the accounting records and returns,
the auditor shall state that fact in his report.

(3) If the auditor fails to obtain all the information and explanations which, to the best of his knowledge and belief, are necessary for the purposes of his audit, he shall state that fact in his report.

(4) If—
(a) the requirements of regulations under section 412 (disclosure of directors' benefits: remuneration, pensions and compensation for loss of office) are not complied with in the annual accounts, or
(b) in the case of a quoted company, the requirements of regulations under section 421 as to information forming the auditable part of the directors' remuneration report are not complied with in that report,
the auditor must include in his report, so far as he is reasonably able to do so, a statement giving the required particulars.

(5) If the directors of the company—
(a) have prepared accounts in accordance with the small companies regime, or
(b) have taken advantage of small companies exemption from the requirement to prepare a strategic report or in preparing the directors' report,
and in the auditor's opinion they were not entitled to do so, the auditor shall state that fact in his report.

498A Auditor's duties in relation to separate corporate governance statement

Where the company is required to prepare a corporate governance statement in respect of a financial year and no such statement is included in the directors' report—
(a) the company's auditor, in preparing his report on the company's annual accounts

for that year, must ascertain whether a corporate governance statement has been prepared, and

(b) if it appears to the auditor that no such statement has been prepared, he must state that fact in his report.

499 Auditor's general right to information

(1) An auditor of a company—

(a) has a right of access at all times to the company's books, accounts and vouchers (in whatever form they are held), and

(b) may require any of the following persons to provide him with such information or explanations as he thinks necessary for the performance of his duties as auditor.

(2) Those persons are—

(a) any officer or employee of the company;

(b) any person holding or accountable for any of the company's books, accounts or vouchers;

(c) any subsidiary undertaking of the company which is a body corporate incorporated in the United Kingdom;

(d) any officer, employee or auditor of any such subsidiary undertaking or any person holding or accountable for any books, accounts or vouchers of any such subsidiary undertaking;

(e) any person who fell within any of paragraphs (a) to (d) at a time to which the information or explanations required by the auditor relates or relate.

(3) A statement made by a person in response to a requirement under this section may not be used in evidence against him in criminal proceedings except proceedings for an offence under section 501.

(4) Nothing in this section compels a person to disclose information in respect of which a claim to legal professional privilege (in Scotland, to confidentiality of communications) could be maintained in legal proceedings.

500 Auditor's right to information from overseas subsidiaries

(1) Where a parent company has a subsidiary undertaking that is not a body corporate incorporated in the United Kingdom, the auditor of the parent company may require it to obtain from any of the following persons such information or explanations as he may reasonably require for the purposes of his duties as auditor.

(2) Those persons are—

(a) the undertaking;

(b) any officer, employee or auditor of the undertaking;

(c) any person holding or accountable for any of the undertaking's books, accounts or vouchers;

(d) any person who fell within paragraph (b) or (c) at a time to which the information or explanations relates or relate.

(3) If so required, the parent company must take all such steps as are reasonably open to it to obtain the information or explanations from the person concerned.

(4) A statement made by a person in response to a requirement under this section may not be used in evidence against him in criminal proceedings except proceedings for an offence under section 501.

(5) Nothing in this section compels a person to disclose information in respect of which a claim to legal professional privilege (in Scotland, to confidentiality of communications) could be maintained in legal proceedings.

501 Auditor's rights to information: offences

(1) A person commits an offence who knowingly or recklessly makes to an auditor of a company a statement (oral or written) that—

(a) conveys or purports to convey any information or explanations which the auditor requires, or is entitled to require, under section 499, and

(b) is misleading, false or deceptive in a material particular.

(2) A person guilty of an offence under subsection (1) is liable—

(a) on conviction on indictment, to imprisonment for a term not exceeding two years or a fine (or both);

(b) on summary conviction—
(i) in England and Wales, to imprisonment for a term not exceeding twelve months or to a fine not exceeding the statutory maximum (or both);
(ii) in Scotland or Northern Ireland, to imprisonment for a term not exceeding six months or to a fine not exceeding the statutory maximum (or both).

(3) A person who fails to comply with a requirement under section 499 without delay commits an offence unless it was not reasonably practicable for him to provide the required information or explanations.

(4) If a parent company fails to comply with section 500, an offence is committed by—
(a) the company, and
(b) every officer of the company who is in default.

(5) A person guilty of an offence under subsection (3) or (4) is liable on summary conviction to a fine not exceeding level 3 on the standard scale.

(6) Nothing in this section affects any right of an auditor to apply for an injunction (in Scotland, an interdict or an order for specific performance) to enforce any of his rights under section 499 or 500.

502 Auditor's rights in relation to resolutions and meetings

(1) In relation to a written resolution proposed to be agreed to by a private company, the company's auditor is entitled to receive all such communications relating to the resolution as, by virtue of any provision of Chapter 2 of Part 13 of this Act, are required to be supplied to a member of the company.

(2) A company's auditor is entitled—
(a) to receive all notices of, and other communications relating to, any general meeting which a member of the company is entitled to receive,
(b) to attend any general meeting of the company, and
(c) to be heard at any general meeting which he attends on any part of the business of the meeting which concerns him as auditor.

(3) Where the auditor is a firm, the right to attend or be heard at a meeting is exercisable by an individual authorised by the firm in writing to act as its representative at the meeting.

Signature of auditor's report

503 Signature of auditor's report

(1) The auditor's report must state the name of the auditor and be signed and dated.

(2) Where the auditor is an individual, the report must be signed by him.

(3) Where the auditor is a firm, the report must be signed by the senior statutory auditor in his own name, for and on behalf of the auditor.

504 Senior statutory auditor

(1) The senior statutory auditor means the individual identified by the firm as senior statutory auditor in relation to the audit in accordance with—
(a) standards issued by the European Commission, or
(b) if there is no applicable standard so issued, any relevant guidance issued by—
(i) the Secretary of State, or
(ii) a body appointed by order of the Secretary of State.

(2) The person identified as senior statutory auditor must be eligible for appointment as auditor of the company in question (see Chapter 2 of Part 42 of this Act).

(3) The senior statutory auditor is not, by reason of being named or identified as senior statutory auditor or by reason of his having signed the auditor's report, subject to any civil liability to which he would not otherwise be subject.

(4) An order appointing a body for the purpose of subsection (1)(b)(ii) is subject to negative resolution procedure.

505 Names to be stated in published copies of auditor's report

(1) Every copy of the auditor's report that is published by or on behalf of the company must—
(a) state the name of the auditor and (where the auditor is a firm) the name of the person who signed it as senior statutory auditor, or
(b) if the conditions in section 506 (circumstances in which names may be omitted) are met, state that a resolution has been passed and notified to the Secretary of State in accordance with that section.

(2) For the purposes of this section a company is regarded as publishing the report if it publishes, issues or circulates it or otherwise makes it available for public inspection in a manner calculated to invite members of the public generally, or any class of members of the public, to read it.

(3) If a copy of the auditor's report is published without the statement required by this section, an offence is committed by—
   (a) the company, and
   (b) every officer of the company who is in default.

(4) A person guilty of an offence under this section is liable on summary conviction to a fine not exceeding level 3 on the standard scale.

506 Circumstances in which names may be omitted

(1) The auditor's name and, where the auditor is a firm, the name of the person who signed the report as senior statutory auditor, may be omitted from—
   (a) published copies of the report, and
   (b) the copy of the report delivered to the registrar under Chapter 10 of Part 15 (filing of accounts and reports),

   if the following conditions are met.

(2) The conditions are that the company—
   (a) considering on reasonable grounds that statement of the name would create or be likely to create a serious risk that the auditor or senior statutory auditor, or any other person, would be subject to violence or intimidation, has resolved that the name should not be stated, and
   (b) has given notice of the resolution to the Secretary of State, stating—
      (i) the name and registered number of the company,
      (ii) the financial year of the company to which the report relates, and
      (iii) the name of the auditor and (where the auditor is a firm) the name of the person who signed the report as senior statutory auditor.

Offences in connection with auditor's report

507 Offences in connection with auditor's report

(1) A person to whom this section applies commits an offence if he knowingly or recklessly causes a report under section 495 (auditor's report on company's annual accounts) to include any matter that is misleading, false or deceptive in a material particular.

(2) A person to whom this section applies commits an offence if he knowingly or recklessly causes such a report to omit a statement required by—
   (a) section 498(2)(b) (statement that company's accounts do not agree with accounting records and returns),
   (b) section 498(3) (statement that necessary information and explanations not obtained), or
   (c) section 498(5) (statement that directors wrongly took advantage of exemption from obligation to prepare group accounts).

(3) This section applies to—
   (a) where the auditor is an individual, that individual and any employee or agent of his who is eligible for appointment as auditor of the company;
   (b) where the auditor is a firm, any director, member, employee or agent of the firm who is eligible for appointment as auditor of the company.

(4) A person guilty of an offence under this section is liable—
   (a) on conviction on indictment, to a fine;
   (b) on summary conviction, to a fine not exceeding the statutory maximum.

508 *omitted*

509 *omitted*

CHAPTER 4
REMOVAL, RESIGNATION, ETC. OF AUDITORS

Removal of auditor

510 Resolution removing auditor from office

(1) The members of a company may remove an auditor from office at any time.

(2) This power is exercisable only—
(a) by ordinary resolution at a meeting, and
(b) in accordance with section 511 (special notice of resolution to remove auditor).

(3) Nothing in this section is to be taken as depriving the person removed of compensation or damages payable to him in respect of the termination—
(a) of his appointment as auditor, or
(b) of any appointment terminating with that as auditor.

(4) An auditor may not be removed from office before the expiration of his term of office except by resolution under this section.

511 Special notice required for resolution removing auditor from office

(1) Special notice is required for a resolution at a general meeting of a company removing an auditor from office.

(2) On receipt of notice of such an intended resolution the company must immediately send a copy of it to the auditor proposed to be removed.

(3) The auditor proposed to be removed may make with respect to the intended resolution representations in writing to the company (not exceeding a reasonable length) and request their notification to members of the company.

(4) The company must (unless the representations are received by it too late for it to do so)—
(a) in any notice of the resolution given to members of the company, state the fact of the representations having been made, and
(b) send a copy of the representations to every member of the company to whom notice of the meeting is or has been sent.

(5) If a copy of any such representations is not sent out as required because received too late or because of the company's default, the auditor may (without prejudice to his right to be heard orally) require that the representations be read out at the meeting.

(6) Copies of the representations need not be sent out and the representations need not be read at the meeting if, on the application either of the company or of any other person claiming to be aggrieved, the court is satisfied that the auditor is using the provisions of this section to secure needless publicity for defamatory matter.
The court may order the company's costs (in Scotland, expenses) on the application to be paid in whole or in part by the auditor, notwithstanding that he is not a party to the application.

512 Notice to registrar of resolution removing auditor from office

(1) Where a resolution is passed under section 510 (resolution removing auditor from office), the company must give notice of that fact to the registrar within 14 days.

(2) If a company fails to give the notice required by this section, an offence is committed by—
(a) the company, and
(b) every officer of it who is in default.

(3) A person guilty of an offence under this section is liable on summary conviction to a fine not exceeding level 3 on the standard scale and, for continued contravention, a daily default fine not exceeding one-tenth of level 3 on the standard scale.

513 Rights of auditor who has been removed from office

(1) An auditor who has been removed by resolution under section 510 has, notwithstanding his removal, the rights conferred by section 502(2) in relation to any general meeting of the company—
(a) at which his term of office would otherwise have expired, or
(b) at which it is proposed to fill the vacancy caused by his removal.

(2) In such a case the references in that section to matters concerning the auditor as auditor shall be construed as references to matters concerning him as a former auditor.

Failure to re-appoint auditor

514 Failure to re-appoint auditor: special procedure required for written resolution

(1) This section applies where a resolution is proposed as a written resolution of a private company whose effect would be to appoint a person as auditor in place of a person (the "outgoing auditor") whose term of office has expired, or is to expire, at the end of the period for appointing auditors.

(2) The following provisions apply if—
(a) no period for appointing auditors has ended since the outgoing auditor ceased to hold office, or
(b) such a period has ended and an auditor or auditors should have been appointed but were not.
(3) The company must send a copy of the proposed resolution to the person proposed to be appointed and to the outgoing auditor.
(4) The outgoing auditor may, within 14 days after receiving the notice, make with respect to the proposed resolution representations in writing to the company (not exceeding a reasonable length) and request their circulation to members of the company.
(5) The company must circulate the representations together with the copy or copies of the resolution circulated in accordance with section 291 (resolution proposed by directors) or section 293 (resolution proposed by members).
(6) Where subsection (5) applies—
(a) the period allowed under section 293(3) for service of copies of the proposed resolution is 28 days instead of 21 days, and
(b) the provisions of section 293(5) and (6) (offences) apply in relation to a failure to comply with that subsection as in relation to a default in complying with that section.
(7) Copies of the representations need not be circulated if, on the application either of the company or of any other person claiming to be aggrieved, the court is satisfied that the auditor is using the provisions of this section to secure needless publicity for defamatory matter.
The court may order the company's costs (in Scotland, expenses) on the application to be paid in whole or in part by the auditor, notwithstanding that he is not a party to the application.
(8) If any requirement of this section is not complied with, the resolution is ineffective.

515 Failure to re-appoint auditor: special notice required for resolution at general meeting

(1) This section applies to a resolution at a general meeting of a company whose effect would be to appoint a person as auditor in place of a person (the "outgoing auditor") whose term of office has ended, or is to end—
(a) in the case of a private company, at the end of the period for appointing auditors;
(b) in the case of a public company, at the end of the next accounts meeting.
(2) Special notice is required of such a resolution if—
(a) in the case of a private company—
(i) no period for appointing auditors has ended since the outgoing auditor ceased to hold office, or
(ii) such a period has ended and an auditor or auditors should have been appointed but were not;
(b) in the case of a public company—
(i) there has been no accounts meeting of the company since the outgoing auditor ceased to hold office, or
(ii) there has been an accounts meeting at which an auditor or auditors should have been appointed but were not.
(3) On receipt of notice of such an intended resolution the company shall forthwith send a copy of it to the person proposed to be appointed and to the outgoing auditor.
(4) The outgoing auditor may make with respect to the intended resolution representations in writing to the company (not exceeding a reasonable length) and request their notification to members of the company.
(5) The company must (unless the representations are received by it too late for it to do so)—
(a) in any notice of the resolution given to members of the company, state the fact of the representations having been made, and
(b) send a copy of the representations to every member of the company to whom notice of the meeting is or has been sent.
(6) If a copy of any such representations is not sent out as required because received too late or because of the company's default, the outgoing auditor may (without prejudice to his right to be heard orally) require that the representations be read out at the meeting.

(7) Copies of the representations need not be sent out and the representations need not be read at the meeting if, on the application either of the company or of any other person claiming to be aggrieved, the court is satisfied that the auditor is using the provisions of this section to secure needless publicity for defamatory matter.
The court may order the company's costs (in Scotland, expenses) on the application to be paid in whole or in part by the outgoing auditor, notwithstanding that he is not a party to the application.

Resignation of auditor

516 Resignation of auditor

(1) An auditor of a company may resign his office by depositing a notice in writing to that effect at the company's registered office.
(2) The notice is not effective unless it is accompanied by the statement required by section 519.
(3) An effective notice of resignation operates to bring the auditor's term of office to an end as of the date on which the notice is deposited or on such later date as may be specified in it.

517 Notice to registrar of resignation of auditor

(1) Where an auditor resigns the company must within 14 days of the deposit of a notice of resignation send a copy of the notice to the registrar of companies.
(2) If default is made in complying with this section, an offence is committed by—
(a) the company, and
(b) every officer of the company who is in default.

Version applying in Scotland

(3) A person guilty of an offence under this section is liable—
(a) on conviction on indictment, to a fine;
(b) on summary conviction, to a fine not exceeding the statutory maximum and, for continued contravention, a daily default fine not exceeding one-tenth of the statutory maximum.

Version applying in England and Wales

(3) A person guilty of an offence under this section is liable on summary conviction to a fine not exceeding level 5 on the standard scale and, for continued contravention, a daily default fine not exceeding one-tenth of the greater of £5,000 or level 4 on the standard scale.

518 Rights of resigning auditor

(1) This section applies where an auditor's notice of resignation is accompanied by a statement of the circumstances connected with his resignation (see section 519).
(2) He may deposit with the notice a signed requisition calling on the directors of the company forthwith duly to convene a general meeting of the company for the purpose of receiving and considering such explanation of the circumstances connected with his resignation as he may wish to place before the meeting.
(3) He may request the company to circulate to its members—
(a) before the meeting convened on his requisition, or
(b) before any general meeting at which his term of office would otherwise have expired or at which it is proposed to fill the vacancy caused by his resignation,
a statement in writing (not exceeding a reasonable length) of the circumstances connected with his resignation.
(4) The company must (unless the statement is received too late for it to comply)—
(a) in any notice of the meeting given to members of the company, state the fact of the statement having been made, and
(b) send a copy of the statement to every member of the company to whom notice of the meeting is or has been sent.
(5) The directors must within 21 days from the date of the deposit of a requisition under this section proceed duly to convene a meeting for a day not more than 28 days after the date on which the notice convening the meeting is given.
(6) If default is made in complying with subsection (5), every director who failed to take all reasonable steps to secure that a meeting was convened commits an offence.
(7) A person guilty of an offence under this section is liable—
(a) on conviction on indictment, to a fine;

(b) on summary conviction to a fine not exceeding the statutory maximum.

(8) If a copy of the statement mentioned above is not sent out as required because received too late or because of the company's default, the auditor may (without prejudice to his right to be heard orally) require that the statement be read out at the meeting.

(9) Copies of a statement need not be sent out and the statement need not be read out at the meeting if, on the application either of the company or of any other person who claims to be aggrieved, the court is satisfied that the auditor is using the provisions of this section to secure needless publicity for defamatory matter.

The court may order the company's costs (in Scotland, expenses) on such an application to be paid in whole or in part by the auditor, notwithstanding that he is not a party to the application.

(10) An auditor who has resigned has, notwithstanding his resignation, the rights conferred by section 502(2) in relation to any such general meeting of the company as is mentioned in subsection (3)(a) or (b) above.

In such a case the references in that section to matters concerning the auditor as auditor shall be construed as references to matters concerning him as a former auditor.

Statement by auditor on ceasing to hold office

519 Statement by auditor to be deposited with company

(1) Where an auditor of an unquoted company ceases for any reason to hold office, he must deposit at the company's registered office a statement of the circumstances connected with his ceasing to hold office, unless he considers that there are no circumstances in connection with his ceasing to hold office that need to be brought to the attention of members or creditors of the company.

(2) If he considers that there are no circumstances in connection with his ceasing to hold office that need to be brought to the attention of members or creditors of the company, he must deposit at the company's registered office a statement to that effect.

(3) Where an auditor of a quoted company ceases for any reason to hold office, he must deposit at the company's registered office a statement of the circumstances connected with his ceasing to hold office.

(4) The statement required by this section must be deposited—

(a) in the case of resignation, along with the notice of resignation;

(b) in the case of failure to seek re-appointment, not less than 14 days before the end of the time allowed for next appointing an auditor;

(c) in any other case, not later than the end of the period of 14 days beginning with the date on which he ceases to hold office.

(5) A person ceasing to hold office as auditor who fails to comply with this section commits an offence.

(6) In proceedings for such an offence it is a defence for the person charged to show that he took all reasonable steps and exercised all due diligence to avoid the commission of the offence.

(7) A person guilty of an offence under this section is liable—

(a) on conviction on indictment, to a fine;

(b) on summary conviction, to a fine not exceeding the statutory maximum.

(8) Where an offence under this section is committed by a body corporate, every officer of the body who is in default also commits the offence.For this purpose—

(a) any person who purports to act as director, manager or secretary of the body is treated as an officer of the body, and

(b) if the body is a company, any shadow director is treated as an officer of the company.

520 Company's duties in relation to statement

(1) This section applies where the statement deposited under section 519 states the circumstances connected with the auditor's ceasing to hold office.

(2) The company must within 14 days of the deposit of the statement either—

(a) send a copy of it to every person who under section 423 is entitled to be sent copies of the accounts, or

(b) apply to the court.

(3) If it applies to the court, the company must notify the auditor of the application.

(4) If the court is satisfied that the auditor is using the provisions of section 519 to secure needless publicity for defamatory matter—
(a) it shall direct that copies of the statement need not be sent out, and
(b) it may further order the company's costs (in Scotland, expenses) on the application to be paid in whole or in part by the auditor, even if he is not a party to the application.

The company must within 14 days of the court's decision send to the persons mentioned in subsection (2)(a) a statement setting out the effect of the order.

(5) If no such direction is made the company must send copies of the statement to the persons mentioned in subsection (2)(a) within 14 days of the court's decision or, as the case may be, of the discontinuance of the proceedings.

(6) In the event of default in complying with this section an offence is committed by every officer of the company who is in default.

(7) In proceedings for such an offence it is a defence for the person charged to show that he took all reasonable steps and exercised all due diligence to avoid the commission of the offence.

(8) A person guilty of an offence under this section is liable—
(a) on conviction on indictment, to a fine;
(b) on summary conviction, to a fine not exceeding the statutory maximum.

521 Copy of statement to be sent to registrar

(1) Unless within 21 days beginning with the day on which he deposited the statement under section 519 the auditor receives notice of an application to the court under section 520, he must within a further seven days send a copy of the statement to the registrar.

(2) If an application to the court is made under section 520 and the auditor subsequently receives notice under subsection (5) of that section, he must within seven days of receiving the notice send a copy of the statement to the registrar.

(3) An auditor who fails to comply with subsection (1) or (2) commits an offence.

(4) In proceedings for such an offence it is a defence for the person charged to show that he took all reasonable steps and exercised all due diligence to avoid the commission of the offence.

(5) A person guilty of an offence under this section is liable—
(a) on conviction on indictment, to a fine;
(b) on summary conviction, to a fine not exceeding the statutory maximum.

(6) Where an offence under this section is committed by a body corporate, every officer of the body who is in default also commits the offence.For this purpose—
(a) any person who purports to act as director, manager or secretary of the body is treated as an officer of the body, and
(b) if the body is a company, any shadow director is treated as an officer of the company.

522 Duty of auditor to notify appropriate audit authority

(1) Where—
(a) in the case of a major audit, an auditor ceases for any reason to hold office, or
(b) in the case of an audit that is not a major audit, an auditor ceases to hold office before the end of his term of office,

the auditor ceasing to hold office must notify the appropriate audit authority.

(2) The notice must—
(a) inform the appropriate audit authority that he has ceased to hold office, and
(b) be accompanied by a copy of the statement deposited by him at the company's registered office in accordance with section 519.

(3) If the statement so deposited is to the effect that he considers that there are no circumstances in connection with his ceasing to hold office that need to be brought to the attention of members or creditors of the company, the notice must also be accompanied by a statement of the reasons for his ceasing to hold office.

(4) The auditor must comply with this section—
(a) in the case of a major audit, at the same time as he deposits a statement at the company's registered office in accordance with section 519;
(b) in the case of an audit that is not a major audit, at such time (not being earlier than the time mentioned in paragraph (a)) as the appropriate audit authority may require.

(5) A person ceasing to hold office as auditor who fails to comply with this section commits an offence.
(6) If that person is a firm an offence is committed by—
(a) the firm, and
(b) every officer of the firm who is in default.
(7) In proceedings for an offence under this section it is a defence for the person charged to show that he took all reasonable steps and exercised all due diligence to avoid the commission of the offence.
(8) A person guilty of an offence under this section is liable—
(a) on conviction on indictment, to a fine;
(b) on summary conviction, to a fine not exceeding the statutory maximum.

523 Duty of company to notify appropriate audit authority

(1) Where an auditor ceases to hold office before the end of his term of office, the company must notify the appropriate audit authority.
(2) The notice must—
(a) inform the appropriate audit authority that the auditor has ceased to hold office, and
(b) be accompanied by—
(i) a statement by the company of the reasons for his ceasing to hold office, or
(ii) if the copy of the statement deposited by the auditor at the company's registered office in accordance with section 519 contains a statement of circumstances in connection with his ceasing to hold office that need to be brought to the attention of members or creditors of the company, a copy of that statement.
(3) The company must give notice under this section not later than 14 days after the date on which the auditor's statement is deposited at the company's registered office in accordance with section 519.
(4) If a company fails to comply with this section, an offence is committed by—
(a) the company, and
(b) every officer of the company who is in default.
(5) In proceedings for such an offence it is a defence for the person charged to show that he took all reasonable steps and exercised all due diligence to avoid the commission of the offence.
(6) A person guilty of an offence under this section is liable—
(a) on conviction on indictment, to a fine;
(b) on summary conviction, to a fine not exceeding the statutory maximum.

524 Information to be given to accounting authorities

(1) The appropriate audit authority on receiving notice under section 522 or 523 of an auditor's ceasing to hold office—
(a) must inform the accounting authorities, and
(b) may if it thinks fit forward to those authorities a copy of the statement or statements accompanying the notice.
(2) The accounting authorities are—
(a) the Secretary of State, and
(b) any person authorised by the Secretary of State for the purposes of section 456 (revision of defective accounts: persons authorised to apply to court).
(3) If either of the accounting authorities is also the appropriate audit authority it is only necessary to comply with this section as regards any other accounting authority.
(4) If the court has made an order under section 520(4) directing that copies of the statement need not be sent out by the company, sections 460 and 461 (restriction on further disclosure) apply in relation to the copies sent to the accounting authorities as they apply to information obtained under section 459 (power to require documents etc).

525 Meaning of "appropriate audit authority" and "major audit"

(1) In sections 522, 523 and 524 "appropriate audit authority" means—
(a) in the case of a major audit (other than one conducted by an Auditor General) —
(i) the Secretary of State, or
(ii) if the Secretary of State has delegated functions under section 1252 to a body whose functions include receiving the notice in question, that body;

(b) in the case of an audit (other than one conducted by an Auditor General) that is not a major audit, the relevant supervisory body;

(c) in the case of an audit conducted by an Auditor General, the Independent Supervisor. "Supervisory body" and "Independent Supervisor" have the same meaning as in Part 42 (statutory auditors) (see sections 1217 and 1228).

(2) In sections 522 and this section "major audit" means a statutory audit conducted in respect of—

(a) a company any of whose securities have been admitted to the official list (within the meaning of Part 6 of the Financial Services and Markets Act 2000), or

(b) any other person in whose financial condition there is a major public interest.

(3) In determining whether an audit is a major audit within subsection (2)(b), regard shall be had to any guidance issued by any of the authorities mentioned in subsection (1).

Supplementary

526 Effect of casual vacancies

If an auditor ceases to hold office for any reason, any surviving or continuing auditor or auditors may continue to act.

CHAPTER 5
QUOTED COMPANIES: RIGHT OF MEMBERS TO RAISE AUDIT CONCERNS AT ACCOUNTS MEETING

527 Members' power to require website publication of audit concerns

(1) The members of a quoted company may require the company to publish on a website a statement setting out any matter relating to—

(a) the audit of the company's accounts (including the auditor's report and the conduct of the audit) that are to be laid before the next accounts meeting, or

(b) any circumstances connected with an auditor of the company ceasing to hold office since the previous accounts meeting,

that the members propose to raise at the next accounts meeting of the company.

(2) A company is required to do so once it has received requests to that effect from—

(a) members representing at least 5% of the total voting rights of all the members who have a relevant right to vote (excluding any voting rights attached to any shares in the company held as treasury shares), or

(b) at least 100 members who have a relevant right to vote and hold shares in the company on which there has been paid up an average sum, per member, of at least £100.

See also section 153 (exercise of rights where shares held on behalf of others).

(3) In subsection (2) a "relevant right to vote" means a right to vote at the accounts meeting.

(4) A request—

(a) may be sent to the company in hard copy or electronic form,

(b) must identify the statement to which it relates,

(c) must be authenticated by the person or persons making it, and

(d) must be received by the company at least one week before the meeting to which it relates.

(5) A quoted company is not required to place on a website a statement under this section if, on an application by the company or another person who claims to be aggrieved, the court is satisfied that the rights conferred by this section are being abused.

(6) The court may order the members requesting website publication to pay the whole or part of the company's costs (in Scotland, expenses) on such an application, even if they are not parties to the application.

528 Requirements as to website availability

(1) The following provisions apply for the purposes of section 527 (website publication of members' statement of audit concerns).

(2) The information must be made available on a website that—

(a) is maintained by or on behalf of the company, and

(b) identifies the company in question.

(3) Access to the information on the website, and the ability to obtain a hard copy of the information from the website, must not be conditional on the payment of a fee or otherwise restricted.

(4) The statement—

(a) must be made available within three working days of the company being required to publish it on a website, and

(b) must be kept available until after the meeting to which it relates.

(5) A failure to make information available on a website throughout the period specified in subsection (4)(b) is disregarded if—

(a) the information is made available on the website for part of that period, and

(b) the failure is wholly attributable to circumstances that it would not be reasonable to have expected the company to prevent or avoid.

529 Website publication: company's supplementary duties

(1) A quoted company must in the notice it gives of the accounts meeting draw attention to—

(a) the possibility of a statement being placed on a website in pursuance of members' requests under section 527, and

(b) the effect of the following provisions of this section.

(2) A company may not require the members requesting website publication to pay its expenses in complying with that section or section 528 (requirements in connection with website publication).

(3) Where a company is required to place a statement on a website under section 527 it must forward the statement to the company's auditor not later than the time when it makes the statement available on the website.

(4) The business which may be dealt with at the accounts meeting includes any statement that the company has been required under section 527 to publish on a website.

530 Website publication: offences

(1) In the event of default in complying with

(a) section 528 (requirements as to website publication), or

(b) section 529 (companies' supplementary duties in relation to request for website publication),

an offence is committed by every officer of the company who is in default.

(2) A person guilty of an offence under this section is liable—

(a) on conviction on indictment, to a fine;

(b) on summary conviction, to a fine not exceeding the statutory maximum.

531 Meaning of "quoted company"

(1) For the purposes of this Chapter a company is a quoted company if it is a quoted company in accordance with section 385 (quoted and unquoted companies for the purposes of Part (15) in relation to the financial year to which the accounts to be laid at the next accounts meeting relate.

(2) The provisions of subsections (4) to (6) of that section (power to amend definition by regulations) apply in relation to the provisions of this Chapter as in relation to the provisions of that Part.

CHAPTER 6
AUDITORS' LIABILITY

Voidness of provisions protecting auditors from liability

532 Voidness of provisions protecting auditors from liability

(1) This section applies to any provision—

(a) for exempting an auditor of a company (to any extent) from any liability that would otherwise attach to him in connection with any negligence, default, breach of duty or breach of trust in relation to the company occurring in the course of the audit of accounts, or

(b) by which a company directly or indirectly provides an indemnity (to any extent) for an auditor of the company, or of an associated company, against any liability attaching to him in connection with any negligence, default, breach of duty or breach of trust in relation to the company of which he is auditor occurring in the course of the audit of accounts.

(2) Any such provision is void, except as permitted by—
  (a) section 533 (indemnity for costs of successfully defending proceedings), or
  (b) sections 534 to 536 (liability limitation agreements).
(3) This section applies to any provision, whether contained in a company's articles or in any contract with the company or otherwise.
(4) For the purposes of this section companies are associated if one is a subsidiary of the other or both are subsidiaries of the same body corporate.

Indemnity for costs of defending proceedings

533 Indemnity for costs of successfully defending proceedings

Section 532 (general voidness of provisions protecting auditors from liability) does not prevent a company from indemnifying an auditor against any liability incurred by him—
  (a) in defending proceedings (whether civil or criminal) in which judgment is given in his favour or he is acquitted, or
  (b) in connection with an application under section 1157 (power of court to grant relief in case of honest and reasonable conduct) in which relief is granted to him by the court.

Liability limitation agreements

534 Liability limitation agreements

(1) A "liability limitation agreement" is an agreement that purports to limit the amount of a liability owed to a company by its auditor in respect of any negligence, default, breach of duty or breach of trust, occurring in the course of the audit of accounts, of which the auditor may be guilty in relation to the company.
(2) Section 532 (general voidness of provisions protecting auditors from liability) does not affect the validity of a liability limitation agreement that—
  (a) complies with section 535 (terms of liability limitation agreement) and of any regulations under that section, and
  (b) is authorised by the members of the company (see section 536).
(3) Such an agreement—
  (a) is effective to the extent provided by section 537, and
  (b) is not subject—
    (i) in England and Wales or Northern Ireland, to section 2(2) or 3(2)(a) of the Unfair Contract Terms Act 1977;
    (ii) in Scotland, to section 16(1)(b) or 17(1)(a) of that Act.

535 Terms of liability limitation agreement

(1) A liability limitation agreement—
  (a) must not apply in respect of acts or omissions occurring in the course of the audit of accounts for more than one financial year, and
  (b) must specify the financial year in relation to which it applies.
(2) The Secretary of State may by regulations—
  (a) require liability limitation agreements to contain specified provisions or provisions of a specified description;
  (b) prohibit liability limitation agreements from containing specified provisions or provisions of a specified description.

"Specified" here means specified in the regulations.
(3) Without prejudice to the generality of the power conferred by subsection (2), that power may be exercised with a view to preventing adverse effects on competition.
(4) Subject to the preceding provisions of this section, it is immaterial how a liability limitation agreement is framed.

In particular, the limit on the amount of the auditor's liability need not be a sum of money, or a formula, specified in the agreement.
(5) Regulations under this section are subject to negative resolution procedure.

536 Authorisation of agreement by members of the company

(1) A liability limitation agreement is authorised by the members of the company if it has been authorised under this section and that authorisation has not been withdrawn.

(2) A liability limitation agreement between a private company and its auditor may be authorised—
  (a) by the company passing a resolution, before it enters into the agreement, waiving the need for approval,
  (b) by the company passing a resolution, before it enters into the agreement, approving the agreement's principal terms, or
  (c) by the company passing a resolution, after it enters into the agreement, approving the agreement.

(3) A liability limitation agreement between a public company and its auditor may be authorised—
  (a) by the company passing a resolution in general meeting, before it enters into the agreement, approving the agreement's principal terms, or
  (b) by the company passing a resolution in general meeting, after it enters into the agreement, approving the agreement.

(4) The "principal terms" of an agreement are terms specifying, or relevant to the determination of—
  (a) the kind (or kinds) of acts or omissions covered,
  (b) the financial year to which the agreement relates, or
  (c) the limit to which the auditor's liability is subject.

(5) Authorisation under this section may be withdrawn by the company passing an ordinary resolution to that effect—
  (a) at any time before the company enters into the agreement, or
  (b) if the company has already entered into the agreement, before the beginning of the financial year to which the agreement relates.

Paragraph (b) has effect notwithstanding anything in the agreement.

537 Effect of liability limitation agreement

(1) A liability limitation agreement is not effective to limit the auditor's liability to less than such amount as is fair and reasonable in all the circumstances of the case having regard (in particular) to—
  (a) the auditor's responsibilities under this Part,
  (b) the nature and purpose of the auditor's contractual obligations to the company, and
  (c) the professional standards expected of him.

(2) A liability limitation agreement that purports to limit the auditor's liability to less than the amount mentioned in subsection (1) shall have effect as if it limited his liability to that amount.

(3) In determining what is fair and reasonable in all the circumstances of the case no account is to be taken of—
  (a) matters arising after the loss or damage in question has been incurred, or
  (b) matters (whenever arising) affecting the possibility of recovering compensation from other persons liable in respect of the same loss or damage.

538 Disclosure of agreement by company

(1) A company which has entered into a liability limitation agreement must make such disclosure in connection with the agreement as the Secretary of State may require by regulations.

(2) The regulations may provide, in particular, that any disclosure required by the regulations shall be made—
  (a) in a note to the company's annual accounts (in the case of its individual accounts) or in such manner as is specified in the regulations (in the case of group accounts), or
  (b) in the directors' report.

(3) Regulations under this section are subject to negative resolution procedure.

538A Meaning of "corporate governance statement" etc.

(1) In this Part "corporate governance statement" means the statement required by rules 7.2.1 to 7.2.11 in the Disclosure Rules and Transparency Rules sourcebook made by the Financial Conduct Authority.

(2) …

(3) A "separate" corporate governance statement means one that is not included in the directors' report.

CHAPTER 7
SUPPLEMENTARY PROVISIONS

539 Minor definitions

In this Part—

"e-money issuer" means—

(a) an electronic money institution, within the meaning of the Electronic Money Regulations 2011, or

(b) a person who has permission under Part 4A of the Financial Services and Markets Act 2000 to carry on the activity of issuing electronic money within the meaning of article 9B of the Financial Services and Markets Act 2000 (Regulated Activities) Order 2001;

"MiFID investment firm" means an investment firm within the meaning of Article 4.1.1 of Directive 2004/39/EC of the European Parliament and of the Council of 21 April 2004 on markets in financial instruments, other than—

(a) a company to which that Directive does not apply by virtue of Article 2 of that Directive,

(b) a company which is an exempt investment firm within the meaning of regulation 4A(3) of the Financial Services and Markets Act 2000 (Markets in Financial Instruments) Regulations 2007, and

(c) any other company which fulfils all the requirements set out in regulation 4C(3) of those Regulations;

"qualified", in relation to an auditor's report (or a statement contained in an auditor's report), means that the report or statement does not state the auditor's unqualified opinion that the accounts have been properly prepared in accordance with this Act or, in the case of an undertaking not required to prepare accounts in accordance with this Act, under any corresponding legislation under which it is required to prepare accounts;

"turnover", in relation to a company, means the amounts derived from the provision of goods and services falling within the company's ordinary activities, after deduction of—

(a) trade discounts,

(b) value added tax, and

(c) any other taxes based on the amounts so derived;

"UCITS management company" has the meaning given by the Glossary forming part of the Handbook made by the Financial Conduct Authority under the Financial Services and Markets Act 2000.

PART 17
A COMPANY'S SHARE CAPITAL

CHAPTER 1
SHARES AND SHARE CAPITAL OF A COMPANY

Shares

540 Shares

(1) In the Companies Acts "share", in relation to a company, means share in the company's share capital.

(2) A company's shares may no longer be converted into stock.

(3) Stock created before the commencement of this Part may be reconverted into shares in accordance with section 620.

(4) In the Companies Acts—

(a) references to shares include stock except where a distinction between share and stock is express or implied, and

(b) references to a number of shares include an amount of stock where the context admits of the reference to shares being read as including stock.

541 Nature of shares

The shares or other interest of a member in a company are personal property (or, in Scotland, moveable property) and are not in the nature of real estate (or heritage).

542 Nominal value of shares

(1) Shares in a limited company having a share capital must each have a fixed nominal value.

(2) An allotment of a share that does not have a fixed nominal value is void.

(3) Shares in a limited company having a share capital may be denominated in any currency, and different classes of shares may be denominated in different currencies.
But see section 765 (initial authorised minimum share capital requirement for public company to be met by reference to share capital denominated in sterling or euros).

(4) If a company purports to allot shares in contravention of this section, an offence is committed by every officer of the company who is in default.

(5) A person guilty of an offence under this section is liable—
(a) on conviction on indictment, to a fine;
(b) on summary conviction, to a fine not exceeding the statutory maximum.

543 Numbering of shares

(1) Each share in a company having a share capital must be distinguished by its appropriate number, except in the following circumstances.

(2) If at any time—
(a) all the issued shares in a company are fully paid up and rank pari passu for all purposes, or
(b) all the issued shares of a particular class in a company are fully paid up and rank pari passu for all purposes,
none of those shares need thereafter have a distinguishing number so long as it remains fully paid up and ranks pari passu for all purposes with all shares of the same class for the time being issued and fully paid up.

544 Transferability of shares

(1) The shares or other interest of any member in a company are transferable in accordance with the company's articles.

(2) This is subject to—
(a) the Stock Transfer Act 1963 or the Stock Transfer Act (Northern Ireland) 1963 (which enables securities of certain descriptions to be transferred by a simplified process), and
(b) regulations under Chapter 2 of Part 21 of this Act (which enable title to securities to be evidenced and transferred without a written instrument).

(3) See Part 21 of this Act generally as regards share transfers.

545 Companies having a share capital

References in the Companies Acts to a company having a share capital are to a company that has power under its constitution to issue shares.

546 Issued and allotted share capital

(1) References in the Companies Acts—
(a) to "issued share capital" are to shares of a company that have been issued;
(b) to "allotted share capital" are to shares of a company that have been allotted.

(2) References in the Companies Acts to issued or allotted shares, or to issued or allotted share capital, include shares taken on the formation of the company by the subscribers to the company's memorandum.

Share capital

547 Called-up share capital

In the Companies Acts—
"called-up share capital", in relation to a company, means so much of its share capital as equals the aggregate amount of the calls made on its shares (whether or not those calls have been paid), together with—
(a) any share capital paid up without being called, and
(b) any share capital to be paid on a specified future date under the articles, the terms of allotment of the relevant shares or any other arrangements for payment of those shares; and
"uncalled share capital" is to be construed accordingly.

548 Equity share capital

In the Companies Acts "equity share capital", in relation to a company, means its issued sharecapital excluding any part of that capital that, neither as respects dividends nor as respects capital, carries any right to participate beyond a specified amount in a distribution.

CHAPTER 2
ALLOTMENT OF SHARES: GENERAL PROVISIONS

Power of directors to allot shares

549 Exercise by directors of power to allot shares etc.

(1) The directors of a company must not exercise any power of the company—
  (a) to allot shares in the company, or
  (b) to grant rights to subscribe for, or to convert any security into, shares in the company,
except in accordance with section 550 (private company with single class of shares) or section 551 (authorisation by company).
(2) Subsection (1) does not apply—
  (a) to the allotment of shares in pursuance of an employees' share scheme, or
  (b) to the grant of a right to subscribe for, or to convert any security into, shares so allotted.
(3) Subsection (1) does not apply to the allotment of shares pursuant to a right to subscribe for, or to convert any security into, shares in the company.
(4) A director who knowingly contravenes, or permits or authorises a contravention of, this section commits an offence.
(5) A person guilty of an offence under this section is liable—
  (a) on conviction on indictment, to a fine;
  (b) on summary conviction, to a fine not exceeding the statutory maximum.
(6) Nothing in this section affects the validity of an allotment or other transaction.

550 Power of directors to allot shares etc: private company with only one class of shares

Where a private company has only one class of shares, the directors may exercise any power of the company—
  (a) to allot shares of that class, or
  (b) to grant rights to subscribe for or to convert any security into such shares, except to the extent that they are prohibited from doing so by the company's articles.

551 Power of directors to allot shares etc: authorisation by company

(1) The directors of a company may exercise a power of the company—
  (a) to allot shares in the company, or
  (b) to grant rights to subscribe for or to convert any security into shares in the company,
if they are authorised to do so by the company's articles or by resolution of the company.
(2) Authorisation may be given for a particular exercise of the power or for its exercise generally, and may be unconditional or subject to conditions.
(3) Authorisation must—
  (a) state the maximum amount of shares that may be allotted under it, and
  (b) specify the date on which it will expire, which must be not more than five years from—
    (i) in the case of authorisation contained in the company's articles at the time of its original incorporation, the date of that incorporation;
    (ii) in any other case, the date on which the resolution is passed by virtue of which the authorisation is given.
(4) Authorisation may—
  (a) be renewed or further renewed by resolution of the company for a further period not exceeding five years, and
  (b) be revoked or varied at any time by resolution of the company.
(5) A resolution renewing authorisation must—
  (a) state (or restate) the maximum amount of shares that may be allotted under the authorisation or, as the case may be, the amount remaining to be allotted under it, and

(b) specify the date on which the renewed authorisation will expire.

(6) In relation to rights to subscribe for or to convert any security into shares in the company, references in this section to the maximum amount of shares that may be allotted under the authorisation are to the maximum amount of shares that may be allotted pursuant to the rights.

(7) The directors may allot shares, or grant rights to subscribe for or to convert any security into shares, after authorisation has expired if—

(a) the shares are allotted, or the rights are granted, in pursuance of an offer or agreement made by the company before the authorisation expired, and

(b) the authorisation allowed the company to make an offer or agreement which would or might require shares to be allotted, or rights to be granted, after the authorisation had expired.

(8) A resolution of a company to give, vary, revoke or renew authorisation under this section may be an ordinary resolution, even though it amends the company's articles.

(9) Chapter 3 of Part 3 (resolutions affecting a company's constitution) applies to a resolution under this section.

Prohibition of commissions, discounts and allowances

552 General prohibition of commissions, discounts and allowances

(1) Except as permitted by section 553 (permitted commission), a company must not apply any of its shares or capital money, either directly or indirectly, in payment of any commission, discount or allowance to any person in consideration of his—

(a) subscribing or agreeing to subscribe (whether absolutely or conditionally) for shares in the company, or

(b) procuring or agreeing to procure subscriptions (whether absolute or conditional) for shares in the company.

(2) It is immaterial how the shares or money are so applied, whether by being added to the purchase money of property acquired by the company or to the contract price of work to be executed for the company, or being paid out of the nominal purchase money or contract price, or otherwise.

(3) Nothing in this section affects the payment of such brokerage as has previously been lawful.

553 Permitted commission

(1) A company may, if the following conditions are satisfied, pay a commission to a person in consideration of his subscribing or agreeing to subscribe (whether absolutely or conditionally) for shares in the company, or procuring or agreeing to procure subscriptions (whether absolute or conditional) for shares in the company.

(2) The conditions are that—

(a) the payment of the commission is authorised by the company's articles; and

(b) the commission paid or agreed to be paid does not exceed—

(i) 10% of the price at which the shares are issued, or

(ii) the amount or rate authorised by the articles, whichever is the less.

(3) A vendor to, or promoter of, or other person who receives payment in money or shares from, a company may apply any part of the money or shares so received in payment of any commission the payment of which directly by the company would be permitted by this section.

Registration of allotment

554 Registration of allotment

(1) A company must register an allotment of shares as soon as practicable and in any event within two months after the date of the allotment.

(2) This does not apply if the company has issued a share warrant in respect of the shares (see section 779).

(3) If a company fails to comply with this section, an offence is committed by—

(a) the company, and

(b) every officer of the company who is in default.

(4) A person guilty of an offence under this section is liable on summary conviction to a fine not exceeding level 3 on the standard scale and, for continued contravention, a daily default fine not exceeding one-tenth of level 3 on the standard scale.

(5) For the company's duties as to the issue of share certificates etc, see Part 21 (certification and transfer of securities).

Return of allotment

555 Return of allotment by limited company

(1) This section applies to a company limited by shares and to a company limited by guarantee and having a share capital.
(2) The company must, within one month of making an allotment of shares, deliver to the registrar for registration a return of the allotment.
(3) The return must—
  (a) contain the prescribed information, and
  (b) be accompanied by a statement of capital.
(4) The statement of capital must state with respect to the company's share capital at the date to which the return is made up—
  (a) the total number of shares of the company,
  (b) the aggregate nominal value of those shares,
  (c) for each class of shares—
    (i) prescribed particulars of the rights attached to the shares,
    (ii) the total number of shares of that class, and
    (iii) the aggregate nominal value of shares of that class, and
  (d) the amount paid up and the amount (if any) unpaid on each share (whether on account of the nominal value of the share or by way of premium).

556 Return of allotment by unlimited company allotting new class of shares

(1) This section applies to an unlimited company that allots shares of a class with rights that are not in all respects uniform with shares previously allotted.
(2) The company must, within one month of making such an allotment, deliver to the registrar for registration a return of the allotment.
(3) The return must contain the prescribed particulars of the rights attached to the shares.
(4) For the purposes of this section shares are not to be treated as different from shares previously allotted by reason only that the former do not carry the same rights to dividends as the latter during the twelve months immediately following the former's allotment.

557 Offence of failure to make return

(1) If a company makes default in complying with—
section 555 (return of allotment of shares by limited company), or
section 556 (return of allotment of new class of shares by unlimited company), an offence is committed by every officer of the company who is in default.

Version applying in Scotland

(2) A person guilty of an offence under this section is liable—
  (a) on conviction on indictment, to a fine;
  (b) on summary conviction, to a fine not exceeding the statutory maximum and, for continued contravention, a daily default fine not exceeding one-tenth of the statutory maximum.

Version applying in England and Wales

(2) A person guilty of an offence under this section is liable on summary conviction to a fine not exceeding level 5 on the standard scale and, for continued contravention, a daily default fine not exceeding one-tenth of the greater of £5,000 or level 4 on the standard scale.
(3) In the case of default in delivering to the registrar within one month after the allotment the return required by section 555 or 556—
  (a) any person liable for the default may apply to the court for relief, and
  (b) the court, if satisfied—
    (i) that the omission to deliver the document was accidental or due to inadvertence, or
    (ii) that it is just and equitable to grant relief,

may make an order extending the time for delivery of the document for such period as the court thinks proper.

Supplementary provisions

558 When shares are allotted

For the purposes of the Companies Acts shares in a company are taken to be allotted when a person acquires the unconditional right to be included in the company's register of members in respect of the shares.

559 Provisions about allotment not applicable to shares taken on formation

The provisions of this Chapter have no application in relation to the taking of shares by the subscribers to the memorandum on the formation of the company.

CHAPTER 3
ALLOTMENT OF EQUITY SECURITIES: EXISTING SHAREHOLDERS' RIGHT OF PRE-EMPTION

Introductory

560 Meaning of "equity securities" and related expressions

(1) In this Chapter—
"equity securities" means—
(a) ordinary shares in the company, or
(b) rights to subscribe for, or to convert securities into, ordinary shares in the company;
"ordinary shares" means shares other than shares that as respects dividends and capital carry a right to participate only up to a specified amount in a distribution.

(2) References in this Chapter to the allotment of equity securities—
(a) include the grant of a right to subscribe for, or to convert any securities into, ordinary shares in the company, and
(b) do not include the allotment of shares pursuant to such a right.

(3) References in this Chapter to the allotment of equity securities include the sale of ordinary shares in the company that immediately before the sale were held by the company as treasury shares.

Existing shareholders' right of pre-emption

561 Existing shareholders' right of pre-emption

(1) A company must not allot equity securities to a person on any terms unless—
(a) it has made an offer to each person who holds ordinary shares in the company to allot to him on the same or more favourable terms a proportion of those securities that is as nearly as practicable equal to the proportion in nominal value held by him of the ordinary share capital of the company, and
(b) the period during which any such offer may be accepted has expired or the company has received notice of the acceptance or refusal of every offer so made.

(2) Securities that a company has offered to allot to a holder of ordinary shares may be allotted to him, or anyone in whose favour he has renounced his right to their allotment, without contravening subsection (1)(b).

...

(4) Shares held by the company as treasury shares are disregarded for the purposes of this section, so that—
(a) the company is not treated as a person who holds ordinary shares, and
(b) the shares are not treated as forming part of the ordinary share capital of the company.

(5) This section is subject to—
(a) sections 564 to 566 (exceptions to pre-emption right),
(b) sections 567 and 568 (exclusion of rights of pre-emption),
(c) sections 569 to 573 (disapplication of pre-emption rights), and
(d) section 576 (saving for certain older pre-emption procedures).

562 Communication of pre-emption offers to shareholders

(1) This section has effect as to the manner in which offers required by section 561 are to be made to holders of a company's shares.

(2) The offer may be made in hard copy or electronic form.
(3) If the holder—
 (a) has no registered address in an EEA State and has not given to the company an address in an EEA State for the service of notices on him, or
 (b) is the holder of a share warrant,
the offer may be made by causing it, or a notice specifying where a copy of it can be obtained or inspected, to be published in the Gazette.
(4) The offer must state a period during which it may be accepted and the offer shall not be withdrawn before the end of that period.
(5) The period must be a period of at least 14 days beginning—
 (a) in the case of an offer made in hard copy form, with the date on which the offer is sent or supplied;
 (b) in the case of an offer made in electronic form, with the date on which the offer is sent;
 (c) in the case of an offer made by publication in the Gazette, with the date of publication.
(6) The Secretary of State may by regulations made by statutory instrument—
 (a) reduce the period specified in subsection (5) (but not to less than 14 days), or
 (b) increase that period.
(7) A statutory instrument containing regulations made under subsection (6) is subject to affirmative resolution procedure.

563 Liability of company and officers in case of contravention

(1) This section applies where there is a contravention of—
 section 561 (existing shareholders' right of pre-emption), or
 section 562 (communication of pre-emption offers to shareholders).
(2) The company and every officer of it who knowingly authorised or permitted the contravention are jointly and severally liable to compensate any person to whom an offer should have been made in accordance with those provisions for any loss, damage, costs or expenses which the person has sustained or incurred by reason of the contravention.
(3) No proceedings to recover any such loss, damage, costs or expenses shall be commenced after the expiration of two years—
 (a) from the delivery to the registrar of companies of the return of allotment, or
 (b) where equity securities other than shares are granted, from the date of the grant.

Exceptions to right of pre-emption

564 Exception to pre-emption right: bonus shares

Section 561(1) (existing shareholders' right of pre-emption) does not apply in relation to the allotment of bonus shares.

565 Exception to pre-emption right: issue for non-cash consideration

Section 561(1) (existing shareholders' right of pre-emption) does not apply to a particular allotment of equity securities if these are, or are to be, wholly or partly paid up otherwise than in cash.

566 Exception to pre-emption right: employees' share scheme

Section 561 (existing shareholders' right of pre-emption) does not apply to the allotment of equity securities that would, apart from any renunciation or assignment of the right to their allotment, be held under or allotted or transferred pursuant to an employees' share scheme.

Exclusion of right of pre-emption

567 Exclusion of requirements by private companies

(1) All or any of the requirements of—
 (a) section 561 (existing shareholders' right of pre-emption), or
 (b) section 562 (communication of pre-emption offers to shareholders) may be excluded by provision contained in the articles of a private company.
(2) They may be excluded—
 (a) generally in relation to the allotment by the company of equity securities, or
 (b) in relation to allotments of a particular description.

(3) Any requirement or authorisation contained in the articles of a private company that is inconsistent with either of those sections is treated for the purposes of this section as a provision excluding that section.

(4) A provision to which section 568 applies (exclusion of pre-emption right: corresponding right conferred by articles) is not to be treated as inconsistent with section 561.

568 Exclusion of pre-emption right: articles conferring corresponding right

(1) The provisions of this section apply where, in a case in which section 561 (existing shareholders' right of pre-emption) would otherwise apply—

(a) a company's articles contain provision ("pre-emption provision") prohibiting the company from allotting ordinary shares of a particular class unless it has complied with the condition that it makes such an offer as is described in section 561(1) to each person who holds ordinary shares of that class, and

(b) in accordance with that provision—

(i) the company makes an offer to allot shares to such a holder, and

(ii) he or anyone in whose favour he has renounced his right to their allotment accepts the offer.

(2) In that case, section 561 does not apply to the allotment of those shares and the company may allot them accordingly.

(3) The provisions of section 562 (communication of pre-emption offers to shareholders) apply in relation to offers made in pursuance of the pre-emption provision of the company's articles.

This is subject to section 567 (exclusion of requirements by private companies).

(4) If there is a contravention of the pre-emption provision of the company's articles, the company, and every officer of it who knowingly authorised or permitted the contravention, are jointly and severally liable to compensate any person to whom an offer should have been made under the provision for any loss, damage, costs or expenses which the person has sustained or incurred by reason of the contravention.

(5) No proceedings to recover any such loss, damage, costs or expenses may be commenced after the expiration of two years—

(a) from the delivery to the registrar of companies of the return of allotment, or

(b) where equity securities other than shares are granted, from the date of the grant.

Disapplication of pre-emption rights

569 Disapplication of pre-emption rights: private company with only one class of shares

(1) The directors of a private company that has only one class of shares may be given power by the articles, or by a special resolution of the company, to allot equity securities of that class as if section 561 (existing shareholders' right of pre-emption)—

(a) did not apply to the allotment, or

(b) applied to the allotment with such modifications as the directors may determine.

(2) Where the directors make an allotment under this section, the provisions of this Chapter have effect accordingly.

570 Disapplication of pre-emption rights: directors acting under general authorisation

(1) Where the directors of a company are generally authorised for the purposes of section 551 (power of directors to allot shares etc: authorisation by company), they may be given power by the articles, or by a special resolution of the company, to allot equity securities pursuant to that authorisation as if section 561 (existing shareholders' right of pre- emption)—

(a) did not apply to the allotment, or

(b) applied to the allotment with such modifications as the directors may determine.

(2) Where the directors make an allotment under this section, the provisions of this Chapter have effect accordingly.

(3) The power conferred by this section ceases to have effect when the authorisation to which it relates—

(a) is revoked, or

(b) would (if not renewed) expire.

But if the authorisation is renewed the power may also be renewed, for a period not longer than that for which the authorisation is renewed, by a special resolution of the company.

(4) Notwithstanding that the power conferred by this section has expired, the directors may allot equity securities in pursuance of an offer or agreement previously made by the company if the power enabled the company to make an offer or agreement that would or might require equity securities to be allotted after it expired.

571 Disapplication of pre-emption rights by special resolution

(1) Where the directors of a company are authorised for the purposes of section 551 (power of directors to allot shares etc: authorisation by company), whether generally or otherwise, the company may by special resolution resolve that section 561 (existing shareholders' right of pre-emption)—

(a) does not apply to a specified allotment of equity securities to be made pursuant to that authorisation, or

(b) applies to such an allotment with such modifications as may be specified in the resolution.

(2) Where such a resolution is passed the provisions of this Chapter have effect accordingly.

(3) A special resolution under this section ceases to have effect when the authorisation to which it relates—

(a) is revoked, or

(b) would (if not renewed) expire.

But if the authorisation is renewed the resolution may also be renewed, for a period not longer than that for which the authorisation is renewed, by a special resolution of the company.

(4) Notwithstanding that any such resolution has expired, the directors may allot equity securities in pursuance of an offer or agreement previously made by the company if the resolution enabled the company to make an offer or agreement that would or might require equity securities to be allotted after it expired.

(5) A special resolution under this section, or a special resolution to renew such a resolution, must not be proposed unless—

(a) it is recommended by the directors, and

(b) the directors have complied with the following provisions.

(6) Before such a resolution is proposed, the directors must make a written statement setting out—

(a) their reasons for making the recommendation,

(b) the amount to be paid to the company in respect of the equity securities to be allotted, and

(c) the directors' justification of that amount.

(7) The directors' statement must—

(a) if the resolution is proposed as a written resolution, be sent or submitted to every eligible member at or before the time at which the proposed resolution is sent or submitted to him;

(b) if the resolution is proposed at a general meeting, be circulated to the members entitled to notice of the meeting with that notice.

572 Liability for false statement in directors' statement

(1) This section applies in relation to a directors' statement under section 571 (special resolution disapplying pre-emption rights) that is sent, submitted or circulated under subsection (7) of that section.

(2) A person who knowingly or recklessly authorises or permits the inclusion of any matter that is misleading, false or deceptive in a material particular in such a statement commits an offence.

(3) A person guilty of an offence under this section is liable—

(a) on conviction on indictment, to imprisonment for a term not exceeding two years or a fine (or both);

(b) on summary conviction—

(i) in England and Wales, to imprisonment for a term not exceeding twelve months or to a fine not exceeding the statutory maximum (or both);

(ii) in Scotland or Northern Ireland, to imprisonment for a term not exceeding six months, or to a fine not exceeding the statutory maximum (or both).

573 Disapplication of pre-emption rights: sale of treasury shares

(1) This section applies in relation to a sale of shares that is an allotment of equity securities by virtue of section 560(3) (sale of shares held by company as treasury shares).

(2) The directors of a company may be given power by the articles, or by a special resolution of the company, to allot equity securities as if section 561 (existing shareholders' right of pre-emption)—
  (a) did not apply to the allotment, or
  (b) applied to the allotment with such modifications as the directors may determine.

(3) The provisions of section 570(2) and (4) apply in that case as they apply to a case within subsection (1) of that section.

(4) The company may by special resolution resolve that section 561—
  (a) shall not apply to a specified allotment of securities, or
  (b) shall apply to the allotment with such modifications as may be specified in the resolution.

(5) The provisions of section 571(2) and (4) to (7) apply in that case as they apply to a case within subsection (1) of that section.

Supplementary

574 References to holder of shares in relation to offer

(1) In this Chapter, in relation to an offer to allot securities required by—
  (a) section 561 (existing shareholders' right of pre-emption), or
  (b) any provision to which section 568 applies (articles conferring corresponding right),

a reference (however expressed) to the holder of shares of any description is to whoever was the holder of shares of that description at the close of business on a date to be specified in the offer.

(2) The specified date must fall within the period of 28 days immediately before the date of the offer.

575 Saving for other restrictions on offer or allotment

(1) The provisions of this Chapter are without prejudice to any other enactment by virtue of which a company is prohibited (whether generally or in specified circumstances) from offering or allotting equity securities to any person.

(2) Where a company cannot by virtue of such an enactment offer or allot equity securities to a holder of ordinary shares of the company, those shares are disregarded for the purposes of section 561 (existing shareholders' right of pre-emption), so that—
  (a) the person is not treated as a person who holds ordinary shares, and
  (b) the shares are not treated as forming part of the ordinary share capital of the company.

576 Saving for certain older pre-emption requirements

(1) In the case of a public company the provisions of this Chapter do not apply to an allotment of equity securities that are subject to a pre-emption requirement in relation to which section 96(1) of the Companies Act 1985 or Article 106(1) of the Companies (Northern Ireland) Order 1986 applied immediately before the commencement of this Chapter.

(2) In the case of a private company a pre-emption requirement to which section 96(3) of the Companies Act 1985 or Article 106(3) of the Companies (Northern Ireland) Order 1986 applied immediately before the commencement of this Chapter shall have effect, so long as the company remains a private company, as if it were contained in the company's articles.

(3) A pre-emption requirement to which section 96(4) of the Companies Act 1985 or Article 106(4) of the Companies (Northern Ireland) Order 1986 applied immediately before the commencement of this section shall be treated for the purposes of this Chapter as if it were contained in the company's articles.

577 Provisions about pre-emption not applicable to shares taken on formation

The provisions of this Chapter have no application in relation to the taking of shares by the subscribers to the memorandum on the formation of the company.

CHAPTER 4
PUBLIC COMPANIES: ALLOTMENT WHERE ISSUE NOT FULLY SUBSCRIBED

578 Public companies: allotment where issue not fully subscribed

(1) No allotment shall be made of shares of a public company offered for subscription unless—
- (a) the issue is subscribed for in full, or
- (b) the offer is made on terms that the shares subscribed for may be allotted—
  - (i) in any event, or
  - (ii) if specified conditions are met (and those conditions are met).

(2) If shares are prohibited from being allotted by subsection (1) and 40 days have elapsed after the first making of the offer, all money received from applicants for shares must be repaid to them forthwith, without interest.

(3) If any of the money is not repaid within 48 days after the first making of the offer, the directors of the company are jointly and severally liable to repay it, with interest at the rate for the time being specified under section 17 of the Judgments Act 1838 from the expiration of the 48th day.
A director is not so liable if he proves that the default in the repayment of the money was not due to any misconduct or negligence on his part.

(4) This section applies in the case of shares offered as wholly or partly payable otherwise than in cash as it applies in the case of shares offered for subscription.

(5) In that case—
- (a) the references in subsection (1) to subscription shall be construed accordingly;
- (b) references in subsections (2) and (3) to the repayment of money received from applicants for shares include—
  - (i) the return of any other consideration so received (including, if the case so requires, the release of the applicant from any undertaking), or
  - (ii) if it is not reasonably practicable to return the consideration, the payment of money equal to its value at the time it was so received;
- (c) references to interest apply accordingly.

(6) Any condition requiring or binding an applicant for shares to waive compliance with any requirement of this section is void.

579 Public companies: effect of irregular allotment where issue not fully subscribed

(1) An allotment made by a public company to an applicant in contravention of section 578 (public companies: allotment where issue not fully subscribed) is voidable at the instance of the applicant within one month after the date of the allotment, and not later.

(2) It is so voidable even if the company is in the course of being wound up.

(3) A director of a public company who knowingly contravenes, or permits or authorises the contravention of, any provision of section 578 with respect to allotment is liable to compensate the company and the allottee respectively for any loss, damages, costs or expenses that the company or allottee may have sustained or incurred by the contravention.

(4) Proceedings to recover any such loss, damages, costs or expenses may not be brought more than two years after the date of the allotment.

CHAPTER 5
PAYMENT FOR SHARES

General rules

580 Shares not to be allotted at a discount

(1) A company's shares must not be allotted at a discount.

(2) If shares are allotted in contravention of this section, the allottee is liable to pay the company an amount equal to the amount of the discount, with interest at the appropriate rate.

581 Provision for different amounts to be paid on shares

A company, if so authorised by its articles, may—
- (a) make arrangements on the issue of shares for a difference between the shareholders in the amounts and times of payment of calls on their shares;
- (b) accept from any member the whole or part of the amount remaining unpaid on any shares held by him, although no part of that amount has been called up;

(c) pay a dividend in proportion to the amount paid up on each share where a larger amount is paid up on some shares than on others.

582 General rule as to means of payment

(1) Shares allotted by a company, and any premium on them, may be paid up in money or money's worth (including goodwill and know-how).

(2) This section does not prevent a company—

(a) from allotting bonus shares to its members, or

(b) from paying up, with sums available for the purpose, any amounts for the time being unpaid on any of its shares (whether on account of the nominal value of the shares or by way of premium).

(3) This section has effect subject to the following provisions of this Chapter (additional rules for public companies).

583 Meaning of payment in cash

(1) The following provisions have effect for the purposes of the Companies Acts.

(2) A share in a company is deemed paid up (as to its nominal value or any premium on it) in cash, or allotted for cash, if the consideration received for the allotment or payment up is a cash consideration.

(3) A "cash consideration" means—

(a) cash received by the company,

(b) a cheque received by the company in good faith that the directors have no reason for suspecting will not be paid,

(c) a release of a liability of the company for a liquidated sum,

(d) an undertaking to pay cash to the company at a future date, or

(e) payment by any other means giving rise to a present or future entitlement (of the company or a person acting on the company's behalf) to a payment, or credit equivalent to payment, in cash.

(4) The Secretary of State may by order provide that particular means of payment specified in the order are to be regarded as falling within subsection (3)(e).

(5) In relation to the allotment or payment up of shares in a company—

(a) the payment of cash to a person other than the company, or

(b) an undertaking to pay cash to a person other than the company, counts as consideration other than cash.

This does not apply for the purposes of Chapter 3 (allotment of equity securities: existing shareholders' right of pre-emption).

(6) For the purpose of determining whether a share is or is to be allotted for cash, or paid up in cash, "cash" includes foreign currency.

(7) An order under this section is subject to negative resolution procedure.

Additional rules for public companies

584 Public companies: shares taken by subscribers of memorandum

Shares taken by a subscriber to the memorandum of a public company in pursuance of an undertaking of his in the memorandum, and any premium on the shares, must be paid up in cash.

585 Public companies: must not accept undertaking to do work or perform services

(1) A public company must not accept at any time, in payment up of its shares or any premium on them, an undertaking given by any person that he or another should do work or perform services for the company or any other person.

(2) If a public company accepts such an undertaking in payment up of its shares or any premium on them, the holder of the shares when they or the premium are treated as paid up (in whole or in part) by the undertaking is liable—

(a) to pay the company in respect of those shares an amount equal to their nominal value, together with the whole of any premium or, if the case so requires, such proportion of that amount as is treated as paid up by the undertaking; and

(b) to pay interest at the appropriate rate on the amount payable under paragraph (a).

(3) The reference in subsection (2) to the holder of shares includes a person who has an unconditional right—
(a) to be included in the company's register of members in respect of those shares, or
(b) to have an instrument of transfer of them executed in his favour.

586 Public companies: shares must be at least one-quarter paid up

(1) A public company must not allot a share except as paid up at least as to one-quarter of its nominal value and the whole of any premium on it.
(2) This does not apply to shares allotted in pursuance of an employees' share scheme.
(3) If a company allots a share in contravention of this section—
(a) the share is to be treated as if one-quarter of its nominal value, together with the whole of any premium on it, had been received, and
(b) the allottee is liable to pay the company the minimum amount which should have been received in respect of the share under subsection (1) (less the value of any consideration actually applied in payment up, to any extent, of the share and any premium on it), with interest at the appropriate rate.
(4) Subsection (3) does not apply to the allotment of bonus shares, unless the allottee knew or ought to have known the shares were allotted in contravention of this section.

587 Public companies: payment by long-term undertaking

(1) A public company must not allot shares as fully or partly paid up (as to their nominal value or any premium on them) otherwise than in cash if the consideration for the allotment is or includes an undertaking which is to be, or may be, performed more than five years after the date of the allotment.
(2) If a company allots shares in contravention of subsection (1), the allottee is liable to pay the company an amount equal to the aggregate of their nominal value and the whole of any premium (or, if the case so requires, so much of that aggregate as is treated as paid up by the undertaking), with interest at the appropriate rate.
(3) Where a contract for the allotment of shares does not contravene subsection (1), any variation of the contract that has the effect that the contract would have contravened the subsection, if the terms of the contract as varied had been its original terms, is void.
This applies also to the variation by a public company of the terms of a contract entered into before the company was re-registered as a public company.
(4) Where—
(a) a public company allots shares for a consideration which consists of or includes (in accordance with subsection (1)) an undertaking that is to be performed within five years of the allotment, and
(b) the undertaking is not performed within the period allowed by the contract for the allotment of the shares,

the allottee is liable to pay the company, at the end of the period so allowed, an amount equal to the aggregate of the nominal value of the shares and the whole of any premium (or, if the case so requires, so much of that aggregate as is treated as paid up by the undertaking), with interest at the appropriate rate.
(5) References in this section to a contract for the allotment of shares include an ancillary contract relating to payment in respect of them.

Supplementary provisions

588 Liability of subsequent holders of shares

(1) If a person becomes a holder of shares in respect of which—
(a) there has been a contravention of any provision of this Chapter, and
(b) by virtue of that contravention another is liable to pay any amount under the provision contravened,

that person is also liable to pay that amount (jointly and severally with any other person so liable), subject as follows.
(2) A person otherwise liable under subsection (1) is exempted from that liability if either—
(a) he is a purchaser for value and, at the time of the purchase, he did not have actual notice of the contravention concerned, or
(b) he derived title to the shares (directly or indirectly) from a person who became a holder of them after the contravention and was not liable under subsection (1).
(3) References in this section to a holder, in relation to shares in a company, include any person who has an unconditional right—

(a) to be included in the company's register of members in respect of those shares, or
(b) to have an instrument of transfer of the shares executed in his favour.

(4) This section applies in relation to a failure to carry out a term of a contract as mentioned in section 587(4) (public companies: payment by long-term undertaking) as it applies in relation to a contravention of a provision of this Chapter.

589 Power of court to grant relief

(1) This section applies in relation to liability under—

section 585(2) (liability of allottee in case of breach by public company of prohibition on accepting undertaking to do work or perform services),

section 587(2) or (4) (liability of allottee in case of breach by public company of prohibition on payment by long-term undertaking), or

section 588 (liability of subsequent holders of shares),

as it applies in relation to a contravention of those sections.

(2) A person who—
(a) is subject to any such liability to a company in relation to payment in respect of shares in the company, or
(b) is subject to any such liability to a company by virtue of an undertaking given to it in, or in connection with, payment for shares in the company,

may apply to the court to be exempted in whole or in part from the liability.

(3) In the case of a liability within subsection (2)(a), the court may exempt the applicant from the liability only if and to the extent that it appears to the court just and equitable to do so having regard to—
(a) whether the applicant has paid, or is liable to pay, any amount in respect of—
(i) any other liability arising in relation to those shares under any provision of this Chapter or Chapter 6, or
(ii) any liability arising by virtue of any undertaking given in or in connection with payment for those shares;
(b) whether any person other than the applicant has paid or is likely to pay, whether in pursuance of any order of the court or otherwise, any such amount;
(c) whether the applicant or any other person—
(i) has performed in whole or in part, or is likely so to perform any such undertaking, or
(ii) has done or is likely to do any other thing in payment or part payment for the shares.

(4) In the case of a liability within subsection (2)(b), the court may exempt the applicant from the liability only if and to the extent that it appears to the court just and equitable to do so having regard to—
(a) whether the applicant has paid or is liable to pay any amount in respect of liability arising in relation to the shares under any provision of this Chapter or Chapter 6;
(b) whether any person other than the applicant has paid or is likely to pay, whether in pursuance of any order of the court or otherwise, any such amount.

(5) In determining whether it should exempt the applicant in whole or in part from any liability, the court must have regard to the following overriding principles—
(a) a company that has allotted shares should receive money or money's worth at least equal in value to the aggregate of the nominal value of those shares and the whole of any premium or, if the case so requires, so much of that aggregate as is treated as paid up;
(b) subject to that, where a company would, if the court did not grant the exemption, have more than one remedy against a particular person, it should be for the company to decide which remedy it should remain entitled to pursue.

(6) If a person brings proceedings against another ("the contributor") for a contribution in respect of liability to a company arising under any provision of this Chapter or Chapter 6 and it appears to the court that the contributor is liable to make such a contribution, the court may, if and to the extent that it appears to it just and equitable to do so having regard to the respective culpability (in respect of the liability to the company) of the contributor and the person bringing the proceedings—
(a) exempt the contributor in whole or in part from his liability to make such a contribution, or
(b) order the contributor to make a larger contribution than, but for this subsection, he would be liable to make.

590 Penalty for contravention of this Chapter

(1) If a company contravenes any of the provisions of this Chapter, an offence is committed by—
  (a) the company, and
  (b) every officer of the company who is in default.

(2) A person guilty of an offence under this section is liable—
  (a) on conviction on indictment, to a fine;
  (b) on summary conviction, to a fine not exceeding the statutory maximum.

591 Enforceability of undertakings to do work etc.

(1) An undertaking given by any person, in or in connection with payment for shares in a company, to do work or perform services or to do any other thing, if it is enforceable by the company apart from this Chapter, is so enforceable notwithstanding that there has been a contravention in relation to it of a provision of this Chapter or Chapter 6.

(2) This is without prejudice to section 589 (power of court to grant relief etc in respect of liabilities).

592 The appropriate rate of interest

(1) For the purposes of this Chapter the "appropriate rate" of interest is 5% per annum or such other rate as may be specified by order made by the Secretary of State.

(2) An order under this section is subject to negative resolution procedure.

CHAPTER 6
PUBLIC COMPANIES: INDEPENDENT VALUATION OF NON-CASH CONSIDERATION

Non-cash consideration for shares

593 Public company: valuation of non-cash consideration for shares

(1) A public company must not allot shares as fully or partly paid up (as to their nominal value or any premium on them) otherwise than in cash unless—
  (a) the consideration for the allotment has been independently valued in accordance with the provisions of this Chapter,
  (b) the valuer's report has been made to the company during the six months immediately preceding the allotment of the shares, and
  (c) a copy of the report has been sent to the proposed allottee.

(2) For this purpose the application of an amount standing to the credit of—
  (a) any of a company's reserve accounts, or
  (b) its profit and loss account,

in paying up (to any extent) shares allotted to members of the company, or premiums on shares so allotted, does not count as consideration for the allotment.

Accordingly, subsection (1) does not apply in that case.

(3) If a company allots shares in contravention of subsection (1) and either—
  (a) the allottee has not received the valuer's report required to be sent to him, or
  (b) there has been some other contravention of the requirements of this section or section 596 that the allottee knew or ought to have known amounted to a contravention,

the allottee is liable to pay the company an amount equal to the aggregate of the nominal value of the shares and the whole of any premium (or, if the case so requires, so much of that aggregate as is treated as paid up by the consideration), with interest at the appropriate rate.

(4) This section has effect subject to—

section 594 (exception to valuation requirement: arrangement with another company), and

section 595 (exception to valuation requirement: merger or division).

594 Exception to valuation requirement: arrangement with another company

(1) Section 593 (valuation of non-cash consideration) does not apply to the allotment of shares by a company ("company A") in connection with an arrangement to which this section applies.

(2) This section applies to an arrangement for the allotment of shares in company A on terms that the whole or part of the consideration for the shares allotted is to be provided by—

(a) the transfer to that company, or
(b) the cancellation,

of all or some of the shares, or of all or some of the shares of a particular class, in another company ("company B").

(3) It is immaterial whether the arrangement provides for the issue to company A of shares, or shares of any particular class, in company B.

(4) This section applies to an arrangement only if under the arrangement it is open to all the holders of the shares in company B (or, where the arrangement applies only to shares of a particular class, to all the holders of shares of that class) to take part in the arrangement.

(5) In determining whether that is the case, the following shall be disregarded—
(a) shares held by or by a nominee of company A;
(b) shares held by or by a nominee of a company which is—
(i) the holding company, or a subsidiary, of company A, or
(ii) a subsidiary of such a holding company;
(c) shares held as treasury shares by company B.

(6) In this section—
(a) "arrangement" means any agreement, scheme or arrangement (including an arrangement sanctioned in accordance with—
(i) Part 26 (arrangements and reconstructions), or
(ii) section 110 of the Insolvency Act 1986 or Article 96 of the Insolvency (Northern Ireland) Order 1989 (liquidator in winding up accepting shares as consideration for sale of company property)), and
(b) "company", except in reference to company A, includes any body corporate.

595 Exception to valuation requirement: merger or division

(1) Section 593 (valuation of non-cash consideration) does not apply to the allotment of shares by a company as part of a scheme to which Part 27 (mergers and divisions of public companies) applies if—
(a) in the case of a scheme involving a merger, an expert's report is drawn up as required by section 909, or
(b) in the case of a scheme involving a division, an expert's report is drawn up as required by section 924.

(2)–(3) …

596 Non-cash consideration for shares: requirements as to valuation and report

(1) The provisions of sections 1150 to 1153 (general provisions as to independent valuation and report) apply to the valuation and report required by section 593 (public company: valuation of non-cash consideration for shares).

(2) The valuer's report must state—
(a) the nominal value of the shares to be wholly or partly paid for by the consideration in question;
(b) the amount of any premium payable on the shares;
(c) the description of the consideration and, as respects so much of the consideration as he himself has valued, a description of that part of the consideration, the method used to value it and the date of the valuation;
(d) the extent to which the nominal value of the shares and any premium are to be treated as paid up—
(i) by the consideration;
(ii) in cash.

(3) The valuer's report must contain or be accompanied by a note by him—
(a) in the case of a valuation made by a person other than himself, that it appeared to himself reasonable to arrange for it to be so made or to accept a valuation so made,
(b) whoever made the valuation, that the method of valuation was reasonable in all the circumstances,
(c) that it appears to the valuer that there has been no material change in the value of the consideration in question since the valuation, and
(d) that, on the basis of the valuation, the value of the consideration, together with any cash by which the nominal value of the shares or any premium payable on them is to be paid up, is not less than so much of the aggregate of the nominal value and

the whole of any such premium as is treated as paid up by the consideration and any such cash.

(4) Where the consideration to be valued is accepted partly in payment up of the nominal value of the shares and any premium and partly for some other consideration given by the company, section 593 and the preceding provisions of this section apply as if references to the consideration accepted by the company included the proportion of that consideration that is properly attributable to the payment up of that value and any premium.

(5) In such a case—

(a) the valuer must carry out, or arrange for, such other valuations as will enable him to determine that proportion, and

(b) his report must state what valuations have been made under this subsection and also the reason for, and method and date of, any such valuation and any other matters which may be relevant to that determination.

597 Copy of report to be delivered to registrar

(1) A company to which a report is made under section 593 as to the value of any consideration for which, or partly for which, it proposes to allot shares must deliver a copy of the report to the registrar for registration.

(2) The copy must be delivered at the same time that the company files the return of the allotment of those shares under section 555 (return of allotment by limited company).

(3) If default is made in complying with subsection (1) or (2), an offence is committed by every officer of the company who is in default.

Version applying in Scotland

(4) A person guilty of an offence under this section is liable—

(a) on conviction on indictment, to a fine;

(b) on summary conviction, to a fine not exceeding the statutory maximum and, for continued contravention, a daily default fine not exceeding one-tenth of the statutory maximum.

Version applying in England and Wales

(4) A person guilty of an offence under this section is liable on summary conviction to a fine not exceeding level 5 on the standard scale and, for continued contravention, a daily default fine not exceeding one-tenth of the greater of £5,000 or level 4 on the standard scale.

(5) In the case of default in delivering to the registrar any document as required by this section, any person liable for the default may apply to the court for relief.

(6) The court, if satisfied—

(a) that the omission to deliver the document was accidental or due to inadvertence, or

(b) that it is just and equitable to grant relief,

may make an order extending the time for delivery of the document for such period as the court thinks proper.

Transfer of non-cash asset in initial period

598 Public company: agreement for transfer of non-cash asset in initial period

(1) A public company formed as such must not enter into an agreement—

(a) with a person who is a subscriber to the company's memorandum,

(b) for the transfer by him to the company, or another, before the end of the company's initial period of one or more non-cash assets, and

(c) under which the consideration for the transfer to be given by the company is at the time of the agreement equal in value to one-tenth or more of the company's issued share capital,

unless the conditions referred to below have been complied with.

(2) The company's "initial period" means the period of two years beginning with the date of the company being issued with a certificate under section 761 (trading certificate).

(3) The conditions are those specified in—

section 599 (requirement of independent valuation), and

section 601 (requirement of approval by members).

(4) This section does not apply where—

(a) it is part of the company's ordinary business to acquire, or arrange for other persons to acquire, assets of a particular description, and

(b) the agreement is entered into by the company in the ordinary course of that business.

(5) This section does not apply to an agreement entered into by the company under the supervision of the court or of an officer authorised by the court for the purpose.

599 Agreement for transfer of non-cash asset: requirement of independent valuation

(1) The following conditions must have been complied with—

(a) the consideration to be received by the company, and any consideration other than cash to be given by the company, must have been independently valued in accordance with the provisions of this Chapter,

(b) the valuer's report must have been made to the company during the six months immediately preceding the date of the agreement, and

(c) a copy of the report must have been sent to the other party to the proposed agreement not later than the date on which copies have to be circulated to members under section 601(3).

(2) The reference in subsection (1)(a) to the consideration to be received by the company is to the asset to be transferred to it or, as the case may be, to the advantage to the company of the asset's transfer to another person.

(3) The reference in subsection (1)(c) to the other party to the proposed agreement is to the person referred to in section 598(1)(a).

If he has received a copy of the report under section 601 in his capacity as a member of the company, it is not necessary to send another copy under this section.

(4) This section does not affect any requirement to value any consideration for purposes of section 593 (valuation of non-cash consideration for shares).

600 Agreement for transfer of non-cash asset: requirements as to valuation and report

(1) The provisions of sections 1150 to 1153 (general provisions as to independent valuation and report) apply to the valuation and report required by section 599 (public company: transfer of non-cash asset).

(2) The valuer's report must state—

(a) the consideration to be received by the company, describing the asset in question (specifying the amount to be received in cash) and the consideration to be given by the company (specifying the amount to be given in cash), and

(b) the method and date of valuation.

(3) The valuer's report must contain or be accompanied by a note by him—

(a) in the case of a valuation made by a person other than himself, that it appeared to himself reasonable to arrange for it to be so made or to accept a valuation so made,

(b) whoever made the valuation, that the method of valuation was reasonable in all the circumstances,

(c) that it appears to the valuer that there has been no material change in the value of the consideration in question since the valuation, and

(d) that, on the basis of the valuation, the value of the consideration to be received by the company is not less than the value of the consideration to be given by it.

(4) Any reference in section 599 or this section to consideration given for the transfer of an asset includes consideration given partly for its transfer.

(5) In such a case—

(a) the value of any consideration partly so given is to be taken as the proportion of the consideration properly attributable to its transfer,

(b) the valuer must carry out or arrange for such valuations of anything else as will enable him to determine that proportion, and

(c) his report must state what valuations have been made for that purpose and also the reason for and method and date of any such valuation and any other matters which may be relevant to that determination.

601 Agreement for transfer of non-cash asset: requirement of approval by members

(1) The following conditions must have been complied with—

(a) the terms of the agreement must have been approved by an ordinary resolution of the company,

(b) copies of the valuer's report must have been circulated to the members entitled to notice of the meeting at which the resolution is proposed, not later than the date on which notice of the meeting is given, and

(c) a copy of the proposed resolution must have been sent to the other party to the proposed agreement.

(2) The reference in subsection (1)(c) to the other party to the proposed agreement is to the person referred to in section 598(1)(a).

602 Copy of resolution to be delivered to registrar

(1) A company that has passed a resolution under section 601 with respect to the transfer of an asset must, within 15 days of doing so, deliver to the registrar a copy of the resolution together with the valuer's report required by that section.

(2) If a company fails to comply with subsection (1), an offence is committed by—

(a) the company, and

(b) every officer of the company who is in default.

(3) A person guilty of an offence under this section is liable on summary conviction to a fine not exceeding level 3 on the standard scale and, for continued contravention, to a daily default fine not exceeding one-tenth of level 3 on the standard scale.

603 Adaptation of provisions in relation to company re-registering as public

The provisions of sections 598 to 602 (public companies: transfer of non-cash assets) apply with the following adaptations in relation to a company re-registered as a public company—

(a) the reference in section 598(1)(a) to a person who is a subscriber to the company's memorandum shall be read as a reference to a person who is a member of the company on the date of re-registration;

(b) the reference in section 598(2) to the date of the company being issued with a certificate under section 761 (trading certificate) shall be read as a reference to the date of re-registration.

604 Agreement for transfer of non-cash asset: effect of contravention

(1) This section applies where a public company enters into an agreement in contravention of section 598 and either—

(a) the other party to the agreement has not received the valuer's report required to be sent to him, or

(b) there has been some other contravention of the requirements of this Chapter that the other party to the agreement knew or ought to have known amounted to a contravention.

(2) In those circumstances—

(a) the company is entitled to recover from that person any consideration given by it under the agreement, or an amount equal to the value of the consideration at the time of the agreement, and

(b) the agreement, so far as not carried out, is void.

(3) If the agreement is or includes an agreement for the allotment of shares in the company, then—

(a) whether or not the agreement also contravenes section 593 (valuation of non-cash consideration for shares), this section does not apply to it in so far as it is for the allotment of shares, and

(b) the allottee is liable to pay the company an amount equal to the aggregate of the nominal value of the shares and the whole of any premium (or, if the case so requires, so much of that aggregate as is treated as paid up by the consideration), with interest at the appropriate rate.

Supplementary provisions

605 Liability of subsequent holders of shares

(1) If a person becomes a holder of shares in respect of which—

(a) there has been a contravention of section 593 (public company: valuation of non-cash consideration for shares), and

(b) by virtue of that contravention another is liable to pay any amount under the provision contravened,

that person is also liable to pay that amount (jointly and severally with any other person so liable), unless he is exempted from liability under subsection (3) below.

(2) If a company enters into an agreement in contravention of section 598 (public company: agreement for transfer of non-cash asset in initial period) and—
(a) the agreement is or includes an agreement for the allotment of shares in the company,
(b) a person becomes a holder of shares allotted under the agreement, and
(c) by virtue of the agreement and allotment under it another person is liable to pay an amount under section 604,
the person who becomes the holder of the shares is also liable to pay that amount (jointly and severally with any other person so liable), unless he is exempted from liability under subsection (3) below.
This applies whether or not the agreement also contravenes section 593.
(3) A person otherwise liable under subsection (1) or (2) is exempted from that liability if either—
(a) he is a purchaser for value and, at the time of the purchase, he did not have actual notice of the contravention concerned, or
(b) he derived title to the shares (directly or indirectly) from a person who became a holder of them after the contravention and was not liable under subsection (1) or (2).
(4) References in this section to a holder, in relation to shares in a company, include any person who has an unconditional right—
(a) to be included in the company's register of members in respect of those shares, or
(b) to have an instrument of transfer of the shares executed in his favour.

606 Power of court to grant relief

(1) A person who—
(a) is liable to a company under any provision of this Chapter in relation to payment in respect of any shares in the company, or
(b) is liable to a company by virtue of an undertaking given to it in, or in connection with, payment for any shares in the company,
may apply to the court to be exempted in whole or in part from the liability.
(2) In the case of a liability within subsection (1)(a), the court may exempt the applicant from the liability only if and to the extent that it appears to the court just and equitable to do so having regard to—
(a) whether the applicant has paid, or is liable to pay, any amount in respect of—
(i) any other liability arising in relation to those shares under any provision of this Chapter or Chapter 5, or
(ii) any liability arising by virtue of any undertaking given in or in connection with payment for those shares;
(b) whether any person other than the applicant has paid or is likely to pay, whether in pursuance of any order of the court or otherwise, any such amount;
(c) whether the applicant or any other person—
(i) has performed in whole or in part, or is likely so to perform any such undertaking, or
(ii) has done or is likely to do any other thing in payment or part payment for the shares.
(3) In the case of a liability within subsection (1)(b), the court may exempt the applicant from the liability only if and to the extent that it appears to the court just and equitable to do so having regard to—
(a) whether the applicant has paid or is liable to pay any amount in respect of liability arising in relation to the shares under any provision of this Chapter or Chapter 5;
(b) whether any person other than the applicant has paid or is likely to pay, whether in pursuance of any order of the court or otherwise, any such amount.
(4) In determining whether it should exempt the applicant in whole or in part from any liability, the court must have regard to the following overriding principles—
(a) that a company that has allotted shares should receive money or money's worth at least equal in value to the aggregate of the nominal value of those shares and the whole of any premium or, if the case so requires, so much of that aggregate as is treated as paid up;
(b) subject to this, that where such a company would, if the court did not grant the exemption, have more than one remedy against a particular person, it should be for the company to decide which remedy it should remain entitled to pursue.

(5) If a person brings proceedings against another ("the contributor") for a contribution in respect of liability to a company arising under any provision of this Chapter or Chapter 5 and it appears to the court that the contributor is liable to make such a contribution, the court may, if and to the extent that it appears to it, just and equitable to do so having regard to the respective culpability (in respect of the liability to the company) of the contributor and the person bringing the proceedings—
(a) exempt the contributor in whole or in part from his liability to make such a contribution, or
(b) order the contributor to make a larger contribution than, but for this subsection, he would be liable to make.

(6) Where a person is liable to a company under section 604(2) (agreement for transfer of non-cash asset: effect of contravention), the court may, on application, exempt him in whole or in part from that liability if and to the extent that it appears to the court to be just and equitable to do so having regard to any benefit accruing to the company by virtue of anything done by him towards the carrying out of the agreement mentioned in that subsection.

607 Penalty for contravention of this Chapter

(1) This section applies where a company contravenes—
section 593 (public company allotting shares for non-cash consideration), or
section 598 (public company entering into agreement for transfer of non-cash asset).

(2) An offence is committed by—
(a) the company, and
(b) every officer of the company who is in default.

(3) A person guilty of an offence under this section is liable—
(a) on conviction on indictment, to a fine;
(b) on summary conviction, to a fine not exceeding the statutory maximum.

608 Enforceability of undertakings to do work etc.

(1) An undertaking given by any person, in or in connection with payment for shares in a company, to do work or perform services or to do any other thing, if it is enforceable by the company apart from this Chapter, is so enforceable notwithstanding that there has been a contravention in relation to it of a provision of this Chapter or Chapter 5.

(2) This is without prejudice to section 606 (power of court to grant relief etc in respect of liabilities).

609 The appropriate rate of interest

(1) For the purposes of this Chapter the "appropriate rate" of interest is 5% per annum or such other rate as may be specified by order made by the Secretary of State.

(2) An order under this section is subject to negative resolution procedure.

CHAPTER 7
SHARE PREMIUMS

The share premium account

610 Application of share premiums

(1) If a company issues shares at a premium, whether for cash or otherwise, a sum equal to the aggregate amount or value of the premiums on those shares must be transferred to an account called "the share premium account".

(2) Where, on issuing shares, a company has transferred a sum to the share premium account, it may use that sum to write off—
(a) the expenses of the issue of those shares;
(b) any commission paid on the issue of those shares.

(3) The company may use the share premium account to pay up new shares to be allotted to members as fully paid bonus shares.

(4) Subject to subsections (2) and (3), the provisions of the Companies Acts relating to the reduction of a company's share capital apply as if the share premium account were part of its paid up share capital.

(5) This section has effect subject to—

section 611 (group reconstruction relief);
section 612 (merger relief);
section 614 (power to make further provisions by regulations).

(6) In this Chapter "the issuing company" means the company issuing shares as mentioned in subsection (1) above.

Relief from requirements as to share premiums

611 Group reconstruction relief

(1) This section applies where the issuing company—
   (a) is a wholly-owned subsidiary of another company ("the holding company"), and
   (b) allots shares—
      (i) to the holding company, or
      (ii) to another wholly-owned subsidiary of the holding company,

   in consideration for the transfer to the issuing company of non-cash assets of a company ("the transferor company") that is a member of the group of companies that comprises the holding company and all its wholly-owned subsidiaries.

(2) Where the shares in the issuing company allotted in consideration for the transfer are issued at a premium, the issuing company is not required by section 610 to transfer any amount in excess of the minimum premium value to the share premium account.

(3) The minimum premium value means the amount (if any) by which the base value of the consideration for the shares allotted exceeds the aggregate nominal value of the shares.

(4) The base value of the consideration for the shares allotted is the amount by which the base value of the assets transferred exceeds the base value of any liabilities of the transferor company assumed by the issuing company as part of the consideration for the assets transferred.

(5) For the purposes of this section—
   (a) the base value of assets transferred is taken as—
      (i) the cost of those assets to the transferor company, or
      (ii) if less, the amount at which those assets are stated in the transferor company's accounting records immediately before the transfer;
   (b) the base value of the liabilities assumed is taken as the amount at which they are stated in the transferor company's accounting records immediately before the transfer.

612 Merger relief

(1) This section applies where the issuing company has secured at least a 90% equity holding in another company in pursuance of an arrangement providing for the allotment of equity shares in the issuing company on terms that the consideration for the shares allotted is to be provided—
   (a) by the issue or transfer to the issuing company of equity shares in the other company, or
   (b) by the cancellation of any such shares not held by the issuing company.

(2) If the equity shares in the issuing company allotted in pursuance of the arrangement in consideration for the acquisition or cancellation of equity shares in the other company are issued at a premium, section 610 does not apply to the premiums on those shares.

(3) Where the arrangement also provides for the allotment of any shares in the issuing company on terms that the consideration for those shares is to be provided—
   (a) by the issue or transfer to the issuing company of non-equity shares in the other company, or
   (b) by the cancellation of any such shares in that company not held by the issuing company,

   relief under subsection (2) extends to any shares in the issuing company allotted on those terms in pursuance of the arrangement.

(4) This section does not apply in a case falling within section 611 (group reconstruction relief).

613 Merger relief: meaning of 90% equity holding

(1) The following provisions have effect to determine for the purposes of section 612 (merger relief) whether a company ("company A") has secured at least a 90% equity holding in

another company ("company B") in pursuance of such an arrangement as is mentioned in subsection (1) of that section.

(2) Company A has secured at least a 90% equity holding in company B if in consequence of an acquisition or cancellation of equity shares in company B (in pursuance of that arrangement) it holds equity shares in company B of an aggregate amount equal to 90% or more of the nominal value of that company's equity share capital.

(3) For this purpose—

(a) it is immaterial whether any of those shares were acquired in pursuance of the arrangement; and

(b) shares in company B held by the company as treasury shares are excluded in determining the nominal value of company B's share capital.

(4) Where the equity share capital of company B is divided into different classes of shares, company A is not regarded as having secured at least a 90% equity holding in company B unless the requirements of subsection (2) are met in relation to each of those classes of shares taken separately.

(5) For the purposes of this section shares held by—

(a) a company that is company A's holding company or subsidiary, or

(b) a subsidiary of company A's holding company, or

(c) its or their nominees,

are treated as held by company A.

614 Power to make further provision by regulations

(1) The Secretary of State may by regulations make such provision as he thinks appropriate—

(a) for relieving companies from the requirements of section 610 (application of share premiums) in relation to premiums other than cash premiums;

(b) for restricting or otherwise modifying any relief from those requirements provided by this Chapter.

(2) Regulations under this section are subject to affirmative resolution procedure.

615 Relief may be reflected in company's balance sheet

An amount corresponding to the amount representing the premiums, or part of the premiums, on shares issued by a company that by virtue of any relief under this Chapter is not included in the company's share premium account may also be disregarded in determining the amount at which any shares or other consideration provided for the shares issued is to be included in the company's balance sheet.

Supplementary provisions

616 Interpretation of this Chapter

(1) In this Chapter—

"arrangement" means any agreement, scheme or arrangement (including an arrangement sanctioned in accordance with—

(a) Part 26 (arrangements and reconstructions), or

(b) section 110 of the Insolvency Act 1986 or Article 96 of the Insolvency (Northern Ireland) Order 1989 (liquidator in winding up accepting shares as consideration for sale of company property));

"company", except in reference to the issuing company, includes any body corporate;

"equity shares" means shares comprised in a company's equity share capital, and "non-equity shares" means shares (of any class) that are not so comprised;

"the issuing company" has the meaning given by section 610(6).

(2) References in this Chapter (however expressed) to—

(a) the acquisition by a company of shares in another company, and

(b) the issue or allotment of shares to, or the transfer of shares to or by, a company,

include (respectively) the acquisition of shares by, and the issue or allotment or transfer of shares to or by, a nominee of that company.

The reference in section 611 to the transferor company shall be read accordingly.

(3) References in this Chapter to the transfer of shares in a company include the transfer of a right to be included in the company's register of members in respect of those shares.

CHAPTER 8
ALTERATION OF SHARE CAPITAL

How share capital may be altered

617 Alteration of share capital of limited company

(1) A limited company having a share capital may not alter its share capital except in the following ways.

(2) The company may—

(a) increase its share capital by allotting new shares in accordance with this Part, or

(b) reduce its share capital in accordance with Chapter 10.

(3) The company may—

(a) sub-divide or consolidate all or any of its share capital in accordance with section 618, or

(b) reconvert stock into shares in accordance with section 620.

(4) The company may redenominate all or any of its shares in accordance with section 622, and may reduce its share capital in accordance with section 626 in connection with such a redenomination.

(5) Nothing in this section affects—

(a) the power of a company to purchase its own shares, or to redeem shares, in accordance with Part 18;

(b) the power of a company to purchase its own shares in pursuance of an order of the court under—

(i) section 98 (application to court to cancel resolution for re-registration as a private company),

(ii) section 721(6) (powers of court on objection to redemption or purchase of shares out of capital),

(iii) section 759 (remedial order in case of breach of prohibition of public offers by private company), or

(iv) Part 30 (protection of members against unfair prejudice);

(c) the forfeiture of shares, or the acceptance of shares surrendered in lieu, in pursuance of the company's articles, for failure to pay any sum payable in respect of the shares;

(d) the cancellation of shares under section 662 (duty to cancel shares held by or for a public company);

(e) the power of a company—

(i) to enter into a compromise or arrangement in accordance with Part 26 (arrangements and reconstructions), or

(ii) to do anything required to comply with an order of the court on an application under that Part;

(f) the cancellation of a share warrant issued by the company and of the shares specified in it by a cancellation order or suspended cancellation order made under paragraph 6 of Schedule 4 to the Small Business, Enterprise and Employment Act 2015 (cancellation where share warrants not surrendered in accordance with that Schedule);

(g) the cancellation of a share warrant issued by the company and of the shares specified in it pursuant to section 1028A(2) or 1032A(2) (cancellation of share warrants on restoration of a company).

Subdivision or consolidation of shares

618 Sub-division or consolidation of shares

(1) A limited company having a share capital may—

(a) sub-divide its shares, or any of them, into shares of a smaller nominal amount than its existing shares, or

(b) consolidate and divide all or any of its share capital into shares of a larger nominal amount than its existing shares.

(2) In any sub-division, consolidation or division of shares under this section, the proportion between the amount paid and the amount (if any) unpaid on each resulting share must be the same as it was in the case of the share from which that share is derived.

(3) A company may exercise a power conferred by this section only if its members have passed a resolution authorising it to do so.

(4) A resolution under subsection (3) may authorise a company—
(a) to exercise more than one of the powers conferred by this section;
(b) to exercise a power on more than one occasion;
(c) to exercise a power at a specified time or in specified circumstances.
(5) The company's articles may exclude or restrict the exercise of any power conferred by this section.

619 Notice to registrar of sub-division or consolidation

(1) If a company exercises the power conferred by section 618 (sub-division or consolidation of shares) it must within one month after doing so give notice to the registrar, specifying the shares affected.
(2) The notice must be accompanied by a statement of capital.
(3) The statement of capital must state with respect to the company's share capital immediately following the exercise of the power—
(a) the total number of shares of the company,
(b) the aggregate nominal value of those shares,
(c) for each class of shares—
(i) prescribed particulars of the rights attached to the shares,
(ii) the total number of shares of that class, and
(iii) the aggregate nominal value of shares of that class, and
(d) the amount paid up and the amount (if any) unpaid on each share (whether on account of the nominal value of the share or by way of premium).
(4) If default is made in complying with this section, an offence is committed by—
(a) the company, and
(b) every officer of the company who is in default.
(5) A person guilty of an offence under this section is liable on summary conviction to a fine not exceeding level 3 on the standard scale and, for continued contravention, a daily default fine not exceeding one-tenth of level 3 on the standard scale.

Reconversion of stock into shares

620 Reconversion of stock into shares

(1) A limited company that has converted paid-up shares into stock (before the repeal by this Act of the power to do so) may reconvert that stock into paid-up shares of any nominal value.
(2) A company may exercise the power conferred by this section only if its members have passed an ordinary resolution authorising it to do so.
(3) A resolution under subsection (2) may authorise a company to exercise the power conferred by this section—
(a) on more than one occasion;
(b) at a specified time or in specified circumstances.

621 Notice to registrar of reconversion of stock into shares

(1) If a company exercises a power conferred by section 620 (reconversion of stock into shares) it must within one month after doing so give notice to the registrar, specifying the stock affected.
(2) The notice must be accompanied by a statement of capital.
(3) The statement of capital must state with respect to the company's share capital immediately following the exercise of the power—
(a) the total number of shares of the company,
(b) the aggregate nominal value of those shares,
(c) for each class of shares—
(i) prescribed particulars of the rights attached to the shares,
(ii) the total number of shares of that class, and
(iii) the aggregate nominal value of shares of that class, and
(d) the amount paid up and the amount (if any) unpaid on each share (whether on account of the nominal value of the share or by way of premium).
(4) If default is made in complying with this section, an offence is committed by—
(a) the company, and
(b) every officer of the company who is in default.

(5) A person guilty of an offence under this section is liable on summary conviction to a fine not exceeding level 3 on the standard scale and, for continued contravention, a daily default fine not exceeding one-tenth of level 3 on the standard scale.

Redenomination of share capital

622 Redenomination of share capital

(1) A limited company having a share capital may by resolution redenominate its share capital or any class of its share capital.
"Redenominate" means convert shares from having a fixed nominal value in one currency to having a fixed nominal value in another currency.

(2) The conversion must be made at an appropriate spot rate of exchange specified in the resolution.

(3) The rate must be either—
(a) a rate prevailing on a day specified in the resolution, or
(b) a rate determined by taking the average of rates prevailing on each consecutive day of a period specified in the resolution.
The day or period specified for the purposes of paragraph (a) or (b) must be within the period of 28 days ending on the day before the resolution is passed.

(4) A resolution under this section may specify conditions which must be met before the redenomination takes effect.

(5) Redenomination in accordance with a resolution under this section takes effect—
(a) on the day on which the resolution is passed, or
(b) on such later day as may be determined in accordance with the resolution.

(6) A resolution under this section lapses if the redenomination for which it provides has not taken effect at the end of the period of 28 days beginning on the date on which it is passed.

(7) A company's articles may prohibit or restrict the exercise of the power conferred by this section.

(8) Chapter 3 of Part 3 (resolutions affecting a company's constitution) applies to a resolution under this section.

623 Calculation of new nominal values

For each class of share the new nominal value of each share is calculated as follows:
Step One
Take the aggregate of the old nominal values of all the shares of that class.
Step Two
Translate that amount into the new currency at the rate of exchange specified in the resolution.
Step Three
Divide that amount by the number of shares in the class.

624 Effect of redenomination

(1) The redenomination of shares does not affect any rights or obligations of members under the company's constitution, or any restrictions affecting members under the company's constitution.
In particular, it does not affect entitlement to dividends (including entitlement to dividends in a particular currency), voting rights or any liability in respect of amounts unpaid on shares.

(2) For this purpose the company's constitution includes the terms on which any shares of the company are allotted or held.

(3) Subject to subsection (1), references to the old nominal value of the shares in any agreement or statement, or in any deed, instrument or document, shall (unless the context otherwise requires) be read after the resolution takes effect as references to the new nominal value of the shares.

625 Notice to registrar of redenomination

(1) If a limited company having a share capital redenominates any of its share capital, it must within one month after doing so give notice to the registrar, specifying the shares redenominated.

(2) The notice must—
(a) state the date on which the resolution was passed, and
(b) be accompanied by a statement of capital.

(3) The statement of capital must state with respect to the company's share capital as redenominated by the resolution—
(a) the total number of shares of the company,
(b) the aggregate nominal value of those shares,
(c) for each class of shares—
(i) prescribed particulars of the rights attached to the shares,
(ii) the total number of shares of that class, and
(iii) the aggregate nominal value of shares of that class, and
(d) the amount paid up and the amount (if any) unpaid on each share (whether on account of the nominal value of the share or by way of premium).
(4) If default is made in complying with this section, an offence is committed by—
(a) the company, and
(b) every officer of the company who is in default.
(5) A person guilty of an offence under this section is liable on summary conviction to a fine not exceeding level 3 on the standard scale and, for continued contravention, a daily default fine not exceeding one-tenth of level 3 on the standard scale.

626 Reduction of capital in connection with redenomination

(1) A limited company that passes a resolution redenominating some or all of its shares may, for the purpose of adjusting the nominal values of the redenominated shares to obtain values that are, in the opinion of the company, more suitable, reduce its share capital under this section.
(2) A reduction of capital under this section requires a special resolution of the company.
(3) Any such resolution must be passed within three months of the resolution effecting the redenomination.
(4) The amount by which a company's share capital is reduced under this section must not exceed 10% of the nominal value of the company's allotted share capital immediately after the reduction.
(5) A reduction of capital under this section does not extinguish or reduce any liability in respect of share capital not paid up.
(6) Nothing in Chapter 10 applies to a reduction of capital under this section.

627 Notice to registrar of reduction of capital in connection with redenomination

(1) A companythat passes a resolution under section 626 (reduction of capital in connection with redenomination) must within 15 days after the resolution is passed give notice to the registrar stating—
(a) the date of the resolution, and
(b) the date of the resolution under section 622 in connection with which it was passed. This is in addition to the copies of the resolutions themselves that are required to be delivered to the registrar under Chapter 3 of Part 3.
(2) The notice must be accompanied by a statement of capital.
(3) The statement of capital must state with respect to the company's share capital as reduced by the resolution—
(a) the total number of shares of the company,
(b) the aggregate nominal value of those shares,
(c) for each class of shares—
(i) prescribed particulars of the rights attached to the shares,
(ii) the total number of shares of that class, and
(iii) the aggregate nominal value of shares of that class, and
(d) the amount paid up and the amount (if any) unpaid on each share (whether on account of the nominal value of the share or by way of premium).
(4) The registrar must register the notice and the statement on receipt.
(5) The reduction of capital is not effective until those documents are registered.
(6) The company must also deliver to the registrar, within 15 days after the resolution is passed, a statement by the directors confirming that the reduction in share capital is in accordance with section 626(4) (reduction of capital not to exceed 10% of nominal value of allotted shares immediately after reduction).
(7) If default is made in complying with this section, an offence is committed by—
(a) the company, and
(b) every officer of the company who is in default.

(8) A person guilty of an offence under this section is liable—
(a) on conviction on indictment to a fine, and
(b) on summary conviction to a fine not exceeding the statutory maximum.

628 Redenomination reserve

(1) The amount by which a company's share capital is reduced under section 626 (reduction of capital in connection with redenomination) must be transferred to a reserve, called "the redenomination reserve".
(2) The redenomination reserve may be applied by the company in paying up shares to be allotted to members as fully paid bonus shares.
(3) Subject to that, the provisions of the Companies Acts relating to the reduction of a company's share capital apply as if the redenomination reserve were paid-up share capital of the company.

CHAPTER 9
CLASSES OF SHARE AND CLASS RIGHTS

Introductory

629 Classes of shares

(1) For the purposes of the Companies Acts shares are of one class if the rights attached to them are in all respects uniform.
(2) For this purpose the rights attached to shares are not regarded as different from those attached to other shares by reason only that they do not carry the same rights to dividends in the twelve months immediately following their allotment.

Variation of class rights

630 Variation of class rights: companies having a share capital

(1) This section is concerned with the variation of the rights attached to a class of shares in a company having a share capital.
(2) Rights attached to a class of a company's shares may only be varied—
(a) in accordance with provision in the company's articles for the variation of those rights, or
(b) where the company's articles contain no such provision, if the holders of shares of that class consent to the variation in accordance with this section.
(3) This is without prejudice to any other restrictions on the variation of the rights.
(4) The consent required for the purposes of this section on the part of the holders of a class of a company's shares is—
(a) consent in writing from the holders of at least three-quarters in nominal value of the issued shares of that class (excluding any shares held as treasury shares), or
(b) a special resolution passed at a separate general meeting of the holders of that class sanctioning the variation.
(5) Any amendment of a provision contained in a company's articles for the variation of the rights attached to a class of shares, or the insertion of any such provision into the articles, is itself to be treated as a variation of those rights.
(6) In this section, and (except where the context otherwise requires) in any provision in a company's articles for the variation of the rights attached to a class of shares, references to the variation of those rights include references to their abrogation.

631 Variation of class rights: companies without a share capital

(1) This section is concerned with the variation of the rights of a class of members of a company where the company does not have a share capital.
(2) Rights of a class of members may only be varied—
(a) in accordance with provision in the company's articles for the variation of those rights, or
(b) where the company's articles contain no such provision, if the members of that class consent to the variation in accordance with this section.
(3) This is without prejudice to any other restrictions on the variation of the rights.
(4) The consent required for the purposes of this section on the part of the members of a class is—
(a) consent in writing from at least three-quarters of the members of the class, or
(b) a special resolution passed at a separate general meeting of the members of that class sanctioning the variation.

(5) Any amendment of a provision contained in a company's articles for the variation of the rights of a class of members, or the insertion of any such provision into the articles, is itself to be treated as a variation of those rights.

(6) In this section, and (except where the context otherwise requires) in any provision in a company's articles for the variation of the rights of a class of members, references to the variation of those rights include references to their abrogation.

632 Variation of class rights: saving for court's powers under other provisions

Nothing in section 630 or 631 (variation of class rights) affects the power of the court under—

section 98 (application to cancel resolution for public company to be re-registered as private),

Part 26 (arrangements and reconstructions), or

Part 30 (protection of members against unfair prejudice).

633 Right to object to variation: companies having a share capital

(1) This section applies where the rights attached to any class of shares in a company are varied under section 630 (variation of class rights: companies having a share capital).

(2) The holders of not less in the aggregate than 15% of the issued shares of the class in question (being persons who did not consent to or vote in favour of the resolution for the variation) may apply to the court to have the variation cancelled.

For this purpose any of the company's share capital held as treasury shares is disregarded.

(3) If such an application is made, the variation has no effect unless and until it is confirmed by the court.

(4) Application to the court—

(a) must be made within 21 days after the date on which the consent was given or the resolution was passed (as the case may be), and

(b) may be made on behalf of the shareholders entitled to make the application by such one or more of their number as they may appoint in writing for the purpose.

(5) The court, after hearing the applicant and any other persons who apply to the court to be heard and appear to the court to be interested in the application, may, if satisfied having regard to all the circumstances of the case that the variation would unfairly prejudice the shareholders of the class represented by the applicant, disallow the variation, and shall if not so satisfied confirm it.

The decision of the court on any such application is final.

(6) References in this section to the variation of the rights of holders of a class of shares include references to their abrogation.

634 Right to object to variation: companies without a share capital

(1) This section applies where the rights of any class of members of a company are varied under section 631 (variation of class rights: companies without a share capital).

(2) Members amounting to not less than 15% of the members of the class in question (being persons who did not consent to or vote in favour of the resolution for the variation) may apply to the court to have the variation cancelled.

(3) If such an application is made, the variation has no effect unless and until it is confirmed by the court.

(4) Application to the court must be made within 21 days after the date on which the consent was given or the resolution was passed (as the case may be) and may be made on behalf of the members entitled to make the application by such one or more of their number as they may appoint in writing for the purpose.

(5) The court, after hearing the applicant and any other persons who apply to the court to be heard and appear to the court to be interested in the application, may, if satisfied having regard to all the circumstances of the case that the variation would unfairly prejudice the members of the class represented by the applicant, disallow the variation, and shall if not so satisfied confirm it.

The decision of the court on any such application is final.

(6) References in this section to the variation of the rights of a class of members include references to their abrogation.

635 Copy of court order to be forwarded to the registrar

(1) The company must within 15 days after the making of an order by the court on an application under section 633 or 634 (objection to variation of class rights) forward a copy of the order to the registrar.

(2) If default is made in complying with this section an offence is committed by—
   (a) the company, and
   (b) every officer of the company who is in default.

(3) A person guilty of an offence under this section is liable on summary conviction to a fine not exceeding level 3 on the standard scale and, for continued contravention, a daily default fine not exceeding one-tenth of level 3 on the standard scale.

Matters to be notified to the registrar

636 Notice of name or other designation of class of shares

(1) Where a company assigns a name or other designation, or a new name or other designation, to any class or description of its shares, it must within one month from doing so deliver to the registrar a notice giving particulars of the name or designation so assigned.

(2) If default is made in complying with this section, an offence is committed by—
   (a) the company, and
   (b) every officer of the company who is in default.

(3) A person guilty of an offence under this section is liable on summary conviction to a fine not exceeding level 3 on the standard scale and, for continued contravention, a daily default fine not exceeding one-tenth of level 3 on the standard scale.

637 Notice of particulars of variation of rights attached to shares

(1) Where the rights attached to any shares of a company are varied, the company must within one month from the date on which the variation is made deliver to the registrar a notice giving particulars of the variation.

(2) If default is made in complying with this section, an offence is committed by—
   (a) the company, and
   (b) every officer of the company who is in default.

(3) A person guilty of an offence under this section is liable on summary conviction to a fine not exceeding level 3 on the standard scale and, for continued contravention, a daily default fine not exceeding one-tenth of level 3 on the standard scale.

638 Notice of new class of members

(1) If a company not having a share capital creates a new class of members, the company must within one month from the date on which the new class is created deliver to the registrar a notice containing particulars of the rights attached to that class.

(2) If default is made in complying with this section, an offence is committed by—
   (a) the company, and
   (b) every officer of the company who is in default.

(3) A person guilty of an offence under this section is liable on summary conviction to a fine not exceeding level 3 on the standard scale and, for continued contravention, a daily default fine not exceeding one-tenth of level 3 on the standard scale.

639 Notice of name or other designation of class of members

(1) Where a company not having a share capital assigns a name or other designation, or a new name or other designation, to any class of its members, it must within one month from doing so deliver to the registrar a notice giving particulars of the name or designation so assigned.

(2) If default is made in complying with this section, an offence is committed by—
   (a) the company, and
   (b) every officer of the company who is in default.

(3) A person guilty of an offence under this section is liable on summary conviction to a fine not exceeding level 3 on the standard scale and, for continued contravention, a daily default fine not exceeding one-tenth of level 3 on the standard scale.

640 Notice of particulars of variation of class rights

(1) If the rights of any class of members of a company not having a share capital are varied, the company must within one month from the date on which the variation is made deliver to the registrar a notice containing particulars of the variation.

(2) If default is made in complying with this section, an offence is committed by—
(a) the company, and
(b) every officer of the company who is in default.
(3) A person guilty of an offence under this section is liable on summary conviction to a fine not exceeding level 3 on the standard scale and, for continued contravention, a daily default fine not exceeding one-tenth of level 3 on the standard scale.

CHAPTER 10
REDUCTION OF SHARE CAPITAL
Introductory

641 Circumstances in which a company may reduce its share capital

(1) A limited company having a share capital may reduce its share capital—
(a) in the case of a private company limited by shares, by special resolution supported by a solvency statement (see sections 642 to 644);
(b) in any case, by special resolution confirmed by the court (see sections 645 to 651).
(2) A company may not reduce its capital under subsection (1)(a) if as a result of the reduction there would no longer be any member of the company holding shares other than redeemable shares.
(2A) A company may not reduce its share capital under subsection (1)(a) or (b) as part of a scheme by virtue of which a person, or a person together with its associates, is to acquire all the shares in the company or (where there is more than one class of shares in a company) all the shares of one or more classes, in each case other than shares that are already held by that person or its associates.
(2B) Subsection (2A) does not apply to a scheme under which—
(a) the company is to have a new parent undertaking,
(b) all or substantially all of the members of the company become members of the parent undertaking, and
(c) the members of the company are to hold proportions of the equity share capital of the parent undertaking in the same or substantially the same proportions as they hold the equity share capital of the company.
(2C) In this section—
"associate"has the meaning given by section 988 (meaning of "associate"), reading references in that section to an offeror as references to the person acquiring the shares in the company;
"scheme" means a compromise or arrangement sanctioned by the court under Part 26 (arrangements and reconstructions).
(3) Subject to subsections (2) to (2B), a company may reduce its share capital under this section in any way.
(4) In particular, a company may—
(a) extinguish or reduce the liability on any of its shares in respect of share capital not paid up, or
(b) either with or without extinguishing or reducing liability on any of its shares—
(i) cancel any paid-up share capital that is lost or unrepresented by available assets, or
(ii) repay any paid-up share capital in excess of the company's wants.
(5) A special resolution under this section may not provide for a reduction of share capital to take effect later than the date on which the resolution has effect in accordance with this Chapter.
(6) This Chapter (apart from subsection (5) above) has effect subject to any provision of the company's articles restricting or prohibiting the reduction of the company's share capital.
(7) In subsection (1)(b), section 91(5)(b)(iii), sections 645 to 651 (except in the phrase "sanctioned by the court under Part 26") and 653 (1) "the court" means, in England and Wales, the High Court.

Private companies: reduction of capital supported by solvency statement

642 Reduction of capital supported by solvency statement

(1) A resolution for reducing share capital of a private company limited by shares is supported by a solvency statement if—
(a) the directors of the company make a statement of the solvency of the company in accordance with section 643 (a "solvency statement") not more than 15 days before the date on which the resolution is passed, and

(b) the resolution and solvency statement are registered in accordance with section 644.

(2) Where the resolution is proposed as a written resolution, a copy of the solvency statement must be sent or submitted to every eligible member at or before the time at which the proposed resolution is sent or submitted to him.

(3) Where the resolution is proposed at a general meeting, a copy of the solvency statement must be made available for inspection by members of the company throughout that meeting.

(4) The validity of a resolution is not affected by a failure to comply with subsection (2) or (3).

643 Solvency statement

(1) A solvency statement is a statement that each of the directors—
   (a) has formed the opinion, as regards the company's situation at the date of the statement, that there is no ground on which the company could then be found to be unable to pay (or otherwise discharge) its debts; and
   (b) has also formed the opinion—
      (i) if it is intended to commence the winding up of the company within twelve months of that date, that the company will be able to pay (or otherwise discharge) its debts in full within twelve months of the commencement of the winding up; or
      (ii) in any other case, that the company will be able to pay (or otherwise discharge) its debts as they fall due during the year immediately following that date.

(2) In forming those opinions, the directors must take into account all of the company's liabilities (including any contingent or prospective liabilities).

(3) The solvency statement must be in the prescribed form and must state—
   (a) the date on which it is made, and
   (b) the name of each director of the company.

(4) If the directors make a solvency statement without having reasonable grounds for the opinions expressed in it, and the statement is delivered to the registrar, an offence is committed by every director who is in default.

(5) A person guilty of an offence under subsection (4) is liable—
   (a) on conviction on indictment, to imprisonment for a term not exceeding two years or a fine (or both);
   (b) on summary conviction—
      (i) in England and Wales, to imprisonment for a term not exceeding twelve months or to a fine not exceeding the statutory maximum (or both);
      (ii) in Scotland or Northern Ireland, to imprisonment for a term not exceeding six months, or to a fine not exceeding the statutory maximum (or both).

644 Registration of resolution and supporting documents

(1) Within 15 days after the resolution for reducing share capital is passed the company must deliver to the registrar—
   (a) a copy of the solvency statement, and
   (b) a statement of capital.

   This is in addition to the copy of the resolution itself that is required to be delivered to the registrar under Chapter 3 of Part 3.

(2) The statement of capital must state with respect to the company's share capital as reduced by the resolution—
   (a) the total number of shares of the company,
   (b) the aggregate nominal value of those shares,
   (c) for each class of shares—
      (i) prescribed particulars of the rights attached to the shares,
      (ii) the total number of shares of that class, and
      (iii) the aggregate nominal value of shares of that class, and
   (d) the amount paid up and the amount (if any) unpaid on each share (whether on account of the nominal value of the share or by way of premium).

(3) The registrar must register the documents delivered to him under subsection (1) on receipt.

(4) The resolution does not take effect until those documents are registered.

(5) The company must also deliver to the registrar, within 15 days after the resolution is passed, a statement by the directors confirming that the solvency statement was—
- (a) made not more than 15 days before the date on which the resolution was passed, and
- (b) provided to members in accordance with section 642(2) or (3).

(6) The validity of a resolution is not affected by—
- (a) a failure to deliver the documents required to be delivered to the registrar under subsection (1) within the time specified in that subsection, or
- (b) a failure to comply with subsection (5).

(7) If the company delivers to the registrar a solvency statement that was not provided to members in accordance with section 642(2) or (3), an offence is committed by every officer of the company who is in default.

(8) If default is made in complying with this section, an offence is committed by—
- (a) the company, and
- (b) every officer of the company who is in default.

(9) A person guilty of an offence under subsection (7) or (8) is liable—
- (a) on conviction on indictment, to a fine;
- (b) on summary conviction, to a fine not exceeding the statutory maximum.

Reduction of capital confirmed by the court

645 Application to court for order of confirmation

(1) Where a company has passed a resolution for reducing share capital, it may apply to the court for an order confirming the reduction.

(2) If the proposed reduction of capital involves either—
- (a) diminution of liability in respect of unpaid share capital, or
- (b) the payment to a shareholder of any paid-up share capital,

section 646 (creditors entitled to object to reduction) applies unless the court directs otherwise.

(3) The court may, if having regard to any special circumstances of the case it thinks proper to do so, direct that section 646 is not to apply as regards any class or classes of creditors.

(4) The court may direct that section 646 is to apply in any other case.

646 Creditors entitled to object to reduction

(1) Where this section applies (see section 645(2) and (4)), every creditor of the company who—
- (a) at the date fixed by the court is entitled to any debt or claim that, if that date were the commencement of the winding up of the company would be admissible in proof against the company, and
- (b) can show that there is a real likelihood that the reduction would result in the company being unable to discharge his debt or claim when it fell due,

is entitled to object to the reduction of capital.

(2) The court shall settle a list of creditors entitled to object.

(3) For that purpose the court—
- (a) shall ascertain, as far as possible without requiring an application from any creditor, the names of those creditors and the nature and amount of their debts or claims, and
- (b) may publish notices fixing a day or days within which creditors not entered on the list are to claim to be so entered or are to be excluded from the right of objecting to the reduction of capital.

(4) If a creditor entered on the list whose debt or claim is not discharged or has not determined does not consent to the reduction, the court may, if it thinks fit, dispense with the consent of that creditor on the company securing payment of his debt or claim.

(5) For this purpose the debt or claim must be secured by appropriating (as the court may direct) the following amount—
- (a) if the company admits the full amount of the debt or claim or, though not admitting it, is willing to provide for it, the full amount of the debt or claim;

(b) if the company does not admit, and is not willing to provide for, the full amount of the debt or claim, or if the amount is contingent or not ascertained, an amount fixed by the court after the like enquiry and adjudication as if the company were being wound up by the court.

647 Offences in connection with list of creditors

(1) If an officer of the company—
  (a) intentionally or recklessly—
    (i) conceals the name of a creditor entitled to object to the reduction of capital, or
    (ii) misrepresents the nature or amount of the debt or claim of a creditor, or
  (b) is knowingly concerned in any such concealment or misrepresentation, he commits an offence.

(2) A person guilty of an offence under this section is liable—
  (a) on conviction on indictment, to a fine;
  (b) on summary conviction, to a fine not exceeding the statutory maximum.

648 Court order confirming reduction

(1) The court may make an order confirming the reduction of capital on such terms and conditions as it thinks fit.

(2) The court must not confirm the reduction unless it is satisfied, with respect to every creditor of the company who is entitled to object to the reduction of capital that either—
  (a) his consent to the reduction has been obtained, or
  (b) his debt or claim has been discharged, or has determined or has been secured.

(3) Where the court confirms the reduction, it may order the company to publish (as the court directs) the reasons for reduction of capital, or such other information in regard to it as the court thinks expedient with a view to giving proper information to the public, and (if the court thinks fit) the causes that led to the reduction.

(4) The court may, if for any special reason it thinks proper to do so, make an order directing that the company must, during such period (commencing on or at any time after the date of the order) as is specified in the order, add to its name as its last words the words "and reduced".
If such an order is made, those words are, until the end of the period specified in the order, deemed to be part of the company's name.

649 Registration of order and statement of capital

(1) The registrar, on production of an order of the court confirming the reduction of a company's share capital and the delivery of a copy of the order and of a statement of capital (approved by the court), shall register the order and statement.
This is subject to section 650 (public company reducing capital below authorised minimum).

(2) The statement of capital must state with respect to the company's share capital as altered by the order—
  (a) the total number of shares of the company,
  (b) the aggregate nominal value of those shares,
  (c) for each class of shares—
    (i) prescribed particulars of the rights attached to the shares,
    (ii) the total number of shares of that class, and
    (iii) the aggregate nominal value of shares of that class, and
  (d) the amount paid up and the amount (if any) unpaid on each share (whether on account of the nominal value of the share or by way of premium).

(3) The resolution for reducing share capital, as confirmed by the court's order, takes effect—
  (a) in the case of a reduction of share capital that forms part of a compromise or arrangement sanctioned by the court under Part 26 (arrangements and reconstructions)—
    (i) on delivery of the order and statement of capital to the registrar, or
    (ii) if the court so orders, on the registration of the order and statement of capital;
  (b) in any other case, on the registration of the order and statement of capital.

(4) Notice of the registration of the order and statement of capital must be published in such manner as the court may direct.

(5) The registrar must certify the registration of the order and statement of capital.

(6) The certificate—

(a) must be signed by the registrar or authenticated by the registrar's official seal, and

(b) is conclusive evidence—

(i) that the requirements of this Act with respect to the reduction of share capital have been complied with, and

(ii) that the company's share capital is as stated in the statement of capital.

Public company reducing capital below authorised minimum

650 Public company reducing capital below authorised minimum

(1) This section applies where the court makes an order confirming a reduction of a public company's capital that has the effect of bringing the nominal value of its allotted share capital below the authorised minimum.

(2) The registrar must not register the order unless either—

(a) the court so directs, or

(b) the company is first re-registered as a private company.

(3) Section 651 provides an expedited procedure for re-registration in these circumstances.

651 Expedited procedure for re-registration as a private company

(1) The court may authorise the company to be re-registered as a private company without its having passed the special resolution required by section 97.

(2) If it does so, the court must specify in the order the changes to the company's name and articles to be made in connection with the re-registration.

(3) The company may then be re-registered as a private company if an application to that effect is delivered to the registrar together with—

(a) a copy of the court's order, and

(b) notice of the company's name, and a copy of the company's articles, as altered by the court's order.

(4) On receipt of such an application the registrar must issue a certificate of incorporation altered to meet the circumstances of the case.

(5) The certificate must state that it is issued on re-registration and the date on which it is issued.

(6) On the issue of the certificate—

(a) the company by virtue of the issue of the certificate becomes a private company, and

(b) the changes in the company's name and articles take effect.

(7) The certificate is conclusive evidence that the requirements of this Act as to re-registration have been complied with.

Effect of reduction of capital

652 Liability of members following reduction of capital

(1) Where a company's share capital is reduced a member of the company (past or present) is not liable in respect of any share to any call or contribution exceeding in amount the difference (if any) between—

(a) the nominal amount of the share as notified to the registrar in the statement of capital delivered under section 644 or 649, 1028A or 1032A of this Act or paragraph 7 of Schedule 4 to the Small Business, Enterprise and Employment Act 2015, and

(b) the amount paid on the share or the reduced amount (if any) which is deemed to have been paid on it, as the case may be.

(2) This is subject to section 653 (liability to creditor in case of omission from list).

(3) Nothing in this section affects the rights of the contributories among themselves.

653 Liability to creditor in case of omission from list of creditors

(1) This section applies where, in the case of a reduction of capital confirmed by the court—

(a) a creditor entitled to object to the reduction of share capital is by reason of his ignorance—

(i) of the proceedings for reduction of share capital, or

(ii) of their nature and effect with respect to his debt or claim, not entered on the list of creditors, and

(b) after the reduction of capital the company is unable to pay the amount of his debt or claim.

(2) Every person who was a member of the company at the date on which the resolution for reducing capital took effect under section 649(3) is liable to contribute for the payment of the debt or claim an amount not exceeding that which he would have been liable to contribute if the company had commenced to be wound up on the day before that date.

(3) If the company is wound up, the court on the application of the creditor in question, and proof of ignorance as mentioned in subsection (1)(a), may if it thinks fit—

(a) settle accordingly a list of persons liable to contribute under this section, and

(b) make and enforce calls and orders on them as if they were ordinary contributories in a winding up.

(4) The reference in subsection (1)(b) to a company being unable to pay the amount of a debt or claim has the same meaning as in section 123 of the Insolvency Act 1986 or Article 103 of the Insolvency (Northern Ireland) Order 1989.

CHAPTER 11
MISCELLANEOUS AND SUPPLEMENTARY PROVISIONS

654 Treatment of reserve arising from reduction of capital

(1) A reserve arising from the reduction of a company's share capital is not distributable, subject to any provision made by order under this section.

(2) The Secretary of State may by order specify cases in which—

(a) the prohibition in subsection (1) does not apply, and

(b) the reserve is to be treated for the purposes of Part 23 (distributions) as a realised profit.

(3) An order under this section is subject to affirmative resolution procedure.

655 Shares no bar to damages against company

A person is not debarred from obtaining damages or other compensation from a company by reason only of his holding or having held shares in the company or any right to apply or subscribe for shares or to be included in the company's register of members in respect of shares.

656 Public companies: duty of directors to call meeting on serious loss of capital

(1) Where the net assets of a public company are half or less of its called-up share capital, the directors must call a general meeting of the company to consider whether any, and if so what, steps should be taken to deal with the situation.

(2) They must do so not later than 28 days from the earliest day on which that fact is known to a director of the company.

(3) The meeting must be convened for a date not later than 56 days from that day.

(4) If there is a failure to convene a meeting as required by this section, each of the directors of the company who—

(a) knowingly authorises or permits the failure, or

(b) after the period during which the meeting should have been convened, knowingly authorises or permits the failure to continue,

commits an offence.

(5) A person guilty of an offence under this section is liable—

(a) on conviction on indictment, to a fine;

(b) on summary conviction, to a fine not exceeding the statutory maximum.

(6) Nothing in this section authorises the consideration at a meeting convened in pursuance of subsection (1) of any matter that could not have been considered at that meeting apart from this section.

657 General power to make further provision by regulations

(1) The Secretary of State may by regulations modify the following provisions of this Part—

sections 552 and 553 (prohibited commissions, discounts and allowances),
Chapter 5 (payment for shares),
Chapter 6 (public companies: independent valuation of non-cash consideration),
Chapter 7 (share premiums),

sections 622 to 628 (redenomination of share capital),
Chapter 10 (reduction of capital), and
section 656 (public companies: duty of directors to call meeting on serious loss of capital).

(2) The regulations may—
   (a) amend or repeal any of those provisions, or
   (b) make such other provision as appears to the Secretary of State appropriate in place of any of those provisions.

(3) Regulations under this section may make consequential amendments or repeals in other provisions of this Act, or in other enactments.

(4) Regulations under this section are subject to affirmative resolution procedure.

PART 18
ACQUISITION BY LIMITED COMPANY OF ITS OWN SHARES

CHAPTER 1
GENERAL PROVISIONS

Introductory

658 General rule against limited company acquiring its own shares

(1) A limited company must not acquire its own shares, whether by purchase, subscription or otherwise, except in accordance with the provisions of this Part.

(2) If a company purports to act in contravention of this section—
   (a) an offence is committed by—
      (i) the company, and
      (ii) every officer of the company who is in default, and
   (b) the purported acquisition is void.

(3) A person guilty of an offence under this section is liable—
   (a) on conviction on indictment, to imprisonment for a term not exceeding two years or a fine (or both);
   (b) on summary conviction—
      (i) in England and Wales, to imprisonment for a term not exceeding twelve months or a fine not exceeding the statutory maximum (or both);
      (ii) in Scotland or Northern Ireland, to imprisonment for a term not exceeding six months or a fine not exceeding the statutory maximum (or both).

659 Exceptions to general rule

(1) A limited company may acquire any of its own fully paid shares otherwise than for valuable consideration.

(2) Section 658 does not prohibit—
   (a) the acquisition of shares in a reduction of capital duly made;
   (b) the purchase of shares in pursuance of an order of the court under—
      (i) section 98 (application to court to cancel resolution for re-registration as a private company),
      (ii) section 721(6) (powers of court on objection to redemption or purchase of shares out of capital),
      (iii) section 759 (remedial order in case of breach of prohibition of public offers by private company), or
      (iv) Part 30 (protection of members against unfair prejudice);
   (c) the forfeiture of shares, or the acceptance of shares surrendered in lieu, in pursuance of the company's articles, for failure to pay any sum payable in respect of the shares.

Shares held by company's nominee

660 Treatment of shares held by nominee

(1) This section applies where shares in a limited company—
   (a) are taken by a subscriber to the memorandum as nominee of the company,
   (b) are issued to a nominee of the company, or

(c) are acquired by a nominee of the company, partly paid up, from a third person.

(2) For all purposes—

(a) the shares are to be treated as held by the nominee on his own account, and

(b) the company is to be regarded as having no beneficial interest in them.

(3) This section does not apply—

(a) to shares acquired otherwise than by subscription by a nominee of a public company, where—

(i) a person acquires shares in the company with financial assistance given to him, directly or indirectly, by the company for the purpose of or in connection with the acquisition, and

(ii) the company has a beneficial interest in the shares;

(b) to shares acquired by a nominee of the company when the company has no beneficial interest in the shares.

661 Liability of others where nominee fails to make payment in respect of shares

(1) This section applies where shares in a limited company—

(a) are taken by a subscriber to the memorandum as nominee of the company,

(b) are issued to a nominee of the company, or

(c) are acquired by a nominee of the company, partly paid up, from a third person.

(2) If the nominee, having been called on to pay any amount for the purposes of paying up, or paying any premium on, the shares, fails to pay that amount within 21 days from being called on to do so, then—

(a) in the case of shares that he agreed to take as subscriber to the memorandum, the other subscribers to the memorandum, and

(b) in any other case, the directors of the company when the shares were issued to or acquired by him,

are jointly and severally liable with him to pay that amount.

(3) If in proceedings for the recovery of an amount under subsection (2) it appears to the court that the subscriber or director—

(a) has acted honestly and reasonably, and

(b) having regard to all the circumstances of the case, ought fairly to be relieved from liability,

the court may relieve him, either wholly or in part, from his liability on such terms as the court thinks fit.

(4) If a subscriber to a company's memorandum or a director of a company has reason to apprehend that a claim will or might be made for the recovery of any such amount from him—

(a) he may apply to the court for relief, and

(b) the court has the same power to relieve him as it would have had in proceedings for recovery of that amount.

(5) This section does not apply to shares acquired by a nominee of the company when the company has no beneficial interest in the shares.

Shares held by or for public company

662 Duty to cancel shares in public company held by or for the company

(1) This section applies in the case of a public company—

(a) where shares in the company are forfeited, or surrendered to the company in lieu of forfeiture, in pursuance of the articles, for failure to pay any sum payable in respect of the shares;

(b) where shares in the company are surrendered to the company in pursuance of section 102C(1)(b) of the Building Societies Act 1986;

(c) where shares in the company are acquired by it (otherwise than in accordance with this Part or Part 30 (protection of members against unfair prejudice)) and the company has a beneficial interest in the shares;

(d) where a nominee of the company acquires shares in the company from a third party without financial assistance being given directly or indirectly by the company and the company has a beneficial interest in the shares; or

(e) where a person acquires shares in the company, with financial assistance given to him, directly or indirectly, by the company for the purpose of or in connection with the acquisition, and the company has a beneficial interest in the shares.

(2) Unless the shares or any interest of the company in them are previously disposed of, the company must—
(a) cancel the shares and diminish the amount of the company's share capital by the nominal value of the shares cancelled, and
(b) where the effect is that the nominal value of the company's allotted share capital is brought below the authorised minimum, apply for re-registration as a private company, stating the effect of the cancellation.

(3) It must do so no later than—
(a) in a case within subsection (1)(a) or (b), three years from the date of the forfeiture or surrender;
(b) in a case within subsection (1)(c) or (d), three years from the date of the acquisition;
(c) in a case within subsection (1)(e), one year from the date of the acquisition.

(4) The directors of the company may take any steps necessary to enable the company to comply with this section, and may do so without complying with the provisions of Chapter 10 of Part 17 (reduction of capital).
See also section 664 (re-registration as private company in consequence of cancellation).

(5) Neither the company nor, in a case within subsection (1)(d) or (e), the nominee or other shareholder may exercise any voting rights in respect of the shares.

(6) Any purported exercise of those rights is void.

663 Notice of cancellation of shares

(1) Where a company cancels shares in order to comply with section 662, it must within one month after the shares are cancelled give notice to the registrar, specifying the shares cancelled.

(2) The notice must be accompanied by a statement of capital.

(3) The statement of capital must state with respect to the company's share capital immediately following the cancellation—
(a) the total number of shares of the company,
(b) the aggregate nominal value of those shares,
(c) for each class of shares—
(i) prescribed particulars of the rights attached to the shares,
(ii) the total number of shares of that class, and
(iii) the aggregate nominal value of shares of that class, and
(d) the amount paid up and the amount (if any) unpaid on each share (whether on account of the nominal value of the share or by way of premium).

(4) If default is made in complying with this section, an offence is committed by—
(a) the company, and
(b) every officer of the company who is in default.

(5) A person guilty of an offence under this section is liable on summary conviction to a fine not exceeding level 3 on the standard scale and, for continued contravention, a daily default fine not exceeding one-tenth of level 3 on the standard scale.

664 Re-registration as private company in consequence of cancellation

(1) Where a company is obliged to re-register as a private company to comply with section 662, the directors may resolve that the company should be so re-registered.
Chapter 3 of Part 3 (resolutions affecting a company's constitution) applies to any such resolution.

(2) The resolution may make such changes—
(a) in the company's name, and
(b) in the company's articles,
as are necessary in connection with its becoming a private company.

(3) The application for re-registration must contain a statement of the company's proposed name on re-registration.

(4) The application must be accompanied by—
(a) a copy of the resolution (unless a copy has already been forwarded under Chapter 3 of Part 3),
(b) a copy of the company's articles as amended by the resolution, and
(c) a statement of compliance.

(5) The statement of compliance required is a statement that the requirements of this section as to re-registration as a private company have been complied with.
(6) The registrar may accept the statement of compliance as sufficient evidence that the company is entitled to be re-registered as a private company.

665 Issue of certificate of incorporation on re-registration

(1) If on an application under section 664 the registrar is satisfied that the company is entitled to be re-registered as a private company, the company shall be re-registered accordingly.
(2) The registrar must issue a certificate of incorporation altered to meet the circumstances of the case.
(3) The certificate must state that it is issued on re-registration and the date on which it is issued.
(4) On the issue of the certificate—
 (a) the company by virtue of the issue of the certificate becomes a private company, and
 (b) the changes in the company's name and articles take effect.
(5) The certificate is conclusive evidence that the requirements of this Act as to re-registration have been complied with.

666 Effect of failure to re-register

(1) If a public company that is required by section 662 to apply to be re-registered as a private company fails to do so before the end of the period specified in subsection (3) of that section, Chapter 1 of Part 20 (prohibition of public offers by private company) applies to it as if it were a private company.
(2) Subject to that, the company continues to be treated as a public company until it is so re- registered.

667 Offence in case of failure to cancel shares or re-register

(1) This section applies where a company, when required to do by section 662—
 (a) fails to cancel any shares, or
 (b) fails to make an application for re-registration as a private company, within the time specified in subsection (3) of that section.
(2) An offence is committed by—
 (a) the company, and
 (b) every officer of the company who is in default.
(3) A person guilty of an offence under this section is liable on summary conviction to a fine not exceeding level 3 on the standard scale and, for continued contravention, a daily default fine not exceeding one-tenth of level 3 on the standard scale.

668 Application of provisions to company re-registering as public company

(1) This section applies where, after shares in a private company—
 (a) are forfeited in pursuance of the company's articles or are surrendered to the company in lieu of forfeiture,
 (b) are acquired by the company (otherwise than by any of the methods permitted by this Part or Part 30 (protection of members against unfair prejudice)), the company having a beneficial interest in the shares,
 (c) are acquired by a nominee of the company from a third party without financial assistance being given directly or indirectly by the company, the company having a beneficial interest in the shares, or
 (d) are acquired by a person with financial assistance given to him, directly or indirectly, by the company for the purpose of or in connection with the acquisition, the company having a beneficial interest in the shares,

the company is re-registered as a public company.
(2) In that case the provisions of sections 662 to 667 apply to the company as if it had been a public company at the time of the forfeiture, surrender or acquisition, subject to the following modification.

(3) The modification is that the period specified in section 662(3)(a), (b) or (c) (period for complying with obligations under that section) runs from the date of the re-registration of the company as a public company.

669 Transfer to reserve on acquisition of shares by public company or nominee

(1) Where—

(a) a public company, or a nominee of a public company, acquires shares in the company, and

(b) those shares are shown in a balance sheet of the company as an asset,

an amount equal to the value of the shares must be transferred out of profits available for dividend to a reserve fund and is not then available for distribution.

(2) Subsection (1) applies to an interest in shares as it applies to shares.

As it so applies the reference to the value of the shares shall be read as a reference to the value to the company of its interest in the shares.

Charges of public company on own shares

670 Public companies: general rule against lien or charge on own shares

(1) A lien or other charge of a public company on its own shares (whether taken expressly or otherwise) is void, except as permitted by this section.

(2) In the case of any description of company, a charge is permitted if the shares are not fully paid up and the charge is for an amount payable in respect of the shares.

(3) In the case of a company whose ordinary business—

(a) includes the lending of money, or

(b) consists of the provision of credit or the bailment (in Scotland, hiring) of goods under a hire-purchase agreement, or both,

a charge is permitted (whether the shares are fully paid or not) if it arises in connection with a transaction entered into by the company in the ordinary course of that business.

(4) In the case of a company that has been re-registered as a public company, a charge is permitted if it was in existence immediately before the application for re-registration.

Supplementary provisions

671 Interests to be disregarded in determining whether company has beneficial interest

In determining for the purposes of this Chapter whether a company has a beneficial interest in shares, there shall be disregarded any such interest as is mentioned in—

section 672 (residual interest under pension scheme or employees' share scheme),
section 673 (employer's charges and other rights of recovery), or
section 674 (rights as personal representative or trustee).

672 Residual interest under pension scheme or employees' share scheme

(1) Where the shares are held on trust for the purposes of a pension scheme or employees' share scheme, there shall be disregarded any residual interest of the company that has not vested in possession.

(2) A "residual interest" means a right of the company to receive any of the trust property in the event of—

(a) all the liabilities arising under the scheme having been satisfied or provided for, or

(b) the company ceasing to participate in the scheme, or

(c) the trust property at any time exceeding what is necessary for satisfying the liabilities arising or expected to arise under the scheme.

(3) In subsection (2)—

(a) the reference to a right includes a right dependent on the exercise of a discretion vested by the scheme in the trustee or another person, and

(b) the reference to liabilities arising under a scheme includes liabilities that have resulted, or may result, from the exercise of any such discretion.

(4) For the purposes of this section a residual interest vests in possession—

(a) in a case within subsection (2)(a), on the occurrence of the event mentioned there (whether or not the amount of the property receivable pursuant to the right is ascertained);

(b) in a case within subsection (2)(b) or (c), when the company becomes entitled to require the trustee to transfer to it any of the property receivable pursuant to that right.

(5) Where by virtue of this section shares are exempt from section 660 or 661 (shares held by company's nominee) at the time they are taken, issued or acquired but the residual interest in question vests in possession before they are disposed of or fully paid up, those sections apply to the shares as if they had been taken, issued or acquired on the date on which that interest vests in possession.

(6) Where by virtue of this section shares are exempt from sections 662 to 668 (shares held by or for public company) at the time they are acquired but the residual interest in question vests in possession before they are disposed of, those sections apply to the shares as if they had been acquired on the date on which the interest vests in possession.

673 Employer's charges and other rights of recovery

(1) Where the shares are held on trust for the purposes of a pension scheme there shall be disregarded—

(a) any charge or lien on, or set-off against, any benefit or other right or interest under the scheme for the purpose of enabling the employer or former employer of a member of the scheme to obtain the discharge of a monetary obligation due to him from the member;

(b) any right to receive from the trustee of the scheme, or as trustee of the scheme to retain, an amount that can be recovered or retained—

(i) under section 61 of the Pension Schemes Act 1993, or otherwise, as reimbursement or partial reimbursement for any contributions equivalent premium paid in connection with the scheme under Part 3 of that Act, or

(ii) under section 57 of the Pension Schemes (Northern Ireland) Act 1993, or otherwise, as reimbursement or partial reimbursement for any contributions equivalent premium paid in connection with the scheme under Part 3 of that Act.

(2) Where the shares are held on trust for the purposes of an employees' share scheme, there shall be disregarded any charge or lien on, or set-off against, any benefit or other right or interest under the scheme for the purpose of enabling the employer or former employer of a member of the scheme to obtain the discharge of a monetary obligation due to him from the member.

674 Rights as personal representative or trustee

Where the company is a personal representative or trustee, there shall be disregarded any rights that the company has in that capacity including, in particular—

(a) any right to recover its expenses or be remunerated out of the estate or trust property, and

(b) any right to be indemnified out of that property for any liability incurred by reason of any act or omission of the company in the performance of its duties as personal representative or trustee.

675 Meaning of "pension scheme"

(1) In this Chapter "pension scheme" means a scheme for the provision of benefits consisting of or including relevant benefits for or in respect of employees or former employees.

(2) In subsection (1) "relevant benefits" means any pension, lump sum, gratuity or other like benefit given or to be given on retirement or on death or in anticipation of retirement or, in connection with past service, after retirement or death.

676 Application of provisions to directors

For the purposes of this Chapter references to "employer" and "employee", in the context of a pension scheme or employees' share scheme, shall be read as if a director of a company were employed by it.

CHAPTER 2
FINANCIAL ASSISTANCE FOR PURCHASE OF OWN SHARES

Introductory

677 Meaning of "financial assistance"

(1) In this Chapter "financial assistance" means—

(a) financial assistance given by way of gift,

(b) financial assistance given—

(i) by way of guarantee, security or indemnity (other than an indemnity in respect of the indemnifier's own neglect or default), or

(ii) by way of release or waiver,

(c) financial assistance given—

(i) by way of a loan or any other agreement under which any of the obligations of the person giving the assistance are to be fulfilled at a time when in accordance with the agreement any obligation of another party to the agreement remains unfulfilled, or

(ii) by way of the novation of, or the assignment (in Scotland, assignation) of rights arising under, a loan or such other agreement, or

(d) any other financial assistance given by a company where—

(i) the net assets of the company are reduced to a material extent by the giving of the assistance, or

(ii) the company has no net assets.

(2) "Net assets" here means the aggregate amount of the company's assets less the aggregate amount of its liabilities.

(3) For this purpose a company's liabilities include—

(a) where the company draws up Companies Act individual accounts, any provision of a kind specified for the purposes of this subsection by regulations under section 396, and

(b) where the company draws up IAS individual accounts, any provision made in those accounts.

Circumstances in which financial assistance prohibited

678 Assistance for acquisition of shares in public company

(1) Where a person is acquiring or proposing to acquire shares in a public company, it is not lawful for that company, or a company that is a subsidiary of that company, to give financial assistance directly or indirectly for the purpose of the acquisition before or at the same time as the acquisition takes place.

(2) Subsection (1) does not prohibit a company from giving financial assistance for the acquisition of shares in it or its holding company if—

(a) the company's principal purpose in giving the assistance is not to give it for the purpose of any such acquisition, or

(b) the giving of the assistance for that purpose is only an incidental part of some larger purpose of the company,

and the assistance is given in good faith in the interests of the company.

(3) Where—

(a) a person has acquired shares in a company, and

(b) a liability has been incurred (by that or another person) for the purpose of the acquisition,

it is not lawful for that company, or a company that is a subsidiary of that company, to give financial assistance directly or indirectly for the purpose of reducing or discharging the liability if, at the time the assistance is given, the company in which the shares were acquired is a public company.

(4) Subsection (3) does not prohibit a company from giving financial assistance if—

(a) the company's principal purpose in giving the assistance is not to reduce or discharge any liability incurred by a person for the purpose of the acquisition of shares in the company or its holding company, or

(b) the reduction or discharge of any such liability is only an incidental part of some larger purpose of the company,

and the assistance is given in good faith in the interests of the company.

(5) This section has effect subject to sections 681 and 682 (unconditional and conditional exceptions to prohibition).

679 Assistance by public company for acquisition of shares in its private holding company

(1) Where a person is acquiring or proposing to acquire shares in a private company, it is not lawful for a public company that is a subsidiary of that company to give financial assistance directly or indirectly for the purpose of the acquisition before or at the same time as the acquisition takes place.

(2) Subsection (1) does not prohibit a company from giving financial assistance for the acquisition of shares in its holding company if—
  (a) the company's principal purpose in giving the assistance is not to give it for the purpose of any such acquisition, or
  (b) the giving of the assistance for that purpose is only an incidental part of some larger purpose of the company,

and the assistance is given in good faith in the interests of the company.

(3) Where—
  (a) a person has acquired shares in a private company, and
  (b) a liability has been incurred (by that or another person) for the purpose of the acquisition,

it is not lawful for a public company that is a subsidiary of that company to give financial assistance directly or indirectly for the purpose of reducing or discharging the liability.

(4) Subsection (3) does not prohibit a company from giving financial assistance if—
  (a) the company's principal purpose in giving the assistance is not to reduce or discharge any liability incurred by a person for the purpose of the acquisition of shares in its holding company, or
  (b) the reduction or discharge of any such liability is only an incidental part of some larger purpose of the company,

and the assistance is given in good faith in the interests of the company.

(5) This section has effect subject to sections 681 and 682 (unconditional and conditional exceptions to prohibition).

680 Prohibited financial assistance an offence

(1) If a company contravenes section 678(1) or (3) or section 679(1) or (3) (prohibited financial assistance) an offence is committed by—
  (a) the company, and
  (b) every officer of the company who is in default.

(2) A person guilty of an offence under this section is liable—
  (a) on conviction on indictment, to imprisonment for a term not exceeding two years or a fine (or both);
  (b) on summary conviction—
    (i) in England and Wales, to imprisonment for a term not exceeding twelve months or to a fine not exceeding the statutory maximum (or both);
    (ii) in Scotland or Northern Ireland, to imprisonment for a term not exceeding six months, or to a fine not exceeding the statutory maximum (or both).

Exceptions from prohibition

681 Unconditional exceptions

(1) Neither section 678 nor section 679 prohibits a transaction to which this section applies.

(2) Those transactions are—
  (a) a distribution of the company's assets by way of—
    (i) dividend lawfully made, or
    (ii) distribution in the course of a company's winding up;
  (b) an allotment of bonus shares;
  (c) a reduction of capital under Chapter 10 of Part 17;
  (d) a redemption of shares under Chapter 3 or a purchase of shares under Chapter 4 of this Part;
  (e) anything done in pursuance of an order of the court under Part 26 (order sanctioning compromise or arrangement with members or creditors);
  (f) anything done under an arrangement made in pursuance of section 110 of the Insolvency Act 1986 or Article 96 of the Insolvency (Northern Ireland) Order 1989 (liquidator in winding up accepting shares as consideration for sale of company's property);
  (g) anything done under an arrangement made between a company and its creditors that is binding on the creditors by virtue of Part 1 of the Insolvency Act 1986 or Part 2 of the Insolvency (Northern Ireland) Order 1989.

682 Conditional exceptions

(1) Neither section 678 nor section 679 prohibits a transaction to which this section applies—
  (a) if the company giving the assistance is a private company, or
  (b) if the company giving the assistance is a public company and—
    (i) the company has net assets that are not reduced by the giving of the assistance, or
    (ii) to the extent that those assets are so reduced, the assistance is provided out of distributable profits.
(2) The transactions to which this section applies are—
  (a) where the lending of money is part of the ordinary business of the company, the lending of money in the ordinary course of the company's business;
  (b) the provision by the company, in good faith in the interests of the company or its holding company, of financial assistance for the purposes of an employees' share scheme;
  (c) the provision of financial assistance by the company for the purposes of or in connection with anything done by the company (or another company in the same group) for the purpose of enabling or facilitating transactions in shares in the first-mentioned company or its holding company between, and involving the acquisition of beneficial ownership of those shares by—
    (i) bona fide employees or former employees of that company (or another company in the same group), or
    (ii) spouses or civil partners, widows, widowers or surviving civil partners, or minor children or step-children of any such employees or former employees;
  (d) the making by the company of loans to persons (other than directors) employed in good faith by the company with a view to enabling those persons to acquire fully paid shares in the company or its holding company to be held by them by way of beneficial ownership.
(3) The references in this section to "net assets" are to the amount by which the aggregate of the company's assets exceeds the aggregate of its liabilities.
(4) For this purpose—
  (a) the amount of both assets and liabilities shall be taken to be as stated in the company's accounting records immediately before the financial assistance is given, and
  (b) "liabilities" includes any amount retained as reasonably necessary for the purpose of providing for a liability the nature of which is clearly defined and that is either likely to be incurred or certain to be incurred but uncertain as to amount or as to the date on which it will arise.
  (5) For the purposes of subsection (2)(c) a company is in the same group as another company if it is a holding company or subsidiary of that company or a subsidiary of a holding company of that company.

Supplementary

683 Definitions for this Chapter

(1) In this Chapter—
"distributable profits", in relation to the giving of any financial assistance—
  (a) means those profits out of which the company could lawfully make a distribution equal in value to that assistance, and
  (b) includes, in a case where the financial assistance consists of or includes, or is treated as arising in consequence of, the sale, transfer or other disposition of a non- cash asset, any profit that, if the company were to make a distribution of that character would be available for that purpose (see section 846); and

"distribution" has the same meaning as in Part 23 (distributions) (see section 829).
(2) In this Chapter—
  (a) a reference to a person incurring a liability includes his changing his financial position by making an agreement or arrangement (whether enforceable or unenforceable, and whether made on his own account or with any other person) or by any other means, and

(b) a reference to a company giving financial assistance for the purposes of reducing or discharging a liability incurred by a person for the purpose of the acquisition of shares includes its giving such assistance for the purpose of wholly or partly restoring his financial position to what it was before the acquisition took place.

CHAPTER 3
REDEEMABLE SHARES

684 Power of limited company to issue redeemable shares

(1) A limited company having a share capital may issue shares that are to be redeemed or are liable to be redeemed at the option of the company or the shareholder ("redeemable shares"), subject to the following provisions.

(2) The articles of a private limited company may exclude or restrict the issue of redeemable shares.

(3) A public limited company may only issue redeemable shares if it is authorised to do so by its articles.

(4) No redeemable shares may be issued at a time when there are no issued shares of the company that are not redeemable.

685 Terms and manner of redemption

(1) The directors of a limited company may determine the terms, conditions and manner of redemption of shares if they are authorised to do so—
 (a) by the company's articles, or
 (b) by a resolution of the company.

(2) A resolution under subsection (1)(b) may be an ordinary resolution, even though it amends the company's articles.

(3) Where the directors are authorised under subsection (1) to determine the terms, conditions and manner of redemption of shares—
 (a) they must do so before the shares are allotted, and
 (b) any obligation of the company to state in a statement of capital the rights attached to the shares extends to the terms, conditions and manner of redemption.

(4) Where the directors are not so authorised, the terms, conditions and manner of redemption of any redeemable shares must be stated in the company's articles.

686 Payment for redeemable shares

(1) Redeemable shares in a limited company may not be redeemed unless they are fully paid.

(2) The terms of redemption of shares in a limited company may provide that the amount payable on redemption may, by agreement between the company and the holder of the shares, be paid on a date later than the redemption date.

(3) Unless redeemed in accordance with a provision authorised by subsection (2), the shares must be paid for on redemption.

687 Financing of redemption

(1) A private limited company may redeem redeemable shares out of capital in accordance with Chapter 5.

(2) Subject to that, redeemable shares in a limited company may only be redeemed out of—
 (a) distributable profits of the company, or
 (b) the proceeds of a fresh issue of shares made for the purposes of the redemption.

(3) Any premium payable on redemption of shares in a limited company must be paid out of distributable profits of the company, subject to the following provision.

(4) If the redeemable shares were issued at a premium, any premium payable on their redemption may be paid out of the proceeds of a fresh issue of shares made for the purposes of the redemption, up to an amount equal to—
 (a) the aggregate of the premiums received by the company on the issue of the shares redeemed, or
 (b) the current amount of the company's share premium account (including any sum transferred to that account in respect of premiums on the new shares),

whichever is the less.

(5) The amount of the company's share premium account is reduced by a sum corresponding (or by sums in the aggregate corresponding) to the amount of any payment made under subsection (4).
(6) This section is subject to section 735(4) (terms of redemption enforceable in a winding up).

688 Redeemed shares treated as cancelled

Where shares in a limited company are redeemed—
- (a) the shares are treated as cancelled, and
- (b) the amount of the company's issued share capital is diminished accordingly by the nominal value of the shares redeemed.

689 Notice to registrar of redemption

(1) If a limited company redeems any redeemable shares it must within one month after doing so give notice to the registrar, specifying the shares redeemed.
(2) The notice must be accompanied by a statement of capital.
(3) The statement of capital must state with respect to the company's share capital immediately following the redemption—
- (a) the total number of shares of the company,
- (b) the aggregate nominal value of those shares,
- (c) for each class of shares—
  - (i) prescribed particulars of the rights attached to the shares,
  - (ii) the total number of shares of that class, and
  - (iii) the aggregate nominal value of shares of that class, and
- (d) the amount paid up and the amount (if any) unpaid on each share (whether on account of the nominal value of the share or by way of premium).

(4) If default is made in complying with this section, an offence is committed by—
- (a) the company, and
- (b) every officer of the company who is in default.

(5) A person guilty of an offence under this section is liable on summary conviction to a fine not exceeding level 3 on the standard scale and, for continued contravention, a daily default fine not exceeding one-tenth of level 3 on the standard scale.

CHAPTER 4
PURCHASE OF OWN SHARES

General provisions

690 Power of limited company to purchase own shares

(1) A limited company having a share capital may purchase its own shares (including any redeemable shares), subject to—
- (a) the following provisions of this Chapter, and
- (b) any restriction or prohibition in the company's articles.

(2) A limited company may not purchase its own shares if as a result of the purchase there would no longer be any issued shares of the company other than redeemable shares or shares held as treasury shares.

691 Payment for purchase of own shares

(1) A limited company may not purchase its own shares unless they are fully paid.
(2) Where a limited company purchases its own shares, the shares must be paid for on purchase.
(3) But subsection (2) does not apply in a case where a private limited company is purchasing shares for the purposes of or pursuant to an employees' share scheme.

692 Financing of purchase of own shares

(1) A private limited company may purchase its own shares out of capital in accordance with Chapter 5.

(1ZA) If authorised to do so by its articles, a private limited company may purchase its own shares out of capital otherwise than in accordance with Chapter 5, up to an aggregate purchase price in a financial year of the lower of—
- (a) £15,000, or
- (b) the nominal value of 5% of its fully paid share capital as at the beginning of the financial year.

(1A) If the share capital of the company is not denominated in sterling, the value in sterling of the share capital shall be calculated for the purposes of subsection (1ZA)(b) at an appropriate spot rate of exchange.

(1B) The rate must be a rate prevailing on a day specified in the resolution authorising the purchase of the shares.

(2) Subject to subsections (1) and (1ZA)—
- (a) a limited company may only purchase its own shares out of—
  - (i) distributable profits of the company, or
  - (ii) the proceeds of a fresh issue of shares made for the purpose of financing the purchase, and
- (b) any premium payable on the purchase by a limited company of its own shares must be paid out of distributable profits of the company, subject to subsection (3).

(3) If the shares to be purchased were issued at a premium, any premium payable on their purchase by the company may be paid out of the proceeds of a fresh issue of shares made for the purpose of financing the purchase, up to an amount equal to—
- (a) the aggregate of the premiums received by the company on the issue of the shares purchased, or
- (b) the current amount of the company's share premium account (including any sum transferred to that account in respect of premiums on the new shares),

whichever is the less.

(4) The amount of the company's share premium account is reduced by a sum corresponding (or by sums in the aggregate corresponding) to the amount of any payment made under subsection (3).

(5) This section has effect subject to section 735(4) (terms of purchase enforceable in a winding up).

Authority for purchase of own shares

693 Authority for purchase of own shares

(1) A limited company may only purchase its own shares—
- (a) by an off-market purchase, authorised in accordance with section 693A or in pursuance of a contract approved in advance in accordance with section 694;
- (b) by a market purchase, authorised in accordance with section 701.

(2) A purchase is "off-market" if the shares either—
- (a) are purchased otherwise than on a recognised investment exchange, or
- (b) are purchased on a recognised investment exchange but are not subject to a marketing arrangement on the exchange.

(3) For this purpose a company's shares are subject to a marketing arrangement on a recognised investment exchange if—
- (a) they are listed under Part 6 of the Financial Services and Markets Act 2000, or
- (b) the company has been afforded facilities for dealings in the shares to take place on the exchange—
  - (i) without prior permission for individual transactions from the authority governing that investment exchange, and
  - (ii) without limit as to the time during which those facilities are to be available.

(4) A purchase is a "market purchase" if it is made on a recognised investment exchange and is not an off-market purchase by virtue of subsection (2)(b).

(5) In this section "recognised investment exchange" means a recognised investment exchange (within the meaning of Part 18 of the Financial Services and Markets Act 2000) other than an overseas exchange (within the meaning of that Part).

693A Authority for off-market purchase for the purposes of or pursuant to an employees' share scheme

(1) A company may make an off-market purchase of its own shares for the purposes of or pursuant to an employees' share scheme if the purchase has first been authorised by a resolution of the company under this section.

(2) That authority—

(a) may be general or limited to the purchase of shares of a particular class or description, and

(b) may be unconditional or subject to conditions.

(3) The authority must—

(a) specify the maximum number of shares authorised to be acquired, and

(b) determine both the maximum and minimum prices that may be paid for the shares.

(4) The authority may be varied, revoked or from time to time renewed by a resolution of the company.

(5) A resolution conferring, varying or renewing authority must specify a date on which it is to expire, which must not be later than five years after the date on which the resolution is passed.

(6) A company may make a purchase of its own shares after the expiry of the time limit specified if—

(a) the contract of purchase was concluded before the authority expired, and

(b) the terms of the authority permitted the company to make a contract of purchase that would or might be executed wholly or partly after its expiration.

(7) A resolution to confer or vary authority under this section may determine the maximum or minimum price for purchase by—

(a) specifying a particular sum, or

(b) providing a basis or formula for calculating the amount of the price (but without reference to any person's discretion or opinion).

(8) Chapter 3 of Part 3 (resolutions affecting a company's constitution) applies to a resolution under this section.

Authority for off-market purchase

694 Authority for off-market purchase

(1) Subject to section 693A, a company may only make an off-market purchase of its own shares in pursuance of a contract approved prior to the purchase in accordance with this section.

(2) Either—

(a) the terms of the contract must be authorised by a resolution of the company before the contract is entered into, or

(b) the contract must provide that no shares may be purchased in pursuance of the contract until its terms have been authorised by a resolution of the company.

(3) The contract may be a contract, entered into by the company and relating to shares in the company, that does not amount to a contract to purchase the shares but under which the company may (subject to any conditions) become entitled or obliged to purchase the shares.

(4) The authority conferred by a resolution under this section may be varied, revoked or from time to time renewed by a resolution of the company.

(5) In the case of a public company a resolution conferring, varying or renewing authority must specify a date on which the authority is to expire, which must not be later than five years after the date on which the resolution is passed.

(6) A resolution conferring, varying, revoking or renewing authority under this section is subject to—

section 695 (exercise of voting rights), and

section 696 (disclosure of details of contract).

695 Resolution authorising off-market purchase: exercise of voting rights

(1) This section applies to a resolution to confer, vary, revoke or renew authority for the purposes of section 694 (authority for off-market purchase of own shares).

(2) Where the resolution is proposed as a written resolution, a member who holds shares to which the resolution relates is not an eligible member.

(3) Where the resolution is proposed at a meeting of the company, it is not effective if—

(a) any member of the company holding shares to which the resolution relates exercises the voting rights carried by any of those shares in voting on the resolution, and

(b) the resolution would not have been passed if he had not done so.

(4) For this purpose—

(a) a member who holds shares to which the resolution relates is regarded as exercising the voting rights carried by those shares not only if he votes in respect of them on a poll on the question whether the resolution shall be passed, but also if he votes on the resolution otherwise than on a poll;

(b) any member of the company may demand a poll on that question;

(c) a vote and a demand for a poll by a person as proxy for a member are the same respectively as a vote and a demand by the member.

696 Resolution authorising off-market purchase: disclosure of details of contract

(1) This section applies in relation to a resolution to confer, vary, revoke or renew authority for the purposes of section 694 (authority for off-market purchase of own shares).

(2) A copy of the contract (if it is in writing) or a memorandum setting out its terms (if it is not) must be made available to members—

(a) in the case of a written resolution, by being sent or submitted to every eligible member at or before the time at which the proposed resolution is sent or submitted to him;

(b) in the case of a resolution at a meeting, by being made available for inspection by members of the company both—

(i) at the company's registered office for not less than 15 days ending with the date of the meeting, and

(ii) at the meeting itself.

(3) A memorandum of contract terms so made available must include the names of the members holding shares to which the contract relates.

(4) A copy of the contract so made available must have annexed to it a written memorandum specifying such of those names as do not appear in the contract itself.

(5) The resolution is not validly passed if the requirements of this section are not complied with

697 Variation of contract for off-market purchase

(1) A company may only agree to a variation of a contract authorised under section 694 (authority for off-market purchase) if the variation is approved in advance in accordance with this section.

(2) The terms of the variation must be authorised by a resolution of the company before it is agreed to.

(3) That authority may be varied, revoked or from time to time renewed by a resolution of the company.

(4) In the case of a public company a resolution conferring, varying or renewing authority must specify a date on which the authority is to expire, which must not be later than five years after the date on which the resolution is passed.

(5) A resolution conferring, varying, revoking or renewing authority under this section is subject to—

section 698 (exercise of voting rights), and

section 699 (disclosure of details of variation).

698 Resolution authorising variation: exercise of voting rights

(1) This section applies to a resolution to confer, vary, revoke or renew authority for the purposes of section 697 (variation of contract for off-market purchase of own shares).

(2) Where the resolution is proposed as a written resolution, a member who holds shares to which the resolution relates is not an eligible member.

(3) Where the resolution is proposed at a meeting of the company, it is not effective if—

(a) any member of the company holding shares to which the resolution relates exercises the voting rights carried by any of those shares in voting on the resolution, and

(b) the resolution would not have been passed if he had not done so.

(4) For this purpose—

(a) a member who holds shares to which the resolution relates is regarded as exercising the voting rights carried by those shares not only if he votes in respect of them on a poll on the question whether the resolution shall be passed, but also if he votes on the resolution otherwise than on a poll;

(b) any member of the company may demand a poll on that question;

(c) a vote and a demand for a poll by a person as proxy for a member are the same respectively as a vote and a demand by the member.

699 Resolution authorising variation: disclosure of details of variation

(1) This section applies in relation to a resolution under section 697 (variation of contract for off-market purchase of own shares).

(2) A copy of the proposed variation (if it is in writing) or a written memorandum giving details of the proposed variation (if it is not) must be made available to members—

(a) in the case of a written resolution, by being sent or submitted to every eligible member at or before the time at which the proposed resolution is sent or submitted to him;

(b) in the case of a resolution at a meeting, by being made available for inspection by members of the company both—

(i) at the company's registered office for not less than 15 days ending with the date of the meeting, and

(ii) at the meeting itself.

(3) There must also be made available as mentioned in subsection (2) a copy of the original contract or, as the case may be, a memorandum of its terms, together with any variations previously made.

(4) A memorandum of the proposed variation so made available must include the names of the members holding shares to which the variation relates.

(5) A copy of the proposed variation so made available must have annexed to it a written memorandum specifying such of those names as do not appear in the variation itself.

(6) The resolution is not validly passed if the requirements of this section are not complied with.

700 Release of company's rights under contract for off-market purchase

(1) An agreement by a company to release its rights under a contract approved under section 694 (authorisation of off-market purchase) is void unless the terms of the release agreement are approved in advance in accordance with this section.

(2) The terms of the proposed agreement must be authorised by a resolution of the company before the agreement is entered into.

(3) That authority may be varied, revoked or from time to time renewed by a resolution of the company.

(4) In the case of a public company a resolution conferring, varying or renewing authority must specify a date on which the authority is to expire, which must not be later than five years after the date on which the resolution is passed.

(5) The provisions of—

section 698 (exercise of voting rights), and

section 699 (disclosure of details of variation),

apply to a resolution authorising a proposed release agreement as they apply to a resolution authorising a proposed variation.

Authority for market purchase

701 Authority for market purchase

(1) A company may only make a market purchase of its own shares if the purchase has first been authorised by a resolution of the company.

(2) That authority—

(a) may be general or limited to the purchase of shares of a particular class or description, and

(b) may be unconditional or subject to conditions.

(3) The authority must—

(a) specify the maximum number of shares authorised to be acquired, and

(b) determine both the maximum and minimum prices that may be paid for the shares.

(4) The authority may be varied, revoked or from time to time renewed by a resolution of the company.

(5) A resolution conferring, varying or renewing authority must specify a date on which it is to expire, which must not be later than five years after the date on which the resolution is passed.

(6) A company may make a purchase of its own shares after the expiry of the time limit specified if—
  (a) the contract of purchase was concluded before the authority expired, and
  (b) the terms of the authority permitted the company to make a contract of purchase that would or might be executed wholly or partly after its expiration.

(7) A resolution to confer or vary authority under this section may determine either or both the maximum and minimum price for purchase by—
  (a) specifying a particular sum, or
  (b) providing a basis or formula for calculating the amount of the price (but without reference to any person's discretion or opinion).

(8) Chapter 3 of Part 3 (resolutions affecting a company's constitution) applies to a resolution under this section.

Supplementary provisions

702 Copy of contract or memorandum to be available for inspection

(1) This section applies where a company has entered into—
  (a) a contract approved under section 694 (authorisation of contract for off-market purchase), or
  (b) a contract for a purchase authorised under section 701 (authorisation of market purchase).

(2) The company must keep available for inspection—
  (a) a copy of the contract, or
  (b) if the contract is not in writing, a written memorandum setting out its terms.

(3) The copy or memorandum must be kept available for inspection from the conclusion of the contract until the end of the period of ten years beginning with—
  (a) the date on which the purchase of all the shares in pursuance of the contract is completed, or
  (b) the date on which the contract otherwise determines.

(4) The copy or memorandum must be kept available for inspection—
  (a) at the company's registered office, or
  (b) at a place specified in regulations under section 1136.

(5) The company must give notice to the registrar—
  (a) of the place at which the copy or memorandum is kept available for inspection, and
  (b) of any change in that place,

unless it has at all times been kept at the company's registered office.

(6) Every copy or memorandum required to be kept under this section must be kept open to inspection without charge—
  (a) by any member of the company, and
  (b) in the case of a public company, by any other person.

(7) The provisions of this section apply to a variation of a contract as they apply to the original contract.

703 Enforcement of right to inspect copy or memorandum

(1) If default is made in complying with section 702(2), (3) or (4) or default is made for 14 days in complying with section 702(5), or an inspection required under section 702(6) is refused, an offence is committed by—
  (a) the company, and
  (b) every officer of the company who is in default.

(2) A person guilty of an offence under this section is liable on summary conviction to a fine not exceeding level 3 on the standard scale and, for continued contravention, a daily default fine not exceeding one-tenth of level 3 on the standard scale.

(3) In the case of refusal of an inspection required under section 702(6) the court may by order compel an immediate inspection.

704 No assignment of company's right to purchase own shares

The rights of a company under a contract authorised under—
  (za) section 693A (authority for off-market purchase for the purposes of or pursuant to an employees' share scheme),
  (a) section 694 (authority for off-market purchase), or

(b) section 701 (authority for market purchase)
are not capable of being assigned.

705 Payments apart from purchase price to be made out of distributable profits

(1) A payment made by a company in consideration of—
(a) acquiring any right with respect to the purchase of its own shares in pursuance of a contingent purchase contract approved under section 694 (authorisation of off-market purchase),
(b) the variation of any contract approved under that section, or
(c) the release of any of the company's obligations with respect to the purchase of any of its own shares under a contract—
(i) approved under section 694, or
(ii) authorised under section 701 (authorisation of market purchase),
must be made out of the company's distributable profits.
(2) If this requirement is not met in relation to a contract, then—
(a) in a case within subsection (1)(a), no purchase by the company of its own shares in pursuance of that contract may be made under this Chapter;
(b) in a case within subsection (1)(b), no such purchase following the variation may be made under this Chapter;
(c) in a case within subsection (1)(c), the purported release is void.

706 Treatment of shares purchased

Where a limited company makes a purchase of its own shares in accordance with this Chapter, then—
(a) if section 724 (treasury shares) applies, the shares may be held and dealt with in accordance with Chapter 6;
(b) if that section does not apply—
(i) the shares are treated as cancelled, and
(ii) the amount of the company's issued share capital is diminished accordingly by the nominal value of the shares cancelled.

707 Return to registrar of purchase of own shares

(1) Where a company purchases shares under this Chapter, it must deliver a return to the registrar within the period of 28 days beginning with the date on which the shares are delivered to it.
(2) The return must distinguish—
(a) shares in relation to which section 724 (treasury shares) applies and shares in relation to which that section does not apply, and
(b) shares in relation to which that section applies—
(i) that are cancelled forthwith (under section 729 (cancellation of treasury shares)), and
(ii) that are not so cancelled.
(3) The return must state, with respect to shares of each class purchased—
(a) the number and nominal value of the shares, and
(b) the date on which they were delivered to the company.
(4) In the case of a public company the return must also state—
(a) the aggregate amount paid by the company for the shares, and
(b) the maximum and minimum prices paid in respect of shares of each class purchased.
(5) Particulars of shares delivered to the company on different dates and under different contracts may be included in a single return.
In such a case the amount required to be stated under subsection (4)(a) is the aggregate amount paid by the company for all the shares to which the return relates.
(6) If default is made in complying with this section an offence is committed by every officer of the company who is in default.

Version applying in Scotland

(7) A person guilty of an offence under this section is liable—
(a) on conviction on indictment, to a fine;
(b) on summary conviction to a fine not exceeding the statutory maximum and, for continued contravention, a daily default fine not exceeding one-tenth of the statutory maximum.

Version applying in England and Wales

(7) A person guilty of an offence under this section is liable on summary conviction to a fine not exceeding level 5 on the standard scale and, for continued contravention, a daily default fine not exceeding one-tenth of the greater of £5,000 or level 4 on the standard scale.

708 Notice to registrar of cancellation of shares

(1) If on the purchase by a company of any of its own shares in accordance with this Part—
 (a) section 724 (treasury shares) does not apply (so that the shares are treated as cancelled), or
 (b) that section applies but the shares are cancelled forthwith (under section 729 (cancellation of treasury shares)),

the company must give notice of cancellation to the registrar, within the period of 28 days beginning with the date on which the shares are delivered to it, specifying the shares cancelled.

(2) The notice must be accompanied by a statement of capital, except where the statement of capital would be the same as a statement of capital that is required to be delivered to the registrar under section 720B(1).

(3) The statement of capital must state with respect to the company's share capital immediately following the cancellation—
 (a) the total number of shares of the company,
 (b) the aggregate nominal value of those shares,
 (c) for each class of shares—
  (i) prescribed particulars of the rights attached to the shares,
  (ii) the total number of shares of that class, and
  (iii) the aggregate nominal value of shares of that class, and
 (d) the amount paid up and the amount (if any) unpaid on each share (whether on account of the nominal value of the share or by way of premium).

(4) If default is made in complying with this section, an offence is committed by—
 (a) the company, and
 (b) every officer of the company who is in default.

(5) A person guilty of an offence under this section is liable on summary conviction to a fine not exceeding level 3 on the standard scale and, for continued contravention, a daily default fine not exceeding one-tenth of level 3 on the standard scale.

CHAPTER 5
REDEMPTION OR PURCHASE BY PRIVATE COMPANY OUT OF CAPITAL

Introductory

709 Power of private limited company to redeem or purchase own shares out of capital

(1) A private limited company may in accordance with this Chapter, but subject to any restriction or prohibition in the company's articles, make a payment in respect of the redemption or purchase of its own shares otherwise than out of distributable profits or the proceeds of a fresh issue of shares.

(2) References below in this Chapter to payment out of capital are to any payment so made, whether or not it would be regarded apart from this section as a payment out of capital.

(3) This Chapter is subject to section 692(1ZA) (purchase of own shares up to annual limit).

The permissible capital payment

710 The permissible capital payment

(1) The payment that may, in accordance with this Chapter, be made by a company out of capital in respect of the redemption or purchase of its own shares is such amount as, after applying for that purpose—
 (a) any available profits of the company, and
 (b) the proceeds of any fresh issue of shares made for the purposes of the redemption or purchase,

is required to meet the price of redemption or purchase.

(2) That is referred to below in this Chapter as "the permissible capital payment" for the shares.

711 Available profits

(1) For the purposes of this Chapter the available profits of the company, in relation to the redemption or purchase of any shares, are the profits of the company that are available for distribution (within the meaning of Part 23).

(2) But the question whether a company has any profits so available, and the amount of any such profits, shall be determined in accordance with section 712 instead of in accordance with sections 836 to 842 in that Part.

712 Determination of available profits

(1) The available profits of the company are determined as follows.

(2) First, determine the profits of the company by reference to the following items as stated in the relevant accounts—
- (a) profits, losses, assets and liabilities,
- (b) provisions of the following kinds—
  - (i) where the relevant accounts are Companies Act accounts, provisions of a kind specified for the purposes of this subsection by regulations under section 396;
  - (ii) where the relevant accounts are IAS accounts, provisions of any kind;
- (c) share capital and reserves (including undistributable reserves).

(3) Second, reduce the amount so determined by the amount of—
- (a) any distribution lawfully made by the company, and
- (b) any other relevant payment lawfully made by the company out of distributable profits,

after the date of the relevant accounts and before the end of the relevant period.

(4) For this purpose "other relevant payment lawfully made" includes—
- (a) financial assistance lawfully given out of distributable profits in accordance with Chapter 2,
- (b) payments lawfully made out of distributable profits in respect of the purchase by the company of any shares in the company, and
- (c) payments of any description specified in section 705 (payments other than purchase price to be made out of distributable profits) lawfully made by the company.

(5) The resulting figure is the amount of available profits.

(6) For the purposes of this section "the relevant accounts" are any accounts that—
- (a) are prepared as at a date within the relevant period, and
- (b) are such as to enable a reasonable judgment to be made as to the amounts of the items mentioned in subsection (2).

(7) In this section "the relevant period" means the period of three months ending with the date on which the solvency statement is made in accordance with section 720A or the directors' statement is made in accordance with section 714.

Requirements for payment out of capital

713 Requirements for payment out of capital

(1) A payment out of capital by a private company for the redemption or purchase of its own shares is not lawful unless the requirements of the following sections are met—

section 714 (directors' statement and auditor's report);
section 716 (approval by special resolution);
section 719 (public notice of proposed payment);
section 720 (directors' statement and auditor's report to be available for inspection).

(2) This is subject to section 720A to any order of the court under section 721 (power of court to extend period for compliance on application by persons objecting to payment).

714 Directors' statement and auditor's report

(1) The company's directors must make a statement in accordance with this section.

(2) The statement must specify the amount of the permissible capital payment for the shares in question.

(3) It must state that, having made full inquiry into the affairs and prospects of the company, the directors have formed the opinion—

(a) as regards its initial situation immediately following the date on which the payment out of capital is proposed to be made, that there will be no grounds on which the company could then be found unable to pay its debts, and
(b) as regards its prospects for the year immediately following that date, that having regard to—
(i) their intentions with respect to the management of the company's business during that year, and
(ii) the amount and character of the financial resources that will in their view be available to the company during that year,

the company will be able to continue to carry on business as a going concern (and will accordingly be able to pay its debts as they fall due) throughout that year.

(4) In forming their opinion for the purposes of subsection (3)(a), the directors must take into account all of the company's liabilities (including any contingent or prospective liabilities).

(5) The directors' statement must be in the prescribed form and must contain such information with respect to the nature of the company's business as may be prescribed.

(6) It must in addition have annexed to it a report addressed to the directors by the company's auditor stating that—
(a) he has inquired into the company's state of affairs,
(b) the amount specified in the statement as the permissible capital payment for the shares in question is in his view properly determined in accordance with sections 710 to 712, and
(c) he is not aware of anything to indicate that the opinion expressed by the directors in their statement as to any of the matters mentioned in subsection (3) above is unreasonable in all the circumstances.

715 Directors' statement: offence if no reasonable grounds for opinion

(1) If the directors make a statement under section 714 without having reasonable grounds for the opinion expressed in it, an offence is committed by every director who is in default.

(2) A person guilty of an offence under this section is liable—
(a) on conviction on indictment, to imprisonment for a term not exceeding two years or a fine (or both);
(b) on summary conviction—
(i) in England and Wales, to imprisonment for a term not exceeding twelve months or a fine not exceeding the statutory maximum (or both);
(ii) in Scotland or Northern Ireland, to imprisonment for a term not exceeding six months or a fine not exceeding the statutory maximum (or both).

716 Payment to be approved by special resolution

(1) The payment out of capital must be approved by a special resolution of the company.

(2) The resolution must be passed on, or within the week immediately following, the date on which the directors make the statement required by section 714.

(3) A resolution under this section is subject to—
section 717 (exercise of voting rights), and
section 718 (disclosure of directors' statement and auditors' report).

717 Resolution authorising payment: exercise of voting rights

(1) This section applies to a resolution under section 716 (authority for payment out of capital for redemption or purchase of own shares).

(2) Where the resolution is proposed as a written resolution, a member who holds shares to which the resolution relates is not an eligible member.

(3) Where the resolution is proposed at a meeting of the company, it is not effective if—
(a) any member of the company holding shares to which the resolution relates exercises the voting rights carried by any of those shares in voting on the resolution, and
(b) the resolution would not have been passed if he had not done so.

(4) For this purpose—
(a) a member who holds shares to which the resolution relates is regarded as exercising the voting rights carried by those shares not only if he votes in respect of them on a poll on the question whether the resolution shall be passed, but also if he votes on the resolution otherwise than on a poll;

(b) any member of the company may demand a poll on that question;

(c) a vote and a demand for a poll by a person as proxy for a member are the same respectively as a vote and a demand by the member.

718 Resolution authorising payment: disclosure of directors' statement and auditor's report

(1) This section applies to a resolution under section 716 (resolution authorising payment out of capital for redemption or purchase of own shares).

(2) A copy of the directors' statement and auditor's report under section 714 must be made available to members—

(a) in the case of a written resolution, by being sent or submitted to every eligible member at or before the time at which the proposed resolution is sent or submitted to him;

(b) in the case of a resolution at a meeting, by being made available for inspection by members of the company at the meeting.

(3) The resolution is ineffective if this requirement is not complied with.

719 Public notice of proposed payment

(1) Within the week immediately following the date of the resolution under section 716 the company must cause to be published in the Gazette a notice—

(a) stating that the company has approved a payment out of capital for the purpose of acquiring its own shares by redemption or purchase or both (as the case may be),

(b) specifying—

(i) the amount of the permissible capital payment for the shares in question, and

(ii) the date of the resolution,

(c) stating where the directors' statement and auditor's report required by section 714 are available for inspection, and

(d) stating that any creditor of the company may at any time within the five weeks immediately following the date of the resolution apply to the court under section 721 for an order preventing the payment.

(2) Within the week immediately following the date of the resolution the company must also either—

(a) cause a notice to the same effect as that required by subsection (1) to be published in an appropriate national newspaper, or

(b) give notice in writing to that effect to each of its creditors.

(3) "An appropriate national newspaper" means a newspaper circulating throughout the part of the United Kingdom in which the company is registered.

(4) Not later than the day on which the company—

(a) first publishes the notice required by subsection (1), or

(b) if earlier, first publishes or gives the notice required by subsection (2),

the company must deliver to the registrar a copy of the directors' statement and auditor's report required by section 714.

720 Directors' statement and auditor's report to be available for inspection

(1) The directors' statement and auditor's report must be kept available for inspection throughout the period—

(a) beginning with the day on which the company—

(i) first publishes the notice required by section 719(1), or

(ii) if earlier, first publishes or gives the notice required by section 719(2), and

(b) ending five weeks after the date of the resolution for payment out of capital.

(2) They must be kept available for inspection—

(a) at the company's registered office, or

(b) at a place specified in regulations under section 1136.

(3) The company must give notice to the registrar—

(a) of the place at which the statement and report are kept available for inspection, and

(b) of any change in that place,

unless they have at all times been kept at the company's registered office.

(4) They must be open to the inspection of any member or creditor of the company without charge.

(5) If default is made for 14 days in complying with subsection (3), or an inspection under subsection (4) is refused, an offence is committed by—
(a) the company, and
(b) every officer of the company who is in default.

(6) A person guilty of an offence under this section is liable on summary conviction to a fine not exceeding level 3 on the standard scale and, for continued contravention, a daily default fine not exceeding one-tenth of level 3 on the standard scale.

(7) In the case of a refusal of an inspection required by subsection (4), the court may by order compel an immediate inspection.

Requirements for payment out of capital: employees' share schemes

720A Reduced requirements for payment out of capital for purchase of own shares for the purposes of or pursuant to an employees' share scheme

(1) Section 713(1) does not apply to the purchase out of capital by a private company of its own shares for the purposes of or pursuant to an employees' share scheme when approved by special resolution supported by a solvency statement.

(2) For the purposes of this section a resolution is supported by a solvency statement if—
(a) the directors of the company make a solvency statement (see section 643) not more than 15 days before the date on which the resolution is passed, and
(b) the resolution and solvency statement are registered in accordance with section 720B.

(3) Where the resolution is proposed as a written resolution, a copy of the solvency statement must be sent or submitted to every eligible member at or before the time at which the proposed resolution is sent or submitted to the member.

(4) Where the resolution is proposed at a general meeting, a copy of the solvency statement must be made available for inspection by members of the company throughout that meeting.

(5) The validity of a resolution is not affected by a failure to comply with subsection (3) or (4).

(6) Section 717 (resolution authorising payment: exercise of voting rights) applies to a resolution under this section as it applies to a resolution under section 716.

720B Registration of resolution and supporting documents for purchase of own shares for the purposes of or pursuant to an employees' share scheme

(1) Within 15 days after the passing of the resolution for a payment out of capital by a private company for the purchase of its own shares for the purposes of or pursuant to an employees' share scheme the company must deliver to the registrar–
(a) a copy of the solvency statement,
(b) a copy of the resolution, and
(c) a statement of capital.

(2) The statement of capital must state with respect to the company's share capital as reduced by the resolution—
(a) the total number of shares of the company,
(b) the aggregate nominal value of those shares,
(c) for each class of shares—
(i) prescribed particulars of the rights attached to the shares,
(ii) the total number of shares of that class, and
(iii) the aggregate nominal value of shares of that class, and
(d) the amount paid up and the amount (if any) unpaid on each share (whether on account of the nominal value of the share of by way of premium).

(3) The registrar must register the documents delivered to him under subsection (1) on receipt.

(4) The resolution does not take effect until those documents are registered.

(5) The company must also deliver to the registrar, within 15 days after the resolution is passed, a statement by the directors confirming that the solvency statement was—
(a) made not more than 15 days before the date on which the resolution was passed, and
(b) provided to members in accordance with section 720A(3) or (4).

(6) The validity of a resolution is not affected by—
(a) a failure to deliver the documents required to be delivered to the registrar under subsection (1) within the time specified in that subsection, or

(b) a failure to comply with subsection (5).

(7) If the company delivers to the registrar a solvency statement that was not provided to members in accordance with section 720A(3) or (4), an offence is committed by every officer of the company who is in default.

(8) If default is made in complying with this section, an offence is committed by–

(a) the company, and

(b) every officer of the company who is in default.

(9) A person guilty of an offence under subsection (7) or (8) is liable–

(a) on conviction on indictment, to a fine;

(b) on summary conviction, to a fine not exceeding the statutory maximum.

Objection to payment by members or creditors

721 Application to court to cancel resolution

(1) Where a private company passes a special resolution approving a payment out of capital for the redemption or purchase of any of its shares—

(a) any member of the company (other than one who consented to or voted in favour of the resolution), and

(b) any creditor of the company,

may apply to the court for the cancellation of the resolution.

(2) The application—

(a) must be made within five weeks after the passing of the resolution, and

(b) may be made on behalf of the persons entitled to make it by such one or more of their number as they may appoint in writing for the purpose.

(3) On an application under this section the court may if it thinks fit—

(a) adjourn the proceedings in order that an arrangement may be made to the satisfaction of the court—

(i) for the purchase of the interests of dissentient members, or

(ii) for the protection of dissentient creditors, and

(b) give such directions and make such orders as it thinks expedient for facilitating or carrying into effect any such arrangement.

(4) Subject to that, the court must make an order either cancelling or confirming the resolution, and may do so on such terms and conditions as it thinks fit.

(5) If the court confirms the resolution, it may by order alter or extend any date or period of time specified—

(a) in the resolution, or

(b) in any provision of this Chapter applying to the redemption or purchase to which the resolution relates.

(6) The court's order may, if the court thinks fit—

(a) provide for the purchase by the company of the shares of any of its members and for the reduction accordingly of the company's capital, and

(b) make any alteration in the company's articles that may be required in consequence of that provision.

(7) The court's order may, if the court thinks fit, require the company not to make any, or any specified, amendments of its articles without the leave of the court.

722 Notice to registrar of court application or order

(1) On making an application under section 721 (application to court to cancel resolution) the applicants, or the person making the application on their behalf, must immediately give notice to the registrar.

This is without prejudice to any provision of rules of court as to service of notice of the application.

(2) On being served with notice of any such application, the company must immediately give notice to the registrar.

(3) Within 15 days of the making of the court's order on the application, or such longer period as the court may at any time direct, the company must deliver to the registrar a copy of the order.

(4) If a company fails to comply with subsection (2) or (3) an offence is committed by—

(a) the company, and

(b) every officer of the company who is in default.

(5) A person guilty of an offence under this section is liable on summary conviction to a fine not exceeding level 3 on the standard scale and, for continued contravention, a daily default fine not exceeding one-tenth of level 3 on the standard scale.

Supplementary provisions

723 Time when payment out of capital to be made or shares to be surrendered

(1) The payment out of capital, if made in accordance with a resolution under section 716 must be made—
- (a) no earlier than five weeks after the date on which the resolution under section 716 is passed, and
- (b) no more than seven weeks after that date.

(1A) Shares to be purchased in accordance with a resolution under section 720A must be surrendered—
- (a) no earlier than five weeks after the date on which the resolution under section 720A is passed, and
- (b) no later than seven weeks after that date.

(2) This is subject to any exercise of the court's powers under section 721(5) (power to alter or extend time where resolution confirmed after objection).

CHAPTER 6
TREASURY SHARES

724 Treasury shares

(1) This section applies where—
- (a) a limited company makes a purchase of its own shares in accordance with Chapter 4, and
- (b) the purchase is made out of distributable profits.

(2) …

(3) Where this section applies the company may—
- (a) hold the shares (or any of them), or
- (b) deal with any of them, at any time, in accordance with section 727 or 729.

(4) Where shares are held by the company, the company must be entered in its register of members as the member holding the shares.

(5) In the Companies Acts references to a company holding shares as treasury shares are to the company holding shares that—
- (a) were (or are treated as having been) purchased by it in circumstances in which this section applies, and
- (b) have been held by the company continuously since they were so purchased (or treated as purchased).

725 …

726 Treasury shares: exercise of rights

(1) This section applies where shares are held by a company as treasury shares.

(2) The company must not exercise any right in respect of the treasury shares, and any purported exercise of such a right is void.
This applies, in particular, to any right to attend or vote at meetings.

(3) No dividend may be paid, and no other distribution (whether in cash or otherwise) of the company's assets (including any distribution of assets to members on a winding up) may be made to the company, in respect of the treasury shares.

(4) Nothing in this section prevents—
- (a) an allotment of shares as fully paid bonus shares in respect of the treasury shares, or
- (b) the payment of any amount payable on the redemption of the treasury shares (if they are redeemable shares).

(5) Shares allotted as fully paid bonus shares in respect of the treasury shares are treated as if purchased by the company, at the time they were allotted, in circumstances in which section 724(1) (treasury shares) applied.

727 Treasury shares: disposal

(1) Where shares are held as treasury shares, the company may at any time—
   (a) sell the shares (or any of them) for a cash consideration, or
   (b) transfer the shares (or any of them) for the purposes of or pursuant to an employees' share scheme.

(2) In subsection (1)(a) "cash consideration" means—
   (a) cash received by the company, or
   (b) a cheque received by the company in good faith that the directors have no reason for suspecting will not be paid, or
   (c) a release of a liability of the company for a liquidated sum, or
   (d) an undertaking to pay cash to the company on or before a date not more than 90 days after the date on which the company agrees to sell the shares, or
   (e) payment by any other means giving rise to a present or future entitlement (of the company or a person acting on the company's behalf) to a payment, or credit equivalent to payment, in cash.

   For this purpose "cash" includes foreign currency.

(3) The Secretary of State may by order provide that particular means of payment specified in the order are to be regarded as falling within subsection (2)(e).

(4) If the company receives a notice under section 979 (takeover offers: right of offeror to buy out minority shareholders) that a person desires to acquire shares held by the company as treasury shares, the company must not sell or transfer the shares to which the notice relates except to that person.

(5) An order under this section is subject to negative resolution procedure.

728 Treasury shares: notice of disposal

(1) Where shares held by a company as treasury shares—
   (a) are sold, or
   (b) are transferred for the purposes of an employees' share scheme,

   the company must deliver a return to the registrar not later than 28 days after the shares are disposed of.

(2) The return must state with respect to shares of each class disposed of—
   (a) the number and nominal value of the shares, and
   (b) the date on which they were disposed of.

(3) Particulars of shares disposed of on different dates may be included in a single return.

(4) If default is made in complying with this section an offence is committed by every officer of the company who is in default.

Version applying in Scotland

(5) A person guilty of an offence under this section is liable—
   (a) on conviction on indictment, to a fine;
   (b) on summary conviction, to a fine not exceeding the statutory maximum and, for continued contravention, a daily default fine not exceeding one-tenth of the statutory maximum.

Version applying in England and Wales

(5) A person guilty of an offence under this section is liable on summary conviction to a fine not exceeding level 5 on the standard scale and, for continued contravention, a daily default fine not exceeding one-tenth of the greater of £5,000 or level 4 on the standard scale.

729 Treasury shares: cancellation

(1) Where shares are held as treasury shares, the company may at any time cancel the shares (or any of them).

(2)–(3) …

(4) If company cancels shares held as treasury shares, the amount of the company's share capital is reduced accordingly by the nominal amount of the shares cancelled.

(5) The directors may take any steps required to enable the company to cancel its shares under this section without complying with the provisions of Chapter 10 of Part 17 (reduction of share capital).

730 Treasury shares: notice of cancellation

(1) Where shares held by a company as treasury shares are cancelled, the company must deliver a return to the registrar not later than 28 days after the shares are cancelled.

   This does not apply to shares that are cancelled forthwith on their acquisition by the company (see section 708).

(2) The return must state with respect to shares of each class cancelled—
(a) the number and nominal value of the shares, and
(b) the date on which they were cancelled.
(3) Particulars of shares cancelled on different dates may be included in a single return.
(4) The notice must be accompanied by a statement of capital.
(5) The statement of capital must state with respect to the company's share capital immediately following the cancellation—
(a) the total number of shares of the company,
(b) the aggregate nominal value of those shares,
(c) for each class of shares—
(i) prescribed particulars of the rights attached to the shares,
(ii) the total number of shares of that class, and
(iii) the aggregate nominal value of shares of that class, and
(d) the amount paid up and the amount (if any) unpaid on each share (whether on account of the nominal value of the share or by way of premium).
(6) If default is made in complying with this section, an offence is committed by—
(a) the company, and
(b) every officer of the company who is in default.
(7) A person guilty of an offence under this section is liable on summary conviction to a fine not exceeding level 3 on the standard scale and, for continued contravention, a daily default fine not exceeding one-tenth of level 3 on the standard scale.

731 Treasury shares: treatment of proceeds of sale

(1) Where shares held as treasury shares are sold, the proceeds of sale must be dealt with in accordance with this section.
(2) If the proceeds of sale are equal to or less than the purchase price paid by the company for the shares, the proceeds are treated for the purposes of Part 23 (distributions) as a realised profit of the company.
(3) If the proceeds of sale exceed the purchase price paid by the company—
(a) an amount equal to the purchase price paid is treated as a realised profit of the company for the purposes of that Part, and
(b) the excess must be transferred to the company's share premium account.
(4) For the purposes of this section—
(a) the purchase price paid by the company must be determined by the application of a weighted average price method, and
(b) if the shares were allotted to the company as fully paid bonus shares, the purchase price paid for them is treated as nil.

732 Treasury shares: offences

(1) If a company contravenes any of the provisions of this Chapter (except section 730 (notice of cancellation)), an offence is committed by—
(a) the company, and
(b) every officer of the company who is in default.
(2) A person guilty of an offence under this section is liable—
(a) on conviction on indictment, to a fine;
(b) on summary conviction to a fine not exceeding the statutory maximum.

CHAPTER 7
SUPPLEMENTARY PROVISIONS

733 The capital redemption reserve

(1) In the following circumstances a company must transfer amounts to a reserve, called the "capital redemption reserve".
(2) Where under this Part shares of a limited company are redeemed or purchased wholly out of the company's profits, the amount by which the company's issued share capital is diminished in accordance with—
(a) section 688(b) (on the cancellation of shares redeemed), or
(b) section 706(b)(ii) (on the cancellation of shares purchased), must be transferred to the capital redemption reserve.

(3) If—
(a) the shares are redeemed or purchased wholly or partly out of the proceeds of a fresh issue, and
(b) the aggregate amount of the proceeds is less than the aggregate nominal value of the shares redeemed or purchased,
the amount of the difference must be transferred to the capital redemption reserve.
This does not apply in the case of a private company if, in addition to the proceeds of the fresh issue, the company applies a payment out of capital under Chapter 5 in making the redemption or purchase.
(4) The amount by which a company's share capital is diminished in accordance with section 729(4) (on the cancellation of shares held as treasury shares) must be transferred to the capital redemption reserve.
(5) The company may use the capital redemption reserve to pay up new shares to be allotted to members as fully paid bonus shares.
(6) Subject to that, the provisions of the Companies Acts relating to the reduction of a company's share capital apply as if the capital redemption reserve were part of its paid up share capital.

734 Accounting consequences of payment out of capital

(1) This section applies where a payment out of capital is made in accordance with Chapter 5 or section 692(1ZA) (redemption or purchase of own shares by private company out of capital).
(1A) In relation to a payment under section 692(1ZA) references to the permissible capital payment are to the purchase price of the shares or (if less) the part of it met out of the payment under section 692(1ZA) and any proceeds of a fresh issue used to make the purchase.
(2) If the permissible capital payment is less than the nominal amount of the shares redeemed or purchased, the amount of the difference must be transferred to the company's capital redemption reserve.
(3) If the permissible capital payment is greater than the nominal amount of the shares redeemed or purchased—
(a) the amount of any capital redemption reserve, share premium account or fully paid share capital of the company, and
(b) any amount representing unrealised profits of the company for the time being standing to the credit of any revaluation reserve maintained by the company,
may be reduced by a sum not exceeding (or by sums not in total exceeding) the amount by which the permissible capital payment exceeds the nominal amount of the shares.
(4) Where the proceeds of a fresh issue are applied by the company in making a redemption or purchase of its own shares in addition to a payment out of capital under Chapter 5 the references in subsections (2) and (3) to the permissible capital payment are to be read as referring to the aggregate of that payment and those proceeds.

735 Effect of company's failure to redeem or purchase

(1) This section applies where a company—
(a) issues shares on terms that they are or are liable to be redeemed, or
(b) agrees to purchase any of its shares.
(2) The company is not liable in damages in respect of any failure on its part to redeem or purchase any of the shares.
This is without prejudice to any right of the holder of the shares other than his right to sue the company for damages in respect of its failure.
(3) The court shall not grant an order for specific performance of the terms of redemption or purchase if the company shows that it is unable to meet the costs of redeeming or purchasing the shares in question out of distributable profits.
(4) If the company is wound up and at the commencement of the winding up any of the shares have not been redeemed or purchased, the terms of redemption or purchase may be enforced against the company.
When shares are redeemed or purchased under this subsection, they are treated as cancelled.

(5) Subsection (4) does not apply if—
(a) the terms provided for the redemption or purchase to take place at a date later than that of the commencement of the winding up, or
(b) during the period—
(i) beginning with the date on which the redemption or purchase was to have taken place, and
(ii) ending with the commencement of the winding up,
the company could not at any time have lawfully made a distribution equal in value to the price at which the shares were to have been redeemed or purchased.
(6) There shall be paid in priority to any amount that the company is liable under subsection (4) to pay in respect of any shares—
(a) all other debts and liabilities of the company (other than any due to members in their character as such), and
(b) if other shares carry rights (whether as to capital or as to income) that are preferred to the rights as to capital attaching to the first-mentioned shares, any amount due in satisfaction of those preferred rights.
Subject to that, any such amount shall be paid in priority to any amounts due to members in satisfaction of their rights (whether as to capital or income) as members.

736 Meaning of "distributable profits"

In this Part (except in Chapter 2 (financial assistance): see section 683) "distributable profits", in relation to the making of any payment by a company, means profits out of which the company could lawfully make a distribution (within the meaning given by section 830) equal in value to the payment.

737 General power to make further provision by regulations

(1) The Secretary of State may by regulations modify the provisions of this Part.
(2) The regulations may—
(a) amend or repeal any of the provisions of this Part, or
(b) make such other provision as appears to the Secretary of State appropriate in place of any of the provisions of this Part.
(3) Regulations under this section may make consequential amendments or repeals in other provisions of this Act, or in other enactments.
(4) Regulations under this section are subject to affirmative resolution procedure.

PART 19
DEBENTURES

General provisions

738 Meaning of "debenture"

In the Companies Acts "debenture" includes debenture stock, bonds and any other securities of a company, whether or not constituting a charge on the assets of the company.

739 Perpetual debentures

(1) A condition contained in debentures, or in a deed for securing debentures, is not invalid by reason only that the debentures are made—
(a) irredeemable, or
(b) redeemable only—
(i) on the happening of a contingency (however remote), or
(ii) on the expiration of a period (however long), any rule of equity to the contrary notwithstanding.
(2) Subsection (1) applies to debentures whenever issued and to deeds whenever executed.

740 Enforcement of contract to subscribe for debentures

A contract with a company to take up and pay for debentures of the company may be enforced by an order for specific performance.

741 Registration of allotment of debentures

(1) A company must register an allotment of debentures as soon as practicable and in any event within two months after the date of the allotment.

(2) If a company fails to comply with this section, an offence is committed by—
   (a) the company, and
   (b) every officer of the company who is in default.

(3) A person guilty of an offence under this section is liable on summary conviction to a fine not exceeding level 3 on the standard scale and, for continued contravention, a daily default fine not exceeding one-tenth of level 3 on the standard scale.

(4) For the duties of the company as to the issue of the debentures, or certificates of debenture stock, see Part 21 (certification and transfer of securities)

742 Debentures to bearer (Scotland)

Notwithstanding anything in the statute of the Scots Parliament of 1696, chapter 25, debentures to bearer issued in Scotland are valid and binding according to their terms.

Register of debenture holders

743 Register of debenture holders

(1) Any register of debenture holders of a company that is kept by the company must be kept available for inspection—
   (a) at the company's registered office, or
   (b) at a place specified in regulations under section 1136.

(2) A company must give notice to the registrar of the place where any such register is kept available for inspection and of any change in that place.

(3) No such notice is required if the register has, at all times since it came into existence, been kept available for inspection at the company's registered office.

(4) If a company makes default for 14 days in complying with subsection (2), an offence is committed by—
   (a) the company, and
   (b) every officer of the company who is in default.

(5) A person guilty of an offence under this section is liable on summary conviction to a fine not exceeding level 3 on the standard scale and, for continued contravention, a daily default fine not exceeding one-tenth of level 3 on the standard scale.

(6) References in this section to a register of debenture holders include a duplicate—
   (a) of a register of debenture holders that is kept outside the United Kingdom, or
   (b) of any part of such a register.

744 Register of debenture holders: right to inspect and require copy

(1) Every register of debenture holders of a company must, except when duly closed, be open to the inspection—
   (a) of the registered holder of any such debentures, or any holder of shares in the company, without charge, and
   (b) of any other person on payment of such fee as may be prescribed.

(2) Any person may require a copy of the register, or any part of it, on payment of such fee as may be prescribed.

(3) A person seeking to exercise either of the rights conferred by this section must make a request to the company to that effect.

(4) The request must contain the following information—
   (a) in the case of an individual, his name and address;
   (b) in the case of an organisation, the name and address of an individual responsible for making the request on behalf of the organisation;
   (c) the purpose for which the information is to be used; and
   (d) whether the information will be disclosed to any other person, and if so—
      (i) where that person is an individual, his name and address,
      (ii) where that person is an organisation, the name and address of an individual responsible for receiving the information on its behalf, and
      (iii) the purpose for which the information is to be used by that person.

(5) For the purposes of this section a register is "duly closed" if it is closed in accordance with provision contained—
   (a) in the articles or in the debentures,
   (b) in the case of debenture stock in the stock certificates, or

(c) in the trust deed or other document securing the debentures or debenture stock.
The total period for which a register is closed in any year must not exceed 30 days.

(6) References in this section to a register of debenture holders include a duplicate—
(a) of a register of debenture holders that is kept outside the United Kingdom, or
(b) of any part of such a register.

745 Register of debenture holders: response to request for inspection or copy

(1) Where a company receives a request under section 744 (register of debenture holders: right to inspect and require copy), it must within five working days either—
(a) comply with the request, or
(b) apply to the court.

(2) If it applies to the court it must notify the person making the request.

(3) If on an application under this section the court is satisfied that the inspection or copy is not sought for a proper purpose—
(a) it shall direct the company not to comply with the request, and
(b) it may further order that the company's costs (in Scotland, expenses) on the application be paid in whole or in part by the person who made the request, even if he is not a party to the application.

(4) If the court makes such a direction and it appears to the court that the company is or may be subject to other requests made for a similar purpose (whether made by the same person or different persons), it may direct that the company is not to comply with any such request.
The order must contain such provision as appears to the court appropriate to identify the requests to which it applies.

(5) If on an application under this section the court does not direct the company not to comply with the request, the company must comply with the request immediately upon the court giving its decision or, as the case may be, the proceedings being discontinued.

746 Register of debenture holders: refusal of inspection or default in providing copy

(1) If an inspection required under section 744 (register of debenture holders: right to inspect and require copy) is refused or default is made in providing a copy required under that section, otherwise than in accordance with an order of the court, an offence is committed by—
(a) the company, and
(b) every officer of the company who is in default.

(2) A person guilty of an offence under this section is liable on summary conviction to a fine not exceeding level 3 on the standard scale and, for continued contravention, a daily default fine not exceeding one-tenth of level 3 on the standard scale.

(3) In the case of any such refusal or default the court may by order compel an immediate inspection or, as the case may be, direct that the copy required be sent to the person requesting it.

747 Register of debenture holders: offences in connection with request for or disclosure of information

(1) It is an offence for a person knowingly or recklessly to make in a request under section 744 (register of debenture holders: right to inspect and require copy) a statement that is misleading, false or deceptive in a material particular.

(2) It is an offence for a person in possession of information obtained by exercise of either of the rights conferred by that section—
(a) to do anything that results in the information being disclosed to another person, or
(b) to fail to do anything with the result that the information is disclosed to another person,
knowing, or having reason to suspect, that person may use the information for a purpose that is not a proper purpose.

(3) A person guilty of an offence under this section is liable—
(a) on conviction on indictment, to imprisonment for a term not exceeding two years or a fine (or both);
(b) on summary conviction—
(i) in England and Wales, to imprisonment for a term not exceeding twelve months or to a fine not exceeding the statutory maximum (or both);
(ii) in Scotland or Northern Ireland, to imprisonment for a term not exceeding six months, or to a fine not exceeding the statutory maximum (or both).

748 Time limit for claims arising from entry in register

(1) Liability incurred by a company—
  (a) from the making or deletion of an entry in the register of debenture holders, or
  (b) from a failure to make or delete any such entry,
is not enforceable more than ten years after the date on which the entry was made or deleted or, as the case may be, the failure first occurred.

(2) This is without prejudice to any lesser period of limitation (and, in Scotland, to any rule that the obligation giving rise to the liability prescribes before the expiry of that period).

Supplementary provisions

749 Right of debenture holder to copy of deed

(1) Any holder of debentures of a company is entitled, on request and on payment of such fee as may be prescribed, to be provided with a copy of any trust deed for securing the debentures.

(2) If default is made in complying with this section, an offence is committed by every officer of the company who is in default.

(3) A person guilty of an offence under this section is liable on summary conviction to a fine not exceeding level 3 on the standard scale and, for continued contravention, a daily default fine not exceeding one-tenth of level 3 on the standard scale.

(4) In the case of any such default the court may direct that the copy required be sent to the person requiring it.

750 Liability of trustees of debentures

(1) Any provision contained in—
  (a) a trust deed for securing an issue of debentures, or
  (b) any contract with the holders of debentures secured by a trust deed,
is void in so far as it would have the effect of exempting a trustee of the deed from, or indemnifying him against, liability for breach of trust where he fails to show the degree of care and diligence required of him as trustee, having regard to the provisions of the trust deed conferring on him any powers, authorities or discretions.

(2) Subsection (1) does not invalidate—
  (a) a release otherwise validly given in respect of anything done or omitted to be done by a trustee before the giving of the release;
  (b) any provision enabling such a release to be given—
    (i) on being agreed to by a majority of not less than 75% in value of the debenture holders present and voting in person or, where proxies are permitted, by proxy at a meeting summoned for the purpose, and
    (ii) either with respect to specific acts or omissions or on the trustee dying or ceasing to act.

(3) This section is subject to section 751 (saving for certain older provisions).

751 Liability of trustees of debentures: saving for certain older provisions

(1) Section 750 (liability of trustees of debentures) does not operate—
  (a) to invalidate any provision in force on the relevant date so long as any person—
    (i) then entitled to the benefit of the provision, or
    (ii) afterwards given the benefit of the provision under subsection (3) below,
  remains a trustee of the deed in question, or
  (b) to deprive any person of any exemption or right to be indemnified in respect of anything done or omitted to be done by him while any such provision was in force.

(2) The relevant date for this purpose is—
  (a) 1st July 1948 in a case where section 192 of the Companies Act 1985 applied immediately before the commencement of this section;
  (b) 1st July 1961 in a case where Article 201 of the Companies (Northern Ireland) Order 1986 then applied.

(3) While any trustee of a trust deed remains entitled to the benefit of a provision saved by subsection (1) above the benefit of that provision may be given either—
  (a) to all trustees of the deed, present and future, or
  (b) to any named trustees or proposed trustees of it,
by a resolution passed by a majority of not less than 75% in value of the debenture holders present in person or, where proxies are permitted, by proxy at a meeting summoned for the purpose.

(4) A meeting for that purpose must be summoned in accordance with the provisions of the deed or, if the deed makes no provision for summoning meetings, in a manner approved by the court.

752 Power to re-issue redeemed debentures

(1) Where a company has redeemed debentures previously issued, then unless—
   (a) provision to the contrary (express or implied) is contained in the company's articles or in any contract made by the company, or
   (b) the company has, by passing a resolution to that effect or by some other act, manifested its intention that the debentures shall be cancelled,

the company may re-issue the debentures, either by re-issuing the same debentures or by issuing new debentures in their place.

This subsection is deemed always to have had effect.

(2) On a re-issue of redeemed debentures the person entitled to the debentures has (and is deemed always to have had) the same priorities as if the debentures had never been redeemed.

(3) The re-issue of a debenture or the issue of another debenture in its place under this section is treated as the issue of a new debenture for the purposes of stamp duty.

It is not so treated for the purposes of any provision limiting the amount or number of debentures to be issued.

(4) A person lending money on the security of a debenture re-issued under this section which appears to be duly stamped may give the debenture in evidence in any proceedings for enforcing his security without payment of the stamp duty or any penalty in respect of it, unless he had notice (or, but for his negligence, might have discovered) that the debenture was not duly stamped.

In that case the company is liable to pay the proper stamp duty and penalty.

753 Deposit of debentures to secure advances

Where a company has deposited any of its debentures to secure advances from time to time on current account or otherwise, the debentures are not treated as redeemed by reason only of the company's account having ceased to be in debit while the debentures remained so deposited.

754 Priorities where debentures secured by floating charge

(1) This section applies where debentures of a company registered in England and Wales or Northern Ireland are secured by a charge that, as created, was a floating charge.

(2) If possession is taken, by or on behalf of the holders of the debentures, of any property comprised in or subject to the charge, and the company is not at that time in the course of being wound up, the company's preferential debts shall be paid out of assets coming to the hands of the persons taking possession in priority to any claims for principal or interest in respect of the debentures.

(3) "Preferential debts" means the categories of debts listed in Schedule 6 to the Insolvency Act 1986 or Schedule 4 to the Insolvency (Northern Ireland) Order 1989.

For the purposes of those Schedules "the relevant date" is the date of possession being taken as mentioned in subsection (2).

(4) Payments under this section shall be recouped, as far as may be, out of the assets of the company available for payment of general creditors.

PART 20
PRIVATE AND PUBLIC COMPANIES

CHAPTER 1
PROHIBITION OF PUBLIC OFFERS BY PRIVATE COMPANIES

755 Prohibition of public offers by private company

(1) A private company limited by shares or limited by guarantee and having a share capital must not—
   (a) offer to the public any securities of the company, or
   (b) allot or agree to allot any securities of the company with a view to their being offered to the public.

(2) Unless the contrary is proved, an allotment or agreement to allot securities is presumed to be made with a view to their being offered to the public if an offer of the securities (or any of them) to the public is made—
  (a) within six months after the allotment or agreement to allot, or
  (b) before the receipt by the company of the whole of the consideration to be received by it in respect of the securities.
(3) A company does not contravene this section if—
  (a) it acts in good faith in pursuance of arrangements under which it is to re-register as a public company before the securities are allotted, or
  (b) as part of the terms of the offer it undertakes to re-register as a public company within a specified period, and that undertaking is complied with.
(4) The specified period for the purposes of subsection (3)(b) must be a period ending not later than six months after the day on which the offer is made (or, in the case of an offer made on different days, first made).
(5) In this Chapter "securities" means shares or debentures.

756 Meaning of "offer to the public"

(1) This section explains what is meant in this Chapter by an offer of securities to the public.
(2) An offer to the public includes an offer to any section of the public, however selected.
(3) An offer is not regarded as an offer to the public if it can properly be regarded, in all the circumstances, as—
  (a) not being calculated to result, directly or indirectly, in securities of the company becoming available to persons other than those receiving the offer, or
  (b) otherwise being a private concern of the person receiving it and the person making it.
(4) An offer is to be regarded (unless the contrary is proved) as being a private concern of the person receiving it and the person making it if—
  (a) it is made to a person already connected with the company and, where it is made on terms allowing that person to renounce his rights, the rights may only be renounced in favour of another person already connected with the company; or
  (b) it is an offer to subscribe for securities to be held under an employees' share scheme and, where it is made on terms allowing that person to renounce his rights, the rights may only be renounced in favour of—
    (i) another person entitled to hold securities under the scheme, or
    (ii) a person already connected with the company.
(5) For the purposes of this section "person already connected with the company" means—
  (a) an existing member or employee of the company,
  (b) a member of the family of a person who is or was a member or employee of the company,
  (c) the widow or widower, or surviving civil partner, of a person who was a member or employee of the company,
  (d) an existing debenture holder of the company, or
  (e) a trustee (acting in his capacity as such) of a trust of which the principal beneficiary is a person within any of paragraphs (a) to (d).
(6) For the purposes of subsection (5)(b) the members of a person's family are the person's spouse or civil partner and children (including step-children) and their descendants.

757 Enforcement of prohibition: order restraining proposed contravention

(1) If it appears to the court—
  (a) on an application under this section, or
  (b) in proceedings under Part 30 (protection of members against unfair prejudice),

that a company is proposing to act in contravention of section 755 (prohibition of public offers by private companies), the court shall make an order under this section.
(2) An order under this section is an order restraining the company from contravening that section.

(3) An application for an order under this section may be made by—
(a) a member or creditor of the company, or
(b) the Secretary of State.

758 Enforcement of prohibition: orders available to the court after contravention

(1) This section applies if it appears to the court—
(a) on an application under this section, or
(b) in proceedings under Part 30 (protection of members against unfair prejudice), that a company has acted in contravention of section 755 (prohibition of public offers by private companies).

(2) The court must make an order requiring the company to re-register as a public company unless it appears to the court—
(a) that the company does not meet the requirements for re-registration as a public company, and
(b) that it is impractical or undesirable to require it to take steps to do so.

(3) If it does not make an order for re-registration, the court may make either or both of the following—
(a) a remedial order (see section 759), or
(b) an order for the compulsory winding up of the company.

(4) An application under this section may be made by—
(a) a member of the company who—
(i) was a member at the time the offer was made (or, if the offer was made over a period, at any time during that period), or
(ii) became a member as a result of the offer,
(b) a creditor of the company who was a creditor at the time the offer was made (or, if the offer was made over a period, at any time during that period), or
(c) the Secretary of State.

759 Enforcement of prohibition: remedial order

(1) A "remedial order" is an order for the purpose of putting a person affected by anything done in contravention of section 755 (prohibition of public offers by private company) in the position he would have been in if it had not been done.

(2) The following provisions are without prejudice to the generality of the power to make such an order.

(3) Where a private company has—
(a) allotted securities pursuant to an offer to the public, or
(b) allotted or agreed to allot securities with a view to their being offered to the public,

a remedial order may require any person knowingly concerned in the contravention of section 755 to offer to purchase any of those securities at such price and on such other terms as the court thinks fit.

(4) A remedial order may be made—
(a) against any person knowingly concerned in the contravention, whether or not an officer of the company;
(b) notwithstanding anything in the company's constitution (which includes, for this purpose, the terms on which any securities of the company are allotted or held);
(c) whether or not the holder of the securities subject to the order is the person to whom the company allotted or agreed to allot them.

(5) Where a remedial order is made against the company itself, the court may provide for the reduction of the company's capital accordingly.

760 Validity of allotment etc not affected

Nothing in this Chapter affects the validity of any allotment or sale of securities or of any agreement to allot or sell securities.

CHAPTER 2

MINIMUM SHARE CAPITAL REQUIREMENT FOR PUBLIC COMPANIES

761 Public company: requirement as to minimum share capital

(1) A company that is a public company (otherwise than by virtue of re-registration as a public company) must not do business or exercise any borrowing powers unless the registrar has issued it with a certificate under this section (a "trading certificate").

(2) The registrar shall issue a trading certificate if, on an application made in accordance with section 762, he is satisfied that the nominal value of the company's allotted share capital is not less than the authorised minimum.
(3) For this purpose a share allotted in pursuance of an employees' share scheme shall not be taken into account unless paid up as to—
(a) at least one-quarter of the nominal value of the share, and
(b) the whole of any premium on the share.
(4) A trading certificate has effect from the date on which it is issued and is conclusive evidence that the company is entitled to do business and exercise any borrowing powers.

762 Procedure for obtaining certificate

(1) An application for a certificate under section 761 must—
(a) state that the nominal value of the company's allotted share capital is not less than the authorised minimum,
(b) specify the amount, or estimated amount, of the company's preliminary expenses,
(c) specify any amount or benefit paid or given, or intended to be paid or given, to any promoter of the company, and the consideration for the payment or benefit, and
(d) be accompanied by a statement of compliance.
(2) The statement of compliance is a statement that the company meets the requirements for the issue of a certificate under section 761.
(3) The registrar may accept the statement of compliance as sufficient evidence of the matters stated in it.

763 The authorised minimum

(1) "The authorised minimum", in relation to the nominal value of a public company's allotted share capital is—
(a) £50,000, or
(b) the prescribed euro equivalent.
(2) The Secretary of State may by order prescribe the amount in euros that is for the time being to be treated as equivalent to the sterling amount of the authorised minimum.
(3) This power may be exercised from time to time as appears to the Secretary of State to be appropriate.
(4) The amount prescribed shall be determined by applying an appropriate spot rate of exchange to the sterling amount and rounding to the nearest 100 euros.
(5) An order under this section is subject to negative resolution procedure.
(6) This section has effect subject to any exercise of the power conferred by section 764 (power to alter authorised minimum).

764 Power to alter authorised minimum

(1) The Secretary of State may by order—
(a) alter the sterling amount of the authorised minimum, and
(b) make a corresponding alteration of the prescribed euro equivalent.
(2) The amount of the prescribed euro equivalent shall be determined by applying an appropriate spot rate of exchange to the sterling amount and rounding to the nearest 100 euros.
(3) An order under this section that increases the authorised minimum may—
(a) require a public company having an allotted share capital of which the nominal value is less than the amount specified in the order to—
(i) increase that value to not less than that amount, or
(ii) re-register as a private company;
(b) make provision in connection with any such requirement for any of the matters for which provision is made by this Act relating to—
(i) a company's registration, re-registration or change of name,
(ii) payment for shares comprised in a company's share capital, and
(iii) offers to the public of shares in or debentures of a company,
including provision as to the consequences (in criminal law or otherwise) of a failure to comply with any requirement of the order;
(c) provide for any provision of the order to come into force on different days for different purposes.
(4) An order under this section is subject to affirmative resolution procedure.

765 Authorised minimum: application of initial requirement

(1) The initial requirement for a public company to have allotted share capital of a nominal value not less than the authorised minimum, that is—
  (a) the requirement in section 761(2) for the issue of a trading certificate, or
  (b) the requirement in section 91(1)(a) for re-registration as a public company,
must be met either by reference to allotted share capital denominated in sterling or by reference to allotted share capital denominated in euros (but not partly in one and partly in the other).

(2) Whether the requirement is met is determined in the first case by reference to the sterling amount and in the second case by reference to the prescribed euro equivalent.

(3) No account is to be taken of any allotted share capital of the company denominated in a currency other than sterling or, as the case may be, euros.

(4) If the company could meet the requirement either by reference to share capital denominated in sterling or by reference to share capital denominated in euros, it must elect in its application for a trading certificate or, as the case may be, for re-registration as a public company which is to be the currency by reference to which the matter is determined.

766 Authorised minimum: application where shares denominated in different currencies etc

(1) The Secretary of State may make provision by regulations as to the application of the authorised minimum in relation to a public company that—
  (a) has shares denominated—
    (i) in more than one currency, or
    (ii) in a currency other than sterling or euros,
  (b) redenominates the whole or part of its allotted share capital, or
  (c) allots new shares.

(2) The regulations may make provision as to the currencies, exchange rates and dates by reference to which it is to be determined whether the nominal value of the company's allotted share capital is less than the authorised minimum.

(3) The regulations may provide that where—
  (a) a company has redenominated the whole or part of its allotted share capital, and
  (b) the effect of the redenomination is that the nominal value of the company's allotted share capital is less than the authorised minimum,
the company must re-register as a private company.

(4) Regulations under subsection (3) may make provision corresponding to any provision made by sections 664 to 667 (re-registration as private company in consequence of cancellation of shares).

(5) Any regulations under this section have effect subject to section 765 (authorised minimum: application of initial requirement).

(6) Regulations under this section are subject to negative resolution procedure.

767 Consequences of doing business etc without a trading certificate

(1) If a company does business or exercises any borrowing powers in contravention of section 761, an offence is committed by—
  (a) the company, and
  (b) every officer of the company who is in default.

(2) A person guilty of an offence under subsection (1) is liable—
  (a) on conviction on indictment, to a fine;
  (b) on summary conviction, to a fine not exceeding the statutory maximum.

(3) A contravention of section 761 does not affect the validity of a transaction entered into by the company, but if a company—
  (a) enters into a transaction in contravention of that section, and
  (b) fails to comply with its obligations in connection with the transaction within 21 days from being called on to do so,
the directors of the company are jointly and severally liable to indemnify any other party to the transaction in respect of any loss or damage suffered by him by reason of the company's failure to comply with its obligations.

(4) The directors who are so liable are those who were directors at the time the company entered into the transaction.

PART 21
CERTIFICATION AND TRANSFER OF SECURITIES

CHAPTER 1
CERTIFICATION AND TRANSFER OF SECURITIES: GENERAL

Share certificates

768 Share certificate to be evidence of title

(1) In the case of a company registered in England and Wales or Northern Ireland, a certificate under the common seal of the company specifying any shares held by a member is prima facie evidence of his title to the shares.

(2) In the case of a company registered in Scotland—

(a) a certificate under the common seal of the company specifying any shares held by a member, or

(b) a certificate specifying any shares held by a member and subscribed by the company in accordance with the Requirements of Writing (Scotland) Act 1995,

is sufficient evidence, unless the contrary is shown, of his title to the shares.

Issue of certificates etc on allotment

769 Duty of company as to issue of certificates etc on allotment

(1) A company must, within two months after the allotment of any of its shares, debentures or debenture stock, complete and have ready for delivery—

(a) the certificates of the shares allotted,

(b) the debentures allotted, or

(c) the certificates of the debenture stock allotted.

(2) Subsection (1) does not apply—

(a) if the conditions of issue of the shares, debentures or debenture stock provide otherwise,

(b) in the case of allotment to a financial institution (see section 778), or

(c) in the case of an allotment of shares if, following the allotment, the company has issued a share warrant in respect of the shares (see section 779).

(3) If default is made in complying with subsection (1) an offence is committed by every officer of the company who is in default.

(4) A person guilty of an offence under subsection (3) is liable on summary conviction to a fine not exceeding level 3 on the standard scale and, for continued contravention, a daily default fine not exceeding one-tenth of level 3 on the standard scale.

Transfer of securities

770 Registration of transfer

(1) A company may not register a transfer of shares in or debentures of the company unless—

(a) a proper instrument of transfer has been delivered to it, or

(b) the transfer—

(i) is an exempt transfer within the Stock Transfer Act 1982, or

(ii) is in accordance with regulations under Chapter 2 of this Part.

(2) Subsection (1) does not affect any power of the company to register as shareholder or debenture holder a person to whom the right to any shares in or debentures of the company has been transmitted by operation of law.

771 Procedure on transfer being lodged

(1) When a transfer of shares in or debentures of a company has been lodged with the company, the company must either—

(a) register the transfer, or

(b) give the transferee notice of refusal to register the transfer, together with its reasons for the refusal,

as soon as practicable and in any event within two months after the date on which the transfer is lodged with it.

(2) If the company refuses to register the transfer, it must provide the transferee with such further information about the reasons for the refusal as the transferee may reasonably request.
This does not include copies of minutes of meetings of directors.

(3) If a company fails to comply with this section, an offence is committed by—
(a) the company, and
(b) every officer of the company who is in default.

(4) A person guilty of an offence under this section is liable on summary conviction to a fine not exceeding level 3 on the standard scale and, for continued contravention, a daily default fine not exceeding one-tenth of level 3 on the standard scale.

(5) This section does not apply—
(a) in relation to a transfer of shares if the company has issued a share warrant in respect of the shares (see section 779);
(b) in relation to the transmission of shares or debentures by operation of law.

772 Transfer of shares on application of transferor

On the application of the transferor of any share or interest in a company, the company shall enter in its register of members the name of the transferee in the same manner and subject to the same conditions as if the application for the entry were made by the transferee.

773 Execution of share transfer by personal representative

An instrument of transfer of the share or other interest of a deceased member of a company—
(a) may be made by his personal representative although the personal representative is not himself a member of the company, and
(b) is as effective as if the personal representative had been such a member at the time of the execution of the instrument.

774 Evidence of grant of probate etc

The production to a company of any document that is by law sufficient evidence of the grant of—
(a) probate of the will of a deceased person,
(b) letters of administration of the estate of a deceased person, or
(c) confirmation as executor of a deceased person,
shall be accepted by the company as sufficient evidence of the grant.

775 Certification of instrument of transfer

(1) The certification by a company of an instrument of transfer of any shares in, or debentures of, the company is to be taken as a representation by the company to any person acting on the faith of the certification that there have been produced to the company such documents as on their face show a prima facie title to the shares or debentures in the transferor named in the instrument.

(2) The certification is not to be taken as a representation that the transferor has any title to the shares or debentures.

(3) Where a person acts on the faith of a false certification by a company made negligently, the company is under the same liability to him as if the certification had been made fraudulently.

(4) For the purposes of this section—
(a) an instrument of transfer is certificated if it bears the words "certificate lodged" (or words to the like effect);
(b) the certification of an instrument of transfer is made by a company if—
(i) the person issuing the instrument is a person authorised to issue certificated instruments of transfer on the company's behalf, and
(ii) the certification is signed by a person authorised to certificate transfers on the company's behalf or by an officer or employee either of the company or of a body corporate so authorised;
(c) a certification is treated as signed by a person if—
(i) it purports to be authenticated by his signature or initials (whether handwritten or not), and

(ii) it is not shown that the signature or initials was or were placed there neither by himself nor by a person authorised to use the signature or initials for the purpose of certificating transfers on the company's behalf.

Issue of certificates etc on transfer

776 Duty of company as to issue of certificates etc. on transfer

(1) A company must, within two months after the date on which a transfer of any of its shares, debentures or debenture stock is lodged with the company, complete and have ready for delivery—
(a) the certificates of the shares transferred,
(b) the debentures transferred, or
(c) the certificates of the debenture stock transferred.
(2) For this purpose a "transfer" means—
(a) a transfer duly stamped and otherwise valid, or
(b) an exempt transfer within the Stock Transfer Act 1982,
but does not include a transfer that the company is for any reason entitled to refuse to register and does not register.
(3) Subsection (1) does not apply—
(a) if the conditions of issue of the shares, debentures or debenture stock provide otherwise,
(b) in the case of a transfer to a financial institution (see section 778), or
(c) in the case of a transfer of shares if, following the transfer, the company has issued a share warrant in respect of the shares (see section 779).
(4) Subsection (1) has effect subject to section 777 (cases where the Stock Transfer Act 1982 applies).
(5) If default is made in complying with subsection (1) an offence is committed by every officer of the company who is in default.
(6) A person guilty of an offence under this section is liable on summary conviction to a fine not exceeding level 3 on the standard scale and, for continued contravention, a daily default fine not exceeding one-tenth of level 3 on the standard scale.

777 Issue of certificates etc: cases within the Stock Transfer Act 1982

(1) Section 776(1) (duty of company as to issue of certificates etc on transfer) does not apply in the case of a transfer to a person where, by virtue of regulations under section 3 of the Stock Transfer Act 1982, he is not entitled to a certificate or other document of or evidencing title in respect of the securities transferred.
(2) But if in such a case the transferee—
(a) subsequently becomes entitled to such a certificate or other document by virtue of any provision of those regulations, and
(b) gives notice in writing of that fact to the company,
section 776 (duty to company as to issue of certificates etc) has effect as if the reference in subsection (1) of that section to the date of the lodging of the transfer were a reference to the date of the notice.

Issue of certificates etc on allotment or transfer to financial institution

778 Issue of certificates etc: allotment or transfer to financial institution

(1) A company—
(a) of which shares or debentures are allotted to a financial institution,
(b) of which debenture stock is allotted to a financial institution, or
(c) with which a transfer for transferring shares, debentures or debenture stock to a financial institution is lodged,
is not required in consequence of that allotment or transfer to comply with section 769(1) or 776(1) (duty of company as to issue of certificates etc).
(2) A "financial institution" means—
(a) a recognised clearing house acting in relation to a recognised investment exchange, or
(b) a nominee of—
(i) a recognised clearing house acting in that way, or
(ii) a recognised investment exchange,

designated for the purposes of this section in the rules of the recognised investment exchange in question.

(3) Expressions used in subsection (2) have the same meaning as in Part 18 of the Financial Services and Markets Act 2000.

Share warrants

779 Prohibition on issue of new share warrants and effect of existing share warrants

(1) A company limited by shares may, if so authorised by its articles, issue with respect to any fully paid shares a warrant (a "share warrant") stating that the bearer of the warrant is entitled to the shares specified in it.

(2) A share warrant issued under the company's common seal or (in the case of a company registered in Scotland) subscribed in accordance with the Requirements of Writing (Scotland) Act 1995 entitles the bearer to the shares specified in it and the shares may be transferred by delivery of the warrant.

(3) A company that issues a share warrant may, if so authorised by its articles, provide (by coupons or otherwise) for the payment of the future dividends on the shares included in the warrant.

(4) No share warrant may be issued by a company (irrespective of whether its articles purport to authorise it to do so) on or after the day on which section 84 of the Small Business, Enterprise and Employment Act 2015 comes into force.

780 ...

781 Offences in connection with share warrants (Scotland)

(1) If in Scotland a person—

(a) with intent to defraud, forges or alters, or offers, utters, disposes of, or puts off, knowing the same to be forged or altered, any share warrant or coupon, or any document purporting to be a share warrant or coupon issued in pursuance of this Act, or

(b) by means of any such forged or altered share warrant, coupon or document—

(i) demands or endeavours to obtain or receive any share or interest in a company under this Act, or

(ii) demands or endeavours to receive any dividend or money payment in respect of any such share or interest,

knowing the warrant, coupon or document to be forged or altered,

he commits an offence.

(2) If in Scotland a person without lawful authority or excuse (of which proof lies on him)—

(a) engraves or makes on any plate, wood, stone, or other material, any share warrant or coupon purporting to be—

(i) a share warrant or coupon issued or made by any particular company in pursuance of this Act, or

(ii) a blank share warrant or coupon so issued or made, or

(iii) a part of such a share warrant or coupon, or

(b) uses any such plate, wood, stone, or other material, for the making or printing of any such share warrant or coupon, or of any such blank share warrant or coupon or of any part of such a share warrant or coupon, or

(c) knowingly has in his custody or possession any such plate, wood, stone, or other material,

he commits an offence.

(3) A person guilty of an offence under subsection (1) is liable on summary conviction to imprisonment for a term not exceeding six months or to a fine not exceeding level 5 on the standard scale (or both).

(4) A person guilty of an offence under subsection (2) is liable—

(a) on conviction on indictment, to imprisonment for a term not exceeding seven years or a fine (or both);

(b) on summary conviction, to imprisonment for a term not exceeding six months or a fine not exceeding the statutory maximum (or both).

Supplementary provisions

782 Issue of certificates etc: court order to make good default

(1) If a company on which a notice has been served requiring it to make good any default in complying with—

(a) section 769(1) (duty of company as to issue of certificates etc on allotment),

(b) section 776(1) (duty of company as to issue of certificates etc on transfer), or

(c) section 780(1) (duty of company as to issue of certificates etc on surrender of share warrant),

fails to make good the default within ten days after service of the notice, the person entitled to have the certificates or the debentures delivered to him may apply to the court.

(2) The court may on such an application make an order directing the company and any officer of it to make good the default within such time as may be specified in the order.

(3) The order may provide that all costs (in Scotland, expenses) of and incidental to the application are to be borne by the company or by an officer of it responsible for the default.

CHAPTER 2
EVIDENCING AND TRANSFER OF TITLE TO SECURITIES WITHOUT WRITTEN INSTRUMENT

Introductory

783 Scope of this Chapter

In this Chapter—

(a) "securities" means shares, debentures, debenture stock, loan stock, bonds, units of a collective investment scheme within the meaning of the Financial Services and Markets Act 2000 and other securities of any description;

(b) references to title to securities include any legal or equitable interest in securities;

(c) references to a transfer of title include a transfer by way of security;

(d) references to transfer without a written instrument include, in relation to bearer securities, transfer without delivery.

784 *omitted*

Powers exercisable

785 Provision enabling procedures for evidencing and transferring title

(1) Provision may be made by regulations for enabling title to securities to be evidenced and transferred without a written instrument.

(2) *omitted*

786–790 *omitted*

PART 22
INFORMATION ABOUT INTERESTS IN A COMPANY'S SHARES

Introductory

791 Companies to which this Part applies

This Part applies only to public companies.

792 Shares to which this Part applies

(1) References in this Part to a company's shares are to the company's issued shares of a class carrying rights to vote in all circumstances at general meetings of the company (including any shares held as treasury shares).

(2) The temporary suspension of voting rights in respect of any shares does not affect the application of this Part in relation to interests in those or any other shares.

Notice requiring information about interests in shares

793 Notice by company requiring information about interests in its shares

(1) A public company may give notice under this section to any person whom the company knows or has reasonable cause to believe—

(a) to be interested in the company's shares, or

(b) to have been so interested at any time during the three years immediately preceding the date on which the notice is issued.

(2) The notice may require the person—

(a) to confirm that fact or (as the case may be) to state whether or not it is the case, and

(b) if he holds, or has during that time held, any such interest, to give such further information as may be required in accordance with the following provisions of this section.

(3) The notice may require the person to whom it is addressed to give particulars of his own present or past interest in the company's shares (held by him at any time during the three year period mentioned in subsection (1)(b)).

(4) The notice may require the person to whom it is addressed, where—

(a) his interest is a present interest and another interest in the shares subsists, or

(b) another interest in the shares subsisted during that three year period at a time when his interest subsisted,

to give, so far as lies within his knowledge, such particulars with respect to that other interest as may be required by the notice.

(5) The particulars referred to in subsections (3) and (4) include—

(a) the identity of persons interested in the shares in question, and

(b) whether persons interested in the same shares are or were parties to—

(i) an agreement to which section 824 applies (certain share acquisition agreements), or

(ii) an agreement or arrangement relating to the exercise of any rights conferred by the holding of the shares.

(6) The notice may require the person to whom it is addressed, where his interest is a past interest, to give (so far as lies within his knowledge) particulars of the identity of the person who held that interest immediately upon his ceasing to hold it.

(7) The information required by the notice must be given within such reasonable time as may be specified in the notice.

794 Notice requiring information: order imposing restrictions on shares

(1) Where—

(a) a notice under section 793 (notice requiring information about interests in company's shares) is served by a company on a person who is or was interested in shares in the company, and

(b) that person fails to give the company the information required by the notice within the time specified in it,

the company may apply to the court for an order directing that the shares in question be subject to restrictions.

For the effect of such an order see section 797.

(2) If the court is satisfied that such an order may unfairly affect the rights of third parties in respect of the shares, the court may, for the purpose of protecting those rights and subject to such terms as it thinks fit, direct that such acts by such persons or descriptions of persons and for such purposes as may be set out in the order shall not constitute a breach of the restrictions.

(3) On an application under this section the court may make an interim order.

Any such order may be made unconditionally or on such terms as the court thinks fit.

(4) Sections 798 to 802 make further provision about orders under this section.

795 Notice requiring information: offences

(1) A person who—

(a) fails to comply with a notice under section 793 (notice requiring information about interests in company's shares), or

(b) in purported compliance with such a notice—

(i) makes a statement that he knows to be false in a material particular, or

(ii) recklessly makes a statement that is false in a material particular,

commits an offence.

(2) A person does not commit an offence under subsection (1)(a) if he proves that the requirement to give information was frivolous or vexatious.

(3) A person guilty of an offence under this section is liable—

(a) on conviction on indictment, to imprisonment for a term not exceeding two years or a fine (or both);
(b) on summary conviction—
(i) in England and Wales, to imprisonment for a term not exceeding twelve months or to a fine not exceeding the statutory maximum (or both);
(ii) in Scotland or Northern Ireland, to imprisonment for a term not exceeding six months, or to a fine not exceeding the statutory maximum (or both).

796 Notice requiring information: persons exempted from obligation to comply

(1) A person is not obliged to comply with a notice under section 793 (notice requiring information about interests in company's shares) if he is for the time being exempted by the Secretary of State from the operation of that section.
(2) The Secretary of State must not grant any such exemption unless—
(a) he has consulted the Governor of the Bank of England, and
(b) he (the Secretary of State) is satisfied that, having regard to any undertaking given by the person in question with respect to any interest held or to be held by him in any shares, there are special reasons why that person should not be subject to the obligations imposed by that section.

Orders imposing restrictions on shares

797 Consequences of order imposing restrictions

(1) The effect of an order under section 794 that shares are subject to restrictions is as follows—
(a) any transfer of the shares is void;
(b) no voting rights are exercisable in respect of the shares;
(c) no further shares may be issued in right of the shares or in pursuance of an offer made to their holder;
(d) except in a liquidation, no payment may be made of sums due from the company on the shares, whether in respect of capital or otherwise.
(2) Where shares are subject to the restriction in subsection (1)(a), an agreement to transfer the shares is void.
This does not apply to an agreement to transfer the shares on the making of an order under section 800 made by virtue of subsection (3)(b) (removal of restrictions in case of court-approved transfer).
(3) Where shares are subject to the restriction in subsection (1)(c) or (d), an agreement to transfer any right to be issued with other shares in right of those shares, or to receive any payment on them (otherwise than in a liquidation), is void.
This does not apply to an agreement to transfer any such right on the making of an order under section 800 made by virtue of subsection (3)(b) (removal of restrictions in case of court-approved transfer).
(4) The provisions of this section are subject—
(a) to any directions under section 794(2) or section 799(3) (directions for protection of third parties), and
(b) in the case of an interim order under section 794(3), to the terms of the order.

798 Penalty for attempted evasion of restrictions

(1) This section applies where shares are subject to restrictions by virtue of an order under section 794.
(2) A person commits an offence if he—
(a) exercises or purports to exercise any right—
(i) to dispose of shares that to his knowledge, are for the time being subject to restrictions, or
(ii) to dispose of any right to be issued with any such shares, or
(b) votes in respect of any such shares (whether as holder or proxy), or appoints a proxy to vote in respect of them, or
(c) being the holder of any such shares, fails to notify of their being subject to those restrictions a person whom he does not know to be aware of that fact but does know to be entitled (apart from the restrictions) to vote in respect of those shares whether as holder or as proxy, or

(d) being the holder of any such shares, or being entitled to a right to be issued with other shares in right of them, or to receive any payment on them (otherwise than in a liquidation), enters into an agreement which is void under section 797(2) or (3).

(3) If shares in a company are issued in contravention of the restrictions, an offence is committed by—
  (a) the company, and
  (b) every officer of the company who is in default.

(4) A person guilty of an offence under this section is liable—
  (a) on conviction on indictment, to a fine;
  (b) on summary conviction, to a fine not exceeding the statutory maximum.

(5) The provisions of this section are subject—
  (a) to any directions under—
  section 794(2) (directions for protection of third parties), or
  section 799 or 800 (relaxation or removal of restrictions), and
  (b) in the case of an interim order under section 794(3), to the terms of the order.

799 Relaxation of restrictions

(1) An application may be made to the court on the ground that an order directing that shares shall be subject to restrictions unfairly affects the rights of third parties in respect of the shares.

(2) An application for an order under this section may be made by the company or by any person aggrieved.

(3) If the court is satisfied that the application is well-founded, it may, for the purpose of protecting the rights of third parties in respect of the shares, and subject to such terms as it thinks fit, direct that such acts by such persons or descriptions of persons and for such purposes as may be set out in the order do not constitute a breach of the restrictions.

800 Removal of restrictions

(1) An application may be made to the court for an order directing that the shares shall cease to be subject to restrictions.

(2) An application for an order under this section may be made by the company or by any person aggrieved.

(3) The court must not make an order under this section unless—
  (a) it is satisfied that the relevant facts about the shares have been disclosed to the company and no unfair advantage has accrued to any person as a result of the earlier failure to make that disclosure, or
  (b) the shares are to be transferred for valuable consideration and the court approves the transfer.

(4) An order under this section made by virtue of subsection (3)(b) may continue, in whole or in part, the restrictions mentioned in section 797(1)(c) and (d) (restrictions on issue of further shares or making of payments) so far as they relate to a right acquired or offer made before the transfer.

(5) Where any restrictions continue in force under subsection (4)—
  (a) an application may be made under this section for an order directing that the shares shall cease to be subject to those restrictions, and
  (b) subsection (3) does not apply in relation to the making of such an order.

801 Order for sale of shares

(1) The court may order that the shares subject to restrictions be sold, subject to the court's approval as to the sale.

(2) An application for an order under subsection (1) may only be made by the company.

(3) Where the court has made an order under this section, it may make such further order relating to the sale or transfer of the shares as it thinks fit.

(4) An application for an order under subsection (3) may be made—
  (a) by the company,
  (b) by the person appointed by or in pursuance of the order to effect the sale, or
  (c) by any person interested in the shares.

(5) On making an order under subsection (1) or (3) the court may order that the applicant's costs (in Scotland, expenses) be paid out of the proceeds of sale.

802 Application of proceeds of sale under court order

(1) Where shares are sold in pursuance of an order of the court under section 801, the proceeds of the sale, less the costs of the sale, must be paid into court for the benefit of the persons who are beneficially interested in the shares.

(2) A person who is beneficially interested in the shares may apply to the court for the whole or part of those proceeds to be paid to him.

(3) On such an application the court shall order the payment to the applicant of—

- (a) the whole of the proceeds of sale together with any interest on them, or
- (b) if another person had a beneficial interest in the shares at the time of their sale, such proportion of the proceeds and interest as the value of the applicant's interest in the shares bears to the total value of the shares.

This is subject to the following qualification.

(4) If the court has ordered under section 801(5) that the costs (in Scotland, expenses) of an applicant under that section are to be paid out of the proceeds of sale, the applicant is entitled to payment of his costs (or expenses) out of those proceeds before any person interested in the shares receives any part of those proceeds.

803 Power of members to require company to act

(1) The members of a company may require it to exercise its powers under section 793 (notice requiring information about interests in shares).

(2) A company is required to do so once it has received requests (to the same effect) from members of the company holding at least 10% of such of the paid-up capital of the company as carries a right to vote at general meetings of the company (excluding any voting rights attached to any shares in the company held as treasury shares).

(3) A request—

- (a) may be in hard copy form or in electronic form,
- (b) must—
  - (i) state that the company is requested to exercise its powers under section 793,
  - (ii) specify the manner in which the company is requested to act, and
  - (iii) give reasonable grounds for requiring the company to exercise those powers in the manner specified, and
- (c) must be authenticated by the person or persons making it.

804 Duty of company to comply with requirement

(1) A company that is required under section 803 to exercise its powers under section 793 (notice requiring information about interests in company's shares) must exercise those powers in the manner specified in the requests.

(2) If default is made in complying with subsection (1) an offence is committed by every officer of the company who is in default.

(3) A person guilty of an offence under this section is liable—

- (a) on conviction on indictment, to a fine;
- (b) on summary conviction, to a fine not exceeding the statutory maximum.

805 Report to members on outcome of investigation

(1) On the conclusion of an investigation carried out by a company in pursuance of a requirement under section 803 the company must cause a report of the information received in pursuance of the investigation to be prepared.

The report must be made available for inspection within a reasonable period (not more than 15 days) after the conclusion of the investigation.

(2) Where—

- (a) a company undertakes an investigation in pursuance of a requirement under section 803, and
- (b) the investigation is not concluded within three months after the date on which the company became subject to the requirement,

the company must cause to be prepared in respect of that period, and in respect of each succeeding period of three months ending before the conclusion of the investigation, an interim report of the information received during that period in pursuance of the investigation.

(3) Each such report must be made available for inspection within a reasonable period (not more than 15 days) after the end of the period to which it relates.

(4) The reports must be retained by the company for at least six years from the date on which they are first made available for inspection and must be kept available for inspection during that time—
  (a) at the company's registered office, or
  (b) at a place specified in regulations under section 1136.

(5) The company must give notice to the registrar—
  (a) of the place at which the reports are kept available for inspection, and
  (b) of any change in that place,

unless they have at all times been kept at the company's registered office.

(6) The company must within three days of making any report prepared under this section available for inspection, notify the members who made the requests under section 803 where the report is so available.

(7) For the purposes of this section an investigation carried out by a company in pursuance of a requirement under section 803 is concluded when—
  (a) the company has made all such inquiries as are necessary or expedient for the purposes of the requirement, and
  (b) in the case of each such inquiry—
    (i) a response has been received by the company, or
    (ii) the time allowed for a response has elapsed.

806 Report to members: offences

(1) If default is made for 14 days in complying with section 805(5) (notice to registrar of place at which reports made available for inspection) an offence is committed by—
  (a) the company, and
  (b) every officer of the company who is in default.

(2) A person guilty of an offence under subsection (1) is liable on summary conviction to a fine not exceeding level 3 on the standard scale and, for continued contravention, a daily default fine not exceeding one-tenth of level 3 on the standard scale.

(3) If default is made in complying with any other provision of section 805 (report to members on outcome of investigation), an offence is committed by every officer of the company who is in default.

(4) A person guilty of an offence under subsection (3) is liable—
  (a) on conviction on indictment, to a fine;
  (b) on summary conviction, to a fine not exceeding the statutory maximum.

807 Right to inspect and request copy of reports

(1) Any report prepared under section 805 must be open to inspection by any person without charge.

(2) Any person is entitled, on request and on payment of such fee as may be prescribed, to be provided with a copy of any such report or any part of it.

The copy must be provided within ten days after the request is received by the company.

(3) If an inspection required under subsection (1) is refused, or default is made in complying with subsection (2), an offence is committed by—
  (a) the company, and
  (b) every officer of the company who is in default.

(4) A person guilty of an offence under this section is liable on summary conviction to a fine not exceeding level 3 on the standard scale and, for continued contravention, a daily default fine not exceeding one-tenth of level 3 on the standard scale.

(5) In the case of any such refusal or default the court may by order compel an immediate inspection or, as the case may be, direct that the copy required be sent to the person requiring it.

Register of interests disclosed

808 Register of interests disclosed

(1) The company must keep a register of information received by it in pursuance of a requirement imposed under section 793 (notice requiring information about interests in company's shares).

(2) A company which receives any such information must, within three days of the receipt, enter in the register—
  (a) the fact that the requirement was imposed and the date on which it was imposed, and

(b) the information received in pursuance of the requirement.

(3) The information must be entered against the name of the present holder of the shares in question or, if there is no present holder or the present holder is not known, against the name of the person holding the interest.

(4) The register must be made up so that the entries against the names entered in it appear in chronological order.

(5) If default is made in complying with this section an offence is committed by—

(a) the company, and

(b) every officer of the company who is in default.

(6) A person guilty of an offence under this section is liable on summary conviction to a fine not exceeding level 3 on the standard scale and, for continued contravention, a daily default fine not exceeding one-tenth of level 3 on the standard scale.

(7) The company is not by virtue of anything done for the purposes of this section affected with notice of, or put upon inquiry as to, the rights of any person in relation to any shares.

809 Register to be kept available for inspection

(1) The register kept under section 808 (register of interests disclosed) must be kept available for inspection—

(a) at the company's registered office, or

(b) at a place specified in regulations under section 1136.

(2) A company must give notice to the registrar of companies of the place where the register is kept available for inspection and of any change in that place.

(3) No such notice is required if the register has at all times been kept available for inspection at the company's registered office.

(4) If default is made in complying with subsection (1), or a company makes default for 14 days in complying with subsection (2), an offence is committed by—

(a) the company, and

(b) every officer of the company who is in default.

(5) A person guilty of an offence under this section is liable on summary conviction to a fine not exceeding level 3 on the standard scale and, for continued contravention, a daily default fine not exceeding one-tenth of level 3 on the standard scale.

810 Associated index

(1) Unless the register kept under section 808 (register of interests disclosed) is kept in such a form as itself to constitute an index, the company must keep an index of the names entered in it.

(2) The company must make any necessary entry or alteration in the index within ten days after the date on which any entry or alteration is made in the register.

(3) The index must contain, in respect of each name, a sufficient indication to enable the information entered against it to be readily found.

(4) The index must be at all times kept available for inspection at the same place as the register.

(5) If default is made in complying with this section, an offence is committed by—

(a) the company, and

(b) every officer of the company who is in default.

(6) A person guilty of an offence under this section is liable on summary conviction to a fine not exceeding level 3 on the standard scale and, for continued contravention, a daily default fine not exceeding one-tenth of level 3 on the standard scale.

811 Rights to inspect and require copy of entries

(1) The register required to be kept under section 808 (register of interests disclosed), and any associated index, must be open to inspection by any person without charge.

(2) Any person is entitled, on request and on payment of such fee as may be prescribed, to be provided with a copy of any entry in the register.

(3) A person seeking to exercise either of the rights conferred by this section must make a request to the company to that effect.

(4) The request must contain the following information—

(a) in the case of an individual, his name and address;

(b) in the case of an organisation, the name and address of an individual responsible for making the request on behalf of the organisation;

(c) the purpose for which the information is to be used; and
(d) whether the information will be disclosed to any other person, and if so—
 (i) where that person is an individual, his name and address,
 (ii) where that person is an organisation, the name and address of an individual responsible for receiving the information on its behalf, and
 (iii) the purpose for which the information is to be used by that person.

812 Court supervision of purpose for which rights may be exercised

(1) Where a company receives a request under section 811 (register of interests disclosed: right to inspect and require copy), it must—
 (a) comply with the request if it is satisfied that it is made for a proper purpose, and
 (b) refuse the request if it is not so satisfied.
(2) If the company refuses the request, it must inform the person making the request, stating the reason why it is not satisfied.
(3) A person whose request is refused may apply to the court.
(4) If an application is made to the court—
 (a) the person who made the request must notify the company, and
 (b) the company must use its best endeavours to notify any persons whose details would be disclosed if the company were required to comply with the request.
(5) If the court is not satisfied that the inspection or copy is sought for a proper purpose, it shall direct the company not to comply with the request.
(6) If the court makes such a direction and it appears to the court that the company is or may be subject to other requests made for a similar purpose (whether made by the same person or different persons), it may direct that the company is not to comply with any such request.
The order must contain such provision as appears to the court appropriate to identify the requests to which it applies.
(7) If the court does not direct the company not to comply with the request, the company must comply with the request immediately upon the court giving its decision or, as the case may be, the proceedings being discontinued.

813 Register of interests disclosed: refusal of inspection or default in providing copy

(1) If an inspection required under section 811 (register of interests disclosed: right to inspect and require copy) is refused or default is made in providing a copy required under that section, otherwise than in accordance with section 812, an offence is committed by—
 (a) the company, and
 (b) every officer of the company who is in default.
(2) A person guilty of an offence under this section is liable on summary conviction to a fine not exceeding level 3 on the standard scale and, for continued contravention, a daily default fine not exceeding one-tenth of level 3 on the standard scale.
(3) In the case of any such refusal or default the court may by order compel an immediate inspection or, as the case may be, direct that the copy required be sent to the person requesting it.

814 Register of interests disclosed: offences in connection with request for or disclosure of information

(1) It is an offence for a person knowingly or recklessly to make in a request under section 811
(register of interests disclosed: right to inspect or require copy) a statement that is misleading, false or deceptive in a material particular.
(2) It is an offence for a person in possession of information obtained by exercise of either of the rights conferred by that section—
 (a) to do anything that results in the information being disclosed to another person, or
 (b) to fail to do anything with the result that the information is disclosed to another person,
knowing, or having reason to suspect, that person may use the information for a purpose that is not a proper purpose.
(3) A person guilty of an offence under this section is liable—

(a) on conviction on indictment, to imprisonment for a term not exceeding two years or a fine (or both);
(b) on summary conviction—
(i) in England and Wales, to imprisonment for a term not exceeding twelve months or to a fine not exceeding the statutory maximum (or both);
(ii) in Scotland or Northern Ireland, to imprisonment for a term not exceeding six months, or to a fine not exceeding the statutory maximum (or both).

815 Entries not to be removed from register

(1) Entries in the register kept under section 808 (register of interests disclosed) must not be deleted except in accordance with—
section 816 (old entries), or
section 817 (incorrect entry relating to third party).
(2) If an entry is deleted in contravention of subsection (1), the company must restore it as soon as reasonably practicable.
(3) If default is made in complying with subsection (1) or (2), an offence is committed by—
(a) the company, and
(b) every officer of the company who is in default.
(4) A person guilty of an offence under this section is liable on summary conviction to a fine not exceeding level 3 on the standard scale and, for continued contravention of subsection (2), a daily default fine not exceeding one-tenth of level 3 on the standard scale.

816 Removal of entries from register: old entries

A company may remove an entry from the register kept under section 808 (register of interests disclosed) if more than six years have elapsed since the entry was made.

817 Removal of entries from register: incorrect entry relating to third party

(1) This section applies where in pursuance of an obligation imposed by a notice under section 793 (notice requiring information about interests in company's shares) a person gives to a company the name and address of another person as being interested in shares in the company.
(2) That other person may apply to the company for the removal of the entry from the register.
(3) If the company is satisfied that the information in pursuance of which the entry was made is incorrect, it shall remove the entry.
(4) If an application under subsection (3) is refused, the applicant may apply to the court for an order directing the company to remove the entry in question from the register.
The court may make such an order if it thinks fit.

818 Adjustment of entry relating to share acquisition agreement

(1) If a person who is identified in the register kept by a company under section 808 (register of interests disclosed) as being a party to an agreement to which section 824 applies (certain share acquisition agreements) ceases to be a party to the agreement, he may apply to the company for the inclusion of that information in the register.
(2) If the company is satisfied that he has ceased to be a party to the agreement, it shall record that information (if not already recorded) in every place where his name appears in the register as a party to the agreement.
(3) If an application under this section is refused (otherwise than on the ground that the information has already been recorded), the applicant may apply to the court for an order directing the company to include the information in question in the register.
The court may make such an order if it thinks fit.

819 Duty of company ceasing to be public company

(1) If a company ceases to be a public company, it must continue to keep any register kept under section 808 (register of interests disclosed), and any associated index, until the end of the period of six years after it ceased to be such a company.
(2) If default is made in complying with this section, an offence is committed by—
(a) the company, and
(b) every officer of the company who is in default.

(3) A person guilty of an offence under this section is liable on summary conviction to a fine not exceeding level 3 on the standard scale and, for continued contravention, a daily default fine not exceeding one-tenth of level 3 on the standard scale.

Meaning of interest in shares

820 Interest in shares: general

(1) This section applies to determine for the purposes of this Part whether a person has an interest in shares.

(2) In this Part—

(a) a reference to an interest in shares includes an interest of any kind whatsoever in the shares, and

(b) any restraints or restrictions to which the exercise of any right attached to the interest is or may be subject shall be disregarded.

(3) Where an interest in shares is comprised in property held on trust, every beneficiary of the trust is treated as having an interest in the shares.

(4) A person is treated as having an interest in shares if—

(a) he enters into a contract to acquire them, or

(b) not being the registered holder, he is entitled—

(i) to exercise any right conferred by the holding of the shares, or

(ii) to control the exercise of any such right.

(5) For the purposes of subsection (4)(b) a person is entitled to exercise or control the exercise of a right conferred by the holding of shares if he—

(a) has a right (whether subject to conditions or not) the exercise of which would make him so entitled, or

(b) is under an obligation (whether subject to conditions or not) the fulfilment of which would make him so entitled.

(6) A person is treated as having an interest in shares if—

(a) he has a right to call for delivery of the shares to himself or to his order, or

(b) he has a right to acquire an interest in shares or is under an obligation to take an interest in shares.

This applies whether the right or obligation is conditional or absolute.

(7) Persons having a joint interest are treated as each having that interest.

(8) It is immaterial that shares in which a person has an interest are unidentifiable.

821 Interest in shares: right to subscribe for shares

(1) Section 793 (notice by company requiring information about interests in its shares) applies in relation to a person who has, or previously had, or is or was entitled to acquire, a right to subscribe for shares in the company as it applies in relation to a person who is or was interested in shares in that company.

(2) References in that section to an interest in shares shall be read accordingly.

822 Interest in shares: family interests

(1) For the purposes of this Part a person is taken to be interested in shares in which—

(a) his spouse or civil partner, or

(b) any infant child or step-child of his,

is interested.

(2) In relation to Scotland "infant" means a person under the age of 18 years.

823 Interest in shares: corporate interests

(1) For the purposes of this Part a person is taken to be interested in shares if a body corporate is interested in them and—

(a) the body or its directors are accustomed to act in accordance with his directions or instructions, or

(b) he is entitled to exercise or control the exercise of one-third or more of the voting power at general meetings of the body.

(2) For the purposes of this section a person is treated as entitled to exercise or control the exercise of voting power if—

(a) another body corporate is entitled to exercise or control the exercise of that voting power, and

(b) he is entitled to exercise or control the exercise of one-third or more of the voting power at general meetings of that body corporate.

(3) For the purposes of this section a person is treated as entitled to exercise or control the exercise of voting power if—
(a) he has a right (whether or not subject to conditions) the exercise of which would make him so entitled, or
(b) he is under an obligation (whether or not subject to conditions) the fulfilment of which would make him so entitled.

824 Interest in shares: agreement to acquire interests in a particular company

(1) For the purposes of this Part an interest in shares may arise from an agreement between two or more persons that includes provision for the acquisition by any one or more of them of interests in shares of a particular public company (the "target company" for that agreement).
(2) This section applies to such an agreement if—
(a) the agreement includes provision imposing obligations or restrictions on any one or more of the parties to it with respect to their use, retention or disposal of their interests in the shares of the target company acquired in pursuance of the agreement (whether or not together with any other interests of theirs in the company's shares to which the agreement relates), and
(b) an interest in the target company's shares is in fact acquired by any of the parties in pursuance of the agreement.
(3) The reference in subsection (2) to the use of interests in shares in the target company is to the exercise of any rights or of any control or influence arising from those interests (including the right to enter into an agreement for the exercise, or for control of the exercise, of any of those rights by another person).
(4) Once an interest in shares in the target company has been acquired in pursuance of the agreement, this section continues to apply to the agreement so long as the agreement continues to include provisions of any description mentioned in subsection (2).
This applies irrespective of—
(a) whether or not any further acquisitions of interests in the company's shares take place in pursuance of the agreement;
(b) any change in the persons who are for the time being parties to it;
(c) any variation of the agreement.
References in this subsection to the agreement include any agreement having effect (whether directly or indirectly) in substitution for the original agreement.
(5) In this section—
(a) "agreement" includes any agreement or arrangement, and
(b) references to provisions of an agreement include—
(i) undertakings, expectations or understandings operative under an arrangement, and
(ii) any provision whether express or implied and whether absolute or not.
References elsewhere in this Part to an agreement to which this section applies have a corresponding meaning.
(6) This section does not apply—
(a) to an agreement that is not legally binding unless it involves mutuality in the undertakings, expectations or understandings of the parties to it; or
(b) to an agreement to underwrite or sub-underwrite an offer of shares in a company, provided the agreement is confined to that purpose and any matters incidental to it.

825 Extent of obligation in case of share acquisition agreement

(1) For the purposes of this Part each party to an agreement to which section 824 applies is treated as interested in all shares in the target company in which any other party to the agreement is interested apart from the agreement (whether or not the interest of the other party was acquired, or includes any interest that was acquired, in pursuance of the agreement).
(2) For those purposes an interest of a party to such an agreement in shares in the target company is an interest apart from the agreement if he is interested in those shares otherwise than by virtue of the application of section 824 (and this section) in relation to the agreement.
(3) Accordingly, any such interest of the person (apart from the agreement) includes for those purposes any interest treated as his under section 822 or 823 (family or corporate interests) or by the application of section 824 (and this section) in relation to any other agreement with respect to shares in the target company to which he is a party.

(4) A notification with respect to his interest in shares in the target company made to the company under this Part by a person who is for the time being a party to an agreement to which section 824 applies must—
(a) state that the person making the notification is a party to such an agreement,
(b) include the names and (so far as known to him) the addresses of the other parties to the agreement, identifying them as such, and
(c) state whether or not any of the shares to which the notification relates are shares in which he is interested by virtue of section 824 (and this section) and, if so, the number of those shares.

Other supplementary provisions

826 Information protected from wider disclosure

(1) Information in respect of which a company is for the time being entitled to any exemption conferred by regulations under section 409(3) (information about related undertakings to be given in notes to accounts: exemption where disclosure harmful to company's business)—
(a) must not be included in a report under section 805 (report to members on outcome of investigation), and
(b) must not be made available under section 811 (right to inspect and request copy of entries).
(2) Where any such information is omitted from a report under section 805, that fact must be stated in the report.

827 Reckoning of periods for fulfilling obligations

Where the period allowed by any provision of this Part for fulfilling an obligation is expressed as a number of days, any day that is not a working day shall be disregarded in reckoning that period.

828 *omitted*

PART 23
DISTRIBUTIONS

CHAPTER 1
RESTRICTIONS ON WHEN DISTRIBUTIONS MAY BE MADE

Introductory

829 Meaning of "distribution"

(1) In this Part "distribution" means every description of distribution of a company's assets to its members, whether in cash or otherwise, subject to the following exceptions.
(2) The following are not distributions for the purposes of this Part—
(a) an issue of shares as fully or partly paid bonus shares;
(b) the reduction of share capital—
(i) by extinguishing or reducing the liability of any of the members on any of the company's shares in respect of share capital not paid up, or
(ii) by repaying paid-up share capital;
(c) the redemption or purchase of any of the company's own shares out of capital (including the proceeds of any fresh issue of shares) or out of unrealised profits in accordance with Chapter 3, 4 or 5 of Part 18;
(d) a distribution of assets to members of the company on its winding up.

General rules

830 Distributions to be made only out of profits available for the purpose

(1) A company may only make a distribution out of profits available for the purpose.
(2) A company's profits available for distribution are its accumulated, realised profits, so far as not previously utilised by distribution or capitalisation, less its accumulated, realised losses, so far as not previously written off in a reduction or reorganisation of capital duly made.

(3) Subsection (2) has effect subject to sections 832 and 835 (investment companies etc: distributions out of accumulated revenue profits).

831 Net asset restriction on distributions by public companies

(1) A public company may only make a distribution—
(a) if the amount of its net assets is not less than the aggregate of its called-up share capital and undistributable reserves, and
(b) if, and to the extent that, the distribution does not reduce the amount of those assets to less than that aggregate.
(2) For this purpose a company's "net assets" means the aggregate of the company's assets less the aggregate of its liabilities.
(3) "Liabilities" here includes—
(a) where the relevant accounts are Companies Act accounts, provisions of a kind specified for the purposes of this subsection by regulations under section 396;
(b) where the relevant accounts are IAS accounts, provisions of any kind.
(4) A company's undistributable reserves are—
(a) its share premium account;
(b) its capital redemption reserve;
(c) the amount by which its accumulated, unrealised profits (so far as not previously utilised by capitalisation) exceed its accumulated, unrealised losses (so far as not previously written off in a reduction or reorganisation of capital duly made);
(d) any other reserve that the company is prohibited from distributing—
(i) by any enactment (other than one contained in this Part), or
(ii) by its articles.

The reference in paragraph (c) to capitalisation does not include a transfer of profits of the company to its capital redemption reserve.
(5) A public company must not include any uncalled share capital as an asset in any accounts relevant for purposes of this section.
(6) Subsection (1) has effect subject to sections 832 and 835 (investment companies etc: distributions out of accumulated revenue profits).

Distributions by investment companies

832 Distributions by investment companies out of accumulated revenue profits

(1) An investment company may make a distribution out of its accumulated, realised revenue profits if the following conditions are met.
(2) It may make such a distribution only if, and to the extent that, its accumulated, realised revenue profits, so far as not previously utilised by a distribution or capitalisation, exceed its accumulated revenue losses (whether realised or unrealised), so far as not previously written off in a reduction or reorganisation of capital duly made.
(3) It may make such a distribution only—
(a) if the amount of its assets is at least equal to one and a half times the aggregate of its liabilities to creditors, and
(b) if, and to the extent that, the distribution does not reduce that amount to less than one and a half times that aggregate.
(4) For this purpose a company's liabilities to creditors include—
(a) in the case of Companies Act accounts, provisions of a kind specified for the purposes of this subsection by regulations under section 396;
(b) in the case of IAS accounts, provisions for liabilities to creditors.
(5) The following conditions must also be met—
(a) the company's shares must be shares admitted to trading on a regulated market;
(b) during the relevant period it must not have—
(i) …
(ii) applied any unrealised profits in paying up debentures or amounts unpaid on its issued shares;
(c) it must have given notice to the registrar under section 833(1) (notice of intention to carry on business as an investment company)—
(i) before the beginning of the relevant period, or
(ii) as soon as reasonably practicable after the date of its incorporation.
(6) For the purposes of this section—
(a) …
(b) the "relevant period" is the period beginning with—

(i) the first day of the accounting reference period immediately preceding that in which the proposed distribution is to be made, or

(ii) where the distribution is to be made in the company's first accounting reference period, the first day of that period,

and ending with the date of the distribution.

(7) The company must not include any uncalled share capital as an asset in any accounts relevant for purposes of this section.

833 Meaning of "investment company"

(1) In this Part an "investment company" means a public company that—

(a) has given notice (which has not been revoked) to the registrar of its intention to carry on business as an investment company, and

(b) since the date of that notice has complied with the following requirement.

(2) The requirement is —

(a) that the business of the company consists of investing its funds in shares, land or other assets, with the aim of spreading investment risk and giving members of the company the benefit of the results of the management of its funds;

(b)–(d) ...

(3) ...

(4) Notice to the registrar under this section may be revoked at any time by the company on giving notice to the registrar that it no longer wishes to be an investment company within the meaning of this section.

(5) On giving such a notice, the company ceases to be such a company.

834, 835 ...

CHAPTER 2
JUSTIFICATION OF DISTRIBUTION BY REFERENCE TO ACCOUNTS

Justification of distribution by reference to accounts

836 Justification of distribution by reference to relevant accounts

(1) Whether a distribution may be made by a company without contravening this Part is determined by reference to the following items as stated in the relevant accounts—

(a) profits, losses, assets and liabilities;

(b) provisions of the following kinds—

(i) where the relevant accounts are Companies Act accounts, provisions of a kind specified for the purposes of this subsection by regulations under section 396;

(ii) where the relevant accounts are IAS accounts, provisions of any kind;

(c) share capital and reserves (including undistributable reserves).

(2) The relevant accounts are the company's last annual accounts, except that—

(a) where the distribution would be found to contravene this Part by reference to the company's last annual accounts, it may be justified by reference to interim accounts, and

(b) where the distribution is proposed to be declared during the company's first accounting reference period, or before any accounts have been circulated in respect of that period, it may be justified by reference to initial accounts.

(3) The requirements of—

section 837 (as regards the company's last annual accounts),
section 838 (as regards interim accounts), and
section 839 (as regards initial accounts),

must be complied with, as and where applicable.

(4) If any applicable requirement of those sections is not complied with, the accounts may not be relied on for the purposes of this Part and the distribution is accordingly treated as contravening this Part.

Requirements applicable in relation to relevant accounts

837 Requirements where last annual accounts used

(1) The company's last annual accounts means the company's individual accounts—

(a) that were last circulated to members in accordance with section 423 (duty to circulate copies of annual accounts and reports).

(2) The accounts must have been properly prepared in accordance with this Act, or have been so prepared subject only to matters that are not material for determining (by reference to the items mentioned in section 836(1)) whether the distribution would contravene this Part.

(3) Unless the company is exempt from audit and the directors take advantage of that exemption, the auditor must have made his report on the accounts.

(4) If that report was qualified—

(a) the auditor must have stated in writing (either at the time of his report or subsequently) whether in his opinion the matters in respect of which his report is qualified are material for determining whether a distribution would contravene this Part, and

(b) a copy of that statement must—

(i) in the case of a private company, have been circulated to members in accordance with section 423, or

(ii) in the case of a public company, have been laid before the company in general meeting.

(5) An auditor's statement is sufficient for the purposes of a distribution if it relates to distributions of a description that includes the distribution in question, even if at the time of the statement it had not been proposed.

838 Requirements where interim accounts used

(1) Interim accounts must be accounts that enable a reasonable judgment to be made as to the amounts of the items mentioned in section 836(1).

(2) Where interim accounts are prepared for a proposed distribution by a public company, the following requirements apply.

(3) The accounts must have been properly prepared, or have been so prepared subject to matters that are not material for determining (by reference to the items mentioned in section 836(1)) whether the distribution would contravene this Part.

(4) "Properly prepared" means prepared in accordance with sections 395 to 397 (requirements for company individual accounts), applying those requirements with such modifications as are necessary because the accounts are prepared otherwise than in respect of an accounting reference period.

(5) The balance sheet comprised in the accounts must have been signed in accordance with section 414.

(6) A copy of the accounts must have been delivered to the registrar.
Any requirement of Part 35 of this Act as to the delivery of a certified translation into English of any document forming part of the accounts must also have been met.

839 Requirements where initial accounts used

(1) Initial accounts must be accounts that enable a reasonable judgment to be made as to the amounts of the items mentioned in section 836(1).

(2) Where initial accounts are prepared for a proposed distribution by a public company, the following requirements apply.

(3) The accounts must have been properly prepared, or have been so prepared subject to matters that are not material for determining (by reference to the items mentioned in section 836(1)) whether the distribution would contravene this Part.

(4) "Properly prepared" means prepared in accordance with sections 395 to 397 (requirements for company individual accounts), applying those requirements with such modifications as are necessary because the accounts are prepared otherwise than in respect of an accounting reference period.

(5) The company's auditor must have made a report stating whether, in his opinion, the accounts have been properly prepared.

(6) If that report was qualified—

(a) the auditor must have stated in writing (either at the time of his report or subsequently) whether in his opinion the matters in respect of which his report is qualified are material for determining whether a distribution would contravene this Part, and

(b) a copy of that statement must have been laid before the company in general meeting.

(7) A copy of the accounts, of the auditor's report and of any auditor's statement must have been delivered to the registrar.
Any requirement of Part 35 of this Act as to the delivery of a certified translation into English of any of those documents must also have been met.

Application of provisions to successive distributions etc.

840 Successive distributions etc by reference to the same accounts

(1) In determining whether a proposed distribution may be made by a company in a case where—
(a) one or more previous distributions have been made in pursuance of a determination made by reference to the same relevant accounts, or
(b) relevant financial assistance has been given, or other relevant payments have been made, since those accounts were prepared,
the provisions of this Part apply as if the amount of the proposed distribution was increased by the amount of the previous distributions, financial assistance and other payments.
(2) The financial assistance and other payments that are relevant for this purpose are—
(a) financial assistance lawfully given by the company out of its distributable profits;
(b) financial assistance given by the company in contravention of section 678 or 679 (prohibited financial assistance) in a case where the giving of that assistance reduces the company's net assets or increases its net liabilities;
(c) payments made by the company in respect of the purchase by it of shares in the company, except a payment lawfully made otherwise than out of distributable profits;
(d) payments of any description specified in section 705 (payments apart from purchase price of shares to be made out of distributable profits).
(3) In this section "financial assistance" has the same meaning as in Chapter 2 of Part 18 (see section 677).
(4) For the purpose of applying subsection (2)(b) in relation to any financial assistance—
(a) "net assets" means the amount by which the aggregate amount of the company's assets exceeds the aggregate amount of its liabilities, and
(b) "net liabilities" means the amount by which the aggregate amount of the company's liabilities exceeds the aggregate amount of its assets,
taking the amount of the assets and liabilities to be as stated in the company's accounting records immediately before the financial assistance is given.
(5) For this purpose a company's liabilities include any amount retained as reasonably necessary for the purposes of providing for any liability—
(a) the nature of which is clearly defined, and
(b) which is either likely to be incurred or certain to be incurred but uncertain as to amount or as to the date on which it will arise.

CHAPTER 3
SUPPLEMENTARY PROVISIONS

Accounting matters

841 Realised losses and profits and revaluation of fixed assets

(1) The following provisions have effect for the purposes of this Part.
(2) The following are treated as realised losses—
(a) in the case of Companies Act accounts, provisions of a kind specified for the purposes of this paragraph by regulations under section 396 (except revaluation provisions);
(b) in the case of IAS accounts, provisions of any kind (except revaluation provisions).
(3) A "revaluation provision" means a provision in respect of a diminution in value of a fixed asset appearing on a revaluation of all the fixed assets of the company, or of all of its fixed assets other than goodwill.
(4) For the purpose of subsections (2) and (3) any consideration by the directors of the value at a particular time of a fixed asset is treated as a revaluation provided—
(a) the directors are satisfied that the aggregate value at that time of the fixed assets of the company that have not actually been revalued is not less than the aggregate amount at which they are then stated in the company's accounts, and

(b) it is stated in a note to the accounts—
(i) that the directors have considered the value of some or all of the fixed assets of the company without actually revaluing them,
(ii) that they are satisfied that the aggregate value of those assets at the time of their consideration was not less than the aggregate amount at which they were then stated in the company's accounts, and
(iii) that accordingly, by virtue of this subsection, amounts are stated in the accounts on the basis that a revaluation of fixed assets of the company is treated as having taken place at that time.

(5) Where—
(a) on the revaluation of a fixed asset, an unrealised profit is shown to have been made, and
(b) on or after the revaluation, a sum is written off or retained for depreciation of that asset over a period,

an amount equal to the amount by which that sum exceeds the sum which would have been so written off or retained for the depreciation of that asset over that period, if that profit had not been made, is treated as a realised profit made over that period.

842 Determination of profit or loss in respect of asset where records incomplete

In determining for the purposes of this Part whether a company has made a profit or loss in respect of an asset where—
(a) there is no record of the original cost of the asset, or
(b) a record cannot be obtained without unreasonable expense or delay,

its cost is taken to be the value ascribed to it in the earliest available record of its value made on or after its acquisition by the company.

843 Realised profits and losses of long-term insurance business

(1) The provisions of this section have effect for the purposes of this Part as it applies in relation to an authorised insurance, other than an insurance special purpose vehicle, company carrying on long-term business.

(2) An amount included in the relevant part of the company's balance sheet that—
(a) represents a surplus in the fund or funds maintained by it in respect of its long-term business, and
(b) has not been allocated to policy holders or, as the case may be, carried forward unappropriated in accordance with asset identification rules made under Part 9A of the Financial Services and Markets Act 2000,

is treated as a realised profit.

(3) For the purposes of subsection (2)—
(a) the relevant part of the balance sheet is that part of the balance sheet that represents accumulated profit or loss;
(b) a surplus in the fund or funds maintained by the company in respect of its long-term business means an excess of the assets representing that fund or those funds over the liabilities of the company attributable to its long-term business, as shown by an actuarial investigation.

(4) A deficit in the fund or funds maintained by the company in respect of its long-term business is treated as a realised loss.
For this purpose a deficit in any such fund or funds means an excess of the liabilities of the company attributable to its long-term business over the assets representing that fund or those funds, as shown by an actuarial investigation.

(5) Subject to subsections (2) and (4), any profit or loss arising in the company's long-term business is to be left out of account.

(6) For the purposes of this section an "actuarial investigation" means an investigation made into the financial condition of an authorised insurance company in respect of its long-term business—
(a) carried out once in every period of twelve months in accordance with rules made under Part 9A of the Financial Services and Markets Act 2000, or
(b) carried out in accordance with a requirement imposed under section 166 of that Act, by an actuary appointed as actuary to the company.

(7) In this section "long-term business" means business that consists of effecting or carrying out contracts of long-term insurance.
This definition must be read with section 22 of the Financial Services and Markets Act 2000, any relevant order under that section and Schedule 2 to that Act.

(8) In this section "insurance special purpose vehicle" means a special purpose vehicle within the meaning of Article 2.1(p) of Directive 2005/68/EC of the European Parliament and of the Council of 16 November 2005 on reinsurance and amending Council Directives 73/239/EEC, 92/49/EEC as well as Directives 98/78/EC and 2002/83/EC.

844 Treatment of development costs

(1) Where development costs are shown or included as an asset in a company's accounts, any amount shown or included in respect of those costs is treated—
  (a) for the purposes of section 830 (distributions to be made out of profits available for the purpose) as a realised loss, and
  (b) for the purposes of section 832 (distributions by investment companies out of accumulated revenue profits) as a realised revenue loss.

This is subject to the following exceptions.

(2) Subsection (1) does not apply to any part of that amount representing an unrealised profit made on revaluation of those costs.

(3) Subsection (1) does not apply if—
  (a) there are special circumstances in the company's case justifying the directors in deciding that the amount there mentioned is not to be treated as required by subsection (1),
  (b) it is stated—
    (i) in the case of Companies Act accounts, in the note required by regulations under section 396 as to the reasons for showing development costs as an asset, or
    (ii) in the case of IAS accounts, in any note to the accounts, that the amount is not to be so treated, and
  (c) the note explains the circumstances relied upon to justify the decision of the directors to that effect.

Distributions in kind

845 Distributions in kind: determination of amount

(1) This section applies for determining the amount of a distribution consisting of or including, or treated as arising in consequence of, the sale, transfer or other disposition by a company of a non-cash asset where—
  (a) at the time of the distribution the company has profits available for distribution, and
  (b) if the amount of the distribution were to be determined in accordance with this section, the company could make the distribution without contravening this Part.

(2) The amount of the distribution (or the relevant part of it) is taken to be—
  (a) in a case where the amount or value of the consideration for the disposition is not less than the book value of the asset, zero;
  (b) in any other case, the amount by which the book value of the asset exceeds the amount or value of any consideration for the disposition.

(3) For the purposes of subsection (1)(a) the company's profits available for distribution are treated as increased by the amount (if any) by which the amount or value of any consideration for the disposition exceeds the book value of the asset.

(4) In this section "book value", in relation to an asset, means—
  (a) the amount at which the asset is stated in the relevant accounts, or
  (b) where the asset is not stated in those accounts at any amount, zero.

(5) The provisions of Chapter 2 (justification of distribution by reference to accounts) have effect subject to this section.

846 Distributions in kind: treatment of unrealised profits

(1) This section applies where—
  (a) a company makes a distribution consisting of or including, or treated as arising in consequence of, the sale, transfer or other disposition by the company of a non-cash asset, and
  (b) any part of the amount at which that asset is stated in the relevant accounts represents an unrealised profit.

(2) That profit is treated as a realised profit—
  (a) for the purpose of determining the lawfulness of the distribution in accordance with this Part (whether before or after the distribution takes place), and

(b) for the purpose of the application, in relation to anything done with a view to or in connection with the making of the distribution, of any provision of regulations under section 396 under which only realised profits are to be included in or transferred to the profit and loss account.

Consequences of unlawful distribution

847 Consequences of unlawful distribution

(1) This section applies where a distribution, or part of one, made by a company to one of its members is made in contravention of this Part.

(2) If at the time of the distribution the member knows or has reasonable grounds for believing that it is so made, he is liable—

(a) to repay it (or that part of it, as the case may be) to the company, or

(b) in the case of a distribution made otherwise than in cash, to pay the company a sum equal to the value of the distribution (or part) at that time.

(3) This is without prejudice to any obligation imposed apart from this section on a member of a company to repay a distribution unlawfully made to him.

(4) This section does not apply in relation to—

(a) financial assistance given by a company in contravention of section 678 or 679, or

(b) any payment made by a company in respect of the redemption or purchase by the company of shares in itself.

Other matters

848 Saving for certain older provisions in articles

(1) Where immediately before the relevant date a company was authorised by a provision of its articles to apply its unrealised profits in paying up in full or in part unissued shares to be allotted to members of the company as fully or partly paid bonus shares, that provision continues (subject to any alteration of the articles) as authority for those profits to be so applied after that date.

(2) For this purpose the relevant date is—

(a) for companies registered in Great Britain, 22nd December 1980;

(b) for companies registered in Northern Ireland, 1st July 1983.

849 Restriction on application of unrealised profits

A company must not apply an unrealised profit in paying up debentures or any amounts unpaid on its issued shares.

850 Treatment of certain older profits or losses

(1) Where the directors of a company are, after making all reasonable enquiries, unable to determine whether a particular profit made before the relevant date is realised or unrealised, they may treat the profit as realised.

(2) Where the directors of a company, after making all reasonable enquiries, are unable to determine whether a particular loss made before the relevant date is realised or unrealised, they may treat the loss as unrealised.

(3) For the purposes of this section the relevant date is—

(a) for companies registered in Great Britain, 22nd December 1980;

(b) for companies registered in Northern Ireland, 1st July 1983.

851 Application of rules of law restricting distributions

(1) Except as provided in this section, the provisions of this Part are without prejudice to any rule of law restricting the sums out of which, or the cases in which, a distribution may be made.

(2) For the purposes of any rule of law requiring distributions to be paid out of profits or restricting the return of capital to members—

(a) section 845 (distributions in kind: determination of amount) applies to determine the amount of any distribution or return of capital consisting of or including, or treated as arising in consequence of the sale, transfer or other disposition by a company of a non-cash asset; and

(b) section 846 (distributions in kind: treatment of unrealised profits) applies as it applies for the purposes of this Part.

(3) In this section references to distributions are to amounts regarded as distributions for the purposes of any such rule of law as is referred to in subsection (1).

852 Saving for other restrictions on distributions

The provisions of this Part are without prejudice to any enactment, or any provision of a company's articles, restricting the sums out of which, or the cases in which, a distribution may be made.

853 Minor definitions

(1) The following provisions apply for the purposes of this Part.

(2) References to profit or losses of any description—

(a) are to profits or losses of that description made at any time, and

(b) except where the context otherwise requires, are to profits or losses of a revenue or capital character.

(3) "Capitalisation", in relation to a company's profits, means any of the following operations (whenever carried out)—

(a) applying the profits in wholly or partly paying up unissued shares in the company to be allotted to members of the company as fully or partly paid bonus shares, or

(b) transferring the profits to capital redemption reserve.

(4) References to "realised profits" and "realised losses", in relation to a company's accounts, are to such profits or losses of the company as fall to be treated as realised in accordance with principles generally accepted at the time when the accounts are prepared, with respect to the determination for accounting purposes of realised profits or losses.

(5) Subsection (4) is without prejudice to—

(a) the construction of any other expression (where appropriate) by reference to accepted accounting principles or practice, or

(b) any specific provision for the treatment of profits or losses of any description as realised.

(6) "Fixed assets" means assets of a company which are intended for use on a continuing basis in the company's activities.

PART 24
A COMPANY'S ANNUAL RETURN

854 Duty to deliver annual returns

(1) Every company must deliver to the registrar successive annual returns each of which is made up to a date not later than the date that is from time to time the company's return date.

(2) The company's return date is—

(a) the anniversary of the company's incorporation, or

(b) if the company's last return delivered in accordance with this Part was made up to a different date, the anniversary of that date.

(3) Each return must—

(a) contain the information required by or under the following provisions of this Part, and

(b) be delivered to the registrar within 28 days after the date to which it is made up.

855 Contents of annual return: general

(1) Every annual return must state the date to which it is made up and contain the following information—

(a) the address of the company's registered office;

(b) the type of company it is and its principal business activities;

(c) the required particulars (see section 855A) of—

(i) the directors of the company, and

(ii) in the case of a private company with a secretary or a public company, the secretary or joint secretaries;

(d) if any company records are (in accordance with regulations under section 1136) kept at a place other than the company's registered office, the address of that place and the records that are kept there;

(2) The information as to the company's type must be given by reference to the classification scheme prescribed for the purposes of this section.

(3) The information as to the company's principal business activities may be given by reference to one or more categories of any prescribed system of classifying business activities.

(4) In this Part—

"DTR5 issuer" means an issuer to which Chapter 5 of the Disclosure Rules and Transparency Rules sourcebook issued by the Financial Conduct Authority applies;

"relevant market" means any of the markets mentioned in article 4(1) of the Financial Services and Markets Act 2000 (Prescribed Markets and Qualifying Investments) Order 2001;

"return period", in relation to an annual return, means the period beginning immediately after the date to which the last return was made up (or, in the case of the first return, with the incorporation of the company) and ending with the date to which the return is made up.

855A Required particulars of directors and secretaries

(1) For the purposes of section 855(1)(c) the required particulars of a director are—

- (a) where the director is an individual, the particulars required by section 163 to be entered in the register of directors (subject to subsection (2) below); and
- (b) where the director is a body corporate or a firm that is a legal person under the law by which it is governed, the particulars required by section 164 to be entered in the register of directors.

(2) The former name of a director who is an individual is a required particular in relation to an annual return only if the director was known by the name for business purposes during the return period.

(3) For the purposes of section 855(1)(c)(ii) the required particulars of a secretary are—

- (a) where a secretary is an individual, the particulars required by section 277 to be entered in the register of secretaries (subject to subsection (4) below); and
- (b) where a secretary is a body corporate or a firm that is a legal person under the law by which it is governed, the particulars required by section 278(1) to be entered in the register of secretaries.

(4) The former name of a secretary who is an individual is a required particular in relation to an annual return only if the secretary was known by the name for business purposes during the return period.

(5) Where all the partners in a firm are joint secretaries, the required particulars are the particulars that would be required to be entered in the register of secretaries if the firm were a legal person and the firm had been appointed secretary.

856 Contents of annual return: information about shares and share capital

(1) The annual return of a company having a share capital must also contain the following information.

(1A) The return must contain a statement of capital.

(2) The statement of capital must state with respect to the company's share capital at the date to which the return is made up—

- (a) the total number of shares of the company,
- (b) the aggregate nominal value of those shares,
- (c) for each class of shares—
  - (i) the voting rights attached to the shares,
  - (ii) the total number of shares of that class, and
  - (iii) the aggregate nominal value of shares of that class, and
- (d) the amount paid up and the amount (if any) unpaid on each share (whether on account of the nominal value of the share or by way of premium).

(2A) The annual return must also state whether any of the company's shares were, at any time during the return period, shares admitted to trading on a relevant market or on any other market which is outside the United Kingdom.

(2B) If any of the company's shares were shares admitted to trading as mentioned in subsection (2A), the annual return must also state whether both of the following conditions were satisfied throughout the return period—
  (a) there were shares of the company which were shares admitted to trading on a relevant market;
  (b) the company was a DTR5 issuer.

856A Contents of annual return: information about shareholders: non-traded companies

(1) This section applies to the annual return of a company none of whose shares were, at any time during the return period, shares admitted to trading on a relevant market or on any other market which is outside the United Kingdom.

(2) The return must also contain the name (as it appears in the company's register of members) of every person who was a member of the company at any time during the return period.
The return must conform to the following requirements for the purpose of enabling the entries relating to any given person to be easily found—
  (a) the entries must be listed in alphabetical order by name; or
  (b) the return must have annexed to it an index that is sufficient to enable the name of the person in question to be easily found.

(3) The return must also state—
  (a) the number of shares of each class held at the end of the cate to which the return is made up by each person who was a member of the company at that time,
  (b) the number of shares of each class transferred during the return period by or to each person who was a member of the company at any t me during that period, and
  (c) the dates of registration of those transfers.

(4) If either of the two immediately preceding returns has given the full particulars required by subsections (2) and (3), the return need only give such particulars as relate—
  (a) to persons who became, or ceased to be, members during the return period, and
  (b) to shares transferred during that period.

856B Contents of annual return: information about shareholders: certain traded companies

(1) This section applies to the annual return of a company any of whose shares were, at any time during the return period, shares admitted to trading on a relevant market or on any other market which is outside the United Kingdom.

(2) But this section does not apply to the annual return of a company if throughout the return period—
  (a) there were shares of the company which were shares admitted to trading on a relevant market, and
  (b) the company was a DTR5 issuer.

(3) The annual return of a company to which this section applies must also state, in respect of each person who held at least 5% of the issued shares of any class of the company at the end of the date to which the return is made up—
  (a) the person's name and address (as they appear in the company's register of members); and
  (b) the number of shares of each class held by the person at that time.

(4) The return must conform to the following requirements for the purpose of enabling entries relating to any given person to be easily found—
  (a) the entries must be listed in alphabetical order by name; or
  (b) the return must have annexed to it an index that is sufficient to enable the name of the person in question to be easily found.

857 Contents of annual return: power to make further provision by regulations

(1) The Secretary of State may by regulations make further provision as to the information to be given in a company's annual return.

(2) The regulations may—

(a) amend or repeal the provisions of sections 855 and 856, and
(b) provide for exceptions from the requirements of those sections as they have effect from time to time.

(3) Regulations under this section are subject to negative resolution procedure.

858 Failure to deliver annual return

(1) If a company fails to deliver an annual return before the end of the period of 28 days after a return date, an offence is committed by—
(a) the company,
(b) subject to subsection (4)—
(i) every director of the company, and
(ii) in the case of a private company with a secretary or a public company, every secretary of the company, and
(c) every other officer of the company who is in default.

For this purpose a shadow director is treated as a director.

(2) A person guilty of an offence under subsection (1) is liable on summary conviction to a fine not exceeding level 5 on the standard scale and, for continued contravention, a daily default fine not exceeding one-tenth of the greater of £5,000 or level 4 on the standard scale.

(3) The contravention continues until such time as an annual return made up to that return date is delivered by the company to the registrar.

(4) It is a defence for a director or secretary charged with an offence under subsection (1)(b) to prove that he took all reasonable steps to avoid the commission or continuation of the offence.

(5) In the case of continued contravention, an offence is also committed by every officer of the company who did not commit an offence under subsection (1) in relation to the initial contravention but is in default in relation to the continued contravention.

A person guilty of an offence under this subsection is liable on summary conviction to a fine not exceeding one-tenth of the greater of £5,000 or level 4 on the standard scale for each day on which the contravention continues and he is in default.

859 ...

PART 25
COMPANY CHARGES

CHAPTER A1
REGISTRATION OF COMPANY CHARGES

Company charge

859A Charges created by a company

(1) Subject to subsection (6), this section applies where a company creates a charge.

(2) The registrar must register the charge if, before the end of the period allowed for delivery, the company or any person interested in the charge delivers to the registrar for registration a section 859D statement of particulars.

(3) Where the charge is created or evidenced by an instrument, the registrar is required to register it only if a certified copy of the instrument is delivered to the registrar with the statement of particulars.

(4) "The period allowed for delivery" is 21 days beginning with the day after the date of creation of the charge (see section 859E), unless an order allowing an extended period is made under section 859F(3).

(5) Where an order is made under section 859F(3) a copy of the order must be delivered to the registrar with the statement of particulars.

(6) This section does not apply to—
(a) a charge in favour of a landlord on a cash deposit given as a security in connection with the lease of land;
(b) a charge created by a member of Lloyd's (within the meaning of the Lloyd's Act 1982) to secure its obligations in connection with its underwriting business at Lloyd's;
(c) a charge excluded from the application of this section by or under any other Act.

(7) In this Part—
"cash" includes foreign currency,
"charge" includes—
(a) a mortgage;
(b) a standard security, assignation in security, and any other right in security constituted under the law of Scotland, including any heritable security, but not including a pledge, and
"company" means a UK-registered company.

859B Charge in series of debentures

(1) This section applies where—
(a) a company creates a series of debentures containing a charge, or giving a charge by reference to another instrument, and
(b) debenture holders of that series are entitled to the benefit of the charge pari passu.
(2) The registrar must register the charge if, before the end of the period allowed for delivery, the company or any person interested in the charge delivers to the registrar for registration, a section 859D statement of particulars which also contains the following—
(a) either—
(i) the name of each of the trustees for the debenture holders, or
(ii) where there are more than four such persons, the names of any four persons listed in the charge instrument as trustees for the debenture holders, and a statement that there are other such persons;
(b) the dates of the resolutions authorising the issue of the series;
(c) the date of the covering instrument (if any) by which the series is created or defined.
(3) Where the charge is created or evidenced by an instrument, the registrar is required to register it only if a certified copy of the instrument is delivered to the registrar with the statement of particulars.
(4) Where the charge is not created or evidenced by an instrument, the registrar is required to register it only if a certified copy of one of the debentures in the series is delivered to the registrar with the statement of particulars.
(5) For the purposes of this section a statement of particulars is taken to be a section 859D statement of particulars even if it does not contain the names of the debenture holders.
(6) "The period allowed for delivery" is—
(a) if there is a deed containing the charge, 21 days beginning with the day after the date on which the deed is executed;
(b) if there is no deed containing the charge, 21 days beginning with the day after the date on which the first debenture of the series is executed.
(7) Where an order is made under section 859F(3) a copy of the order must be delivered to the registrar with the statement of particulars.
(8) In this section "deed" means—
(a) a deed governed by the law of England and Wales or Northern Ireland, or
(b) an instrument governed by a law other than the law of England and Wales or Northern Ireland which requires delivery under that law in order to take effect.

859C Charges existing on property or undertaking acquired

(1) This section applies where a company acquires property or undertaking which is subject to a charge of a kind which would, if it had been created by the company after the acquisition of the property or undertaking, have been capable of being registered under section 859A.
(2) The registrar must register the charge if the company or any person interested in the charge delivers to the registrar for registration a section 859D statement of particulars.
(3) Where the charge is created or evidenced by an instrument, the registrar is required to register it only if a certified copy of the instrument is delivered to the registrar with the statement of particulars.

859D Particulars to be delivered to registrar

(1) A statement of particulars relating to a charge created by a company is a "section 859D statement of particulars" if it contains the following particulars—
(a) the registered name and number of the company;
(b) the date of creation of the charge and (if the charge is one to which section 859C applies) the date of acquisition of the property or undertaking concerned;
(c) where the charge is created or evidenced by an instrument, the particulars listed in subsection (2);

(d) where the charge is not created or evidenced by an instrument, the particulars listed in subsection (3).

(2) The particulars referred to in subsection (1)(c) are—
(a) any of the following—
(i) the name of each of the persons in whose favour the charge has been created or of the security agents or trustees holding the charge for the benefit of one or more persons; or,
(ii) where there are more than four such persons, security agents or trustees, the names of any four such persons, security agents or trustees listed in the charge instrument, and a statement that there are other such persons, security agents or trustees;
(b) whether the instrument is expressed to contain a floating charge and, if so, whether it is expressed to cover all the property and undertaking of the company;
(c) whether any of the terms of the charge prohibit or restrict the company from creating further security that will rank equally with or ahead of the charge;
(d) whether (and if so, a short description of) any land, ship, aircraft or intellectual property that is registered or required to be registered in the United Kingdom, is subject to a charge (which is not a floating charge) or fixed security included in the instrument;
(e) whether the instrument includes a charge (which is not a floating charge) or fixed security over—
(i) any tangible or corporeal property, or
(ii) any intangible or incorporeal property, not described in paragraph (d).

(3) The particulars referred to in subsection (1)(d) are—
(a) a statement that there is no instrument creating or evidencing the charge;
(b) the names of each of the persons in whose favour the charge has been created or the names of any security agents or trustees holding the charge for the benefit of one or more persons;
(c) the nature of the charge;
(d) a short description of the property or undertaking charged;
(e) the obligations secured by the charge.

(4) In this section "fixed security" has the meaning given in section 486(1) of the Companies Act 1985.

(5) In this section "intellectual property" includes—
(a) any patent, trade mark, registered design, copyright or design right;
(b) any licence under or in respect of any such right.

859E Date of creation of charge

(1) For the purposes of this Part, a charge of the type described in column 1 of the Table below is taken to be created on the date given in relation to it in column 2 of that Table.

1 Type of charge	*2 When charge created*
Standard security	The date of its recording in the Register of Sasines or its registration in the Land Register of Scotland
Charge other than a standard security, where created or evidenced by an instrument	Where the instrument is a deed that has been executed and has immediate effect on execution and delivery, the date of delivery
	Where the instrument is a deed that has been executed and held in escrow, the date of delivery into escrow
	Where the instrument is a deed that has been executed and held as undelivered, the date of delivery
	Where the instrument is not a deed and has immediate effect on execution, the date of execution

	Where the instrument is not a deed and does not have immediate effect on execution, the date on which the instrument takes effect
Charge other than a standard security, where not created or evidenced by an instrument	The date on which the charge comes into effect.

(2) Where a charge is created or evidenced by an instrument made between two or more parties, references in the Table in subsection (1) to execution are to execution by all the parties to the instrument whose execution is essential for the instrument to take effect as a charge.

(3) This section applies for the purposes of this Chapter even if further forms, notices, registrations or other actions or proceedings are necessary to make the charge valid or effectual for any other purposes.

(4) For the purposes of this Chapter, the registrar is entitled without further enquiry to accept a charge as created on the date given as the date of creation of the charge in a section 859D statement of particulars.

(5) In this section "deed" means—

(a) a deed governed by the law of England and Wales or Northern Ireland, or

(b) an instrument governed by a law other than the law of England and Wales or Northern Ireland which requires delivery under that law in order to take effect.

(6) References in this section to delivery, in relation to a deed, include delivery as a deed where required.

859F Extension of period allowed for delivery

(1) Subsection (3) applies if the court is satisfied that—

(a) neither the company nor any other person interested in the charge has delivered to the registrar the documents required under section 859A or (as the case may be) 859B before the end of the period allowed for delivery under the section concerned, and

(b) the requirement in subsection (2) is met.

(2) The requirement is—

(a) that the failure to deliver those documents—

(i) was accidental or due to inadvertence or to some other sufficient cause, or

(ii) is not of a nature to prejudice the position of creditors or shareholders of the company, or

(b) that on other grounds it is just and equitable to grant relief.

(3) The court may, on the application of the company or a person interested, and on such terms and conditions as seem to the court just and expedient, order that the period allowed for delivery be extended.

859G Personal information etc in certified copies

(1) The following are not required to be included in a certified copy of an instrument or debenture delivered to the registrar for the purposes of any provision of this Chapter—

(a) personal information relating to an individual (other than the name of an individual);

(b) the number or other identifier of a bank or securities account of a company or individual;

(c) a signature.

(2) The registrar is entitled without further enquiry, to accept the certified copy of an instrument whether or not any of the information in subsection (1) is contained within the instrument.

859H Consequence of failure to deliver charges

(1) This section applies if—

(a) a company creates a charge to which section 859A or 859B applies, and

(b) the documents required by section 859A or (as the case may be) 859B are not delivered to the registrar by the company or another person interested in the charge before the end of the relevant period allowed for delivery.

(2) "The relevant period allowed for delivery" is—

(a) the period allowed for delivery under the section in question, or
(b) if an order under section 859F(3) has been made, the period allowed by the order.

(3) Where this section applies, the charge is void (so far as any security on the company's property or undertaking is conferred by it) against—
(a) a liquidator of the company,
(b) an administrator of the company, and
(c) a creditor of the company.

(4) Subsection (3) is without prejudice to any contract or obligation for repayment of the money secured by the charge; and when a charge becomes void under this section, the money secured by it immediately becomes payable.

The register

859I Entries on the register

(1) This section applies where a charge is registered in accordance with a provision of this Chapter.

(2) The registrar must—
(a) allocate to the charge a unique reference code and place a note in the register recording that reference code; and
(b) include in the register any documents delivered under section 859A(3) or (5), 859B(3), (4) or (7), or 859C(3).

(3) The registrar must give a certificate of the registration of the charge to the person who delivered to the registrar a section 859D statement of particulars relating to the charge.

(4) The certificate must state—
(a) the registered name and number of the company in respect of which the charge was registered; and
(b) the unique reference code allocated to the charge.

(5) The certificate must be signed by the registrar or authenticated by the registrar's official seal.

(6) In the case of registration under section 859A or 859B, the certificate is conclusive evidence that the documents required by the section concerned were delivered to the registrar before the end of the relevant period allowed for delivery.

(7) "The relevant period allowed for delivery" is—
(a) the period allowed for delivery under the section in question, or
(b) if an order under section 859F(3) has been made, the period allowed by the order.

859J Company holding property or undertaking as trustee

(1) Where a company is acting as trustee of property or undertaking which is the subject of a charge delivered for registration under this Chapter, the company or any person interested in the charge may deliver to the registrar a statement to that effect.

(2) A statement delivered after the delivery for registration of the charge must include—
(a) the registered name and number of the company; and
(b) the unique reference code allocated to the charge.

859K Registration of enforcement of security

(1) Subsection (2) applies where a person—
(a) obtains an order for the appointment of a receiver or manager of a company's property or undertaking, or
(b) appoints such a receiver or manager under powers contained in an instrument.

(2) The person must, within 7 days of the order or of the appointment under those powers—
(a) give notice to the registrar of that fact, and
(b) if the order was obtained, or the appointment made, by virtue of a registered charge held by the person give the registrar a notice containing—
(i) in the case of a charge created before 6th April 2013, the information specified in subsection (4);
(ii) in the case of a charge created on or after 6th April 2013, the unique reference code allocated to the charge.

(3) Where a person appointed receiver or manager of a company's property or undertaking under powers contained in an instrument ceases to act as such a receiver or manager, the person must, on so ceasing—

(a) give notice to the registrar of that fact, and
(b) give the registrar a notice containing—
(i) in the case of a charge created before 6th April 2013, the information specified in subsection (4), or
(ii) in the case of a charge created on or after 6th April 2013, the unique reference code allocated to the charge.

(4) The information referred to in subsections (2)(b)(i) and (3)(b)(i) is—
(a) the date of the creation of the charge;
(b) a description of the instrument (if any) creating or evidencing the charge;
(c) short particulars of the property or undertaking charged.

(5) The registrar must include in the register—
(a) a fact of which notice is given under subsection (2)(a), and
(b) a fact of which notice is given under subsection (3)(a).

(6) A person who makes default in complying with the requirements of subsections (2) or (3) of this section commits an offence.

(7) A person guilty of an offence under this section is liable on summary conviction to a fine not exceeding level 3 on the standard scale and, for continued contravention, a daily default fine not exceeding one-tenth of level 3 on the standard scale.

(8) This section applies only to a receiver or manager appointed—
(a) by a court in England and Wales or Northern Ireland, or
(b) under an instrument governed by the law of England and Wales or Northern Ireland.

(9) This section does not apply to a receiver appointed under Chapter 2 of Part 3 of the Insolvency Act 1986 (receivers (Scotland)).

859L Entries of satisfaction and release

(1) Subsection (5) applies if the statement set out in subsection (2) and the particulars set out in subsection (4) are delivered to the registrar with respect to a registered charge.

(2) The statement referred to in subsection (1) is a statement to the effect that—
(a) the debt for which the charge was given has been paid or satisfied in whole or in part, or
(b) all or part of the property or undertaking charged—
(i) has been released from the charge, or
(ii) has ceased to form part of the company's property or undertaking.

(3) Where a statement within subsection (2)(b) relates to part only of the property or undertaking charged, the statement must include a short description of that part.

(4) The particulars referred to in subsection (1) are—
(a) the name and address of the person delivering the statement and an indication of their interest in the charge;
(b) the registered name and number of the company that—
(i) created the charge (in a case within section 859A or 859B), or
(ii) acquired the property or undertaking subject to the charge (in a case within section 859C);
(c) in respect of a charge created before 6th April 2013—
(i) the date of creation of the charge;
(ii) a description of the instrument (if any) by which the charge is created or evidenced;
(iii) short particulars of the property or undertaking charged;
(d) in respect of a charge created on or after 6th April 2013, the unique reference code allocated to the charge.

(5) The registrar must include in the register—
(a) a statement of satisfaction in whole or in part, or
(b) a statement of the fact that all or part of the property or undertaking has been released from the charge or has ceased to form part of the company's property or undertaking (as the case may be).

859M Rectification of register

(1) Subsection (3) applies if the court is satisfied that—
(a) there has been an omission or mis-statement in any statement or notice delivered to the registrar in accordance with this Chapter, and

(b) the requirement in subsection (2) is met.

(2) The requirement is that the court is satisfied—

(a) that the omission or mis-statement—

(i) was accidental or due to inadvertence or to some other sufficient cause, or

(ii) is not of a nature to prejudice the position of creditors or shareholders of the company, or

(b) that on other grounds it is just and equitable to grant relief.

(3) The court may, on the application of the company or a person interested, and on such terms and conditions as seem to the court just and expedient, order that the omission or mis-statement be rectified.

(4) A copy of the court's order must be sent by the applicant to the registrar for registration.

859N Replacement of instrument or debenture

(1) Subsection (2) applies if the court is satisfied that—

(a) a copy of an instrument or debenture delivered to the registrar under this Chapter contains material which could have been omitted under section 859G;

(b) the wrong instrument or debenture was delivered to the registrar; or

(c) the copy was defective.

(2) The court may, on the application of the company or a person interested, and on such terms and conditions as seem to the court just and expedient, order that the copy of the instrument or debenture be removed from the register and replaced.

(3) A copy of the court's order must be sent by the applicant to the registrar for registration.

859O Notification of addition to or amendment of charge

(1) This section applies where, after the creation of a charge, the charge is amended by adding or amending a term that—

(a) prohibits or restricts the creation of any fixed security or any other charge having priority over, or ranking pari passu with, the charge; or

(b) varies, or otherwise regulates the order of, the ranking of the charge in relation to any fixed security or any other charge.

(2) Either the company that created the charge or the person taking the benefit of the charge (or another charge referred to in subsection (1)(b)) may deliver to the registrar for registration—

(a) a certified copy of the instrument effecting the amendment, variation or regulation, and

(b) a statement of the particulars set out in subsection (3).

(3) The particulars to be included in the statement are—

(a) the registered name and number of the company;

(b) in the case of a charge created before 6th April 2013—

(i) the date of creation of the charge;

(ii) a description of the instrument (if any) by which the charge was created or evidenced;

(iii) short particulars of the property or undertaking charged as set out when the charge was registered;

(c) in the case of a charge created on or after 6th April 2013, (where allocated) the unique reference code allocated to the charge.

(4) Subsections (1) to (3) do not affect the continued application of section 466 of the Companies Act 1985.

(5) In this section "fixed security" has the meaning given in section 486(1) of the Companies Act 1985.

859P Companies to keep copies of instruments creating and amending charges

(1) A company must keep available for inspection a copy of every—

(a) instrument creating a charge capable of registration under this Chapter, and

(b) instrument effecting any variation or amendment of such a charge.

(2) In the case of a charge contained in a series of uniform debentures, a copy of one of the debentures of the series is sufficient for the purposes of subsection (1)(a).

(3) If the particulars referred to in section 859D(1) or the particulars of the property or undertaking charged are not contained in the instrument creating the charge, but are instead contained in other documents which are referred to in or otherwise incorporated into the instrument, then the company must also keep available for inspection a copy of those other documents.

(4) It is sufficient for the purposes of subsection (1)(a) if the company keeps a copy of the instrument in the form delivered to the registrar under section 859A(3), 859B(3) or (4) or 859C(3).
(5) Where a translation has been delivered to the registrar in accordance with section 1105, the company must keep available for inspection a copy of the translation.

859Q Instruments creating charges to be available for inspection

(1) This section applies to documents required to be kept available for inspection under section 859P (copies of instruments creating and amending charges).
(2) The documents must be kept available for inspection—
 (a) at the company's registered office, or
 (b) at a place specified in regulations under section 1136.
(3) The company must give notice to the registrar—
 (a) of the place at which the documents are kept available for inspection, and
 (b) of any change in that place,
 unless they have at all times been kept at the company's registered office.
(4) The documents must be open to the inspection—
 (a) of any creditor or member of the company, without charge, and
 (b) of any other person, on payment of such fee as may be prescribed.
(5) If default is made for 14 days in complying with subsection (3) or an inspection required under subsection (4) is refused, an offence is committed by—
 (a) the company, and
 (b) every officer of the company who is in default.
(6) A person guilty of an offence under this section is liable on summary conviction to a fine not exceeding level 3 on the standard scale and, for continued contravention, a daily default fine not exceeding one-tenth of level 3 on the standard scale.
(7) If an inspection required under subsection (4) is refused the court may by order compel an immediate inspection.
(8) Where the company and a person wishing to carry out an inspection under subsection (4) agree, the inspection may be carried out by electronic means.

CHAPTERS 1–3...

PART 26
ARRANGEMENTS AND RECONSTRUCTIONS

Application of this Part

895 Application of this Part

(1) The provisions of this Part apply where a compromise or arrangement is proposed between a company and—
 (a) its creditors, or any class of them, or
 (b) its members, or any class of them.
(2) In this Part—
 "arrangement" includes a reorganisation of the company's share capital by the consolidation of shares of different classes or by the division of shares into shares of different classes, or by both of those methods; and
 "company"—
 (a) in section 900 (powers of court to facilitate reconstruction or amalgamation) means a company within the meaning of this Act, and
 (b) elsewhere in this Part means any company liable to be wound up under the Insolvency Act 1986 or the Insolvency (Northern Ireland) Order 1989.
(3) The provisions of this Part have effect subject to Part 27 (mergers and divisions of public companies) where that Part applies (see sections 902 and 903).

Meeting of creditors or members

896 Court order for holding of meeting

(1) The court may, on an application under this section, order a meeting of the creditors or class of creditors, or of the members of the company or class of members (as the case may be), to be summoned in such manner as the court directs.

(2) An application under this section may be made by—
  (a) the company,
  (b) any creditor or member of the company,
  (c) if the company is being wound up, the liquidator, or
  (d) if the company is in administration, the administrator.

(3) Section 323 (representation of corporations at meetings) applies to a meeting of creditors under this section as to a meeting of the company (references to a member of the company being read as references to a creditor).

897 Statement to be circulated or made available

(1) Where a meeting is summoned under section 896—
  (a) every notice summoning the meeting that is sent to a creditor or member must be accompanied by a statement complying with this section, and
  (b) every notice summoning the meeting that is given by advertisement must either—
    (i) include such a statement, or
    (ii) state where and how creditors or members entitled to attend the meeting may obtain copies of such a statement.

(2) The statement must—
  (a) explain the effect of the compromise or arrangement, and
  (b) in particular, state—
    (i) any material interests of the directors of the company (whether as directors or as members or as creditors of the company or otherwise), and
    (ii) the effect on those interests of the compromise or arrangement, in so far as it is different from the effect on the like interests of other persons.

(3) Where the compromise or arrangement affects the rights of debenture holders of the company, the statement must give the like explanation as respects the trustees of any deed for securing the issue of the debentures as it is required to give as respects the company's directors.

(4) Where a notice given by advertisement states that copies of an explanatory statement can be obtained by creditors or members entitled to attend the meeting, every such creditor or member is entitled, on making application in the manner indicated by the notice, to be provided by the company with a copy of the statement free of charge.

(5) If a company makes default in complying with any requirement of this section, an offence is committed by—
  (a) the company, and
  (b) every officer of the company who is in default. This is subject to subsection (7) below.

(6) For this purpose the following are treated as officers of the company—
  (a) a liquidator or administrator of the company, and
  (b) a trustee of a deed for securing the issue of debentures of the company.

(7) A person is not guilty of an offence under this section if he shows that the default was due to the refusal of a director or trustee for debenture holders to supply the necessary particulars of his interests.

(8) A person guilty of an offence under this section is liable—
  (a) on conviction on indictment, to a fine;
  (b) on summary conviction, to a fine not exceeding the statutory maximum.

898 Duty of directors and trustees to provide information

(1) It is the duty of—
  (a) any director of the company, and
  (b) any trustee for its debenture holders,

  to give notice to the company of such matters relating to himself as may be necessary for the purposes of section 897 (explanatory statement to be circulated or made available).

(2) Any person who makes default in complying with this section commits an offence.

(3) A person guilty of an offence under this section is liable on summary conviction to a fine not exceeding level 3 on the standard scale.

Court sanction for compromise or arrangement

899 Court sanction for compromise or arrangement

(1) If a majority in number representing 75% in value of the creditors or class of creditors or members or class of members (as the case may be), present and voting either in person or by proxy at the meeting summoned under section 896, agree a compromise or arrangement, the court may, on an application under this section, sanction the compromise or arrangement.

(2) An application under this section may be made by—

(a) the company,

(b) any creditor or member of the company,

(c) if the company is being wound up, the liquidator, or

(d) if the company is in administration, the administrator.

(3) A compromise or arrangement sanctioned by the court is binding on—

(a) all creditors or the class of creditors or on the members or class of members (as the case may be), and

(b) the company or, in the case of a company in the course of being wound up, the liquidator and contributories of the company.

(4) The court's order has no effect until a copy of it has been delivered to the registrar.

(5) Section 323 (representation of corporations at meetings) applies to a meeting of creditors under this section as to a meeting of the company (references to a member of the company being read as references to a creditor).

Reconstructions and amalgamations

900 Powers of court to facilitate reconstruction or amalgamation

(1) This section applies where application is made to the court under section 899 to sanction a compromise or arrangement and it is shown that—

(a) the compromise or arrangement is proposed for the purposes of, or in connection with, a scheme for the reconstruction of any company or companies, or the amalgamation of any two or more companies, and

(b) under the scheme the whole or any part of the undertaking or the property of any company concerned in the scheme ("a transferor company") is to be transferred to another company ("the transferee company").

(2) The court may, either by the order sanctioning the compromise or arrangement or by a subsequent order, make provision for all or any of the following matters—

(a) the transfer to the transferee company of the whole or any part of the undertaking and of the property or liabilities of any transferor company;

(b) the allotting or appropriation by the transferee company of any shares, debentures, policies or other like interests in that company which under the compromise or arrangement are to be allotted or appropriated by that company to or for any person;

(c) the continuation by or against the transferee company of any legal proceedings pending by or against any transferor company;

(d) the dissolution, without winding up, of any transferor company;

(e) the provision to be made for any persons who, within such time and in such manner as the court directs, dissent from the compromise or arrangement;

(f) such incidental, consequential and supplemental matters as are necessary to secure that the reconstruction or amalgamation is fully and effectively carried out.

(3) If an order under this section provides for the transfer of property or liabilities—

(a) the property is by virtue of the order transferred to, and vests in, the transferee company, and

(b) the liabilities are, by virtue of the order, transferred to and become liabilities of that company.

(4) The property (if the order so directs) vests freed from any charge that is by virtue of the compromise or arrangement to cease to have effect.

(5) In this section—

"property" includes property, rights and powers of every description; and "liabilities" includes duties.

(6) Every company in relation to which an order is made under this section must cause a copy of the order to be delivered to the registrar within seven days after its making.

(7) If default is made in complying with subsection (6) an offence is committed by—
  (a) the company, and
  (b) every officer of the company who is in default.

(8) A person guilty of an offence under subsection (7) is liable on summary conviction to a fine not exceeding level 3 on the standard scale and, for continued contravention, a daily default fine not exceeding one-tenth of level 3 on the standard scale.

Obligations of company with respect to articles etc

901 Obligations of company with respect to articles etc.

(1) This section applies—
  (a) to any order under section 899 (order sanctioning compromise or arrangement), and
  (b) to any order under section 900 (order facilitating reconstruction or amalgamation) that alters the company's constitution.

(2) If the order amends—
  (a) the company's articles, or
  (b) any resolution or agreement to which Chapter 3 of Part 3 applies (resolution or agreement affecting a company's constitution),

the copy of the order delivered to the registrar by the company under section 899(4) or section 900(6) must be accompanied by a copy of the company's articles, or the resolution or agreement in question, as amended.

(3) Every copy of the company's articles issued by the company after the order is made must be accompanied by a copy of the order, unless the effect of the order has been incorporated into the articles by amendment.

(4) In this section—
  (a) references to the effect of the order include the effect of the compromise or arrangement to which the order relates; and
  (b) in the case of a company not having articles, references to its articles shall be read as references to the instrument constituting the company or defining its constitution.

(5) If a company makes default in complying with this section an offence is committed by—
  (a) the company, and
  (b) every officer of the company who is in default.

(6) A person guilty of an offence under this section is liable on summary conviction to a fine not exceeding level 3 on the standard scale.

PART 27
OMITTED

PART 28
TAKEOVERS ETC

CHAPTER 1
THE TAKEOVER PANEL

The Panel and its rules

942 The Panel

(1) The body known as the Panel on Takeovers and Mergers ("the Panel") is to have the functions conferred on it by or under this Chapter.

(2) The Panel may do anything that it considers necessary or expedient for the purposes of, or in connection with, its functions.

(3) The Panel may make arrangements for any of its functions to be discharged by—
  (a) a committee or sub-committee of the Panel, or
  (b) an officer or member of staff of the Panel, or a person acting as such.

This is subject to section 943(4) and (5).

943 Rules

(1) The Panel must make rules giving effect to Articles 3.1, 4.2, 5, 6.1 to 6.3, 7 to 9 and 13 of the Takeovers Directive.

(2) Rules made by the Panel may also make other provision—

(a) for or in connection with the regulation of—

(i) takeover bids,

(ii) merger transactions, and

(iii) transactions (not falling within sub-paragraph (i) or (ii)) that have or may have, directly or indirectly, an effect on the ownership or control of companies;

(b) for or in connection with the regulation of things done in consequence of, or otherwise in relation to, any such bid or transaction;

(c) about cases where—

(i) any such bid or transaction is, or has been, contemplated or apprehended, or

(ii) an announcement is made denying that any such bid or transaction is intended.

(3) The provision that may be made under subsection (2) includes, in particular, provision for a matter that is, or is similar to, a matter provided for by the Panel in the City Code on Takeovers and Mergers as it had effect immediately before the passing of this Act.

(4) In relation to rules made by virtue of section 957 (fees and charges), functions under this section may be discharged either by the Panel itself or by a committee of the Panel (but not otherwise).

(5) In relation to rules of any other description, the Panel must discharge its functions under this section by a committee of the Panel.

(6) Section 1 (meaning of “company”) does not apply for the purposes of this section.

(7) In this section “takeover bid” includes a takeover bid within the meaning of the Takeovers Directive.

(8) In this Chapter “the Takeovers Directive” means Directive 2004/25/EC of the European Parliament and of the Council.

(9) A reference to rules in the following provisions of this Chapter is to rules under this section.

944 *omitted*

945 Rulings

(1) The Panel may give rulings on the interpretation, application or effect of rules.

(2) To the extent and in the circumstances specified in rules, and subject to any review or appeal, a ruling has binding effect.

946 Directions

Rules may contain provision conferring power on the Panel to give any direction that appears to the Panel to be necessary in order—

(a) to restrain a person from acting (or continuing to act) in breach of rules;

(b) to restrain a person from doing (or continuing to do) a particular thing, pending determination of whether that or any other conduct of his is or would be a breach of rules;

(c) otherwise to secure compliance with rules.

Information

947 Power to require documents and information

(1) The Panel may by notice in writing require a person—

(a) to produce any documents that are specified or described in the notice;

(b) to provide, in the form and manner specified in the notice, such information as may be specified or described in the notice.

(2) A requirement under subsection (1) must be complied with—

(a) at a place specified in the notice, and

(b) before the end of such reasonable period as may be so specified.

(3) This section applies only to documents and information reasonably required in connection with the exercise by the Panel of its functions.

(4) The Panel may require—
 (a) any document produced to be authenticated, or
 (b) any information provided (whether in a document or otherwise) to be verified, in such manner as it may reasonably require.
(5) The Panel may authorise a person to exercise any of its powers under this section.
(6) A person exercising a power by virtue of subsection (5) must, if required to do so, produce evidence of his authority to exercise the power.
(7) The production of a document in pursuance of this section does not affect any lien that a person has on the document.
(8) The Panel may take copies of or extracts from a document produced in pursuance of this section.
(9) A reference in this section to the production of a document includes a reference to the production of—
 (a) a hard copy of information recorded otherwise than in hard copy form, or
 (b) information in a form from which a hard copy can be readily obtained.
(10) A person is not required by this section to disclose documents or information in respect of which a claim to legal professional privilege (in Scotland, to confidentiality of communications) could be maintained in legal proceedings.

948 Restrictions on disclosure

(1) This section applies to information (in whatever form)—
 (a) relating to the private affairs of an individual, or
 (b) relating to any particular business,

that is provided to the Panel in connection with the exercise of its functions.
(2) No such information may, during the lifetime of the individual or so long as the business continues to be carried on, be disclosed without the consent of that individual or (as the case may be) the person for the time being carrying on that business.
(3) Subsection (2) does not apply to any disclosure of information that—
 (a) is made for the purpose of facilitating the carrying out by the Panel of any of its functions,
 (b) is made to a person specified in Part 1 of Schedule 2,
 (c) is of a description specified in Part 2 of that Schedule, or
 (d) is made in accordance with Part 3 of that Schedule.
(4) The Secretary of State may amend Schedule 2 by order subject to negative resolution procedure.
(5) An order under subsection (4) must not—
 (a) amend Part 1 of Schedule 2 by specifying a person unless the person exercises functions of a public nature (whether or not he exercises any other function);
 (b) amend Part 2 of Schedule 2 by adding or modifying a description of disclosure unless the purpose for which the disclosure is permitted is likely to facilitate the exercise of a function of a public nature;
 (c) amend Part 3 of Schedule 2 so as to have the effect of permitting disclosures to be made to a body other than one that exercises functions of a public nature in a country or territory outside the United Kingdom.
(6) Subsection (2) does not apply to—
 (a) the disclosure by an authority within subsection (7) of information disclosed to it by the Panel in reliance on subsection (3);
 (b) the disclosure of such information by anyone who has obtained it directly or indirectly from an authority within subsection (7).
(7) The authorities within this subsection are—
 (a) the Financial Conduct Authority;
 (aa) the Prudential Regulation Authority;
 (ab) the Bank of England;
 (b) an authority designated as a supervisory authority for the purposes of Article 4.1 of the Takeovers Directive;
 (c) any other person or body that exercises functions of a public nature, under legislation in an EEA State other than the United Kingdom, that are similar to the Panel's functions or those of the Financial Conduct Authority or the Prudential Regulation Authority or similar to the regulatory functions of the Bank of England.

(8) This section does not prohibit the disclosure of information if the information is or has been available to the public from any other source.

(9) Nothing in this section authorises the making of a disclosure in contravention of the Data Protection Act 1998.

949 Offence of disclosure in contravention of section 948

(1) A person who discloses information in contravention of section 948 is guilty of an offence, unless—

- (a) he did not know, and had no reason to suspect, that the information had been provided as mentioned in section 948(1), or
- (b) he took all reasonable steps and exercised all due diligence to avoid the commission of the offence.

(2) A person guilty of an offence under this section is liable—

- (a) on conviction on indictment, to imprisonment for a term not exceeding two years or a fine (or both);
- (b) on summary conviction—
  - (i) in England and Wales, to imprisonment for a term not exceeding twelve months or to a fine not exceeding the statutory maximum (or both);
  - (ii) in Scotland or Northern Ireland, to imprisonment for a term not exceeding six months, or to a fine not exceeding the statutory maximum (or both).

(3) Where a company or other body corporate commits an offence under this section, an offence is also committed by every officer of the company or other body corporate who is in default.

Co-operation

950 Panel's duty of co-operation

(1) The Panel must take such steps as it considers appropriate to co-operate with—

- (a) the Financial Conduct Authority;
- (aa) the Prudential Regulation Authority;
- (ab) the Bank of England;
- (b) an authority designated as a supervisory authority for the purposes of Article 4.1 of the Takeovers Directive;
- (c) any other person or body that exercises functions of a public nature, under legislation in any country or territory outside the United Kingdom, that appear to the Panel to be similar to its own functions or those of the Financial Conduct Authority or the Prudential Regulation Authority or similar to the regulatory functions of the Bank of England.

(2) Co-operation may include the sharing of information that the Panel is not prevented from disclosing.

Hearings and appeals

951 Hearings and appeals

(1) Rules must provide for a decision of the Panel to be subject to review by a committee of the Panel (the "Hearings Committee") at the instance of such persons affected by the decision as are specified in the rules.

(2) Rules may also confer other functions on the Hearings Committee.

(3) Rules must provide for there to be a right of appeal against a decision of the Hearings Committee to an independent tribunal (the "Takeover Appeal Board") in such circumstances and subject to such conditions as are specified in the rules.

(4) Rules may contain—

- (a) provision as to matters of procedure in relation to proceedings before the Hearings Committee (including provision imposing time limits);
- (b) provision about evidence in such proceedings;
- (c) provision as to the powers of the Hearings Committee dealing with a matter referred to it;
- (d) provision about enforcement of decisions of the Hearings Committee and the Takeover Appeal Board.

(5) Rules must contain provision—

(a) requiring the Panel, when acting in relation to any proceedings before the Hearings Committee or the Takeover Appeal Board, to do so by an officer or member of staff of the Panel (or a person acting as such);
(b) preventing a person who is or has been a member of the committee mentioned in section 943(5) from being a member of the Hearings Committee or the Takeover Appeal Board;
(c) preventing a person who is a member of the committee mentioned in section 943(5), of the Hearings Committee or of the Takeover Appeal Board from acting as mentioned in paragraph (a).

Contravention of rules etc

952 Sanctions

(1) Rules may contain provision conferring power on the Panel to impose sanctions on a person who has—
(a) acted in breach of rules, or
(b) failed to comply with a direction given by virtue of section 946.
(2) Subsection (3) applies where rules made by virtue of subsection (1) confer power on the Panel to impose a sanction of a kind not provided for by the City Code on Takeovers and Mergers as it had effect immediately before the passing of this Act.
(3) The Panel must prepare a statement (a "policy statement") of its policy with respect to—
(a) the imposition of the sanction in question, and
(b) where the sanction is in the nature of a financial penalty, the amount of the penalty that may be imposed.

An element of the policy must be that, in making a decision about any such matter, the Panel has regard to the factors mentioned in subsection (4).
(4) The factors are—
(a) the seriousness of the breach or failure in question in relation to the nature of the rule or direction contravened;
(b) the extent to which the breach or failure was deliberate or reckless;
(c) whether the person on whom the sanction is to be imposed is an individual.
(5) The Panel may at any time revise a policy statement.
(6) The Panel must prepare a draft of any proposed policy statement (or revised policy statement) and consult such persons about the draft as the Panel considers appropriate.
(7) The Panel must publish, in whatever way it considers appropriate, any policy statement (or revised policy statement) that it prepares.
(8) In exercising, or deciding whether to exercise, its power to impose a sanction within subsection (2) in the case of any particular breach or failure, the Panel must have regard to any relevant policy statement published and in force at the time when the breach or failure occurred.

953 Failure to comply with rules about bid documentation

(1) This section applies where a takeover bid is made for a company that has securities carrying voting rights admitted to trading on a regulated market in the United Kingdom.
(2) Where an offer document published in respect of the bid does not comply with offer document rules, an offence is committed by—
(a) the person making the bid, and
(b) where the person making the bid is a body of persons, any director, officer or member of that body who caused the document to be published.
(3) A person commits an offence under subsection (2) only if—
(a) he knew that the offer document did not comply, or was reckless as to whether it complied, and
(b) he failed to take all reasonable steps to secure that it did comply.
(4) Where a response document published in respect of the bid does not comply with response document rules, an offence is committed by any director or other officer of the company referred to in subsection (1) who—
(a) knew that the response document did not comply, or was reckless as to whether it complied, and
(b) failed to take all reasonable steps to secure that it did comply.

(5) Where an offence is committed under subsection (2)(b) or (4) by a company or other body corporate ("the relevant body")—
   (a) subsection (2)(b) has effect as if the reference to a director, officer or member of the person making the bid included a reference to a director, officer or member of the relevant body;
   (b) subsection (4) has effect as if the reference to a director or other officer of the company referred to in subsection (1) included a reference to a director, officer or member of the relevant body.
(6) A person guilty of an offence under this section is liable—
   (a) on conviction on indictment, to a fine;
   (b) on summary conviction, to a fine not exceeding the statutory maximum.
(7) Nothing in this section affects any power of the Panel in relation to the enforcement of its rules.
(8) Section 1 (meaning of "company") does not apply for the purposes of this section.
(9) In this section—
"designated" means designated in rules;
"offer document" means a document required to be published by rules giving effect to Article 6.2 of the Takeovers Directive;
"offer document rules" means rules designated as rules that give effect to Article 6.3 of that Directive;
"response document" means a document required to be published by rules giving effect to Article 9.5 of that Directive;
"response document rules" means rules designated as rules that give effect to the first sentence of Article 9.5 of that Directive;
"securities" means shares or debentures;
"takeover bid" has the same meaning as in that Directive;
"voting rights" means rights to vote at general meetings of the company in question, including rights that arise only in certain circumstances.

954 Compensation

(1) Rules may confer power on the Panel to order a person to pay such compensation as it thinks just and reasonable if he is in breach of a rule the effect of which is to require the payment of money.
(2) Rules made by virtue of this section may include provision for the payment of interest (including compound interest).

955 Enforcement by the court

(1) If, on the application of the Panel, the court is satisfied—
   (a) that there is a reasonable likelihood that a person will contravene a rule-based requirement, or
   (b) that a person has contravened a rule-based requirement or a disclosure requirement,
the court may make any order it thinks fit to secure compliance with the requirement.
(2) In subsection (1) "the court" means the High Court or, in Scotland, the Court of Session.
(3) Except as provided by subsection (1), no person—
   (a) has a right to seek an injunction, or
   (b) in Scotland, has title or interest to seek an interdict or an order for specific performance,
to prevent a person from contravening (or continuing to contravene) a rule-based requirement or a disclosure requirement.
(4) In this section—
"contravene" includes fail to comply;
"disclosure requirement" means a requirement imposed under section 947; "rule-based requirement" means a requirement imposed by or under rules.

956 No action for breach of statutory duty etc.

(1) Contravention of a rule-based requirement or a disclosure requirement does not give rise to any right of action for breach of statutory duty.

(2) Contravention of a rule-based requirement does not make any transaction void or unenforceable or (subject to any provision made by rules) affect the validity of any other thing.

(3) In this section—

(a) "contravention" includes failure to comply;

(b) "disclosure requirement" and "rule-based requirement" have the same meaning as in section 955.

Funding

957 Fees and charges

(1) Rules may provide for fees or charges to be payable to the Panel for the purpose of meeting any part of its expenses.

(2) A reference in this section or section 958 to expenses of the Panel is to any expenses that have been or are to be incurred by the Panel in, or in connection with, the discharge of its functions, including in particular—

(a) payments in respect of the expenses of the Takeover Appeal Board;

(b) the cost of repaying the principal of, and of paying any interest on, any money borrowed by the Panel;

(c) the cost of maintaining adequate reserves.

958 Levy

(1) For the purpose of meeting any part of the expenses of the Panel, the Secretary of State may by regulations provide for a levy to be payable to the Panel—

(a) by specified persons or bodies, or persons or bodies of a specified description, or

(b) on transactions, of a specified description, in securities on specified markets.

In this subsection "specified" means specified in the regulations.

(2) The power to specify (or to specify descriptions of) persons or bodies must be exercised in such a way that the levy is payable only by persons or bodies that appear to the Secretary of State—

(a) to be capable of being directly affected by the exercise of any of the functions of the Panel, or

(b) otherwise to have a substantial interest in the exercise of any of those functions.

(3) Regulations under this section may in particular—

(a) specify the rate of the levy and the period in respect of which it is payable at that rate;

(b) make provision as to the times when, and the manner in which, payments are to be made in respect of the levy.

(4) In determining the rate of the levy payable in respect of a particular period, the Secretary of State—

(a) must take into account any other income received or expected by the Panel in respect of that period;

(b) may take into account estimated as well as actual expenses of the Panel in respect of that period.

(5) The Panel must—

(a) keep proper accounts in respect of any amounts of levy received by virtue of this section;

(b) prepare, in relation to each period in respect of which any such amounts are received, a statement of account relating to those amounts in such form and manner as is specified in the regulations.

Those accounts must be audited, and the statement certified, by persons appointed by the Secretary of State.

(6) Regulations under this section—

(a) are subject to affirmative resolution procedure if subsection (7) applies to them;

(b) otherwise, are subject to negative resolution procedure.

(7) This subsection applies to—

(a) the first regulations under this section;

(b) any other regulations under this section that would result in a change in the persons or bodies by whom, or the transactions on which, the levy is payable.

(8) If a draft of an instrument containing regulations under this section would, apart from this subsection, be treated for the purposes of the Standing Orders of either House of

Parliament as a hybrid instrument, it is to proceed in that House as if it were not such an instrument.

959 Recovery of fees, charges or levy

An amount payable by any person or body by virtue of section 957 or 958 is a debt due from that person or body to the Panel, and is recoverable accordingly.

Miscellaneous and supplementary

960 Panel as party to proceedings

The Panel is capable (despite being an unincorporated body) of—

(a) bringing proceedings under this Chapter in its own name;

(b) bringing or defending any other proceedings in its own name.

961 Exemption from liability in damages

(1) Neither the Panel, nor any person within subsection (2), is to be liable in damages for anything done (or omitted to be done) in, or in connection with, the discharge or purported discharge of the Panel's functions.

(2) A person is within this subsection if—

(a) he is (or is acting as) a member, officer or member of staff of the Panel, or

(b) he is a person authorised under section 947(5).

(3) Subsection (1) does not apply—

(a) if the act or omission is shown to have been in bad faith, or

(b) so as to prevent an award of damages in respect of the act or omission on the ground that it was unlawful as a result of section 6(1) of the Human Rights Act 1998 (acts of public authorities incompatible with Convention rights).

962 Privilege against self-incrimination

(1) A statement made by a person in response to—

(a) a requirement under section 947(1), or

(b) an order made by the court under section 955 to secure compliance with such a requirement,

may not be used against him in criminal proceedings in which he is charged with an offence to which this subsection applies.

(2) Subsection (1) applies to any offence other than an offence under one of the following provisions (which concern false statements made otherwise than on oath)—

(a) section 5 of the Perjury Act 1911;

(b) section 44(2) of the Criminal Law (Consolidation) (Scotland) Act 1995;

(c) Article 10 of the Perjury (Northern Ireland) Order 1979.

963 Annual reports

(1) After the end of each financial year the Panel must publish a report.

(2) The report must—

(a) set out how the Panel's functions were discharged in the year in question;

(b) include the Panel's accounts for that year;

(c) mention any matters the Panel considers to be of relevance to the discharge of its functions.

964, 965 *omitted*

CHAPTER 2
IMPEDIMENTS TO TAKEOVERS

Opting in and opting out

966 Opting in and opting out

(1) A company may by special resolution (an "opting-in resolution") opt in for the purposes of this Chapter if the following three conditions are met in relation to the company.

(2) The first condition is that the company has voting shares admitted to trading on a regulated market.

(3) The second condition is that—

(a) the company's articles of association—

(i) do not contain any such restrictions as are mentioned in Article 11 of the Takeovers Directive, or

(ii) if they do contain any such restrictions, provide for the restrictions not to apply at a time when, or in circumstances in which, they would be disapplied by that Article,

and

(b) those articles do not contain any other provision which would be incompatible with that Article.

(4) The third condition is that—

(a) no shares conferring special rights in the company are held by—

(i) a minister,

(ii) a nominee of, or any other person acting on behalf of, a minister, or

(iii) a company directly or indirectly controlled by a minister,

and

(b) no such rights are exercisable by or on behalf of a minister under any enactment.

(5) A company may revoke an opting-in resolution by a further special resolution (an "opting-out resolution").

(6) For the purposes of subsection (3), a reference in Article 11 of the Takeovers Directive to Article 7.1 or 9 of that Directive is to be read as referring to rules under section 943(1) giving effect to the relevant Article.

(7) In subsection (4) "minister" means—

(a) the holder of an office in Her Majesty's Government in the United Kingdom;

(b) the Scottish Ministers;

(c) a Minister within the meaning given by section 7(3) of the Northern Ireland Act 1998;

(d) the Welsh Ministers;

and for the purposes of that subsection "minister" also includes the Treasury, the Board of Trade and the Defence Council.

(8) The Secretary of State may by order subject to negative resolution procedure provide that subsection (4) applies in relation to a specified person or body that exercises functions of a public nature as it applies in relation to a minister.

"Specified" means specified in the order.

967 Further provision about opting-in and opting-out resolutions

(1) An opting-in resolution or an opting-out resolution must specify the date from which it is to have effect (the "effective date").

(2) The effective date of an opting-in resolution may not be earlier than the date on which the resolution is passed.

(3) The second and third conditions in section 966 must be met at the time when an opting-in resolution is passed, but the first one does not need to be met until the effective date.

(4) An opting-in resolution passed before the time when voting shares of the company are admitted to trading on a regulated market complies with the requirement in subsection (1) if, instead of specifying a particular date, it provides for the resolution to have effect from that time.

(5) An opting-in resolution passed before the commencement of this section complies with the requirement in subsection (1) if, instead of specifying a particular date, it provides for the resolution to have effect from that commencement.

(6) The effective date of an opting-out resolution may not be earlier than the first anniversary of the date on which a copy of the opting-in resolution was forwarded to the registrar.

(7) Where a company has passed an opting-in resolution, any alteration of its articles of association that would prevent the second condition in section 966 from being met is of no effect until the effective date of an opting-out resolution passed by the company.

Consequences of opting in

968 Effect on contractual restrictions

(1) The following provisions have effect where a takeover bid is made for an opted-in company.

(2) An agreement to which this section applies is invalid in so far as it places any restriction—
 (a) on the transfer to the offeror, or at his direction to another person, of shares in the company during the offer period;
 (b) on the transfer to any person of shares in the company at a time during the offer period when the offeror holds shares amounting to not less than 75% in value of all the voting shares in the company;
 (c) on rights to vote at a general meeting of the company that decides whether to take any action which might result in the frustration of the bid;
 (d) on rights to vote at a general meeting of the company that—
  (i) is the first such meeting to be held after the end of the offer period, and
  (ii) is held at a time when the offeror holds shares amounting to not less than 75% in value of all the voting shares in the company.

(3) This section applies to an agreement—
 (a) entered into between a person holding shares in the company and another such person on or after 21st April 2004, or
 (b) entered into at any time between such a person and the company,

and it applies to such an agreement even if the law applicable to the agreement (apart from this section) is not the law of a part of the United Kingdom.

(4) The reference in subsection (2)(c) to rights to vote at a general meeting of the company that decides whether to take any action which might result in the frustration of the bid includes a reference to rights to vote on a written resolution concerned with that question.

(5) For the purposes of subsection (2)(c), action which might result in the frustration of a bid is any action of that kind specified in rules under section 943(1) giving effect to Article 9 of the Takeovers Directive.

(6) If a person suffers loss as a result of any act or omission that would (but for this section) be a breach of an agreement to which this section applies, he is entitled to compensation, of such amount as the court considers just and equitable, from any person who would (but for this section) be liable to him for committing or inducing the breach.

(7) In subsection (6) "the court" means the High Court or, in Scotland, the Court of Session.

(8) A reference in this section to voting shares in the company does not include—
 (a) debentures, or
 (b) shares that, under the company's articles of association, do not normally carry rights to vote at its general meetings (for example, shares carrying rights to vote that, under those articles, arise only where specified pecuniary advantages are not provided).

969 Power of offeror to require general meeting to be called

(1) Where a takeover bid is made for an opted-in company, the offeror may by making a request to the directors of the company require them to call a general meeting of the company if, at the date at which the request is made, he holds shares amounting to not less than 75% in value of all the voting shares in the company.

(2) The reference in subsection (1) to voting shares in the company does not include—
 (a) debentures, or
 (b) shares that, under the company's articles of association, do not normally carry rights to vote at its general meetings (for example, shares carrying rights to vote that, under those articles, arise only where specified pecuniary advantages are not provided).

(3) Sections 303 to 305 (members' power to require general meetings to be called) apply as they would do if subsection (1) above were substituted for subsections (1) to (3) of section 303, and with any other necessary modifications.

Supplementary

970 Communication of decisions

(1) A company that has passed an opting-in resolution or an opting-out resolution must notify—
 (a) the Panel, and
 (b) where the company—
  (i) has voting shares admitted to trading on a regulated market in an EEA State other than the United Kingdom, or

(ii) has requested such admission,

the authority designated by that state as the supervisory authority for the purposes of Article 4.1 of the Takeovers Directive.

(2) Notification must be given within 15 days after the resolution is passed and, if any admission or request such as is mentioned in subsection (1)(b) occurs at a later time, within 15 days after that time.

(3) If a company fails to comply with this section, an offence is committed by—

(a) the company, and

(b) every officer of it who is in default.

(4) A person guilty of an offence under this section is liable on summary conviction to a fine not exceeding level 3 on the standard scale and, for continued contravention, a daily default fine not exceeding one-tenth of level 3 on the standard scale.

971 Interpretation of this Chapter

(1) In this Chapter—

"offeror" and "takeover bid" have the same meaning as in the Takeovers Directive;

"offer period", in relation to a takeover bid, means the time allowed for acceptance of the bid by—

(a) rules under section 943(1) giving effect to Article 7.1 of the Takeovers Directive, or

(b) where the rules giving effect to that Article which apply to the bid are those of an EEA State other than the United Kingdom, those rules;

"opted-in company" means a company in relation to which—

(a) an opting-in resolution has effect, and

(b) the conditions in section 966(2) and (4) continue to be met;

"opting-in resolution" has the meaning given by section 966(1);

"opting-out resolution" has the meaning given by section 966(5);

"the Takeovers Directive" means Directive 2004/25/EC of the European Parliament and of the Council;

"voting rights" means rights to vote at general meetings of the company in question, including rights that arise only in certain circumstances;

"voting shares" means shares carrying voting rights.

(2) For the purposes of this Chapter—

(a) securities of a company are treated as shares in the company if they are convertible into or entitle the holder to subscribe for such shares;

(b) debentures issued by a company are treated as shares in the company if they carry voting rights.

972, 973 *omitted*

CHAPTER 3

"SQUEEZE-OUT" AND "SELL-OUT"

Takeover offers

974 Meaning of "takeover offer"

(1) For the purposes of this Chapter an offer to acquire shares in a company is a "takeover offer" if the following two conditions are satisfied in relation to the offer.

(2) The first condition is that it is an offer to acquire—

(a) all the shares in a company, or

(b) where there is more than one class of shares in a company, all the shares of one or more classes,

other than shares that at the date of the offer are already held by the offeror. Section 975 contains provision supplementing this subsection.

(3) The second condition is that the terms of the offer are the same—

(a) in relation to all the shares to which the offer relates, or

(b) where the shares to which the offer relates include shares of different classes, in relation to all the shares of each class.

Section 976 contains provision treating this condition as satisfied in certain circumstances.

(4) In subsections (1) to (3) "shares" means shares, other than relevant treasury shares, that have been allotted on the date of the offer (but see subsection (5)).

(5) A takeover offer may include among the shares to which it relates—

(a) all or any shares that are allotted after the date of the offer but before a specified date;

(b) all or any relevant treasury shares that cease to be held as treasury shares before a specified date;

(c) all or any other relevant treasury shares.

(6) In this section—

"relevant treasury shares" means shares that—

(a) are held by the company as treasury shares on the date of the offer, or

(b) become shares held by the company as treasury shares after that date but before a specified date;

"specified date" means a date specified in or determined in accordance with the terms of the offer.

(7) Where the terms of an offer make provision for their revision and for acceptances on the previous terms to be treated as acceptances on the revised terms, then, if the terms of the offer are revised in accordance with that provision—

(a) the revision is not to be regarded for the purposes of this Chapter as the making of a fresh offer, and

(b) references in this Chapter to the date of the offer are accordingly to be read as references to the date of the original offer.

975 Shares already held by the offeror etc.

(1) The reference in section 974(2) to shares already held by the offeror includes a reference to shares that he has contracted to acquire, whether unconditionally or subject to conditions being met.

This is subject to subsection (2).

(2) The reference in section 974(2) to shares already held by the offeror does not include a reference to shares that are the subject of a contract—

(a) intended to secure that the holder of the shares will accept the offer when it is made, and

(b) entered into—

(i) by deed and for no consideration,

(ii) for consideration of negligible value, or

(iii) for consideration consisting of a promise by the offeror to make the offer.

(3) In relation to Scotland, this section applies as if the words "by deed and" in subsection (2)(b)(i) were omitted.

(4) The condition in section 974(2) is treated as satisfied where—

(a) the offer does not extend to shares that associates of the offeror hold or have contracted to acquire (whether unconditionally or subject to conditions being met), and

(b) the condition would be satisfied if the offer did extend to those shares.

(For further provision about such shares, see section 977(2)).

976 Cases where offer treated as being on same terms

(1) The condition in section 974(3) (terms of offer to be the same for all shares or all shares of particular classes) is treated as satisfied where subsection (2) or (3) below applies.

(2) This subsection applies where—

(a) shares carry an entitlement to a particular dividend which other shares of the same class, by reason of being allotted later, do not carry,

(b) there is a difference in the value of consideration offered for the shares allotted earlier as against that offered for those allotted later,

(c) that difference merely reflects the difference in entitlement to the dividend, and

(d) the condition in section 974(3) would be satisfied but for that difference.

(3) This subsection applies where—

(a) the law of a country or territory outside the United Kingdom—

(i) precludes an offer of consideration in the form, or any of the forms, specified in the terms of the offer ("the specified form"), or

(ii) precludes it except after compliance by the offeror with conditions with which he is unable to comply or which he regards as unduly onerous,

(b) the persons to whom an offer of consideration in the specified form is precluded are able to receive consideration in another form that is of substantially equivalent value, and

(c) the condition in section 974(3) would be satisfied but for the fact that an offer of consideration in the specified form to those persons is precluded.

977 Shares to which an offer relates

(1) Where a takeover offer is made and, during the period beginning with the date of the offer and ending when the offer can no longer be accepted, the offeror—

(a) acquires or unconditionally contracts to acquire any of the shares to which the offer relates, but

(b) does not do so by virtue of acceptances of the offer,

those shares are treated for the purposes of this Chapter as excluded from those to which the offer relates.

(2) For the purposes of this Chapter shares that an associate of the offeror holds or has contracted to acquire, whether at the date of the offer or subsequently, are not treated as shares to which the offer relates, even if the offer extends to such shares.

In this subsection "contracted" means contracted unconditionally or subject to conditions being met.

(3) This section is subject to section 979(8) and (9).

978 Effect of impossibility etc of communicating or accepting offer

(1) Where there are holders of shares in a company to whom an offer to acquire shares in the company is not communicated, that does not prevent the offer from being a takeover offer for the purposes of this Chapter if—

(a) those shareholders have no registered address in the United Kingdom,

(b) the offer was not communicated to those shareholders in order not to contravene the law of a country or territory outside the United Kingdom, and

(c) either—

(i) the offer is published in the Gazette, or

(ii) the offer can be inspected, or a copy of it obtained, at a place in an EEA State or on a website, and a notice is published in the Gazette specifying the address of that place or website.

(2) Where an offer is made to acquire shares in a company and there are persons for whom, by reason of the law of a country or territory outside the United Kingdom, it is impossible to accept the offer, or more difficult to do so, that does not prevent the offer from being a takeover offer for the purposes of this Chapter.

(3) It is not to be inferred—

(a) that an offer which is not communicated to every holder of shares in the company cannot be a takeover offer for the purposes of this Chapter unless the requirements of paragraphs (a) to (c) of subsection (1) are met, or

(b) that an offer which is impossible, or more difficult, for certain persons to accept cannot be a takeover offer for those purposes unless the reason for the impossibility or difficulty is the one mentioned in subsection (2).

"Squeeze-out"

979 Right of offeror to buy out minority shareholder

(1) Subsection (2) applies in a case where a takeover offer does not relate to shares of different classes.

(2) If the offeror has, by virtue of acceptances of the offer, acquired or unconditionally contracted to acquire—

(a) not less than 90% in value of the shares to which the offer relates, and

(b) in a case where the shares to which the offer relates are voting shares, not less than 90% of the voting rights carried by those shares,

he may give notice to the holder of any shares to which the offer relates which the offeror has not acquired or unconditionally contracted to acquire that he desires to acquire those shares.

(3) Subsection (4) applies in a case where a takeover offer relates to shares of different classes.

(4) If the offeror has, by virtue of acceptances of the offer, acquired or unconditionally contracted to acquire—
   (a) not less than 90% in value of the shares of any class to which the offer relates, and
   (b) in a case where the shares of that class are voting shares, not less than 90% of the voting rights carried by those shares,

   he may give notice to the holder of any shares of that class to which the offer relates which the offeror has not acquired or unconditionally contracted to acquire that he desires to acquire those shares.

(5) In the case of a takeover offer which includes among the shares to which it relates—
   (a) shares that are allotted after the date of the offer, or
   (b) relevant treasury shares (within the meaning of section 974) that cease to be held as treasury shares after the date of the offer,

   the offeror's entitlement to give a notice under subsection (2) or (4) on any particular date shall be determined as if the shares to which the offer relates did not include any allotted, or ceasing to be held as treasury shares, on or after that date.

(6) Subsection (7) applies where—
   (a) the requirements for the giving of a notice under subsection (2) or (4) are satisfied, and
   (b) there are shares in the company which the offeror, or an associate of his, has contracted to acquire subject to conditions being met, and in relation to which the contract has not become unconditional.

(7) The offeror's entitlement to give a notice under subsection (2) or (4) shall be determined as if—
   (a) the shares to which the offer relates included shares falling within paragraph (b) of subsection (6), and
   (b) in relation to shares falling within that paragraph, the words "by virtue of acceptances of the offer" in subsection (2) or (4) were omitted.

(8) Where—
   (a) a takeover offer is made,
   (b) during the period beginning with the date of the offer and ending when the offer can no longer be accepted, the offeror—
      (i) acquires or unconditionally contracts to acquire any of the shares to which the offer relates, but
      (ii) does not do so by virtue of acceptances of the offer, and
   (c) subsection (10) applies,

   then for the purposes of this section those shares are not excluded by section 977(1) from those to which the offer relates, and the offeror is treated as having acquired or contracted to acquire them by virtue of acceptances of the offer.

(9) Where—
   (a) a takeover offer is made,
   (b) during the period beginning with the date of the offer and ending when the offer can no longer be accepted, an associate of the offeror acquires or unconditionally contracts to acquire any of the shares to which the offer relates, and
   (c) subsection (10) applies,

   then for the purposes of this section those shares are not excluded by section 977(2) from those to which the offer relates.

(10) This subsection applies if—
   (a) at the time the shares are acquired or contracted to be acquired as mentioned in subsection (8) or (9) (as the case may be), the value of the consideration for which they are acquired or contracted to be acquired ("the acquisition consideration") does not exceed the value of the consideration specified in the terms of the offer, or
   (b) those terms are subsequently revised so that when the revision is announced the value of the acquisition consideration, at the time mentioned in paragraph (a), no longer exceeds the value of the consideration specified in those terms.

980 Further provision about notices given under section 979

(1) A notice under section 979 must be given in the prescribed manner.

(2) No notice may be given under section 979(2) or (4) after the end of—

(a) the period of three months beginning with the day after the last day on which the offer can be accepted, or

(b) the period of six months beginning with the date of the offer, where that period ends earlier and the offer is one to which subsection (3) below applies.

(3) This subsection applies to an offer if the time allowed for acceptance of the offer is not governed by rules under section 943(1) that give effect to Article 7 of the Takeovers Directive.

In this subsection "the Takeovers Directive" has the same meaning as in section 943.

(4) At the time when the offeror first gives a notice under section 979 in relation to an offer, he must send to the company—

(a) a copy of the notice, and

(b) a statutory declaration by him in the prescribed form, stating that the conditions for the giving of the notice are satisfied.

(5) Where the offeror is a company (whether or not a company within the meaning of this Act) the statutory declaration must be signed by a director.

(6) A person commits an offence if—

(a) he fails to send a copy of a notice or a statutory declaration as required by subsection (4), or

(b) he makes such a declaration for the purposes of that subsection knowing it to be false or without having reasonable grounds for believing it to be true.

(7) It is a defence for a person charged with an offence for failing to send a copy of a notice as required by subsection (4) to prove that he took reasonable steps for securing compliance with that subsection.

(8) A person guilty of an offence under this section is liable—

(a) on conviction on indictment, to imprisonment for a term not exceeding two years or a fine (or both);

(b) on summary conviction—

(i) in England and Wales, to imprisonment for a term not exceeding twelve months or to a fine not exceeding the statutory maximum (or both) and, for continued contravention, a daily default fine not exceeding one-fiftieth of the greater of £5,000 or the amount corresponding to level 4 on the standard scale for summary offences,

(ii) in Scotland or Northern Ireland, to imprisonment for a term not exceeding six months, or to a fine not exceeding the statutory maximum (or both) and, for continued contravention, a daily default fine not exceeding one-fiftieth of the statutory maximum.

981 Effect of notice under section 979

(1) Subject to section 986 (applications to the court), this section applies where the offeror gives a shareholder a notice under section 979.

(2) The offeror is entitled and bound to acquire the shares to which the notice relates on the terms of the offer.

(3) Where the terms of an offer are such as to give the shareholder a choice of consideration, the notice must give particulars of the choice and state—

(a) that the shareholder may, within six weeks from the date of the notice, indicate his choice by a written communication sent to the offeror at an address specified in the notice, and

(b) which consideration specified in the offer will apply if he does not indicate a choice.

The reference in subsection (2) to the terms of the offer is to be read accordingly.

(4) Subsection (3) applies whether or not any time-limit or other conditions applicable to the choice under the terms of the offer can still be complied with.

(5) If the consideration offered to or (as the case may be) chosen by the shareholder—

(a) is not cash and the offeror is no longer able to provide it, or

(b) was to have been provided by a third party who is no longer bound or able to provide it,

the consideration is to be taken to consist of an amount of cash, payable by the offeror, which at the date of the notice is equivalent to the consideration offered or (as the case may be) chosen.

(6) At the end of six weeks from the date of the notice the offeror must immediately—
(a) send a copy of the notice to the company, and
(b) pay or transfer to the company the consideration for the shares to which the notice relates.
Where the consideration consists of shares or securities to be allotted by the offeror, the reference in paragraph (b) to the transfer of the consideration is to be read as a reference to the allotment of the shares or securities to the company.
(7) If the shares to which the notice relates are registered, the copy of the notice sent to the company under subsection (6)(a) must be accompanied by an instrument of transfer executed on behalf of the holder of the shares by a person appointed by the offeror.
On receipt of that instrument the company must register the offeror as the holder of those shares.
(8) If the shares to which the notice relates are transferable by the delivery of warrants or other instruments, the copy of the notice sent to the company under subsection (6)(a) must be accompanied by a statement to that effect.
On receipt of that statement the company must issue the offeror with warrants or other instruments in respect of the shares, and those already in issue in respect of the shares become void.
(9) The company must hold any money or other consideration received by it under subsection (6)(b) on trust for the person who, before the offeror acquired them, was entitled to the shares in respect of which the money or other consideration was received.
Section 982 contains further provision about how the company should deal with such money or other consideration.

982 Further provision about consideration held on trust under section 981(9)

(1) This section applies where an offeror pays or transfers consideration to the company under section 981(6).
(2) The company must pay into a separate bank account that complies with subsection (3)—
(a) any money it receives under paragraph (b) of section 981(6), and
(b) any dividend or other sum accruing from any other consideration it receives under that paragraph.
(3) A bank account complies with this subsection if the balance on the account—
(a) bears interest at an appropriate rate, and
(b) can be withdrawn by such notice (if any) as is appropriate.
(4) If—
(a) the person entitled to the consideration held on trust by virtue of section 981(9) cannot be found, and
(b) subsection (5) applies,
the consideration (together with any interest, dividend or other benefit that has accrued from it) must be paid into court.
(5) This subsection applies where—
(a) reasonable enquiries have been made at reasonable intervals to find the person, and
(b) twelve years have elapsed since the consideration was received, or the company is wound up.
(6) In relation to a company registered in Scotland, subsections (7) and (8) apply instead of subsection (4).
(7) If the person entitled to the consideration held on trust by virtue of section 981(9) cannot be found and subsection (5) applies—
(a) the trust terminates,
(b) the company or (if the company is wound up) the liquidator must sell any consideration other than cash and any benefit other than cash that has accrued from the consideration, and
(c) a sum representing—
(i) the consideration so far as it is cash,
(ii) the proceeds of any sale under paragraph (b), and
(iii) any interest, dividend or other benefit that has accrued from the consideration,
must be deposited in the name of the Accountant of Court in a separate bank account complying with subsection (3) and the receipt for the deposit must be transmitted to the Accountant of Court.

(8) Section 58 of the Bankruptcy (Scotland) Act 1985 (c. 66) (so far as consistent with this Act) applies (with any necessary modifications) to sums deposited under subsection (7) as it applies to sums deposited under section 57(1)(a) of that Act.

(9) The expenses of any such enquiries as are mentioned in subsection (5) may be paid out of the money or other property held on trust for the person to whom the enquiry relates.

"Sell-out"

983 Right of minority shareholder to be bought out by offeror

(1) Subsections (2) and (3) apply in a case where a takeover offer relates to all the shares in a company.
For this purpose a takeover offer relates to all the shares in a company if it is an offer to acquire all the shares in the company within the meaning of section 974.

(2) The holder of any voting shares to which the offer relates who has not accepted the offer may require the offeror to acquire those shares if, at any time before the end of the period within which the offer can be accepted—
- (a) the offeror has by virtue of acceptances of the offer acquired or unconditionally contracted to acquire some (but not all) of the shares to which the offer relates, and
- (b) those shares, with or without any other shares in the company which he has acquired or contracted to acquire (whether unconditionally or subject to conditions being met)—
  - (i) amount to not less than 90% in value of all the voting shares in the company (or would do so but for section 990(1)), and
  - (ii) carry not less than 90% of the voting rights in the company (or would do so but for section 990(1)).

(3) The holder of any non-voting shares to which the offer relates who has not accepted the offer may require the offeror to acquire those shares if, at any time before the end of the period within which the offer can be accepted—
- (a) the offeror has by virtue of acceptances of the offer acquired or unconditionally contracted to acquire some (but not all) of the shares to which the offer relates, and
- (b) those shares, with or without any other shares in the company which he has acquired or contracted to acquire (whether unconditionally or subject to conditions being met), amount to not less than 90% in value of all the shares in the company (or would do so but for section 990(1)).

(4) If a takeover offer relates to shares of one or more classes and at any time before the end of the period within which the offer can be accepted—
- (a) the offeror has by virtue of acceptances of the offer acquired or unconditionally contracted to acquire some (but not all) of the shares of any class to which the offer relates, and
- (b) those shares, with or without any other shares of that class which he has acquired or contracted to acquire (whether unconditionally or subject to conditions being met)—
  - (i) amount to not less than 90% in value of all the shares of that class, and
  - (ii) in a case where the shares of that class are voting shares, carry not less than 90% of the voting rights carried by the shares of that class,

the holder of any shares of that class to which the offer relates who has not accepted the offer may require the offeror to acquire those shares.

(5) For the purposes of subsections (2) to (4), in calculating 90% of the value of any shares, shares held by the company as treasury shares are to be treated as having been acquired by the offeror.

(6) Subsection (7) applies where—
- (a) a shareholder exercises rights conferred on him by subsection (2), (3) or (4),
- (b) at the time when he does so, there are shares in the company which the offeror has contracted to acquire subject to conditions being met, and in relation to which the contract has not become unconditional, and
- (c) the requirement imposed by subsection (2)(b), (3)(b) or (4)(b) (as the case may be) would not be satisfied if those shares were not taken into account.

(7) The shareholder is treated for the purposes of section 985 as not having exercised his rights under this section unless the requirement imposed by paragraph (b) of subsection (2), (3) or (4) (as the case may be) would be satisfied if—

(a) the reference in that paragraph to other shares in the company which the offeror has contracted to acquire unconditionally or subject to conditions being met were a reference to such shares which he has unconditionally contracted to acquire, and
(b) the reference in that subsection to the period within which the offer can be accepted were a reference to the period referred to in section 984(2).

(8) A reference in subsection (2)(b), (3)(b), (4)(b), (6) or (7) to shares which the offeror has acquired or contracted to acquire includes a reference to shares which an associate of his has acquired or contracted to acquire.

984 Further provision about rights conferred by section 983

(1) Rights conferred on a shareholder by subsection (2), (3) or (4) of section 983 are exercisable by a written communication addressed to the offeror.

(2) Rights conferred on a shareholder by subsection (2), (3) or (4) of that section are not exercisable after the end of the period of three months from—
(a) the end of the period within which the offer can be accepted, or
(b) if later, the date of the notice that must be given under subsection (3) below.

(3) Within one month of the time specified in subsection (2), (3) or (4) (as the case may be) of that section, the offeror must give any shareholder who has not accepted the offer notice in the prescribed manner of—
(a) the rights that are exercisable by the shareholder under that subsection, and
(b) the period within which the rights are exercisable.
If the notice is given before the end of the period within which the offer can be accepted, it must state that the offer is still open for acceptance.

(4) Subsection (3) does not apply if the offeror has given the shareholder a notice in respect of the shares in question under section 979.

(5) An offeror who fails to comply with subsection (3) commits an offence.
If the offeror is a company, every officer of that company who is in default or to whose neglect the failure is attributable also commits an offence.

(6) If an offeror other than a company is charged with an offence for failing to comply with subsection (3), it is a defence for him to prove that he took all reasonable steps for securing compliance with that subsection.

Version applying in Scotland

(7) A person guilty of an offence under this section is liable—
(a) on conviction on indictment, to a fine;
(b) on summary conviction, to a fine not exceeding the statutory maximum and, for continued contravention, a daily default fine not exceeding one-fiftieth of the statutory maximum.

Version applying in England and Wales

(7) A person guilty of an offence under this section is liable–
(a) on conviction on indictment, to a fine;
(b) on summary conviction, to a fine not exceeding the statutory maximum and, for continued contravention, a daily default fine not exceeding one-fiftieth of the greater of £5,000 or the amount corresponding to level 4 on the standard scale for summary offences.

985 Effect of requirement under section 983

(1) Subject to section 986, this section applies where a shareholder exercises his rights under section 983 in respect of any shares held by him.

(2) The offeror is entitled and bound to acquire those shares on the terms of the offer or on such other terms as may be agreed.

(3) Where the terms of an offer are such as to give the shareholder a choice of consideration—
(a) the shareholder may indicate his choice when requiring the offeror to acquire the shares, and
(b) the notice given to the shareholder under section 984(3)—
(i) must give particulars of the choice and of the rights conferred by this subsection, and
(ii) may state which consideration specified in the offer will apply if he does not indicate a choice.
The reference in subsection (2) to the terms of the offer is to be read accordingly.

(4) Subsection (3) applies whether or not any time-limit or other conditions applicable to the choice under the terms of the offer can still be complied with.

(5) If the consideration offered to or (as the case may be) chosen by the shareholder—
(a) is not cash and the offeror is no longer able to provide it, or
(b) was to have been provided by a third party who is no longer bound or able to provide it,
the consideration is to be taken to consist of an amount of cash, payable by the offeror, which at the date when the shareholder requires the offeror to acquire the shares is equivalent to the consideration offered or (as the case may be) chosen.

Supplementary

986 Applications to the court

(1) Where a notice is given under section 979 to a shareholder the court may, on an application made by him, order—
(a) that the offeror is not entitled and bound to acquire the shares to which the notice relates, or
(b) that the terms on which the offeror is entitled and bound to acquire the shares shall be such as the court thinks fit.
(2) An application under subsection (1) must be made within six weeks from the date on which the notice referred to in that subsection was given.
If an application to the court under subsection (1) is pending at the end of that period, section 981(6) does not have effect until the application has been disposed of.
(3) Where a shareholder exercises his rights under section 983 in respect of any shares held by him, the court may, on an application made by him or the offeror, order that the terms on which the offeror is entitled and bound to acquire the shares shall be such as the court thinks fit.
(4) On an application under subsection (1) or (3)—
(a) the court may not require consideration of a higher value than that specified in the terms of the offer ("the offer value") to be given for the shares to which the application relates unless the holder of the shares shows that the offer value would be unfair;
(b) the court may not require consideration of a lower value than the offer value to be given for the shares.
(5) No order for costs or expenses may be made against a shareholder making an application under subsection (1) or (3) unless the court considers that—
(a) the application was unnecessary, improper or vexatious,
(b) there has been unreasonable delay in making the application, or
(c) there has been unreasonable conduct on the shareholder's part in conducting the proceedings on the application.
(6) A shareholder who has made an application under subsection (1) or (3) must give notice of the application to the offeror.
(7) An offeror who is given notice of an application under subsection (1) or (3) must give a copy of the notice to—
(a) any person (other than the applicant) to whom a notice has been given under section 979;
(b) any person who has exercised his rights under section 983.
(8) An offeror who makes an application under subsection (3) must give notice of the application to—
(a) any person to whom a notice has been given under section 979;
(b) any person who has exercised his rights under section 983.
(9) Where a takeover offer has not been accepted to the extent necessary for entitling the offeror to give notices under subsection (2) or (4) of section 979 the court may, on an application made by him, make an order authorising him to give notices under that subsection if it is satisfied that—
(a) the offeror has after reasonable enquiry been unable to trace one or more of the persons holding shares to which the offer relates,
(b) the requirements of that subsection would have been met if the person, or all the persons, mentioned in paragraph (a) above had accepted the offer, and
(c) the consideration offered is fair and reasonable. This is subject to subsection (10).

(10) The court may not make an order under subsection (9) unless it considers that it is just and equitable to do so having regard, in particular, to the number of shareholders who have been traced but who have not accepted the offer.

987 Joint offers

(1) In the case of a takeover offer made by two or more persons jointly, this Chapter has effect as follows.

(2) The conditions for the exercise of the rights conferred by section 979 are satisfied—

(a) in the case of acquisitions by virtue of acceptances of the offer, by the joint offerors acquiring or unconditionally contracting to acquire the necessary shares jointly;

(b) in other cases, by the joint offerors acquiring or unconditionally contracting to acquire the necessary shares either jointly or separately.

(3) The conditions for the exercise of the rights conferred by section 983 are satisfied—

(a) in the case of acquisitions by virtue of acceptances of the offer, by the joint offerors acquiring or unconditionally contracting to acquire the necessary shares jointly;

(b) in other cases, by the joint offerors acquiring or contracting (whether unconditionally or subject to conditions being met) to acquire the necessary shares either jointly or separately.

(4) Subject to the following provisions, the rights and obligations of the offeror under sections 979 to 985 are respectively joint rights and joint and several obligations of the joint offerors.

(5) A provision of sections 979 to 986 that requires or authorises a notice or other document to be given or sent by or to the joint offerors is complied with if the notice or document is given or sent by or to any of them (but see subsection (6)).

(6) The statutory declaration required by section 980(4) must be made by all of the joint offerors and, where one or more of them is a company, signed by a director of that company.

(7) In sections 974 to 977, 979(9), 981(6), 983(8) and 988 references to the offeror are to be read as references to the joint offerors or any of them.

(8) In section 981(7) and (8) references to the offeror are to be read as references to the joint offerors or such of them as they may determine.

(9) In sections 981(5)(a) and 985(5)(a) references to the offeror being no longer able to provide the relevant consideration are to be read as references to none of the joint offerors being able to do so.

(10) In section 986 references to the offeror are to be read as references to the joint offerors, except that—

(a) an application under subsection (3) or (9) may be made by any of them, and

(b) the reference in subsection (9)(a) to the offeror having been unable to trace one or more of the persons holding shares is to be read as a reference to none of the offerors having been able to do so.

Interpretation

988 Associates

(1) In this Chapter "associate", in relation to an offeror, means—

(a) a nominee of the offeror,

(b) a holding company, subsidiary or fellow subsidiary of the offeror or a nominee of such a holding company, subsidiary or fellow subsidiary,

(c) a body corporate in which the offeror is substantially interested,

(d) a person who is, or is a nominee of, a party to a share acquisition agreement with the offeror, or

(e) (where the offeror is an individual) his spouse or civil partner and any minor child or step-child of his.

(2) For the purposes of subsection (1)(b) a company is a fellow subsidiary of another body corporate if both are subsidiaries of the same body corporate but neither is a subsidiary of the other.

(3) For the purposes of subsection (1)(c) an offeror has a substantial interest in a body corporate if—

(a) the body or its directors are accustomed to act in accordance with his directions or instructions, or

(b) he is entitled to exercise or control the exercise of one-third or more of the voting power at general meetings of the body.

Subsections (2) and (3) of section 823 (which contain provision about when a person is treated as entitled to exercise or control the exercise of voting power) apply for the purposes of this subsection as they apply for the purposes of that section.

(4) For the purposes of subsection (1)(d) an agreement is a share acquisition agreement if—

(a) it is an agreement for the acquisition of, or of an interest in, shares to which the offer relates,

(b) it includes provisions imposing obligations or restrictions on any one or more of the parties to it with respect to their use, retention or disposal of such shares, or their interests in such shares, acquired in pursuance of the agreement (whether or not together with any other shares to which the offer relates or any other interests of theirs in such shares), and

(c) it is not an excluded agreement (see subsection (5)).

(5) An agreement is an "excluded agreement"—

(a) if it is not legally binding, unless it involves mutuality in the undertakings, expectations or understandings of the parties to it, or

(b) if it is an agreement to underwrite or sub-underwrite an offer of shares in a company, provided the agreement is confined to that purpose and any matters incidental to it.

(6) The reference in subsection (4)(b) to the use of interests in shares is to the exercise of any rights or of any control or influence arising from those interests (including the right to enter into an agreement for the exercise, or for control of the exercise, of any of those rights by another person).

(7) In this section—

(a) "agreement" includes any agreement or arrangement;

(b) references to provisions of an agreement include—

(i) undertakings, expectations or understandings operative under an arrangement, and

(ii) any provision whether express or implied and whether absolute or not.

989 Convertible securities

(1) For the purposes of this Chapter securities of a company are treated as shares in the company if they are convertible into or entitle the holder to subscribe for such shares. References to the holder of shares or a shareholder are to be read accordingly.

(2) Subsection (1) is not to be read as requiring any securities to be treated—

(a) as shares of the same class as those into which they are convertible or for which the holder is entitled to subscribe, or

(b) as shares of the same class as other securities by reason only that the shares into which they are convertible or for which the holder is entitled to subscribe are of the same class.

990 Debentures carrying voting rights

(1) For the purposes of this Chapter debentures issued by a company to which subsection (2) applies are treated as shares in the company if they carry voting rights.

(2) This subsection applies to a company that has voting shares, or debentures carrying voting rights, which are admitted to trading on a regulated market.

(3) In this Chapter, in relation to debentures treated as shares by virtue of subsection (1)—

(a) references to the holder of shares or a shareholder are to be read accordingly;

(b) references to shares being allotted are to be read as references to debentures being issued.

991 Interpretation

(1) In this Chapter—

"the company" means the company whose shares are the subject of a takeover offer;

"date of the offer" means—

(a) where the offer is published, the date of publication;

(b) where the offer is not published, or where any notices of the offer are given before the date of publication, the date when notices of the offer (or the first such notices) are given;

and references to the date of the offer are to be read in accordance with section 974(7) (revision of offer terms) where that applies;

"non-voting shares" means shares that are not voting shares;

"offeror" means (subject to section 987) the person making a takeover offer;

"voting rights" means rights to vote at general meetings of the company, including rights that arise only in certain circumstances;

"voting shares" means shares carrying voting rights.

(2) For the purposes of this Chapter a person contracts unconditionally to acquire shares if his entitlement under the contract to acquire them is not (or is no longer) subject to conditions or if all conditions to which it was subject have been met.

A reference to a contract becoming unconditional is to be read accordingly.

992 *omitted*

PART 29
FRAUDULENT TRADING

993 Offence of fraudulent trading

(1) If any business of a company is carried on with intent to defraud creditors of the company or creditors of any other person, or for any fraudulent purpose, every person who is knowingly a party to the carrying on of the business in that manner commits an offence.

(2) This applies whether or not the company has been, or is in the course of being, wound up.

(3) A person guilty of an offence under this section is liable—

(a) on conviction on indictment, to imprisonment for a term not exceeding ten years or a fine (or both);

(b) on summary conviction—

(i) in England and Wales, to imprisonment for a term not exceeding twelve months or a fine not exceeding the statutory maximum (or both);

(ii) in Scotland or Northern Ireland, to imprisonment for a term not exceeding six months or a fine not exceeding the statutory maximum (or both).

PART 30
PROTECTION OF MEMBERS AGAINST UNFAIR PREJUDICE

Main provisions

994 Petition by company member

(1) A member of a company may apply to the court by petition for an order under this Part on the ground—

(a) that the company's affairs are being or have been conducted in a manner that is unfairly prejudicial to the interests of members generally or of some part of its members (including at least himself), or

(b) that an actual or proposed act or omission of the company (including an act or omission on its behalf) is or would be so prejudicial.

(1A) For the purposes of subsection (1)(a), a removal of the company's auditor from office—

(a) on grounds of divergence of opinions on accounting treatments or audit procedures, or

(b) on any other improper grounds, shall be treated as being unfairly prejudicial to the interests of some part of the company's members.

(2) The provisions of this Part apply to a person who is not a member of a company but to whom shares in the company have been transferred or transmitted by operation of law as they apply to a member of a company.

(3) In this section, and so far as applicable for the purposes of this section in the other provisions of this Part, "company" means—

(a) a company within the meaning of this Act.

995 Petition by Secretary of State

(1) This section applies to a company in respect of which—

(a) the Secretary of State has received a report under section 437 of the Companies Act 1985 (inspector's report);

(b) the Secretary of State has exercised his powers under section 447 or 448 of that Act (powers to require documents and information or to enter and search premises);
(c) the Secretary of State, the Financial Conduct Authority, the Prudential Regulation Authority or the Bank of England has exercised his or its powers under Part 11 of the Financial Services and Markets Act 2000 (information gathering and investigations); or
(d) the Secretary of State has received a report from an investigator appointed by him or the Financial Services Authority under that Part.

(2) If it appears to the Secretary of State that in the case of such a company—
(a) the company's affairs are being or have been conducted in a manner that is unfairly prejudicial to the interests of members generally or of some part of its members, or
(b) an actual or proposed act or omission of the company (including an act or omission on its behalf) is or would be so prejudicial,

he may apply to the court by petition for an order under this Part.

(3) The Secretary of State may do this in addition to, or instead of, presenting a petition for the winding up of the company.

(4) In this section, and so far as applicable for the purposes of this section in the other provisions of this Part, "company" means any body corporate that is liable to be wound up under the Insolvency Act 1986 or the Insolvency (Northern Ireland) Order 1989.

996 Powers of the court under this Part

(1) If the court is satisfied that a petition under this Part is well founded, it may make such order as it thinks fit for giving relief in respect of the matters complained of.

(2) Without prejudice to the generality of subsection (1), the court's order may—
(a) regulate the conduct of the company's affairs in the future;
(b) require the company—
(i) to refrain from doing or continuing an act complained of, or
(ii) to do an act that the petitioner has complained it has omitted to do;
(c) authorise civil proceedings to be brought in the name and on behalf of the company by such person or persons and on such terms as the court may direct;
(d) require the company not to make any, or any specified, alterations in its articles without the leave of the court;
(e) provide for the purchase of the shares of any members of the company by other members or by the company itself and, in the case of a purchase by the company itself, the reduction of the company's capital accordingly.

Supplementary provisions

997 Application of general rule-making powers

The power to make rules under section 411 of the Insolvency Act 1986 or Article 359 of the Insolvency (Northern Ireland) Order 1989, so far as relating to a winding-up petition, applies for the purposes of a petition under this Part.

998 Copy of order affecting company's constitution to be delivered to registrar

(1) Where an order of the court under this Part—
(a) alters the company's constitution, or
(b) gives leave for the company to make any, or any specified, alterations to its constitution,

the company must deliver a copy of the order to the registrar.

(2) It must do so within 14 days from the making of the order or such longer period as the court may allow.

(3) If a company makes default in complying with this section, an offence is committed by—
(a) the company, and
(b) every officer of the company who is in default.

(4) A person guilty of an offence under this section is liable on summary conviction to a fine not exceeding level 3 on the standard scale and, for continued contravention, a daily default fine not exceeding one-tenth of level 3 on the standard scale.

999 Supplementary provisions where company's constitution altered

(1) This section applies where an order under this Part alters a company's constitution.

(2) If the order amends—

(a) a company's articles, or
(b) any resolution or agreement to which Chapter 3 of Part 3 applies (resolution or agreement affecting a company's constitution),

the copy of the order delivered to the registrar by the company under section 998 must be accompanied by a copy of the company's articles, or the resolution or agreement in question, as amended.

(3) Every copy of a company's articles issued by the company after the order is made must be accompanied by a copy of the order, unless the effect of the order has been incorporated into the articles by amendment.

(4) If a company makes default in complying with this section an offence is committed by—
(a) the company, and
(b) every officer of the company who is in default.

(5) A person guilty of an offence under this section is liable on summary conviction to a fine not exceeding level 3 on the standard scale.

PART 31
DISSOLUTION AND RESTORATION TO THE REGISTER

CHAPTER 1
STRIKING OFF

Registrar's power to strike off defunct company

1000 Power to strike off company not carrying on business or in operation

(1) If the registrar has reasonable cause to believe that a company is not carrying on business or in operation, the registrar may send to the company a communication inquiring whether the company is carrying on business or in operation.

(2) If the registrar does not within one month of sending the communication receive any answer to it, the registrar must within 14 days after the expiration of that month send to the company a second communication referring to the first communication and stating—
(a) that no answer to it has been received, and
(b) that if an answer is not received to the second communication within one month from its date, a notice will be published in the Gazette with a view to striking the company's name off the register.

(3) If the registrar—
(a) receives an answer to the effect that the company is not carrying on business or in operation, or
(b) does not within one month after sending the second communication receive any answer,

the registrar may publish in the Gazette, and send to the company, a notice that at the expiration of three months from the date of the notice the name of the company mentioned in it will, unless cause is shown to the contrary, be struck off the register and the company will be dissolved.

(4) At the expiration of the time mentioned in the notice the registrar may, unless cause to the contrary is previously shown by the company, strike its name off the register.

(5) The registrar must publish notice in the Gazette of the company's name having been struck off the register.

(6) On the publication of the notice in the Gazette the company is dissolved.

(7) However—
(a) the liability (if any) of every director, managing officer and member of the company continues and may be enforced as if the company had not been dissolved, and
(b) nothing in this section affects the power of the court to wind up a company the name of which has been struck off the register.

1001 Duty to act in case of company being wound up

(1) If, in a case where a company is being wound up—
(a) the registrar has reasonable cause to believe—
(i) that no liquidator is acting, or
(ii) that the affairs of the company are fully wound up, and
(b) the returns required to be made by the liquidator have not been made for a period of six consecutive months,

the registrar must publish in the Gazette and send to the company or the liquidator (if any) a notice that at the expiration of three months from the date of the notice the name of the company mentioned in it will, unless cause is shown to the contrary, be struck off the register and the company will be dissolved.

(2) At the expiration of the time mentioned in the notice the registrar may, unless cause to the contrary is previously shown by the company, strike its name off the register.

(3) The registrar must publish notice in the Gazette of the company's name having been struck off the register.

(4) On the publication of the notice in the Gazette the company is dissolved.

(5) However—

(a) the liability (if any) of every director, managing officer and member of the company continues and may be enforced as if the company had not been dissolved, and

(b) nothing in this section affects the power of the court to wind up a company the name of which has been struck off the register.

1002 Supplementary provisions as to service of communication or notice

(1) If the registrar is not able to send a communication or notice under section 1000 or 1001 to a company in accordance with Schedule 4, the communication may be sent to an officer of the company at an address for that officer that has been notified to the registrar by the company.

(2) If there is no officer of the company whose name and address are known to the registrar, the communication or notice may be sent to each of the persons who subscribed the memorandum (if their addresses are known to the registrar).

(3) A notice to be sent to a liquidator under section 1001 may be sent to the address of the liquidator's last known place of business or to an address specified by the liquidator to the registrar for the purpose of receiving notices, or notices of that kind.

(4) In this section "address" has the same meaning as in section 1148(1).

Voluntary striking off

1003 Striking off on application by company

(1) On application by a company, the registrar of companies may strike the company's name off the register.

(2) The application—

(a) must be made on the company's behalf by its directors or by a majority of them, and

(b) must contain the prescribed information.

(3) The registrar may not strike a company off under this section until after the expiration of three months from the publication by the registrar in the Gazette of a notice—

(a) stating that the registrar may exercise the power under this section in relation to the company, and

(b) inviting any person to show cause why that should not be done.

(4) The registrar must publish notice in the Gazette of the company's name having been struck off.

(5) On the publication of the notice in the Gazette the company is dissolved.

(6) However—

(a) the liability (if any) of every director, managing officer and member of the company continues and may be enforced as if the company had not been dissolved, and

(b) nothing in this section affects the power of the court to wind up a company the name of which has been struck off the register.

1004 Circumstances in which application not to be made: activities of company

(1) An application under section 1003 (application for voluntary striking off) on behalf of a company must not be made if, at any time in the previous three months, the company has—

(a) changed its name,

(b) traded or otherwise carried on business,

(c) made a disposal for value of property or rights that, immediately before ceasing to trade or otherwise carry on business, it held for the purpose of disposal for gain in the normal course of trading or otherwise carrying on business, or

(d) engaged in any other activity, except one which is—

(i) necessary or expedient for the purpose of making an application under that section, or deciding whether to do so,
(ii) necessary or expedient for the purpose of concluding the affairs of the company,
(iii) necessary or expedient for the purpose of complying with any statutory requirement, or
(iv) specified by the Secretary of State by order for the purposes of this sub-paragraph.

(2) For the purposes of this section, a company is not to be treated as trading or otherwise carrying on business by virtue only of the fact that it makes a payment in respect of a liability incurred in the course of trading or otherwise carrying on business.

(3) The Secretary of State may by order amend subsection (1) for the purpose of altering the period in relation to which the doing of the things mentioned in paragraphs (a) to (d) of that subsection is relevant.

(4) An order under this section is subject to negative resolution procedure.

(5) It is an offence for a person to make an application in contravention of this section.

(6) In proceedings for such an offence it is a defence for the accused to prove that he did not know, and could not reasonably have known, of the existence of the facts that led to the contravention.

(7) A person guilty of an offence under this section is liable—
(a) on conviction on indictment, to a fine;
(b) on summary conviction, to a fine not exceeding the statutory maximum.

1005 Circumstances in which application not to be made: other proceedings not concluded

(1) An application under section 1003 (application for voluntary striking off) on behalf of a company must not be made at a time when—
(a) an application to the court under Part 26 has been made on behalf of the company for the sanctioning of a compromise or arrangement and the matter has not been finally concluded;
(b) a voluntary arrangement in relation to the company has been proposed under Part 1 of the Insolvency Act 1986 or Part 2 of the Insolvency (Northern Ireland) Order 1989 and the matter has not been finally concluded;
(c) the company is in administration under Part 2 of that Act or Part 3 of that Order;
(d) paragraph 44 of Schedule B1 to that Act or paragraph 45 of Schedule B1 to that Order applies (interim moratorium on proceedings where application to the court for an administration order has been made or notice of intention to appoint administrator has been filed);
(e) the company is being wound up under Part 4 of that Act or Part 5 of that Order, whether voluntarily or by the court, or a petition under that Part for winding up of the company by the court has been presented and not finally dealt with or withdrawn;
(f) there is a receiver or manager of the company's property;
(g) the company's estate is being administered by a judicial factor.

(2) For the purposes of subsection (1)(a), the matter is finally concluded if—
(a) the application has been withdrawn,
(b) the application has been finally dealt with without a compromise or arrangement being sanctioned by the court, or
(c) a compromise or arrangement has been sanctioned by the court and has, together with anything required to be done under any provision made in relation to the matter by order of the court, been fully carried out.

(3) For the purposes of subsection (1)(b), the matter is finally concluded if—
(a) no meetings are to be summoned under section 3 of the Insolvency Act 1986 or Article 16 of the Insolvency (Northern Ireland) Order 1989,
(b) meetings summoned under that section or Article fail to approve the arrangement with no, or the same, modifications,
(c) an arrangement approved by meetings summoned under that section, or in consequence of a direction under section 6(4)(b) of that Act or Article 19(4)(b) of that Order, has been fully implemented, or
(d) the court makes an order under section 6(5) of that Act or Article 19(5) of that Order revoking approval given at previous meetings and, if the court gives any directions under section 6(6) of that Act or Article 19(6) of that Order, the company has done whatever it is required to do under those directions.

(4) It is an offence for a person to make an application in contravention of this section.

(5) In proceedings for such an offence it is a defence for the accused to prove that he did not know, and could not reasonably have known, of the existence of the facts that led to the contravention.

(6) A person guilty of an offence under this section is liable—

(a) on conviction on indictment, to a fine;

(b) on summary conviction, to a fine not exceeding the statutory maximum.

1006 Copy of application to be given to members, employees, etc.

(1) A person who makes an application under section 1003 (application for voluntary striking off) on behalf of a company must secure that, within seven days from the day on which the application is made, a copy of it is given to every person who at any time on that day is—

(a) a member of the company,

(b) an employee of the company,

(c) a creditor of the company,

(d) a director of the company,

(e) a manager or trustee of any pension fund established for the benefit of employees of the company, or

(f) a person of a description specified for the purposes of this paragraph by regulations made by the Secretary of State.

Regulations under paragraph (f) are subject to negative resolution procedure.

(2) Subsection (1) does not require a copy of the application to be given to a director who is a party to the application.

(3) The duty imposed by this section ceases to apply if the application is withdrawn before the end of the period for giving the copy application.

(4) A person who fails to perform the duty imposed on him by this section commits an offence. If he does so with the intention of concealing the making of the application from the person concerned, he commits an aggravated offence.

(5) In proceedings for an offence under this section it is a defence for the accused to prove that he took all reasonable steps to perform the duty.

(6) A person guilty of an offence under this section (other than an aggravated offence) is liable—

(a) on conviction on indictment, to a fine;

(b) on summary conviction, to a fine not exceeding the statutory maximum.

(7) A person guilty of an aggravated offence under this section is liable—

(a) on conviction on indictment, to imprisonment for a term not exceeding seven years or a fine (or both);

(b) on summary conviction—

(i) in England and Wales, to imprisonment for a term not exceeding twelve months or to a fine not exceeding the statutory maximum (or both);

(ii) in Scotland or Northern Ireland, to imprisonment for a term not exceeding six months, or to a fine not exceeding the statutory maximum (or both).

1007 Copy of application to be given to new members, employees, etc.

(1) This section applies in relation to any time after the day on which a company makes an application under section 1003 (application for voluntary striking off) and before the day on which the application is finally dealt with or withdrawn.

(2) A person who is a director of the company at the end of a day on which a person (other than himself) becomes—

(a) a member of the company,

(b) an employee of the company,

(c) a creditor of the company,

(d) a director of the company,

(e) a manager or trustee of any pension fund established for the benefit of employees of the company, or

(f) a person of a description specified for the purposes of this paragraph by regulations made by the Secretary of State,

must secure that a copy of the application is given to that person within seven days from that day.

Regulations under paragraph (f) are subject to negative resolution procedure.

(3) The duty imposed by this section ceases to apply if the application is finally dealt with or withdrawn before the end of the period for giving the copy application.

(4) A person who fails to perform the duty imposed on him by this section commits an offence. If he does so with the intention of concealing the making of the application from the person concerned, he commits an aggravated offence.

(5) In proceedings for an offence under this section it is a defence for the accused to prove—
- (a) that at the time of the failure he was not aware of the fact that the company had made an application under section 1003, or
- (b) that he took all reasonable steps to perform the duty.

(6) A person guilty of an offence under this section (other than an aggravated offence) is liable—
- (a) on conviction on indictment, to a fine;
- (b) on summary conviction, to a fine not exceeding the statutory maximum.

(7) A person guilty of an aggravated offence under this section is liable—
- (a) on conviction on indictment, to imprisonment for a term not exceeding seven years or a fine (or both);
- (b) on summary conviction—
  - (i) in England and Wales, to imprisonment for a term not exceeding twelve months or to a fine not exceeding the statutory maximum (or both);
  - (ii) in Scotland or Northern Ireland, to imprisonment for a term not exceeding six months, or to a fine not exceeding the statutory maximum (or both).

1008 Copy of application: provisions as to service of documents

(1) The following provisions have effect for the purposes of—
section 1006 (copy of application to be given to members, employees, etc), and
section 1007 (copy of application to be given to new members, employees, etc).

(2) A document is treated as given to a person if it is—
- (a) delivered to him, or
- (b) left at his proper address, or
- (c) sent by post to him at that address.

(3) For the purposes of subsection (2) and section 7 of the Interpretation Act 1978 (service of documents by post) as it applies in relation to that subsection, the proper address of a person is—
- (a) in the case of a firm incorporated or formed in the United Kingdom, its registered or principal office;
- (b) in the case of a firm incorporated or formed outside the United Kingdom—
  - (i) if it has a place of business in the United Kingdom, its principal office in the United Kingdom, or
  - (ii) if it does not have a place of business in the United Kingdom, its registered or principal office;
- (c) in the case of an individual, his last known address.

(4) In the case of a creditor of the company a document is treated as given to him if it is left or sent by post to him—
- (a) at the place of business of his with which the company has had dealings by virtue of which he is a creditor of the company, or
- (b) if there is more than one such place of business, at each of them.

1009 Circumstances in which application to be withdrawn

(1) This section applies where, at any time on or after the day on which a company makes an application under section 1003 (application for voluntary striking off) and before the day on which the application is finally dealt with or withdrawn—
- (a) the company—
  - (i) changes its name,
  - (ii) trades or otherwise carries on business,
  - (iii) makes a disposal for value of any property or rights other than those which it was necessary or expedient for it to hold for the purpose of making, or proceeding with, an application under that section, or
  - (iv) engages in any activity, except one to which subsection (4) applies;
- (b) an application is made to the court under Part 26 on behalf of the company for the sanctioning of a compromise or arrangement;
- (c) a voluntary arrangement in relation to the company is proposed under Part 1 of the Insolvency Act 1986 or Part 2 of the Insolvency (Northern Ireland) Order 1989;

(d) an application to the court for an administration order in respect of the company is made under paragraph 12 of Schedule B1 to that Act or paragraph 13 of Schedule B1 to that Order;
(e) an administrator is appointed in respect of the company under paragraph 14 or 22 of Schedule B1 to that Act or paragraph 15 or 23 of Schedule B1 to that Order, or a copy of notice of intention to appoint an administrator of the company under any of those provisions is filed with the court;
(f) there arise any of the circumstances in which, under section 84(1) of that Act or Article 70 of that Order, the company may be voluntarily wound up;
(g) a petition is presented for the winding up of the company by the court under Part 4 of that Act or Part 5 of that Order;
(h) a receiver or manager of the company's property is appointed; or
(i) a judicial factor is appointed to administer the company's estate.

(2) A person who, at the end of a day on which any of the events mentioned in subsection (1) occurs, is a director of the company must secure that the company's application is withdrawn forthwith.

(3) For the purposes of subsection (1)(a), a company is not treated as trading or otherwise carrying on business by virtue only of the fact that it makes a payment in respect of a liability incurred in the course of trading or otherwise carrying on business.

(4) The excepted activities referred to in subsection (1)(a)(iv) are—
(a) any activity necessary or expedient for the purposes of—
(i) making, or proceeding with, an application under section 1003 (application for voluntary striking off),
(ii) concluding affairs of the company that are outstanding because of what has been necessary or expedient for the purpose of making, or proceeding with, such an application, or
(iii) complying with any statutory requirement;
(b) any activity specified by the Secretary of State by order for the purposes of this subsection.

An order under paragraph (b) is subject to negative resolution procedure.

(5) A person who fails to perform the duty imposed on him by this section commits an offence.

(6) In proceedings for an offence under this section it is a defence for the accused to prove—
(a) that at the time of the failure he was not aware of the fact that the company had made an application under section 1003, or
(b) that he took all reasonable steps to perform the duty.

(7) A person guilty of an offence under this section is liable—
(a) on conviction on indictment, to a fine;
(b) on summary conviction, to a fine not exceeding the statutory maximum.

1010 Withdrawal of application

An application under section 1003 is withdrawn by notice to the registrar.

1011 Meaning of "creditor"

In this Chapter "creditor" includes a contingent or prospective creditor.

CHAPTERS 2, 3
OMITTED

PARTS 32–34
OMITTED

PART 35
THE REGISTRAR OF COMPANIES

Scheme of this Part

1059A Scheme of this Part

(1) The scheme of this Part is as follows.

(2) The following provisions apply generally (to the registrar, to any functions of the registrar, or to documents delivered to or issued by the registrar under any enactment, as the case may be)—

sections 1060(1) and (2) and 1061 to 1063 (the registrar),
sections 1068 to 1071 (delivery of documents to the registrar),
sections 1072 to 1076 (requirements for proper delivery),
sections 1080(1), (4) and (5) and 1092 (keeping and production of records),
section 1083 (preservation of original documents),
section 1084A (recording optional information on register),
sections 1108 to 1110 (language requirements: transliteration),
sections 1111 and 1114 to 1119 (supplementary provisions).

(3) The following provisions apply in relation to companies (to companies or for the purposes of the Companies Acts, as the case may be)—
section 1060(3) and (4) (references to the registrar in the Companies Acts),
sections 1064 and 1065 (certificates of incorporation),
section 1066 (companies' registered numbers),
sections 1077 to 1079A (public notice of certain information),
sections 1080(2) and (3), 1081, 1082 and 1084 (the register),
sections 1085 to 1091 (inspection of the register),
sections 1093 to 1098 (correction or removal of material on the register),
section 1106 (voluntary filing of translations),
sections 1112 and 1113 (supplementary provisions).

(4) The following provisions apply as indicated in the provisions concerned—
section 1067 (registered numbers of UK establishments of overseas companies),
sections 1099 to 1101 (the registrar's index of company names),
sections 1102 to 1105 and 1107 (language requirements: translation).

(5) Unless the context otherwise requires, the provisions of this Part apply to an overseas company as they apply to a company as defined in section 1.

The registrar

1060 The registrar

(1) There shall continue to be—
(a) a registrar of companies for England and Wales,
(b) a registrar of companies for Scotland, and
(c) a registrar of companies for Northern Ireland.

(2) The registrars shall be appointed by the Secretary of State.

(3) In the Companies Acts "the registrar of companies" and "the registrar" mean the registrar of companies for England and Wales, Scotland or Northern Ireland, as the case may require.

(4) References in the Companies Acts to registration in a particular part of the United Kingdom are to registration by the registrar for that part of the United Kingdom.

1061 The registrar's functions

(1) The registrar shall continue—
(a) to perform the functions conferred on the registrar by or under the Companies Acts or any other enactment, and
(b) to perform such functions on behalf of the Secretary of State, in relation to the registration of companies or other matters, as the Secretary of State may from time to time direct.

...

(3) References in this Act to the functions of the registrar are to functions within subsection (1)(a) or (b).

1062, 1063 *omitted*

Certificates of incorporation

1064 Public notice of issue of certificate of incorporation

(1) The registrar must cause to be published—
(a) in the Gazette, or
(b) in accordance with section 1116 (alternative means of giving public notice), notice of the issue by the registrar of any certificate of incorporation of a company.

(2) The notice must state the name and registered number of the company and the date of issue of the certificate.

(3) This section applies to a certificate of incorporation issued under—
  (a) section 80 (change of name),
  (b) section 88 (Welsh companies), or
  (c) any provision of Part 7 (re-registration),

as well as to the certificate issued on a company's formation.

1065 Right to certificate of incorporation

Any person may require the registrar to provide him with a copy of any certificate of incorporation of a company, signed by the registrar or authenticated by the registrar's seal.

Registered numbers

1066 Company's registered numbers

(1) The registrar shall allocate to every company a number, which shall be known as the company's registered number.

(2) Companies' registered numbers shall be in such form, consisting of one or more sequences of figures or letters, as the registrar may determine.

(3) The registrar may on adopting a new form of registered number make such changes of existing registered numbers as appear necessary.

(4) A change of a company's registered number has effect from the date on which the company is notified by the registrar of the change.

(5) For a period of three years beginning with that date any requirement to disclose the company's registered number imposed by regulations under section 82 or section 1051 (trading disclosures) is satisfied by the use of either the old number or the new.

(6) In this section "company" includes an overseas company whose particulars have been registered under section 1046, other than a company that appears to the registrar not to be required to register particulars under that section.

1067–1070 *omitted*

1071 Document not delivered until received

(1) A document is not delivered to the registrar until it is received by the registrar.

(2) Provision may be made by registrar's rules as to when a document is to be regarded as received.

Requirements for proper delivery

1072 Requirements for proper delivery

(1) A document delivered to the registrar is not properly delivered unless all the following requirements are met—
  (a) the requirements of the provision under which the document is to be delivered to the registrar as regards—
    (i) the contents of the document, and
    (ii) form, authentication and manner of delivery;
  (b) any applicable requirements under—
      section 1068 (registrar's requirements as to form, authentication and manner of delivery),
      section 1069 (power to require delivery by electronic means), or section 1070 (agreement for delivery by electronic means);
  (c) any requirements of this Part as to the language in which the document is drawn up and delivered or as to its being accompanied on delivery by a certified translation into English;
  (d) in so far as it consists of or includes names and addresses, any requirements of this Part as to permitted characters, letters or symbols or as to its being accompanied on delivery by a certificate as to the transliteration of any element;
  (e) any applicable requirements under section 1111 (registrar's requirements as to certification or verification);

(f) any requirement of regulations under section 1082 (use of unique identifiers);
(g) any requirements as regards payment of a fee in respect of its receipt by the registrar.

(2) A document that is not properly delivered is treated for the purposes of the provision requiring or authorising it to be delivered as not having been delivered, subject to the provisions of section 1073 (power to accept documents not meeting requirements for proper delivery).

1073 Power to accept documents not meeting requirements for proper delivery

(1) The registrar may accept (and register) a document that does not comply with the requirements for proper delivery.
(2) A document accepted by the registrar under this section is treated as received by the registrar for the purposes of section 1077 (public notice of receipt of certain documents).
(3) No objection may be taken to the legal consequences of a document's being accepted (or registered) by the registrar under this section on the ground that the requirements for proper delivery were not met.
(4) The acceptance of a document by the registrar under this section does not affect—
(a) the continuing obligation to comply with the requirements for proper delivery, or
(b) subject as follows, any liability for failure to comply with those requirements.
(5) For the purposes of—
(a) section 453 (civil penalty for failure to file accounts and reports), and
(b) any enactment imposing a daily default fine for failure to deliver the document,
the period after the document is accepted does not count as a period during which there is default in complying with the requirements for proper delivery.
(6) But if, subsequently—
(a) the registrar issues a notice under section 1094(4) in respect of the document (notice of administrative removal from the register), and
(b) the requirements for proper delivery are not complied with before the end of the period of 14 days after the issue of that notice,
any subsequent period of default does count for the purposes of those provisions.

1074 Documents containing unnecessary material

(1) This section applies where a document delivered to the registrar contains unnecessary material.
(2) "Unnecessary material" means material that—
(a) is not necessary in order to comply with an obligation under any enactment, and
(b) is not specifically authorised to be delivered to the registrar.
(3) For this purpose an obligation to deliver a document of a particular description, or conforming to certain requirements, is regarded as not extending to anything that is not needed for a document of that description or, as the case may be, conforming to those requirements.
(4) If the unnecessary material cannot readily be separated from the rest of the document, the document is treated as not meeting the requirements for proper delivery.
(5) If the unnecessary material can readily be separated from the rest of the document, the registrar may register the document either—
(a) with the omission of the unnecessary material, or
(b) as delivered.

1075 Informal correction of document

(1) A document delivered to the registrar may be corrected by the registrar if it appears to the registrar to be incomplete or internally inconsistent.
(2) This power is exercisable only—
(a) on instructions, and
(b) if the company (or other body) to which the document relates has given (and has not withdrawn) its consent to instructions being given under this section.
(3) The following requirements must be met as regards the instructions—
(a) the instructions must be given in response to an enquiry by the registrar;
(b) the registrar must be satisfied that the person giving the instructions is authorised to do so—
(i) by the person by whom the document was delivered, or
(ii) by the company (or other body) to which the document relates;

(c) the instructions must meet any requirements of registrar's rules as to—
(i) the form and manner in which they are given, and
(ii) authentication.

(4) The consent of the company (or other body) to instructions being given under this section (and any withdrawal of such consent)—
(a) may be in hard copy or electronic form, and
(b) must be notified to the registrar.

(5) This section applies in relation to documents delivered under Part 25 (company charges) by a person other than the company (or other body) as if the references to the company (or other body) were to the company (or other body) or the person by whom the document was delivered.

(6) A document that is corrected under this section is treated, for the purposes of any enactment relating to its delivery, as having been delivered when the correction is made.

(7) The power conferred by this section is not exercisable if the document has been registered under section 1073 (power to accept documents not meeting requirements for proper delivery).

1076 Replacement of document not meeting requirements for proper delivery

(1) The registrar may accept a replacement for a document previously delivered that—
(a) did not comply with the requirements for proper delivery, or
(b) contained unnecessary material (within the meaning of section 1074).

(2) A replacement document must not be accepted unless the registrar is satisfied that it is delivered by—
(a) the person by whom the original document was delivered, or
(b) the company or other body to which the original document relates, and that it complies with the requirements for proper delivery.

(3) The power of the registrar to impose requirements as to the form and manner of delivery includes power to impose requirements as to the identification of the original document and the delivery of the replacement in a form and manner enabling it to be associated with the original.

(4) This section does not apply where the original document was delivered under Part 25 (company charges) (but see section 859M (rectification of register of charges)).

Public notice of receipt of certain documents

1077 Public notice of receipt of certain documents

(1) The registrar must cause to be published—
(a) in the Gazette, or
(b) in accordance with section 1116 (alternative means of giving public notice),
notice of the receipt by the registrar of any document that, on receipt, is subject to the Directive disclosure requirements (see section 1078).

(2) The notice must state the name and registered number of the company, the description of document and the date of receipt.

(3) The registrar is not required to cause notice of the receipt of a document to be published before the date of incorporation of the company to which the document relates.

1078 Documents subject to Directive disclosure requirements

(1) The documents subject to the "Directive disclosure requirements" are as follows.
The requirements referred to are those of Article 3 of the Directive 2009/101/EC, as amended, extended and applied.

(2) In the case of every company—

Constitutional documents

1. The company's memorandum and articles.
2. Any amendment of the company's articles (including every resolution or agreement required to be embodied in or annexed to copies of the company's articles issued by the company).
3. After any amendment of the company's articles, the text of the articles as amended.
4. Any notice of a change of the company's name.

Directors
1. The statement of proposed officers required on formation of the company.
2. Notification of any change among the company's directors.
3. Notification of any change in the particulars of directors required to be delivered to the registrar.

Accounts, reports and returns
1. All documents required to be delivered to the registrar under section 441 (annual accounts and reports).
1A. All documents delivered to the registrar under sections 394A(2)(e), 448A(2)(e) and 479A(2)(e) (qualifying subsidiary companies: conditions for exemption from the audit, preparation and filing of individual accounts).
2. The company's annual return.

Registered office
Notification of any change of the company's registered office.

Winding up
1. Copy of any winding-up order in respect of the company.
2. Notice of the appointment of liquidators.
3. Order for the dissolution of a company on a winding up.
4. Return by a liquidator of the final meeting of a company on a winding up.

(3) In the case of a public company—

Share capital
1. Any statement of capital and initial shareholdings.
2. Any return of allotment and the statement of capital accompanying it.
3. Copy of any resolution under section 570 or 571 (disapplication of pre-emption rights).
4. Copy of any report under section 593 or 599 as to the value of a non-cash asset.
5. Statement of capital accompanying notice given under section 625 (notice by company of redenomination of shares).
6. Statement of capital accompanying notice given under section 627 (notice by company of reduction of capital in connection with redenomination of shares).
7. Notice delivered under section 636 (notice of new name of class of shares) or 637 (notice of variation of rights attached to shares).
8. Statement of capital accompanying order delivered under section 649 (order of court confirming reduction of capital).
9. Notification (under section 689) of the redemption of shares and the statement of capital accompanying it.
10. Statement of capital accompanying return delivered under section 708 (notice of cancellation of shares on purchase of own shares) or 730 (notice of cancellation of shares held as treasury shares).
11. Any statement of compliance delivered under section 762 (statement that company meets conditions for issue of trading certificate).

Mergers and divisions
1. Copy of any draft of the terms of a scheme required to be delivered to the registrar under section 906 or 921.
2. Copy of any order under section 899 or 900 in respect of a compromise or arrangement to which Part 27 (mergers and divisions of public companies) applies.

(4) Where a private company re-registers as a public company (see section 96)—
(a) the last statement of capital relating to the company received by the registrar under any provision of the Companies Acts becomes subject to the Directive disclosure requirements, and
(b) section 1077 (public notice of receipt of certain documents) applies as if the statement had been received by the registrar when the re-registration takes effect.

(4A) Where a company is required by regulation 14 of the Reports on Payments to Governments Regulations 2014 to deliver to the registrar a report or consolidated report on payments to governments, that report or consolidated report.

(4B) Where a company is required by regulation 15 of the Reports on Payments to Governments Regulations 2014 to deliver to the registrar information on payments to governments which is contained in a report or consolidated report prepared in accordance with equivalent reporting requirements (within the meaning of those Regulations), that information.

(5) In the case of an overseas company, such particulars, returns and other documents required to be delivered under Part 34 as may be specified by the Secretary of State by regulations.

(6) Regulations under subsection (5) are subject to negative resolution procedure.

1079 Effect of failure to give public notice

(1) A company is not entitled to rely against other persons on the happening of any event to which this section applies unless—

(a) the event has been officially notified at the material time, or

(b) the company shows that the person concerned knew of the event at the material time.

(2) The events to which this section applies are—

(a) an amendment of the company's articles,

(b) a change among the company's directors,

(c) (as regards service of any document on the company) a change of the company's registered office,

(d) the making of a winding-up order in respect of the company, or

(e) the appointment of a liquidator in a voluntary winding up of the company.

(3) If the material time falls—

(a) on or before the 15th day after the date of official notification, or

(b) where the 15th day was not a working day, on or before the next day that was,

the company is not entitled to rely on the happening of the event as against a person who shows that he was unavoidably prevented from knowing of the event at that time.

(4) "Official notification" means—

(a) in relation to an amendment of the company's articles, notification in accordance with section 1077 (public notice of receipt by registrar of certain documents) of the amendment and the amended text of the articles;

(b) in relation to anything else stated in a document subject to the Directive disclosure requirements, notification of that document in accordance with that section;

(c) in relation to the appointment of a liquidator in a voluntary winding up, notification of that event in accordance with section 109 of the Insolvency Act 1986 or Article 95 of the Insolvency (Northern Ireland) Order 1989.

1079A Provision of information for publication on European e-Justice portal

(1) The registrar must provide the information required by Article 3a(1) of Directive 2009/101/EC for publication on the European e-Justice portal in accordance with the portal's rules and technical requirements.

(2) In this section, "the European e-Justice portal" means the single European electronic access point for legal information, judicial and administrative institutions, registers, databases and other services referred to in Directive 2009/101/EC.

(3) The references in this section to Directive 2009/101/EC and Article 3a of that Directive are to that Directive, and that provision, as amended from time to time.

The register

1080 The register

(1) The registrar shall continue to keep records of—

(a) the information contained in documents delivered to the registrar under any enactment, and

(b) certificates issued by the registrar under any enactment.

(2) The records relating to companies are referred to collectively in the Companies Acts as "the register".

(3) Information deriving from documents subject to the Directive disclosure requirements (see section 1078) that are delivered to the registrar on or after 1st January 2007 must be kept by the registrar in electronic form.
(4) Subject to that, information contained in documents delivered to the registrar may be recorded and kept in any form the registrar thinks fit, provided it is possible to inspect it and produce a copy of it.
This is sufficient compliance with any duty of the registrar to keep, file or register the document or to record the information contained in it.
(5) The records kept by the registrar must be such that information relating to a company or other registered body is associated with that body, in such manner as the registrar may determine, so as to enable all the information relating to the body to be retrieved.

1081 Annotation of the register

(1) The registrar must place a note in the register recording—
(a) the date on which a document is delivered to the registrar;
(b) if a document is corrected under section 1075, the nature and date of the correction;
(c) if a document is replaced (whether or not material derived from it is removed), the fact that it has been replaced and the date of delivery of the replacement;
(d) if material is removed—
(i) what was removed (giving a general description of its contents),
(ii) under what power, and
(iii) the date on which that was done;
(e) if a document is rectified under section 859M, the nature and date of rectification;
(f) if a document is replaced under section 859N, the fact that it has been replaced and the date of delivery of the replacement.
(2) The Secretary of State may make provision by regulations—
(a) authorising or requiring the registrar to annotate the register in such other circumstances as may be specified in the regulations, and
(b) as to the contents of any such annotation.
(3) No annotation is required in the case of a document that by virtue of section 1072(2) (documents not meeting requirements for proper delivery) is treated as not having been delivered.
(4) A note may be removed if it no longer serves any useful purpose.
(5) Any duty or power of the registrar with respect to annotation of the register is subject to the court's power under section 1097 (powers of court on ordering removal of material from the register) to direct—
(a) that a note be removed from the register, or
(b) that no note shall be made of the removal of material that is the subject of the court's order.
(6) Notes placed in the register in accordance with subsection (1), or in pursuance of regulations under subsection (2), are part of the register for all purposes of the Companies Acts.
(7) Regulations under this section are subject to negative resolution procedure.

1082–1084 *omitted*

Inspection etc of the register

1085 Inspection of the register

(1) Any person may inspect the register.
(2) The right of inspection extends to the originals of documents delivered to the registrar in hard copy form if, and only if, the record kept by the registrar of the contents of the document is illegible or unavailable.
The period for which such originals are to be kept is limited by section 1083(1).
(3) This section has effect subject to section 1087 (material not available for public inspection).

1086 Right to copy of material on the register

(1) Any person may require a copy of any material on the register.

(2) The fee for any such copy of material derived from a document subject to the Directive disclosure requirements (see section 1078), whether in hard copy or electronic form, must not exceed the administrative cost of providing it.

(3) This section has effect subject to section 1087 (material not available for public inspection).

1087 Material not available for public inspection

(1) The following material must not be made available by the registrar for public inspection—

(a) the contents of any document sent to the registrar containing views expressed pursuant to section 56 (comments on proposal by company to use certain words or expressions in company name);

(b) protected information within section 242(1) (directors' residential addresses: restriction on disclosure by registrar) or any corresponding provision of regulations under section 1046 (overseas companies);

(ba) representations received by the registrar in response to a notice under—

(i) section 245(2) (notice of proposal to put director's usual residential address on the public record), or

(ii) any corresponding provision of regulations under section 1046 (overseas companies);

(c) any application to the registrar under section 1024 (application for administrative restoration to the register) that has not yet been determined or was not successful;

(d) any document received by the registrar in connection with the giving or withdrawal of consent under section 1075 (informal correction of documents);

(e) any application or other document delivered to the registrar under section 1088 (application to make address unavailable for public inspection) and any address in respect of which such an application is successful;

(f) any application or other document delivered to the registrar under section 1095 (application for rectification of register);

(g) any court order under section 1096 (rectification of the register under court order) that the court has directed under section 1097 (powers of court on ordering removal of material from the register) is not to be made available for public inspection;

(ga) any application or other document delivered to the registrar under section 1097A (rectification of company registered office) other than an order or direction of the court;

(h) …

(i) any e-mail address, identification code or password deriving from a document delivered for the purpose of authorising or facilitating electronic filing procedures or providing information by telephone;

(j) the contents of any documents held by the registrar pending a decision of the Regulator of Community Interest Companies under—

(i) section 36A of the Companies (Audit, Investigations and Community Enterprise) Act 2004 (eligibility for registration as community interest company),

(ii) section 38 of that Act (eligibility for conversion to community interest company), or

(iii) section 55 of that Act (eligibility for conversion from community interest company to charity),

and that the registrar is not later required to record;

(k) any other material excluded from public inspection by or under any other enactment.

(2) A restriction applying by reference to material deriving from a particular description of document does not affect the availability for public inspection of the same information contained in material derived from another description of document in relation to which no such restriction applies.

(3) Material to which this section applies need not be retained by the registrar for longer than appears to the registrar reasonably necessary for the purposes for which the material was delivered to the registrar.

1088–1098 *omitted*

The registrar's index of company names

1099 The registrar's index of company names

(1) The registrar of companies must keep an index of the names of the companies and other bodies to which this section applies.
This is "the registrar's index of company names".

(2) This section applies to—
  (a) UK-registered companies;
  (b) any body to which any provision of the Companies Acts applies by virtue of regulations under section 1043 (unregistered companies); and
  (c) overseas companies that have registered particulars with the registrar under section 1046, other than companies that appear to the registrar not to be required to do so.

(3) This section also applies to—
  (a) limited partnerships registered in the United Kingdom;
  (b) limited liability partnerships incorporated in the United Kingdom;
  (c) European Economic Interest Groupings registered in the United Kingdom;
  (d) open-ended investment companies authorised in the United Kingdom;
  (e) societies registered under the Co-operative and Community Benefit Societies Act 2014 or the Industrial and Provident Societies Act (Northern Ireland) 1969.

(4) The Secretary of State may by order amend subsection (3)—
  (a) by the addition of any description of body;
  (b) by the deletion of any description of body.

(5) Any such order is subject to negative resolution procedure.

1100 Right to inspect index

Any person may inspect the registrar's index of company names.

1101 *omitted*

Language requirements: translation

1102, 1103 *omitted*

1104 Documents relating to Welsh companies

(1) Documents relating to a Welsh company may be drawn up and delivered to the registrar in Welsh.

(2) On delivery to the registrar any such document must be accompanied by a certified translation into English, unless it is—
  (a) of a description excepted from that requirement by regulations made by the Secretary of State, or
  (b) in a form prescribed in Welsh (or partly in Welsh and partly in English) by virtue of section 26 of the Welsh Language Act 1993.

(3) Where a document is properly delivered to the registrar in Welsh without a certified translation into English, the registrar must obtain such a translation if the document is to be available for public inspection.
The translation is treated as if delivered to the registrar in accordance with the same provision as the original.

(4) A Welsh company may deliver to the registrar a certified translation into Welsh of any document in English that relates to the company and is or has been delivered to the registrar.

(5) Section 1105 (which requires certified translations into English of documents delivered to the registrar in another language) does not apply to a document relating to a Welsh company that is drawn up and delivered in Welsh.

1105 Documents that may be drawn up and delivered in other languages

(1) Documents to which this section applies may be drawn up and delivered to the registrar in a language other than English, but when delivered to the registrar they must be accompanied by a certified translation into English.

(2) This section applies to—
  (a) agreements required to be forwarded to the registrar under Chapter 3 of Part 3 (agreements affecting the company's constitution);

(b) documents required to be delivered under section 400(2)(e) or section 401(2)(f) (company included in accounts of larger group: required to deliver copy of group accounts);
(c) certified copies required to be delivered under Part 25 (company charges);
(d) documents of any other description specified in regulations made by the Secretary of State.

(3) Regulations under this section are subject to negative resolution procedure.

1006–1011 *omitted*

1112 General false statement offence

(1) It is an offence for a person knowingly or recklessly—
(a) to deliver or cause to be delivered to the registrar, for any purpose of the Companies Acts, a document, or
(b) to make to the registrar, for any such purpose, a statement, that is misleading, false or deceptive in a material particular.

(2) A person guilty of an offence under this section is liable—
(a) on conviction on indictment, to imprisonment for a term not exceeding two years or a fine (or both);
(b) on summary conviction—
(i) in England and Wales, to imprisonment for a term not exceeding twelve months or to a fine not exceeding the statutory maximum (or both);
(ii) in Scotland or Northern Ireland, to imprisonment for a term not exceeding six months, or to a fine not exceeding the statutory maximum (or both).

1113 Enforcement of company's filing obligations

(1) This section applies where a company has made default in complying with any obligation under the Companies Acts—
(a) to deliver a document to the registrar, or
(b) to give notice to the registrar of any matter.

(2) The registrar, or any member or creditor of the company, may give notice to the company requiring it to comply with the obligation.

(3) If the company fails to make good the default within 14 days after service of the notice, the registrar, or any member or creditor of the company, may apply to the court for an order directing the company, and any specified officer of it, to make good the default within a specified time.

(4) The court's order may provide that all costs (in Scotland, expenses) of or incidental to the application are to be borne by the company or by any officers of it responsible for the default.

(5) This section does not affect the operation of any enactment making it an offence, or imposing a civil penalty, for the default.

1114 Application of provisions about documents and delivery

(1) In this Part—
(a) "document" means information recorded in any form, and
(b) references to delivering a document include forwarding, lodging, registering, sending, producing or submitting it or (in the case of a notice) giving it.

(2) Except as otherwise provided, this Part applies in relation to the supply to the registrar of information otherwise than in documentary form as it applies in relation to the delivery of a document.

1115–1120 *omitted*

PART 36
OFFENCES UNDER THE COMPANIES ACTS

Liability of officer in default

1121 Liability of officer in default

(1) This section has effect for the purposes of any provision of the Companies Acts to the effect that, in the event of contravention of an enactment in relation to a company, an offence is committed by every officer of the company who is in default.

(2) For this purpose "officer" includes—
(a) any director, manager or secretary, and
(b) any person who is to be treated as an officer of the company for the purposes of the provision in question.
(3) An officer is "in default" for the purposes of the provision if he authorises or permits, participates in, or fails to take all reasonable steps to prevent, the contravention.

1122 Liability of company as officer in default

(1) Where a company is an officer of another company, it does not commit an offence as an officer in default unless one of its officers is in default.
(2) Where any such offence is committed by a company the officer in question also commits the offence and is liable to be proceeded against and punished accordingly.
(3) In this section "officer" and "in default" have the meanings given by section 1121.

1123 Application to bodies other than companies

(1) Section 1121 (liability of officers in default) applies to a body other than a company as it applies to a company.
(2) As it applies in relation to a body corporate other than a company—
(a) the reference to a director of the company shall be read as referring—
(i) where the body's affairs are managed by its members, to a member of the body,
(ii) in any other case, to any corresponding officer of the body, and
(b) the reference to a manager or secretary of the company shall be read as referring to any manager, secretary or similar officer of the body.
(3) As it applies in relation to a partnership—
(a) the reference to a director of the company shall be read as referring to a member of the partnership, and
(b) the reference to a manager or secretary of the company shall be read as referring to any manager, secretary or similar officer of the partnership.
(4) As it applies in relation to an unincorporated body other than a partnership—
(a) the reference to a director of the company shall be read as referring—
(i) where the body's affairs are managed by its members, to a member of the body,
(ii) in any other case, to a member of the governing body, and
(b) the reference to a manager or secretary of the company shall be read as referring to any manager, secretary or similar officer of the body.

1124 *omitted*

General provisions

1125 Meaning of "daily default fine"

(1) This section defines what is meant in the Companies Acts where it is provided that a person guilty of an offence is liable on summary conviction to a fine not exceeding a specified amount "and, for continued contravention, a daily default fine" not exceeding a specified amount.
(2) This means that the person is liable on a second or subsequent summary conviction of the offence to a fine not exceeding the latter amount for each day on which the contravention is continued (instead of being liable to a fine not exceeding the former amount).

1126 Consents required for certain prosecutions

(1) This section applies to proceedings for an offence under any of the following provisions—
section 458, 460 or 949 of this Act (offences of unauthorised disclosure of information);
section 953 of this Act (failure to comply with rules about takeover bid documents);
section 448, 449, 450, 451 or 453A of the Companies Act 1985 (offences in connection with company investigations);
section 798 of this Act or section 455 of the Companies Act 1985 (offence of attempting to evade restrictions on shares).
(2) No such proceedings are to be brought in England and Wales except by or with the consent of—
(a) in the case of an offence under—

(i) section 458, 460 or 949 of this Act,
(ii) section 953 of this Act, or
(iii) section 448, 449, 450, 451 or 453A of the Companies Act 1985, the Secretary of State or the Director of Public Prosecutions;
(b) in the case of an offence under section 798 of this Act or section 455 of the Companies Act 1985, the Secretary of State.

(3) No such proceedings are to be brought in Northern Ireland except by or with the consent of—
(a) in the case of an offence under—
(i) section 458, 460 or 949 of this Act,
(ii) section 953 of this Act, or
(iii) section 448, 449, 450, 451 or 453A of the Companies Act 1985,
the Secretary of State or the Director of Public Prosecutions for Northern Ireland;
(b) in the case of an offence under section 798 of this Act or section 455 of the Companies Act 1985, the Secretary of State.

1127 Summary proceedings: venue

(1) Summary proceedings for any offence under the Companies Acts may be taken—
(a) against a body corporate, at any place at which the body has a place of business, and
(b) against any other person, at any place at which he is for the time being.

(2) This is without prejudice to any jurisdiction exercisable apart from this section.

1128 Summary proceedings: time limit for proceedings

(1) An information relating to an offence under the Companies Acts that is triable by a magistrates' court in England and Wales may be so tried if it is laid—
(a) at any time within three years after the commission of the offence, and
(b) within twelve months after the date on which evidence sufficient in the opinion of the Director of Public Prosecutions or the Secretary of State (as the case may be) to justify the proceedings comes to his knowledge.

(2) Summary proceedings in Scotland for an offence under the Companies Acts—
(a) must not be commenced after the expiration of three years from the commission of the offence;
(b) subject to that, may be commenced at any time—
(i) within twelve months after the date on which evidence sufficient in the Lord Advocate's opinion to justify the proceedings came to his knowledge, or
(ii) where such evidence was reported to him by the Secretary of State, within twelve months after the date on which it came to the knowledge of the latter.

Section 136(3) of the Criminal Procedure (Scotland) Act 1995 (c. 46) (date when proceedings deemed to be commenced) applies for the purposes of this subsection as for the purposes of that section.

(3) A magistrates' court in Northern Ireland has jurisdiction to hear and determine a complaint charging the commission of a summary offence under the Companies Acts provided that the complaint is made—
(a) within three years from the time when the offence was committed, and
(b) within twelve months from the date on which evidence sufficient in the opinion of the Director of Public Prosecutions for Northern Ireland or the Secretary of State (as the case may be) to justify the proceedings comes to his knowledge.

(4) For the purposes of this section a certificate of the Director of Public Prosecutions, the Lord Advocate, the Director of Public Prosecutions for Northern Ireland or the Secretary of State (as the case may be) as to the date on which such evidence as is referred to above came to his notice is conclusive evidence.

1129 Legal professional privilege

In proceedings against a person for an offence under the Companies Acts, nothing in those Acts is to be taken to require any person to disclose any information that he is entitled to refuse to disclose on grounds of legal professional privilege (in Scotland, confidentiality of communications).

1130 Proceedings against unincorporated bodies

(1) Proceedings for an offence under the Companies Acts alleged to have been committed by an unincorporated body must be brought in the name of the body (and not in that of any of its members).

(2) For the purposes of such proceedings—
   (a) any rules of court relating to the service of documents have effect as if the body were a body corporate, and
   (b) the following provisions apply as they apply in relation to a body corporate—
      (i) in England and Wales, section 33 of the Criminal Justice Act 1925 and Schedule 3 to the Magistrates' Courts Act 1980,
      (ii) in Scotland, sections 70 and 143 of the Criminal Procedure (Scotland) Act 1995,
      (iii) in Northern Ireland, section 18 of the Criminal Justice Act (Northern Ireland) 1945 and Article 166 of and Schedule 4 to the Magistrates' Courts (Northern Ireland) Order 1981.
(3) A fine imposed on an unincorporated body on its conviction of an offence under the Companies Acts must be paid out of the funds of the body.

1131 *omitted*

Production and inspection of documents

1132 Production and inspection of documents where offence suspected

(1) An application under this section may be made—
   (a) in England and Wales, to a judge of the High Court by the Director of Public Prosecutions, the Secretary of State or a chief officer of police;
   (b) in Scotland, to one of the Lords Commissioners of Justiciary by the Lord Advocate;
   (c) in Northern Ireland, to the High Court by the Director of Public Prosecutions for Northern Ireland, the Department of Enterprise, Trade and Investment or a chief superintendent of the Police Service of Northern Ireland.
(2) If on an application under this section there is shown to be reasonable cause to believe—
   (a) that any person has, while an officer of a company, committed an offence in connection with the management of the company's affairs, and
   (b) that evidence of the commission of the offence is to be found in any documents in the possession or control of the company,

   an order under this section may be made.
(3) The order may—
   (a) authorise any person named in it to inspect the documents in question, or any of them, for the purpose of investigating and obtaining evidence of the offence, or
   (b) require the secretary of the company, or such other officer of it as may be named in the order, to produce the documents (or any of them) to a person named in the order at a place so named.
   (4) This section applies also in relation to documents in the possession or control of a person carrying on the business of banking, so far as they relate to the company's affairs, as it applies to documents in the possession or control of the company, except that no such order as is referred to in subsection (3)(b) may be made by virtue of this subsection.
(5) The decision under this section of a judge of the High Court, any of the Lords Commissioners of Justiciary or the High Court is not appealable.
(6) In this section "document" includes information recorded in any form.

1133 *omitted*

PART 37
COMPANIES: SUPPLEMENTARY PROVISIONS

Company records

1134 Meaning of "company records"

In this Part "company records" means—
   (a) any register, index, accounting records, agreement, memorandum, minutes or other document required by the Companies Acts to be kept by a company, and
   (b) any register kept by a company of its debenture holders.

1135 Form of company records

(1) Company records—
  (a) may be kept in hard copy or electronic form, and
  (b) may be arranged in such manner as the directors of the company think fit, provided the information in question is adequately recorded for future reference.

(2) Where the records are kept in electronic form, they must be capable of being reproduced in hard copy form.

(3) If a company fails to comply with this section, an offence is committed by every officer of the company who is in default.

(4) A person guilty of an offence under this section is liable on summary conviction to a fine not exceeding level 3 on the standard scale and, for continued contravention, a daily default fine not exceeding one-tenth of level 3 on the standard scale.

(5) Any provision of an instrument made by a company before 12th February 1979 that requires a register of holders of the company's debentures to be kept in hard copy form is to be read as requiring it to be kept in hard copy or electronic form.

1136 Regulations about where certain company records to be kept available for inspection

(1) The Secretary of State may make provision by regulations specifying places other than a company's registered office at which company records required to be kept available for inspection under a relevant provision may be so kept in compliance with that provision.

(2) The "relevant provisions" are—
  section 114 (register of members);
  section 162 (register of directors);
  section 228 (directors' service contracts);
  section 237 (directors' indemnities);
  section 275 (register of secretaries);
  section 358 (records of resolutions etc);
  section 702 (contracts relating to purchase of own shares);
  section 720 (documents relating to redemption or purchase of own shares out of capital by private company);
  section 743 (register of debenture holders);
  section 805 (report to members of outcome of investigation by public company into interests in its shares);
  section 809 (register of interests in shares disclosed to public company);
  section 859Q (instruments creating charges).

(3) The regulations may specify a place by reference to the company's principal place of business, the part of the United Kingdom in which the company is registered, the place at which the company keeps any other records available for inspection or in any other way.

(4) The regulations may provide that a company does not comply with a relevant provision by keeping company records available for inspection at a place specified in the regulations unless conditions specified in the regulations are met.

(5) The regulations—
  (a) need not specify a place in relation to each relevant provision;
  (b) may specify more than one place in relation to a relevant provision.

(6) A requirement under a relevant provision to keep company records available for inspection is not complied with by keeping them available for inspection at a place specified in the regulations unless all the company's records subject to the requirement are kept there.

(7) Regulations under this section are subject to negative resolution procedure.

1137 Regulations about inspection of records and provision of copies

(1) The Secretary of State may make provision by regulations as to the obligations of a company that is required by any provision of the Companies Acts—
  (a) to keep available for inspection any company records, or
  (b) to provide copies of any company records.

(2) A company that fails to comply with the regulations is treated as having refused inspection or, as the case may be, having failed to provide a copy.

(3) The regulations may—
  (a) make provision as to the time, duration and manner of inspection, including the circumstances in which and extent to which the copying of information is permitted in the course of inspection, and

(b) define what may be required of the company as regards the nature, extent and manner of extracting or presenting any information for the purposes of inspection or the provision of copies.

(4) Where there is power to charge a fee, the regulations may make provision as to the amount of the fee and the basis of its calculation.

(5) Nothing in any provision of this Act or in the regulations shall be read as preventing a company—

(a) from affording more extensive facilities than are required by the regulations, or

(b) where a fee may be charged, from charging a lesser fee than that prescribed or none at all.

(6) Regulations under this section are subject to negative resolution procedure.

1138 Duty to take precautions against falsification

(1) Where company records are kept otherwise than in bound books, adequate precautions must be taken—

(a) to guard against falsification, and

(b) to facilitate the discovery of falsification.

(2) If a company fails to comply with this section, an offence is committed by every officer of the company who is in default.

(3) A person guilty of an offence under this section is liable on summary conviction to a fine not exceeding level 3 on the standard scale and, for continued contravention, a daily default fine not exceeding one-tenth of level 3 on the standard scale.

(4) This section does not apply to the documents required to be kept under—

(a) section 228 (copy of director's service contract or memorandum of its terms); or

(b) section 237 (qualifying indemnity provision).

Service addresses

1139 Service of documents on company

(1) A document may be served on a company registered under this Act by leaving it at, or sending it by post to, the company's registered office.

(2) A document may be served on an overseas company whose particulars are registered under section 1046—

(a) by leaving it at, or sending it by post to, the registered address of any person resident in the United Kingdom who is authorised to accept service of documents on the company's behalf, or

(b) if there is no such person, or if any such person refuses service or service cannot for any other reason be effected, by leaving it at or sending by post to any place of business of the company in the United Kingdom.

(3) For the purposes of this section a person's "registered address" means any address for the time being shown as a current address in relation to that person in the part of the register available for public inspection.

(4) Where a company registered in Scotland or Northern Ireland carries on business in England and Wales, the process of any court in England and Wales may be served on the company by leaving it at, or sending it by post to, the company's principal place of business in England and Wales, addressed to the manager or other head officer in England and Wales of the company.

Where process is served on a company under this subsection, the person issuing out the process must send a copy of it by post to the company's registered office.

(5) Further provision as to service and other matters is made in the company communications provisions (see section 1143).

1140 Service of documents on directors, secretaries and others

(1) A document may be served on a person to whom this section applies by leaving it at, or sending it by post to, the person's registered address.

(2) This section applies to—

(a) a director or secretary of a company;

(b) in the case of an overseas company whose particulars are registered under section 1046, a person holding any such position as may be specified for the purposes of this section by regulations under that section;

(c) a person appointed in relation to a company as—

(i) a judicial factor (in Scotland),

(ii) an interim manager appointed under section 76 of the Charities Act 2011 or section 33 of the Charities Act (Northern Ireland) 2008, or

(iii) a manager appointed under section 47 of the Companies (Audit, Investigations and Community Enterprise) Act 2004.

(3) This section applies whatever the purpose of the document in question.
It is not restricted to service for purposes arising out of or in connection with the appointment or position mentioned in subsection (2) or in connection with the company concerned.

(4) For the purposes of this section a person's "registered address" means any address for the time being shown as a current address in relation to that person in the part of the register available for public inspection.

(5) If notice of a change of that address is given to the registrar, a person may validly serve a document at the address previously registered until the end of the period of 14 days beginning with the date on which notice of the change is registered.

(6) Service may not be effected by virtue of this section at an address—

(a) if notice has been registered of the termination of the appointment in relation to which the address was registered and the address is not a registered address of the person concerned in relation to any other appointment;

(b) in the case of a person holding any such position as is mentioned in subsection (2)(b), if the overseas company has ceased to have any connection with the United Kingdom by virtue of which it is required to register particulars under section 1046.

(7) Further provision as to service and other matters is made in the company communications provisions (see section 1143).

(8) Nothing in this section shall be read as affecting any enactment or rule of law under which permission is required for service out of the jurisdiction.

1141 Service addresses

(1) In the Companies Acts a "service address", in relation to a person, means an address at which documents may be effectively served on that person.

(2) The Secretary of State may by regulations specify conditions with which a service address must comply.

(3) Regulations under this section are subject to negative resolution procedure.

1142 Requirement to give service address

Any obligation under the Companies Acts to give a person's address is, unless otherwise expressly provided, to give a service address for that person.

Sending or supplying documents or information

1143 The company communications provisions

(1) The provisions of sections 1144 to 1148 and Schedules 4 and 5 ("the company communications provisions") have effect for the purposes of any provision of the Companies Acts that authorises or requires documents or information to be sent or supplied by or to a company.

(2) The company communications provisions have effect subject to any requirements imposed, or contrary provision made, by or under any enactment.

(3) In particular, in their application in relation to documents or information to be sent or supplied to the registrar, they have effect subject to the provisions of Part 35.

(4) For the purposes of subsection (2), provision is not to be regarded as contrary to the company communications provisions by reason only of the fact that it expressly authorises a document or information to be sent or supplied in hard copy form, in electronic form or by means of a website.

1144 Sending or supplying documents or information

(1) Documents or information to be sent or supplied to a company must be sent or supplied in accordance with the provisions of Schedule 4.

(2) Documents or information to be sent or supplied by a company must be sent or supplied in accordance with the provisions of Schedule 5.

(3) The provisions referred to in subsection (2) apply (and those referred to in subsection (1) do not apply) in relation to documents or information that are to be sent or supplied by one company to another.

1145 Right to hard copy version

(1) Where a member of a company or a holder of a company's debentures has received a document or information from the company otherwise than in hard copy form, he is entitled to require the company to send him a version of the document or information in hard copy form.

(2) The company must send the document or information in hard copy form within 21 days of receipt of the request from the member or debenture holder.

(3) The company may not make a charge for providing the document or information in that form.

(4) If a company fails to comply with this section, an offence is committed by the company and every officer of it who is in default.

(5) A person guilty of an offence under this section is liable on summary conviction to a fine not exceeding level 3 on the standard scale and, for continued contravention, a daily default fine not exceeding one-tenth of level 3 on the standard scale.

1146 Requirement of authentication

(1) This section applies in relation to the authentication of a document or information sent or supplied by a person to a company.

(2) A document or information sent or supplied in hard copy form is sufficiently authenticated if it is signed by the person sending or supplying it.

(3) A document or information sent or supplied in electronic form is sufficiently authenticated—

(a) if the identity of the sender is confirmed in a manner specified by the company, or

(b) where no such manner has been specified by the company, if the communication contains or is accompanied by a statement of the identity of the sender and the company has no reason to doubt the truth of that statement.

(4) Where a document or information is sent or supplied by one person on behalf of another, nothing in this section affects any provision of the company's articles under which the company may require reasonable evidence of the authority of the former to act on behalf of the latter.

1147 Deemed delivery of documents and information

(1) This section applies in relation to documents and information sent or supplied by a company.

(2) Where—

(a) the document or information is sent by post (whether in hard copy or electronic form) to an address in the United Kingdom, and

(b) the company is able to show that it was properly addressed, prepaid and posted,

it is deemed to have been received by the intended recipient 48 hours after it was posted.

(3) Where—

(a) the document or information is sent or supplied by electronic means, and

(b) the company is able to show that it was properly addressed,

it is deemed to have been received by the intended recipient 48 hours after it was sent.

(4) Where the document or information is sent or supplied by means of a website, it is deemed to have been received by the intended recipient—

(a) when the material was first made available on the website, or

(b) if later, when the recipient received (or is deemed to have received) notice of the fact that the material was available on the website.

(5) In calculating a period of hours for the purposes of this section, no account shall be taken of any part of a day that is not a working day.

(6) This section has effect subject to—

(a) in its application to documents or information sent or supplied by a company to its members, any contrary provision of the company's articles;

(b) in its application to documents or information sent or supplied by a company to its debentures holders, any contrary provision in the instrument constituting the debentures;

(c) in its application to documents or information sent or supplied by a company to a person otherwise than in his capacity as a member or debenture holder, any contrary provision in an agreement between the company and that person.

1148 Interpretation of company communications provisions

(1) In the company communications provisions—

"address" includes a number or address used for the purposes of sending or receiving documents or information by electronic means;
"company" includes any body corporate;
"document" includes summons, notice, order or other legal process and registers.

(2) References in the company communications provisions to provisions of the Companies Acts authorising or requiring a document or information to be sent or supplied include all such provisions, whatever expression is used, and references to documents or information being sent or supplied shall be construed accordingly.

(3) References in the company communications provisions to documents or information being sent or supplied by or to a company include references to documents or information being sent or supplied by or to the directors of a company acting on behalf of the company.

Requirements as to independent valuation

1149 Application of valuation requirements

The provisions of sections 1150 to 1153 apply to the valuation and report required by—

section 93 (re-registration as public company: recent allotment of shares for non-cash consideration);
section 593 (allotment of shares of public company in consideration of non-cash asset);
section 599 (transfer of non-cash asset to public company).

1150 Valuation by qualified independent person

(1) The valuation and report must be made by a person ("the valuer") who—
- (a) is eligible for appointment as a statutory auditor (see section 1212), and
- (b) meets the independence requirement in section 1151.

(2) However, where it appears to the valuer to be reasonable for the valuation of the consideration, or part of it, to be made by (or for him to accept a valuation made by) another person who—
- (a) appears to him to have the requisite knowledge and experience to value the consideration or that part of it, and
- (b) is not an officer or employee of—
  - (i) the company, or
  - (ii) any other body corporate that is that company's subsidiary or holding company or a subsidiary of that company's holding company,

  or a partner of or employed by any such officer or employee,

he may arrange for or accept such a valuation, together with a report which will enable him to make his own report under this section.

(3) The references in subsection (2)(b) to an officer or employee do not include an auditor.

(4) Where the consideration or part of it is valued by a person other than the valuer himself, the latter's report must state that fact and shall also—
- (a) state the former's name and what knowledge and experience he has to carry out the valuation, and
- (b) describe so much of the consideration as was valued by the other person, and the method used to value it, and specify the date of that valuation.

1151 The independence requirement

(1) A person meets the independence requirement for the purposes of section 1150 only if—
- (a) he is not—
  - (i) an officer or employee of the company, or
  - (ii) a partner or employee of such a person, or a partnership of which such a person is a partner;
- (b) he is not—
  - (i) an officer or employee of an associated undertaking of the company, or
  - (ii) a partner or employee of such a person, or a partnership of which such a person is a partner; and
- (c) there does not exist between—
  - (i) the person or an associate of his, and
  - (ii) the company or an associated undertaking of the company,

a connection of any such description as may be specified by regulations made by the Secretary of State.

(2) An auditor of the company is not regarded as an officer or employee of the company for this purpose.

(3) In this section—

"associated undertaking" means—

(a) a parent undertaking or subsidiary undertaking of the company, or

(b) a subsidiary undertaking of a parent undertaking of the company; and "associate" has the meaning given by section 1152.

(4) Regulations under this section are subject to negative resolution procedure.

1152 Meaning of "associate"

(1) This section defines "associate" for the purposes of section 1151 (valuation: independence requirement).

(2) In relation to an individual, "associate" means—

(a) that individual's spouse or civil partner or minor child or step-child,

(b) any body corporate of which that individual is a director, and

(c) any employee or partner of that individual.

(3) In relation to a body corporate, "associate" means—

(a) any body corporate of which that body is a director,

(b) any body corporate in the same group as that body, and

(c) any employee or partner of that body or of any body corporate in the same group.

(4) In relation to a partnership that is a legal person under the law by which it is governed, "associate" means—

(a) any body corporate of which that partnership is a director,

(b) any employee of or partner in that partnership, and

(c) any person who is an associate of a partner in that partnership.

(5) In relation to a partnership that is not a legal person under the law by which it is governed, "associate" means any person who is an associate of any of the partners.

(6) In this section, in relation to a limited liability partnership, for "director" read "member".

1153 Valuer entitled to full disclosure

(1) A person carrying out a valuation or making a report with respect to any consideration proposed to be accepted or given by a company, is entitled to require from the officers of the company such information and explanation as he thinks necessary to enable him to—

(a) carry out the valuation or make the report, and

(b) provide any note required by section 596(3) or 600(3) (note required where valuation carried out by another person).

(2) A person who knowingly or recklessly makes a statement to which this subsection applies that is misleading, false or deceptive in a material particular commits an offence.

(3) Subsection (2) applies to a statement—

(a) made (whether orally or in writing) to a person carrying out a valuation or making a report, and

(b) conveying or purporting to convey any information or explanation which that person requires, or is entitled to require, under subsection (1).

(4) A person guilty of an offence under subsection (2) is liable—

(a) on conviction on indictment, to imprisonment for a term not exceeding two years or a fine (or both);

(b) on summary conviction—

(i) in England and Wales, to imprisonment for a term not exceeding twelve months or to a fine not exceeding the statutory maximum (or both);

(ii) in Scotland or Northern Ireland, to imprisonment for a term not exceeding six months, or to a fine not exceeding the statutory maximum (or both).

Notice of appointment of certain officers

1154 Duty to notify registrar of certain appointments etc

(1) Notice must be given to the registrar of the appointment in relation to a company of—

(a) a judicial factor (in Scotland),

(b) an interim manager appointed under section 18 of the Charities Act 1993 orsection 33 of the Charities Act (Northern Ireland) 2008, or

(c) a manager appointed under section 47 of the Companies (Audit, Investigations and Community Enterprise) Act 2004.

(2) The notice must be given—
  (a) in the case of appointment of a judicial factor, by the judicial factor;
  (b) in the case of appointment of an interim manager under section 76 of the Charities Act 2011, by the Charity Commission;
  (bb) in the case of appointment of a receiver or manager under section 33 of the Charities Act (Northern Ireland) 2008, by the Charity Commission for Northern Ireland;
  (c) in the case of appointment of a manager under section 47 of the Companies (Audit, Investigations and Community Enterprise) Act 2004, by the Regulator of Community Interest Companies.

(3) The notice must specify an address at which service of documents (including legal process) may be effected on the person appointed.
Notice of a change in the address for service may be given to the registrar by the person appointed.

(4) Where notice has been given under this section of the appointment of a person, notice must also be given to the registrar of the termination of the appointment.
This notice must be given by the person specified in subsection (2).

1155 Offence of failure to give notice

(1) If a judicial factor fails to give notice of his appointment in accordance with section 1154 within the period of 14 days after the appointment he commits an offence.

(2) A person guilty of an offence under this section is liable on summary conviction to a fine not exceeding level 5 on the standard scale and, for continued contravention, a daily default fine not exceeding one-tenth of level 5 on the standard scale.

Courts and legal proceedings

1156 Meaning of "the court"

(1) Except as otherwise provided, in the Companies Acts "the court" means—
  (a) in England and Wales, the High Court or the county court;
  (b) in Scotland, the Court of Session or the sheriff court;
  (c) in Northern Ireland, the High Court.

(2) The provisions of the Companies Acts conferring jurisdiction on "the court" as defined above have effect subject to any enactment or rule of law relating to the allocation of jurisdiction or distribution of business between courts in any part of the United Kingdom.

1157 Power of court to grant relief in certain cases

(1) If in proceedings for negligence, default, breach of duty or breach of trust against—
  (a) an officer of a company, or
  (b) a person employed by a company as auditor (whether he is or is not an officer of the company),

it appears to the court hearing the case that the officer or person is or may be liable but that he acted honestly and reasonably, and that having regard to all the circumstances of the case (including those connected with his appointment) he ought fairly to be excused, the court may relieve him, either wholly or in part, from his liability on such terms as it thinks fit.

(2) If any such officer or person has reason to apprehend that a claim will or might be made against him in respect of negligence, default, breach of duty or breach of trust—
  (a) he may apply to the court for relief, and
  (b) the court has the same power to relieve him as it would have had if it had been a court before which proceedings against him for negligence, default, breach of duty or breach of trust had been brought.

(3) Where a case to which subsection (1) applies is being tried by a judge with a jury, the judge, after hearing the evidence, may, if he is satisfied that the defendant (in Scotland, the defender) ought in pursuance of that subsection to be relieved either in whole or in part from the liability sought to be enforced against him, withdraw the case from the jury and forthwith direct judgment to be entered for the defendant (in Scotland, grant decree of absolvitor) on such terms as to costs (in Scotland, expenses) or otherwise as the judge may think proper.

PART 38
COMPANIES: INTERPRETATION

Meaning of "UK-registered company"

1158 Meaning of "UK-registered company"

In the Companies Acts "UK-registered company" means a company registered under this Act. The expression does not include an overseas company that has registered particulars under section 1046.

Meaning of "subsidiary" and related expressions

1159 Meaning of "subsidiary" etc.

(1) A company is a "subsidiary" of another company, its "holding company", if that other company—
 (a) holds a majority of the voting rights in it, or
 (b) is a member of it and has the right to appoint or remove a majority of its board of directors, or
 (c) is a member of it and controls alone, pursuant to an agreement with other members, a majority of the voting rights in it,

 or if it is a subsidiary of a company that is itself a subsidiary of that other company.

(2) A company is a "wholly-owned subsidiary" of another company if it has no members except that other and that other's wholly-owned subsidiaries or persons acting on behalf of that other or its wholly-owned subsidiaries.

(3) Schedule 6 contains provisions explaining expressions used in this section and otherwise supplementing this section.

(4) In this section and that Schedule "company" includes any body corporate.

1160 *Omitted*

Meaning of "undertaking" and related expressions

1161 Meaning of "undertaking" and related expressions

(1) In the Companies Acts "undertaking" means—
 (a) a body corporate or partnership, or
 (b) an unincorporated association carrying on a trade or business, with or without a view to profit.

(2) In the Companies Acts references to shares—
 (a) in relation to an undertaking with capital but no share capital, are to rights to share in the capital of the undertaking; and
 (b) in relation to an undertaking without capital, are to interests—
  (i) conferring any right to share in the profits or liability to contribute to the losses of the undertaking, or
  (ii) giving rise to an obligation to contribute to the debts or expenses of the undertaking in the event of a winding up.

(3) Other expressions appropriate to companies shall be construed, in relation to an undertaking which is not a company, as references to the corresponding persons, officers, documents or organs, as the case may be, appropriate to undertakings of that description. This is subject to provision in any specific context providing for the translation of such expressions.

(4) References in the Companies Acts to "fellow subsidiary undertakings" are to undertakings which are subsidiary undertakings of the same parent undertaking but are not parent undertakings or subsidiary undertakings of each other.

(5) In the Companies Acts "group undertaking", in relation to an undertaking, means an undertaking which is—
 (a) a parent undertaking or subsidiary undertaking of that undertaking, or
 (b) a subsidiary undertaking of any parent undertaking of that undertaking.

1162 Parent and subsidiary undertakings

(1) This section (together with Schedule 7) defines "parent undertaking" and "subsidiary undertaking" for the purposes of the Companies Acts.

(2) An undertaking is a parent undertaking in relation to another undertaking, a subsidiary undertaking, if—
(a) it holds a majority of the voting rights in the undertaking, or
(b) it is a member of the undertaking and has the right to appoint or remove a majority of its board of directors, or
(c) it has the right to exercise a dominant influence over the undertaking—
(i) by virtue of provisions contained in the undertaking's articles, or
(ii) by virtue of a control contract, or
(d) it is a member of the undertaking and controls alone, pursuant to an agreement with other shareholders or members, a majority of the voting rights in the undertaking.

(3) For the purposes of subsection (2) an undertaking shall be treated as a member of another undertaking—
(a) if any of its subsidiary undertakings is a member of that undertaking, or
(b) if any shares in that other undertaking are held by a person acting on behalf of the undertaking or any of its subsidiary undertakings.

(4) An undertaking is also a parent undertaking in relation to another undertaking, a subsidiary undertaking, if—
(a) it has the power to exercise, or actually exercises, dominant influence or control over it, or
(b) it and the subsidiary undertaking are managed on a unified basis.

(5) A parent undertaking shall be treated as the parent undertaking of undertakings in relation to which any of its subsidiary undertakings are, or are to be treated as, parent undertakings; and references to its subsidiary undertakings shall be construed accordingly.

(6) Schedule 7 contains provisions explaining expressions used in this section and otherwise supplementing this section.

(7) In this section and that Schedule references to shares, in relation to an undertaking, are to allotted shares.

Other definitions

1163 "Non-cash asset"

(1) In the Companies Acts "non-cash asset" means any property or interest in property, other than cash.
For this purpose "cash" includes foreign currency.

(2) A reference to the transfer or acquisition of a non-cash asset includes—
(a) the creation or extinction of an estate or interest in, or a right over, any property, and
(b) the discharge of a liability of any person, other than a liability for a liquidated sum.

1164 Meaning of "banking company" and "banking group"

(1) This section defines "banking company" and "banking group" for the purposes of the Companies Acts.

(2) "Banking company" means a person who has permission under Part 4A of the Financial Services and Markets Act 2000 to accept deposits, other than—
(a) a person who is not a company, and
(b) a person who has such permission only for the purpose of carrying on another regulated activity in accordance with permission under that Part.

(3) The definition in subsection (2) must be read with section 22 of that Act, any relevant order under that section and Schedule 2 to that Act.

(4) References to a banking group are to a group where the parent company is a banking company or where—
(a) the parent company's principal subsidiary undertakings are wholly or mainly credit institutions, and
(b) the parent company does not itself carry on any material business apart from the acquisition, management and disposal of interests in subsidiary undertakings.
"Group" here means a parent undertaking and its subsidiary undertakings.

(5) For the purposes of subsection (4)—
(a) a parent company's principal subsidiary undertakings are the subsidiary undertakings of the company whose results or financial position would principally affect the figures shown in the group accounts, and
(b) the management of interests in subsidiary undertakings includes the provision of services to such undertakings.

1165 Meaning of "insurance company" and related expressions

(1) This section defines "insurance company", "authorised insurance company", "insurance group" and "insurance market activity" for the purposes of the Companies Acts.

(2) An "authorised insurance company" means a person (whether incorporated or not) who has permission under Part 4A of the Financial Services and Markets Act 2000 to effect or carry out contracts of insurance.

(3) An "insurance company" means—

(a) an authorised insurance company, or

(b) any other person (whether incorporated or not) who—

(i) carries on insurance market activity, or

(ii) may effect or carry out contracts of insurance under which the benefits provided by that person are exclusively or primarily benefits in kind in the event of accident to or breakdown of a vehicle.

(4) Neither expression includes a friendly society within the meaning of the Friendly Societies Act 1992.

(5) References to an insurance group are to a group where the parent company is an insurance company or where—

(a) the parent company's principal subsidiary undertakings are wholly or mainly insurance companies, and

(b) the parent company does not itself carry on any material business apart from the acquisition, management and disposal of interests in subsidiary undertakings.

"Group" here means a parent undertaking and its subsidiary undertakings.

(6) For the purposes of subsection (5)—

(a) a parent company's principal subsidiary undertakings are the subsidiary undertakings of the company whose results or financial position would principally affect the figures shown in the group accounts, and

(b) the management of interests in subsidiary undertakings includes the provision of services to such undertakings.

(7) "Insurance market activity" has the meaning given in section 316(3) of the Financial Services and Markets Act 2000.

(8) References in this section to contracts of insurance and to the effecting or carrying out of such contracts must be read with section 22 of that Act, any relevant order under that section and Schedule 2 to that Act.

1166 "Employees' share scheme"

For the purposes of the Companies Acts an employees' share scheme is a scheme for encouraging or facilitating the holding of shares in or debentures of a company by or for the benefit of—

(a) the bona fide employees or former employees of—

(i) the company,

(ii) any subsidiary of the company, or

(iii) the company's holding company or any subsidiary of the company's holding company, or

(b) the spouses, civil partners, surviving spouses, surviving civil partners, or minor children or step-children of such employees or former employees.

1167 Meaning of "prescribed"

In the Companies Acts "prescribed" means prescribed (by order or by regulations) by the Secretary of State.

1168 Hard copy and electronic form and related expressions

(1) The following provisions apply for the purposes of the Companies Acts.

(2) A document or information is sent or supplied in hard copy form if it is sent or supplied in a paper copy or similar form capable of being read.

References to hard copy have a corresponding meaning.

(3) A document or information is sent or supplied in electronic form if it is sent or supplied—

(a) by electronic means (for example, by e-mail or fax), or

(b) by any other means while in an electronic form (for example, sending a disk by post). References to electronic copy have a corresponding meaning.

(4) A document or information is sent or supplied by electronic means if it is—
(a) sent initially and received at its destination by means of electronic equipment for the processing (which expression includes digital compression) or storage of data, and
(b) entirely transmitted, conveyed and received by wire, by radio, by optical means or by other electromagnetic means.
References to electronic means have a corresponding meaning.
(5) A document or information authorised or required to be sent or supplied in electronic form must be sent or supplied in a form, and by a means, that the sender or supplier reasonably considers will enable the recipient—
(a) to read it, and
(b) to retain a copy of it.
(6) For the purposes of this section, a document or information can be read only if—
(a) it can be read with the naked eye, or
(b) to the extent that it consists of images (for example photographs, pictures, maps, plans or drawings), it can be seen with the naked eye.
(7) The provisions of this section apply whether the provision of the Companies Acts in question uses the words "sent" or "supplied" or uses other words (such as "deliver", "provide", "produce" or, in the case of a notice, "give") to refer to the sending or supplying of a document or information.

1169 Dormant companies

(1) For the purposes of the Companies Acts a company is "dormant" during any period in which it has no significant accounting transaction.
(2) A "significant accounting transaction" means a transaction that is required by section 386 to be entered in the company's accounting records.
(3) In determining whether or when a company is dormant, there shall be disregarded—
(a) any transaction arising from the taking of shares in the company by a subscriber to the memorandum as a result of an undertaking of his in connection with the formation of the company;
(b) any transaction consisting of the payment of—
(i) a fee to the registrar on a change of the company's name,
(ii) a fee to the registrar on the re-registration of the company,
(iii) a penalty under section 453 (penalty for failure to file accounts), or
(iv) a fee to the registrar for the registration of an annual return.
(4) Any reference in the Companies Acts to a body corporate other than a company being dormant has a corresponding meaning.

1170 Meaning of "EEA State" and related expressions

In the Companies Acts–
"EEA State" has the meaning given by Schedule 1 to the Interpretation Act 1978;
"EEA company" and "EEA undertaking" mean a company or undertaking governed by the law of an EEA State.

1170A Receiver or manager and certain related references

(1) Any reference in the Companies Acts to a receiver or manager of the property of a company, or to a receiver of it, includes a receiver or manager or (as the case may be) a receiver of part only of that property and a receiver only of the income arising from the property or from part of it.
(2) Any reference in the Companies Acts to the appointment of a receiver or manager under powers contained in an instrument includes an appointment made under powers that by virtue of an enactment are implied in and have effect as if contained in an instrument.

1170B Meaning of "contributory"

(1) In the Companies Acts "contributory" means every person liable to contribute to the assets of a company in the event of its being wound up.
(2) For the purposes of all proceedings for determining, and all proceedings prior to the final determination of, the persons who are to be deemed contributories, the expression includes any person alleged to be a contributory.
(3) The reference in subsection (1) to persons liable to contribute to the assets does not include a person so liable by virtue of a declaration by the court under—

(a) section 213 of the Insolvency Act 1986 or Article 177 of the Insolvency (Northern Ireland) Order 1989 (fraudulent trading), or
(b) section 214 of that Act or Article 178 of that Order (wrongful trading).

1171 The former Companies Acts

In the Companies Acts—

"the former Companies Acts" means—
(a) the Joint Stock Companies Acts, the Companies Act 1862, the Companies (Consolidation) Act 1908, the Companies Act 1929, the Companies Act (Northern Ireland) 1932, the Companies Acts 1948 to 1983, the Companies Act (Northern Ireland) 1960, the Companies (Northern Ireland) Order 1986 and the Companies Consolidation (Consequential Provisions) (Northern Ireland) Order 1986, and
(b) the provisions of the Companies Act 1985 and the Companies Consolidation (Consequential Provisions) Act 1985 that are no longer in force;

"the Joint Stock Companies Acts" means the Joint Stock Companies Act 1856, the Joint Stock Companies Acts 1856, 1857, the Joint Stock Banking Companies Act 1857, and the Act to enable Joint Stock Banking Companies to be formed on the principle of limited liability, but does not include the Joint Stock Companies Act 1844.

General

1172 References to requirements of this Act

References in the company law provisions of this Act to the requirements of this Act include the requirements of regulations and orders made under it.

1173 Minor definitions: general

(1) In the Companies Acts—

"body corporate" and "corporation" include a body incorporated outside the United Kingdom, but do not include—
(a) a corporation sole, or
(b) a partnership that, whether or not a legal person, is not regarded as a body corporate under the law by which it is governed;

"credit institution" means a credit institution as defined in Article 4(1)(1) of Regulation (EU) No 575/2013;

"financial institution" means a financial institution within the meaning of Article 1.1 of the Council Directive on the obligations of branches established in a Member State of credit and financial institutions having their head offices outside that Member State regarding the publication of annual accounting documents (the Bank Branches Directive, 89/117/EEC);

"firm" means any entity, whether or not a legal person, that is not an individual and includes a body corporate, a corporation sole and a partnership or other unincorporated association;

"the Gazette" means—
(a) as respects companies registered in England and Wales, the London Gazette,
(b) as respects companies registered in Scotland, the Edinburgh Gazette, and
(c) as respects companies registered in Northern Ireland, the Belfast Gazette;

"hire-purchase agreement" has the same meaning as in the Consumer Credit Act 1974;

"officer", in relation to a body corporate, includes a director, manager or secretary;

"parent company" means a company that is a parent undertaking (see section 1162 and Schedule 7);

"regulated activity" has the meaning given in section 22 of the Financial Services and Markets Act 2000;

"regulated market" has the same meaning as in Directive 2004/39/EC of the European Parliament and of the Council on markets in financial instruments (see Article 4.1(14));

"transferable securities" means anything which is a transferable security for the purposes of Directive 2004/39/EC of the European Parliament and of the Council on markets in financial instruments;

"working day", in relation to a company, means a day that is not a Saturday or Sunday, Christmas Day, Good Friday or any day that is a bank holiday under the Banking and Financial Dealings Act 1971 in the part of the United Kingdom where the company is registered.

(2) In relation to an EEA State that has not implemented Directive 2004/39/EC of the European Parliament and of the Council on markets in financial instruments, the following definition of "regulated market" has effect in place of that in subsection (1)—
"regulated market" has the same meaning as it has in Council Directive 93/22/EEC on investment services in the securities field.

1174 Index of defined expressions

Schedule 8 contains an index of provisions defining or otherwise explaining expressions used in the Companies Acts.

1175–1181 *omitted*

PART 40

COMPANY DIRECTORS: FOREIGN DISQUALIFICATION ETC

Introductory

1182 Persons subject to foreign restrictions

(1) This section defines what is meant by references in this Part to a person being subject to foreign restrictions.
(2) A person is subject to foreign restrictions if under the law of a country or territory outside the United Kingdom—
(a) he is, by reason of misconduct or unfitness, disqualified to any extent from acting in connection with the affairs of a company,
(b) he is, by reason of misconduct or unfitness, required—
(i) to obtain permission from a court or other authority, or
(ii) to meet any other condition,
before acting in connection with the affairs of a company, or
(c) he has, by reason of misconduct or unfitness, given undertakings to a court or other authority of a country or territory outside the United Kingdom—
(i) not to act in connection with the affairs of a company, or
(ii) restricting the extent to which, or the way in which, he may do so.
(3) The references in subsection (2) to acting in connection with the affairs of a company are to doing any of the following—
(a) being a director of a company,
(b) acting as receiver of a company's property, or
(c) being concerned or taking part in the promotion, formation or management of a company.
(4) In this section—
(a) "company" means a company incorporated or formed under the law of the country or territory in question, and
(b) in relation to such a company—
"director" means the holder of an office corresponding to that of director of a UK company; and
"receiver" includes any corresponding officer under the law of that country or territory.

1183 Meaning of "the court" and "UK company"

In this Part—
"the court" means—
(a) in England and Wales, the High Court or the county court;
(b) in Scotland, the Court of Session or the sheriff court;
(c) in Northern Ireland, the High Court;
"UK company" means a company registered under this Act.

Power to disqualify

1184 Disqualification of persons subject to foreign restrictions

(1) The Secretary of State may make provision by regulations disqualifying a person subject to foreign restrictions from—
(a) being a director of a UK company,
(b) acting as receiver of a UK company's property, or

(c) in any way, whether directly or indirectly, being concerned or taking part in the promotion, formation or management of a UK company.

(2) The regulations may provide that a person subject to foreign restrictions—

(a) is disqualified automatically by virtue of the regulations, or

(b) may be disqualified by order of the court on the application of the Secretary of State.

(3) The regulations may provide that the Secretary of State may accept an undertaking (a "disqualification undertaking") from a person subject to foreign restrictions that he will not do anything which would be in breach of a disqualification under subsection (1).

(4) In this Part—

(a) a "person disqualified under this Part" is a person—

(i) disqualified as mentioned in subsection (2)(a) or (b), or

(ii) who has given and is subject to a disqualification undertaking;

(b) references to a breach of a disqualification include a breach of a disqualification undertaking.

(5) The regulations may provide for applications to the court by persons disqualified under this Part for permission to act in a way which would otherwise be in breach of the disqualification.

(6) The regulations must provide that a person ceases to be disqualified under this Part on his ceasing to be subject to foreign restrictions.

(7) Regulations under this section are subject to affirmative resolution procedure.

1185 Disqualification regulations: supplementary

(1) Regulations under section 1184 may make different provision for different cases and may in particular distinguish between cases by reference to—

(a) the conduct on the basis of which the person became subject to foreign restrictions;

(b) the nature of the foreign restrictions;

(c) the country or territory under whose law the foreign restrictions were imposed.

(2) Regulations under section 1184(2)(b) or (5) (provision for applications to the court)—

(a) must specify the grounds on which an application may be made;

(b) may specify factors to which the court shall have regard in determining an application.

(3) The regulations may, in particular, require the court to have regard to the following factors—

(a) whether the conduct on the basis of which the person became subject to foreign restrictions would, if done in relation to a UK company, have led a court to make a disqualification order on an application under the Company Directors Disqualification Act 1986 or the Company Directors Disqualification (Northern Ireland) Order 2002;

(b) in a case in which the conduct on the basis of which the person became subject to foreign restrictions would not be unlawful if done in relation to a UK company, the fact that the person acted unlawfully under foreign law;

(c) whether the person's activities in relation to UK companies began after he became subject to foreign restrictions;

(d) whether the person's activities (or proposed activities) in relation to UK companies are undertaken (or are proposed to be undertaken) outside the United Kingdom.

(4) Regulations under section 1184(3) (provision as to undertakings given to the Secretary of State) may include provision allowing the Secretary of State, in determining whether to accept an undertaking, to take into account matters other than criminal convictions notwithstanding that the person may be criminally liable in respect of those matters.

(5) Regulations under section 1184(5) (provision for application to court for permission to act) may include provision—

(a) entitling the Secretary of State to be represented at the hearing of the application, and

(b) as to the giving of evidence or the calling of witnesses by the Secretary of State at the hearing of the application.

1186 Offence of breach of disqualification

(1) Regulations under section 1184 may provide that a person disqualified under this Part who acts in breach of the disqualification commits an offence.

(2) The regulations may provide that a person guilty of such an offence is liable—
(a) on conviction on indictment, to imprisonment for a term not exceeding two years or a fine (or both);
(b) on summary conviction—
(i) in England and Wales, to imprisonment for a term not exceeding twelve months or to a fine not exceeding the statutory maximum (or both);
(ii) in Scotland or Northern Ireland, to imprisonment for a term not exceeding six months, or to a fine not exceeding the statutory maximum (or both).
(3) In relation to an offence committed before the commencement of section 154(1) of the Criminal Justice Act 2003, for "twelve months" in subsection (2)(b)(i) substitute "six months".

Power to make persons liable for company's debts

1187 Personal liability for debts of company

(1) The Secretary of State may provide by regulations that a person who, at a time when he is subject to foreign restrictions—
(a) is a director of a UK company, or
(b) is involved in the management of a UK company,
is personally responsible for all debts and other liabilities of the company incurred during that time.
(2) A person who is personally responsible by virtue of this section for debts and other liabilities of a company is jointly and severally liable in respect of those debts and liabilities with—
(a) the company, and
(b) any other person who (whether by virtue of this section or otherwise) is so liable.
(3) For the purposes of this section a person is involved in the management of a company if he is concerned, whether directly or indirectly, or takes part, in the management of the company.
(4) The regulations may make different provision for different cases and may in particular distinguish between cases by reference to—
(a) the conduct on the basis of which the person became subject to foreign restrictions;
(b) the nature of the foreign restrictions;
(c) the country or territory under whose law the foreign restrictions were imposed.
(5) Regulations under this section are subject to affirmative resolution procedure.

Power to require statements to be sent to the registrar of companies

1188 Statements from persons subject to foreign restrictions

(1) The Secretary of State may make provision by regulations requiring a person who—
(a) is subject to foreign restrictions, and
(b) is not disqualified under this Part,
to send a statement to the registrar if he does anything that, if done by a person disqualified under this Part, would be in breach of the disqualification.
(2) The statement must include such information as may be specified in the regulations relating to—
(a) the person's activities in relation to UK companies, and
(b) the foreign restrictions to which the person is subject.
(3) The statement must be sent to the registrar within such period as may be specified in the regulations.
(4) The regulations may make different provision for different cases and may in particular distinguish between cases by reference to—
(a) the conduct on the basis of which the person became subject to foreign restrictions;
(b) the nature of the foreign restrictions;
(c) the country or territory under whose law the foreign restrictions were imposed.
(5) Regulations under this section are subject to affirmative resolution procedure.

1189 Statements from persons disqualified

(1) The Secretary of State may make provision by regulations requiring a statement or notice sent to the registrar of companies under any of the provisions listed below that relates (wholly or partly) to a person who—
(a) is a person disqualified under this Part, or

(b) is subject to a disqualification order or disqualification undertaking under the Company Directors Disqualification Act 1986 or the Company Directors Disqualification (Northern Ireland) Order 2002,

to be accompanied by an additional statement.

(2) The provisions referred to above are—

(a) section 12 (statement of a company's proposed officers),

(b) section 167(2) (notice of person having become director), and

(c) section 276 (notice of a person having become secretary or one of joint secretaries).

(3) The additional statement is a statement that the person has obtained permission from a court, on an application under section 1184(5) or (as the case may be) for the purposes of section 1(1)(a) of the Company Directors Disqualification Act 1986 or Article 3(1) of the Company Directors Disqualification (Northern Ireland) Order 2002, to act in the capacity in question.

(4) Regulations under this section are subject to affirmative resolution procedure.

1190 Statements: whether to be made public

(1) Regulations under section 1188 or 1189 (statements required to be sent to registrar) may provide that a statement sent to the registrar of companies under the regulations is to be treated as a record relating to a company for the purposes of section 1080 (the companies register).

(2) The regulations may make provision as to the circumstances in which such a statement is to be, or may be—

(a) withheld from public inspection, or

(b) removed from the register.

(3) The regulations may, in particular, provide that a statement is not to be withheld from public inspection or removed from the register unless the person to whom it relates provides such information, and satisfies such other conditions, as may be specified.

(4) The regulations may provide that section 1081 (note of removal of material from the register) does not apply, or applies with such modifications as may be specified, in the case of material removed from the register under the regulations.

(5) In this section "specified" means specified in the regulations.

1191 Offences

(1) Regulations under section 1188 or 1189 may provide that it is an offence for a person—

(a) to fail to comply with a requirement under the regulations to send a statement to the registrar;

(b) knowingly or recklessly to send a statement under the regulations to the registrar that is misleading, false or deceptive in a material particular.

(2) The regulations may provide that a person guilty of such an offence is liable—

(a) on conviction on indictment, to imprisonment for a term not exceeding two years or a fine (or both);

(b) on summary conviction—

(i) in England and Wales, to imprisonment for a term not exceeding twelve months or to a fine not exceeding the statutory maximum (or both);

(ii) in Scotland or Northern Ireland, to imprisonment for a term not exceeding six months, or to a fine not exceeding the statutory maximum (or both).

(3) In relation to an offence committed before the commencement of section 154(1) of the Criminal Justice Act 2003, for "twelve months" in subsection (2)(b)(i) substitute "six months".

PART 41
BUSINESS NAMES

CHAPTER 1
RESTRICTED OR PROHIBITED NAMES

Introductory

1192 Application of this Chapter

(1) This Chapter applies to any person carrying on business in the United Kingdom.

(2) The provisions of this Chapter do not prevent—
(a) an individual carrying on business under a name consisting of his surname without any addition other than a permitted addition, or
(b) individuals carrying on business in partnership under a name consisting of the surnames of all the partners without any addition other than a permitted addition.
(3) The following are the permitted additions—
(a) in the case of an individual, his forename or initial;
(b) in the case of a partnership—
(i) the forenames of individual partners or the initials of those forenames, or
(ii) where two or more individual partners have the same surname, the addition of "s" at the end of that surname;
(c) in either case, an addition merely indicating that the business is carried on in succession to a former owner of the business.

Sensitive words or expressions

1193 Name suggesting connection with government or public authority

(1) A person must not, without the approval of the Secretary of State, carry on business in the United Kingdom under a name that would be likely to give the impression that the business is connected with—
(a) Her Majesty's Government, any part of the Scottish administration, the Welsh Government or Her Majesty's Government in Northern Ireland,
(b) any local authority, or
(c) any public authority specified for the purposes of this section by regulations made by the Secretary of State.
(2) For the purposes of this section— "local authority" means—
(a) a local authority within the meaning of the Local Government Act 1972, the Common Council of the City of London or the Council of the Isles of Scilly,
(b) a council constituted under section 2 of the Local Government etc. (Scotland) Act 1994, or
(c) a district council in Northern Ireland;
"public authority" includes any person or body having functions of a public nature.
(3) Regulations under this section are subject to affirmative resolution procedure.
(4) A person who contravenes this section commits an offence.
(5) Where an offence under this section is committed by a body corporate, an offence is also committed by every officer of the body who is in default.
(6) A person guilty of an offence under this section is liable on summary conviction to a fine not exceeding level 3 on the standard scale and, for continued contravention, a daily default fine not exceeding one-tenth of level 3 on the standard scale.

1194 Other sensitive words or expressions

(1) A person must not, without the approval of the Secretary of State, carry on business in the United Kingdom under a name that includes a word or expression for the time being specified in regulations made by the Secretary of State under this section.
(2) Regulations under this section are subject to approval after being made.
(3) A person who contravenes this section commits an offence.
(4) Where an offence under this section is committed by a body corporate, an offence is also committed by every officer of the body who is in default.
(5) A person guilty of an offence under this section is liable on summary conviction to a fine not exceeding level 3 on the standard scale and, for continued contravention, a daily default fine not exceeding one-tenth of level 3 on the standard scale.

1195 Requirement to seek comments of government department or other relevant body

(1) The Secretary of State may by regulations under—
(a) section 1193 (name suggesting connection with government or public authority), or
(b) section 1194 (other sensitive words or expressions),
require that, in connection with an application for the approval of the Secretary of State under that section, the applicant must seek the view of a specified Government department or other body.

(2) Where such a requirement applies, the applicant must request the specified department or other body (in writing) to indicate whether (and if so why) it has any objections to the proposed name.
(3) He must submit to the Secretary of State a statement that such a request has been made and a copy of any response received from the specified body.
(4) If these requirements are not complied with, the Secretary of State may refuse to consider the application for approval.
(5) In this section "specified" means specified in the regulations.

1196 Withdrawal of Secretary of State's approval

(1) This section applies to approval given for the purposes of—
section 1193 (name suggesting connection with government or public authority), or
section 1194 (other sensitive words or expressions).
(2) If it appears to the Secretary of State that there are overriding considerations of public policy that require such approval to be withdrawn, the approval may be withdrawn by notice in writing given to the person concerned.
(3) The notice must state the date as from which approval is withdrawn.

Misleading names

1197 Name containing inappropriate indication of company type or legal form

(1) The Secretary of State may make provision by regulations prohibiting a person from carrying on business in the United Kingdom under a name consisting of or containing specified words, expressions or other indications—
(a) that are associated with a particular type of company or form of organisation, or
(b) that are similar to words, expressions or other indications associated with a particular type of company or form of organisation.
(2) The regulations may prohibit the use of words, expressions or other indications—
(a) in a specified part, or otherwise than in a specified part, of a name;
(b) in conjunction with, or otherwise than in conjunction with, such other words, expressions or indications as may be specified.
(3) In this section "specified" means specified in the regulations.
(4) Regulations under this section are subject to negative resolution procedure.
(5) A person who uses a name in contravention of regulations under this section commits an offence.
(6) Where an offence under this section is committed by a body corporate, an offence is also committed by every officer of the body who is in default.
(7) A person guilty of an offence under this section is liable on summary conviction to a fine not exceeding level 3 on the standard scale and, for continued contravention, a daily default fine not exceeding one-tenth of level 3 on the standard scale.

1198 Name giving misleading indication of activities

(1) A person must not carry on business in the United Kingdom under a name that gives so misleading an indication of the nature of the activities of the business as to be likely to cause harm to the public.
(2) A person who uses a name in contravention of this section commits an offence.
(3) Where an offence under this section is committed by a body corporate, an offence is also committed by every officer of the body who is in default.
(4) A person guilty of an offence under this section is liable on summary conviction to a fine not exceeding level 3 on the standard scale and, for continued contravention, a daily default fine not exceeding one-tenth of level 3 on the standard scale.

Supplementary

1199 Savings for existing lawful business names

(1) This section has effect in relation to—
sections 1192 to 1196 (sensitive words or expressions), and
section 1197 (inappropriate indication of company type or legal form).
(2) Those sections do not apply to the carrying on of a business by a person who—
(a) carried on the business immediately before the date on which this Chapter came into force, and

(b) continues to carry it on under the name that immediately before that date was its lawful business name.

(3) Where—

(a) a business is transferred to a person on or after the date on which this Chapter came into force, and

(b) that person carries on the business under the name that was its lawful business name immediately before the transfer,

those sections do not apply in relation to the carrying on of the business under that name during the period of twelve months beginning with the date of the transfer.

(4) In this section "lawful business name", in relation to a business, means a name under which the business was carried on without contravening—

(a) section 2(1) of the Business Names Act 1985 or Article 4(1) of the Business Names (Northern Ireland) Order 1986, or

(b) after this Chapter has come into force, the provisions of this Chapter.

CHAPTER 2
DISCLOSURE REQUIRED IN CASE OF INDIVIDUAL OR PARTNERSHIP

Introductory

1200 Application of this Chapter

(1) This Chapter applies to an individual or partnership carrying on business in the United Kingdom under a business name.

References in this Chapter to "a person to whom this Chapter applies" are to such an individual or partnership.

(2) For the purposes of this Chapter a "business name" means a name other than—

(a) in the case of an individual, his surname without any addition other than a permitted addition;

(b) in the case of a partnership—

(i) the surnames of all partners who are individuals, and

(ii) the corporate names of all partners who are bodies corporate,

without any addition other than a permitted addition.

(3) The following are the permitted additions—

(a) in the case of an individual, his forename or initial;

(b) in the case of a partnership—

(i) the forenames of individual partners or the initials of those forenames, or

(ii) where two or more individual partners have the same surname, the addition of "s" at the end of that surname;

(c) in either case, an addition merely indicating that the business is carried on in succession to a former owner of the business.

1201 Information required to be disclosed

(1) The "information required by this Chapter" is—

(a) in the case of an individual, the individual's name;

(b) in the case of a partnership, the name of each member of the partnership;

and, in relation to each person so named, an address at which service of any document relating in any way to the business will be effective.

(2) If the individual or partnership has a place of business in the United Kingdom, the address must be in the United Kingdom.

(3) If the individual or partnership does not have a place of business in the United Kingdom, the address must be an address at which service of documents can be effected by physical delivery and the delivery of documents is capable of being recorded by the obtaining of an acknowledgement of delivery.

Disclosure requirements

1202 Disclosure required: business documents etc

(1) A person to whom this Chapter applies must state the information required by this Chapter, in legible characters, on all—

(a) business letters,

(b) written orders for goods or services to be supplied to the business,

(c) invoices and receipts issued in the course of the business, and

(d) written demands for payment of debts arising in the course of the business.

This subsection has effect subject to section 1203 (exemption for large partnerships if certain conditions met).

(2) A person to whom this Chapter applies must secure that the information required by this Chapter is immediately given, by written notice, to any person with whom anything is done or discussed in the course of the business and who asks for that information.

(3) The Secretary of State may by regulations require that such notices be given in a specified form.

(4) Regulations under this section are subject to negative resolution procedure.

1203 Exemption for large partnerships if certain conditions met

(1) Section 1202(1) (disclosure required in business documents) does not apply in relation to a document issued by a partnership of more than 20 persons if the following conditions are met.

(2) The conditions are that—

(a) the partnership maintains at its principal place of business a list of the names of all the partners,

(b) no partner's name appears in the document, except in the text or as a signatory, and

(c) the document states in legible characters the address of the partnership's principal place of business and that the list of the partners' names is open to inspection there.

(3) Where a partnership maintains a list of the partners' names for the purposes of this section, any person may inspect the list during office hours.

(4) Where an inspection required by a person in accordance with this section is refused, an offence is committed by any member of the partnership concerned who without reasonable excuse refused the inspection or permitted it to be refused.

(5) A person guilty of an offence under subsection (4) is liable on summary conviction to a fine not exceeding level 3 on the standard scale and, for continued contravention, a daily default fine not exceeding one-tenth of level 3 on the standard scale.

1204 Disclosure required: business premises

(1) A person to whom this Chapter applies must, in any premises—

(a) where the business is carried on, and

(b) to which customers of the business or suppliers of goods or services to the business have access,

display in a prominent position, so that it may easily be read by such customers or suppliers, a notice containing the information required by this Chapter.

(2) The Secretary of State may by regulations require that such notices be displayed in a specified form.

(3) Regulations under this section are subject to negative resolution procedure.

Consequences of failure to make required disclosure

1205 Criminal consequences of failure to make required disclosure

(1) A person who without reasonable excuse fails to comply with the requirements of—

section 1202 (disclosure required: business documents etc), or

section 1204 (disclosure required: business premises),

commits an offence.

(2) Where an offence under this section is committed by a body corporate, an offence is also committed by every officer of the body who is in default.

(3) A person guilty of an offence under this section is liable on summary conviction to a fine not exceeding level 3 on the standard scale and, for continued contravention, a daily default fine not exceeding one-tenth of level 3 on the standard scale.

(4) References in this section to the requirements of section 1202 or 1204 include the requirements of regulations under that section.

1206 Civil consequences of failure to make required disclosure

(1) This section applies to any legal proceedings brought by a person to whom this Chapter applies to enforce a right arising out of a contract made in the course of a business in respect of which he was, at the time the contract was made, in breach of section 1202(1)

or (2) (disclosure in business documents etc) or section 1204(1) (disclosure at business premises).

(2) The proceedings shall be dismissed if the defendant (in Scotland, the defender) to the proceedings shows—
(a) that he has a claim against the claimant (pursuer) arising out of the contract that he has been unable to pursue by reason of the latter's breach of the requirements of this Chapter, or
(b) that he has suffered some financial loss in connection with the contract by reason of the claimant's (pursuer's) breach of those requirements,
unless the court before which the proceedings are brought is satisfied that it is just and equitable to permit the proceedings to continue.

(3) References in this section to the requirements of this Chapter include the requirements of regulations under this Chapter.

(4) This section does not affect the right of any person to enforce such rights as he may have against another person in any proceedings brought by that person.

CHAPTER 3
SUPPLEMENTARY

1207 Application of general provisions about offences

The provisions of sections 1121 to 1123 (liability of officer in default) and 1125 to 1131 (general provisions about offences) apply in relation to offences under this Part as in relation to offences under the Companies Acts.

1208 Interpretation

In this Part—
"business" includes a profession;
"initial" includes any recognised abbreviation of a name; "partnership" means—
(a) a partnership within the Partnership Act 1890, or
(b) a limited partnership registered under the Limited Partnerships Act 1907,
or a firm or entity of a similar character formed under the law of a country or territory outside the United Kingdom;
"surname", in relation to a peer or person usually known by a British title different from his surname, means the title by which he is known.

PART 42
STATUTORY AUDITORS

CHAPTER 1
INTRODUCTORY

1209 Main purposes of Part

The main purposes of this Part are—
(a) to secure that only persons who are properly supervised and appropriately qualified are appointed as statutory auditors, and
(b) to secure that audits by persons so appointed are carried out properly, with integrity and with a proper degree of independence.

1210 Meaning of "statutory auditor" etc

(1) In this Part "statutory auditor" means—
(a) a person appointed as auditor under Part 16 of this Act,
(b)–(h) *omitted*
and the expressions "statutory audit" and "statutory audit work" are to be construed accordingly.

(2) In this Part "audited person" means the person in respect of whom a statutory audit is conducted.

(3) *omitted*

(4) An order under this section is subject to negative resolution procedure.

1211 Eligibility for appointment as a statutory auditor: overview

A person is eligible for appointment as a statutory auditor only if the person is so eligible—
(a) by virtue of Chapter 2 (individuals and firms), or
(b) by virtue of Chapter 3 (Comptroller and Auditor General, etc).

CHAPTER 2
INDIVIDUALS AND FIRMS

Eligibility for appointment

1212 Individuals and firms: eligibility for appointment as a statutory auditor

(1) An individual or firm is eligible for appointment as a statutory auditor if the individual or firm—
- (a) is a member of a recognised supervisory body, and
- (b) is eligible for appointment under the rules of that body.

(2) In the cases to which section 1222 applies (individuals retaining only 1967 Act authorisation) a person's eligibility for appointment as a statutory auditor is restricted as mentioned in that section.

1213 Effect of ineligibility

(1) No person may act as statutory auditor of an audited person if he is ineligible for appointment as a statutory auditor.

(2) If at any time during his term of office a statutory auditor becomes ineligible for appointment as a statutory auditor, he must immediately—
- (a) resign his office (with immediate effect), and
- (b) give notice in writing to the audited person that he has resigned by reason of his becoming ineligible for appointment.

(3) A person is guilty of an offence if—
- (a) he acts as a statutory auditor in contravention of subsection (1), or
- (b) he fails to give the notice mentioned in paragraph (b) of subsection (2) in accordance with that subsection.

(4) A person guilty of an offence under subsection (3) is liable—
- (a) on conviction on indictment, to a fine;
- (b) on summary conviction, to a fine not exceeding the statutory maximum.

(5) A person is guilty of an offence if—
- (a) he has been convicted of an offence under subsection (3)(a) or this subsection, and
- (b) he continues to act as a statutory auditor in contravention of subsection (1) after the conviction.

(6) A person is guilty of an offence if—
- (a) he has been convicted of an offence under subsection (3)(b) or this subsection, and
- (b) he continues, after the conviction, to fail to give the notice mentioned in subsection (2)(b).

Version applying in Scotland

(7) A person guilty of an offence under subsection (5) or (6) is liable—
- (a) on conviction on indictment, to a fine;
- (b) on summary conviction, to a fine not exceeding one-tenth of the statutory maximum for each day on which the act or the failure continues.

Version applying in England and Wales

(7) A person guilty of an offence under this section is liable on summary conviction to a fine not exceeding level 5 on the standard scale and, for continued contravention, a daily default fine not exceeding one-tenth of the greater of £5,000 or level 4 on the standard scale.

(8) In proceedings against a person for an offence under this section it is a defence for him to show that he did not know and had no reason to believe that he was, or had become, ineligible for appointment as a statutory auditor.

Independence requirement

1214 Independence requirement

(1) A person may not act as statutory auditor of an audited person if one or more of subsections (2), (3) and (4) apply to him.

(2) This subsection applies if the person is—
- (a) an officer or employee of the audited person, or
- (b) a partner or employee of such a person, or a partnership of which such a person is a partner.

(3) This subsection applies if the person is—
(a) an officer or employee of an associated undertaking of the audited person, or
(b) a partner or employee of such a person, or a partnership of which such a person is a partner.
(4) This subsection applies if there exists, between—
(a) the person or an associate of his, and
(b) the audited person or an associated undertaking of the audited person,
a connection of any such description as may be specified by regulations made by the Secretary of State.
(5) An auditor of an audited person is not to be regarded as an officer or employee of the person for the purposes of subsections (2) and (3).
(6) In this section "associated undertaking", in relation to an audited person, means—
(a) a parent undertaking or subsidiary undertaking of the audited person, or
(b) a subsidiary undertaking of a parent undertaking of the audited person.
(7) Regulations under subsection (4) are subject to negative resolution procedure.

1215 Effect of lack of independence

(1) If at any time during his term of office a statutory auditor becomes prohibited from acting by section 1214(1), he must immediately—
(a) resign his office (with immediate effect), and
(b) give notice in writing to the audited person that he has resigned by reason of his lack of independence.
(2) A person is guilty of an offence if—
(a) he acts as a statutory auditor in contravention of section 1214(1), or
(b) he fails to give the notice mentioned in paragraph (b) of subsection (1) in accordance with that subsection.
(3) A person guilty of an offence under subsection (2) is liable—
(a) on conviction on indictment, to a fine;
(b) on summary conviction, to a fine not exceeding the statutory maximum.
(4) A person is guilty of an offence if—
(a) he has been convicted of an offence under subsection (2)(a) or this subsection, and
(b) he continues to act as a statutory auditor in contravention of section 1214(1) after the conviction.
(5) A person is guilty of an offence if—
(a) he has been convicted of an offence under subsection (2)(b) or this subsection, and
(b) after the conviction, he continues to fail to give the notice mentioned in subsection (1)(b).

Version applying in Scotland

(6) A person guilty of an offence under subsection (4) or (5) is liable—
(a) on conviction on indictment, to a fine;
(b) on summary conviction, to a fine not exceeding one-tenth of the statutory maximum for each day on which the act or the failure continues.

Version applying in England and Wales

(6) A person guilty of an offence under subsection (4) or (5) is liable–
(a) on conviction on indictment, to a fine;
(b) on summary conviction, to a fine not exceeding one-tenth of the greater of £5,000 or the amount corresponding to level 4 on the standard scale for summary offences for each day on which the act or the failure continues.
(7) In proceedings against a person for an offence under this section it is a defence for him to show that he did not know and had no reason to believe that he was, or had become, prohibited from acting as statutory auditor of the audited person by section 1214(1).

Effect of appointment of a partnership

1216 Effect of appointment of a partnership

(1) This section applies where a partnership constituted under the law of—
(a) England and Wales,
(b) Northern Ireland, or
(c) any other country or territory in which a partnership is not a legal person, is by virtue of this Chapter appointed as statutory auditor of an audited person.

(2) Unless a contrary intention appears, the appointment is an appointment of the partnership as such and not of the partners.
(3) Where the partnership ceases, the appointment is to be treated as extending to—
(a) any appropriate partnership which succeeds to the practice of that partnership, or
(b) any other appropriate person who succeeds to that practice having previously carried it on in partnership.
(4) For the purposes of subsection (3)—
(a) a partnership is to be regarded as succeeding to the practice of another partnership only if the members of the successor partnership are substantially the same as those of the former partnership, and
(b) a partnership or other person is to be regarded as succeeding to the practice of a partnership only if it or he succeeds to the whole or substantially the whole of the business of the former partnership.
(5) Where the partnership ceases and the appointment is not treated under subsection (3) as extending to any partnership or other person, the appointment may with the consent of the audited person be treated as extending to an appropriate partnership, or other appropriate person, who succeeds to—
(a) the business of the former partnership, or
(b) such part of it as is agreed by the audited person is to be treated as comprising the appointment.
(6) For the purposes of this section, a partnership or other person is "appropriate" if it or he—
(a) is eligible for appointment as a statutory auditor by virtue of this Chapter, and
(b) is not prohibited by section 1214(1) from acting as statutory auditor of the audited person.

Supervisory bodies

1217 Supervisory bodies
(1) In this Part a "supervisory body" means a body established in the United Kingdom (whether a body corporate or an unincorporated association) which maintains and enforces rules as to—
(a) the eligibility of persons for appointment as a statutory auditor, and
(b) the conduct of statutory audit work,
which are binding on persons seeking appointment or acting as a statutory auditor because they are members of that body.
(1A) The rules referred to in paragraphs 9(3)(b) (confidentiality of information) and 10C(3)(a) and (b) (bar on appointment as director or other officer) of Schedule 10 must also be binding on persons who—
(a) have sought appointment or acted as a statutory auditor, and
(b) have been members of the body at any time after the commencement of this Part.
(2) In this Part references to the members of a supervisory body are to the persons who, whether or not members of the body, are subject to its rules in seeking appointment or acting as a statutory auditor.
(3) In this Part references to the rules of a supervisory body are to the rules (whether or not laid down by the body itself) which the body has power to enforce and which are relevant for the purposes of this Part.
This includes rules relating to the admission or expulsion of members of the body, so far as relevant for the purposes of this Part.
(4) Schedule 10 has effect with respect to the recognition of supervisory bodies for the purposes of this Part.

1218 Exemption from liability for damages
(1) No person within subsection (2) is to be liable in damages for anything done or omitted in the discharge or purported discharge of functions to which this subsection applies.
(2) The persons within this subsection are—
(a) any recognised supervisory body,
(b) any officer or employee of a recognised supervisory body, and
(c) any member of the governing body of a recognised supervisory body.

(3) Subsection (1) applies to the functions of a recognised supervisory body so far as relating to, or to matters arising out of, any of the following—
(a) rules, practices, powers and arrangements of the body to which the requirements of Part 2 of Schedule 10 apply;
(b) the obligations with which paragraph 20 of that Schedule requires the body to comply;
(c) any guidance issued by the body;
(d) the obligations imposed on the body by or by virtue of this Part.

(4) The reference in subsection (3)(c) to guidance issued by a recognised supervisory body is a reference to any guidance or recommendation which is—
(a) issued or made by it to all or any class of its members or persons seeking to become members, and
(b) relevant for the purposes of this Part,

including any guidance or recommendation relating to the admission or expulsion of members of the body, so far as relevant for the purposes of this Part.

(5) Subsection (1) does not apply—
(a) if the act or omission is shown to have been in bad faith, or
(b) so as to prevent an award of damages in respect of the act or omission on the ground that it was unlawful as a result of section 6(1) of the Human Rights Act 1998 (c. 42) (acts of public authorities incompatible with Convention rights).

Professional qualifications

1219 Appropriate qualifications

(1) A person holds an appropriate qualification for the purposes of this Chapter if and only if—
(a) he holds a recognised professional qualification obtained in the United Kingdom,
(b) immediately before the commencement of this Chapter, he—
(i) held an appropriate qualification for the purposes of Part 2 of the Companies Act 1989 (eligibility for appointment as company auditor) by virtue of section 31(1)(a) or (c) of that Act, or
(ii) was treated as holding an appropriate qualification for those purposes by virtue of section 31(2), (3) or (4) of that Act,
(c) immediately before the commencement of this Chapter, he—
(i) held an appropriate qualification for the purposes of Part III of the Companies (Northern Ireland) Order 1990 by virtue of Article 34(1)(a) or (c) of that Order, or
(ii) was treated as holding an appropriate qualification for those purposes by virtue of Article 34(2), (3) or (4) of that Order,
(d) he is within subsection (2), or
...
(f) subject to any direction under section 1221(5), he is regarded for the purposes of this Chapter as holding an approved third country qualification.

(2) A person is within this subsection if—
(a) before 1st January 1990, he began a course of study or practical training leading to a professional qualification in accountancy offered by a body established in the United Kingdom,
(b) he obtained that qualification on or after 1st January 1990 and before 1st January 1996, and
(c) the Secretary of State approves his qualification as an appropriate qualification for the purposes of this Chapter.

(3) The Secretary of State may approve a qualification under subsection (2)(c) only if he is satisfied that, at the time the qualification was awarded, the body concerned had adequate arrangements to ensure that the qualification was awarded only to persons educated and trained to a standard equivalent to that required, at that time, in the case of a recognised professional qualification under Part 2 of the Companies Act 1989 (eligibility for appointment as company auditor).

1220 Qualifying bodies and recognised professional qualifications

(1) In this Part a "qualifying body" means a body established in the United Kingdom (whether a body corporate or an unincorporated association) which offers a professional qualification in accountancy.

(2) In this Part references to the rules of a qualifying body are to the rules (whether or not laid down by the body itself) which the body has power to enforce and which are relevant for the purposes of this Part.

This includes, so far as so relevant, rules relating to—

(a) admission to or expulsion from a course of study leading to a qualification,

(b) the award or deprivation of a qualification, or

(c) the approval of a person for the purposes of giving practical training or the withdrawal of such approval.

(3) Schedule 11 has effect with respect to the recognition for the purposes of this Part of a professional qualification offered by a qualifying body.

1221 Approval of third country qualifications

(1) The Secretary of State may declare that the following are to be regarded for the purposes of this Chapter as holding an approved third country qualification—

(a) persons who are qualified to audit accounts under the law of a specified third country, or

(b) persons who hold a specified professional qualification in accountancy obtained in a specified third country.

(1A) A declaration under subsection (1)(a) or (b) must be expressed to be subject to the requirement that any person to whom the declaration relates must pass an aptitude test in accordance with subsection (7A), unless an aptitude test is not required (see subsection (7B)).

(2) A declaration under subsection (1)(b) may be expressed to be subject to the satisfaction of any specified requirement or requirements.

(3) The Secretary of State may make a declaration under subsection (1) only if he is satisfied that—

(a) in the case of a declaration under subsection (1)(a), the fact that the persons in question are qualified to audit accounts under the law of the specified third country, or

(b) in the case of a declaration under subsection (1)(b), the specified professional qualification taken with any requirement or requirements to be specified under subsection (2), affords an assurance of professional competence equivalent to that afforded by a recognised professional qualification.

(4) The Secretary of State may make a declaration under subsection (1) only if he is satisfied that the treatment that the persons who are the subject of the declaration will receive as a result of it is comparable to the treatment which is, or is likely to be, afforded in the specified third country or a part of it to—

(a) in the case of a declaration under subsection (1)(a), some or all persons who are eligible to be appointed as a statutory auditor, and

(b) in the case of a declaration under subsection (1)(b), some or all persons who hold a corresponding recognised professional qualification.

(5) The Secretary of State may direct that persons holding an approved third country qualification are not to be treated as holding an appropriate qualification for the purposes of this Chapter unless they hold such additional educational qualifications as the Secretary of State may specify for the purpose of ensuring that such persons have an adequate knowledge of the law and practice in the United Kingdom relevant to the audit of accounts.

(6) The Secretary of State may give different directions in relation to different approved third country qualifications.

(7) The Secretary of State may, if he thinks fit, having regard to the considerations mentioned in subsections (3) and (4), withdraw a declaration under subsection (1) in relation to—

(a) persons becoming qualified to audit accounts under the law of the specified third country after such date as he may specify, or

(b) persons obtaining the specified professional qualification after such date as he may specify.

(7A) An aptitude test required for the purposes of subsection (1A)—
(a) must test the person's knowledge of subjects—
(i) that are covered by a recognised professional qualification,
(ii) that are not covered by the professional qualification already held by the person, and
(iii) the knowledge of which is essential for the pursuit of the profession of statutory auditor;
(b) may test the person's knowledge of rules of professional conduct;
(c) must not test the person's knowledge of any other matters.
(7B) No aptitude test is required for the purposes of subsection (1A) if the subjects that are covered by a recognised professional qualification and the knowledge of which is essential for the pursuit of the profession of statutory auditor are covered by the professional qualification already held by the person.
(8) The Secretary of State may, if he thinks fit, having regard to the considerations mentioned in subsections (3) and (4), vary or revoke a requirement specified under subsection (2) from such date as he may specify.

1222 Eligibility of individuals retaining only 1967 Act authorisation

(1) A person whose only appropriate qualification is based on his retention of an authorisation originally granted by the Board of Trade or the Secretary of State under section 13(1) of the Companies Act 1967 is eligible only for appointment as auditor of an unquoted company.
(2) A company is "unquoted" if, at the time of the person's appointment, neither the company, nor any parent undertaking of which it is a subsidiary undertaking, is a quoted company within the meaning of section 385(2).
(3) References to a person eligible for appointment as a statutory auditor by virtue of this Part in enactments relating to eligibility for appointment as auditor of a person other than a company do not include a person to whom this section applies.

Information

1223 Matters to be notified to the Secretary of State

(1) The Secretary of State may require a recognised supervisory body or a recognised qualifying body—
(a) to notify him immediately of the occurrence of such events as he may specify in writing and to give him such information in respect of those events as is so specified;
(b) to give him, at such times or in respect of such periods as he may specify in writing, such information as is so specified.
(2) The notices and information required to be given must be such as the Secretary of State may reasonably require for the exercise of his functions under this Part.
(3) The Secretary of State may require information given under this section to be given in a specified form or verified in a specified manner.
(4) Any notice or information required to be given under this section must be given in writing unless the Secretary of State specifies or approves some other manner.

1223A Notification of matters relevant to other EEA States

(1) A recognised supervisory body must notify the Secretary of State of—
(a) any withdrawal of a notifiable person's eligibility for appointment as a statutory auditor; and
(b) the reasons for the withdrawal.
(2) A recognised supervisory body must also notify the Secretary of State of any reasonable grounds it has for suspecting that—
(a) a person has contravened the law of the United Kingdom, or any other EEA State or part of an EEA State, implementing the Audit Directive, and
(b) the act or omission constituting that contravention took place on the territory of an EEA State other than the United Kingdom.
(3) In this section "notifiable person" means a member of the recognised supervisory body in question—
(a) who is also an EEA auditor; and
(b) in respect of whom the EEA competent authority is not the recognised supervisory body itself.

1224 The Secretary of State's power to call for information

(1) The Secretary of State may by notice in writing require a person within subsection (2) to give him such information as he may reasonably require for the exercise of his functions under this Part.

(2) The persons within this subsection are—

(a) any recognised supervisory body,

(b) any recognised qualifying body, and

(c) any person eligible for appointment as a statutory auditor by virtue of this Chapter.

(3) The Secretary of State may require that any information which he requires under this section is to be given within such reasonable time and verified in such manner as he may specify.

1224A Restrictions on disclosure

(1) This section applies to information (in whatever form)—

(a) relating to the private affairs of an individual, or

(b) relating to any particular business,

that is provided to a body to which this section applies in connection with the exercise of its functions under this Part or sections 522 to 524 (notification to appropriate audit authority of resignation or removal of auditor).

(2) This section applies to—

(a) a recognised supervisory body,

(b) a recognised qualifying body,

(c) a body performing functions for the purposes of arrangements within paragraph 23(1) (independent monitoring of certain audits), paragraph 23(A)(1) (independent monitoring of third country audits) or paragraph 24(1) (independent investigation of public interest cases) of Schedule 10,

(d) the Independent Supervisor,

(e) the Secretary of State, and

(f) a body designated by the Secretary of State under section 1252 (delegation of the Secretary of State's functions).

(3) No such information may, during the lifetime of the individual or so long as the business continues to be carried on, be disclosed without the consent of that individual or (as the case may be) the person for the time being carrying on that business.

(4) Subsection (3) does not apply to any disclosure of information that—

(a) is made for the purpose of facilitating the carrying out by the body of any of its functions,

(b) is made to a person specified in Part 1 of Schedule 11A,

(c) is of a description specified in Part 2 of that Schedule, or

(d) is made in accordance with Part 3 of that Schedule.

(5) Subsection (3) does not apply to—

(a) the disclosure by an EEA competent authority of information disclosed to it by the body in reliance on subsection (4);

(b) the disclosure of such information by anyone who has obtained it directly or indirectly from an EEA competent authority.

(6) This section does not prohibit the disclosure of information if the information is or has been available to the public from any other source.

(7) Nothing in this section authorises the making of a disclosure in contravention of the Data Protection Act 1998.

1224B Offence of disclosure in contravention of section 1224A

(1) A person who discloses information in contravention of section 1224A (restrictions on disclosure) is guilty of an offence, unless—

(a) he did not know, and had no reason to suspect, that the information had been provided as mentioned in section 1224A(1), or

(b) he took all reasonable steps and exercised all due diligence to avoid the commission of the offence.

(2) A person guilty of an offence under this section is liable—

(a) on conviction on indictment, to imprisonment for a term not exceeding two years or a fine (or both);

(b) on summary conviction—
(i) in Scotland, to imprisonment for a term not exceeding 12 months or to a fine not exceeding the statutory maximum, or to both;
(ii) in England and Wales or Northern Ireland, to imprisonment for a term not exceeding three months or to a fine not exceeding the statutory maximum, or to both.

Enforcement

1225 Enforcement: general

(1) This section applies if at any time it appears to the Secretary of State—
(a) in the case of a recognised supervisory body, that any requirement of Part 2 or 3 of Schedule 10 is not satisfied,
(b) in the case of a recognised professional qualification offered by a recognised qualifying body, that any requirement of Part 2 of Schedule 11 is not satisfied, or
(c) that a recognised supervisory body or a recognised qualifying body has not complied with an obligation imposed on it by or by virtue of this Part (other than an obligation to pay a financial penalty under section 1225D).
(2) The Secretary of State may do any one or more of the following—
(a) give a direction to the body under section 1225A;
(b) make an application to the court in respect of the body under section 1225C;
(c) impose a financial penalty on the body under section 1225D.
(3) Subsection (2) is without prejudice to the powers of the Secretary of State under paragraph 3 of Schedule 10 and paragraph 3 of Schedule 11 (revocation of recognition orders).

1225A–1225G *omitted*

CHAPTERS 3–5
OMITTED

CHAPTER 6
SUPPLEMENTARY AND GENERAL

Power to require second company audit

1248 Secretary of State's power to require second audit of a company

(1) This section applies where a person appointed as statutory auditor of a company was not an appropriate person for any part of the period during which the audit was conducted.
(2) The Secretary of State may direct the company concerned to retain an appropriate person—
(a) to conduct a second audit of the relevant accounts, or
(b) to review the first audit and to report (giving his reasons) whether a second audit is needed.
(3) For the purposes of subsections (1) and (2) a person is "appropriate" if he—
(a) is eligible for appointment as a statutory auditor or, if the person is an Auditor General, for appointment as statutory auditor of the company, and
(b) is not prohibited by section 1214(1) (independence requirement) from acting as statutory auditor of the company.
(4) The Secretary of State must send a copy of a direction under subsection (2) to the registrar of companies.
(5) The company is guilty of an offence if—
(a) it fails to comply with a direction under subsection (2) within the period of 21 days beginning with the date on which it is given, or
(b) it has been convicted of a previous offence under this subsection and the failure to comply with the direction which led to the conviction continues after the conviction.
(6) The company must—
(a) send a copy of a report under subsection (2)(b) to the registrar of companies, and
(b) if the report states that a second audit is needed, take such steps as are necessary for the carrying out of that audit.

(7) The company is guilty of an offence if—
(a) it fails to send a copy of a report under subsection (2)(b) to the registrar within the period of 21 days beginning with the date on which it receives it,
(b) in a case within subsection (6)(b), it fails to take the steps mentioned immediately it receives the report, or
(c) it has been convicted of a previous offence under this subsection and the failure to send a copy of the report, or take the steps, which led to the conviction continues after the conviction.

Version applying in England and Wales

(8) A company guilty of an offence under this section is liable on summary conviction—
(a) in a case within subsection (5)(a) or (7)(a) or (b), to a fine not exceeding level 5 on the standard scale, and
(b) in a case within subsection (5)(b) or (7)(c), to a fine not exceeding one-tenth of level 5 on the standard scale for each day on which the failure continues.

Version applying in Scotland

(8) A company guilty of an offence under this section is liable on summary conviction—
(a) in a case within subsection (5)(a) or (7)(a) or (b), to a fine not exceeding level 5 on the standard scale, and
(b) in a case within subsection (5)(b) or (7)(c), to a fine not exceeding one-tenth of the greater of £5,000 or level 4 on the standard scale for each day on which the failure continues.

(9) In this section "registrar of companies" has the meaning given by section 1060.

1249 Supplementary provision about second audits

(1) If a person accepts an appointment, or continues to act, as statutory auditor of a company at a time when he knows he is not an appropriate person, the company may recover from him any costs incurred by it in complying with the requirements of section 1248.
For this purpose "appropriate" is to be construed in accordance with subsection (3) of that section.
(2) Where a second audit is carried out under section 1248, any statutory or other provision applying in relation to the first audit applies also, in so far as practicable, in relation to the second audit.
(3) A direction under section 1248(2) is, on the application of the Secretary of State, enforceable by injunction or, in Scotland, by an order under section 45 of the Court of Session Act 1988.

False and misleading statements

1250 Misleading, false and deceptive statements

(1) A person is guilty of an offence if—
(a) for the purposes of or in connection with any application under this Part, or
(b) in purported compliance with any requirement imposed on him by or by virtue of this Part,
he knowingly or recklessly furnishes information which is misleading, false or deceptive in a material particular.
(2) It is an offence for a person whose name does not appear on the register of auditors kept under regulations under section 1239 in an entry made under subsection (1)(a) of that section to describe himself as a registered auditor or so to hold himself out as to indicate, or be reasonably understood to indicate, that he is a registered auditor.
(3) It is an offence for a person whose name does not appear on the register of auditors kept under regulations under that section in an entry made under subsection (1)(b) of that section to describe himself as a registered third country auditor or so to hold himself out as to indicate, or be reasonably understood to indicate, that he is a registered third country auditor.
(4) It is an offence for a body which is not a recognised supervisory body or a recognised qualifying body to describe itself as so recognised or so to describe itself or hold itself out as to indicate, or be reasonably understood to indicate, that it is so recognised.
(5) A person guilty of an offence under subsection (1) is liable—
(a) on conviction on indictment, to imprisonment for a term not exceeding two years or to a fine (or both);

(b) on summary conviction—
  (i) in England and Wales, to imprisonment for a term not exceeding twelve months or to a fine not exceeding the statutory maximum (or both),
  (ii) in Scotland or Northern Ireland, to imprisonment for a term not exceeding six months or to a fine not exceeding the statutory maximum (or both).

In relation to an offence committed before the commencement of section 154(1) of the Criminal Justice Act 2003, for "twelve months" in paragraph (b)(i) substitute "six months".

(6) Subject to subsection (7), a person guilty of an offence under subsection (2), (3) or (4) is liable on summary conviction—
  (a) in England and Wales, to imprisonment for a term not exceeding 51 weeks or to a fine not exceeding level 5 on the standard scale (or both),
  (b) in Scotland or Northern Ireland, to imprisonment for a term not exceeding six months or to a fine not exceeding level 5 on the standard scale (or both).

In relation to an offence committed before the commencement of section 281(5) of the Criminal Justice Act 2003, for "51 weeks" in paragraph (a) substitute "six months".

(7) Where a contravention of subsection (2), (3) or (4) involves a public display of the offending description, the maximum fine that may be imposed is an amount equal to level 5 on the standard scale multiplied by the number of days for which the display has continued.

(8) It is a defence for a person charged with an offence under subsection (2), (3) or (4) to show that he took all reasonable precautions and exercised all due diligence to avoid the commission of the offence.

1251–1259 *omitted*

Interpretation

1260 Meaning of "associate"

(1) In this Part "associate", in relation to a person, is to be construed as follows.

(2) In relation to an individual, "associate" means—
  (a) that individual's spouse, civil partner or minor child or step-child,
  (b) any body corporate of which that individual is a director, and
  (c) any employee or partner of that individual.

(3) In relation to a body corporate, "associate" means—
  (a) any body corporate of which that body is a director,
  (b) any body corporate in the same group as that body, and
  (c) any employee or partner of that body or of any body corporate in the same group.

(4) In relation to a partnership constituted under the law of Scotland, or any other country or territory in which a partnership is a legal person, "associate" means—
  (a) any body corporate of which that partnership is a director,
  (b) any employee of or partner in that partnership, and
  (c) any person who is an associate of a partner in that partnership.

(5) In relation to a partnership constituted under the law of England and Wales or Northern Ireland, or the law of any other country or territory in which a partnership is not a legal person, "associate" means any person who is an associate of any of the partners.

(6) In subsections (2)(b), (3)(a) and (4)(a), in the case of a body corporate which is a limited liability partnership, "director" is to be read as "member".

1261 Minor definitions

(1) In this Part, unless a contrary intention appears—

"address" means—
  (a) in relation to an individual, his usual residential or business address;
  (b) in relation to a firm, its registered or principal office in the United Kingdom;

"the Audit Directive" means Directive 2006/43/EC of the European Parliament and of the Council on statutory audits of annual accounts and consolidated accounts, amending Council Directives 78/660/EEC and 83/349/EEC and repealing Council Directive 84/253/EEC, as amended at any time before 1st January 2009;

"audit working papers" means any documents which—
  (a) are or have been held by a statutory auditor, an EEA auditor or a third country auditor, and
  (b) are related to the conduct of an audit conducted by that auditor;

"company" means any company or other body the accounts of which must be audited in accordance with Part 16;

"director", in relation to a body corporate, includes any person occupying in relation to it the position of a director (by whatever name called) and any person in accordance with whose directions or instructions (not being advice given in a professional capacity) the directors of the body are accustomed to act;

"EEA auditor" means an individual who is approved in accordance with the Audit Directive by an EEA competent authority to carry out audits of annual accounts or consolidated accounts required by Community law;

"EEA competent authority" means a competent authority within the meaning of Article 2.10 of the Audit Directive of an EEA State other than the United Kingdom;]

"firm" means any entity, whether or not a legal person, which is not an individual and includes a body corporate, a corporation sole and a partnership or other unincorporated association;

"group", in relation to a body corporate, means the body corporate, any other body corporate which is its holding company or subsidiary and any other body corporate which is a subsidiary of that holding company;

"holding company" and "subsidiary" are to be read in accordance with section 1159 and Schedule 6;

"officer", in relation to a body corporate, includes a director, a manager, a secretary or, where the affairs of the body are managed by its members, a member;

"parent undertaking" and "subsidiary undertaking" are to be read in accordance with section 1162 and Schedule 7;

"third country" means a country or territory that is not an EEA State or part of an EEA State;

"third country auditor" means a person, other than a person eligible for appointment as a statutory auditor, who is eligible to conduct audits of the accounts of bodies corporate incorporated or formed under the law of a third country in accordance with the law of that country;

"third country competent authority" means a body established in a third country exercising functions related to the regulation or oversight of auditors.

"transfer", in relation to audit working papers, includes physical and electronic transfer and allowing access to such papers.

(2) For the purposes of this Part a body is to be regarded as "established in the United Kingdom" if and only if—
  (a) it is incorporated or formed under the law of the United Kingdom or a part of the United Kingdom, or
  (b) its central management and control are exercised in the United Kingdom;

and any reference to a qualification "obtained in the United Kingdom" is to a qualification obtained from such a body.

(2A) For the purposes of this Part, Gibraltar shall be treated as if it were an EEA State.

(3) The Secretary of State may by regulations make such modifications of this Part as appear to him to be necessary or appropriate for the purposes of its application in relation to any firm, or description of firm, which is not a body corporate or a partnership.

(4) Regulations under subsection (3) are subject to negative resolution procedure.

1262 Index of defined expressions

The following Table shows provisions defining or otherwise explaining expressions used in this Part (other than provisions defining or explaining an expression used only in the same section)—

Expression	Provision
address	section 1261(1)
appropriate qualification	section 1219
approved third country competent authority	section 1253D(2)
associate	section 1260
Audit Directive	section 1261(1)
audit working papers	section 1261(1)
audited person	section 1210(2)
Auditor General	section 1226(1)
company	section 1261(1)
delegation order	section 1252(1)
director (of a body corporate)	section 1261(1)
EEA auditor	section 1261(1)

EEA competent authority	section 1261(1)
enactment	section 1293
established in the United Kingdom	section 1261(2)
firm	section 1261(1)
group (in relation to a body corporate)	section 1261(1)
holding company	section 1261(1)
main purposes of this Part	section 1209
member (of a supervisory body)	section 1217(2)
obtained in the United Kingdom	section 1261(2)
officer	section 1261(1)
parent undertaking	section 1261(1)
qualifying body	section 1220(1)
recognised, in relation to a professional qualification	section 1220(3) and Schedule 11
recognised, in relation to a qualifying body	paragraph 1(2) of Schedule 11
recognised, in relation to a supervisory body	section 1217(4) and Schedule 10
registered third country auditor	section 1241(1)
rules of a qualifying body	section 1220(2)
rules of a supervisory body	section 1217(3)
statutory auditor, statutory audit and statutory audit work	section 1210(1)
subsidiary	section 1261(1)
supervisory body	section 1217(1)
subsidiary undertaking	section 1261(1)
third country	section 1261(1)
third country auditor	section 1261(1)
third country competent authority	section 1261(1)
transfer (in relation to audit working papers)	section 1261(1)
UK-traded non-EEA company	section 1241(2)

Miscellaneous and general

1263 Power to make provision in consequence of changes affecting accountancy bodies

(1) The Secretary of State may by regulations make such amendments of enactments as appear to him to be necessary or expedient in consequence of any change of name, merger or transfer of engagements affecting—

(a) a recognised supervisory body or recognised qualifying body, or

(b) a body of accountants referred to in, or approved, authorised or otherwise recognised for the purposes of, any other enactment.

(2) Regulations under this section are subject to negative resolution procedure.

1264 Consequential amendments

Schedule 14 contains consequential amendments relating to this Part.

PART 43

OMITTED

PART 44

MISCELLANEOUS PROVISIONS

1274–1276 *omitted*

Information as to exercise of voting rights by institutional investors

1277 Power to require information about exercise of voting rights

(1) The Treasury or the Secretary of State may make provision by regulations requiring institutions to which this section applies to provide information about the exercise of voting rights attached to shares to which this section applies.

(2) This power is exercisable in accordance with—

section 1278 (institutions to which information provisions apply),

section 1279 (shares to which information provisions apply), and

section 1280 (obligations with respect to provision of information).

(3) In this section and the sections mentioned above—
 (a) references to a person acting on behalf of an institution include—
  (i) any person to whom authority has been delegated by the institution to take decisions as to any matter relevant to the subject matter of the regulations, and
  (ii) such other persons as may be specified; and
 (b) "specified" means specified in the regulations.
(4) The obligation imposed by regulations under this section is enforceable by civil proceedings brought by—
 (a) any person to whom the information should have been provided, or
 (b) a specified regulatory authority.
(5) Regulations under this section may make different provision for different descriptions of institution, different descriptions of shares and for other different circumstances.
(6) Regulations under this section are subject to affirmative resolution procedure.

1278 Institutions to which information provisions apply

(1) The institutions to which section 1277 applies are—
 (a) unit trust schemes within the meaning of the Financial Services and Markets Act 2000 in respect of which an order is in force under section 243 of that Act;
 (b) open-ended investment companies incorporated by virtue of regulations under section 262 of that Act;
 (c) companies approved for the purposes of Chapter 4 of Part 24 of the Corporation Tax Act 2010 (investment trusts);
 (d) pension schemes as defined in section 1(5) of the Pension Schemes Act 1993 or the Pension Schemes (Northern Ireland) Act 1993;
 (e) undertakings authorised under the Financial Services and Markets Act 2000 to carry on long-term insurance business (that is, the activity of effecting or carrying out contracts of long-term insurance within the meaning of the Financial Services and Markets (Regulated Activities) Order 2001;
(2) Regulations under that section may—
 (a) provide that the section applies to other descriptions of institution;
 (b) provide that the section does not apply to a specified description of institution.
(3) The regulations must specify by whom, in the case of any description of institution, the duty imposed by the regulations is to be fulfilled.

1279 Shares to which information provisions apply

(1) The shares to which section 1277 applies are shares—
 (a) of a description traded on a specified market, and
 (b) in which the institution has, or is taken to have, an interest.
 Regulations under that section may provide that the section does not apply to shares of a specified description.
(2) For this purpose an institution has an interest in shares if the shares, or a depositary certificate in respect of them, are held by it, or on its behalf.
 A "depositary certificate" means an instrument conferring rights (other than options)—
 (a) in respect of shares held by another person, and
 (b) the transfer of which may be effected without the consent of that person.
(3) Where an institution has an interest—
 (a) in a specified description of collective investment scheme (within the meaning of the Financial Services and Markets Act 2000), or
 (b) in any other specified description of scheme or collective investment vehicle,
 it is taken to have an interest in any shares in which that scheme or vehicle has or is taken to have an interest.
(4) For this purpose a scheme or vehicle is taken to have an interest in shares if it would be regarded as having such an interest in accordance with subsection (2) if it was an institution to which section 1277 applied.

1280 Obligations with respect to provision of information

(1) Regulations under section 1277 may require the provision of specified information about—
 (a) the exercise or non-exercise of voting rights by the institution or any person acting on its behalf,

(b) any instructions given by the institution or any person acting on its behalf as to the exercise or non-exercise of voting rights, and
(c) any delegation by the institution or any person acting on its behalf of any functions in relation to the exercise or non-exercise of voting rights or the giving of such instructions.

(2) The regulations may require information to be provided in respect of specified occasions or specified periods.

(3) Where instructions are given to act on the recommendations or advice of another person, the regulations may require the provision of information about what recommendations or advice were given.

(4) The regulations may require information to be provided—
(a) in such manner as may be specified, and
(b) to such persons as may be specified, or to the public, or both.

(5) The regulations may provide—
(a) that an institution may discharge its obligations under the regulations by referring to information disclosed by a person acting on its behalf, and
(b) that in such a case it is sufficient, where that other person acts on behalf of more than one institution, that the reference is to information given in aggregated form, that is—
(i) relating to the exercise or non-exercise by that person of voting rights on behalf of more than one institution, or
(ii) relating to the instructions given by that person in respect of the exercise or non-exercise of voting rights on behalf of more than one institution, or
(iii) relating to the delegation by that person of functions in relation to the exercise or non-exercise of voting rights, or the giving of instructions in respect of the exercise or non-exercise of voting rights, on behalf of more than one institution.

(6) References in this section to instructions are to instructions of any description, whether general or specific, whether binding or not and whether or not acted upon.

1281–1283 *omitted*

PART 45
NORTHERN IRELAND

1284 Extension of Companies Acts to Northern Ireland

(1) The Companies Acts as defined by this Act (see section 2) extend to Northern Ireland.

(2) The Companies (Northern Ireland) Order 1986, the Companies Consolidation (Consequential Provisions) (Northern Ireland) Order 1986 and Part 3 of the Companies (Audit, Investigations and Community Enterprise) Order 2005 shall cease to have effect accordingly.

1285 Extension of GB enactments relating to SEs

(1) The enactments in force in Great Britain relating to SEs extend to Northern Ireland.

(2) The following enactments shall cease to have effect accordingly—
(a) the European Public Limited-Liability Company Regulations (Northern Ireland) 2004, and
(b) the European Public Limited-Liability Company (Fees) Regulations (Northern Ireland) 2004.

(3) In this section "SE" means a European Public Limited-Liability Company (or Societas Europaea) within the meaning of Council Regulation 2157/2001/EC of 8 October 2001 on the Statute for a European Company.

1286 Extension of GB enactments relating to certain other forms of business organisation

(1) The enactments in force in Great Britain relating to—
(a) limited liability partnerships,
(b) limited partnerships,
(c) open-ended investment companies, and
(d) European Economic Interest Groupings, extend to Northern Ireland.

(2) The following enactments shall cease to have effect accordingly—
   (a) the Limited Liability Partnerships Act (Northern Ireland) 2002;
   (b) the Limited Partnerships Act 1907 as it formerly had effect in Northern Ireland;
   (c) the Open-Ended Investment Companies Act (Northern Ireland) 2002;
   (d) the European Economic Interest Groupings Regulations (Northern Ireland) 1989.

1287 Extension of enactments relating to business names

(1) The provisions of Part 41 of this Act (business names) extend to Northern Ireland.
(2) The Business Names (Northern Ireland) Order 1986 shall cease to have effect accordingly.

PART 46
GENERAL SUPPLEMENTARY PROVISIONS

Regulations and orders

1288 Regulations and orders: statutory instrument

Except as otherwise provided, regulations and orders under this Act shall be made by statutory instrument.

1289 Regulations and orders: negative resolution procedure

Where regulations or orders under this Act are subject to "negative resolution procedure" the statutory instrument containing the regulations or order shall be subject to annulment in pursuance of a resolution of either House of Parliament.

1290 Regulations and orders: affirmative resolution procedure

Where regulations or orders under this Act are subject to "affirmative resolution procedure" the regulations or order must not be made unless a draft of the statutory instrument containing them has been laid before Parliament and approved by a resolution of each House of Parliament.

1291 Regulations and orders: approval after being made

(1) Regulations or orders under this Act that are subject to "approval after being made"—
   (a) must be laid before Parliament after being made, and
   (b) cease to have effect at the end of 28 days beginning with the day on which they were made unless during that period they are approved by resolution of each House.
(2) In reckoning the period of 28 days no account shall be taken of any time during which Parliament is dissolved or prorogued or during which both Houses are adjourned for more than four days.
(3) The regulations or order ceasing to have effect does not affect—
   (a) anything previously done under them or it, or
   (b) the making of new regulations or a new order.

1292 Regulations and orders: supplementary

(1) Regulations or orders under this Act may—
   (a) make different provision for different cases or circumstances,
   (b) include supplementary, incidental and consequential provision, and
   (c) make transitional provision and savings.
(2) Any provision that may be made by regulations under this Act may be made by order; and any provision that may be made by order under this Act may be made by regulations.
(3) Any provision that may be made by regulations or order under this Act for which no Parliamentary procedure is prescribed may be made by regulations or order subject to negative or affirmative resolution procedure.
(4) Any provision that may be made by regulations or order under this Act subject to negative resolution procedure may be made by regulations or order subject to affirmative resolution procedure.

Meaning of "enactment"

1293 Meaning of "enactment"

In this Act, unless the context otherwise requires, "enactment" includes—
   (a) an enactment contained in subordinate legislation within the meaning of the Interpretation Act 1978,

(aa) an enactment contained in, or in an instrument made under, a Measure or Act of the National Assembly for Wales,
(b) an enactment contained in, or in an instrument made under, an Act of the Scottish Parliament, and
(c) an enactment contained in, or in an instrument made under, Northern Ireland legislation within the meaning of the Interpretation Act 1978.

1294–1296 *omitted*

1297 Continuity of the law

(1) This section applies where any provision of this Act re-enacts (with or without modification) an enactment repealed by this Act.
(2) The repeal and re-enactment does not affect the continuity of the law.
(3) Anything done (including subordinate legislation made), or having effect as if done, under or for the purposes of the repealed provision that could have been done under or for the purposes of the corresponding provision of this Act, if in force or effective immediately before the commencement of that corresponding provision, has effect thereafter as if done under or for the purposes of that corresponding provision.
(4) Any reference (express or implied) in this Act or any other enactment, instrument or document to a provision of this Act shall be construed (so far as the context permits) as including, as respects times, circumstances or purposes in relation to which the corresponding repealed provision had effect, a reference to that corresponding provision.
(5) Any reference (express or implied) in any enactment, instrument or document to a repealed provision shall be construed (so far as the context permits), as respects times, circumstances and purposes in relation to which the corresponding provision of this Act has effect, as being or (according to the context) including a reference to the corresponding provision of this Act.
(6) This section has effect subject to any specific transitional provision or saving contained in this Act.
(7) References in this section to this Act include subordinate legislation made under this Act.
(8) In this section "subordinate legislation" has the same meaning as in the Interpretation Act 1978.

PART 47
FINAL PROVISIONS

1298 Short title

The short title of this Act is the Companies Act 2006.

1299 Extent

Except as otherwise provided (or the context otherwise requires), the provisions of this Act extend to the whole of the United Kingdom.

1300 Commencement

(1) The following provisions come into force on the day this Act is passed—
   (a) Part 43 (transparency obligations and related matters), except the amendment in paragraph 11(2) of Schedule 15 of the definition of "regulated market" in Part 6 of the Financial Services and Markets Act 2000,
   (b) in Part 44 (miscellaneous provisions)—
   section 1274 (grants to bodies concerned with actuarial standards etc), and section 1276 (application of provisions to Scotland and Northern Ireland),
   (c) Part 46 (general supplementary provisions), except section 1295 and Schedule 16 (repeals), and
   (d) this Part.
(2) The other provisions of this Act come into force on such day as may be appointed by order of the Secretary of State or the Treasury

SCHEDULES **Sections 254 and 255**

SCHEDULE 1
CONNECTED PERSONS: REFERENCES TO AN INTEREST IN SHARES OR DEBENTURES

Introduction

1. (1) The provisions of this Schedule have effect for the interpretation of references in sections 254 and 255 (directors connected with or controlling a body corporate) to an interest in shares or debentures.
   (2) The provisions are expressed in relation to shares but apply to debentures as they apply to shares.

General provisions

2. (1) A reference to an interest in shares includes any interest of any kind whatsoever in shares.
   (2) Any restraints or restrictions to which the exercise of any right attached to the interest is or may be subject shall be disregarded.
   (3) It is immaterial that the shares in which a person has an interest are not identifiable.
   (4) Persons having a joint interest in shares are deemed each of them to have that interest.

Rights to acquire shares

3. (1) A person is taken to have an interest in shares if he enters into a contract to acquire them.
   (2) A person is taken to have an interest in shares if—
      (a) he has a right to call for delivery of the shares to himself or to his order, or
      (b) he has a right to acquire an interest in shares or is under an obligation to take an interest in shares,

   whether the right or obligation is conditional or absolute.
   (3) Rights or obligations to subscribe for shares are not to be taken for the purposes of sub-paragraph (2) to be rights to acquire or obligations to take an interest in shares.
   (4) A person ceases to have an interest in shares by virtue of this paragraph—
      (a) on the shares being delivered to another person at his order—
         (i) in fulfilment of a contract for their acquisition by him, or
         (ii) in satisfaction of a right of his to call for their delivery;
      (b) on a failure to deliver the shares in accordance with the terms of such a contract or on which such a right falls to be satisfied;
      (c) on the lapse of his right to call for the delivery of shares.

Right to exercise or control exercise of rights

4. (1) A person is taken to have an interest in shares if, not being the registered holder, he is entitled—
      (a) to exercise any right conferred by the holding of the shares, or
      (b) to control the exercise of any such right.
   (2) For this purpose a person is taken to be entitled to exercise or control the exercise of a right conferred by the holding of shares if he—
      (a) has a right (whether subject to conditions or not) the exercise of which would make him so entitled, or
      (b) is under an obligation (whether or not so subject) the fulfilment of which would make him so entitled.
   (3) A person is not by virtue of this paragraph taken to be interested in shares by reason only that—
      (a) he has been appointed a proxy to exercise any of the rights attached to the shares, or
      (b) he has been appointed by a body corporate to act as its representative at any meeting of a company or of any class of its members.

Bodies corporate

5. (1) A person is taken to be interested in shares if a body corporate is interested in them and—
      (a) the body corporate or its directors are accustomed to act in accordance with his directions or instructions, or

(b) he is entitled to exercise or control the exercise of more than one-half of the voting power at general meetings of the body corporate.

(2) For the purposes of sub-paragraph (1)(b) where—

(a) a person is entitled to exercise or control the exercise of more than one-half of the voting power at general meetings of a body corporate, and

(b) that body corporate is entitled to exercise or control the exercise of any of the voting power at general meetings of another body corporate,

the voting power mentioned in paragraph (b) above is taken to be exercisable by that person.

Trusts

6. (1) Where an interest in shares is comprised in property held on trust, every beneficiary of the trust is taken to have an interest in shares, subject as follows.

(2) So long as a person is entitled to receive, during the lifetime of himself or another, income from trust property comprising shares, an interest in the shares in reversion or remainder or (as regards Scotland) in fee shall be disregarded.

(3) A person is treated as not interested in shares if and so long as he holds them—

(a) under the law in force in any part of the United Kingdom, as a bare trustee or as a custodian trustee, or

(b) under the law in force in Scotland, as a simple trustee.

(4) There shall be disregarded any interest of a person subsisting by virtue of—

(a) an authorised unit trust scheme (within the meaning of section 237 of the Financial Services and Markets Act 2000);

(b) a scheme made under section 22 or 22A of the Charities Act 1960, section 25 of the Charities Act (Northern Ireland) 1964 or section 24 or 25 of the Charities Act 1993, or section 96 or 100 of the Charities Act 2011 section 11 of the Trustee Investments Act 1961 or section 42 of the Administration of Justice Act 1982; or

(c) the scheme set out in the Schedule to the Church Funds Investment Measure 1958.

(5) There shall be disregarded any interest—

(a) of the Church of Scotland General Trustees or of the Church of Scotland Trust in shares held by them;

(b) of any other person in shares held by those Trustees or that Trust otherwise than as simple trustees.

"The Church of Scotland General Trustees" are the body incorporated by the order confirmed by the Church of Scotland (General Trustees) Order Confirmation Act 1921, and "the Church of Scotland Trust" is the body incorporated by the order confirmed by the Church of Scotland Trust Order Confirmation Act 1932.

SCHEDULES 2, 3
OMITTED

SCHEDULE 4 **Section 1144(1)**
DOCUMENTS AND INFORMATION SENT OR SUPPLIED TO A COMPANY

PART 1
INTRODUCTION

Application of Schedule

1. (1) This Schedule applies to documents or information sent or supplied to a company.

(2) It does not apply to documents or information sent or supplied by another company (see section 1144(3) and Schedule 5).

PART 2
COMMUNICATIONS IN HARD COPY FORM

Introduction

2. A document or information is validly sent or supplied to a company if it is sent or supplied in hard copy form in accordance with this Part of this Schedule.

Method of communication in hard copy form

3. (1) A document or information in hard copy form may be sent or supplied by hand or by post to an address (in accordance with paragraph 4).
(2) For the purposes of this Schedule, a person sends a document or information by post if he posts a prepaid envelope containing the document or information.

Address for communications in hard copy form

4. A document or information in hard copy form may be sent or supplied—
(a) to an address specified by the company for the purpose;
(b) to the company's registered office;
(c) to an address to which any provision of the Companies Acts authorises the document or information to be sent or supplied.

PART 3
COMMUNICATIONS IN ELECTRONIC FORM

Introduction

5. A document or information is validly sent or supplied to a company if it is sent or supplied in electronic form in accordance with this Part of this Schedule.

Conditions for use of communications in electronic form

6. A document or information may only be sent or supplied to a company in electronic form if—
(a) the company has agreed (generally or specifically) that the document or information may be sent or supplied in that form (and has not revoked that agreement), or
(b) the company is deemed to have so agreed by a provision in the Companies Acts.

Address for communications in electronic form

7. (1) Where the document or information is sent or supplied by electronic means, it may only be sent or supplied to an address—
(a) specified for the purpose by the company (generally or specifically), or
(b) deemed by a provision in the Companies Acts to have been so specified.
(2) Where the document or information is sent or supplied in electronic form by hand or by post, it must be sent or supplied to an address to which it could be validly sent if it were in hard copy form.

PART 4
OTHER AGREED FORMS OF COMMUNICATION

8. A document or information that is sent or supplied to a company otherwise than in hard copy form or electronic form is validly sent or supplied if it is sent or supplied in a form or manner that has been agreed by the company.

SCHEDULE 5 **Section 1144(2)**
COMMUNICATIONS BY A COMPANY

PART 1
INTRODUCTION

Application of this Schedule

1. This Schedule applies to documents or information sent or supplied by a company.

PART 2
COMMUNICATIONS IN HARD COPY FORM

Introduction

2. A document or information is validly sent or supplied by a company if it is sent or supplied in hard copy form in accordance with this Part of this Schedule.

Method of communication in hard copy form

3. (1) A document or information in hard copy form must be—
(a) handed to the intended recipient, or
(b) sent or supplied by hand or by post to an address (in accordance with paragraph 4).
(2) For the purposes of this Schedule, a person sends a document or information by post if he posts a prepaid envelope containing the document or information.

Address for communications in hard copy form

4. (1) A document or information in hard copy form may be sent or supplied by the company—
(a) to an address specified for the purpose by the intended recipient;
(b) to a company at its registered office;
(c) to a person in his capacity as a member of the company at his address as shown in the company's register of members;
(d) to a person in his capacity as a director of the company at his address as shown in the company's register of directors;
(e) to an address to which any provision of the Companies Acts authorises the document or information to be sent or supplied.
(2) Where the company is unable to obtain an address falling within sub-paragraph (1), the document or information may be sent or supplied to the intended recipient's last address known to the company.

PART 3
COMMUNICATIONS IN ELECTRONIC FORM

Introduction

5. A document or information is validly sent or supplied by a company if it is sent in electronic form in accordance with this Part of this Schedule.

Agreement to communications in electronic form

6. A document or information may only be sent or supplied by a company in electronic form—
(a) to a person who has agreed (generally or specifically) that the document or information may be sent or supplied in that form (and has not revoked that agreement), or
(b) to a company that is deemed to have so agreed by a provision in the Companies Acts.

Address for communications in electronic form

7. (1) Where the document or information is sent or supplied by electronic means, it may only be sent or supplied to an address—
(a) specified for the purpose by the intended recipient (generally or specifically), or
(b) where the intended recipient is a company, deemed by a provision of the Companies Acts to have been so specified.
(2) Where the document or information is sent or supplied in electronic form by hand or by post, it must be—
(a) handed to the intended recipient, or
(b) sent or supplied to an address to which it could be validly sent if it were in hard copy form.

PART 4
COMMUNICATIONS BY MEANS OF A WEBSITE

Use of website

8. A document or information is validly sent or supplied by a company if it is made available on a website in accordance with this Part of this Schedule.

Agreement to use of website

9. A document or information may only be sent or supplied by the company to a person by being made available on a website if the person—
   (a) has agreed (generally or specifically) that the document or information may be sent or supplied to him in that manner, or
   (b) is taken to have so agreed under—
      (i) paragraph 10 (members of the company etc), or
      (ii) paragraph 11 (debenture holders),

and has not revoked that agreement.

Deemed agreement of members of company etc to use of website

10. (1) This paragraph applies to a document or information to be sent or supplied to a person—
   (a) as a member of the company, or
   (b) as a person nominated by a member in accordance with the company's articles to enjoy or exercise all or any specified rights of the member in relation to the company, or
   (c) as a person nominated by a member under section 146 to enjoy information rights.

(2) To the extent that—
   (a) the members of the company have resolved that the company may send or supply documents or information to members by making them available on a website, or
   (b) the company's articles contain provision to that effect,

a person in relation to whom the following conditions are met is taken to have agreed that the company may send or supply documents or information to him in that manner.

(3) The conditions are that—
   (a) the person has been asked individually by the company to agree that the company may send or supply documents or information generally, or the documents or information in question, to him by means of a website, and
   (b) the company has not received a response within the period of 28 days beginning with the date on which the company's request was sent.

(4) A person is not taken to have so agreed if the company's request—
   (a) did not state clearly what the effect of a failure to respond would be, or
   (b) was sent less than twelve months after a previous request made to him for the purposes of this paragraph in respect of the same or a similar class of documents or information.

(5) Chapter 3 of Part 3 (resolutions affecting a company's constitution) applies to a resolution under this paragraph.

Deemed agreement of debenture holders to use of website

11. (1) This paragraph applies to a document or information to be sent or supplied to a person as holder of a company's debentures.

(2) To the extent that—
   (a) the relevant debenture holders have duly resolved that the company may send or supply documents or information to them by making them available on a website, or
   (b) the instrument creating the debenture in question contains provision to that effect,

a debenture holder in relation to whom the following conditions are met is taken to have agreed that the company may send or supply documents or information to him in that manner.

(3) The conditions are that—
   (a) the debenture holder has been asked individually by the company to agree that the company may send or supply documents or information generally, or the documents or information in question, to him by means of a website, and
   (b) the company has not received a response within the period of 28 days beginning with the date on which the company's request was sent.

(4) A person is not taken to have so agreed if the company's request—
   (a) did not state clearly what the effect of a failure to respond would be, or
   (b) was sent less than twelve months after a previous request made to him for the purposes of this paragraph in respect of the same or a similar class of documents or information.

(5) For the purposes of this paragraph—

(a) the relevant debenture holders are the holders of debentures of the company ranking pari passu for all purposes with the intended recipient, and
(b) a resolution of the relevant debenture holders is duly passed if they agree in accordance with the provisions of the instruments creating the debentures.

Availability of document or information

12. (1) A document or information authorised or required to be sent or supplied by means of a website must be made available in a form, and by a means, that the company reasonably considers will enable the recipient—
(a) to read it, and
(b) to retain a copy of it.
(2) For this purpose a document or information can be read only if—
(a) it can be read with the naked eye, or
(b) to the extent that it consists of images (for example photographs, pictures, maps, plans or drawings), it can be seen with the naked eye.

Notification of availability

13. (1) The company must notify the intended recipient of—
(a) the presence of the document or information on the website,
(b) the address of the website,
(c) the place on the website where it may be accessed, and
(d) how to access the document or information.
(2) The document or information is taken to be sent—
(a) on the date on which the notification required by this paragraph is sent, or
(b) if later, the date on which the document or information first appears on the website after that notification is sent.

Period of availability on website

14. (1) The company must make the document or information available on the website throughout—
(a) the period specified by any applicable provision of the Companies Acts, or
(b) if no such period is specified, the period of 28 days beginning with the date on which the notification required under paragraph 13 is sent to the person in question.
(2) For the purposes of this paragraph, a failure to make a document or information available on a website throughout the period mentioned in sub-paragraph (1) shall be disregarded if—
(a) it is made available on the website for part of that period, and
(b) the failure to make it available throughout that period is wholly attributable to circumstances that it would not be reasonable to have expected the company to prevent or avoid.

PART 5
OTHER AGREED FORMS OF COMMUNICATION

15. A document or information that is sent or supplied otherwise than in hard copy or electronic form or by means of a website is validly sent or supplied if it is sent or supplied in a form or manner that has been agreed by the intended recipient.

PART 6
SUPPLEMENTARY PROVISIONS

Joint holders of shares or debentures

16. (1) This paragraph applies in relation to documents or information to be sent or supplied to joint holders of shares or debentures of a company.
(2) Anything to be agreed or specified by the holder must be agreed or specified by all the joint holders.
(3) Anything authorised or required to be sent or supplied to the holder may be sent or supplied either—
(a) to each of the joint holders, or
(b) to the holder whose name appears first in the register of members or the relevant register of debenture holders.

(4) This paragraph has effect subject to anything in the company's articles.

Death or bankruptcy of holder of shares

17. (1) This paragraph has effect in the case of the death or bankruptcy of a holder of a company's shares.
(2) Documents or information required or authorised to be sent or supplied to the member may be sent or supplied to the persons claiming to be entitled to the shares in consequence of the death or bankruptcy—
(a) by name, or
(b) by the title of representatives of the deceased, or trustee of the bankrupt, or by any like description,
at the address in the United Kingdom supplied for the purpose by those so claiming.
(3) Until such an address has been so supplied, a document or information may be sent or supplied in any manner in which it might have been sent or supplied if the death or bankruptcy had not occurred.
(4) This paragraph has effect subject to anything in the company's articles.
(5) References in this paragraph to the bankruptcy of a person include—
(a) the sequestration of the estate of a person;
(b) a person's estate being the subject of a protected trust deed (within the meaning of the Bankruptcy (Scotland) Act 1985).
In such a case the reference in sub-paragraph (2)(b) to the trustee of the bankrupt is to be read as the permanent or interim trustee (within the meaning of that Act) on the sequestrated estate or, as the case may be, the trustee under the protected deed.

SCHEDULE 6 **Section 1159**
MEANING OF "SUBSIDIARY" ETC: SUPPLEMENTARY PROVISIONS

Introduction

1. The provisions of this Part of this Schedule explain expressions used in section 1159 (meaning of "subsidiary" etc) and otherwise supplement that section.

Voting rights in a company

2. In section 1159(1)(a) and (c) the references to the voting rights in a company are to the rights conferred on shareholders in respect of their shares or, in the case of a company not having a share capital, on members, to vote at general meetings of the company on all, or substantially all, matters.

Right to appoint or remove a majority of the directors

3. (1) In section 1159(1)(b) the reference to the right to appoint or remove a majority of the board of directors is to the right to appoint or remove directors holding a majority of the voting rights at meetings of the board on all, or substantially all, matters.
(2) A company shall be treated as having the right to appoint to a directorship if—
(a) a person's appointment to it follows necessarily from his appointment as director of the company, or
(b) the directorship is held by the company itself.
(3) A right to appoint or remove which is exercisable only with the consent or concurrence of another person shall be left out of account unless no other person has a right to appoint or, as the case may be, remove in relation to that directorship.

Rights exercisable only in certain circumstances or temporarily incapable of exercise

4. (1) Rights which are exercisable only in certain circumstances shall be taken into account only—
(a) when the circumstances have arisen, and for so long as they continue to obtain, or
(b) when the circumstances are within the control of the person having the rights.
(2) Rights which are normally exercisable but are temporarily incapable of exercise shall continue to be taken into account.

Rights held by one person on behalf of another

5. Rights held by a person in a fiduciary capacity shall be treated as not held by him.

6. (1) Rights held by a person as nominee for another shall be treated as held by the other.
(2) Rights shall be regarded as held as nominee for another if they are exercisable only on his instructions or with his consent or concurrence.

Rights attached to shares held by way of security

7. Rights attached to shares held by way of security shall be treated as held by the person providing the security—
(a) where apart from the right to exercise them for the purpose of preserving the value of the security, or of realising it, the rights are exercisable only in accordance with his instructions, and
(b) where the shares are held in connection with the granting of loans as part of normal business activities and apart from the right to exercise them for the purpose of preserving the value of the security, or of realising it, the rights are exercisable only in his interests.

Rights attributed to holding company

8. (1) Rights shall be treated as held by a holding company if they are held by any of its subsidiary companies.
(2) Nothing in paragraph 6 or 7 shall be construed as requiring rights held by a holding company to be treated as held by any of its subsidiaries.
(3) For the purposes of paragraph 7 rights shall be treated as being exercisable in accordance with the instructions or in the interests of a company if they are exercisable in accordance with the instructions of or, as the case may be, in the interests of—
(a) any subsidiary or holding company of that company, or
(b) any subsidiary of a holding company of that company.

Disregard of certain rights

9. The voting rights in a company shall be reduced by any rights held by the company itself.

Supplementary

10. References in any provision of paragraphs 5 to 9 to rights held by a person include rights falling to be treated as held by him by virtue of any other provision of those paragraphs but not rights which by virtue of any such provision are to be treated as not held by him.

SCHEDULE 7 **Section 1162**

PARENT AND SUBSIDIARY UNDERTAKINGS: SUPPLEMENTARY PROVISIONS

Introduction

1. The provisions of this Schedule explain expressions used in section 1162 (parent and subsidiary undertakings) and otherwise supplement that section.

Voting rights in an undertaking

2. (1) In section 1162(2)(a) and (d) the references to the voting rights in an undertaking are to the rights conferred on shareholders in respect of their shares or, in the case of an undertaking not having a share capital, on members, to vote at general meetings of the undertaking on all, or substantially all, matters.
(2) In relation to an undertaking which does not have general meetings at which matters are decided by the exercise of voting rights the references to holding a majority of the voting rights in the undertaking shall be construed as references to having the right under the constitution of the undertaking to direct the overall policy of the undertaking or to alter the terms of its constitution.

Right to appoint or remove a majority of the directors

3. (1) In section 1162(2)(b) the reference to the right to appoint or remove a majority of the board of directors is to the right to appoint or remove directors holding a majority of the voting rights at meetings of the board on all, or substantially all, matters.

(2) An undertaking shall be treated as having the right to appoint to a directorship if—
(a) a person's appointment to it follows necessarily from his appointment as director of the undertaking, or
(b) the directorship is held by the undertaking itself.
(3) A right to appoint or remove which is exercisable only with the consent or concurrence of another person shall be left out of account unless no other person has a right to appoint or, as the case may be, remove in relation to that directorship.

Right to exercise dominant influence

4. (1) For the purposes of section 1162(2)(c) an undertaking shall not be regarded as having the right to exercise a dominant influence over another undertaking unless it has a right to give directions with respect to the operating and financial policies of that other undertaking which its directors are obliged to comply with whether or not they are for the benefit of that other undertaking.
(2) A "control contract" means a contract in writing conferring such a right which—
(a) is of a kind authorised by the articles of the undertaking in relation to which the right is exercisable, and
(b) is permitted by the law under which that undertaking is established.
(3) This paragraph shall not be read as affecting the construction of section 1162(4)(a).

Rights exercisable only in certain circumstances or temporarily incapable of exercise

5. (1) Rights which are exercisable only in certain circumstances shall be taken into account only—
(a) when the circumstances have arisen, and for so long as they continue to obtain, or
(b) when the circumstances are within the control of the person having the rights.
(2) Rights which are normally exercisable but are temporarily incapable of exercise shall continue to be taken into account.

Rights held by one person on behalf of another

6. Rights held by a person in a fiduciary capacity shall be treated as not held by him.
7. (1) Rights held by a person as nominee for another shall be treated as held by the other.
(2) Rights shall be regarded as held as nominee for another if they are exercisable only on his instructions or with his consent or concurrence.

Rights attached to shares held by way of security

8. Rights attached to shares held by way of security shall be treated as held by the person providing the security—
(a) where apart from the right to exercise them for the purpose of preserving the value of the security, or of realising it, the rights are exercisable only in accordance with his instructions, and
(b) where the shares are held in connection with the granting of loans as part of normal business activities and apart from the right to exercise them for the purpose of preserving the value of the security, or of realising it, the rights are exercisable only in his interests.

Rights attributed to parent undertaking

9. (1) Rights shall be treated as held by a parent undertaking if they are held by any of its subsidiary undertakings.
(2) Nothing in paragraph 7 or 8 shall be construed as requiring rights held by a parent undertaking to be treated as held by any of its subsidiary undertakings.
(3) For the purposes of paragraph 8 rights shall be treated as being exercisable in accordance with the instructions or in the interests of an undertaking if they are exercisable in accordance with the instructions of or, as the case may be, in the interests of any group undertaking.

Disregard of certain rights

10. The voting rights in an undertaking shall be reduced by any rights held by the undertaking itself.

Supplementary

11. References in any provision of paragraphs 6 to 10 to rights held by a person include rights falling to be treated as held by him by virtue of any other provision of those paragraphs but not rights which by virtue of any such provision are to be treated as not held by him.

SCHEDULE 8 **Section 1174**

INDEX OF DEFINED EXPRESSIONS

accounting reference date and accounting reference period	section 391
accounting standards (in Part 15)	section 464
accounts meeting	section 437(3)
acquisition, in relation to a non-cash asset	section 1163(2)
address	
— generally in the Companies Acts	section 1142
— in the company communications provisions	section 1148(1)
affirmative resolution procedure, in relation to regulations and orders	section 1290
allotment (time of)	section 558
allotment of equity securities (in Chapter 3 of Part 17)	section 560(2) and (3)
allotted share capital and allotted shares	section 546(1)(b) and (2)
annual accounts (in Part 15)	section 471
annual accounts and reports (in Part 15)	section 471
annual general meeting	section 336
annual return	section 854
appropriate audit authority (in sections 522, 523 and 524)	section 525(1)
appropriate rate of interest	
— in Chapter 5 of Part 17	section 592
— in Chapter 6 of Part 17	section 609
approval after being made, in relation to regulations and orders	section 1291
arrangement	
— in Chapter 7 of Part 17	section 616(1)
— in Part 26	section 895(2)
articles	section 18
associate (in Chapter 3 of Part 28)	section 988
associated bodies corporate and associated company (in Part 10)	section 256
authenticated, in relation to a document or information sent or supplied to a company	section 1146
authorised group, of members of a company (in Part 14)	section 370(3)
authorised insurance company	section 1165(2)
authorised minimum (in relation to share capital of public company)	section 763
available profits (in Chapter 5 of Part 18)	sections 711 and 712
banking company and banking group	section 1164
body corporate	section 1173(1)
called-up share capital	section 547
capital redemption reserve	section 733
capitalisation in relation to a company's profits (in Part 23)	section 853(3)
cash (in relation to paying up or allotting shares)	section 583
cause of action, in relation to derivative proceedings (in Chapter 2 of Part 11)	section 265(7)
certified translation (in Part 35)	section 1107
charge (in Chapter A1 of Part 25)	section 859A(7)
circulation date, in relation to a written resolution (in Part 13)	section 290
class of shares	section 629
the Companies Acts	section 2

Companies Act accounts	sections 395(1)(a) and 403(2)(a)
Companies Act group accounts	section 403(2)(a)
Companies Act individual accounts	section 395(1)(a)
companies involved in the division (in Part 27)	section 919(2)
company	
— generally in the Companies Acts	section 1
— in Chapter 7 of Part 17	section 616(1)
— in Chapter A1 of Part 25	section 859A(7)
— in Part 26	section 895(2)
— in Chapter 3 of Part 28	section 991(1)
— in the company communications provisions	section 1148(1)
the company communications provisions	section 1143
the company law provisions of this Act	section 2(2)
company records (in Part 37)	section 1134
connected with, in relation to a director (in Part 10)	sections 252 to 254
constitution, of a company	
— generally in the Companies Acts	section 17
— in Part 10	section 257
contributory	section 1170B
controlling, of a body corporate by a director (in Part 10)	section 255
corporate governance statement and separate corporate governance statement	
— in Part 15	section 472A
— in Part 16	section 538A
corporation	section 1173(1)
the court	section 1156
credit institution	section 1173(1)
credit transaction (in Chapter 4 of Part 10)	section 202
creditor (in Chapter 1 of Part 31)	section 1011
daily default fine	section 1125
date of the offer (in Chapter 3 of Part 28)	section 991(1)
debenture	section 738
derivative claim (in Chapter 1 of Part 11)	section 260
derivative proceedings (in Chapter 2 of Part 11)	section 265
Directive disclosure requirements	section 1078
director	
— generally in the Companies Acts	section 250
— in Chapter 8 of Part 10	section 240(3)
— in Chapter 1 of Part 11	section 260(5)
— in Chapter 2 of Part 11	section 265(7)
— in Part 14	section 379(1)
directors' remuneration report	section 420
directors' report	section 415
distributable profits	
— in Chapter 2 of Part 18	section 683(1)
— elsewhere in Part 18	section 736
distribution	
— in Chapter 2 of Part 18	section 683(1)
— in Part 23	section 829
division (in Part 27)	section 919
document	
— in Part 35	section 1114(1)
— in the company communications provisions	section 1148(1)
directors remuneration policy (in Chapter 4A of Part 10)	section 226A(1)
dormant, in relation to a company or other body corporate	section 1169
EEA State and related expressions	section 1170
electronic form, electronic copy, electronic means	

— generally in the Companies Acts	section 1168(3) and (4)
— in relation to communications to a company	Part 3 of Schedule 4
— in relation to communications by a company	Part 3 of Schedule 5
eligible members, in relation to a written resolution	section 289
e-money issuer	
— in Part 15	section 474(1)
— in Part 16	section 539
employees' share scheme	section 1166
employer and employee (in Chapter 1 of Part 18)	section 676
enactment	section 1293
equity securities (in Chapter 3 of Part 17)	section 560(1)
equity share capital	section 548
equity shares (in Chapter 7 of Part 17)	section 616(1)
establishment of an overseas company (in Part 35)	section 1067(6)
existing company (in Part 27)	section 902(2)
fellow subsidiary undertakings	section 1161(4)
financial assistance (in Chapter 2 of Part 18)	section 677
financial institution	section 1173(1)
financial year, of a company	section 390
firm	section 1173(1)
fixed assets (in Part 23)	section 853
the former Companies Acts	section 1171
the Gazette	section 1173(1)
group (in Part 15)	section 474(1)
group undertaking	section 1161(5)
hard copy form and hard copy	
— generally in the Companies Acts	section 1168(2)
— in relation to communications to a company	Part 2 of Schedule 4
— in relation to communications by a company	Part 2 of Schedule 5
hire-purchase agreement	section 1173(1)
holder of shares (in Chapter 3 of Part 17)	section 574
holding company	section 1159 (and see section 1160 and Schedule 6)
IAS accounts	sections 395(1)(b) and 403(1) and (2)(b)
IAS group accounts	section 403(1) and (2)(b)
IAS individual accounts	section 395(1)(b)
IAS Regulation (in Part 15)	section 474(1)
included in the consolidation, in relation to group accounts (in Part 15)	section 474(1)
individual accounts	section 394
information rights (in Part 9)	section 146(3)
insurance company	section 1165(3)
insurance group	section 1165(5)
insurance market activity	section 1165(7)
interest in shares (for the purposes of Part 22)	sections 820 to 825
international accounting standards (in Part 15)	section 474(1)
investment company (in Part 23)	section 833
issued share capital and issued shares	section 546(1)(a) and (2)
the issuing company (in Chapter 7 of Part 17)	section 610(6)
the Joint Stock Companies Acts	section 1171
liabilities (in Part 27)	section 941
liability, references to incurring, reducing or discharging (in Chapter 2 of Part 18)	section 683(2)
limited by guarantee	section 3(3)
limited by shares	section 3(2)
limited company	section 3
the main register (of members) (in Chapter 3 of Part 8)	section 131(1)
major audit (in sections 522 and 525)	section 525(2)

market purchase, by a company of its own shares (in Chapter 4 of Part 18)	section 693(4)
member, of a company	
— generally in the Companies Acts	section 112
— in Chapter 1 of Part 11	section 260(5)
— in Chapter 2 of Part 11	section 265(7)
memorandum of association	section 8
merger (in Part 27)	section 904
merging companies (in Part 27)	section 904(2)
merger by absorption (in Part 27)	section 904(1)(a)
merger by formation of a new company (in Part 27)	section 904(1)(b)
MiFID Investment Firm	
— in Part 15	section 474(1)
— in Part 16	section 539
negative resolution procedure, in relation to regulations and orders	section 1289
net assets (in Part 7)	section 92
new company (in Part 27)	section 902(2)
non-cash asset	section 1163
non-voting shares (in Chapter 3 of Part 28)	section 991(1)
number, in relation to shares	section 540(4)(b)
off-market purchase, by a company of its own shares (in Chapter 4 of Part 18)	section 693(2)
offer period (in Chapter 2 of Part 28)	section 971(1)
offer to the public (in Chapter 1 of Part 20)	section 756
offeror	
— in Chapter 2 of Part 28	section 971(1)
— in Chapter 3 of Part 28	section 991(1)
officer, in relation to a body corporate	section 1173(1)
officer in default	section 1121
official seal, of registrar	section 1062
opted-in company (in Chapter 2 of Part 28)	section 971(1)
opting-in resolution (in Chapter 2 of Part 28)	section 966(1)
opting-out resolution (in Chapter 2 of Part 28)	section 966(5)
ordinary resolution	section 282
ordinary shares (in Chapter 3 of Part 17)	section 560(1)
organisation (in Part 14)	section 379(1)
other relevant transactions or arrangements (in Chapter 4 of Part 10)	section 210
overseas company	section 1044
overseas branch register	section 129(1)
paid up	section 583
the Panel (in Part 28)	section 942
parent company	section 1173(1)
parent undertaking	section 1162 (and see Schedule 7)
payment for loss of office (in Chapter 4 of Part 10)	section 215
payment for loss of office (in Chapter 4A of Part 10)	section 226A(1)
pension scheme (in Chapter 1 of Part 18)	section 675
period for appointing auditors, in relation to a private company	section 485(2)
period for filing, in relation to accounts and reports for a financial year	section 442
permissible capital payment (in Chapter 5 of Part 18)	section 710
political donation (in Part 14)	section 364
political expenditure (in Part 14)	section 365
political organisation (in Part 14)	section 363(2)
prescribed	section 1167
private company	section 4
profit and loss account (in Part 15)	section 474(1) and (2)
profits and losses (in Part 23)	section 853(2)

profits available for distribution (for the purposes of Part 23)	section 830(2)
property (in Part 27)	section 941
protected information (in Chapter 8 of Part 10)	section 240
provision for entrenchment, in relation to a company's articles	section 22
public company	section 4
publication, in relation to accounts and reports (in sections 433 to 435)	section 436
qualified, in relation to an auditor's report etc	
(in Part 15)	section 474(1)
(in Part 16)	section 539
qualifying shares (in Chapter 6 of Part 18)	section 724(2)
qualifying third party indemnity provision (in Chapter 7 of Part 10)	section 234
qualifying pension scheme indemnity provision (in Chapter 7 of Part 10)	section 235
quasi-loan (in Chapter 4 of Part 10)	section 199
quoted company	
— in Chapter 4A of Part 10	section 226A(1)
— in Part 13	section 361
— in Part 15	section 385
— in Chapter 5 of Part 16	section 531 (and section 385)
realised profits and losses (in Part 23)	section 853(4)
receiver or manager (and certain related references)	section 1170A
redeemable shares	section 684(1)
redenominate	section 622(1)
redenomination reserve	section 628
the register	section 1080
register of directors	section 162
register of directors' residential addresses	section 165
register of members	section 113
register of secretaries	section 275
registered number, of a company (or an overseas company)	section 1066 (and section 1059A(5))
registered number, of a UK establishment of an overseas company	section 1067
registered office, of a company	section 86
registrar and registrar of companies	section 1060
registrar's index of company names	section 1099
registrar's rules	section 1117
registration in a particular part of the United Kingdom	section 1060(4)
regulated activity	
— generally in the Companies Acts	section 1173(1)
— in Part 15	section 474(1)
regulated market	section 1173(1)
relevant accounts (in Part 23)	section 836(2)
remuneration payment in Chapter 4A of Part 10	section 226A(1)
requirements for proper delivery (in Part 35)	section 1072 (and see section 1073)
requirements of this Act	section 1172
return period (in Part 24)	section 855(4)
securities (and related expressions)	
— in Chapter 1 of Part 20	section 755(5)
— in Chapter 2 of Part 21	section 783
senior statutory auditor	section 504
sent or supplied, in relation to documents or information (in the company communications provisions)	section 1148(2) and (3)
service address	section 1141

service contract, of a director (in Part 10)	section 227
shadow director	section 251
share	
— generally in the Companies Acts	section 540 (and see section 1161(2))
— in Part 22	section 792
— in section 1162 and Schedule 7	section 1162(7)
share capital, company having a	section 545
share exchange ratio	
— in Chapter 2 of Part 27	section 905(2)
— in Chapter 3 of Part 27	section 920(2)
share premium account	section 610(1)
share warrant	section 779(1)
small companies exemption (in relation to directors' report)	section 415A
small companies regime, for accounts	section 381
solvency statement (in sections 641 to 644)	section 643
special notice, in relation to a resolution	section 312
special resolution	section 283
statutory accounts	section 434(3)
subsidiary	section 1159 (and see section 1160 and Schedule 6)
subsidiary undertaking	section 1162 (and see Schedule 7)
takeover bid (in Chapter 2 of Part 28)	section 971(1)
takeover offer (in Chapter 3 of Part 28)	section 974
the Takeovers Directive	
— in Chapter 1 of Part 28	section 943(8)
— in Chapter 2 of Part 28	section 971(1)
traded company	
— in Part 13	section 360C
— in Part 15	section 474(1)
trading certificate	section 761(1)
transfer, in relation to a non-cash asset	section 1163(2)
transferable securities	section 1173(1)
treasury shares	section 724(5)
turnover	
— in Part 15	section 474(1)
— in Part 16	section 539
UCITS management company	
— in Part 15	section 474(1)
— in Part 16	section 539
UK establishment of an overseas company (in Part 35)	section 1067(6)
UK-registered company	section 1158
uncalled share capital	section 547
unconditional, in relation to a contract to acquire shares (in Chapter 3 of Part 28)	section 991(2)
undistributable reserves	section 831(4)
undertaking	section 1161(1)
unique identifier	section 1082
unlimited company	section 3
unquoted company (in Part 15)	section 385
voting rights	
— in Chapter 2 of Part 28	section 971(1)
— in Chapter 3 of Part 28	section 991(1)
— in section 1159 and Schedule 6	paragraph 2 of Schedule 6
— in section 1162 and Schedule 7	paragraph 2 of Schedule 7
voting shares	
— in Chapter 2 of Part 28	section 971(1)
— in Chapter 3 of Part 28	section 991(1)

website, communication by a company by means of	Part 4 of Schedule 5
Welsh company	section 88
wholly-owned subsidiary	section 1159(2) (and see section 1160 and Schedule 6)
working day, in relation to a company	section 1173(1)
written resolution	section 288

CORPORATE MANSLAUGHTER AND CORPORATE HOMICIDE ACT 2007 (2007, c. 19)

Corporate manslaughter and corporate homicide

1 The offence

(1) An organisation to which this section applies is guilty of an offence if the way in which its activities are managed or organised—
  (a) causes a person's death, and
  (b) amounts to a gross breach of a relevant duty of care owed by the organisation to the deceased.

(2) The organisations to which this section applies are—
  (a) a corporation;
  (b) a department or other body listed in Schedule 1;
  (c) a police force;
  (d) a partnership, or a trade union or employers' association, that is an employer.

(3) An organisation is guilty of an offence under this section only if the way in which its activities are managed or organised by its senior management is a substantial element in the breach referred to in subsection (1).

(4) For the purposes of this Act—
  (a) "relevant duty of care" has the meaning given by section 2, read with sections 3 to 7;
  (b) a breach of a duty of care by an organisation is a "gross" breach if the conduct alleged to amount to a breach of that duty falls far below what can reasonably be expected of the organisation in the circumstances;
  (c) "senior management", in relation to an organisation, means the persons who play significant roles in—
    (i) the making of decisions about how the whole or a substantial part of its activities are to be managed or organised, or
    (ii) the actual managing or organising of the whole or a substantial part of those activities.

(5) The offence under this section is called—
  (a) corporate manslaughter, in so far as it is an offence under the law of England and Wales or Northern Ireland;
  (b) corporate homicide, in so far as it is an offence under the law of Scotland.

(6) An organisation that is guilty of corporate manslaughter or corporate homicide is liable on conviction on indictment to a fine.

(7) The offence of corporate homicide is indictable only in the High Court of Justiciary.

Relevant duty of care

2 Meaning of "relevant duty of care"

(1) A "relevant duty of care", in relation to an organisation, means any of the following duties owed by it under the law of negligence—
  (a) a duty owed to its employees or to other persons working for the organisation or performing services for it;
  (b) a duty owed as occupier of premises;
  (c) a duty owed in connection with—
    (i) the supply by the organisation of goods or services (whether for consideration or not),

(ii) the carrying on by the organisation of any construction or maintenance operations,
(iii) the carrying on by the organisation of any other activity on a commercial basis, or
(iv) the use or keeping by the organisation of any plant, vehicle or other thing;
(d) a duty owed to a person who, by reason of being a person within subsection (2), is someone for whose safety the organisation is responsible.

(2) A person is within this subsection if—
(a) he is detained at a custodial institution or in a custody area at a court or police station;
(aa) he is detained in service custody premises;
(b) he is detained at a removal centre or short-term holding facility, a short-term holding facility or in pre-departure accommodation;
(c) he is being transported in a vehicle, or being held in any premises, in pursuance of prison escort arrangements or immigration escort arrangements;
(d) he is living in secure accommodation in which he has been placed;
(e) he is a detained patient.

(3) Subsection (1) is subject to sections 3 to 7.

(4) A reference in subsection (1) to a duty owed under the law of negligence includes a reference to a duty that would be owed under the law of negligence but for any statutory provision under which liability is imposed in place of liability under that law.

(5) For the purposes of this Act, whether a particular organisation owes a duty of care to a particular individual is a question of law.
The judge must make any findings of fact necessary to decide that question.

(6) For the purposes of this Act there is to be disregarded—
(a) any rule of the common law that has the effect of preventing a duty of care from being owed by one person to another by reason of the fact that they are jointly engaged in unlawful conduct;
(b) any such rule that has the effect of preventing a duty of care from being owed to a person by reason of his acceptance of a risk of harm.

(7) In this section—
"construction or maintenance operations" means operations of any of the following descriptions—
(a) construction, installation, alteration, extension, improvement, repair, maintenance, decoration, cleaning, demolition or dismantling of—
(i) any building or structure,
(ii) anything else that forms, or is to form, part of the land, or
(iii) any plant, vehicle or other thing;
(b) operations that form an integral part of, or are preparatory to, or are for rendering complete, any operations within paragraph (a);

"custodial institution" means a prison, a young offender institution, a secure college, a secure training centre, a young offenders institution, a young offenders centre, a juvenile justice centre or a remand centre;

"customs premises" means premises wholly or partly occupied by persons designated under section 3 (general customs officials) or 11 (customs revenue officials) of the Borders, Citizenship and Immigration Act 2009;

"detained patient" means—
(a) a person who is detained in any premises under—
(i) Part 2 or 3 of the Mental Health Act 1983 ("the 1983 Act"), or
(ii) Part 2 or 3 of the Mental Health (Northern Ireland) Order 1986 ("the 1986 Order");
(b) a person who (otherwise than by reason of being detained as mentioned in paragraph (a)) is deemed to be in legal custody by—
(i) section 137 of the 1983 Act,
(ii) Article 131 of the 1986 Order, or
(iii) article 11 of the Mental Health (Care and Treatment) (Scotland) Act 2003 (Consequential Provisions) Order 2005;
(c) a person who is detained in any premises, or is otherwise in custody, under the Mental Health (Care and Treatment) (Scotland) Act 2003 or Part 6 of the Criminal Procedure (Scotland) Act 1995 or who is detained in a hospital under section 200 of that Act of 1995;

"immigration escort arrangements" means arrangements made under section 156 of the Immigration and Asylum Act 1999;

"the law of negligence" includes—

(a) in relation to England and Wales, the Occupiers' Liability Act 1957, the Defective Premises Act 1972 and the Occupiers' Liability Act 1984;

(b) in relation to Scotland, the Occupiers' Liability (Scotland) Act 1960;

(c) in relation to Northern Ireland, the Occupiers' Liability Act (Northern Ireland) 1957, the Defective Premises (Northern Ireland) Order 1975, the Occupiers' Liability (Northern Ireland) Order 1987 and the Defective Premises (Landlord's Liability) Act (Northern Ireland) 2001;

"prison escort arrangements" means arrangements made under section 80 of the Criminal Justice Act 1991 or under section 102 or 118 of the Criminal Justice and Public Order Act 1994;

"removal centre" and "pre-departure accommodation" have the meaning given by section 147 of the Immigration and Asylum Act 1999;

"secure accommodation" means accommodation, not consisting of or forming part of a custodial institution, provided for the purpose of restricting the liberty of persons under the age of 18;

"service custody premises" has the meaning given by section 300(7) of the Armed Forces Act 2006.

3–7 *omitted*

Gross breach

8 Factors for jury

(1) This section applies where—

(a) it is established that an organisation owed a relevant duty of care to a person, and

(b) it falls to the jury to decide whether there was a gross breach of that duty.

(2) The jury must consider whether the evidence shows that the organisation failed to comply with any health and safety legislation that relates to the alleged breach, and if so—

(a) how serious that failure was;

(b) how much of a risk of death it posed.

(3) The jury may also—

(a) consider the extent to which the evidence shows that there were attitudes, policies, systems or accepted practices within the organisation that were likely to have encouraged any such failure as is mentioned in subsection (2), or to have produced tolerance of it;

(b) have regard to any health and safety guidance that relates to the alleged breach.

(4) This section does not prevent the jury from having regard to any other matters they consider relevant.

(5) In this section "health and safety guidance" means any code, guidance, manual or similar publication that is concerned with health and safety matters and is made or issued (under a statutory provision or otherwise) by an authority responsible for the enforcement of any health and safety legislation.

Remedial orders and publicity orders

9 Power to order breach etc to be remedied

(1) A court before which an organisation is convicted of corporate manslaughter or corporate homicide may make an order (a "remedial order") requiring the organisation to take specified steps to remedy—

(a) the breach mentioned in section 1(1) ("the relevant breach");

(b) any matter that appears to the court to have resulted from the relevant breach and to have been a cause of the death;

(c) any deficiency, as regards health and safety matters, in the organisation's policies, systems or practices of which the relevant breach appears to the court to be an indication.

(2) A remedial order may be made only on an application by the prosecution specifying the terms of the proposed order.
Any such order must be on such terms (whether those proposed or others) as the court considers appropriate having regard to any representations made, and any evidence adduced, in relation to that matter by the prosecution or on behalf of the organisation.
(3) Before making an application for a remedial order the prosecution must consult such enforcement authority or authorities as it considers appropriate having regard to the nature of the relevant breach.
(4) A remedial order—
(a) must specify a period within which the steps referred to in subsection (1) are to be taken;
(b) may require the organisation to supply to an enforcement authority consulted under subsection (3), within a specified period, evidence that those steps have been taken.
A period specified under this subsection may be extended or further extended by order of the court on an application made before the end of that period or extended period.
(5) An organisation that fails to comply with a remedial order is guilty of an offence, and liable on conviction on indictment to a fine.

10 Power to order conviction etc to be publicised

(1) A court before which an organisation is convicted of corporate manslaughter or corporate homicide may make an order (a "publicity order") requiring the organisation to publicise in a specified manner—
(a) the fact that it has been convicted of the offence;
(b) specified particulars of the offence;
(c) the amount of any fine imposed;
(d) the terms of any remedial order made.
(2) In deciding on the terms of a publicity order that it is proposing to make, the court must—
(a) ascertain the views of such enforcement authority or authorities (if any) as it considers appropriate, and
(b) have regard to any representations made by the prosecution or on behalf of the organisation.
(3) A publicity order—
(a) must specify a period within which the requirements referred to in subsection (1) are to be complied with;
(b) may require the organisation to supply to any enforcement authority whose views have been ascertained under subsection (2), within a specified period, evidence that those requirements have been complied with.
(4) An organisation that fails to comply with a publicity order is guilty of an offence, and liable on conviction on indictment to a fine.

Application to particular categories of organisation

11–13 *omitted*

14 Application to partnerships

(1) For the purposes of this Act a partnership is to be treated as owing whatever duties of care it would owe if it were a body corporate.
(2) Proceedings for an offence under this Act alleged to have been committed by a partnership are to be brought in the name of the partnership (and not in that of any of its members).
(3) A fine imposed on a partnership on its conviction of an offence under this Act is to be paid out of the funds of the partnership.
(4) This section does not apply to a partnership that is a legal person under the law by which it is governed.

Miscellaneous

15 Procedure, evidence and sentencing

(1) Any statutory provision (whenever made) about criminal proceedings applies, subject to any prescribed adaptations or modifications, in relation to proceedings under this Act against—

(a) a department or other body listed in Schedule 1,
(b) a police force,
(c) a partnership,
(d) a trade union, or
(e) an employers' association that is not a corporation,

as it applies in relation to proceedings against a corporation.

(2) In this section—

"prescribed" means—

(a) in relation to proceedings under this Act in England and Wales, prescribed by an order made by the Secretary of State;
(b) in relation to proceedings under this Act in Northern Ireland, prescribed by an order made by the Department of Justice in Northern Ireland;

"provision about criminal proceedings" includes—

(a) provision about procedure in or in connection with criminal proceedings;
(b) provision about evidence in such proceedings;
(c) provision about sentencing, or otherwise dealing with, persons convicted of offences;

"statutory" means contained in, or in an instrument made under, any Act or any Northern Ireland legislation.

(3) A reference in this section to proceedings (except in the definition of "prescribed" in subsection (2)) is to proceedings in England and Wales or Northern Ireland.

(4) An order of the Secretary of State under this section is subject to negative resolution procedure.

16 *omitted*

17 DPP's consent required for proceedings

Proceedings for an offence of corporate manslaughter—

(a) may not be instituted in England and Wales without the consent of the Director of Public Prosecutions;
(b) may not be instituted in Northern Ireland without the consent of the Director of Public Prosecutions for Northern Ireland.

18 No individual liability

(1) An individual cannot be guilty of aiding, abetting, counselling or procuring the commission of an offence of corporate manslaughter.

This subsection applies only in England and Wales

(1A) An individual cannot be guilty of an offence under Part 2 of the Serious Crime Act 2007 (encouraging or assisting crime) by reference to an offence of corporate manslaughter.

(2) An individual cannot be guilty of aiding, abetting, counselling or procuring, or being art and part in, the commission of an offence of corporate homicide.

19 Convictions under this Act and under health and safety legislation

(1) Where in the same proceedings there is—

(a) a charge of corporate manslaughter or corporate homicide arising out of a particular set of circumstances, and
(b) a charge against the same defendant of a health and safety offence arising out of some or all of those circumstances,

the jury may, if the interests of justice so require, be invited to return a verdict on each charge.

(2) An organisation that has been convicted of corporate manslaughter or corporate homicide arising out of a particular set of circumstances may, if the interests of justice so require, be charged with a health and safety offence arising out of some or all of those circumstances.

(3) In this section "health and safety offence" means an offence under any health and safety legislation.

20 Abolition of liability of corporations for manslaughter at common law

The common law offence of manslaughter by gross negligence is abolished in its application to corporations, and in any application it has to other organisations to which section 1 applies.

General and supplemental

21–24 *omitted*

25 Interpretation

In this Act—

"armed forces" has the meaning given by section 12(1);

"corporation" does not include a corporation sole but includes any body corporate wherever incorporated;

"employee" means an individual who works under a contract of employment or apprenticeship (whether express or implied and, if express, whether oral or in writing), and related expressions are to be construed accordingly; see also sections 11(3)(a), 12(2) and 13(3) (which apply for the purposes of section 2);

"employers' association" has the meaning given by section 122 of the Trade Union and Labour Relations (Consolidation) Act 1992 or Article 4 of the Industrial Relations (Northern Ireland) Order 1992;

"enforcement authority" means an authority responsible for the enforcement of any health and safety legislation;

"health and safety legislation" means any statutory provision dealing with health and safety matters, including in particular provision contained in the Health and Safety at Work etc. Act 1974 or the Health and Safety at Work (Northern Ireland) Order 1978 and provision dealing with health and safety matters contained in Part 3 of the Energy Act 2013 (nuclear regulation);

"member", in relation to the armed forces, is to be read in accordance with section 12(3);

"partnership" means—

(a) a partnership within the Partnership Act 1890, or

(b) a limited partnership registered under the Limited Partnerships Act 1907,

or a firm or entity of a similar character formed under the law of a country or territory outside the United Kingdom;

"police force" has the meaning given by section 13(1); "premises" includes land, buildings and moveable structures;

"public authority" has the same meaning as in section 6 of the Human Rights Act 1998 (disregarding subsections (3)(a) and (4) of that section);

"publicity order" means an order under section 10(1); "remedial order" means an order under section 9(1);

"statutory provision", except in section 15, means provision contained in, or in an instrument made under, any Act, any Act of the Scottish Parliament or any Northern Ireland legislation;

"trade union" has the meaning given by section 1 of the Trade Union and Labour Relations (Consolidation) Act 1992 or Article 3 of the Industrial Relations (Northern Ireland) Order 1992.

26 *omitted*

27 Commencement and savings

(1) The preceding provisions of this Act come into force in accordance with provision made by order by the Secretary of State.

(1A) The power in subsection (1) is exercisable by the Department of Justice in Northern Ireland (and not by the Secretary of State) for the purposes of the law of Northern Ireland.

(2) An order bringing into force paragraph (d) of section 2(1) is subject to affirmative resolution procedure.

(3) Section 1 does not apply in relation to anything done or omitted before the commencement of that section.

(4) Section 20 does not affect any liability, investigation, legal proceeding or penalty for or in respect of an offence committed wholly or partly before the commencement of that section.

(5) For the purposes of subsection (4) an offence is committed wholly or partly before the commencement of section 20 if any of the conduct or events alleged to constitute the offence occurred before that commencement.

28 Extent and territorial application

(1) Subject to subsection (2), this Act extends to England and Wales, Scotland and Northern Ireland.

(2) An amendment made by this Act extends to the same part or parts of the United Kingdom as the provision to which it relates.

(3) Section 1 applies if the harm resulting in death is sustained in the United Kingdom or—

(a) within the seaward limits of the territorial sea adjacent to the United Kingdom;
(b) on a ship registered under Part 2 of the Merchant Shipping Act 1995;
(c) on a British-controlled aircraft as defined in section 92 of the Civil Aviation Act 1982;
(d) on a British-controlled hovercraft within the meaning of that section as applied in relation to hovercraft by virtue of provision made under the Hovercraft Act 1968;
(e) in any place to which an Order in Council under section 10(1) of the Petroleum Act 1998 applies (criminal jurisdiction in relation to offshore activities).

(4) For the purposes of subsection (3)(b) to (d) harm sustained on a ship, aircraft or hovercraft includes harm sustained by a person who—
(a) is then no longer on board the ship, aircraft or hovercraft in consequence of the wrecking of it or of some other mishap affecting it or occurring on it, and
(b) sustains the harm in consequence of that event.

29 Short title

This Act may be cited as the Corporate Manslaughter and Corporate Homicide Act 2007.

BRIBERY ACT 2010
(2010, c. 23)

General bribery offences

1 Offences of bribing another person

(1) A person ("P") is guilty of an offence if either of the following cases applies.
(2) Case 1 is where—
(a) P offers, promises or gives a financial or other advantage to another person, and
(b) P intends the advantage—
(i) to induce a person to perform improperly a relevant function or activity, or
(ii) to reward a person for the improper performance of such a function or activity.
(3) Case 2 is where—
(a) P offers, promises or gives a financial or other advantage to another person, and
(b) P knows or believes that the acceptance of the advantage would itself constitute the improper performance of a relevant function or activity.
(4) In case 1 it does not matter whether the person to whom the advantage is offered, promised or given is the same person as the person who is to perform, or has performed, the function or activity concerned.
(5) In cases 1 and 2 it does not matter whether the advantage is offered, promised or given by P directly or through a third party.

2 Offences relating to being bribed

(1) A person ("R") is guilty of an offence if any of the following cases applies.
(2) Case 3 is where R requests, agrees to receive or accepts a financial or other advantage intending that, in consequence, a relevant function or activity should be performed improperly (whether by R or another person).
(3) Case 4 is where—
(a) R requests, agrees to receive or accepts a financial or other advantage, and
(b) the request, agreement or acceptance itself constitutes the improper performance by R of a relevant function or activity.
(4) Case 5 is where R requests, agrees to receive or accepts a financial or other advantage as a reward for the improper performance (whether by R or another person) of a relevant function or activity.
(5) Case 6 is where, in anticipation of or in consequence of R requesting, agreeing to receive or accepting a financial or other advantage, a relevant function or activity is performed improperly—
(a) by R, or
(b) by another person at R's request or with R's assent or acquiescence.
(6) In cases 3 to 6 it does not matter—
(a) whether R requests, agrees to receive or accepts (or is to request, agree to receive or accept) the advantage directly or through a third party,
(b) whether the advantage is (or is to be) for the benefit of R or another person.

(7) In cases 4 to 6 it does not matter whether R knows or believes that the performance of the function or activity is improper.

(8) In case 6, where a person other than R is performing the function or activity, it also does not matter whether that person knows or believes that the performance of the function or activity is improper.

3 Function or activity to which bribe relates

(1) For the purposes of this Act a function or activity is a relevant function or activity if—
  (a) it falls within subsection (2), and
  (b) meets one or more of conditions A to C.

(2) The following functions and activities fall within this subsection—
  (a) any function of a public nature,
  (b) any activity connected with a business,
  (c) any activity performed in the course of a person's employment,
  (d) any activity performed by or on behalf of a body of persons (whether corporate or unincorporate).

(3) Condition A is that a person performing the function or activity is expected to perform it in good faith.

(4) Condition B is that a person performing the function or activity is expected to perform it impartially.

(5) Condition C is that a person performing the function or activity is in a position of trust by virtue of performing it.

(6) A function or activity is a relevant function or activity even if it—
  (a) has no connection with the United Kingdom, and
  (b) is performed in a country or territory outside the United Kingdom.

(7) In this section "business" includes trade or profession.

4 Improper performance to which bribe relates

(1) For the purposes of this Act a relevant function or activity—
  (a) is performed improperly if it is performed in breach of a relevant expectation, and
  (b) is to be treated as being performed improperly if there is a failure to perform the function or activity and that failure is itself a breach of a relevant expectation.

(2) In subsection (1) "relevant expectation"—
  (a) in relation to a function or activity which meets condition A or B, means the expectation mentioned in the condition concerned, and
  (b) in relation to a function or activity which meets condition C, means any expectation as to the manner in which, or the reasons for which, the function or activity will be performed that arises from the position of trust mentioned in that condition.

(3) Anything that a person does (or omits to do) arising from or in connection with that person's past performance of a relevant function or activity is to be treated for the purposes of this Act as being done (or omitted) by that person in the performance of that function or activity.

5 Expectation test

(1) For the purposes of sections 3 and 4, the test of what is expected is a test of what a reasonable person in the United Kingdom would expect in relation to the performance of the type of function or activity concerned.

(2) In deciding what such a person would expect in relation to the performance of a function or activity where the performance is not subject to the law of any part of the United Kingdom, any local custom or practice is to be disregarded unless it is permitted or required by the written law applicable to the country or territory concerned.

(3) In subsection (2) "written law" means law contained in—
  (a) any written constitution, or provision made by or under legislation, applicable to the country or territory concerned, or
  (b) any judicial decision which is so applicable and is evidenced in published written sources.

Bribery of foreign public officials

6 Bribery of foreign public officials

(1) A person ("P") who bribes a foreign public official ("F") is guilty of an offence if P's intention is to influence F in F's capacity as a foreign public official.

(2) P must also intend to obtain or retain—
(a) business, or
(b) an advantage in the conduct of business.
(3) P bribes F if, and only if—
(a) directly or through a third party, P offers, promises or gives any financial or other advantage—
(i) to F, or
(ii) to another person at F's request or with F's assent or acquiescence, and
(b) F is neither permitted nor required by the written law applicable to F to be influenced in F's capacity as a foreign public official by the offer, promise or gift.
(4) References in this section to influencing F in F's capacity as a foreign public official mean influencing F in the performance of F's functions as such an official, which includes—
(a) any omission to exercise those functions, and
(b) any use of F's position as such an official, even if not within F's authority.
(5) "Foreign public official" means an individual who—
(a) holds a legislative, administrative or judicial position of any kind, whether appointed or elected, of a country or territory outside the United Kingdom (or any subdivision of such a country or territory),
(b) exercises a public function—
(i) for or on behalf of a country or territory outside the United Kingdom (or any subdivision of such a country or territory), or
(ii) for any public agency or public enterprise of that country or territory (or subdivision), or
(c) is an official or agent of a public international organisation.
(6) "Public international organisation" means an organisation whose members are any of the following—
(a) countries or territories,
(b) governments of countries or territories,
(c) other public international organisations,
(d) a mixture of any of the above.
(7) For the purposes of subsection (3)(b), the written law applicable to F is—
(a) where the performance of the functions of F which P intends to influence would be subject to the law of any part of the United Kingdom, the law of that part of the United Kingdom,
(b) where paragraph (a) does not apply and F is an official or agent of a public international organisation, the applicable written rules of that organisation,
(c) where paragraphs (a) and (b) do not apply, the law of the country or territory in relation to which F is a foreign public official so far as that law is contained in—
(i) any written constitution, or provision made by or under legislation, applicable to the country or territory concerned, or
(ii) any judicial decision which is so applicable and is evidenced in published written sources.
(8) For the purposes of this section, a trade or profession is a business.

Failure of commercial organisations to prevent bribery

7 Failure of commercial organisations to prevent bribery

(1) A relevant commercial organisation ("C") is guilty of an offence under this section if a person ("A") associated with C bribes another person intending—
(a) to obtain or retain business for C, or
(b) to obtain or retain an advantage in the conduct of business for C.
(2) But it is a defence for C to prove that C had in place adequate procedures designed to prevent persons associated with C from undertaking such conduct.
(3) For the purposes of this section, A bribes another person if, and only if, A—
(a) is, or would be, guilty of an offence under section 1 or 6 (whether or not A has been prosecuted for such an offence), or
(b) would be guilty of such an offence if section 12(2)(c) and (4) were omitted.
(4) See section 8 for the meaning of a person associated with C and see section 9 for a duty on the Secretary of State to publish guidance.
(5) In this section—
"partnership" means—

(a) a partnership within the Partnership Act 1890, or
(b) a limited partnership registered under the Limited Partnerships Act 1907,
or a firm or entity of a similar character formed under the law of a country or territory outside the United Kingdom,
"relevant commercial organisation" means—
(a) a body which is incorporated under the law of any part of the United Kingdom and which carries on a business (whether there or elsewhere),
(b) any other body corporate (wherever incorporated) which carries on a business, or part of a business, in any part of the United Kingdom,
(c) a partnership which is formed under the law of any part of the United Kingdom and which carries on a business (whether there or elsewhere), or
(d) any other partnership (wherever formed) which carries on a business, or part of a business, in any part of the United Kingdom,
and, for the purposes of this section, a trade or profession is a business.

8 Meaning of associated person

(1) For the purposes of section 7, a person ("A") is associated with C if (disregarding any bribe under consideration) A is a person who performs services for or on behalf of C.
(2) The capacity in which A performs services for or on behalf of C does not matter.
(3) Accordingly A may (for example) be C's employee, agent or subsidiary.
(4) Whether or not A is a person who performs services for or on behalf of C is to be determined by reference to all the relevant circumstances and not merely by reference to the nature of the relationship between A and C.
(5) But if A is an employee of C, it is to be presumed unless the contrary is shown that A is a person who performs services for or on behalf of C.

9 Guidance about commercial organisations preventing bribery

(1) The Secretary of State must publish guidance about procedures that relevant commercial organisations can put in place to prevent persons associated with them from bribing as mentioned in section 7(1).
(2) The Secretary of State may, from time to time, publish revisions to guidance under this section or revised guidance.
(3) The Secretary of State must consult the Scottish Ministers and the Department of Justice in Northern Ireland before publishing anything under this section.
(4) Publication under this section is to be in such manner as the Secretary of State considers appropriate.
(5) Expressions used in this section have the same meaning as in section 7.

Prosecution and penalties

10 Consent to prosecution

(1) No proceedings for an offence under this Act may be instituted in England and Wales except by or with the consent of—
(a) the Director of Public Prosecutions,
(b) the Director of the Serious Fraud Office, or
(c) ...
(2) No proceedings for an offence under this Act may be instituted in Northern Ireland except by or with the consent of—
(a) the Director of Public Prosecutions for Northern Ireland, or
(b) the Director of the Serious Fraud Office.
(3) No proceedings for an offence under this Act may be instituted in England and Wales or Northern Ireland by a person—
(a) who is acting—
(i) under the direction or instruction of the Director of Public Prosecutions or the Director of the Serious Fraud Office, or
(ii) on behalf of such a Director, or
(b) to whom such a function has been assigned by such a Director, except with the consent of the Director concerned to the institution of the proceedings.
(4) The Director of Public Prosecutions, the Director of the Serious Fraud Office and the Director of Revenue and Customs Prosecutions must exercise personally any function under subsection (1), (2) or (3) of giving consent.

(5) The only exception is if—
(a) the Director concerned is unavailable, and
(b) there is another person who is designated in writing by the Director acting personally as the person who is authorised to exercise any such function when the Director is unavailable.
(6) In that case, the other person may exercise the function but must do so personally.
(7) Subsections (4) to (6) apply instead of any other provisions which would otherwise have enabled any function of the Director of Public Prosecutions or the Director of the Serious Fraud Office under subsection (1), (2) or (3) of giving consent to be exercised by a person other than the Director concerned.
(8) No proceedings for an offence under this Act may be instituted in Northern Ireland by virtue of section 36 of the Justice (Northern Ireland) Act 2002 (delegation of the functions of the Director of Public Prosecutions for Northern Ireland to persons other than the Deputy Director) except with the consent of the Director of Public Prosecutions for Northern Ireland to the institution of the proceedings.
(9) The Director of Public Prosecutions for Northern Ireland must exercise personally any function under subsection (2) or (8) of giving consent unless the function is exercised personally by the Deputy Director of Public Prosecutions for Northern Ireland by virtue of section 30(4) or (7) of the Act of 2002 (powers of Deputy Director to exercise functions of Director).
(10) Subsection (9) applies instead of section 36 of the Act of 2002 in relation to the functions of the Director of Public Prosecutions for Northern Ireland and the Deputy Director of Public Prosecutions for Northern Ireland under, or (as the case may be) by virtue of, subsections (2) and (8) above of giving consent.

11 Penalties

(1) An individual guilty of an offence under section 1, 2 or 6 is liable—
(a) on summary conviction, to imprisonment for a term not exceeding 12 months, or to a fine not exceeding the statutory maximum, or to both,
(b) on conviction on indictment, to imprisonment for a term not exceeding 10 years, or to a fine, or to both.
(2) Any other person guilty of an offence under section 1, 2 or 6 is liable—
(a) on summary conviction, to a fine not exceeding the statutory maximum,
(b) on conviction on indictment, to a fine.
(3) A person guilty of an offence under section 7 is liable on conviction on indictment to a fine.
(4) The reference in subsection (1)(a) to 12 months is to be read—
(a) in its application to England and Wales in relation to an offence committed before the commencement of section 154(1) of the Criminal Justice Act 2003, and
(b) in its application to Northern Ireland, as a reference to 6 months.

Other provisions about offences

12 Offences under this Act: territorial application

(1) An offence is committed under section 1, 2 or 6 in England and Wales, Scotland or Northern Ireland if any act or omission which forms part of the offence takes place in that part of the United Kingdom.
(2) Subsection (3) applies if—
(a) no act or omission which forms part of an offence under section 1, 2 or 6 takes place in the United Kingdom,
(b) a person's acts or omissions done or made outside the United Kingdom would form part of such an offence if done or made in the United Kingdom, and
(c) that person has a close connection with the United Kingdom.
(3) In such a case—
(a) the acts or omissions form part of the offence referred to in subsection (2)(a), and
(b) proceedings for the offence may be taken at any place in the United Kingdom.
(4) For the purposes of subsection (2)(c) a person has a close connection with the United Kingdom if, and only if, the person was one of the following at the time the acts or omissions concerned were done or made—
(a) a British citizen,
(b) a British overseas territories citizen,
(c) a British National (Overseas),

(d) a British Overseas citizen,
(e) a person who under the British Nationality Act 1981 was a British subject,
(f) a British protected person within the meaning of that Act,
(g) an individual ordinarily resident in the United Kingdom,
(h) a body incorporated under the law of any part of the United Kingdom,
(i) a Scottish partnership.

(5) An offence is committed under section 7 irrespective of whether the acts or omissions which form part of the offence take place in the United Kingdom or elsewhere.

(6) Where no act or omission which forms part of an offence under section 7 takes place in the United Kingdom, proceedings for the offence may be taken at any place in the United Kingdom.

(7) Subsection (8) applies if, by virtue of this section, proceedings for an offence are to be taken in Scotland against a person.

(8) Such proceedings may be taken—
(a) in any sheriff court district in which the person is apprehended or in custody, or
(b) in such sheriff court district as the Lord Advocate may determine.

(9) In subsection (8) "sheriff court district" is to be read in accordance with section 307(1) of the Criminal Procedure (Scotland) Act 1995.

13 Defence for certain bribery offences etc

(1) It is a defence for a person charged with a relevant bribery offence to prove that the person's conduct was necessary for—
(a) the proper exercise of any function of an intelligence service, or
(b) the proper exercise of any function of the armed forces when engaged on active service.

(2)–(6) *omitted*

14 Offences under sections 1, 2 and 6 by bodies corporate etc

(1) This section applies if an offence under section 1, 2 or 6 is committed by a body corporate or a Scottish partnership.

(2) If the offence is proved to have been committed with the consent or connivance of—
(a) a senior officer of the body corporate or Scottish partnership, or
(b) a person purporting to act in such a capacity,
the senior officer or person (as well as the body corporate or partnership) is guilty of the offence and liable to be proceeded against and punished accordingly.

(3) But subsection (2) does not apply, in the case of an offence which is committed under section 1, 2 or 6 by virtue of section 12(2) to (4), to a senior officer or person purporting to act in such a capacity unless the senior officer or person has a close connection with the United Kingdom (within the meaning given by section 12(4)).

(4) In this section—
"director", in relation to a body corporate whose affairs are managed by its members, means a member of the body corporate,
"senior officer" means—
(a) in relation to a body corporate, a director, manager, secretary or other similar officer of the body corporate, and
(b) in relation to a Scottish partnership, a partner in the partnership.

15 Offences under section 7 by partnerships

(1) Proceedings for an offence under section 7 alleged to have been committed by a partnership must be brought in the name of the partnership (and not in that of any of the partners).

(2), (3) *omitted*

(4) In this section "partnership" has the same meaning as in section 7.

Supplementary and final provisions

16 Application to Crown

This Act applies to individuals in the public service of the Crown as it applies to other individuals.

17 Consequential provision

(1) The following common law offences are abolished—
(a) the offences under the law of England and Wales and Northern Ireland of bribery and embracery,

(b) the offences under the law of Scotland of bribery and accepting a bribe.

(2)–(10) *omitted*

18 Extent

(1) ... this Act extends to England and Wales, Scotland and Northern Ireland.

(2)–(5) *omitted*

19 *omitted*

20 Short title

This Act may be cited as the Bribery Act 2010.

PARTNERSHIPS (PROSECUTION) (SCOTLAND) ACT 2013
(2013, c. 21)

Prosecution after dissolution

1 Prosecution of dissolved partnership

(1) This section and sections 2 and 3 apply where—
- (a) a partnership is dissolved, and
- (b) an offence is alleged to have been committed by the partnership before dissolution.

(2) The partnership may be prosecuted, or continue to be prosecuted, for the offence as if it had not been dissolved.

(3) But it is not competent to commence proceedings against the partnership by virtue of subsection (2) if a period of more than 5 years has elapsed since the partnership was dissolved.

(4) For the purposes of subsection (3), proceedings are commenced on the date on which an indictment or, as the case may be, a complaint is served on the partnership.

(5) Subsection (3) is without prejudice to section 136 of the Criminal Procedure (Scotland) Act 1995 (time limit for certain offences).

(6) Where a partnership is convicted of an offence by virtue of subsection (2), any enactment or rule of law relating to the liability of partners on the conviction of a partnership applies as if the partnership had not been dissolved.

(7) But subsection (6) is subject to section 3 (which disapplies provisions restricting payment of fines to partnership assets).

2 Dissolution of partnership: proceedings against former partner or other person

(1) A person, who could have been prosecuted for the offence committed by the partnership had it not been dissolved, may be prosecuted, or may continue to be prosecuted, despite the dissolution.

(2) Subsection (1) applies irrespective of whether the partnership has been or is prosecuted for the offence but not where the partnership has been so prosecuted and acquitted.

(3) In proceedings against a person by virtue of subsection (1), evidence led may include evidence as to the commission of the offence by the partnership.

3 Payment of fine where dissolved partnership convicted

An enactment, in so far as it restricts to payment out of a partnership's assets the payment of a fine imposed on the partnership on its conviction of an offence, does not apply in the case of a partnership which has been dissolved.

Prosecution after change in membership

4 Prosecution of partnership after change in membership

(1) This section and section 5 apply where—
- (a) there is a change in the membership of a partnership,
- (b) the partnership continues to carry on business after the change, and

(c) an offence is alleged to have been committed by the partnership before the change.

(2) The partnership may be prosecuted, or continue to be prosecuted, for the offence.

(3) For the purposes of this section and section 5, any enactment or rule of law, by virtue of which a change in membership of a partnership results in a new partnership being constituted, does not apply.

(4) In this section and section 5, there is a change in the membership of a partnership where—

(a) a partner dies or, if not an individual, ceases to exist,

(b) a partner resigns, retires or is expelled from the partnership, or

(c) a person is admitted as a partner into the partnership.

5 Change in membership of partnership: proceedings against partner or other person

(1) A person, who could have been prosecuted for the offence committed by the partnership had there not been a change in membership, may be prosecuted, or may continue to be prosecuted, for the offence despite the change in membership.

(2) Subsection (1) applies irrespective of whether the partnership has been or is prosecuted for the offence but not where the partnership has been so prosecuted and acquitted.

(3) In proceedings against a person by virtue of subsection (1), evidence led may include evidence as to the commission of the offence by the partnership.

General and miscellaneous

7 Interpretation

In this Act—

(a) references to an offence, in relation to its commission or alleged commission by a partnership, are references to an offence that the partnership is, by virtue of an enactment or rule of law, capable of committing separately from its partners,

(b) "enactment" includes an enactment contained—

(i) in subordinate legislation (within the meaning of the Interpretation Act 1978), or

(ii) in, or in an instrument made under, an Act of the Scottish Parliament.

8 Short title, commencement and extent

(1) This Act may be cited as the Partnerships (Prosecution) (Scotland) Act 2013.

(2) This Act comes into force on the day after the day on which this Act is passed.

(3) This Act applies where the partnership is dissolved or there is a change in the membership of the partnership on or after the day on which this Act comes into force.

(4) This Act (other than section 3)—

(a) applies irrespective of when the offence mentioned in section 1(1)(b) or 4(1)(c) is alleged to have been committed,

(b) applies to any proceedings in relation to such an offence which are ongoing on the day this Act comes into force as it applies in relation to proceedings commenced after that day.

(5) This Act extends only to Scotland.

(6) But the amendment made by section 6(2), and any amendment made by an order under section 6(6), has the same extent as the enactment (or the relevant part of the enactment) to which it relates.

PART II
STATUTORY INSTRUMENTS

INSOLVENCY PROCEEDINGS (MONETARY LIMITS) ORDER 1986 (SI 1986, No. 1996)

4 The amount prescribed for the purposes of paragraphs 9 and 12 of Schedule 6 to the Act (maximum amount for preferential status of employees' claims for remuneration and under the Reserve Forces (Safeguard of Employment) Act 1985) is £800.

FINANCIAL SERVICES AND MARKETS ACT 2000 (PRESCRIBED MARKETS AND QUALIFYING INVESTMENTS) ORDER 2001 (SI 2001, No. 996)

1 Citation

This Order may be cited as the Financial Services and Markets Act 2000 (Prescribed Markets and Qualifying Investments) Order 2001.

2 Commencement

This Order comes into force on the day on which section 123 of the Act (power to impose penalties in cases of market abuse) comes into force.

3 Interpretation

In this Order—

"the Act" means the Financial Services and Markets Act 2000;

"regulated market" has the meaning given in Article 4.1.14 of the markets in financial instruments directive; and

"auctioned products" has the meaning given in Article 4 of Commission Regulation (EU) No 1031/2010 on the timing, administration and other aspects of auctioning of greenhouse gas emission allowances pursuant to Directive 2003/87/EC of the European Parliament and of the Council establishing a scheme for greenhouse gas emission allowances trading within the Community;

"emission allowance auctioning regulation" means Commission Regulation (EU) No 1031/2010 of 12 November 2010 on the timing, administration and other aspects of auctioning of greenhouse gas emission allowances pursuant to the emission allowance trading directive;

"recognised auction platform" means a recognised investment exchange in relation to which there is in force a recognition order made under regulation 2 of the Recognised Auction Platforms Regulations 2011 (recognition orders);

"UK recognised investment exchange" means a body corporate or unincorporated association in respect of which there is in effect a recognition order made under section 290(1)(a) of the Act (recognition orders in respect of investment exchanges other than overseas investment exchanges).

4 Prescribed Markets and auction platforms

(1) There are prescribed, as markets to which subsections (2), (3), (5), (6) and (7) of section 118 apply—
   (a) all markets which are established under the rules of a UK recognised investment exchange,
   (b) the market known as OFEX,
   (c) all other markets which are regulated markets.

(2) There are prescribed, as markets to which subsections (4) and (8) of section 118 apply—
   (a) all markets which are established under the rules of a UK recognised investment exchange;
   (b) the market known as OFEX.

(3) There are prescribed, as auction platforms to which subsections (2), (3), (5), (6) and (7) of section 118 (as modified by the Recognised Auction Platform Regulations 2011) apply, all recognised auction platforms, and all other auction platforms which have been appointed under the emission allowance auctioning regulation.

(4) There are prescribed, as auction platforms to which subsections (4) and (8) of section 118 (as modified by the Recognised Auction Platform Regulations 2011) apply, all recognised auction platforms.

(5) There are prescribed, as auction platforms to which subsection (8A) of section 118 as inserted by the modifications made to that section by the Recognised Auction Platforms Regulations 2011 applies, all auction platforms which have been appointed under the emission allowance auctioning regulation.

5 Qualifying Investments

(1) There are prescribed, as qualifying investments in relation to the markets prescribed by article 4(1) and (2), all financial instruments within the meaning given in Article 1(3) of Directive 2003/6/EC of the European Parliament and the Council of 28 January 2003 on insider dealing and market manipulation (market abuse) as modified by Article 69 of Directive 2004/39/EC on markets in financial instruments.

(2) There are prescribed, as qualifying investments in relation to the auction platforms prescribed by article 4(3) and (4), all auctioned products which are financial instruments within the meaning given in Article 4.1(17) of the market in financial instruments directive.

(3) There are prescribed, as qualifying investments in relation to the auction platforms prescribed by article 4(5), all auctioned products which are not financial instruments within the meaning given in Article 4.1(17) of the market in financial instruments directive.

FINANCIAL SERVICES AND MARKETS ACT 2000 (OFFICIAL LISTING OF SECURITIES) REGULATIONS 2001 (SI 2001, No. 2956)

PART 1
GENERAL

1 Citation and commencement

These Regulations may be cited as the Financial Services and Markets Act 2000 (Official Listing of Securities) Regulations 2001 and come into force on the day on which section 74(1) comes into force.

2 Interpretation

(1) In these Regulations—

"the Act" means the Financial Services and Markets Act 2000;

"the Financial Promotion Order" means the Financial Services and Markets Act 2000 (Financial Promotion) Order 2001;

"issuer" has the same meaning as is given, for the purposes of section 103(1), in regulation 4 below;

"non-listing prospectus" has the meaning given in section 87(2); and

"the Regulated Activities Order" means the Financial Services and Markets Act 2000 (Regulated Activities) Order 2001.

(2) Any reference in these Regulations to a section or Schedule is, unless otherwise stated or unless the context otherwise requires, a reference to that section of or Schedule to the Act.

PART 2
MISCELLANEOUS MATTERS PRESCRIBED FOR THE PURPOSES OF PART VI OF THE ACT

3 Bodies whose securities may not be listed

For the purposes of section 75(3) (which provides that no application for listing may be entertained in respect of securities issued by a body of a prescribed kind) there are prescribed the following kinds of body—

(a) where the securities are securities within the meaning of the Regulated Activities Order, a private company within the meaning of section 4(1) of the Companies Act 2006;

(b) an old public company within the meaning of section 1 of the Companies Consolidation (Consequential Provisions) Act 1985 or article 3 of the Companies Consolidation (Consequential Provisions) (Northern Ireland) Order 1986.

4 Meaning of "issuer"

(1) For the purposes of section 103(1), "issuer" has the meaning given in this regulation.

(2) In relation to certificates or other instruments falling within article 80 of the Regulated Activities Order (certificates representing certain securities), "issuer" means—

(a) …

(b) for all other purposes, the person who issued or is to issue the securities to which the certificates or instruments relate.

(3) In relation to any other securities, "issuer" means the person by whom the securities have been or are to be issued.

5 Meaning of "approved exchange"

For the purposes of paragraph 9 of Schedule 10, "approved exchange" means a recognised investment exchange approved by the Treasury for the purposes of the Public Offers of Securities Regulations 1995 (either generally or in relation to dealings in securities).

PART 3

PERSONS RESPONSIBLE FOR LISTING PARTICULARS, PROSPECTUSES AND NON-LISTING PROSPECTUSES

6 Responsibility for listing particulars

(1) Subject to the following provisions of this Part, for the purposes of Part VI of the Act the persons responsible for listing particulars (including supplementary listing particulars) are—

(a) the issuer of the securities to which the particulars relate;

(b) where the issuer is a body corporate, each person who is a director of that body at the time when the particulars are submitted to the FCA;

(c) where the issuer is a body corporate, each person who has authorised himself to be named, and is named, in the particulars as a director or as having agreed to become a director of that body either immediately or at a future time;

(d) each person who accepts, and is stated in the particulars as accepting, responsibility for the particulars;

(e) each person not falling within any of the foregoing sub-paragraphs who has authorised the contents of the particulars.

(2) A person is not to be treated as responsible for any particulars by virtue of paragraph (1)(b) above if they are published without his knowledge or consent and on becoming aware of their publication he forthwith gives reasonable public notice that they were published without his knowledge or consent.

(3) When accepting responsibility for particulars under paragraph (1)(d) above or authorising their contents under paragraph (1)(e) above, a person may state that he does so only in relation to certain specified parts of the particulars, or only in certain specified respects, and in such a case he is responsible under paragraph (1)(d) or (e) above—

(a) only to the extent specified; and

(b) only if the material in question is included in (or substantially in) the form and context to which he has agreed.

(4) Nothing in this regulation is to be construed as making a person responsible for any particulars by reason of giving advice as to their contents in a professional capacity.

(5) Where by virtue of this regulation the issuer of any shares pays or is liable to pay compensation under section 90 for loss suffered in respect of shares for which a person has subscribed no account is to be taken of that liability or payment in determining any question as to the amount paid on subscription for those shares or as to the amount paid up or deemed to be paid up on them.

7 Securities issued in connection with takeovers and mergers

(1) This regulation applies where—

(a) listing particulars relate to securities which are to be issued in connection with—

(i) an offer by the issuer (or by a wholly-owned subsidiary of the issuer) for securities issued by another person ("A");

(ii) an agreement for the acquisition by the issuer (or by a wholly-owned subsidiary of the issuer) of securities issued by another person ("A"); or

(iii) any arrangement whereby the whole of the undertaking of another person ("A") is to become the undertaking of the issuer (or of a wholly-owned subsidiary of the issuer, or of a body corporate which will become such a subsidiary by virtue of the arrangement); and

(b) each of the specified persons is responsible by virtue of regulation 6(1)(d) above for any part ("the relevant part") of the particulars relating to A or to the securities or undertaking to which the offer, agreement or arrangement relates.

(2) In paragraph (1)(b) above the "specified persons" are—

(a) A; and

(b) where A is a body corporate—

(i) each person who is a director of A at the time when the particulars are submitted to the FCA; and

(ii) each other person who has authorised himself to be named, and is named, in the particulars as a director of A.

(3) Where this regulation applies, no person is to be treated as responsible for the relevant part of the particulars under regulation 6(1)(a), (b) or (c) above but without prejudice to his being responsible under regulation 6(1)(d).

(4) In this regulation—

(a) "listing particulars" includes supplementary listing particulars; and

(b) "wholly-owned subsidiary" is to be construed in accordance with section 1159 of the Companies Act 2006 (and, in relation to an issuer which is not a body corporate, means a body corporate which would be a wholly-owned subsidiary of the issuer within the meaning of that section if the issuer were a body corporate).

8 Successor companies under legislation relating to electricity

(1) Where—

(a) the same document contains listing particulars relating to the securities of—

(i) two or more successor companies within the meaning of Part II of the Electricity Act 1989, or

(ii) two or more successor companies within the meaning of Part III of the Electricity (Northern Ireland) Order 1992; and

(b) the responsibility of any person for any information included in the document ("the relevant information") is stated in the document to be confined to its inclusion as part of the particulars relating to the securities of any one of those companies,

that person is not to be treated as responsible, by virtue of regulation 6 above, for the relevant information in so far as it is stated in the document to form part of the particulars relating to the securities of any other of those companies.

(2) "Listing particulars" includes supplementary listing particulars.

9 Specialist securities

(1) This regulation applies where listing particulars relate to securities of a kind specified by listing rules for the purposes of section 82(1)(c), other than securities which are to be issued in the circumstances mentioned in regulation 7(1)(a) above.

(2) No person is to be treated as responsible for the particulars under regulation 6(1)(a), (b) or (c) above but without prejudice to his being responsible under regulation 6(1)(d).

(3) "Listing particulars" includes supplementary listing particulars.

INSOLVENCY ACT 1986 (PRESCRIBED PART) ORDER 2003 (SI 2003, No. 2097)

1 Citation, Commencement and Interpretation

(1) This Order may be cited as the Insolvency Act 1986 (Prescribed Part) Order 2003 and shall come into force on 15th September 2003.

(2) In this order "the 1986 Act" means the Insolvency Act 1986.

2 Minimum value of the company's net property

For the purposes of section 176A(3)(a) of the 1986 Act the minimum value of the company's net property is £10,000.

3 **Calculation of prescribed part**

(1) The prescribed part of the company's net property to be made available for the satisfaction of unsecured debts of the company pursuant to section 176A of the 1986 Act shall be calculated as follows—

(a) where the company's net property does not exceed £10,000 in value, 50% of that property;

(b) subject to paragraph (2), where the company's net property exceeds £10,000 in value the sum of—

(i) 50% of the first £10,000 in value; and

(ii) 20% of that part of the company's net property which exceeds £10,000 in value.

(2) The value of the prescribed part of the company's net property to be made available for the satisfaction of unsecured debts of the company pursuant to section 176A shall not exceed £600,000.

COMPANIES (REGISTRATION) REGULATIONS 2008 (SI 2008, No. 3014)

1 **Citation, commencement and interpretation**

(1) These Regulations may be cited as the Companies (Registration) Regulations 2008 and come into force on 1st October 2009.

(2) In these Regulations "the Act" means the Companies Act 2006.

2 **Memorandum of association**

For the purposes of section 8 of the Act—

(a) the memorandum of association of a company having a share capital shall be in the form set out in Schedule 1; and

(b) the memorandum of association of a company not having a share capital shall be in the form set out in Schedule 2.

3 **Statement of capital and initial shareholdings**

For the purposes of section 10(3) of the Act, the statement of capital and initial shareholdings shall contain the name and address of each subscriber to the memorandum of association.

4 **Statement of guarantee**

For the purposes of section 11(2) of the Act, the statement of guarantee shall contain the name and address of each subscriber to the memorandum of association.

5 **Form of assent for re-registration of private limited company as unlimited**

The form set out in Schedule 3 is the form prescribed for the purposes of section 103(2)(a) of the Act.

6 **Form of assent for re-registration of public company as private and unlimited**

The form set out in Schedule 4 is the form prescribed for the purposes of section 110(2)(a) of the Act.

SCHEDULE 1 **Regulation 2(a)**

COMPANY HAVING A SHARE CAPITAL

Memorandum of association of [*insert name of company*]

Each subscriber to this memorandum of association wishes to form a company under the Companies Act 2006 and agrees to become a member of the company and to take at least one share.

Name of each subscriber	*Authentication by each subscriber*

Dated

SCHEDULE 2 **Regulation 2(b)**
COMPANY HAVING A SHARE CAPITAL

Memorandum of association of [*insert name of company*]
Each subscriber to this memorandum of association wishes to form a company under the Companies Act 2006 and agrees to become a member of the company.

Name of each subscriber	*Authentication by each subscriber*

Dated

SCHEDULES 3 AND 4
OMITTED

COMPANIES (MODEL ARTICLES) REGULATIONS 2008 (SI 2008, No. 3229)

1 Citation and Commencement
These Regulations may be cited as the Companies (Model Articles) Regulations 2008 and come into force on 1st October 2009.

2 Model articles for private companies limited by shares
Schedule 1 to these Regulations prescribes the model articles of association for private companies limited by shares.

3 Model articles for private companies limited by guarantee
Schedule 2 to these Regulations prescribes the model articles of association for private companies limited by guarantee.

4 Model articles for public companies
Schedule 3 to these Regulations prescribes the model articles of association for public companies.

SCHEDULE 1 **Regulation 2**
MODEL ARTICLES FOR PRIVATE COMPANIES LIMITED BY SHARES

PART 1
INTERPRETATION AND LIMITATION OF LIABILITY

1 Defined terms
In the articles, unless the context requires otherwise—

"articles" means the company's articles of association;

"bankruptcy" includes individual insolvency proceedings in a jurisdiction other than England and Wales or Northern Ireland which have an effect similar to that of bankruptcy;

"chairman" has the meaning given in article 12;

"chairman of the meeting" has the meaning given in article 39;

"Companies Acts" means the Companies Acts (as defined in section 2 of the Companies Act 2006), in so far as they apply to the company;

"director" means a director of the company, and includes any person occupying the position of director, by whatever name called;

"distribution recipient" has the meaning given in article 31;

"document" includes, unless otherwise specified, any document sent or supplied in electronic form;

"electronic form" has the meaning given in section 1168 of the Companies Act 2006;

"fully paid" in relation to a share, means that the nominal value and any premium to be paid to the company in respect of that share have been paid to the company;

"hard copy form" has the meaning given in section 1168 of the Companies Act 2006;

"holder" in relation to shares means the person whose name is entered in the register of members as the holder of the shares;

"instrument" means a document in hard copy form;
"ordinary resolution" has the meaning given in section 282 of the Companies Act 2006;
"paid" means paid or credited as paid;
"participate", in relation to a directors' meeting, has the meaning given in article 10;
"proxy notice" has the meaning given in article 45;
"shareholder" means a person who is the holder of a share;
"shares" means shares in the company;
"special resolution" has the meaning given in section 283 of the Companies Act 2006;
"subsidiary" has the meaning given in section 1159 of the Companies Act 2006;
"transmittee" means a person entitled to a share by reason of the death or bankruptcy of a shareholder or otherwise by operation of law; and
"writing" means the representation or reproduction of words, symbols or other information in a visible form by any method or combination of methods, whether sent or supplied in electronic form or otherwise.

Unless the context otherwise requires, other words or expressions contained in these articles bear the same meaning as in the Companies Act 2006 as in force on the date when these articles become binding on the company.

2 Liability of members

The liability of the members is limited to the amount, if any, unpaid on the shares held by them.

PART 2
DIRECTORS

DIRECTORS' POWERS AND RESPONSIBILITIES

3 Directors' general authority

Subject to the articles, the directors are responsible for the management of the company's business, for which purpose they may exercise all the powers of the company.

4 Shareholders' reserve power

(1) The shareholders may, by special resolution, direct the directors to take, or refrain from taking, specified action.
(2) No such special resolution invalidates anything which the directors have done before the passing of the resolution.

5 Directors may delegate

(1) Subject to the articles, the directors may delegate any of the powers which are conferred on them under the articles—
  (a) to such person or committee;
  (b) by such means (including by power of attorney);
  (c) to such an extent;
  (d) in relation to such matters or territories; and
  (e) on such terms and conditions; as they think fit.
(2) If the directors so specify, any such delegation may authorise further delegation of the directors' powers by any person to whom they are delegated.
(3) The directors may revoke any delegation in whole or part, or alter its terms and conditions.

6 Committees

(1) Committees to which the directors delegate any of their powers must follow procedures which are based as far as they are applicable on those provisions of the articles which govern the taking of decisions by directors.
(2) The directors may make rules of procedure for all or any committees, which prevail over rules derived from the articles if they are not consistent with them.

DECISION-MAKING BY DIRECTORS

7 Directors to take decisions collectively

(1) The general rule about decision-making by directors is that any decision of the directors must be either a majority decision at a meeting or a decision taken in accordance with article 8.

(2) If—
(a) the company only has one director, and
(b) no provision of the articles requires it to have more than one director,
the general rule does not apply, and the director may take decisions without regard to any of the provisions of the articles relating to directors' decision-making.

8 Unanimous decisions

(1) A decision of the directors is taken in accordance with this article when all eligible directors indicate to each other by any means that they share a common view on a matter.
(2) Such a decision may take the form of a resolution in writing, copies of which have been signed by each eligible director or to which each eligible director has otherwise indicated agreement in writing.
(3) References in this article to eligible directors are to directors who would have been entitled to vote on the matter had it been proposed as a resolution at a directors' meeting.
(4) A decision may not be taken in accordance with this article if the eligible directors would not have formed a quorum at such a meeting.

9 Calling a directors' meeting

(1) Any director may call a directors' meeting by giving notice of the meeting to the directors or by authorising the company secretary (if any) to give such notice.
(2) Notice of any directors' meeting must indicate—
(a) its proposed date and time;
(b) where it is to take place; and
(c) if it is anticipated that directors participating in the meeting will not be in the same place, how it is proposed that they should communicate with each other during the meeting.
(3) Notice of a directors' meeting must be given to each director, but need not be in writing.
(4) Notice of a directors' meeting need not be given to directors who waive their entitlement to notice of that meeting, by giving notice to that effect to the company not more than 7 days after the date on which the meeting is held. Where such notice is given after the meeting has been held, that does not affect the validity of the meeting, or of any business conducted at it.

10 Participation in directors' meetings

(1) Subject to the articles, directors participate in a directors' meeting, or part of a directors' meeting, when—
(a) the meeting has been called and takes place in accordance with the articles, and
(b) they can each communicate to the others any information or opinions they have on any particular item of the business of the meeting.
(2) In determining whether directors are participating in a directors' meeting, it is irrelevant where any director is or how they communicate with each other.
(3) If all the directors participating in a meeting are not in the same place, they may decide that the meeting is to be treated as taking place wherever any of them is.

11 Quorum for directors' meetings

(1) At a directors' meeting, unless a quorum is participating, no proposal is to be voted on, except a proposal to call another meeting.
(2) The quorum for directors' meetings may be fixed from time to time by a decision of the directors, but it must never be less than two, and unless otherwise fixed it is two.
(3) If the total number of directors for the time being is less than the quorum required, the directors must not take any decision other than a decision—
(a) to appoint further directors, or
(b) to call a general meeting so as to enable the shareholders to appoint further directors.

12 Chairing of directors' meetings

(1) The directors may appoint a director to chair their meetings.
(2) The person so appointed for the time being is known as the chairman.
(3) The directors may terminate the chairman's appointment at any time.
(4) If the chairman is not participating in a directors' meeting within ten minutes of the time at which it was to start, the participating directors must appoint one of themselves to chair it.

13 Casting vote

(1) If the numbers of votes for and against a proposal are equal, the chairman or other director chairing the meeting has a casting vote.
(2) But this does not apply if, in accordance with the articles, the chairman or other director is not to be counted as participating in the decision-making process for quorum or voting purposes.

14 Conflicts of interest

(1) If a proposed decision of the directors is concerned with an actual or proposed transaction or arrangement with the company in which a director is interested, that director is not to be counted as participating in the decision-making process for quorum or voting purposes.
(2) But if paragraph (3) applies, a director who is interested in an actual or proposed transaction or arrangement with the company is to be counted as participating in the decision-making process for quorum and voting purposes.
(3) This paragraph applies when—
 (a) the company by ordinary resolution disapplies the provision of the articles which would otherwise prevent a director from being counted as participating in the decision-making process;
 (b) the director's interest cannot reasonably be regarded as likely to give rise to a conflict of interest; or
 (c) the director's conflict of interest arises from a permitted cause.
(4) For the purposes of this article, the following are permitted causes—
 (a) a guarantee given, or to be given, by or to a director in respect of an obligation incurred by or on behalf of the company or any of its subsidiaries;
 (b) subscription, or an agreement to subscribe, for shares or other securities of the company or any of its subsidiaries, or to underwrite, sub-underwrite, or guarantee subscription for any such shares or securities; and
 (c) arrangements pursuant to which benefits are made available to employees and directors or former employees and directors of the company or any of its subsidiaries which do not provide special benefits for directors or former directors.
(5) For the purposes of this article, references to proposed decisions and decision-making processes include any directors' meeting or part of a directors' meeting.
(6) Subject to paragraph (7), if a question arises at a meeting of directors or of a committee of directors as to the right of a director to participate in the meeting (or part of the meeting) for voting or quorum purposes, the question may, before the conclusion of the meeting, be referred to the chairman whose ruling in relation to any director other than the chairman is to be final and conclusive.
(7) If any question as to the right to participate in the meeting (or part of the meeting) should arise in respect of the chairman, the question is to be decided by a decision of the directors at that meeting, for which purpose the chairman is not to be counted as participating in the meeting (or that part of the meeting) for voting or quorum purposes.

15 Records of decisions to be kept

The directors must ensure that the company keeps a record, in writing, for at least 10 years from the date of the decision recorded, of every unanimous or majority decision taken by the directors.

16 Directors' discretion to make further rules

Subject to the articles, the directors may make any rule which they think fit about how they take decisions, and about how such rules are to be recorded or communicated to directors.

APPOINTMENT OF DIRECTORS

17 Methods of appointing directors

(1) Any person who is willing to act as a director, and is permitted by law to do so, may be appointed to be a director—
 (a) by ordinary resolution, or
 (b) by a decision of the directors.
(2) In any case where, as a result of death, the company has no shareholders and no directors, the personal representatives of the last shareholder to have died have the right, by notice in writing, to appoint a person to be a director.

(3) For the purposes of paragraph (2), where 2 or more shareholders die in circumstances rendering it uncertain who was the last to die, a younger shareholder is deemed to have survived an older shareholder.

18 Termination of director's appointment

A person ceases to be a director as soon as—

(a) that person ceases to be a director by virtue of any provision of the Companies Act 2006 or is prohibited from being a director by law;
(b) a bankruptcy order is made against that person;
(c) a composition is made with that person's creditors generally in satisfaction of that person's debts;
(d) a registered medical practitioner who is treating that person gives a written opinion to the company stating that that person has become physically or mentally incapable of acting as a director and may remain so for more than three months;
(e) ...
(f) notification is received by the company from the director that the director is resigning from office, and such resignation has taken effect in accordance with its terms.

19 Directors' remuneration

(1) Directors may undertake any services for the company that the directors decide.
(2) Directors are entitled to such remuneration as the directors determine—
(a) for their services to the company as directors, and
(b) for any other service which they undertake for the company.
(3) Subject to the articles, a director's remuneration may—
(a) take any form, and
(b) include any arrangements in connection with the payment of a pension, allowance or gratuity, or any death, sickness or disability benefits, to or in respect of that director.
(4) Unless the directors decide otherwise, directors' remuneration accrues from day to day.
(5) Unless the directors decide otherwise, directors are not accountable to the company for any remuneration which they receive as directors or other officers or employees of the company's subsidiaries or of any other body corporate in which the company is interested.

20 Directors' expenses

The company may pay any reasonable expenses which the directors properly incur in connection with their attendance at—

(a) meetings of directors or committees of directors,
(b) general meetings, or
(c) separate meetings of the holders of any class of shares or of debentures of the company,

or otherwise in connection with the exercise of their powers and the discharge of their responsibilities in relation to the company.

PART 3
SHARES AND DISTRIBUTIONS

SHARES

21 All shares to be fully paid up

(1) No share is to be issued for less than the aggregate of its nominal value and any premium to be paid to the company in consideration for its issue.
(2) This does not apply to shares taken on the formation of the company by the subscribers to the company's memorandum.

22 Powers to issue different classes of share

(1) Subject to the articles, but without prejudice to the rights attached to any existing share, the company may issue shares with such rights or restrictions as may be determined by ordinary resolution.

(2) The company may issue shares which are to be redeemed, or are liable to be redeemed at the option of the company or the holder, and the directors may determine the terms, conditions and manner of redemption of any such shares.

23 Company not bound by less than absolute interests

Except as required by law, no person is to be recognised by the company as holding any share upon any trust, and except as otherwise required by law or the articles, the company is not in any way to be bound by or recognise any interest in a share other than the holder's absolute ownership of it and all the rights attaching to it.

24 Share certificates

(1) The company must issue each shareholder, free of charge, with one or more certificates in respect of the shares which that shareholder holds.

(2) Every certificate must specify—

- (a) in respect of how many shares, of what class, it is issued;
- (b) the nominal value of those shares;
- (c) that the shares are fully paid; and
- (d) any distinguishing numbers assigned to them.

(3) No certificate may be issued in respect of shares of more than one class.

(4) If more than one person holds a share, only one certificate may be issued in respect of it.

(5) Certificates must—

- (a) have affixed to them the company's common seal, or
- (b) be otherwise executed in accordance with the Companies Acts.

25 Replacement share certificates

(1) If a certificate issued in respect of a shareholder's shares is—

- (a) damaged or defaced, or
- (b) said to be lost, stolen or destroyed,

that shareholder is entitled to be issued with a replacement certificate in respect of the same shares.

(2) A shareholder exercising the right to be issued with such a replacement certificate—

- (a) may at the same time exercise the right to be issued with a single certificate or separate certificates;
- (b) must return the certificate which is to be replaced to the company if it is damaged or defaced; and
- (c) must comply with such conditions as to evidence, indemnity and the payment of a reasonable fee as the directors decide.

26 Share transfers

(1) Shares may be transferred by means of an instrument of transfer in any usual form or any other form approved by the directors, which is executed by or on behalf of the transferor.

(2) No fee may be charged for registering any instrument of transfer or other document relating to or affecting the title to any share.

(3) The company may retain any instrument of transfer which is registered.

(4) The transferor remains the holder of a share until the transferee's name is entered in the register of members as holder of it.

(5) The directors may refuse to register the transfer of a share, and if they do so, the instrument of transfer must be returned to the transferee with the notice of refusal unless they suspect that the proposed transfer may be fraudulent.

27 Transmission of shares

(1) If title to a share passes to a transmittee, the company may only recognise the transmittee as having any title to that share.

(2) A transmittee who produces such evidence of entitlement to shares as the directors may properly require—

- (a) may, subject to the articles, choose either to become the holder of those shares or to have them transferred to another person, and
- (b) subject to the articles, and pending any transfer of the shares to another person, has the same rights as the holder had.

(3) But transmittees do not have the right to attend or vote at a general meeting, or agree to a proposed written resolution, in respect of shares to which they are entitled, by reason of the holder's death or bankruptcy or otherwise, unless they become the holders of those shares.

28 Exercise of transmittees' rights

(1) Transmittees who wish to become the holders of shares to which they have become entitled must notify the company in writing of that wish.

(2) If the transmittee wishes to have a share transferred to another person, the transmittee must execute an instrument of transfer in respect of it.

(3) Any transfer made or executed under this article is to be treated as if it were made or executed by the person from whom the transmittee has derived rights in respect of the share, and as if the event which gave rise to the transmission had not occurred.

29 Transmittees bound by prior notices

If a notice is given to a shareholder in respect of shares and a transmittee is entitled to those shares, the transmittee is bound by the notice if it was given to the shareholder before the transmittee's name has been entered in the register of members.

DIVIDENDS AND OTHER DISTRIBUTIONS

30 Procedure for declaring dividends

(1) The company may by ordinary resolution declare dividends, and the directors may decide to pay interim dividends.

(2) A dividend must not be declared unless the directors have made a recommendation as to its amount. Such a dividend must not exceed the amount recommended by the directors.

(3) No dividend may be declared or paid unless it is in accordance with shareholders' respective rights.

(4) Unless the shareholders' resolution to declare or directors' decision to pay a dividend, or the terms on which shares are issued, specify otherwise, it must be paid by reference to each shareholder's holding of shares on the date of the resolution or decision to declare or pay it.

(5) If the company's share capital is divided into different classes, no interim dividend may be paid on shares carrying deferred or non-preferred rights if, at the time of payment, any preferential dividend is in arrear.

(6) The directors may pay at intervals any dividend payable at a fixed rate if it appears to them that the profits available for distribution justify the payment.

(7) If the directors act in good faith, they do not incur any liability to the holders of shares conferring preferred rights for any loss they may suffer by the lawful payment of an interim dividend on shares with deferred or non-preferred rights.

31 Payment of dividends and other distributions

(1) Where a dividend or other sum which is a distribution is payable in respect of a share, it must be paid by one or more of the following means—

(a) transfer to a bank or building society account specified by the distribution recipient either in writing or as the directors may otherwise decide;

(b) sending a cheque made payable to the distribution recipient by post to the distribution recipient at the distribution recipient's registered address (if the distribution recipient is a holder of the share), or (in any other case) to an address specified by the distribution recipient either in writing or as the directors may otherwise decide;

(c) sending a cheque made payable to such person by post to such person at such address as the distribution recipient has specified either in writing or as the directors may otherwise decide; or

(d) any other means of payment as the directors agree with the distribution recipient either in writing or by such other means as the directors decide.

(2) In the articles, "the distribution recipient" means, in respect of a share in respect of which a dividend or other sum is payable—

(a) the holder of the share; or

(b) if the share has two or more joint holders, whichever of them is named first in the register of members; or

(c) if the holder is no longer entitled to the share by reason of death or bankruptcy, or otherwise by operation of law, the transmittee.

32 No interest on distributions

The company may not pay interest on any dividend or other sum payable in respect of a share unless otherwise provided by—

(a) the terms on which the share was issued, or

(b) the provisions of another agreement between the holder of that share and the company.

33 Unclaimed distributions

(1) All dividends or other sums which are—

(a) payable in respect of shares, and

(b) unclaimed after having been declared or become payable,

may be invested or otherwise made use of by the directors for the benefit of the company until claimed.

(2) The payment of any such dividend or other sum into a separate account does not make the company a trustee in respect of it.

(3) If—

(a) twelve years have passed from the date on which a dividend or other sum became due for payment, and

(b) the distribution recipient has not claimed it,

the distribution recipient is no longer entitled to that dividend or other sum and it ceases to remain owing by the company.

34 Non-cash distributions

(1) Subject to the terms of issue of the share in question, the company may, by ordinary resolution on the recommendation of the directors, decide to pay all or part of a dividend or other distribution payable in respect of a share by transferring non-cash assets of equivalent value (including, without limitation, shares or other securities in any company).

(2) For the purposes of paying a non-cash distribution, the directors may make whatever arrangements they think fit, including, where any difficulty arises regarding the distribution—

(a) fixing the value of any assets;

(b) paying cash to any distribution recipient on the basis of that value in order to adjust the rights of recipients; and

(c) vesting any assets in trustees.

35 Waiver of distributions

Distribution recipients may waive their entitlement to a dividend or other distribution payable in respect of a share by giving the company notice in writing to that effect, but if—

(a) the share has more than one holder, or

(b) more than one person is entitled to the share, whether by reason of the death or bankruptcy of one or more joint holders, or otherwise,

the notice is not effective unless it is expressed to be given, and signed, by all the holders or persons otherwise entitled to the share.

CAPITALISATION OF PROFITS

36 Authority to capitalise and appropriation of capitalised sums

(1) Subject to the articles, the directors may, if they are so authorised by an ordinary resolution—

(a) decide to capitalise any profits of the company (whether or not they are available for distribution) which are not required for paying a preferential dividend, or any sum standing to the credit of the company's share premium account or capital redemption reserve; and

(b) appropriate any sum which they so decide to capitalise (a "capitalised sum") to the persons who would have been entitled to it if it were distributed by way of dividend (the "persons entitled") and in the same proportions.

(2) Capitalised sums must be applied—

(a) on behalf of the persons entitled, and

(b) in the same proportions as a dividend would have been distributed to them.

(3) Any capitalised sum may be applied in paying up new shares of a nominal amount equal to the capitalised sum which are then allotted credited as fully paid to the persons entitled or as they may direct.
(4) A capitalised sum which was appropriated from profits available for distribution may be applied in paying up new debentures of the company which are then allotted credited as fully paid to the persons entitled or as they may direct.
(5) Subject to the articles the directors may—
 (a) apply capitalised sums in accordance with paragraphs (3) and (4) partly in one way and partly in another;
 (b) make such arrangements as they think fit to deal with shares or debentures becoming distributable in fractions under this article (including the issuing of fractional certificates or the making of cash payments); and
 (c) authorise any person to enter into an agreement with the company on behalf of all the persons entitled which is binding on them in respect of the allotment of shares and debentures to them under this article.

PART 4
DECISION-MAKING BY SHAREHOLDERS

ORGANISATION OF GENERAL MEETINGS

37 Attendance and speaking at general meetings

(1) A person is able to exercise the right to speak at a general meeting when that person is in a position to communicate to all those attending the meeting, during the meeting, any information or opinions which that person has on the business of the meeting.
(2) A person is able to exercise the right to vote at a general meeting when—
 (a) that person is able to vote, during the meeting, on resolutions put to the vote at the meeting, and
 (b) that person's vote can be taken into account in determining whether or not such resolutions are passed at the same time as the votes of all the other persons attending the meeting.
(3) The directors may make whatever arrangements they consider appropriate to enable those attending a general meeting to exercise their rights to speak or vote at it.
(4) In determining attendance at a general meeting, it is immaterial whether any two or more members attending it are in the same place as each other.
(5) Two or more persons who are not in the same place as each other attend a general meeting if their circumstances are such that if they have (or were to have) rights to speak and vote at that meeting, they are (or would be) able to exercise them.

38 Quorum for general meetings

No business other than the appointment of the chairman of the meeting is to be transacted at a general meeting if the persons attending it do not constitute a quorum.

39 Chairing general meetings

(1) If the directors have appointed a chairman, the chairman shall chair general meetings if present and willing to do so.
(2) If the directors have not appointed a chairman, or if the chairman is unwilling to chair the meeting or is not present within ten minutes of the time at which a meeting was due to start—
 (a) the directors present, or
 (b) (if no directors are present), the meeting,

must appoint a director or shareholder to chair the meeting, and the appointment of the chairman of the meeting must be the first business of the meeting.
(3) The person chairing a meeting in accordance with this article is referred to as "the chairman of the meeting".

40 Attendance and speaking by directors and non-shareholders

(1) Directors may attend and speak at general meetings, whether or not they are shareholders.
(2) The chairman of the meeting may permit other persons who are not—
 (a) shareholders of the company, or

(b) otherwise entitled to exercise the rights of shareholders in relation to general meetings,

to attend and speak at a general meeting.

41 Adjournment

(1) If the persons attending a general meeting within half an hour of the time at which the meeting was due to start do not constitute a quorum, or if during a meeting a quorum ceases to be present, the chairman of the meeting must adjourn it.

(2) The chairman of the meeting may adjourn a general meeting at which a quorum is present if—

(a) the meeting consents to an adjournment, or

(b) it appears to the chairman of the meeting that an adjournment is necessary to protect the safety of any person attending the meeting or ensure that the business of the meeting is conducted in an orderly manner.

(3) The chairman of the meeting must adjourn a general meeting if directed to do so by the meeting.

(4) When adjourning a general meeting, the chairman of the meeting must—

(a) either specify the time and place to which it is adjourned or state that it is to continue at a time and place to be fixed by the directors, and

(b) have regard to any directions as to the time and place of any adjournment which have been given by the meeting.

(5) If the continuation of an adjourned meeting is to take place more than 14 days after it was adjourned, the company must give at least 7 clear days' notice of it (that is, excluding the day of the adjourned meeting and the day on which the notice is given)—

(a) to the same persons to whom notice of the company's general meetings is required to be given, and

(b) containing the same information which such notice is required to contain.

(6) No business may be transacted at an adjourned general meeting which could not properly have been transacted at the meeting if the adjournment had not taken place.

VOTING AT GENERAL MEETINGS

42 Voting: general

A resolution put to the vote of a general meeting must be decided on a show of hands unless a poll is duly demanded in accordance with the articles.

43 Errors and disputes

(1) No objection may be raised to the qualification of any person voting at a general meeting except at the meeting or adjourned meeting at which the vote objected to is tendered, and every vote not disallowed at the meeting is valid.

(2) Any such objection must be referred to the chairman of the meeting, whose decision is final.

44 Poll votes

(1) A poll on a resolution may be demanded—

(a) in advance of the general meeting where it is to be put to the vote, or

(b) at a general meeting, either before a show of hands on that resolution or immediately after the result of a show of hands on that resolution is declared.

(2) A poll may be demanded by—

(a) the chairman of the meeting;

(b) the directors;

(c) two or more persons having the right to vote on the resolution; or

(d) a person or persons representing not less than one tenth of the total voting rights of all the shareholders having the right to vote on the resolution.

(3) A demand for a poll may be withdrawn if—

(a) the poll has not yet been taken, and

(b) the chairman of the meeting consents to the withdrawal.

(4) Polls must be taken immediately and in such manner as the chairman of the meeting directs.

45 Content of proxy notices

(1) Proxies may only validly be appointed by a notice in writing (a "proxy notice") which—

(a) states the name and address of the shareholder appointing the proxy;
(b) identifies the person appointed to be that shareholder's proxy and the general meeting in relation to which that person is appointed;
(c) is signed by or on behalf of the shareholder appointing the proxy, or is authenticated in such manner as the directors may determine; and
(d) is delivered to the company in accordance with the articles and any instructions contained in the notice of the general meeting to which they relate.

(2) The company may require proxy notices to be delivered in a particular form, and may specify different forms for different purposes.

(3) Proxy notices may specify how the proxy appointed under them is to vote (or that the proxy is to abstain from voting) on one or more resolutions.

(4) Unless a proxy notice indicates otherwise, it must be treated as—
(a) allowing the person appointed under it as a proxy discretion as to how to vote on any ancillary or procedural resolutions put to the meeting, and
(b) appointing that person as a proxy in relation to any adjournment of the general meeting to which it relates as well as the meeting itself.

46 Delivery of proxy notices

(1) A person who is entitled to attend, speak or vote (either on a show of hands or on a poll) at a general meeting remains so entitled in respect of that meeting or any adjournment of it, even though a valid proxy notice has been delivered to the company by or on behalf of that person.

(2) An appointment under a proxy notice may be revoked by delivering to the company a notice in writing given by or on behalf of the person by whom or on whose behalf the proxy notice was given.

(3) A notice revoking a proxy appointment only takes effect if it is delivered before the start of the meeting or adjourned meeting to which it relates.

(4) If a proxy notice is not executed by the person appointing the proxy, it must be accompanied by written evidence of the authority of the person who executed it to execute it on the appointor's behalf.

47 Amendments to resolutions

(1) An ordinary resolution to be proposed at a general meeting may be amended by ordinary resolution if—
(a) notice of the proposed amendment is given to the company in writing by a person entitled to vote at the general meeting at which it is to be proposed not less than 48 hours before the meeting is to take place (or such later time as the chairman of the meeting may determine), and
(b) the proposed amendment does not, in the reasonable opinion of the chairman of the meeting, materially alter the scope of the resolution.

(2) A special resolution to be proposed at a general meeting may be amended by ordinary resolution, if—
(a) the chairman of the meeting proposes the amendment at the general meeting at which the resolution is to be proposed, and
(b) the amendment does not go beyond what is necessary to correct a grammatical or other non-substantive error in the resolution.

(3) If the chairman of the meeting, acting in good faith, wrongly decides that an amendment to a resolution is out of order, the chairman's error does not invalidate the vote on that resolution.

PART 5
ADMINISTRATIVE ARRANGEMENTS

48 Means of communication to be used

(1) Subject to the articles, anything sent or supplied by or to the company under the articles may be sent or supplied in any way in which the Companies Act 2006 provides for documents or information which are authorised or required by any provision of that Act to be sent or supplied by or to the company.

(2) Subject to the articles, any notice or document to be sent or supplied to a director in connection with the taking of decisions by directors may also be sent or supplied by

the means by which that director has asked to be sent or supplied with such notices or documents for the time being.

(3) A director may agree with the company that notices or documents sent to that director in a particular way are to be deemed to have been received within a specified time of their being sent, and for the specified time to be less than 48 hours.

49 Company seals

(1) Any common seal may only be used by the authority of the directors.

(2) The directors may decide by what means and in what form any common seal is to be used.

(3) Unless otherwise decided by the directors, if the company has a common seal and it is affixed to a document, the document must also be signed by at least one authorised person in the presence of a witness who attests the signature.

(4) For the purposes of this article, an authorised person is—

(a) any director of the company;

(b) the company secretary (if any); or

(c) any person authorised by the directors for the purpose of signing documents to which the common seal is applied.

50 No right to inspect accounts and other records

Except as provided by law or authorised by the directors or an ordinary resolution of the company, no person is entitled to inspect any of the company's accounting or other records or documents merely by virtue of being a shareholder.

51 Provision for employees on cessation of business

The directors may decide to make provision for the benefit of persons employed or formerly employed by the company or any of its subsidiaries (other than a director or former director or shadow director) in connection with the cessation or transfer to any person of the whole or part of the undertaking of the company or that subsidiary.

DIRECTORS' INDEMNITY AND INSURANCE

52 Indemnity

(1) Subject to paragraph (2), a relevant director of the company or an associated company may be indemnified out of the company's assets against—

(a) any liability incurred by that director in connection with any negligence, default, breach of duty or breach of trust in relation to the company or an associated company,

(b) any liability incurred by that director in connection with the activities of the company or an associated company in its capacity as a trustee of an occupational pension scheme (as defined in section 235(6) of the Companies Act 2006),

(c) any other liability incurred by that director as an officer of the company or an associated company.

(2) This article does not authorise any indemnity which would be prohibited or rendered void by any provision of the Companies Acts or by any other provision of law.

(3) In this article—

(a) companies are associated if one is a subsidiary of the other or both are subsidiaries of the same body corporate, and

(b) a "relevant director" means any director or former director of the company or an associated company.

53 Insurance

(1) The directors may decide to purchase and maintain insurance, at the expense of the company, for the benefit of any relevant director in respect of any relevant loss.

(2) In this article—

(a) a "relevant director" means any director or former director of the company or an associated company,

(b) a "relevant loss" means any loss or liability which has been or may be incurred by a relevant director in connection with that director's duties or powers in relation to the company, any associated company or any pension fund or employees' share scheme of the company or associated company, and

(c) companies are associated if one is a subsidiary of the other or both are subsidiaries of the same body corporate.

SCHEDULE 2
OMITTED

SCHEDULE 3
MODEL ARTICLES FOR PUBLIC COMPANIES

PART 1
INTERPRETATION AND LIMITATION OF LIABILITY

1 Defined terms

In the articles , unless the context requires otherwise—

"alternate" or "alternate director" has the meaning given in article 25; "appointor" has the meaning given in article 25;
"articles" means the company's articles of association;
"bankruptcy" includes individual insolvency proceedings in a jurisdiction other than England and Wales or Northern Ireland which have an effect similar to that of bankruptcy;
"call" has the meaning given in article 54;
"call notice" has the meaning given in article 54;
"certificate" means a paper certificate (other than a share warrant) evidencing a person's title to specified shares or other securities;
"certificated" in relation to a share, means that it is not an uncertificated share or a share in respect of which a share warrant has been issued and is current;
"chairman" has the meaning given in article 12;
"chairman of the meeting" has the meaning given in article 31;
"Companies Acts" means the Companies Acts (as defined in section 2 of the Companies Act 2006), in so far as they apply to the company;
"company's lien" has the meaning given in article 52;
"director" means a director of the company, and includes any person occupying the position of director, by whatever name called;
"distribution recipient" has the meaning given in article 72;
"document" includes, unless otherwise specified, any document sent or supplied in electronic form;
"electronic form" has the meaning given in section 1168 of the Companies Act 2006;
"fully paid" in relation to a share, means that the nominal value and any premium to be paid to the company in respect of that share have been paid to the company;
"hard copy form" has the meaning given in section 1168 of the Companies Act 2006;
"holder" in relation to shares means the person whose name is entered in the register of members as the holder of the shares, or, in the case of a share in respect of which a share warrant has been issued (and not cancelled), the person in possession of that warrant; "instrument" means a document in hard copy form;
"lien enforcement notice" has the meaning given in article 53;
"member" has the meaning given in section 112 of the Companies Act 2006;
"ordinary resolution" has the meaning given in section 282 of the Companies Act 2006;
"paid" means paid or credited as paid;
"participate", in relation to a directors' meeting, has the meaning given in article 9;
"partly paid" in relation to a share means that part of that share's nominal value or any premium at which it was issued has not been paid to the company;
"proxy notice" has the meaning given in article 38; "securities seal" has the meaning given in article 47; "shares" means shares in the company;
"special resolution" has the meaning given in section 283 of the Companies Act 2006;
"subsidiary" has the meaning given in section 1159 of the Companies Act 2006;
"transmittee" means a person entitled to a share by reason of the death or bankruptcy of a shareholder or otherwise by operation of law;
"uncertificated" in relation to a share means that, by virtue of legislation (other than section 778 of the Companies Act 2006) permitting title to shares to be evidenced and transferred without a certificate, title to that share is evidenced and may be transferred without a certificate; and

"writing" means the representation or reproduction of words, symbols or other information in a visible form by any method or combination of methods, whether sent or supplied in electronic form or otherwise.

Unless the context otherwise requires, other words or expressions contained in these articles bear the same meaning as in the Companies Act 2006 as in force on the date when these articles become binding on the company.

2 Liability of members

The liability of the members is limited to the amount, if any, unpaid on the shares held by them.

PART 2
DIRECTORS

DIRECTORS' POWERS AND RESPONSIBILITIES

3 Directors' general authority

Subject to the articles, the directors are responsible for the management of the company's business, for which purpose they may exercise all the powers of the company.

4 Members' reserve power

(1) The members may, by special resolution, direct the directors to take, or refrain from taking, specified action.

(2) No such special resolution invalidates anything which the directors have done before the passing of the resolution.

5 Directors may delegate

(1) Subject to the articles, the directors may delegate any of the powers which are conferred on them under the articles—

(a) to such person or committee;

(b) by such means (including by power of attorney);

(c) to such an extent;

(d) in relation to such matters or territories; and

(e) on such terms and conditions; as they think fit.

(2) If the directors so specify, any such delegation may authorise further delegation of the directors' powers by any person to whom they are delegated.

(3) The directors may revoke any delegation in whole or part, or alter its terms and conditions.

6 Committees

(1) Committees to which the directors delegate any of their powers must follow procedures which are based as far as they are applicable on those provisions of the articles which govern the taking of decisions by directors.

(2) The directors may make rules of procedure for all or any committees, which prevail over rules derived from the articles if they are not consistent with them.

DECISION-MAKING BY DIRECTORS

7 Directors to take decisions collectively

Decisions of the directors may be taken—

(a) at a directors' meeting, or

(b) in the form of a directors' written resolution.

8 Calling a directors' meeting

(1) Any director may call a directors' meeting.

(2) The company secretary must call a directors' meeting if a director so requests.

(3) A directors' meeting is called by giving notice of the meeting to the directors.

(4) Notice of any directors' meeting must indicate—

(a) its proposed date and time;

(b) where it is to take place; and

(c) if it is anticipated that directors participating in the meeting will not be in the same place, how it is proposed that they should communicate with each other during the meeting.

(5) Notice of a directors' meeting must be given to each director, but need not be in writing.
(6) Notice of a directors' meeting need not be given to directors who waive their entitlement to notice of that meeting, by giving notice to that effect to the company not more than 7 days after the date on which the meeting is held. Where such notice is given after the meeting has been held, that does not affect the validity of the meeting, or of any business conducted at it.

9 Participation in directors' meetings

(1) Subject to the articles, directors participate in a directors' meeting, or part of a directors' meeting, when—
 (a) the meeting has been called and takes place in accordance with the articles, and
 (b) they can each communicate to the others any information or opinions they have on any particular item of the business of the meeting.
(2) In determining whether directors are participating in a directors' meeting, it is irrelevant where any director is or how they communicate with each other.
(3) If all the directors participating in a meeting are not in the same place, they may decide that the meeting is to be treated as taking place wherever any of them is.

10 Quorum for directors' meetings

(1) At a directors' meeting, unless a quorum is participating, no proposal is to be voted on, except a proposal to call another meeting.
(2) The quorum for directors' meetings may be fixed from time to time by a decision of the directors, but it must never be less than two, and unless otherwise fixed it is two.

11 Meetings where total number of directors less than quorum

(1) This article applies where the total number of directors for the time being is less than the quorum for directors' meetings.
(2) If there is only one director, that director may appoint sufficient directors to make up a quorum or call a general meeting to do so.
(3) If there is more than one director—
 (a) a directors' meeting may take place, if it is called in accordance with the articles and at least two directors participate in it, with a view to appointing sufficient directors to make up a quorum or calling a general meeting to do so, and
 (b) if a directors' meeting is called but only one director attends at the appointed date and time to participate in it, that director may appoint sufficient directors to make up a quorum or call a general meeting to do so.

12 Chairing directors' meetings

(1) The directors may appoint a director to chair their meetings.
(2) The person so appointed for the time being is known as the chairman.
(3) The directors may appoint other directors as deputy or assistant chairmen to chair directors' meetings in the chairman's absence.
(4) The directors may terminate the appointment of the chairman, deputy or assistant chairman at any time.
(5) If neither the chairman nor any director appointed generally to chair directors' meetings in the chairman's absence is participating in a meeting within ten minutes of the time at which it was to start, the participating directors must appoint one of themselves to chair it.

13 Voting at directors' meetings: general rules

(1) Subject to the articles, a decision is taken at a directors' meeting by a majority of the votes of the participating directors.
(2) Subject to the articles, each director participating in a directors' meeting has one vote.
(3) Subject to the articles, if a director has an interest in an actual or proposed transaction or arrangement with the company—
 (a) that director and that director's alternate may not vote on any proposal relating to it, but
 (b) this does not preclude the alternate from voting in relation to that transaction or arrangement on behalf of another appointor who does not have such an interest.

14 Chairman's casting vote at directors' meetings

(1) If the numbers of votes for and against a proposal are equal, the chairman or other director chairing the meeting has a casting vote.

(2) But this does not apply if, in accordance with the articles, the chairman or other director is not to be counted as participating in the decision-making process for quorum or voting purposes.

15 Alternates voting at directors' meetings

A director who is also an alternate director has an additional vote on behalf of each appointor who is—

(a) not participating in a directors' meeting, and
(b) would have been entitled to vote if they were participating in it.

16 Conflicts of interest

(1) If a directors' meeting, or part of a directors' meeting, is concerned with an actual or proposed transaction or arrangement with the company in which a director is interested, that director is not to be counted as participating in that meeting, or part of a meeting, for quorum or voting purposes.

(2) But if paragraph (3) applies, a director who is interested in an actual or proposed transaction or arrangement with the company is to be counted as participating in a decision at a directors' meeting, or part of a directors' meeting, relating to it for quorum and voting purposes.

(3) This paragraph applies when—
(a) the company by ordinary resolution disapplies the provision of the articles which would otherwise prevent a director from being counted as participating in, or voting at, a directors' meeting;
(b) the director's interest cannot reasonably be regarded as likely to give rise to a conflict of interest; or
(c) the director's conflict of interest arises from a permitted cause.

(4) For the purposes of this article, the following are permitted causes—
(a) a guarantee given, or to be given, by or to a director in respect of an obligation incurred by or on behalf of the company or any of its subsidiaries;
(b) subscription, or an agreement to subscribe, for shares or other securities of the company or any of its subsidiaries, or to underwrite, sub-underwrite, or guarantee subscription for any such shares or securities; and
(c) arrangements pursuant to which benefits are made available to employees and directors or former employees and directors of the company or any of its subsidiaries which do not provide special benefits for directors or former directors.

(5) Subject to paragraph (6), if a question arises at a meeting of directors or of a committee of directors as to the right of a director to participate in the meeting (or part of the meeting) for voting or quorum purposes, the question may, before the conclusion of the meeting, be referred to the chairman whose ruling in relation to any director other than the chairman is to be final and conclusive.

(6) If any question as to the right to participate in the meeting (or part of the meeting) should arise in respect of the chairman, the question is to be decided by a decision of the directors at that meeting, for which purpose the chairman is not to be counted as participating in the meeting (or that part of the meeting) for voting or quorum purposes.

17 Proposing directors' written resolutions

(1) Any director may propose a directors' written resolution.

(2) The company secretary must propose a directors' written resolution if a director so requests.

(3) A directors' written resolution is proposed by giving notice of the proposed resolution to the directors.

(4) Notice of a proposed directors' written resolution must indicate—
(a) the proposed resolution, and
(b) the time by which it is proposed that the directors should adopt it.

(5) Notice of a proposed directors' written resolution must be given in writing to each director.

(6) Any decision which a person giving notice of a proposed directors' written resolution takes regarding the process of adopting that resolution must be taken reasonably in good faith.

18 Adoption of directors' written resolutions

(1) A proposed directors' written resolution is adopted when all the directors who would have been entitled to vote on the resolution at a directors' meeting have signed one or more copies of it, provided that those directors would have formed a quorum at such a meeting.

(2) It is immaterial whether any director signs the resolution before or after the time by which the notice proposed that it should be adopted.

(3) Once a directors' written resolution has been adopted, it must be treated as if it had been a decision taken at a directors' meeting in accordance with the articles.

(4) The company secretary must ensure that the company keeps a record, in writing, of all directors' written resolutions for at least ten years from the date of their adoption.

19 Directors' discretion to make further rules

Subject to the articles, the directors may make any rule which they think fit about how they take decisions, and about how such rules are to be recorded or communicated to directors.

APPOINTMENT OF DIRECTORS

20 Methods of appointing directors

Any person who is willing to act as a director, and is permitted by law to do so, may be appointed to be a director—

(a) by ordinary resolution, or
(b) by a decision of the directors.

21 Retirement of directors by rotation

(1) At the first annual general meeting all the directors must retire from office.

(2) At every subsequent annual general meeting any directors—

(a) who have been appointed by the directors since the last annual general meeting, or
(b) who were not appointed or reappointed at one of the preceding two annual general meetings,

must retire from office and may offer themselves for reappointment by the members.

22 Termination of director's appointment

A person ceases to be a director as soon as—

(a) that person ceases to be a director by virtue of any provision of the Companies Act 2006 or is prohibited from being a director by law;
(b) a bankruptcy order is made against that person;
(c) a composition is made with that person's creditors generally in satisfaction of that person's debts;
(d) a registered medical practitioner who is treating that person gives a written opinion to the company stating that that person has become physically or mentally incapable of acting as a director and may remain so for more than three months;
(e) ...
(f) notification is received by the company from the director that the director is resigning from office as director, and such resignation has taken effect in accordance with its terms.

23 Directors' remuneration

(1) Directors may undertake any services for the company that the directors decide.

(2) Directors are entitled to such remuneration as the directors determine—

(a) for their services to the company as directors, and
(b) for any other service which they undertake for the company.

(3) Subject to the articles, a director's remuneration may—

(a) take any form, and
(b) include any arrangements in connection with the payment of a pension, allowance or gratuity, or any death, sickness or disability benefits, to or in respect of that director.

(4) Unless the directors decide otherwise, directors' remuneration accrues from day to day.

(5) Unless the directors decide otherwise, directors are not accountable to the company for any remuneration which they receive as directors or other officers or employees of the company's subsidiaries or of any other body corporate in which the company is interested.

24 Directors' expenses

The company may pay any reasonable expenses which the directors properly incur in connection with their attendance at—

(a) meetings of directors or committees of directors,
(b) general meetings, or
(c) separate meetings of the holders of any class of shares or of debentures of the company,

or otherwise in connection with the exercise of their powers and the discharge of their responsibilities in relation to the company.

ALTERNATE DIRECTORS

25 Appointment and removal of alternates

(1) Any director (the "appointor") may appoint as an alternate any other director, or any other person approved by resolution of the directors, to—
(a) exercise that director's powers, and
(b) carry out that director's responsibilities,
in relation to the taking of decisions by the directors in the absence of the alternate's appointor.
(2) Any appointment or removal of an alternate must be effected by notice in writing to the company signed by the appointor, or in any other manner approved by the directors.
(3) The notice must—
(a) identify the proposed alternate, and
(b) in the case of a notice of appointment, contain a statement signed by the proposed alternate that the proposed alternate is willing to act as the alternate of the director giving the notice.

26 Rights and responsibilities of alternate directors

(1) An alternate director has the same rights, in relation to any directors' meeting or directors' written resolution, as the alternate's appointor.
(2) Except as the articles specify otherwise, alternate directors—
(a) are deemed for all purposes to be directors;
(b) are liable for their own acts and omissions;
(c) are subject to the same restrictions as their appointors; and
(d) are not deemed to be agents of or for their appointors.
(3) A person who is an alternate director but not a director—
(a) may be counted as participating for the purposes of determining whether a quorum is participating (but only if that person's appointor is not participating), and
(b) may sign a written resolution (but only if it is not signed or to be signed by that person's appointor).
No alternate may be counted as more than one director for such purposes.
(4) An alternate director is not entitled to receive any remuneration from the company for serving as an alternate director except such part of the alternate's appointor's remuneration as the appointor may direct by notice in writing made to the company.

27 Termination of alternate directorship

An alternate director's appointment as an alternate terminates—

(a) when the alternate's appointor revokes the appointment by notice to the company in writing specifying when it is to terminate;
(b) on the occurrence in relation to the alternate of any event which, if it occurred in relation to the alternate's appointor, would result in the termination of the appointor's appointment as a director;
(c) on the death of the alternate's appointor; or
(d) when the alternate's appointor's appointment as a director terminates, except that an alternate's appointment as an alternate does not terminate when the appointor retires by rotation at a general meeting and is then re-appointed as a director at the same general meeting.

PART 3
DECISION-MAKING BY MEMBERS

ORGANISATION OF GENERAL MEETINGS

28 Members can call general meeting if not enough directors

If—

(a) the company has fewer than two directors, and
(b) the director (if any) is unable or unwilling to appoint sufficient directors to make up a quorum or to call a general meeting to do so,

then two or more members may call a general meeting (or instruct the company secretary to do so) for the purpose of appointing one or more directors.

29 Attendance and speaking at general meetings

(1) A person is able to exercise the right to speak at a general meeting when that person is in a position to communicate to all those attending the meeting, during the meeting, any information or opinions which that person has on the business of the meeting.
(2) A person is able to exercise the right to vote at a general meeting when—
(a) that person is able to vote, during the meeting, on resolutions put to the vote at the meeting, and
(b) that person's vote can be taken into account in determining whether or not such resolutions are passed at the same time as the votes of all the other persons attending the meeting.
(3) The directors may make whatever arrangements they consider appropriate to enable those attending a general meeting to exercise their rights to speak or vote at it.
(4) In determining attendance at a general meeting, it is immaterial whether any two or more members attending it are in the same place as each other.
(5) Two or more persons who are not in the same place as each other attend a general meeting if their circumstances are such that if they have (or were to have) rights to speak and vote at that meeting, they are (or would be) able to exercise them.

30 Quorum for general meetings

No business other than the appointment of the chairman of the meeting is to be transacted at a general meeting if the persons attending it do not constitute a quorum.

31 Chairing general meetings

(1) If the directors have appointed a chairman, the chairman shall chair general meetings if present and willing to do so.
(2) If the directors have not appointed a chairman, or if the chairman is unwilling to chair the meeting or is not present within ten minutes of the time at which a meeting was due to start—
(a) the directors present, or
(b) (if no directors are present), the meeting,
must appoint a director or member to chair the meeting, and the appointment of the chairman of the meeting must be the first business of the meeting.
(3) The person chairing a meeting in accordance with this article is referred to as "the chairman of the meeting".

32 Attendance and speaking by directors and non-members

(1) Directors may attend and speak at general meetings, whether or not they are members.
(2) The chairman of the meeting may permit other persons who are not—
(a) members of the company, or
(b) otherwise entitled to exercise the rights of members in relation to general meetings,
to attend and speak at a general meeting.

33 Adjournment

(1) If the persons attending a general meeting within half an hour of the time at which the meeting was due to start do not constitute a quorum, or if during a meeting a quorum ceases to be present, the chairman of the meeting must adjourn it.
(2) The chairman of the meeting may adjourn a general meeting at which a quorum is present if—

(a) the meeting consents to an adjournment, or
(b) it appears to the chairman of the meeting that an adjournment is necessary to protect the safety of any person attending the meeting or ensure that the business of the meeting is conducted in an orderly manner.

(3) The chairman of the meeting must adjourn a general meeting if directed to do so by the meeting.

(4) When adjourning a general meeting, the chairman of the meeting must—
(a) either specify the time and place to which it is adjourned or state that it is to continue at a time and place to be fixed by the directors, and
(b) have regard to any directions as to the time and place of any adjournment which have been given by the meeting.

(5) If the continuation of an adjourned meeting is to take place more than 14 days after it was adjourned, the company must give at least 7 clear days' notice of it (that is, excluding the day of the adjourned meeting and the day on which the notice is given)—
(a) to the same persons to whom notice of the company's general meetings is required to be given, and
(b) containing the same information which such notice is required to contain.

(6) No business may be transacted at an adjourned general meeting which could not properly have been transacted at the meeting if the adjournment had not taken place.

VOTING AT GENERAL MEETINGS

34 Voting: general

A resolution put to the vote of a general meeting must be decided on a show of hands unless a poll is duly demanded in accordance with the articles.

35 Errors and disputes

(1) No objection may be raised to the qualification of any person voting at a general meeting except at the meeting or adjourned meeting at which the vote objected to is tendered, and every vote not disallowed at the meeting is valid.

(2) Any such objection must be referred to the chairman of the meeting whose decision is final.

36 Demanding a poll

(1) A poll on a resolution may be demanded—
(a) in advance of the general meeting where it is to be put to the vote, or
(b) at a general meeting, either before a show of hands on that resolution or immediately after the result of a show of hands on that resolution is declared.

(2) A poll may be demanded by—
(a) the chairman of the meeting;
(b) the directors;
(c) two or more persons having the right to vote on the resolution; or
(d) a person or persons representing not less than one tenth of the total voting rights of all the members having the right to vote on the resolution.

(3) A demand for a poll may be withdrawn if—
(a) the poll has not yet been taken, and
(b) the chairman of the meeting consents to the withdrawal.

37 Procedure on a poll

(1) Subject to the articles, polls at general meetings must be taken when, where and in such manner as the chairman of the meeting directs.

(2) The chairman of the meeting may appoint scrutineers (who need not be members) and decide how and when the result of the poll is to be declared.

(3) The result of a poll shall be the decision of the meeting in respect of the resolution on which the poll was demanded.

(4) A poll on—
(a) the election of the chairman of the meeting, or
(b) a question of adjournment, must be taken immediately.

(5) Other polls must be taken within 30 days of their being demanded.

(6) A demand for a poll does not prevent a general meeting from continuing, except as regards the question on which the poll was demanded.
(7) No notice need be given of a poll not taken immediately if the time and place at which it is to be taken are announced at the meeting at which it is demanded.
(8) In any other case, at least 7 days' notice must be given specifying the time and place at which the poll is to be taken.

38 Content of proxy notices

(1) Proxies may only validly be appointed by a notice in writing (a "proxy notice") which—
(a) states the name and address of the member appointing the proxy;
(b) identifies the person appointed to be that member's proxy and the general meeting in relation to which that person is appointed;
(c) is signed by or on behalf of the member appointing the proxy, or is authenticated in such manner as the directors may determine; and
(d) is delivered to the company in accordance with the articles and any instructions contained in the notice of the general meeting to which they relate.
(2) The company may require proxy notices to be delivered in a particular form, and may specify different forms for different purposes.
(3) Proxy notices may specify how the proxy appointed under them is to vote (or that the proxy is to abstain from voting) on one or more resolutions.
(4) Unless a proxy notice indicates otherwise, it must be treated as—
(a) allowing the person appointed under it as a proxy discretion as to how to vote on any ancillary or procedural resolutions put to the meeting, and
(b) appointing that person as a proxy in relation to any adjournment of the general meeting to which it relates as well as the meeting itself.

39 Delivery of proxy notices

(1) Any notice of a general meeting must specify the address or addresses ("proxy notification address") at which the company or its agents will receive proxy notices relating to that meeting, or any adjournment of it, delivered in hard copy or electronic form.
(2) A person who is entitled to attend, speak or vote (either on a show of hands or on a poll) at a general meeting remains so entitled in respect of that meeting or any adjournment of it, even though a valid proxy notice has been delivered to the company by or on behalf of that person.
(3) Subject to paragraphs (4) and (5), a proxy notice must be delivered to a proxy notification address not less than 48 hours before the general meeting or adjourned meeting to which it relates.
(4) In the case of a poll taken more than 48 hours after it is demanded, the notice must be delivered to a proxy notification address not less than 24 hours before the time appointed for the taking of the poll.
(5) In the case of a poll not taken during the meeting but taken not more than 48 hours after it was demanded, the proxy notice must be delivered—
(a) in accordance with paragraph (3), or
(b) at the meeting at which the poll was demanded to the chairman, secretary or any director.
(6) An appointment under a proxy notice may be revoked by delivering a notice in writing given by or on behalf of the person by whom or on whose behalf the proxy notice was given to a proxy notification address.
(7) A notice revoking a proxy appointment only takes effect if it is delivered before—
(a) the start of the meeting or adjourned meeting to which it relates, or
(b) (in the case of a poll not taken on the same day as the meeting or adjourned meeting) the time appointed for taking the poll to which it relates.
(8) If a proxy notice is not signed by the person appointing the proxy, it must be accompanied by written evidence of the authority of the person who executed it to execute it on the appointor's behalf.

40 Amendments to resolutions

(1) An ordinary resolution to be proposed at a general meeting may be amended by ordinary resolution if—
(a) notice of the proposed amendment is given to the company secretary in writing by a person entitled to vote at the general meeting at which it is to be proposed not less

than 48 hours before the meeting is to take place (or such later time as the chairman of the meeting may determine), and

(b) the proposed amendment does not, in the reasonable opinion of the chairman of the meeting, materially alter the scope of the resolution.

(2) A special resolution to be proposed at a general meeting may be amended by ordinary resolution, if—

(a) the chairman of the meeting proposes the amendment at the general meeting at which the resolution is to be proposed, and

(b) the amendment does not go beyond what is necessary to correct a grammatical or other non-substantive error in the resolution.

(3) If the chairman of the meeting, acting in good faith, wrongly decides that an amendment to a resolution is out of order, the chairman's error does not invalidate the vote on that resolution.

RESTRICTIONS ON MEMBERS' RIGHTS

41 No voting of shares on which money owed to company

No voting rights attached to a share may be exercised at any general meeting, at any adjournment of it, or on any poll called at or in relation to it, unless all amounts payable to the company in respect of that share have been paid.

APPLICATION OF RULES TO CLASS MEETINGS

42 Class meetings

The provisions of the articles relating to general meetings apply, with any necessary modifications, to meetings of the holders of any class of shares.

PART 4
SHARES AND DISTRIBUTIONS

ISSUE OF SHARES

43 Powers to issue different classes of share

(1) Subject to the articles, but without prejudice to the rights attached to any existing share, the company may issue shares with such rights or restrictions as may be determined by ordinary resolution.

(2) The company may issue shares which are to be redeemed, or are liable to be redeemed at the option of the company or the holder, and the directors may determine the terms, conditions and manner of redemption of any such shares.

44 Payment of commissions on subscription for shares

(1) The company may pay any person a commission in consideration for that person—

(a) subscribing, or agreeing to subscribe, for shares, or

(b) procuring, or agreeing to procure, subscriptions for shares.

(2) Any such commission may be paid—

(a) in cash, or in fully paid or partly paid shares or other securities, or partly in one way and partly in the other, and

(b) in respect of a conditional or an absolute subscription.

INTERESTS IN SHARES

45 Company not bound by less than absolute interests

Except as required by law, no person is to be recognised by the company as holding any share upon any trust, and except as otherwise required by law or the articles, the company is not in any way to be bound by or recognise any interest in a share other than the holder's absolute ownership of it and all the rights attaching to it.

SHARE CERTIFICATES

46 Certificates to be issued except in certain cases

(1) The company must issue each member with one or more certificates in respect of the shares which that member holds.

(2) This article does not apply to—
  (a) uncertificated shares;
  (b) shares in respect of which a share warrant has been issued; or
  (c) shares in respect of which the Companies Acts permit the company not to issue a certificate.
(3) Except as otherwise specified in the articles, all certificates must be issued free of charge.
(4) No certificate may be issued in respect of shares of more than one class.
(5) If more than one person holds a share, only one certificate may be issued in respect of it.

47 Contents and execution of share certificates

(1) Every certificate must specify—
  (a) in respect of how many shares, of what class, it is issued;
  (b) the nominal value of those shares;
  (c) the amount paid up on them; and
  (d) any distinguishing numbers assigned to them.
(2) Certificates must—
  (a) have affixed to them the company's common seal or an official seal which is a facsimile of the company's common seal with the addition on its face of the word "Securities" (a "securities seal"), or
  (b) be otherwise executed in accordance with the Companies Acts.

48 Consolidated share certificates

(1) When a member's holding of shares of a particular class increases, the company may issue that member with—
  (a) a single, consolidated certificate in respect of all the shares of a particular class which that member holds, or
  (b) a separate certificate in respect of only those shares by which that member's holding has increased.
(2) When a member's holding of shares of a particular class is reduced, the company must ensure that the member is issued with one or more certificates in respect of the number of shares held by the member after that reduction. But the company need not (in the absence of a request from the member) issue any new certificate if—
  (a) all the shares which the member no longer holds as a result of the reduction, and
  (b) none of the shares which the member retains following the reduction, were, immediately before the reduction, represented by the same certificate.
(3) A member may request the company, in writing, to replace—
  (a) the member's separate certificates with a consolidated certificate, or
  (b) the member's consolidated certificate with two or more separate certificates representing such proportion of the shares as the member may specify.
(4) When the company complies with such a request it may charge such reasonable fee as the directors may decide for doing so.
(5) A consolidated certificate must not be issued unless any certificates which it is to replace have first been returned to the company for cancellation.

49 Replacement share certificates

(1) If a certificate issued in respect of a member's shares is—
  (a) damaged or defaced, or
  (b) said to be lost, stolen or destroyed,

that member is entitled to be issued with a replacement certificate in respect of the same shares.

(2) A member exercising the right to be issued with such a replacement certificate—
  (a) may at the same time exercise the right to be issued with a single certificate or separate certificates;
  (b) must return the certificate which is to be replaced to the company if it is damaged or defaced; and
  (c) must comply with such conditions as to evidence, indemnity and the payment of a reasonable fee as the directors decide.

SHARES NOT HELD IN CERTIFICATED FORM

50 Uncertificated shares

(1) In this article, "the relevant rules" means—
  (a) any applicable provision of the Companies Acts about the holding, evidencing of title to, or transfer of shares other than in certificated form, and
  (b) any applicable legislation, rules or other arrangements made under or by virtue of such provision.

(2) The provisions of this article have effect subject to the relevant rules.

(3) Any provision of the articles which is inconsistent with the relevant rules must be disregarded, to the extent that it is inconsistent, whenever the relevant rules apply.

(4) Any share or class of shares of the company may be issued or held on such terms, or in such a way, that—
  (a) title to it or them is not, or must not be, evidenced by a certificate, or
  (b) it or they may or must be transferred wholly or partly without a certificate.

(5) The directors have power to take such steps as they think fit in relation to—
  (a) the evidencing of and transfer of title to uncertificated shares (including in connection with the issue of such shares);
  (b) any records relating to the holding of uncertificated shares;
  (c) the conversion of certificated shares into uncertificated shares; or
  (d) the conversion of uncertificated shares into certificated shares.

(6) The company may by notice to the holder of a share require that share—
  (a) if it is uncertificated, to be converted into certificated form, and
  (b) if it is certificated, to be converted into uncertificated form, to enable it to be dealt with in accordance with the articles.

(7) If—
  (a) the articles give the directors power to take action, or require other persons to take action, in order to sell, transfer or otherwise dispose of shares, and
  (b) uncertificated shares are subject to that power, but the power is expressed in terms which assume the use of a certificate or other written instrument,

the directors may take such action as is necessary or expedient to achieve the same results when exercising that power in relation to uncertificated shares.

(8) In particular, the directors may take such action as they consider appropriate to achieve the sale, transfer, disposal, forfeiture, re-allotment or surrender of an uncertificated share or otherwise to enforce a lien in respect of it.

(9) Unless the directors otherwise determine, shares which a member holds in uncertificated form must be treated as separate holdings from any shares which that member holds in certificated form.

(10) A class of shares must not be treated as two classes simply because some shares of that class are held in certificated form and others are held in uncertificated form.

51 Share warrants

(1) The directors may issue a share warrant in respect of any fully paid share.

(2) Share warrants must be—
  (a) issued in such form, and
  (b) executed in such manner, as the directors decide.

(3) A share represented by a share warrant may be transferred by delivery of the warrant representing it.

(4) The directors may make provision for the payment of dividends in respect of any share represented by a share warrant.

(5) Subject to the articles, the directors may decide the conditions on which any share warrant is issued. In particular, they may—
  (a) decide the conditions on which new warrants are to be issued in place of warrants which are damaged or defaced, or said to have been lost, stolen or destroyed;
  (b) decide the conditions on which bearers of warrants are entitled to attend and vote at general meetings;
  (c) decide the conditions subject to which bearers of warrants may surrender their warrant so as to hold their shares in certificated or uncertificated form instead; and
  (d) vary the conditions of issue of any warrant from time to time,

and the bearer of a warrant is subject to the conditions and procedures in force in relation to it, whether or not they were decided or specified before the warrant was issued.

(6) Subject to the conditions on which the warrants are issued from time to time, bearers of share warrants have the same rights and privileges as they would if their names had been included in the register as holders of the shares represented by their warrants.

(7) The company must not in any way be bound by or recognise any interest in a share represented by a share warrant other than the absolute right of the bearer of that warrant to that warrant.

PARTLY PAID SHARES

52 Company's lien over partly paid shares

(1) The company has a lien ("the company's lien") over every share which is partly paid for any part of—

(a) that share's nominal value, and

(b) any premium at which it was issued,

which has not been paid to the company, and which is payable immediately or at some time in the future, whether or not a call notice has been sent in respect of it.

(2) The company's lien over a share—

(a) takes priority over any third party's interest in that share, and

(b) extends to any dividend or other money payable by the company in respect of that share and (if the lien is enforced and the share is sold by the company) the proceeds of sale of that share.

(3) The directors may at any time decide that a share which is or would otherwise be subject to the company's lien shall not be subject to it, either wholly or in part.

53 Enforcement of the company's lien

(1) Subject to the provisions of this article, if—

(a) a lien enforcement notice has been given in respect of a share, and

(b) the person to whom the notice was given has failed to comply with it, the company may sell that share in such manner as the directors decide.

(2) A lien enforcement notice—

(a) may only be given in respect of a share which is subject to the company's lien, in respect of which a sum is payable and the due date for payment of that sum has passed;

(b) must specify the share concerned;

(c) must require payment of the sum payable within 14 days of the notice;

(d) must be addressed either to the holder of the share or to a person entitled to it by reason of the holder's death, bankruptcy or otherwise; and

(e) must state the company's intention to sell the share if the notice is not complied with.

(3) Where shares are sold under this article—

(a) the directors may authorise any person to execute an instrument of transfer of the shares to the purchaser or a person nominated by the purchaser, and

(b) the transferee is not bound to see to the application of the consideration, and the transferee's title is not affected by any irregularity in or invalidity of the process leading to the sale.

(4) The net proceeds of any such sale (after payment of the costs of sale and any other costs of enforcing the lien) must be applied—

(a) first, in payment of so much of the sum for which the lien exists as was payable at the date of the lien enforcement notice,

(b) second, to the person entitled to the shares at the date of the sale, but only after the certificate for the shares sold has been surrendered to the company for cancellation or a suitable indemnity has been given for any lost certificates, and subject to a lien equivalent to the company's lien over the shares before the sale for any money payable in respect of the shares after the date of the lien enforcement notice.

(5) A statutory declaration by a director or the company secretary that the declarant is a director or the company secretary and that a share has been sold to satisfy the company's lien on a specified date—

(a) is conclusive evidence of the facts stated in it as against all persons claiming to be entitled to the share, and

(b) subject to compliance with any other formalities of transfer required by the articles or by law, constitutes a good title to the share.

54 Call notices

(1) Subject to the articles and the terms on which shares are allotted, the directors may send a notice (a "call notice") to a member requiring the member to pay the company a specified sum of money (a "call") which is payable in respect of shares which that member holds at the date when the directors decide to send the call notice.

(2) A call notice—

(a) may not require a member to pay a call which exceeds the total sum unpaid on that member's shares (whether as to the share's nominal value or any amount payable to the company by way of premium);

(b) must state when and how any call to which it relates it is to be paid; and

(c) may permit or require the call to be paid by instalments.

(3) A member must comply with the requirements of a call notice, but no member is obliged to pay any call before 14 days have passed since the notice was sent.

(4) Before the company has received any call due under a call notice the directors may—

(a) revoke it wholly or in part, or

(b) specify a later time for payment than is specified in the notice,

by a further notice in writing to the member in respect of whose shares the call is made.

55 Liability to pay calls

(1) Liability to pay a call is not extinguished or transferred by transferring the shares in respect of which it is required to be paid.

(2) Joint holders of a share are jointly and severally liable to pay all calls in respect of that share.

(3) Subject to the terms on which shares are allotted, the directors may, when issuing shares, provide that call notices sent to the holders of those shares may require them—

(a) to pay calls which are not the same, or

(b) to pay calls at different times.

56 When call notice need not be issued

(1) A call notice need not be issued in respect of sums which are specified, in the terms on which a share is issued, as being payable to the company in respect of that share (whether in respect of nominal value or premium)—

(a) on allotment;

(b) on the occurrence of a particular event; or

(c) on a date fixed by or in accordance with the terms of issue.

(2) But if the due date for payment of such a sum has passed and it has not been paid, the holder of the share concerned is treated in all respects as having failed to comply with a call notice in respect of that sum, and is liable to the same consequences as regards the payment of interest and forfeiture.

57 Failure to comply with call notice: automatic consequences

(1) If a person is liable to pay a call and fails to do so by the call payment date—

(a) the directors may issue a notice of intended forfeiture to that person, and

(b) until the call is paid, that person must pay the company interest on the call from the call payment date at the relevant rate.

(2) For the purposes of this article—

(a) the "call payment date" is the time when the call notice states that a call is payable, unless the directors give a notice specifying a later date, in which case the "call payment date" is that later date;

(b) the "relevant rate" is—

(i) the rate fixed by the terms on which the share in respect of which the call is due was allotted;

(ii) such other rate as was fixed in the call notice which required payment of the call, or has otherwise been determined by the directors; or

(iii) if no rate is fixed in either of these ways, 5 per cent per annum.

(3) The relevant rate must not exceed by more than 5 percentage points the base lending rate most recently set by the Monetary Policy Committee of the Bank of England in connection with its responsibilities under Part 2 of the Bank of England Act 1998(2).

(4) The directors may waive any obligation to pay interest on a call wholly or in part.

58 Notice of intended forfeiture

A notice of intended forfeiture—

(a) may be sent in respect of any share in respect of which a call has not been paid as required by a call notice;
(b) must be sent to the holder of that share or to a person entitled to it by reason of the holder's death, bankruptcy or otherwise;
(c) must require payment of the call and any accrued interest by a date which is not less than 14 days after the date of the notice;
(d) must state how the payment is to be made; and
(e) must state that if the notice is not complied with, the shares in respect of which the call is payable will be liable to be forfeited.

59 Directors' power to forfeit shares

If a notice of intended forfeiture is not complied with before the date by which payment of the call is required in the notice of intended forfeiture, the directors may decide that any share in respect of which it was given is forfeited, and the forfeiture is to include all dividends or other moneys payable in respect of the forfeited shares and not paid before the forfeiture.

60 Effect of forfeiture

(1) Subject to the articles, the forfeiture of a share extinguishes—
  (a) all interests in that share, and all claims and demands against the company in respect of it, and
  (b) all other rights and liabilities incidental to the share as between the person whose share it was prior to the forfeiture and the company.
(2) Any share which is forfeited in accordance with the articles—
  (a) is deemed to have been forfeited when the directors decide that it is forfeited;
  (b) is deemed to be the property of the company; and
  (c) may be sold, re-allotted or otherwise disposed of as the directors think fit.
(3) If a person's shares have been forfeited—
  (a) the company must send that person notice that forfeiture has occurred and record it in the register of members;
  (b) that person ceases to be a member in respect of those shares;
  (c) that person must surrender the certificate for the shares forfeited to the company for cancellation;
  (d) that person remains liable to the company for all sums payable by that person under the articles at the date of forfeiture in respect of those shares, including any interest (whether accrued before or after the date of forfeiture); and
  (e) the directors may waive payment of such sums wholly or in part or enforce payment without any allowance for the value of the shares at the time of forfeiture or for any consideration received on their disposal.
(4) At any time before the company disposes of a forfeited share, the directors may decide to cancel the forfeiture on payment of all calls and interest due in respect of it and on such other terms as they think fit.

61 Procedure following forfeiture

(1) If a forfeited share is to be disposed of by being transferred, the company may receive the consideration for the transfer and the directors may authorise any person to execute the instrument of transfer.
(2) A statutory declaration by a director or the company secretary that the declarant is a director or the company secretary and that a share has been forfeited on a specified date—
  (a) is conclusive evidence of the facts stated in it as against all persons claiming to be entitled to the share, and
  (b) subject to compliance with any other formalities of transfer required by the articles or by law, constitutes a good title to the share.
(3) A person to whom a forfeited share is transferred is not bound to see to the application of the consideration (if any) nor is that person's title to the share affected by any irregularity in or invalidity of the process leading to the forfeiture or transfer of the share.
(4) If the company sells a forfeited share, the person who held it prior to its forfeiture is entitled to receive from the company the proceeds of such sale, net of any commission, and excluding any amount which—

(a) was, or would have become, payable, and
(b) had not, when that share was forfeited, been paid by that person in respect of that share,

but no interest is payable to such a person in respect of such proceeds and the company is not required to account for any money earned on them.

62 Surrender of shares

(1) A member may surrender any share—
(a) in respect of which the directors may issue a notice of intended forfeiture;
(b) which the directors may forfeit; or
(c) which has been forfeited.
(2) The directors may accept the surrender of any such share.
(3) The effect of surrender on a share is the same as the effect of forfeiture on that share.
(4) A share which has been surrendered may be dealt with in the same way as a share which has been forfeited.

TRANSFER AND TRANSMISSION OF SHARES

63 Transfers of certificated shares

(1) Certificated shares may be transferred by means of an instrument of transfer in any usual form or any other form approved by the directors, which is executed by or on behalf of—
(a) the transferor, and
(b) (if any of the shares is partly paid) the transferee.
(2) No fee may be charged for registering any instrument of transfer or other document relating to or affecting the title to any share.
(3) The company may retain any instrument of transfer which is registered.
(4) The transferor remains the holder of a certificated share until the transferee's name is entered in the register of members as holder of it.
(5) The directors may refuse to register the transfer of a certificated share if—
(a) the share is not fully paid;
(b) the transfer is not lodged at the company's registered office or such other place as the directors have appointed;
(c) the transfer is not accompanied by the certificate for the shares to which it relates, or such other evidence as the directors may reasonably require to show the transferor's right to make the transfer, or evidence of the right of someone other than the transferor to make the transfer on the transferor's behalf;
(d) the transfer is in respect of more than one class of share; or
(e) the transfer is in favour of more than four transferees.
(6) If the directors refuse to register the transfer of a share, the instrument of transfer must be returned to the transferee with the notice of refusal unless they suspect that the proposed transfer may be fraudulent.

64 Transfer of uncertificated shares

A transfer of an uncertificated share must not be registered if it is in favour of more than four transferees.

65 Transmission of shares

(1) If title to a share passes to a transmittee, the company may only recognise the transmittee as having any title to that share.
(2) Nothing in these articles releases the estate of a deceased member from any liability in respect of a share solely or jointly held by that member.

66 Transmittees' rights

(1) A transmittee who produces such evidence of entitlement to shares as the directors may properly require—
(a) may, subject to the articles, choose either to become the holder of those shares or to have them transferred to another person, and
(b) subject to the articles, and pending any transfer of the shares to another person, has the same rights as the holder had.

(2) But transmittees do not have the right to attend or vote at a general meeting in respect of shares to which they are entitled, by reason of the holder's death or bankruptcy or otherwise, unless they become the holders of those shares

67 Exercise of transmittees' rights

(1) Transmittees who wish to become the holders of shares to which they have become entitled must notify the company in writing of that wish.

(2) If the share is a certificated share and a transmittee wishes to have it transferred to another person, the transmittee must execute an instrument of transfer in respect of it.

(3) If the share is an uncertificated share and the transmittee wishes to have it transferred to another person, the transmittee must—

(a) procure that all appropriate instructions are given to effect the transfer, or

(b) procure that the uncertificated share is changed into certificated form and then execute an instrument of transfer in respect of it.

(4) Any transfer made or executed under this article is to be treated as if it were made or executed by the person from whom the transmittee has derived rights in respect of the share, and as if the event which gave rise to the transmission had not occurred.

68 Transmittees bound by prior notices

If a notice is given to a member in respect of shares and a transmittee is entitled to those shares, the transmittee is bound by the notice if it was given to the member before the transmittee's name has been entered in the register of members.

CONSOLIDATION OF SHARES

69 Procedure for disposing of fractions of shares

(1) This article applies where—

(a) there has been a consolidation or division of shares, and

(b) as a result, members are entitled to fractions of shares.

(2) The directors may—

(a) sell the shares representing the fractions to any person including the company for the best price reasonably obtainable;

(b) in the case of a certificated share, authorise any person to execute an instrument of transfer of the shares to the purchaser or a person nominated by the purchaser; and

(c) distribute the net proceeds of sale in due proportion among the holders of the shares.

(3) Where any holder's entitlement to a portion of the proceeds of sale amounts to less than a minimum figure determined by the directors, that member's portion may be distributed to an organisation which is a charity for the purposes of the law of England and Wales, Scotland or Northern Ireland.

(4) The person to whom the shares are transferred is not obliged to ensure that any purchase money is received by the person entitled to the relevant fractions.

(5) The transferee's title to the shares is not affected by any irregularity in or invalidity of the process leading to their sale.

DISTRIBUTIONS

70 Procedure for declaring dividends

(1) The company may by ordinary resolution declare dividends, and the directors may decide to pay interim dividends.

(2) A dividend must not be declared unless the directors have made a recommendation as to its amount. Such a dividend must not exceed the amount recommended by the directors.

(3) No dividend may be declared or paid unless it is in accordance with members' respective rights.

(4) Unless the members' resolution to declare or directors' decision to pay a dividend, or the terms on which shares are issued, specify otherwise, it must be paid by reference to each member's holding of shares on the date of the resolution or decision to declare or pay it.

(5) If the company's share capital is divided into different classes, no interim dividend may be paid on shares carrying deferred or non-preferred rights if, at the time of payment, any preferential dividend is in arrear.

(6) The directors may pay at intervals any dividend payable at a fixed rate if it appears to them that the profits available for distribution justify the payment.
(7) If the directors act in good faith, they do not incur any liability to the holders of shares conferring preferred rights for any loss they may suffer by the lawful payment of an interim dividend on shares with deferred or non-preferred rights.

71 Calculation of dividends

(1) Except as otherwise provided by the articles or the rights attached to shares, all dividends must be—
  (a) declared and paid according to the amounts paid up on the shares on which the dividend is paid, and
  (b) apportioned and paid proportionately to the amounts paid up on the shares during any portion or portions of the period in respect of which the dividend is paid.
(2) If any share is issued on terms providing that it ranks for dividend as from a particular date, that share ranks for dividend accordingly.
(3) For the purposes of calculating dividends, no account is to be taken of any amount which has been paid up on a share in advance of the due date for payment of that amount.

72 Payment of dividends and other distributions

(1) Where a dividend or other sum which is a distribution is payable in respect of a share, it must be paid by one or more of the following means—
  (a) transfer to a bank or building society account specified by the distribution recipient either in writing or as the directors may otherwise decide;
  (b) sending a cheque made payable to the distribution recipient by post to the distribution recipient at the distribution recipient's registered address (if the distribution recipient is a holder of the share), or (in any other case) to an address specified by the distribution recipient either in writing or as the directors may otherwise decide;
  (c) sending a cheque made payable to such person by post to such person at such address as the distribution recipient has specified either in writing or as the directors may otherwise decide; or
  (d) any other means of payment as the directors agree with the distribution recipient either in writing or by such other means as the directors decide.
(2) In the articles, "the distribution recipient" means, in respect of a share in respect of which a dividend or other sum is payable—
  (a) the holder of the share; or
  (b) if the share has two or more joint holders, whichever of them is named first in the register of members; or
  (c) if the holder is no longer entitled to the share by reason of death or bankruptcy, or otherwise by operation of law, the transmittee.

73 Deductions from distributions in respect of sums owed to the company

(1) If—
  (a) a share is subject to the company's lien, and
  (b) the directors are entitled to issue a lien enforcement notice in respect of it,

  they may, instead of issuing a lien enforcement notice, deduct from any dividend or other sum payable in respect of the share any sum of money which is payable to the company in respect of that share to the extent that they are entitled to require payment under a lien enforcement notice.
(2) Money so deducted must be used to pay any of the sums payable in respect of that share.
(3) The company must notify the distribution recipient in writing of—
  (a) the fact and amount of any such deduction;
  (b) any non-payment of a dividend or other sum payable in respect of a share resulting from any such deduction; and
  (c) how the money deducted has been applied.

74 No interest on distributions

The company may not pay interest on any dividend or other sum payable in respect of a share unless otherwise provided by—

(a) the terms on which the share was issued, or
(b) the provisions of another agreement between the holder of that share and the company.

75 Unclaimed distributions

(1) All dividends or other sums which are—
(a) payable in respect of shares, and
(b) unclaimed after having been declared or become payable,
may be invested or otherwise made use of by the directors for the benefit of the company until claimed.
(2) The payment of any such dividend or other sum into a separate account does not make the company a trustee in respect of it.
(3) If—
(a) twelve years have passed from the date on which a dividend or other sum became due for payment, and
(b) the distribution recipient has not claimed it,
the distribution recipient is no longer entitled to that dividend or other sum and it ceases to remain owing by the company.

76 Non-cash distributions

(1) Subject to the terms of issue of the share in question, the company may, by ordinary resolution on the recommendation of the directors, decide to pay all or part of a dividend or other distribution payable in respect of a share by transferring non-cash assets of equivalent value (including, without limitation, shares or other securities in any company).
(2) If the shares in respect of which such a non-cash distribution is paid are uncertificated, any shares in the company which are issued as a non-cash distribution in respect of them must be uncertificated.
(3) For the purposes of paying a non-cash distribution, the directors may make whatever arrangements they think fit, including, where any difficulty arises regarding the distribution—
(a) fixing the value of any assets;
(b) paying cash to any distribution recipient on the basis of that value in order to adjust the rights of recipients; and
(c) vesting any assets in trustees.

77 Waiver of distributions

Distribution recipients may waive their entitlement to a dividend or other distribution payable in respect of a share by giving the company notice in writing to that effect, but if—
(a) the share has more than one holder, or
(b) more than one person is entitled to the share, whether by reason of the death or bankruptcy of one or more joint holders, or otherwise,
the notice is not effective unless it is expressed to be given, and signed, by all the holders or persons otherwise entitled to the share.

CAPITALISATION OF PROFITS

78 Authority to capitalise and appropriation of capitalised sums

(1) Subject to the articles, the directors may, if they are so authorised by an ordinary resolution—
(a) decide to capitalise any profits of the company (whether or not they are available for distribution) which are not required for paying a preferential dividend, or any sum standing to the credit of the company's share premium account or capital redemption reserve; and
(b) appropriate any sum which they so decide to capitalise (a "capitalised sum") to the persons who would have been entitled to it if it were distributed by way of dividend (the "persons entitled") and in the same proportions.
(2) Capitalised sums must be applied—
(a) on behalf of the persons entitled, and
(b) in the same proportions as a dividend would have been distributed to them.

(3) Any capitalised sum may be applied in paying up new shares of a nominal amount equal to the capitalised sum which are then allotted credited as fully paid to the persons entitled or as they may direct.

(4) A capitalised sum which was appropriated from profits available for distribution may be applied—

(a) in or towards paying up any amounts unpaid on existing shares held by the persons entitled, or

(b) in paying up new debentures of the company which are then allotted credited as fully paid to the persons entitled or as they may direct.

(5) Subject to the articles the directors may—

(a) apply capitalised sums in accordance with paragraphs (3) and (4) partly in one way and partly in another;

(b) make such arrangements as they think fit to deal with shares or debentures becoming distributable in fractions under this article (including the issuing of fractional certificates or the making of cash payments); and

(c) authorise any person to enter into an agreement with the company on behalf of all the persons entitled which is binding on them in respect of the allotment of shares and debentures to them under this article.

PART 5
MISCELLANEOUS PROVISIONS

COMMUNICATIONS

79 Means of communication to be used

(1) Subject to the articles, anything sent or supplied by or to the company under the articles may be sent or supplied in any way in which the Companies Act 2006 provides for documents or information which are authorised or required by any provision of that Act to be sent or supplied by or to the company.

(2) Subject to the articles, any notice or document to be sent or supplied to a director in connection with the taking of decisions by directors may also be sent or supplied by the means by which that director has asked to be sent or supplied with such notices or documents for the time being.

(3) A director may agree with the company that notices or documents sent to that director in a particular way are to be deemed to have been received within a specified time of their being sent, and for the specified time to be less than 48 hours.

80 Failure to notify contact details

(1) If—

(a) the company sends two consecutive documents to a member over a period of at least 12 months, and

(b) each of those documents is returned undelivered, or the company receives notification that it has not been delivered,

that member ceases to be entitled to receive notices from the company.

(2) A member who has ceased to be entitled to receive notices from the company becomes entitled to receive such notices again by sending the company—

(a) a new address to be recorded in the register of members, or

(b) if the member has agreed that the company should use a means of communication other than sending things to such an address, the information that the company needs to use that means of communication effectively.

ADMINISTRATIVE ARRANGEMENTS

81 Company seals

(1) Any common seal may only be used by the authority of the directors.

(2) The directors may decide by what means and in what form any common seal or securities seal is to be used.

(3) Unless otherwise decided by the directors, if the company has a common seal and it is affixed to a document, the document must also be signed by at least one authorised person in the presence of a witness who attests the signature.

(4) For the purposes of this article, an authorised person is—
(a) any director of the company;
(b) the company secretary; or
(c) any person authorised by the directors for the purpose of signing documents to which the common seal is applied.

(5) If the company has an official seal for use abroad, it may only be affixed to a document if its use on that document, or documents of a class to which it belongs, has been authorised by a decision of the directors.

(6) If the company has a securities seal, it may only be affixed to securities by the company secretary or a person authorised to apply it to securities by the company secretary.

(7) For the purposes of the articles, references to the securities seal being affixed to any document include the reproduction of the image of that seal on or in a document by any mechanical or electronic means which has been approved by the directors in relation to that document or documents of a class to which it belongs.

82 Destruction of documents

(1) The company is entitled to destroy—
(a) all instruments of transfer of shares which have been registered, and all other documents on the basis of which any entries are made in the register of members, from six years after the date of registration;
(b) all dividend mandates, variations or cancellations of dividend mandates, and notifications of change of address, from two years after they have been recorded;
(c) all share certificates which have been cancelled from one year after the date of the cancellation;
(d) all paid dividend warrants and cheques from one year after the date of actual payment; and
(e) all proxy notices from one year after the end of the meeting to which the proxy notice relates.

(2) If the company destroys a document in good faith, in accordance with the articles, and without notice of any claim to which that document may be relevant, it is conclusively presumed in favour of the company that—
(a) entries in the register purporting to have been made on the basis of an instrument of transfer or other document so destroyed were duly and properly made;
(b) any instrument of transfer so destroyed was a valid and effective instrument duly and properly registered;
(c) any share certificate so destroyed was a valid and effective certificate duly and properly cancelled; and
(d) any other document so destroyed was a valid and effective document in accordance with its recorded particulars in the books or records of the company.

(3) This article does not impose on the company any liability which it would not otherwise have if it destroys any document before the time at which this article permits it to do so.

(4) In this article, references to the destruction of any document include a reference to its being disposed of in any manner.

83 No right to inspect accounts and other records

Except as provided by law or authorised by the directors or an ordinary resolution of the company, no person is entitled to inspect any of the company's accounting or other records or documents merely by virtue of being a member.

84 Provision for employees on cessation of business

The directors may decide to make provision for the benefit of persons employed or formerly employed by the company or any of its subsidiaries (other than a director or former director or shadow director) in connection with the cessation or transfer to any person of the whole or part of the undertaking of the company or that subsidiary.

DIRECTORS' INDEMNITY AND INSURANCE

85 Indemnity

(1) Subject to paragraph (2), a relevant director of the company or an associated company may be indemnified out of the company's assets against—

(a) any liability incurred by that director in connection with any negligence, default, breach of duty or breach of trust in relation to the company or an associated company,

(b) any liability incurred by that director in connection with the activities of the company or an associated company in its capacity as a trustee of an occupational pension scheme (as defined in section 235(6) of the Companies Act 2006),

(c) any other liability incurred by that director as an officer of the company or an associated company.

(2) This article does not authorise any indemnity which would be prohibited or rendered void by any provision of the Companies Acts or by any other provision of law.

(3) In this article—

(a) companies are associated if one is a subsidiary of the other or both are subsidiaries of the same body corporate, and

(b) a "relevant director" means any director or former director of the company or an associated company.

86 Insurance

(1) The directors may decide to purchase and maintain insurance, at the expense of the company, for the benefit of any relevant director in respect of any relevant loss.

(2) In this article—

(a) a "relevant director" means any director or former director of the company or an associated company,

(b) a "relevant loss" means any loss or liability which has been or may be incurred by a relevant director in connection with that director's duties or powers in relation to the company, any associated company or any pension fund or employees' share scheme of the company or associated company, and

(c) companies are associated if one is a subsidiary of the other or both are subsidiaries of the same body corporate.

PART III
EU LEGISLATION

COUNCIL REGULATION (EC) No. 2157/2001 of 8 October 2001 on the Statute for a European company (SE)

THE COUNCIL OF THE EUROPEAN UNION,

Having regard to the Treaty establishing the European Community, and in particular Article 308 thereof,

Having regard to the proposal from the Commission,

Having regard to the opinion of the European Parliament,

Having regard to the opinion of the Economic and Social Committee,

Whereas:

(1) The completion of the internal market and the improvement it brings about in the economic and social situation throughout the Community mean not only that barriers to trade must be removed, but also that the structures of production must be adapted to the Community dimension. For that purpose it is essential that companies the business of which is not limited to satisfying purely local needs should be able to plan and carry out the reorganisation of their business on a Community scale.

(2) Such reorganisation presupposes that existing companies from different Member States are given the option of combining their potential by means of mergers. Such operations can be carried out only with due regard to the rules of competition laid down in the Treaty.

(3) Restructuring and cooperation operations involving companies from different Member States give rise to legal and psychological difficulties and tax problems. The approximation of Member States' company law by means of Directives based on Article 44 of the Treaty can overcome some of those difficulties. Such approximation does not, however, release companies governed by different legal systems from the obligation to choose a form of company governed by a particular national law.

(4) The legal framework within which business must be carried on in the Community is still based largely on national laws and therefore no longer corresponds to the economic framework within which it must develop if the objectives set out in Article 18 of the Treaty are to be achieved. That situation forms a considerable obstacle to the creation of groups of companies from different Member States.

(5) Member States are obliged to ensure that the provisions applicable to European companies under this Regulation do not result either in discrimination arising out of unjustified different treatment of European companies compared with public limited-liability companies or in disproportionate restrictions on the formation of a European company or on the transfer of its registered office.

(6) It is essential to ensure as far as possible that the economic unit and the legal unit of business in the Community coincide. For that purpose, provision should be made for the creation, side by side with companies governed by a particular national law, of companies formed and carrying on business under the law created by a Community Regulation directly applicable in all Member States.

(7) The provisions of such a Regulation will permit the creation and management of companies with a European dimension, free from the obstacles arising from the disparity and the limited territorial application of national company law.

(8) The Statute for a European public limited-liability company (hereafter referred to as "SE") is among the measures to be adopted by the Council before 1992 listed in the Commission's White Paper on completing the internal market, approved by the European Council that met in Milan in June 1985. The European Council that met in Brussels in 1987 expressed the wish to see such a Statute created swiftly.

(9) Since the Commission's submission in 1970 of a proposal for a Regulation on the Statute for a European public limited-liability company, amended in 1975, work on the approximation of national company law has made substantial progress, so that on those points where the functioning of an SE does not need uniform Community rules reference may be made to the law governing public limited-liability companies in the Member State where it has its registered office.

(10) Without prejudice to any economic needs that may arise in the future, if the essential objective of legal rules governing SEs is to be attained, it must be possible at least to create such a company as a means both of enabling companies from different Member States to merge or to create a holding company and of enabling companies and other legal persons carrying on economic activities and governed by the laws of different Member States to form joint subsidiaries.

(11) In the same context it should be possible for a public limited-liability company with a registered office and head office within the Community to transform itself into an SE without going into liquidation, provided it has a subsidiary in a Member State other than that of its registered office.

(12) National provisions applying to public limited-liability companies that offer their securities to the public and to securities transactions should also apply where an SE is formed by means of an offer of securities to the public and to SEs wishing to utilise such financial instruments.

(13) The SE itself must take the form of a company with share capital, that being the form most suited, in terms of both financing and management, to the needs of a company carrying on business on a European scale. In order to ensure that such companies are of reasonable size, a minimum amount of capital should be set so that they have sufficient assets without making it difficult for small and medium-sized undertakings to form SEs.

(14) An SE must be efficiently managed and properly supervised. It must be borne in mind that there are at present in the Community two different systems for the administration of public limited-liability companies. Although an SE should be allowed to choose between the two systems, the respective responsibilities of those responsible for management and those responsible for supervision should be clearly defined.

(15) Under the rules and general principles of private international law, where one undertaking controls another governed by a different legal system, its ensuing rights and obligations as regards the protection of minority shareholders and third parties are governed by the law governing the controlled undertaking, without prejudice to the obligations imposed on the controlling undertaking by its own law, for example the requirement to prepare consolidated accounts.

(16) Without prejudice to the consequences of any subsequent coordination of the laws of the Member States, specific rules for SEs are not at present required in this field. The rules and general principles of private international law should therefore be applied both where an SE exercises control and where it is the controlled company.

(17) The rule thus applicable where an SE is controlled by another undertaking should be specified, and for this purpose reference should be made to the law governing public limited-liability companies in the Member State in which the SE has its registered office.

(18) Each Member State must be required to apply the sanctions applicable to public limited-liability companies governed by its law in respect of infringements of this Regulation.

(19) The rules on the involvement of employees in the European company are laid down in Directive 2001/86/EC, and those provisions thus form an indissociable complement to this Regulation and must be applied concomitantly.

(20) This Regulation does not cover other areas of law such as taxation, competition, intellectual property or insolvency. The provisions of the Member States' law and of Community law are therefore applicable in the above areas and in other areas not covered by this Regulation.

(21) Directive 2001/86/EC is designed to ensure that employees have a right of involvement in issues and decisions affecting the life of their SE. Other social and labour legislation questions, in particular the right of employees to information and consultation as regulated in the Member States, are governed by the national provisions applicable, under the same conditions, to public limited-liability companies.

(22) The entry into force of this Regulation must be deferred so that each Member State may incorporate into its national law the provisions of Directive 2001/86/EC and set up in advance the necessary machinery for the formation and operation of SEs with registered offices within its territory, so that the Regulation and the Directive may be applied concomitantly.

(23) A company the head office of which is not in the Community should be allowed to participate in the formation of an SE provided that company is formed under the law of a Member State, has its registered office in that Member State and has a real and continuous link with a Member State's economy according to the principles established in the 1962

General Programme for the abolition of restrictions on freedom of establishment. Such a link exists in particular if a company has an establishment in that Member State and conducts operations therefrom.

(24) The SE should be enabled to transfer its registered office to another Member State. Adequate protection of the interests of minority shareholders who oppose the transfer, of creditors and of holders of other rights should be proportionate. Such transfer should not affect the rights originating before the transfer.

(25) This Regulation is without prejudice to any provision which may be inserted in the 1968 Brussels Convention or in any text adopted by Member States or by the Council to replace such Convention, relating to the rules of jurisdiction applicable in the case of transfer of the registered offices of a public limited-liability company from one Member State to another.

(26) Activities by financial institutions are regulated by specific directives and the national law implementing those directives and additional national rules regulating those activities apply in full to an SE.

(27) In view of the specific Community character of an SE, the "real seat" arrangement adopted by this Regulation in respect of SEs is without prejudice to Member States' laws and does not pre-empt any choices to be made for other Community texts on company law.

(28) The Treaty does not provide, for the adoption of this Regulation, powers of action other than those of Article 308 thereof.

(29) Since the objectives of the intended action, as outlined above, cannot be adequately attained by the Member States in as much as a European public limited-liability company is being established at European level and can therefore, because of the scale and impact of such company, be better attained at Community level, the Community may take measures in accordance with the principle of subsidiarity enshrined in Article 5 of the Treaty. In accordance with the principle of proportionality as set out in the said Article, this Regulation does not go beyond what is necessary to attain these objectives,

HAS ADOPTED THIS REGULATION:

TITLE I
GENERAL PROVISIONS

Article 1

1. A company may be set up within the territory of the Community in the form of a European public limited-liability company (Societas Europaea or SE) on the conditions and in the manner laid down in this Regulation.
2. The capital of an SE shall be divided into shares. No shareholder shall be liable for more than the amount he has subscribed.
3. An SE shall have legal personality.
4. Employee involvement in an SE shall be governed by the provisions of Directive 2001/86/EC.

Article 2

1. Public limited-liability companies such as referred to in Annex I, formed under the law of a Member State, with registered offices and head offices within the Community may form an SE by means of a merger provided that at least two of them are governed by the law of different Member States.
2. Public and private limited-liability companies such as referred to in Annex II, formed under the law of a Member State, with registered offices and head offices within the Community may promote the formation of a holding SE provided that each of at least two of them:
   (a) is governed by the law of a different Member State, or
   (b) has for at least two years had a subsidiary company governed by the law of another Member State or a branch situated in another Member State.
3. Companies and firms within the meaning of the second paragraph of Article 48 of the Treaty and other legal bodies governed by public or private law, formed under the law of a Member State, with registered offices and head offices within the Community may form a subsidiary SE by subscribing for its shares, provided that each of at least two of them:
   (a) is governed by the law of a different Member State, or
   (b) has for at least two years had a subsidiary company governed by the law of another Member State or a branch situated in another Member State.

4. A public limited-liability company, formed under the law of a Member State, which has its registered office and head office within the Community may be transformed into an SE if for at least two years it has had a subsidiary company governed by the law of another Member State.
5. A Member State may provide that a company the head office of which is not in the Community may participate in the formation of an SE provided that company is formed under the law of a Member State, has its registered office in that Member State and has a real and continuous link with a Member State's economy.

Article 3

1. For the purposes of Article 2(1), (2) and (3), an SE shall be regarded as a public limited-liability company governed by the law of the Member State in which it has its registered office.
2. An SE may itself set up one or more subsidiaries in the form of SEs. The provisions of the law of the Member State in which a subsidiary SE has its registered office that require a public limited-liability company to have more than one shareholder shall not apply in the case of the subsidiary SE. The provisions of national law implementing the twelfth Council Company Law Directive (89/667/EEC) of 21 December 1989 on single-member private limited-liability companies shall apply to SEs mutatis mutandis.

Article 4

1. The capital of an SE shall be expressed in euro.
2. The subscribed capital shall not be less than EUR 120000.
3. The laws of a Member State requiring a greater subscribed capital for companies carrying on certain types of activity shall apply to SEs with registered offices in that Member State.

Article 5

Subject to Article 4(1) and (2), the capital of an SE, its maintenance and changes thereto, together with its shares, bonds and other similar securities shall be governed by the provisions which would apply to a public limited-liability company with a registered office in the Member State in which the SE is registered.

Article 6

For the purposes of this Regulation, "the statutes of the SE" shall mean both the instrument of incorporation and, where they are the subject of a separate document, the statutes of the SE.

Article 7

The registered office of an SE shall be located within the Community, in the same Member State as its head office. A Member State may in addition impose on SEs registered in its territory the obligation of locating their head office and their registered office in the same place.

Article 8

1. The registered office of an SE may be transferred to another Member State in accordance with paragraphs 2 to 13. Such a transfer shall not result in the winding up of the SE or in the creation of a new legal person.
2. The management or administrative organ shall draw up a transfer proposal and publicise it in accordance with Article 13, without prejudice to any additional forms of publication provided for by the Member State of the registered office. That proposal shall state the current name, registered office and number of the SE and shall cover:
   (a) the proposed registered office of the SE;
   (b) the proposed statutes of the SE including, where appropriate, its new name;
   (c) any implication the transfer may have on employees' involvement;
   (d) the proposed transfer timetable;
   (e) any rights provided for the protection of shareholders and/or creditors.
3. The management or administrative organ shall draw up a report explaining and justifying the legal and economic aspects of the transfer and explaining the implications of the transfer for shareholders, creditors and employees.
4. An SE's shareholders and creditors shall be entitled, at least one month before the general meeting called upon to decide on the transfer, to examine at the SE's registered office the transfer proposal and the report drawn up pursuant to paragraph 3 and, on request, to obtain copies of those documents free of charge.

5. A Member State may, in the case of SEs registered within its terr tory, adopt provisions designed to ensure appropriate protection for minority shareholders who oppose a transfer.
6. No decision to transfer may be taken for two months after publication of the proposal. Such a decision shall be taken as laid down in Article 59.
7. Before the competent authority issues the certificate mentioned in paragraph 8, the SE shall satisfy it that, in respect of any liabilities arising prior to the publication of the transfer proposal, the interests of creditors and holders of other rights in respect of the SE (including those of public bodies) have been adequately protected in accordance with requirements laid down by the Member State where the SE has its registered office prior to the transfer.
   A Member State may extend the application of the first subparagraph to liabilities that arise (or may arise) prior to the transfer.
   The first and second subparagraphs shall be without prejudice to the application to SEs of the national legislation of Member States concerning the satisfaction or securing of payments to public bodies.
8. In the Member State in which an SE has its registered office the court, notary or other competent authority shall issue a certificate attesting to the completion of the acts and formalities to be accomplished before the transfer.
9. The new registration may not be effected until the certificate referred to in paragraph 8 has been submitted, and evidence produced that the formalities required for registration in the country of the new registered office have been completed.
10. The transfer of an SE's registered office and the consequent amendment of its statutes shall take effect on the date on which the SE is registered, in accordance with Article 12, in the register for its new registered office.
11. When the SE's new registration has been effected, the registry for its new registration shall notify the registry for its old registration. Deletion of the old registration shall be effected on receipt of that notification, but not before.
12. The new registration and the deletion of the old registration shall be publicised in the Member States concerned in accordance with Article 13.
13. On publication of an SE's new registration, the new registered office may be relied on as against third parties. However, as long as the deletion of the SE's registration from the register for its previous registered office has not been publicised, third parties may continue to rely on the previous registered office unless the SE proves that such third parties were aware of the new registered office.
14. The laws of a Member State may provide that, as regards SEs registered in that Member State, the transfer of a registered office which would result in a change of the law applicable shall not take effect if any of that Member State's competent authorities opposes it within the two-month period referred to in paragraph 6. Such opposition may be based only on grounds of public interest.
    Where an SE is supervised by a national financial supervisory authority according to Community directives the right to oppose the change of registered office applies to this authority as well.
    Review by a judicial authority shall be possible.
15. An SE may not transfer its registered office if proceedings for winding up, liquidation, insolvency or suspension of payments or other similar proceedings have been brought against it.
16. An SE which has transferred its registered office to another Member State shall be considered, in respect of any cause of action arising prior to the transfer as determined in paragraph 10, as having its registered office in the Member States where the SE was registered prior to the transfer, even if the SE is sued after the transfer.

Article 9

1. An SE shall be governed:
   (a) by this Regulation,
   (b) where expressly authorised by this Regulation, by the provisions of its statutes or
   (c) in the case of matters not regulated by this Regulation or, where matters are partly regulated by it, of those aspects not covered by it, by:

(i) the provisions of laws adopted by Member States in implementation of Community measures relating specifically to SEs;
(ii) the provisions of Member States' laws which would apply to a public limited-liability company formed in accordance with the law of the Member State in which the SE has its registered office;
(iii) the provisions of its statutes, in the same way as for a public limited-liability company formed in accordance with the law of the Member State in which the SE has its registered office.

2. The provisions of laws adopted by Member States specifically for the SE must be in accordance with Directives applicable to public limited-liability companies referred to in Annex I.
3. If the nature of the business carried out by an SE is regulated by specific provisions of national laws, those laws shall apply in full to the SE.

Article 10

Subject to this Regulation, an SE shall be treated in every Member State as if it were a public limited-liability company formed in accordance with the law of the Member State in which it has its registered office.

Article 11

1. The name of an SE shall be preceded or followed by the abbreviation SE.
2. Only SEs may include the abbreviation SE in their name.
3. Nevertheless, companies, firms and other legal entities registered in a Member State before the date of entry into force of this Regulation in the names of which the abbreviation SE appears shall not be required to alter their names.

Article 12

1. Every SE shall be registered in the Member State in which it has its registered office in a register designated by the law of that Member State in accordance with Article 3 of the first Council Directive (68/151/EEC) of 9 March 1968 on coordination of safeguards which, for the protection of the interests of members and others, are required by Member States of companies within the meaning of the second paragraph of Article 58 of the Treaty, with a view to making such safeguards equivalent throughout the Community.
2. An SE may not be registered unless an agreement on arrangements for employee involvement pursuant to Article 4 of Directive 2001/86/EC has been concluded, or a decision pursuant to Article 3(6) of the Directive has been taken, or the period for negotiations pursuant to Article 5 of the Directive has expired without an agreement having been concluded.
3. In order for an SE to be registered in a Member State which has made use of the option referred to in Article 7(3) of Directive 2001/86/EC, either an agreement pursuant to Article 4 of the Directive must have been concluded on the arrangements for employee involvement, including participation, or none of the participating companies must have been governed by participation rules prior to the registration of the SE.
4. The statutes of the SE must not conflict at any time with the arrangements for employee involvement which have been so determined. Where new such arrangements determined pursuant to the Directive conflict with the existing statutes, the statutes shall to the extent necessary be amended.
   In this case, a Member State may provide that the management organ or the administrative organ of the SE shall be entitled to proceed to amend the statutes without any further decision from the general shareholders meeting.

Article 13

Publication of the documents and particulars concerning an SE which must be publicised under this Regulation shall be effected in the manner laid down in the laws of the Member State in which the SE has its registered office in accordance with Directive 68/151/EEC.

Article 14

1. Notice of an SE's registration and of the deletion of such a registration shall be published for information purposes in the Official Journal of the European Communities after publication in accordance with Article 13. That notice shall state the name, number, date

and place of registration of the SE, the date and place of publication and the title of publication, the registered office of the SE and its sector of activity.

2. Where the registered office of an SE is transferred in accordance with Article 8, notice shall be published giving the information provided for in paragraph 1, together with that relating to the new registration.
3. The particulars referred to in paragraph 1 shall be forwarded to the Office for Official Publications of the European Communities within one month of the publication referred to in Article 13.

TITLE II
FORMATION

Section 1: General

Article 15

1. Subject to this Regulation, the formation of an SE shall be governed by the law applicable to public limited-liability companies in the Member State in which the SE establishes its registered office.
2. The registration of an SE shall be publicised in accordance with Article 13.

Article 16

1. An SE shall acquire legal personality on the date on which it is registered in the register referred to in Article 12.
2. If acts have been performed in an SE's name before its registration in accordance with Article 12 and the SE does not assume the obligations arising out of such acts after its registration, the natural persons, companies, firms or other legal entities which performed those acts shall be jointly and severally liable therefor, without l mit, in the absence of agreement to the contrary.

Section 2: Formation by merger

Article 17

1. An SE may be formed by means of a merger in accordance with Article 2(1).
2. Such a merger may be carried out in accordance with:
   (a) the procedure for merger by acquisition laid down in Article 3(1) of the third Council Directive (78/855/EEC) of 9 October 1978 based on Article 54(3)(g) of the Treaty concerning mergers of public limited-liability companies or
   (b) the procedure for merger by the formation of a new company laid down in Article 4(1) of the said Directive.

   In the case of a merger by acquisition, the acquiring company shall take the form of an SE when the merger takes place. In the case of a merger by the formation of a new company, the SE shall be the newly formed company.

Article 18

For matters not covered by this section or, where a matter is partly covered by it, for aspects not covered by it, each company involved in the formation of an SE by merger shall be governed by the provisions of the law of the Member State to which it is subject that apply to mergers of public limited-liability companies in accordance with Directive 78/855/EEC.

Article 19

The laws of a Member State may provide that a company governed by the law of that Member State may not take part in the formation of an SE by merger if any of that Member State's competent authorities opposes it before the issue of the certificate referred to in Article 25(2). Such opposition may be based only on grounds of public interest. Review by a judicial authority shall be possible.

Article 20

1. The management or administrative organs of merging companies shall draw up draft terms of merger. The draft terms of merger shall include the following particulars:
   (a) the name and registered office of each of the merging companies together with those proposed for the SE;

(b) the share-exchange ratio and the amount of any compensation;
(c) the terms for the allotment of shares in the SE;
(d) the date from which the holding of shares in the SE will entitle the holders to share in profits and any special conditions affecting that entitlement;
(e) the date from which the transactions of the merging companies will be treated for accounting purposes as being those of the SE;
(f) the rights conferred by the SE on the holders of shares to which special rights are attached and on the holders of securities other than shares, or the measures proposed concerning them;
(g) any special advantage granted to the experts who examine the draft terms of merger or to members of the administrative, management, supervisory or controlling organs of the merging companies;
(h) the statutes of the SE;
(i) information on the procedures by which arrangements for employee involvement are determined pursuant to Directive 2001/86/EC.

2. The merging companies may include further items in the draft terms of merger.

Article 21

For each of the merging companies and subject to the additional requirements imposed by the Member State to which the company concerned is subject, the following particulars shall be published in the national gazette of that Member State:

(a) the type, name and registered office of every merging company;
(b) the register in which the documents referred to in Article 3(2) of Directive 68/151/EEC are filed in respect of each merging company, and the number of the entry in that register;
(c) an indication of the arrangements made in accordance with Article 24 for the exercise of the rights of the creditors of the company in question and the address at which complete information on those arrangements may be obtained free of charge;
(d) an indication of the arrangements made in accordance with Article 24 for the exercise of the rights of minority shareholders of the company in question and the address at which complete information on those arrangements may be obtained free of charge;
(e) the name and registered office proposed for the SE.

Article 22

As an alternative to experts operating on behalf of each of the merging companies, one or more independent experts as defined in Article 10 of Directive 78/855/EEC, appointed for those purposes at the joint request of the companies by a judicial or administrative authority in the Member State of one of the merging companies or of the proposed SE, may examine the draft terms of merger and draw up a single report to all the shareholders.

The experts shall have the right to request from each of the merging companies any information they consider necessary to enable them to complete their function.

Article 23

1. The general meeting of each of the merging companies shall approve the draft terms of merger.
2. Employee involvement in the SE shall be decided pursuant to Directive 2001/86/EC. The general meetings of each of the merging companies may reserve the right to make registration of the SE conditional upon its express ratification of the arrangements so decided.

Article 24

1. The law of the Member State governing each merging company shall apply as in the case of a merger of public limited-liability companies, taking into account the cross-border nature of the merger, with regard to the protection of the interests of:

(a) creditors of the merging companies;
(b) holders of bonds of the merging companies;
(c) holders of securities, other than shares, which carry special rights in the merging companies.

2. A Member State may, in the case of the merging companies governed by its law, adopt provisions designed to ensure appropriate protection for minority shareholders who have opposed the merger.

Article 25

1. The legality of a merger shall be scrutinised, as regards the part of the procedure concerning each merging company, in accordance with the law on mergers of public limited-liability companies of the Member State to which the merging company is subject.
2. In each Member State concerned the court, notary or other competent authority shall issue a certificate conclusively attesting to the completion of the pre-merger acts and formalities.
3. If the law of a Member State to which a merging company is subject provides for a procedure to scrutinise and amend the share-exchange ratio, or a procedure to compensate minority shareholders, without preventing the registration of the merger, such procedures shall only apply if the other merging companies situated in Member States which do not provide for such procedure explicitly accept, when approving the draft terms of the merger in accordance with Article 23(1), the possibility for the shareholders of that merging company to have recourse to such procedure. In such cases, the court, notary or other competent authorities may issue the certificate referred to in paragraph 2 even if such a procedure has been commenced. The certificate must, however, indicate that the procedure is pending. The decision in the procedure shall be binding on the acquiring company and all its shareholders.

Article 26

1. The legality of a merger shall be scrutinised, as regards the part of the procedure concerning the completion of the merger and the formation of the SE, by the court, notary or other authority competent in the Member State of the proposed registered office of the SE to scrutinise that aspect of the legality of mergers of public limited-liability companies.
2. To that end each merging company shall submit to the competent authority the certificate referred to in Article 25(2) within six months of its issue together with a copy of the draft terms of merger approved by that company.
3. The authority referred to in paragraph 1 shall in particular ensure that the merging companies have approved draft terms of merger in the same terms and that arrangements for employee involvement have been determined pursuant to Directive 2001/86/EC.
4. That authority shall also satisfy itself that the SE has been formed in accordance with the requirements of the law of the Member State in which it has its registered office in accordance with Article 15.

Article 27

1. A merger and the simultaneous formation of an SE shall take effect on the date on which the SE is registered in accordance with Article 12.
2. The SE may not be registered until the formalities provided for in Articles 25 and 26 have been completed.

Article 28

For each of the merging companies the completion of the merger shall be publicised as laid down by the law of each Member State in accordance with Article 3 of Directive 68/151/EEC.

Article 29

1. A merger carried out as laid down in Article 17(2)(a) shall have the following consequences ipso jure and simultaneously:
   (a) all the assets and liabilities of each company being acquired are transferred to the acquiring company;
   (b) the shareholders of the company being acquired become shareholders of the acquiring company;
   (c) the company being acquired ceases to exist;
   (d) the acquiring company adopts the form of an SE.
2. A merger carried out as laid down in Article 17(2)(b) shall have the following consequences ipso jure and simultaneously:
   (a) all the assets and liabilities of the merging companies are transferred to the SE;
   (b) the shareholders of the merging companies become shareholders of the SE;
   (c) the merging companies cease to exist.

3. Where, in the case of a merger of public limited-liability companies, the law of a Member State requires the completion of any special formalities before the transfer of certain assets, rights and obligations by the merging companies becomes effective against third parties, those formalities shall apply and shall be carried out either by the merging companies or by the SE following its registration.
4. The rights and obligations of the participating companies on terms and conditions of employment arising from national law, practice and individual employment contracts or employment relationships and existing at the date of the registration shall, by reason of such registration be transferred to the SE upon its registration.

Article 30

A merger as provided for in Article 2(1) may not be declared null and void once the SE has been registered.

The absence of scrutiny of the legality of the merger pursuant to Articles 25 and 26 may be included among the grounds for the winding-up of the SE.

Article 31

1. Where a merger within the meaning of Article 17(2)(a) is carried out by a company which holds all the shares and other securities conferring the right to vote at general meetings of another company, neither Article 20(1)(b), (c) and (d), Article 29(1)(b) nor Article 22 shall apply. National law governing each merging company and mergers of public limited- liability companies in accordance with Article 24 of Directive 78/855/EEC shall nevertheless apply.
2. Where a merger by acquisition is carried out by a company which holds 90 % or more but not all of the shares and other securities conferring the right to vote at general meetings of another company, reports by the management or administrative body, reports by an independent expert or experts and the documents necessary for scrutiny shall be required only to the extent that the national law governing either the acquiring company or the company being acquired so requires.

Member States may, however, provide that this paragraph may apply where a company holds shares conferring 90 % or more but not all of the voting rights.

Section 3: Formation of a holding SE

Article 32

1. A holding SE may be formed in accordance with Article 2(2).
   A company promoting the formation of a holding SE in accordance with Article 2(2) shall continue to exist.
2. The management or administrative organs of the companies which promote such an operation shall draw up, in the same terms, draft terms for the formation of the holding SE. The draft terms shall include a report explaining and justifying the legal and economic aspects of the formation and indicating the implications for the shareholders and for the employees of the adoption of the form of a holding SE. The draft terms shall also set out the particulars provided for in Article 20(1)(a), (b), (c), (f), (g), (h) and (i) and shall fix the minimum proportion of the shares in each of the companies promoting the operation which the shareholders must contribute to the formation of the holding SE. That proportion shall be shares conferring more than 50 % of the permanent voting rights.
3. For each of the companies promoting the operation, the draft terms for the formation of the holding SE shall be publicised in the manner laid down in each Member State's national law in accordance with Article 3 of Directive 68/151/EEC at least one month before the date of the general meeting called to decide thereon.
4. One or more experts independent of the companies promoting the operation, appointed or approved by a judicial or administrative authority in the Member State to which each company is subject in accordance with national provisions adopted in implementation of Directive 78/855/EEC, shall examine the draft terms of formation drawn up in accordance with paragraph 2 and draw up a written report for the shareholders of each company. By agreement between the companies promoting the operation, a single written report may be drawn up for the shareholders of all the companies by one or more independent experts, appointed or approved by a judicial or administrative authority in the Member State to which one of the companies promoting the operation or the proposed SE is

subject in accordance with national provisions adopted in implementation of Directive 78/855/EEC.

5. The report shall indicate any particular difficulties of valuation and state whether the proposed share-exchange ratio is fair and reasonable, indicating the methods used to arrive at it and whether such methods are adequate in the case in question.
6. The general meeting of each company promoting the operation shall approve the draft terms of formation of the holding SE.
   Employee involvement in the holding SE shall be decided pursuant to Directive 2001/86/EC. The general meetings of each company promoting the operation may reserve the right to make registration of the holding SE conditional upon its express ratification of the arrangements so decided.
7. These provisions shall apply mutatis mutandis to private limited-liability companies.

Article 33

1. The shareholders of the companies promoting such an operation shall have a period of three months in which to inform the promoting companies whether they intend to contribute their shares to the formation of the holding SE. That period shall begin on the date upon which the terms for the formation of the holding SE have been finally determined in accordance with Article 32.
2. The holding SE shall be formed only if, within the period referred to in paragraph 1, the shareholders of the companies promoting the operation have assigned the minimum proportion of shares in each company in accordance with the draft terms of formation and if all the other conditions are fulfilled.
3. If the conditions for the formation of the holding SE are all fulfilled in accordance with paragraph 2, that fact shall, in respect of each of the promoting companies, be publicised in the manner laid down in the national law governing each of those companies adopted in implementation of Article 3 of Directive 68/151/EEC.
   Shareholders of the companies promoting the operation who have not indicated whether they intend to make their shares available to the promoting companies for the purpose of forming the holding SE within the period referred to in paragraph 1 shall have a further month in which to do so.
4. Shareholders who have contributed their securities to the formation of the SE shall receive shares in the holding SE.
5. The holding SE may not be registered until it is shown that the formalities referred to in Article 32 have been completed and that the conditions referred to in paragraph 2 have been fulfilled.

Article 34

A Member State may, in the case of companies promoting such an operation, adopt provisions designed to ensure protection for minority shareholders who oppose the operation, creditors and employees.

Section 4: Formation of a subsidiary SE

Article 35

An SE may be formed in accordance with Article 2(3).

Article 36

Companies, firms and other legal entities participating in such an operation shall be subject to the provisions governing their participation in the formation of a subsidiary in the form of a public limited-liability company under national law.

Section 5: Conversion of an existing public limited-liability company into an SE

Article 37

1. An SE may be formed in accordance with Article 2(4).
2. Without prejudice to Article 12 the conversion of a public limited-liability company into an SE shall not result in the winding up of the company or in the creation of a new legal person.
3. The registered office may not be transferred from one Member State to another pursuant to Article 8 at the same time as the conversion is effected.

4. The management or administrative organ of the company in question shall draw up draft terms of conversion and a report explaining and justifying the legal and economic aspects of the conversion and indicating the implications for the shareholders and for the employees of the adoption of the form of an SE.
5. The draft terms of conversion shall be publicised in the manner laid down in each Member State's law in accordance with Article 3 of Directive 68/151/EEC at least one month before the general meeting called upon to decide thereon.
6. Before the general meeting referred to in paragraph 7 one or more independent experts appointed or approved, in accordance with the national provisions adopted in implementation of Article 10 of Directive 78/855/EEC, by a judicial or administrative authority in the Member State to which the company being converted into an SE is subject shall certify in compliance with Directive 77/91/EEC mutatis mutandis that the company has net assets at least equivalent to its capital plus those reserves which must not be distributed under the law or the Statutes.
7. The general meeting of the company in question shall approve the draft terms of conversion together with the statutes of the SE. The decision of the general meeting shall be passed as laid down in the provisions of national law adopted in implementation of Article 7 of Directive 78/855/EEC.
8. Member States may condition a conversion to a favourable vote of a qualified majority or unanimity in the organ of the company to be converted within which employee participation is organised.
9. The rights and obligations of the company to be converted on terms and conditions of employment arising from national law, practice and individual employment contracts or employment relationships and existing at the date of the registration shall, by reason of such registration be transferred to the SE.

TITLE III
STRUCTURE OF THE SE

Article 38

Under the conditions laid down by this Regulation an SE shall comprise:

(a) a general meeting of shareholders and
(b) either a supervisory organ and a management organ (two-tier system) or an administrative organ (one-tier system) depending on the form adopted in the statutes.

Section 1: Two-tier system

Article 39

1. The management organ shall be responsible for managing the SE. A Member State may provide that a managing director or managing directors shall be responsible for the current management under the same conditions as for public limited-liability companies that have registered offices within that Member State's territory.
2. The member or members of the management organ shall be appointed and removed by the supervisory organ.
   A Member State may, however, require or permit the statutes to provide that the member or members of the management organ shall be appointed and removed by the general meeting under the same conditions as for public limited-liability companies that have registered offices within its territory.
3. No person may at the same time be a member of both the management organ and the supervisory organ of the same SE. The supervisory organ may, however, nominate one of its members to act as a member of the management organ in the event of a vacancy. During such a period the functions of the person concerned as a member of the supervisory organ shall be suspended. A Member State may impose a time limit on such a period.
4. The number of members of the management organ or the rules for determining it shall be laid down in the SE's statutes. A Member State may, however, fix a minimum and/or a maximum number.

5. Where no provision is made for a two-tier system in relation to public limited-liability companies with registered offices within its territory, a Member State may adopt the appropriate measures in relation to SEs.

Article 40

1. The supervisory organ shall supervise the work of the management organ. It may not itself exercise the power to manage the SE.
2. The members of the supervisory organ shall be appointed by the general meeting. The members of the first supervisory organ may, however, be appointed by the statutes. This shall apply without prejudice to Article 47(4) or to any employee participation arrangements determined pursuant to Directive 2001/86/EC.
3. The number of members of the supervisory organ or the rules for determining it shall be laid down in the statutes. A Member State may, however, stipulate the number of members of the supervisory organ for SEs registered within its territory or a minimum and/or a maximum number.

Article 41

1. The management organ shall report to the supervisory organ at least once every three months on the progress and foreseeable development of the SE's business.
2. In addition to the regular information referred to in paragraph 1, the management organ shall promptly pass the supervisory organ any information on events likely to have an appreciable effect on the SE.
3. The supervisory organ may require the management organ to provide information of any kind which it needs to exercise supervision in accordance with Article 40(1). A Member State may provide that each member of the supervisory organ also be entitled to this facility.
4. The supervisory organ may undertake or arrange for any investigations necessary for the performance of its duties.
5. Each member of the supervisory organ shall be entitled to examine all information submitted to it.

Article 42

The supervisory organ shall elect a chairman from among its members. If half of the members are appointed by employees, only a member appointed by the general meeting of shareholders may be elected chairman.

Section 2: The one-tier system

Article 43

1. The administrative organ shall manage the SE. A Member State may provide that a managing director or managing directors shall be responsible for the day-to-day management under the same conditions as for public limited-liability companies that have registered offices within that Member State's territory.
2. The number of members of the administrative organ or the rules for determining it shall be laid down in the SE's statutes. A Member State may, however, set a minimum and, where necessary, a maximum number of members.

The administrative organ shall, however, consist of at least three members where employee participation is regulated in accordance with Directive 2001/86/EC.

3. The member or members of the administrative organ shall be appointed by the general meeting. The members of the first administrative organ may, however, be appointed by the statutes. This shall apply without prejudice to Article 47(4) or to any employee participation arrangements determined pursuant to Directive 2001/86/EC.
4. Where no provision is made for a one-tier system in relation to public limited-liability companies with registered offices within its territory, a Member State may adopt the appropriate measures in relation to SEs.

Article 44

1. The administrative organ shall meet at least once every three months at intervals laid down by the statutes to discuss the progress and foreseeable development of the SE's business.
2. Each member of the administrative organ shall be entitled to examine all information submitted to it.

Article 45

The administrative organ shall elect a chairman from among its members. If half of the members are appointed by employees, only a member appointed by the general meeting of shareholders may be elected chairman.

Section 3: Rules common to the one-tier and two-tier systems

Article 46

1. Members of company organs shall be appointed for a period laid down in the statutes not exceeding six years.
2. Subject to any restrictions laid down in the statutes, members may be reappointed once or more than once for the period determined in accordance with paragraph 1.

Article 47

1. An SE's statutes may permit a company or other legal entity to be a member of one of its organs, provided that the law applicable to public limited-liability companies in the Member State in which the SE's registered office is situated does not provide otherwise. That company or other legal entity shall designate a natural person to exercise its functions on the organ in question.
2. No person may be a member of any SE organ or a representative of a member within the meaning of paragraph 1 who:
   (a) is disqualified, under the law of the Member State in which the SE's registered office is situated, from serving on the corresponding organ of a public limited-liability company governed by the law of that Member State, or
   (b) is disqualified from serving on the corresponding organ of a public limited-liability company governed by the law of a Member State owing to a judicial or administrative decision delivered in a Member State.
3. An SE's statutes may, in accordance with the law applicable to public limited-liability companies in the Member State in which the SE's registered office is situated, lay down special conditions of eligibility for members representing the shareholders.
4. This Regulation shall not affect national law permitting a minority of shareholders or other persons or authorities to appoint some of the members of a company organ.

Article 48

1. An SE's statutes shall list the categories of transactions which require authorisation of the management organ by the supervisory organ in the two-tier system or an express decision by the administrative organ in the one-tier system.
   A Member State may, however, provide that in the two-tier system the supervisory organ may itself make certain categories of transactions subject to authorisation.
2. A Member State may determine the categories of transactions which must at least be indicated in the statutes of SEs registered within its territory.

Article 49

The members of an SE's organs shall be under a duty, even after they have ceased to hold office, not to divulge any information which they have concerning the SE the disclosure of which might be prejudicial to the company's interests, except where such disclosure is required or permitted under national law provisions applicable to public limited-liability companies or is in the public interest.

Article 50

1. Unless otherwise provided by this Regulation or the statutes, the internal rules relating to quorums and decision-taking in SE organs shall be as follows:
   (a) quorum: at least half of the members must be present or represented;
   (b) decision-taking: a majority of the members present or represented.
2. Where there is no relevant provision in the statutes, the chairman of each organ shall have a casting vote in the event of a tie. There shall be no provision to the contrary in the statutes, however, where half of the supervisory organ consists of employees' representatives.
3. Where employee participation is provided for in accordance with Directive 2001/86/EC, a Member State may provide that the supervisory organ's quorum and decision-making shall, by way of derogation from the provisions referred to in paragraphs 1 and 2, be

subject to the rules applicable, under the same conditions, to public limited-liability companies governed by the law of the Member State concerned.

Article 51

Members of an SE's management, supervisory and administrative organs shall be liable, in accordance with the provisions applicable to public limited-liability companies in the Member State in which the SE's registered office is situated, for loss or damage sustained by the SE following any breach on their part of the legal, statutory or other obligations inherent in their duties.

Section 4: General meeting

Article 52

The general meeting shall decide on matters for which it is given sole responsibility by:

(a) this Regulation or

(b) the legislation of the Member State in which the SE's registered office is situated adopted in implementation of Directive 2001/86/EC.

Furthermore, the general meeting shall decide on matters for which responsibility is given to the general meeting of a public limited-liability company governed by the law of the Member State in which the SE's registered office is situated, either by the law of that Member State or by the SE's statutes in accordance with that law.

Article 53

Without prejudice to the rules laid down in this section, the organisation and conduct of general meetings together with voting procedures shall be governed by the law applicable to public limited-liability companies in the Member State in which the SE's registered office is situated.

Article 54

1. An SE shall hold a general meeting at least once each calendar year, within six months of the end of its financial year, unless the law of the Member State in which the SE's registered office is situated applicable to public limited-liability companies carrying on the same type of activity as the SE provides for more frequent meetings. A Member State may, however, provide that the first general meeting may be held at any time in the 18 months following an SE's incorporation.
2. General meetings may be convened at any time by the management organ, the administrative organ, the supervisory organ or any other organ or competent authority in accordance with the national law applicable to public limited-liability companies in the Member State in which the SE's registered office is situated.

Article 55

1. One or more shareholders who together hold at least 10 % of an SE's subscribed capital may request the SE to convene a general meeting and draw up the agenda therefor; the SE's statutes or national legislation may provide for a smaller proportion under the same conditions as those applicable to public limited-liability companies.
2. The request that a general meeting be convened shall state the items to be put on the agenda.
3. If, following a request made under paragraph 1, a general meeting is not held in due time and, in any event, within two months, the competent judicial or administrative authority within the jurisdiction of which the SE's registered office is situated may order that a general meeting be convened within a given period or authorise either the shareholders who have requested it or their representatives to convene a general meeting. This shall be without prejudice to any national provisions which allow the shareholders themselves to convene general meetings.

Article 56

One or more shareholders who together hold at least 10 % of an SE's subscribed capital may request that one or more additional items be put on the agenda of any general meeting. The procedures and time limits applicable to such requests shall be laid down by the national law of the Member State in which the SE's registered office is situated or, failing that, by the SE's statutes. The above proportion may be reduced by the statutes or by the law of the Member State in which the SE's registered office is situated under the same conditions as are applicable to public limited-liability companies.

Article 57

Save where this Regulation or, failing that, the law applicable to public limited-liability companies in the Member State in which an SE's registered office is situated requires a larger majority, the general meeting's decisions shall be taken by a majority of the votes validly cast.

Article 58

The votes cast shall not include votes attaching to shares in respect of which the shareholder has not taken part in the vote or has abstained or has returned a blank or spoilt ballot paper.

Article 59

1. Amendment of an SE's statutes shall require a decision by the general meeting taken by a majority which may not be less than two thirds of the votes cast, unless the law applicable to public limited-liability companies in the Member State in which an SE's registered office is situated requires or permits a larger majority.
2. A Member State may, however, provide that where at least half of an SE's subscribed capital is represented, a simple majority of the votes referred to in paragraph 1 shall suffice.
3. Amendments to an SE's statutes shall be publicised in accordance with Article 13.

Article 60

1. Where an SE has two or more classes of shares, every decision by the general meeting shall be subject to a separate vote by each class of shareholders whose class rights are affected thereby.
2. Where a decision by the general meeting requires the majority of votes specified in Article 59(1) or (2), that majority shall also be required for the separate vote by each class of shareholders whose class rights are affected by the decision.

TITLE IV
ANNUAL ACCOUNTS AND CONSOLIDATED ACCOUNTS

Article 61

Subject to Article 62 an SE shall be governed by the rules applicable to public limited-liability companies under the law of the Member State in which its registered office is situated as regards the preparation of its annual and, where appropriate, consolidated accounts including the accompanying annual report and the auditing and publication of those accounts.

Article 62

1. An SE which is a credit or financial institution shall be governed by the rules laid down in the national law of the Member State in which its registered office is situated in implementation of Directive 2000/12/EC of the European Parliament and of the Council of 20 March 2000 relating to the taking up and pursuit of the business of credit institutions as regards the preparation of its annual and, where appropriate, consolidated accounts, including the accompanying annual report and the auditing and publication of those accounts.
2. An SE which is an insurance undertaking shall be governed by the rules laid down in the national law of the Member State in which its registered office is situated in implementation of Council Directive 91/674/EEC of 19 December 1991 on the annual accounts and consolidated accounts of insurance undertakings as regards the preparation of its annual and, where appropriate, consolidated accounts including the accompanying annual report and the auditing and publication of those accounts.

TITLE V
WINDING UP, LIQUIDATION, INSOLVENCY AND CESSATION OF PAYMENTS

Article 63

As regards winding up, liquidation, insolvency, cessation of payments and similar procedures, an SE shall be governed by the legal provisions which would apply to a public limited-liability company formed in accordance with the law of the Member State in which its registered office is situated, including provisions relating to decision-making by the general meeting.

Article 64

1. When an SE no longer complies with the requirement laid down in Article 7, the Member State in which the SE's registered office is situated shall take appropriate measures to oblige the SE to regularise its position within a specified period either:
   (a) by re-establishing its head office in the Member State in which its registered office is situated or
   (b) by transferring the registered office by means of the procedure laid down in Article 8.
2. The Member State in which the SE's registered office is situated shall put in place the measures necessary to ensure that an SE which fails to regularise its position in accordance with paragraph 1 is liquidated.
3. The Member State in which the SE's registered office is situated shall set up a judicial remedy with regard to any established infringement of Article 7. That remedy shall have a suspensory effect on the procedures laid down in paragraphs 1 and 2.
4. Where it is established on the initiative of either the authorities or any interested party that an SE has its head office within the territory of a Member State in breach of Article 7, the authorities of that Member State shall immediately inform the Member State in which the SE's registered office is situated.

Article 65

Without prejudice to provisions of national law requiring additional publication, the initiation and termination of winding up, liquidation, insolvency or cessation of payment procedures and any decision to continue operating shall be publicised in accordance with Article 13.

Article 66

1. An SE may be converted into a public limited-liability company governed by the law of the Member State in which its registered office is situated. No decision on conversion may be taken before two years have elapsed since its registration or before the first two sets of annual accounts have been approved.
2. The conversion of an SE into a public limited-liability company shall not result in the winding up of the company or in the creation of a new legal person.
3. The management or administrative organ of the SE shall draw up draft terms of conversion and a report explaining and justifying the legal and economic aspects of the conversion and indicating the implications of the adoption of the public limited-liability company for the shareholders and for the employees.
4. The draft terms of conversion shall be publicised in the manner laid down in each Member State's law in accordance with Article 3 of Directive 68/151/EEC at least one month before the general meeting called to decide thereon.
5. Before the general meeting referred to in paragraph 6, one or more independent experts appointed or approved, in accordance with the national provisions adopted in implementation of Article 10 of Directive 78/855/EEC, by a judicial or administrative authority in the Member State to which the SE being converted into a public limited-liability company is subject shall certify that the company has assets at least equivalent to its capital.
6. The general meeting of the SE shall approve the draft terms of conversion together with the statutes of the public limited-liability company. The decision of the general meeting shall be passed as laid down in the provisions of national law adopted in implementation of Article 7 of Directive 78/855/EEC.

TITLE VI
ADDITIONAL AND TRANSITIONAL PROVISIONS

Article 67

1. If and so long as the third phase of economic and monetary union (EMU) does not apply to it each Member State may make SEs with registered offices within its territory subject to the same provisions as apply to public limited-liability companies covered by its legislation as regards the expression of their capital. An SE may, in any case, express its capital in euro as well. In that event the national currency/euro conversion rate shall be that for the last day of the month preceding that of the formation of the SE.

2. If and so long as the third phase of EMU does not apply to the Member State in which an SE has its registered office, the SE may, however, prepare and publish its annual and, where appropriate, consolidated accounts in euro. The Member State may require that the SE's annual and, where appropriate, consolidated accounts be prepared and published in the national currency under the same conditions as those laid down for public limited- liability companies governed by the law of that Member State. This shall not prejudge the additional possibility for an SE of publishing its annual and, where appropriate, consolidated accounts in euro in accordance with Council Directive 90/604/EEC of 8 November 1990 amending Directive 78/60/EEC on annual accounts and Directive 83/349/EEC on consolidated accounts as concerns the exemptions for small and medium- sized companies and the publication of accounts in ecu.

TITLE VII
FINAL PROVISIONS

Article 68

1. The Member States shall make such provision as is appropriate to ensure the effective application of this Regulation.
2. Each Member State shall designate the competent authorities within the meaning of Articles 8, 25, 26, 54, 55 and 64. It shall inform the Commission and the other Member States accordingly.

Article 69

Five years at the latest after the entry into force of this Regulation, the Commission shall forward to the Council and the European Parliament a report on the application of the Regulation and proposals for amendments, where appropriate. The report shall, in particular, analyse the appropriateness of:

(a) allowing the location of an SE's head office and registered office in different Member States;

(b) broadening the concept of merger in Article 17(2) in order to admit also other types of merger than those defined in Articles 3(1) and 4(1) of Directive 78/855/EEC;

(c) revising the jurisdiction clause in Article 8(16) in the light of any provision which may have been inserted in the 1968 Brussels Convention or in any text adopted by Member States or by the Council to replace such Convention;

(d) allowing provisions in the statutes of an SE adopted by a Member State in execution of authorisations given to the Member States by this Regulation or laws adopted to ensure the effective application of this Regulation in respect to the SE which deviate from or are complementary to these laws, even when such provisions would not be authorised in the statutes of a public limited-liability company having its registered office in the Member State.

Article 70

This Regulation shall enter into force on 8 October 2004.

This Regulation shall be binding in its entirety and directly applicable in all Member States.

Done at Luxembourg, 8 October 2001.

ANNEX I
PUBLIC LIMITED-LIABILITY COMPANIES REFERRED TO IN ARTICLE 2(1)
UNITED KINGDOM:

public companies limited by shares
public companies limited by guarantee having a share capital

ANNEX II
PUBLIC AND PRIVATE LIMITED-LIABILITY COMPANIES
REFERRED TO IN ARTICLE 2(2)
UNITED KINGDOM:

public companies limited by shares
public companies limited by guarantee having a share capital

DIRECTIVE 2003/6/EC OF THE EUROPEAN PARLIAMENT AND OF THE COUNCIL of 28 January 2003 on insider dealing and market manipulation (market abuse)

THE EUROPEAN PARLIAMENT AND THE COUNCIL OF THE EUROPEAN UNION,

Having regard to the Treaty establishing the European Community, and in particular Article 95 thereof,

Having regard to the proposal from the Commission,

Having regard to the opinion of the European Economic and Social Committee, Having regard to the opinion of the European Central Bank,

Acting in accordance with the procedure laid down in Article 251,

Whereas:

(1) A genuine Single Market for financial services is crucial for economic growth and job creation in the Community.

(2) An integrated and efficient financial market requires market integrity. The smooth functioning of securities markets and public confidence in markets are prerequisites for economic growth and wealth. Market abuse harms the integrity of financial markets and public confidence in securities and derivatives.

(3) The Commission Communication of 11 May 1999 entitled "Implementing the framework for financial markets: action plan" identifies a series of actions that are needed in order to complete the single market for financial services. The Lisbon European Council of April 2000 called for the implementation of that action plan by 2005. The action plan stresses the need to draw up a Directive against market manipulation.

(4) At its meeting on 17 July 2000, the Council set up the Committee of Wise Men on the Regulation of European Securities Markets. In its final report, the Committee of Wise Men proposed the introduction of new legislative techniques based on a four-level approach, namely framework principles, implementing measures, cooperation and enforcement. Level 1, the Directive, should confine itself to broad general "framework" principles while Level 2 should contain technical implementing measures to be adopted by the Commission with the assistance of a committee.

(5) The Resolution adopted by the Stockholm European Council of March 2001 endorsed the final report of the Committee of Wise Men and the proposed four-level approach to make the regulatory process for Community securities legislation more efficient and transparent.

(6) The Resolution of the European Parliament of 5 February 2002 on the implementation of financial services legislation also endorsed the Committee of Wise Men's report, on the basis of the solemn declaration made before Parliament the same day by the Commission and the letter of 2 October 2001 addressed by the Internal Market Commissioner to the chairman of Parliament's Committee on Economic and Monetary Affairs with regard to the safeguards for the European Parliament's role in this process.

(7) The measures necessary for the implementation of this Directive should be adopted in accordance with Council Decision 1999/468/EC of 28 June 1999 laying down the procedures for the exercise of implementing powers conferred on the Commission.

(8) According to the Stockholm European Council, Level 2 implementing measures should be used more frequently, to ensure that technical provisions can be kept up to date with market and supervisory developments, and deadlines should be set for all stages of Level 2 work.

(9) The European Parliament should be given a period of three months from the first transmission of draft implementing measures to allow it to examine them and to give its opinion. However, in urgent and duly justified cases, this period may be shortened. If, within that period, a resolution is passed by the European Parliament, the Commission should re-examine the draft measures.

(10) New financial and technical developments enhance the incentives, means and opportunities for market abuse: through new products, new technologies, increasing cross-border activities and the Internet.

(11) The existing Community legal framework to protect market integrity is incomplete. Legal requirements vary from one Member State to another, leaving economic actors often uncertain over concepts, definitions and enforcement. In some Member States there is no legislation addressing the issues of price manipulation and the dissemination of misleading information.

(12) Market abuse consists of insider dealing and market manipulation. The objective of legislation against insider dealing is the same as that of legislation against market manipulation: to ensure the integrity of Community financial markets and to enhance investor confidence in those markets. It is therefore advisable to adopt combined rules to combat both insider dealing and market manipulation. A single Directive will ensure throughout the Community the same framework for allocation of responsibilities, enforcement and cooperation.

(13) Given the changes in financial markets and in Community legislation since the adoption of Council Directive 89/592/EEC of 13 November 1989 coordinating regulations on insider dealing, that Directive should now be replaced, to ensure consistency with legislation against market manipulation. A new Directive is also needed to avoid loopholes in Community legislation which could be used for wrongful conduct and which would undermine public confidence and therefore prejudice the smooth functioning of the markets.

(14) This Directive meets the concerns expressed by the Member States following the terrorist attacks on 11 September 2001 as regards the fight against financing terrorist activities.

(15) Insider dealing and market manipulation prevent full and proper market transparency, which is a prerequisite for trading for all economic actors in integrated financial markets.

(16) Inside information is any information of a precise nature which has not been made public, relating, directly or indirectly, to one or more issuers of financial instruments or to one or more financial instruments. Information which could have a significant effect on the evolution and forming of the prices of a regulated market as such could be considered as information which indirectly relates to one or more issuers of financial instruments or to one or more related derivative financial instruments.

(17) As regards insider dealing, account should be taken of cases where inside information originates not from a profession or function but from criminal activities, the preparation or execution of which could have a significant effect on the prices of one or more financial instruments or on price formation in the regulated market as such.

(18) Use of inside information can consist in the acquisition or disposal of financial instruments by a person who knows, or ought to have known, that the information possessed is inside information. In this respect, the competent authorities should consider what a normal and reasonable person would know or should have known in the circumstances. Moreover, the mere fact that market-makers, bodies authorised to act as counterparties, or persons authorised to execute orders on behalf of third parties with inside information confine themselves, in the first two cases, to pursuing their legitimate business of buying or selling financial instruments or, in the last case, to carrying out an order dutifully, should not in itself be deemed to constitute use of such inside information.

(19) Member States should tackle the practice known as “front running”, including “front running” in commodity derivatives, where it constitutes market abuse under the definitions contained in this Directive.

(20) A person who enters into transactions or issues orders to trade which are constitutive of market manipulation may be able to establish that his reasons for entering into such transactions or issuing orders to trade were legitimate and that the transactions and orders to trade were in conformity with accepted practice on the regulated market concerned. A sanction could still be imposed if the competent authority established that there was another, illegitimate, reason behind these transactions or orders to trade.

(21) The competent authority may issue guidance on matters covered by this Directive, e.g. definition of inside information in relation to derivatives on commodities or implementation of the definition of accepted market practices relating to the definition of market manipulation. This guidance should be in conformity with the provisions of the Directive and the implementing measures adopted in accordance with the comitology procedure.

(22) Member States should be able to choose the most appropriate way to regulate persons producing or disseminating research concerning financial instruments or issuers of financial instruments or persons producing or disseminating other information recommending or suggesting investment strategy, including appropriate mechanisms for self-regulation, which should be notified to the Commission.

(23) Posting of inside information by issuers on their internet sites should be in accordance with the rules on transfer of personal data to third countries as laid down in Directive 95/46/EC of the European Parliament and of the Council of 24 October 1995 on the protection of individuals with regard to the processing of personal data and on the movement of such data.

(24) Prompt and fair disclosure of information to the public enhances market integrity, whereas selective disclosure by issuers can lead to a loss of investor confidence in the integrity of financial markets. Professional economic actors should contribute to market integrity by various means. Such measures could include, for instance, the creation of "grey lists", the application of "window trading" to sensitive categories of personnel, the application of internal codes of conduct and the establishment of "Chinese walls". Such preventive measures may contribute to combating market abuse only if they are enforced with determination and are dutifully controlled. Adequate enforcement control would imply for instance the designation of compliance officers within the bodies concerned and periodic checks conducted by independent auditors.

(25) Modern communication methods make it possible for financial market professionals and private investors to have more equal access to financial information, but also increase the risk of the spread of false or misleading information.

(26) Greater transparency of transactions conducted by persons discharging managerial responsibilities within issuers and, where applicable, persons closely associated with them, constitutes a preventive measure against market abuse. The publication of those transactions on at least an individual basis can also be a highly valuable source of information to investors.

(27) Market operators should contribute to the prevention of market abuse and adopt structural provisions aimed at preventing and detecting market manipulation practices. Such provisions may include requirements concerning transparency of transactions concluded, total disclosure of price-regularisation agreements, a fair system of order pairing, introduction of an effective atypical-order detection scheme, sufficiently robust financial instrument reference price-fixing schemes and clarity of rules on the suspension of transactions.

(28) This Directive should be interpreted, and implemented by Member States, in a manner consistent with the requirements for effective regulation in order to protect the interests of holders of transferable securities carrying voting rights in a company (or which may carry such rights as a consequence of the exercise of rights or conversion) when the company is subject to a public take-over bid or other proposed change of control. In particular, this Directive does not in any way prevent a Member State from putting or having in place such measures as it sees fit for these purposes.

(29) Having access to inside information relating to another company and using it in the context of a public take-over bid for the purpose of gaining control of that company or proposing a merger with that company should not in itself be deemed to constitute insider dealing.

(30) Since the acquisition or disposal of financial instruments necessarily involves a prior decision to acquire or dispose taken by the person who undertakes one or other of these operations, the carrying out of this acquisition or disposal should not be deemed in itself to constitute the use of inside information.

(31) Research and estimates developed from publicly available data should not be regarded as inside information and, therefore, any transaction carried out on the basis of such research or estimates should not be deemed in itself to constitute insider dealing within the meaning of this Directive.

(32) Member States and the European System of Central Banks, national central banks or any other officially designated body, or any person acting on their behalf, should not be restricted in carrying out monetary, exchange-rate or public debt management policy.

(33) Stabilisation of financial instruments or trading in own shares in buy-back programmes can be legitimate, in certain circumstances, for economic reasons and should not, therefore, in themselves be regarded as market abuse. Common standards should be developed to provide practical guidance.

(34) The widening scope of financial markets, the rapid change and the range of new products and developments require a wide application of this Directive to financial instruments and techniques involved, in order to guarantee the integrity of Community financial markets.

(35) Establishing a level playing field in Community financial markets requires wide geographical application of the provisions covered by this Directive. As regards derivative instruments not admitted to trading but falling within the scope of this Directive, each Member State should be competent to sanction actions carried out on its territory or abroad which concern underlying financial instruments admitted to trading on a regulated

market situated or operating within its territory or for which a request for admission to trading on such a regulated market has been made. Each Member State should also be competent to sanction actions carried out on its territory which concern underlying financial instruments admitted to trading on a regulated market in a Member State or for which a request for admission to trading on such a market has been made.

(36) A variety of competent authorities in Member States, having different responsibilities, may create confusion among economic actors. A single competent authority should be designated in each Member State to assume at least final responsibility for supervising compliance with the provisions adopted pursuant to this Directive, as well as international collaboration. Such an authority should be of an administrative nature guaranteeing its independence of economic actors and avoiding conflicts of interest. In accordance with national law, Member States should ensure appropriate financing of the competent authority. That authority should have adequate arrangements for consultation concerning possible changes in national legislation such as a consultative committee composed of representatives of issuers, financial services providers and consumers, so as to be fully informed of their views and concerns.

(37) A common minimum set of effective tools and powers for the competent authority of each Member State will guarantee supervisory effectiveness. Market undertakings and all economic actors should also contribute at their level to market integrity. In this sense, the designation of a single competent authority for market abuse does not exclude collaboration links or delegation under the responsibility of the competent authority, between that authority and market undertakings with a view to guaranteeing efficient supervision of compliance with the provisions adopted pursuant to this Directive.

(38) In order to ensure that a Community framework against market abuse is sufficient, any infringement of the prohibitions or requirements laid down pursuant to this Directive will have to be promptly detected and sanctioned. To this end, sanctions should be sufficiently dissuasive and proportionate to the gravity of the infringement and to the gains realised and should be consistently applied.

(39) Member States should remain alert, in determining the administrative measures and sanctions, to the need to ensure a degree of uniformity of regulation from one Member State to another.

(40) Increasing cross-border activities require improved cooperation and a comprehensive set of provisions for the exchange of information between national competent authorities. The organisation of supervision and of investigatory powers in each Member State should not hinder cooperation between the competent national authorities.

(41) Since the objective of the proposed action, namely to prevent market abuse in the form of insider dealing and market manipulation, cannot be sufficiently achieved by the Member States and can therefore, by reason of the scale and effects of the measures, be better achieved at Community level, the Community may adopt measures, in accordance with the principle of subsidiarity as set out in Article 5 of the Treaty. In accordance with the principle of proportionality, as set out in that Article, this Directive does not go beyond what is necessary in order to achieve that objective.

(42) Technical guidance and implementing measures for the rules laid down in this Directive may from time to time be necessary to take account of new developments on financial markets. The Commission should accordingly be empowered to adopt implementing measures, provided that these do not modify the essential elements of this Directive and the Commission acts according to the principles set out in this Directive, after consulting the European Securities Committee established by Commission Decision 2001/528/EC.

(43) In exercising its implementing powers in accordance with this Directive, the Commission should respect the following principles:

- the need to ensure confidence in financial markets among investors by promoting high standards of transparency in financial markets,
- the need to provide investors with a wide range of competing investments and a level of disclosure and protection tailored to their circumstances,
- the need to ensure that independent regulatory authorities enforce the rules consistently, especially as regards the fight against economic crime,
- the need for high levels of transparency and consultation with all market participants and with the European Parliament and the Council,
- the need to encourage innovation in financial markets if they are to be dynamic and efficient,

- the need to ensure market integrity by close and reactive monitoring of financial innovation,
- the importance of reducing the cost of, and increasing access to, capital,
- the balance of costs and benefits to market participants on a long-term basis (including small and medium-sized businesses and small investors) in any implementing measures,
- the need to foster the international competitiveness of EU financial markets without prejudice to a much-needed extension of international cooperation,
- the need to achieve a level playing field for all market participants by establishing EU- wide regulations every time it is appropriate,
- the need to respect differences in national markets where these do not unduly impinge on the coherence of the single market,
- the need to ensure coherence with other Community legislation in this area, as imbalances in information and a lack of transparency may jeopardise the operation of the markets and above all harm consumers and small investors.

(44) This Directive respects the fundamental rights and observes the principles recognised in particular by the Charter of Fundamental Rights of the European Union and in particular by Article 11 thereof and Article 10 of the European Convention on Human Rights. In this regard, this Directive does not in any way prevent Member States from applying their constitutional rules relating to freedom of the press and freedom of expression in the media,

HAVE ADOPTED THIS DIRECTIVE:

Article 1

For the purposes of this Directive:

1. "Inside information" shall mean information of a precise nature which has not been made public, relating, directly or indirectly, to one or more issuers of financial instruments or to one or more financial instruments and which, if it were made public, would be likely to have a significant effect on the prices of those financial instruments or on the price of related derivative financial instruments.
   In relation to derivatives on commodities, "inside information" shall mean information of a precise nature which has not been made public, relating, directly or indirectly, to one or more such derivatives and which users of markets on which such derivatives are traded would expect to receive in accordance with accepted market practices on those markets. For persons charged with the execution of orders concerning financial instruments, "inside information" shall also mean information conveyed by a client and related to the client's pending orders, which is of a precise nature, which relates directly or indirectly to one or more issuers of financial instruments or to one or more financial instruments, and which, if it were made public, would be likely to have a significant effect on the prices of those financial instruments or on the price of related derivative financial instruments.
2. "Market manipulation" shall mean:
   (a) transactions or orders to trade:
      - which give, or are likely to give, false or misleading signals as to the supply of, demand for or price of financial instruments, or
      - which secure, by a person, or persons acting in collaboration, the price of one or several financial instruments at an abnormal or artificial level,

      unless the person who entered into the transactions or issued the orders to trade establishes that his reasons for so doing are legitimate and that these transactions or orders to trade conform to accepted market practices on the regulated market concerned;

   (b) transactions or orders to trade which employ fictitious devices or any other form of deception or contrivance;

   (c) dissemination of information through the media, including the Internet, or by any other means, which gives, or is likely to give, false or misleading signals as to financial instruments, including the dissemination of rumours and false or misleading news, where the person who made the dissemination knew, or ought to have known, that the information was false or misleading. In respect of journalists when they act in their professional capacity such dissemination of information is to be assessed, without prejudice to Article 11, taking into account the rules governing their profession, unless those persons derive, directly or indirectly, an advantage or profits from the dissemination of the information in question.

In particular, the following instances are derived from the core definition given in points (a), (b) and (c) above:

- conduct by a person, or persons acting in collaboration, to secure a dominant position over the supply of or demand for a financial instrument which has the effect of fixing, directly or indirectly, purchase or sale prices or creating other unfair trading conditions,
- the buying or selling of financial instruments at the close of the market with the effect of misleading investors acting on the basis of closing prices,
- taking advantage of occasional or regular access to the traditional or electronic media by voicing an opinion about a financial instrument (or indirectly about its issuer) while having previously taken positions on that financial instrument and profiting subsequently from the impact of the opinions voiced on the price of that instrument, without having simultaneously disclosed that conflict of interest to the public in a proper and effective way.

The definitions of market manipulation shall be adapted so as to ensure that new patterns of activity that in practice constitute market manipulation can be included.

3. "Financial instrument" shall mean:
   - transferable securities as defined in Council Directive 93/22/EEC of 10 May 1993 on investment services in the securities field,
   - units in collective investment undertakings,
   - money-market instruments,
   - financial-futures contracts, including equivalent cash-settled instruments,
   - forward interest-rate agreements,
   - interest-rate, currency and equity swaps,
   - options to acquire or dispose of any instrument falling into these categories, including equivalent cash-settled instruments. This category includes in particular options on currency and on interest rates,
   - derivatives on commodities,
   - any other instrument admitted to trading on a regulated market in a Member State or for which a request for admission to trading on such a market has been made.
4. "Regulated market" shall mean a market as defined by Article 1(13) of Directive 93/22/EEC.
5. "Accepted market practices" shall mean practices that are reasonably expected in one or more financial markets and are accepted by the competent authority in accordance with guidelines adopted by the Commission in accordance with the procedure laid down in Article 17(2).

   The European Supervisory Authority (European Securities and Markets Authority) (hereinafter "ESMA"), established by Regulation (EU) No 1095/2010 of the European Parliament and of the Council may develop draft implementing technical standards to ensure uniform conditions of application of the acts adopted by the Commission in accordance with this Article in relation to accepted market practices.

   Power is conferred on the Commission to adopt the implementing technical standards referred to in the second subparagraph in accordance with Article 15 of Regulation (EU) No 1095/2010.
6. "Person" shall mean any natural or legal person.
7. "Competent authority" shall mean the competent authority designated in accordance with Article 11.

   In order to take account of developments on financial markets and to ensure uniform application of this Directive in the Community, the Commission, shall adopt implementing measures concerning points 1, 2 and 3 of this Article. Those measures, designed to amend non-essential elements of this Directive by supplementing it, shall be adopted in accordance with the regulatory procedure with scrutiny referred to in Article 17(2a).

Article 2

1. Member States shall prohibit any person referred to in the second subparagraph who possesses inside information from using that information by acquiring or disposing of, or by trying to acquire or dispose of, for his own account or for the account of a third party, either directly or indirectly, financial instruments to which that information relates.

The first subparagraph shall apply to any person who possesses that information:

(a) by virtue of his membership of the administrative, management or supervisory bodies of the issuer; or
(b) by virtue of his holding in the capital of the issuer; or
(c) by virtue of his having access to the information through the exercise of his employment, profession or duties; or
(d) by virtue of his criminal activities.

2. Where the person referred to in paragraph 1 is a legal person, the prohibition laid down in that paragraph shall also apply to the natural persons who take part in the decision to carry out the transaction for the account of the legal person concerned.
3. This Article shall not apply to transactions conducted in the discharge of an obligation that has become due to acquire or dispose of financial instruments where that obligation results from an agreement concluded before the person concerned possessed inside information.

Article 3

Member States shall prohibit any person subject to the prohibition laid down in Article 2 from:

(a) disclosing inside information to any other person unless such disclosure is made in the normal course of the exercise of his employment, profession or duties;
(b) recommending or inducing another person, on the basis of inside information, to acquire or dispose of financial instruments to which that information relates.

Article 4

Member States shall ensure that Articles 2 and 3 also apply to any person, other than the persons referred to in those Articles, who possesses inside information while that person knows, or ought to have known, that it is inside information.

Article 5

Member States shall prohibit any person from engaging in market manipulation.

Article 6

1. Member States shall ensure that issuers of financial instruments inform the public as soon as possible of inside information which directly concerns the said issuers.
Without prejudice to any measures taken to comply with the provisions of the first subparagraph, Member States shall ensure that issuers, for an appropriate period, post on their Internet sites all inside information that they are required to disclose publicly.
2. An issuer may under his own responsibility delay the public disclosure of inside information, as referred to in paragraph 1, such as not to prejudice his legitimate interests provided that such omission would not be likely to mislead the public and provided that the issuer is able to ensure the confidentiality of that information. Member States may require that an issuer shall without delay inform the competent authority of the decision to delay the public disclosure of inside information.
3. Member States shall require that, whenever an issuer, or a person acting on his behalf or for his account, discloses any inside information to any third party in the normal exercise of his employment, profession or duties, as referred to in Article 3(a), he must make complete and effective public disclosure of that information, simultaneously in the case of an intentional disclosure and promptly in the case of a non-intentional disclosure.
The provisions of the first subparagraph shall not apply if the person receiving the information owes a duty of confidentiality, regardless of whether such duty is based on a law, on regulations, on articles of association or on a contract.
Member States shall require that issuers, or persons acting on their behalf or for their account, draw up a list of those persons working for them, under a contract of employment or otherwise, who have access to inside information. Issuers and persons acting on their behalf or for their account shall regularly update this list and transmit it to the competent authority whenever the latter requests it.
4. Persons discharging managerial responsibilities within an issuer of financial instruments and, where applicable, persons closely associated with them, shall, at least, notify to the competent authority the existence of transactions conducted on their own account relating to shares of the said issuer, or to derivatives or other financial instruments linked to them. Member States shall ensure that public access to information concerning such transactions, on at least an individual basis, is readily available as soon as possible.

5. Member States shall ensure that there is appropriate regulation in place to ensure that persons who produce or disseminate research concerning financial instruments or issuers of financial instruments and persons who produce or disseminate other information recommending or suggesting investment strategy, intended for distribution channels or for the public, take reasonable care to ensure that such information is fairly presented and disclose their interests or indicate conflicts of interest concerning the financial instruments to which that information relates. Details of such regulation shall be notified to the Commission.
6. Member States shall ensure that market operators adopt structural provisions aimed at preventing and detecting market manipulation practices.
7. With a view to ensuring compliance with paragraphs 1 to 5, the competent authority may take all necessary measures to ensure that the public is correctly informed.
8. Public institutions disseminating statistics liable to have a significant effect on financial markets shall disseminate them in a fair and transparent way.
9. Member States shall require that any person professionally arranging transactions in financial instruments who reasonably suspects that a transaction might constitute insider dealing or market manipulation shall notify the competent authority without delay.
10. In order to take account of technical developments on financial markets and to ensure uniform application of this Directive, the Commission shall adopt implementing measures concerning:
    — the technical modalities for appropriate public disclosure of inside information as referred to in paragraphs 1 and 3,
    — the technical modalities for delaying the public disclosure of inside information as referred to in paragraph 2,
    — the technical modalities designed to favour a common approach in the implementation of the second sentence of paragraph 2,
    — the conditions under which issuers, or entities acting on their behalf, are to draw up a list of those persons working for them and having access to inside information, as referred to in paragraph 3, together with the conditions under which such lists are to be updated,
    — the categories of persons who are subject to a duty of disclosure as referred to in paragraph 4 and the characteristics of a transaction, including its size, which trigger that duty, and the technical arrangements for disclosure to the competent authority,
    — technical arrangements, for the various categories of person referred to in paragraph 5, for fair presentation of research and other information recommending investment strategy and for disclosure of particular interests or conflicts of interest as referred to in paragraph 5. Such arrangements shall take into account the rules, including self-regulation, governing the profession of journalist,
    — technical arrangements governing notification to the competent authority by the persons referred to in paragraph 9.

    Those measures, designed to amend non-essential elements of this Directive by supplementing it, shall be adopted in accordance with the regulatory procedure with scrutiny referred to in Article 17(2a).
11. ESMA may develop draft implementing technical standards to ensure uniform conditions of application of the acts adopted by the Commission in accordance with the sixth indent of the first subparagraph of paragraph 10. Power is conferred on the Commission to adopt the implementing technical standards referred to in the first subparagraph in accordance with Article 15 of Regulation (EU) No 1095/2010.

Article 7

This Directive shall not apply to transactions carried out in pursuit of monetary, exchange-rate or public debt-management policy by a Member State, by the European System of Central Banks, by a national central bank or by any other officially designated body, or by any person acting on their behalf. Member States may extend this exemption to their federated States or similar local authorities in respect of the management of their public debt.

Article 8

1. The prohibitions provided for in this Directive shall not apply to trading in own shares in 'buy-back' programmes or to the stabilisation of a financial instrument provided such trading is carried out in accordance with implementing measures. Those measures,

designed to amend non-essential elements of this Directive by supplementing it, shall be adopted in accordance with the regulatory procedure with scrutiny referred to in Article 17(2a).

2. ESMA may develop draft implementing technical standards to ensure uniform conditions of application of acts adopted by the Commission in accordance with paragraph 1. Power is conferred on the Commission to adopt the implementing technical standards referred to in the first subparagraph in accordance with Article 15 of Regulation (EU) No 1095/2010.

Article 9

This Directive shall apply to any financial instrument admitted to trading on a regulated market in at least one Member State, or for which a request for admission to trading on such a market has been made, irrespective of whether or not the transaction itself actually takes place on that market.

Articles 2, 3 and 4 shall also apply to any financial instrument not admitted to trading on a regulated market in a Member State, but whose value depends on a financial instrument as referred to in paragraph 1.

Article 6(1) to (3) shall not apply to issuers who have not requested or approved admission of their financial instruments to trading on a regulated market in a Member State.

Article 10

Each Member State shall apply the prohibitions and requirements provided for in this Directive to:

(a) actions carried out on its territory or abroad concerning financial instruments that are admitted to trading on a regulated market situated or operating within its territory or for which a request for admission to trading on such market has been made;

(b) actions carried out on its territory concerning financial instruments that are admitted to trading on a regulated market in a Member State or for which a request for admission to trading on such market has been made.

Article 11

Without prejudice to the competences of the judicial authorities, each Member State shall designate a single administrative authority competent to ensure that the provisions adopted pursuant to this Directive are applied.

Member States shall establish effective consultative arrangements and procedures with market participants concerning possible changes in national legislation. These arrangements may include consultative committees within each competent authority, the membership of which should reflect as far as possible the diversity of market participants, be they issuers, providers of financial services or consumers.

Article 12

1. The competent authority shall be given all supervisory and investigatory powers that are necessary for the exercise of its functions. It shall exercise such powers:
   (a) directly; or
   (b) in collaboration with other authorities or with the market undertakings; or
   (c) under its responsibility by delegation to such authorities or to the market undertakings; or
   (d) by application to the competent judicial authorities.
2. Without prejudice to Article 6(7), the powers referred to in paragraph 1 of this Article shall be exercised in conformity with national law and shall include at least the right to:
   (a) have access to any document in any form whatsoever, and to receive a copy of it;
   (b) demand information from any person, including those who are successively involved in the transmission of orders or conduct of the operations concerned, as well as their principals, and if necessary, to summon and hear any such person;
   (c) carry out on-site inspections;
   (d) require existing telephone and existing data traffic records;
   (e) require the cessation of any practice that is contrary to the provisions adopted in the implementation of this Directive;
   (f) suspend trading of the financial instruments concerned;
   (g) request the freezing and/or sequestration of assets;
   (h) request temporary prohibition of professional activity.
3. This Article shall be without prejudice to national legal provisions on professional secrecy.

Article 13

The obligation of professional secrecy shall apply to all persons who work or who have worked for the competent authority or for any authority or market undertaking to whom the competent authority has delegated its powers, including auditors and experts instructed by the competent authority. Information covered by professional secrecy may not be disclosed to any other person or authority except by virtue of provisions laid down by law.

Article 14

1. Without prejudice to the right of Member States to impose criminal sanctions, Member States shall ensure, in conformity with their national law, that the appropriate administrative measures can be taken or administrative sanctions be imposed against the persons responsible where the provisions adopted in the implementation of this Directive have not been complied with. Member States shall ensure that these measures are effective, proportionate and dissuasive.
2. In accordance with the procedure laid down in Article 17(2), the Commission shall, for information, draw up a list of the administrative measures and sanctions referred to in paragraph 1.
3. Member States shall determine the sanctions to be applied for failure to cooperate in an investigation covered by Article 12.
4. Member States shall provide that the competent authority may disclose to the public every measure or sanction that will be imposed for infringement of the provisions adopted in the implementation of this Directive, unless such disclosure would seriously jeopardise the financial markets or cause disproportionate damage to the parties involved.
5. Member States shall provide ESMA annually with aggregated information regarding all administrative measures and sanctions imposed in accordance with paragraphs 1 and 2. Where the competent authority has disclosed an administrative measure or a sanction to the public, it shall contemporaneously report that fact to ESMA.
   Where a published sanction relates to an investment firm authorised in accordance with Directive 2004/39/EC, ESMA shall add a reference to the published sanction in the register of investment firms established under Article 5(3) of Directive 2004/39/EC.

Article 15

Member States shall ensure that an appeal may be brought before a court against the decisions taken by the competent authority.

Article 15a

1. The competent authorities shall cooperate with ESMA for the purposes of this Directive, in accordance with Regulation (EU) No 1095/2010.
2. The competent authorities shall, without delay, provide ESMA with all information necessary to carry out its duties, in accordance with Article 35 of Regulation (EU) No 1095/2010.

Article 16

1. Competent authorities shall cooperate with each other whenever necessary for the purpose of carrying out their duties, making use of their powers whether set out in this Directive or in national law. Competent authorities shall render assistance to competent authorities of other Member States. In particular, they shall exchange information and cooperate in investigation activities.
2. Competent authorities shall, on request, immediately supply any information required for the purpose referred to in paragraph 1. Where necessary, the competent authorities receiving any such request shall immediately take the necessary measures in order to gather the required information. If the requested competent authority is not able to supply the required information immediately, it shall notify the requesting competent authority of the reasons. Information thus supplied shall be covered by the obligation of professional secrecy to which the persons employed or formerly employed by the competent authorities receiving the information are subject.
   The competent authorities may refuse to act on a request for information where:
   - communication might adversely affect the sovereignty, security or public policy of the Member State addressed,
   - judicial proceedings have already been initiated in respect of the same actions and against the same persons before the authorities of the Member State addressed, or

– where a final judgment has already been delivered in relation to such persons for the same actions in the Member State addressed.

In any such case, they shall notify the requesting competent authority accordingly, providing as detailed information as possible on those proceedings or the judgment. Without prejudice to Article 226 of the Treaty, a competent authority whose request for information is not acted upon within a reasonable time or whose request for information is rejected may bring that non-compliance to the attention of the Committee of European Securities Regulators, where discussion will take place in order to reach a rapid and effective solution.

Without prejudice to Article 258 of the Treaty on the Functioning of the European Union (TFEU), a competent authority whose request for information is not acted upon within a reasonable time or whose request for information is rejected may refer that rejection or absence of action within a reasonable timeframe to ESMA. In the situations referred to in the first sentence, ESMA may act in accordance with Article 19 of Regulation (EU) No 1095/2010, without prejudice to the possibilities for refusing to act on a request for information provided for in the second subparagraph of this paragraph and to the possibility of ESMA acting in accordance with Article 17 of Regulation (EU) No 1095/2010.

3. Where a competent authority is convinced that acts contrary to the provisions of this Directive are being, or have been, carried out on the territory of another Member State or that acts are affecting financial instruments traded on a regulated market situated in another Member State, it shall give notice of that fact in as specific a manner as possible to the competent authority of the other Member State. The competent authority of the other Member State shall take appropriate action. It shall inform the notifying competent authority of the outcome and, so far as possible, of significant interim developments. This paragraph shall not prejudice the competences of the competent authority that has forwarded the information. The competent authorities of the various Member States that are competent for the purposes of Article 10 shall consult each other on the proposed follow-up to their action.

4. A competent authority of one Member State may request that an investigation be carried out by the competent authority of another Member State, on the latter's territory.

It may further request that members of its own personnel be allowed to accompany the personnel of the competent authority of that other Member State during the course of the investigation.

The investigation shall, however, be subject throughout to the overall control of the Member State on whose territory it is conducted.

The competent authorities may refuse to act on a request for an investigation to be conducted as provided for in the first subparagraph, or on a request for its personnel to be accompanied by personnel of the competent authority of another Member State as provided for in the second subparagraph, where such an investigation might adversely affect the sovereignty, security or public policy of the State addressed, or where judicial proceedings have already been initiated in respect of the same actions and against the same persons before the authorities of the State addressed or where a final judgment has already been delivered in relation to such persons for the same actions in the State addressed. In such case, they shall notify the requesting competent authority accordingly, providing information, as detailed as possible, on those proceedings or judgment. Without prejudice to Article 258 TFEU, a competent authority whose application to open an inquiry or whose request for authorisation for its officials to accompany those of the other Member State's competent authority is not acted upon within a reasonable time or is rejected may refer that rejection or absence of action within a reasonable timeframe to ESMA. In the situations referred to in the first sentence, ESMA may act in accordance with Article 19 of Regulation (EU) No 1095/2010, without prejudice to the possibilities for refusing to act on a request for information provided in the fourth subparagraph of this paragraph and to the possibility of ESMA acting in accordance with Article 17 of Regulation (EU) No 1095/2010.

5. In order to ensure uniform conditions of application of paragraphs 2 and 4, ESMA may develop draft implementing technical standards on the procedures and forms for exchange of information and for cross-border inspections as referred to in this Article.

Power is conferred on the Commission to adopt the implementing technical standards referred to in the first subparagraph in accordance with Article 15 of Regulation (EU) No 1095/2010.

Article 17

1. The Commission shall be assisted by the European Securities Committee instituted by Decision 2001/528/EC (hereinafter referred to as the "Committee").
2. Where reference is made to this paragraph, Articles 5 and 7 of Decision 1999/468/EC shall apply, having regard to the provisions of Article 8 thereof, provided that the implementing measures adopted according to this procedure do not modify the essential provisions of this Directive.
   The period laid down in Article 5(6) of Decision 1999/468/EC shall be set at three months.

2a. Where reference is made to this paragraph, Article 5a(1) to (4) and Article 7 of Decision 1999/468/EC shall apply, having regard to the provisions of Article 8 thereof.

3. By 31 December 2010, and, thereafter, at least every three years, the Commission shall review the provisions concerning its implementing powers and present a report to the European Parliament and to the Council on the functioning of those powers. The report shall examine, in particular, the need for the Commission to propose amendments to this Directive in order to ensure the appropriate scope of the implementing powers conferred on the Commission. The conclusion as to whether or not amendment is necessary shall be accompanied by a detailed statement of reasons. If necessary, the report shall be accompanied by a legislative proposal to amend the provisions conferring implementing powers on the Commission.
4. Without prejudice to the implementing measures already adopted, on the expiry of a four- year period following the entry into force of this Directive, the application of its provisions requiring the adoption of technical rules and decisions in accordance with paragraph 2 shall be suspended. On a proposal from the Commission, the European Parliament and the Council may renew the provisions concerned in accordance with the procedure laid down in Article 251 of the Treaty and, to that end, they shall review them prior to the expiry of the period referred to above.

Article 17a

By 1 December 2011 the Commission shall review Articles 1, 6, 8, 14, and 16 and present any appropriate legislative proposals in order to allow the full application of the delegated acts under Article 290 TFEU and implementing acts under Article 291 TFEU in respect of this Directive. Without prejudice to implementing measures already adopted, the powers conferred on the Commission in Article 17 to adopt implementing measures that remain after the entry into force of the Lisbon Treaty shall cease to apply on 1 December 2012.

Article 18

Member States shall bring into force the laws, regulations and administrative provisions necessary to comply with this Directive not later than 12 October 2004. They shall forthwith inform the Commission thereof.

When Member States adopt those measures, they shall contain a reference to this Directive or be accompanied by such a reference on the occasion of their official publication. Member States shall determine how such reference is to be made.

Article 19

Article 11 shall not prejudge the possibility for a Member State to make separate legal and administrative arrangements for overseas European territories for whose external relations that Member State is responsible.

Article 20

Directive 89/592/EEC and Article 68(1) and Article 81(1) of Directive 2001/34/EC of the European Parliament and of the Council of 28 May 2001 on the admission of securities to official stock exchange listing and on information to be published on those securities shall be repealed with effect from the date of entry into force of this Directive.

Article 21

This Directive shall enter into force on the day of its publication in the Official Journal of the European Union.

Article 22

This Directive is addressed to the Member States.

Done at Brussels, 28 January 2003.

DIRECTIVE 2004/39/EC OF THE EUROPEAN PARLIAMENT AND OF THE COUNCIL of 21 April 2004 on markets in financial instruments amending Council Directives 85/611/EEC and 93/6/EEC and Directive 2000/12/EC of the European Parliament and of the Council and repealing Council Directive 93/22/EEC

Article 4 Definitions

1. For the purposes of this Directive, the following definitions shall apply:

(1) "Investment firm" means any legal person whose regular occupation or business is the provision of one or more investment services to third parties and/or the performance of one or more investment activities on a professional basis;

Member States may include in the definition of investment firms undertakings which are not legal persons, provided that:

(a) their legal status ensures a level of protection for third parties' interests equivalent to that afforded by legal persons, and

(b) they are subject to equivalent prudential supervision appropriate to their legal form.

However, where a natural person provides services involving the holding of third parties' funds or transferable securities, he may be considered as an investment firm for the purposes of this Directive only if, without prejudice to the other requirements imposed in this Directive and in Directive 93/6/EEC, he complies with the following conditions:

(a) the ownership rights of third parties in instruments and funds must be safeguarded, especially in the event of the insolvency of the firm or of its proprietors, seizure, set-off or any other action by creditors of the firm or of its proprietors;

(b) the firm must be subject to rules designed to monitor the firm's solvency and that of its proprietors;

(c) the firm's annual accounts must be audited by one or more persons empowered, under national law, to audit accounts;

(d) where the firm has only one proprietor, he must make provision for the protection of investors in the event of the firm's cessation of business following his death, his incapacity or any other such event;

(2) "Investment services and activities" means any of the services and activities listed in Section A of Annex I relating to any of the instruments listed in Section C of Annex I;

The Commission shall determine:

– the derivative contracts mentioned in Section C 7 of Annex I that have the characteristics of other derivative financial instruments, having regard to whether, inter alia, they are cleared and settled through recognised clearing houses or are subject to regular margin calls

– the derivative contracts mentioned in Section C 10 of Annex I that have the characteristics of other derivative financial instruments, having regard to whether, inter alia, they are traded on a regulated market or an MTF, are cleared and settled through recognised clearing houses or are subject to regular margin calls;

...

(13) "Market operator" means a person or persons who manages and/or operates the business of a regulated market. The market operator may be the regulated market itself;

(14) "Regulated market" means a multilateral system operated and/or managed by a market operator, which brings together or facilitates the bringing together of multiple third-party buying and selling interests in financial instruments – in the system and in accordance with its non-discretionary rules – in a way that results in a contract, in respect of the financial instruments admitted to trading under its rules and/or systems, and which is authorised and functions regularly and in accordance with the provisions of Title III;

(15) "Multilateral trading facility (MTF)" means a multilateral system, operated by an investment firm or a market operator, which brings together multiple third-party buying and selling interests in financial instruments – in the system and in accordance with non-discretionary rules – in a way that results in a contract in accordance with the provisions of Title II;

...

(17) "Financial instrument" means those instruments specified in Section C of Annex I;

(18) "Transferable securities" means those classes of securities which are negotiable on the capital market, with the exception of instruments of payment, such as:

(a) shares in companies and other securities equivalent to shares in companies, partnerships or other entities, and depositary receipts in respect of shares;

(b) bonds or other forms of securitised debt, including depositary receipts in respect of such securities;

(c) any other securities giving the right to acquire or sell any such transferable securities or giving rise to a cash settlement determined by reference to transferable securities, currencies, interest rates or yields, commodities or other indices or measures;

(19) "Money-market instruments" means those classes of instruments which are normally dealt in on the money market, such as treasury bills, certificates of deposit and commercial papers and excluding instruments of payment;

ANNEX I

LIST OF SERVICES AND ACTIVITIES AND FINANCIAL INSTRUMENTS

Section A: Investment services and activities

(1) Reception and transmission of orders in relation to one or more financial instruments.

(2) Execution of orders on behalf of clients.

(3) Dealing on own account.

(4) Portfolio management.

(5) Investment advice.

(6) Underwriting of financial instruments and/or placing of financial instruments on a firm commitment basis.

(7) Placing of financial instruments without a firm commitment basis

(8) Operation of Multilateral Trading Facilities.

Section B: Ancillary services

(1) Safekeeping and administration of financial instruments for the account of clients, including custodianship and related services such as cash/collateral management;

(2) Granting credits or loans to an investor to allow him to carry out a transaction in one or more financial instruments, where the firm granting the credit or loan is involved in the transaction;

(3) Advice to undertakings on capital structure, industrial strategy and related matters and advice and services relating to mergers and the purchase of undertakings;

(4) Foreign exchange services where these are connected to the provision of investment services;

(5) Investment research and financial analysis or other forms of general recommendation relating to transactions in financial instruments;

(6) Services related to underwriting.

(7) Investment services and activities as well as ancillary services of the type included under Section A or B of Annex 1 related to the underlying of the derivatives included under Section C–5, 6, 7 and 10 — where these are connected to the provision of investment or ancillary services.

Section C: Financial Instruments

(1) Transferable securities;

(2) Money-market instruments;

(3) Units in collective investment undertakings;

(4) Options, futures, swaps, forward rate agreements and any other derivative contracts relating to securities, currencies, interest rates or yields, or other derivatives instruments, financial indices or financial measures which may be settled physically or in cash;

(5) Options, futures, swaps, forward rate agreements and any other derivative contracts relating to commodities that must be settled in cash or may be settled in cash at the option of one of the parties (otherwise than by reason of a default or other termination event);

(6) Options, futures, swaps, and any other derivative contract relating to commodities that can be physically settled provided that they are traded on a regulated market and/or an MTF;

(7) Options, futures, swaps, forwards and any other derivative contracts relating to commodities, that can be physically settled not otherwise mentioned in C.6 and not being for commercial purposes, which have the characteristics of other derivative financial instruments, having regard to whether, inter alia, they are cleared and settled through recognised clearing houses or are subject to regular margin calls;

(8) Derivative instruments for the transfer of credit risk;

(9) Financial contracts for differences.

(10) Options, futures, swaps, forward rate agreements and any other derivative contracts relating to climatic variables, freight rates, emission allowances or inflation rates or other official economic statistics that must be settled in cash or may be settled in cash at the option of one of the parties (otherwise than by reason of a default or other termination event), as well as any other derivative contracts relating to assets, rights, obligations, indices and measures not otherwise mentioned in this Section, which have the characteristics of other derivative financial instruments, having regard to whether, inter alia, they are traded on a regulated market or an MTF, are cleared and settled through recognised clearing houses or are subject to regular margin calls.

INDEX

Printed and bound by CPI Group (UK) Ltd, Croydon, CR0 4YY